BATTLE OF WATERLOO.

A HISTORY OF ALL NATIONS,

FROM

THE EARLIEST PERIODS TO THE PRESENT TIME;

OR,

UNIVERSAL HISTORY:

IN WHICH THE HISTORY OF

EVERY NATION, ANCIENT AND MODERN,

IS SEPARATELY GIVEN.

ILLUSTRATED BY 70 STYLOGRAPHIC MAPS, AND 700 ENGRAVINGS.

REVISED EDITION,

BROUGHT DOWN TO THE LATEST PERIOD,

BY S. G. GOODRICH,

AUTHOR OF "PARLEY'S CABINET LIBRARY," "PARLEY'S TALES," "RECOLLECTIONS OF A LIFETIME," &c. &c.

VOL. II.

FURNISHED ONLY TO SUBSCRIBERS.

NEW YORK:

J. C. DERBY & N. C. MILLER,

PUBLISHERS OF SUBSCRIPTION BOOKS,

NO. 5 SPRUCE ST. (TRIBUNE BUILDINGS).

18[illegible]4.

PUBLISHERS' ADVERTISEMENT TO THE REVISED EDITION.

THIRTY-SIX THOUSAND COPIES of this elaborate work have already been sold! The flattering confidence indicated by this liberal patronage, has induced the author and publishers, to revise the work thoroughly, to bring it down to the latest period. and to introduce

NEW AND SUPERIOR ILLUSTRATIONS.

Thus improved and perfected, it is believed that no other Universal History, extant, can compare with this for the fullness and accuracy of its statements, the convenience of its arrangement, the amount of blended interest and instruction which it contains, or for the strength, durability and neatness of its mechanical execution.

The Work hereafter will be regularly Revised,

and can therefore, at all times, be relied upon as containing the latest important events, connected with the progress of mankind, in politics, society, arts, science,
—in all that belongs to civilization—
and in a form convenient,
cheap and durable.

C. A. ALVORD, PRINTER,
No 15 Vandewater Street, N. Y

CONTENTS OF VOL. II.

Europe.

Introductory.

Greece.

Italy.

Ancient Rome.

Modern Italy.

Malta.

The Byzantine Empire.

Ragusa.

Turkey in Europe.

Spain.

Portugal.

France.

The British Empire.

Germany.

Empire of Austria.

Prussia.

Minor German States.

Switzerland.

Holland.

Belgium.

Denmark.

Sweden.

Norway.

Lapland.

Finland.

The Russian Empire.

Poland.

Hungary.

America.

North America.

Polar Regions.

British America.

United States.

Mexico.

Guatimala.

The West Indies.

South America.

New Grenada. Venezuela. Equador.

Peru and Bolivia.

Chili and Patagonia.

United Provinces of La Plata.

Paraguay and Uruguay.

Brazil and Guiana.

Oceanica.

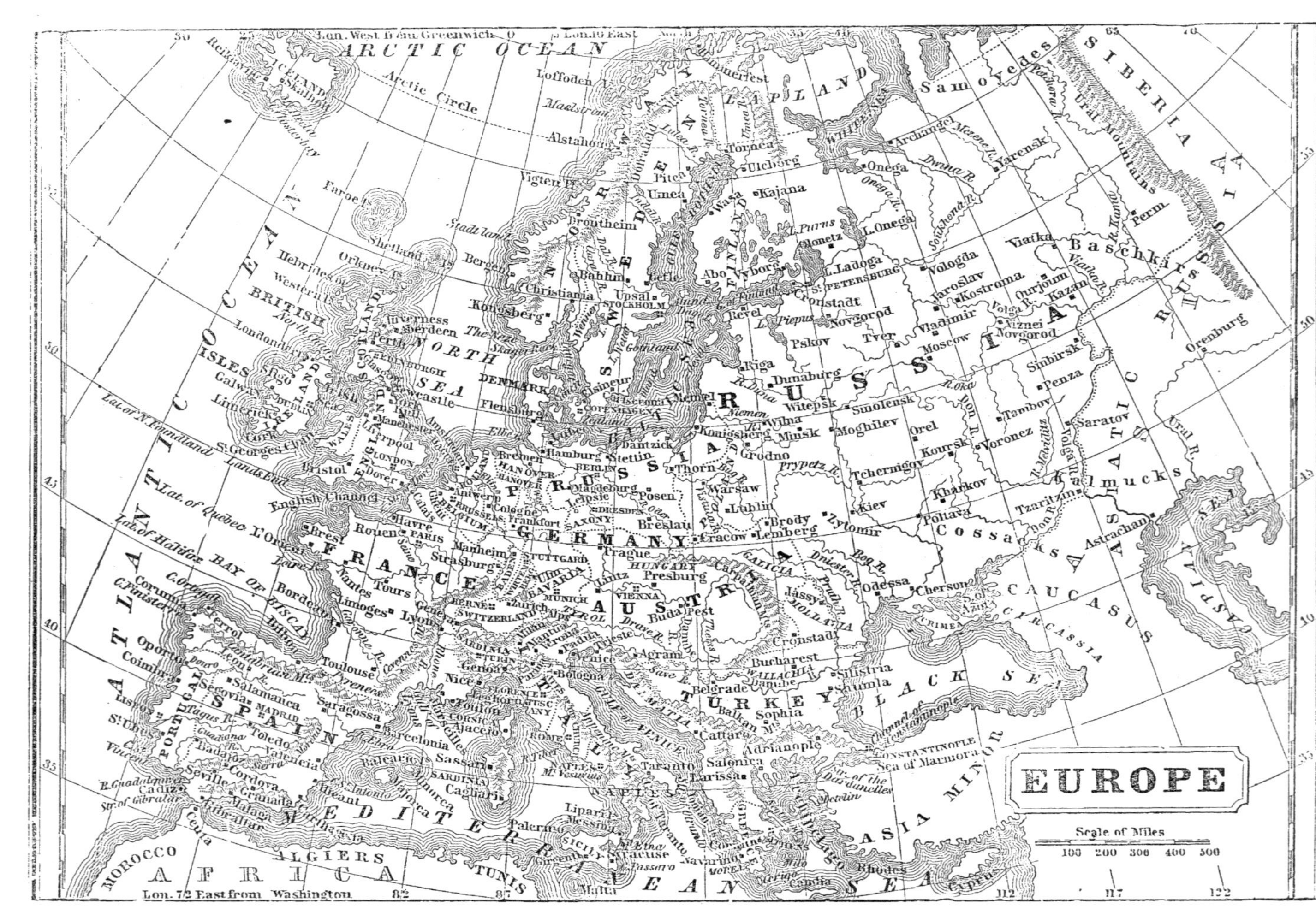
EUROPE
Scale of Miles
100 200 300 400 500
Lon. West from Greenwich
Lon. East
Lon. 72 East from Washington
ARCTIC OCEAN
Arctic Circle
ATLANTIC OCEAN
NORTH SEA
BALTIC SEA
BAY OF BISCAY
English Channel
MEDITERRANEAN SEA
BLACK SEA
CASPIAN SEA
Sea of Marmora
Archipelago
WHITE SEA
Gulf of Bothnia
Gulf of Finland
Gulf of Venice
Skager Rack
Cattegat
St. Georges Chan.
Str. of Gibraltar
Lat. of N. Foundland
Lat. of Quebec
Lat. of Halifax
ICELAND
Faroe Is.
Shetland Is.
Orkney Is.
Hebrides
LAPLAND
NORWAY
SWEDEN
FINLAND
RUSSIA
Samoyedes
SIBERIA
Ural Mountains
Baschkirs
Kalmucks
Cossacks
CAUCASUS
CIRCASSIA
ASIATIC RUSSIA
ASIA MINOR
BRITISH ISLES
SCOTLAND
IRELAND
ENGLAND
WALES
DENMARK
PRUSSIA
GERMANY
FRANCE
AUSTRIA
HUNGARY
GALICIA
MOLDAVIA
WALLACHIA
TURKEY
GREECE
ITALY
SARDINIA
CORSICA
SICILY
SPAIN
PORTUGAL
AFRICA
MOROCCO
ALGIERS
TUNIS
Loffoden Is.
Maelstrom
Hammerfest
Tornea
Uleaborg
Archangel
Onega
Yarensk
Perm
Viatka
Kazan
Orenburg
St. Petersburg
Cronstadt
Novgorod
Moscow
Tver
Pskov
Riga
Dunaburg
Witepsk
Smolensk
Wilna
Minsk
Grodno
Warsaw
Moghilev
Orel
Koursk
Voronez
Tambov
Penza
Simbirsk
Saratov
Tzaritzin
Astrachan
Kiev
Kharkov
Poltava
Odessa
Cherson
Stockholm
Upsal
Christiania
Bergen
Drontheim
Gottenburg
Copenhagen
Elsinore
Abo
Wasa
Kajana
Umea
Pitea
Altenburg
Hamburg
Lubec
Stettin
Dantzick
Konigsberg
Memel
Berlin
Hanover
Bremen
Magdeburg
Leipsic
Dresden
Breslau
Posen
Thorn
Frankfort
Cologne
Stuttgard
Munich
Prague
Vienna
Presburg
Buda
Pest
Cracow
Lemberg
Brody
Zytomir
Jassy
Bucharest
Silistria
Shumla
Belgrade
Sophia
Adrianople
Constantinople
Salonica
Larissa
Cattaro
Paris
Havre
Rouen
Brest
Nantes
Tours
Bordeaux
Limoges
Lyons
Toulouse
Marseilles
Toulon
Strasburg
Manheim
Geneva
Berne
Zurich
Milan
Turin
Genoa
Nice
Venice
Trieste
Florence
Leghorn
Rome
Naples
Taranto
Palermo
Messina
Syracuse
Malta
Cagliari
Sassari
Ajaccio
Madrid
Toledo
Salamanca
Segovia
Saragossa
Barcelona
Valencia
Alicant
Carthagena
Malaga
Granada
Cordova
Seville
Cadiz
Gibraltar
Ceuta
Lisbon
Oporto
Coimbra
Corunna
Ferrol
Bilboa
Edinburgh
Glasgow
Aberdeen
Inverness
Perth
Newcastle
York
Hull
Manchester
Liverpool
London
Dover
Bristol
Lands End
Dublin
Cork
Limerick
Galway
Sligo
Londonderry
Amsterdam
Antwerp
Brussels
Calais
Danube R.
Volga R.
Don R.
Dnieper R.
Dniester R.
Ural R.
Dwina R.
Rhone R.
Ebro R.
Tagus R.
Loire R.
Elbe R.
Vistula R.
L. Ladoga
L. Onega
L. Peipus
Balearic Is.
Minorca
Majorca
Rhodes
Candia
Cyprus
Crimea
Pyrenees Mts.
Carpathian Mts.
Balkan Mts.
Apennine Mts.

CHAPTER CCCXI.

Preliminary Sketch of Europe.

EUROPE forms a peninsular prolongation of Asia, from which it is separated by the River Kara, the Ural Mountains, the Ural River, and the Caspian Sea, and on the south by the mountain chain of the Caucasus. On all other sides it is bounded by seas, gulfs, and straits.

The greatest length of Europe, from Astrakan, in Russia, to Brest, in France, is 2,400 miles; the extreme width, from Cape North, in Russia, to Cape Matapan, in Greece, is 2,360 miles. Its whole extent is about 3,500,000 square miles—its entire population is now (1863) somewhat over two hundred and eighty millions. Three-fourths of its surface are covered by mountains and high lands: one-fourth by plains. The peninsulas occupy one-fourth of the territory, and the islands about one-twentieth. The indentation of Europe, by numerous seas and gulfs, connecting it with the sea, has doubtless had a powerful influence in stimulating commercial enterprise, and in connection therewith, every other kind of industry. We may thus see that while geographical circumstances have raised human society to the highest pitch of civilization here—that Africa, influenced also by geographical circumstances, adverse to the development of human energies, inasmuch as it is a solid mass of land, affording little stimulus to commerce, and few facilities for intercourse with the rest of the world, remains from generation to generation in a state of social and mental degradation.

Though Europe was the latest portion of the Eastern Continent to receive the light of science, yet it must now be regarded as the centre of civilization, refinement, and the arts. Though small in extent compared with Asia and Africa, not on the whole fertile by nature, neither abounding in minerals, nor the precious metals, yet it is now the richest and most productive portion of the earth. It has grown rich on the treasures of other countries; it has brought the silk-worm from India, fine wool from Africa, the peach from Persia, the Orange from China, and the potato from America. Such is the power of human skill and industry, that a barren, rugged, and wild region, which nature had only covered with forests, has been completely changed by its inhabitants. Europe, in which the beaver a few centuries ago built its habitation in security on the banks of solitary rivers, has become the seat of powerful empires. Its fields yield rich harvests, its commerce brings the luxuries of every climate, its cities are adorned with palaces, it is the lawgiver of the world, and, with the exception of our own country, it extends its sway over a great part of the rest of the earth. Already has one whole continent been peopled by its colonies. A large portion of Asia is under its dominion, and Africa cannot long resist the efforts which are making to let in the light upon her dark and hidden regions.

The principal ranges of mountains are the Scandinavian or Dofrafield range, the Pyrenees, Alps, Apennines, and Carpathian Mountains. The Scandinavian chain commences at the southern extremity of Norway, and running north, soon becomes the boundary between Sweden and Norway. The Pyrenees run in an easterly direction from the southern part of the Bay of Biscay to the Mediterranean, forming the boundary between France and Spain. The Alps, the loftiest mountains in Europe, form the western boundary of Italy, separating it from France, Switzerland, and Germany. The Apennines commence near the Mediterranean, at the southwestern extremity, and pursuing an easterly course around the Gulf of Genoa, turn to the southeast, and pass in that direction to the southern extremity of Italy. The Carpathian Mountains encircle Hungary on three sides, separating it from Germany on the northwest, from Galicia on the northeast, and from Turkey on the southeast. At the southern extremity of the range, a branch proceeds in a southerly direction across the Danube to the centre

Fallow Deer.

Wild Boar.

Lynx

of European Turkey, connecting the Carpathian Mountains with the great eastern branch of the Alps.

Norway and Sweden are mountainous. The countries included in the three southern peninsulas, viz., Spain, Italy, and Turkey, are also traversed by mountain ranges. The same description applies to a large portion of Hungary and the southern part of Germany, nearly the whole of Switzerland, and the southeastern part of France. All the northern and western parts of France are hilly. The rest of continental Europe, comprising the Netherlands, Denmark, the northern part of Germany, Prussia, and Russia, consists chiefly of plains.

TABLE OF MOUNTAINS.

Names.	*Height.*	*Names.*	*Height.*
Alps, Switzerland..	15,732	Balkan, Turkey	10,000
Pyrenees, Spain ...	11,500	Pindus, Greece	7,700
Apennines, Italy...	9,521	Carpathian, Hungary	10,000
Etna, Sicily	11,000	Ben Nevis, Scotland	4,380
Corsican	10,000	Snowdon, Wales....	3,570

The islands of Europe include Spitzbergen and Nova Zembla on the north, in the Arctic Ocean; the British Isles, of which Great Britain and Ireland are the principal; the Azores, in the Atlantic, with various small islands in the Mediterranean.

TABLE OF ISLANDS.

Names.	*Sq. Ms.*	*Names.*	*Sq. Ms.*
Great Britain	84,700	Sardinia............	9,120
Ireland	32,000	Corsica.............	3,888
Iceland	40,000	Malta	188
Sicily	12,500	Candia.............	4,026

The rivers of Europe are inferior to those of America. The largest is the Volga, and the only one which reaches two thousand miles in length. The following embraces the principal:

TABLE OF RIVERS.

Names.	*Length.*	*Names.*	*Length.*
Volga, Russia........	2,000	Rhone, France	540
Danube, Austria.....	1,680	Seine, do..........	480
Dneiper, Russia	1,050	Douro, Spain	450
Don, do........	860	Po, Italy.............	380
Rhine, Germany.....	830	Thames, England.....	240
Vistula...............	650	Shannon, Ireland.....	220
Loire, France........	620	Tiber, Italy	210

The following embraces the principal lakes:

TABLE OF LAKES.

Names.	*Sq. Ms.*	*Names.*	*Sq. Ms.*
Ladoga, Russia	6,350	Leman, or L. of Geneva	380
Onega, do.......	2,300	Maggiore, Italy.......	150
Wener, Sweden	2,150	Neufchatel, Switzerl'd.	115

The precious metals are not found in large quantities in Europe. The more useful minerals, however, abound, as coal, iron, lead, tin, copper, and salt. In some parts mercury and quicksilver are met with; in the Ural Mountains, gold, silver, and platina are obtained.

The climate of Europe is affected by various circumstances, rendering some parts more temperate, and others colder or warmer than might be expected from their latitude. The eastern portion of Europe, including two-thirds of Russia in Europe, is rendered colder by the winds which sweep over it, chilled by the immense masses of snow and ice embosomed in the mountains of Central Asia. The southern parts of Europe are rendered warmer by the hot winds which visit them from the burning deserts and plains of Africa. The extremes both of heat and cold are diminished in those countries which border upon the Atlantic by the constant action of the sea-air. These appear to be the three great causes which modify the climate of Europe, and render it so different in some parts from what it is in others of the same latitude, and so different from the climate of those portions of America which lie in the same parallels.

There is another fact to be taken into consideration, in comparing the climate of the Atlantic part of Europe with that of the Atlantic part of North America. In Greenland, and the adjacent regions, there are immense masses of snow and ice, which accumulate from year to year, or are broken up, in the form of icebergs, sometimes reaching the tropics before they are melted. On the contrary, along the borders of Europe, such accumulations do not take place. The gulfs of Norway are almost always open, while the coast of Greenland, exactly opposite, is frequently rendered inaccessible, from fixed or floating barriers of ice.

These considerations will be sufficient to account for most of the contrasts, which we observe between our own climate and that of the Atlantic parts of Europe. The climate of England, being surrounded by the sea, is rendered by the sea air much more temperate. The winters in that country are less extreme than those of the southern parts of New England. Newfoundland, also, surrounded by the sea, and further south than England, swept by the winds which come from the icy regions of the north, and the adjacent countries, experiences a winter so intense, as almost to render it uninhabitable. Spain, Italy, and Turkey in Europe, illustrate the influence of the warm winds of Africa. Situated in the latitude of Massachusetts and New York, they produce oranges, lemons, figs, and grapes, which, in our country, are the products of regions at least twelve degrees further south.

The American, in turning from the natural to the artificial features of Europe, discovers certain marked and prominent peculiarities. In the first place, the number of populous cities is much greater in Europe than in America; and in these there is a greater display of public buildings. The pride or policy of most of the European princes has led them to establish in their cities, universities, hospitals, museums, libraries, and other institutions, the buildings for which are usually magnificent. The churches, being generally built by the aid of the governments, are numerous, and many of them costly. Besides these, in the great capitals, as London, Paris, and others, there are usually splendid palaces, occupied by the royal family. Most of these towns are embellished with parks or gardens, which are laid out with walks, ornamented with trees, and refreshed with fountains. Many of the great cities on the continent are surrounded by walls, which are employed for defence in time of war, and the gates, by which they are entered, being under the direction of the government, render it easy

The Four-horned Sheep.

The Ibex

The Marten.

Common Lizard.

Adder.

Leech.

to watch and control the people in time of peace.

One of the most remarkable distinctions between our own and European countries, is the union in the latter of civil with religious matters. For the purpose of increasing their power, the sovereigns usually establish some particular form of worship, the ministers of which are directly or indirectly paid by the crown. Thus dependent, these ministers necessarily become attached to the cause of their sovereign, and are thus his sure and zealous supporters. Possessing a powerful influence over the minds of the people, through the dignity of their office, their general intelligence, and the nature of their intercourse with them, they become the most efficient pillars of the government, which it is their supposed duty and certain interest to sustain. It is this powerful combination of the Church and the State, that has enabled the despotic rulers of Europe so long to keep their subjects imprisoned in monarchical institutions.

The natural history of a country is important to be known, and to be kept in view, as it throws light upon its climate, and frequently enters into the manners and customs of nations. The chase of the wild-boar is one of the sports of France and Germany; that of the chamois, occupies the hunter of Switzerland; the Savoyard boy often wanders over Southern Europe, with no other companion, and no other stock in trade than a marmot. The abundance of fish along the seacoasts of Europe, gives occupation to a large number of people in these regions. The most remarkable fact, however, in regard to the animal kingdom of Europe is, that nearly all the domestic animals are of foreign origin. The horse is from Asia, the ass and mule from Asia or Africa. The domestic cattle are probably from the original wild bull of Europe; sheep are doubtless from eastern breeds; the cock is from India, the pheasant from Asia Minor, the turkey from America. These facts indicate that enterprise in the inhabitants of Europe which has led them to make all other parts of the world tributary to their wants. The progress of civilization has also had an influence in extirpating some of the larger and more formidable wild animals of Europe, as the lion and tiger, which were doubtless natives of that country, ages ago.

The Animal Kingdom. There is considerable resemblance between the animals of Northern Europe and Northern Asia: in the southern portion of the latter, however, there are several remarkable specimens not now to be found in Europe; such as the lion, tiger, elephant, rhinoceros, &c.

The aurochs, or wild-bull, which was anciently spread over Europe, is now chiefly confined to the forests of Poland; the moufflon, which partakes of the qualities of the deer and the goat, is found in parts of Greece, and in the islands of Sardinia and Corsica. The ibex, a species of goat, is very timid, and is approached by the hunters with difficulty. It is met with in the high Alps, and also in the island of Candia. The chamois is common in Switzerland, and the pursuit of it is one of the peculiar sports of that country. It is also found in other parts of Europe.

The elk, resembling our moose, as well as the reindeer, is found in the north; the stag and red deer are met with in the forests of Middle and Northern Europe; the fallow-deer is more extensively distributed. The roebuck is met with in the Highlands of Scotland, and some other mountainous portions of Europe.

The wild-boar is the original of our common swine, and is found in France, Germany, Italy, Spain, and other parts; the lynx, wild-cat, weasel, stoat, pine-weasel, marten, sable, pole-cat, badger, glutton, are all more or less common.

The brown bear, always savage and solitary, is widely diffused; the black bear and the white bear are confined to the more northern regions; several species of foxes are met with; the wolf is common in France, and other continental countries, but has been extirpated in the British Isles. The jackal, a creature hunting in packs, and uttering a doleful cry, is found in Greece. The hare and the rabbit are widely distributed.

Squirrels are of various kinds, and in most parts are numerous. The marmot is found in Poland and the Alps; the hamster in parts of Germany and Poland; the souslik, beaver, hedgehog, otter, and other small quadrupeds, are found in various localities.

Birds in general are less restricted to particular regions than quadrupeds, and most of those of Europe are, therefore, common to the other continents of the eastern hemisphere, and a few even to the western hemisphere. Many species of eagles, vultures, hawks, owls, and other nocturnal and diurnal birds of prey, abound, but chiefly in mountainous or wooded regions. The lammergeir is a large species of vulture found in the Alps. The falcon, a species of hawk, was formerly trained to pursue game. The various species of lark, thrush, and warbler are distinguished for their song; to the latter belongs the nightingale. Of the gallinaceous birds there are several valuable species, such as the grouse, including the black-cock, the moor-hen, and the ptarmigan, the pheasant, the partridge, quail, &c. The great bustard is one of the largest of the European land birds, measuring four feet in length; it has, however, become very rare. The crane and the stork are common; the latter breeds chiefly in cities, where its presence is considered desirable; it may be seen unmolested in the streets and upon the houses, and is serviceable as a scavenger. The ortolan is a little bird, highly esteemed as a luxury. The water fowls are various and numerous. The domestic fowls are the same as in this country.

The reptiles and insects are not so numerous as in the other quarters of the globe. The adder is one of the most poisonous of the serpents; the lizards are harmless and of small size. The leech abounds in the south, and is made an article of commerce.

Eagle.

Falc n.

Partridges.

Races of Men. To trace and define the original races of mankind, as we do those of the inferior animals, is everywhere difficult, in consequence of the nice shades of distinction which prevail among some of those which approach nearest to each other. But this difficulty is greater in Europe than in any other quarter of the globe, because of the mixture of races, which has taken place here, through conquest, emigration, and other circumstances. The multiplicity of languages, which existed here in former times—seventy, for instance, in France alone—attest this diversity. The great mass of the population, however, evidently belong to the Caucasian race; but this is so broken into varieties and shades of varieties, as to present a subject of great perplexity if we attempt to go beyond a very general classification. The following brief summary will be sufficient for the purpose of this preliminary sketch.

The inhabitants of Europe belong to twenty different races; but five of these comprise the great bulk of the population. 1. The *German* or *Teutonic* race comprises the Germans, Dutch, Danes, Swedes, Norwegians, English, and a part of the Swiss: these people speak Teutonic dialects. 2. The *Greco-Latin* race comprises the Greeks, Albanians, Wallachians, Italians, French, Spaniards, and Portuguese, with a part of the Swiss. 3. The *Sclavonic* race embraces the Russians, Poles, Lithuanians, Bohemians, Servians, Bosnians, Dalmatians, Bulgarians, with the Wends of Prussia, the Sorbians of Prussia and Saxony, the Lettes of Russia, &c. These three races are the most numerous. 4. To the Uralian or *Finnic* race belong the Finns, Laplanders, Esthonians, Magyars or Hungarians, and some smaller tribes in Russia. 5. The *Turkish* race comprises the Ottoman Turks or ruling people of Turkey, the Turcomans of the same empire, and several tribes often called *Tartars* in Russia.

Beside these principal races are the Biscayans of Spain; the Celts, comprising the Highlanders of Scotland, the native Irish, the Welsh, and the Bretons of Western France; the Samoides; the Mongols, of whom the only tribe are the Kalmucks of Russia; Jews; Armenians; Gypsies, &c. The Gypsies, called *Bohemians* in France, *Gitanos* in Spain, and *Zigeuner* in Germany, are a roving tribe, supposed to be originally from Hindostan; they are scattered all over Europe, and their number is estimated at from six to eight hundred thousand. They live sometimes in tents, often in caves, or in huts half under ground, and covered with sods. They rarely pursue any regular trade, but are often jugglers, fortune-tellers, &c. They have a peculiar language, but no religion. In Spain, many of them have become settled people.

There are three great monotheistical systems of religious belief predominant in Europe, viz.: I. CHRISTIANITY, of which the principal seat and centre, though not its birthplace, is Europe. The Christian nations in Europe are divided into three leading sects, viz.: 1. The *Greek Catholic*, or Eastern church, which prevails in Greece, part of Albania and Bulgaria, in Servia, Sclavonia, Croatia, Wallachia, Moldavia, Russia, &c. 2. The Latin, or *Roman Catholic* church, of which the pope, one of the sovereign powers of Europe, is the head. This creed is predominant in Italy, Spain, Portugal, France, Austria, the half of Germany and of Switzerland, Belgium, Poland, and Ireland, and numbers some adherents in Great Britain, Holland, and Turkey. 3. The *Protestant church*, which predominates, under different creeds, in Denmark, Sweden, Norway, Great Britain, Prussia, a part of Germany and of Switzerland. This faith has also numerous professors in Hungary, Transylvania, and France. Its principal branches are the Lutheran, the Presbyterian or Reformed, and the Episcopalian churches.

II. MAHOMETANISM, or Islamism, is professed by the Turks. III. The Mosaic or Jewish religion. There are about two millions five hundred thousand Jews scattered throughout Europe. They are not tolerated in Spain, Portugal, and Norway. In the Austrian states they have few privileges. In Russia the laws relating to them have recently become very intolerant. In the states of the German confederation, in France, Prussia, and the Low Countries, they enjoy the rights of citizens, and, in Poland, they are eligible to public employments. The Kalmucks and many of the Samoides are pagans.

In almost every European state we find the citizens divided into four distinct classes. The first is that of the nobility, which exists in nearly every state, with the exception of France, Norway, and the Turkish empire. Nobility is, in most cases, viewed in Europe as a hereditary rank; but it can be acquired by the will of the sovereign, and, in some instances, purchased by money. The clergy form the second class of the community. The third is that of the citizens, or inhabitants of towns, which, in most countries, enjoys peculiar rights and privileges. The fourth and lowest class includes the peasants, and forms the mass of the population in every country. These distinctions have been much modified within the last twenty years, and changes, tending to greater equality, are constantly taking place.

With the exception of the Kalmucks, Nogays, Laponians, and Samoides, in Russia, who yet lead the life of herdsmen or hunters, all the nations of Europe have been permanently settled for many centuries. The cultivation of the soil has, therefore, been carried to great perfection in this part of the earth. Husbandry is pursued with the greatest industry in the British empire, the Netherlands, Belgium, Switzerland, Germany, some parts of Italy, Denmark, and Sweden. The agriculture of the east of England and Scotland, the Netherlands, Belgium, Germany, and the northern parts of France and Italy, is most distinguished; although Russia, Hungary, and Poland, whose agriculture is not nearly so advanced, are the granaries of Europe. The raising of cattle is, in some countries, pursued only in connection with agriculture; in the mountainous districts alone it forms the principal branch of rural industry.

The cultivation of fruits belongs to the temperate districts, particularly France and Germany; but the finer fruits can only be extensively reared in the southern parts of Europe. The manufacture of wine is most considerable in France, the south of Germany, Hungary, Spain, Portugal, Italy, and the Turkish empire. The finest kinds are produced in Hungary, near Tokay; in Champagne, and Burgundy, upon the banks of the Rhine, Rhone, Moselle, and Garonne; in Spain, the Two Sicilies, the banks of the Upper Douro, and some islands of the Ægean Sea. The olive belongs to the warmer regions, particularly Naples, Greece, and Spain; other vegetable oils are produced in the temperate parts of Europe. The breeding of silkworms is also peculiar to warmer climates, and is chiefly carried on in Lombardy. The cultivation of forests has been greatly neglected in most countries, and in many, a want of wood begins to be felt, although Europe is, on the whole, well stocked with wood.

The fisheries are important to the coast nations of Europe, who take herrings, tunnies, anchovies, mackerels, and other fish, from the surrounding seas. Hunting forms a principal occupation only of a few small tribes in Russia. Mining is conducted with great skill in England, Germany, Hungary, and Sweden. The river fisheries are also important.

European industry is rivalled by no other part of the world, either in the diversity or the extent of its productions, although the Japanese and Chinese have cultivated some branches of art for many thousand years. Europe not only manufactures its own raw produce, but also that of almost every other region of the earth. The principal seats of European industry are Great Britain, the Netherlands, Belgium, France, Germany, and Switzerland. The best woollen fabrics are made in England and France; cotton in England, Saxony, and France; linen in Germany; lace in Brabant; silks in France; paper in Holland and Switzerland; leather in Turkey and Russia; china in Germany; earthen-ware in England and France; glass in Bohemia and England; hardware in England; straw hats in Italy; and jewelry work in France, Germany, and England.

The internal commerce of Europe is carried on in all countries with considerable animation, and is facilitated by well-constructed high roads, canals, and railroads, which are particularly good in the British empire, the Netherlands, Belgium, France, Lombardy, Prussia, and Russia. The British, French, Danes, Dutch, and Swedes are most distinguished in commercial navigation. But no nation can in this respect be compared with Great Britain, whose fleets are in every sea, and colonies in almost every region of the earth. As a medium of exchange, all European states coin money. Many states likewise support a paper-currency, the value of which is maintained by public credit.

The following table shows the political divisions of Europe, with the principal cities, and their population:—

POLITICAL DIVISIONS.

Principal Countries.	*Square miles.*	*Population.* 1862.	*Pop. s. m.*	*Religion.*	*Capitals.*	*Population.* 1862.
Nor'n Europe.						
Denmark........	21,615	2,605,024	124	Protest.	Copenhagen...	155,143
Sweden and Norway... ..	292,104	5,290,622	18	..do ...	Stockholm....	112,391
Russia..........	2,041,000	65,810,752	32	Greek...	St. Petersburg.	520,131
Cent'l Europe.						
G. Britain and Ireland......	122,150	29,307,199	252	Pr. & Ca	London	2,803,034
Holland	11,470	3,569,456	324	Protest.	Hague	81,893
Belgium	12,569	4,731,957	393	Catholic	Brussels......	174,829
France..........	207,252	37,472,732	180	..do....	Paris.........	1,696,141
Switzerland......	17,208	2,510,494	148	Pr. & Ca	Berne	29,016
Austrian Emp...	255,000	35,019,058	137	Catholic	Vienna	476,222
Prussian Kingd..	106,000	18,500,446	174	Protest.	Berlin........	547,571
Germany excl. of Austria & Prussia......	98,104	17,308,643	168	Pr. & Ca	Frankfort	71,452
South Europe.						
Spain...........	176,480	16,560,813	95	Catholic	Madrid.......	475,785
Portugal.........	34,500	3,923,410	115	..do....	Lisbon.......	275,286
Italy, exclusive of Austrian States.......	100,879	22,610,269	226	..do....	Rome	194,587
Greece	16,000	1,096,810	68	Greek..	Athens.......	41,298
Turkey..........	153,140	15,500,000	85	Mahom	Const'ntinople	700,000

The following table may be found convenient for reference:—

DISTANCES FROM LONDON.

Names.	*Miles.*	*Names.*	*Miles*
Paris, ...	225	Rome, ...	800
Amsterdam, ...	240	Madrid, ...	700
Copenhagen,...........	600	Athens, ...	1500
St. Petersburg,.........	1140	Constantinople, ...	1700
Vienna, ...	660	Berne,.................	650

As an illustration of the influence of physical circumstances in determining the fortune of nations, we may properly direct the attention of the reader to the position of Europe in respect to the Mediterranean Sea. The length of this is about two thousand miles; but the winding coast on the European side measures at least twice that distance. Three peninsulas — those of Greece, Italy, and Spain — project wholly or in part into this sea, and upon these were the first seats of European civilization. The whole border of the Mediterranean is historical ground. Nearly every promontory, cape, headland, island, and bay, within its circuit, has been the site of some renowned city, or is associated with memorable events in the annals of mankind. It would be easy to trace the career of Phœnicia in Asia, of Carthage in Africa, of Greece and Rome in Europe, to their maritime position, and to show how the facilities afforded to early commerce by the Mediterranean, rendered its borders, for two thousand years, the great centre of the world's civilization. In comparing the coasts of Africa with those of Europe, as displayed upon a map, we are struck with the remarkable difference. Those of the former have an even outline, with few projections or indentations: we see a solid mass of land, intersected by no great bays, or seas, or navigable rivers; and hence Africa, affording little facility to navigation, remains either an unknown land, or is occupied by agricultural and nomadic races, who continue, from age to age, in barbaric darkness. Europe, on the contrary, is edged by a coast presenting a succession of capes, bays, headlands, inlets, and islands, inviting the people to commerce, which is the great source of enterprise, knowledge, and improvement. It is reasonable to assign a portion of national character to races, and a portion, also, to climate; but position, in relation to the sea, has an influence upon nations, even more transforming than these. Had the negroes been planted in Greece, they might have led the world in arts and arms; had the Greeks been confined to Nigritia, they would doubtless have continued, from age to age, mere nomads. Since the first empires sprung up in the valleys of the Euphrates and the Nile, no nation of mere agriculturists has become permanently enlightened, refined, or powerful. The plough, the spade, and the mattock teach the mind but little: human nature dwindles, when it is absorbed in mere tillage of the soil. The merchant, who visits various countries, has his mind enlarged, and his enterprise quickened; the mariner, stimulated by difficulty, and roused by danger, has his faculties sharpened, his courage elevated, and his resources, mental and physical, indefinitely multiplied. Under the influence of these, every kind of productive skill is fostered; and thus a civilized state which consists in the diffusion of diversified arts and varied knowledge in the community, is attained. It is a mistake, then, manifest from the example of Europe to consider agriculture as the chief source of human progress. The land feeds mankind, but the sea has civilized them. Agricultural nations may be productive, but commercial countries will govern them: the first may live, but the countries combining the two will

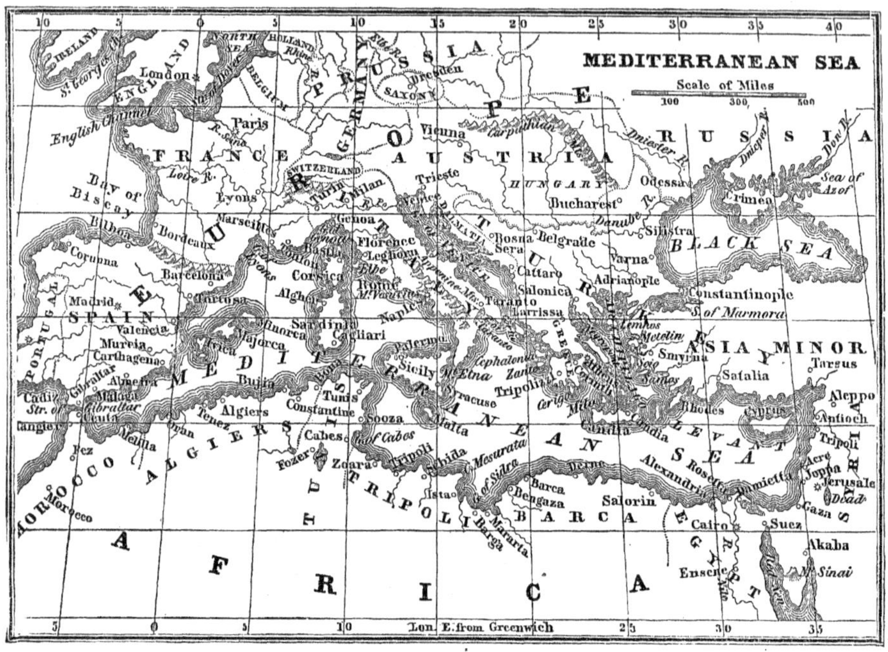

be rich, intelligent, enterprising, and powerful. Europe, a maritime country, and little favorable to agriculture, is the centre of wealth, power, and intelligence — making the old world tributary to it, and, in fact, controlling almost the entire products of the eastern hemisphere; while the vast interior plateaus of Asia and Africa, formed for agriculture alone, continue as they were three thousand years ago — the domain of barbarians, without towns, cities, books, or permanent institutions.

Such is a brief view of the modern geography of Europe; the details of its ancient geography will best be exhibited as we treat successively of the several countries. It may be remarked, that the geographical names, which were used in ancient times, are, for the most part, in use at the present day, especially those which were applied to countries, as the following table will show: —

Ancient Names.	*Modern Names.*
Greece,	Greece.
Italy,	Italy.
Hispania,	Spain and Portugal.
Gaul,	France.
Britain,	Britain.
Hibernia,	Ireland.
Caledonia,	Scotland.
Germany,	Germany.
Helvetia,	Switzerland.
Sarmatia,	Poland and part of Russia.
Scandinavia,	Norway, Sweden and Denmark.
Flanders,	Belgium.
Batavia,	Holland.
Sicily,	Sicily.

We have here given the English names, but most of them are derived from the Romans, who used the Latin language. The difference between the English and Latin names was often only in the termination; as, *Britannia*, for *Britain*; *Grecia*, for *Greece*, &c. The ancient Latin or Greek names are called *classical.*

The following is the order in which the several topics of European history will be presented: —

1. Greece, Ancient and Modern. 2. Ancient Rome. 3. Modern Italy. 4. The Greek Empire. 5. Ragusa. 6. Turkey in Europe. 7. Spain. 8. Portugal. 9. France. 10. Great Britain. 11. Germany. 12. Austria. 13. Prussia. 14. Smaller German States. 15. Switzerland. 16. Holland. 17. Belgium. 18. Denmark. 19. Sweden. 20. Norway. 21. Lapland. 22. Finland. 23. Russia. 24. Poland. 25. Hungary.

CHAPTER CCCXII.

Historical Sketch of Europe.

THE name of Europe is supposed to be derived from *Europa*, the daughter of an ancient king of Tyre; but in what particular manner, does not appear. Though by far the smallest of the four quarters of the globe, and the last portion of the old world to be settled, it is manifest, from the preceding sketch, that it is the first in respect to the intelligence, skill, wealth, and power of its inhabitants. It has, indeed, long been the seat and centre of civilization, from which light and knowledge have radiated over the world. At no period of human history has any country displayed such progress in the arts, such advances in science such diffusion of knowledge, as are now witnessed among the leading nations of Europe.

Asia being the nursery of mankind, Europe, as well

as Africa, received its first inhabitants from that quarter. But the history of the original settlements in Europe must ever remain shrouded in obscurity. About two thousand years before Christ, certain bands of emigrants, from the Asiatic borders of the Mediterranean Sea, began to visit Greece, which they found already occupied by various tribes of savages. These were called *Pelasgians*, and lived in caves, fed upon roots and wild fruit, and clothed themselves in the skins of wild beasts.

About 763 B. C., we are told that Romulus founded Rome, in the centre of Italy; but already the country around was occupied by various tribes, and one of these, the *Etruscans*, who possessed the territory now called *Tuscany*, had made considerable progress in civilization. About eight centuries previous to the Christian era, the Carthaginians had colonies in Spain, and were accustomed to visit Britain and Ireland, all of which countries were peopled at that early period.

In the days of Julius Cæsar, sixty years before Christ, not only the portions of Europe which lay along the Mediterranean Sea, but the central and northern sections, were thickly inhabited. Gaul was in the possession of a great and powerful nation, consisting of Celts, who presented a most formidable opposition to the great Roman leader. For nine campaigns they resisted his legions; and it was not till more than a million of men had fallen, that they yielded to the conqueror. At this period, it appears that the whole of Europe was peopled, and many portions of it seem to have been swarming with inhabitants.

From this hasty view, we are able to trace the general current of events in relation to the first settlement of Europe. It would appear that, at least two thousand years before Christ, portions of emigrants began to set off from the thickly-settled coasts of Asia Minor and Africa, to seek their fortunes in the yet unexplored regions which lay along the northern border of the Mediterranean Sea. These parties went by water, and, at first, in small boats, or vessels; and consisted, doubtless, of the restless, dissatisfied, and daring portion of the community. In all its essential features, it is probable that the emigration of this period resembled that of our own time — in which the hardy and resolute adventurers plunge into the wilderness, to contend with difficulties, and conquer a subsistence from the savage inhabitants, and equally inhospitable nature, in a new country. As these parties started from different points, and consisted of different races, they laid the foundation of so many different tribes, which, as they extended, and began to approach each other, fell into frequent acts of hostility; for it seems that man, in the early stages of society, is the most pugnacious of animals.

Thus it would appear, that the southern maritime parts of Europe were settled by emigration from the civilized portions of Asia and Africa, lying at the eastern extremity of the Mediterranean Sea; that these emigrants went chiefly by water, and carried with them the arts known to the countries from which they sprung; and that this movement had begun at least as early as one thousand eight hundred and fifty years before Christ.

But while this process was going on, another stream of emigration was setting in from Asia, upon Europe, farther to the north. This consisted of various tribes, who either passed between the Caspian and Black Seas, and crossed the Don, or, taking a more northerly route, crossed the Volga. The general direction of this movement was to the north-west. The countries from which these people came, were probably Scythia or Tartary, and the regions round the Caucasian Mountains.

The southern nations of Europe, such as the Greeks and Romans, settled down in cities, and cultivated the arts; they had a knowledge of letters, and had thus the means of recording events. Of these we have, therefore, some accounts, and are able to trace the main current of history far back, till it blends in the distance with the mists of fable. With the northern nations, it is otherwise. These were entirely in a savage or barbarous state; for centuries they had no permanent abodes. They flowed onward like an inundation — wave following wave, but leaving no record behind. After the lapse of centuries, we find the whole country occupied, even to the remotest limit of Britain; we see that the great valley of the north is insufficient for the flood of population, and that it even bursts over the Alps, and flows over like lava upon the plains of Northern Italy. From these facts, we can deduce inferences, and in the absence of precise records, the imagination can aid us to fill up the mighty picture. We can see, that for ages there was a constant outpouring of nations from Asia upon Europe; we can see that these were restless, roving tribes, half herdsmen and half robbers; living partly by plunder, and partly by the pasturage of cattle; till, at last, one by one, they fixed upon some favored spot, and became a settled people. So much we know; and though we cannot give name and place to particular events, it requires no stretch of fancy to conclude, that this is the history of the first settlement of Middle and Northern Europe. When Cæsar, about sixty years before Christ, crossed the Alps, and began his campaigns in Gaul, he kept a record of what he saw. From that period, we have a continuous history of leading events; but for the two thousand years preceding, during which these portions of Europe were becoming settled, we have hardly any other guide than inference or conjecture.

The emigration into Middle and Northern Europe appears to have continued for a series of ages; and it is probable that, in some instances, whole nations, amounting to hundreds of thousands, broke from their foundations, moving in one overwhelming torrent to the north and west, in search of a new abode. Among these emigrant people, the Celts appear to have been one of the most numerous and ancient. At the earliest periods of history, they already occupied a great part of Central and Western Europe. Prior to the Christian era, these people, under the name of *Gauls*, had possessed Northern Italy; and in the year 389 B. C., a host of them burst over the Alps, and directing their way to Rome, laid that city in ashes. A vast multitude of these people invaded Macedonia and Greece, where they obtained immense booty.

It would appear that the power of the Gauls in Europe was on the decline, even before the time of Cæsar's conquest. They were pressed by enemies on all sides, and, though still numerous and formidable, had evidently lost that ascendency which they had maintained for many centuries before. At this period, they occupied the northern part of Italy, Spain, France, Britain, and Ireland; and the present inhabitants of these several countries have a mixture of Celtic blood in their veins. Their language is still preserved, with considerable purity, among the Irish, who are, in fact, a Celtic nation. Ireland had the singular fortune never to be conquered by Rome, nor indeed by any of the tribes that overran the northern portions of Europe. The Irish, therefore, are the oldest nation in Europe, and present to us not only the language of their Celtic ancestors, but, perhaps, an example of their physical and moral characteristics.

The Celts, or Gauls, as described by Cæsar, were men of large size, fair complexion, reddish hair, and fierce aspect. They could bear cold and rain, but neither heat nor thirst; they were vain and boastful, clamorous and impatient of control, and quarrelsome among themselves. Their first onset was formidable; but if once repulsed, they easily gave way and dispersed. Their swords were long and unwieldy, and being made of copper, bent before the steel armor of the Romans. They fought naked down to the waist. Their shields were large and oblong, but slight and ill contrived for protection.

Their government was aristocratic. The nobles formed the senate, or supreme council. The common people appear to have had no political rights, and were in a state of vassalage. The Druids were the priests, and formed a powerful hierarchy. They were interpreters of the law, and judges in civil and criminal matters. Their sacerdotal character was hereditary, though young men of noble families were occasionally adopted into the order.

The Germanic family, though divided into several branches, formed one of the mighty waves of population which poured forth upon Europe from the western portions of Asia. These spread themselves to the north, and occupied Germany, Denmark, Sweden and Norway, and a part of Russia and Poland. In the latter regions, they met with Tartars from Asiatic Scythia, and the mixture of these races produced the Sclavonic nations.

The decline of the Roman power, in the fourth and fifth centuries, tempted the northern tribes from their cold and less fertile regions, and they rushed down like an avalanche, overspreading the countries which lay before them. The Danes and Saxons seized upon England, and various other tribes obtained a footing in France, Spain, Italy, Greece, and Carthage. The present language of Germany, England, Holland, Denmark, and Sweden has a basis derived from the great Germanic stock. The language of France, Spain, and Italy has a basis derived from the Latin tongue.

Robust forms, light hair, blue eyes, florid complexion, and large, broad-fronted heads constitute the chief physical characteristics of the pure Germanic family; while morally and intellectually, they stand preëminent above all the other tribes of mankind. They are conspicuous, in particular, for what may be called the *industrial virtues*, exhibiting a degree of indomitable perseverance in all improving pursuits, which has rendered them the great inventors of the human race. The mixture of German and Tartar blood in the north-eastern nations of Europe, has given to these darker hair and complexions than the pure Germans, and has also lessened their propensity to intellectual cultivation. The effects of the Tartar conquest of Russia, in the twelfth century, by Zingis Khan, whose successors held the country for two hundred years, will probably be observable in the career of this people for ages to come, and, indeed, perhaps as long as the race exists.

The history of Europe may be divided into three periods—*Ancient History*, the *Middle Ages*, and *Modern History*. The first of these periods begins with the settlement of Inachus in Greece, in the year 1856 B. C., and ends with the fall of Rome in the year 476 A. D. During this period, none of the present kingdoms of Europe were founded, and the whole space is occupied with the history of Greece and Rome, embracing, however, many countries which formed dependencies of the latter.

The middle or dark ages, extending from the fall of Rome to the year 1400, comprise a long and remarkable period in the history of the human race, and exhibit many wonderful phenomena of human nature. It was during this period that most of the present kingdoms of Europe had their foundation; it was during this period that the feudal system took its rise, that the crusades ran their wild career, that the troubadours sung their lays of love and war, and that the fantastic institution of chivalry, with most of the orders of knighthood, had their beginning and end. It

Knight Errant.

was during this period, also, for the most part, that Christianity was disseminated throughout Europe, that the present languages of Europe were formed, and that a commingling of races took place, which seemed indispensable to a high and permanent civilization. We may refer to this period, also, for the germs of many of the arts and institutions, which contribute to the present improved condition of mankind.

The recorded history of the middle ages is occupied chiefly with the doings of kings, princes, and potentates. We hear little of the common people, but their slaughter in war. They were, indeed, regarded but as ingenious animals, made to serve the privileged classes to live, suffer, or perish, as might serve the interest pleasure, or caprice of their masters. As they had no political rights, so they had few domestic comforts. They had, in their mud dwellings, no chairs or chimneys; a heap of straw served for a bed, and a billet of wood was the only pillow. The houses of the rich, at this period, afforded, indeed, a striking contrast to those of the present day. Few of them contained more than four beds. The walls, which were of stone, were generally bare, without wainscot, or even plaster. In a few instances, they were decorated with hangings.

In the twelfth century, a large proportion of England was stagnating with bog, or darkened by native forests, where the wild ox, the roe, the stag, and the wolf, had hardly learned the supremacy of man. The culture of land was so imperfect, that nine or ten bushels of corn to the acre was an average crop. The average annual rent of an acre of land was from sixpence to a shilling. In the reign of Edward I., (1272,) a quarter of wheat was sold for four shillings sterling. The price of a sheep was a shilling, that of an ox ten shillings. It appears that in **1301**, a set of carpenter's tools was sold for one shilling.

At this period, the living of even the highest nobility of England afforded a striking contrast to that of their luxurious descendants. They drank little wine, which was then sold only by the apothecaries. They rarely kept male servants, except for husbandry, and still more rarely travelled beyond their native country. An income of ten or twenty pounds was reckoned a competent estate for a gentleman; at least, the lord of a single manor seldom enjoyed more. A knight who possessed one hundred and fifty pounds a year, passed for extremely rich. Sir John Fortescue speaks of five pounds a year as "a fair living for a yeoman;" and we read that the same sum served for the annual expenses of a scholar attending the university. Modern lawyers must be surprised at the following, which Mr. Hallam extracts from the churchwarden's accounts of St. Margaret, Westminster, for **1476**, "Also, paid to Roger Fylpot, learned in the law, for his counsel-giving, three shillings eight pence, with four-pence for his dinner."

In an inventory of the goods of "John Poet, late the king's servant," who died about **1524**, we find that this gentleman's house consisted of a hall, parlor, buttery, and kitchen, with five bedsteads, two chambers, three garrets, and some minor accommodations. From this, it may be inferred that Mr. Poet was rather an important man in his day, for very few individuals at that time could boast of such accommodations.

Notwithstanding these aspects of the middle ages, we shall still find in their history many topics which strongly excite the imagination; hence, as we know, it is the favorite era of poetry and romance. We shall have occasion to give more ample details upon this and other topics, here only glanced at in order to prepare the reader for our sketches of the several countries which follow our general views of Europe.

We may consider the middle ages as extending to the beginning of the fifteenth century. From this period, we can trace a series of remarkable events, all tending to aid in that sunrise of civilization which followed the dark ages. The use of gunpowder in projecting heavy bodies is said to have been discovered by Berthold Schwartz, a monk of Mayence, about the year **1300**. It was not much used for military purposes till **1350**; and indeed, it was not generally adopted till near a century after. Its ultimate effect has been to modify the art of war; to render it more dependent on science and intellectual combinations, and less a conflict of animal strength and courage. It has sunk the mere hero of muscle into insignificance, and given ascendency to the leader who combines intellect with skill. It has, at the same time, served to render wars less bloody, and has given opportunity to soften, with certain amenities, even the harsh and revolting aspect of the field of battle.

The invention of printing, about the year **1444**, by Guttenberg, also of Mayence, was the crowning art of modern times. Prior to this, all books were written with a pen. A copy of the Bible required four years of labor, even for an expert writer, and its value was equal to that of a house and farm. Few, indeed, could possess such a treasure. At the present time, a single day's labor of a common workman will purchase two copies of this sacred volume. In the production of books, Guttenberg's invention has increased the power of man probably five thousand fold. It now serves not only to record every passing event, every useful invention, every discovery in art and science, but it has also written down and multiplied, in a thousand forms, all that is left of the past history of mankind. Thus all human knowledge is placed upon record scattered over the four quarters of the globe, and rendered indestructible by any event less extensive than the devastation of the entire surface of the earth. Nor is even this all: knowledge, with its illuminating power, is diffused among all classes of men; it is every where shedding light upon the darkened minds of the mass; it is bursting open the doors of prisons, sundering the fetters of tyranny, spreading abroad the equalizing power of Christianity, and teaching even kings and princes to look upon their subjects as their fellow-men, with rights as sacred as their own, in the eye of reason and of God.

The revival of letters had commenced in the thirteenth century. Dante was born in **1265**, Petrarch in **1304**, and Boccaccio in **1313**. These shining lights were but forerunners of others that soon followed. The discovery or revival of Justinian's code of Roman law, in the twelfth century, served to modify the barbarism of the middle ages, and to make preparation for the dawn of a brighter era. The invention of the mariner's compass, though the date of it is lost in obscurity, was applied to maritime purposes about the year **1403**; and the enlargement of navigation, and the discovery of America, in **1492**, were the important consequences.

During the middle ages, the head of the Romish church had acquired and exercised a powerful ascendency over the minds of all classes of men — simple and sage, the plebeian and the prince. However our present notions of religious liberty may be shocked at this dominion, we cannot deny that we owe much to the monks of this period. Whatever of Christian piety existed, was excited and cherished by them; copies of the sacred Scriptures were chiefly preserved and multiplied in the monasteries, and the remains of classical literature have been handed down to us through the same channel.

But the period at last arrived, when the temporal power of the pope was to receive a decisive check, and the church over which he presided was to undergo a fiery trial. Luther, a Saxon monk, began his attack in **1517**, and thus commenced that mighty movement which is known in history as the *Reformation.* The result of this was to strip the see of Rome of its claims to dominion in secular matters, and to diffuse among the people, at large, the consciousness of a right, before denied, to exercise their private judgment in religious concerns.

From this period, we can see a rapid advance in the march of civilization, and even amidst the violent agitations of society. In **1648**, Charles the First, of England, was brought to the block for the exercise of power which had been more harshly employed, without opposition, by his predecessors. In **1789**, the first French revolution commenced, and a heavy reckoning was rendered for bygone years of tyranny, profligacy, and crime. The nineteenth century dawned upon a new era of improvement, such as the world had never seen: but the details of its history do not belong to this preliminary view.

Greece.

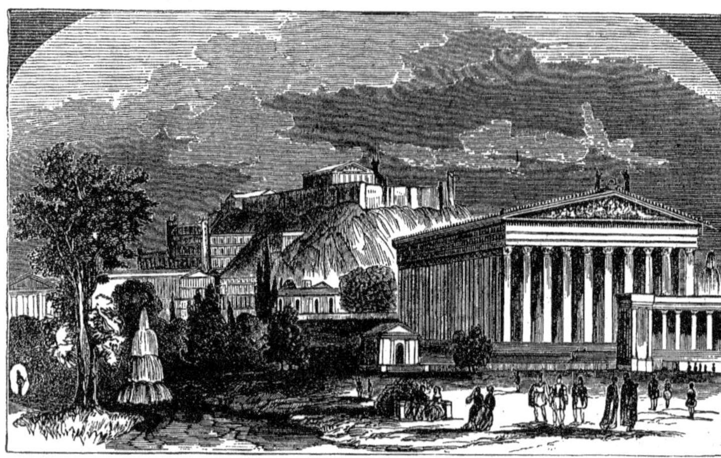

View of Athens Restored. The Temple of Jupiter.

CHAPTER CCCXIII.

Geographical Sketch — Ancient and Modern — Founding of the Grecian States — Early Historical Incidents.

We are now about to enter upon one of the most interesting and instructive portions of human knowledge — the history of Greece. This carries us back to a remote period of time, when mankind had but recently started in their career, and exhibits the spectacle of a people beginning in barbarism, and advancing through every stage of improvement, till they reached the highest degree of civilization which was known to antiquity.

The Greeks were a remarkable people, of a lively temper, and richly endowed with mental and personal advantages. At the same time, they occupied a country at once beautiful to the eye, and admirably suited to the development of genius such as they possessed. Their history, therefore, is the history of a favored portion of the human race, working out their destiny beneath the fairest skies, and amid the loveliest landscapes to be found on the earth.

Before we proceed with our account, it may be well to take a hasty retrospect of the state of the world at the period when our story begins. As we have seen, nearly two thousand years before the birth of Christ, the people of Assyria, Babylonia, and Egypt had advanced so far in improvement as to have established regular governments, built towns and cities, and possessed many of the elements of civilization. Letters, the great instrument of improvement, the key that first unlocked the human mind, were invented in Egypt; and here science had its birth and earliest development. Here, also, was the cradle of a multitude of arts, which afterwards passed into Greece, and have since come down to us beautified by hands that embellished whatever they touched. It was at this early period, about the time that Jacob migrated into Egypt, and when the Phœnicians were beginning their commercial career, that Grecian history commences As a preparation for this, we must glance at the ancient, as well as modern, geography of the country.

Greece is situated on the northern side of the Mediterranean. It consists of a peninsula projecting southward into the sea. This is about three hundred miles in length, but modern Greece occupies little more than two thirds of this territory. The present extent of the kingdom of Greece is about sixteen thousand square miles, or nearly twice as great as that of the state of Massachusetts. Its population is over one million; but little beyond that of the city of New York. The coasts are exceedingly irregular, and present a multitude of capes and bays, which, in all ages, have invited the people to maritime enterprises.

On the west is the Ionian Sea, in which are several islands, now forming the Ionian republic which is

Grecian Costumes.

under the protection of Great Britain. The names of these are as follows: —

Modern Names.	*Ancient Names.*	*Present Capitals.*
Corfu,	Corcyra,	Corfu.
Paxo,	Paxos,	Gago.
St. Maura,	Leucadia,	Santa Maura.
Theaki,	Ithaca,	Vathi.
Cephalonia,	Cephalonia,	Argostoli.
Zante,	Zacynthus,	Zante.
Cerigo,	Cytheria,	Moson.

East of Greece is the Ægean Sea, now called the Archipelago, and studded with numerous islands. Forty of these are deemed considerable. The following table exhibits the most important: —

Modern Names	*Ancient Names.*	*Present Capitals.*
Negropont,	Eubœa,	Negropont.
Stalaminè,	Lemnos.	
Hydra,	Hydrea,	Hydra.
Paros,	Paros.	
Antiparos,	Olearos.	
Naxia,	Naxos,	Naxos.
Delos,	Delos,	Delos.
Santorin,	Thera.	
Milo,	Melos.	
Argentera,	Cimolas.	
Salamis,	Salamis.	
Syra,	Syros.	
Andros,	Andros.	
Tine, or Tinos,	Tenos.	

To the south of Greece is Crete, now *Candia*, the largest island in the Mediterranean, and conspicuous in history. At present it is subject to Egypt. Along the coast of Asia Minor are Cyprus, Rhodes, Cos, Samos, Chios, &c.

Modern Names.	*Ancient Names.*	*Present Capitals.*
Tenedos,	Tenedos.	
Mitylene,	Lesbos.	
Chios,	Scio.	
Samos,	Samos.	
Patmos,	Palmo.	
Rhodes,	Rhodes.	
Cyprus,	Cyprus,	Cyprus.

All these, except Candia, properly belong to Asia, and their history has been already given with that of Asia Minor; it is, however, intimately connected with that of Greece.

This country is in the same latitude as Virginia, and its climate is similar, though somewhat warmer. It is exceedingly mountainous, and some of its peaks

Grecian Costumes.

are covered with perpetual snow. Yet the valleys and slopes are fertile, producing wheat, grapes, figs oranges, &c. Greece has ever been celebrated for the picturesque beauty of its landscapes, and its sublime mountains, fancied by the ancient inhabitants to be the abode of gods. Its valleys, assigned to the nymphs and naiads of the forest and the wave; its charming bays, its crystal rivers, and above all its heavenly atmosphere, robing every object in unwonted charms, combined to make it the chosen seat of poetry, and music, and art, in ancient times, and still render it an object of interest to the most indifferent observer.

Lord Byron, who visited the country in 1810, before the late revolution, seems to have been struck with the mingled aspect of loveliness and desolation which the country then presented. He compares it to a human form, from which life had just departed —

> "Before decay's effacing fingers
> Have swept the lines where beauty lingers;"

and he finally exclaims,

> "Sad is the aspect of this shore —
> 'Tis Greece, but living Greece no more!" *

The present inhabitants of this renowned country are, like their famous ancestors, swarthy in complexion, with black eyes and black hair. Taken together, they are an uncommonly beautiful race. They are quick-minded and sagacious; but having been long subjected to the despotic sway of the Turks, they had imbibed some of the vices which spring from a state of servitude.

In 1821, they rose in resistance to their masters, and after a bloody struggle of twelve years, they achieved their independence. The country was erected into a kingdom, and Otho, a German prince, became its chief ruler. Athens, the most renowned city of ancient Greece, is the present capital.

Ancient Greece, in its widest extent, embraced not

* It would appear that Byron's imagination derived from his visit to Greece some of those fine associations which give to his poetry such richness and depth: at the same time, it is not impossible that his stirring appeals to the heroic days and deeds of their ancestors may have contributed to waken that spirit in the modern Greeks which has resulted in their independence. The following is one of the many glowing passages in which he recalls the past glories of their ances-

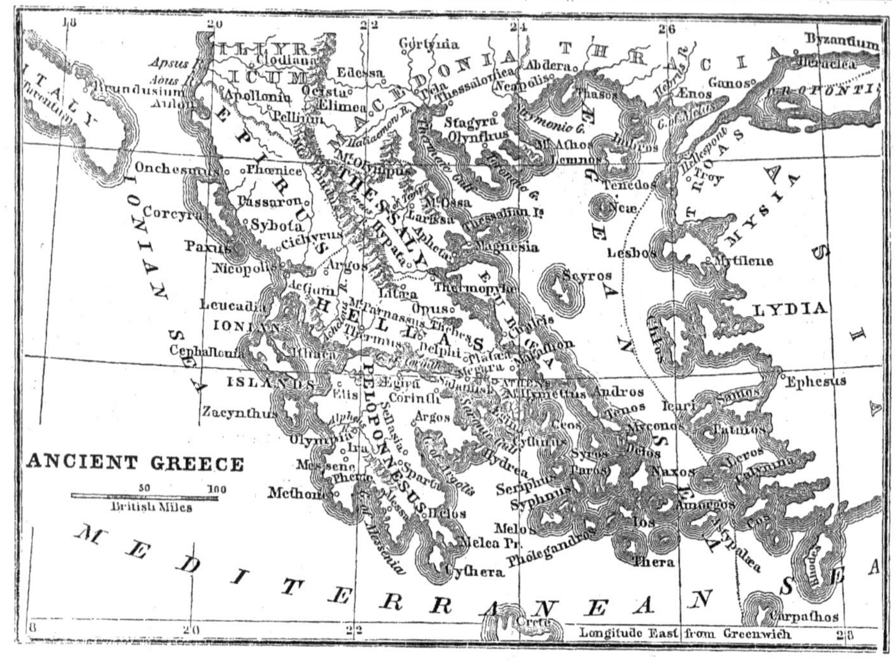

Ancient Greece.

only the territory of modern Greece, but the northern portion of the peninsula, as well as territory still farther north. Its utmost length, including Macedonia, was about four hundred miles, and its extent about forty thousand square miles. The southern part of the peninsula, now styled the *Morea*, and anciently *Peloponnesus*, was about equal in extent to Massachusetts. It included several small states, as Laconia, of which Sparta was the capital; Argolis, Achaia, Arcadia, Elis, and Messene. The middle portion, now called *Livadia*, was anciently *Hellas*. Its whole extent is about equal to that of Connecticut and Rhode Island. Its chief divisions were the states of Acarnania, Ætolia, Doris, Locris, Phocis, Bœotia, Attica, and Megaris. The chief cities were Athens, in Attica, and Thebes, in Bœotia. The northern portion of Greece, and lying on the Adriatic, now called *Albania*, was formerly named *Epirus:* the contiguous territory of *Thessaly* is still known by the same name. In this portion was the city of Larissa. Here also was Mount Olympus, the fancied abode of the fabled Jove, and the vale of Tempe, celebrated in song as one of the most lovely spots to be found in the world.

The islands, lying as well in the Ionian as the Ægean Sea, constituted a fourth division of what was usually considered Greece. In after times, Macedon lying to the north, was regarded as a part of the country.

To the east of Macedon was Thrace, these two being now called *Roumelia*. Thrace was not properly a portion of Greece, and was occupied by a distinct nation; yet it was conquered by Philip of Macedonia, and constituted a portion of the empire of his son Alexander. Many individuals, also, who settled in Greece, and became connected with its fame, were of Thracian birth.

Although the territory of Greece was small, — less, in its widest extent, than one of our larger states, — it is supposed to have had a population of three or four millions in its most flourishing period — that is, in the time of Pericles, about 450 B. C. Its mountains, its rivers, its valleys, its islands, are all diminutive in comparison with others that are found in different parts of the world; yet associated with the name and fame of the ancient Greeks, they are touched with an interest that can never die.

Besides these natural objects, which possess a claim upon the sympathies of every intelligent mind, there are some vestiges of ancient art which still bespeak the genius of their founders, such as the ruins of the temples of Theseus and Minerva at Athens, of Apollo

tors to the remembrance of the people — then sunk in slavery to the Turks: —

"Clime of the unforgotten brave!
Whose land, from plain to mountain-cave,
Was Freedom's home or Glory's grave!
Shrine of the mighty! can it be
That this is all remains of thee?
Approach, thou craven, crouching slave:
Say, is not this Thermopylæ?
These waters blue that round you lave,
O servile offspring of the free —
Pronounce what sea, what shore is this?
The gulf, the rock of Salamis!
These scenes — their story not unknown —
Arise, and make again your own;
Snatch from the ashes of your sires
The embers of your former fires;
And he who in the strife expires
Will add to theirs a name of fear
That Tyranny shall quake to hear,
And leave his sons a hope, a fame,
They too will rather die than shame:
For Freedom's battle once begun,
Bequeathed by bleeding sire to son,
Though baffled oft is ever won."

in the Morea, and many others scattered over the country. Some of the sculptures of ancient Greece exist in the collections of Italy, and are the admiration of the world. Its literature, though preserved but in part, still constitutes a rich portion of the treasures accumulated by human genius.

CHAPTER CCCXIV.

2000 to 1193 B. C.

Poetical and Traditionary History of Greece — Inachus — Cecrops, &c.

GRECIAN history commences above eighteen hundred years before Christ. The thousand years preceding 875 B. C., when Lycurgus gave laws to Sparta, are considered as not strictly historical, the events which distinguished them being commemorated chiefly by tradition and poetry. Yet, however mingled with fable, the history of this long period is not unworthy of notice, seeing that the Greeks themselves believed in it, and made its incidents and heroes the theme of perpetual allusion in their poetry, and even a part of their religion. According to the Greek poets, the original inhabitants of the country, denominated *Pelasgians*, were a race of savages, who lived in caves, fed on nuts and roots, disputed the dominion of the forest with the lion and the bear, and clothed themselves with the skins of wild beasts. These people were spread not only over the territory of Greece, but over other parts of Europe, and in some countries they surpassed others in improvement. At length Uranus, an Egyptian prince, is said to have landed in Greece, and became the father of a family of giants, named *Titans*, who rebelled against him and dethroned him. His son Saturn, who reigned in his stead, in order to prevent a similar fate to himself, ordered all his own children to be put to death as soon as they were born. But one, named *Jupiter*, was concealed by the mother, and reared in the Island of Crete, from which, in time, he returned, and deposed his father. The Titans, jealous of this new prince, rebelled against him, but were vanquished and expelled from Greece.

Jupiter divided his dominions with his brothers Neptune and Pluto. The countries which he reserved to himself he governed with great wisdom, holding his court on Olympus, a mountain in Thessaly, seven thousand feet in height, and the loftiest in Greece. It is quite probable that all these fables had their origin in realities; but any truth which there might be in the story of the Titans and their princes was completely disguised by the poets, and the popular imagination. Saturn, Jupiter, Neptune, and Pluto, came to be regarded not as mortals, but as deities; and the top of Mount Olympus was supposed to be the heavenly residence of the gods, by whom the affairs of mortals were governed. Thus, for ages after the dawn of philosophy, these deified sons of Saturn, and a multitude of others connected with them, were the objects of national worship, not only among the Greeks, but also among the Romans.

At an uncertain but very early date, an Asiatic people, named the *Hellenes*, immigrated into Greece, in some cases expelling the Pelasgi, and in others intermingling with them, so that, in process of time, all the inhabitants of Greece were called Hellenes. They were, however, divided into several races, the principal of which were named *Dorians*, *Æolians*, and *Ionians*. Each of these spoke a dialect differing, in some respects, from those made use of by the others. These dialects were named the *Doric*, *Æolic*, and *Ionic*, in reference to the tribes which used them; and a fourth, which was afterwards formed from the Ionic was named the *Attic*, from its being spoken by the inhabitants of Attica.

Inachus founding the City of Argos.

In the year 1856 B. C., *Inachus*, a Phœnician adventurer, is said to have arrived in Greece, at the head of a small band of his countrymen. On their arrival in Greece, Inachus founded the city of Argos, at the head of what is now called the Gulf of Napoli, in the Peloponnesus.

Three hundred years after this event, (1556 B. C.,) a colony, led by an Egyptian named *Cecrops*, arrived in Attica, and founded the celebrated city of Athens fortifying a high rock, — since called the *Acropolis*, — which rose precipitously above the site afterwards occupied by the town.

Acropolis of Athens.

He placed his rocky fastness under the protection of an Egyptian goddess, from whose Greek name *Athena* — afterwards changed by the Latins into *Minerva* — the city received its title. Being endowed with knowledge and a spirit of enterprise, he effected a union and established a regular government among the rude nations. He divided his province into twelve districts, in each of which there was a principal town, where the affairs of the district were to be transacted,

He instituted marriage, enacted laws, and arranged a system of defence against the Bœotians, the enemies of his people. Thus began the most celebrated of all the Grecian states. Of this Athens was the capital.

At a subsequent period, *Danaus* arrived at Argos with a fresh colony from Egypt. The Argians often suffered for want of water. He first taught them to dig wells; and, by this and similar services, he won special favor. Laying claim to the kingdom, his popularity effected his election; and such were his power and fame, that, long after his death, the southern Greeks still went by he name of *Danaans*. Pelops, an adventurer from Phrygia, in Asia Minor, founded a dynasty, which was destined to succeed that of Danaus, and to have a more extensive sway. The southern peninsula was ever after called by his name, *Peloponnesus*, "the Island of Pelops." At a later period, the names of *Eurysthenes*, *Atreus*, and *Agamemnon*, adorn the annals of Argos, and the neighboring city of Mycenæ. The power of the king, Agamemnon, extended over all Peloponnesus, and several of the Grecian islands.

Cadmus.

About thirty years after the foundation of Athens, a division of Phrygians, who, on account of some troubles in their country, emigrated to the islands of Crete, Rhodes, Eubœa, and to several parts of Greece, founded the celebrated city of Thebes. They had the name of *Cadmeians*, but were a portion of people who were called by the more general names of *Curetes*, *Corybantes*, and others. They brought with them letters, music, the art of working in metals, and a more accurate method of computing time than had hitherto been adopted. *Cadmus*, the leader of the colony that founded Thebes, has the fame of introducing letters into Greece, but it belongs to him only in common with the other chiefs of the Curetes. Crete, one of these Phrygian settlements, presented a masterpiece of political wisdom in its institutions and government. It was a masterpiece — considered in view of its object,— which was the training up of the citizens in the habits of a well-disciplined army, rather than in those of a peaceful commonwealth.

While thus the Phrygian adventurers had brought to their settlements much useful knowledge, nearly at the same time corn and the art of tillage were made known to Attica by Ceres, who was probably a priestess of the Phœnician goddess, Astarte. But improvement was retarded by continual rapine, war, and emigration. One community encroached on another, especially if the latter people possessed a rich soil. The people also on the coast, became addicted to piracy. This was held to be honorable, as it has been so deemed at some period by every barbarous nation; and it is a singular fact that the feeling lasted, in certain parts of Greece, for several centuries, and was not quite extinct until after the time of Thucydides. These evils were checked by the power of Minos at Crete, whose wise institutions, together with the happy situation of his island, had made him the greatest potentate of Greece. He first built a navy, which, besides its usual useful purposes, cleared the Ægean, as far as practicable, of pirates. In the period of tranquillity thus afforded, many cities increased in wealth and power so far as to surround themselves with walls.

The peaceful state of Attica, during the troubled condition of the rest of Greece, some time before this was owing to the apparent disadvantages of its situation. It was a rocky, rugged territory, of a thin and light soil, and hence none coveted it. The quiet and security of Athens made it a refuge to wealthy and powerful men, who were obliged to fly from their homes by war or sedition. Its prosperity was aided by an early reform in its institutions. The twelve cities into which Cecrops had assembled the Atticans retained, under his successors, each its separate magistrates and prytaneum, (town hall,) and were governed independently by their several councils, though they acknowledged a superiority in the king of Athens. When Theseus came to the throne, he completely remodelled its political state. He was the son of Ægeus, king of Athens, but brought up at the court of his father-in-law, king of a small town in Peloponnesus. When grown to manhood, his mother sent him to Athens. He was a man of more than the prodigious strength and agility of the age, and aspired to imitate the exploits and acquire the renown of Hercules. He took his way through the Isthmus of Corinth, the only passage between Peloponnesus and Northern Greece. The route was infested by powerful marauders; but all who attacked him were slain or defeated, and he arrived at Athens, having delivered his country from some of its most terrible savages. Both the king, his father, and the people, favored him on account of his exploits.

In a war with Minos, king of Crete, the Athenians had purchased peace by a yearly tribute of seven youths and seven virgins as slaves — a tribute which was felt to be exceedingly burdensome. The captives had hitherto been drawn by lot from the people. Theseus offered himself as one. His adventure, however, disguised by fable, would seem to have been very successful, as, instead of becoming a slave, he was received with honor, procured the remission of the tribute, and finally obtained Ariadne, the daughter of Minos, in marriage. The patriotism and daring of Theseus raised him to the highest popularity among his countrymen. He succeeded to the government without opposition on the death of Ægeus, notwithstanding the expectations of the nephews of the old king. Through his personal influence, he effected a great political change; for he persuaded the inhabitants to give up their separate councils and magistracies, and submit to a common jurisdiction. Every man was to hold his dwelling and his property as before; but justice was to be administered, and all public affairs transacted, at Athens. These and other important regulations, by which all Attica was joined in a lasting union, brought to Athens its early prosperity and civilization, its subsequent eminence in the arts of peace and war, and its importance in history, to which the extent and value of its territory bore no proportion. This union in Attica produced such a degree of quiet and order, that the Athenians were the first people in Greece who left off the habit of carrying arms, and adopted the garb of peace.

CHAPTER CCCXV.

1193 to 724 B. C.

The Trojan War — Sparta, or Lacedæmon — General Events to the End of the Second Messenian War.

The Wooden Horse. — (See p. 268.)

THE Trojan war, so embellished by poetry and distorted by fable, was doubtless a real occurrence, and deserves a place in Grecian history. We have, however, given so full an account of it under Asia Minor, that we shall only present a brief outline of it here. It owed its existence to the spirit of piracy so common in these early ages, and which resulted in wars or other disastrous events among mankind. The famous voyage of the Argonauts, which took place some years before, was doubtless a piratical expedition to the shores of the Euxine, remarkable for its daring and the number of distinguished personages engaged in it. Jason, its commander, consummated his object in carrying away with him Medea, the daughter of the Colchian king.

The origin of the Trojan war was a similar outrage committed against Greece, though it was followed by more extensive mischiefs. Paris, son of Priam, king of Troy, undertaking an expedition of this kind, arrived at Sparta, and was hospitably entertained by Menelaus, the brother of Agamemnon. The result of his visit was that he became enamored of Helen, the wife of his host, and carried her off. Menelaus and Agamemnon were powerful princes, particularly the latter; and they found no difficulty in uniting Greece for the overthrow of Troy, actuated as the parties were by resentment of aggression, the love of war, and the hope of plunder.

It was the latter part of the twelfth century B. C. that the combined Grecian fleet was assembled at Aulis, in Bœotia. Here it was so long detained by contrary winds, supposed to be occasioned by the anger of Diana, that Agamemnon's army is said to have compelled him to sacrifice his daughter Iphigenia to the goddess. The Trojans, the objects of vengeance and rapine, were a people who differed little from the Greeks in origin, habits, language, or civilization. They were less powerful than the united strength of Greece; but the resources of the latter country were unequal to the maintenance of an army at a distance It was therefore obliged to support itself by plunder from the neighboring cities, and by other means, which consumed the time, thus protracting the war through ten years. At the end of this period, Troy was taken, and suffered the horrible fate common to captured cities — massacre and devastation. This war, as has been stated, is the subject of the Iliad of

Homer.

Homer, which depicts, in its own inimitable way, the horrors of national contention. The picture of Grecian manners, too, at this early age, is most admirable, as contained in the Iliad, and its sequel, the Odyssey.

Upon their return from Troy, the Grecian chiefs found every thing changed during their absence. A new generation, growing to manhood, had adopted leaders of its own, and the heroes of the war found their places occupied by strangers, their property taken, and their families impoverished and cast out. Struggles ensued, in which some regained their proper place in the community; others were obliged to seek for settlements elsewhere. Ulysses found his wife Penelope, a paragon of beauty and virtue, wooed by several suitors, whom she put off from time to time. Agamemnon, on his return, was murdered by his wife, Clytemnestra, and his cousin Ægisthus, for whom she had conceived an adulterous passion. This was followed by their murder by Orestes, son of Agamemnon, who eventually recovered the throne.

In the reign of Tisamenus, the son of Orestes, a change took place in the ruling population, through nearly the whole of Peloponnesus. This revolution is commonly known as the return of the Heraclidæ, or sons of Hercules. This most renowned of the Grecian heroes was great grandson to Perseus, king of Argos, the founder of Mycenæ. Some of his posterity were princes of Doris, and here they constantly claimed the royalty of Argos, from the time when it passed from the line of Perseus to that of Pelops. They made two unsuccessful attempts upon Peloponnesus, but, in the third attempt, they gained their object. This was eighty years after the Trojan war, (1113 B. C.,) when the Dorians invaded the peninsula under Temenus, Cresphontes, and Aristodemus, all descended from Hercules. The most of the territory was parcelled among the invaders. It happened that Aristodemus, to whom the province of Laconia, and its capital, Sparta, were assigned, died. His twin sons, Eurystheus and Procles, were made joint kings of the same. As they were each a founder of a royal house, from their time two kings continued to reign over Sparta, or *Lacedæmon*, as the state was called, one from each family. The oppressions which flowed from this revolution were severe, as the chiefs were obliged to recompense their followers, and their demands could be satisfied only by the general spoliation of the old inhabitants. Great numbers emigrated; the remainder were mostly made slaves. A considerable part of Messenia was left to its rightful owners. Civilization was put back by this irruption of the rude Dorians, and the country was constantly distracted with disputes arising from the partition of the conquered territory.

The government established by the Heraclidæ was the same which then universally prevailed in Greece — an irregular mixture of monarchy and oligarchy, with a slight infusion of democracy; but there was a constant tendency to the increase of the latter elements. In the age which followed the Dorian conquest of Peloponnesus, the power of the king had diminished, and was at length abolished. All authority was engrossed by the wealthy landholders, who abused their ascendency in crushing the poor. Argos was the first to abolish royalty, or to render it insignificant. Corinth, though suffering several revolutions, was more quiet than the other republics of the peninsula, and was ruled with the most equity and moderation. Lacedæmon had one source of dissension peculiar to itself — its divided royalty. The two kings were ever at variance, and each had his respective and warm partisans. More or less anarchy existed with unmitigated oppression to the many. Such was the state of Lacedæmon, when the death of Polydectes, the fifth from Procles, gave the crown to Lycurgus, his brother.

Lycurgus.

Lycurgus, soon after, discovering the late king's widow to be with child, immediately declared that he held the crown only as protector for the infant, if a boy, as the event proved. The measures which Lycurgus took to secure his nephew on the throne, procured him the highest esteem; and, though he was once banished from Sparta by his enemies, he was at length invited back to legislate for the state, (864 B. C.) When he returned, he had his plan of government already formed, its leading principles being adopted from Crete, where he had passed much of his exile. Having procured the sanction of the oracle at Delphi, he had sufficient influence to establish his scheme of government. He began his labors by instituting a senate to make laws, and see that they were executed. This senate was composed of thirty members, the kings being of the number, and acting as presidents. The latter, also, had the priesthood and the command of the army.

But, in after times, the most important magistracy was that of the Ephori, who are said to have been either instituted or made prominent by Theopompus, above one hundred years after Lycurgus. Their number was first taken annually from the people, and their office was to watch over all the other inhabitants, whether magistrates or private persons. They were empowered to fine, imprison, depose from office, or bring to an immediate trial, any person, from the king to the meanest citizen, unrestrained by any precise law. As was to be expected, in the course of time they gained a power nearly despotic. Lycurgus next made a division of the lands, so that all the Spartans shared it fairly between them. When he endeavored to do the same with the furniture, clothes, &c., he found the rich very averse to his proposals. He therefore pursued another course. He substituted iron for gold and silver as a medium of exchange. As this iron money was of no account among the neighboring countries the Spartans could no longer indulge in luxury by freely purchasing costly articles. The necessary arts of life he allowed to be practised only by slaves.

The legislator having thus banished the desire of gain, his object was to occupy the mind with love of praise and emulation in patriotism and courage, and to educate the citizens in the best manner for war. The education of the children, and the habits of the men, were equally regulated by public authority, and care was taken that all family ties should be weaker than that which bound the citizen to the commonwealth. The boys were reckoned as belonging less to their parents than to the state, and were taken to the former to be educated in bands under appointed governors. They were bred to military exercises and the uncomplaining endurance of hardships; practised in combats with each other, and kept on scanty fare, but encouraged to mend it by whatever they could take undiscovered from the messes of the men. By this they were formed to enterprise and circumspection, being liable, if detected, to heavy punishment for their awkwardness. It was a regulation that all persons, even the kings, should eat at public tables, and that these tables should be served only with plain food. This regulation, more than any other, at first offended the rich citizens. In time, however, these dinners, which consisted of a kind of soup called *black broth*, came to be much relished, and very agreeable discourse often attended them.

The Lacedæmonians were made a most formidable people, through the principles and discipline in which they were thus trained. They were disgraced forever, if they gave way to fear in the most hopeless situation. After a defeat in war, amidst the general mourning, the kindred of those who had been slain were required to put on the appearance of joy, because their relatives had not shared the reproach of flight. Their motto was, to perish rather than yield; and it was an unwonted occurrence for a Lacedæmonian detachment to surrender to the most overwhelming force. The object aimed at in the institutions of Lycurgus was reached; but it was a limited excellence, and almost entirely warlike. Very little regard was bestowed on any who were without the circle of the commonwealth.

The impulse given to the Lacedæmonian spirit and ambition soon showed itself in their attacks on the bordering states, especially on Messenia. Inflamed by wrongs both done and suffered in the second generation after Lycurgus, (743 B. C.,) the Lacedæmonians resolved to make a sudden attack on that province without any declaration of war, and bound themselves by oath not to return home till they had conquered the Messenians. But they found it a difficult undertaking, and prolonged probably beyond all their expectations. The Messenians, by avoiding battles and defending towns, were able to maintain the conflict for many years, till the Lacedæmonians feared for the existence of the state, through the want of children to supply the waste of war and natural decay. In this exigency, they sent orders to the marriageable virgins to recruit the population by a promiscuous intercourse with the young men, who, being children when the war began, had not taken the oath. The offspring of this singular and indecent order were denominated *Partheniæ*, or "sons of virgins." When the war was ended, the Partheniæ were permitted to settle out of Peloponnesus, as they became restive and dangerous through the slight which was put upon them on account of their origin. They accordingly migrated to Italy, and founded the city of Tarentum.

The submission of Messenia continued through forty years. But so grievous was the oppression of the inhabitants, and so undying was the Grecian spirit of independence, that they only wanted a leader; and a leader they found in Aristomenes, a youth of the regal line. Joined by the Arcadians and others, the most

The Messenian War.

heroic deeds were achieved by the Messenians under Aristomenes. In one engagement, it is related, that he was knocked down and taken, with about fifty of his band. The prisoners were thrown as rebels into a deep cavern, and all were killed by the fall except Aristomenes, who was wonderfully preserved, and enabled to escape. Returning to Eira, a stronghold near the sea, which the Lacedæmonians had besieged, he soon gave proof to the enemy of his presence, by his accustomed valor and discretion. The siege was protracted till the eleventh year, when the Lacedæmonian commander, one stormy night, learning that a post in the fort had been quitted by its guard, succeeded in occupying it with his own troops. Aristomenes, flying to the spot, commenced a vigorous defence, aided by the women, who mixed in the fight. But they were oppressed by the numbers of the foe and by the boisterous weather. Cold, wet, sleepless, jaded, and hungry, they kept up the struggle during three nights and two days: at length, when all was hopeless, they formed their column, placing in the middle their women and children, and resolved to make their way out of the place. The enemy, unwilling to resist the effects of their despair, granted the passage which had been demanded. The Arcadians received them with kindness, and gave them allotments of land.

The Messenians, who fell under the power of Lacedæmon, were reduced to the condition of slaves or Helots. From other parts of the peninsula, a colony was formed under a son of Aristomenes, which settled in Sicily. Aristomenes himself determined never to quit his country, so that he might always make war on Lacedæmon as opportunity offered. But he sought the means of further hostilities in vain, and was induced to retire to Rhodes, where his remaining days were passed in tranquillity. The character of Aristomenes is one of the most beautiful among the warriors of antiquity He conducted the struggle in which he was engaged with uniform obedience to the laws of war, sparing the vanquished, and manifesting a clemency and gentleness peculiarly rare in so warlike an age.

CHAPTER CCCXVI.

1193 to 506 B. C.

Athens, from the Trojan War to the First Interference of Persia in the Affairs of Greece.

Codrus devoting himself to Death.

THE institutions which Theseus established in Athens kept the city tranquil, even amidst the general convulsions which followed the return of the Greeks from Troy. Hence it became a desirable place of resort to refugees from other provinces. The reception at

Athens of inhabitants from Achaia, who were compelled, by being over populated, to migrate, became the occasion of a war between Doris and Athens. The Delphian oracle had promised victory to the Dorians if they avoided killing the Athenian king. Codrus, who was then king, resolved to devote himself for his people, and, accordingly, entering the enemy's camp in the habit of a peasant, he provoked a quarrel, in which he was killed. When the invaders learned that the Athenian king was killed, they at once retreated.

The succession at Athens was disputed between the sons of Codrus; the oracle decided in favor of Medon, the eldest son, who was lame. It was, however, only a compromise, it being determined that after Codrus none could be worthy of the title of king. Medon became only the first magistrate, with the title of *archon*, which was to be hereditary. These events happened B. C. 804. About this time, Attica, being too full of inhabitants, sent forth a colony to Asia Minor, under Androclus and Neleus, sons of Codrus. At different periods in Grecian history, the business of colonization was vigorously carried on, so that nearly all the adjacent coasts and islands were studded with towns and cities of the Greeks. The settlements were almost all along the sea, as inland territories were rarely coveted; consequently they were enabled to communicate readily with one another, and with the parent state.

Twelve archons followed Medon in hereditary succession. The last was Alcmæon, at whose death, about one hundred and sixty years after that of Codrus, Charops was made archon for ten years, and six succeeded under the same term of time. Afterwards, the duration of the office was reduced to a year, and its duties divided among nine persons, taken at first by suffrage, and afterwards by lot from the *eupatridæ*, or nobles. Among the nine, one was chief; the second had the title of *king*, who was also the high priest; the third was called *polemarch*, meaning the military commander; and the other six presided as judges. The nine together formed the *council of state*. Legislation alone was in the people. Under such a political arrangement, Athens was torn by the clashing ambition of factious nobles. The most powerful family was that of the Alcmæonidæ, descended from the last perpetual archon, and through him from Codrus. But their influence was resisted, particularly by Cylon, a man of high nobility and great power, who attempted to make himself *tyrant* of Athens — the name by which the Greeks denoted a man who had brought under his dominion a state, of which the legal government was republican. Cylon's attempt, however, proved disastrous to him and his followers.

The disorders consequent on this state of things required a remedy, and Draco was called to legislate for Athens. Though he did not alter the political constitution, he established a penal code absurdly severe; every crime, great and small, was made capital, on the ground that every breach of a positive law was treason to the state. The necessary result was, that all crimes, except the greatest, went unpunished, as few would undertake either prosecution or conviction. Aristotle tells us that Herodicus used to say that "Draco's institutions seemed rather to come from a dragon than a man." The evils under which the state suffered still continued, heightened by the revolt of Salamis, an island which was subject to Athens. Solon had once reduced the island, and was possessed of a reputation both for wisdom and valor; and, having devised a form of government with Epimenides, a Cretan philosopher, he was looked to as the only man capable of settling the distracted commonwealth.

In the year 562 B. C., Solon was accordingly appointed archon, with peculiar powers for reforming the state. The task he executed with great success, both in respect to the political constitution and the code of civil and criminal law. The latter proved to be so excellent, that the Romans formed their law upon it;

Solon.

and, through them, it has become the basis of the laws now existing in most of Europe. The peculiar system of the government which he established will be exhibited in another place.* It is only to be remarked that his friends advised him to procure the regal authority; but he absolutely refused it, alleging that "tyranny resembled a fair garden; a beautiful spot while we are within, but it wants a way to get out." Resolving to give the Athenians the best laws they were capable of receiving, where he found things tolerable in the constitution, he refused to change them, as he disliked unnecessary innovations, and he laid it down as a maxim, that "those laws will best be observed which power and justice equally support."

After the laws of Solon had been promulgated, he was so frequently applied to for explanations and alterations by the weak or captious, that, wearied with their importunities, and wishing to give to his great work a degree of solidity, he determined to travel. Having bound the Athenians by an oath that his institutions should be changed in no part for the space of ten years, he departed on his journey. He survived some twelve years after this, having returned to Athens upon the expiration of the ten, and endeavoring in vain to compose the dissensions that had taken place during his absence. He died at Cyprus, in the eightieth year of his age. After his death, the Athenians, becoming probably more tranquil, paid him the highest honors, and erected in the forum and at Salamis a statue of him in brass, with his hand in his gown — the posture in which he was accustomed to address the people. In addition to his talents for legis-

* See General Views.

'ation, Solon was an eloquent speaker, and excelled in poetry.

Not long after the laws of Solon had been adopted, Athens was distracted by contentions. The old factions of the *mountains*, the *valleys*, and the *coast* renewed their struggle; they inflamed the minds of the Athenians against one another, and endeavored to subvert and usurp the government. Lycurgus was at the head of the country people; Megacles was the chief of the inhabitants of the sea-coast, and Pisistratus, in order, as he alleged, to protect those in the high lands from tyranny, declared himself their leader. The last was the democratic party. All three were men of high birth, without which, at this time, there was little chance of greatness at Athens. Pisistratus was distinguished for his eloquence and military talents; and, by mildness of character and affability of manners, had become the most popular man in the city. A remark of Solon, however, shows what he thought or feared respecting Pisistratus. He was wont to say to the latter, "Sir, were it not for your ambition, you would be the best citizen in Athens."

One day, Pisistratus came in a chariot into the market-place wounded and bloody, and complained that he had been waylaid by his enemies, and with difficulty escaped alive. In after times, the story has been commonly disbelieved; but, as it was long supposed to be true, and no account has come down to us to the contrary, and as the history is told by persons hostile to Pisistratus, there is no difficulty in receiving it as true. A guard was appointed for him, and with it he seized the Acropolis. He was supported by his party, and those of his opponents who would not submit to him were forced into exile. From this period, Pisistratus was generally considered as tyrant of Athens, though his friends denied the charge, asserting that the constitution was unaltered, and that he even obeyed a citation from the Areopagus.

As it was, Pisistratus at once enjoyed the reality of power, while he avoided, in a measure, the odium of usurpation. His control of the government was not, however, uninterrupted. Twice was he banished from the city, and twice he returned: he at last died at an advanced period, while in the administration of Athens. His ability was great, and his liberality and moderation were uncommon in the existing state of society. He was a patron of learning and the arts, and is said to have founded the first public library known to the world. The earliest collection and arrangement of the poems of Homer, which had been before brought by Lycurgus into Greece, are ascribed to him. As an illustration of his kindness of disposition, the following incident is related: It happened that Pisistratus, who, as prince of Athens, received the tenth part of every man's rents and of the fruits of his ground, perceived once an old man gathering something among the rocks; he inquired of him what he was doing, and what were the fruits of his labors. "Troubles and a few plants of wild sage," replied he; "and of these Pisistratus must have a tenth." The ruler said no more, but, when he returned to the city, he exempted the man from paying his tax.

Hippias and Hipparchus, sons of Pisistratus, succeeded to the government, and inherited the influence as well as the power of their father. Their measures were characterized by a wisdom and moderation similar to his. Hippias chiefly conducted the civil administration, while Hipparchus was engaged in measures with a view to enlighten the minds and cultivate the tastes of the citizens. In patronizing learning and learned men, he invited Anacreon and Simonides to Athens, and maintained them there; and, that he might extend a degree of instruction to those who, in an age when books were few and costly, had neither means nor leisure for study, he erected in the streets and highways marble columns, with heads of Mercury, having short moral sentences engraved on their sides. Hipparchus also directed the rhapsodists to recite the poems of Homer at the great feast of Panathenæa, or "all Athens," that the people might be instructed in the sciences and the moral conduct of life.

Hipparchus was slain by means of a conspiracy. The cause of this is somewhat obscure; but it is certain that the motives which impelled the perpetrators to this act were of a private, not of a public nature. The main conspirators were two friends, Harmodius and Aristogeiton, from the middle rank of citizens. They both perished, however, in the attempt. The effect of this fatal plot was to render the survivor, Hippias, suspicious and revengeful. From this time forward, his government became jealous and severe. He renounced all confidence in popularity, and endeavored to secure himself by the death of the objects of his suspicions. His tyranny lasted four years after the death of his brother. The Alcmæonidæ, who had been ejected some years before by the father of Hippias, were unceasingly watchful for an opportunity to return. This was eventually effected by the aid of the Lacedæmonians, who, under their king Cleomenes, besieged Athens, and obliged the Pisistratidæ to surrender the city and quit the territory. Hippias and his partisans retired to Sigeium, on the Hellespont, (510 B. C.) The Pisistratidæ held the ascendency in Athens for fifty years, dating from the occupation of the citadel. It was under this family that Athens first became remarkable for the splendor of its public buildings.

The direction of affairs in Athens was now disputed between Isagoras and Clisthenes the acknowledged head of the Alcmæonidæ. The latter, having courted the favor of the populace, gained the ascendant, by which means some changes were made in the constitution, tending to render it more democratical. He opened public offices to all the citizens. Isagoras, having secured the aid of the Spartan king Cleomenes, had with him only a small band of soldiers, and made the most exorbitant demands upon the Athenians, supposing that no one would dispute the will of the Spartan king. He found, however, that Athens was not fallen so low as to endure this insolence of usurpation. The people flew to arms, and Isagoras and his party were defeated. The direction of government now fell into the hands of Clisthenes and his friends; and, as a war with Lacedæmon was expected, it was natural for the Athenians to look for aid wherever it might be obtained. Accordingly they sent ambassadors to Sardis, the capital of Lydia, then a Persian province, to propose an alliance. The satrap, or governor, asked the ambassadors who the Athenians were, and where they dwelt; when he heard the answer, he scornfully rejected the proposed alliance with so insignificant a state, unless they would give earth and water to King Darius, in token of subjection. The demand was complied with on the part of the ambassadors, but the Athenian people disowned the act.

Meanwhile Cleomenes entered Attica with a power

ful army; but, owing principally to the defection of the Corinthians, who composed a part of his forces, he was obliged to abandon his object of attacking Attica. The Athenians, thus left at liberty, proceeded to chastise the Bœotians and others, who had invaded Attica in another quarter. These enemies were immediately subdued. But Athens was destined, at length, to combat a foe whose resources were infinitely greater than any with which she had hitherto been called to contend. Hippias, still an exile, having been disappointed in the assistance expected from the Lacedæmonians, went to Sardis, and persuaded the satrap Artaphernes to make war upon his country, engaging that, upon the event of being restored to the sovereignty, he would hold it as a vassal to the Persian monarch. On hearing this, the Athenians sent ambassadors to the satrap to dissuade him from granting the request of Hippias. They, however, received for answer an imperious order to submit at their peril to Hippias, and, refusing obedience, they thenceforth considered themselves as at war with Persia.

In the mean time, the events which followed the expulsion of Hippias had popularized the Athenian government. Continually appealed to by their present leaders, the Alcmæonidæ, the people became versed in public affairs, and were henceforth practically as well as legally supreme. The result was an increasing vigor and spirit in the government, and a great improvement as to internal quiet and security. Though jealous and violent in troublous times, and sometimes hurried into acts the most foolish and iniquitous, — always defective as a means of discovering truth, — the popular courts were generally honest in intention and did justice in all disputes between the rich and poor with an impartiality elsewhere little known in Greece.

Burning of Athens by the Persians.

CHAPTER CCCXVII.

506 to 479 B. C.

Transactions from the First Persian Interference to the Conclusion of the Persian Invasion.

The Grecian colonies on the coast of Asia Minor, having been invaded by the Persians, were, some of them, broken up, and the inhabitants, sailing to parts of Europe even as far as Gaul, founded other colonies. During this state of things in Asia Minor, the Ionians sent to Athens to request assistance, which was readily obtained. With the help of a fleet of ships, great exploits were performed, and the Ionians sacked Sardis. When Darius heard of this, he declared himself the enemy of Athens, and earnestly desired some opportunity to revenge the injury. The Ionians were soon after reduced to subjection.

When the news arrived that Darius had in view the conquest of Greece, the Athenians and inhabitants of Ægina, with others of the Grecian states, wisely compromised some differences that had arisen amongst them, and which had produced some unimportant conflicts, that they might exert all their force against the common enemy

In prosecution of the enterprise which had now been resolved upon, Mardonius, who had lately married a daughter of Darius, was sent with a large army and fleet, avowedly to punish Athens for the burning of Sardis. He crossed the Hellespont. Thrace was already subject to the Persians, excepting a portion of the savage mountaineers; and Macedonia, having formerly submitted to deliver earth and water, did not now venture to refuse a demanded tribute. But the Persian fleet, in doubling the promontory of Athos, lost, in a violent tempest, three hundred ships and above twenty thousand men; and of the army many were slain in consequence of a night attack from a band of Thracians. Although the latter were defeated, the season was then so far advanced, that it was thought best by the Persian leader to return, and pass the winter in Asia.

Darius, now wishing to know which of the Grecian states he might consider as friends or foes, despatched heralds to the several communities of Greece, to demand of them the accustomed token of submission — "earth and water." Many towns on the continent, and most of the islands, did not see fit to refuse it; but at Athens and Sparta, not only was a determined refusal given, but the public indignation was vented against the Persian heralds, who, at one place being thrown into a cavern, and at the other into a well, were told there to take their earth and water.

A Persian Herald thrown into a Well.

As there was now an interval of suspense, the Greeks were kept with difficulty from being embroiled with one another. Indeed, at one time, Cleomenes led an army against the Argians, and surprised and routed them with much slaughter. A war also arose between Athens and Ægina. While Greece was in this state of turbulence, Persia was again preparing for its conquest. Mardonius was recalled, and his command given to Artaphernes, joined with Datis, a Median nobleman, probably more experienced. The Persian armament was increased to five hundred ships, and to five hundred thousand men.

This expedition accordingly set sail, and Hippias, now in advanced life, served as guide and conductor. To avoid the circuitous and dangerous route by Thrace and Macedonia, it was determined to cross the Ægean, reducing the islands on the way. Naxos and several other islands submitted. As soon, however, as the Persian fleet was descried by the inhabitants of Eretria, they sent to demand the assistance of Athens. The four thousand Athenians who had been settled on the territory of Chalcis were ordered to assist them. Little, however, was effected by their interposition, for the Eretrians were divided among themselves; and after resisting the enemy six days, the place was betrayed to the Persians, who pillaged and burnt the city, and sold the inhabitants for slaves. The Athenians returned home, having reserved themselves for the defence of their native country. The Persians, now masters of Eubœa, crossed into Attica, and landed, at the suggestion of Hippias, on the narrow plain of Marathon, 490 B. C., six years from the period in which the Persian invasion first commenced.

It happened that Athens had a commander equal to the emergency in Miltiades, the son of Cimon. He had been appointed one of the ten generals who regularly directed the armies of the state; but so conscious were his colleagues of his superior ability, that four of them made over to him their days of command. The generals were equally divided in opinion whether to risk a battle or defend the city; but the decision rested with the polemarch Callimachus. He acceded to the views of Miltiades, that a battle should be risked; and the army accordingly marched to Marathon, where, on his own day of command, he led it into action. The Athenians were joined by the few troops that could be gathered in Platæa, a little commonwealth of Bœotia. The united force may have amounted to about fourteen thousand heavy-armed troops, with about an equal number of light-armed men. The Persian army brought into the field is stated at one hundred thousand.

No ground could have been more favorable to the Athenians, situated as they were, with a vast inferiority as to numbers. It was neither among hills, where their heavy phalanx would have been unable to keep its ranks unbroken and available against the expert archery of the enemy, nor on a wide plain, where it would have been surrounded by numbers. In the narrow plain of Marathon, the ground favored the movements of the phalanx, while its small area precluded the evolutions of the hostile cavalry, which was excellent. Still limited as the space was, Miltiades only presented a front equal to that of the enemy, at the same time purposely weakening the centre of his force. Then, with the strength of the army in its wings, with a view to leave as little opportunity of action as possible to the Persian horse and archery, he ordered the troops to advance running, and engage at once in close fight. The conflict was fierce. The weak centre of the Athenians was broken and pursued into the country; but their powerful wings routed those who were opposed to them, and, being immediately recalled from pursuit, were led against the conquering centre of the Persian army, defeated it, and, following to the shore the fleeing enemy, made dreadful havoc among them. According to Herodotus, six thousand three hundred of the enemy were slain, and only one hundred and ninety-two of the Athenians and Platæans, among whom was the polemarch Callimachus — with many other eminent men. Seven ships were taken on the shore.

"The Athenians who fought at Marathon," says the Greek historian, "were the first among the Greeks known to have adopted running for the purpose of coming at once to close fight; and they were the first who withstood — in the field — even the sight of the Median dress, and of the men who wore it; for hitherto the very name of the Medes and Persians had been a terror to the Greeks." Cynegirus, the brother of the poet Æschylus, is reported to have performed prodigies of valor, and was finally killed holding on by his teeth to a ship which was ready to sail, after both his hands had been cut off. According to Justin, Hippias, who expected to have been restored to the sovereignty of Athens by the power of the Persians, perished in the engagement.

The Persian army, on its embarkation, sailed immediately toward Athens, hoping to reach it before the return of its defenders; but in this they were disappointed, and they set sail for Asia. The success of Miltiades gave him unbounded popularity and influence. Presuming on his favor with the people, he requested a fleet of seventy ships, on the pretext that he would bring great riches to Athens, but really with a design of revenging a personal injury. He led them to the Isle of Paros, as if to punish its people for their forced service in the Persian fleet, and for this purpose demanded of the latter one hundred talents, as the price of his retreat. The Parians, however, refused, and resisted him with spirit; and it happening that Miltiades received a wound, they were delivered from the danger which impended over them by his return to Athens.

Here Miltiades was brought to trial for his life by

Xanthippus, a man of high consideration, on account of the failure of his promises made to the people. There was some ground for the process against him, as he was guilty of an atrocious abuse of the public authority, for the gratification of individual revenge; but neither can the act of the Athenians be excused, in intrusting such an armament to the sole pleasure of a popular man. The memory of his services, however, with pity for his present situation, prevailed on the people to absolve him on the capital charge; but he was fined fifty talents—about fifty thousand dollars. Miltiades died soon after from the mortification of his wound; but the fine was paid by Cimon, his son.

Four years after the battle of Marathon, Egypt revolted from the Persians, and the death of Darius shortly followed. Xerxes, his son and successor, recovered that country, and immediately after, commenced his attempt to subdue such Greek states as persisted in their independence. He brought together the most powerful armament, both by land and sea, which history has recorded. The preparations cost him the labor of four years. The number of the ships of war was stated at twelve hundred, and that of ships of burden three thousand. The former were of greater strength and size than any before seen in the ancient world. The army consisted of one million seven hundred thousand foot, and eighty thousand horse—beside an immense retinue of attendants. In the fifth year of the preparation, he moved toward the Hellespont with this overwhelming force, and crossed it on a bridge of boats, occupying seven days and nights in the crossing. He passed through Thrace and Macedonia, and moved toward Athens. Most of the Grecian states desisted from their mutual quarrels, and joined against the invaders, Lacedæmon taking the lead.

It became the Lacedæmonians to be on the alert in this instance, inasmuch, as on the occasion of the former Persian invasion, their selfish and timid, or superstitious policy, delayed their succors to the Athenians till the danger was past. The Argians stood aloof, refusing to be commanded by the Lacedæmonians, from whom they had lately suffered severely in war, and the Thebans eventually joined the Persians. The first resistance which the enemy encountered was at Thermopylæ, a mountain pass on the coast connecting Thessaly and Phocis, the only tolerable outlet southward from Thessaly. Here were posted rather more than five thousand regular troops, under the Spartan king Leonidas, the brother of Cleomenes. Their purpose was to maintain the passage, till the whole strength of the different states could be sent out. This small body of Greeks checked the whole Persian force for several days. They had been at first requested by the messenger, whom the king sent to them, to lay down their arms: the short and brave reply was, "Let Xerxes come and take them."

At length, Xerxes was told of a pass by which the troops might be led across the mountains. He accordingly sent round a strong detachment to attack the Greeks in the rear, while his main army advanced on their front. This movement effected their destruction. Leonidas and a chosen few determined to perish, knowing the value of a great example of self-devotion, and moved by the voice of the oracle, that either Sparta or her king must perish. Dismissing, therefore, the rest of his army, he retained three hundred Spartans who were with him. The Thespians, amounting to seven hundred, declared their resolution to share his fate. Leonidas detained the four hundred Thebans in the army against their will, as hostages for the doubtful faith of their countrymen. With this insignificant force, the Greeks advanced to meet the enemy and fighting with the resolution inspired by despair, they made vast slaughter. The advantage continued to be theirs, till the Persian detachment came up in their rear; they then retreated to a hillock, and forming on the top, prolonged the struggle. When their spears were broken, they fought with their swords, and if these failed, with their hands and teeth, till the Spartans and Thespians were all slain to a man. The Thebans surrendered in a body, as soon as, by the retreat of their companions to the hillock, they were permitted to do as they pleased.

After all the exertions that had been made, the Athenians at home, finding that they were deserted by their allies, and that they could not preserve their city unless by submission, immediately resolved to abandon it on the approach of Xerxes. The fleet from Artemisium was assembled at Salamis to assist in their removal. Their wives, children, and servants, were transported to Salamis, Trœzen, and Ægina, while the able-bodied men were mostly serving in the ships, a few only, principally poor men, being left behind. The Persians advanced on Athens, after burning Thespia and Platæa. They entered the city; but the few Athenians in the Acropolis made an obstinate defence, and the citadel was with great difficulty taken and burnt. The defenders were slaughtered.

The Persian fleet, besides suffering from storms, had met with a severe check at Artemisium, and was now destined to be completely defeated at Salamis, (480 B. C.) The Persians had considerably more than one thousand triremes, while the Greeks had but three hundred and seventy-eight, of which one hundred and eighty were Athenian. The whole Persian army, with Xerxes at its head, was drawn up on the Attic shore to view the engagement. The great disparity of the forces caused at first a general movement of fear on the part of the Greeks; but at length their onset became steady and orderly, after the manner taught them by Themistocles, to strike with the heads of their ships the enemy's broadside. The Greeks were completely victorious, and the hostile armament was ruined. The discomfiture of his fleet struck Xerxes with dismay, and he soon returned to Asia; but he left a powerful army behind him, under Mardonius, whose ambition was flattered with the idea of becoming the conqueror of Greece.

In the spring of 479 B. C., the first important measure of Mardonius was an attempt to detach the Athenians from the Grecian confederacy. But all the powerful considerations which he urged were unavailing, and he accordingly straightway advanced on Athens. The inhabitants, failing to receive the assistance which they expected from their allies, passed over into Salamis, and left him the empty city, which he occupied. The Spartans delayed sending assistance to the Athenians, until they had reason to think that their own liberties were endangered by the Persian power in Greece. They finally despatched five thousand men, and the whole of Lacedæmon five thousand in addition. The Athenians crossed from Salamis, and the confederate army, being assembled at Eleusis, advanced to Erythræ, on the border of Bœotia, where i took up a position at the base of Mount Cithæron

The heavy-armed troops of the Grecian army amounted to thirty-eight thousand. Of the five thousand Spartans from the city, each of them was attended by seven light-armed helots. The other light-armed troops swelled the whole number of the allied army to about one hundred and ten thousand. The army was led by Pausanias, the Spartan commander. The Athenian force, consisting of eight thousand

Aristides.

heavy-armed troops was led by Aristides, known in history as The Just. The army of Mardonius consisted of three hundred thousand Asiatics and about fifty thousand Greeks.

When Mardonius left Athens, he burnt and demolished what remained of the city. The first attack was made by the Persian cavalry, who, by riding up in small parties, discharged their arrows and then retired. This annoyance was borne for a time; at length a desperate charge, made by three hundred picked Athenians, brought the cavalry into a general engagement. The heavy-armed Athenians coming up, repulsed them with great slaughter. After various changes of position, and successful manœuvres on the part of the Greeks, he general battle was begun at Platæa. The Persians fought with great bravery; but neither this nor vast superiority in numbers could make up for their inferiority in arms and discipline. They were at length defeated with great slaughter, Mardonius being killed. Of the Grecian auxiliaries in the ranks of the Persian army, a portion were not hearty in the cause, and these rendered but little assistance to the invaders.

The Persian fugitives who escaped into their intrenched camp, were in time to close the gates, and man the walls against the Lacedæmonians and Tegeans. These, being unskilled in the attack of fortifications, made no impression on the enemy; but on the arrival of the Athenians, the works were soon carried. The passions of the Athenians, inflamed by long distress and danger, were indulged in a manner too sanguinary to be justified. Of the three hundred thousand men who were left with Mardonius, scarcely three thousand escaped, exclusive of forty thousand who retreated under Artabazus. When the latter perceived that all was lost, he marched with great expedition to Thrace, and passed over the Hellespont into Asia. "The mind revolts from such sweeping destruction, even amidst its exultation on viewing the deliverance of a great people from unprincipled aggression. It were indeed to be wished that an outraged nation would remember mercy in the moment of vengeance, and refrain from needlessly visiting on the miserable tools of despotism, the crimes of their employers."

This battle, in its results, not only freed the Grecians from the terrors of servitude, but made them possessors of immense wealth. When Xerxes left the army for Asia, he gave most of his riches and valuable furniture to Mardonius, as he was his brother-in-law. The rest he divided among his subordinate favorites. Couches magnificently embroidered; tables of gold and silver; golden bowls and goblets; stalls and mangers of brass; chains, bracelets; cimeters, some of solid gold, others set with precious stones and many chests of Persian money, which constituted the currency of Greece from that time, and continued to do so for several years,—all came into the possession of the conquerors.

The battle of Platæa, it is said, happened on the 22d of September. On the same day, another battle, neither less glorious nor less decisive, was fought between the same nations at the promontory of Mycale, in Ionia, opposite to the Isle of Samos. A Persian fleet and army were destroyed there by a Greek fleet that had been sent to the Ionian coast under the command of Leotychides, the Spartan king. An army of sixty thousand Persians was on the shore; but both suffered the same fate, from the valor of the Greeks. The Ionians of the islands having been liberated from the Persian dominion, joined the Greeks. When the slaughter had ceased, the Persian ships and camp, and all the valuable treasures contained in them, became the prize of the victors. Ionia regained its freedom, and the Asiatic coast was abandoned by the Persian monarch. When every thing of value was taken out of the enemy's camp and fleet, the Greeks reduced the ships to ashes.

After this signal blow, which not only completed the ruin of the Persian expedition against Europe, but restored liberty to the fairest portion of Asia, the Grecian fleet went to Samos, and, after some other adventures by a part of it, eventually returned to Greece. Macedonia had renounced the connection with Persia immediately after the battle of Platæa. About the same time, probably, Thrace threw off its dependence.

Thus ended, after two campaigns, this memorable expedition of a powerful monarch against a brave nation. The result must be attributed to the independent spirit of the Greeks, and especially to the generous perseverance of the Athenians, who refused very advantageous offers from Xerxes after the loss of their city, and whose abandonment of the common cause would doubtless have determined the subjugation of Greece.

CHAPTER CCCXVIII.

479 to 431 B. C.

Athenian Ascendency.

Immediately after the battle of Platæa, the Athnians had begun to bring back their families, and to rebuild their city and ramparts. This measure was most unreasonably displeasing to the Lacedæmonians. To the latter, the command in the war, both by land and sea, had been intrusted; but although they were the most distinguished military Greek nation, the Athenian fleet had been more numerous, and the power and spirit which Athens displayed, had made a forcible impression on all minds. The Lacedæmonians, consistently with their narrow and jealous policy, attempted to prevent the Athenians from erecting fortifications for the protection of their city, and endeavored to embarrass their measures for repairing the heavy loss which they had sustained in their own cause and in that of Greece. They even had the effrontery, through an embassy, to urge the Athenians not to proceed with the ramparts, but rather, if possible, to reduce the walls of all other cities out of the Peloponnesus, that the enemy might never more have any strong place to fix his quarters in, as recently in Thebes. Had the demand been complied with, Athens would have become entirely subject to Lacedæmon.

The Lacedæmonian intrigues were defeated by the address of Themistocles, the Athenian. He contrived, through purposed delays in negotiation, to deceive the Lacedæmonians in regard to building the walls; and when they were raised to the requisite height, he informed that people that Athens was already sufficiently fortified, and henceforth, if they and their allies had any thing to propose, they must do it to persons able to judge both of the common interest and their own. Meanwhile the war was prosecuted against Persia, the allies maintaining a strong navy in the Ægean Sea. But the confederacy was partly broken up by the arrogance of Pausanias, the Lacedæmonian, who was secretly engaged in a personal negotiation with Xerxes, promising the latter, for his daughter in marriage, the subjugation of Greece. A favorable answer raised his pride to such a degree, that he treated the allies with the utmost haughtiness and severity.

At this crisis, Pausanias was called home under a charge of treason; and immediately the whole fleet, excepting the Peloponnesians, took the Athenians for leaders. Dorcis was sent out to replace Pausanias; but the allies refusing him obedience, he withdrew with his squadron from the fleet. Athens was from this time destined to be the head of a confederacy consisting of the Greeks of the Ægean Islands, Asia Minor, and Thrace. The consequence was, not merely the liberation of the Greek colonies, but the acquisition by Athens of a high degree of power. The confederates were permitted to supply money instead of ships, the latter being provided by Athens; and thus the former shortly found themselves reduced to the condition of tributaries to that state. She certainly did not use her power with much moderation.

The beginning of the Athenian ascendency took place about the year 477 B. C. A few more details, leading to this result, must be given. The Athenians, being acknowledged as leaders by the Greeks of Asia and the islands, proceeded regularly to organize the confederacy. By common consent, Aristides was appointed to make the assessment, determining how much each city was to contribute to the support of the war. This he executed with the greatest impartiality, and in such a manner that the justice of the proportions appears to have been questioned by none. The whole annual amount of the tribute was four hundred and sixty talents — not far from half a million of dollars. The war was successfully carried on under Cimon, the son of Miltiades, against those places in Europe which still held out for the Persian king.

But the allies grew weary of the contest, and began to refuse their services. The Athenians, being conscious of their strength, became haughtier in their conduct, and more harsh in enforcing the stipulated services, which came to be less punctually rendered. Hence Athens had wars with the delinquents; and as she uniformly prevailed, the fleet of the conquered city was taken from it, and a heavier tribute levied. In this way, from the leader, she became the mistress of her allies. Not far from this time, (469 B. C.,) the forces of the Athenian league, under Cimon, won two great victories, on the same day, from the Persians, by sea and then by land, at the mouth of the River Eurymedon, in Pamphylia.

In the aggressions made by the Athenians on some of the neighboring islands, the Lacedæmonians were appealed to, who secretly prepared to invade Attica. 464 B. C. But they were prevented by an earthquake, by which a great part of Sparta was overthrown, and twenty thousand persons perished. The helots, who were nearly all of Grecian blood, and chiefly descended from the conquered Messenians, took this opportunity to revolt, and for ten years gave great trouble to Lacedæmon. This people were finally received by the Athenians, who established them at Naupactus on the Corinthian Gulf.

A quarrel taking place between Megara and Corinth, the former revolted from the Lacedæmonian confederacy, and connected itself with Athens — 458 B. C. This was a fortunate occurrence to the latter. A war ensued against the Peloponnesians, in which Athens gained many successes both by land and sea. Its most active enemies by land were the Corinthians; by sea, the Æginetans; but the Athenians were victorious. About the same time, they began the construction of their long walls, by which the city and its port, Piræus, were connected, in such a way, that as long as they could command the sea and defend the walls, the most powerful land force could endanger neither.

In the present state of things, it was the policy of Lacedæmon to raise up Thebes as a check upon Athens; but little was effected by this means, as the successes of the latter in a short time brought all Bœotia into alliance with it. The Eastern Locrians were now brought to submission under the Athenian Myronides, and about the same period Ægina submitted to give up its fleet, demolish its walls, and pay a tribute. Thus this "eyesore of Piræus," as it was called, ceased to give trouble to Athens from its maritime strength and ever-active hostility. The war continued about four years longer, generally in favor of Athens. It was then suspended by a five years' truce with the Peloponnesians, B. C. 450.

The empire of Athens had now attained its greatest magnitude, extending over most of the islands of the Ægean, including Eubœa; over the Grecian towns of Thrace and Macedonia, and those of Asia. The terms of subjection were various; in some more, in others less, absolute. The Athenian power was extensive also on the continent of Greece. It controlled Megaris, Bœotia, Phocis, and Eastern Locris; from Pegæ and Naupactus, it commanded the Corinthian Gulf; in Peloponnesus, Trœzen was subject to it; its influence was predominant in Achaia, and Argos was connected with it by interest. From this enlargement of external influence, proceeded important changes in the internal government of the city. The poorer citizens ascended somewhat in the scale of society, and became comparatively enlightened.

After the fall of Themistocles, who had been ban

ished by ostracism, Cimon was long the first man in Athens. He possessed great abilities, wealth, and integrity, and was profusely liberal. The fences of his gardens and orchards he threw down, and permitted all to partake of their produce. A table for many of the poorer citizens was spread every day, and he was always ready to give or lend money to the indigent. His magnificence was also displayed in the public works with which he adorned the city,—porticoes, groves, and gardens,—the expense of which was derived partly from his own funds, and partly from the wealth which his victories had brought into the public treasury. But as Cimon was aristocratical in his political bias, and courted the friendship of Sparta, he at length fell under the ban of a party who obtained the ascendency, and procured his banishment—also by ostracism. The ostensible leader of this party was Ephialtes; but Pericles, the son of Xanthippus, was rapidly gaining the chief influence.

Pericles was at this period young; his birth was noble, and his abilities great. He possessed some military distinction, but was principally noted as an accomplished statesman and speaker. The force, polish, and elegance of his oratory were such as Athens had never known before. Every natural endowment was improved to the utmost by education, and by converse with philosophers and men of letters. The new government, with a view to gratify the multitude who missed the bounty of Cimon, sought the necessary means for this purpose, and was so fortunate as to curtail the aristocratic council of Areopagus, by the eloquence and influence of Pericles. In consequence of this change, the power of directing the issues from the public treasury without control, fell into the hands of the assembly.

Since the Persian war, Athens had become the seat of philosophy and art. Their growth had been liberally encouraged under the administrations of Themistocles and Cimon, and that of Pericles advanced yet further in the same career. The city was adorned with the masterpieces of sculpture, painting, and architecture. Contests of poetry and music accompanied the religious festivals. Tragedy and comedy, brought forth by the great masters of the passions and the heart, eagerly engaged the attention of the people. Many distinguished philosophers were resident in Athens, and their discourses in porticoes and other places of public resort commanded crowds of enthusiastic auditors. The consequence was, that the citizens were gratified, sometimes instructed and refined, but generally they became frivolous, critical, fastidious, and capricious. They lived rather upon excitement, than upon any steady and effectual application to some particular pursuit.

Hence arose a throng of profligate demagogues, who always made it an object to cater to the popular taste, at any cost of justice and humanity. What wonder, then, that we shall hereafter find the sway of the people as jealous as oppressive, and in case of the revolt of allies, their vengeance as cruel as their rule had been iniquitous?

Shortly after the rise of Pericles, an Athenian armament was despatched to Egypt to assist the inhabitants of that country in a revolt conducted by Inaros against the Persian authority. But it proved to be a failure; and after a contest of five years' duration, the rebellion was suppressed, its leader crucified, and most of his Grecian auxiliaries destroyed—454 B. C. About this time, the two great parties in Athens were reconciled, and Cimon was recalled at the motion of Pericles, having completed only five years of his term of banishment. His restoration probably facilitated the conclusion of the truce with Lacedæmon, before spoken of; and till his death Athens was undisturbed by internal contests. Some employment was furnished the people, who had become unaccustomed to peaceful industry, in colonizing the Thracian Chersonese; and at length the popular thirst of conquest was gratified for a short time in an attempt to add Cyprus to the Athenian confederacy. Cimon died during this enterprise, of which he was the leader; and this, with the want of provisions made it necessary for the armament to return.

After the termination of the five years' truce with Lacedæmon, difficulties again arose between that state and Athens; but by the address of Pericles, they were arrested without any fatal issue. Bribery is said to have been employed to procure the retreat of Pleistoanax, the youthful king of Lacedæmon, who had invaded Attica with an army. Athens, however, was at the same time in trouble from other quarters; the extent of her empire facilitated revolts, which brought her into contests; and becoming weary with such a state of things, and unable to maintain her empire in its present vastness, she now concluded with the Peloponnesians a truce for thirty years. By this act, besides Bœotia and Megara, which were already lost, she gave up Nisæa, Pegæ, and Trœzen, with the influence which they had hitherto exercised in Achaia. B. C. 445.

After the death of Cimon, a new opponent to Pericles was put forward by the aristocratical party, in the person of Thucydides, the brother-in-law of Cimon. But Pericles, who had yielded the palm to Cimon, would not give place to any other, and he obtained the entire ascendency in directing the affairs of the government. Through his influence, Thucydides, his rival, was soon banished by ostracism. A quarrel between Samos and Miletus, both allies of Athens, induced the Athenians to undertake the reduction of the former, which was effected in the ninth month of the siege. This took place six years from the commencement of the thirty years' truce.

Three years after the reduction of Samos, a dispute between Corinth and Corcyra, a colony of Corinth, gave rise to the most general, lasting, and pernicious war with which Greece had been hitherto afflicted. Corinth obtained aid from several of the Peloponnesian states, to reduce the inhabitants of Corcyra to subjection; while Corcyra, on the other hand, formed a defensive alliance with Athens, from which she received a fleet for her defence. The effect of these measures was obvious from the beginning. War raged among most of the Grecian states, and at length the great contest between Lacedæmon and Athens sprang up, which is to be detailed in the following chapter.

CHAPTER CCCXIX.

431 to 404 B. C.

The Peloponnesian War.

Matters being in the situation already stated, the Thebans, who were the most powerful and adventurous of the Spartan allies, undertook a military enterprise against the republic of Platæa. They entered the town, and were partially successful at first, but were at length overcome, and nearly two hundred prisoners falling into the hands of the Platæans, were all put to the sword. The Athenians, to whom Platæa had been remarkably faithful, espoused the part of the latter in this contest

The league being now broken between the Athenians and the Peloponnesians, each party prepared for war. Both the Lacedæmonians and Athenians solicited the aid of Persia, and both summoned their confederates in arms. Nearly all the Grecian states and islands embarked in the war on the one side or the other. Such was the ardor of preparation, that only a few weeks after the affair at Platæa, the Lacedæmonians and their associates assembled an army of sixty thousand men at the Isthmus of Corinth. Archidamus, the Spartan king, was intrusted with the general conduct of the war. They soon entered Attica, and, meeting with no opposition, advanced along its eastern coast, burning the towns and ravaging the country in their course. The Athenians, in the mean time, had, by the advice of Pericles, brought into the city their families and furniture, and sent their cattle to Eubœa and the other adjacent islands. This, however, was done reluctantly, for they were, beyond all other Greeks, attached to a country life, and the cessation of income from their country estates brought many of them from competence to poverty. Accommodations failed, too, in the city, for so vast a multitude. Nevertheless, they applied themselves vigorously to warlike preparations, and a fleet of one hundred ships was made ready to act against the enemy at home.

With this fleet, joined by several from Corcyra and other places, the Athenians sailed round Peloponnesus, and wasted much of its western coast. Passing on, they took Astacus, in Acarnania, expelled its tyrant, and, establishing democracy, admitted it to an alliance. Without any act of hostility, they brought the large island of Cephalonia over to their interest. Archidamus, vainly seeking a general battle with the Athenians, and finding his provisions not likely to hold out, returned home by way of Bœotia. This marauding expedition was repeated the next year by the Spartan king, but with no more decisive result, as Pericles adhered to the same policy in avoiding a direct engagement with his enemy on land.

But it exceeded the power of this great man to meet another enemy that was sent upon him and his people: that was a pestilence, which at this time attacked the unfortunate Athenians — having originated in Ethiopia, and afflicted Egypt and many parts of Asia. "It began with heats in the head, and inflammation in the eyes; the tongue and throat were bloody, the breath fetid; then came sneezing, then laborious coughing, then excessive evacuations in all ways, followed by violent hickups and spasms. The skin was reddish, and full of ulcers, but not outwardly hot, though the internal fever was such, that the patient could not bear the slightest covering, and many threw themselves into the wells for relief. Thirst was unquenchable, and sleep there was none; yet the sufferers were less weakened than might have been expected. The fever lasted from seven to nine days; but many who survived it perished by the ulceration of the bowels, and the flax which followed. The disease passed from the head through the whole body, and finally fixed in the extremities, which many lost. Some were totally deprived of memory, and recovered, not knowing their nearest friends, nor even themselves." Many other circumstances might be mentioned, were there space, showing the fearful character and effects of this pestilential fever. We must state that the moral recklessness of men, in the feeling that death was inevitable, almost surpasses belief. Many, laying their hands on every thing they could reach, revelled in debauchery and intemperance. The laws were impotent, since no one expected that he should live to suffer their sentence.

The spirit of the Athenians was broken. They made proposals of peace, which were haughtily refused; and the shame of failure concurred with previous sufferings to heighten their anger against Pericles, as the author of their misery. Pericles ably defended himself before an assembly which was called for the purpose. His arguments persuaded them to maintain the war; but their indignation for their individual losses did not subside till they had fined him heavily. He died soon after, (429 B. C.,) a victim of the pestilence, having first buried the last of his children, on which occasion his fortitude completely gave way.

The war continued without interruption for seven years following the death of Pericles, producing much individual loss and suffering, but with no decisive advantage to either of the contending states. The continental dependencies of Athens were attacked. Platæa fell after a noble defence. Most of the island of Lesbos revolted, but was in the end reduced to subjection. The states of Greece generally, at this period, became subject to internal commotions and seditions. In every republic, and in almost every city, the ambitious and intriguing found means of procuring the assistance of Sparta or of Athens, according as they espoused and favored the aristocratical or democratical interest. In this state of things, the most unnatural crimes were committed. The prodigal assassin freed himself from the clamors and the threats of his creditor. The parent with great cruelty punished the extravagance and dissipation of the son: the son avenged by parricide the severity of the parent. Public assemblies, meeting to consult the welfare of the state, decided their debates by the sword. Men thirsted for the blood of one another; and this general disorder overwhelmed all laws, human and divine.

In the seventh year of the war, the Lacedæmonians found themselves obliged to sue for peace; but the terms offered by the Athenians were too severe for their acceptance; however, in the eighth year, a truce for one year was concluded between Athens and Lacedæmon, together with a part of the Peloponnesian confederacy. But hostilities were still carried on in Thrace, where Bracidas, the Lacedæmonian, had, in the preceding year, captured Amphipolis, an Athenian colony of great importance; and soon after the expiration of the truce, the Athenians received a severe defeat, in attempting to recover it. A fifty years' truce was concluded between Athens and Lacedæmon, (421 B. C.,) to which, however, a great number of the Peloponnesian confederates refused to be parties. By its terms, Athens and Lacedæmon were placed nearly in the same situation as at the commencement of hostilities; but the interests of the several states of the Peloponnesian confederacy were entirely neglected.

A general dissatisfaction prevailed among the allies of Lacedæmon, who found themselves abandoned by the head of the confederacy at the first moment at which her interest ceased to be identical with theirs. Other causes of complaint existed against Lacedæmon, and there were also many disputes between the subordinate allies. A peculiar complicity attended the politics of Greece; and Athens became at one time actually at the head of a confederacy of Peloponnesian states. The war between Lacedæmon and Athens soon revived, and events speedily occurred which gave it a more decided character than before.

At the beginning of the Peloponnesian war, the superiority of Syracuse over the other states of Sicily had become nearly complete. The city was democratical, which inclined it to unite its interests with Athens; but on the other hand, its Dorian origin created a connection with Sparta. The Leontines, an Ionian people of Sicily, with many smaller states, endeavored to emancipate themselves from the authority of Syracuse; but being hard pressed in the war which ensued, they applied to Athens for assistance. This was granted, and soon after a general peace was concluded among the Sicilian states. But new disputes arose; and at length, the people of Egesta having implored the Athenians to protect them from Syracuse, the largest armament that the Athenians had ever despatched for foreign conquest, sailed from Athens.

Alcibiades.

This was the result of the counsels of Alcibiades, the Athenian, who had begun some time before to take a part in public affairs. He was the son of Clinias, a person of the highest birth in Athens, and early became master of a vast inheritance. His talents were as brilliant as his ambition was unbounded. Surrounded by flatterers, his confident temper was so far inflamed, that he meditated, contrary to the Athenian custom, speaking in the assembly before his twelfth year. From this purpose he was diverted by the great and wise Socrates, who, observing his superior abilities, took a special interest in him. A mutual friendship ensued; but the influence of Socrates could not permanently overcome the temptations which beset his young disciple. He became but too frequently the slave of voluptuousness and passion.

In fitting out the armament spoken of, Alcibiades afterwards declared his plans to have extended far beyond the immediate object of the expedition. He proposed, he said, to make the conquest of Sicily itself a step to that of the Greek states in Italy, and then to conquer Carthage; after this, the communication with Spain would enable Athens to raise mercenaries sufficient to insure the conquest of Peloponnesus. Alcibiades himself, having been forced by a party intrigue to fly from Athens, went to Lacedæmon, and by explaining these views, induced the Lacedæmonians to send aid to Syracuse. The succors arrived just in time to prevent its capture. The event of the expedition was, that the Athenian armament, as well as another of nearly equal force, which was sent to its support, was totally destroyed.

By this deviation from the policy recommended by Pericles, the Athenians lost that superiority which it had cost them so much to attain, and of which nothing but their own imprudence could have deprived them. The disaster occurred in the nineteenth year of the war, B. C. 413. The Athenians had soon to contend for the dominion of the sea: their allies began to leave them; and Persia gave her assistance to the Peloponnesians. The Athenian constitution underwent more than one change, and Alcibiades returned to his country. His talents enabled the Athenians, in some degree, to recover their superiority; but he was shortly after banished. Finally, in the twenty-sixth year of the war, the Athenian fleet was almost entirely captured in the battle of Ægospotami, and in the spring of the year 404 B. C. the city surrendered to the Lacedæmonians.

The subordinate allies urged the conquerors to execute a dreadful vengeance on their enemy; but the Lacedæmonians, whose views of self-interest were seldom impeded by any violent passions, perceived the wisdom of preserving Athens, and satisfied themselves with destroying the fortifications and the navy, reducing Athens to the condition of a subject ally, and establishing an oligarchy of thirty, in place of the splendid and energetic democracy which had rendered Athens so formidable to all the states of Greece. Athens submitted unwillingly, but unavoidably. Lysander, who had commanded the Lacedæmonian fleet in the engagement before referred to, entered the harbor; the exiles from the city returned, and the demolition of the walls was begun to the sound of festive music; for that day, says Xenophon, was thought the beginning of freedom to Greece. The general opinion, as the event showed, was erroneous, the weaker states gaining little by the change of masters. The war, which had lasted nearly twenty-seven years, was concluded, 403 B. C.

Death of Alcibiades.

Alcibiades was not among the exiles restored. He remained on his Thracian lordship, whither he had previously repaired, an object of jealousy both to Lacedæmon and to the new government of Athens. At last, to escape the former, he went into Asia.

When residing there, his house was attacked by a tumultuous assembly of people, at whose instigation is uncertain. The house was set on fire; Alcibiades sallied out with his servants, and none dared to meet him hand to hand — such was his personal prowess; but he was overwhelmed from a distance with darts and arrows, and thus slain before he had reached his fortieth year.

Death of Socrates.

CHAPTER CCCXX.

404 to 338 B. C.

Lacedæmonian and Theban Ascendency.

The elasticity which habits of freedom had given to the Athenian spirit, soon enabled the people to throw off the dominion of the oligarchy of thirty, or the thirty tyrants. These were Lacedæmonian captains, to whom the government of Athens was delegated by Lysander. Their administration was at first popular, but at length became excessively unjust and despotic. Many of the citizens were put to death through personal enmity, and many for their wealth; and it was actually voted that each one of the thirty should select one man, according to his pleasure, from the foreign sojourners in Athens; and that all so chosen should be put to death, and their property transferred to the treasury. These and other barbarities could not long be endured. Thrasybulus, who was then residing in Bœotia, was encouraged by the multitude of exiles to strike a blow against the despots. In this enterprise he succeeded, and the ancient constitution was reëstablished.

About three years after the restoration of democracy, Athens was disgraced by the condemnation of the most excellent man she ever produced — the philosopher Socrates. He was impeached before the popular court for reviling the gods which Athens acknowledged, for preaching other gods, and for corrupting the youth. He triumphantly repelled the accusations; but his accusers were powerful, and his judges prejudiced. He had mortally offended the sophists and atheists, and indeed all the followers of Democritus, the atomic philosopher, by his keen and pungent exposure of their errors. The popular sentiment was, doubtless, against Socrates, and the court but too evidently sympathized with it. His danger was increased by the manner of his defence. The judges were displeased at his denying them the accustomed homage of supplication and tears, which the philosopher considered as equally unworthy of himself, and really disrespectful to the tribunal. He was, therefore, condemned to suffer death.

Socrates again addressed his judges, declaring his innocence, and observing that the charges against him even if proved, did not amount to a capital crime. "But," he said, in conclusion, "it is time to depart; I to die, you to live; but which for the greatest good, God only knows." The execution of the sentence was respited for thirty days, on account of the absence of the sacred ship of Theseus,* during which it was not lawful to put malefactors to death. For this period, the friends of the philosopher had free access to him in prison. Means were contrived for his escape; the jailer was bribed, a vessel made ready, and a retreat in Thessaly provided. But Socrates, having always taught the duty of obedience to the laws, would not consent to set the example of breaking them. He waited the return of the ship, passed his last morning in calmly reasoning with his friends on the immortality of the soul, and the happiness derived from virtue, took the poisonous cup of hemlock, and died.

A few years anterior to the fall of Athens and the prevalence of the Spartan power, Amyrtæus, who had held a precarious freedom in the marshes of Egypt for forty years, established the independence of that country, in the reign of Darius Nothus, king of Persia. The embarrassments in which this and other revolts involved the Persian monarchy, had in a great measure checked her efforts in favor of Lacedæmon, during the

* On the eve of the day when Socrates was condemned, this ship was sent with offerings of thanksgiving to Apollo at Delos.

Peloponnesian war. Darius died soon after its conclusion, and was succeeded by Artaxerxes Mnemon.

A little subsequent to this, Cyrus, a younger brother of Artaxerxes, attempted to seize the sovereignty. The western parts of the Persian dominions, comprehending the Grecian Asiatic states, were in a very insubordinate state, and some in actual rebellion. This afforded a pretext for Cyrus to raise a body of mercenary Greek troops. With these and a large body of Asiatics, he marched toward Babylon. A battle took place at Cunaxa (400 B. C.,) not far from Babylon, in which Cyrus was slain, and the Asiatic part of his army defeated.

The Greeks, who had themselves been successful, were now left alone in the heart of a great empire. They amounted in number to about ten thousand. The generals were cut off by a treacherous stratagem of the Persians; but by their perfect discipline, assisted by the discretion and courage of Xenophon, the celebrated Athenian historian, they effected their retreat to the shores of the Euxine, which they reached at Trapezus, and passing along the southern coast, crossed over the Thracian Bosphorus into Europe. This remarkable achievement, which we have before described, is called "The Retreat of the Ten Thousand." "This expedition," says Sir Walter Raleigh, "as in all ages it was glorious, so did it both discover the secrets of Asia, and stir up the Greeks to think upon greater enterprises than ever their forefathers had undertaken."

The Greek army afterwards entered into the service of the Lacedæmonian confederacy, which had engaged in a war with Persia for the purpose of enabling the Asiatic Greeks to assert their independence. Dercyllidas, who was at the head of the Greeks, compelled the Persian commanders to conclude a treaty, by which all the Greek states of Asia were declared independent, 397 B. C. But this treaty not being ratified by the king of Persia, the Lacedæmonians renewed the war, though they were troubled at home by the reluctance which the Greek states showed to submit to their supremacy. Agesilaus, king of Lacedæmon, passed over into Asia with a Grecian army. His measures were marked with ability, and, in some degree, attended with success; but in the mean time, Athens entered into an alliance with Thebes against Lacedæmon. They were soon joined by the Corinthians, and Argians, and others of the inferior states of Greece.

Enagoras, governor of Cyprus, under the Persian authority or patronage, effected a union between Persia and this confederacy. The allied fleet defeated that of the Lacedæmonians at Cnidus, 394 B. C. The Athenian fortifications were soon afterwards restored, and that state began to recover its importance under Conon and Iphicrates.

In 387 B. C., the peace of Antalcidas — so called from the Lacedæmonian negotiator — was concluded, by which all the continental Greeks of Asia, with the Islands of Clazomenæ and Cyprus, became again subject to Persia. The European states of Greece were all to be independent. The supremacy of Lacedæmon was not so much impaired as her reputation was blemished by this disgraceful treaty. She was soon again at the head of a confederacy of dependent states, and owed the loss of her ascendency at last to the hostility produced by an extraxagant act of injustice, as will be mentioned in its place.

The change from the Athenian to the Lacedæmonian scendency "was, in some respects, a happy one, but not upon the whole. The smaller states were indeed released from the grinding tributes which had been wrung from them to support the navy of Athens, and to feed and amuse its idle and luxurious people. But the democratical governments were generally changed into oligarchies of the narrowest kind, dependent for existence, not on the willing acquiescence of the people, but on Lacedæmon. Many states were made the residence of Spartan governors, who were generally oppressive and arbitrary. Bred up in contempt for all mankind except their own fellow-citizens, they considered as rebellious all opposition to the will of a Spartan officer. Their tempers were harsh, their manners rude. Their notions of law were entirely derived from the institutions of Lacedæmon; and as popular complaint was never there allowed against any measure of persons in authority, they would put down all remonstrance, however moderate and lawful, by the most violent means. Athenian officers were commonly men of milder temper and more polished manners, and more accustomed to respect the feelings of the persons under their command. A proverb was current in Greece, that the Athenians were better as individuals, the Lacedæmonians as a government; and it illustrates the conduct of the two states toward their subjects."

The tranquillity which had now existed for a few years was interrupted from a new quarter. Olynthus, a Greek town on the coast of Macedonia, had become the head of a sort of federation of republics. Some towns which had refused to join the league, and were threatened with war, applied to Lacedæmon for protection. The Lacedæmonians were at present in the zenith of their power; Bœotia was completely theirs, Corinth firm in their friendship, Argos was reduced and Athens without allies. The Lacedæmonian confederates sent troops in aid of the towns which had asked for aid against Olynthus. A part of these, as they passed through Bœotia, were applied to for assistance by a political party in Thebes, then out of power. The Lacedæmonian commander suddenly seized the Cadmea, the citadel of Thebes; and in this notable treachery he was supported by King Agesilaus and the Spartan government; for such treachery it was, being a flagrant breach of that treaty establishing the independence of all Grecian towns, to which they had solemnly sworn.

This measure at first strengthened the Lacedæmonian power in the south of Greece; and soon afterward the Olynthians submitted, and formed part of the confederacy, subject to Lacedæmon. But it proved the beginning of a train of misfortunes which broke the power of the latter forever; in the opinion of Xenophon, it was a deserved punishment, suited to the perfidy and violence before mentioned. The era of the Olynthian subjection was 379 B. C.; but in the same year, the Thebans drove out the Lacedæmonians from the Cadmea. A war now ensued between Lacedæmon and Thebes. A Lacedæmonian general attempted to seize Athens in the midst of a profound peace—an act of perfidy, which, although unsuccessful, the Lacedæmonian government readily forgave. The Athenians, on this occurrence, immediately joined the Thebans; and the ensuing events of the war were unfavorable to the Lacedæmonians. But the Athenians afterwards withdrew from the contest, and finally gave their assistance to the Lacedæmonians.

At this time, Thebes, a state which produced few distinguished men, possessed two extraordinary citizens—Epaminondas and Pelopidas. The former was a man of consummate ability, but of retired and studious habits and limited fortune. He had hitherto taken little part in public affairs, and had remained undisturbed in Thebes under the usurping government. Pelopidas was active, prompt, and daring, possessing great dexterity and ready invention. He had been an exile, and was one of the seven conspirators who began the revolution. These men were mutual friends, and it was their fortune to inflict a dreadful defeat on the Lacedæmonians at Leuctra, 371 B. C.

This was a battle in which an important improvement in the Grecian science of war was made by Epaminondas. Heretofore the entire fronts of contending armies had commonly been brought into action at once, and the contest decided in every portion of the line by superior numbers or prowess. The Thebans had sometimes charged in column, when otherwise unable to break the opposing phalanx; but it was reserved for Epaminondas, to select, from the first, one point on which to make the decisive attack, and, while he withheld the weaker parts of his line from immediately closing, to unite in the attacking column such a body, that, though weaker in numbers on the whole, he might be decidedly stronger at the decisive point. On both sides, the battle was commenced by the horse, and that of the Lacedæmonians was quickly driven back on the infantry. Their phalanx was formed twelve deep; and Epaminondas directed his column fifty deep against the right wing, where stood Cleombrotus, the king, with most of the Spartans. Epaminondas considered that, if this were routed, the rest would be an easy conquest. The unequal struggle was maintained a while by the chosen band around the Spartan king; but the pressure was too severe; the king was slain, with many of the noblest Spartans; the remainder of the line speedily followed; and the proud Lacedæmonians with astonishment saw themselves overcome in a pitched battle with inferior numbers—an occurrence unknown for ages—371 B. C.

It appears that the remains of the army were saved principally by a truce effected through the mediation of Jason, then holding the supreme authority in Thessaly, which had acquired a short-lived importance. The Thebans now became the leading power of Greece; the Peloponnesus was repeatedly invaded by them; and they even attempted to establish, by the assistance of Persia, a general Greek confederacy, of which they themselves aspired to be leaders. This scheme proved abortive; and the several states of Greece were involved in a variety of political relations much too complicated to admit of explanation here.

Lacedæmon soon after experienced a further crippling of her power by the independence of Messenia, which the assistance of Thebes was the means of effecting. This event took place 369 B. C. At last, in 362 B. C., a battle was fought at Mantinea, in Arcadia, in which the Thebans were successful, but Epaminondas was killed. He fell just at the critical moment of the fight. He lived to know that his army was victorious; then fainted on the extraction of the weapon, and died, it is said, with an expression of joy that he had not lived to taste of defeat. No one attempted to improve the victory. Pelopidas was already dead, and the whole result of the day was completely indecisive.

With this event terminated the superiority of the Thebans, but that of the Lacedæmonians never revived. A general peace ensued, to which, however the Lacedæmonians were not expressly parties. The effect of the temporary superiority of the Thebans was thus permanently beneficial to the general freedom of Greece, by destroying, or at least interrupting, the system under which one leading state had been accustomed to compel many others, under the title of allies, to follow its lead, whether in peace or war.

At this period of Greek history, a state became important, which hitherto had scarcely been considered as belonging to Greece. Macedonia was chiefly surrounded, on the land side, by barbarians of a warlike character; and her sea-coast was planted with ancient Grecian colonies. The foundation of her monarchy dates from about 596 B. C. It had been tributary to the Persian power, but emancipated itself soon after the failure of the expedition of Xerxes. It had occasionally taken part in the wars of the leading states of the south; but little can be said favorably of its policy or good faith. The country itself was frequently harassed by civil wars between different branches of the royal family. In one of the most marked eras of such discord, Philip, the son of Amyntas, became king, 359 B. C. In addition to the civil broils he found the kingdom endangered by the barbarous tribes of Illyria and Pœonia, and by the hostility of the Thracians and Athenians, each of whom supported a pretender to the crown. It seems probable, too, that it was actually at war with Olynthus, which was now recovering its importance.

The first success of Philip was against the Athenians, whose army was forced to capitulate and quit the country; and immediately after this, he obtained a great victory over the Pœonians and Illyrians, together with a large accession of territory. He obtained peace, or, as some think, alliance with the Athenians by measures of conciliation; but a dispute arising respecting Amphipolis—a city which had once been among the most valuable possessions of Athens, now under the power of Philip—and negotiation failing, the quarrel between Macedonia and Athens was renewed. About this time, Rhodes, Chios, Byzantium, and Cos, four states of the Athenian confederacy, declared themselves independent. A contest commenced, commonly called the *social war;* and Philip, uniting himself with the Olynthians, declared war against Athens, and carried it on with success. At the same time, the Athenians were involved in hostilities in Thrace, and with the Thebans. At last they were under the necessity of acknowledging the independence of their revolted allies—355 B. C.

At the instigation of the Thebans, the Amphictyonic council condemned the Lacedæmonians and Phocians to pay a fine. The former were mulcted in the sum of five hundred talents, on account of their seizure of the Cadmea; and, refusing to pay, the fine was doubled, according to the law of that council. The Phocians were fined for ploughing up some land said to have been consecrated to the Delphian Apollo. The two states resisted the authority of the council, and the Phocians seized the temple of Delphi, where immense treasures were accumulated. The war against Phocis, usually called the *Phocian Sacred War*, was waged by Thebes, at the head of an Amphictyonic confederacy, comprehending many Locrian and Thessalian tribes. These were aided by the Macedonians. Phocis was assisted by Lacedæmon, Athens, and their confederates.

In the mean time, the Macedonian king extended

his dominion, or, at any rate, his influence, over the greater part of Illyria on one side, and Thrace on the other. Athens, however, acquired the Thracian Chersonese, and afterwards succeeded in detaching Olynthus from the alliance of Macedonia; but the result was, that Philip reduced Olynthus, and added the territory to his dominions. Peace was at length concluded between Athens and Macedonia — 346 B. C. The party in Athens which had been most adverse to

Demosthenes.

Philip, was headed by the illustrious orator Demosthenes, who, nevertheless, concurred in advising this peace. This individual, the most renowned in eloquence whether of ancient or modern times, was now a young man, rising to eminence as a professional lawyer. From his father he had inherited a considerable fortune; but this he rapidly dissipated, and then, at the age of twenty-five, betook himself to a profession by which many had arisen to wealth and importance in Athens — that of writing speeches for suitors in the courts of judicature. At the time now spoken of, he had become a leading speaker in the assembly, and had embarked himself in a party hostile to Philip. Notwithstanding a disadvantageous voice and person, and a harsh temper, he became, by the force of application and ability, the first man of Athens — her most finished orator, and most powerful political leader.

The sacred war terminated, soon after the peace between Athens and Macedonia, by a complete conquest of the Phocians, on whom a heavy fine was imposed. Beside this, all the towns were destroyed except three, and their fortifications were dismantled. The people were removed into villages, their military stores taken from them, and their voice in the Amphictyonic council transferred to the Macedonian king. This punishment was inflicted in the room of that which was allotted to sacrilege by the Amphictyonic law, viz., the throwing of the people of the guilty district from the cliffs of the sacred mountain. The latter course had been advised in regard to the Phocians, but more moderate counsels prevailed.

The influence and dominion acquired by Philip were extended from time to time, especially in parts of Thrace which were yet unsubdued. He was considered, beside, as the head of a league formed by many of the Thessalian nations. On the other hand, the party of Demosthenes, in addition to their alarm at the increase of Philip's power, were anxious for war with Macedonia, as the most effectual means of holding the political power at Athens. Their opponents were headed, also, by a person of singular ability in debate, second only to Demosthenes; this was Æschines. The charges preferred, each against the other were almost equally well sustained, though Demosthenes prevailed in the end. The sounder opinion respecting the war was probably entertained by Æschines, as the Athenians, acting as the allies of Philip, might perhaps have moderated the proceedings of the confederacy, and secured the continuance of peace on their part.

Hostilities between the two countries recommenced partially, without an actual declaration of war. The confederacy against Philip was a powerful one. The people of Chios, Rhodes, and Cos were strong at sea, and closely connected with Byzantium. The power of Athens alone was most formidable, and there was an abundance of supplies, for the Athenians had secured the alliance of Persia. The first commander of their armament in the Hellespont was Chares. Under him it sustained a defeat; but Phocion, a man of superior abilities, superseding him, restored the face of affairs by his success against the enemy, and his justice and liberality toward the confederates. The system of operations was ably projected by Demosthenes, and was carried into effect by Phocion with no less ability. The success of the measures adopted by the latter was materially affected by the weight of his character. Philip now abandoned the hope of reducing the adverse towns of the Thracian shore, and came to a compromise with his enemies. Hence another interval of peace ensued.

Yet another sacred war broke out soon after the termination of the preceding. The inhabitants of Amphissa, a town of the Ozolian Locrians, having, like the Phocians, used in tillage some of the land consecrated to the Delphian Apollo, they resisted the judgment passed against them by the Amphictyonic council, and war ensued. That council chose Philip as the commander of its army, and the Athenians declared in favor of the Amphissians. In a short time, the latter were reduced. But Athens was at the head of a confederacy consisting of Athenians, Corinthians, Megarians, and Acarnanians; and by the address of Demosthenes, the Thebans were detached from the Amphictyonic league, and united themselves with Athens. A battle took place at Chæronea in Bœotia, between the army of the Athenian confederacy and that of the Amphictyonic league. The aggregate force of the former appears to have considerably exceeded that of Philip; but the advantage was balanced by the latter being united under one able commander. The Athenian generals were Chares and Lysicles. The names of the Theban commanders have not been preserved. The battle was hard fought and decisive, and was gained by the Macedonian king — 338 B. C. This, finally, threw Greece into the hands of the conqueror.

The news filled Athens with dismay. Demosthenes, the adviser of the war, had borne arms in the battle, and for more rapid flight had thrown away his shield — an action deemed the most disgraceful proof of cowardice. The sense of his political failure and his military dishonor, prevented him from showing himself in the first burst of popular indignation; and he procured a mission by which he withdrew a while from Athens. The leaders of the war party had the address, after having escaped condemnation themselves through the moderation of their adversaries to divert the popular fury against the generals

Lysicles was the victim selected: he was condemned and executed.

Philip, however, chose not to treat his enemy as a conquered people. The separate governments retained their independence, subject only, in their national acts, to the control of the king. A garrison of the victorious army was placed in the Cadmea, — the citadel of Thebes, — and a general peace was established.

CHAPTER CCCXXI.

338 to 280 B. C.

Macedonian Ascendency.

Alexander.

PHILIP was now, without question, the first potentate of Greece. His kingdom was flourishing; his enemies reduced; his allies many and powerful, and entirely under his direction. Macedonia thus took her place as the leading state in Greece. The extraordinary genius of Philip was no doubt the principal cause of his success; but much, also, was owing to the peculiar circumstances of the internal politics of Athens. "The party which principally opposed his projects found themselves, for the preservation of their power, under the necessity of stimulating the democracy by violent and precipitate measures: of these circumstances Philip always availed himself with perfect skill and temper; and even if we fully admit the truth of the charge commonly made against him, of grasping and unscrupulous ambition in his general policy, we must acknowledge, on the other hand, that in almost every single point of dispute between himself and his adversaries, strict and liberal justice, according to Greek notions, was on his side."

At the instance of Philip, a general congress was assembled at Corinth. His projects for the invasion of Persia were approved, and he was elected captain-general of Greece. In the midst of his preparations, he was assassinated by a Macedonian of rank. This was in the second year after the victory at Chæronea. But Philip's plans of conquest, though interrupted for the present, did not perish with himself; for he left a son, — the celebrated Alexander, — of talents not inferior, and ambition more unbounded. The news of Philip's death was received by the party of Demosthenes at Athens with the most unmanly exultation. The murderer had been slain, but high honors were voted to his memory. This was not only disgraceful in itself, but was stamped with a character of peculiar ingratitude, in view of Philip's leniency towards the city.

Philip was succeeded in the sovereignty of Macedonia by Alexander. The latter was intrusted with the authority which his father had held in Thessaly; and he was elected leader of the Greek confederacy against Persia, at a congress held at Corinth. Lacedæmon alone dissented from the choice, its deputies protesting "that their national inheritance was not to follow, but to lead." Alexander was eminently fitted for the high station to which he was called. His great natural endowments had been improved by the best instructions which the age could supply. As a patron of letters, Philip manifested both liberality and discernment. His court was the resort of many eminent philosophers; but the education of his son had been chiefly intrusted to Aristotle, the most distinguished of them all.

Massacre at Thebes.

Macedonia was attacked by the Illyrians and some Thracian tribes, but under its new king successfully resisted the attack, whose army advanced even to the north of the Ister. These wars are said to have been excited by the party of Demosthenes at Athens, who are also accused of communicating with Persia, as indeed almost every Greek state had been within the last eighty years. The Thebans alone broke out into actual conflict, and attacked the Amphictyonic garrison in the Cadmea. No other state was subjected to so galling a mark of defeat as that which ensued. It was not long before Alexander took the city: a dreadful massacre followed; all who survived were sold for slaves; and the city was utterly destroyed. This terrible catastrophe occurred in the year 335 B. C. All opposition was abandoned on the part of the Athenians, and a general peace ensued in Greece.

The confederacy, now collected their resources for the invasion of the Persian empire. There was little or no cause of quarrel between Greece and Persia, but the notions of international justice were very loose in those days, and especially among the Greeks. Nations paid respect to treaties, and regarded those nations to whom they were bound by treaty; but other communities seem hardly to have been considered as possessing any rights whatever. The invasion of the East was an affair rather of ancient enmity, and, so far as Alexander was concerned, of unscrupulous ambition. As we have already given an account of Alexander's conquests, we shall but briefly notice them here.

His army passed into Asia by the Hellespont in 334 B. C., and defeated the Persians at the River Granicus, in Mysia. The same year, Alexander conquered the provinces on the western coast of Asia Minor. In the following year, he proceeded still farther eastward, and although endangered by the activity of the Persian fleet in the Ægean Sea, and by a union between Lacedæmon and Persia, he penetrated to the borders of Syria, and in the autumn of the same year, he entirely defeated an immense army, headed by the Persian king Darius himself, at Issus, in Cilicia.

This was immediately followed by the conquest of Syria, though Tyre was not reduced till after a siege of seven months. Alexander next proceeded to Egypt, whose conquest was effected, or rather whose submission was received, without delay. By these events, the Persians were cut off from all communication with Egypt. Here he commenced a permanent and useful monument of his greatness, in founding the city of Alexandria, 332 B. C.

Alexander then crossed Syria and Mesopotamia, passed the Tigris, and in 331 B. C., met and defeated the enemy at Gangamela, near Arbela, on the eastern bank of the river. He was now master of Persia. Darius escaped into Bactria, where he was slain by Bessus. The latter now declared himself the king of Asia; but Alexander's army having crossed the Oxus, Bessus was delivered up to him by his associates, and was put to death as a murderer and traitor. The Macedonian advanced northward as far as the Jaxartes, and defeated a tribe of Scythians dwelling on the north-eastern frontier of the Persian empire. The reduction of Sogdiana (328 B. C.) completed the conquest of the Persian monarchy.

The next measure of Alexander was the invasion of India; for the lust of conquest increased in proportion to the increase of his dominions. After returning victorious from this expedition, he spent the short remainder of his life in the improvement of Babylon, which he chose for the seat of his government. He attempted to bring back the province of Babylonia to its ancient fruitfulness and prosperity, by reconstructing the ancient canals, dams, and other works, which were designed to irrigate the region, by carrying through it and diffusing the waters of the Tigris and Euphrates. While he was overlooking these works, with his wonted activity and carelessness of his person, in an open boat, among the unwholesome marshes,—and at the same time being addicted to excessive debauchery,—he was seized with a fever, and shortly after died, in the thirty-third year of his age, and in the thirteenth of his reign. B. C. 323.

Alexander left his vast empire to be torn in pieces by the greedy and impatient soldiers who had aided him in the acquisition of his prey. A period of confusion, bloodshed, and crime ensued, to which the history of civilized nations scarcely furnishes a parallel.

During the latter years of Alexander, Greece was generally quiet, and little remarkable occurred, except some party struggles in Athens. The proposal, on the part of Ctesiphon, to honor Demosthenes with a golden crown, caused a ferment in Athens, and the latter was attacked in a speech of great ability by Æschines. This brought out Demosthenes in defence, whose oration, still extant, is the most remarkable on record. Ctesiphon, who was prosecuted for making the proposal, was acquitted, and the accusers, failing to obtain a fifth of the votes, became liable to a heavy fine; so far had Æschines underrated the power of his opponent's eloquence or interest. Unable to pay the fine, or perhaps unwilling to live under his triumphant enemies, Æschines departed from Athens, and made his residence at Rhodes.

Not long before the death of Alexander, Demosthenes also went into banishment. The cause of it was the prosecution brought against him, on a charge of being bribed to espouse the cause of Harpalus, who had rebelled against the Macedonian monarch. Demosthenes, probably finding the popular current strong against him, and wishing therefore to take his trial before a more impartial tribunal, procured a decree to refer the matter to the Areopagus. The court pronounced against him, and Demosthenes, being fined in the sum of fifty talents, withdrew to Ægina.

We have already given a rapid sketch of the events which followed the death of Alexander; but it is necessary to glance again at this subject. Difficulties immediately arose as to the succession in the empire. It was believed that on his death-bed the conqueror had given his ring and signet to Perdiccas, one of his most eminent generals. The army made choice of Philip Aridæus, an illegitimate son of Philip; and one of Alexander's wives having borne a son soon after the monarch's death, he was named from the father, and associated in the kingdom with Aridæus. The latter was a youth of feeble intellect. Perdiccas was appointed regent in conjunction with Leonatus, one of the Macedonian generals. Meleager, another general, who was afterward associated with them, was put to death soon after his elevation. Perdiccas had the actual sway under these circumstances.

The several departments of the empire were committed to the government of different officers. The most important arrangements were the following: Antipater and Craterus took the Macedonian provinces; Ptolemy Soter took Egypt; Thrace was assigned to Lysimachus; Cappadocia and Paphlagonia to Eumenes; the Greater Phrygia to Perdiccas; the Lesser, with Pamphylia and Lycia, to Antigonus; Persis to Peucestes; Media to Python; and Syria, Cilicia, and Babylon to Seleucus Nicanor. There were some twenty-three other generals, to whom less considerable portions of the empire were consigned. As was to have been expected, these generals contended among themselves in bloody wars and massacres—a calamity which might possibly have been avoided had Alexander expressly appointed a successor. Their contentions issued, in 312 B. C., in the establishment of four of the number over the whole empire, in their separate divisions, which constituted four considerable monarchies.

The names of these generals were Ptolemy, Lysimachus, Cassander, and Seleucus. Egypt, Libya Arabia, and Palestine, were assigned to Ptolemy Macedonia and Greece, to Cassander; Bithynia and Thrace, to Lysimachus; but the remaining territories in Asia, as far as the River Indus, which were called the *kingdom of Syria*, to Seleucus. The most powerful of these divisions was that of Syria, under Seleucus and his descendants, called *Seleucidæ*, and that of Egypt, under the Ptolemies. Only Ptolemy and Seleucus transmitted their empires to their children.

Of the relatives of Alexander, his brother Aridæus, and his son Alexander, before spoken of, were soon destroyed. Another son, named Hercules, with his mother, Barsine, and Cleopatra, the only sister of Alexander, shared the same fate not long afterwards

Thus his whole family became extinct—a remarkable instance of the vanity of human grandeur.

The contests among these generals enabled some of the Asiatic provinces to assert their independence and the kingdoms of Bithynia, Cappadocia, Pontus, and Pergamus, appear to have originated not far from this period. Egypt and its dependencies remained under the dominion of Ptolemy's descendants; Seleucus's family maintained the kingdom of Syria; and Macedonia was subjected for a time to a series of hapless revolutions.

"Such," it has been remarked, "were the results of Alexander's conquests, and of his early death. There is some reason for believing that the prolongation of his life might have been productive of good. Undoubtedly he had discovered views of policy much more enlarged and liberal than those commonly entertained by ancient conquerors. At the time of his death, he was strenuously endeavoring to remove the prejudices of his countrymen, and to obtain for the inhabitants of the conquered districts a recognition of their rights, and a compliance with their national feelings, to a degree which had already shocked the arrogant and exclusive feelings of his Grecian followers. The civilization of some countries of the East, and especially of Egypt, gained a considerable advance from Alexander's conquest; and the foundation of Alexandria produced advantages of which he had a distinct foresight; though their magnitude must have far exceeded any degree of success which he had contemplated from his measure.

"Here, however, his merits terminate; and had these alone been known to historians, he never would have obtained from them the surname of *Great*, which he owed entirely to his military renown. Yet, if we confine our attention to his warlike career, we shall find him to have been, perhaps, the cause of more misery to mankind than any human being whose name makes a part of history. Other conquerors, it is true, have shed more blood; many have waged war on a much more cruel system; and he exhibited some instances of forbearance, which were rare and unexpected in those times, although in modern warfare, a contrary conduct would have been more remarkable. But no one ever bestowed such fatal brilliancy upon the hateful lust of conquest. His extraordinary abilities, his daring spirit, and the unparalleled splendor of his successes, have been the more mischievous in their example from the amiable qualities which he united to his military propensities."

Such is the stern but just verdict of reason upon the career of Alexander. His achievements were, however, stupendous. He crossed the Propontis in 334, and died in 323. It was in the brief space of eleven years, as has been before remarked, that he accomplished the deeds of which we have given a naked outline. Nor was he a mere warrior. He displayed great talents as a statesman, and many of the traits of a gentleman. His whole life, indeed, was founded upon an atrocious wrong—that one man may sacrifice millions of lives for his own ambition. But this was the error of the age. As before intimated, considered in the light of Christianity, he was a monster; yet, according to the heathen model, he was a hero, and almost a god.

In seeking for the motives which impelled Alexander forward in his meteor-like career, we shall see that it was the love of glory—an inspiration like that of the chase, in which the field is an empire, and the game nothing less than kings. In this wild ambition, he was stimulated by the Iliad of Homer; and it was his darling dream to match the bloody deeds of its heroes—Ajax and Achilles. It is impossible to see in his conduct any thing which shows a regard to the permanent happiness of mankind. He makes war as if might were the only test of right; and he sacrifices nations to his thirst of conquest with as little question of the rectitude of his conduct as is entertained by the lion when he slays the antelope, or the sportsman when he brings down his game.

Although we see many noble traits in Alexander, the real selfishness of his character is evinced in his famous letter to Aristotle. The latter, having published some of his works, is sharply rebuked by the conqueror, who says to him, "Now that you have done this, what advantage have I, your pupil, over the rest of mankind, since you have put it in the power of others to possess the knowledge which before was only imparted to me?" What can be more narrow and selfish than this? Even the current standard of morals in Alexander's time would condemn it as excessive meanness.

We must not omit to record the last days of one that figures in Alexander's annals, and is hardly less famous than the conqueror himself: we mean his noble horse, Bucephalus. This animal, more renowned than any other of his race, died on the banks of the Hydaspes. Craterus was ordered to superintend the building of two cities, one on each side of this river. The object was to secure the passage in future. That on the left bank was called *Nicæa*, the other *Bucephala*, in honor of the favorite horse, which expired in battle without a wound, being worn out by age, heat, and over-exertion. He was then thirty years old. He was a large, powerful, and spirited horse, and would allow no one but Alexander to mount him. From a mark of a bull's head imprinted on him, he derived his name, *Bucephalus;* though some say that he was so called in consequence of having in his forehead a white mark resembling a bull's head.

Once this famous charger, whose duties were restricted to the field of battle, was intercepted, and fell into the hands of the Uxians. Alexander caused a proclamation to be made, that, if Bucephalus were not restored, he would wage a war of extirpation against the whole nation. The restoration of the animal instantly followed the receipt of this notification; so great was Alexander's regard for his horse, and so great the terror of his name among the barbarians. "Thus far," writes Arrian, "let Bucephalus be honored by me, for the sake of his master."

CHAPTER CCCXXII.

280 to 146 B. C.

Decline and Fall of the States, or Roman Conquest.

A FURTHER account of the successors of Alexander is not required here; and indeed their history presents only a series of uninteresting revolutions. The Grecian people had now lost their political distinction. A few efforts only were made to revive the expiring spirit of liberty. Demosthenes had labored somewhat to this effect, and to arouse his countrymen to shake off the yoke of Macedon; but it was too late. The pacific counsels of Phocion suited far better the timid and languid temper of the people. When Antipater governed Greece, subsequently to Alexander's death, he demanded that Demosthenes should be delivered up to him. But this Demosthenes prevented, by resorting to suicide. Among the efforts made to vindicate the national freedom, and indeed the last one, was the formation of the *Achæan league*, which was a union of twelve of the smaller states, for this object. But before we speak more particularly of this, a short notice must be taken of the irruption of the Gauls into Greece.

A body of this people had emigrated into Pannonia, the part of Hungary immediately south and west of the Danube, at the same time that another horde crossed the Alps, and planted themselves in Cisalpine Gaul. The portion which settled in Pannonia afterwards extended their sway as far as the borders of Thrace, under the command of Cambaules. Subsequently to this period, three bodies of invaders went forth, one of which, under its leader, Bolgius, attacked Macedonia and Illyricum. They were encountered by Ptolemy Ceraunus, who was overcome and slain 280 B. C., a few months after the death of Seleucus. Following this event, the Gauls retired; but in the next year, Brennus and Acichorius, who had in the preceding year commanded the army which attacked Pæonia, led a vast body of Gauls, both infantry and cavalry, against Greece.

They were checked for some time at Thermopylæ, by a powerful Grecian army, assembled to oppose them, headed by the Athenians. The barbarians had no defensive armor, except a shield; their weapons were a javelin and a large, pointless, cutting sword; their mode of fighting was irregular; and they strove in vain to penetrate the firm barrier of Grecian spears that stretched entirely across the narrow valley. This pass, however, they eventually turned, by drawing off a portion of the Grecian forces in defence of a town of the Ætolian territory, which the Gauls had reached in another quarter, and where they had committed the most dreadful excesses upon its inhabitants.

After this, they attacked the temple of Apollo at Delphi, in Phocis. Here they were repulsed with great loss by the natives, aided by the strength of the position, and by the superstitious terrors attached to the spot. Of this circumstance the Phocians availed themselves with great dexterity, having learned beforehand the response of the oracle, that "the god would protect his own." The miserable remnant of the army under Brennus arrived at length in the encampment of their countrymen, when their commander, who had been dangerously wounded, is said to have wilfully hastened his death through shame. Before the passage at Thermopylæ had been won, a body of Gauls had ravaged Ætolia, whence they were compelled to retreat. The whole invading army was finally destroyed at the River Sperchius, in Thessaly.

The Achæan league was formed 280 B. C., at first by four Achæan states. Soon afterward it was joined by other cities of Achaia. These all combined for the purposes of reciprocal defence and common regulation. About thirty years after its origin, Aratus having headed a revolution in Sicyon, united that important city to the league, and was subsequently general or president of the confederation.

The citadel of Corinth, one of the strongest fortresses in Greece, was the most important of all to any person ambitious of empire, being set on a lofty mountain in the isthmus. It gave to its possessor not only the command of the rich and populous Corinth, but also the power of impeding all land passage between the peninsula and the continent of Greece. This citadel, which was in the possession of Antigonus Gonatas was surprised and taken by Aratus, and the result was, that much of Southern Greece was relieved from the ascendency of Macedonia. In this contest the Achæan league was assisted by Ptolemy Philadelphus, the king of Egypt.

But in the year 226 B. C., Cleomenes, who had become king of Sparta after that state had been subjected to several severe contests, determined to assert the predominance of his country in Greece, and made war upon the Achæans. He obtained some important victories, and won Argos and Corinth from the league. They were, however, taken from him not long afterward, in a battle which was obstinately contested; but at length the Lacedæmonian force was irrecoverably broken and put to rout. Sparta was captured, but the Lacedæmonians were left by the conquerors in the possession of their independence.

Macedonia and Greece were now preparing to follow the fate of all the nations within the grasp of Roman ambition. Their period of conquest was ended, and that of their subjugation was at hand. The Romans had become the most powerful of the contemporary nations, and were fast extending their conquests toward the East. The occasion of the introduction of the Romans into Greece, was an invitation from the Ætolians to interfere in a quarrel they had with Macedonia. Roman commissioners were appointed, who decided against Philip V., the Macedonian king. He yielded to the decision, and died soon after. He was succeeded by Perseus, his son. The Romans declared war against this prince, upon pretexts which are now scarcely intelligible.

The Achæans had suppressed a revolt at Lacedæmon, and had put an end to the institutions of Lycurgus, in 189 B. C. They had also been able to suppress an attempt of the Messenians to separate themselves from the league. In every transaction in Greece, whether invited or not, the Romans now claimed and exercised the right of interference; and their dispute with Perseus seems to have commenced on the same principle. He had endeavored to conciliate the favor of the Achæans, who had for a long time shown to the Macedonians every symptom of hatred short of actual war. The Romans encouraged the Achæans to persevere in this policy.

War was declared by the Romans against Macedon 172 B. C. Perseus was at first joined by the Bœotians; but their courage failing them, they abandoned the cause. They were not saved from the vengeance of Romans by this movement. That people punished such individuals as had been active against them, and broke up the Bœotian confederacy. In the early part of the contest, Perseus obtained some successes, upon which he offered to make peace on the same terms with those which had been exacted from Philip; but the Roman general demanded that he should submit to the discretion of the senate, thus acting upon the avowed Roman principle of increasing the arrogance of their tone upon any defeat, and manifesting moderation only in success — a base and contemptible principle.

In the fifth year of the war, Perseus was completely

routed at Pydna by Paulus Æmilius. He was shortly after made prisoner, conveyed to Rome, and exhibited in triumph, after which he died in prison from ill usage. His kingdom was broken up into districts, which were allowed to elect their own magistrates, but were made tributary to Rome. The inhabitants of each district were forbidden to contract marriages, or make bargains, in reference to land, with those of any other, and no timber was allowed to be cut for ship-building. This settlement was completed in the year 167 B. C.

The Illyrians, having joined Perseus at the end of the war, were totally subdued. But an exploit, most characteristic of the Romans, was performed in Epirus. The Epirotes had commenced hostilities against Rome, during the war of Perseus, in consequence of the oppressive treatment which they received; but they were shortly compelled to submit. After their submission had been accepted, troops were introduced, under false pretences, into their towns; the towns, to the number of seventy, were plundered and destroyed, and their inhabitants, to the amount of one hundred and fifty thousand men, women, and children, were sold as slaves.

The Rhodians had been put in possession of Lycia and Caria by the Romans. The Lycians refused to submit, and they were encouraged by Rome against the Rhodians, who, however, succeeded in reducing them. Subsequently, the Rhodians had offered to arrange a peace, as mediators between Rome and Perseus. For these offences, they were obliged to put to death all who had spoken against Rome, and to give up both Lycia and Caria to the all-grasping power of that state.

The reward of the Achæans for their unfailing fidelity as allies of Rome, was that, as soon as the Romans were strong enough to dispense with their voluntary services, they strove to weaken them as much as possible, that they might be the less able to withstand oppression. Three years after the return of the Roman general Æmilius to Italy, C. Sulpicius Gallus was sent into Greece, and instructed to sever as many cities as possible from the Achæan league. This object was, to some extent, effected.

Some time previously to the subjugation of Greece, Philopœmen was selected to command the forces of the Achæan cities. He was an admirable man; but in one instance he stained his character by his conduct toward the Spartans, numbers of whom he cruelly butchered when the city of Sparta was taken by him. He was, however, called to suffer in his turn; for, at the age of seventy years, he was taken prisoner when besieging Messene. The Messenians were so rejoiced to possess this illustrious man in bondage, that they dragged him in chains to the public theatre, for crowds to gaze upon him. At night, he was put into a dungeon, and the jailer carried to him a dose of poison. He calmly received the cup, and having learned that most of his friends had escaped by flight, he said, "Then I find we are not entirely unfortunate," and drinking off the fatal draught without one murmur, laid himself down and expired.

The Romans had, in effect, conquered Greece by their arts, before they made use of their arms. They had corrupted many of the principal Greeks, and on specious pretences they marched their legions against this once renowned people. The consul Mummius completed the war which Metellus commenced. The former, arriving with a powerful army, sent Metellus and his forces back into Macedonia. He then engaged in the siege of Corinth, which Metellus had before approached. In that city, Diæus, the Achæan leader, had shut himself up. The besiegers were careless through the confidence of strength, and the Achæans, making a sudden sally, drove in their outposts, and killed and wounded numbers of them. Encouraged by this success, they came out and offered battle. The consul eagerly embraced it. The Achæan cavalry fled at the first onset, but the foot maintained the fight with desperate resolution against an enemy superior in strength. At length they were broken by an attack in flank, and finally routed. Had Diæus now retreated into Corinth, assembled the relics of the vanquished army, and prepared for a resolute defence, he might probably have obtained some tolerable terms for his country, from the eager desire of Mummius to finish the war before the expiration of his command. Instead of this, he fled to Megalopolis, where he killed his wife to save her from captivity, and then ended his own life by poison.

Abandoned by their leader, the Achæans made no attempt at defence. They silently withdrew in the following night, and most of the Corinthians did the same. The gates were left open; but Mummius delayed for a time to enter, from fear of an ambuscade. On the third day after the engagement, he entered the city. He cruelly slaughtered most of the men whom he found there, sold the women and children, and pillaged and burnt the place, after selecting the most celebrated works of art, and shipping them for Rome. The pretence for all this destruction was the insult offered to the Roman commissioners, who had been sent, ten in number, to assist the consul in settling the affairs of Greece. The true motive was the wish to deprive the Achæans of a fortress important both from its strength and situation.

From this time forward, Greece, with the exception of Thessaly, was reduced to a Roman province, under the name of *Achaia*, and a Roman magistrate was sent out each year to govern it. Thessaly, as well as Epirus, was included in the province of Macedonia 146 B. C.

CHAPTER CCCXXIII.

146 B. C. to A. D. 1454.

Roman Dominion.

After the fall of the Achaian confederacy, the history of Greece was, for a lengthened period, that of an oppressed and degraded province. The form of government in most of the states was nominally republican, but constituted according to the pleasure of the Romans, and not according to the wishes or interests of the people. The wealthier classes retained all the authority in their hands; and if any person was aggrieved by a decision of the magistrates, the appeal was not to a tribunal of a more popular character, but to the Roman governor. This condition of dependency continued for more than four succeeding centuries. The evils of oppression and rapine were thus long endured, to a greater or less extent, by a people, who always superior in arts and literature, had at one period been the terror of the Oriental world, by their military prowess.

Some benefits resulted from the Roman sway over

Greece, such as protection against foreign war, and the diminution of civil broils. These were considerable, but hardly sufficient to counterbalance the evils. 'So far as the characters of men are determined by the government under which they live, we need not doubt that the Roman conquest was most pernicious to that of the Greeks; nor that, even though we exclude the positive oppression and spoliation they so often suffered, the stagnation of energy resulting from their servitude was more destructive, both to virtue and happiness, than the storms of their turbulent independence."

But though Greece had lost all political importance, it was not the less, under the empire of Rome, the intellectual head of the civilized world, the centre of art, philosophy, and literature. The influence of Grecian models produced whatever of excellence was attained in these departments by the Romans. No Roman youth, of high birth or wealth, was thought to have received an accomplished education, without a visit to Athens, and a course of instruction under its professors of eloquence. But whatever aid Greece afforded to the leading minds of other countries, it gave birth to few or none during this period of its existence.

The political subjection of the Greeks produced a subserviency among the mass which was deeply to be deplored. The acute and versatile genius of the nation enabled them, as they led the way in all the more liberal arts, to be also singularly successful in devising the most ingenious methods of self-debasement. Depraved and impoverished as they were by the manner of their government, they poured out swarms of adventurers to seek their fortunes as buffoons, as parasites, as ready instruments of every low and contemptible service. The favor of the proconsul, in particular, was to be courted by flattery and corrupt fawning, and to be maintained in its exclusiveness by defamation of all rivals.

Great as were the mischiefs springing from the grasping policy of Rome, it does not, therefore, follow, that her conquests were, upon the whole, to be lamented by the world. We may not see the end of a mighty scheme of action carried through at a vast expense of blood and suffering; yet we may reasonably conclude that a beneficent Providence has an end in view, justifying the expenditure at which it is reached. We cannot doubt that the successive conquests made by Macedonia and Rome over Greece, were the appointed, as they were the most effectual means, of preparing for the diffusion of the Christian faith. The one furnished a common language, the other established a common government; and by the joint working of both, an easy and unrestricted communication was insured, through all that portion of the world which was then civilized. In the lifetime of a single person, Christianity was preached from Syria to Spain; though it seems to have been in Grecian Asia that churches arose most rapidly, and in the greatest numbers.

As the fortunes of Greece, from this time, merge in those of Rome, so its history is more properly that of Rome, not merely until the extinction of the Western Empire of Rome, A. D. 476, but until the overthrow of the Byzantine, or Eastern Empire by the Turks, A. D. 1454. It is true that, after the seat of dominion was transferred from Rome to the Grecian city of Byzantium, the sceptre came gradually again into the hands of the Grecian race; but still the story of the Eastern Empire is best treated as a sequel to that of Rome. That empire, long sunk in debility and corruption, gave way, at last, to the power of the Turks, a formidable Asiatic tribe, who gained a footing in Europe in the fourteenth century. All the provinces of the empire, to the south of the Danube, inclusive of Greece, received from the conquerors the name of *Turkey in Europe*. Having now sketched the political history of the ancient Greeks, we shall briefly mention the principal islands, and then give a view of the social state of this renowned people, in early days

CHAPTER CCCXXIV.

The Greek Islands — Macedon — Thrace.

The islands embraced in the Ægean Sea, now the *Archipelago*, were grouped by the ancients under two heads — the *Cyclades* and *Sporades*. The former were so called from being arranged in a circular manner around the Island of Delos. These lay between Eubœa and Crete. The Sporades are the various other islands *scattered* along the coast of Asia Minor and Europe; the latter were called the *Northern Sporades* and the former the *Southern Sporades*. The *Ionian Islands* have been mentioned as being to the west of Greece, in the Ionian Sea. We shall begin our account of the islands, with those which lie east of Greece, and proceed thence to Crete; we shall then speak of the Ionian Islands. The Southern Sporades have been sufficiently noticed.

Thasos, now *Thaso*, or *Tasso*, is on the coast of Thrace, about forty miles in circumference, and was anciently proverbial for its fertility. Its wine was famous, and its marble quarries in high repute. The capital of the island had the same name. According to ancient legends, long before the time of Hercules, a company of Phœnicians came hither, led by Thasos, in search of his sister Europa, who had been carried off by Jupiter. The island was afterward colonized by settlers from Paros. There were gold mines here, and the people became so rich as to tempt the Milesians to besiege them, 492 B. C. They were afterward reduced by the Persians under Mardonius, and subsequently received the army of Xerxes, upon which ceremony they expended four hundred talents of silver. The island passed successively to the Athenians, Macedonians, and Romans. It has long been held by the Turks, who govern it by means of an aga. The population is about six thousand, chiefly Greeks. It is still fertile, producing oil, maize, honey, and timber, with large herds of cattle and sheep.

Samothrace, now *Samotraki*, thirty-eight miles from the coast of Thrace, and twenty miles in circumference, is famous in ancient history for a deluge, which happened before the time of the Argonauts, and inundated the country, reaching the very tops of the mountains. It was probably first peopled by Thracians, and subsequently by Pelasgian settlers. The people were very religious, and the place was esteemed sacred. It was the chief seat of the worship of the *Cabiri*, which was attended with such obscenities that many of the old authors, finding it impossible to describe them, declared them to be mysteries which it was unlawful to reveal. The island was a safe asylum for fugitives. The people were first governed by kings, but afterward the government was democratic. They joined the army of Xerxes, and one of their ships was distinguished for its exploits in the battle of Salamis. The island is said to contain a mountain so high that the plains of Troy may be seen from the top. At present it belongs to Turkey.

Imbros, now *Imbro*, is eighteen miles south-east of Samothrace, and twenty-two north-east of Lemnos. It is hilly and well wooded. The population consists of four thousand Greeks. It was early governed by its own laws, but was taken by the Persians 508 B. C. It was afterward subject to Athens, Macedon, Pergamus, and the Romans. In modern times, it has been held by the Turks.

Lemnos, now *Stalimene*, has an area of about one hundred and fifty square miles, and a population of eight thousand Greeks. It is hilly, and produces wine, corn, hemp, flax, and fruits. It is known in ancient mythology as the island on which Vulcan fell, on being kicked out of heaven for his impudence. He was the god of fire, and established his forges in Lemnos, for he was also a blacksmith. There was once a volcano on the island, which probably gave rise to this fable. A terrible story is related of the women of this place, who are said, in ancient days, to have murdered all the men except Troas, the king. Afterward, the Pelasgi being driven out of Attica, went to Lemnos, carrying off with them some Athenian women. These had children, who despised their half brethren, born of Pelasgian women; and hence the Pelasgians murdered both their children and their mothers. On account of these atrocities, Lemnos had a bad name in ancient times. The island was taken by the Athenians under Miltiades. Here was a famous labyrinth, some ruins of which existed in the time of Pliny. The island is noted for a kind of chalk, called *Lemnian earth*, supposed to have wonderful medicinal properties.

Eubœa, now *Negropont*, lay along the coast of Attica and Bœotia, from which it was separated by the narrow channel of Euripus. This is only sixteen feet across at one point, and here a bridge has been thrown over it. The island is ninety miles long, and from five to thirty wide. The land is generally elevated. Some of the mountains are quite lofty; several are four thousand feet high, and that of Delphi is seven thousand two hundred and sixty-six feet. The country produces olives and wines, the latter being kept in pigskins. The island has seventy thousand inhabitants, mostly Greeks. They are much annoyed by pirates. At Cape Therma there are hot springs. On the northern side there are several small islands. In the mountains are wild deer and boar, and the plains are overrun with hares and rabbits. There is not a stream deserving the name of river in the whole island. The town of Egripos, anciently *Chalcis*, is defended with walls: it has narrow streets and capacious houses. Outside of the town is a suburb devoted to trade, which consists chiefly in fruits. This city is capable of becoming an important commercial site.

The first inhabitants of Eubœa were probably Pelasgians, who, doubtless, settled most of the islands of the Ægean, as well as the main land of Greece, before historic times. Chalcis and Eretria were founded by the Athenians, before the Trojan war. At a very early date, these were independent but allied towns, which had advanced to a high degree of prosperity, holding dominion over Andros, Tenos, and Ceos, and sending colonies to the coasts of Macedon and Thrace, and even to Sicily and Italy. A war took place between Chalcis and Eretria, which Thucydides regards as one of the oldest on record. It seems not to have lasted long, for in the sixth century B. C., the people were still flourishing, being governed by their wealthier citizens. After this, they provoked the hostility of the Athenians, who invaded the island, captured it, inflicted great severities upon the inhabitants, and reduced it to a state of dependence on Attica. In the wars with Darius and Xerxes, the Eubœans took part with the Greeks. They revolted from the Athenians 445 B. C., but were soon reduced by Pericles. They came successively under the control of Philip of Macedon, of the Romans, the Venetians, and finally the Turks. The people took part in the late revolution against Turkey, and the island now forms an independent portion of the kingdom of Greece. Its barbarous modern name seems to be a corruption of *Egripos*.

We come now to the Cyclades. *Andros*, now *Andro*, six miles south-east of Negropont, is very mountainous, and some peaks are covered with snow a great part of the year. It is twenty-one miles long and eight broad; the population is eighteen thousand. Andros, or Castro, is the chief town: beside this, there are sixty-six villages. The soil is fertile, and the fine gardens produce lemons, oranges, pomegranates, &c. Six thousand pounds of silk are annually exported. Wheat and barley are sown together, and bread is made of the mixed grains. This island received its name from the son of one of its kings, who lived in the time of the Trojan war.

Tenos, now *Tino*, is fifteen miles in circuit. It is mountainous, and produces wine greatly esteemed by the ancients. The chief town is called *Tenos*. Ceos, now *Zeos*, or *Zeo*, thirteen miles from Cape Colonna, is fourteen miles long and ten wide. It consists of a mountain called *St. Elias*, sloping gradually to the sea. It produces wine, barley, cotton, silk, and sheep. It has five thousand inhabitants. Anciently, this island had four considerable cities, of which one was Iulus, the remains of which are yet visible. Several eminent Greeks were natives of Ceos, among whom was Simonides. It appears that the people were Ionians from Athens; they furnished some vessels to the Greek fleet at the battle of Salamis. *Gyaros*, now *Ghioura* is four miles long and three wide. It is, at present, only inhabited by fishermen. The Romans used it as a place of banishment. *Syros*, now *Syra*, is east of Delos, is twenty miles in circumference, and fertile in corn and wine. The inhabitants anciently lived to a great age, on account of the salutairy of the air. *Myconus*, now *Myconi*, separated from Delos by a narrow channel, is ten miles long and two to six wide. It is mountainous, and not fertile, yet it produces some corn and cotton. Population, four thousand. Ancient fable represents the Centaur, killed by Hercules, as buried here; hence the proverb, to *put all things under one Myconus*. The people were poor, and had the reputation of being parasitical to the rich; hence, *Mycenian guests* was a term for people who invited themselves to dinner.

Delos, now *Delo*, is deemed the central island of the Cyclades. The ancient legend represents it as originally a floating island, raised from the sea by Neptune. It was celebrated for the worship of Apollo and Diana, who were said to have been born there.

> "Latona once, on Delo's isle,
> Gave to the world a matchless pair —
> Apollo, who makes nature smile,
> Whose shoulders glow with golden hair;

And Dian, goddess of the chase,
Whose shafts unerring ever fly,
Sole sovereign of the female race,
Nocturnal empress of the sky."

The temple of Apollo at Delos was very celebrated. It was held in such veneration, that the Persians, who had pillaged and profaned most of the other temples of Greece, never once offered violence to this, but regarded it with the most awful reverence. The island came into the possession of the Athenians in the time of Pisistratus; they ordained that no one should die or be buried there. They instituted a festival called the *Delia*, which returned every fifth year. The general of Mithridates desolated the island, and it is now little more than a mass of bare rock.

Cythnus, now *Thermia*, was near Ceos, and famous for its cheese. *Seriphus*, now *Serpho*, was barren and uncultivated. The Romans banished criminals to this island. Here Cassius Severus was exiled, and here he died. The frogs of this place were said never to croak till taken to some other spot, when they became very noisy and clamorous. *Siphnos*, now *Siphanto*, has fine harbors, and produces excellent fruit. The inhabitants were noted for their depravity. They, however, manifested spirit in the time of Darius, and refused to give the homage of earth and water. They had gold mines, till, refusing a tribute to Apollo, these were inundated and disappeared. The air is so wholesome, that many of the natives live to be one hundred and twenty years old.

Paros, now *Paro*, is about thirty-six miles in circumference; population, four thousand. The mountain of Marpessus abounds in the celebrated white marble used by the ancient sculptors. The island was colonized by the Cretans, and attained great prosperity. It submitted to Darius, and furnished sailors for the Persian fleet. It was afterwards made tributary to Athens. It became subject to the Ptolemies, then to the Romans, and, like the other Cyclades, to the Venetians, in the fourteenth century. Toward the close of the eighteenth century, the Russians made it the station of their fleet. The celebrated Greek Chronicle, now in the museum of Oxford, was found here. *Antiparos* is a small island, near to Paros. It is chiefly celebrated for its wonderful grotto, discovered about two centuries ago.

Naxos, now *Naxia*, six miles from Paros, is one of the largest of the Cyclades, being one hundred and five miles in circumference. It is very fertile, and produces corn, oil, fruit, silk, and abounds in game. It has forty villages and ten thousand inhabitants. Bacchus was anciently the chief deity of the island. The capital was called Naxos. The island was colonized by the Corsicans: the people were governed by kings, but afterward exchanged their government for a republic. Pisistratus subjected them to Athens, and the island, in later times, experienced many vicissitudes.

Melos, now *Milo*, is sixty miles in circumference. It was colonized by the Lacedæmonians at an early date, and enjoyed its independence for seven hundred years. Having offended the Athenians, the island was taken, the men slain, the women and children made slaves, and the country left a scene of desolation. It was repeopled by the Athenians, and the original inhabitants, in part, returned. The other islands in this quarter—*Amorgos*, now *Amerigo; Astypalaia*, now *Stamphalia; Ios*, now *Nio; Thera*, now *Santorin;* and some others, are of no particular note or celebrity. *Carpathos*, now *Scarpanto*, lies between Rhodes and Crete: it is mentioned by Homer, but its history is little known.

Crete, now *Candia*, is the largest of the Greek islands and one of the largest in the Mediterranean, being one hundred and sixty miles long and six to thirty wide. It is very fertile, producing wheat, wine, oil, sugar, honey, gums, lemons, oranges, and various other fruits. The chief town is Candia, strongly fortified; it has twelve hundred inhabitants; population of the island two hundred and eighty thousand. In the time of Homer, it was very populous, and had one hundred cities. It is traversed by mountains, the loftiest of which is Psilorite, or Monte Jova, the ancient *Ida*, which is covered a great part of the year with snow. It is said that Jupiter was educated here by the Corybantes, the priests of Cybele, and the Cretans boasted that they could show his tomb. About 1400 B. C., Minos, said to be the son of Jupiter and Europa, whom the latter carried off from Phœnicia, was king of Crete and was celebrated for his excellent laws, his justice and his moderation. He was called the "favorite of the gods," the "confidant of Jupiter," and the "wise legislator." After death, the poets assigned him the office of supreme judge in the infernal regions.

Theseus and the Athenian Youths before Minos.

We have already spoken of Theseus, who was sent by the Athenians, with six other youths and seven maidens, as their annual tribute to Minos, to be devoured by the Minotaur, a dreadful monster, who dwelt in a labyrinth. Ariadne, the daughter of Minos, fell in love with Theseus, and gave him a thread when he entered the labyrinth, by means of which he found his way out, after having killed the Minotaur. He persuaded Minos to give up the tribute, and returned, with his companions, safely to Athens. Crete came into the possession of the Romans, and was long subject to the Byzantine empire. In A. D. 823, it was taken by the Saracens, and was afterwards subject to the Venetians for four centuries. In 1669, it was taken by the Turks the capital having been invested for twenty years—the longest siege in modern times. About fifteen years since, it was given by the sultan of Turkey to Mehemet Ali, and it is now a dependency of Egypt.

The *Ionian Islands*, in the Ionian Sea, to the west of Greece, have been noticed in the geographical view of that country. *Corcyra*, now *Corfu*, is on the east of Epirus. It was early colonized from Colchis. Here Homer places the shipwreck of Ulysses. *Paxus*, now *Paxo*, lies eight miles south-east of Corfu, and is nearly covered with olive trees. It has some com merce, and a population of four thousand. *Santa Maura*, the ancient *Leucadia*, is celebrated for the promontory called the "Lover's Leap," from whence Sappho plunged into the sea. *Cephalonia* is the largest of the group, being forty miles in length. Oil, muscadine wine, cotton, and honey are its principal productions. Its inhabitants accompanied Ulysses to the Trojan war. *Ithaka*, now *Theaki*, lies between Cephalonia and the continent. Homer makes this a part of the kingdom and the residence of Ulysses. *Zante*, the ancient *Zacynthus*, produces currants, of which it exports annually nearly eight million pounds. *Cerigo*, the ancient *Cythera*, abounds with hares, quails, turtle, and falcon. Here was a famous temple to Venus, it being supposed that this goddess rose from the sea on the shore. In 1815 these islands were formed into an independent state, called the *Ionian Republic*, under the protection of Great Britain.

Macedonia has been already mentioned, and we need only add a few particulars. It was situated between Thrace, Epirus, and Greece. Its boundaries varied at different times. The kingdom was founded by Caranus, a descendant of Hercules, 814 B. C. Philip was one of his descendants. This sovereign, who was one of the ablest men of ancient times, extended his dominions by conquering the adjacent tribes, and Pliny says his territories included one hundred and fifty nations. His capital was at Pella. The people of this country were naturally warlike, and the "Macedonian phalanx" was deemed almost invincible in the time of Philip and Alexander. When Greece was threatened by the Romans, (B. C. 279,) Pyrrhus, king of Macedon, displayed great talents, making two expeditions to Italy. Macedon was taken, at last, by the Romans, and reduced to a Roman province.

Thrace lay to the east of Macedon. The soil is for the most part barren. The people were warlike, but deemed cruel and barbarous — sacrificing their enemies on the altars of their gods. The first inhabitants lived on milk and the flesh of sheep, and were addicted to plunder. Their earliest government was monarchical. Many Greeks settled here, and Thrace was deemed, at one period, a part of Greece. It was conquered by Alexander, and afterward passed to the Romans, and lastly to the Turks, who still hold it. This, with a part of the ancient Macedon, Thessaly, and Albania, are now called *Roumelia*. The Islands of Thasos, Samothrace, and Imbros belonged to Thrace.

CHAPTER CCCXXV.

General Views. — *Extent, Divisions, Population, &c. — Cities of Ancient Greece.*

The extent of Greece has been mentioned in the preceding narrative. As it was at no time one compact empire, but different portions of it were subject to the several states successively, as they rose into power, it is not easy to define its limits when at the highest point of its dominion. When Athens was in the ascendant, Greece was perhaps the greatest in territorial extent, unless the conquests of Alexander may properly be considered as defining its boundaries. In this case, it would include not only Macedonia, but several countries in Asia and Africa.

But Greece, strictly speaking, was a more limited country. It embraced more territory, indeed, than modern Greece; but even including Macedonia, it was, as we have said, only about four hundred miles in length, and contained an area of not more than forty thousand square miles.

The population of Greece, in its most flourishing period, — that is, in the time of Pericles, — is supposed to have been three or four million. Its military power which was famous throughout the world, and the terror of the adjacent nations, was constituted rather by the bravery and discipline of its troops, than by its numbers. The institutions, both of Athens and Lacedæmon, and particularly of the latter, were directly adapted and formed to make fighting citizens, or soldiers. This was the case with several other of the Grecian states or cities. The aggregate military force of Greece, was about four hundred thousand men.

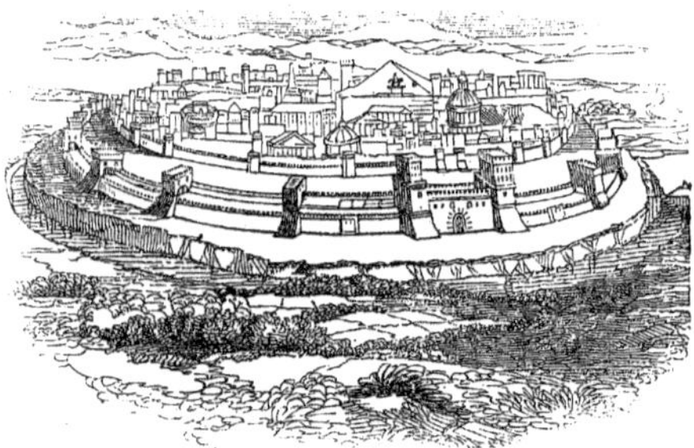

Ancient Walled City.

Athens, so frequently mentioned in the history of Greece, and itself furnishing much of its history, was the principal city of Greece. From its origin to the time of its subjection to the Romans, and indeed subsequently, by means of its splendid ruins, it has been a theme of interest to the scholar, the antiquarian, the artist, and the man of taste. At the height of its prosperity, no city of the ancient world could vie with it in the beauty and elegance of its public buildings, its delectable groves and haunts of philosophy, its statuary, and other works of art. It still retains in its ruins some traces of its past greatness, particularly in the Parthenon, the temple of Neptune, and the temple of Jupiter Olympus.

Athens was situated about five miles from the Gulf of Ægina: the modern Athens occupies only the northern and central parts of the ancient. The Acropolis, or citadel, stood upon a high rock, and was capable of strong defence; within it was the Pantheon; to the west was the Areopagus, or Mars' Hill; below, to the east, stood the temple of Jupiter Olympus, which was one of the largest in Greece. The only considerable elevation of land was the rock or mount on which the citadel was erected, as Athens was in fact situated in a large plain. In its most flourishing state, it was twenty-five miles in circumference. It was divided into two separate parts — the upper city, or citadel, and the lower city. The inhabitants of both amounted to four hundred and forty thousand, of whom the greater part were slaves. The upper city was sixteen miles in circumference, and was surrounded by a strong wall, adorned by nine gates, to one of which, called the *Grand Entrance*, the Athenians ascended by steps covered with white marble. The lower city contained all the buildings that surrounded the citadel, and was encompassed by substantial walls.

Among the public structures not named above

which the city contained in the long course of its existence, were the Temple of Theseus; the octagonal Tower of the Winds; the monument of Philopappus, near which was the Pnyx, or the place in which the popular assemblies were held, and whence the Athenian orators "thundered over Greece;" the choraic monument of Lysicratus, called also the *Lantern of Demosthenes;* Adrian's Gate, and many others — some of the proudest efforts of art and genius that the world ever saw.

Sparta was the capital of the province of Laconia. It was built upon the banks of the River Eurotas, and at the foot of Mount Taygetus. Its form was circular, and its circumference measured only six miles. The houses were not built close together, or in the usual compact form of cities, but divided into different villages, according to the ancient manner of the Greeks. Of these villages there were five, built round an eminence at different distances, each of which was occupied by one of the five tribes of Sparta. The prevailing simple and austere manners of the inhabitants were hostile to external splendor, and on this account their houses were destitute of ornaments. The great square, or forum, however, in which several streets terminated, was embellished with temples and statuary. It also contained the public edifices, in which the meetings of the various bodies of magistrates were held.

The city was adorned also with a large number of monuments in honor of the gods and ancient heroes. Religious reverence was shown to the memory of Hercules, Tyndarus, Castor, Pollux, Leonidas, and others. In the environs of Sparta were courses for horse and foot races, and places of exercises for youth, embowered by beautiful plane-trees. Indeed, this city was surrounded, to a great extent, with vineyards, olive and plane trees, gardens, and summer-houses. It was destitute of walls till it fell under the dominion of tyrants, after the time of Alexander. The breasts of its brave citizens were deemed an adequate defence. The modern *Misitra*, the capital of Laconia, is situated near the ancient Sparta. Some of the ruins of the latter are still visible.

Ruins at Corinth.

Corinth was the capital of Achaia, and situated on the isthmus which separates the Morea from Attica. It was founded in 1520 B. C. Lying between two seas, it had two ports, one on each coast. It was long and justly celebrated. It stood at the foot of a high hill, on which was built the citadel, the hill bearing the name of *Acrocorinthus*. This city was one of the best peopled and most wealthy in Greece. Including the citadel, it was about ten miles in circumference. The navigation round the capes of Malea and Tænarus was reckoned so dangerous, on account of storms and pirates, that merchants generally transported their goods over the isthmus, whence Corinth became the mart of Europe and Asia.

The natives of this city were distinguished for their skill in working metals. The Corinthian brass, — a mixture of copper with some small quantity of gold and silver — formed a composition extremely brilliant and durable. The ornaments on pottery ware are known to have been executed here with inimitable art. That peculiarly chaste and beautiful order of pillars which are used at this day, in the decoration of buildings, took from this city the name of *Corinthian* pillars. Its citizens made high pretensions to politeness, philosophy, and learning.

Corinth enjoyed its liberty and an immense traffic till B. C. 146, when it was taken and burnt by the Romans. It was then deemed the strongest city in the world, and was a distinguished seat of opulence and the fine arts. After lying in ruins for many years, it was rebuilt by Julius Cæsar. In removing the rubbish, an immense quantity of vessels of brass and earthen ware was found and conveyed to Rome.

Since the time of Cæsar, the city had been often burnt, plundered, and subjugated, till under the tyranny of the Turks it was so decayed, that the population did not exceed fifteen hundred souls — one half Mahometans, and the other half Christians. Since the revolution, it is rapidly recovering from the disasters of the war. In the mind of the Christian scholar and disciple, Corinth is delightfully associated with the labors of the apostle Paul there, and the foundation of a large and flourishing Christian church by means of those labors.

Thebes, the capital of Bœotia, was built by Cadmus, who first introduced letters into Greece. It was situated on the River Ismenus, and had seven gates, with walls upwards of seven miles in circumference. The other states of Greece were for a long time indignant against the inhabitants of Thebes for their perfidy in joining the Persians, and for this they were severely punished. Under Pelopidas and Epaminondas, however, Thebes became the most powerful city in Greece. It was destroyed by Alexander the Great after a terrible carnage of its citizens, six thousand of them having been slain, and thirty thousand sold for slaves. The house in which the famous lyric poet Pindar was born and educated was ordered to be spared while all the rest were ordered to be demolished.

The city was afterwards rebuilt by Cassander; but in Strabo's time, (about 20 A. D.,) Thebes was only an inconsiderable village. There are remains of its ruins still visible.

Argos was the principal city in the district of Argolis, and supposed to be the favorite residence of Juno It was situated on the River Inachus, and was defended by two citadels. The inhabitants were called *Argivi* — a name by which the Greeks in general were frequently denominated It is thought to have been the most ancient of the Grecian cities, having been founded by Inachus, who arrived in Greece from Phœnicia, 1856 years B. C., as before stated.

Nauplia was the harbor of Argos, and to the south of this was the Lake of Lerna, where Hercules slew the monstrous hydra. To the north of Argos stood Mycenæ, the city of Agamemnon, after whose death it gradually declined, till at last it was destroyed by the Argians. The Cyclopean walls found in the vicinity of Argos and the neighboring places, composed of large blocks of stone, are of remote, but unknown antiquity. The modern capital of Argolis, Napoli di Romania, in the vicinity of the ancient city, is the most important town of the Morea, and the strongest fortress in Greece.

There were other cities of ancient Greece, but none of commanding importance. Several of them were distinguished as the scenes of battles, or birthplaces of great men, or the locality of extraordinary events, but are not otherwise specially deserving of notice.

CHAPTER CCCXXVI.

Government — Military Affairs.

Greece, as a whole, possessed no common form of government. Its separate states were distinguished each by its peculiar constitution, or acknowledged plan for the regulation of affairs. This constitution, or plan, varied at different periods; sometimes it was democratic, at other times it partook of the monarchical or aristocratic element. The democratic form was, perhaps, the more prevailing feature in the government of the several states. They frequently entered into leagues and confederacies with each other, and in this respect bore some distant resemblance to the present government of the United States of America. The greater prevalence of the monarchical or oligarchic principle was in the earlier period of the state; that of the democratic or republican principle was in the latter period.

At the time of the return of the Heraclidæ, which was about 1100 B. C., the government most common in Greece was an irregular mixture of monarchy and oligarchy, with a slight infusion of democracy. "In a people recently emerged from barbarism, the power is always chiefly in the landholders. If the lordships be large, the proprietors are sovereign on their own estates; and though, for the military advantages of union, they may acknowledge a king, he is little more than the head of a confederacy. But when the lordships are too small for independent defence, the proprietors are forced to a stricter union; they assemble, therefore, in towns, and the king is the chief magistrate, as well as the military leader, the power being principally in the landholders, but exercised by them as a body over the people, and not as lords over their respective vassals. This was the first political order of Greece.

"The judicial power, with the general regulation of affairs, was in the council of the principal persons, under the titles of *elders*, *chiefs*, or *princes*; the king was military commander, president of the council, and priest. The assembly of the people had little to do with the ordinary direction of the state, being paramount, indeed, when called together, but only called on unusual occasions, and principally to decide the contests of the king and chiefs. The king was weak, the people scattered; the great proprietors were strong and united, and gradually monopolized the powers of the state, till the towns almost universally passed into oligarchical republics."

As the wealth was nearly all engrossed by the oligarchs, whose possession of the land gave them the possession of almost every other species of property in the end, the poorer classes were ever looking for an opportunity to enrich and avenge themselves by the spoliation of their oppressors. Such an opportunity was frequently afforded, when the oligarchy happened to be divided within itself, and the weaker party made common cause with the people against their oppressors. Hence proceeded the series of bloody commotions which runs through all the history of Greece.

In some states, a middle class arose, in consequence of the growth of commerce. This class became favorable to a regular government, having otherwise much to lose. With the prevalence of such an order of men we see the establishment of a comparatively mild and regular oligarchy, and sometimes a permanent democracy.

Argos was the first to abolish royalty, or to reduce it to insignificance; but the government which was substituted for it did not render the people at all happy. Contentions between the rich and poor, as also seditions, were frequent and violent; the dominion of Argos, anciently the most extensive in Greece, was curtailed by the revolt of numerous towns. Many of these succeeded in maintaining their independence.

Corinth, although it underwent several revolutions, was commonly the most quiet of the Peloponnesian republics, and that whose government was characterized by the greatest equity. Its situation was propitious to trade, and that produced a middle class, which in some degree protected the poor against oppression, and the rich against evils which would otherwise have resulted from their own excesses.

The government of Athens was at first monarchical, but after the death of Codrus, it became in a degree democratic. The Athenians were divided into three classes — citizens or freemen, foreigners or sojourners, and slaves. To each class were assigned peculiar offices, privileges, or services. The classes were in general preserved distinct, though there might be a passing from the one to the other, in certain cases. Poverty might reduce a free-born citizen to servitude, at least to a species of it; and merit or money might raise the slave to the dignity of freedom.

The usual government of Athens was carried on by the archons, the senate of five hundred, and assemblies of the people. The archons held the supreme executive power. They were elected annually by lot They were decorated by garlands of myrtle, were protected from violence and insult, and were exempted from certain taxes. The senate of five hundred was elected annually by lot from the different tribes. The business of this body was to consider all proposals intended to come before the people, and to see that nothing improper should be submitted. The assemblies of the people were convened for the purpose of consulting on what was most beneficial to the commonwealth. The right of attending was enjoyed by all the freemen of Athens. Strangers, slaves women, and persons who had received an infamous punishment were excluded. These assemblies were held four times every thirty-five days, and also in cases of peculiar emergency.

The smallest number of which an assembly could consist, according to law, was six thousand citizens. There was the arena in which the intellectual contests of the great men of Athens were exhibited — in which the orators shone, swaying the popular will and heart by an irresistible eloquence. It is not to be denied, however, that the noble art which was there so admirably cultivated, was often perverted to base and profligate purposes.

There were also other bodies occasionally concerned in the government of Athens, as various courts, particularly that celebrated one called *Areopagus.* The name of the court was taken from the place where it was held, viz., Mars' Hill. It commanded the most profound respect throughout all Greece, in view of the wisdom and justice of its proceedings. It took cognizance of crimes, abuses, and innovations, either in religion or government. It inspected the laws and public manners. The greatest decorum marked its deliberations and doings.

A singular and most unjust mode of procedure marked the government of Athens in one particular; that was *ostracism*, a kind of popular judgment, so called from *ostrakon*, a shell, or tile, on which votes were written. The form in which that judgment was expressed is thus described: "The people being assembled, each citizen, writing on a shell the name of the individual most obnoxious to him, without the allegation of a crime, carried it to a certain part of the market-place fixed for the purpose, and deposited it there. These shells were numbered in the gross by the archons. If they did not amount to six thousand, the ostracism was void. If they amounted to this number, the archons, laying every name by itself, pronounced him, whose name was written by the major part, banished for ten years, with leave to enjoy his estate." This is sufficient to account for the disgraceful fact, that so many citizens, distinguished by their virtues and public services, suffered from the ingratitude or the spleen of the Athenian populace.

In Lacedæmon, the inhabitants consisted of two classes only — citizens and slaves, the latter otherwise called *helots.* The citizens, however, were divided into two classes, the *homoii* and the *hypomiones.* The privileges of these varied; the former were eligible to office; the latter, consisting of the poorer citizens, the freedmen and their sons, were allowed only to vote at the elections. The helots were much more numerous than the citizens. Their services were like those of servants in general, though less severe than those assigned to that class elsewhere in Greece.

The republic of Lacedæmon had two magistrates, called *kings*, but they differed from those of most other nations. They possessed few of the peculiar prerogatives of kings. They formed a check upon each other, and their power otherwise was very limited. Every month, they took an oath that they would rule according to the laws. One of them commanded the army on military expeditions, while the other usually remained at home to administer the laws. As first citizens of the state, they presided in the senate; but their peculiar prerogative was to superintend the religion of the state.

The senate of Sparta consisted, together with the two kings, of twenty-eight members, who were above sixty years of age, and elected to the office for life, and on account of their virtues. Their duty was to consider all questions respecting peace or war, and other important affairs of the republic. Sparta had another body of men, called *ephori*, who were five magistrates elected annually by the citizens to inspect the education of the youth and the administration of justice. Together with these appliances of government, they had public assemblies. These were held to decide on matters laid before them by the senate. There were two of these bodies; one was called the *general assembly*, attended by all the freemen of Laconia; the other, the *lesser assembly*, composed of Spartans only, who exceeded thirty years of age. Of these bodies, the kings, as well as the other magistrates, constituted a component part.

Pertaining to the government of the Greeks, as a confederated body, was the *Amphictyonic council.* This was an assembly composed at first of a few states in the northern parts of Greece, but afterwards of twelve states, the object of which was the decision of all differences between cities, and to try such offences as openly violated the laws of nations. The number of

Greek Armor.

deputies usually sent to this council was two from each state. It met twice a year. The vernal assembly was held at Delphi, and the autumnal at Thermopylæ. Each deputy took an oath, purporting that he would never injure any Amphictyonic city, and that, if any attempts of the kind were made by others, he would oppose them by force of arms. He further swore that, if any outrage was inflicted on the sacred territory of

Delphi, or any designs were formed against the temple by others, he would use his utmost efforts to bring the offenders to punishment.

The armies of the different Grecian states consisted, for the most part, of citizens and armed slaves, whom the laws obliged, at a certain age, to become enrolled and equipped ready for service at the summons of the magistrate. It was not their policy to have hired or standing armies. The main body of their forces was composed of infantry. The rest rode in chariots, upon horseback, or upon elephants. The use of these, which was at first indulged in by their chiefs and famous warriors, was at length abandoned, except that cavalry was continued to be employed in warfare. The officers and upper classes usually fought on horseback.

The infantry were divided into two classes, respectively termed the heavy-armed and the light-armed. The citizens constituted the first of these divisions; the slaves belonged to the other. The armor of each division corresponded with its designation; the former wearing helmets of brass or iron upon their heads, and cuirasses and greaves of the same metal on other parts of the body; the latter using bows, javelins, slings, and the like.

The Greek arms were at first made of brass, the boots and some other portions being of tin. Iron became afterward the chief material. The *defensive* arms were a helmet, a breastplate, and a plate for the back, greaves to defend the legs, guards for the hands, a sort of belt which covered a part of the body in front, and a shield. The *offensive* arms were the spear or pike, the sword, the pole-axe, a club of wood or iron, the bow and arrow, darts or javelins, and slings.

The Greeks, notwithstanding their bravery in the field, were very inefficient in undertaking the siege of walled towns. The engines of war for battering down walls and towers were not to be compared with modern artillery. Yet, at times, strongly fortified places were greatly annoyed, and effectually carried by assault, by the use of the battering-ram, moving tower, catapulta, and similar engines.

Every citizen was liable to be summoned for the defence of the state, between the ages of twenty and sixty; but those of advanced years were exempted from foreign service. The Athenians had a custom of appointing ten generals to every army, one being chosen from each of the ten wards of Attica. But the evils of this measure caused, in time, its abandonment so far, as that only one of the ten was appointed to the actual command, the remaining nine serving generally as his counsellors.

The severest punishments were inflicted, by the Lacedæmonians, on deserters, or cowards who fled from battle. They forfeited all the privileges and honors of citizens; it was a disgrace to intermarry with them; they might be beaten by any who met them, without the liberty of self-defence; and they wore some distinguishing dress as a mark of infamy.

The Greek *ships* consisted chiefly of three sorts: ships of war, those of burden, and those of passage. At an early period, their ships of war were merely large open boats, and generally propelled by oars. They were capable of holding from fifty to one hundred and twenty men. The rowers at first sat in a single line along each side of the vessel; but afterwards the Corinthians invented the *trireme*, a species of galley, which had three benches, or tiers of rowers. These were not fixed in a vertical line, over each other but back of each other, ascending gradually, in the form of stairs. In their fights, the soldiers or marines

Grecian Galley.

stood on the deck of the ship, and assailed the enemy with darts or javelins; and when the vessels came close to each other, they fought hand to hand with the sword and spear.

CHAPTER CCCXXVII.

Religion — Literature and Science — Arts

Ruins of an Ancient Temple.

THE religion of the Greeks was a product of the imagination rather than of reason. It had little to do with moral improvement, but very much by way of pleasing the fancy. It thus agreed with the poetic genius of the people. Fiction was its life and its charm.

The gods and demigods, whom the Greeks worshipped, were divided into three classes — *celestial marine*, and *infernal*. They were all subject to Jupiter, who was considered the father of gods and men The above classes are according to their degrees of dignity. As the Greeks had no sacred books, the fictions of their poets on these topics, sanctioned also by the priests and legislators, were the only authority for the popular belief. In the hands of the poet, the national religion could not fail to be an elegant and fascinating, though a wild and corrupt system.

The celestial deities were Jupiter, Apollo, Mars, Mercury, Bacchus, Vulcan, Juno, Minerva, Venus, Diana Ceres, and Vesta. The marine deities consisted of Neptune and his wife Amphitrite, Oceanus and his wife Thetys, Triton, Proteus, Nereus, and his sister and consort Doris, &c. The names of the infernal deities were Pluto and his consort Proserpine, Plutus

Charon, the Furies, Fates, and the three judges, Minos, Æacus, and Rhadamanthus. There were many other divinities of various characters and descriptions; as, Cupid, the god of love; the Muses, who presided over poetry, music, dancing, and the liberal arts; the Graces; and Pan, Sylvanus, Priapus, Aristæus, Terminus, and others, under the title of *moral* deities. We may enumerate also the Sirens, Gorgons, Harpies, Dryads, Naiads, Nereids, Tritons, Lares, Penates, Fauns, Satyrs, Pales, and a vast number of Nymphs.

The worship of these divinities was conducted by priests dressed in costly habits, who offered sacrifices of animals, fruits, perfumes, and occasionally human victims. The sacrifices were sometimes accompanied by prayers, music, dancing, processions, games, dramatic entertainments, feasting, and masquerading. In the worship of Bacchus, in particular, every species of indecency and uproar was practised.

The objects of religious worship among the Greeks were almost innumerable. The imagination of the ancients filled all nature with an invisible and poetic creation. To them, the dark grove, the shady valley, the cool rivulet, and every solitary scene, appeared the haunt of those half-divine beings, whose existence formed a mysterious link between gods and men; more beautiful than mortals, less sacred than the gods.

In the deep gloom of the forests the Dryads dwelt; while the Hamadryad lived in the oak, with which she was born, and with which she died. The Oread roamed over the mountains in pursuit of the swift stag, or the young Naiad leaned upon her urn, bending over the cool fountain which reflected her divine image.

When the shepherd wandered through the shady groves of Arcadia, his imagination represented these airy beings around him. He heard their soft voices whispering through the leaves; or if, fainting from the heat of the noonday sun, a spot more peculiarly favored by nature met his view, — a cluster of shady trees, or a clear brook, whose bubbling waters sparkled over the flowery turf, — a mysterious charm seemed to invest the solitary scene; and fancy pictured the white feet of the retreating nymphs, glancing through the dark foliage.

When the huntsman, in the keen excitement of the chase, followed the deer over the lonely mountains, and the shades of night began to veil the surrounding objects, the fleet Oread with bow and quiver bounded past him. He saw her, with step more than mortal, spring down the steep descent, and join the train of the huntress queen.

Then, beside the lonely rock, in the dark and mystic recess, the ear was startled by the discordant laugh of the half-human Satyr or the mocking Faun. The credulous peasant, as he fled affrighted from the sound, believed that he beheld a band of these grotesque creatures dancing under the spreading oak, with their features expressive of mockery, and their human shape disfigured by the horns and feet of a goat, forming the link which connected the brute creation with the human family.

Every river, grove, and valley, was animate with life. The silent shores of the sea were peopled by the green-haired Nereids. In grottoes and rocky caves, where bright spars and colored shells were arranged in fantastic variety, these sea-nymphs were accustomed to dwell. Altars smoked in their honor along the sea-coast, and offerings of milk, oil, and honey were laid

Apollo. Jupiter.

Neptune. Pluto.

Mars. Mercury.

Hercules. Vulcan.

there by the mariner, who came to implore their favor and protection.

At night, their light forms glided along the shore, with coral and pearls glittering in their long tresses. But when Triton blew a blast upon his silver sounding shell, they plunged into the blue waters, and dived into the deep to attend the car of Amphitrite.

> "At eventide, when the shore is dim,
> And bubbling wreaths with the billows swim,
> They rise on the wing of the freshened breeze,
> And flit with the wind o'er the rolling seas."

While the enlightened mind rejects these fantastic superstitions, it cannot but allow that the credulous worshipper of the heathen gods, to whom all nature seemed replete with divine beings, was superior to the modern unbeliever, who can behold the wonders of the universe with an unmoved eye; who can view the sun sinking on the bosom of the ocean; the blue sky spangled with stars; all that creation has of the beautiful and terrible, without tracing that sublimity and beauty to a divine source; without feeling that

> "There is a power whose care
> Teaches thy way along that pathless coast,
> The desert and illimitable air,
> Lone wandering, but not lost."

The divinities of Greece were not held by the people to be mere passive phantoms. They are supposed to mingle not only in the extraordinary but the common incidents of life. The thunder was the voice of Jupiter, and the lightning his spear. The breeze of summer was the impulse given by the wing of Zephyr, and the echo of the forest was the voice of a goddess. The affection of lovers was decreed by Venus, and the anxiety of the enamored bosom was the smart inflicted by Cupid's arrow.

In battle, Mars led the way, while the several gods took part in the strife, furnishing their favorites with charmed arms, and endowing them with supernatural skill and power. On the sea, Neptune was supposed to be a vigilant observer of events; and when the billows raged, it was imagined to be a manifestation of his fury.

If the winds arose, Æolus was the author of the blast; if a cloud sailed through the sky, it was the chariot of Jupiter. The morning was introduced by the rosy-fingered Aurora; the rainbow indicated the presence of Iris. All earth was a kind of heaven, and heaven was upon earth.

Thus the Greek mythology, formed upon imagination, was a beautiful, though in some respects a fearful dream, where there was much meaning and connection. In it allegory and true history were mixed and blended together; and although it was neither founded upon reason nor revelation, yet it shadowed forth sublime truths in dark and mysterious images.

It must be admitted, however, that the physical was much more prominent than the moral, in the divinities shaped out by the imagination of the Greeks. Their gods, represented as mingling in the affairs of mortals, frequently lent their superior power and intelligence to the promotion of schemes of vice and villany. They were animated by envy, malice, and all the evil passions to which men are subject, and they did not hesitate to adopt any measures, however base, to gratify their nefarious purposes. Even Jupiter, the king of heaven, is described as acting a very profligate part on earth.

Yet, strange as it may seem, most of the Greeks appear to have been impressed with sincere religious feelings. The stories of their gods had come down to them with the authority of antiquity, and habit made them bow to beings whose characters their reason could not approve. It seems impossible, however, that the sages, philosophers, and other persons of cultivated intellect, who flourished in Greece, could have reposed faith in the tissue of gross and extravagant fables, of which this mythology was composed; and, in reality, it is known that Socrates and others of the wisest men of antiquity rejected the popular belief, and, observing the unity of design which is apparent in all the works of nature, rightly concluded that the whole universe must have been created by one omnipotent and omniscient GOD, the Sovereign and Ruler of all.

The Greeks believed in the immortality of the soul, and a future state of rewards and punishments. They imagined, that, after death, the souls of men descended to the shores of a dismal and pestilential stream, called the *Styx*, where Charon, a grim-looking personage, acted as ferryman, and rowed the spirits of the dead across the melancholy river, the boundary of the dominions of Pluto.

Charon, the Ferryman to Hell.

To obtain a passage in Charon's boat, it was necessary that the deceased should have been buried. Those who were drowned at sea, or who were in any other manner deprived of the customary rites of sepulture, were compelled to wander about on the banks of the Styx for a hundred years, before being permitted to cross it.

After quitting the vessel of Charon, the trembling shades advanced to the palace of Pluto, the gate of which was guarded by a monstrous dog, named *Cerberus*, which had three heads, and a body covered with snakes instead of hair. They then appeared before Minos, Rhadamanthus, and Œacus, the three judges of the infernal regions, by whom the wicked were condemned to torments, and the good rewarded with heavenly pleasures.

Tartarus, the place of punishment, was the abode of darkness and horror. There Tantalus, for a vile crime done in life, remained perpetually surrounded with water, which fled from his lips whenever he attempted to quench his burning thirst; while over his head hung branches laden with the most inviting fruits, which shrunk from his grasp as often as he stretched out his hand to pluck them.

There also was Ixion bound with serpents to the rim of a wheel, which, constantly revolving, allowed no cessation of his agonies. Another variety of punishment was allotted to Sisyphus, who was condemned to the endless task of rolling a huge stone up the side of a steep mountain, which he had no sooner accomplished than it rolled down again to its former place. On one side criminals were writhing under the merciless lash of the avenging Furies, and on another were to be seen wretches surrounded with unquenchable flames.

Elysium, the abode of the blessed, was a region of surpassing loveliness and pleasure. Groves of the richest verdure, and streams of silvery clearness, were to be met with on every side. The air was pure, serene, and temperate; the birds continually warbled in the woods, and a brighter light than that of the sun was diffused throughout that happy land. No cares nor sorrow could disturb its inhabitants, who spent their time in the enjoyment of those pleasures they had loved on earth, or in admiring the wisdom and power of the gods.

Chariot Race.

With the religion of the Greeks were connected their temples, oracles, and games. Their principal temples were those of Diana at Ephesus, of Apollo in the city of Miletus, of Ceres and Proserpine at Eleusis, and that of Olympian Jove at Athens. They were all built of marble, and adorned with the most beautiful ornaments. The most celebrated Grecian temple, however, was that of Apollo at Delphos, which was revered and resorted to by all the surrounding nations. Oracles were consulted by the Greeks on every important occasion, and their decisions were held sacred and inviolable. This was on the supposition or belief that the gods communicated with men, and by oracular responses revealed the secrets of futurity. The most celebrated oracles were those of Apollo at Delphi and Delos, the oracle of Jupiter at Dodona, and that of Trophonius, at Lebadea. They were, however, little more than systems of deceit, imposition, or equivocation.

The public and solemn games in Greece were the Olympic, Pythian, Nemean, and Isthmian. The con-

Victor at the Olympic Games.

ests at these several games were running, leaping, throwing the quoit, boxing, and wrestling. Horse races and chariot races were also held in repute. Besides these, there were contests in which musicians, poets, artists, and philosophers engaged for victory. The victors were crowned with olive leaves, and carried about in triumphal processions. These occasions, in which the utmost emulation was excited, brought together a vast concourse of Greeks and strangers, and operated favorably on the national spirit.

The Greeks were eminently an intellectual people, and so far as their engagements in war and other active enterprises permitted, were devoted to literary pursuits. The productions which they have left behind them are some of the most finished specimens of genius and taste which the world has ever known. To this day they continue to be standards of excellence, and are studied as models by the scholars of every civilized nation. The departments of intellectual effort in which they chiefly excelled were poetry, the drama, oratory, history, and philosophy.

As in most other countries, poetry flourished in Greece earlier than prose. At a very remote period, Linus, Orpheus, and Musæus are said to have composed poetry; but although some verses attributed to them are still extant, it is now generally admitted that these must have been the production of more modern times. Homer, the most ancient of the Grecian poets whose works have been preserved, is understood to have existed in the tenth century before Christ, or about three centuries previous to the appearance of any known prose writers in that country. The biographers of Homer represent him as a blind old minstrel, who went from place to place, reciting or singing his verses for a livelihood.

The Iliad and Odyssey of Homer are long narrative poems, illustrative of events connected with the Trojan war. At the time when the Iliad opens, the tenth and last year of the siege has already arrived, and the remaining incidents and final result of the contest are successively described with great poetical power. This is the whole subject of the twenty-four books or sections of the Iliad; yet the characters and scenes portrayed in the poem are so numerous as to add the strong charm of variety to its other beauties. The immortal gods are represented as not only feeling a deep interest, but even making themselves active parties, in the war; which intermixture of divine and human agency in the poem, has, of course, the effect of taking from it all natural probability; yet, leaving this objection aside, there is much in the Iliad to engage the attention of an inquirer into the early history of mankind. It abounds with descriptions and incidents which throw a light upon either the time of action in the poem, or the time of its composition. Heroes are represented as, in those days, yoking their own cars; queens and princesses are busied in spinning; and Achilles kills his mutton with his own hand, and dresses his own dinner. Yet these operations, tame and commonplace, if not vulgar, as they are, do not, in the hands of Homer, detract in the slightest degree from the dignified grandeur of the characters who perform them.

The general tone of the poem is grave and lofty and it occasionally rises into sublimity. In the language there is often a surprising felicity — insomuch that one word will sometimes fill the mind of the reader with a perfect and delightful picture. But the great merit of the work lies in the strength of thought, and the singular ardor of imagination, which it displays. "No poet was ever more happy," says Dr

90

Blair, "in the choice of his subject, or more successful in painting his historical and descriptive pieces. There is a considerable resemblance in the style to that of some parts of the Bible, — for instance, Isaiah, — which is not to be wondered at, seeing that the writings of the Old Testament are productions of nearly the same age, and of a part of the world not far from the alleged birthplace of Homer."

The following passage from the Iliad, which describes part of an interview between Hector, one of the brave defenders of Troy, and his wife, Andromache, is full of truth and beauty, and may serve as a specimen of the poem. It is copied from Pope's translation.

"Too daring prince! ah, whither dost thou run?
Ah, too forgetful of thy wife and son!
And think'st thou not how wretched we shall be,
A widow I, an helpless orphan he?
For sure such courage length of life denies,
And thou must fall, thy virtue's sacrifice.
Greece in her single heroes strove in vain;
Now, hosts oppose thee, and thou must be slain!
O, grant me, gods, ere Hector meets his doom, —
All I can ask of Heaven, — an early tomb!
So shall my days in one sad tenor run,
And end with sorrows, as they first begun.
No parent now remains, my griefs to share,
No father's aid, no mother's tender care;
The fierce Achilles wrapped our walls in fire,
Laid Thebé waste, and slew my warlike sire!
His fate compassion in the victor bred;
Stern as he was, he yet revered the dead;
His radiant arms preserved from hostile spoil,
And laid him decent on the funeral pile;
Then raised a mountain where his bones were burned:
The mountain nymphs the rural tomb adorned.
Jove's sylvan daughters bade their elms bestow
A barren shade, and in his honor grow."

The Odyssey has been said to resemble a work called forth by the success of a previous one, and ranks, as a whole, below the Iliad. It relates to the adventures which befell Ulysses, king of the Island of Ithaca, on his way home from the Trojan war. Both this poem and the Iliad have continued for more than two thousand years to enjoy the admiration of mankind; and it is certainly a proof of surpassing merit, that no effort in the same style of poetry, though made under circumstances much more advantageous than those of the blind old minstrel, has ever been in nearly the same degree successful.

Sappho was a lyrical poetess, whose genius was so much admired by the Greeks, that they honored her with the title of "the Tenth Muse." The following fragment will serve to show the poetic feeling and fancy which characterize the productions of this celebrated woman.

THE ROSE.

"Would Jove appoint some flower to reign
In matchless beauty on the plain,
The rose — mankind will all agree —
The rose the queen of flowers should be:
The pride of plants, the grace of bowers,
The blush of meads, the eye of flowers,
Its beauties charm the gods above;
Its fragrance is the breath of love;
Its foliage wantons in the air,
Luxuriant, like the flowing hair;
It shines in blooming splendor gay,
While zephyrs on its bosom play."

The remaining works of Anacreon consist of odes and sonnets, chiefly referring to the subjects of love and wine. His style is graceful, sprightly, and mellifluous, but he can only be considered as an inspired voluptuary The Athenians, in his own spirit, reared a monument to him in the shape of a drunkard singing — an expressive proof of the blindness of the ancients to the vicious and degrading nature of intemperance.

The following piece exhibits a fair specimen of the poetry of Anacreon: —

ON HIS LYRE.

"'Wake, O lyre, thy silent strings:
Celebrate the brother kings, —
Sons of Athens, famed afar, —
Cadmus, and the Theban war!'
Rapt, I strike the vocal shell —
Hark! — the trembling chords rebel;
All averse to arms they prove,
Warbling only strains of love.
Late I strung anew my lyre —
'Heavenly muse, my breast inspire,
While the swelling notes resound
Hercules, for toils renowned!'
Still the chords rebellious prove,
Answering only strains of love.
Farewell, heroes, farewell, kings!
Love alone shall tune my strings."

The drama arose in the sixth century before the Christian era, under Thespis, a native of Icaria, in Attica. From a rude beginning, in the Grecian custom of celebrating the praises of Bacchus by joyous dancing and the singing of hymns, it soon arose to a regular art, and some of the most eminent Greek authors of an early period are known as dramatists.

Oratory was signally cultivated among the Greeks, particularly the Athenians, whose institutions were rather more free than was elsewhere the case in Greece. It became an object of attention soon after the Persian invasion, about 480 B. C. It was cultivated with wonderful success — was marked by boldness and vehemence at first, but afterwards by greater refinement and elegance.

History, after those earlier ages in which poetry was the vehicle of recorded events, was attended to with an interest and success demanded by its importance. It took its rise more especially in the fifth century before the Christian era. The fanciful and often merely fabulous compositions of the bard, and the uncertain voice of tradition, were, previous to this period, the only records of the past, with the exception of the sacred Scriptures. The historians of Greece attained to various and surprising excellence in a comparatively short period.

Philosophy, which flourished greatly among the Greeks, was divided into various schools or sects. Professors of philosophy arose from the early rhapsodists — men who recited the poems of Homer and others at the public games, commenting at the same time upon them; and who, having established schools, were dignified by the name of *sophists*, or teachers of wisdom. The Grecian philosophy was, however, merely speculative, and seldom based upon facts. The spirit of mystery which prevailed in religion, extended itself into philosophy; and the object of the earliest Grecian moralists was not so much to instruct the people, as to compose, for a narrow circle of scholars, a discipline which should raise them above the common level of mankind. Such were the instructions of Pythagoras who imposed a long and arduous probation before a man could be received as his disciple; and many philosophers made a distinction between the doctrines which they publicly taught, and those reserved for a few more favored hearers.

The principal sects of philosophy in Greece were the Ionic, the most ancient, founded by Thales: the

Italian, by Pythagoras; the Socratic, by Socrates; the Cynic, by Antisthenes; the Academic, by Plato; the Peripatetic, by Aristotle; the Sceptical, by Pyrrho: the Stoic, by Zeno, and the Epicurean, by Epicurus. These sects were distinguished by certain peculiarities of doctrine; as, for instance, the Italian taught the transmigration of souls; the Socratic insisted on the excellence of virtue; the Cynic condemned all society, knowledge, and the arts of life; the Academic dealt in ideal forms and mystical theogony; the Peripatetic exhibited the model of a perfect logic; the Sceptical inculcated universal doubt; the Stoic decried all weakness, and made insensibility a virtue; and the Epicurean pointed to pleasure as the supreme good. The system taught by Aristotle has exerted the greatest influence over the human mind. It reigned in the schools through sixteen hundred years. That inculcated by Socrates was the most correct. It was purer and loftier than even that of Pythagoras, whose morality and religion greatly excelled what was then current in Greece. The Socratic scheme maintained, with ability, the being of a God, together with the incorporeal nature and immortality of the soul.

In respect to the sciences, strictly so called, the Greeks were not undistinguished, although the boundaries of exact knowledge have been greatly extended since their day. This might naturally be expected, as the advancement of such learning essentially depends on accurate, various, and long-continued observation. In Greece, the field of mathematical science did not lie waste. Thales, of Miletus, in the time of Solon, had brought from Egypt some important truths in geometry and astronomy. He disclosed many properties of triangles and circles, asserted the roundness of the earth, explained the nature of eclipses, and actually foretold an eclipse of the sun. His disciples, the Ionic philosophers, pursued his discoveries.

Pythagoras also, however devoted to ethics and theology, did not overlook mathematics or physics. He enlarged the bounds of geometry, and introduced the sciences of numbers and music, though his arithmetical speculations were perverted by the fanciful idea of mysterious virtue in certain numbers and combinations. In applying the sciences of arithmetic and geometry to nature, the Pythagoreans seem to have been less happy. Nevertheless they lighted on some truths as to the system of the world, which their successors rejected, such as that the earth moves round its axis, and both it and the planets round the sun.

Mathematical studies were pursued by Plato, and many of his followers, in a spirit which resembled that of the Pythagoreans. He himself is said to have invented the method of analysis, which ascertains the truth or falsehood of a proposition, by examining that which will follow from the supposition that it is true. By means of this and other discoveries, among which were the leading properties of the three conic sections, the school of Plato much advanced the science of geometry. But, like the Pythagoreans, they were indifferent observers of nature, and wedded to notions of symmetry and numerical resemblances. They were less accurate in respect to astronomy, holding that the sun, planets, and the heavenly sphere, all revolved around the earth. In this they agreed with Aristotle and his disciples, who seem, however, to have been better observers and reasoners on nature, though not equalling the Platonists in pure mathematics.

The most famous seat of this science in after time was the Greek colony of Alexandria. The extensive commerce of the city, concurred with the munificence of its princes in attracting thither men of learning who had their fortunes to seek. All sects were alike welcome, and every question that divided the Athenian schools was discussed with no less ability in the capital of Egypt. Under the Ptolemies arose the famous library, by far the first in the world. Every study was here encouraged; but those f. which the Alexandrine school was most especiall; distinguished, beside mathematics, were criticism philology, and antiquities.

The seven wise men of Greece, who were found in the ranks of philosophy, were Thales, of Miletus; Solon, of Athens; Bias, of Priene; Chilo, of Lacedæmon; Cleobulus, of Lindos; Pittacus, of Mitylene; and Periander, of Corinth. The sayings which they are recorded as having uttered and enforced on many occasions, embody the results of sound sense and varied experience. Among many others, we may select one from each of these men, as a specimen. Pittacus says, "The possession of power discovers a man's true character." Bias says, "Form your plans with deliberation, but execute them with vigor." Solon says, "Do not consider the present pleasure, but the ultimate good." Cleobulus says, "Endeavor always to employ your thoughts on something worthy." Periander says, "The intention of crime is as sinful as the act." Chilo says, "The three most difficult things are, to keep a secret, to employ time properly, and to bear an injury." Thales says, "The same measure of gratitude which we show to our parents, we may expect from our children." Other aphorisms of this last philosopher will be found in our sketch of his life, under the head of Miletus.

In a people so endowed with the love of the grand and beautiful as were the Greeks, we naturally look for exquisite productions in the imitative or fine arts; and we are not disappointed. Greece, in the age of Pericles, (about 430 B. C.,) abounded in architects, sculptors, and painters. It was then in the zenith of its glory in literature as well as the arts. The taste of the public mind conformed to this state of things till after the death of Alexander. Even to this day, Greece, particularly Athens, is the instructress of the world by means of those monuments of its art and genius that yet remain.

The Greek taste in art commenced in the colony of Ionia. We find that as far back as the eighth century B. C., when the parent country was still immersed in barbarism, the cities of Ionia had already become the seats of refinement. There architecture arose into grandeur and elegance. There painting and sculpture, of a refined character, may be said to have been first practised and cultivated. But these arts, together with poetry and philosophy, gradually found their way into European Greece, and flourished there in the highest perfection. At the period above referred to, the area of the citadel of Athens, in which the Parthenon stands, was adorned with numerous magnificent porticoes, and other public buildings, and the whole of its space, although more than six miles in circumference, was so diversified by works of painting and statuary, that it is described as exhibiting one continued scene of enchantment and beauty. In other parts of Greece, also, there were not wanting specimens of the same perfection, in architecture, statuary, and painting.

Ruins of Arch of Adrian, near Athens.

The Greeks invented that system of architecture, which is universally considered as the most finished and perfect. It consisted of three distinct orders, the Doric, the Ionic, and the Corinthian. The Doric was distinguished by a masculine grandeur and sublime plainness. The Ionic was characterized by gracefulness and elegance. The Corinthian affected the highest magnificence and ornament, by uniting the peculiar excellences of all the orders.

The same appreciation of beauty and taste, and the same power of executing the fair ideal, were manifested in the Grecian mind, in regard to sculpture, as in architecture. Specimens of their art in this branch are perfect models. The Dying Gladiator, the Venus, and the Laocoon, of the Greek sculptors, have a world-wide fame. In painting, though very few specimens have come down to us, the Greeks are supposed to have greatly excelled. The ancient writers speak with high admiration of the works of Zeuxis, Apelles, Parrhasius, Protogenes, and Timanthes—which have perished in the lapse of time. In music, the Greeks appear to have been less distinguished than several modern nations.

In the useful and necessary arts of life, the Greeks never made any great proficiency. Agriculture, manufactures, and commerce, were left for other nations to perfect. The Romans surpassed the Greeks in agriculture, and probably also in the mechanic arts. In the time of the ancient Greeks, several important inventions or discoveries, which seem to be essential to comfort, in the modern acceptation of that term, were unknown. They were unacquainted with street pavements, in all probability, for although the most minute accounts have been transmitted of the buildings in many of the Grecian cities, yet we hear nothing of the pavement of any of them. They paid particular attention to the construction of their roads, but suffered all the inconvenience of their streets being filled with dirt and mire. Their modes of conveying intelligence were very imperfect, as public criers were chiefly employed. The Greeks were unacquainted with linen and glass, as also with the lighting of their cities in the night. They were wholly ignorant of the art of constructing clocks. To say nothing of the extraordinary discoveries or inventions of modern ages, as the art of printing, and the magnetic needle, and in more recent times of the application of steam in manufacturing, in sailing, and in travelling on land—the ancient Greeks, as well as the other contemporary nations, were ignorant of many arts and contrivances now deemed indispensable, not only to convenience and comfort, but almost to life itself.

CHAPTER CCCXXVIII.

Manners, Customs, and Domestic Life

Greek Vases.

The Greeks, in personal appearance, were prepossessing, and their women, in many instances, were particularly beautiful. The characteristics of the Grecian face were dark complexion, and black hair and eyes. With their fine forms, enchanting expression, and intellectual preëminence, they seem to have been altogether a favored race. Their habits of life corresponded with their external condition and constitutional endowments. Lively, ardent, and curious, they were fond of gay and imposing amusements.

In their dress, they, in common with other ancient nations, differed much from that of most modern ones. As their climate was peculiarly mild and agreeable, the costume of the people was light and simple, intended rather as a graceful covering of the body, than as a defence against the weather.

The men wore an inner garment, called *tunic*, which descended to the middle of the leg, and over which they cast a mantle. On their heads, after they began to use a covering for them, they wore a sort of hat, which was tied under the chin. On their feet they wore shoes or sandals, which were fastened with thongs or cords.

The women, particularly in Athens, wore a white tunic of woollen, which was closely bound at the waist by a broad sash, and descended in flowing folds down to the heels. Above this they wore a shorter robe, confined round the waist with a ribbon, and bordered at the bottom by stripes of various colors. The ribbon was generally saffron-colored. Over the above they sometimes put on a robe, which was worn gathered up like a scarf. The Greek women always had their heads covered, their hair being curled and braided in a very tasteful manner. At Athens, they wore in their hair golden grasshoppers, which were an emblem of the antiquity of their nation, and an intimation that they were sprung from the earth. Earrings and bracelets of gold were also in use; and in the times of Athenian luxury, the ladies of Athens were wont to paint their cheeks and eyebrows, and employ other artificial means to heighten the charms of beauty.

In Sparta, the kings, magistrates, and citizens were

but little distinguished by external appearance. The military costume was of a red color. The Greeks in general placed a high value on scarlet, and a still greater on purple.

The classes into which the Greeks were generally divided were two, namely, freemen and slaves. In Sparta, as has been mentioned, all mechanical, agricultural, and menial labors were performed by the latter, while the freemen bestowed their attention exclusively on war, politics, and the education of the young. The case was somewhat different in Athens and the other Grecian states. In these, the citizens were disposed to engage in mechanical trades, as well as in the pursuits of commerce, the slaves in the mean while attending to their appropriate labors.

The ordinary amusements of the people consisted in conversing together, or listening to the orators in the market-place, walking in the public gardens, attending the lectures and disputations of the philosophers, and rendering assistance in the numerous processions, games, and festivities, which took place in honor of the gods.

There was a variety of trades and occupations in Greece, connected with the necessary arts of life, but not so large a number as modern inventions, and our minute subdivision of labor, have rendered indispensable. In Athens, multitudes of citizens had no private, regular occupation whatever, but subsisted on the pay they received for their attendance in the political and judicial assemblies, on the allowance of provisions made to them at the public festivals, and on occasional donations of money from the public treasury, or from the funds of opulent individuals. The Greeks were a highly commercial people, and in some of the states a large part of the inhabitants were occupied, directly or indirectly, with commerce. Numerous colonies were planted by the Greeks in Asia Minor, in Sicily, Italy, Spain, and Gaul. Their vessels were small, usually with a single sail.

Greek Vessel.

The private houses in the Grecian cities were, for the mass of the people, extremely mean in aspect, being built of clay or unbaked bricks, and arranged in irregular lines along the sides of narrow streets. But men of wealth had large and handsome establishments. Their dwellings were divided into several apartments, with two or more stories, mounted by staircases.

In front was a large gate, outside of which was a heap of manure left there by the horses and mules. Here a number of dogs and pigs were accustomed to assemble. The first rooms seen on entering were decorated with paintings. There were separate apartments for the men, the visitors, and strangers. There was also a remote room for the girls, who were kept under lock and key.

The houses of the wealthier class abounded in paintings, sculptures, vases, and ornamental works of art. The walls were plastered and finished with joiner's work. The sides and ceilings were adorned with paintings: gold and ivory set off the furniture. Screens of rich tapestry were in use.

Street in Athens.

Among the articles of household furniture, we may enumerate chairs, beds of geese feathers, bedsteads, bedsteads with musquito nets, lambskin blankets, tables, candelabras, carpets, footstools, lamps, chafing-dishes, vases of various forms; baskets, basins, bellows, brooms, cisterns, ovens, frying-pans, hand-mills, knives, soup-ladles, lanterns, mirrors, mortars, sieves, spits, and, in short, most of the articles, or substitutes for them, now in use.

The public buildings of Greece have never been equalled, much less surpassed, in any country of the world, for combined magnificence and durability Formed of polished stone, or of the finest marble, and exhibiting in their construction the admirable proportions and beauty of the three Grecian orders, already mentioned — the Doric, Ionic, and Corinthian — these temples and edifices have long been justly reckoned among the wonders of human art. Though in ruins, they are yet the objects of imitation to the most refined and tasteful nations of the earth. Far from hoping to excel them, the modern architect esteems himself fortunate when he has been successful in copying their distinguishing excellences.

The meals of the Greeks were usually four in number. Breakfast was taken about the rising of the sun; the next meal at midday; then came the afternoon repast; and lastly, the supper, which was the principal meal. At table, their custom, like that so common among the Orientals, was to recline on cushions, or couches, instead of sitting upright. This was more especially the case as luxury began to prevail. In the primitive ages, the people fed on fruits and roots; but afterward, their fare became more varied and rich, animal food of several kinds being served up, and many delicacies of cookery being known.

In the earliest ages, convivial entertainments were generally acts of public devotion; but afterward they seem to have been adopted in private life. There were also political feasts, in which a whole city, tribe, or other division, met together. Water and wine were used for drinking. Perfumed wines were introduced at the tables of the rich. Every thing capable of sustaining life, or gratifying the taste, was employed as food. The Greeks generally had a liking for the products of the water. Hot baths were very numerous, and bathing in them, and anointing the body, with a change of clean clothes, were usual in preparing for a feast. When guests were invited, men and women were never invited together.

Ornamented Vases.

The education of children was carefully attended to by the Greeks, and a judicious, comprehensive system seems to have been followed in the schools. The Spartan plan of training was limited very much to the physical powers. These were strengthened by an appropriate discipline, while exercises were adapted to accustom the mind to fortitude. The Lacedæmonians deemed the pursuits of literature too enervating, or effeminate. The Athenians, and those in the other states who took Athens as a model, gave their youth a much more enlarged education. They did not, indeed, neglect physical training; but they connected with this, instructions in reading, writing, grammar, music, and recitation, and, in later times, an induction into philosophy and oratory.

The marriages among the Greeks were generally formed at an early age, as Grecian women were marriageable about their fourteenth year; but they were lawful only as the consent of parents, or other relatives, could be obtained. This institution was greatly encouraged in all parts of Greece. Want of esteem, and sometimes the infliction of punishment, attended the failure of entering into the connubial state. Though nuptial engagements were entered into with many formalities, they were very easily set aside. All that was to be done, in that case, was, that the parties should furnish the archon with a written certificate of their consent to separate from each other.

Polygamy was allowed only after times of great calamity, such as war, or pestilence. Socrates married a second wife on this account. Violations of the marriage contract, though the punishment was severe, were often committed. The Grecian women seldom appeared in strange company, but were confined to the remote parts of the house, into which no male visitants were admitted. Their time was spent in spinning, weaving, baking bread, and superintending the labors of their female slaves. When they appeared in public, as during solemn festivals, they walked in procession, with downcast eyes, surrounded by their slaves and attendant maidens, or proceeded unostentatiously to the place in which their presence was allowed. The lower classes, however, were practically exempted from these restrictions; and even females of rank contrived, on some occasions, to evade them. The case was wholly different with the Lacedæmonian women, who were obliged, by the laws of Lycurgus, to exhibit themselves in public.

In some parts of Greece, parents might expose their children, in certain cases. Children were required to maintain their parents, in old age; but, according to the laws of Solon, if a person did not bring up his children to some useful employment, they were to be released from such an obligation.

The funerals of the Greeks were attended with many ceremonies, showing that they considered the duties belonging to the dead as of the highest importance. In their view, it was the most dreadful of all imprecations, to wish that a person might die without the honors of a funeral. The dead body, as the will of the deceased, or of the kindred, directed, was either committed to the grave or consumed upon a funeral pile; the ashes being, in the latter case, afterward gathered, and placed in an urn. The urn was buried in the earth.

CHAPTER CCCXXIX.

Celebrated Characters.

Grecian history abounds in great men; and many of these, in the productions left behind them, have become the instructors of mankind in every subsequent age. Among these we must first reckon *Homer*, the father of poetry, and the greatest of poets, who has already been noticed in the history of Asia Minor. He is supposed to have been preceded by others in the Grecian poetic annals; but on this subject we have no authentic information. His are the earliest works of the kind which have survived the ravages of time; and he is, therefore, justly styled the most ancient of profane classical authors.

Hesiod differed from Homer, and was greatly inferior to him; yet he deserves a record by his side. He, too, comes down from a venerable antiquity, for he is generally supposed to have been contemporaneous with the father of Greek poetry. He was born at Ascra, in Bœotia, and was the author of several poems of considerable merit, two of which are extant. These are entitled the *Theogony*, or the *Generation of the Gods*, and the *Works and Days*. The former gives a faithful account of the gods of antiquity. The latter being on agriculture, contains refined moral reflections, which mingle with his instructions for cultivating fields. Hesiod is admired for elegance and sweetness. Cicero highly commends him; and the Greeks were so partial to his moral instructions, that they required their children to commit them all to memory. He is reported to have spent his youthful years in tending his father's flocks, on the sides of Mount Helicon.

Lycurgus, the legislator, flourished about 884 years B. C. He was regent of Sparta, until Charilaus, his nephew, had attained to mature years. Then, leaving Sparta, he travelled into Asia and Egypt, for the purpose of improving his mind, and observing the manners, customs, and political institutions of different nations. At this period, there was a deplorable state of things in his native country. Intestine divisions and factious contentions rose so high, that the laws fell into contempt, the authority of the kings was disregarded, and all was anarchy and confusion. The conviction became general, that a reform in the national institutions was indispensable; and the eyes of the

Lacedæmonians turned to Lycurgus, as a man whose experience, wisdom, and probity preëminently qualified him for the task of preparing a new constitution for his country.

At this crisis he returned, and, as has been stated in the narrative, he reformed the abuses of the state, banished luxury, and brought forward a system which gave rise to all the magnanimity, fortitude, and intrepidity, which distinguished the Lacedæmonian people. Having established his laws, and engaged the citizens not to alter them until his return, he left his country, and, by a voluntary death, rendered that event impossible; thus securing, as far as in his power, the perpetuity of his institutions.

Solon, the legislator and philosopher, was born at Salamis, and educated at Athens, and consecrated his life to the good of his country. By his descent, as well as by his talents and virtues, he was one of the noblest of the Greeks. By his father's side, he derived his origin from King Codrus. After he had devoted part of his time to philosophical and political studies, Solon travelled over the greatest part of Greece; but at his return, he was distressed with the dissensions which prevailed among his countrymen. All fixed their eyes upon him as a deliverer, and he was unanimously elected archon and sovereign legislator. It was now in his power to have made himself absolute; but he refused the dangerous office of king of Athens, and, in the capacity of lawgiver, he commenced and carried through a reformation in every department.

The sanguinary laws of Draco were all cancelled by Solon, except that against murder, and the punishment denounced against each offender was proportioned to his crime; but he made no law against parricide or sacrilege. The former of these crimes, he said, was too horrible to human nature for a man to be guilty of it; and the latter could never be committed, because the history of Athens, hitherto, had not furnished a single instance. Yet human wickedness, as we are forced to admit, has frequently ventured to these extremes. Solon instituted the Areopagus, and regulated the Prytaneum. His excellent code of laws flourished through a period of four hundred years. He died, as some report, in Cyprus, in the eightieth year of his age, about 558 B. C.

Solon possessed a genius for poetry, as well as philosophy and legislation. To the writing of verses he was addicted more especially in his youth. Plato says of him, that if he had finished all his poems, and particularly his History of the Atlantic Island which he brought out of Egypt, and had taken time to revise and correct them, as others did, neither Homer, Hesiod, nor any other ancient poet, would have been more famous.

Thales, *Anaximander*, *Pythagoras*, and *Anacreon*, are noticed in our sketch of Asia Minor. Of the works of *Simonides*, only some fragments are extant. He is said chiefly to have excelled in elegiac composition, but he was successful, also, in other kinds of poetry. He attempted several epics, one of which was on Cambyses, king of Persia. The prevailing characteristic of his poetry was tenderness and plaintive sweetness. He enjoyed the powers of his mind and body till a very advanced age, and gained a prize for poetical composition in his eightieth year. After this, he lived ten years, and finally died in the Island of Sicily. He flourished about 538 B. C.

Æschylus was the first eminent dramatic poet of Greece. He had the reputation of being a brave soldier, but a far more desirable name as a great poet. Of tragedy, strictly speaking, he was deemed the father; such were the improvements which he effected on the Athenian stage. He wrote ninety tragedies, forty of which were rewarded with the public prize but only seven are extant. His productions are characterized by an uncommon boldness and originality his style is concise, and too often obscure, having a mixture both of the sublime and bombastic. His supremacy in dramatic composition was at length contested by the youthful Sophocles, and with success. The works of this rival being preferred, he withdrew from the scene of his triumphs into Sicily, where he lived under the patronage of Hiero, king of Syracuse. He died on the island, in the sixty-ninth year of his age, 456 B. C.; his death having been caused, it is said, by the singular circumstance of the fall, on his head, of a tortoise from the talons of an eagle.

Sophocles, the dramatist, was born at Colonos, in the vicinity of Athens, about 497 B. C. He distinguished himself for statesmanship as well as poetry. He commanded the Athenian armies, and in several instances he shared the supreme command with Pericles. The commencement of his poetic course reflects great honor on the abilities of Sophocles. In a yearly contest for tragedy, which was instituted by the Athenians on account of taking the Island of Scyros, he obtained the prize over many competitors, in the number of whom was Æschylus, as already mentioned. Each was admired for his peculiar qualities; Sophocles for his sublimity and majesty, Æschylus for his tenderness and pathos. Their contentions, though at first honorable, at length degenerated into jealousy and rivalship.

Seven only remain of the one hundred and twenty tragedies which Sophocles composed. Twenty times did the theatrical judges confer upon him the crown of victory; and, according to some accounts, he died of excess of joy, in consequence of having obtained his twentieth poetical prize at the Olympic games.

The ingratitude of the children of the poet is well known. They wished to become immediate possessors of their father's estate, and therefore, impatient of his long life, they accused him before the Areopagus of insanity or dotage. The only defence which Sophocles made, was to read his tragedy of Œdipus at Colonos, which he had recently finished; and then he asked his judges whether the author of such a performance could be justly taxed with insanity or imbecility. It was a triumphant and successful appeal. He died in the ninety-first year of his age, 406 B. C.

Euripides was also a celebrated tragic poet, born at Salamis, 480 B. C. His teachers were men of eminence in the several branches to which he attended—Prodicus in eloquence, Socrates in ethics, and Anaxagoras in philosophy. Betaking himself to authorship, after his prolonged studies, his writings became so much the admiration of his countrymen, that the Greeks who had accompanied Nicias on his expedition against Syracuse were freed from slavery in consequence of being able to repeat some verses from the plays of Euripides. He was the rival of Sophocles. The jealousy between these eminent poets was made the subject of successful ridicule by the comic poet Aristophanes. Euripides sought retirement from the world, and often confined himself in a solitary cave near Salamis, where he wrote and finished his most excellent tragedies.

Admired as he was, he also had his enemies. Their ridicule and envy he felt so keenly, that he at last removed from Athens. The remainder of his days he spent at the court of Archelaus, king of Macedonia, where he received the highest marks of royal munificence and friendship. His death is said to have been occasioned by the king's dogs, which met him in his solitary walks, and tore him to pieces. He died in his seventy-eighth year. A greater number of his tragedies are extant than of those of his rivals, viz., nineteen out of seventy-five. This poet is peculiarly happy in expressing the passion of love. He is characterized by an uncommon tenderness and pathos. Occasionally he rises into sublimity. The most familiar expressions have received a perfect polish from his pen. He abounds also in what is still better—fine moral and philosophical sentiments; though the Athenians thought that there was occasionally a spice of impiety in his writings.

Aristophanes was a native of Athens, and the most celebrated of the comic writers of Greece. He has been called the prince of the ancient comedy, as is Menander of the new. Eleven of his fifty-four comedies have come down to us. He severely lashed the vices of the age; nor did he spare, at times, the feelings of the wise and good. His attack upon the venerable Socrates, in his play called *Nubes*, has always been censured, and that with justice. His wit is admirable, but we find it too often in connection with obscenity. It is said that St. Chrysostom used to keep the comedies of Aristophanes under his pillow, on account of the brilliancy of the composition. He flourished 434 B. C.

Pindar was one of the greatest of the Grecian poets. He was a native of Thebes; but his countrymen did not at first appreciate his poetic talents. After his death, however, they erected a statue to his memory; for it was found that all Greece was filled with admiration of his genius. His compositions were quoted by statesmen and princes, and his hymns were repeated in the temples, at the celebration of the festivals. The greatest part of his works have perished. The odes that are extant are admirable for sublimity of sentiment, grandeur of expression, energy and magnificence of style, boldness of imagery, harmony of numbers, and elegance of diction. He seemed to fulfil the prognostic by which his early youth was marked, viz., the settling of a swarm of bees on his lips, and the formation of a honey-comb there, as he lay upon the grass asleep. It could be no other than an augury of his future greatness, and the sweetness of his song! He died 435 B. C., at the age, as is said, of eighty-six years.

Herodotus was born at Halicarnassus, one of the Dorian Greek cities of Asia Minor, in the account of which we have sketched his life.

Thucydides, the historian whose early aspirations after excellence in the composition of history appeared, as he burst into tears when he heard Herodotus at the Olympic games, even surpassed the object of his emulation, in some of the attributes of that species of writing. He stands unrivalled for the fire, conciseness, and energy of his narrative. He is considered also highly authentic, as he was himself interested in the events which he narrated. The history of Thucydides was so admired, that Demosthenes, to perfect himself as an orator, transcribed it eight different times, and read it with such attention, that he could almost repeat it from memory. This historian died at Athens where he was born, but from which he had been banished. He was, however, recalled, at length, to the place of his birth, where he passed the remainder of his days. He lived to his eightieth year, 394 B. C.

Hippocrates, the father of medicine was born in the Island of Cos, situated on the coast of Asia Minor, in the history of which we have given his life. He studied physic with his grandfather, Nebrus, and improved himself by reading the tablets in the temples of the gods, where each individual had written down the diseases under which he had labored, and the means of his recovery. His knowledge was daily increased by the experiments he made upon the human frame, and from his accurate observations he learned how to regulate his own life, as well as to prescribe to his fellow-men. He died in the ninety-ninth year of his age, 361 B. C., free from the infirmities incident to age; and after death he received the name of *Great*. His writings, few of which remain, procured for him also the epithet of *Divine*. According to Galen, his opinion is as respectable as the voice of an oracle.

Socrates was the most eminent of the heathen moralists. He was the father of nearly all the sects of philosophy which sprung up in after times. There were few that did not rejoice to trace their origin to him, so signal was the influence of his character and abilities. All that may be called the Socratic sects were employed, like him, in instituting inquiries respecting the nature of good and evil, of happiness and misery.

Socrates was a native of Athens. He followed, for some time, the occupation of his father, who was a statuary. He was called away from this inferior employment, of which, however, he was never ashamed, by the urgency of a friend; and philosophy soon became his study. He appeared, like the rest of his countrymen, in the field of battle, and he fought with boldness and intrepidity. But his character as a soldier and patriot has been utterly forgotten in the world-wide estimation he has received as a sage and moralist. He was fond of labor, bore injuries with patience, and acquired that serenity of mind and firmness of countenance which would not be affected by any dangers, however alarming, or any calamities, however great.

The philosophy of Socrates was wholly promulgated in conversation, not in writing; but his doctrines and character have been handed down to posterity by two of his most gifted disciples, Plato and Xenophon, who are soon to be noticed. He spoke with freedom on every subject, religious as well as civil. This independence of spirit, and the visible superiority of mind and genius over the rest of his countrymen, created him many enemies, and at length they condemned him to death, on the false accusation of corrupting the Athenian youth, of making innovations in the religion of the Greeks, and of ridiculing the gods whom the Athenians worshipped. He drank the poisonous cup in the seventieth year of his age, and died, 401 B. C.

Socrates is said to have brought down Philosophy from the clouds, and made her converse with men. Ever earnest in recommending piety and virtue, and showing that man's happiness and dignity are determined by his mind, and not by his fortunes; by virtue and wisdom, not by rank and wealth; his own life was the best example of his precepts. When forced into public office, he manifested unbending uprightness, and his private conduct was no less exemplary. Barefooted and poorly clad, he associated with the rich and gay, as with the poor, in the same spirit of good will. His advice and instructions were given to all without fee or reward, for his temper was rigidly independent, and if he possessed little of the world's goods, he wanted even less.

Xenophanes was the originator of the *eclectic* school of philosophy, which was a modification of the Italian school, founded by Pythagoras. He was a native of Colophon, one of the cities of Ionia, and lived to the great age of one hundred years.

Parmenides was the pupil of the preceding philosopher, and embraced substantially the same theory in regard to God and the universe.

Zeno, the philosopher, was a native of Elea, and a disciple of Parmenides. In his opinions, he mainly followed the teachings of his predecessors. He was a zealous supporter of popular rights, and is said to have been put to death with the most cruel torments, by the tyrant of his native city, for having attempted the deposition of the latter. Among his particular doctrines, he maintained the impossibility of motion, and called in question the existance of the material universe.

One of Zeno's disciples was Leucippus. He was the author of what is called the *atomic theory*, and a *vacuum*, which was afterward more fully explained by Democritus and Epicurus. He taught that all things are composed of very minute, indivisible atoms; that these possess in themselves the principle of motion, and that the universe was formed in consequence of their falling into a vacuum. He flourished about 428 B. C. His theory has had many supporters.

Xenophon, the celebrated general, historian, and philosopher, was an Athenian by birth. He was bred in the school of Socrates, and acquired great literary distinction. His account of the life and doctrines of Socrates is characterized by sobriety of mind and practical good sense, and probably gives a better idea of the original than that of Plato.

Xenophon served in the army of Cyrus the younger, and superintended the retreat of the ten thousand, after the battle of Cunaxa, as we have related in the history of Persia. He afterwards followed the fortunes of Agesilaus, and acquired riches in his expeditions. In his subsequent retirement at Elea, under the patronage of Agesilaus, he composed and wrote for the information of posterity, and died at Corinth, in his ninetieth year, 359 B. C. Beside his *Memorabilia* of Socrates, he continued the history of Thucydides, wrote a life of Cyrus the Great, and produced other works of high interest. The simplicity and elegance of Xenophon's style induced Quintilian to say, that "the Graces dictated his language, and that the goddess of Persuasion dwelt upon his lips." His religious sentiments were among the most correct of the Grecian school.

Plato, the most illustrious of the disciples of Socrates, was an Athenian by descent, but born in the Island of Ægina. He was, during eight years, the pupil of that great man; after whose death, he travelled into foreign countries. When he had finished his travels, he retired to the groves of Academus, a spot which had been the property of a citizen of that name, and from which it was ever after called the *Academy*. Here he was attended by a crowd of noble and illustrious pupils. He continued, with few intervals, to teach in Athens till the time of his death, which occurred about the eightieth year of his age.

Plato.

The learning and virtues of this philosopher were topics of conversation in every part of Greece. He was elegant in his manners, and partook freely of innocent pleasures and amusements. His works are numerous, consisting of thirty-nine dialogues and thirteen epistles. These embrace a vast variety of subjects,—ethical, physical, logical, and political,—and are written with singular elegance, melody, and sweetness of expression.

Plato possessed a mind almost unrivalled for its completeness at all points, and uniting the greatest acuteness, vigor, and comprehension of understanding, with a most glowing and poetical imagination, and matchless dignity, power, and beauty of style. But his genius was too original and peculiar to fit him for the mere reporter of another's opinions; and much of what he has written under the name of Socrates must be considered as his own. The bias of his mind was to abstract speculation—to the discovery of the principles of morality, rather than the application of its precepts to particular cases. In his fondness for lofty contemplation, he sometimes slides into mysticism and obscurity—a tendency which is not observable in the discourses of Socrates given by his other celebrated disciple, Xenophon. The deep and subtile speculations of Plato's Socrates on the nature of moral goodness and beauty, however admirable in themselves, appear to be characteristic of the writer, rather than his master.

Plato concurred with many others of antiquity in conceiving two principles—God and matter—to have coëxisted in the universe from eternity. He viewed the Deity as an intelligent cause, the origin of all spiritual being, and the framer of the material world.

Aristotle. This philosopher is often called the *Stagirite*, from the place of his birth, Stagira. He possessed an understanding at once the most comprehensive and the most discriminating. He was the father of philosophical criticism, the ablest of Grecian speculative politicians, and an acute and curious observer of all remarkable phenomena, whether in the material or intellectual world.

His writings treat of almost every branch of knowledge of his time. Moral and natural philosophy metaphysics, mechanics, grammar, criticism, and politics, all occupied his pen. His vast and varied erudition, and wonderful subtilty and acuteness, were, however joined with a somewhat dogmatical temper, and a strong desire to give to his treatment of every subject an air of scientific completeness. Hence it comes that while the individual reputation of Aristotle was almost unrivalled, his school was comparatively barren of emi-

Aristotle.

nent men. Among his followers, improvement has ever been retarded by the opinion that they had in his works a perfect system of human knowledge. This made them consent to explain and enforce his conclusions, without pursuing them further, or inquiring into the evidence upon which they rested.

His power of systematic arrangement was indeed extraordinary, and the talent was accompanied with the disposition to carry it to excess. This is peculiarly striking in his ethics, in reading which we can hardly fail to be impressed with the idea that, while Plato teaches men to feel and act, the object of Aristotle is rather to instruct them how to define and classify their actions. He died in the sixty-third year of his age, 322 B. C.; but the cause of his death is not certainly known, some saying that he drowned himself in the Euripus, inasmuch as he could not find out the cause of its flux and reflux; and others, that he died of a colic at Athens.

Demosthenes, the prince of orators, whose career forms a part of the history of his country, and as such has been already exhibited, was by birth an Athenian. He was an heir to property; but being only seven years old when his father died, and his guardians proving unfaithful to their trust, his youth was marked by misfortune, want, and neglect of education. He was therefore indebted afterward to his own industry and application for the discipline of his mind, and preparation for the duties of life. By unwearied efforts, and by overcoming the greatest obstacles, such as weakness of the lungs, difficulty of pronunciation, and awkward habits of body, he perfected himself in the art of speaking.

The orations called *Philippics*, from being directed against Philip, are generally referred to as the most powerful specimens of the oratory of Demosthenes. Various others are extant whose eloquence is scarcely inferior; and amongst these may be particularly mentioned the orations for the Olynthians, and the orator's defence of himself against Æschines. No public speaker can be said to have expressed the various passions of hatred, resentment, or indignation, with more energy than he. His great rival compared him to a siren, from the melody of his expressions.

Æschines. The rival above spoken of was Æschines, who flourished 342 B. C. When the Athenians wished to reward the patriotic labors of Demosthenes with a golden crown, Æschines impeached Ctesiphon, who proposed it; and to their subsequent dispute posterity is indebted for the two celebrated orations concerning the crown. Æschines was defeated by his rival's superior eloquence, and banished to Rhodes; but as he departed from Athens, Demosthenes followed him, and nobly forced him to accept a present of silver. Æschines wrote three orations, and nine epistles, of which the orations only are extant.

Antisthenes. This philosopher was the head of a sect which made it their boast to discard all prejudices, all arbitrary likings and dislikings, and to live by the dictates of pure reason, without regard to the customs and opinions of men. They ridiculed those who placed their happiness in the ostentation of riches; yet they were no less vainly boastful in the display of their rags and filthiness: they ridiculed all who lived according to other men's opinions, and not to their own; and they pursued their maxims even to the disregard of the most natural and necessary decencies. From their rude and slovenly manner of life, and their snarling moroseness, they were known by the name of *Cynics*, or dog-philosophers. Of this sect was the celebrated Diogenes, whom we have noticed in our history of Asia Minor.

Zeno, a native of Cyprus, was the founder of the sect called *Stoics*, who somewhat resembled the Cynics. The term is derived from *stoa*, a portico, the customary resort of Zeno. He was austere in his manners, but his life was an example of moderation and sobriety. Offended at the degree of importance allowed by the Academy to outward things, Zeno endeavored to found his system on loftier principles. In this he was not altogether successful. His views appear, when broadly stated, to agree with the doctrine of Pyrrho, who held that virtue was the only good, vice the only evil, and that all other things, such as health or sickness, pleasure or pain, were so utterly indifferent, that a wise man would not have even a choice between them. If he modified this doctrine to some extent, he only fell in with the views of the Academy, which regarded worldly good as possessing substantial value, but yet of so inferior a kind, that the greatest amount of it could not be weighed against a single point of moral worth or intellectual accomplishment. Zeno, in his maxims, used to say, that with virtue, men could live happily under the most pressing calamities: that nature had given us two ears, and only one mouth, to tell us that we ought to listen more than speak.

Epicurus. Few names of antiquity are more familiar than that of Epicurus, not on account of any remarkable discrimination of intellect or goodness of heart, but as being the founder of a famous school of philosophy known by his name. His most remarkable tenet was, that pleasure was the only good, and pain the only evil. These were the terms in which his tenet was expressed, although he and his followers explained it in such a manner as to render it comparatively harmless. This was, however, at some expense of consistency and clearness. His opinions speedily became extremely popular, as might be supposed from the moral corruption of human nature, especially as they were represented, though wrongly, as countenancing sensual indulgence of every kind.

Euclid. This distinguished mathematician belonged to Alexandria. He flourished about 300 B. C. He is the author of the well-known Elements of Geometry, a treatise yet unmatched in clearness, precision, and logical strictness of deduction. Beside arranging, and consecutively proving, the fundamental truths of the science, he did much to enlarge its scope. His attention was turned chiefly to pure mathematics.

Archimedes. This mathematician, who was born at Syracuse, not only outstripped all his contemporaries, but went near to anticipate some of the discoveries which have done most honor to modern science. He extended the boundaries of geometry in every direction, but especially where it treats of curvilinear figures and solids. If he was great as a geometer, he was to the full as eminent as a mechanician. Before his time, mechanics and hydrostatics could hardly be deemed to exist as sciences; he established both on sure grounds, and enriched them with many valuable discoveries.

At the siege of Syracuse, by the Roman general Marcellus, the beleaguering army was baffled for a long time merely by the genius of Archimedes. His skill disconcerted all the projects of the hostile engineers, while they were unable to guard against his more formidable engines. The city was ultimately taken by surprise. Archimedes perished in the tumult of the storm, against the wish and command of the Roman leader, 208 B. C.

Theocritus. This individual flourished at Syracuse about 270 B. C. He distinguished himself by his poetic compositions, of which thirty idyls and some epigrams are extant, written in the Doric dialect, and admired for their beauty, elegance, and simplicity. He excelled in pastorals. He stands at the head in this department of poetry, Virgil himself imitating and borrowing from him. It is said he wrote some invectives against Hiero, king of Syracuse, who ordered him to be strangled.

Polybius. This learned author, who wrote the history of the Greeks and Romans, properly succeeds Xenophon among the Grecian historians. He was a native of Arcadia, and was born 205 B. C. Having lived in Rome, and being acquainted with the prominent men of his time, his history is distinguished by comprehensiveness, and by the admirable accuracy and impartiality of the narrator. His history was written in Greek, divided into forty books, which began with the first Punic war, and finished with "the conquest of Macedonia by Paulus." The greatest part of this valuable work is lost. Five books and many fragments only remain. He died in his eighty-second year, 124 B. C.

Eratosthenes. This individual, who was called a second Plato, was a native of Cyrene. He was an eminent geometer and astronomer, a rhetorician and poet, an antiquary, and the father of the common system of early chronology. He attempted to calculate the size of the earth by observing the zenith distance of the sun at Alexandria at noon on a midsummer day, when upright objects cast no shadow at Syene. He thus ascertained the difference of latitude, from which, the distance of places being known, it was easy to compute the circumference of the globe. He left many valuable works, which are mostly lost, both in astronomy and pure mathematics.

Plutarch. This illustrious man was born at Chæronea. He died at an advanced age, in his native place, about A. D. 140. Having travelled, in quest of knowledge, through Egypt and Greece, he retired to Rome, where he opened a school, with great reputation. After a residence in that city of about forty years, he removed to Chæronea, and in that delightful retirement composed the greatest part of his works.

His Lives of Illustrious Men is the most esteemed of his productions. His precision and fidelity are remarkable. His style is energetic and animated, though not distinguished for purity or elegance. With a few deficiencies, he is still the most entertaining, instructive, and interesting of all the writers of ancient history. It has been remarked, that "were a man of true taste and judgment asked what book he wished to save from destruction, of all the profane compositions of antiquity, he would, probably, without hesitation reply, the Lives of Plutarch."

CHAPTER CCCXXX.

A. D. 1454 to 1863.

*History of Modern Greece — **Revolution.***

After the overthrow of the Byzantine empire, in 1454, a long period of oppression and misery followed under the rule of the semi-barbarous Turks. It presents, however, but a barren field for history. The Grecian people were but the slaves of strangers, whose creed and language were wholly dissimilar to their own. The two races, therefore, never became homogeneous; the relation of conquerors and conquered continued century after century; the Greeks, instead of being governed, were plundered and oppressed by pachas, or lieutenants, who were placed over them in various parts of the country. It was a state of things far more intolerable than even the degraded condition of the Greeks under the Byzantine emperors.

The story of the ancestors of this oppressed people was the delight of the civilized world, and the rude and cruel Turks were sufficiently detested by every scholar and patriot; but no effective sympathy had been exerted in reference to this land of heroes among the Christian nations of Europe. Through more than three centuries, they writhed and suffered under the heavy yoke of savage domination. They were left, indeed, to work out the problem of their deliverance from amidst themselves. The commencement of the revolution which issued in their independence was their own work. The spirit of resistance and the desire for nationality sprang up toward the close of the eighteenth century. At that time, several secret societies were formed, and schemes were devised for effecting the liberation of the country. Money was also contributed for the same object through numerous associations.

It was a dark and deeply-cherished wrong, which the whole Greek nation felt, as they looked back upon ages of plunder, and poverty, and oppression. The scenes before their eyes harrowed up their souls — their fields successively stripped of their harvests, their flocks and herds driven off to satiate the appetite of strangers, their sons forced into foreign wars, their daughters selected as victims of privileged lust, their temples and shrines piled into ruins, and their religion rendered the object of mockery and scorn. As they brooded over these things, they made up their minds, at last, to perish rather than submit longer to exactions so cruel and a degradation so painful. Such an inheritance of bondage and shame they could not think of transmitting any longer to those who should come after them. Hence their desperate though unequal contest with their haughty oppressor. They encountered him with a force that made their resistance, at first, more a subject of derision than alarm.

"But courage and decided patriotism seldom reckon nicely upon numbers. They had that within them which no superiority of strength could subdue — a spirit resolutely resolved on freedom! They had no arms, ammunition, or system of operation; no disciplined legions to force the enemy from his strong positions; no fleet to prevent the access of hostile squadrons: they rose as each man's sense of duty prompted, and seized such weapons as were within their reach; it might be a bludgeon, but it was wielded by an arm true to its trust; it might be a boat, but it was armed with concealed fire; it might be a rock, but it went on its precipitous course with unerring aim; or it might be a fragment of a column, but, like the pillars of Gaza, it crushed the insulters with the insulted."

The spirit which had been enkindled manifested itself on several occasions, but too feebly or partially to effect much until the year 1821, when a secret society, under the name of *Hetairists*, issued their proclamation of a design to emancipate Greece. In their call upon the friends of freedom for assistance, they were answered from every nook and corner of the land, and preparations were forthwith made for active warfare. The spirit of insurrection soon became violent, and correspondent measures were taken by the Turkish sultan to check it at once. An act of shocking cruelty was committed by him, with a view to strike terror into the hearts of the Greeks. Their venerable patriarch, Gregory, he caused to be dragged from the church to the palace, and his body to be hung for two days over the principal entrance, as a spectacle to every passer-by. Nine bishops were afterward hung with him, adding terror to the view. At the same time, a general massacre of the Greeks in the Turkish capital took place. Men, women, and children, in great numbers, were indiscriminately butchered. Churches and temples were made scenes of pillage and impious desecration.

These events were soon followed by the siege of Tripolitza, a Turkish city in the heart of the Morea. Hither had fled many Turkish soldiers and citizens, who had been pursued by the enraged Greeks. The hills around the city having been taken possession of, the city itself was effectually encircled by the invading army. The besieged, thus having no access to a supply of provisions from without, had exhausted those within at the end of six months, during which the siege continued. All the horrors of starvation were now before them. Pestilence, the usual accompaniment of scarcity, soon added to the sufferings of the inhabitants.

As matters could not long continue in this state, proposals of capitulation were made to the Greeks, through some of the wealthiest citizens deputed for this purpose. But all that was effected by the measure was, that a few days' truce took place, with a view to an easier decision of the terms of surrender. Before the termination of the truce, however, a party of the besiegers mounted an unguarded portion of the walls, which they happened to observe, and there displayed their flag. At this sight, a rush was made from every quarter, the Greeks at once scaling the walls and the Turks retiring. At the same time, the gates were opened, and every Turk that appeared was shot or hewed down. Though the latter fought with the utmost bravery, the onset of the Greeks was too fierce to be withstood, and the city was accordingly taken. The loss of the Turks, by famine and the carnage of battle, was no less than fifteen thousand men.

The Greeks, now justly encouraged by their victory, scattered themselves about the country, and engaged the Turks wherever an opportunity was presented. Thus the whole extent of Greece became one vast battle-field. During the struggle, their warfare was carried on in an erratic manner. There was little regular combination of forces; small bodies were banded together, under what were called *capitani*, or chiefs many of whom distinguished themselves by their moral or heroic qualities.

It was at the breaking out of the revolution that events occurred at the island of Scio, of a character among the most mournful that history records. The inhabitants of the island, from various reasons, but particularly from the complicated character of their commerce and natural quietness of disposition, declined involving themselves in the confederation. They felt that too much was at stake to embark in an enterprise which was yet so uncertain in its issue, and which, if it should terminate unfavorably, would involve them in utter ruin.

At length, however, the aga, or military governor, began to suspect them of a disposition to favor the spirit of revolt that was abroad, put an end to the peculiar privileges they enjoyed, and adopted a system of the most oppressive violence. But to these atrocious measures they unresistingly submitted, till their wrongs, increasing with their forbearance, became at last insupportable. Their chief men and opulent citizens were cast into prison as hostages, their fields ravaged and dwellings plundered by mercenary soldiers, and the sanctity of virtue wantonly outraged. Still they were slow to adopt the desperate alternative of open resistance, and hesitated, in torturing suspense, till roused by the reckless zeal of a few wandering Samians.

They adopted no organized system of operation, and were destitute of the advantages of discipline or the implements of war; but, arming themselves with such weapons as their forests furnished, they rose on their oppressors. Under all their disadvantages, Providence for a time seemed to favor their perilous determination; but the alarm having been given to the admiral of the Turkish fleet, who was supposed at the time to be much farther off from the place, he immediately anchored in the bay with a force of forty sail, and opened all their batteries on the devoted town. The scene that followed has few parallels in the history of warfare. It was not the suppression of a rebellion, but the extinction of a people, who had ever been characterized for their amiable and forgiving spirit. The town was taken, sacked, and demolished; the priests and elders who had been cast into prison as hostages were brought out and impaled alive; and the inhabitants of every age and condition, without regard to sex, were hunted down in every retreat, and massacred in cold blood, till at last the entire island, so recently teeming with life and radiant with beauty became a field of desolation, groans, and blood.

A similar fate attended Ipsara, a small island of wild, rugged peaks, and rock-bound coast. Its inhabtants, in their struggle for independence, exhibited a heroism worthy of the days of Leonidas. After contending with their numerous foes till every ray of hope was extinguished, they blew up their fortifications, overwhelming themselves and thousands of their enemies in instant death. They who were not within the works, to escape the vengeance or lust of the Turks, threw themselves into the sea. On every cliff the mother might be seen clasping her infant to her bosom, and plunging into the wave, with her shrieking, despairing daughters at her side. The bodies of beautiful women and youth were seen for days floating around the isle on their watery bier — a sight which might have excited pity in wild beasts, but which the Mussulman looked upon with infernal triumph and gratification. The island soon became a blackened ruin.

For two years after the capture of Tripolitza, the contest between the Greeks and their oppressors continued with varying success. The insurgents never yielded to despair, although they sought in vain the countenance and assistance of the various European powers. Indirect aid was imparted to them from many parts of Europe and the United States, but no open governmental encouragement till in the subsequent period of the revolution. After the exploit of Marco Bozzaris, in attacking a Turkish pacha in his camp, in 1823, and utterly defeating a force of twelve thousand Turks, the attention of Europe, as well as America, was more effectually turned toward the affairs of Greece. It was so striking an instance of valor and patriotism, that the world could not but note and admire it. On the 30th of August, coming suddenly upon the pacha, who was reposing in perfect unconsciousness of danger, he penetrated to his very tent before the Turks could recover from the panic into which they were thrown. Blood was profusely spilt on both sides, but the victory was not doubtful. At the moment of entering the pacha's tent, Bozzaris received a mortal wound, and, being borne from the field, soon after expired. His last words were, "Could a Suliot leader die a nobler death?"

The fate of Bozzaris has been the theme of a beautiful poem by our countryman Halleck, from which we extract a single verse: —

"They fought like brave men, long and well;
They piled that ground with Moslem slain;
They conquered; but Bozzaris fell,
Bleeding at every vein.
His few surviving comrades saw
His smile when rang their proud hurrah,
And the red field was won.
They saw in death his eyelids close,
Calmly, as to a night's repose,
Like flowers at set of sun."

Roused by this instance of successful daring, as well as by the general character of the contest, many private individuals from France, Russia, England, and the United States, now sought the classic soil of Greece, and devoted their lives to the cause on account of which that country was bleeding at every pore. A good service was rendered to Greece by these disinterested and heroic men. Among them Lord Byron, who arrived at Missolonghi in June, 1824, was conspicuous. In two or three months, however, he was carried off by disease, after having made great personal and pecuniary sacrifices.

Missolonghi was the principal stronghold of the Greeks in Ætolia, and around it the force of the Turks was now centred. A siege of four months and a half was sustained by the Greeks, during which a spirit of bravery and endurance was eminently displayed.

Lord Byron in Greece.

The Turks lost nine thousand men in the course of the siege; but, their army being at length reënforced by the arrival of Ibrahim Pacha with a numerous Egyptian army, it was impossible much longer to defend the place, and the enemy in a short space of time reduced it to a heap of ruins.

A portion of the heroic garrison, however, effected their escape by forcing a passage through the besiegers. This was attempted about eight o'clock in the evening, under the conduct of Noto Bozzaris, the uncle of Marco, who brought out about eighteen hundred men in safety. Arrangements had been previously made on the part of the sick, aged, and wounded, with many women who remained behind in a mill, to blow up the building with powder as soon as it should be entered by the Turks. This office was performed by an old wounded soldier, who, taking his seat on a mine, fired it upon their entrance into the place.

The immediate effect, on the Greeks, of the fall of Missolonghi, and the arrival of Ibrahim Pacha's army, was dispiriting; but the remoter bearing of these events was highly propitious to the cause of Greece. No sooner had Europe heard the news of Grecian valor and patriotism, equalling the renown of her earlier days, than the liveliest interest began to be manifested in her struggle. France led the way in the expression of an effective sympathy. Some of her most prominent men were connected with the Philhellenian Society, whose object was to aid the cause of Greece. Germany then followed. King Louis of Bavaria signed the Greek subscription, and gave his soldiers permission to fight for the Greeks. Greek children, who became orphans, were, in several instances, gratuitously educated in Germany, France, and Switzerland. The effect of these manifestations of interest, was greatly to cheer the desponding Greeks.

In the mean while, Ibrahim Pacha's army overran almost all parts of the Peloponnesus, carrying with it fire, carnage, and desolation. No submission, however, was obtained from the people, though their country was turned into a desert. No extremity of famine and want could induce them to enter into a treaty with their inhuman oppressors.

After Greece had been thoroughly devastated, and the determination of her people not to submit to the Mussulman power been evinced by the endurance of every horror which war and slaughter could bring, the governments of Russia, France, and England, moved by humanity, thought fit to interfere between the parties. The negotiations for peace would, perhaps, have resulted in nothing, but for a fortunate blunder of the

Battle of Navarino.

British admiral, who, not appreciating the delicacy of his undertaking, attacked the Turks at Navarino, and annihilated their marine at a blow. This event occurred on the 20th of October, 1827, in the bay before that place. With the fleet of England, those of France and Russia were combined. The Turkish-Egyptian fleet consisted of one hundred and ten ships, of which a part were burnt, part driven on shore, and the rest disabled.

Great as this disaster was to the Turks, it did not at once deter them from the fell purpose of crushing their revolted province. Though their power was diminished, their rage increased, and they contrived to carry on the contest two years longer. Still they were unable to make head against the Greeks. The independence of the latter was, in effect, established, from the time of the great naval fight; for the allied governments, finding themselves fairly committed in the business, persisted, until the court of Constantinople was brought to terms. Particularly were the Turks disposed to yield, as the Russians attacked them by land. On the 14th of September, 1829, the sultan of Turkey acknowledged the independence of Greece, on the condition that a million and a half of piastres be paid annually to the Porte.

Two years before this event, in 1827, the Greeks called together a national assembly, at Ægina, and chose a president for the nation. The object of their choice was Count John Capo d'Istria, a Russian. The allied powers sanctioned the appointment, and Capo d'Istria entered upon the administration of government. His personal qualifications were of a high order, but he was injudicious in the choice of his advisers, and therefore became obnoxious to a party. These caused him to be assassinated, before the term of seven years, for which he was chosen, had expired. He succeeded, however, in establishing an efficient government.

It was now resolved, by Russia, France, and England, to give the Greeks a prince connected by the ties of relationship with some royal family of Europe. Prince Leopold, of Saxe-Coburg, was selected, on the 20th of February, 1830; and he accepted the offer, "as sovereign prince of Greece." He continued in this station not more than three months, having

Otho, King of Greece.

resigned it from choice. Otho, a young prince of the house of Bavaria, was then elected king, and reigned till 1862, when he resigned. No successor has yet (1863) been appointed.

CHAPTER CCCXXXI.

Present State of Greece.

View of Athens: the Parthenon.

The extent and physical geography of Greece have been already given. The government is a constitutional monarchy, hereditary in the Bavarian line of Otho, the present king. The country is divided into ten districts, or *nomoi*, as follows: —

Nomoi.	*Capitals.*
Argolis, (Corinth, Hydra, Spetzia, Poros,)	Napoli, or Nauplia.
Achaia and Elis,	Patras.
Messenia,	Cyparissa, or Arcadia.
Arcadia,	Tripolitza.

Nomoi.	*Capitals.*
Laconia,	Misitra.
Acarnania and Ætolia,	Vrachori.
Phocis and Locris,	Salona, or Amphissa.
Attica, (Bœotia, Ægina,)	Athens.
Eubœa, (with Northern Sporades,)	Chalcis.
Cyclades,	Hermopolis in Syra.

The vine and olive have always been the most important articles of cultivation in Greece. The mulberry-trees have long been carefully cultivated for the breeding of silkworms. The rich, aromatic herbs, with which the country abounds supply food for innumerable bees, whose honey and wax afford a considerable source of trade. The long ravages of the late revolutionary war desolated a great part of the country; but wine, oil, silk, raisins, currants, figs, oranges, maize, sugar, drugs, &c., are exported; and the commercial activity of the natives, combined with the central position of the country, and its numerous harbors, is gradually restoring its ancient prosperity.

Athens, the capital, about five miles from the Gulf of Ægina, anciently decorated with innumerable masterpieces of architecture and sculpture, still retains, in its ruins, some traces of its past splendor; but it has suffered much during the war of the revolution, having been several times attacked by the contending parties. The modern city occupies only the northern and central parts of the ancient Athens. Some vestiges of the former walls are visible. The Acropolis, or citadel, stands upon a high rock, and is still susceptible of defence, but its walls have often been renewed; within is the Parthenon, the Temple of Athene or Minerva, now in ruins; to the west is the Areopagus, or Mars' Hill — the place where the Apostle Paul made his

Paul preaching at Athens.

celebrated address to the Athenians. Below, to the east, stand the remains of the once splendid Temple of Jupiter Olympus, which was one of the largest in Greece, combining Attic elegance with Oriental magnificence; it contained a famous colossal statue of Jupiter, made of gold and ivory. The Temple of Theseus; the octagonal Tower of the Winds; the choragic mon-

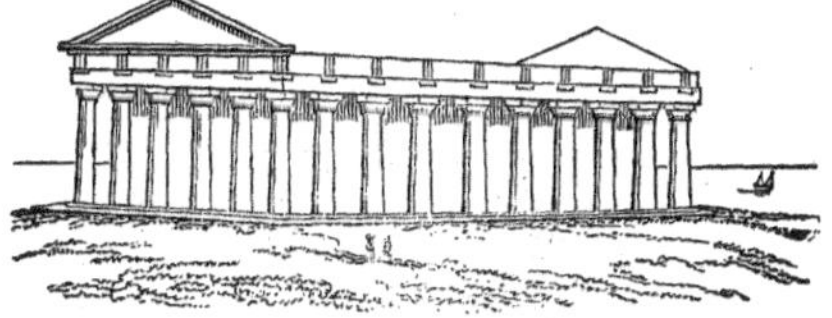

Ruins of the Temple of Theseus.

ument of Lysicrates, called also the *Lantern of Demosthenes;* Adrian's Gate, and some other edifices, are in a more or less complete state of preservation. The population of Athens, before the late war, was about fifteen thousand, but is now 41,298. In the neighborhood are Lepsina, the ancient *Eleusis;* Marathon, a small village, upon the plains of which the Persians were defeated by the Athenians under Miltiades, and Megaris, before the late war a flourishing town, with twelve thousand inhabitants, but now deserted.

Livadia, near the Lake Copais, was completely ruined by the war, previous to which it was a busy place, with ten thousand inhabitants. In its vicinity are the ruins of the ancient Thebes, once one of the most important cities of Greece. Salona, in Phocis, situated near Parnassus, has some manufacturing industry, with from five thousand to eight thousand inhabitants. In the neighborhood, at the foot of Parnassus, is Castri, the ancient Delphi, which contained the oracle of Apollo, resorted to in ancient times from all parts of the world. Here is the fountain of Castalia. Lepanto, Missolonghi, and Anatolico, are in Acarnania and Ætolia, of which the capital is Vrachori. Nauplia, or Napoli di Romania, the capital of Argolis, is the most important town of the Morea; but its situation is unhealthy. It is the strongest fortress in Greece; its vast citadel is called the Gibraltar of the Archipelago. The town is meanly built and dirty. Population, twelve thousand. In the neighborhood are the ruins of Argos, Mycenæ, Tyrinthus, and Trœzene. The Cyclopean walls, found in the vicinity of these places, composed of large blocks of stone, are of a remote but unknown antiquity. Tripolitza, capital of Arcadia, was the residence of the Turkish authorities, and the capital of the Morea, previous to the revolution; but its mosques, its seraglio, and castle have been destroyed, and its population reduced to two thousand or one thousand five hundred souls. In the vicinity are the ruins of Tegæa and Megalopolis, ancient capitals of Arcadia, and of Mantinea, celebrated for the victory gained by Epaminondas over the Spartans.

Mistra, or Misitra, the capital of Laconia, was reduced to a heap of ruins by the Egyptian forces during the revolution. It is picturesquely situated at the foot of Mount Taygetus, and its citadel is still standing. The population does not exceed two thousand souls. The ruins of Sparta are in its vicinity. Near these is the beautiful country in which Amyclæ, the birthplace of the heroes Castor and Pollux, was situated. This spot is still noted for its fertility. Monembasia, or Napoli di Malvasia, important for its port and its fortifications, is noted for its excellent wines called *Malmsey.* Modon, in the nomos of Messenia, is a small town, but has a good harbor, and is strongly fortified. Near it is the village of Navarino, in whose harbor the Turco-Egyptian fleet was destroyed by the Russian, English, and French fleet, as before stated. Calamata, in the same province, has hardly risen from its ruins, since the desolating campaign of the Egyptians in the Morea. Coron, which is also situated in Messenia, has a good harbor, and is strongly fortified. Pyrgos, like Calamata, is beginning to recover from its late desolation. Near it are the ruins of Olympia, in which the Olympic games were celebrated: here was the magnificent temple of Jupiter Olympus, containing the colossal statue of the god, sixty feet high, made of gold and ivory by Phidias.

Castor and Pollux

Patras, the capital of Achaia, stands upon the shore of a gulf which bears its name. It is the centre of the commercial relations of the Morea with the rest of Europe, and contains eight thousand inhabitants. The monastery of Megaspilæon, in the neighborhood, is celebrated for its riches, its fortifications, and vast vaults; it contains two hundred monks. Calavrita, to the south-east, is a small town. Corinth, situated upon the isthmus of the same name, between two seas, once proverbial for its wealth and luxury, is now an inconsiderable place, but is rapidly recovering from the disasters of the war. Its citadel, or Acrocorinth, is a fortress of great strength. In the neighboring district stand the ruins of the ancient Nemæa and Sicyon. Egripo, in Negropont, situated on the straits of the same name, is an important commercial town, with ten thousand inhabitants.

Syra, on the island of the same name, is the capital of the Cyclades, and the principal commercial place in Greece. The commerce of Turkey, Europe, and Egypt, with the whole kingdom centres here: the almonds of Scio, the wines of Naxos, the grapes of Patras, the oil and silk of the Morea, the wool of Romelia, the rice of Alexandria, &c., are collected in its harbor, thronged with vessels. Here also the pirates, that long infested these seas, disposed of their ill-gotten, but rich merchandise. Population, twenty-five thousand. Naxia, a small town on the Island of Naxos, Milos, and Tinos, are the other principal towns of the Cyclades.

Hydra, on the island of the same name, is a well-built town, with handsome houses and quays, clean streets, and twenty thousand inhabitants. It formerly carried on an extensive commerce, which, though injured by the war, is still considerable. The island, a barren rock without water, was settled by a number of fugitive Albanians, who became remarkable for their commercial enterprise and naval skill. The Island of Spetzia, of a similar character, and settled by the same nation, acquired similar commercial importance; and the Hydriots and Spetziots formed the chief naval force of the Greeks during the revolution.

Inhabitants of Greece.

The present inhabitants of Greece are chiefly natives of the country, with some Albanians, Jews, and Armenians. The Greeks are distinguished for their personal beauty; their complexion is dark and clear, and their eyes are large and brilliant. There is a great national similarity among all the Greeks, however widely scattered. The features of their ancestors, which have come down to us in medals and statues, are clearly preserved in the faces of the moderns. Among the amusements of this people, the dance seems to stand foremost. They scarcely meet without this entertainment. The dances are often accompanied by songs. Foot races, wrestling, and throwing the disc — undoubtedly handed down from antiquity — still maintain their places among the youth. The people sit cross-legged, in the Turkish fashion; smoke with long pipes, write with the left hand, salute, sleep, loiter about, all *à la Turque*. Their religion is that of the Greek church, which, in its doctrines, rites, ceremonies, and government, resembles that of the Roman Catholic; their language, called the *Romaic*, is derived from that noblest of idioms, the ancient Greek.

In character, the Greeks have shown the influences of political circumstances. All of them retain the ingenuity, the intelligence, and the versatile temperament of their ancestors; some have kept alive their indomitable spirit of liberty in the mountains, and are fierce, warlike, and independent; while others, in the plains or the cities, have been oppressed by barbarian conquerors, and have become artful, obsequious, mean, and treacherous. The great body of them are ignorant, and too often immoral. The long oppression of Turkish despotism, and the sanguinary and desolating war of the revolution, have at length been succeeded by a gleam of peace and freedom; but the wounds of this unhappy country can be healed only by a permanent enjoyment of those blessings. Order is now restored, commerce revived, industry protected, institutions of education are established, and the religion of Christ has again become that of the government: in their train will doubtless follow peace, virtue, wealth, arts, and civilization.

Italy.

View of Modern Rome.

CHAPTER CCCXXXII.

Geographical Description of Italy.

ITALY, which was the centre of the Roman empire, ... the most powerful empire of all antiquity, — is a large peninsula on the northern side of the Mediterranean, having the Adriatic Sea on the east, and the Tyrrhene or Tuscan Sea on the west. It is bounded on the north by the lofty mountain chain of the Alps, and is traversed through its whole length by the Apennines.

The surface of the country is very diversified. The southern part is mountainous. In the north is a great plain extending in an unbroken level from the Alps and Apennines to the Adriatic, and watered by the Po and its tributaries. This is the most fertile plain in Europe. The soil of Italy is fruitful, producing plentiful crops of grain, fruits, wine, and oil. The amenity of its climate, and its picturesque scenery, render it one of the most delightful regions in the world.

The Alps occupy the northern and north-western border of Italy. The Apennines extend through the whole peninsula, from the valley of Savona to the Strait of Messina, sending off a branch to Otranto. They nowhere rise to the limit of perpetual ice, but are covered with snow in winter, and are crowned to their summits with trees. The highest mountains are Mount Corno, or the Gran Sasso, nine thousand five hundred and twenty feet, and Mount Velino, eight thousand one hundred and eighty-three feet, high.

The only considerable river is the Po, which drains nearly the whole of the northern part. Most of the other streams rise in the Apennines, whose vicinity to the sea on both sides prevents their having a long course.

On the north-east is an arm of the Mediterranean, called the *Adriatic Sea*, or the *Gulf of Venice*. It is about six hundred miles long, and one hundred and fifty wide, and its narrow entrance is commanded by the Island of Corfu. It has several good harbors, but in some parts the coast is dangerous. Its principal bays are the Gulfs of Trieste and Manfredonia. To the south-east of Italy, between Sicily and Greece, is the Ionian Sea, which is connected by the Strait or Faro of Messina with the Sicilian Sea, lying between Naples and Sicily, and containing the Lipari Isles. The part of the sea between the Islands of Corsica and Sardinia and the Tuscan shore, is often called the *Tuscan* or *Tyrrhenian Sea*, and between Nice and Lucca is the Gulf of Genoa. The principal islands are Sicily, Sardinia, and Corsica. To the south of Sicily is the Maltese group, comprising Malta, Gozzo, and Comino, and belonging to Great Britain. The chief lakes of Italy are Maggiore, Como, Gardo, and Celano, all celebrated for their beauty.

Italy was called *Hesperia* by the Greeks, on account of its lying *westward* of Greece. In very remote ages, it was also known by the names of *Saturnia*, *Ausonia*, and *Œnotria*. The designation of *Italy* was not generally adopted till about the commencement of our era. It was, until the years 1860–61, divided as follows: Lombardy and Venice, Sardinia, Parma, Modena, Lucca, States of the Church, San Marino, Tuscany, and Naples, or the Two Sicilies. The extent of the territory is about one hundred and eighteen thou-

sand square miles; the population, nearly 23,000,000.

PRESENT DIVISIONS OF ITALY.

Divisions.	*Rank.*	*Pop.* 1860.	*Cities.*	*Pop.*
Lombardy	All these states and provinces were united under Victor E'manuel in the years 1859–61, under the title of "Kingdom of Italy."	3,039,085	Milan	177,968
Sardinia		4,080,009	Turin	179,635
Parma, Modena, Lucca, Bologna, Ferrara, Ravenna, Massa, &c		2,117,782	Parma	45,673
			Modena	81,868
			Lucca	22,000
			Ferrara	25,586
Ancona and Pesaro		902,079	Ancona	28,814
Umbria		491,745	Perouse	18,000
Tuscany		1,826,830	Florence	114,500
Naples		7,146,864	Naples	417,436
Sicily		2,315,925	Palermo	186,170
States of the Church	Papacy	690,000	Rome	194,587
Total		22,610,269		

The divisions of modern Italy correspond, in some degree, to the ancient ones; the various cities bear marks of different degrees of antiquity. At Rome, and in other places, are many ruins which date back for two thousand years. The people of Italy are generally of a swarthy complexion, and though considerable differences are found between those of different districts, and though they have all lost the vigor of their ancestors, they are still distinguished by the same general characteristics, and by a high order of genius.

Italy abounds in cities famous for their history, and interesting for the monuments of art which they contain. Rome, which was the centre of the Roman empire, and is often called the *Eternal City*, from its antiquity, stands upon both sides of the Tiber, fifteen miles from the sea. It is situated on several low hills, and is sixteen miles in circumference, comprehending, however, within this space much open ground, gardens, vineyards, and fie ls. Once the capital of an empire which embraced nearly the whole of the known world, and for centuries the residence of the popes, who have adorned it with all the splendors of painting, sculpture, and architecture, there is no place that can compare with Rome in its majestic ruins, its associations with the past, the solemn grandeur of its churches and palaces, and its endless treasures of art. At present, it has only one hundred and fifty thousand inhabitants, but in former times it contained four millions. Naples is the largest city in Italy. Venice, Milan, Genoa, Florence, are all celebrated.

In Italy are the most splendid and perfect monuments of architecture. The churches are the most costly and magnificent; the monasteries capacious, and the palaces unrivalled. Many of these latter, however, are suffered to decay and some have been razed for the sake of the materials. Architecture, painting, sculpture, and other arts are exhausted on the churches. Many of them have a minuteness of finish that is truly wonderful. The pillars of some are encrusted with mosaic pictures of precious stones, the walls are covered with frescoes, the doors inimitably carved in bronze, and the interior and exterior profusely adorned with exquisite statues in marble or bronze. The dwelling-houses of the rich and noble are vast palaces, which in many places are quite deserted, or occupied by foreign residents. In Florence, the houses resemble fortresses — a feature indicative of that time when the city was convulsed by the violence and feuds of its factions. In the northern countries, they are commonly provided with projecting porticoes or arcades, stretching uninterruptedly from one end of a city to another. In the Roman and Neapolitan territories, they are almost universally without chimneys, as the mildness of the climate renders a fire rarely necessary for comfort.

CHAPTER CCCXXXIII.

Ancient Geography of Italy — Glance at its Early History.

Ancient Italy comprised three great divisions — *Cisalpine Gaul*, in the north; *Italy Proper*, in the centre; and *Magna Græcia*, in the south. *Cisalpine Gaul* was divided by the River Padus, now called the *Po*, into two separate territories, called *Gallia Transpadana*, and *Gallia Cispadana*. The whole country was, after the Roman conquest, also termed *Gallia Togata*, in allusion to the people having adopted the use of the Roman *toga*, or cloak. Venetia was in the north-east, and Liguria in the south-west of this region.

Italy Proper extended southward from Gallia Cispadana to the Rivers Silaurus and Trento, comprehending modern Tuscany, the Papal States, and the northern part of the kingdom of Naples. The ancient divisions were Etruria, Latium, Umbria, Picenum, Campania, Samnium, and the territory of the Sabines.

Etruria was a highly-civilized country at an early

date. Its inhabitants had made great advances in science and the arts before the foundation of Rome. Many of their sculptured gems, vases, and paintings still exist. The walls of their ancient cities are to be seen at the present day at Cortona, Perugia, Fiesole, and other places. The Etruscans formed a confederation of twelve states, each of which was an independent community with regard to its domestic policy.

Latium lay on the western coast of Italy, between the Tiber and the Liris. In early times, it was inhabited by various tribes, called Latins, Ausones, Rutuli, Sabines, Volsci, &c.

Campania extended along the western coast from the Liris to the Silaurus, and comprised the territory around the city of Naples. This country has always been famous for its beauty and fertility. It suffered more frequent changes of inhabitants in early times, than any other part of Italy. Attracted by the fertility of the soil and the mildness of the climate, one horde of invaders poured in after another, and established their dominion here, until the Roman conquest secured the tranquillity of the country.

Magna Græcia was settled at an early period by colonies from Greece, who brought with them the arts and institutions of that country. It was divided into Apulia, Calabria, Lucania, and Bruttium. The most important city in Magna Græcia was Tarentum, the inhabitants of which were remarkable for their wealth and luxurious habits. Brundusium, in Calabria, was connected with Rome by the road called the *Appian Way:* here the Romans usually set sail for Greece. The ruins of Pæstum, in Lucania, form a great object of attraction to the modern tourist.

Tabular View of Ancient Italy.

CISALPINE GAUL.

Ancient Divisions	*Modern Names.*	*Chief Cities.*	*Modern Names.*
Venetia,	Venice.	Tergeste, Patavium,	Trieste. Padua.
Lingones,		Ravenna,	Ravenna.
Boii,	Modena.	Mutina,	Modena.
Liguria,	Parma & Southern part of Sardinia.	Genua, Nicœe,	Genoa. Nice.
Taurini,	Northern part of Sardinia.	Augusta Taurinorum,	Turin.
Insubres,	Lombardy.	Mediolanum, Ticinium,	Milan. Pavia.

ITALY PROPER.

Ancient Divisions.	*Modern Names.*	*Chief Cities.*	*Modern Names.*
Etruria,	Tuscany.	Florentia, Portus Herculeus,	Florence Leghorn.
Latium, Picenum,	States of the Church.	Rome, Tibur, Spoletium,	Rome. Tivoli. Spoletto
Campania,	Part of the Kingdom of Naples.	Neapolis, Capua,	Naples. Capua.

MAGNA GRÆCIA.

Ancient Divisions.	*Modern Names.*	*Chief Cities.*	*Modern Names.*
Apulia, Lucania, Calabria, Bruttium,	Kingdom of Naples.	Venusia, Pæstum, Tarentum, Brundusium, Hydruntum, Rhegium,	Venosa Pesti. Taranto. Brindisi. Otranto. Reggio.

By the light of the earliest historical records, it appears that Italy, between one and two thousand years before the Christian era, was inhabited by two races of people, differing from each other in language and manners. One race dwelt on the coast and the plains adjacent, and the other on the mountains in the interior.

The former were probably a part of the great Pelasgic tribe or family, which also inhabited Greece and Asia Minor in very ancient times. Of the latter, we know nothing previous to their appearance in the mountain regions of Italy, where they may be regarded as indigenous or native. The Pelasgians of Italy seem to have been similar in character to those of Greece, though more advanced in knowledge. They were here an agricultural people, and built towns with Cyclopean walls of unhammered stone. Probably they came into Italy as conquerors or colonists; but after having been long settled here, it seems that the aboriginal mountaineers descended into their territories and subjugated them. We then find the south of Italy occupied by a people calling themselves *Œnotrians;* the region in the neighborhood of the Tiber by the Siculi, who afterwards invaded the Island of Trinacria, and gave it the name of *Sicily;* and Etruria, inhabited by the Tyrrhenians.

Other names appear shortly afterward in history. The Latins, according to tradition, were driven down the River Anio by the Sabines; and the latter, in their turn, expelled the Siculi, who proceeded south and crossed over the Strait of Messina. About one thousand years before Christ, the Greeks began to found colonies in the south of Italy. The Chalcidians and Eretrians, from the Island of Eubœa, built the cities of Cuma and Naples in Campania, and Rhegium on the strait. The Achæans built Sybaris, Crotona, and Metapontum. In Sicily, the Dorian Greeks founded Messana, Syracuse, Hybla, Gela, and Agrigentum. The Ionians founded Naxus, Catana, and Himera. There were also Greek colonies in Corsica and Sardinia.

Ancient Rome.

Ruins of the Roman Forum.

CHAPTER CCCXXXIV.

1184 to 508 B. C.

Early Legends — Æneas — Romulus and Remus — The Seven Kings — Downfall of the Monarchy.

THE history of Rome may be conveniently divided into three periods — the first, extending from its foundation, in 753 B. C., to the last of the kings, 508 B. C.; the second, during which Rome was a republic, reaching to the establishment of the power of Augustus, 30 B. C.; and the third, that of the empire, the most brilliant in Roman history, which ceases in A. D. 476, with the downfall of the Roman dominion, and the overthrow of the Empire of the West.

In the history of almost every country, whose early records are lost in the twilight of antiquity tradition and legend supply the place of authenticated facts. In the history of ancient Rome, during the period preceding the foundation of the city, and during its rise from obscurity, fables and romantic tales are so interwoven with what is historical, that it is extremely difficult to separate the true from the false. It is probable that these legends, in which the foundation of Rome is traced to an illustrious source, and in which the gods descend from Mount Olympus to take part in the concerns of the imperial city, were invented by the Romans themselves, at a period when Rome had acquired some importance as a capital, for the purpose of flattering their national pride. How many generations passed away before these legends became incorporated in the popular belief as true history, we have no means of discovering. Though we may sometimes pause, says an old writer, when reading the early annals of Rome, and hesitate what judgment to pass on many of the events which are there recorded, there are landmarks enough to prevent us from straying too far from our course, and to lead us on safely to the *terra firma* of history.

The early legends of Rome relate that the nation had its origin from Æneas, a Trojan prince, who, with his father and a large train of followers, fled from the ruins of Troy, 1184 years before Christ. He carried his household gods with him, in search of a new home in the west. They were guided by a star, and the will of the gods was made known to them by oracles. They settled in Latium, one of the countries of ancient Italy. The king, Latinus, gave his daughter Lavinia in marriage to Æneas, and the rest of the Trojans formed matrimonial alliances with the Latins. Civil wars followed, however, and in one of these Æneas was killed. The Trojans concealed his body, and asserted that he had ascended to heaven. His son Ascanius built the city of Alba Longa upon a neighboring hill, to which the Trojans removed. The history of this city remains in comparative obscurity till the reign of Procas, several centuries later. This king had two sons, Numitor and Amulius. Numitor, the eldest, should have succeeded to the throne at his father's death; but he was removed by Amulius, who usurped the sceptre himself. To prevent the power from reverting to his brother's family, he caused his only son to be slain, and made his daughter Sylvia a vestal virgin, whose duty it was to watch the ever-burning fire of the goddess Vesta. She had, however, been secretly married, or, according to the legend, been violated, by the god Mars, and bore twin sons. By order of Amulius, they were thrown into the Tiber: the rising waters of the river, however, carried the basket which contained them safely to shore, and landed them under a wild fig-tree. A she-wolf, who came down to the river to drink, saw them, and carried them to her den, where she suckled them, and where, some time afterward, they were found by Faustulus, the king's herdsman.

Romulus and Remus

The twins were brought up with the children of the shepherd, and were called *Romulus* and *Remus*. When they grew up, they were made leaders in many expeditions against robbers and rival tribes, and in exploits which required courage and ability. In one of these, Remus, fighting with some of the people belonging to the household of the king, fell into an ambush, and, being made prisoner, was carried before Amulius. The king, struck by his appearance and bearing, hesitated to pronounce sentence upon him, but asked him who he was. He had hardly heard his history, and recognized him as the grandson of his brother, than the palace was attacked by Romulus and his friends, who had hastened to the rescue of Remus. Amulius was put to death, and Numitor, the rightful king, was called from his farm, and placed upon the throne.

As a reward for their services, the two brothers asked permission to build a city on the Palatine Hill, in whose vicinity they had been brought up. Their request was granted, and the proposed walls soon began to rise from the ground. A dispute occurred between the brothers as to which should give his name to the city, and they agreed to consult the gods by augury, and to abide by the result. As they were watching the heavens at sunrise,—the usual practice in such cases,—Remus saw six vultures, and immediately after, Romulus saw twelve, and was adjudged victor. From that day to the present, the spot on which the wild fig-tree grew, and where the twin children were nursed by a she-wolf, has been called ROME. The foundations of the city were marked out with a plough, the furrow was turned inward, and the plough was lifted over the spaces intended for gates. When the walls had arisen a few feet from the earth, Remus scornfully leaped over them, saying, "Will such defences as these keep out an enemy?" As he did this, the person charged with the building of the walls struck him a blow with the spade he held in his hand, and killed him on the spot. The laying the foundation of Rome is supposed to have occurred in the year 753 B. C. The Romans reckoned from this event, taking it as the starting point in their chronology, always saying that such an occurrence happened in such a year A. U. C., i. e., *Anno ab Urbe Condita*— "in the year from the foundation of the city."

When the city was finished, it consisted of about a thousand dwellings irregularly arranged. Romulus was chosen king, and devoted himself to the formation of laws, and the establishment of good order among his subjects. Finding that the population was not sufficiently numerous, he invited strangers from all countries to come and settle there, and even set apart an asylum, to which any man might flee from the neighboring communities, and be safe from pursuit. This rapidly increased the population of the city, and Rome became filled with desperadoes and fugitives of all descriptions. A natural consequence of this was, that the Romans were disliked and feared by the surrounding people, who would neither give them their daughters for wives, nor deal with them as traders, nor associate with them as neighbors. Romulus, who feared that the effect of this isolated position would be to diminish the numbers of his subjects more than any thing he had done would do to increase them, resolved to employ a stratagem, and to provide the citizens with wives by force. The senate approved of his plan, and it was carried into execution.

A feast was proclaimed in honor of Neptune, and invitations were extended to the inhabitants of the neighboring towns. Crowds flocked from all quarters; for once the people overcame their scruples, and filled the squares and open places of Rome. They came from Cænina, and Antemnæ, and from the country of the Sabines. Men and women, boys and girls, old and young, were there to see the show. Hardly, however, had the ceremonies begun, when at a given signal, the Roman youth rushed among the crowd, seized the most beautiful girls, and carried them home for wives. The Sabines, who were the greatest sufferers on this occasion, swore a terrible vengeance upon the treacherous Romans. Their king, Titus Tatius, raised a large army, and encamping under the walls of Rome, laid siege to the city. Many battles ensued between the hostile nations. In one of these, it is said, a certain gate of Rome opened of its own accord, leaving the entrance free to the Sabine army. It was shut by the inhabitants, but again swung open, as if moved by some invisible hand. As the enemy poured into the city through the passage thus provided, thinking that the gods were working a miracle in their favor, a stream of water burst from the temple of Janus, and swept them away in its torrents. From this time, the temple, though shut during peace, was always left open in time of war, that the god might be ready with his resistless floods to destroy the enemies of Rome. Further hostilities between the two people were checked by the interference of the Sabine girls themselves, who had become reconciled to their lot, and found that their husbands were not the barbarians they thought: a truce was agreed upon, a treaty of peace was subsequently made, and the two nations were combined into one. Romulus reigned alone after the death of Tatius; and thus was the first step toward the extension of the Roman dominion consummated.

Romulus reigned for forty years, beloved and revered by his subjects. As, according to the legend, he was of divine descent, and claimed Mars for his father, and the daughter of a king for his mother, it could hardly be expected that the fable would allow him to die a natural death. Demigods never return to their native clay, and tradition always removes the bodies of heroes, before they have time to moulder into dust. So the fable takes Romulus up to heaven, in the midst of a storm of thunder and rain, and at the close of a review of his troops. It was believed that Mars had carried him to Mount Olympus in his chariot. He was afterwards worshipped as a god, and sacrifices were offered to him, in a temple erected in his honor. Such is the traditional account of the life of one whom later historians believe never to have existed. His history is regarded by many as a fable from beginning to end. The whole first period of Roman history is uncertain, for the reason that there were no regular historians in those days, — their place being supplied by the chief pontiff or priest, whose duty it was to keep a register of the events of each year on a white table: these notes were afterward collected into books, and were the only record of public transactions. Beside being imperfect and superficial in themselves, they were in part destroyed when the Gauls took the city of Rome, many centuries later; and thus the thread of Roman history was interrupted. New annals were composed by the priests from such materials as remained; and these, mixed probably with a strong leaven of conjecture and with popular traditions, were arranged by the pontiffs so as to form the semblance of a history. Seven kings only are stated to have reigned during the period that the monarchy lasted — a period of two hundred and forty-five years; — and this, in itself, is sufficient to throw doubt over the whole. To assign a reign of thirty-five years to seven successive sovereigns, is contrary to all probability, in times of rapine and violence, and in a kingdom where the throne was elective, where each monarch is represented as being of mature age when he commenced his reign, and of whom four are said to have me with violent deaths. The number of kings is stated to have been seven, probably because the annalists could discover no traces of any more. They may be, perhaps, the types of whole races of sovereigns, each king standing for the line which he founded, or for the virtue or vice most conspicuous in his character. Numa Pompilius may thus receive credit for the wisdom and integrity of some dozen successors, while upon the head of Tarquinius Superbus are heaped the crimes of a long series of monarchs. However this may be, we have no other guide than the distorted records which have been handed down to us, and which we shall be obliged to follow, till we arrive at a period where the path is clearer and history more certain.

The death of Romulus left the Romans without a king; and the senate, upon whom devolved the duty of choosing another, failed to make a choice, but divided themselves into committees of ten, each body holding the kingly power for ten days in rotation. This species of interregnum lasted a year, when the senate yielded to the clamors and importunities of the people, and invested *Numa Pompilius*, a Sabine of high character, with the royal dignity. Rome prospered during his reign, which lasted forty-three years, and was spent in fostering and encouraging the arts of peace. The temple of Janus remained shut, for no war, offensive or defensive, laid waste and desolated the country. A temple was built to Faith, and honesty and fair-dealing were worshipped as divine. The citizens were divided into classes, according to their trades and pursuits. Agriculture was especially favored, and the arts of husbandry promoted; the territories which the Romans had acquired in war, were divided equally among the people. Numa loved tranquillity, and wished that every man might live happily upon his own estate. He forbade costly sacrifices and the shedding of blood upon the altars of the gods. The fruits of the earth, cakes of flour or parched corn, were deemed sufficient to propitiate an offended divinity. The religious worship of the Romans was entirely remodelled by Numa. He assumed himself the dignity of high priest, and to him is ascribed the institution of all the priestly offices. He created four *pontiffs*, who presided at religious ceremonies; three *flamens*, who were devoted to the worship of the three principal gods — Jupiter, Mars, and Romulus; four *augurs*, who were supposed to be able to foretell events, and to discover the will of the gods by certain signs; twelve *Salians*, or priests of Mars, who sang and danced at the festivals of that god; and the *Vestal Virgins*, or priestesses of Vesta, who watched over the fire that was kept perpetually burning in the temple of the goddess. The sacred fire was considered emblematical of the existence of the state, and to suffer it to go out was to endanger the country. Once a year, however, it was extinguished, and rekindled from the rays of the sun. In all his acts of legislation, Numa professed to be guided by the goddess Egeria. He spent his hours of leisure in her company in a sacred grove near Rome, where, for a long time afterward, the memory of Numa and his divine instructress was held in respect and veneration. He died at the age of eighty, B. C. 670.

He was succeeded by *Tullus Hostilius*, an impetuous and warlike prince, who spent his life in the camp. He soon had an occasion to prove his valor: the borderers along the Roman and Alban territory began to rob and plunder each other, and this brought on hos tilities. The two armies met, but their angry feelings were cooled by the recollection of their ties of consanguinity, and they ultimately refused to fight. It was finally determined to leave the dispute to six champions, three to be selected from each army. In the Roman army were three brothers born at one birth, named *Horatii*: in the Alban army were three others like them, named *Curiatii*. These were fixed upon for the champions, and they advanced to the contest amid the hopes and anxieties of the two armies; for it had been agreed that the victorious nation was to rule over the other. The spectators held their breath, as the champions approached and brandished their burnished arms in the air. At the first attack, the three Albans were severely wounded, while two of the Romans fell dead under their blows, and the remaining one took to flight, pursued by his antagonists. The Albans thought the day was won, and a cry of wailing ran through the Roman ranks. Exultation and despair were, however, premature, for the Roman champion, turning suddenly upon his foes, who had been separated from each other in the ardor of pursuit, despatched them one after another, and remained alone upon the field. Alba was given to the Roman dominion, and was bound to obey her conqueror. But in a war which soon sprung up between the Romans and the Fidenates, the Alban general, Mettus Fuffetius, refused to lead his army to battle, intending to side with the victors, after the day was decided. The Romans, who came off conquerors, determined to punish this act of treachery; they took Mettus, and bound him between two chariots, and driving the horses different ways, tore his body asunder. They then went to Alba, destroyed the city, and compelled the inhabitants to emigrate to Rome. This is all that history tells us of the administration of Tullus: he reigned thirty-three years, and it is said that his house was struck by lightning, and that he was burned with it to ashes, for having neglected the worship of the gods.

Ancus Marcius was the fourth king of Rome, and is stated to have been the grandson of Numa Pompilius. He began his reign in 638 B. C. Several Latin cities were taken by the Romans during his reign, and their inhabitants were brought to Rome, where the Aventine Hill was given them to dwell upon. He is said to have been the founder of the colony of Ostia, a town at the mouth of the Tiber, which was the port or harbor of Rome, and the oldest Roman colony known in after ages. He was succeeded, at the expiration of twenty-nine years, by *Tarquinius Priscus*, whose history is extremely doubtful, and is even believed by some to be a sheer fabrication. He is represented as a wealthy Etruscan, who came as a stranger to settle at Rome, and who, by his liberality and the splendor in which he lived, obtained great popularity with the people. Ancus Marcius, at his death, made him the guardian of his children, and he was chosen king, 609 B. C. Many splendid works, traces and remains of which exist at the present day, are ascribed to him; among these are the *cloacæ*,—or great public sewers, to carry off the water and refuse,—the circus or race course and the forum or market-place. That these works were built about this time, is evident from the fact that the stone used in the construction of the *cloacæ* is a volcanic substance, found in many places about Rome, but which was never used for building purposes, subsequently to the establishment of the republic. These vast works are supposed to have been accomplished, as in Egypt, by forced labor; and it is not an unfair inference to suppose, that the government which could effect such great undertakings by task-work, must have been both powerful and despotic.

Among the wonderful tales which embellish the poetical legend of Tarquinius Priscus, is one which was undoubtedly invented by the priests to inspire the people with a stronger belief in the mysteries of augury. The king, says the story, was contemplating some plan, to which the augurs were opposed, on the ground that it was contrary to the will of the gods. Tarquin, who had but little faith in divination, wished to put the science to the test, and told Attius Nævius, one of the augurs, that if he could tell him whether the idea he had in his mind were possible or not, he would, in future give more credit to his art. "It is possible," said Nævius. "Then," said the king, "cut this whetstone with a knife, for it was that that I was thinking of." The augur took the knife, and cut through the stone with the greatest ease, and the king believed in his counsels ever afterward. Images of the gods were first introduced into the Roman worship during the period ascribed to the reign of Tarquin I.; and the sacrifice of animals, which had been forbidden by Numa Pompilius, was added to the more simple offerings of corn and fruit. Two more Vestal virgins were appointed, making their number six, instead of four; and the rites of religion were altogether performed with more splendor than in the earlier period of the monarchy.

A singular instance of the inaccuracy of the Roman traditions is presented in the commonly received account of the death, by assassination, of Tarquinius Priscus. He is said to have been murdered after a reign of thirty-three years; and it is also stated, that the assassins were employed by the sons of Ancus Marcius, who contended that they had a right to the throne. This is evidently false; for, in the first place, the throne was not hereditary; therefore the sons of Ancus Marcius had no more right to it than any body else. Why, too, did they wait thirty-three years before asserting their claim? Again, if Tarquin had reigned thirty years, he must have been nearly seventy at the time of his death; yet we are told that his sons had not arrived at the age of manhood. The whole story of this monarch is probably a fable;—all that can be asserted with certainty is, that under the dominion of the later kings, whoever they were, the power and extent of their territory was far greater than it ever was before, and that even at that early day, Rome merited the title she afterwards bore—that of "the Imperial City."

Tarquin I. was succeeded, in the year 576 B. C., by *Servius Tullius*, celebrated for his good deeds and wise laws. He added the Esquiline and Viminal hills to the city, which now included seven—the two just mentioned, the Palatine, the Capitoline, the Aventine the Cœlian, and the Quirinal. He built walls around them, and these continued to be the walls of Rome for eight hundred years, till the time of the emperor Aurelian. He made many laws to screen the poor from the oppressions of the rich, and to bring the plebeians nearer to an equality with the patricians. As an instance of this, we may state as follows: It had been the custom for the patricians to fight on horseback, or in chariots, and for the common men to fight on foo. The latter had always been so badly armed and ill disciplined, that they were of little consideration in the army. Under Servius, however, the richest of the commons were selected to form new companies of horsemen, and were obliged to arm themselves according to the extent of their property. Servius is said to have reigned forty-four years, and to have come to his death by violence and treachery, in which one of his daughters, and her husband, son of the late king Tarquin, were the principal actors. The aged monarch, says the story, was murdered by Lucius Tarquinius, husband of his eldest daughter; and as his body lay bleeding in the street, the inhuman woman ordered her charioteer to drive over the corpse. The street where this unnatural deed was done, was called *Via Scelerata*, or the "Wicked Way." *Lucius Tarquinius* thus became king, in 532 B. C. He is known in history as *Tarquinius Superbus*, or "Tarquin the Proud." His story is generally regarded as fabulous, partly because usurpation is impossible, by assassination or any other means, where the power is conferred by the senate, who would not be apt thus to recompense crime, by raising a murderer to the supreme power; and partly because Lucius, being a son of Tarquin I., must have been nearly of the same age as Servius Tullius, whom he dethroned; that is, about seventy. After his usurpation, he reigned twenty-four years, and, on the establishment of a republic, and the downfall of the monarchy, carried on wars for the recovery of his throne, for fifteen years longer. The last king of Rome, who passes in the legend as Tarquinius Superbus, was undoubtedly a tyrant, whose chief object seems to have been to degrade the commons, and draw the line still broader between them and the patricians. He built the great temple and fortress called the *Capitol*, on the Capitoline Hill. This edifice was constructed of hewn stone, with gates of brass. The Sibylline books were kept in this temple, under ground, and were guarded by priests appointed for the purpose. They contained a great number of prophecies, written in Greek, on palm leaves, and were consulted by the augurs on all extraordinary occasions. A legend connected with these oracles may account for the veneration in which they were held, even to a late period.

The story is, that an old woman, of singular appearance, and dressed in weird attire, presented herself before Tarquinius, with nine books, purporting to contain the prophecies of the Sibyl, for which she demanded a large sum of money. The king refused to buy them, for the reason that he did not know who the lady was, nor what her books contained. The weird woman went away, and burnt three of her books, and then returned with the remaining six; the price continuing the same as for the whole nine. Tarquin again refused; on which the ancient dame departed a second time, and burnt three more of the volumes. On her reappearance with the three which were left, Tarquin consulted with the augurs, who advised him to purchase the books, not forgetting to reprimand him for the six which he had allowed to be destroyed. Tarquin bought the oracles, and the old woman disappeared, and was seen no more. These volumes became the oracles of Rome, and, as we have stated, were guarded with extraordinary care.

In the twenty-fourth year of the reign of Tarquin, 508 B. C., a revolution occurred, in which the people rose against the tyranny and despotism of the government, and overthrowing the monarchical form, established a republic on its ruins. How this revolution was brought about is not known with any certainty for the accounts of it are not authentic. The legend which here, as elsewhere, supplies the place of history, gives the following narrative: Titus, Aruns, and Sextus, the three sons of the king, with their cousin Collatinus, were supping in the camp under the walls of Ardea, a city to which the Roman army was laying siege. When their brains were a little elevated with wine, they fell into a vein of bravado; and finding nothing better worthy of a wager than the conduct of their respective wives, they agreed to mount their horses, and repair to Rome, and decide the question from personal observation. The three princes found their wives making merry around a well-filled board, and rejoicing at the continued absence of their liege lords. Lucretia, the wife of Collatinus, was found working with her maids at the loom. With this lady Sextus fell violently in love, and, some time afterward he behaved in so brutal a manner toward her, that Lucretia, unable to survive her dishonor, stabbed herself to the heart. Lucius Junius Brutus, who is said to have feigned insanity for the purpose of evading the cruelty of Tarquin, and who was present at her death, now threw off the mask, and drawing the knife from the wound, swore, by the blood upon it, to be avenged upon the tyrant and his offspring.

The people were wrought up to the highest pitch of excitement by the outrage. Tarquin, who was absent, was declared by the senate to be expelled from the throne. The gates of the city were shut. The body of Lucretia was exposed to public view, and Brutus harangued the people, exhorting them to aid in expelling the tyrant. A meeting was called in the field of Mars, to form a new government. The fall of the monarchy was pronounced, and the chief power was placed in the hands of two *prætors*, or *consuls*, to be elected annually. Brutus and Collatinus were the first consuls. Thus the title of "king of Rome" became extinct, at least for a time; for it was only resuscitated, two thousand years later, in the person of the duke of Reichstadt, son of Napoleon Bonaparte.

CHAPTER CCCXXXV.

Manners and Customs of the Romans during the Monarchy.

Very little is known, with certainty, of the manners and customs of the Romans, during the time of the kings. Rome was decidedly a military state, and the people were all trained to arms; but it was also an agricultural nation, and the whole of the commonalty consisted of farmers, who cultivated their lands in time of peace, and took the field when their services were required as soldiers. Foreign commerce was probably in the hands of the nobles, and retail trade was held in such low estimation, that the free commons were forbidden by law to engage in it.

The manner of living was extremely simple. The principal food of all classes consisted of bread and pottage, with herbs, roots, and fruits; the chief beverage was the milk of goats. The great fared no better than the humble — despising luxurious habits as unworthy a warlike nation. The houses at Rome, in those early times, were mere cottages, one story high, and built of wood. They had neither chimneys nor windows. Candles, made either of wax or tallow, were used to illuminate the rooms. The furniture probably corresponded with the rudeness and simplicity of the dwellings. The domestic servants, both male and female, were slaves.

The distinguishing part of the Roman costume was the toga, or mantle. This was a large woollen shawl, in the form of a semicircle, usually white, but sometimes bordered with scarlet or crimson. It was probably worn over a loose robe, without sleeves, as the arms were bare, except as they were covered by the toga. The togas of slaves and poor people were of a dark color. They were worn, at this period, by both sexes. The Romans had various coverings for the feet, but they were chiefly of two kinds — the one a shoe, not unlike ours, and the other a slipper, or sandal, fastened with leather thongs.

The power of a father over his children was so absolute, that he might even sell them for slaves, or put them to death; nor were they free, at any age, from parental authority, unless the father himself emancipated them. In every private house, the hearth was consecrated to the *lares*, or household gods, and was the centre of union to the members of the family. The common hearth of the whole people — the symbol of their union as a nation — was the altar in the temple of Vesta. Poems, in praise of princes and popular heroes, were recited at banquets, to a flute accompaniment. When any great person died, verses commemorating his virtues were sung at his funeral. The Romans buried or burned the bodies of the dead. The artists employed at Rome, during this period, came from Etruria, which was now at the height of its greatness. At Veii, an Etruscan city, was made a celebrated ornament for the top of the Capitol; being a chariot, with four horses, wrought in *terra cotta*, or baked clay, and regarded as a fine work of art. Bronze was not used till a later period, nor is there any mention made of paintings in the time of the monarchy.

During the time of Romulus, the whole Roman people consisted of the patricians, or patrons, and their clients. These clients were bondmen; but how they became so is not exactly known. The patricians were the original citizens or nobility of Rome, and it is probable that the common people were placed under their protection, and that thus the latter became the lord or patron of a number of attached followers, wholly devoted to the interests of his house. In the course of time, there arose another class, distinct from either of these two; namely, the free commons, or plebeians, the great mass of whom were conquered Latins, who were admitted as subjects, not citizens of Rome. They were excluded from any share in the government, but could hold property, and were protected by the laws. They could not marry into patrician families, and thus the line of distinction between citizens and subjects was carefully preserved.

The senate consisted at first of two hundred members; but, at a later period, the number was increased to three hundred. These, however, had no power to pass laws, without the sanction of the general assembly of the citizens, who held their meetings in the Comitium, or place of public assembly. Questions proposed in the senate were here decided by vote, and the will of the majority ruled. The power of the king was limited. He was commander-in-chief of the army, but could make no laws without the consent of the citizens. He had the disposal of the spoils and lands acquired by war, so that the sovereign possessed extensive domains, and a numerous train of dependants. The government of Rome, therefore, at this period, was what we should call, in our day, a constitutional monarchy.

CHAPTER CCCXXXVI.

508 to 451 B. C.

Attempts of Tarquin to recover the Throne — Revolt of the Plebeians — Coriolanus — Cincinnatus — A Roman Triumph.

THE substitution of republican for monarchical institutions having been resolved upon, the consuls set about securing the permanency of the liberal government. The consuls were each to exercise the sovereign power for one month, by turn, during which they were to be invested with all the insignia of royalty except the crown. They did not perform the great sacrifices however, as the kings had done: a *rex sacrorum*, or chief pontiff, was chosen to administer the religious affairs of the state. The expulsion of Tarquin was confirmed, and many of the useful laws of Servius Tullius were revised and reënacted. The plebeians recovered some of the rights of which they had been deprived by the late sovereign. Lands were granted to them out of the royal property, in lots of about four acres, and some of the wealthiest members among them were admitted to the senate. The plebeian senators were chosen from among those who had been raised by the constitution of Servius to the rank of knights, or horse soldiers; and to distinguish them from the patrician members of the senate, they were called *conscript.*

The beginning of the new government was disturbed by the attempts of the deposed monarch to recover his throne. He, with his family, had taken refuge with his son Sextus, king of the Gabii. Through his intrigues, a conspiracy was formed in his favor in Rome itself. Tradition relates that the plot was laid by some of the nobles who were discontented with the concessions made to the plebeians, and that among the conspirators were two sons of Brutus, who, with others, on the discovery of the scheme, were condemned to death by their father in his character of consul. The story goes on to say, that having passed the fatal sentence on his guilty children, Brutus had the firmness to sit calmly by and see it executed. This famous story has immortalized the name of Brutus; but collateral evidence and comparisons of dates forbid us to regard it as any thing more than a fiction, invented, or perhaps borrowed from the legends of other countries, to personify justice, or to add lustre to the name of distinguished Romans. Brutus is represented by the ancient historians as being a child when Tarquinius ascended the throne: yet when that prince was deposed, only twenty-five years afterward, we are told that his sons were of an age to take part in a conspiracy against the government. The fact, or supposition, that the plot was laid by the nobles to crush the newly-acquired liberties of the plebeians, would seem to preclude the possibility of the sons of Brutus, evidently of plebeian origin themselves, joining in any enterprise against their own freedom. The history of the first years of the commonwealth is as uncertain as that of the kings, and for the same reason — that most of the records of that period were lost when Rome was plundered by the Gauls

In consequence of the conspiracy just mentioned, a decree of banishment was pronounced against the whole of the royal family; and this sentence was so strictly enforced, that not even Collatinus, the consul, who was Tarquin's nephew, was excepted. His place was filled by Publius Valerius, a patrician, who obtained the name of *Poplicola*, because he supported the rights of the people. Tarquin, notwithstanding the failure of his plot, persuaded the Etruscans to attempt his restoration by force of arms. In a battle which ensued, between the Etruscans under Tarquin, and the Romans under Brutus, the latter was killed by Aruns, son of Tarquin; Aruns himself fell mortally wounded. It is said that in the middle of the night after the contest, a voice issued from a neighboring wood, proclaiming that the Etruscans had lost one man more than the Romans. At this sound, the Etruscans, who were very superstitious, were struck with awe, and immediately marched home. Valerius, the surviving consul, ruled alone for the rest of the year, and administered the authority with great applause. Tarquin, however, was not idle, and the repeated failure of his attempts to regain the crown seemed only to increase his zeal. He went to Clusium, a city in the most distant part of Etruria, and induced Porsenna, its king, to assist him. A large army was raised, and Porsenna marched against Rome. The poets and romancers, who have undertaken to fill the gap here created by the absence of authentic records seem to have drawn largely upon their imagination, for their facts. The city, it is said, was saved by three warriors, who, alone and single-handed, defended a bridge across which the Etruscans were pursuing the flying Romans. They kept the enemy at bay till their companions had cut the bridge asunder, when one of them, Horatius Cocles, leaped into the river, and, amid showers of javelins, swam safely to shore. For this gallant act he was honored with a statue in the forum, and the gift of as much land as he could drive his plough round in the course of a day.

The Etruscans, though repulsed, were not discouraged, and laying siege to Rome, endeavored to reduce the inhabitants by famine. In this extremity, it is said, Caius Mucius, a young patrician, undertook to rid his country from so terrible an enemy as King Porsenna; and having entered the Etruscan camp in disguise, he saw a princely-looking personage sitting in state, distributing pay to the soldiers. Thinking this must be the king, Mucius stabbed him to the heart; on which he was seized and carried before Porsenna, to whom he boldly avowed his purpose. Being threatened with torture unless he avowed the whole plot, he thrust his right hand into a fire that was burning near, and held it there till it was consumed, thus proving his indifference to threats. The sequel of the story is, that Porsenna, struck with his courage, generously gave him his life, and that Mucius, out of gratitude, told him to be continually on his guard, as three hundred Roman youth had sworn to take his life. Without pursuing further this account, we may state that the character of Porsenna is believed to be fabulous; but there is no reason to doubt, that about this time, though the exact date is not certain, Rome was conquered by the Etruscans, and that the city was surrendered. The Romans even gave up their arms, and were forbidden to use iron except for the purposes of agriculture. It is stated that they even sent the conquering prince, personified in the legend by Porsenna, an ivory throne and sceptre, a golden crown and triumphal robe, besides paying, as tribute, a tenth of the produce of the land. It is not certain that this war was undertaken at the instigation of Tarquin; it was more probably an invasion of the Etruscans, with a view to conquest.

The indefatigable Tarquin, says the story, still nourished the hope of regaining the throne of Rome; and excited by him, the Latins invaded the Roman territory. They were totally defeated, and a truce succeeded. Hostility broke out afresh, however, and the armies meeting near Lake Regillus, about 496 B. C., a furious combat ensued. The Romans were yielding, and were on the point of flying, when their general made a solemn vow that he would raise a temple to the twin gods Castor and Pollux, if they would lend him their assistance at this critical moment. Suddenly there appeared two horsemen of gigantic height, mounted on milk white steeds: they placed themselves at the head of the Roman legions, and followed by the cavalry and foot-soldiers, into whom the presence of the twin brothers had breathed new courage, forced their way through the Latin ranks, and dividing and isolating the enemy, easily put them to flight. When the victory was won, no vestige remained of the white horsemen, except the deep mark of a horse's hoof in a hard black rock near by. But on the evening of the same day, as the sun was going down, and as the inhabitants of Rome were waiting under their porticoes and in the streets for some tidings of the engagement, two horsemen made their appearance in the forum. Their arms were stained with blood, and their horses were covered with foam. Alighting near the temple of Vesta, where a spring of water bubbles from the ground, they washed away the stains of the conflict, and the people crowded around them, asking the news. The mysterious knights told them how the battle had been fought and won by the Romans, and then mounting their steeds, suddenly disappeared. They were believed to be Castor and Pollux, and according to the vow of the general, a temple was built and dedicated to their worship. There is so much of the fanciful in the Roman legends of the exiled king's attempts to recover his throne, and the poet's hand is so evident in the account of the war with Porsenna, and the battle of the Regillus, that Niebuhr supposes it to be the concluding portion of some epic poem, entitled probably the "Lay of the Tarquins."

After the loss of this battle, the Latins abandoned the cause of Tarquin, who retired to Cumæ, in Campania, where he shortly after died. Thus Rome was freed from fear of foreign domination. No sooner, however, were they relieved from external disturbances, than they began to have troubles at home. The patricians and plebeians formed two distinct classes, and it appears to have been the special object of the former to depress and enslave the laboring portion. The many privileges restored or granted to the latter, in the beginning of the commonwealth, were, one by one, taken away; the lands which had been given them were resumed; the taxes were increased; and the consulship was no longer shared by the two orders; but both consuls were chosen from among the patricians. The people began to feel that it was as hard to be ruled by an overbearing aristocracy, as by a tyrannical king. When reading of the distresses of the plebeians at this period, we are to understand that numerous class of small farmers which constituted by far the greater proportion of the Roman commonalty. The chief cause of their increasing poverty was, that they were burdened with taxes far beyond their means, and in order to pay them, were obliged to borrow money at exorbitant interest, so that they became involved in debts which they could not discharge; and then, according to the Roman laws, they became the slaves of their creditors. Such children and grandchildren of the debtor as were still under his authority shared the same fate, and became the property of the creditor. The creditors were generally the patricians, the debtors the plebeians; so that, in fact, one part of the population belonged entirely to the other. The patricians, having the government now exclusively in their own hands, managed to obtain exemption from the tithes for the lands which they held, while, on the other hand, the taxes were rigorously exacted from the plebeians. To add to these distresses, the loss of the territory beyond the Tiber, on the Etruscan side, had reduced many families to absolute beggary; and the poorer classes were excluded by the wealthier from all use of the public pastures. A new magistrate, called the *dictator*, had also been created: this officer was elected for six months, during which he had the power of an absolute sovereign within the city, and one mile beyond it. The consulship still existed, but the dictator was a higher magistrate; and whatever the real object of the institution of this office, ts immediate effect was, by a rigorous enforcement of the law relative to debtors, to reduce them to a state of slavery. The misery of the plebeians was still further augmented by the basest injustice. They were all soldiers, and those who were pledged for debt were obliged to serve in the field as well as others; yet their share of the spoils, which might have helped them to pay their debts, was withheld from them, while the debts themselves were becoming larger and larger, by the addition of the interest. From all these causes the lower classes became hopelessly in debt, and were driven to despair by the rigor of their creditors.

In this posture of affairs, a single spark kindled a great conflagration. During the consulship of Appius Claudius and Publius Servilius, (493 B. C.,) an old man, covered with rags and filth, pale and emaciated, with squalid hair and neglected beard, rushed into the forum, and, with outstretched arms, implored the aid of the people. He exhibited the scars and the wounds which he had received in twenty-eight battles with the enemies of Rome. He was recognized by several persons as a captain in the army, and on being asked the cause of his wretched appearance, said that the sentence of the law had been passed upon him as a debtor, and that he and his two sons had been cast into prison. He had fallen into debt, because, while serving in the army, his farm had been plundered and his house burnt by the enemy: taxes had nevertheless been exacted from him, to pay which he had been obliged to borrow money: compound interest had eaten up what little property remained to him, and he soon became the bondman of his creditor. Imprisonment and stripes had been his portion from that day. He had made his escape from confinement, and besought protection and support. Whether this be, or not, an exact account of what actually took place, it is certain that this or some other incident occasioned a violent tumult: the multitude crowded the streets, clamoring for relief; the senators were struck with consternation, and hardly dared assemble for public business. The two consuls were divided as to the measures to be pursued, and the city seemed doomed to witness the horrors of bloodshed and civil war. At this moment, the news arrived that the Volscians were in arms against Rome, and were almost under its very walls.

This intelligence was received as glad tidings by the plebeians. Throwing their caps in the air, they exclaimed, that the patricians might go and fight their own battles, and resolutely refused to enlist. The senate empowered Servilius to treat with them. He issued an edict, proclaiming that all who were in bondage for debt, might, if they chose, quit their prisons to join the army, and that, as long as a man was under arms, no one should touch his property, or keep his children in bondage. The effect was immediate; the prisons were emptied, and the escaped convicts swelled the ranks of the army. After an easy victory, the consul Servilius led home his conquering troops, full of hope for the future; but a bitter disappointment awaited all, when the iron-hearted Appius, colleague of Servilius, ordered the debtors back to their prisons. Dreadful clamors and disturbances ensued; the people held nocturnal meetings on the Aventine and Esquiline Hills, to concert measures of relief. Again the Roman territory was invaded — the Sabines were already ravaging its borders. In this emergency, Marcus Valerius was appointed dictator, and being a favorite, the people, long suffering, and slow to wrath, readily enlisted under his banner, and followed him to the field. Success was on their side, for they returned a second time triumphant and laden with spoils. Valerius now attempted to obtain from the senate a redress of the popular grievances, but in vain. The plebeians, seeing no chance of legal relief, withdrew from the city, and established their camp on a hill beyond the Anio. Here they resolved to found an independent city, unless a plan for mutual accommodation could be decided upon. At last, the patricians deputed ten senators to visit the plebeian camp and propose terms of peace.

One of these, Menenius Agrippa, addressed to the people the following apologue "In ancient times, when the human body was not, as at present, an individual whole, but every member had its own separate plans, purposes, will, and language, it happened that on a certain emergency, the limbs fell into a quarrel with the stomach. They complained that this member remained idle in the midst of them, doing nothing but enjoying itself. To gratify their enmity, they agreed that they would no longer labor for it. The hands therefore, refused to convey food to the mouth; the mouth refused to open, and the teeth to chew. But while they thus attempted to starve the stomach, they were starving themselves; and when they were reduced to the most deplorable state of feebleness, they discovered that the stomach is by no means useless. that it gives, as well as receives, nourishment, distributing to all parts of the body life and health."

But it appears that the plebeians, who had had experience enough in false promises and treacherous hopes, demanded something more solid than fables, and seemed to think that moral lessons, however pointed, came with an ill grace from persons who regarded them so little themselves. So a treaty was made, after considerable discussion, and its articles were signed and sworn to by the two orders. The principal stipulations of this instrument were, the restoration of the law by which the property, and not the person, of a debtor should be liable for his debts; and the creation of two magistrates, chosen from among the plebeians, to be called *tribunes of the people*, whose duty it should be to protect their liberties, and whose persons should be held sacred under all circumstances: outlawry was to be pronounced upon any one who should injure them. The institution of the tribunes was the greatest step yet made toward the freedom of the people. All who were in bondage for debt were set free; those who had pledged themselves were released from the obligation of becoming slaves. The houses of the tribunes remained open day and night, that the injured might, at any time, seek protection from injustice or contempt of the laws. The hill where the plebeians had encamped, and where they had offered sacrifices to Jupiter, received the name of the *Sacred Mount*. The popular or democratic constitution of Rome may be properly dated from this period — 493 B. C.

At this time, an excellent man and patriotic citizen, named *Spurius Cassius*, was consul. During his administration, treaties were formed with the Latins and Hernici; and thus the confederacy to which Rome owed her greatness under the later kings was reorganized. He also proposed an agrarian law, to the effect that land should be given to all those plebeians who had none, and that the patricians should pay, as formerly, tithes upon the lands occupied by them. This law was passed after a violent opposition, but the succeeding consuls took care that it should never be carried into effect: so the commons continued to suffer all the miseries attendant on poverty and the oppressions of a tyrannical government. Spurius Cassius was, at the expiration of his year of office, charged with treason, and beheaded. The feuds of the nobles appear to have been carried on with a ferocious spirit that marks the barbarism of the age. The conflicts and the crimes which accompanied them were not noted in the annals of the times; but we are able to infer, from some notices which have been discovered, with what bitterness political animosities were indulged.

The commons, finding that the passage of the agrarian law was becoming every day more problematical, refused to serve as soldiers; and soon after, the neglect of agriculture, caused by the numerous wars of the Romans, occasioned a severe famine. Disturbances took place in consequence, and the senate and people became highly inflamed against each other. Some sympathizing Greek prince, or, as it is stated by other annalists, Gelon, king of Sicily, sent at this period a supply of corn to Rome, which it was proposed to distribute at once among the people. This benevolent plan was strongly opposed by Caius Marcius Coriolanus, a hero, whose history, above all others, the poets have delighted to embellish. He was haughty and violent, and besides hating the people as a patrician would hate the plebeians, he thoroughly detested them for having refused to confirm his election to the consulate. The contemptuous and bitter language which Shakspeare puts into his mouth, would perhaps seem too strong, did we not remember that no wars are more bloody than those of class, and no feuds more deadly than those springing from division into castes: —

. . . . "What would you have, you curs,
That like nor peace nor war? The one affrights you,
The other makes you proud. He that trusts you,
Where he should find you lions, finds you hares;
Where foxes, geese. You are no surer, no,
Than is the coal of fire upon the ice,
Or hailstone in the sun. Who deserves greatness
Deserves your hate; and your affections are
A sick man's appetite, who desires most that
Which would increase his evil. He that depends
Upon your favors, swims with fins of lead,
And hews down oaks with rushes. Hang ye! Trust ye?
With every minute you do change a mind,
And call him noble that was now your hate,
Him vile that was your garland. What's the matter,
That in these several places of the city
You cry against the noble senate, who,
Under the gods, keep you in awe, which else
Would feed on one another? What's your seeking?"

He carried his hatred so far as to persuade the consuls to refuse to assent to a division of the corn. For this act he was indicted by the tribunes of the people, the ostensible charge being that he aspired to the sovereign authority. He was banished from Rome, and took refuge among the Volscians, who, before long, became involved in a war with Rome. They met with success every where, and marching through the Roman territories, under the guidance of Coriolanus and their king Tullus, laid waste all the lands belonging to the commons, sparing only the property of the patricians. They then surrounded the city, and closely besieged it Within the walls, nothing was heard but cries of lamentation and distress; the women ran to the temples of the gods to pray for mercy; it was the darkest day that Rome had ever known; for the enemy was the most formidable that had ever attacked it, while the disaffection of the people destroyed her means of defence. A deputation which was sent to Coriolanus was received with chilling indifference, and was told to expect peace on no other conditions than the returning to the Volscians all the lands which had been taken from them, the recall of all Roman exiles, and the restoration of their property. The senate refused to accede to these terms An embassy of ten senators next appeared before Coriolanus, humbly suing for peace on less stringent conditions: but the haughty leader was inflexible. Then all the priests came in

Mother of Coriolanus addressing him.

solemn procession, but with no better success. At last, the noble matrons, dressed in mourning and headed by the wife, mother, and children of the stern exile, proceeded to his camp. The Volscian soldiers, who guarded his tent, silently made way for the sad procession, and the whole camp seemed touched by this afflicting evidence of the misfortunes of Rome. As the mother of the exile appeared before her son, she said, in a voice half choked with sobs, "Must it be thus, that Rome would have escaped the dishonor of beholding an enemy's camp under her walls, had I never borne a son? that if I had remained childless

I should have died a free woman in a free city?" Coriolanus wrung his hands, looked at his army and the walls of his native city, now humbled before him, and exclaimed, "O mother, what hast thou done! Thine is the victory — Rome is saved, but shame and ruin await thy son." He then embraced his wife and children, and giving them a safe-conduct back to Rome, made a precipitate retreat with his army. He never returned, but passed his life in exile. According to another version of the story, he was assassinated by the Volscians, who considered that, in sparing Rome, he had betrayed their interests. The date of these events, though uncertain, is usually fixed at 458 B. C.

Rome and the neighboring states were not in a very prosperous condition at this period. The ravages of warfare were every where visible. Many towns were in ruins; much of the country was laid waste; the vines and fruit-trees had been destroyed; and whole villages were in ashes. Added to the miseries of war were those of the plague; and the scarcity of corn, and the neglect of agriculture, were the cause of a severe famine. The year following the peace with the Volscians, the Æquians broke into the Roman territory; and this incursion was so formidable, that it threatened Rome with dissolution in its weak condition. An army sent against them was decoyed into a narrow pass, with steep, bare hills on each side. They could neither advance nor retreat. There was neither food for the men, nor grass for the horses, and they were in danger of starving, if the enemy, who were surrounding them on every side, did not despatch them by a more summary means. Five horsemen broke out of the lines before the rear was quite closed up, and carried the disheartening news to Rome. With one accord, Cincinnatus, "the curly-headed," who had formerly been consul, was chosen dictator, and an embassy was sent to his farm to require his immediate presence at Rome. He was found ploughing in the field, with no clothing but his kilt. As he arrived in the city, the senators and the patricians went out to meet him, and he was conducted to the capital by twenty-four lictors with their rods and axes, the multitude crowding round him to see the man who was to be their deliverer.

Roman Triumphal Procession.

He was invested with supreme power for six months. His first step was to order every man to shut his shop. The courts of law were closed, and directions were given that until the army was delivered, no man must attend to any private business. Every citizen of age to bear arms was next ordered to appear in the Field of Mars before sunset, with provisions for five days, and a dozen stout stakes. The city was now alive, and nothing was heard but the clashing of arms and the hewing of trees. At sunset, a large and fully-equipped army left the walls of Rome, and proceeded toward Mount Algidus, where the enemy were posted. They arrived here at midnight, and forming themselves into a column, completely surrounded the mountain. When all was ready, they gave one long, tremendous shout, which echoed and reverberated from rock to rock, filling the enemy with surprise and terror, and inspiring their countrymen with new hope, as they recognized the well known Roman hurrah. These shouted back again, and began to assail the enemy. Their friends without, in the mean time, dug a ditch round the mountain, and fenced it with a rampart of stakes and turf. When the morning came, the astonished Æquians found themselves completely enclosed, and offered Cincinnatus his own terms. The victorious Romans, after stripping them of their arms, baggage, and every thing valuable, and making them pass under a yoke formed of their spears marched home in triumph. As Cincinnatus entered Rome, he was honored with a golden crown; tables were set out at every door, laden with meat and drink, and the soldiers and the people feasted together with songs and rejoicing. A triumphal procession was decreed to Cincinnatus, who, having held the power a fortnight, and saved the Roman army from destruction, abdicated, and returned to his plough.

Such is the legend of Cincinnatus. Much of it is doubtful, except the fact of his having been dictator and having gained a victory over the Æquians. It is not certain that he enjoyed the glory of a triumph but as this honor was conferred upon many Roman generals in after times, it may be proper to describe it here. It was the greatest military honor that could be attained in the Roman state. It was a solemn procession, in which the victorious general and his army proceeded through the city to the Capitol. The procession was formed in the Field of Mars, and passed through the most public streets, which were strewed with flowers, while incense was burning on altars raised in different places. First came the musicians, playing and singing triumphal songs; next, the oxen for sacrifice, adorned with flowers; then the spoils taken from the enemy, drawn in wagons; then came the captives of rank in chains, and after them walked the lictors, who were followed by a troop of musicians and dancers. The general himself, crowned with laurel, rode in a circular chariot, drawn by four horses, and his children usually accompanied him. The consuls and senators walked before him, during the republic; but in the time of the emperors, they followed the chariot on foot. The soldiers closed the procession. A part of the spoils was offered to Jupiter; the sacrifices were performed; and then the general gave a sumptuous entertainment to his friends and the chief citizens in the Capitol.

CHAPTER CCCXXXVII.

451 to 274 B. C.

The Laws of the Twelve Tables — The Decemvirs — The Censorship — The Invasion of the Gauls — The Samnite Wars — The Invasion of Pyrrhus — Condition of the People — Public Works — Literature.

The agrarian law, and the discussions concerning it, soon began again to agitate the contending factions. The senate and people were both weary of these endless disputes, and all parties concurred in the opinion that the existing evils might be removed by the enactment of a body of wholesome laws. Three commissioners were accordingly sent to Greece to examine the legal institutions of that country, and select such laws as were suitable to the Romans. Ten magistrates were appointed to administer these new laws. They superseded the consuls and tribunes, and exercised the supreme power by turns. They were called *decemviri*, and the whole body was styled a *decemvirate.* The old laws and usages were amended by many alterations and additions, and were formed into a regular code; these were engraved on twelve tables of brass, and were hung up in the Comitium. The *Laws of the Twelve Tables* were the basis of all Roman law till the time of the emperors. By this famous code, the distinction between patrician and plebeian tribes was abolished, and all were called indiscriminately, *Roman citizens.* The laws in relation to debt were not altered, but it is probable that as the times grew better, there was less occasion to borrow, and their severity was less felt. The first decemvirs governed uprightly, and at the expiration of the year, no objection was made to a continuation of the same form of government. Appius Claudius, one of the first, was reëlected, with four new patricians and five plebeians, who soon began to display the state and authority of kings. They became tyrannical and despotic, and at the end of their term of office, refused to resign Having tasted the sweets of power, they were unwilling to return to the rank of simple citizens. The melancholy story of Virginia, which is unhappily no fiction, sufficiently exemplifies the violence and oppression to which the people were subjected under the second decemvirate.

Appius Claudius, one of the decemvirs, and an old man, conceived a violent passion for Virginia, the daughter of a centurion named Virginius. This young lady was about fifteen years of age, and very beautiful. Appius bribed a creature of his, named Claudius, to claim her as his slave. The cause was tried before Appius, who adjudged her to Claudius. Virginius, who guessed at the designs of the tyrant, asked permission to take a last farewell of his daughter; when, pretending to embrace her, he snatched a knife from a butcher's stall, and stabbed her to the heart. Then brandishing the weapon in the air, he exclaimed, "By this blood, Appius, I devote thy head to the infernal gods!" Virginius returned to the camp with the bloody knife in his hand, and a multitude of the citizens in his company. This tragedy was the drop that made the bucket overflow. The army had already been excited to madness by the cowardly murder of Licinius Dentatus, by order of the decemvirs. He had boldly pleaded the cause of the people, and for this was marked out for destruction. Under pretence of doing him honor, he was sent with a convoy of supplies for the army, which was encamped outside the city in expectation of an attack, with a body-guard of one hundred and fifty soldiers, who had received orders to assassinate him in the woods. Passing through a ravine among the hills, they fell suddenly upon him The brave old soldier, who had fought in a hundred and twenty battles, set his back against a rock, and defended himself till fifteen of his assailants had fallen, and till he had wounded thirty others. He then kept off their javelins with his shield, but was at last crushed by huge stones thrown upon him from the top of the rock. The outrage upon Virginius was more than the army could bear; and plucking up their standards, they marched upon Rome. The commons and the remainder of the soldiers joined with them, and formed an encampment on the Sacred Mount, where they remained till the patricians yielded, and the decemvirs resigned.

The commons now came into possession of more rights and privileges than ever before. Two consuls were again chosen, and the people again elected tribunes, to whom they might appeal in case of injustice: several laws were passed for their future security. A most important office, which sprung from the dissolution of the decemvirate, was the censorship. The duties of the censors, of whom there were two, holding the office for five years, were the taking a register of the citizens and their property, for the purpose of levying the taxes in due proportion; the management of all the property from which the government revenues were derived; and the supervision of the public morals. Another privilege obtained at this period by the plebeians was the right of intermarriage with the patrician houses, which had never before been permitted. A period of comparative tranquillity followed these concessions, which lasted till the year 404 B. C.

At this time, the people of Veii — the richest city of Etruria, and a dangerous rival to the Roman republic — gave the Romans so much annoyance, that the latter resolved to destroy it. They accordingly laid siege to the city, and remained ten years under its walls, vainly endeavoring to undermine the foundations, or in some way to force an entrance. At the close of the tenth year, Furius Camillus was chosen dictator, and by his directions it is said that a mine was dug from the Roman camp into the citadel of Veii, through which an entrance was effected, and the city taken. The plunder was shared by the soldiers. The inhabitants were enslaved or ransomed, and the images of the gods transferred to Rome. Camillus, who won the victory, soon experienced the ingratitude of his countrymen. He was charged with having appropriated to his private purposes a part of the plunder of Veii, and unwilling to expose himself to the ignominy of a public trial, went into voluntary exile As he was going out of the gates, he is said to have turned round, and uttered a prayer to the gods that his countrymen might one day be made sensible of his innocence and their own ingratitude — a wish, says the account, which was speedily realized by the invasion of the Gauls.

These people were the ancient inhabitants of France. They were uncivilized and warlike, depending for their victories on personal strength and their destructive mode of warfare. They had already crossed the Alps, and in the year of the city 364, and 389 B. C., penetrated over the Apennines into Etruria, whose cities they laid waste. These barbarians created terror by their fierce aspect, and the deafening noise of innumerable horns and trumpets. Finding themselves but feebly resisted, they pressed onward toward Rome, where the utmost alarm prevailed, as the city was totally unprepared against so formidable a foe. A body of Roman troops took post near the River Allia, about eleven miles from Rome, where they were immediately attacked and dispersed by the Gauls. The routed army was pursued with dreadful slaughter to the very gates of Rome; and had not the victors paused to gather the spoil, that day would have put an end to the Roman name and nation. The affrighted Romans found it impossible to defend the city against such an enemy, and the mass of the population dispersed themselves over the surrounding country, after having garrisoned the Capitol with about one thousand troops. About eighty of the chief patricians, preferring to die than survive the republic, put on their robes of ceremony and sat down in the Forum in their curule chairs, to await the coming of the enemy.

When the Gauls broke into the city, they found it as silent as the grave. Every house was shut; not a human being appeared in the streets; and when they came to the Forum, and saw the priests and senators sitting in deathlike stillness, they began to think that these were the Roman gods, and that they had come to save the city. But the illusion soon vanished: the self-devoted patriots fell victims to their attachment to their home and country, and were slaughtered by the ruthless invaders. The latter then gave themselves up to plunder. They broke into the houses, and set the city on fire in different places. With the exception of a few buildings, Rome was reduced to a heap of ashes. It was then that most of the records of its history were destroyed; and hence arise the many doubts that are thrown upon all that is related of the times that preceded the invasion of the Gauls. The latter now laid siege to the Capitol; but as it held out longer than they expected, they made an attempt to capture it by surprise in the dead of the night. The Roman sentinels were all asleep, and the Gaul who was climbing the rampart at the head of his countrymen was just gaining the summit, when some geese, that were sacred to Juno, and were kept in the temple, gave warning of the danger by screaming and flapping their wings. The tribune, Marcus Manlius, rushed to the spot, and hurled backward the foremost intruder, who bore down in his fall those who were mounting the hill.

Thus the Capitol was saved; but the sufferings of the besieged from famine induced them to enter into an agreement with the Gauls, and ransom the city and its territory for one thousand pounds weight of gold. The Roman account of the close of this mortifying episode in their history is quite magniloquent, and by its very grandeur induces the belief that the records therein given are mere fables, designed to gloss over the defeat and humiliation of the Romans. In these it is stated that, as the gold was being weighed, Camillus, whose return had been solicited by his repentant countrymen, entered the Forum at the head of an army, and ordered the gold to be carried back to the Capitol. It is also stated that a battle ensued in consequence, that the Gauls suffered a total defeat, and were driven from Rome without the treasure. The story goes on to say that, when on their retreat, they were attacked and defeated a second time, when all the booty they were carrying off was taken from them, and their chief made prisoner. It is more probable that the Gauls went away with the gold they had obtained, and that Camillus was recalled, with many other exiles, to supply the place of the citizens who had perished during this destructive invasion.

The city was now to be rebuilt; and this was no easy task for a people so impoverished as were the Romans at this period. The citizens shrank from the idea, and proposed to emigrate in a body to Veii. This project was strenuously opposed by the patricians, who appealed to the people not to desert the memorable seat of their ancestors. Every encouragement was given them, which could assist in restoring the city; they were allowed to hew stone and cut wood wherever they could find them, and to erect their habitations on any spot and in any manner they chose. To prevent the possibility of settling at Veii, the houses there were pulled down to furnish materials for the new city. The result of these concessions was an incongruous mass of buildings, which, however, sufficed to preserve the site and name of ancient Rome. The distress of the lower classes was very great, and Manlius, the tribune, who had saved the Capitol, came forward as the champion of their sufferings. He sold his estate to buy them bread, and became the idol of the multitude. Like Coriolanus, he was accused of aspiring to the supreme power, and being invited to a conference on the hill where stood the Capitol, was treacherously thrown from the Tarpeian Rock.

In this manner the Romans went on, a mixture of turbulence and superstition within their walls, and successful enterprises without; for they were at this period engaged in a variety of petty wars. Their armies were constantly in the field against the Gauls or the Etruscans; but as the relation of wars that led to no particular result is extremely uninteresting, we only speak of them at all, in order to show that the Romans were seldom at peace. The famous legend of Marcus Curtius belongs to this period, and though evidently a story having no foundation in truth is too remarkable to be omitted. It is said that during an earthquake, a yawning gulf opened in the Forum, threatening to swallow up houses and temples in its abyss. Burnt-offerings and prayers were of no avail; he gulf continued gaping in the heart of the city. The augurs declared that it would not close till the most precious thing in Rome had been thrown into it. Marcus Curtius arrayed himself in complete armor, mounted his finest charger, and saying that patriotism and military virtue were the most precious qualities a state could possess, leaped boldly into the chasm, in the presence of the priests, the senate, and the people. The abyss, concludes the story, closed over him, and he was seen no more.

The patricians now gradually acquired the principal influence in the state, and it was evident that the plebeians, ground down by oppression and worn out by suffering, were losing their spirit and courage. Rome was on the point of degenerating into a miserable oligarchy, and her name would have come down to us shorn of its ancient glories, had not her decline been arrested by two men, whose appearance changed the fate of their country and the world. These men, Licinius and Sextus, were tribunes of the people; Licinius brought forward three bills: the first opened the consulship to plebeians; the second prohibited any one from occupying more than five hundred acres of land; and the third provided that those who were pledged for debt should be released from the obligation of paying interest, and should be allowed three years to refund the principal. The patricians resisted the passing of these laws for five years, when the people took up arms, and stationed themselves on Mount Aventine. To avoid civil war, Camillus, the dictator, advised concession, and the three bills were passed. This arrangement (366 B. C.) settled all affairs for the time amicably.

In the year 342 B. C., a war commenced between the Romans and Samnites, inhabitants of a province in Lower Italy. Hostilities were brought about by an application on the part of the Campanians, who were oppressed by the Samnites, to the Romans against their enemies. Valerius Corvus, the Roman consul, marched against the Samnites, and forced them to retreat, after a bloody engagement, to their own borders. At the same time, another Roman army invaded the country of the Samnites, and after a doubtful contest, gained a victory by the heroic conduct of their general, Publius Decius. The vanquished nation was obliged to sue for peace, but maintained it only till they recovered from their defeat. Twenty-two years after, (320 B. C.,) a new war broke out, more bloody than the preceding, which was prosecuted with greater obstinacy, as the other states in Lower Italy came to the aid of the Samnites. Though the Romans were generally victorious, yet in the year 313 B. C., their army was drawn by treachery into a narrow defile near the city of Caudium, and being surrounded on every side by the forces of the enemy, was compelled to submit to the ignominy of passing under the yoke. This was done by setting up two spears, with a third across them at the top. Under this every man of the army passed, having previously been stripped of all his arms and clothes, except a single garment. The Romans, disarmed, half naked, and burning with shame at this dishonor, found a refuge in the city of Capua, an ally of Rome.

The Roman senate refused to ratify the treaty which the Samnites had forced their humbled foes to sign, and delivering up to them the consuls who had made it, sent other commanders to prosecute the war. Papirius Cursor succeeded in avenging the disgrace which his countrymen had suffered, by inflicting a similar ignominy upon the enemy. The war was still prosecuted with fury; but the power of the Samnites declined every day, while that of the Romans gained fresh vigor from each new victory. The Samnites, being now hard pressed, determined to call a foreign power to their assistance. At the entreaty of the city of Tarentum, Pyrrhus, king of Epirus, took up arms against the Romans, 279 B. C. He sent an advanced guard of three thousand men, and soon followed with a force of twenty thousand foot, three thousand cavalry, and twenty elephants, the first that had ever been seen in Italy. In the battle which ensued, the troops on each side advanced and receded seven times, without deciding the conflict. Pyrrhus then brought his elephants into action, the sight of which struck both horses and men with terror and the Romans broke their ranks; the rout was general, and the Roman army fled. Their valor, however, seems to have inspired Pyrrhus with admiration, for he is stated to have exclaimed, while viewing the field of battle the next day, "Had I such soldiers as the Romans, the world would be mine; had the Romans such a general as I, the world would be theirs."

The Romans refused to listen to any accommodation or amicable arrangement for peace, but sent an embassy to treat for an exchange of prisoners. Fabricius, an old senator, was at the head of the deputation. The Epirote king, knowing his reputation for integrity, determined to try him, and offered him gold and rich presents; but they were all sternly refused. The next day, Pyrrhus ordered one of his largest elephants to be placed behind a curtain, which at a signal was drawn, and discovered the animal raising his trunk in a threatening manner. Fabricius stood unterrified, and then, turning to the king, said, "Neither your gold yesterday, nor your big beast to-day, can move *me*." Pyrrhus, enchanted to find such firmness in a *barbarian*, as the Greeks called every one but themselves, released the prisoners. The Romans soon recovered from the effects of this defeat, and as the panic occasioned by the elephants passed away, a large army took the field. While the two forces were approaching each other, a letter was brought to Fabricius from the physician of Pyrrhus, offering to poison the king for a proper reward. Fabricius, fired with indignation at this treacherous proposal, sent the letter to Pyrrhus. The king, struck with amazement, exclaimed, "Admirable Fabricius, it is as easy to turn the sun from his course as thee from the path of honor." Then, clothing and releasing all his Roman prisoners, he embarked his army for Sicily, where, in two years, he made himself master of the island. The Romans, during his absence, retrieved their affairs, and when, in 274 B. C., Pyrrhus, at the solicitation of his allies, again took the field against the Romans, he found it no longer possible to gain a single advantage over them. He abandoned the Samnites and Tarentines, and returned to Epirus with the remains of his shattered forces. The allied nations could no longer resist the conquering career of the Romans, who emerged from this last contest, called the *fourth Samnite war*, the rulers of all Italy south of Cisalpine Gaul. Almost every town in the peninsula now contained a Roman garrison. The conquered nations were in general left in possession of their own laws, and at liberty to elect their own magistrates They were called allies, and though they paid no land tax to the Roman government, were obliged to furnish a certain number of soldiers to the state, and to clothe and pay them. The Romans, however, gained by these conquests, new territories, with forests, rivers, and harbors, from which large revenues were derived, that enriched the state, and consequently the people.

As we are now considerably advanced in the history of Rome, it may be proper to glance briefly at the condition of the people, their manners and customs, their public works, and literary attainments, at this period. The Romans were progressing towards that state of luxurious refinement, which they afterward carried to a height that has never been surpassed. The spoils of Greek and Etruscan cities had made them familiar with luxuries that were unknown to their ancestors. All classes of the citizens were enriched by these victories, and the increasing extent of the Roman dominions rendered the patronage of the government so great, that thousands were supported from the public treasury. It was at this period that the first silver coinage was issued; but it is unknown whether it was a right confined to the government, or allowed to private individuals.

About this time, Appius the Blind, distinguished himself, when censor, by the construction of a military road which extended from Rome to Brundusium, a distance of three hundred and sixty miles. It was paved with lava, and was called the *Appian Way*. He likewise built the first aqueduct at Rome. Prisoners taken in the Samnite wars, besides hired laborers, were employed on these works. Tiles were introduced, instead of boards, as a material for roofing houses, which were now much better built than in the first years after the invasion of the Gauls. The city was beginning also to be embellished with good streets, fine stone buildings, bronze statues, and other works of art. Something like literature and oratory begins to be visible at this time. Brief, dry chronicles of public events were kept. It was the custom to sing heroic poems, and to recite comic dialogues, at banquets. Ballads of Romulus and Remus formed the entertainment of the common people. Combats of gladiators were now first introduced. This barbarous spectacle was at first considered as a sacrifice in honor of the dead, and the gladiators, it is supposed, were criminals, or captives condemned to death; but in later times great numbers of slaves were bought and trained for the purpose.

CHAPTER CCCXXXVIII.

274 to 62 B. C.

The Punic Wars — Conquest of Greece — Revolt at Rome — Jugurtha — Inroads of the Barbarians — The Social War — Marius and Sylla — Spartacus — Conspiracy of Catiline.

Our history now approaches the memorable era of the *Punic wars*, a contest for supremacy between the two greatest republics in existence. Rome was now prosperous and rich. Her very prosperity, added to the knowledge that it arose from success in war, made the people anxious to find another enemy, with whose spoils to fill the Roman coffers, and of whose citizens they might make slaves. Casting their eyes across the Mediterranean, whose waters were not broad enough to conceal the glory and magnificence which appeared on the African shore, or deep enough to quench the fires of ambition and rivalry in their breasts, they beheld the republic of Carthage, whose dominion of the seas and superiority in naval strength, pouring the most unbounded wealth into the lap of the queen of the western seas, excited the jealousy and cupidity of the Romans.

Once resolved upon war, they were never long in finding an occasion for commencing it, though the cause of it in this case was not very honorable to either party. In the year 264 B. C., a company of brigands in Sicily, called *Mamertines*, from the place of their origin, seized the town of Messina, and butchered the citizens. The Syracusans were about to take vengeance upon them; but the Mamertines divided into two parties — the one seeking the aid of the Carthaginians, the other that of the Romans: thus the two republics were brought into collision. The Carthaginians were enraged at the interference of the Romans, — for Sicily was theirs by right of conquest, — and hired, for the contest, a vast number of mercenary troops in Gaul, Liguria, and Spain.

The Romans laid siege to Agrigentum, in Sicily, which was a great naval depot of the Carthaginians, and captured it, 262 B. C. They had no ships of war, while their powerful rival was the acknowledged mistress of the ocean. It happened that a Carthaginian ship was driven upon their shore, which furnished them with a model for building. They soon equipped a fleet of one hundred and thirty ships, and, to their own astonishment, achieved, in 260, a naval victory, capturing fifty of the enemy's fleet. This being the first sea fight in which they had ever engaged, caused an immense exultation in the capital; and the Romans were so far encouraged by their success, that they crossed the Mediterranean, and landed in Africa. We have described more particularly the events of this campaign and the tragical fate of Regulus, in the history of Carthage. After various successes on both sides, the Romans so effectually crippled the Carthaginian power, that her naval strength was utterly annihilated. The first Punic war ended 242 B. C., and it is a somewhat extraordinary fact that the temple of Janus was now shut for the second time since the foundation of Rome. It will be remembered that this happened only in time of peace, and we may judge from this how completely the military character inspired the whole Roman policy: a state of hostility seemed to be the permanent and natural relation between Rome and her neighbors.

In 218 B. C., the second Punic war commenced. For an account of this most formidable contest, we must again refer the reader to the history of Carthage, where the career of Hannibal, and his invasion of Italy, are given in full. In the battle of Lake Thrasymenus, of which we have already spoken, it is said that a terrible earthquake took place, which overthrew city after city, and buried them deep in the bowels of the earth. Yet so intent were the combatants upon the battle, that not one of them was sensible of this great convulsion of nature.

"Such the storm of battle on that day,
And such the fury, whose convulsion blinds
To all save carnage, that, beneath the fray,
An earthquake rolled unheededly away;
None felt stern nature rocking at his feet,
And yawning forth a grave for those who lay
Upon their bucklers for a winding-sheet.
Such is th' absorbing hate when warring nations meet."

As we have stated in the story of Hannibal's career, he arrived under the walls of Rome, and seemed on the point of humbling the imperial city. But the Romans were so far from despairing, that at this very moment they sent out, by the opposite gates, a reënforcement of men for their armies in Spain. Hannibal was mortified at this evidence of their self-confidence and resolution; but still more so when he heard that the ground on which his army lay encamped had been put up at auction, while he was there, in Rome, and sold at its full value. He took his revenge by offering for sale the shops round the Roman Forum. Without doing more than threaten the city, Hannibal was recalled to Africa, in 201 B. C., to oppose the Roman forces under Scipio, who had transported his army across the Mediterranean. The battle of Zama soon followed, by the results of which Carthage was completely prostrated at the feet of her enemy. Her exulting rival imposed on her the harshest terms, stripping her of her fleet, her elephants, and all her territories out of Africa. Thus, after a duration of seventeen years, ended the second Punic war, 201 B. C.

Rome had now become a great military republic, supreme in Western Europe, and exercising a predominant influence in the East, where the kingdoms formed from the fragments of Alexander's empire had sunk into weakness, from the exhaustion of mutual wars. The Athenians, exposed to the attacks of Philip V., king of Macedon, sought the protection of the Romans, which was readily granted, as the senate had been anxious to find a pretext for meddling in the affairs of Greece. War was accordingly declared against Philip, and an army was sent into Macedonia. The Macedonians were irretrievably overthrown in a battle fought at Cynoscephalæ, (197 B. C.,) and forced to submit. A second Macedonian war was soon after proclaimed against Perseus, the son and successor of Philip. Paulus Æmilius took the command of the Roman forces, and in 167 B. C., completely routed the enemy. By this victory, Macedonia, Epirus, and Illyricum, were reduced to the condition of Roman provinces.

The third Punic war ensued, 149 B. C. Three years after, Carthage was destroyed by fire, by the army of Scipio Æmilianus, and the civilization, and arts, and literature, accumulated during seven hundred years, were ruthlessly blotted out of existence. The very ruins of the city were levelled to the ground, and heavy curses were pronounced on any one who should attempt to rebuild it. If we are to believe that nations are to be governed by the same rules of justice which have been given to individuals, and that national crimes will meet with as sure a retribution as is visited upon single acts of disobedience, we cannot but feel that the Romans had now entered upon that career of relentless cruelty, and of rapacious lust of dominion, which, in time, brought down upon them, as a means of divine vengeance, the barbarian hordes of the north. As we pursue their history, and follow their brutal and hard-hearted policy, which visited all r als with extermination, and wasted with fire and sword all lands that were fairer than their own, we can hardly fail to be convinced that the incursions of the Goths and Vandals were as much the execution of a divine command as when "the fountains of the great deep were broken up, and the windows of heaven were opened, and the rain was upon the earth forty days and forty nights." Even Scipio, as he surveyed the ruins of the city which had fallen before him, was impressed with some anticipation of the kind, and could not refrain from tears. In his commiseration for the melancholy fate of his country's rival, he repeated these lines of Homer: —

"Yet come it will: the day decreed by fates —
How my heart trembles while my tongue relates!
The day when thou, imperial Troy, must bend,
And see thy warriors fall, thy glories end!"

Polybius, the historian, interrogated him as to his meaning. He replied, that his thoughts were fixed on his own country, which he foresaw must also submit to the vicissitudes which attend all human things.

In the mean time, a rebellion had broken out in Greece, excited by an impostor named Andriscus, who pretended to be the son of Philip. The war which followed in this country proved fatal to its liberties. The Achæans, stimulated by some factious leaders, took up arms, but were subdued by the Romans, under the consul Mummius. Corinth, one of the most opulent cities of antiquity, was plundered of its statues and other works of art, and then destroyed. Thebes and Chalcis shared a similar fate. The fall of Corinth was a means of introducing a taste for the fine arts among the Romans, which, if we are to believe an anecdote related of Mummius, had not yet penetrated into the country. It is said, that this general, on shipping his plunder to Italy, bargained with the shipmaster that in case the statues and paintings were lost, he should furnish others as good in their stead, and at his own price.

At this period, the government of Rome was not conducted in a manner calculated to preserve its republican institutions. The numerous class of small farmers that formerly constituted the strength of the commonwealth, had become nearly extinct; having left their farms for the camp, and become altogether devoted to a military life. Most of the small farms had been sold or given up, so that the rich possessed immense estates, and the poor had for the most part no land at all. There were beside large companies of wealthy men at Rome, who contracted for different branches of the revenue; that is, they paid so much a year to the government for the right of collecting the taxes, and duties of every description; whatever they received beyond what they had engaged to pay was their own: it was evidently their interest to extort as much as possible from the people. The republic seemed indeed verging to its fall. In this state of things, two brothers, Tiberius and Caius Gracchus, tribunes of the people, resolved to attempt the restoration of the Licinian law against holding large tracts of land. Great opposition was made to this proposal by the nobles. The death of Attalus, king of Pergamus, afforded the elder Gracchus a new opportunity for espousing the cause of the people. This king, who died without heirs, left all his territories and treasures to Rome, and Gracchus proposed that the land should be divided among the people, and the treasures spent in purchasing agricultural implements. This caused greater disturbances than ever, 132 B. C. In a riot which followed, Gracchus was struck dead by a piece of a broken bench, and three hundred of his partisans were killed. Twelve years afterward, Caius, who had attempted to complete what was begun by his brother, was declared an outlaw, and it was promised that whoever should bring his head to the consul should receive its weight in gold. In a street fight that ensued, three thousand of his followers were slain, and the head of Gracchus was cut from his living body. Septimuleius, one of his intimate friends, obtained possession of it, and carried it home, where he took out the brain and filled the cavity with lead, to increase its weight. He received of the consul seventeen pounds of gold in consequence.

With the Gracchi perished the real freedom of Rome. From this time, the power of the state was wielded by a corrupt and insolent aristocracy. The senate was now essentially changed from that venerable assembly whom we have seen overthrowing Pyrrhus and Hannibal, as much by their virtues as their arms. It was no longer composed of those men who, when the Gauls burst into the city, seemed the tutelary deities of Rome. The senators were now only distinguished from the rest of the people by their luxurious habits. Their profligacy and corruption soon became strikingly manifest. In the misunderstanding with Jugurtha, which happened at this time, and of which we have spoken at length in the history of Numidia, the senate was several times bribed by this most unprincipled usurper; and the senators were, in fact, open to the offers of the highest bidder. Their venality was so outrageous, that Jugurtha was allowed to assassinate, with impunity, Adherbal, the heir to the Numidian throne; and, still later, in the streets of Rome, he murdered his cousin Massiva; while the senate, bought over to his side, failed to take notice of the outrage. It was this atrocity, however, that at last cost him his life and kingdom; for an army was subsequently sent out to Numidia, under Metellus, where the Roman arms prevailed, and where Jugurtha was finally captured, 106 B. C.

While these events were passing, tribes of northern barbarians, known as *Cimbri* and *Teutones*, directed their march toward the Roman provinces, and seriously menaced Western Italy. They ravaged a part of Gaul, where several battles were fought with them by the Romans. One, more terrible than the rest, in which eighty thousand Roman soldiers and forty thousand camp attendants were cut to pieces, excited the greatest consternation at Rome. Caius Marius, being deemed the fittest man to oppose an army of barbarians, in case they should cross the Alps, was four successive times elected consul. The whole available force of the republic was placed under his command. He trained his soldiers to endure extreme hardships, and marched against the Teutones, who were now actually entering Italy, by two different passes. One of these bands was intercepted, and entirely routed by Marius; but the other effected an entrance into Cisalpine Gaul, now Lombardy, where for some time they made frightful ravages; but at length a decisive victory was gained over them by the united forces of the two consuls, Marius and Catullus, and the invasion was completely crushed, 101 B. C. A second servile war, in Sicily, was concluded about this time, by the annihilation of the insurgents.

The great question which now occupied the ruling classes at Rome, and also created violent factions in the state, was, whether the Italians should be admitted to the Roman franchise. The nobles took part against the Italian allies, who, excited to hostility, formed a combination against Rome, and established an independent republic. Thus commenced the contest known as the *social war*, which lasted for three years, and drenched every part of Italy with blood. At the end of the third year, fortune was every where adverse to the allies; one by one they lost their best generals, and the spirit of resistance gradually died away. The senate now came to the conclusion that it would be better to yield to the demands of the Italian people, and granted the privileges of citizenship to the inhabitants of those cities who laid down their arms. Thus ended the social or Marsic war, which cost Italy the loss of three hundred thousand of the flower of her population, in the concessions which might have obviated it; and, from that time, all the people of Italy may be regarded as Roman. This event took place 88 B. C.

The old disputes between the patrician and plebeian factions now commenced with greater ferocity than ever, under the auspices of Sylla and Marius. The former was supported by the nobles; the latter by the popular party. A war with Mithridates, king of Pontus, afforded a cause of contention to the two rivals. This prince, having made himself master of Asia Minor, now menaced the possessions of Rome. Sylla was elected consul, for the purpose of taking the command; for Marius was now seventy years of age. The latter endeavored to obtain the office by intrigue; but being exposed, he, his son, and nine others, were outlawed, and took to flight. The adventures of the aged warrior, during his exile, are romantic and interesting. He was cast ashore on the coast of Italy, during a storm, and having put to sea in an open boat, a party of soldiers, in pursuit of him, galloped up, and called to the sailors to return, while Marius urged them to sail away with all speed. They did so; but, being afraid of the consequences, soon put him on shore again, and left him. He concealed himself for a time among the marshes, but, being discovered, was thrown into a dungeon at Minturnæ. The inhabitants, not venturing to put him openly to death, sent a public slave to kill him. This man, a Cimbrian by birth, could not face the destroyer of his nation, though unarmed, and in the seventieth year of his age. The terrible countenance of Marius appalled him. He fled from the dungeon; and the magistrates of Minturnæ, supposing such an effect could only be produced by the will of the gods, set the aged general at liberty, and furnished him with a vessel to carry him to Africa. But he had no sooner landed at Carthage, than Sextilius, the Roman governor of the province, sent word to him, that unless he quitted Africa, he should treat him as a public enemy. "Go, tell thy master," he replied to the messenger, "thou sawest Caius Marius sitting, an exile, amid the ruins of Carthage." In the following year, however, he returned to Rome.

Sylla had, in the mean time, left Italy with his army, to carry on the war with Mithridates. The latter was compelled to solicit peace, which was readily granted by Sylla, who desired to return to Rome, where his party had suffered the most cruel treatment from Marius, who, having raised an army of slaves and mercenaries, had gained possession of the city. The principal senators of the faction of Sylla were murdered, and Marius seized the consulship, which he held till his death, 86 B. C. Sylla now returned, and commenced an indiscriminate slaughter of all who had opposed him. He was joined by great numbers of partisans, amongst whom was a young man named *Pompeius*, afterward Pompey the Great. He ordered the execution of eight thousand prisoners, and then prepared a proscriptive list; that is, made a written statement of all suspicious persons, and set a price upon their heads. Many persons took advantage of this, to circulate false information against their enemies, or even creditors, so as to have the names of these put upon the list. Not only in Rome, but in all the cities of Italy, was this decimation of the population put in practice. The few who were able to escape, fled to Spain, where the Marian party was the strongest. Sylla was now invested with supreme power, for an indefinite period. He only exercised it three years; abdicating at the end of that time. He retired to the country, where he wrote his own memoirs, and soon after died. The Marian faction exciting disturbances in Spain, Pompey was sent, with a large army, to quell them, in which undertaking he was successful.

Five years after the death of Sylla, a Thracian, of the name of *Spartacus*, with a number of gladiators, escaped from a barrack, or fencing-school, at Capua, and took refuge in the crater of Mount Vesuvius. Here he was joined by vast numbers of slaves, gladiators, and robbers; and defeated, in succession, four consular armies, and plundered and ravaged the surrounding country. His forces soon increased to one hundred and twenty thousand men, and he was fired with the idea of taking Rome, and ruling all Italy. Approaching the capital, he was met by a large army, under the prætor Crassus. His forces were utterly routed, after a desperate and bloody action, he and forty thousand of his followers being killed. Those who escaped death on the field, were taken prisoners, and slain in cold blood, some time after. Spartacus died like a hero; and, though a slave and gladiator, seems not to have been destitute of noble qualities. When wounded in the leg, he fought upon his knees, covering himself with his buckler, and wielding his sword with his other hand; and when he fell, overpowered by superior numbers, he breathed his last upon a heap of Romans, who had fallen beneath his sword.

Pompey and Crassus were now appointed consuls. Pompey was admired for his personal character; and the wealth of Crassus obtained a consideration which his own merits could not have inspired. He sought to acquire popularity by largesses to the poorer classes, and even fed the greater part of the citizens, for three months. Pompey paid his court to the people, by restoring the tribunitial power, and repealing the most unpopular of the laws of Sylla. He was soon after placed at the head of an expedition against the freebooters on the Mediterranean Sea, where piracy had been practised from the earliest ages. In a few months, such were his skill and perseverance, this powerful band of marauders was broken up, and the prisoners were distributed as colonists in Asia Minor. Pompey now marched against Mithridates, king of Pontus, who had again declared war; he subdued and routed his armies, and established the Roman dominion over the greater part of Western Asia. Returning to Rome, he was honored with the most splendid triumphal procession that ever entered its gates. In this were exhibited the names of fifteen conquered kingdoms, eight hundred captured cities, one thousand castles subjugated, and twenty-nine cities repeopled.

But in the midst of this magnificence and apparent security, while the republic was thus adding distant territories to its dominions, Rome itself narrowly escaped destruction, from a deeply-laid plot, known as the conspiracy of Catiline. This person was a man of high birth, but his naturally bad character had been degraded and vilified by connection with the most profligate and dissipated associates. His ambition, which was insatiable and persevering, had been fired by the examples of Marius and Sylla, and he aspired to the supreme sovereignty of Rome. He found but little difficulty in gaining partisans, among that class of persons who have nothing to lose, and who are sure to be gainers by any social revolution. He represented them as oppressed by tyrants, who ground the mass for their own pleasure and profit; and held out to them, as incentives to rebellion, the abolition of debts, the proscription of the wealthy, and plunder and rapine for all his party. The plot was to have ramifications throughout Italy, the different parts of which were assigned to different leaders. The great obstacle to the success of the conspiracy, was the vigilance of

Cicero.

Cicero, the celebrated orator, and at that time consul. His murder was deemed a necessary preliminary to the undertaking. In this attempt, however, the assassins were foiled. Rome was now filled with the most alarming rumors; and in the midst of the general consternation, Catiline had the hardihood to present himself in the senate-house. Cicero, unable to restrain his indignation at the sight of the hardened traitor, poured forth upon him such a torrent of invective, that Catiline, overwhelmed with confusion, was unable to reply, but abruptly fled, declaring open war as he hastened from the Forum. The energy of Cicero, however, saved the country; the principal leaders were discovered and strangled; and an army sent against Catiline hemmed his forces in among the passes of the Apennines, where they were all slain, fighting with desperation to the last. The suppression of this conspiracy took place 62 B. C., and was the most glorious act in the life of Cicero. The senate bestowed upon him, in consequence, the honorable title of *Father of his Country.*

CHAPTER CCCXXXIX.

62 to 31 B. C.

Rise and Fall of Julius Cæsar — Brutus and Cassius — The Second Triumvirate — Battle of Actium — Octavius Cæsar sole Master of Rome.

Julius Cæsar, whom we have already mentioned, and whose abilities were, at this period, known and valued, began now to attract notice. Observing the growing jealousy of Pompey and Crassus, he resolved to turn their rivalry to his own advantage. He had warmly espoused the popular interests, and had become a great favorite with the people. To further his own schemes, he applied himself to reconcile the enmity existing between the two great leaders. In this he was successful. The three then joined in a scheme for dividing the provinces among themselves, and holding — each one in his own portion — the supreme authority. This union was called the *first triumvirate*, and was established 59 B. C. Pompey took Spain for his portion; Crassus, Syria for his; and Cæsar, Cisalpine Gaul for his. Pompey, who preferred remaining at Rome, in order to take advantage of any circumstance that might favor his views, sent a lieutenant to represent him in Spain. Cæsar and Crassus repaired to their provinces. The progress and fate of the latter we have already described, in the history of Parthia. Cæsar's victorious career in Gaul lasted nearly eight years; during which time, he invaded Britain twice, and actually conquered the southern part of the island. The Romans gained nothing, however, by the invasion, except some little knowledge of the country. Cæsar's exploits in Gaul, which will be more fully referred to in the history of that country, resulted in its complete subjection, 50 B. C.

The death of Crassus left the field of competition open to Pompey and Cæsar. Their former good will toward each other was now exchanged for open rivalry. The senate, who favored Pompey's interests, passed a decree, in 49 B. C., commanding Cæsar, who was still in Gaul, to disband his army before a specified day. Indignant at this treatment, after his long services in the camp, he resolved to overturn the faction by whom the republic was governed. The rapidity of his movements disconcerted his enemies, and his army soon reached the banks of the Rubicon, a small river, which divided Italy from Cisalpine Gaul. Struck with the gravity and importance of the step he was about to take, whose results could be nothing less than civil war and bloodshed in his own country, he is said to have paused, debating in his own mind whether to advance or recede. The stream of the Rubicon the Romans had ever been taught to regard as the sacred boundary of their domestic empire. "If I pass this river," said Cæsar, "what misery shall I bring upon my country! and if I stop where I am, I am undone!" He hesitated still; when, as if yielding to an irresistible impulse, and exclaiming, "*Alea jacta est!*" — The die is cast! — spurred his horse into the water. His army followed, and advanced into the heart of the country. Pompey's genius and usual good fortune seemed now to forsake him; his troops deserted by thousands; the senate and his most attached partisans abandoned Rome; and Pompey himself fled to Greece.

Cæsar overran all Italy in less than two months, and, after a stay of six days in Rome, departed to attack Pompey's lieutenant in Spain. He subdued the whole of that country in forty days, and immediately commenced preparations for following Pompey and giving him battle. The latter was aware of his intention, however, and collected an immense army from the various provinces of the East. He had a fleet of five hundred ships; and often in his camp were to be seen from one to two hundred senators, among whom were Cicero and Cato. Cæsar's army of twenty-three thousand men crossed the Adriatic, from Brundusium to Dyrrachium. He himself crossed in an open fishing boat, with a single sailor, who was ignorant of the name of his passenger: the roughness of the weather seeming to intimidate the fisherman, Cæsar encouraged him with the words which have since become famous "Fear nothing: you carry Cæsar and his fortunes.' The confidence of Pompey's army, which consisted of fifty-two thousand men, was raised to the highest pitch on seeing the inferior number of the enemy. They looked upon victory as certain, and the officers disputed about dividing the spoils before the battle was fought. They disposed of all the offices and dignities in the republic, and elected the consuls for several years to come. The most confident even sent to Rome to hire houses suitable to the offices which they expected to enjoy after the victory.

The memorable battle of Pharsalia followed; the effeminate and unskilled recruits who formed the bulk of Pompey's army were, however, no match for the long-tried and hardy veterans, who, under their great leader's guidance, hardly knew what it was to suffer defeat. Pompey's rout was overwhelming and irretrievable, and his flying squadrons were slaughtered in large numbers. The auxiliary troops were put to the sword, but the Romans laid down their arms and received quarter. Pompey fled to Mitylene, from whence he sailed for Egypt, hoping to find protection at the court of that country, as he had been of service to the father of the king then on the throne; but it happened that this prince, who was very young, was at open war with his sister Cleopatra, who was desirous of gaining sole possession of the throne. The young king's ministers represented to him that, in order to secure the alliance of Cæsar, it would be more politic to put Pompey to death than to afford him the protection he was coming to seek. The king consented, and Pompey was assassinated before he reached the shore. Such was the end of Pompey the Great, a man of commanding talents and of most amiable character. But all his virtues were overwhelmed by his vanity and ambition, which led him to put his fate and that of the republic into the scale against the fortunes of Cæsar. He was a better man than his antagonist, but not so well fitted for empire, as he had not his rival's energy to restrain the violence of his followers. Incapable of sustaining himself at the height which he had reached, he fell rapidly, and lost much of his fame by the manner of his fall.

Cæsar soon arrived in Egypt; and his next task was

to arrange the disputed succession of the Egyptian crown, Cleopatra and her brother being the rival candidates. Cæsar was seduced by the charms of the Eastern princess, and, contrary to the expectations of the king's party, decided in her favor. A struggle followed, in which Cæsar was ultimately victorious, leaving Cleopatra in peaceful possession of the throne. The conqueror now set out for Syria, where Pharnaces, the son of Mithridates, had raised an insurrection against the Roman government. Cæsar crushed the revolt so easily, that he described the campaign in three words: "*Veni, vidi, vici*"—I came, I saw, I conquered. Having thus settled the affairs of Egypt and Syria, he returned to Rome, where the greatest confusion reigned, caused by the quarrels of Mark Antony and Dolabella. The former had been intrusted with the management of affairs during Cæsar's absence, and the latter was tribune. Their disagreements were with some difficulty reconciled, and Cæsar then applied himself to the war now breaking out in Africa, under the direction of Cato, governor of Utica, and the sons of Pompey. A league was formed by these individuals against Cæsar, which was strengthened by an alliance with Juba, king of Numidia. But the great Roman general, who never gave his enemies time to concert their plans, embarked with a large army for Africa, gained a decisive victory over Juba, and then, marching upon Utica, compelled it to surrender. The submission of this town is memorable on account of the voluntary death of Cato. He calmly put an end to his own existence, rather than witness the final overthrow of the republic. Retiring to his chamber, on the night of the surrender of Utica, he composed himself to read Plato's dialogue on the immortality of the soul. He then lay down, and slept soundly for a few hours. Toward morning, he rose and stabbed himself with his sword, dying, as he had lived, a Stoic. He foresaw that Cæsar would become the sole and absolute ruler of the Roman empire, unless some great effort were made by the republicans. In his attempts to preserve the free constitution he failed, and died rather than survive it. He was afterward called *Cato Uticensis*, from the place of his death.

The return of Cæsar to Rome was hailed with tumultuous joy, and was followed by a season of festivity. The senate granted him the dictatorship for ten years, and caused a statue of him to be erected, bearing the inscription, "Cæsar the Demigod." Four triumphs were decreed to him: one for Gaul, one for Egypt, one for Pontus, and the last for Numidia. In one of these, two thousand eight hundred and twenty-two golden crowns were borne in the triumphal procession. Cæsar gave a banquet to the people of Rome at twenty-two thousand tables, placed in the streets, and provided entertainments for them at the theatres. As he returned home from the banquet, lights were borne on each side of him by forty elephants. But he was soon called from these festivities to suppress a rebellion in Spain, headed by the sons of Pompey. The war lasted several months, but resulted in Cæsar's gaining a decided victory on the plains of Munda, which put an end to the civil wars. He was made dictator for life on his arrival at Rome, and became an absolute sovereign in every thing but the title. He now turned his thoughts to legislation, of which we can say but little, as his plans for the improvement of the state were frustrated by his premature death. He projected many vast designs for the benefit of the republic which he was not allowed to carry into execution. He contemplated the rebuilding of several cities, the draining of the Pomptine Marshes, the formation of a new channel for the Tiber, and of a capacious harbor at its mouth, and the cutting of a canal across the Isthmus of Corinth. He made his famous reform of the calendar about this period, which exists to the present day, and of which a word or two will not be out of place. The old Roman months had never made a complete year, so that, from time to time, it became necessary to insert, or "intercalate," as it was called, an additional month, to bring the seasons into their proper places. Cæsar remedied all this by making the months correspond to the real length of the year, which he made to consist of three hundred and sixty-five days, beginning on the first of January; but, finding that there were really about six hours more than three hundred and sixty-five days in a year, he ordered that one day should be added to every fourth year, which is what we call *leap year*. It was discovered, many centuries later, that there was a trifling error in this calculation, and that a year consists of three hundred and sixty-five days, five hours, and forty-nine minutes. A mistake of eleven minutes a year had, therefore, been made, which, as time advanced, threatened again to throw the calendar into confusion. This error was rectified, in all Catholic countries, in the sixteenth century: in England, in the year 1752, in consequence of this trifling miscalculation, the almanacs were ten days in advance of the seasons; so that ten days were omitted in the year, to bring them right again. With these alterations, the calendar remains as Cæsar arranged it; and the year of three hundred and sixty-five days is called the *Julian year*.

It must be confessed that the chief acts of Cæsar, when he became perpetual dictator, were of a somewhat despotic nature; for he assumed the right of disposing of half the offices of state, and of recommending candidates for the rest. He gave places in the senate to whom he pleased, and largely increased the number of senators. He looked upon himself not as the chief of a republic, but as the sovereign lord of a people who were to be ruled by his will. But his exercise of power was marked with great clemency and wisdom: he granted the freedom of the city to all physicians and professors of the liberal arts; he confined the judicial power to the senators and knights; and ordered that no freeman, between twenty and forty years of age, should remain more than three years out of Italy. But all his genius could not compensate, in the minds of his countrymen, for the crime of elevating himself upon the ruins of the republic. He possessed already the full authority of a monarch; but the Romans were more willing to grant the power than the title. The name of *king* was insufferably odious to them; and the belief that Cæsar was aiming at a crown led to the formation of a conspiracy for his destruction. Sixty senators were implicated in it many of them his personal friends. Brutus and Cassius, whose lives he had spared at the battle of Pharsalia, were at the head of the plot, which was to be put in execution on the ides of March. He is said to have been aware of this conspiracy; but, saying that he would rather die at once than live in fear of assassination, he entered the senate-house as usual, and took his customary seat. This was the 15th of March, 44 B. C. At a concerted signal, the conspirators rushed upon him, and one, named Casca, stabbed him in the shoulder. Cæsar turned upon him, and, with his stylus, or steel writing rod, wounded him in the arm. The assailants now gathered round him; but he repulsed them, and stood his ground firmly till he saw Brutus among the conspirators: from that moment he made no attempt to save himself; he muffled his face in his cloak, and, casting upon Brutus a look of reproach, and saying simply, "And thou too, Brutus!" sank down at the base of Pompey's statue, pierced by twenty-three wounds.

Thus perished, in his fifty-sixth year, Julius Cæsar—the greatest man in all Roman history. His talents were only equalled by his ambition. He sought glory always by worthy means when possible, but did not hesitate to reach the accomplishment of his towering wishes by trampling upon life and liberty. In private affairs, he was extravagant of money, his debts at one time amounting to over a million of dollars; but, in public concerns, he did not appear greedy of wealth. It was said of him that he could at the same time employ his ear to listen, his eye to read, his hand to write, and his mind to dictate. He sought dominion as if impelled by fate; and once said to the inhabitants of a village, "I would rather be first here than second in Rome." He left behind him an account of his battles, written from day to day. These Commentaries, beside furnishing a fund of authentic narrative for history, are admired for their elegance of style. He was courageous, self-possessed, clement, and generous; and, though of slender make and of delicate constitution, was able to make long marches, and seldom stopped for repose, sleeping on the way in a litter or chariot. As a general, he was equal to the greatest and most admired commanders the world ever produced; indeed, hardly one can be compared with him, with the exception, perhaps, of Hannibal. As an orator, he was second to Cicero alone. In appearance, he was tall and commanding, with an open countenance, fair complexion, and fine, dark eyes: he was even reported to be the handsomest man in Rome. According to the old Valerian law, Cæsar was legally put to death; yet the consequences of this act were in the highest degree pernicious to the Roman people, and began to be manifested before the blood in Cæsar's veins had grown cold.

Julius Cæsar writing his Commentaries.

The senators, frightened at their own act, fled terrified to their homes. The people, worked upon by the arts of Mark Antony, who seized this opportunity of gratifying his own ambition, under the pretence of promoting justice, stormed the senate-house, and tore up the benches to make a funeral pile for Cæsar's body. The conspirators took refuge in the Capitol, which they garrisoned with gladiators. Their houses were set on fire with flaming brands, and they themselves soon fled, seeing that they were no longer safe. A second triumvirate was now formed by Antony, in conjunction with Lepidus, an intriguing demagogue, and Octavius, the heir of Cæsar. These three conspirators against the liberties of Rome met on an island in one of the branches of the Po, 43 B. C. A partition of the whole Roman world was made, Antony taking Gaul, Lepidus Spain, and Octavius Africa and the islands of the Mediterranean. Italy and the eastern provinces were to remain in common. Each one of the triumvirs bound himself to give up his most intimate friend, in case his death should be deemed necessary by the others. It was also settled that Lepidus should take charge of the capital, while Octavius and Antony should march against Brutus and Cassius, who had collected two powerful armies in Macedonia and Syria, and had united them at Smyrna. These plans met with no opposition at Rome, and thus was established the second triumvirate.

One of the first acts of these remorseless conspirators was to publish a proscription; and all the horrors of the reign of Sylla were acted over again. Lepidus gave up his brother Paulus, Antony sacrificed his uncle Lucius, and Octavius allowed Cicero to be murdered. Two hundred senators, two thousand knights and citizens, were massacred the same year. They were hunted from place to place, and all that escaped fled to Brutus's camp, trusting their fate to the issue of the coming war. The triumvirs, having satisfied their desire for bloodshed, raised a formidable army, of which Antony and Octavius, as previously agreed, took the command. They passed into Greece, and met the forces of Brutus and Cassius on the plains of Philippi, in Macedonia, 42 B. C. The republican army consisted of eighty thousand foot and twenty thousand horse; that of the triumvirs amounted to a hundred thousand foot and thirteen thousand horse. The Roman world looked on in breathless suspense; for the fate of the republic depended on the result of a single battle. The contest began with marked success on the part of Brutus's army; but fortune soon deserted him, and the soldiers every where began to yield. Cassius made every possible effort to rally his infantry, stopping those who fled, and seizing the standards with his own hand. But the unfortunate commander was unable to inspire the timorous fugitives with courage, and was found soon after dead in his tent. The rout now became general, and the whole army, seized by a sudden panic, gave way at once. Brutus threw himself upon his sword; and with him expired the last hope of Roman liberty.

The triumvirs were now masters of the civilized world, and made a cruel use of their victory. They put to death, without mercy, all their political opponents, literally extirpating the republicans. Octavius distributed lands in Italy among his soldiers, for the purpose of attaching them to his interest, so that, whenever he should find an opportunity to get rid of his two colleagues in the triumvirate, he might be assured of the support of the veteran troops. Antony paid a visit to

Greece, where he was received with flattery and attention. From thence he passed into Asia, where all the monarchs of the East who acknowledged the Roman power came to pay him obeisance. He proceeded from kingdom to kingdom, attended by a succession of sovereigns, exacting contributions, distributing favors, and giving away crowns as he pleased. When at Tarsus, in Cilicia, he summoned Cleopatra to attend his court, and account for her having furnished assistance to Cassius at the battle of Pharsalia: she came, and as we have related in the history of Egypt, in her company Antony forgot his schemes of ambition, and his hopes of empire. Following her to Egypt, he neglected all public affairs, and his duties as master of half the Roman empire. The Romans blushed to see him a slave to the caprices of an abandoned woman. His best friends deserted him, and he lost reputation and name. His wife, Octavia, sister of Octavius, went to Egypt in the hope of reclaiming him; but the infatuated Antony refused to see her, and dismissed her ignominiously from the country. Octavius, fired with this insult, made a formal declaration of war against Antony, and both sides prepared for a contest which was to place the fortunes of Rome in the hands of a single master.

Antony's force comprised all the military strength of the East: his land army numbered one hundred thousand foot, and twelve thousand horse; and his flee amounted to five hundred ships of war. Octavius's forces were inferior in number, but much superior in discipline, to those of Antony. The rival powers at length assembled near Actium, on the Greek coas' of the Adriatic, 31 B. C. For several months they remained in view of each other without coming to an engagement. At length, Antony, instigated by Cleopatra, who had followed him in the campaign, resolved to trust his fate to the issue of a naval battle. The fight was long and severe: success was doubtful, when Cleopatra, struck with a sudden panic, fled with her squadron from the engagement. This turned the fortune of the day; for Antony, regardless of his character and name, fled after her; his fate, and that of Cleopatra, have been elsewhere detailed.

Thus ended the Roman republic, in the elevation to the supreme power of the first of its emperors. The people, weary of the oppressions of the aristocracy gladly sought shelter in the sway of a single master. The city was inhabited by a motley population, collected from all quarters of the world, and speaking diverse languages; and being thus deficient in patriotic principles, was better fitted for a monarchy than a republic.

ROMAN EMPIRE.

CHAPTER CCCXL.

30 B. C. to A. D. 81.

Emperors of Rome from Augustus to Titus — Destruction of Herculaneum and Pompeii.

We must here pause to take a survey of the Roman empire, which, under Augustus, had attained its greatest splendor and territorial extension. It comprised the following countries, in Europe; Italy, Gaul as far as he Rhine, nearly all Spain, Rhœtia, Noricum, Illyricum, Macedonia, Epirus, Greece, Thrace, Mœsia, Dacia, Pannonia, and part of Britain; in Asia, Colchis, Iberia, Albania, Syria, Palestine, Arabia, the Bosphorus, and the several states of Asia Minor; in Africa, nearly the whole of its northern coast, including Mauritania, Numidia, the territory of Carthage, Cyrenaica, and Egypt. The whole extent of the empire from north to south was eighteen hundred miles, and up wards of three thousand from east to west. It includ ed the finest portions of the old world, and was more than equal in extent to modern Europe, its population being estimated at one hundred and twenty million.

Throughout this huge assemblage of races and communities, national feelings and recollections were obliterated, or merged beneath the overshadowing influence of imperial Rome. The Latin language was spoken in Italy, Gaul, and Africa; Greek in nearly all the East; and Celtic in Britain and the north of Gaul; Syrian, Coptic, and Armenian, &c., in other parts of the empire. The great mass of the rural population preserved, however, their provincial dialects. Six classes of inhabitants are distinguishable at this period. 1. The senatorial families; 2. The inhabitants of large towns, living on the luxury of the rich, and sharing in their corruption; 3. The inhabitants of small towns, poor and despised; 4. Husbandmen; 5. Slaves; 6. Banditti, occupying the woods and mountains, and living by robbery.

Under Augustus, the city of Rome was unsurpassed for magnificence, wealth, and luxury. Its architectural splendor properly dates from the reign of Augustus, who boasted that he "found it of brick, and left it of marble." The palaces, triumphal arches, columns, porticos, obelisks, fountains, baths, temples, theatres and circuses, were almost without number; and their ruins at the present day strike the beholder with amazement. Thirty-one great roads centred in Rome. These, issuing from the Forum, traversed Italy, pervaded the provinces, and terminated on the frontiers of the empire. The Tiber was spanned by eight bridges, and travellers entered the city by thirty gates. The whole plain between the Quirinal Hill and the river was one mass of temples, arcades, and places of amusement, uninterrupted by any private habitations.

Amid all the adulation of the senate and people, Augustus did not forget that he owed his elevation to the army. He therefore exerted himself to attach the soldiers to his interests. He dispersed his veterans over Italy in thirty-two colonies, often dispossessing the former occupants to make way for the new settlers. He maintained seventeen legions in Europe, and eight in Asia and Africa. The emperor's person was protected by a body of nine thousand men, called the *prætorian guard.* Two powerful fleets were established, one at Ravenna, to guard the Adriatic, and one at Micenum, near Naples, to protect the western part of the Mediterranean. The revenues of the empire amounted to two hundred millions of dollars; and this sum was hardly sufficient to defray the expenses of the government. The character of Augustus changed very much on the assumption of supreme power. He became distinguished for clemency and moderation, and his administration displayed him as truly anxious to insure the happiness of the people intrusted to his charge. He assumed the dignity of chief pontiff; so that, like the ancient kings, he was at the head of the state religion. The people were not directly taxed for the vast improvements undertaken during his reign, which were made at the expense of Augustus himself, and wealthy persons who were stimulated by his example.

Roman civilization was rapidly disseminated through the empire. Learning was cultivated; the country improved; new towns were built; villas and ornamental gardens constructed; and the people taught many useful arts, of which they were till then ignorant. The agriculture of Europe was much ameliorated by the introduction of the flowers and fruits of the East, and of the cultivation of flax from Egypt. Glass was manufactured at Alexandria, and sent to Rome. Paper was also made in large quantities from the papyrus plant. Tapestry was made at Padua, and steel goods of all kinds at Como. Ice and cheese were brought to Rome from the Alpine districts; pork, geese, and salt from Gaul; spices, perfumes, and precious stones from the East; and an abundance of gold, silver, and iron, as tribute from conquered nations. The Romans purchased also manufactured silk of a people who came to their Eastern dominions from some unknown country beyond: it is generally supposed, however, to have been Western China. This was so rare, that it was sold for its weight in gold, and the thicker kinds were often unwoven for the purpose of manufacturing slighter ones. The reign of Augustus is considered the era of learning and the fine arts, and is often called the *Augustan age.* The poets, romancers, and historians were patronized by the emperor: among these were Horace, Virgil, Ovid, and Livy.

Although the emperor concentrated nearly all the authority in his own person, yet he was easy of access, and gained great applause for his affability and condescension. On one occasion, having been informed that a certain knight squandered his patrimony in an unworthy manner, he summoned him to appear before him; but finding the charge false, he acquitted the knight, upon which the latter said, "Another time, Cæsar, before you listen to an accusation against an honest man, take care that your informant be honest." Augustus recognized the existing laws, and gave them their proper course, though by his word alone he could condemn or acquit whom he pleased; he even plead in person for those whom he desired to protect. One of his soldiers entreated his assistance in a cause which was about to be heard, and Augustus bade him apply to an advocate. "Ah," replied the veteran, "it was not by proxy that I served you at the battle of Actium." Cæsar was so struck by the answer, that he pleaded the soldier's cause, and gained it. These instances may serve to show the familiarity to which the emperor admitted his subjects, notwithstanding his possession of the sovereign power, and his freedom from all responsibility.

In the reign of Augustus, a great part of Germany was brought under the dominion of Rome. The German wars, which occurred about nineteen years after the battle of Actium, were conducted by Tiberius and Drusus, the sons-in-law of the emperor. Very little is known of these contests, except that the Germans were usually defeated, while their lands were ravaged, and great numbers of women and children carried away for slaves. Eventually, however, they partly recovered their independence by the destruction of a large Roman army under Varus. This defeat Augustus did not long survive. In the seventy-fourth year of his age, he began to think of withdrawing from the fatigues of government, and of making Tiberius his partner in the empire. This he did, and named him as his successor. He then ordered the census of Rome to be taken, which showed the population of the city to be four million one hundred and thirty-seven thousand. He was shortly after taken ill, and died at Nola, in Campania. His death caused general and unfeigned grief throughout the empire, and the honors paid to his memory seem to have had no bounds. Temples were erected to his name, and it was asserted that he had been seen ascending to heaven.

Tiberius, the successor of Augustus, had hitherto

lived in a state of profound dissimulation, and had concealed his real character from the emperor. His natural disposition was arbitrary, suspicious, and cruel, and he proved a most tyrannical sovereign. His jealousy was soon aroused by the popularity of his nephew, Germanicus, whom he had been compelled, by Augustus, to declare his heir. He appointed him governor of the Eastern provinces, and at the same time gave orders to have him poisoned on his arrival at his destination. He then abandoned himself to all kinds of profligacy and vice. In order to have more leisure for the indulgence of his pleasures, he retired to the beautiful Island of Capreæ, near Naples, leaving the cares of government in the hands of his prime minister, Sejanus, whose depravity was equal to his own. He soon obtained the entire control of the empire, and, to aid in this, employed hosts of spies and informers. He put to death many of the most eminent Romans, after making them undergo the mockery of a trial. His most important act was that of increasing the number of the prætorian guards, who formed the military force of the capital and the body-guard of the emperor. In time they became so powerful, that they took upon themselves to set up and depose the emperors at pleasure. They were not very unlike the janizaries of the Turkish empire. The sway of Sejanus was unlimited, and the number of statues erected to him exceeded those of the emperor: he was more dreaded than the tyrant who actually wore the purple.

Tiberius soon grew jealous of his minister, and caused him to be put to death on a charge of conspiracy; and a new favorite, Macro, was chosen to supply his place. This minister, in his turn, conspired against the life of his master, and assassinated him in the twenty-third year of his reign, A. D. 37. The accession of *Caligula*, the son of Germanicus, whom Tiberius had named his successor, was hailed with great joy both by the senate and the people. By some concessions which he made, and other acts of generosity, he became so popular, that, when he was attacked by sickness soon after, sacrifices were offered in every temple for his recovery. It is probable that his brain was disordered during his illness, for his subsequent acts were those of a madman, whose insanity displayed itself in reckless cruelty and extravagance. His brief reign of four years is one of the most frightful periods of Roman history. He ordered all the prisoners in Rome to be thrown to wild beasts without trial, and put a large number of senators to death. Every ten days, he sent supplies of human victims to his menagerie, which he called "clearing his accounts." He once said that he wished the Roman people had but one neck, that he might despatch them all at a single blow. He erected a temple to himself, and established a college of priests to superintend his own worship. He had a favorite horse, named *Incitatus*, to whom he frequently sent invitations to dine at the royal table, where he was fed on gilded oats, and drank wine from jewelled goblets. He was on the point of raising this quadruped to the consulship, when Incitatus died, and received a magnificent funeral. The Romans soon became weary of a monster equally wicked and contemptible, and a successful conspiracy terminated his existence, A. D. 41.

Claudius, uncle to Caligula, was raised to the throne by the conspirators. He was of weak intellect, and suffered himself to be guided by unprincipled favorites. Notwithstanding his imbecility, however, he undertook a war against Britain; and the campaigns thus commenced, led to the complete subjugation of the southern part of the island. A large aqueduct was constructed at this period, which supplied Rome with water down to the middle ages. Claudius had one son; but he had married a second wife, named *Agrippina*, who had also a son, known in history by the name of *Nero*. The empress, who was ambitious and crafty, prevailed upon Claudius to name her son as his successor, in preference to his own son, Britannicus. She then poisoned him, that he might not have an opportunity to alter his will, A. D. 54. Thus died the unfortunate Claudius, who was, perhaps, more to be pitied than condemned.

Nero.

Nero was but seventeen years old at his accession, and possessed great natural talents, but a character perverted by bad examples and by familiarity with vice. For five years, he governed with moderation and justice; but soon became weary under the restraint imposed upon him by his mother, who, finding herself neglected, threatened to transfer the throne to Britannicus. This threat, by inspiring Nero with fear, broke the feeble restraints that withheld the young tyrant from crime. He resolved that his brother should perish, and committed his first murder with all the coolness of an accomplished assassin. He invited the young Britannicus to a feast: the unfortunate prince had scarcely touched with his lips the fatal cup, when the subtle poison chilled his senses. He fell back on the couch and expired. The corpse was carried out, the funeral rites were performed in haste and without pomp, the body being painted white to conceal the change of color effected by the poison. But the rain, falling from heaven in torrents, rendered the artifice useless, and exposed the crime. Agrippina was soon after murdered in her bed. Nero then made a tour through Italy, and appeared on the stage at Naples, as an opera singer. His passion for music amounted to an absolute mania, and his greatest ambition was, to be thought the finest singer in the world. Soon after his return to Rome, a dreadful conflagration broke out, which lasted six days and seven nights, and destroyed the greater part of the city. It was said that the emperor himself was the author of this terrible calamity. This is not certain, though it is well known that he showed no anxiety to avert the flames, but watched them from a tower, where he sang the "Taking of Ilium," accompanying himself upon the harp. Many libraries and works of art perished in the fire, which is an important event in the history of Rome, as the city was rebuilt upon an improved plan. The Christians, who were at this period beginning to attract notice, were charged by Nero with having fired the city; and the persecution raised against them on this account was dreadful in the extreme. Some were covered with the skins of wild beasts, and, in that disguise, devoured by dogs. Some were crucified, and others burnt alive. "When the day was not sufficient for their tortures," says Tacitus, "the flames in which they perished served to illuminate the night."

The crimes of Nero now became so atrocious, that a conspiracy was formed against him, in which a great number of the nobles were engaged; but it was discovered, and all concerned were put to death. Among the victims were Lucan the poet and Seneca the philosopher. About this time, Nero killed his wife Poppæa by a kick. He made a visit to Greece, to display his skill at the Olympic games. While thus engaged, the rebellion, of which we have spoken in detail in the history of the Jews, broke out in Palestine, which led, in the end, to the dispersion of the Jewish nation. A general revolt now took place in Gaul and Spain, and the soldiers in the latter country proclaimed as emperor *Servius Galba*, a general over seventy years of age, who marched to Rome at the head of the insurgent army. Nero received the account of Galba's revolt while he was at supper in Rome, and was so struck with terror, that he overturned the table with his foot. From that moment he considered his ruin as certain. The miserable emperor endeavored to poison himself, but was baffled: the revolt became general: he ran from house to house, but every door was shut. He called upon his gladiators to kill him, but none would obey. Then rushing desperately forth, he seemed bent upon throwing himself into the Tiber; but his courage failed. One of his freedmen, named Phaon, taking pity on his distress, offered to conceal him in his own country house, about four miles distant, and Nero accepted the offer with joy. He started with four domestics. The journey, though short, was crowded with adventures. An earthquake shook the ground as he passed along, and thunder and lightning accompanied his steps. He heard confused noises from the camp, and the cries of the people invoking curses and breathing vengeance upon him. A traveller meeting him on the way said, "There go men in pursuit of Nero." His horse soon after took fright at a dead body that lay in the road; and Nero, dropping the handkerchief that concealed his face, was recognized by a soldier who was passing. He fled into a thicket, and from thence gained the house of Phaon. He here made several ineffectual attempts to put an end to his life, but finally, with the assistance of his secretary, placed a dagger at his throat and inflicted a mortal wound, as the pursuing soldiers entered the room. His body was privately, though honorably interred, and many of the lower ranks, whose love he had won by his prodigality, lamented his loss and brought flowers to his tomb. *Galba*, his successor, was proclaimed emperor A. D. 68.

This event was followed by the greatest confusion imaginable, four persons being raised to the throne in the short space of eighteen months. It would be useless to recount the scenes of violence and bloodshed which followed. Galba reigned but seven months. His niggardly economy procured him the resentment of the prætorian guard, who murdered him, and proclaimed emperor a very rich man, named *Otho*. In the mean time, the German legions, stationed on the frontiers of the Rhine, had chosen their commander, *Vitellius*, emperor, and marched with all speed upon Rome, to depose Otho. A battle was fought between the two rivals, near the town of Cremona, where Otho was defeated, and put an end to his own existence, having held the supreme power during the space of three months. Vitellius occupied the throne just long enough to become celebrated throughout the world for his gluttony. One of his favorite dishes was an olio, composed of the sounds of the fish called *scarrus*, the brains of woodcocks, the tongues of peacocks, and the spawn of lampreys from the Caspian Sea. This luxurious combination was called the "shield of Minerva." The Roman troops in the East, having heard of the defeat of Otho, had proclaimed their general, *Vespasian*, as his successor, and an insurrection broke out in Rome, in which Vitellius was murdered. Vespasian ascended the throne A. D. 69. He is described as a very excellent man, plain in his manners, upright in his conduct, and free from tyranny. He governed wisely, and soon restored order at Rome. His son Titus was left to carry on the war against the Jews, and the siege of Jerusalem soon commenced. Vespasian invited to Rome the most celebrated masters and artificers from every part of the world. He built the celebrated amphitheatre, known by the name of the

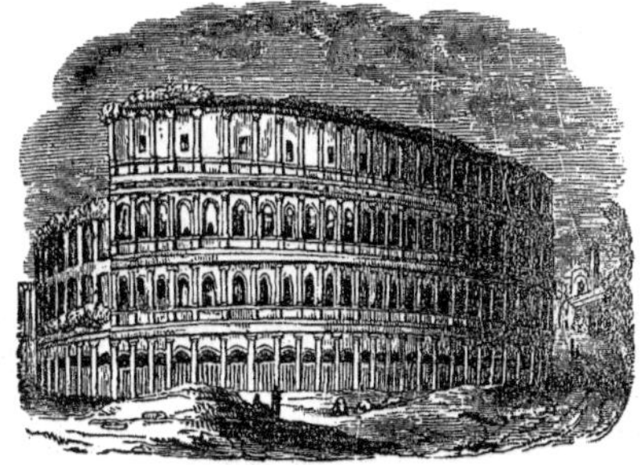

The Coliseum.

Coliseum. He founded new cities, and repaired the old ones, which had suffered from the devastations of his predecessors. He died after a reign of ten years, in Campania, A. D. 79.

He was succeeded by his son *Titus*, who was called by his subjects "the love and delight of human kind." In his youth, he had been fond of pleasure and dissipation, but he reformed his habits on ascending the throne, and became a pattern of regularity and moderation. Having called to mind one evening that he had done no beneficent act within the last twenty-four hours, he exclaimed, "I have lost a day!" His reign was short and marked by public calamities: fire consumed a great part of the city; a pestilence thinned the population, and an eruption of Mount Vesuvius caused the ruin of Herculaneum and Pompeii. This calamity was not so destructive of human life as many earthquakes and inundations that have since happened; but it has a degree of interest peculiar to itself, as having been the means of preserving to our times, entire and unchanged, two towns of the ancient Romans exactly as they were in the times of Titus Cæsar. In this catastrophe, Pliny the elder perished, and his nephew, Pliny the younger, has given a most interesting account of the event, from which we extract the following passage: —

"My uncle was at that time, with the fleet under his command, at Misenum. On the 24th of August, about one in the afternoon, my mother desired him to observe a cloud which appeared, of a very unusual size and shape. He had just returned from enjoying the benefit of the sun, and after bathing in cold water and taking a slight repast, had retired to his study. He immediately rose, and went out upon an eminence, from which he might more distinctly view this very singular phenomenon. It was not at that distance discernible from what mountain this cloud issued, but it was found afterward to proceed from Vesuvius. I cannot give a more exact description of its figure, than by comparing it to that of a pine-tree; for it shot up to a great height, in the form of a tall trunk, which spread at the top into a sort of branches, occasioned, I suppose, either by the force of the internal vapor which impelled the cloud upward, decreasing in strength as it advanced, or by the cloud being pressed back by its own weight, and thus expanding. It appeared sometimes bright, and sometimes dark and spotted, apparently more or less impregnated with earth and cinders.

"This uncommon appearance excited my uncle's philosophical curiosity to take a nearer view of it. He accordingly ordered a light vessel to be prepared, and offered me the liberty, if I thought proper, to attend him. I rather chose to continue the employment in which I was engaged, for it happened that he had given me a certain writing to copy. As he was going out of the house with his tablets in his hand, he was met by the sailors belonging to the galleys stationed at Retina, from which they had fled in the utmost terror, for, that port being situated at the foot of Vesuvius, they had no other way to escape than by sea. They conjured him, therefore, not to proceed and expose his life to such imminent danger. He altered his intention, and instead of gratifying his philosophical spirit, he resigned it to the more magnanimous principle of aiding the distressed.

"With this view, he ordered the fleet immediately to put to sea, and went himself on board, with an intention of assisting not only Retina, but the other towns which stood thick upon that beautiful coast. Hastening to the place, therefore, from which others fled with the utmost terror, he steered his direct course to the point of danger, and with so much calmness and presence of mind as to be able to make and dictate his observations upon the appearance and progress of that dreadful scene. He was now so near the mountain, that the cinders, which grew thicker and hotter the more he advanced, fell into the ships, together with pumice-stones and black pieces of burning rock. They were likewise in danger, not only of being left aground by the sudden retreat of the sea, but also from the vast fragments which rolled down from the mountain and obstructed all the shore. Here he stopped to consider whether he should return back, to which the pilot advising him, 'Fortune,' said he, 'befriends the brave: steer to Pomponianus.'

"Pomponianus was then at Stabiæ, separated by a gulf, which the sea, after many windings, forms upon that shore. Pomponianus had already sent his baggage on board; for though he was not at that time in actual danger, yet being extremely near, he was determined, if it should increase, to put to sea as soon as the wind should change. It was favorable, however, for carrying my uncle to Pomponianus, whom he found in the greatest consternation; and embracing him with tenderness, he encouraged and exhorted him to keep up his spirits. The more to dissipate his fears, he ordered his servants, with an air of unconcern, to carry him to the baths; and after having bathed, he sat down to supper with cheerfulness, or at least the appearance of it.

"In the mean while, the fire of Vesuvius flamed forth from several parts of the mountain with great violence, which the darkness of the night contributed to render still more visible and dreadful. But my uncle, in order to calm the apprehensions of his friend, assured him it was only the conflagration of the villages which the country people had abandoned. After this, he retired to rest, and was so little discomposed as to fall into a deep sleep. The court which led to his apartment being now almost filled with stones and ashes, it would have been impossible, if he had delayed much longer, for him to have made his way out; it was, therefore, thought proper to awaken him. He got up, and joined Pomponianus and the rest of the company. They consulted together whether it would be most prudent to trust to the houses, which now shook from side to side with violent convulsions, or flee to the open fields, where the stones and cinders fell in large showers, and threatened them with instant destruction.

"In this distress, they resolved for the fields, as the less dangerous of the two — a resolution which, while the rest of the company were hurried into by their fears, my uncle embraced upon cool and deliberate consideration. They went out, having pillows tied upon their heads with napkins, as a defence against the storm of stones which rained round them.

"It was now day every where else, but *there* a deeper darkness prevailed than in the blackest night; they had, however, torches and other lights. They thought it expedient to go down farther upon the shore, in order to observe if they might safely put out to sea, but they found the waves still running excessively high. There, my uncle, having drunk a draught or two of cold water, laid himself down upon a sailcloth, when immediately the flames, preceded by a strong smell of sulphur, dispersed the rest of the company and forced him to rise. He raised himself up with the assistance of two of his servants, and instantly fell down dead. He was suffocated, as I conjecture, by some noxious vapor, having always had weak lungs, and being frequently subject to a difficulty of breathing. As soon as it was light again, which was not till the third day after, his body was found entire, and without any marks of violence, exactly in the posture in which he fell, and looking more like a man asleep than dead."

This is the only account of the fate of any individual who perished by this awful visitation; and the ancient writers mention the fact of the destruction of these cities so slightly, that the statement might have been doubted, but for their accidental discovery in sinking a well in the early part of the last century. Streets and squares have since been laid open, houses examined, cellars excavated, and the whole manner of living in those ancient times been brought to light.

The remains of human beings have been found in situations which show how instantaneously death must have overtaken them. The mass formed by the ashes and lava that issued from the volcano, was from seventy to one hundred and twelve feet deep, so that the new surface was so much higher than the old one, which, with its towns and detached habitations, parks, gardens, meadows, and vineyards, were all buried beneath.

CHAPTER CCCXLI.

A. D. 81 to 337.

Emperors of Rome from Domitian to Constantine the Great.

TITUS died in the third year of his reign, (A. D. 81,) and was succeeded by his brother *Domitian.* This sovereign began well, and soon gained the character of a liberal and wise prince. But these fair promises were speedily blighted, and he became the most complete despot that ever governed the Roman empire. He was more hateful than either Caligula or Nero, for his tyranny proceeded from a bad heart, while theirs was, perhaps, the result of disordered intellect. He put to death those who were good and noble for no other reason than because they were so; and was often present at the tortures of his victims. From these scenes of blood, he would retire to his apartment, and pass his time in catching flies, and stabbing them with a bodkin. He persecuted the Jews and Christians with unrelenting cruelty. His wars were unsuccessful, and the Romans had the more cause to rejoice at his death, as it placed upon the throne the first of the five good emperors. Domitian, the last of the Cæsars, was assassinated in his palace A. D. 96, after a reign of fifteen years.

His successor, *Cocceius Nerva*, was born in Spain, of an illustrious Roman family, and was chosen emperor by the senate on the very day of the death of Domitian. He was already in advanced age, and was much beloved for the mildness of his manners and the benevolence of his disposition. His reign was short, and undistinguished by any remarkable occurrence. His life was twice attempted; but he still died quietly in his bed, A. D. 98. He had designated *Trajan*, then governor of Upper Germany, as his successor. The new emperor soon arrived at Rome, and was received with every demonstration of joy. His reputation in the country where he governed had reached even distant Rome, where his qualities as a soldier, and as a legislator, were already well known. He had always lived in the most unassuming style, performing long marches on foot with his troops, and sharing with them the fatigues and dangers of war. He knew all the old soldiers by name, and conversed familiarly with them. He possessed an amiable disposition, great experience in war, and many moral and intellectual qualifications. His personal appearance corresponded with his mind, and as he entered Rome in the vigor of manhood, he inspired his subjects with a respect which they never ceased to attach to his name

Hardly had he mounted the throne, than he was called upon to check the insolence of the Dacians, who had ravaged part of the empire, and demanded tribute from the Roman people. This nation was effectually humbled, and its territory reduced to a Roman province. The famous column of Trajan at Rome, which exists to this day, was erected to commemorate this event. The emperor's attention was now claimed by the calls of peace, and to these he devoted himself with energy and zeal. He reformed many abuses in the government, at the same time lessening the taxes. His empress, Plotina, exerted herself to produce a change in the manners of the ladies, who were noted for their levity and fondness for pleasure. Trajan enforced rigorously the laws which had been enacted against those who dissented from the established religion, and for this reason is numbered among the persecutors of Christianity. He died in Cilicia, A. D. 117, having reigned nineteen years. His body was burnt, and his ashes were placed in a golden urn, and deposited beneath his column at Rome.

Adrian, the nephew of Trajan, next occupied the palace of the Cæsars. He was a man of great talent and learning, but made no conquests; on the contrary, he gave up some of those acquired by his predecessor, judging them a detriment, rather than an advantage to the empire. He was the first Roman emperor that made a tour of the provinces. He visited Gaul, Germany, Britain, Spain, Greece, and all the countries of Asia and Africa that were under his dominion. He greatly improved every region through which he passed. The empire was not disturbed by any war of importance during his reign, except one that was occasioned by an insurrection of the Jews. He ruled twenty-two years, and died of a lingering disease at Baiæ, near Naples, A. D. 139. He had previously named as his successor *Antoninus Pius*, a man of noble birth, and highly esteemed for his many virtues.

This prince has been pronounced by historians, the most noble character that ever sat upon a throne. His mild and merciful reign was probably the most tranquil and happy the Roman empire ever enjoyed. The prosperity of this period is best proved by the fact that we know very little of it, few details having come down to us; it seems to have passed in peace and happiness, and we have every reason to suppose that the temple of Janus was shut. Antoninus died in the twenty-second year of his reign, (A. D. 161,) bequeathing nothing but his private fortune to his family. During the greater part of the ensuing century, the sovereign deemed it essential to his popularity to assume the surname of *Antoninus.* The foreign trade of Rome appears to have been very flourishing at this period. Furs were brought from Siberia, and large quantities of amber, which was used for drinking cups, were sent from the shores of the Baltic. The rich productions of the East were conveyed to Alexandria by caravans, and from thence to Rome. Various manufactures were extensively carried on at Alexandria, but more especially those of linen, cotton, and glass.

Marcus Aurelius succeeded to the empire, but for some reason not well understood, his power was shared by Lucius Verus, to whom he had given his daughter in marriage. Aurelius had all the virtues of Antoninus and his colleague all the vices of Nero. The former took an early opportunity of sending his partner at the head of an army against the Parthians. During his absence, Aurelius governed mildly and beneficently. The return of the army brought a dreadful calamity upon the empire. The soldiers came back infected by the plague, which quickly spread through

Italy and the provinces. The ravages of this pestilence were dreadful beyond description, and the Germans took advantage of the weakness occasioned by it, to revolt against the Romans. In conjunction with the northern nations, they advanced even to the frontiers of Italy, and for nearly thirteen years, with one short interval of peace, Aurelius was engaged in conducting the war against them in Germany. He died fighting on the frontiers, A. D. 180. The glory of the empire may be said to have expired with him. The personal character of the emperor had but little influence over the events of his inauspicious reign, in which began first to appear those evidences of declining power that foretold the dissolution of the empire. The invasion of the Germans exhibited the first symptoms of the great migration of nations which eventually overwhelmed Rome.

Commodus, the son of Aurelius, was the next occupant of the throne. He was a brutal tyrant, equally detestable as a man and a sovereign. His cruelties rivalled those of Domitian, and he was detested by all except the soldiers, whose favor he preserved by bestowing money on them with a lavish hand. To detail the vices and cruelties of this monster, would detract from the dignity of history. An instance or two will suffice to place his character in a true light. When only twelve years old, he ordered the overseer of his bath to be thrown into the furnace, because he had made the water too hot. On one occasion, while walking in the street, he cut a fat man in two, that he might have the satisfaction of seeing his entrails fall upon the ground. He was endowed with extraordinary strength, and often, in imitation of Hercules, went abroad dressed in a lion's skin, and armed with a knotted club. To display his strength and skill in arms, he appeared publicly in the amphitheatre: he is said to have fought in this way seven hundred and thirty-five times, and always to have been victorious. The military events of his reign were a disgrace to the Roman name. A plague broke out in the city, and lasted two years, carrying off, at times, two thousand persons in a day. Rome was also set on fire by lightning, and a large part of it burnt. This calamity was followed by a famine, supposed to have been caused by the prime minister, who bought up the corn on speculation. A conspiracy was formed against Commodus in his own household, and poison was administered to him by one of his female favorites. The poison operated too slowly, however, and he was strangled by the hands of Narcissus, his favorite gladiator, A. D. 192. He had reigned twelve years. His body was thrown into the Tiber, and his statues were demolished.

Helvius Pertinax next ascended the vacant throne. The life of this person had been so crowded with adventures, that he was familiarly called *Fortune's tennis ball*. He was born a slave, and followed for some time the trade of a charcoal burner. He afterwards turned shopkeeper, and still later, became a schoolmaster, and taught Latin and Greek. Turning his attention to the law, he distinguished himself at the bar, which he in turn abandoned, and took up the profession of arms. He obtained the command of a legion under Aurelius, and under Commodus became prefect of Rome. He was chosen emperor by the assassins of Commodus, and this choice was confirmed by the people. The hopes which had been formed respecting him were not disappointed He attended all the meetings of the senate, and paid such devotion to business that the meanest petitioner could always obtain access to him. He melted down all the silver statues which had been erected to Commodus, and was thus able to abolish many oppressive taxes. He endeavored to restrain the licentiousness of the prætorian bands, and thus excited the hatred of this arrogant soldiery. They met him in the street, and attacked him; but he boldly faced the insurgents, and by his courage and determination so intimidated them, that they fell back, and seemed inclined to retreat. But he was struck in the breast by a lance, and fell, muffling his head in his robe, A. D. 193.

A scene of degradation hitherto unparalleled was now exhibited. The empire was put up at auction to the highest bidder, by the prætorian guards. *Didius Julianus*, a senator, was the successful competitor, having promised twenty-five thousand sesterces to each prætorian, a sum amounting in all to about ten millions of dollars. He did not long enjoy his dearly-purchased dignity, for the soldiers in different provinces had elected three other emperors, one of whom, *Septimius Severus*, marched direct to Rome, and entered the city unopposed. The wretched Didius, who had purchased a comfortless and disgraceful reign of three months, was dragged from his throne, and his head was struck off by the common executioner. The senate acknowledged Severus, the new claimant. The senate, at this period, was very differently constituted from what it was in former times, for the Roman franchise had been so extended, that half the world were Roman citizens, and people of all countries were found among the senators. Severus disarmed the prætorians, and banished them to the distance of one hundred miles from the city. He was the first emperor that afforded favor and protection to the Christians. The first four years of his reign were occupied in war with the two rivals, who had been proclaimed emperors at the same time with himself. During this period, the great city of Byzantium, on the site of which Constantinople now stands, was taken and destroyed. Niger and Albinus, the two competitors for the purple, were both slain, and Severus reigned alone. He extended the dominions of the empire, and died at York, in Britain, A. D. 211, after a reign of eighteen years.

His sons, *Caracalla* and Geta quarrelled about the division of the empire, until the latter was slain by Caracalla in the arms of his mother. The assassin who now mounted the throne, proved the worst tyrant that had yet disgraced it. He did not confine his cruelty to Rome, as the other emperors had done, but made every province a scene of bloodshed and extortion. He travelled from place to place, accompanied by a portion of the prætorian guards. He caused the senate to rank his murdered brother in the number of the gods. He ordered a general massacre of the inhabitants of Alexandria, because an allusion had been made to the violent death of Geta in one of their theatres. He gave himself up to the society of buffoons and gladiators, many of whom he raised to high offices, and upon whom he squandered the public money. At length, a conspiracy was formed against the tyrant, headed by Macrinus, a person of some influence at Rome, and Caracalla was assassinated in the sixth year of his reign, A. D. 217. *Macrinus* was proclaimed emperor, but held the power only three months, being slain in a battle against a pretender to the throne of the name of *Heliogabalus*, and an illegitimate son of Caracalla.

Heliogabalus was raised to the throne, and was another of those princes whose characters are a disgrace to history. He appointed his mother and grandmother colleagues in the empire, and created a senate of women, whose business it was to arrange the fashions of dress which were to prevail in the kingdom. What Caligula had been unable to do, he accomplished: he made his horse consul and fed him on gilded oats. He engaged openly in such brutal and infamous debaucheries, that his name has become a term to express disgust and reproach above all others. He compelled the Romans to worship a black stone, and raised temples to this as a deity. Some of his suppers cost sixty thousand dollars each, and he never wore the same dress twice. Finding himself hated and despised, and fearing treachery, he erected a tower with steps of gold and mother-of-pearl, from which he might, in the last extremity, cast himself down. He kept within reach cords of purple silk and gold, with which to strangle himself, and golden swords and daggers. But he was not destined to perish by his own hand, for his soldiers mutinied, and pursued him through the rooms of his palace. They dragged him from an obscure corner, put him to death, and threw his body into the Tiber, A. D. 222.

His cousin, *Alexander Severus*, succeeded him, and proved an excellent sovereign in an age, and upon a throne, where virtues were more dangerous than vices. During his reign, a great revolution took place in the East. The Parthian kings had long held dominion over Persia, but the Persian empire was restored by a prince named *Artaxerxes*, who became its sovereign, and laid claim to extensive countries possessed by the Romans. This demand led to a war which was conducted by Alexander in person. The particulars are not well known, but there is reason to believe that the Romans were unsuccessful, and that they made peace, by giving up many parts of their Eastern possessions. The emperor again took the field against the Northern Germans, who had invaded the Roman territory. He here fell a victim to the discontents of his soldiers. The spirit of sedition was fomented by one of the generals, named *Maximin*, and in a riot which followed, the emperor was slain, A. D. 225. Maximin was immediately named his successor. His only qualifications were his gigantic stature and his prodigious strength. He was eight feet high, and could draw a load which a yoke of oxen could not move. The senate refused to ratify his election, but he determined to reign without their concurrence. He put to death every one whom he disliked, and condemned rich men to execution, for the purpose of confiscating their estates. He continued the war against the Germans, cut down their standing corn, and wasted their country to an extent of four hundred and fifty miles. Two noble Romans, named *Gordian*, father and son, were declared joint emperors at Rome. They were both murdered, however, and two senators, *Maximus* and *Balbinus*, were chosen in their stead. The former took the command against Maximin, who was advancing toward Italy, while the latter remained at Rome to conduct the administration there. But Maximin was slain by his own soldiers before the hostile armies met, and Maximus returned to Rome in triumph. The prætorians were dissatisfied with the emperors, who had been elected without their sanction. They determined upon effecting a change in the government, and attacked the palace; they seized the two sovereigns who were returning from the Capitoline games, and put them to death. *Gordian*, grandson of the elder of the two emperors of that name, and only twelve years of age, was proclaimed emperor in their stead.

It is an ungrateful task to pass in review the emperors who filled the throne during this period; for the most part their reigns were of short duration, and their acts are of little importance in history. We only notice them to show to what degree of degradation the Roman people had fallen: the sovereign, in almost every case, gained his power by bribery, and lost it by assassination. The prætorian guard held the whole sway, and used it for their own pleasure and emolument; while the people looked on, calm and unmoved, at the atrocities which were committed in their midst, and which were destined to pass down to posterity as common characteristics of a Roman emperor. The Roman dominion was fast declining; partly in consequence of the high pitch to which the luxurious splendor and profligate effeminacy of private and public life had been carried, and partly because the quick succession of emperors produced a fatal neglect in the administration of the state. No individual talent, and no high example of virtue, could any longer suffice to arrest the progress of corruption or prevent the downfall of Rome. The empire was collapsing within, while the growing insolence of the barbarian hordes of the north threatened its destruction from without. Gordian, after a reign of six years, was assassinated by *Philippus*, who then assumed the purple, and was followed, in quick succession, by *Decius*, *Gallus*, *Æmilianus*, *Valerian*, *Gallienus*, *Claudius*, and *Quintillius*. Their reigns are characterized by the customary scenes of persecution of the Christians, invasions of the barbarians, profligacy, and assassination. Nearly all these emperors died violent deaths.

Quintillius was succeeded, in A. D. 270, by *Aurelian*, a native of Pannonia, and the son of a peasant. He secured the tranquillity of Europe, and then marched into the East, against Zenobia. The fate of this Eastern queen has been detailed in our history of Palmyra. Aurelian restored to the empire some portion of its former greatness; but his career was terminated, in less than eight years, by assassination. A tranquil interregnum of more than half a year ensued; not a single general coming forward to seize the imperial crown. The reckless ambition of the soldiers seems to have been awed by the wretched fate of the preceding emperors. *Tacitus*, a descendant of the historian of that name, succeeded to the throne. He was a good ruler, but survived his honors only six months. *Probus*, a Pannonian, was the next sovereign, and enjoyed a prosperous but warlike reign of six years. He was assassinated by his soldiers, who complained of his severities. His successor was *Aurelius Carus*, prefect of the prætorian guards. A flash of lightning terminated his brief career. A distinguished commander, named *Diocletian*, who had risen from an humble station, was next proclaimed emperor, A. D. 284.

The accession of this prince is the beginning of a new era in the history of Rome, as he introduced a novel system of government, by which the empire was divided into four parts; each division having its own sovereign, and its own capital. Two of these sovereigns were emperors, and bore the title of Augustus while the other two, who might be called their viceroys, bore that of Cæsar. Diocletian took upon himself the government of the eastern provinces, fixing his capital at Nicomedia, a famous city of Bithynia. His colleague, Maximian, a skilful soldier, but a ferocious barbarian, ruled over Italy, Africa, and the islands, holding his court at Milan. The two Cæsars were Constantius and Galerius; to the former were assigned Gaul, Britain, and Spain; to the latter, Illyricum, and all the countries bordering on the Danube. Diocletian obtained many brilliant successes over the Persians; but sullied his triumphs by persecution of the Christians, which surpassed all others which had preceded it in severity. After a reign of twenty years, he determined to resign the imperial power, and persuaded Maximian to do the same. The ceremony of abdication was performed, the same day, at Nicomedia and at Milan — May the 1st, A. D. 305. Diocletian survived this act nine years, and never regretted the loss of his throne. Maximian and others wrote to him, advising him to resume the sceptre; but he replied, by letter, "If you could see the cabbages I raise in my garden, you would not ask me to take a throne!"

The two Cæsars succeeded to the throne they vacated. Constantius died, the year following his accession, at the imperial palace at York, his British capital. His son, *Constantine*, was immediately proclaimed Augustus by the soldiers; but his election was opposed by Galerius, while the senate and prætorians, at Rome, raised to the vacant dignity *Maxentius*, son of the late emperor Maximian. Great confusion resulted from these conflicting claims; and it was evident that the plan of succession marked out by Diocletian, would not answer the expectations he had formed. At one period, there were six Augusti, and not a single Cæsar. In the midst of these disturbances, Galerius died, and Constantine went to war with Maxentius, who was ruling over Italy in a most tyrannical manner. He set out from Britain for Rome, with an army of one hundred thousand men, and met Maxentius, without the gates of the city, where a fierce and bloody battle was fought. The prætorian guard were destroyed by repeated charges of the Gallic horse, and Maxentius was drowned in the Tiber. Constantine thus became emperor of the west; Licinius, the successor of Galerius, holding the provinces of the east. The two emperors were soon engaged in a struggle for the superiority; and Licinius, being defeated in two severe battles, was taken prisoner at Nicomedia, and put to death — A. D. 324. Constantine became thus sole master of the Roman empire.

The new emperor removed the great source of the calamities which had befallen Rome, by disbanding the prætorian guards. During his reign, the controversies in the church led to the convocation of the celebrated council of Nice, (A. D. 325,) in which the doctrine of the Trinity was fixed and defined. He revoked the edicts which had been issued against the Christians, and was loaded with insult and execration, by the populace, for so doing. His rage at this treatment is said greatly to have influenced him in removing the seat of government from Rome to Byzantium. The new city was situated on the Thracian Bosphorus, and possessed great advantages for commerce and defence. It was three years in building, and received the name of *Constantinople*. Enormous sums were spent in embellishing the metropolis, which was divided into fourteen wards, and adorned with a capitol, amphitheatre, palaces, and churches. Many of the senators and wealthy families followed the court, and fixed their residence at Constantinople, where all kinds of luxuries and pleasures abounded. Rome was now no longer the first city in the world. It was at this period that the emperor openly professed Christianity. All pagan rites were prohibited in the new city; while the majority of the people at Rome still adhered to the ancient faith. Constantine adopted Oriental manners, and affected the gorgeous attire of the Persian monarchs. The court was maintained with extreme splendor; and flowing robes of silk, embroidered with flowers, were substituted for the austere garb of Rome. The whole empire was divided into four portions, called *prefectures*. Rome and Constantinople had each its separate prefect. Constantine, who received the title of the *Great*, died in the year 337, having reigned thirty-three years. He has been much blamed for dividing the empire, but its dominions were too extensive and scattered to remain in the possession of a single dynasty. By founding another capital in the east, he probably did not hasten the fall of the west; while, at the same time, he established a second empire, which lasted for more than a thousand years after his death; though, it must be admitted, with little benefit to the world or glory to the Roman name.

CHAPTER CCCXLII.

A. D. 337 to 476.

Decline of Rome — Theodosius the Great — Alaric, Attila, and Genseric — Final Overthrow of the Empire of the West.

The sixty years that followed the death of Constantine the Great are chiefly marked by the decline of the Roman power, and the progress of the barbarians, by whom it was finally destroyed. The late emperor divided the empire among his three sons, Constantine II., Constantius, and Constans; but they were not content with their respective portions. In a civil war which broke out soon afterward, the eldest and youngest were slain; leaving *Constantius*, the second brother, sole emperor. He was a weak sovereign. He established his court at Constantinople, and gave the government of the western provinces to his cousin Julian. The latter fixed his residence at Paris, then called *Lutetia*, being a mere military station. He was a brave general, and soon excited the jealousy of Constantius, by his victorious campaigns against the Germans. A civil war was on the point of breaking out, when Constantius died, leaving *Julian* master of the whole empire — A. D. 361.

This emperor stands out in strong relief from among the numerous imbecile sovereigns who occupied the throne about this period. In most respects, his conduct merits high praise. He was just, merciful, and tolerant. He had been educated a Christian, but abandoned that religion for paganism; and, by this step, acquired in history the surname of "the Apostate." But he would never inflict punishment for difference of opinion, and allowed his subjects that freedom of worship which he claimed for himself. One of his failings was a desire to be thought a philosopher; and in order to acquire the title, he disregarded some of the common decencies of life. A treatise is still extant, from his pen, in which he expatiates with singu ar complacency on the neglected state of his beard, he length of his nails, and the inky blackness of his hands. He reigned but two years; falling on the battle-field, in an unsuccessful campaign against the Persians, A. D. 363. An individual called *Jovian* was named emperor by the army, who had advanced into the heart of the enemy's country without sufficient resources. The only important act of this sovereign was to extricate the troops from their difficulties, and secure them a safe retreat. He died on the way homeward, A. D. 364.

Valentinian, his successor, chosen by the council of ministers and generals, was a distinguished soldier, and a professor of the Christian doctrines. He chose his brother Valens as his partner, and gave him the dominion of the east, reserving to himself that of the west, comprising Italy, Gaul, Spain, Britain, Africa, and Illyricum. His capital was Milan; that of Valens, Constantinople. From this period, the annals of the Byzantine empire form a separate history, though the two governments had occasional connection for a few years afterward. Valentinian displayed his military skill against the barbarians of Africa and Gaul, and while in the act of upbraiding their troops for their treacherous conduct, burst a blood-vessel, and expired, A. D. 375. Valens was killed, three years later, in a battle fought at Adrianople, against the Goths, and in which the Romans were defeated. *Gratian*, who had succeeded his father, Valentinian, in the west, gave the provinces of the east to *Theodosius*, one of his most able generals, and well fitted to keep the barbarians in check.

Through the able administration of these emperors, both the eastern and western empires were beginning once more to enjoy peace and tranquillity; when a people more barbarous and ferocious than any previously known, appeared in the north-eastern portion. They were supposed by the Goths to be the offspring of witches and infernal spirits in the deserts of Scythia; an opinion that forcibly expressed how unsightly was their appearance, and how tremendous their hostility. These were the Huns, who had never been seen by the Romans till this period. Their life was devoted to war and hunting: they built no cities, and erected no houses. A place surrounded by walls they looked upon as a sepulchre, and they never believed themselves in safety beneath a roof. They invaded the territory of the Goths, and made a horrible carnage of all upon whom they could lay their hands, regarding neither age nor sex. The whole Gothic nation was now reduced to despair; their warriors, who had so often maintained a fierce struggle against the Roman legions, now appeared as suppliants on the banks of the Danube, begging for permission to cultivate the waste lands of Thrace. The request was granted, on condition that they would resign their arms; but they avoided complying with this stipulation, which brought down upon them the avenging battalions of Theodosius. The Goths were thoroughly chastised, and resolved never more to molest the Romans, but guarded the banks of the Danube from further invasion. After several revolutions, the details of which would be uninteresting here, Theodosius became master of the whole Roman world. His reign is distinguished by the total abolition of the heathen idolatry, and the establishment of the Christian religion throughout the empire. He was well aware that the division of the kingdom into east and west had now become a permanent necessity. He therefore, by will, appointed *Arcadius*, his elder son, emperor of the *East*, and *Honorius*, the younger, emperor of the *West*. He soon after died of the dropsy, at Milan, A. D. 395. The two divisions were now considered as separate empires: nor were they ever after united. Theodosius was the last great emperor of Rome. From the time of his death, the western provinces only can be termed the Roman empire; and all these were soon overrun by different nations of barbarians, who possessed themselves of one country after another, till the Romans, who had ruled the world for so many ages, were superseded by a new people, and gradually became blended with their conquerors.

Under Arcadius and Honorius, their respective subjects began to regard each other not only as foreigners, but as enemies; and this too at a moment when union and harmony could alone save them from the ruin which was impending over them. The Goths, who had remained quiet during the reign of Theodosius, disdained submission to his imbecile successors. They raised the standard of revolt, and chose for their

Alaric.

leader *Alaric*,* the most formidable foe that the Romans had yet encountered. In this state of things, the latter voluntarily abandoned Britain, being no longer able to keep possession of a distant province, while they were losing ground every where, and were scarcely masters even of their own homes. The barbarians, under Alaric, now invaded Italy, and a war of ten years duration succeeded. Rome was besieged three times, was once ransomed, but was finally taken and sacked in the year 410. The churches were spared, as well as those who had fled thither for refuge. For six days the city was in the ruthless hands of the Goths, and the once proud mistress of the world experienced a terrible retribution for the sufferings she had caused to so many cities, countries, and nations. The treasures collected during a thousand years, from all quarters, became the prey of the barbarians. Hardly had they evacuated Rome when Alaric died, and the world enjoyed a moment of peace. Rome and Italy celebrated public festivals on the occasion.

But the march of desolation was soon renewed. The barbarians had learned the way to Rome: Alaric, king of the Goths, taught them the weakness of the former queen of the world, and Attila, king of the

* Alaric was king of a southern tribe, who settled in Thrace in the time of Theodosius, and are known in history by the title of *Visigoths*.

Huns, prepared himself to profit by the knowledge they obtained. Honorius died A. D. 423, and his nephew, Valentinian III., succeeded him as emperor of the west. He was scarcely seated on the throne when

Attila

the Huns invaded the eastern empire, and forced the emperor to cede them a large territory south of the Danube, and agree to pay an annual tribute. Attila now directed his views to Gaul. With an immense army, he crossed the Rhine, the Moselle, and the Seine. He met the army of the Romans at Chalons. Anxious for the result of the battle, he consulted the soothsayers, and was assured by them of a terrible defeat. He concealed his alarm, rode through the ranks of his warriors, reminded them of their deeds, spoke of his joy at the prospect of a battle, and at the thought that their valor was to be rewarded. "One half the inhabitants of the world were now face to face — here the element of a world ready to perish, there the element of a world ready to be born." The most bloody contest ever fought in Europe followed, between the Huns and the Romans under Ætius. Attila is said to have lost more than two hundred thousand men, and with those that remained escaped across the Rhine.

"If we may believe the old men," says Jornandes, a writer almost contemporary, "a little rivulet that crossed this memorable plain was suddenly so swollen, not with rain, but blood, that it became a rapid torrent; and the wounded soldiers, parched with thirst, who dragged themselves to its brink, swallowed with avidity the revolting mixture, which their own veins had helped to pollute."

Some years later, with recruited forces, and a burning desire for vengeance, Attila attacked Italy with dreadful fury. The emperor trembled, but supplicated in vain. Attila conquered and destroyed Aquileia, Padua, Verona, and laid waste the plains of Lombardy. The inhabitants fled to the Alps and the Apennines, and to the shallows of the Adriatic, where they built Venice. The emperor had no army to oppose the destroyer; so the pope, Leo I., went to his camp, and succeeded in negotiating a peace. This result was so unexpected to the despairing Romans, that they looked upon their preservation as a miracle, and ascribed it to St. Peter. The death of Attila soon after, and the civil war among his followers, delayed the utter ruin of the empire. But Ætius, the Roman general, was murdered by Valentinian, his ungrateful master, and the unchecked ravages of the barbarians speedily filled all the provinces with misery and despair.

"Could we suppose," — says an eminent historian,* in view of the state of the Roman empire, now threatened by the barbarian hordes around it, — "could we suppose a philosopher to have lived at this period of the world, elevated by benevolence, and enlightened by learning and reflection, concerned for the happiness of mankind, and capable of comprehending it, we can conceive nothing more interesting than would to him have appeared the situations and fortunes of the human race. The civilized world, he would have said, is sinking in the west before these endless tribes of savages from the north. What can be the consequence? Will the world be lost in the darkness of ignorance and ferocity? Sink, never to emerge? Or will the wrecks of literature and the arts, that may survive the storm, be fitted to strike the attention of these rude conquerors, or sufficient to enrich their minds with the seeds of future improvement? Or lastly, and on the other hand, may not this extended and dreadful convulsion of Europe be, after all, favorable to the human race? Some change is necessary; the civilized world is no longer to be respected; its manners are corrupted, its literature, its religion, is lost in controversy, or debased by superstition. There is no genius, no liberty, no virtue; surely the human race will be improved by the renewal which it will receive from the influx of these freeborn warriors; mankind, fresh from the hand of nature, and regenerated by this new infusion of youth and vigor, will no longer exhibit the vices and weakness of this decrepitude of humanity; their aspect will be erect, their step firm, their character manly.

"There are not wanting the means to advance them to perfection; the Roman law is at hand to connect them with each other, Christianity to unite them to their Creator; they are already free. The world will indeed begin anew; but it will start to a race of happiness and glory. Such, we may conceive, *might* have been the apposite speculations of any enlightened reasoner at that critical period. But with what eagerness would he have wished to penetrate into futurity! How would he have sighed to lift up that awful veil which no hand can remove, no eye can pierce! With what intensity of curiosity would he have longed to gaze upon the scenes that were in reality to approach.

"And, could such an anticipation of the subsequent history of the world have been indeed allowed him, with what variety of emotions would he have surveyed the strange and shifting drama that was afterward exhibited by the conflicting reason and passions of mankind; the licentious warrior, the gloomy monk, the military prophet, the priestly despot, the shuddering devotee, the iron baron, the ready vassal, the courteous knight, the princely merchant, the fearless navigator, the patient scholar, the munificent patron, the bold reformer, the relentless bigot, the consuming martyr, the poet, the artist, and the philosopher, the legislator, the statesman, and the sage, *all* that were by their united virtues and labors to assist the progress of the human race, *all* that were at last to advance society to the state which, during the greater part of the last century, it so happily had reached — the state of balanced power, of diffused humanity and knowledge of political dignity, of private and public happiness."

* Smith's Lectures, vol. i. p. 33

The last enemies of Rome were the Vandals, under Genseric, who had founded a kingdom at Carthage, in Africa. In A. D. 455, he appeared with an immense fleet at the mouth of the Tiber. The gates of the city were opened without resistance, and its temples, churches, palaces, and firesides were again ransacked by the rude hands of barbarian invaders. They were allowed fourteen days of license to destroy, plunder, enslave, or assassinate. The buildings that the Goths had spared, they razed to the ground: all of value that the former had left, they stowed on board the hundreds of ships that constituted their fleet. Thousands of Roman citizens were carried captives into Africa, where they were sold for slaves to the Moors. Genseric continued to wage war against the Romans till the fall of the empire, twenty years after his first invasion. During this period, eight emperors were successively raised to the throne; but their acts were not of sufficient importance to entitle them to mention here. The last of these, named *Augustulus*, was dethroned in 476, by a German chief, named *Odoacer*, who abolished the name and office of *emperor*, and assumed that of *king of Italy*. The ancient history of Rome terminates with this event, and here begins the history of modern Italy. Such was the end of the Roman empire of the west; although the descendants of Constantine continued to hold the empire of the east for nearly a thousand years longer.

The Romans at length became extinct as a nation, or rather blended with their barbarian conquerors, both in Italy and the provinces. This great catastrophe was not the work of a few years, but was accomplished by the operation of causes which had been gathering strength and force for many centuries. The barbarians became an instrument of retribution for the aggressions and cruelties of the descendants of Romulus and Remus. The emperors could no longer defend the provinces which they still affected to rule. It is impossible to calculate the millions of human beings that perished before the downfall of Rome was accomplished. The calamities which afflicted the human race exceed, in extent of desolation, in the number of victims, and in intensity of suffering, every thing else that history presents to an affrighted imagination.*

We cannot better conclude this brief history of the rise and fall of the Roman empire, than by the following passage from the pen of Dumas.† It occurs in a rapid and summary view of the events which are chronicled in the present chapter:—

"The Roman empire, too vast to be held in subjection by one man, dropped from the dying hands of Theodosius the Great; and, breaking in two parts, rolled on either side of his coffin—forming, under Arcadius and Honorius, the two Christian empires of the east and the west.

"Those streams of nations, however, which had thrown themselves into the great Roman flood, brought with them more slime than pure water. The empire gained, indeed, their science and civilization, but it was forced to take, in connection with these, their concomitant and inseparable vices. Corruption entered the court; debauchery, the cities; and supineness, the camps. Men drooped under the weight of mantles so light that the breeze would lift them from their shoulders. Soldiers, unarmed, reposed on couches beneath painted tents, and drank from cups heavier than their swords. All things had become venal—the integrity of citizens, the honor of wives, the service of warriors. A nation is near its fall when its *lares* are statues of gold. The young and pure morality of the gospel was not in harmony with this worn-out and corrupted world. The primitive race, fallen into impiety, was destroyed by water: the second, steeped in corruption, was now to be purified by fire and the sword.

"Accordingly, from the heart of countries unknown to this degenerate people, from the north, the east, and the south, with great tumult of arms, arose innumerable hordes of barbarians. They rushed over the land in irregular masses; some on foot; some on horses; some on camels; and some on sleds drawn by the reindeer. They crossed rivers by floating on their bucklers; they traversed the sea in frail barks. They went onward, driving the inhabitants before them with their swords, as the shepherd drives the flock with his crook. They overturned nation after nation, as if the voice of God had said, I will mingle the people of the earth as the whirlwind mingles the dust, until from their contact the sparks of the Christian faith shall be kindled over the face of the earth; and ancient times and memorials shall be forgotten, and all things shall become new.

"There was, however, order in destruction; for

* We give the following recapitulation of the emperors of Rome, to enable the reader to see at a glance the line of sovereigns who successively swayed the destinies of the ancient masters of the world:—

Emperor	From	To
Augustus,	from 30 B. C.	to A. D. 14
Tiberius,	from A. D. 14	to 37
Caligula,	37	41
Claudius,	41	54
Nero,	54	68
Galba, Otho, Vitellius,	68	69
Vespasian,	69	79
Titus,	79	81
Domitian,	81	96
Nerva,	96	98
Trajan,	98	117
Adrian,	117	139
Antoninus Pius,	139	161
Marcus Aurelius,	161	180
Commodus,	180	192
Pertinax,	from A. D. 192	to 193
Didius Julianus,		
Septimius Severus,	193	211
Caracalla,	211	217
Macrinus,		
Heliogabalus,	217	222
Alexander Severus,	222	235
Maximin,	235	238
Gordian,	238	244
Philippus,	244	249
Decius,	249	251
Gallus,	251	253
Æmilianus,		
Valerian,	253	260
Gallienus,	260	268
Claudius,	from A. D. 268	to 270
Quintillius,		
Aurelian,	270	275
Tacitus,	275	276
Probus,	276	282
Carus,	282	284
Diocletian and Maximian,	284	305
Constantius and Galerius,	305	306
Constantine,	306	337
Constantius, (Constantine II., Constans,)	337	361
Julian,	361	363
Jovian,	363	364
Valentinian, Valens, Gratian, Valentinian II.,	364	378
Theodosius and Gratian,	378	395

At this period, the empire was divided into the eastern and western divisions. We shall here give only the emperors who ruled over the latter portion, the eastern sovereigns belonging to the history of the Byzantine or Greek empire.

Emperor	From	To
Honorius,	from A. D. 395	to 423
Joannes,	424	425
Valentinian III.,	425	455
Maximus,	455	
Avitus,	from A. D. 455	to 456
Majorianus,	457	461
Severus,	461	465
Procopius,	467	472
Glycerius,	from A. D. 473	to 474
Nepos,	474	475
Augustulus,	475	476

† From "The Progress of Democracy. By Alexander Dumas. Translated by an American."

from this chaos a new world was to emerge. Each actor in the drama had his part assigned him; God having apportioned to each his task, as the husbandman designates to his laborers the fields they are to harrow.

"First, Alaric, at the head of the Goths, overran Italy, impelled by the breath of Jehovah, as a vessel is driven by the tempest. He goes not in his own strength merely; but seems urged and sustained by a mighty, yet invisible power. A monk met him in the midst of his career, and conjured him to turn back. 'It is not in my power,' replied the barbarian: 'an irresistible impulse forces me onward to the overthrow of Rome.' Three times he surrounded the Eternal City with his sea of soldiers; and three times, like the ebbing tide, he retired from it. An embassy of citizens was at length despatched to his camp, recommending him to abandon his enterprise, and assuring him that he would else encounter an army thrice as numerous as his own.

"'So much the better,' replied this reaper of men; 'the thicker the grass, the more easily is it mown.'

"At length, however, he acceded to their request, on condition of receiving, as a recompense for his clemency, all the gold, silver, precious stones, and barbarian slaves that the city contained.

"'And what, then, will remain to the inhabitants?' demanded the ambassadors.

"'Life,' replied Alaric.

"The Romans, of necessity, submitted to the severe terms of the conqueror, and delivered to him five thousand pounds' weight of gold, thirty thousand pounds of silver, four thousand tunics of silk, three thousand scarlet skins, and three thousand pounds of pepper. The vanquished inhabitants, for their ransom, had melted the golden statue of Courage, which they called the *Martial Virtue.*

"Genseric, at the head of the Vandals, passed into Africa, and marched toward Carthage, where the wrecks of Rome had taken refuge. He arrived before the city; and while his troops were mounting the ramparts, the people were descending to the circus. Without was the tumult of arms; and within, the resounding echoes of the games: at the foot of the walls were the shrieks and curses of those who slipped in gore and fell in the *mêlée;* on the steps of the amphitheatre, were the songs of musicians and the sound of accompanying flutes.

"After taking full possession of the city, Genseric presented himself at the circus, and commanded its guards to open the gates.

"'To whom?' said they.

"'To the king of the earth and the sea,' replied the conqueror.

"Not content with the subjugation of Carthage, Genseric now prepared for further victories. He did not know what people dwelt on the earth, but he panted to destroy them. He embarked his army on the sea, and when the pilot demanded what course he should steer, his answer was,—

"'Where God pleases to send me.'

"'Against what nation do you make war?'

"'Against that which God wills to punish.'

"The last of this trio of conquerors was Attila, whose destination was Gaul. Wherever he encamped, his army covered the space of three cities. A captive king mounted guard at the tent of each of his generals; and, at his own tent, one of his own generals stood sentinel. He disdained the gold and silver vessels of Greece, and feasted on raw flesh served in dishes of wood. He swept like a torrent over the eastern empire, making Leo II. and Zeno Isauricus his tributaries. He strode with disdain through Rome, already ruined by Alaric, and at length planted his foot on that portion of the earth which is now called France. Here his devastating progress left but two cities standing, Troyes and Paris. By day, the earth was crimsoned with blood; and at night, the blazing homes of the slaughtered inhabitants illumined and reddened the firmament. Children were suspended by the leg to trees, and abandoned, alive, to birds of prey. Maidens were crushed under chariot-wheels. Old men were fastened to the necks of goaded horses that rushed with them to destruction. Five hundred blazing cities designated the march of the king of the Huns across the world, and a desolate wilderness occupied the intervals between them.

"'The grass itself will not grow,' said the exterminator, 'after the steed of Attila has trampled it!'

"Every thing concerning these envoys of celestial vengeance is extraordinary.

"Alaric, when about to embark for Sicily, died at Cosentia. His soldiers, aided by their army of prisoners, turned the course of the Busento, and dug a deep trench for his corpse in the midst of the channel. They then heaped over the body gold, and jewels, and precious stuffs, turned back the current of the river to its original bed, and massacred the slaves who had aided in the task, that the secret of the sepulture might remain untold.

"Attila expired in the arms of his bride, Ildico; and the Huns made incisions beneath their eyes with the points of their swords, that with the blood of men, and not the tears of women, they might bewail the loss of their conquering chieftain. The flower of his soldiers kept watch during the day over his body, chanting war like songs. At night, they enclosed the corpse in three coffins,—one of gold, another of silver, and the last of iron,—and buried it privately on a bed of arms, flags, and precious stones; and, as in the case of Alaric, to prevent the secret of this sepulchral wealth from transpiring, the grave-diggers were pushed into the tomb, and interred alive with the dead.

"Thus passed away these men, who, instructed in their mission by a savage instinct, forestalled the judgment of the world; entitling themselves the 'Hammer of the Universe,' or the 'Scourge of God.'

"When the wind had dispersed the dust of these countless armies; when the smoke of these blazing cities had ascended to the sky; when the vapors, arising from these murderous battle-fields, had returned to the earth in fertilizing dews; when, in short, the eye could penetrate to this immense chaos through the veil of dust, smoke, and vapor that enveloped it, a young and renewed people were seen pressing around a few old men, who held the gospel in one hand and the cross in the other. These old men were the fathers of the church. These young people were our forefathers, as the Hebrews had been our ancestors—living springs which gushed pure from the earth at the very spot where the corrupted waters were ingulfed.

"These were the Franks, the Burgunds, and the Visigoths, who divided Gaul; the Ostrogoths, the Langobardi, and the Gepidæ, who spread themselves over Italy; the Alans, the Vandals, and the Suevi, who took possession of Spain; the Picts, the Scots, and the

Anglo-Saxons, who disputed among themselves for Great Britain. And in the midst of these new and barbarous races stood some few old Roman colonies, scattered here and there — a kind of columns, long ago planted by civilization, and now astonished to find themselves standing in the midst of barbarism, while they bore upon their sides the half-effaced names of the first possessors of the world."

CHAPTER CCCXLIII.

Manners and Customs of the Ancient Romans.

General. Soldier.

As war was the great business of the Romans, we find that they carried the various arts connected with it to a high degree of perfection. The army was arranged in divisions called *legions.* A Roman legion was drawn up in three ranks — the *hastati*, the *principes*, and the *triarii*. In addition to these, there were light troops, who detached themselves from the main body at the beginning of a battle, and skirmished with missile weapons.

A legion consisted of about five thousand men. The weapons of the troops differed according to the rank of the soldier. The *hastati* had a large shield of wood, leather, and iron, a short, pointed sword, two javelins, an iron or brazen helmet, and a coat of mail. The *principes* and *triarii* used weapons of the same kind. The light troops had a small, round shield, a javelin, and a helmet of leather. Each shield was marked with the name of the soldier, and whoever returned from the fight without it forfeited his life.

When a Roman army moved to battle, the light-armed troops went in advance; then followed the heavy-armed, foot and horse, then the pioneers, then the general's baggage and horses, then the general himself, then the tribunes; after these, followed the standards, the choice men of the army, the servants and drivers of beasts.

No part of Roman discipline was more admirable than that which related to the encampment. However fatigued the soldiers might be by a long march or a severe battle, the camp was regularly measured out and fortified by a ditch before any one was allowed sleep or refreshment. It was an exact square of four hundred feet, with a rampart of earth and stakes three feet high, surrounded by a ditch nine feet wide and seven deep. Careful watch was kept during the night, and, as all the soldiers knew their proper places, if an alarm occurred, they could easil find the rallying point. They were constantly exercised in walking, running, leaping, swimming, shooting arrows, hurling javelins, while in complete armor; while on a march, they were obliged to carry sixty pounds weight of provisions and utensils.

In attacking fortified towns, battering-rams were used. The soldiers were drawn up in a *testudo*, or tortoise: this was an arrangement in which they stood close together, raising their shields, so as to form a compact covering over them, like the scales of a tortoise.

Roman Galley.

The Roman ships were of three kinds — the war galley, the transport, and the ships of burden. The first was propelled chiefly by oars, the second was often towed by the war galley, and the third depended on her sails. Ships of war had sometimes five rows of oars. Some had turrets for soldiers and warlike engines. Others had sharp prows, covered with brass, for the purpose of dashing against their enemies. The naval tactics of the ancients were very simple, the ships coming immediately to close action, and the battle being a contest between single vessels.

The Roman religion was founded on the mytho logical system of the Greeks. A plurality of deities superintending human concerns was the prevailing creed. All these had priests, ministers, sacrifices, and oblations. They had the same gods as the Greeks, to which they added some of their own. The most remarkable festivals were the *Lupercalia* and *Saturnalia.* White goats were sacrificed on some altars, and on others, the fruits of the earth were offered up. Chariot races, and combats of wild beasts, and gladiatorial exhibitions were viewed with transport by the Romans during their solemn festivals. The latter were held in the circus, or amphitheatre. Nothing can more strongly evince that brutality, which, even in the progress of refinement, never deserted the Roman character, than the love of these combats. Such exhibitions could only please a people who had a strong tincture of ferocity.

The persons who offered sacrifices purified themselves by certain rites, which were supposed to have secret virtue for cleansing the heart. The priest was clad in white, and on his brow he wore a chaplet made from the tree sacred to the divinity he was about to propitiate. On some occasions, however, the hair was dishevelled. The ceremony opened with vows and prayers; the victim was then brought; silence

Battering Ram

was proclaimed by the herald; the idlers and the impious were driven from the temple; a cake was thrown on the victim; wine was brought and tasted both by the priest and all present; what remained was poured between the horns of the victim, and was called a *libation*. The fire was now lighted; the incense was burnt; the inferior priests, half naked, brought forward the victim; one, called *cultarius*, struck it with a hatchet, and then cut its throat; the blood was received into vases, and poured on the altar; the carcass was laid on the consecrated table, and was either wholly burnt as an offering to the gods, or a portion only was consumed, while the rest was roasted and eaten by the attendants. When this was finished, the sacrificers washed their hands, repeated some prayers, and made new libations, when the *Formula*, or *Extemplo*, dismissed the spectators.

The fifth day after the birth of an infant was celebrated by a festival. The parents and friends made presents to the child, and an entertainment followed. In education, the Romans imitated the Greeks, who paid great attention to the bringing up of children. They were first taught to swim and dive, and then to read. If the father was poor, the child was brought up to a trade; if rich, he was taught the fine arts, grammar, geography, ethics, arms, dancing, &c. From school the children went to the gymnasia, where they practised wrestling, running, and leaping. They played many games of skill and strength, and some which prevail at the present day — blind-man's-buff, rolling hoop, hide and seek, &c. At the age of eighteen, the boys were enrolled among the youths capable of military duty, and at twenty they were considered men.

Lovers in ancient times seem to have been as fantastic as in our day. They were accustomed to seek omens in the crackling of leaves in the fire, and apple seeds pressed between the thumb and finger. A lover often walked before the door of his mistress in the evening, coughing or whistling, to attract her notice. If the fair one did not appear, he struck the door, or perhaps burst forth in an amatory song. If all this failed, he cut upon the door posts, or suspended over the threshold, the history of his love and his anguish. Sometimes he would address the door post, as if it could sympathize with him, or he would perfume it, or anoint it with oil, cover it with flowers, or moisten it with libations of wine. The lovers in those days had good constitutions, for they often roamed abroad all night in their amatory devotions, even during the coldest weather.

Betrothal, among the Romans, was a curious ceremony. The woman placed herself, before ten witnesses, in the arms of the man she was to marry. they then ate together a cake, composed of farina, salt, and water, which had been blessed by the priest. These three materials, kneaded together and baked, so that the parts could no longer be separated, were intended to show the indissoluble connection of marriage. On the day of the union, the bride was taken from her parents, dressed in a veil and robe, and, carrying a distaff in her hand, she stepped over the threshold of her new residence, supported by two youths, and lighted by a third with a torch. She then placed herself upon a sheep-skin spread before the entrance, and called to the bridegroom, who came immediately and offered her the key of the house. The husband and wife then touched fire and water, as symbols of purity and nuptial fidelity. Music, singing, and feasting followed, and the husband, after supper, scattered nuts among the boys.

The art of agriculture was held in the highest esteem by the Romans. The operations of the field commenced at daylight; the meals were cooked and eaten in the open air, and the labor was conducted amid rustic songs. Mules and oxen were used in the plough The vintage and harvest were seasons of mirth and gladness, and festivals in honor of Ceres and Bacchus were universal, the first fruits being laid upon their altars. The Romans paid great attention to horses, and the stables were well constructed. They had also pigsties, poultry yards, ox-stalls, dove-cots, and parks for boars, goats, and other animals. Ponds were constructed for fish at vast expense, as they were considered a great delicacy.

The Romans carried on the mechanical arts chiefly

by slaves as journeymen. We read of basket makers, carpenters, dyers, enamellers, farmers, founders, glass manufacturers, globe makers, goldsmiths, joiners, tanners, wax chandlers, fresco painters, &c., &c.

The Romans were indebted for their early skill in architecture to the Etrurians. Their temples were generally crowned with cupolas, and were mostly circular, and very splendid. Great skill and industry were conspicuous in the construction of aqueducts,

Roman Aqueduct.

which were of great length and extent. Architecture, sculpture, and painting exhausted their refinements on the establishment of baths, which, for their vast extent, were compared to cities. Those of Caracalla had accommodations for three thousand persons; and the present church of the Carthusians is in one of the halls of the bath of Diocletian. The Roman roads were better than those of any other people, being paved with flint stones, and cemented with mortar.

Painting, among the Romans, did not arrive at any degree of perfection. Julius Cæsar expended great sums in purchasing pictures of the old Greek masters, and Augustus encouraged the art, but with little success. Sculpture was introduced early into Rome, but the representations were very unskilful. It may be here remarked that, after the conquest of Greece, the Romans were greatly indebted to that country for their progress in the fine arts, in literature, and philosophy. Greek architecture especially, though somewhat modified, was adopted by the Romans in their public buildings. Many of the finest specimens of sculpture and painting in Greece were taken to Rome by the conquering generals, and became models for the artists there.

The superior Roman houses were of different kinds — town houses, or rather winter houses, suburban villas, and subterraneous houses used in the heat of summer. The former were often very elegant — specimens of which may be seen at Pompeii. In general, however, the Roman houses were deficient in taste. The streets of the city of Rome were very irregular, and, though the public buildings were magnificent, many private dwellings were mean. They had no chimneys; they were unacquainted with glass for windows, and used horn, flakes of mica, and linen. The outer door was supplied with a bell: the hall was guarded by a slave in chains. They had often portable furnaces instead of fireplaces.

The bedsteads were six feet long and three broad; there were two in each room, one for sleeping and the other for lounging. The Romans are represented as taking a nap after dinner. The beds consisted of mattresses, stuffed with straw, wool, or dried vegetables. In ancient times, the Romans slept upon straw and dried leaves. They had, in later times, down beds from Egypt. The blankets were skins of sheep, with the wool on. The furniture of the room consisted of wash-basins, chairs, slippers, clothes-chests, and sometimes mirrors, of gold, silver, or other metals, were hung around the walls. The articles in the women's room were instruments for spinning and weaving, scales and weights, a large and small mask, a broad brimmed hat, an umbrella, fan, sandal cases, a mirror, and trinkets of various kinds.

The tools in use among the Romans were axes of stone, bronze, iron, and silver; saws of stone and iron, picks, trowels, compasses, chisels, wedges, bars, rules, rollers, pulleys, weights, cranes, rods for drawing lines, files, &c. These were generally of iron, though some were of lead, and some of stone. Ploughshares, hoes, and spades were of iron.

Wine was the beverage chiefly used by the Romans, of which they had great variety. Scarcely any thing seems to have been more important to the wealthy Roman, in all his arrangements for comfort, than to be well furnished with choice and approved wines. At the suppers of the rich, there were usually three courses. The first consisted of eggs, salad, radishes, &c., to whet the appetite; with this they drank mead, or a mixture of honey. The second course formed the essential part of the meal, and consisted of substantial viands. The third consisted of fruits, pastry, and confectionary. The Romans reclined at their meals, and nine persons usually sat at table

A woollen *toga*, full for the rich, and scanty for the poor, was the distinctive dress of the Roman people. A tunic, fastened around with a belt, afterward came into use for both sexes. In the progress of refinement, females had three garments; the outer one was called *stola*, richly embroidered, and clasped with gold. The kings wore a white robe with a purple border, and the emperors used one entirely of purple. The people generally had neither hat nor cap; they wore sandals upon their feet.

The Toga.

In early times, there was no public library in Rome though private individuals had collections of books in their houses. As the love of letters became more general, the inhabitants of the capital required books; and Augustus founded three libraries: by degrees twenty-nine were established for the accommodation of the public. They were placed in the temples and in the baths. The books were, however, more select than numerous. Those which were condemned as injurious or seditious were publicly burnt, as a rebuke to their authors.

For the space of nearly five hundred years from the foundation of the city, the Romans had nothing that deserved the name of literature. Ennius, though a Greek by birth, was the first who taught them to write their language with ease and elegance, about 200 B. C. About half a century after, philosophy was introduced from Athens; and it soon became the fashion for well-educated Romans to read, speak, and even write the Greek language. From this period learned Greeks resorted to Rome, where they became teachers, and instructed most of the eminent Romans who were distinguished in literature at the close of the century preceding the Christian era. This was the most brilliant epoch of Roman literature. The writings of Cicero brought the language to perfection, and almost every species of composition was cultivated with success. The Augustine age is, proverbially, that in which the light of learning blazed forth with peculiar brilliancy, and the glory of which time and change have been unable to obscure. It was during this period that Virgil, Horace, Ovid, and Tibullus — the greatest names associated with Roman poetry — appeared; and, as their works have come down to us nearly entire, we are able to share in the fruition of that era of genius.

Juvenal was born at a later period, and flourished during the reign of Nero. Sixteen of his satires are extant. His shafts were levelled not only at the vices of the times, but against mankind at large — thus seeming to make virtue an impossibility in actual life. His writings, therefore, are more likely to injure than benefit the cause of morality. The historians Sallust, Livy, Tacitus, Polybius, and Diodorus, have been mentioned in the introduction to this work. In the second century of the Christian era, Roman literature appears to have declined, and a false taste to have vitiated the great bulk of the community. Oratory continued to form the chief study in the education of the higher classes; yet sophistry in argument and declamation in style, were characteristics of the age. The art of the rhetorician is visible in the prose of Seneca and Pliny, as well as in the poems of Lucan and Valerius Flaccus. All these abandoned nature, and seemed only striving for effect.

In later periods, when civil commotions prevailed, literary pursuits were nearly extinguished. The Roman people at large had never appreciated the great works of their countrymen, and when the patronage of the educated and wealthy was withdrawn, there was no encouragement to literary exertions. By degrees, the poets dwindled into mere versifiers, and the historians became only chroniclers of events. All kinds of barbarisms and corruptions crept into the language, and the stream of Roman literature at last disappeared within the monastic shadows of the church.

In taking a retrospect of Roman poetry, we cannot but be struck with its external and physical character. It deals almost wholly in sensible objects, or the direct associations which spring from them. There is no delving into the caverns of the soul, no roaming on the shoreless sea of spiritual life. While it is occupied with material nature, it lacks the sparkling freshness, the bounding mirth and hilarity, of Grecian song. When compared with the deep, thoughtful, spiritual productions of our own time, it appears bald, and almost puerile. It may be said of Roman literature, as of that of the Greeks, that it is to be admired, in a great degree, from a consideration of the time and circumstances in which it was produced; should any author of our day write a poem of equal merit, and in the same vein as the best that Roman antiquity has handed down to us, it would be received with indifference, if not contempt. It is not, therefore, the positive merit of these renowned productions which extorts the praise of mankind; it is, at least in part, the associated charm of antiquity that bestows upon them their power

The history of Rome is less distinguished by the names of remarkable individuals than that of Greece; yet it is by no means barren of these. *Cincinnatus Fabius*, *Scipio*, *Cato*, *Sylla*, *Marius*, *Pompey*, and *Cæsar*, were all great men; the last, one of the greatest that the world has known. Had he lived to carry out his schemes, he might have proved a benefactor to his country and mankind. Who would not like to know what Cæsar's genius and Cæsar's ambition would have wrought with the boundless resources of the Roman empire in his hands? But it has rarely happened that conquerors are spared to complete their plans. The very condition of their existence seems to forbid the calm and continued exercise of their power. Alexander, Cæsar, Napoleon, and Cromwell, were all struck down in the midst of their unfinished schemes.

Of the celebrated Romans we have mentioned, no one exercised great influence beyond the age in which he lived. But it was different with Cicero — the most exalted character presented by Roman history. He lived not merely for his day; he was not a warrior — writing his annals in blood, to be effaced by the plough or the seasons — or, if remembered, to be only famous in proportion as he was a destroyer. Cicero was a philosopher, in the best sense of the term — a *lover of truth;* and he was endowed with a rare capacity, not only for its discovery, but for its communication to mankind. A large part of his writings are extant in our day. These relate to a great variety of subjects, and there is hardly any important field of inquiry upon which he has not shed imperishable light.

Cicero was born of a wealthy family in Apulia, in the year 107 B. C. He was educated with that sedulous care customary among the enlightened Romans of the period. When advanced to manhood, having determined to be an orator, he trained himself for that high vocation with great industry — at once storing his mind with every species of knowledge, and acquiring those arts and that manner of delivery, which so largely contribute to success.

Possessing genius of a high order, and thus disciplined, we might easily predict Cicero's triumph; but it must be further stated that he was a man of great magnanimity of soul. This was the true secret of his preeminence. It was his patriotism, his love of mankind, his passion for truth, that gave vigor and direction to his genius. These are the qualifications that have rendered him the friend, teacher, and benefactor of the world. As a mere artist in the profession of oratory, Demosthenes was his superior; as a missionary of truth, for every age and country, Cicero was infinitely beyond him.

The career of Cicero has been sketched in the preceding pages, and need not be repeated. Nor need we again advert to Virgil, Horace, Juvenal, and other names which shine in the pages of Roman literature But we must not take leave of our subject without a brief comparison between the two greatest nations of antiquity, and those which have most mingled their spirit and institutions with our own.

In looking back upon the history of Greece and Rome, it is perhaps difficult to decide which bequeathed to after ages the greatest benefits. We are indeed indebted to the former for the finest specimens of various arts, and the most elegant models of literature, and also for a large amount of instruction in politics, derived as well from their institutions as their experience. But on the other hand, the *Civil Law* which forms the basis of all law throughout Christendom, is derived from the Romans. It is believed that the rudiments of this wonderful code* were in existence before the foundation of Rome, especially in what relates to families, relationship, marriage, testaments, succession to intestates, ownership, &c.; but it grew into a complete system under the fostering genius of the Romans, and was finally collected and remodelled by Justinian. As it has thus come down to us under the title of the *Pandects*, containing five hundred and thirty-four decisions of eminent judges and lawyers, it is an imperishable monument of the wisdom of this ancient nation. "Unjust to every other people," says an eloquent writer, "they were yet the firm adherents of law and justice among themselves. They went to war with religious preliminaries. The military oath was their sacrament, in which they engaged for a real presence; and though it was to be a presence in veritable blood, it was yet so religiously fulfilled as to be a bond of virtue. They, at first, sent forth their legions to make war, more, it would seem, because they loved the discipline, than because they wanted the plunder. The tramp of their victorious legions was heard, resounding at the gates of cities and across the borders of nations; their leaders were returning, every few months, with triumphal entries into the city, that a most just people might enjoy and glory in the spectacle of their own public wrongs; till at last, debauched by the plunder of their victories, they may be said to have conquered, on the same day, both the world and their own virtue together. Nor is even this exactly true; for it is remarkable, that they gave back to the subject nations the justice denied them in their conquest, and set up the tribunals of Roman law on the fields of Roman lawlessness! Equally remarkable is it that in the most dissolute age of the empire, the power of scientific law could not be eradicated from the hearts of this wonderful people. While the monster Commodus sits upon the throne, Papinian and Ulpian occupy the bench, adding to the civil code the richest contributions of legal science. And even the signatures of Caracalla and his ministers will be found, not seldom, inscribed on the purest materials of the Pandects!

"What, then, if Rome did not excel in literature? Had she not another talent in her bosom quite as rich and powerful—the sublime talent of law? In her civil code, she has erected the mightiest monument of reason and of moral power that has ever yet been raised by human genius. The honest pride of Cicero was not misplaced when he said, 'How admirable is the wisdom of our ancestors! We alone are masters of civil prudence, and our superiority is the more conspicuous, if we deign to cast our eyes on the rude and almost ridiculous jurisprudence of Draco, Solon, and Lycurgus.'

"Little, however, did he understand, when he thus spake, what gift his country was here preparing for the human race. Could he have pierced the magnificent future, when this same Roman law should have its full scientific embodiment; could he have seen, at the distance of twenty centuries, the barbarians of Northern and Western Europe compacted into great civilized nations, and, after having vanquished the Roman arms and empire, all quietly sheltered under the Roman jurisprudence; a new continent rising to view, beyond the lost Atlantis, to be fostered in its bosom; a spirit of law infused into the whole realm of civilized mind, and revealing its energy now in the common law of England, now in the commercial code, and, last of all, in the international—all matured in the pervading light and warmth of the Roman; liberty secured by the security of justice; the fire of the old Roman virtue burning still in the bosom of legal science, and imparting a character of intellectual and moral gravity to the literature, opinions, and life of all cultivated nations; and then, to crown the whole, the visible certainty that the Roman law has only just begun its career, that it must enter more and more widely into the fortunes of the race, and extend its benign sway wherever law extends, till the globe, with all its peoples, becomes a second Roman empire, and time itself the only date of its sovereignty;—seeing all this, the great orator must have confessed, that every conception he had before entertained of the majesty and grandeur of the Roman jurisprudence, was weak, and even null. Our minds, even now, can but faintly conceive the same."

In contrast to this aspect of the *Roman* character, the same writer says, "The first thing to be observed in the *Greek* literature, is its want of a moral tone. A mere incidental remark of Schlegel touches what might rather be made the staple of criticism, in the works of this wonderful people. 'Even in those cases,' he says, 'where the most open expression of deep feeling, morality, or conscience might have been expected, the Greek authors are apt to view the subject of which they treat, as a mere appearance of the life, with a certain perfect, undisturbed, and elaborate equability.' How could it be otherwise, where an Aristotle, endowed with the most gigantic and powerful intellect ever given to man, could only define virtue itself as the middle point between two extremes, and every moral evil as being either too much or too little? Socrates and his splendid disciple, it is true, had a warmer and more adequate idea of virtue; though it will escape the notice of no thoughtful scholar, that they were charmed with virtue, rather as the Fair than as the Right. This is specially true of Plato. He draws her forth out of his own intellectual beauty, as Pygmalion his ivory statue, and, as this was quickened into life by the word of Venus, so his notion of virtue takes its life from him, from the charms in which it is invested. Evil and vice, too, connect, in his mind, rather with deformity and mortification than with remorse.

On the whole, there is, perhaps, no civilized people whose morality is more earthly and cold than that of the Greeks. At the same time, their sense of beauty in forms, their faculty of outward criticism, is perfect. Their temples and statues are forms of perfect art. Their poets and philosophers chisel their thoughts into groups of marble. Their religion or mythology is scarcely more than a gallery of artistic shapes—exquisitely sensual. They alone, of all people, in fact, have a religion without a moral—gods for the zest of comedy, gay divinities that go hunting, frolicking, and thundering over sea and land. Genius only worships.

* Of the *Laws of the Twelve Tables*, of which we have given an account at p. 742, only scanty fragments remain. They seem to have contained a set of rules, both civil and religious, public and private. They prescribed laws respecting marriage, theft, homicide, interments, inheritance, persons of unsound minds, &c. The basis of these laws, which Cicero deemed worthy of unbounded applause, was derived from nations more ancient than the Romans.

The chisel is the true incense, to hold a place in epic machinery, the true circle of Providence. Every thing done or written, is subtile, ethereal, beautiful, and cold; even the fire is cold — a combustion of icicles. There can be no true heat where there is no moral life. They love their country, but they do not love it well enough to suffer justice to be done in it, or to endure the presence of virtue. Their bravery is cunning, their patriotism an elegant selfishness. In their ostracism, they make public envy a public right, and faction constitutional. We look up and down their history, survey their temples without a religion, their streets lined with chiselled divinities, set up for ornamental effect; we listen to their orators; we open the shining rolls of their literature, and exclaim, 'Splendid sensuality! elegant faction! ornamental religion! a nation perfect in outward criticism, but blind, as yet, to the real nature and power of the moral element'

Modern Italy.

Italian Costumes.

CHAPTER CCCXLIV.

A. D. 466 to 774.

THE GOTHIC AND LOMBARD KINGDOMS OF ITALY. — *Condition of Italy at the Downfall of the Western Empire — Odoacer — Theodoric — Belisarius — The Lombards — Alboin — Astulphus — The Franks — Overthrow of the Lombard Kingdom.*

IN the preceding chapters, we have given an outline of the history of Rome, which, passing through various stages, as a Kingdom, a Republic, and at last an Empire, overspread the civilized world. At the time of its overthrow, it embraced all Italy; but in the progress of centuries, this portion of Europe became divided into separate states, and these were often rivals of each other. It is the rise and progress of these states, which have been noticed in our geographical sketch of Modern Italy, the history of which we are now about to present.

The revolution of 476, which put an end to the Roman Empire in the West, forms one of the most strongly-marked epochs in the history of the world. But this event, so important in our eyes, was so disguised in its character from the view of its contemporaries, that they foresaw none of its mighty consequences. Odoacer compelled the senate of Rome to send away the imperial insignia to Zeno, emperor of Constantinople, declaring that one ruler was sufficient to govern the whole empire. He was not himself aware of the immense change which had been wrought in the great fabric of government in the West. His own power was a secret to him. He sent a modest request to the emperor that he might be allowed to govern the diocese of Italy under the title of *Patrician.* He assumed, it is true, the name of *king;* but this was a barbaric dignity, which often signified no more than the command of an army, or the government of a province. It rather denoted a ruler of men than of territory, and was conferred on Odoacer by his soldiers. Among these the Heruli were the most numerous; whence he is often represented as king of the Heruli.

The forms of the imperial government were little changed from what they had been during a century previous. The power was completely in the hands of armed barbarians, while at the same time the senate of Rome continued to assemble as usual. The consuls were appointed yearly, one by the Byzantine emperor, the other by the king of Italy. The imperial laws were proclaimed in Italy, and respected as before, and none of the municipal or provincial authorities were changed. It is difficult to discover what that public opinion was, and under what form it was expressed, which had still power to prevent the actual monarch of Italy from taking upon himself the title of Roman emperor, and to convince him that he was too weak to attempt the suppression of the rights and claims of an ancient sovereignty — which was, in reality, nothing but a shadow. Odoacer was independent without daring to appear so.

The Roman inhabitants of Italy were nearly extinct. The ancient population had been swept away by every scourge under heaven — war, pestilence, famine, public tyranny, and domestic slavery. For a century preceding the fall of the empire, the existence of the people had been altogether artificial. They were principally supported by the distribution of corn which the emperor had made regularly at Rome, Milan, and other large cities where the court resided. These bounties had been discontinued with the loss of Africa and the ruin of Sicily, and Odoacer did not attempt to renew them. In the mean time, most of the landed proprietors had ceased to cultivate their estates. There was little encouragement to raise corn when it was given away in the market-place. The rearing of cattle had for a time superseded the cultivation of grain; but both the herds and the slaves who tended them had been carried off by the barbarians. The desolation of Italy is frequently described in simple but affecting language in the contemporary letters of the ecclesiastics. Pope Gelasius, in 496, speaks of Tuscany and other provinces in which the human race was almost extinct. Saint Ambrose describes the cities of Bologna, Modena, Reggio, and Piacenza, with the country around them, as a desert.

A rupture soon took place between Odoacer and Zeno. The latter invited Theodoric, a prince of the Ostrogoths, to invade Italy. Odoacer defended that country better than it had been done for many centuries; but Theodoric defeated him in several battles, and besieged him three years in his capital of Ravenna. A treaty was at last made, by which the two sovereigns agreed to rule jointly and equally; but Theodoric assassinated his rival at a feast, and became sole king of Italy, A. D. 493. Notwithstanding this treacherous deed, Theodoric established in his dominions the wisest and most equitable institutions which any northern conqueror had ever granted to the conquered countries of the south. Instead of oppressing one people by means of the other, he strove to hold the balance fairly between them. He adopted and established the entire structure of the Germanic liberties of the Goths, and introduced the practice of agriculture among them by granting them lands, which they held on the ancient German tenure of military service. He indulged his Roman subjects in what they called their liberties; that is to say, the names of the republic, the senate, the consuls, the magistracy, and the laws. He restored the spirit of commerce and manufactures, and maintained peace and plenty throughout Italy. He was illiterate, and unable to write his name except by drawing a pen through lines cut in a plate of gold; yet he favored learning and patronized learned men.

Theodoric did not take up his residence in the ancient capital, but divided his time between Ravenna, the most important fortress in the kingdom, and Verona, from which he was best enabled to provide for the defence of Italy. He designed to restore the glory of the Roman senate, and to attach it to his monarchy. The senators were still distinguished by their immense wealth, and their pride in the antiquity of their race. They still believed themselves to be ancient Romans, not only the descendants, but the equals of the masters of the world. They dreamed of liberty without equality, public strength, or courage; and they entered into conspiracies to restore, not the republic, but the empire. Theodoric, who grew suspicious and irritable in his declining years, punished these men with great severity. The end of his reign was sullied by the condemnation of Boethius and Symmachus, both of whom were senators, and men of consular dignity, and eminently fitted to do honor to the last age of Rome.

Theodoric died in 526. His grandson Athalaric, who was only four or five years old, succeeded him, the government being administered by his mother, Amalasontha. The minority of a Gothic king, and the regency of a female, could not fail to produce wars, intrigues, and internal discords. Six kings reigned from the death of Theodoric to the middle of the sixth century. The disordered state of Italy tempted Justinian, the emperor of the East, to make an effort for the recovery of the peninsula. Belisarius, his general, the greatest captain of the age, after having overthrown the Vandal empire in Africa, invaded Italy with a large army. Rome and Naples fell into his hands. The conquest of Italy was completed by the successor of Belisarius, the consul Narses: the Ostrogothic kingdom was overthrown, and the greater part of Italy was annexed to the Eastern empire for nearly two hundred years; during which time it was governed by a Byzantine viceroy, bearing the title of *exarch.*

The Gothic dominion in Northern Italy was followed by that of the Lombards, or Langobardæ, a people who are supposed to have come from the banks of the Elba, and to have received their name from their long spears. They fought their way from the north to the south, like other barbarous tribes, and appeared on the banks of the Danube about the middle of the sixth century. Here their forces were augmented by the addition of twenty thousand Saxons, and the united masses poured down from the Alps, and spread themselves over Northern Italy, in 568. The leader of the Lombards was *Alboin*, a chief equally renowned for savage vices and virtues. He had conquered the king of the Gepidæ, a barbarous people north of the Danube, and married his daughter Rosamond, making a drinking-cup of his skull. After conquering Northern Italy, he held a great carousal, in the manner of his people and times. At this feast, he filled the skeleton-cup with wine, and sent it to his wife, ordering her to drink its contents, and rejoice with the master of Italy. Rosamond, stung by this insult, caused her husband to be assassinated. She attempted to place her favorite and accomplice, Helmichis, on the throne; but this project failing, she fled with him and her treasures to Constantinople. In this city, she attracted the attention of Longinus, an officer of high rank, who was disposed to make her his wife. Her lover was an obstacle to this union, but she resolved to remove him by poison. She attended him to the bath, and, as he came out, offered him a goblet, of which he drank; but immediately suspecting treachery, he presented his sword to her breast, and compelled her to drink the remainder. The guilty couple ended their lives in mutual reproaches. Their story is a pertinent illustration of the manners of the age.

Alboin was succeeded on the throne of the Lombards by *Clepho*, who was chosen king in 573. At the end of a reign of a year and a half, he was murdered, and a period of turbulence ensued, at the end of which the kingdom became more tranquil, under the sway of *Antharis*, the son of Clepho, who successfully resisted an invasion of the Franks, and at the close of the sixth century, extended his conquests to the extreme south of Italy The divisions and subdivisions of this country were very numerous in the two centuries which followed the first conquest by Alboin. It was the policy of the Lombards, as of most of the barbarian conquerors, to parcel out their territory. Over the divisions chiefs were placed, who exercised a mixed authority, civil and military, having subordinate officers under them. From these territorial divisions arose the Italian titles of nobility. The dukedoms became sovereignties under their dukes, and as such, occupy an important place in Italian history.

The Lombards were slow in changing their rude habits for those which are acquired by intellectual and moral improvement. They engaged in neither commerce nor agriculture. When they were not occupied in wars, councils, or domestic broils, they devoted themselves to feasting and hunting. Among the amusements, new to the Italians, was hawking. The hawk, or falcon, was capable of receiving a tuition which enabled it to know the voice and obey the commands of its master while moving in the air. The noble Lombard regarded his falconry and the use of his sword as equally valuable accomplishments.

There are certain periods in the history of the world, when a thick veil appears to overspread the earth; when all authentic documents and impartial witnesses disappear, and we have no clew by which to trace the course of events. The seventh century is one of those periods. During this time, the historians of the Eastern and Western empires are silent. Vast revolutions were in preparation, or drawing toward their catastrophe, without any recorded facts which exhibit their progressive steps. The principal historical luminary of the West, after the overthrow of the Roman empire, was Gregory, bishop of Tours. His ecclesiastical history, which is brought down to the year 591, four years before his death, is a confused narrative, showing a writer of great ignorance and bigotry; yet this is the only source from which we can gather any knowledge of the manners, opinions, and forms of government which prevailed during the period of which he treats. After Gregory, another author, far more barbarous and more concise, whose name is supposed to be *Fredegaire*, continued the history of the Franks to the year 641. Like his predecessor, he has shed a feeble light, not only upon Gaul, but upon Germany, Italy, and Spain. After Fredegaire, nothing is to be found which deserves the name of history, till the time of Charlemagne. A century and a half passed away, during which we know little of the history of Western Europe, except what is furnished by dates and conjectures.

This long and almost unknown period was not, however, without its importance. Italy slowly recovered from its calamities. The Lombard kings, who were at first elective, and afterward hereditary, showed some respect for the liberty of their subjects, whether of Roman or Teutonic origin. Their laws, considered as the laws of a barbarous people, were wise and equitable. Their dukes, or provincial rulers, early acquired a sentiment of pride and independence, which induced them to seek support in the affection of their subjects. The population of Italy began once more to increase: the race of the conquerors took root, and throve in the soil without entirely superseding that of the conquered natives, whose language still prevailed. The rural districts were cultivated anew, and the towns rebuilt. It was peculiar to the Lombards, that they did not permit the priesthood to take part in political affairs. The church of Rome had not established its power among them. The character of the Lombards compares very favorably with that of most of the other barbarous nations who had possessed themselves of Europe.

During the reign of Astulphus, (A. D. 751 to 756,) the kingdom of the Lombards reached the summit of its greatness. He subdued the exarchate of Ravenna, and erected it into a new dukedom. He then marched against Rome, which was, at that time, nominally subject to the Byzantine emperor, but really governed by the pope. Alarmed at his danger, the pontiff, Stephen, applied for aid to the emperor; but finding that the Byzantine court cared little for Italy, he negotiated with Pepin, the first monarch of the Carlovingian dynasty in France. Pepin immediately crossed the Alps with a powerful army, besieged Astulphus in Pavia, and compelled him to purchase peace, by the cession not only of the places which he had seized in the Roman dukedom, but also by the transfer of the exarchate and the territories of Ancona to the holy see. Pepin withdrew from Italy, but Astulphus was so reluctant to fulfil the terms of the treaty, that a second invasion was necessary to accomplish this work. Astulphus once more submitted, but secretly resolved to renew the war on a more favorable opportunity. Before his preparations were completed, however, he was killed by a fall from his horse, and the Lombard kingdom became distracted by a disputed succession.

By the interference of the pope, the Lombard crown was awarded to Desiderius. This monarch subsequently found himself exposed to the jealousy of the pope, and attempted to strengthen his influence by giving his daughters in marriage to Charles and Carloman, the sons of Pepin. This step led to the downfall of the Lombard monarchy. Charles divorced his wife, and Desiderius in revenge, endeavored to persuade the pope to anoint Carloman's children monarchs of the Franks. Adrian I., who then occupied the pontifical chair, steadily refused. Desiderius invaded his dominions, and the pope, unable to make any resistance, placed himself under the protection of Charles who crossed the Alps with an army, and, after a brief war, put an end to the kingdom of the Lombards, by the capture of Pavia, A. D. 774. Desiderius and his family were sent to France, where they died in obscurity; and Charles the conqueror, better known as *Charlemagne*, received the *iron crown* of Lombardy.

CHAPTER CCCXLV.

A. D. 800 to 1863.

THE LOMBARDO-VENETIAN KINGDOM. — *Lombardy — Milan — Frederic Barbarossa — The Lombard League — Republics of the Middle Ages — The Dukes of Milan — The Austrian Dominions.*

THIS division of the Austrian empire comprised, until recently, the northern part of Italy, including the ancient kingdom of the Lombards, the Milanese territory, and Venice. It is bounded north by Switzerland and the Tyrol, east by the Adriatic, south and west by the kingdom of Sardinia. It is a level country, watered by the Po and its tributary streams. The soil is generally fertile and well cultivated. The western portion contains several beautiful lakes, as Como, Maggiore, Gardo, &c. This kingdom comprised eighteen thousand two hundred and ninety square miles, and four million four hundred thousand inhabitants.

After the ancient kingdom of the Lombards had been subdued by Charlemagne and annexed to the great Frankish empire, it received the name of the *Kingdom of Italy*. The golden diadem worn by the monarch of this country was called the *iron crown*, in consequence of its containing a slender hoop of iron, supposed to have been made from a nail of the true cross. It is preserved to this day in the town of Monza, which has a prescriptive claim to the possession of this celebrated relic of antiquity.

From the year 900 to the middle of the eleventh century, the history of Northern Italy is lost; there were no historians, or their writings have perished. During this period, the cities in this quarter appear to have grown rich and populous; most of them were surrounded by walls and defended by strong citadels. Compared with the extent of the country, the number of cities was very great, and the castles and strongholds were more numerous than even in Germany. What was the exact state of dependence on the German empire at this time cannot be stated; but sentiments of republican freedom are supposed to have arisen and been extensively diffused during the tenth century. The inhabitants of the cities elected their own magistrates and bishops, and this privilege led them to conclude that all just political power emanated from the people.

There appear to have been many wars and revolutions in Northern Italy during this obscure period of history. The claims of the German emperors to the sovereignty of this country were continued, though the utmost military force of the empire was incompetent to enforce them. Frederic Barbarossa, in the twelfth century, was the first emperor who violated the charter granted by his predecessors, by attempting to establish absolute power in the Italian cities. Milan was, at this time, the most important city in Lombardy. The inhabitants resisted the encroachments of the emperor, who raised a large army, and invaded Italy A. D. 1158. He laid siege to Milan, which was compelled to surrender by famine. Frederic disregarded the conditions of the surrender, and behaved with great tyranny. The Milanese revolted. The city was again besieged, and reduced by famine. Frederic took a cruel and barbarous revenge upon the inhabitants by utterly destroying Milan, leaving not one stone upon another, A. D. 1162.

Other Italian cities also felt the severities of the emperor; some were given to the flames, others were abandoned to the pillage of the German soldiery. These outrages led to the Lombard league, in which a number of the cities of this country combined to resist the encroachments of the emperor, A. D. 1167. The Milanese received assistance from their neighbors; their city rose again from its ruins, and was soon prepared to resist the armies of Frederic. The whole of that emperor's reign, from 1152 to 1190, was devoted to a ruinous and unsuccessful war with the Lombards. He crossed the Alps six times with large armies. In 1176, a desperate battle was fought between the Milanese and the army of Frederic, in the neighborhood of Milan. At first, the imperial troops had the advantage; but a body of nine hundred young Milanese, seeing the battle about to be lost, fell on their knees, uttered a prayer to Heaven, and then rushed desperately upon the enemy. This example animated their countrymen, and turned the tide of victory. The Germans were completely overthrown; the emperor fled from the field of battle, and escaped across the Alps in disguise.

A truce of six years followed, at the end of which a treaty was signed, by which Frederic acknowledged the independence of the Lombard republics, on the condition of the annual payment of a small sum of money. Thus, after a desolating war of a third of a century, the cities of Northern Italy, Milan, Bologna, Modena, Parma, Pavia, Verona, Mantua, Brescia, Bergamo, Ferrara, Venice, Lodi, Novara, Como, Vercelli, and some others, threw off their dependence upon the emperor of Germany. This treaty was made at Constance, in Switzerland, June 25, 1183, and deserves notice as the first recorded instance of a treaty between a monarch and his subjects, in which the right of independent self-government was established.

Various forms of popular government were adopted in the Lombard cities. The people sought security against the abuse of power in frequent election and rotation in office. But sudden and violent revolutions were of frequent occurrence. To guard against these, the expedient of an annual chief magistrate was adopted in most cities. This officer was named the *podesta*, and he exercised military and judicial power almost amounting to despotism. Councils of citizens were sometimes chosen to regulate or control the authority of the podesta; but the Italians were never able to balance political power in such a manner as to secure themselves against usurpation and tyranny. The legislative, the judicial, and the executive authorities were so united in the same individual or body, that no check upon the one or the other existed, and the arbitrary use of power was inevitable. The contests of the *Guelfs* and *Ghibellines* tended still further to introduce factions and animosities. In the thirteenth century, there were more than two hundred political communities in Italy, exercising the right of government independently of each other; and the transactions of these separate states render the history of this period a confused mass of details, which cannot be reduced to the form of a connected narrative.

The wars between these communities were carried on by bodies of militia, and all the population of the cities had a military organization. In every city there was a heavy car drawn by oxen, called the *carroccio*, and used for the purpose of displaying the flags and armorial insignia of the place. A tall staff was raised in the middle of the car, on which the standard was hoisted; and an altar was placed in front, at which the priest daily performed religious ceremonies. In the rear were seated the trumpeters, who sounded the charge or retreat. The carroccio was held sacred, and regarded as the rallying point of the troops, who all felt it a duty to do their utmost for its defence.

Milan was regarded as the leading city in Northern Italy. It had several minor cities and villages attached to its government. In the thirteenth century, Milan contained two hundred thousand inhabitants—a larger population than it possesses at the present day. Its well-paved streets and well-built houses, its stone bridges, its public monuments, and its palaces, gave it an appearance wholly distinct from that of the cities in the north and west of Europe. Its territory, which included Pavia, Bergamo, Lodi, and Como, beside one hundred and fifty villages and as many castles, maintained a body of eight hundred knights, and could raise an army of two hundred and forty thousand men. The population of Milan consisted of Guelf and Ghibelline nobles, with their followers, and of merchants, mechanics, and laborers. For a long time, the two noble families of Visconti and Della Torre contended for the chief influence in this city. In the middle of the fourteenth century, the Visconti were almost the absolute sovereigns of Milan and its dependencies. They ruled over sixteen cities of Lombardy, which had been independent republics, and threatened to become masters of Florence. Pope Urban V. attempted to oppose the usurpations of these rulers, who were extending their power into Tuscany. He issued a bull of excommunication against them. Barnabas Visconti, to whom the pope's legate presented the bull, ordered that messenger to *eat* the parchment document with its strings and leaden seals, which the legate was compelled to do with a sword at his throat.

Toward the close of the fourteenth century, through the influence of the emperor Wenceslaus, the Milanese territory was erected into a duchy, and conferred on a prince of the Visconti. The sovereignty passed by marriage to Francesco Sforza, who, from the condition of a common laborer, rose by his talents and courage to be duke of Milan. When the family became extinct, Milan fell under the dominion of the emperor Charles V.; and it was governed as a dependency of the Spanish monarchy till the year 1700, when it became absorbed in the Austrian empire.

Austria remained in quiet possession of the Milanese territory till the period of the French revolution. In 1796, a French army, under Bonaparte, invaded the north of Italy. Within two years, he made himself master of nearly all the large cities, and established the French power throughout the peninsula. The Venetian territory, the duchy of Milan, that of Modena, and a portion of the Papal States, were formed into a new government, called the *Cisalpine Republic*, which, after Napoleon became emperor, was transformed into the *Kingdom of Italy*. The crown was assumed by Napoleon, but the government was administered by his son-in-law, Eugene Beauharnois, as viceroy. After the overthrow of Napoleon, the territories of Milan, Mantua, Venice, and the Valteline, were assigned to Austria by the congress of Vienna. These constituted the Lombardo-Venetian kingdom. The Austrian rule was detested by the Italians, and in 1848, shortly after the expulsion of Louis Philippe from France, they rose in insurrection, and expelled the Austrian garrisons from Milan, Venice, and other cities. They were unable, however, to maintain their independence, and the Austrian dominion was restored in the following year. A large part of Lombardy was ceded to the new "Kingdom of Italy," in 1859, by the treaty of Villafranca. It belongs to the dominions of Victor Emmanuel.

Milan, once the capital of this part of the territory, has no antique structures, the ancient city having been totally destroyed in the twelfth century, as we have already stated. The *Duomo*, or Cathedral of Milan, is a magnificent Gothic edifice of white marble. The great theatre of the *Scala* is esteemed the finest in Italy. Several of the squares of Milan are very spacious. The population is somewhat over one hundred and seventy-five thousand.

CHAPTER CCCXLVI.

A. D. 500 to 1863.

VENICE. — *Commerce of the Middle Ages — Prosperity of the Venetian Republic — Changes in the Government — Rivalry with Genoa — Decline and Fall of the Republic.*

View in Venice.

VENICE is one of the most remarkable places in the world. Its situation is totally unlike that of any other great city. It surpassed all other cities of the middle ages for its commerce, its riches, and its maritime grandeur. It has been no less distinguished for its singular government and its peculiar, self-devoted policy. It is the only capital city of Europe that was not entered by an enemy from the downfall of the Roman empire to the period of the French revolution, and it preserved the name of a republic longer than any other city or nation in the world.

This city is built in the sea, near the north-western shores of the Adriatic. On those shores dwelt, in ancient times, a tribe called the *Heneti*, or *Veneti*. Their descendants continued to bear this name in the fifth century, when the Goths, under Alaric, invaded Italy. To escape from the ravages of these invaders, the Veneti fled to the marshes and sandy islets of the Adriatic, formed by the deposits of the many rivers which fall into the sea at the head of that gulf. Here they founded two small towns called *Rivoalto* or *Rialto* and *Malamocco*. In this retreat they were protected by the difficulty of approaching their abodes. The distance from the shore secured them from enemies on land, and the shallowness of the water hindered the approach of ships from the sea.

These people were first employed in making salt and in fishing. The sea was their only resource, and they soon engaged in maritime traffic. As early as the seventh century, the Venetians were known as traders at Constantinople, in the Levant, and in Egypt. In the year 809, Venice had increased so much that it occupied ninety small islands, all of which were connected by bridges. In 828, a fleet of Venetian merchantmen were driven, by a storm, into the port of Alexandria, in Egypt. In gratitude to Heaven for their deliverance, the crews obtained the body of St. Mark, or what was believed to be such and transported it to

A VIEW OF VENICE

their city. This apostle thus became the tutelary saint of Venice.

Venetian Fishermen.

The Venetians, from their situation, became expert navigators, and extended their trading voyages into every part of the Mediterranean. They established mercantile factories at Rome and Constantinople, where they obtained commercial privileges from the government. By these means, the city increased in wealth, population, and influence. The authority of the republic soon extended beyond the islands round the Rialto, and successive conquests added territories in Istria and Dalmatia to the rising empire. As early as the wars with the Saracens, in the ninth century, the Venetians had become skilled in naval warfare by their struggles with the piratical fleets which then infested the Mediterranean. In 997, the cities of Dalmatia put themselves under the protection of this people.

The most ancient form of government at Venice appears to have been republican. As early as the year 697, the inhabitants elected their chief magistrate, to whom they gave the title of *doge*, the Venetian word for *duke*. This privilege was granted to them by the Byzantine emperor, Leontius, who, at that time, exercised a nominal sovereignty over the territories on the Adriatic. There was a legislative power residing in the people, and an executive power vested in a body of nobles or leading men. The early political history of Venice is marked by a succession of violent tumults arising from the encroachments of the executive power on one hand, and the vindictive reaction of the people on the other. The crusades contributed greatly to the prosperity of Venice, and made it not only the richest, but most powerful city in Lombardy, where almost all the wealth of the East was concentrated. It was owing principally to the Venetians, that Constantinople was taken by the crusaders in 1204. A part of that city and its territory were, in consequence, added to the Venetian dominions. The doge, who had before this assumed the title of *duke of Dalmatia*, was now styled *duke of Three Eighths of the Roman Empire;* a singular, but not inaccurate title. The power and commerce of the Venetians were subsequently augmented by the acquisition of Candia, most of the islands in the Archipelago, and the Ionian group, and the establishment of commercial houses in Palestine and Egypt.

The naval superiority and maritime taste of the Venetians were exemplified by a remarkable state ceremony, annually performed on the festival of the Ascension. This was called the *Marriage of the Adriatic.* The doge, with a splendid train of attendants, and every accompaniment of pomp and parade, went on board the Bucentaur, or state galley, and threw a ring into

Wedding the Adriatic.

the sea with great formalities. By this ceremony, the republic was considered to have espoused the Adriatic. The custom is said to have taken its rise in the twelfth century, during the wars of Frederic Barbarossa, when Pope Alexander III. made a formal grant of the sovereignty of the Adriatic Sea, to the republic of Venice, in return for services rendered by that power to the pontiff; it ceased with the overthrow of the government, in 1797.

Toward the close of the thirteenth century, the college of nobles or tribunes who shared the government with the doge, and had been elected annually, made an effort to perpetuate their power. A violent opposition was made by the people, but the government prevailed, and declared that the members who then composed the grand council should hold their places during life, and be succeeded in office by their descendants, without the formality of an election. Thus an hereditary aristocracy was introduced into the republic. Conspiracies and insurrections were the first fruits of this change in the government, and in 1311 the celebrated *Council of Ten* was established. This was a secret conclave, which employed spies and informers, and ruled the state by terror and mystery. Secret denunciations were received from anonymous accusers and informers, who dropped their letters into a box styled the *Lion's Mouth.* This detestable establishment must be regarded as one of the causes which finally led to the ruin of the state.

From the origin of Venice to its overthrow, it bore the name of a republic; yet its government in latter times was arbitrary and tyrannical. Its social state was no less remarkable than its political constitution. The citizens of the republic were divided into five classes. First were the nobles, thirteen hundred in number, though not all of the same rank. They comprised four classes. The highest comprehended the descendants of those who assisted in the election of the first doge, in the sixth century; those, of course were the oldest noble families in Europe. The second rank consisted of those who were of the grand council when that body became perpetual and hereditary in 1310. The names of those were inscribed in a book called the *Golden Volume*, in which also the names of their descendants were recorded. The third rank comprehended those who purchased nobility and hereditary rights at the price of one hundred thousand Venetian ducats, about two hundred and forty thousand dollars, at a time when the government was in great need of money. The fourth rank consisted of counts and marquises, who bore these titles, but enjoyed no political distinction, and were not employed in the public service. The fifth rank comprehended all other persons, whose vocation was to obey, and never to act, speak, or think on public affairs, but as they were commanded. It is evident, therefore, that the republic of Venice was founded upon no principle of equality. The aristocracy exercised all the functions of government; the doge had very little executive power.

The republics of Genoa and Pisa were the commercial rivals of Venice. They engaged in the most obstinate and long-continued wars, in which many naval battles were fought with various success. The war of Chioggia, in 1378, brought Venice to the brink of ruin. The Genoese blockaded the city, and its surrender appeared inevitable; but the Venetians rescued themselves by immense efforts of courage and perseverance. Early in the fifteenth century, they were seized with an ambition of conquering Northern Italy. This involved them in new wars, which, though prosperous for a time, ultimately plunged them into great embarrassment and suffering. At this period, the republic was powerful and prosperous in a high degree. The commercial capital of Venice equalled thirty millions of dollars; the real estate, twenty millions; the ships amounted to over three thousand, and the sailors to twenty thousand. The doge, Mocenigo, who died at this time, advised the government not to go to war with Milan, a city from which the Venetians obtained every year a million and a half of dollars in the profits of trade. "You may become masters of all the gold in Christendom, by remaining at peace," said the doge; "but war, unjust war, will inevitably lead to ruin. You have men of probity and experience among you: choose one of them, but beware of Francis Foscari. If he is doge, you will have war, and war will bring poverty and dishonor." — Mocenigo died, and Foscari was elected.

As Mocenigo had predicted, a war with Milan followed. The Venetians conquered, and retained possession of several territories on the north of the Po. The members of the reigning families whom they subdued, were carried to Venice, and put to death, as the most certain mode of preventing revolt. It is said, however, that the Venetians proved lenient masters, and that the conquered people lost nothing by the change of sovereignty. The Venetian territory, on the continent, extended from the Adriatic to the River Adda, and from the Po to the Alps, comprising the cities of Verona, Padua, Vicenza, Bassano, Feltre, Belluno, Friuli, Brescia, Bergamo, and Crema. In addition to these conquests, the beautiful and fertile island of Cyprus came into the possession of the republic in 1486, in consequence of the death of Catharine Cornaro, a Venetian lady, the widow of James, king of that island. Venice then became the commanding political power in Christendom, and its citizens the most civilized people on earth — not only opulent and energetic, but devoted to the arts and sciences. Other states made the government of Venice their model, and even solicited Venetian counsellors and leaders. But the seeds of decay and ruin were lurking in the midst of this power and splendor. The territorial acquisitions of the republic drew her into the convulsive politics of Italy, and led the way to irretrievable disasters. From the close of the fifteenth century, the fortunes of the republic began to decline. Her political wisdom degenerated into petty prudence and cunning. Her wars and political entanglements materially reduced her population and wealth. The Venetian commerce was destroyed by a change in the route of trade to the East, occasioned by the discovery of the passage to India around the Cape of Good Hope. This threw the commerce of the East almost entirely into the hands of the Portuguese. The Turks, after capturing Constantinople in 1453, conquered, by degrees, all the Venetian possessions in the Archipelago and on the peninsula of Greece. In 1571, they subdued Cyprus, and in 1699, Candia. From this time, Venice took little part in general politics, and was satisfied with preserving her antiquated constitution, and her territories on the shores of the Adriatic. The invasion of Italy by Bonaparte, in 1796, put an end to the republic of Venice. It was compelled to follow the fortunes of the Cisalpine republic, the kingdom of Italy, and the Lombardo-Venetian kingdom as already related. It became involved in the agitations which followed the French revolution of 1848, and having revolted from Austria, sustained a long and rigorous siege, which terminated by its surrender August 22, 1849.

The Rialto.

Venice is still a magnificent city, though for many years it has been declining. No place in the world is more remarkably situated. It appears to rise out of the sea, to the eye of the distant spectator. It has no streets, but is traversed by an infinite number of canals, on which the inhabitants sail in gondolas. The architecture of the city exhibits a mixture of Greek, Gothic and Saracenic. The bridge of the Rialto consists of a single arch, one hundred and eighty seven feet long. The Square of St. Mark is the most magnificent in Italy. Fine paintings are abundant in this city. The population is about one hundred thousand.

CHAPTER CCCXLVII.

Parma. — Modena. — Massa. — Lucca.

The duchies of Parma, Modena, and Massa, lying in a group together, in the north of Italy, were, until 1860, nominally independent, but now belong, as provinces, to the kingdom of Italy, under Victor Emmanuel.

PARMA lies south of the Milanese, between Modena and the Sardinian territory. This city, and Placentia, or Piacenza, were long in possession of the popes; but, toward the close of the middle ages, they became republics. Civil wars, and the quarrels of the Guelfs and Ghibellines, caused them to fluctuate between one master and another; and, in 1512, Pope Julius II. established his authority over these cities. Pope Paul III. gave them to his son, Lewis Farnese, from whose descendants they passed to the king of Spain. In 1805, they were united to the French empire. After the overthrow of Napoleon, they were given, by the congress of Vienna, to Maria Louisa, his wife; she being a daughter of the emperor of Austria. As sovereign of these territories, she took the title of *duchess of Parma;* and died in 1847.

MODENA lies between Parma and the Roman territories. It has belonged successively to the emperor of Germany, the Venetians, the pope, the duke of Milan, and other powers. In the thirteenth century, it was annexed to the possessions of the house of Este, which reigned at Ferrara. In 1796, it was united to the Cisalpine republic; and afterward to the kingdom of Italy. In 1814, it was assigned to the archduke Francis of Austria.—The small city of MASSA was once a dependency of Modena; but its territory was added to the principality of Lucca and Piombino, which was governed, during the time of the French empire, by Eliza Bacciochi, the sister of Napoleon. It was erected into a duchy in 1814.—LUCCA was an independent republic, in the twelfth century; but it became gradually subjected to the authority of the German emperors, and Lewis of Bavaria erected it into a duchy in 1316. Its government was often changed, but it preserved its freedom from the fifteenth century till the time of Napoleon, who gave it to his sister Eliza. In 1815, it was transferred to the ducal family of Parma; and in 1847, it was annexed to the grand duchy of Tuscany.

CHAPTER CCCXLVIII.

A. D. 1000 to 1863.

THE KINGDOM OF SARDINIA.—*Origin of the House of Savoy—Sardinia—Genoa—Modern Revolutions.*

THIS kingdom comprised not only the island of that name, but the continental territories of Piedmont, Genoa, and Savoy. The continental portion is bounded north by Switzerland, east by Lombardy, south by the Mediterranean, and west by France. The Island of Sardinia lies to the south of Corsica, about midway between Italy and Africa. The whole kingdom comprised about twenty-nine thousand square miles, and contained, in the year 1860, considerably over four million inhabitants. Savoy, the south part of Piedmont, and the territory of Genoa, are mountainous, but the central portion of Piedmont consists of a level plain, watered by the Po and its tributaries. The Island of Sardinia is mountainous, with a tolerably fertile soil, but badly cultivated.

The house of Savoy, now the reigning family in this kingdom, ranks among the oldest in Europe, and may be traced to Humbert, a chief of the eleventh century. The counts of Savoy obtained their territories by the dissolution of the kingdom of Burgundy, the Frankish monarchy, and other governments of the middle ages. In 1482, the house of Savoy acquired, by marriage, a claim to the kingdom of Cyprus, which caused the kings of Sardinia, at a later period, to assume the title of *King of Cyprus and Jerusalem.* Victor Amadeus II., duke of Savoy, was the founder of the Sardinian monarchy. By the treaty of Utrecht, in 1713, he was allowed to add the Island of Sicily to his continental dominions, with the title of *king.* In 1720, he was compelled to exchange this island for Sardinia, which, since that period, has given its name to the kingdom.

Sardinia was one of the earliest conquests of the Carthaginians. The Greeks called this island *Ichnousa* and *Sandaliotis,* from its resemblance to the shape of the human foot. The Romans expelled the Carthaginians, but found the island so unhealthy that they made little attempt to improve it. The Vandals conquered it in the seventh century: the Pisans and Genoese succeeded them in the eleventh. In the thirteenth century, the pope obtained a cession of the island from the Pisans, but it did not long remain attached to the States of the Church. James II., king of Arragon took possession of it in the fourteenth century, and it continued under the government of Spain till 1708, when the British seized the island in the name of the emperor of Germany. In 1720, it was granted to the duke of Savoy, as above stated.

The history of Genoa is more interesting and rich in historical events than that of any other portion of the Sardinian monarchy. When the power of the Germans in Italy was overthrown by the extinction of the Carlovingian race, in the tenth century, Genoa rose to the rank of a republic, and first attracted notice by its wars with the Saracens, who had taken possession of the large islands in the Mediterranean. Till the eleventh century, it appears to have been politically connected with Lombardy. The situation of the city was favorable for commerce, and it engaged in the trade of the Levant, even earlier than Venice. In the twelfth century, Genoa appears in the crusades, and conspicuously in the commerce of the East. In the latter part of this century, its government extended over Montferrat, Monaco, Nice, Marseilles, nearly all the coast of Provence, and the Island of Corsica. The acquisitions of the Genoese on the continent gave rise to violent contentions with their rivals of Pisa, who were then powerful at sea. This quarrel lasted more than two centuries, when the naval strength of the Pisans was broken at the battle of Meloria, in 1282. In this battle, the Pisan fleet was captured, and eleven thousand prisoners carried to Genoa, where they languished in prison for many years, refusing to be liberated on the terms prescribed by their conquerors. Pisa never afterward appeared as a naval power, and its harbor was ruined.

Genoa was also the commercial rival of Venice. The Genoese aided the Greeks in recovering the throne of Constantinople from the Latins, who had seized it by the help of the Venetians. For this service they were rewarded by the gift of Pera, a suburb of Constantinople, on the northern point of the Golden Horn, or harbor of that city. Here the Genoese strengthened themselves by fortifications, and extended their commerce into the Black Sea. Their principal port on this sea was Caffa in the Crimea, from which they received, by the way of the Caspian, the products of the East. In the wars between Genoa and Venice, the Genoese sometimes equipped fleets of one hundred and fifty galleys, carrying forty thousand men. In the fourteenth century, they blockaded Venice, and were very near capturing the city; but by a sudden turn of fortune the Venetians recovered their superiority.

The commercial prosperity, power, and enterprise of the Genoese were such that, had they adopted a wise colonial system, and united all their dependencies by the tie of a common interest, they might have maintained the first rank among the commercial nations of Europe to the end of the middle ages, and prevented the conquest of Constantinople by the Turks. But they exhausted their strength by a profitless contention with their rival, Venice, and became a prey to civil discord and party spirit. By pursuing an unwise policy, they lost their commerce and territories in the Levant; and after the capture of Constantinople, the Genoese power rapidly declined. The form of government became changed from republican to aristocratical, and the people sometimes submitted to a foreign yoke in order to obtain relief from anarchy. One by one, all the colonies and dependencies were lost. Corsica, the last of all, revolted in 1730, and after a long war for its independence, was united to France in 1768.

In the wars which followed the French revolution, Genoa, Savoy, and Piedmont were overrun by the French armies. Savoy and Genoa were for a time annexed to France; but after various changes, these territories were, in 1814, combined with Sardinia into a kingdom. This union was distasteful to the Genoese, who sighed for their ancient independence. Amid the general overturn which followed the French revolution of 1848, Charles Albert, king of Sardinia, attempted to put himself at the head of the Italian revolutionary party, in opposition to the dominion of Austria. In this design he failed. His armies were defeated, and he was compelled to abdicate the crown in favor of his son. The Genoese, in the mean time, attempted to establish an independent government, but without success; and the Sardinian authority was restored. In 1860, after the battle of Solferino, a treaty, made between France and Austria, gave Sardinia to the King of Italy, and Savoy and Nice to France.

Turin, once the capital, is beautifully situated in the valley of the Po, surrounded by an amphitheatre of vine-clad hills, with lofty mountains in the distance. Turin is regularly built, with straight and spacious streets, ornamented with lines of porticos, and opening at their terminations to fine views over the surrounding country. The architecture of the city is very showy, and it may be termed a city of palaces. It has, also, several fine bridges across the Po, and its tributary, the Dora. The population of Turin is about one hundred and eighty thousand.

Genoa, formerly surnamed the *Lordly*, on account of its wealth and its magnificent palaces, now exhibits but a shadow of its former greatness. The main street is the most splendid in the world, being a continued series of palaces and magnificent buildings. The other streets are for the most part narrow and dark. Genoa has still some commerce, and manufactures of rich velvets, damasks, and satins. The neighborhood of the city is rocky and destitute of trees, but abounds with handsome villas and country houses. The population of Genoa is one hundred and twenty thousand.

Cagliari, the capital of the Island of Sardinia, is a place of considerable trade, but crowded, ill-built, and ill-paved. The population is about thirty thousand.

CHAPTER CCCXLIX.

544 B. C. to A. D. 1795.

CORSICA. — *Ancient Corsica — The Carthaginians — The Romans — The Byzantines — The Saracens — The Pisans — The Genoese — King Theodore — Conquest by the British — Annexation of Corsica to France.*

CORSICA lies north of Sardinia, from which it is separated by the Straits of Bonifacio. It is about one hundred and sixteen miles in length from north to south, and fifty in breadth. Its distance from the French coast is about one hundred and twenty miles, and from the coast of Italy about sixty. The face of the island is much diversified. A chain of mountains traverses the whole of its extent from north to south. Fertile valleys extend from this ridge to the east and west. The loftiest of the mountain heights are covered with snow during the greater part of the year. The climate is mild, but violent storms are not uncommon in the winter months. The air in general is clear and salubrious, though in certain parts there are marshy spots producing unwholesome exhalations. The Romans esteemed Corsica an unhealthy region. The soil is rich, but poorly cultivated, the inhabitants being indolent and careless of husbandry. The olive grows wild here, and the vine is cultivated to some extent. Various sorts of grain are raised. Population, 250,000.

The ancient Greeks called this island *Kyrnos;* and according to Herodotus, it was first settled by a body of Phoceans from Asia Minor, who fled before the conquering army of Cyrus, King of Persia, 544 B. C. Of the early history of Corsica, however, we have hardly any distinct knowledge. The troops of this island are mentioned as forming part of the Carthaginian armies in Sicily in the fifth century B. C., and it appears probable that the Carthaginians had conquered a part or the whole of Corsica. After the overthrow of Carthage, the Romans took possession of Corsica, and imposed a tribute of two hundred thousand pounds of wax upon the inhabitants — a curious fact, which serves to indicate what was the staple production of the island in early times. It was used by the Romans as a place of banishment, and here Seneca spent some time in exile.

On the downfall of the Roman empire, Corsica was seized by the Vandals, and subsequently by the Goths. But the successes of Belisarius compelled the latter to abandon the island; and it was annexed to the exarchate of Ravenna, as a dependency of the Byzantine empire. Early in the eighth century, the Saracens conquered this island; but the decline of their power in the west, and the attacks of the French and Arragonese compelled them to abandon it, and Corsica became the subject of contention between the pope and the republics of Pisa and Genoa. At length, the Genoese, having crushed the maritime power of their rivals of Pisa, made themselves masters of Corsica, which they ruled with a rod of iron.

In 1359, a national assembly of the Corsicans, the first of the kind recorded in the history of this island, was held, for the purpose of resisting the domination of foreigners, and the oppression of the native nobility, who, in some parts of the island, assumed the despotic authority of kings. The Genoese, at this time, held a considerable part of the island in subjection. In other parts, the Pisans and Arragonese had recovered portions of the territory. For a long time, the Corsicans maintained a struggle against the invaders. At intervals, they were compelled to submit to the Genoese, the Neapolitans, the Milanese, and the French. At the close of the fifteenth century, they placed themselves under the dominion of the lord of Piombino, by whom the island was sold to the Bank of St. George of Genoa. The bank officers governed Corsica for some years; but their dominion was disliked by the inhabitants, and led to insurrections. The French, who were at that time enemies to the Genoese, assisted the Corsicans in breaking their chains, and a furious war devastated the island. Neither party gave the other any quarter, and such as escaped the sword in battle, were sold as slaves to the Turkish corsairs which hovered about the island. These destructive hostilities continued for many years. The Corsicans offered this island to Louis XIV. of France, but he declined the gift. They next applied for aid to Austria, but without success. Still they continued to carry on the war against the Genoese for the independence of their country.

Matters were in this condition in 1736, when a vessel arrived at Corsica from Tunis, under the English flag, laden with munitions of war, clothing, and money, and bringing a person of noble exterior, richly dressed in the Turkish fashion, who professed to be a grandee of various countries, and made the most magnificent promises of foreign aid. This person was Theodore, baron of Neuhof in Westphalia, a Frenchman by birth, who, after a life of romantic adventures, aspired to be king of Corsica, and had secretly negotiated with some of the chiefs of the island for that purpose. The Corsicans, struck with his personal appearance, dazzled by his promises, and looking upon his opportune arrival as little less than miraculous, willingly chose him for their king. He exercised the regal power for some months, coined money, distributed patents of nobility, instituted an order of knighthood, and, to display his firmness in the maintenance of authority, put to death three persons, members of distinguished families. Being well supported by the Corsicans in the first moments of their enthusiasm, he captured several fortresses from the Genoese, who put a price upon his head. But as his promises of assistance from foreign countries failed, he lost popularity, and was at length compelled to abandon his kingdom. He visited successively Italy, France, and Holland; at Amsterdam he was arrested for debt, but liberated by a Jew, who furnished him with funds to fit out four ships, with which he appeared off Corsica again, A. D. 1738.

The Genoese had by this time obtained the assistance of the French, and reconquered a great part of the island. Theodore found it unsafe to land, and withdrew. The whole of Corsica submitted to the French and Genoese in 1739. Theodore appeared off the island a third time, in 1742; but the inhabitants showed no inclination to receive him. He afterward went to London, where he was imprisoned for debt, but obtained his release through the kind interference of Horace Walpole, and made over the kingdom of Corsica for the security of his creditors. He died at London, in 1756.

On the withdrawal of the French troops in 1742, the Corsicans rose again in insurrection against the Genoese. In 1745, a British fleet gave them some assistance by bombarding the city of Bastia, which was then held by the Genoese forces. The Corsicans were headed by General Paoli, and for some time carried on the war with success. At last, the Genoese, despairing of being able to subdue the island, ceded it to the French in 1768, the same year in which Napoleon Bonaparte was born at Ajaccio — a small seaport in the south-western part.

The French quickly reduced the Corsicans to submission, and Paoli fled to England. The French revolution, in 1789, gave the Corsicans some hope of regaining their independence. At first, the island was admitted to a free participation in the common rights of French citizens; it formed a department of France, and sent deputies to the national assembly. But in 1793, Paoli and some other leading men, being dissatisfied with the proceedings of the French convention, declared Corsica independent of France, and applied to the British for assistance. The French were driven out by a British fleet in 1794, and Corsica was annexed to the empire of Great Britain. A constitution was established, and the government was administered by a British viceroy. The Corsicans and the British, however, could not agree, and a strong party still existed in the island favorable to the French. After a possession of two years, the British abandoned Corsica, in 1798, and it was reannexed to France, in which connection it still remains.

Bastia, on the north-east coast, Ajaccio on the south-west, and Corte in the interior, are the chief towns: none of these are large. The Corsicans partake somewhat of the Italian character; but they are the descendants of so many nations, that they bear no close resemblance to any of the races around them. They are impulsive and revengeful in temper, and much addicted to robbery and assassination. Their courage is undoubted, and they have given birth to the greatest warrior of modern times.

CHAPTER CCCL.

A. D. 476 to 1347.

THE ROMAN STATES. — *Origin of the Papal Power — The Forged Donation of Constantine — Hildebrand's Usurpations — The Crusades — The Jubilee — The Residence at Avignon — Picture of Rome in the Middle Ages.*

THE territory belonging to the government of modern Rome comprises the central part of Italy. It is bounded north by the Lombardo-Venetian territory; east by the Adriatic and Naples, and south and west by Tuscany and the Mediterranean. It is the most fertile part of Italy, and was once the most populous region in Europe; but many portions of it are now deserted, or covered with ruins. The southern part comprises ancient Latium. It contains, since the establishment of the kingdom of Italy, in 1860, less than seven hundred thousand inhabitants.

When the Empire of the West was overthrown, the city of Rome retained the forms of its ancient government, but fell under the dominion of various powers, as we have related in the preceding chapters. This part of its history is enveloped in much obscurity. At length, the authority of the popes began to acquire preponderance at Rome, and the annals of the city become more distinct. For many centuries, its history is little more than the history of the papal power, and it is impossible to separate politics from theology. Small and obscure beginnings laid the foundation of the papal dominion, nor is it possible to fix the precise date of its commencement. The worship of images threw the Byzantine empire into great convulsions in the eighth century. The emperor took the side of the *Iconoclasts*, or image-breakers. Gregory III., bishop of Rome, took the opposite side, and endeavored to arouse a national feeling among the Italians against the Iconoclasts and the emperor. This was a movement toward independence. The Lombards embraced the religious pretext to expel the Byzantines from Italy; but the pontiff, finding that the conquerors were about to impose their own yoke upon him, invoked the assistance of the Franks. Supported by the arms of Pepin and Charlemagne, the bishops of Rome maintained the independence of the Roman territories, and were thus raised to the rank of temporal princes. The proper history of the papacy begins at this point. Adrian I., bishop of Rome, was the pontiff who first combined the elements of the papacy into a system — A. D. 772.

Church of St. Peter's, at Rome.

This dominion was founded upon a forgery. Pepin and Charlemagne, having been favored by the pope in the establishment of their power in France, made a grant to him of the Roman territories, which they had wrested from the exarchate of Ravenna. To secure and give a color of justice to these acquisitions, the popes produced a forged deed, which purported to be from the hand of the emperor Constantine. This document conferred on the popes the sovereignty over Rome, Italy, and the western provinces. Thus the gift of the French monarch was made to appear the restitution of ancient possessions; and the temporal power of the popes, while yet in its infancy, was invested with the sanction of remote antiquity. The forgery is notorious, and is now admitted even by Catholic writers; but in the early days of the papal power, the donation of Constantine was universally received as genuine, and it was long regarded as the legal instrument by which the dominion of the popes was established.

At first, the power of the pope was subordinate to that of the emperor, and confined within very narrow limits. The right of appointing the pope was vested in the emperor; but the power of the former constantly increased, till the ecclesiastical authority of the emperors was almost annihilated. For a long time, political power in Italy was unsettled; a great struggle arose between the popes and the emperors of Germany. The feudal lords of Italy aimed at independence, and the large cities tried to establish freedom. Sometimes the emperor combined with the pope against the people of Rome. Sometimes rival popes struggled for the supremacy. The papal authority greatly flourished during the tenth and eleventh centuries; but from the time of Leo IX., (A. D. 1048,) the popes employed every means which ambition could suggest to render their dominion complete and universal They not only aspired to the character of supreme legislators in the church, but asserted themselves to be the lords of the universe, the arbiters of the fate of empires, and supreme rulers over the kings and princes of the earth.

The papacy derived its greatest strength in the eleventh century, from its opposition to feudalism. Hildebrand, or Gregory VII., (A. D. 1073,) was the first who perceived the tendency of this, and he made the most adroit use of the discovery. In breaking down the imperial authority, and the power of the Italian nobles, he built up the papal dominion to an extraordinary height. He considered the Roman pontiff in his capacity of Christ's vicegerent on earth, as the king of kings and the whole universe as his lawful domain. Under this most arrogant pretension, he claimed tribute from France, Spain, England, Denmark, Poland, and Germany, requiring the kings and princes of those countries to do homage to the Roman pontiff, to make a secure grant of their kingdoms and territories to him, and to hold them under his jurisdiction. The disorganized state of Europe offered a fair prospect of realizing this scheme of dominion; and if the success of Hildebrand had corresponded to the extent of his ambitious views, all the kingdoms of Europe would have been at this day tributary to the Roman see, and its princes the soldiers and vassals of the pope. Many parts of Hildebrand's policy succeeded, and from the time of his pontificate, the face of Europe underwent a considerable change. The prerogatives of the emperors, and other sovereign princes, were necessarily diminished. The crusades increased the papal authority, which may be said to have attained to its height about the close of the thirteenth century.

By the crusades, the popes obtained the privilege of interfering in the internal management of the Christian states. They compelled emperors and kings to assume the cross and lead their armies to the Holy Land. They levied taxes, at their discretion, on the clergy throughout Christendom for the support of these wars. They took under their immediate protection the persons and property of those who enlisted, and these individuals frequently bequeathed large estates to the church. While the papal power thus increased, that of monarchs declined. At first, the pope wore a single crown. Boniface (A. D. 1298) claimed to be both pope and emperor, and is said to be the first pontiff who wore a double crown. Urban V. (A. D. 1362) added the third. Boniface founded the *Jubilee* in 1299. This institution was borrowed, perhaps, from the jubilee of the Hebrews, but it was applied to a very different purpose. Plenary indulgence was granted to all who should appear at Rome during its continuance, confess their sins, partake of the sacrament, and visit certain churches. This was a contrivance to enrich the papal treasury, and proved so successful that the original term of fifty years for its return, was shortened by successive popes to thirty-three, and then to twenty-five years. More than a million of pilgrims resorted to Rome on these occasions, and priests were continually in attendance at the churches, with rakes and shovels, to gather into heaps the money contributed by these immense crowds.

The papal power sensibly declined in the fourteenth century. Philip the Fair, king of France, by a series of artful intrigues, procured the election of the archbishop of Bourdeaux — a creature of his own — to the papacy. The seat of the papal government was removed, in 1307, to Avignon, in France, where it continued till 1378. Clement V. was the first of the popes of Avignon. The transfer of the papal empire to France was injurious to the power of the pope in Italy, though that country remained under his dominion. There were three parties at Rome, headed by three powerful families — the Orsini, the Savelli, and the Colonna. Nearly all the castles and strong places in the Roman territory belonged to these families, who carried on a perpetual warfare with each other, and kept in their pay bands of armed men, who were little better than banditti. The country people, attracted by the hope of plunder, joined these turbulent chiefs, and abandoned their agricultural occupations for the uncertain gains of war, so that the fields were neglected, and the country around Rome was the worst cultivated part of Italy. The want of a proper government tended to increase these disorders, and sometimes there was a long interregnum between the death of one pontiff and the election of another. When a pope died, it was customary for the chief magistrate of Rome to send men with muffled drums through the streets, and order the gates to be thrown open. The inhabitants of every house were obliged to burn lamps all night in their windows, and a watch was held in every parish.

The German emperors, during the middle ages, were crowned at Rome; and, on such occasions, there were commonly scenes of great turbulence and disorder in the city. In the case of rival chiefs contending for the honors of the coronation, battles were fought in the streets, and churches were garrisoned and fortified. The fall of houses, conflagration, slaughter, the ringing of bells in all the churches, the shouts of the combatants, the clang of arms, and the rush of people from every quarter, formed a universal uproar, which was the common prelude to the coronation of a German emperor in Rome.

The people of Rome, throughout the middle ages, were very little disposed to acquiesce in the temporal government of the pope. His pretensions and rights were indefinite and unconfined by positive law; the people, generally, desired to be free. Beside the common causes of insubordination and anarchy among the Italians, which applied equally to the capital city, other sentiments, peculiar to Rome, preserved an influence for many centuries. There still remained enough in the wreck of their vast inheritance to swell the bosoms of her citizens with a consciousness of their own dignity. They bore the venerable name of *Roman;* they contemplated the monuments of art and empire, and sometimes forgot, in the illusions of national pride, that the sceptre of universal empire had departed forever. Yet several of the popes were expelled from Rome by the people during the twelfth century. Lucius II. died of wounds received in a tumult, and the government was vested in fifty-six senators, annually chosen by the people. This constitution lasted nearly half a century. In the twelfth and thirteenth centuries, the senators exercised one distinguishing attribute of sovereignty — that of coining money. Some of their coins still exist, with inscriptions in a very republican tone. The temporal authority of the popes, in respect to Rome, varied, at different periods, according to their personal character.

CHAPTER CCCLI.

A. D. 1347 to 1863.

Rienzi — The Bannerets — The Schism — Capture of Rome by the Constable of Bourbon — Paul IV. — Gregory XII. — Spectacles at Rome — Deposition of the Pope by the French — Restoration — Revolution of 1849. — The Roman Republic — Capture of Rome by General Oudinot.

Pope Pius IX.

An interesting episode in the history of Rome is furnished by the achievements of Cola Rienzi. This person was the son of a Roman citizen in humble life. He was distinguished in early youth by extraordinary talent, an ardent imagination, and an enthusiastic admiration of the liberties enjoyed by the ancient Romans in the days of the republic. Carried away by the strength of his feelings, he imagined that the glory of those days might be renewed, and he seized every opportunity of impressing his own sentiments on the minds of the people. While the popes resided at Avignon, frequent opportunities occurred for making changes in the government of Rome; and in 1347, Rienzi seized an occasion to bring about a revolution. During the absence from the city of Stephen Colonna, the ruling senator, Rienzi excited a revolt among the citizens. They took up arms, expelled the nobles from Rome, and established a republican gov ernment, called the *Good Estate.* Rienzi was chosen chief magistrate, with the title of *tribune.* He made use of his power to repress the nobles, and secure popular privileges. But his sudden success, and the multiplicity of business which overwhelmed him, disordered his brain. He ceased to act with moderation, and was at length assassinated in a popular tumult. The Good Estate of Rome perished with Rienzi. The nobles returned to the city, the Colonnas were reinstated in the government, and the old quarrels of the rival families were renewed.

Not long after the death of Rienzi, the freedom of Rome revived again in republican institutions. Magistrates, called *bannerets*, chosen from the thirteen districts of the city, with a militia of three thousand citizens at their command, were placed at the head of the commonwealth. The great object of this new organization was to intimidate the Roman nobility, whose outrages, in the total absence of government, had grown intolerable. Several of them were hanged the first year by order of the bannerets. How long this form of government continued is not known. At length Pope Gregory XI., at the earnest solicitation of the people of Rome, removed from Avignon to that city, in 1378.

This event caused a great schism in the Catholic church, which lasted forty years. The French cardinals elected a Frenchman for pope, who resided at Avignon. The Italian cardinals made choice of an Italian, who fixed his seat at Rome. All Christendom was divided between these two pontiffs, who reigned, at the same time, for thirty-eight years. In 1409, a third pope was set up; and the schism was not terminated till 1417, when Martin V., a Roman, was made sole pontiff by the council of Constance. The papal authority was much weakened by this long schism, and the scandalous behavior of many of the rivals. The political history of the popes is, indeed, little more than a history of intrigues. At this period, the Roman state had not much significance in Italy, separate from its ecclesiastical character.

During the wars of the emperor Charles V., Rome was taken and sacked, (A. D. 1527,) by the imperial troops, under the command of the constable of Bourbon. For nine months the city continued in their power, and was exposed to all the outrages which the unlicensed brutalities of a horde of barbarous German and Spanish mercenaries could inflict on the inhabitants. The churches and palaces were pillaged; statues and columns were overthrown; and the halls of the Vatican, and the frescoes of Raffael, still bear the marks of these calamities.

Some of the popes ruled with mildness, and were much beloved; others were very arbitrary, and sometimes, by their severity, occasioned tumults in the city. One of the latter was Paul IV., a proud man, ambitious of ruling over other princes, as the popes of old had done. He obtained the papal throne in 1555. But the state of society had undergone an essential change since the flourishing days of ecclesiastical despotism. The pontiff had now little authority out of his own dominions, except in such affairs of the church as came under his special jurisdiction; nor could he expect any homage from the rulers of other states, beyond that which was due to his sacerdotal character. Paul IV. was highly unpopular at Rome; he imposed heavy taxes on the people, and augmented the power of the inquisition, in consequence of which, the prisons of that tribunal were filled with people suspected of heresy. On his death, the people broke open the dungeons, and released the prisoners.

One of the most distinguished of the popes was Gregory XIII., who was elected in 1572. He was much beloved for his mild government; and it was by his authority that the calendar was altered, and the reckoning, called the *New Style*, introduced. This was adopted by all Catholic countries in 1582, but the Protestants did not receive it till many years later.

In the sixteenth century, the power of Rome received a great shock from the Protestant Reformation, but this important event will form a separate portion of our history. From the period of the reformation down to the close of the eighteenth century, Rome affords very little matter for political history.

The city has always exhibited a spectacle of extraordinary gayety and show on the occasion of the coronation of the pope, which continues to be a very magnificent ceremony. It was usually performed in the church of St. John de Lateran, one of the most ancient of all the sacred edifices of Rome. After the pope had been elected by the cardinals, a splendid procession marched from his palace, the Vatican, to the church. The cardinals all attended on horseback, in their purple robes and scarlet hats. The nobles of Rome, in full dress, followed, each attended by four pages in rich array. The pope himself rode on a white mule, preceded by his Swiss guards, in coats of mail, and caps adorned with large plumes of feathers.

In this order the procession traversed the whole length of the city to the Lateran Church, where the pope was duly crowned. After this ceremony, he proceeded to the Capitol, where crowds of the common people thronged around him to beg his blessing. The evening was devoted to illuminations, fireworks, and other public rejoicings. The most striking feature in the public festivities at Rome, at the present day, is the illumination of the great dome of St. Peter's, which has a brilliant effect, as seen against the clear deep blue of an Italian sky.

The invasion of Italy by the French, under Bonaparte, in 1796, led the way to important revolutions in the government of Rome. The pope was at first inclined to be hostile toward the French; but their repeated victories in the north of Italy gave them a decided predominance of power throughout the peninsula; and the pope, Pius VI., was glad to make a treaty with Bonaparte, by which he surrendered to the French a large number of the finest pictures and statues in Rome. The good understanding between the two nations, however, was but of short duration. A popular tumult occurred at Rome, in which the French secretary of legation was killed. The French directory, either irritated at this result, or eager for a pretext for interfering, immediately resolved to depose the pope. Accordingly, in 1798, on a day of public rejoicing at Rome, being the anniversary of the pope's election, two French officers entered the chapel where he was attending the ceremonies, and announced to him that his power was at an end. His Swiss guards were dismissed, and he was placed under the protection of the soldiers of the French republic. The cardinals were all deprived of their authority, and a new government was formed, consisting of consuls ministers of state, and deputies from the provinces The government, however, remained under the influence of the French, and the pope retired to Florence from which place he removed to France, where he died.

After Bonaparte had placed himself at the head of the government of France, and reconquered Italy by the campaign of Marengo, in 1800, he allowed the new pope, who had been elected at Paris, with the title of Pius VII., to assume the pontifical chair at Rome. In July, 1800, he made his entry into the city. He was a man of mild temper, and endeavored to restore every thing to its former state. But his political authority was merely nominal, for he could do nothing without the sanction of the French. In 1804, the pope was required by Bonaparte to attend the ceremony of his coronation, at Paris, when he became emperor of the French. In 1808, Napoleon determined to deprive the pope of all political power. He accordingly wrote to him, desiring that he would resign the sovereign authority of Rome, and content himself with the office of bishop of that city. The pope did not willingly submit; and a French army was sent to Rome, which took him prisoner, and removed him to the north of Italy. Rome was united to the French empire. The convents were all broken up, the monks and nuns sent to their homes, and a new government organized. Both the city of Rome and its territory were much improved under the French government. Manufactures and agriculture were encouraged, the cultivation of silk, cotton, the olive, &c., promoted, and the general condition of the people improved. Rome continued under the government of the French till 1814, when Napoleon, perceiving his own fortunes declining, set the pope at liberty. The overthrow of Napoleon, which followed shortly after, restored the papal government at Rome, and the old order of things was reëstablished in every respect.

Pius VII. died in 1823. His successor, Leo XII., reigned six years, and was followed by Pius VIII., who, being very old, and in feeble health, lived only a few months after his election, and died in 1831. He was succeeded by Gregory XVI. His reign was not distinguished by any remarkable event. Pius IX. succeeded him in 1846. He began his reign by an attempt to introduce reforms into his government, and took measures to establish a system of popular representation. The overthrow of Louis Philippe, in France, in 1848, excited the hopes of the revolutionary party throughout Italy, and the pope hesitated to grant the full measure of popular privileges demanded by his subjects. The people of Rome rose in insurrection, and the pope, in 1849, fled to Gaeta, in the kingdom of Naples. The Romans proclaimed a republic, and organized a government under three triumvirs. The government of Louis Bonaparte, in France, took the side of the pope against the Roman republicans, and sent an army, under General Oudinot, against them. Rome was besieged and bombarded for several weeks. The inhabitants, under Mazzini, Garibaldi, and other energetic leaders, made a resolute defence, but abandoned it in July, 1849. The French took possession of Rome,* and the authority of the pope was restored. The formation of the kingdom of Italy, in 1860, however, deprived him of more than half of his temporal dominions.

Rome, the capital of the Papal States, stands upon the Tiber, about fifteen miles from its mouth. Its walls comprise a circuit of sixteen miles; but a part of the enclosure is waste. Modern Rome is a dull. though interesting city, abounding in palaces, churches, and public buildings. The streets are, in general, narrow and crooked, but some are regular and spacious. Many of the squares are very fine. The great architectural wonder of Rome is the church of St. Peter, which may be regarded as the most sumptuous edifice ever reared by the hand of man. The venerable and imposing ruins of ancient Rome are too numerous to specify; but we will mention a few of the most interesting. These ruins may be divided into three classes, with respect to age — 1. Those of the ancient kings of Rome; 2. Those of the republic; 3. Those of the empire. Those which remain of the first class are very few. One of the most remarkable is the

Mamertine Prison.

Mamertine prison, supposed to be the work of Ancus Martius, or Mamertius, the fourth king of Rome, who flourished about the year 600 B. C. There is a Catholic legend that the apostle Paul or Peter was confined in its dungeons, and that a spring of water miraculously sprung up from the floor, to enable him to baptize the jailer, whom he had converted. The antiquities of the republican age are also few: they comprise a massy square triumphal arch, dedicated to the four-fronted Janus, the relics of a theatre, some tombs, and the foundations of certain structures on the Capitol. The ruins of the era of the empire are abundant, and comprise almost every species of edifice known to ancient architecture. The most imposing of these is the Coliseum, an enormous building, erected by Vespasian and Titus, for the exhibition of public shows. It was capable of containing eighty thousand specta-

* These events are too recent to be judged without caution. France had been a republic but little more than a year, when she interfered to suppress the republican government of Rome, and to restore to dominion that power which has long been regarded as the chief security and support of legitimist opinions and institutions in Europe. The grounds of this intervention were, that France had a right thus to secure the share of influence which was her due in the "balance of Europe;" and, moreover, it was better for the Romans, and for Italy, that she should be the instrument of restoration than the Austrians and Neapolitans, who, at the time, were threatening the insurgent republicans with overthrow. How far these were the true reasons, how far they are just, and what will be the issue of a course so extraordinary, must be left to the judgment and the developments of time.

tors, and, although houses and palaces almost without number have been built from its ruins, it still remains an enormous pile of dilapidated magnificence, to strike every beholder with astonishment.

Ruins of the Palace of the Cæsars.

The remains of the palace of the Cæsars, on the Palatine, still exhibit an immense mass of walls and arches, among which are scattered and broken columns, sculptured marbles, and countless other architectural relics, which belonged, perhaps, to the Golden House of Nero. The remains of the ancient baths of Rome cannot be viewed without admiration; and the same may be said of the aqueducts, some of which still serve the purpose of conveying water to the city. Nearly one half the space contained within the walls of Rome is strown with ruins. Notwithstanding this, the ancient capital of the world is an agreeable residence. The pictures, statuary, libraries, &c., of Rome are the wonder and delight of every traveller. Among

Head of the Apollo Belvidere.

its treasures are the statues of the Apollo Belvidere and the Venus de Medicis, deemed the finest specimens of sculpture in the world. The present population of Rome is about one hundred and ninety thousand.

Bologna stands on the eastern side of the Apennines. It is one of the most ancient cities in Italy. Its university, which once contained ten thousand students, and its school of painting, have raised it to high distinction as a seat of learning and art. It is a well-built city, with long lines of arches and columns, affording sheltered walks to foot passengers. The palaces are spacious, and distinguished for their architectural beauty, and the works of art which they contain. The population is about sixty-five thousand.

Ancona, on the Adriatic, is the most important seaport in the papal territory. The harbor is protected by a magnificent mole erected by the emperor Trajan. Ferrara, on the northern boundary, is a city of grass-grown streets and abandoned palaces. Loreto, on the Adriatic, is famous for its Holy House, a chapel which, according to the Catholic legends, was transported through the air from Palestine to this place. Civita Vecchia, on the Mediterranean, is a seaport, with some small commerce.

The republic of San Marino is a small district, completely enclosed in the papal territory. It consists of a steep mountain, covering an area of about five miles square, near the shore of the Adriatic. The town of San Marino stands on the top of the mountain, and contains about seven thousand inhabitants. The history of this little community can be traced backward as far as the fifth century, when a Dalmatian stonecutter, named *Marino*, built a hermitage in this neighborhood. His religious zeal procured for him the title of *saint*, and a town rose gradually near this spot, which governed itself by its own laws, and was, in every respect, except political strength, an independent state. Small as this community was, it did not escape the convulsions caused by the contention of the Guelfs and Ghibellines, but took sides with the latter. At that time, San Marino appears to have had no political connection with the pope. It maintained its independence till 1739, when the pope seized it; but the emperor of Germany compelled him to restore it to freedom.

San Marino was the only part of Italy that was not revolutionized by Napoleon. The great conqueror spared this little republic, and even made the inhabitants an offer of additional territory, which they had the wisdom to refuse. The independence of San Marino was confirmed on the restoration of the pope, in 1814; and the government of this republic is now vested in a council of three hundred ancients, and a senate composed of twenty patricians, twenty burgesses, and twenty peasants. The chief executive officer has the title of *gonfalonier*, and is elected every three months.

CHAPTER CCCLII.

A. D. 476 to 1348.

Tuscany. — *Ancient Etruria — Charlemagne — The Guelfs and Ghibellines — Popular Government of Florence — Famine of* 1347 *— Great Plague — Boccaccio's Description.*

The modern Grand Duchy of Tuscany is bounded north and east by the Papal States, south and west by that part of the Mediterranean which is sometimes called the *Tyrrhene* or *Tuscan Sea*. It is more mountainous than the papal dominions, being traversed through its whole extent by the Apennines. It is, however, more productive, from the general industry and skill of the inhabitants. Its climate is mild, and, in most parts, salubrious. The vine, the olive, and the mulberry are cultivated with great success. The oil and the wine of Tuscany are the best in all Italy, and its manufactures of silk and straw braid are equally preëminent. Its cities are handsome, well built, and remarkably clean. Tuscany may be regarded, in many important points, as bearing the same rank in Italy that New England does in the United States. It contains, including Lucca, eight thousand seven hundred square miles, and one million nine hundred and fifty thousand inhabitants.

This country was comprised within the limits of the ancient Etruria. Its inhabitants were civilized, and dwelt in well-built and flourishing cities before the foundation of Rome. Some of these are flourishing still, as Cortona, Perugia, Siena, Volterra, &c. They were generally built on the tops of steep hills, and were surrounded by thick walls, constructed of blocks of stone of immense size. Some of these walls still remain, very little impaired by the lapse of three thousand years. The Etruscans were a very powerful nation. In the reign of Porsenna, in the fifth century before Christ, they captured Rome, and compelled the inhabitants to deliver up all their weapons, and stipulate not to make use of iron tools or implements. They long resisted the attacks of the Romans, and were not finally subdued till the third century before the Christian era. A considerable part of the Etruscan religion was incorporated into that of the Romans, such as augury, soothsaying, &c.

Florence, at present the largest city and capital of Tuscany, is not of Etruscan origin. It appears to have been founded by the Romans, in the time of Sulla, about half a century before Christ. It was destroyed by the barbarians who overthrew the Roman empire; but, in the time of Charlemagne, it reappeared. This monarch erected Tuscany into a duchy, and attached it to his empire. It was governed by marquises or dukes, who, in course of time, made themselves independent. At the close of the tenth century, the race of Charlemagne lost their dominion in Italy, and the cities of Tuscany became republics, each governed by a duke and senators. The Italian cities, at this period, were very different from those of any other country. They remained, for the most part, such as they existed in the time of the Romans, inhabited by free citizens, who elected their own magistrates, and made their own municipal laws. In other countries, the cities and towns belonged to the estates of the feudal lords, and their inhabitants were the vassals of those lords, and had no right to make laws for themselves, till they were enabled to do so by charters granted at various times by different sovereigns. There were no free towns or cities in France or Germany at this period, so that the citizens were little better than slaves; and those who exercised any kind of trade were treated with contempt, and liable to be deprived of their profits by their feudal superiors. But, in Italy, the citizens were a free and opulent class of people, and commerce was regarded as an honorable calling.

All Italy was at this time, and long after, divided into two parties, called *Guelfs* and *Ghibellines*, from two ancient German families, bearing these names. The Ghibellines usually took the side of the German emperor against the pope. The Guelfs sided with the pope against the empero. The Guelfs are commonly regarded as the champions of popular liberty; but they appear to have been, when in power, quite as fond of arbitrary measures as their opponents. Both parties were composed of noble families, and fought mainly for their own interests. The conflict between the popes and the emperors arose from a dispute as to the nominal sovereignty over the Italian cities, although these cities were in reality free. Most of the Ghibelline nobles lived in castles among the mountains, where they kept numerous bands of retainers, and exercised a sort of sovereignty over the surrounding country. They adhered to the emperor because it was convenient for them to live under nominal subjection to a prince whose absence from the country left them at liberty to do as they pleased. The common people were in general Guelfs, because they looked to the pope for the protection of their rights against the encroachments of the emperors.

Many Ghibelline nobles, however, found it convenient to live under the laws of the republics, and make their home within the precincts of the towns, where, to defend themselves from the opposite party, they erected fortified dwellings, with thick walls, strong towers, high narrow windows, and heavy doors of oak, secured by massive bolts and bars. The Guelf nobles followed the example of fortifying their houses. All their castles were crowded with knights, esquires, and dependants of inferior rank, forming little armies ready for action. Thus a regular system of civil war was established. At every public festival or assembly of any kind, some altercation was sure to arise between a Guelf and a Ghibelline. A war-cry was instantly raised, and the fiery-tempered Italians, rushing forth with drawn swords at the sound, challenged all they met, to know whether they were friends or foes. In Shakspeare's Romeo and Juliet, this state of society, and its tragical effects, are very strikingly depicted.

When Florence begins to be the subject of historical notice, about the middle of the twelfth century, we find it a turbulent republic, with the Guelfs and Ghibellines in perpetual conflict. The Florentines had long been distinguished by their arts and commerce, and they very justly regarded the higher class of citizens, who attained wealth and honors by their talents and industry, as superior to the nobles, many of whom lived by plunder. They therefore excluded the nobility from their council of government, and formed it from among the citizens of certain trades or professions. No one could be a magistrate, or hold any office of importance, unless his name was registered as belonging to some trade. Sometimes a chief magistrate was appointed, with the title of *gonfalonier*, because he carried the *gonfalon*, or banner of state. When this banner was displayed, the citizens were obliged to assemble and obey the orders of the gonfalonier. Many persons of rank were banished from Florence in these troubled times, and among others, Dante, the great poet, who had been one of the city council of Florence. He was expelled from the city with his party, in **1302**, and passed the remainder of his life in exile, principally at Verona and Ravenna. In his banishment, he composed his great poem of the *Divina Commedia*, which abounds with allusions to the political history and leading characters of that age.

The middle of the fourteenth century was marked by dreadful calamities in Italy. First came a famine caused by excessive rains, which prevented the ripening of the crops. The humane and considerate character of the Florentines appears to great advantage in this emergency. In **1347**, the number of persons in Florence who received bread daily at the public cost was ninety-four thousand. No poor person or stranger was left without provision. The suffering, nevertheless, was so great, that the collection of debts was universally suspended. In the next year appeared the great plague. It originated in the East, and spread over all Europe, continuing its ravages for two years. The first European country which it visited was Italy, to which it was brought from the Levant by the trading-ships of the Pisans, the Genoese, and the Catalonians. It quickly extended to Florence, and spread through Tuscany, from which it pursued its desolating course over all Italy.

Villani, the historian, who has given us a description of the commencement of this terrible scourge, was not able to finish it, falling himself a victim to the disorder. The celebrated Boccaccio, one of the fathers of the Tuscan tongue, was more fortunate. He had retired from Florence, with a select society, to breathe the salubrious air upon the delightful hills in the neighborhood, spending his time in mirth and gayety, out of sight of the general calamities in which the city was involved. The manner in which this society passed their lives, recounting, by turns, stories, anecdotes, and jests, has given birth to a book, called the *Decameron*, considered the finest in the Tuscan language. From the history of this malady, which serves as a preface to the Decameron, we learn that it had been attended, in the Levant, with a bleeding at the nose and mouth, which were the fatal symptoms that appeared in the great plague of the year 543. In Florence, the disease was indicated by swellings either in the groin or under the arms, and afterward in other parts of the body; these were succeeded by black or livid spots, which, as soon as they were visible, were considered a certain sign of death within the third or fourth day. Whole families dropped off in a few days, and the immense number of the dead who were daily borne through the streets to the burial-ground, filled all ranks of persons with such horror, that both public and private business became suspended. The fields, destitute of laborers, were left untilled, and the ripe crops wasted uncut. The authority of the laws being no longer exercised, an unbridled licentiousness reigned among those abandoned wretches who, undaunted in the midst of calamity, chose this scene for the indulgence of their propensity to crime. It appears that, since the great pestilence in the days of Justinian, the greatest within the memory of mankind, there has not been a more fatal one than this of 1348. In six months, from March to September, one hundred thousand persons were said to have died within the walls of Florence.

CHAPTER CCCLIII.

A. D. 1378 to 1863.

Rivalry of Pisa and Florence — The Medici — The Pazzi — Decline of the Republic — Modern History of Tuscany.

The city of Pisa, which was situated at the mouth of the Arno, and was distinguished for its maritime enterprise, was long the rival of Florence; and the two republics carried on the most destructive wars, during many years, for the supremacy in Tuscany. The Florentines had no seaport, but they defeated the Pisans on land, and, at length, collected a navy, by hiring ships of the Genoese. For the first time, the Florentine flag was displayed on the ocean, A. D. 1361. Pisa was attacked from the sea; the great iron chain which protected the mouth of the harbor was broken, and the city was captured. The chain was sent to Florence as a trophy, where a portion of it may be seen at the present day suspended in one of the public squares.

Shortly after this victory, the Medici family began to rise into notice at Florence. They were originally physicians, as their name denotes; and the memory of this was preserved, when they rose to power, by the exhibition of a number of pills on their coat of arms. They first acquired influence by the wealth which they obtained in trade. Cosmo de' Medici, born in 1389, was at the head of a commercial establishment which had counting-houses in all the great cities of Europe. He lived in a magnificent palace at Florence, where he was constantly surrounded by poets, artists, and learned men, who enjoyed his patronage and liberality. He was the richest private man in Europe, and rose to be the chief magistrate of Florence, which he ruled like a prince. The Florentines at this time had the finest manufactures in the world, among which were those of gold, silver, and woollen stuffs, which were carried to great perfection. The adjoining territory was well cultivated, and the peasants were industrious and happy. Such was the munificence of Cosmo, that he gave away for public and charitable uses a sum equal to six millions of dollars. The Florentines ordered his tomb to be inscribed with the words, "*The Father of his Country.*" Cosmo's grandson, Lorenzo, surnamed the *Magnificent*, inherited both his wealth and political power. He was also largely engaged in commerce, and imitated his ancestor in his patronage of literature and learned men.

In 1478, the Pazzi, a Florentine family, the enemies of the Medici, formed a plot to seize the government of the city by assassinating their rivals. Pope Sixtus V. and the archbishop of Pisa entered into this conspiracy. The assassins made their attempt on the 26th of April, in the cathedral of Florence, during the celebration of mass. Lorenzo defended himself, and saved his life; but his brother Giulio was murdered on the spot. The people of the city rose to defend their benefactors; the assassins were torn in pieces by the populace, and the archbishop was hanged from a window in the great square. The pope was not in Florence at the time, but he took his revenge for the failure of the plot by excommunicating the inhabitants. This had little effect. The Florentines defied his power; they gained the protection of Louis XI. of France, and the pope was compelled to retract his excommunication.

The glory of Florence was at its height under the administration of Lorenzo the Magnificent; but the government of the Medici appears to have had the effect of destroying the republican institutions of the state. Lorenzo died in 1492. His successors found little difficulty in establishing arbitrary and hereditary rule in place of popular rights. The chief magistrate soon assumed the title of *prince;* and finally, in 1569, Cosmo de' Medici was formally constituted grand duke of Tuscany. The very name of the Florentine republic was at an end, and their power lost its preeminence in Italy. The princes and grand dukes of

Tuscany did nothing to deserve mention in history. The family of the Medici became extinct in 1737, and the sovereignty of Tuscany passed to the duke of Lorraine; it became absorbed into the house of Austria, in 1745, by the elevation of the grand duke to the imperial throne of Germany.

Tuscany became subjected to the changes which affected all the Italian powers on the conquest of that country by Bonaparte. At first, it was erected into a kingdom, with the name of *Etruria*, and the crown was bestowed by Bonaparte, while consul, upon the duke of Parma. The kingdom of Etruria, however, had but a short existence. The crown was offered by Napoleon to his brother Lucien, who declined it. The kingdom was then united to the French empire, and continued in this connection till the overthrow of Napoleon, when it was restored to the Austrian family which succeeded to the Medici, and the Island of Elba was included in its government. In 1849, the Florentines rose in insurrection, and attempted to establish a republic; but this attempt was crushed by the Austrians, and the authority of the grand duke restored. Tuscany was attached to the "kingdom of Italy" in 1860.

Florence, the capital of Tuscany, is esteemed the neatest and most beautiful city in Italy. It is finely situated on the Arno, surrounded by hills covered with gardens, vineyards, olive groves, and neat villas and country houses. The architecture of the city is of a peculiar character, and is marked by rugged strength rather than classic beauty. The pictures and statuary of the Florentine gallery form a great attraction to strangers. The population is about one hundred and ten thousand.

Leaning Tower of Pisa.

Pisa, on the Arno, near its mouth, was once the rival of Florence in wealth and population. It is now a decayed place, with deserted streets. Its great curiosity is the leaning tower, a work of the middle ages. This edifice is nearly two hundred feet high, and overhangs its base fourteen feet; yet it has stood for many centuries without any tendency toward a fall. Pisa has twenty thousand inhabitants.

Leghorn is the chief seaport of Tuscany. It has considerable trade, but nothing remarkable in architecture or antiquity. Population, eighty thousand.

CHAPTER CCCLIV.

A. D. 537 to 1380.

NAPLES. — *The Exarchate — The Saracens — The Republics of Naples, Gaeta, and Amalfi — The Normans — The House of Swabia — Charles of Anjou — Queen Joanna.*

Vesuvius.

THE kingdom of Naples comprises all the southern portion of the Italian peninsula. It is bounded northwest by the States of the Church, and in every other part by the sea. In connection with the Island of Sicily, it forms a monarchy, called the *kingdom of the Two Sicilies*. It is the largest and most populous of all the Italian states, containing above eight millions of inhabitants, three fourths of whom are in the continental part.

This country is the *Magna Græcia* of ancient history, and exhibits to this day the ruins of ancient Greek cities, which were founded here before the city of Rome. On the overthrow of the western empire, it fell under the dominion of the Goths. From these barbarians it was conquered by Belisarius, A. D. 537 and, although retaken by Totila, the Gothic leader, it was reconquered by Narses, the Byzantine general, in 555, and formed a part of the eastern empire. The chief magistrate was appointed by the Greek emperor or his viceroy, the exarch of Ravenna. When the exarchate was overthrown by the Lombards, the authority of the emperor began to decline in the south of Italy; and the history of this country becomes so obscure, that we have little satisfactory knowledge of its government. In the eleventh century, the city of Naples was governed by a duke, who appears to have been elected by the people. For many centuries, this city possessed a free government, though it was continually obliged to defend itself against the Lombard dukes of Benevento, whose territories surrounded it on all sides.

The Saracens, having conquered the Island of Sicily, passed over to the continent, in the ninth century, and laid siege to Gaeta. The Neapolitans drove them from that city, and carried on a war against them at sea. In consequence of the number of Saracen corsairs that continually infested the Mediterranean at that period, the republics of Naples, Gaeta, and Amalfi were compelled, in their own defence, to devote much attention to naval affairs. In this manner they made such proficiency in the art of navigation, as to become the chief naval powers in the Mediterranean, and their sailors were for many years regarded as the best in Europe. The mariner's compass was long supposed to have been invented by Flavio Gioia of Amalfi; and, although this is not the fact, it is probable that the Amalfitans were the first people of Europe who made use of it. The compass was known in China long before the time of Gioia.

The Normans, who had settled in the north of France, continued to cherish their original spirit of heroic adventure, and, after their conversion to Christianity, this spirit found gratification in pilgrimages to the Holy Land. Combined with this enthusiasm was the hope of conquest and plunder by military force, and all were thoroughly trained to arms. About the year 1025, a company of forty of these Norman adventurers, on their return from Jerusalem, arrived at Amalfi. They were ready for any enterprise which promised glory or profit. The neighboring principalities were then involved in wars, and the Normans were easily induced to enter into the pay of the Italian princes. They became very formidable from their valor, and the success which crowned their labors attracted other adventurers from Normandy. Their numbers increased to such a degree, that they were enabled to make themselves masters of a large portion of the south of Italy, including the city of Naples. Roger II., the chief leader of the Normans, captured this city, and, under the sanction of Pope Innocent III., assumed the title of *king*.

A quarrel broke out between the Normans and Pope Leo IX., in 1053, and the pontiff so far forgot his pacific character as to march with an army against his enemies. The Normans defeated him in battle, and then threw themselves at his feet to supplicate forgiveness for their sin in warring against him. The result was a treaty between the two parties, by which the pope bestowed the sovereignty of Naples and its territories upon the Normans, who, for many centuries afterward, continued to hold this kingdom as a dependency of the pope: the right of the latter, however, to bestow this sovereignty was a mere pretension.

Among the Normans who distinguished themselves in Italy, one family attained to great power, and from this proceeded a race of kings, which became associated, by intermarriages, with most of the royal families of Europe. Tancred of Hauteville, a castle in Normandy, had twelve sons, ten of whom went to Italy. Robert, surnamed *Guiscard* — the "cunning," or "sharp," — was preëminent over all the others for his lofty stature, military talent, and strength of mind. The brothers formed the republic of Apulia in the north-east part of the present kingdom of Naples. Robert was the sovereign of this republic, with the title of *duke*. He added to his dominions, under the sanction of the pope, nearly all the south of Italy, including Amalfi. He attempted also to conquer the Greek empire, and made two expeditions against Constantinople, in the second of which he died.

In 1061, Roger, the youngest brother, undertook the romantic enterprise of conquering Sicily, with a small body of Norman volunteers. The Saracens in that island were broken up into many petty states, and discouraged by the losses of their nation in Spain and Sardinia. After many years of war, Roger became sole master of Sicily, and took the title of *count*. The son of this prince, upon the extinction of Robert Guiscard's posterity, united the two Norman sovereignties of Naples and Sicily into one kingdom, A. D. 1127. The political and social condition of this kingdom, for many centuries, depended on the accidents of marriage, birth, inheritance, gift by will, usurpation, and conquest. No country in Europe was subjected to a greater variety of masters in the same space of time, nor was any one more miserable, though it was one of the most fertile and beautiful regions upon earth.

Roger was harassed during his reign by the turbulence of his barons, and by a war with the emperor of Germany, instigated by the pope. He died in 1154, and was succeeded by his son William the Bad. A person of low origin, named *Mayon*, whom William had raised to high offices, conspired, with a bishop, to dethrone him. Mayon was to usurp the crown, and the bishop was to receive a suitable reward. Mayon, having nearly secured his object, wished to remove his accomplice in the plot, and caused a slow poison to be administered to the bishop. The latter, finding himself ill, and suspecting the cause of his disease, requested Mayon to visit him, and improved the opportunity to assassinate him. Both expired within a few hours of each other. William died in 1160, leaving his crown in such a position as to involve the country in war, and the sovereignty passed by marriage to the German princes of the house of Swabia, in 1196.

Frederic I., at his death, left two sons, Conrad, legitimate, and Manfred, illegitimate. The crown was bequeathed to the former, to revert to the latter, in case of the death of Conrad without heirs. He died, after a reign of four years; and Manfred, supposing that Conradin, the son of Conrad, had died in Germany, claimed the crown. Pope Innocent IV., however, put in a claim of his own, and bestowed the kingdom upon Charles of Anjou, son of the king of France. This prince marched into Italy with an army; a battle was fought, Manfred was slain, and Charles was crowned, by the pope, king of Naples. A. D. 1266. In the following year, Conradin appeared with an army from Germany. Another battle was fought at Benevento. Conradin was defeated and taken prisoner. He was carried to Naples, and beheaded in the market place. While on the scaffold, he addressed the multitude, and threw among them his glove, desiring that it might be taken up by any one who would become his avenger. It was accepted by a Spaniard and carried to Peter, king of Arragon.

The house of Swabia was extinguished by the death of Conradin; and Charles soon acquired the name of the "Tyrant of the Two Sicilies." The rebellion of John of Procida, and the catastrophe of the Sicilian vespers deprived him of the sovereignty of that island. Sicily was separated from Naples in 1282, and continued under the dominion of the Arragonese princes till 1435. But although Sicily was lost, the kingdom of Naples was extended in other quarters. The Anjou kings of Naples became sovereigns of Provence, in the south of France, and from thence easily encroached upon Piedmont. Robert, the third of these kings aspired to the sovereignty of Italy. During the wars between the Guelfs and Ghibellines, he assisted many of the Guelf cities, and compelled them to acknowledge him as their master. Florence twice bestowed upon him a temporary dictatorship; and in 1314, he was acknowledged lord of Lucca, Florence, Pavia, Alessandria, Bergamo, and the cities of Romagna. In 1318, Genoa acknowledged the dominion of the king of Naples. The reign of Robert was long and glorious. His court was the resort of men of genius and learning, among whom was Petrarch, who was honored by the peculiar friendship of the monarch, and was treated with great distinction as long as he chose to make the court of Naples his residence.

Robert died in 1343, leaving the crown to his granddaughter Joanna, then only sixteen years of age. This is the princess so famous in Neapolitan history. She had been married, at the early age of five years, to her cousin Andrew, son of the king of Hungary, who was only two years older than herself. He was educated at the Neapolitan court; but he possessed very little natural talent, and as he grew up, his manners were more like those of the rude Hungarians than the polished Italians. Joanna was remarkable for her wit, grace, and beauty. On the death of her father, the oath of allegiance was taken to her, but not to her husband, who was not popular, and was not to be admitted to any share in the government. On the day previous to that fixed for the coronation, the youthful pair paid a visit to the castle of Aversa, one of the royal residences, situated in a lonely spot, but extremely attractive, on account of its beautiful gardens. On that night Andrew was murdered by strangling. Joanna was suspected of being privy to the deed; and although the pope declared her innocent, there remains evidence sufficient to leave a deep suspicion of the crime upon her memory.

Louis, king of Hungary, the brother of Andrew, went to Rome, and accused Joanna of the murder, before the tribunal of Rienzi, who did not feel competent to decide upon the matter; whereupon Louis prepared to invade Naples. The queen, who had strengthened the suspicions of her guilt by marrying a nobleman who was supposed to be one of her husband's assassins, fled to Provence, and Louis took possession of Naples. One of his first acts was to put to death Prince Charles Durazzo, the brother-in-law of Joanna, who was known to have been concerned in the murder of Andrew. The method taken by Louis to accomplish this act of retribution was singular. Disguising his knowledge of Charles's guilt, he contrived to draw him to the castle of Aversa, and asked him to point out the spot where his brother fell. The prince, having no suspicion of his design, led him to a balcony, when Louis instantly stabbed him to the heart.

CHAPTER CCCLV.

A. D. 1380 to 1863.

The Spanish Dominion in Naples — Invasion of Charles VIII. of France — Insurrection of Masaniello — The Napoleon Dynasty — Modern Revolutions.

Joanna took shelter in Provence, of which country she was countess in her own right; and here she went through a formal trial before the pope, who then resided at Avignon. Being pronounced innocent of the murder of her husband, she returned with her new consort to Naples. The plague had broken out in Italy, and raged with such violence that many towns were half depopulated. The king of Hungary lost so many of his troops that he found it difficult to maintain his footing in the kingdom. He, therefore, made a treaty with Joanna, and she was crowned queen of Naples. She reigned many years in peace, and, having no children of her own, adopted a nephew of the prince of Durazzo, who had been put to death by Louis. He married her niece Margaret, and was declared heir to the throne; but he proved ungrateful. In his impatience for the crown, he conspired against the queen, dethroned and imprisoned her, and after some months caused her to be put to death. Such was the close of the career of Joanna of Naples, who, in her beauty, her crimes, and her tragical end, offers a remarkable counterpart to the history of Mary, queen of Scots. Charles of Durazzo was crowned at Naples in 1382, but did not long enjoy the throne he had usurped, being assassinated in Hungary four years afterward.

From this time, the sovereignty of Naples became a subject of contention between two foreign powers, the one on the opposite side of the Adriatic, and the other beyond the Alps. The princes of the house of Anjou repeatedly invaded Italy, and for more than a century sacrificed great sums of money, and many lives, in unsuccessful attempts to regain the crown of Naples. The title to this crown passed down by inheritance, gift, or purchase, among the French princes, to the end of the fifteenth century. In the mean time, the real sovereignty of Naples was transferred to the Spanish house of Arragon in 1435, and thus Naples and Sicily were again united under one monarch.

Charles VIII. of France, on his accession to the throne, determined to assert his claim to the crown of Naples, and in 1494 crossed the Alps with a formidable army. He found no difficulty in marching triumphantly to Naples, and made his entry into that city in February, 1495. The kingdom submitted without a struggle, and Charles abandoned himself to feasting and amusements, in the belief that it would be as easy to preserve, as it had been to conquer, his new acquisition. But, at the end of three months, he learnt that a powerful league was formed in the north of Italy, for the purpose of expelling him from the country. This league comprised the pope, the emperor, Ferdinand and Isabella of Spain, the duke of Milan, and the republic of Venice. Charles knew it would be impossible to contend with such a host of enemies, and therefore departed hastily for home, with a portion of his army, leaving the rest to defend Naples as well as they could. In a valley, at the foot of the Apennines, he met the army of the allies, under the command of the marquis of Mantua. A battle was fought, in which the French gained the victory, though with serious loss. Charles returned to France, where he died about two years afterward. His garrisons in Naples were expelled or captured, and the former government restored. The expedition of Charles VIII. into Italy forms a distinguishing epoch in the history of that country. It unsettled the whole policy of the peninsula, broke up the governments of the free states, and made Italy the seat of long-continued and desolating wars.

In 1504, the kingdom of the Two Sicilies became an appendage to the Spanish crown, under Ferdinand the Catholic. Naples was governed by a Spanish viceroy for above two hundred years. This dominion was highly injurious to the country. All national spirit was extinguished among the people; superstition, bigotry, and priestly influence had full sway; commerce, manufactures, and agriculture languished, and the population of the kingdom sensibly declined.

The most remarkable event of this period is the insurrection of Masaniello, which, in its sudden and surprising turns of fortune, has hardly been equalled even by the popular overturns which have distinguished our own times. This revolt arose, like most of the political disturbances of Europe, from the arbitrary oppressions of the government. In the year 1647, the viceroy imposed a heavy duty on the fruit which was brought into the city of Naples, causing the people to pay, at the city gates, a toll upon the oranges, apples, grapes, figs, and garden stuff, which constituted the principal food of the lower classes. This naturally caused a great murmuring; and every time the viceroy appeared in the streets, he was assailed by the cries of men, women, and children, who called out to him to repeal the odious tax. The viceroy, to appease them, promised that he would do so; but some of the officers of the government, who made a profit by the tax, persuaded him to break his word. The murmurs of the people now waxed louder and louder, and the excitement was raised to so high a pitch, that nothing but a leader was wanting to rouse the populace into open rebellion. This leader soon appeared.

Masaniello.

There was a young fisherman of Naples, named Thomas Aniello, or, in the vulgar dialect of that city, *Masaniello*. He was a great favorite among the lower classes, on account of his lively temper, engaging manners, courage, and activity. At the time of the fruit tax, his wife was imprisoned for smuggling a little meal into the city. Masaniello also was fined for the offence of his wife, and compelled to sell all the furniture of his little hut to pay the money. He was greatly exasperated by this severe treatment, and laid a plan, with some of his companions, to raise a tumult in the market place, and assault the revenue officers, when the duty was collected. The plot succeeded, and the rioters were joined by thousands of the populace, who forced their way into the palace, and took possession of it, while the viceroy fled for safety to a convent. Masaniello and his followers were now in complete possession of the city. The viceroy attempted to pacify them by offering to repeal the obnoxious taxes, and to grant Masaniello a pension. But this person, elated by his extraordinary and unexpected success, was carried away by ambition, and thought of establishing an independent government. He therefore refused the offer; and being supported by the great mass of the people, he assumed the authority of chief ruler, and, by his orders, several of the noblemen were seized and beheaded.

Dreadful tumults ensued, in which many lives were lost, and several palaces set on fire; while Masaniello, at the head of a numerous band, rode about the city, and issued his commands as a sovereign prince. He even held a conference with the viceroy, who, in order to put a stop to the outrages of the mob, agreed to let him retain the government, and signed a treaty to that effect. Masaniello, now the acknowledged lord of Naples, appeared in a splendid dress of cloth of silver, wearing a cap adorned with jewels and feathers, and mounted on a horse richly caparisoned. But, although he was brave and patriotic, he had not sufficient self-command to behave with proper moderation in the exercise of the great power with which he had been thus unexpectedly intrusted. Success, in fact turned his head, and his behavior was little better than that of a madman. After a few days of absolute rule, he was assassinated by some of his own party, and the insurrection was quelled as speedily as it had been raised.

But although the rebellion of Masaniello was completely crushed, the dominion of the Spaniards in Naples being disliked, there were frequent outbreaks afterward. None of these led to any important results. At length, the Spanish monarchy became involved in ruinous wars with England and Austria, the consequence of which was the transfer of the kingdom of Naples, in 1713, to the house of Austria, and the annexation of Sicily to the dominions of the duke of Savoy. This arrangement, however, was not permanent, and in 1735, Naples and Sicily reverted to Spain. In 1759, the Two Sicilies became an independent kingdom, under a Spanish prince.

Naples remained without any essential change till the period of the French revolution. The invasion of Italy by Bonaparte led the way to political disturbances in 1799, and a popular government was organized at Naples, called the *Parthenopean Republic.* This, however, was of short continuance, and its overthrow was accompanied by terrible massacres. In 1806, Napoleon despatched his brother Joseph, with an army, to invade Naples. The people could offer no effective resistance; the kingdom was conquered by the French, and Joseph was crowned king. The old royal family escaped to Sicily, which was then defended by an English fleet and army. Joseph reigned about two years, when he resigned the crown, and was made king of Spain. Joachim Murat, one of Napoleon's generals, who had married Caroline Bonaparte the sister of the emperor, was placed on the throne of Naples. He preserved his crown after the overthrow of Napoleon in 1814; but on the return of the emperor from Elba, in 1815, Murat attempted to excite an insurrection against the Austrians, in the north of Italy. In consequence of this, he was driven from Naples by an Austrian army, and, on his attempting to return, he was taken prisoner, and shot by order of Ferdinand, the restored sovereign.

The kingdom remained tranquil till 1820, when an

insurrection broke out at Naples, for the purpose of establishing a constitution. The king made a promise to grant the popular request, but the distrust of the people compelled him to resign. The prince, his son, assumed the crown, and sanctioned the constitution. These changes, however, were not approved by the Austrians, whose influence has been predominant in Italy ever since the downfall of Napoleon. An Austrian army invaded Naples in 1821, overthrew the constitution, and restored Ferdinand to the throne.

In 1848, another insurrection commenced at Naples; and another constitution was set up. Sicily revolted, and attempted to establish a constitutional and independent government. After a struggle of more than a year, in which much blood was shed, and the cities of Catania and Messina were almost totally destroyed by the Neapolitan troops, the rebellion was suppressed; the constitutions, both in Naples and Sicily, were overthrown, and the king was restored to absolute power. In 1859, Ferdinand was succeeded by his son Francis II. Sicily, instigated by Garibaldi, immediately revolted, being determined to join the kingdom of Italy, under Victor Emmanuel. Francis was obliged to flee from Naples. On the 21st of October, 1860, the two Sicilies voted almost unanimously to join the kingdom of Italy.

Naples, the largest city in Italy, stands on the shore of a fine bay, which extends 16 miles, with the glorious height of Mount Vesuvius rising above all. The architecture of Naples is characterized rather by showiness than correct taste, and exhibits an immensity of marble, gildings, and decoration. The population of the city is remarkable for its bustle and liveliness, being almost constantly out of doors. The environs of Naples abound in antiquities, and curiosities of all sorts. Among the most interesting of these, are the ancient cities of Herculaneum and Pompeii, which were buried by an eruption of Mount Vesuvius, (A. D. 79,) and have since been laid open to sight, by means of which, great light has been thrown upon the manners, customs, and domestic life of the ancient Romans. The population of Naples is four hundred and twenty thousand.

Salerno is beautifully situated at the bottom of the gulf of that name, south of Naples. The city is more remarkable for the grand and picturesque views in its neighborhood than for the splendor of its architecture. A few miles from Salerno, in a plain near the shore, are the ruins of Pæstum, consisting chiefly of three temples, which form the purest and most perfect specimens extant of the Doric order of architecture. These ruins were antiquities in the time of the emperor Augustus, who paid them a visit from curiosity. This city was anciently called *Posidonium*, and is supposed to have been settled long before the foundation of Rome by a colony of Dorian Greeks.

Capua, in ancient times the most voluptuous city in Italy, and which disputed with Rome the title of *capital*, is now an ordinary town. It has a strong castle and near it are the remains of an ancient amphitheatre. Gaëta is beautifully situated on a promontory jutting into the sea. It is so strongly fortified as to be almost impregnable. Here Pope Pius IX. took refuge when he was expelled from Rome by the populace in 1849. Gallipoli, in the south, is a seaport, from which the oil of this part of the peninsula is exported.

View of Sicily — Mount Æ na in the Interior.

CHAPTER CCCLVI.

1000 B. C. to A. D. 534.

Sicily. — *Ancient Fables of Sicily — The Cyclops — The Sicanians — The Siculi — The Greek Colonies — Syracuse — Gelon — Dionysius the Tyrant — Agathocles — Pyrrhus — Archimedes.*

Sicily lies at the south-western extremity of Italy. It is of a triangular shape, and on this account was originally named *Triquetra* or *Trinacria*. Its later name of *Sicily* was derived from the *Sicani* and *Siculi*, two Italian tribes or nations who emigrated to this island from the continent. It is separated from Italy by a narrow strait, remarkable for the rapidity of its current. In the narrowest part of this strait is a spot which was very dangerous to the navigators of antiquity, owing to the rock Scylla and the whirlpool Charybdis. It is little dreaded in modern times. Sicily is the largest island in the Mediterranean, being nearly double the size of the state of Massachusetts. It is a very beautiful and fertile spot, the face of the country being greatly diversified with mountains and valleys. In the eastern part is Mount Ætna, a lofty volcano, which has been perpetually burning from the earliest period of history. The climate of the island is warm and pleasant, the heat of the summer being tempered by sea breezes.

The first mention of Trinacria is in the Odyssey of Homer, which gives a marvellous account of the adventures of Ulysses and his companions on the shores of this island. The Greeks of Homer's time appear to have known very little of this part of the Mediterranean, and what little they had heard of it was highly embellished with wonders. Homer calls the inhabitants of Trinacria *Cyclops* and *Læstrigons*. They are described as notorious for their inhumanity toward strangers. The Cyclops were believed to be giants, with one eye placed in the middle of the forehead. It was supposed that they fed on human flesh, and forged thunderbolts for Jupiter.

The Sicanians have a more historical character. They appear to have been driven across the strait from Italy by the conquests of the Pelasgi, though, according to some authorities, they came from Spain. They settled in the western part of Sicily, and are said to have joined the Trojan exiles in building the cities of Eryx and Egesta. They appear to have made themselves complete masters of Sicily. After some ages of dominion, they were attacked by the Siculi, an ancient people of Italy, who drove them into a small district of the island, and changed its name from *Sicania* to *Sicily*. Some centuries after this revolution, Greek colonies began to settle on the Sicilian coast. The Corinthians founded Syracuse, 935 B. C. The Siculi had, by this time, become a formidable nation. They were first united under a king named *Æolus*, who is a half-fabulous personage, and was believed to have kept the winds tied in a bag. This story probably arose from the circumstance that he resided on the strait of Messina, which is subject to furious blasts and sudden squalls.

The Greek settlers at Syracuse were harassed with wars carried on against them by the Siculi, who were led by their king, Deucetius. At length the Greeks prevailed, and took him prisoner. Triquetra, the chief city of the Siculi, was captured and destroyed. Deucetius was sent to Corinth, where he passed the remainder of his life. With the conquest of the Siculi, the Greek colonies were extended all over the island. Agrigentum, Panormus, Catana, Messana, and other cities, were founded, and soon became rich and powerful. Syracuse, however, excelled them all in wealth, population, and magnificence. For two or three centuries, these cities possessed democratic governments; but afterwards some of them fell under the tyranny of ambitious individuals. In the fifth century before Christ, Syracuse was governed by an aristocracy which cruelly oppressed the people, and provoked them to insurrection. The tyrannical nobles were driven into exile, 485 B. C.

The expelled nobles fled to *Gelon*, the tyrant or usurping sovereign of the city of Gela. He espoused their cause, and under color of restoring them to their homes, made himself master of Syracuse. He was a skilful politician as well as warrior. Under his government, Syracuse increased rapidly in wealth and importance. The Carthaginians, in their attempts to subjugate Sicily, were utterly defeated by him. The Athenians and Spartans sought his aid in their war against the Persians. Gelon reigned prosperously, and, after his death, (477 B. C.,) was deified by his subjects. *Hiero*, his brother, succeeded him. He subdued Catana and Naxus, and gained a great victory over the Etrurian pirates near Cumæ, which put an end to their depredations. The people of Agrigentum placed themselves under his protection. On his death, (459 B. C.,) he was succeeded by his brother *Thrasybulus*, whose tyranny provoked a rebellion. He was dethroned, and the republican constitution restored. But the people gained little by the change. A system of secret voting, called *petalism*, similar to the Athenian *ostracism*, was introduced, and most of the leading men were banished by the giddy populace. It was at this period that the Athenians made an attempt to conquer Syracuse, which ended in the total defeat of the invaders.

Dionysius I. became ruler of Syracuse, 405 B. C. He was a person of humble origin, but able and courageous. The confusion in which the government was involved, enabled him to seize the sovereign power. He was three times expelled for his tyranny, yet as often found means to regain his authority. The greater part of his reign was passed in wars with Carthage and the Greek states of Italy, as well as with the ancient race of the Siculi. His reign, though tyrannical, was prosperous. He was cut off by poison, (368 B. C.,) and was succeeded by his son, *Dionysius II.*, commonly called the *Tyrant*. This prince had been carefully educated under the guardianship of the virtuous Dio and the philosopher Plato; but, on attaining to supreme power, he quickly forgot all the good that had been taught him, and abandoned himself to every bad passion and indulgence. He banished Dio; but the latter raised an army, expelled the tyrant, and conducted the government for some years with justice and ability. This excellent ruler fell by assassination, and Syracuse became the prey of sanguinary factions. Dionysius, after ten years' exile, took advantage of these troubles to return and recover his throne.

Misfortune had not taught him wisdom or moderation, and he oppressed his subjects with greater tyranny than ever. It was during this part of his life that he is said to have confined suspected persons in a dungeon constructed in the shape of a human ear, where the slightest whisper could be overheard in a particular recess, in which he was accustomed to place himself. Among the ruins of Syracuse, at the present day, may be seen a large chamber, hollowed out of the rock, which corresponds exactly with the description given of the Ear of Dionysius. The Syracusans at length became weary of his oppressions, and solicited the aid of the Corinthians to dethrone him. *Timoleon*, the famous commander, was sent by the Corinthians to Syracuse. He overthrew Dionysius, and the tyrant was banished to Corinth, where he turned schoolmaster, and, it is said, took great pleasure in flogging his pupils.

After the death of Timoleon, (337 B. C.,) *Agathocles*, a man of low rank, raised himself to supreme power by the aid of the Carthaginians. This led to wars with that nation in Sicily, accompanied with great loss and suffering to the Syracusans. Pyrrhus, king of Epirus invaded the island, (276 B. C.,) and, for a short time held it in complete subjection. But he was soon expelled, and the Syracusans, wearied with anarchy conferred their government on *Hiero II.*, who was descended from the ancient royal family of Gelon. Under this prince the city enjoyed peace and prosperity during the wars between Rome and Carthage, in which he took the Roman side. But after his death, the Carthaginian party acquired supremacy in Syracuse, and made a profligate use of their power. A war soon broke out with the Romans, and the consul Marcellus was sent with a fleet and army against Syracuse. He laid siege to the city; but it was defended for a long time by the wonderful skill of the mathematician Archimedes, who invented a number of ingenious machines for destroying the Roman ships, and is said even to have set them on fire by concave mirrors of brass, which reflected the sun's rays. All his ingenuity, however, was unavailing in the end, and Syracuse was taken by storm, 212 B. C.

The death of Archimedes was characteristic of his life. Marcellus, who admired his extraordinary abilities, wished to save him in the storming of the city, and gave orders to the soldiers accordingly, but without effect. Amidst the tumult and confusion of the capture, the philosopher was so absorbed in study, that he was not aware of what was taking place, till a Roman soldier rushed into his apartment, and commanded him to follow him. Archimedes desired him to wait a moment, till he had solved the problem on which he was laboring. The soldier, either from impatience or misunderstanding, killed him on the spot.

Most of the other Greek cities of Sicily were involved in the fortune of Syracuse. Agrigentum, the second city of the island in wealth and importance, was used as a naval station by the Carthaginians in the first Punic war, and was seized by the Romans, 262 B. C. After the fall of Syracuse, the island was made a Roman province, and from its fertility was regarded as the granary of the Roman empire. The manner in which it was governed may be learned from Cicero's orations against Verres, who was prætor or governor of Sicily for many years, and has left a name behind him infamous for rapacity and oppression. Christianity spread early in this island, and the converts were persecuted by Nero. In the fifth century, Sicily was exposed to the ravages of the Vandals; and it subsequently formed a part of the Gothic kingdom of Theodoric. In the year 534, Belisarius conquered the island from Justinian, and it continued to be a dependency of the Byzantine empire for some centuries. The government was administered by an officer with the title of *patrician*, who was sent from Constantinople.

CHAPTER CCCLVII.

A. D. 534 to 1863.

The Saracens in Sicily — The Normans — The French — The Sicilian Vespers — The Spanish Dominion — Modern Revolution.

Under the dominion of the Byzantine emperors, the Sicilians relinquished all martial pursuits for a long series of generations, and turned their attention solely to the arts of peace and the labors of agriculture. Their position in the centre of the Roman empire, preserved them both from civil war and foreign foes; but the rapacity of their governors was a constant and serious evil. In this condition, Sicily remained till the seventh century, when the Saracens began to disturb the tranquillity of the island. The barbarous nations of the north had before invaded and ravaged its coasts, but did not long retain possession of any territory. The Saracens were more fortunate. In 827, they availed themselves of certain quarrels, in which the Sicilians were engaged, to subdue the island. Palermo was chosen for their capital, and the Mahometan dominion prevailed in Sicily for two hundred years. At length, the Greek emperor made an attempt to recover this part of the Byzantine inheritance. An army under George Maniaces landed in Sicily, A. D. 1038, and by the help of a body of Norman auxiliaries, gained important advantages over the Saracens. Maniaces, however, repaid the services of the Normans with ingratitude, and by his injudicious conduct, gave the Saracens a chance to retrieve their losses. The two Norman leaders, Robert and Roger de Hauteville, subsequently conquered Sicily on their own account, and the Saracens, after ten years' struggle, resigned the dominion of the island forever.

Robert resigned his claims to his brother Roger, who assumed the title of *Great Earl of Sicily*. He ruled the island with wisdom, and ranks deservedly with the greatest characters in history. He raised himself from the humble station of a younger son of a private gentleman, to the exalted dignity of a powerful monarch. He was succeeded by his son Simon, whose reign was short, and followed by that of the second son, called *Roger II.* In 1127, this prince added to his Sicilian possessions the whole inheritance of Robert Guiscard, and assumed the title of *king of the Two Sicilies*. The greater part of his reign was occupied in quelling revolts in Italy; but Sicily enjoyed a profound peace. In 1154, his son William ascended the throne, and passed his life in war and confusion. The Saracens were frequently in insurrection under the reign of his successors, and, at length, to establish the tranquillity of the island, they were removed to Apulia, in the northern part of the kingdom of Naples, in the twelfth century, about four hundred years after the conquest of the island by their ancestors. The joint history of Sicily and Naples, down to the accession of Charles of Anjou, has been related in the preceding chapters.

Charles of Anjou soon acquired and deserved the surname of *Tyrant of the Two Sicilies*. He received into his dominions and employed multitudes of Frenchmen, who were permitted to rule without restraint, and to subject the inhabitants of the country to every species of oppression and indignity. A day of severe retribution was at hand, prepared by the persevering industry of one man, known as *John of Procida*. This person was the feudal lord of the little island of Procida, in the Bay of Naples, and a zealous partisan of the house of Swabia. Animated with an intense hatred of the French dominion, he disguised himself as a monk, and visited Sicily, Rome, Spain, and even Constantinople, to excite the enemies of Charles against him. At this time, Peter II. was king of Arragon. He had married Constantia, the daughter of Manfred, whom Charles had expelled from the throne of Naples. John of Procida applied to Peter in behalf of the suffering inhabitants of Sicily and Naples, and appealed to his sense of duty and justice, by referring to the death of Conradin, who had called upon him from the scaffold to avenge his wrongs. Procida suggested a revolt in Sicily, which Peter promised to assist with a body of troops.

In the mean time, all the people of Sicily being subjected to the despotism of the French, were ready for any measure, however desperate, that promised relief. Procida had been successful in sustaining the hope of this relief, and the desire of vengeance. At length, on Easter Day, 1282, the revolt broke out. It is said, by some authors, that the time was agreed upon beforehand, and the secret faithfully kept, though intrusted to thousands of persons. Others affirm that the explosion was accidental, and occasioned by an insult offered by a French officer to a Sicilian lady of Palermo. This point has never been cleared up. What is certain is, that on the ringing of the vesper bell at Palermo on that day, the populace burst suddenly into insurrection, and massacred all the French. Even the Sicilians who had intermarried with that nation were not spared. The movement extended throughout the whole island, and only one Frenchman escaped. This was William de Porcelet, a Provençal, and governor of a small town in Sicily, who had acquired the high esteem of the inhabitants by his benevolent character and upright conduct. He was allowed to depart, with his family, to France.

This transaction is known in history by the name of the *Sicilian vespers.* The number of French who were put to death is computed at eight thousand. The exasperated Charles gathered his forces, and proceeded to Sicily to take vengeance on the revolters. But Peter of Arragon was there before him to defend the island. In the fleet which Charles sent against him, was his son, who bore the title of *Prince of Palermo.* A battle took place between this fleet and that of Peter, in which the prince was taken prisoner; and most of his ships were captured or destroyed. Three years afterward, in 1285, Charles, having met with a constant succession of defeats and reverses, died of chagrin, or, as some historians affirm, by suicide.

By the revolution of the Sicilian vespers, the island was separated from Naples, and transferred to the dominion of the Spanish or Arragonese princes. It was not reannexed to the continental monarchy of Naples till 1435, after which it shared the fate of that kingdom, both in its independence and its subjection to the Spanish princes.

Upon the death of Charles II. of Spain, in 1701, his dominions became an object of eager contention among the leading powers of Europe, and, at the peace of Utrecht, in 1713, Sicily was assigned to the duke of Savoy, who afterward was compelled by the emperor Charles V. to relinquish it and take Sardinia as an equivalent. The Spaniards, however, had no concern in these bargains, and made an attempt in the same year to recover Sicily, in which they failed through the enterprise of the English admiral Byng, who destroyed their fleet, and compelled the Spanish court to abandon the scheme for a season. But in 1734 the attempt was renewed with success. A Spanish army, under the infanta Charles, expelled the German troops, and he was crowned king of the Two Sicilies, at Palermo. He afterward, on becoming king of Spain, transferred the Sicilian crown to his son Ferdinand; and this family have continued to govern the kingdom of the Two Sicilies to the present day, with the exception of the period of Napoleon's supremacy, when Sicily and Naples were separated.

In 1806, on the invasion of Naples by the French, and the assumption of the crown by Joseph Bonaparte, King Ferdinand, of Naples, escaped to Sicily. The French were unable to subdue this island, which was defended by a British fleet. In 1812, a representative constitution, upon a liberal scale, was proclaimed in Sicily, and feudality was abolished by the vote of the Sicilian barons, in parliament assembled. After the overthrow of Murat in Naples, and the restoration of Ferdinand, in 1816, to the throne of the Two Sicilies, he abolished the Sicilian constitution, and combined the legislative and administrative systems of both parts of the kingdom into one. Thus, Sicilian liberty was overthrown. When the revolution of 1820 broke out at Naples, the people of Sicily proclaimed their independence; but this attempt was speedily crushed. In 1848, the same scenes were renewed: but after the suppression of the constitutional party in Naples, the armies of the king invaded Sicily, bombarded and nearly destroyed the cities of Catania and Messina, and in 1849 restored the Neapolitan dominion in the island. The revolution of 1859, which, as we have said, ended in the annexation of the Two Sicilies to the kingdom of Italy in 1860, commenced in this island.

Palermo, the capital, is well built, though it has neither monuments of antiquity nor modern classical edifices. The streets are broad and straight, crossing each other at right angles. Population, one hundred and eighty-six thousand. Messina, on the strait of that name, was, before the recent insurrection, a very fine city, with a flourishing commerce. In the eighteenth century it was desolated by a plague and an earthquake, but recovered in a great degree from these calamities. In 1849, as we have already stated, it was bombarded and nearly destroyed by the Neapolitans. The population is (1863) about ninety-five thousand. Catania, at the foot of Mount Ætna, was the finest city in Sicily before the insurrection of 1848. In the seventeenth century, it was repeatedly devastated by earthquakes and eruptions of Ætna.

CHAPTER CCCLVIII.

Government, Population, Manners, Customs, Languages, Literature, Manufactures, Arts, Education, Religion, &c., of the Italians.

ITALY, in its political relations,* is divided chiefly among five potentates—1. The emperor of Austria, who holds Lombardy and Venice, with Parma and Piacenza, the appanage of Maria Louisa; 2. The king of Sardinia, who has Piedmont, Savoy, and Genoa; 3. The grand duke of Tuscany; 4. The pope, the temporal ruler of the States of the Church; and 5. The king of Naples. Besides these, the duchy of Modena, the principality of Monaco, in Piedmont, and the republic of San Marino, form separate, though they can hardly deserve the name of independent states. The constitutions or governments of all these sovereignties are despotic, the will of the rulers operating unchecked by any legal or constitutional barrier. Neither the great civic nobles of the commercial states, nor the feudal nobility of the country, have any effective influence in the administration. Some few of them exercise, by their immense fortunes, a pernicious influence in checking the operations of justice, throwing all the public burdens upon the industrious classes. The police, in many parts of Italy, is in a most imper-

* These divisions, as well as the views expressed, have been considerably modified by the formation of the Kingdom of Italy, in 1860.

Picture Seller in Rome.

fect state, and bands of licensed robbers have long occupied the mountain districts.

The only tie between the separate governments of which Italy is composed is, or rather has been,—for at the moment when we write this, the state of politics in Italy is quite uncertain,—the paramount influence of Austria; that power which, beyond all others, has opposed, in the most obstinate spirit, every political reform. All the reigning families in Italy, the pope excepted, have family connections with Austria. What is of more consequence, the Austrian armies are generally in a position to crush all attempts at any change not agreeable to the court of Vienna. What the influence of France may hereafter accomplish in Italy, it would be useless at present to conjecture.

Divided as she is, at present, into kingdoms and principalities of the second and third orders, Italy is without any central point; nor can any one of her cities be regarded as the capital. The short-lived kingdom of Italy, which flourished for a while under Napoleon, was an abortive attempt to unite under one crown a country which seems hardly susceptible of political consolidation. Although, in religion, language, and manners, the people of Italy appear as one nation, they have never been united by the bond of a common national feeling. The name of *Italian* is lost in the civic or provincial appellatives by which the natives are distinguished and severed from each other. Italy may possibly recover her independence, but she can scarcely ever again become one kingdom or one republic. Something like a federal union may be possible, and this has been a favorite scheme with some political writers.

The Italian population consists of two classes, the nobles, and the inferior class, comprising the peasantry, artisans, shopkeepers, traders, &c. There is scarcely any intervening class between the upper and the lower. The mass of the Italians is formed of the lower rank. The Italians, taken as a whole, are in some respects the most polished and refined people in the world. The lower ranks show in a very extensive degree the refined taste and manners of the nobles. The common shopkeepers of Florence and Rome possess a knowledge of the fine arts, and sometimes a taste for poetry, which are unknown to the most refined nations beyond the Alps. They delight also in conversation, which they support with peculiar liveliness and eloquence, and with gesticulations the most varied and expressive of any European people. The peasants are, on the whole, a poor, quiet, contented, orderly race, spending all their little savings in finery for their wives and daughters. The populace of the great cities display a character peculiarly idle and tumultuary. The *lazzaroni*, or lower class of Naples, formerly constituted a huge ragged regiment, existing almost out of the pale of regular society, hardly wearing clothes, and living on a handful of macaroni a day. Their condition at the present time, however, is much improved, and the old-fashioned *lazzaroni* can now hardly be said to exist.

The Italian nobles, for some centuries past, have been excluded from all participation in the government of the country, and in this manner have become estranged from all habits of manly and energetic action. Idleness and elegant enjoyment have been regarded among them as the main business of life. The title and rank of a noble descend to all his posterity; and thus the number has greatly increased, and reduced the nobility, generally, to a condition of proud and miserable poverty. It is no uncommon thing for a traveller in Naples, Rome, or Venice, to be accosted by begging counts and marquises. In the palaces, the most superb equipages and apartments are let out to strangers; and many of the palaces have little shops on the ground floor, where the lordly proprietor retails wine and oil by the quart.

The fine arts in Italy have attained a splendor quite unrivalled in any other country, and have flourished in that region as their chosen and peculiar soil. The collections of painting and sculpture are almost endless; and although all the rest of the civilized world have been supplied with these articles from Italy, the country still surpasses every other in the number and excellence of precious relics, in her possession.

The architecture of Italy is the wonder and delight of every traveller. The dwellings of the Italians are celebrated for the splendor and art displayed, both in their form and interior decoration. The houses of the

The Olive Tree.

nobility in Rome, Florence, Venice, and Genoa, are usually dignified with the name of *palaces;* and their classic exterior, spacious apartments, and the works of painting and sculpture with which they are adorned, render them often more interesting to the spectator than those of the greatest monarchs beyond the Alps. They are maintained, however, rather for show than for use; all the finest apartments being employed as galleries of exhibition, while those in which the family reside are of small dimensions in the upper stories. The taste for architectural beauty descends even to the lower ranks. The houses of the farmers and villagers in Tuscany and Lombardy are adorned with porticos and colonnades, and often display a beautiful and classic aspect.

The dress of the Italians does not appear to have any features peculiar, or strictly national. Among the upper ranks, French fashions prevail. The costumes of many of the interior communities, particularly those of the mountainous districts, display a picturesque variety, which, being accompanied with good taste, produces often a very pleasing effect. The shepherds wear the skins of their flocks, with the wool outward in summer, and inward in winter. Their garments are rudely formed, and have only holes pierced for the head and arms. In diet, the Italians are exceedingly temperate; macaroni is the article of food chiefly characteristic of the country. Soups and pottages are common here, as in France. A great variety of excellent wines are produced in Italy, and it is almost every where very cheap, sometimes selling for one or two cents a bottle; yet an Italian is hardly ever seen intoxicated.

Agriculture was practised scientifically in Italy at a very early age, and many parts of the country, particularly in the north, are cultivated like a garden. The most industrious and successful agriculturists are those of Lombardy and Tuscany. The vine, the olive, manna, and rich fruits are among the products of Italy. Food is abundant, and living cheap. Lands are generally cultivated by farmers at the halves, the proprietors furnishing half the stock. A good tenant is seldom removed by his landlord. The manufactures of Italy, once so remarkable for their elegance and variety, are now every where in a state of decay, and present only specimens on a small scale of what formerly existed. Silk was at one time the grand staple,

View in San Marino.

particularly in the form of velvets and damasks, rich adorned with gold and silver embroidery. This ma ufacture still exists in most of the great cities, thou on a reduced scale. Woollen, linen, and cotton clot also continue to be manufactured; and the muslins Taranto enjoy a high reputation. Glass was once celebrated and admired article of manufacture at Ve ice, where it is still fabricated into mirrors, tubes, a beads. The Tuscan manufacture of straw hats affor abundant and profitable employment to the countr girls of that territory, and yields a produce of abo half a million of dollars annually.

The Italian language is founded on the Latin, wi but a small mixture of words from beyond the Alp It has a great variety of dialects, the chief of whi are the Tuscan, the Neapolitan, the Sicilian the V netian, the Milanese, and the Genoese. In all thes the grammatical construction is the same, or deviat but slightly from one standard. The Tuscan is t master dialect. It is spoken in its greatest purity Siena and Florence, but it is the written Italian the whole peninsula. This preëminence has be owing to the extraordinary genius of the early Flo entine writers, Dante, Petrarch, Boccaccio, Boiard Pulci, Poliziano, Macchiavelli, and others, who, by the admirable compositions, gave a universality to t Tuscan dialect, which has made it necessary to eve Italian writer who wishes to be read out of his ov city or province. It is also the common language Rome, where it is spoken with more softness than its native district. The Italians have a proverb whic says, the sweetest sounds upon earth are produce by the "Tuscan tongue in a Roman mouth." Near all the dialects have printed books, but these are chief confined to ballads, tales, and popular literature of t humblest class.

The literature of the Italians is rich in many depar ments. Dante, the earliest of all the great mode poets, was born in 1265. His *Divina Commedia* a poem of great genius and originality, partly religio and partly political. Next to Shakspeare, he is r garded as the greatest of modern poets. Petrarc and Boccaccio succeeded him in the following centur and contributed, the former by his sonnets, and the la ter by his prose tales, to refine and polish the Tusca tongue. Ariosto and Tasso have obtained a unive sal celebrity by their heroic poems. Macchiavel Villani, Guicciardini, Giannone, Botta, and others, hav written valuable historical works. Goldoni, Metastasi and Alfieri, have excelled in dramatic writing; Beccaria and Filangieri, in politics.

During a century and a half which followed the age of Boccaccio and Petrarch, the ablest writers and orators of Europe were the secretaries of state at Florence or Rome, or the tutors and friends of the Medici. Among these were Coluccio, a Florentine secretary of state, of whom the duke of Milan complained that he had done him more injury with his pen than fifteen hundred Florentine knights. Leonardo Aretino was preëminent for his scholarship, and wrote Greek and Latin like one of the ancients. He was also one of the earliest of the good historians of Italy. Poggio was one of the restorers of learning, and his letters abound with antique wisdom. Bembo, Giovio, and others, also distinguished themselves by their scholarship and elegant writings during this period.

At a later date, Italy became distinguished for painting and sculpture. The individuals who excelled in these arts are very numerous. Cimabue and Giotto, who flourished in the thirteenth century, may be regarded as the fathers of Italian painting, which was subsequently carried to the highest point of perfection by Raffael, Michael Angelo, Domenichino, Leonardo da Vinci, Guido, Titian, Paul Veronese, Salvator Rosa, and others. Sculpture has had many distinguished disciples in Italy, the chief of which are Michael Angelo, Donatello, Bandinelli, and in our own days, Canova.

In the philosophical sciences, Italy has many eminent names. Galileo, who invented the telescope, and made various discoveries in astronomy and other departments of physical science, was sent to the Inquisition for affirming that the earth was round; and he was liberated only on the recantation of his opinion. Torricelli, who made some of the earliest experiments on the weight of the atmosphere, was an Italian. Galvani, whose name has been given to a particular department of the science of electricity, was also a native of this country.

In architecture, Italy can boast the names of Palladio Lapo, Bramante, Bernini, Fontana, and others. In music, she has produced Rossini, Cimarosa, Paesiello, Salieri, Cherubini, Spontini, and Paganini. In very recent times, the medical and physical sciences have been illustrated by Spallanzani, Fontana, and others; while Maio and Rosellini have distinguished themselves in the departments of classical literature and antiquarian studies.

In education, Italy exhibits great contrasts. The country abounds with universities, libraries, and aids to learning; yet millions of the inhabitants are utterly illiterate. A single street in Naples will be found to contain more people ignorant of writing and reading, than the whole state of Massachusetts. Except in certain districts, no pains are taken to educate the lower classes. Religion forms a prominent feature of society in Italy, which is the centre of that great spiritual dominion that for so many ages held unbounded sway over Europe. All Italy is Roman Catholic; but the power of the pope has been declining for many years, and the revolutions of 1848 and 1860 have left the country in so unsettled a state that it is impossible to conjecture at the present moment to what extent the papal power will be reëstablished.

Malta.

CHAPTER CCCLIX.

1000 B. C. to A. D. 1814.

Ancient Malta — The Knights of St. John — War with the Turks — Capture of Malta by the French — Downfall of the Order of Knights — Capture by the British — Annexation to Great Britain.

The Island of Malta, the ancient *Melita*, lies fifty-four miles to the south of Sicily. It is twenty miles long and twelve broad, and consists entirely of rock, with a very thin layer of soil, which is kept from washing away by terraces of stone built by the industrious inhabitants in every part of the island. It is very diligently cultivated, and supports a population of sixty thousand. In its neighborhood are three smaller islands — Gozo, Comino, and Cominotto. Malta is supposed to be the *Ogygia* of Homer's Odyssey, where Calypso entertained Ulysses. Its original inhabitants were the Phæacians, who were expelled by the Phœnicians. Afterward the island was successively occupied by the Greeks, the Carthaginians, and the Romans. It was little noticed by the writers of antiquity, and when St. Paul was shipwrecked upon it, the inhabitants were described as "barbarous;" but this epithet was given in that age to all people who were not Greeks or Romans.

In the decline of the Roman empire, Malta fell into the hands of the Goths; after which the Saracens made themselves masters of it. The Normans from Sicily took it from the Saracens in 1190, and it continued attached to the government of that island till 1525, when Charles V. made a grant of it to the Knights of St. John of Jerusalem, who had been expelled from Rhodes by the Turks. These warriors, after establishing themselves in their new residence, took the title of *Knights of Malta.*

The knights of St. John constituted an order which originated in a hospital founded at Jerusalem by permission of the Saracen khalif, about the middle of the eleventh century. This hospital was designed to receive pilgrims from Europe who visited the holy sepulchre. It was annexed to a chapel dedicated to St. John the Almoner, and was at first kept by Benedictine monks. When Palestine was conquered by the Seljukian Turks, who drove away the Arabian and Egyptian Saracens, in 1065, the Christians found these new masters much worse than the first, and the hospital of St. John was plundered. Some time afterward, a Frenchman, named *Gerard*, a pilgrim to the holy city, undertook the management of the establishment. After the conquest of Jerusalem by the crusaders, many of the conquerors, through pious fervor, determined to join him, and devote the rest of their lives to the service of the pilgrims. Some of the French knights endowed the establishment with their property: this example was followed by several other princes; and thus the hospital became possessed of lands in almost every part of Europe, as well as in Palestine. The dress assumed by the Knights Hospitallers was black, with a white cross having eight points on the left breast

Pope Pascal II. sanctioned the new institution, the members of which bound themselves by solemn vows of chastity, individual poverty, and obedience. To these duties was afterward added that of being al-

Knights.

ways ready to "fight the Mussulmans, and all others who forsake the true religion." A splendid church was erected by Gerard near the old hospital, and dedicated to St. John the Baptist, with extensive buildings for the Hospitallers as well as the pilgrims, who were there entertained at free cost. Gerard and his successors established, in various maritime towns of Europe, hospitals in imitation of that of Jerusalem, which served as resting-places for the pilgrims, who were there provided with the means of embarking for Palestine. These houses were called *commanderies*. Gerard died in 1118; and the Hospitallers elected, as grand master, his brother Raymond Dupuy, who drew up a body of statutes or regulations of discipline for the order. The knights, as they increased rapidly in numbers, were classed into seven divisions, according to *languages*, namely, Provence, Auvergne, France, Italy, Arragon, Germany, and England.

For nearly two centuries, the Knights Hospitallers, together with the Templars, were the firmest support of the Christians in the East. When Acre, the last bulwark of Christendom in Palestine, was taken by the Mussulmans in 1291, the remains of the order withdrew to Cyprus, where the town of Limisso was assigned to them as their residence. In 1310, having lost all hope of recovering Palestine, they equipped a fleet, and, being joined by a body of crusaders from Italy, made an attack on the Island of Rhodes, which was then possessed by a band of Greek and Saracen pirates. These the knights defeated, and took possession of Rhodes, Cos, and the neighboring islands. They were now known as the *Knights of Rhodes*. They strengthened their new acquisition with fortifications, and carried on a bold naval warfare against the Mussulmans, especially the Ottoman Turks, who were at that time very powerful in Asia Minor. Some of the Turkish sultans were glad to purchase a temporary peace with the knights. The remainder of their history, while they resided at Rhodes, will be found in the chapter upon that island.

After a long and obstinate resistance to the Ottoman arms, the knights were finally expelled from Rhodes by Sultan Solyman, in 1523. They withdrew to Italy, and resided for a few years at Orvieto. At length, in 1530, Charles V. granted them the Island of Malta and its dependencies. At this time, Malta contained about twelve thousand, and Gozo about five thousand inhabitants, who were in a miserable state. Malta was hardly in a condition to afford a shelter to those who dwelt upon it, and the cultivation of the island had been nearly abandoned from its exposure to the piratical rovers of the Mediterranean. Under the government of the knights, the island soon began to recover from its state of destitution. Their first object was to protect it against the incursions of its piratical enemies For this purpose, the knights began the construction of those stupendous fortifications which remain to this day the astonishment of every beholder, and a monument of the perseverance and military power of the order.

From their stronghold of Malta the knights renewed their warfare against the Turks, who, after suffering much by their attacks, equipped an expedition to drive them from this retreat. In May, 1565, an army of thirty thousand Turks, under Mustapha Pacha, landed in Malta, and laid siege to the city. The knights had but a very inferior force to oppose to the besiegers, but they defended themselves with such desperate bravery, that the Turks were compelled to quit the island with the loss, it is said, of twenty-five thousand men. Shortly after this victory, the grand master, La Vallette, who had commanded the knights during the siege, determined to found a new city. The first stone of it was laid in March, 1566. The name of *Valletta* was given to the city, which is now one of the handsomest of its size in the world.

The knights, now secure in the possession of Malta, continued to cruise against the Ottomans, whom they greatly annoyed. But the discipline of the order relaxed as the objects of their original institution gradually became of secondary importance, and Malta, which was safe against all attack, became a place of luxury and pleasure, rather than of austerity and mortification.

When the French revolution broke out, the knights exhibited a hostile spirit toward the new republic, which led to the downfall of the order. In 1798, a French fleet of thirty-six ships of war and four hundred transports, with an army of forty thousand men on board, under Bonaparte, and destined for the invasion of Egypt, appeared off the Island of Malta. The grand master, Hompesch, was a Frenchman, and many of the knights were of that nation. Owing to these circumstances, little resistance was made, and at length Malta was formally surrendered. Bonaparte, on entering Valletta, was astonished at the strength of the fortifications, and declared it was fortunate for the French that somebody was inside to open the gates for them, as otherwise they would never have gained entrance. With the capture of Malta, the order became extinct, though many noblemen in Europe continue to bear the title of knights of Malta.

The French retained possession of the island · but in the following year they were blockaded by an English fleet. Valletta was closely besieged, and in September, 1800 the garrison and inhabitants being reduced to the last extremity by famine, surrendered. At the general peace of Amiens, in 1802, Great Britain agreed to deliver up Malta to the knights; but this stipulation was not fulfilled, and war broke out again in consequence. The British kept possession of the island, and at the peace of Paris in 1814, it was formally guarantied to Great Britain. It has continued under the dominion of that power to the present day.

Malta is a crown colony of Great Britain; its affairs are under the direction of a governor and eighteen councillors. Valletta, the capital and chief port, enjoys a most advantageous situation between two harbors which are among the finest in the Mediterranean. The city is regularly built of stone, in a highly ornamented and imposing style of architecture. The Church of St. John, in this city, has the most splendid pavement in the world. The palace of the grand master is noted for its magnificent halls and staircases. Valletta is an admirable naval station, deriving great importance from its situation in the heart of the Mediterranean. It serves also, especially during war, as a commercial depot, from which goods may be introduced into Italy and the Levant. Its streets exhibit the most picturesque mixture of population, perhaps, in the world; all the nations bordering on the Mediterranean resorting hither as to a common centre. Citta Vecchia, in the interior of the island, is an ancient place, where the traveller is shown catacombs, in the solid rock, of remarkable extent, and of which the history is entirely lost.

The native Maltese are one of the most primitive races now to be found in the Mediterranean or its neighborhood. They speak a language exclusively their own, and which possibly may be a dialect of the ancient Phœnicians or Carthaginians, though this is a disputed point among philologists. They are dark-skinned, athletic, hardy, and robust, and make excellent sailors. The females are rather below the middle size, well made and graceful, with regular features and delicate limbs. Although of dark complexion, many of them are quite handsome. All classes are industrious, and education is making considerable progress among them. Their religion is Roman Catholic. Almost all the Maltese engaged in trade speak English and Italian in addition to their native tongue.

The Byzantine Empire.

CHAPTER CCCLX.

A. D. 476 to 565.

Geographical View — Fall of the Western Empire — Revolutions of the Byzantine Government — Loss of Italy — Reign of Justin — Accession of Justinian — Factions of the Circus — Insurrection of the Blue and Green Factions — Conflagration in Constantinople — Danger of Justinian — Firmness of the Empress Theodora — The Insurrection suppressed — The Vandal and Persian Wars.

In our history of ancient Rome, we have noticed the division of the empire into the *East* and *West*, and traced the fortunes of the latter till its overthrow in 476. The former, which continued to exist, under the various names of the *Eastern Empire*, the *Greek Empire*, and the *Byzantine Empire*,* for a thousand years later, till it was overturned by the Turks, now claims our attention.

The capital of the Eastern Empire, called *Constantinople*, from its founder, Constantine, was built in part upon the site of an ancient city called *Byzantium*. This was the chief town of the Byzantines, who were a colony of Dorian Greeks, and who established themselves here about 658 B. C. The place became a mart for the ships trading with the Euxine. It was taken by Darius Hystaspes, by the Lacedæmonians, and afterward by the Athenians under Pericles. It was restored to the Lacedæmonians, who held it when Xenophon returned with the ten thousand Greeks. It was greatly harassed by the Gauls, (270 B. C.,) and finally came to the Romans with the conquest of Greece.

The ancient inhabitants of Byzantium were Greeks, and distinguished for debauchery and idleness. The city was thronged with fishermen, sailors, and merchants; many of the latter being foreigners. The government seems to have been democratic, and it is said that some demagogue, being asked what was the law in a particular case, replied, "What I please." The admirable situation of the place* attracted the attention of the emperor Constantine, and he resolved to build a new city there. In three years it was finished, and dedicated to the Virgin Mary, May, 330.

We have already given an account of the Eastern Empire, of which Constantinople continued to be the capital, down to the fall of the Western Empire; but it may be well, before we proceed with the history subsequent to that event, to glance at its situation and extent at this period. In general, it may be remarked that the Eastern Empire comprised the eastern portion of the great Roman Empire. Its territories included countries in Europe, Africa, and Asia, coinciding nearly with the Turkish dominions at the beginning of the present century. The following table will show at a glance its several divisions: —

* Some confusion arises from this diversity of names, and it is increased by the fact that the people of Constantinople are often called in history both *Greeks* and *Romans*. It will be understood that the central part of the Byzantine territory consisted of countries formerly under the government of the Greeks, and the people of which were mainly of this race. Hence the Eastern Empire naturally took the title of the *Greek* Empire; but as Constantinople had been the capital of the Great Roman Empire, as many Romans had settled there, and as the people were proud of the name, the Constantinopolitans often called themselves *Romans*, and the empire itself was called the *Roman* Empire.

* Perhaps no place in the world possesses so many advantages, from position, as Constantinople. Its connection with the several seas give it unrivalled resources for supplies of fish; the adjacent territories are among the most fertile in the world, and the products of the populous countries around the Mediterranean and Black Seas are borne, by water, to its gates, with a miraculous facility. Constantinople is also in the path of the armies that have passed from Asia into Europe or from Europe into Asia, and hence its history is connected with the movements which have agitated these regions for past ages.

Dominions of the Eastern Empire.

IN EUROPE.

Ancient Name.	*Modern Name.*	*To whom now subject.*	*Chief Towns.*	*Ancient Name.*
Thrace	Part of Roumelia	Turkey	Constantinople	Byzantium.
Macedon	Part of Roumelia	Turkey.		
Greece	Greece	Independent Kingdom	Athens	Athens.
Illyricum	Dalmatia, and parts of Croatia, Illyria, and Styria	Austria	Laybach, Trieste	Æmona. Tergeste,
Noricum	Parts of Austria, Bavaria, Croatia, &c.	Austria	Salzburg, Innstadt	Juvanum, Boiodurum.
Pannonia	Sclavonia and parts of Hungary, Austria, Styria, and Croatia.	Austria and Hungary	Vienna, Buda	Vindobona. Aquincum.
Dacia	Transylvania, Moldavia, Wallachia, and Bessarabia	Austria, Turkey, Russia	....	Ulpia Trajani.
Mœsia	Servia, Bulgaria	Turkey	Belgrade	Singidunum.

IN AFRICA.

Ancient Name.	*Modern Name.*	*To whom now subject.*	*Chief Towns.*	*Ancient Name.*
Egypt	Egypt	Formerly subject to Turkey, now independent	Alexandria	Alexandria.
Ethiopia	Nubia	Egypt	Axum	Axum.
Libya, Africa, Numidia, Mauritania	Barbary States	Formerly subject to Turkey, now for the most part independent	Tripoli, Tunis, Algiers, Morocco	Tripoli. Tunis, Algiers, Morocco.

IN ASIA.

Ancient Name.	*Modern Name.*	*To whom now subject.*	*Chief Towns.*	*Ancient Name.*
Colchis, Iberia, Albania	Mingrelia, Georgia, Georgia	Russia.	Teflis.	
Asia Minor	Natolia	Turkey	Smyrna	Smyrna,
Armenia	Armenia	Turkey and Russia.		
Syria	Syria, Palestine, Phœnicia	Turkey	Damascus, Jerusalem	Damascus. Jerusalem. Tyre.
Babylonia, Chaldæa, Mesopotamia, Assyria	Mesopotamia, Koordistan	Turkey	Bagdad, Bassora.	

The four last named countries in Europe, viz., *Noricum*, *Pannonia*, *Dacia*, and *Mœsia*, were never thoroughly subdued by the Romans, and, after the division of the empire, neither portion could claim them as actual possessions. They were the seats of the Gauls, Goths, Huns, and other barbarians, who desolated the Western empire, and often threatened the Eastern kingdom with destruction. They are now all comprised within the limits of Turkey, Austria, Hungary, and Russia.

After the fall of the Roman empire in the West, the court of Constantinople sunk into obscurity, from which it did not emerge for half a century, when its supremacy was restored during the memorable reign of Justinian. The Isaurian Zeno, raised to the purple by his marriage with the princess Ariadne, in the latter part of the fifth century, was compelled to fly into the mountains by a fierce revolt, instigated by his mother-in-law. Zeno was restored to his throne chiefly by the aid of Theodoric, king of the Ostrogoths, who had been carefully educated as a hostage at the court of Constantinople. The turbulence of the Goths, and the faithlessness of the Byzantines, soon destroyed the amity of the two sovereigns. After a sanguinary war, Zeno purchased peace by ceding to Theodoric his right over Italy. This chieftain invaded that country, and made himself master of it, (A. D. 493,) as we have already stated.

The emperor *Justin* ascended the throne of Constantinople in the year 518. He was originally a Dacian peasant, who travelled on foot to the capital to seek his fortune. By his bravery and talent, he rose gradually to the command of the household troops of the emperor Leo, and at the death of this monarch, Justin, by bribing the guard, procured his own elevation to the vacant throne. Totally illiterate himself, he was not insensible of the value of education. He made his nephew Justinian his associate in the empire; and as this prince had been instructed in all the learning of the times, he soon obtained the whole power of the state. After the death of Justin, in 527, *Justinian* ruled alone; but his first exercise of authority fixed a lasting stigma on his reign. He chose for his empress Theodora, a woman of mean birth and infamous character, whose vices had disgusted even a capital so licentious as Constantinople. There is no moral degradation which is not laid to her charge.

Among the most singular and disgraceful follies of the great capital of the East, were the factions of the circus, which arose from the colors worn by the charioteers, who contended for the prize of swiftness. The Green and Blue were the most remarkable for their inveterate hostility, though the White and Red were the most ancient. Justinian was a partisan of the Blues; his favor toward them provoked the hostility of the opposite faction, and led to a sedition, which almost laid Constantinople in ashes. The disturbances first broke forth in the circus. Justinian ordered the rioters to be secured; both factions immediately turned against the monarch. The soldiers were called out, but they were unable to contend against the citizens in the narrow streets. Assailed from the tops of the houses, the barbarian mercenaries flung about firebrands in revenge, and thus kindled a dreadful conflagration, which destroyed a vast number of public and private edifices. The Church of St. Sophia, and part of the imperial palace, were consumed.

Justinian prepared to escape into Asia, and assembled his council to consult upon the means of safety. All advised him to fly except Theodora. If the words ascribed to her be her genuine language on this occasion, she has a claim, whatever her morals may have been, to be ranked as a heroine. "If flight," said she, "were the only means of safety, yet I should disdain to fly. Death is the condition of our birth. I adhere to the maxim of antiquity, that the throne is a glorious sepulchre." This firmness saved Justinian. The Blues and the Greens had come to a sort of armistice, and were assembled in the Hippodrome. Three thousand chosen troops attacked them, and put thirty thousand of the multitude to the sword. Justinian and Theodora were then reinstated in their power, after the city had been several days at the mercy of the rioters.

While the internal state of the empire was thus disturbed by faction, an expensive and unprofitable war was waged against the Persians, until the emperor purchased a disgraceful and precarious truce, which both he and the Persian king chose to designate as an *Endless Peace.*

The usurpation of the throne of the Vandals in Africa by Gelimer, induced Justinian to despatch an invading army into that country, under the command of Belisarius. This general, the most able warrior of his age, landed in Africa in 533. He advanced toward Carthage, defeating the Vandals on his march, and became master of the city with little opposition. Gelimer made one effort to save his kingdom, but it was unsuccessful. His army was irretrievably ruined, and he was closely besieged in a castle on the mountain of Papua, where he sought refuge. The unfortunate Gelimer, after having borne the most dreadful extremities of famine, was forced to surrender unconditionally. He was carried captive to Constantinople, where he was led in the triumphal procession that honored the return of Belisarius. The dethroned monarch showed no sorrow for his fall, but consoled himself by Solomon's reflection on the instability of human greatness, as we have remarked in a previous chapter.

CHAPTER CCCLXI.

A. D. 535 to 542.

The Gothic War — Invasion of Italy by Belisarius — Capture of Rome — Siege of Rome by the Goths — Sale of the Papacy by the Empress Theodora — Disgrace and Beggary of Belisarius — Justinian's Laws — His Edifices — Building of the Church of St. Sophia.

THE murder of Amalasontha, queen of the Goths, by her ungrateful husband, Theodotus, afforded Belisarius a pretext for invading the kingdom of Italy. He sailed from Constantinople for Sicily in 535, and easily conquered that important island. Theodotus, in great terror, hastened to avert the danger by declaring himself the vassal of Justinian. But hearing, immediately afterward, that two Byzantine generals had been defeated in Dalmatia by the Gothic troops, he passed suddenly from the extreme of despair to the height of presumption, and withdrew his allegiance. Belisarius soon appeared to chastise his perfidy. He crossed the Strait of Messina, overran the south of Italy, and captured the city of Naples, while Theodotus, secure within the walls of Rome, made no effort to protect his subjects. At length, the Goths, disgusted with the incapacity and weakness of their sovereign, removed him from the throne, and chose Vitiges for their king. He abandoned Rome, and Belisarius took possession of the city, A. D. 537.

During the ensuing winter, the Goths assembled from every quarter, to save, if possible, their kingdom in Italy. A powerful army, animated by a dauntless spirit, was soon collected, and Vitiges led his followers to the siege of Rome. Belisarius concentrated his forces in the city, and defended it with equal skill and bravery; but famine soon appeared within the walls, and the citizens became anxious for a capitulation. A conspiracy was formed, under the sanction of the pope Sylverius, for betraying the city to the Goths; but it was discovered by an intercepted letter. Belisarius sent Sylverius into banishment, and ordered the bishops to elect a new pontiff. But, before a synod could be convened, Antonia, the general's wife, sold the papacy to Vigilius for two hundred pounds weight of gold. Reënforcements soon arrived from the East, and the Goths were compelled to raise the siege of Rome.

Belisarius finished the war in Italy, by taking prisoner the Gothic king Vitiges, A. D. 539. He returned in triumph to Constantinople, and was next sent to conduct the war against the Persians; but he was soon recalled, and disgraced by the ungrateful Justinian

Belisarius.

While the conquests of Belisarius were restoring the western provinces to the empire, hordes of barbarians ravaged the north-eastern frontiers. Unable to meet them in the field, Justinian entered into an alliance with the Lombards, who had just thrown off the yoke of the

Heruli. To secure this alliance, he gave them settlements in Pannonia. Although Belisarius had contributed so greatly to the glory of Justinian, and, by his talents and popularity, might have placed himself on the throne, he could not escape calumny and suspicion. He was charged with a conspiracy, deprived of his command, imprisoned in his own house, and fined one hundred and twenty thousand pieces of gold. The story commonly related of him is, that his eyes were put out, and he walked the streets as a beggar, saying, "Give a penny to Belisarius the general." Whatever truth there may be in this anecdote, he lived to an advanced age, and died in 565.

The great fame of Justinian is owing to his reform of the Roman law. Notwithstanding all the efforts of preceding emperors and jurists to reduce the Roman jurisprudence to a satisfactory form and system, the vast variety of laws, decisions, and constitutions, involved the subject in great confusion and perplexity. Justinian undertook the task of reducing the whole to order. He employed, for this purpose, the most eminent lawyers of the age, with the celebrated Tribonian at their head. The work, when completed, consisted of three parts, the *Pandects*, the *Institutes*, and the *Novels*. This code of laws remained in force in the Eastern empire until its overthrow by the Turks in 1453. It is now the basis of the civil law among the nations of Europe, and is highly respected in England and the United States. It is often quoted in courts of justice in both countries.

It is to Justinian, also, that Constantinople owes the magnificent church of St. Sophia, now a mosque. Ten thousand men were employed in its construction, and in little less than six years it was completed. "I have vanquished thee, O Solomon!" was the exclamation of the monarch, when he saw the structure finished. Beside this immense pile, Justinian erected twenty-five magnificent churches in and near the city, together with a great number of bridges, aqueducts, and fortifications, throughout the empire. The historian Procopius has left us an entire work on the Edifices of Justinian.

CHAPTER CCCLXII.

A. D. 526 to 565.

Calamities of Justinian's Reign — Comets — Earthquake at Antioch and Berytus — Great Plague — Description of Procopius — Origin and Progress of the Pestilence — Strange Phenomena attending its Appearance — Sufferings of the Victims — Mortality at Constantinople — Singular Mode of intombing the Dead.

The reign of Justinian was marked also by great calamities. The superstitious people were appalled by the appearance of comets of prodigious magnitude. Earthquakes and pestilence added their real scourges to these terrors. In 526, an earthquake at Antioch destroyed two hundred and fifty thousand persons. In 31, the ancient and noble city of Berytus was shaken to the earth. Constantinople suffered severely, and a part of the church of St. Sophia was thrown down.

In 542, a terrible plague, which originated in Egypt, swept over the whole known world, and continued its ravages more than fifty years. It is said there was not a spot upon the earth, even to the mountain tops, that was not visited by this dreadful scourge. During three months, the mortality at Constantinople was from five thousand to ten thousand daily. Many districts in Asia, depopulated by this visitation, have remained waste to the present day. As this is the most widespread and destructive pestilence that ever visited the earth, as far as we are able to learn from history, we subjoin the description of it furnished by Procopius, who resided at Constantinople, who was an eye-witness of this terrible calamity, and, from his connection with the Byzantine government, possessed the means of learning all that could be known of its origin, progress, and effects. The account of this writer is as follows: —

"At this time (A. D. 542) arose a pestilence which almost destroyed the whole human species. It traversed the whole world, attacking all nations and tribes of men, and sparing neither sex nor age. No diversity of climate, latitude, diet, habits, or mode of life obstructed the progress of the pestilence; all varieties of mankind fell prostrate before its sweeping march. Some countries were ravaged in summer, others laid waste in winter.

"It first arose in Egypt, among the inhabitants of Pelusium, from whence, proceeding in two separate routes, it ravaged Alexandria and the rest of Egypt, on one hand, and on the other, extended into Palestine, from which country it spread over the entire world, advancing with uniform rapidity throughout the whole of its progress. It did not suddenly exhaust its venom in any spot, but proceeded with regular steps, and continued in every place along its route a certain space of time, marching thus deliberately to the very extremities of the earth, as if determined that not the most remote corner of the universe should escape its ravaging search. Not even an island, a cavern, or a mountain-top was spared. If any spot was passed over lightly on its first visit, the pestilence was sure to return, and fall with fatal malignity upon the people whom it had first spared, not leaving them till it had swept away the full proportion. It always began on the sea-coasts, and spread into the interior.

"In its second year, about the middle of spring, it reached Constantinople, where I happened to be at that time. The plague broke out in this manner: Multitudes of diabolical spectres were seen, having the shapes of some human figure. Whoever met one of these spectres seemed to be struck on some part of his body, and was on the instant taken sick. At first, the persons who saw these spectres attempted, by prayers and devotions, to free themselves from their attacks; but all in vain, for in the very temples to which they ran for succor, they fell down dead. Then they shut themselves up in their houses, and if their friends called at the door, they refused to see them: not the loudest knocking would be answered, for every one feared that some demon was in pursuit of him. Some were attacked in another way: they fancied in their sleep that they beheld these apparitions, or heard voices crying out that they were numbered with the dead, and straightway they were attacked by the pestilence. Others neither saw the spectres nor dreamed of them, but felt the disease approach in a sudden fever on awaking from sleep; some were seized walking, others while they were about their occupations: they did not change color, nor feel a violent heat or inflammation; but from morning till evening, the fever wore so mild a character, that neither the patient nor physician was alarmed. But on the first day, or the second, or not long after, swellings arose in the abdomen, under the arms, behind the ears, and on the thighs. These particulars were common to all who were attacked by the plague; but there were diversities in the action of the disease, owing either to the different habits of body in different individuals, or to the sovereign power of Him who sent the calamity.

"Some fell into a heavy lethargy, others were seized with a furious madness. In their lethargy, they seemed to have forgotten every thing, like persons buried in eternal sleep; and, unless attendants were constantly at hand to supply them with food, they died of starvation. In their madness, they never slept, but were continually frightened with apparitions, and fears of being murdered: they uttered horrid cries, and ran hither and thither, to save themselves by flight. If the sufferings of the sick were dreadful, those of their friends were hardly less so, for they were distracted with the labor and anxiety of watching over the miserable patients.

"The disease was not propagated by contagion; for neither physicians nor other persons caught it by touching the bodies of those infected; and multitudes, who nursed the sick and buried the dead, escaped its attacks, while others, who were in no way exposed, took it and died. In their delirious ravings, they rolled themselves on the ground, threw themselves from the house-tops, and plunged into the sea, not from thirst, but impelled by an ungovernable fury. Many, unattended, perished from hunger. Those who escaped the lethargy and delirium were carried off by excruciating pains in the swellings.

"The physicians, ignorant of the nature of the disorder, imagined the cause to lie in the swellings, and therefore dissected these tumors in the bodies of those who had died, to discover the secret of the malady. They found them to consist of coals, or black lumps, containing so malignant a poison, that many of them died immediately from the effects of it. Some found their bodies covered with black pustules: these died within an hour. Many were killed by sudden vomitings of blood. Some, after living in great extremity, and being given over by their physicians, recovered, to the astonishment of every one; others, who seemed quite safe, and were assured of their recovery, unexpectedly died. Human skill and human wisdom seemed utterly at fault, for all things were at contradiction. If one man was helped by the use of the bath, another was killed by it. If some perished in an extraordinary manner, others escaped as wonderfully. No remedy for the disorder, no preventive against it, could be found. When a man took the infection, it seemed by chance; when he escaped, it happened he knew not how. Children born of infected mothers were sure to die.

"The plague prevailed four months at Constantinople, and during three months it raged terribly. At first, the number of deaths was but little above the ordinary proportion; but, as the epidemic grew more active, they increased to five thousand a day, and afterward to ten thousand a day, and even more. At first, every one buried those of his own household and such dead bodies as were found here and there; but afterward every thing was left to chance and disorder; for servants were left without masters, and masters without servants. Houses were left desolate, and the tenants remained unburied. All the tombs in the city being filled with bodies, men were sent into the fields in the neighborhood to bury the dead there; but the number of the corpses increasing more and more, they became tired of digging graves, and piled up the bodies in the towers of the city wall, by taking off the roofs and throwing in the bodies, till the towers were full, when the roofs were replaced. A foul air was thus driven by the winds over the city, and added to the infection.

"No funeral offices were performed over the dead: people thought it sufficient, if they were able, to carry the bodies to the shore, cast them by loads into boats, and let the waves transport them wherever chance might direct. All factions and dissensions were hushed in the city; people assisted one another, and buried one another, without thinking of their enmities. Vicious and abandoned men, struck with horror at the awful death which menaced them, became suddenly penitent and devout; yet, as the danger passed away, and their fears abated, they returned to their old ways, and surpassed their old deeds in iniquity; so that it might be said, and not without truth, that the pestilence, either by chance or the will of Providence, had spared the very worst part of mankind."

CHAPTER CCCLXIII.

A. D. 565 to 641.

Reigns of Justin II., Tiberius, and Maurice — Usurpation and Cruelties of Phocas — Calamitous Fate of Maurice — Pope Gregory acknowledged Universal Bishop by Phocas — Overthrow and Death of Phocas — Accession of Heraclius — Persian War — Victories of Khosrou — Conquest of Jerusalem and Asia Minor — Danger of Constantinople — Campaigns of Heraclius — First Appearance of the Saracens.

The reign of *Justin II.*, the nephew and successor of Justinian, was remarkable only for disgrace abroad and misery at home. At his death, in 578, he bequeathed the empire to *Tiberius*, whose virtues amply justified the preference given him. But his reign lasted only four years, and he was succeeded by *Maurice*, who inherited many of his predecessor's virtues. He sent an army, under the eunuch Narses, to the aid of *Khosrou*, king of Persia, who had been driven from his throne by a usurper. This enterprise was crowned with success. Freed from all danger on the side of Persia, Maurice resolved to turn his arms against the Avars, a Tartar nation, who threatened the eastern frontier. But the incapacity of his generals and his own avarice provoked a mutiny of the soldiers. They marched to Constantinople under Phocas, one of their centurions. Had the city continued faithful, this sedition might easily have been quelled; but the licentious populace, disgusted with the parsimony of their sovereign, assaulted him as he walked in a religious procession, and compelled him to seek safety in his palace.

The unfortunate emperor was forced to abdicate: *Phocas* was tumultuously invested with the purple, and welcomed into Constantinople with the acclamations of a thoughtless people. The emperor commenced his reign by dragging Maurice from the sanctuary where he had sought refuge, murdering his five sons successively before his eyes, and then putting the deposed monarch to death by torture. One of the royal nurses attempted to save the prince intrusted to her charge, by presenting her own child to the executioners in his stead. But Maurice refused to sanction the deceit; and, as each blow of the axe fell on the necks of his children, he exclaimed, with pious resignation, "Righteous art thou, O Lord, and just are thy judgments!"

The usurpation of Phocas was basely sanctioned by Pope Gregory, who received in return for his adulation the title of *Universal Bishop*. But the pontiff's flatteries could not save the tyrant from the resentment of his own subjects, who soon discovered their error in preferring such a miscreant to the virtuous Maurice. Heraclius, the exarch, or viceroy, of Africa, invited by the unanimous voice of the empire, sailed to Constantinople, A. D. 610. Scarcely had his fleet appeared in the Hellespont, when the citizens and imperial guards entered the palace, bound Phocas in chains, and sent him a helpless captive to his rival. Heraclius reproached him with his manifold vices, to which the fallen tyrant simply replied, "Wilt thou govern better?" These were the last words of Phocas. After suffering insult and torture, he was beheaded, and his mangled body thrown into the sea.

But the death of Phocas did not deliver the empire from the calamities which his crimes had produced. Khosrou had no sooner learned the fate of his benefactor, Maurice, than he assembled the entire strength of Persia to avenge his murder. The unwise system of persecution which had been gradually established by the Byzantine prelates and emperors, supplied the invader with allies in every province. The Jews, the Nestorians, and the Jacobites* believed, with reason, that the worshippers of fire were more tolerant than the orthodox Christians. Scarcely had the Persians crossed the Euphrates when insurrections were raised in their favor throughout Syria. Khosrou, victorious in two decisive battles, was encouraged to undertake the restoration of the Persian empire as it existed in the age of Cyrus the Great. *Heraclius* had scarcely ascended the throne, when he received intelligence of the fall of Antioch. This was soon followed (A. D. 614) by the storming of Jerusalem, where the Jews, encouraged by the Persians, wreaked dreadful vengeance on the heads of their Christian persecutors. The fugitives from Palestine sought refuge in Egypt, where they were hospitably entertained by the bishop of Alexandria. But Egypt itself, where the din of arms had not been heard since the reign of Diocletian, was invaded, conquered, and, for a time, annexed to the Persian empire, A. D. 616.

Asia Minor was subdued with equal facility. In a single campaign, the Persian armies advanced from the banks of the Euphrates to the Thracian Bosphorus, and, during ten years, their hostile camp was in sight of the towers of Constantinople. The city was, at the same time, so closely pressed by the Avars, that Heraclius was on the point of abandoning the capital, and seeking refuge, with his treasures, in Carthage. He was with difficulty dissuaded from this dishonorable measure by the entreaties of the patriarch. But his prospects appeared to become darker every hour. The Avars, by a treacherous attack, had nearly seized the capital; and the ambassadors sent to supplicate peace and pardon from Khosrou were dismissed with contumely and reproach, the Persian despot declaring that he would not grant peace until Heraclius was brought, bound in chains, to his footstool, or had abjured Christianity, and embraced the Magian religion.

For about twelve years, Heraclius had patiently witnessed the calamities of the empire, without making any effort to protect his subjects. But this last insult roused his slumbering energies, and he entered on a career as glorious as his former inactivity had been disgraceful. He made six successful campaigns against the Persians, and, in the year 627, defeated an army of five hundred thousand men near the site of ancient Nineveh. After reconquering all the provinces which had been overrun by the Persians, Heraclius returned to Constantinople, bringing with him the wood of the "true cross," which Khosrou had taken at Jerusalem—a precious relic, which was deemed a more splendid trophy of his victories than all his spoils and conquests. But victory itself was fatal to Heraclius. The best and bravest of his soldiers had perished in these sanguinary wars. The treasury was empty. Taxes were levied with difficulty in the desolated provinces; and the emperor himself, as if exhausted by his great efforts, sunk into hopeless lethargy.

While Heraclius was enjoying the empty honors of a triumph, the Saracens appeared on the frontiers of Syria. From this moment, the Greek empire sunk rapidly before their fanatic valor, and, in the last eight years of his reign, the emperor lost, by their victories, all that he had rescued from the Persians.

CHAPTER CCCLXIV.

A. D. 641 to 867.

Character of the Byzantine History after the Death of Heraclius — Sieges of Constantinople by the Saracens — Invention of the Greek Fire — Rise of the Iconoclasts — Fortunes of the Empress Irene — Reigns of the Basilian Emperors — Wealth and Luxury of the Greek Empire — State of Europe — Silk.

Heraclius died in 641, at an advanced age. During the greater part of the following century, the history of the empire discloses only a series of crimes among his successors, in their contests for the throne. Murder by the steel or poison, mutilation by cutting off the nose and pulling out the tongue, factious cabals, insurrections, and ecclesiastical tyrannies—such are the materials which fill up the pages of the Byzantine annals at this period!

In 672, during the reign of Constantine Pogonatus, the Saracens besieged Constantinople for five months, but were repelled. They returned for seven years in succession, but were each time defeated, not so much by the able generalship of the garrison as by the help of the Greek fire, which had been invented by Callinicus. With this liquid flame, the ships of the Saracens were set on fire, as we have already related. Though the composition of this is not certainly known, it is supposed to have consisted chiefly of petroleum, mixed

* The Jacobites were a sect of Christians who were united by a Syrian monk named *Jacobus* Bardai, in the sixth century, A. D. They had various communities in Syria, Egypt, and Mesopotamia, and being separated from the Catholic church, obtained protection from the Saracens.

with sulphur and the pitch of green firs. Wherever it lighted, it spread with wonderful rapidity. Water, instead of extinguishing, only scattered and quickened the flame. Nothing could check it except sand, wine, or vinegar. The composition of this powerful agent of destruction was kept as a secret of state by the Greeks for upwards of four hundred years. At length the Mahometans are said to have obtained a knowledge of it, and used it in their wars against the Christians, till the invention of gunpowder.

Leo the Isaurian became emperor in 718. He was originally a grazier. Entering the army, he rose to distinction, and was raised to the throne by the soldiers. He is principally distinguished by his zeal against the worship of images, which, in his time, had become almost universal in the church. The party of which he was the head, obtained the name of *Iconoclasts*, or image-breakers. *Constantine VI.*, a child under the guardianship of his mother Irene, began his reign in 780. Irene restored the worship of images, and went as far in the persecution of the Iconoclasts as Leo had gone in support of them. This unnatural mother dethroned her son, and put out his eyes. She moved through the streets of Constantinople, drawn by four milk-white steeds, in a golden chariot. She, however, fell from this proud eminence, and ended her life in banishment, at the Island of Lesbos, where she earned an humble subsistence by the labor of her own hands.

Basil I. was originally an humble Macedonian adventurer, who, on his first visit to Constantinople, slept at night on the steps of a church. He found employment with one of the retinue of the palace, and rose to be an officer of the imperial stables. He attracted the notice of the emperor Michael, and, by successive gradations, became associated with him in the imperial authority. He ascended the throne by causing Michael to be put to death. Notwithstanding this usurpation, Basil has been ranked among the most able and honorable of all the Byzantine monarchs. His private life was respectable, and his public administration useful and advantageous to the empire. He reformed abuses, and selected the most virtuous and competent men for his agents. Though he did not lead armies himself, he gave the command to deserving men, and the enemies of the empire were once more compelled to respect the majesty of the Roman name.

The descendants of Basil held the throne for nearly two centuries, with the interruption of two usurpations. This succession was attended by many murders and other acts of cruelty. The possession of the throne depended upon various contingencies. The son, or daughter, or brother, or nephew, might succeed as heir, or the monarch might nominate a successor. The army, the officers of the palace, the populace, or the widow of the deceased emperor, might obtain the vacant throne by violence or intrigue. The most common method of removing the sovereign, was by assassination, poisoning, banishment, imprisonment, mutilation, or some more cruel act, perpetrated by a revengeful and successful aspirant. The power of the emperor seems to have been absolute. The offence, the law, the condemnation, and punishment, came in rapid succession, and all but the offence from the emperor's will. A single fact may be cited as an example of the atrocious practices of those days. The barbarians near the Danube had taken twelve thousand prisoners; their noses were cut off, and they were sent back to Constantinople thus mutilated. The emperor sent back to the barbarians some thousands of captives, divided into companies of one hundred each. All their eyes were put out with the exception of one eye to each company, the possessor of which served for a guide to the rest. The materials for this portion of the Byzantine history are very meagre. The greater part of such as existed, were probably destroyed in the great fire at Constantinople, when that city was taken by the Latins in 1204. Perhaps this loss is not much to be regretted, for such atrocities as we have noticed, occupied a large space in the events of the period.

The wealth and luxury of the Greek empire at this date must have been very great. An evidence of this may be given in the condition of a female named *Danielis*, of Patras, in the Peloponnesus. This matron is represented to have been a patroness of Basil in his humble fortunes, and he appears to have enjoyed her favor and bounty after he became emperor. Among her presents to him were a carpet of wool, wrought of exceeding fineness, of a pattern which imitated the spots of a peacock's tail, and of a size equal to the floor of a church. She gave him, also, six hundred pieces of silk and linen. The silk was colored with the Tyrian dye, and adorned with the labors of the needle. The linen was so exquisitely fine, that an entire piece might be rolled in the hollow of a cane. Another of her presents to Basil consisted of three hundred young men as slaves. When she visited the emperor at Constantinople, she was carried the whole distance, five hundred miles, in a litter, attended by three hundred slaves. At her decease, she bequeathed to Leo, the son of Basil, the residue of her estates, which comprised eighty farms and three thousand slaves! We have no means of knowing how a private female, in the ninth century, could have acquired such an amount of wealth, nor how the arts attained to such perfection, in that age and that quarter of the empire. This period is accounted the darkest and most barbarous era in the history of Western Europe, the only exception to the general gloom, being the transient and ineffectual attempt of Charlemagne in the cause of learning and civilization.

During this period, the Byzantine empire was the only part of the world, except China, where the cultivation and manufacture of silk were carried on. This article had been known in Europe for many centuries, but it was not till the reign of Justinian that the eggs of the silkworm were brought from China in the hollow walking-sticks of two Persian monks, who had visited that country in the character of Christian missionaries. From these have proceeded all the silkworms now in Europe. The Byzantine Greeks were the only Europeans who possessed them for six hundred years from the time of Justinian. In the twelfth century, the cultivation of silk was introduced into Sicily, and from thence it extended to Italy, Spain, and France.

CHAPTER CCCLXV.

A. D. 867 to 1057.

Character of the Greeks during this Period — The Empire new modelled — Loss of the Italian Provinces — Extent of the Empire — Description of Constantinople — Theological Disputes, &c.

DURING this period, the inhabitants of the Byzantine empire showed themselves a degenerate race, in comparison with what they had formerly been. Yet they were at least on an equality with the first nations of Europe. Their degeneracy was rather in moral and intellectual qualities than in external show and importance. There remained among them much of ancient pomp and splendor. In the tenth century, the provinces that still acknowledged the authority of the successors of Constantine had been cast into a new form by the institution of the *themes*, or military governments. Of these there were twenty-nine, namely, twelve in Europe, and seventeen in Asia. The victories of a few of the emperors had enlarged the boundaries of the Roman dominions, but, in the eleventh century, the prospect was darkened. The relics of Greek dominion in Italy were swept away by the Norman adventurers, while the Turks had removed many of the Asiatic props of the empire. Still, the spacious provinces of Thrace, Macedonia, and Greece were obedient to the Byzantine sceptre. Cyprus, Rhodes, and Crete, with the fifty islands of the Ægean Sea, also acknowledged its authority.

The subjects of the empire were more ingenious and dexterous than any other people of Europe; and, in their support and restoration of the arts, their patient and peaceful temper, and their refined taste, they challenge our esteem and respect. The first demand of the public revenue was the pomp and pleasure of the emperors. The coasts and islands of Asia and Europe were covered with their magnificent villas. The great palace of Constantinople, the centre of imperial residence, was enlarged and decorated by the wealth of successive sovereigns, and the long series of apartments were adorned with a profusion of gold, silver, and precious stones. No city in the world, probably, surpassed Constantinople in wealth and splendor during the middle ages.

But, in the mean time, theological disputes about questions that pass the limits of human knowledge, and a jealous rivalry between the patriarch of Constantinople and the pope of Rome, produced a division between the Eastern and Western Churches, which the disputes respecting the Bulgarians aggravated into a formal schism. These barbarians were converted to Christianity by Greek and Latin missionaries. The patriarch and the pope contended for the patronage of the new ecclesiastical establishments. The Greeks prevailed in the contest, and banished their Latin adversaries. The court of Rome took revenge by anathematizing the Greeks.

It is a singular fact that, in the long lapse of one thousand years, there seems not to have been any material change in the character of the government, the people, the religion, the commerce, or the occupations, current in the Greek empire. Even under the dominion of the Latin emperors during the period of the crusades, the same course of events continued.

Constantine VII., during his minority, (A. D. 911,) devoted himself to the works of the ancients, and the study of the constitution and political relations of the empire, on which subjects he has left valuable writings. *Nicephorus Phocas*, in 964, was the restorer of the Byzantine power by his own exploits in Crete, and by victories obtained under his generals in the wars with the Saracens in Asia Minor and Syria. *John Zimisces*, in 969, defended the empire against the arms of the Russians under Swaroslav. *Basilius II.* and *Constantine IX.*, in 975, ascended the throne together, and so shared it between them that all the labors of the government fell to the lot of the former and its enjoyments to his associate.

Under these princes, the empire enjoyed a period of good fortune. Basilius broke the power of the Bulgarians, which had long been formidable, in several battles, and subdued them from the mouths of the Danube to the borders of ancient Epirus. After a reign of fifty years, distinguished by every imperial virtue, Basil left the sole possession of the throne to his brother, A. D. 1025.

Constantine IX. governed without capacity, and with a severity which was the effect of fear. He bequeathed the empire, with his daughter Zoe, to the patrician *Romanus Argyrus*, who suffered a defeat from the Saracens, near Aleppo. Zoe was attracted by the beauty of a more youthful lover, and her passion cost her husband his life, and ruined her own fortunes; for scarcely had her paramour obtained the crown, under the name of *Michael IV.*, when his mind became a prey to remorse. Incapable of consolation, so long as the fruit of his crime remained in his possession, he abandoned the throne, and sought to appease the stings of conscience by immuring himself in a cloister, A. D. 1041. The empress raised his cousin, *Michael Calaphates*, to the throne, but soon removed him, and her sister put out his eyes. Zoe then married *Constantius Monomachus*, and lived to old age, through a tranquil reign.

We may observe, in a survey of the ninth, tenth, and eleventh centuries, that, while most of the emperors were vicious and contemptible, several of them appear to have been worthy successors of the best of the old Cæsars. To maintain the luxurious empire of Constantinople against the Saracens, Turks, Bulgarians, and Russians, was a most arduous task, requiring abilities of the highest order. In the capital, a fund of literature was preserved during these times, which was destined to employ the labor of scholars a thousand years afterward.

CHAPTER CCCLXVI.

A. D. 1057 to 1185.

End of the Basilian Dynasty — Accession of the Comneni — Reign of Alexius — State of Literature in Constantinople — Anna Comnena — The Crusades — Extraordinary Adventures of Andronicus — He ascends the Throne — His bloody Reign — Insurrection at Constantinople — Overthrow and tragica Death of Andronicus.

The Basilian or Macedonian dynasty was succeeded on the throne of Constantinople by the race of the Comneni, in 1057. *Alexius Comnenus*, who began to reign in 1081, was a prince of great experience and uncommon endowments. During the thirty-seven years of his administration, he gave to the imperial throne a degree of stability which the external circumstances of the empire had never more urgently required. The power of the Seljukian Turks was advancing with the rapid fortune peculiar to a new founded dynasty, while several provinces of the empire were convulsed with the crusades, and the Russians pressed on its northern frontier. Alexius, with the art of a statesman, withstood every foe. He found an historian in his daughter, Anna Comnena, a female who raised herself above the character of her age. She possessed a genius worthy of her father, and employed the hours which were abstracted from the affairs of government in composing the *Alexiad*, a history of her father's life. We may remark that, about the same period, the old book of Hindoo philosophy, containing the fables of Pilpay, was translated into Greek at Constantinople, and that learning was cultivated by many as the path to dignity and fame.

The history of the crusaders, in their connection with the Byzantine empire, will be chiefly reserved for another portion of this work. After the Comneni had reigned at Constantinople more than a century, with greater glory than any preceding dynasty, they gave occasion for their own ruin, and the subversion of the government. This was accomplished in the person of *Andronicus*, whose adventures are so extraordinary that they merit a detailed narrative. This person was the grandson of Alexius I. He is represented as brave, eloquent, accomplished, of singular grace and beauty, and temperate in an extraordinary degree, "with a heart to resolve, a head to contrive, and a hand to execute." The sister of the empress became his spouse without the sanction of the legal authority. For attempting to assassinate the emperor Manuel, he was punished by an imprisonment which continued twelve years.

At length, he discovered a part of the wall in his prison where the bricks might be removed, and replaced so as not to change their usual appearance. Adjoining this wall was a recess, in which a person might be concealed, but beyond which he could not go. Andronicus removed the bricks, and, having passed into the recess, replaced them, so as to occasion no suspicion. Not being found in his cell the next day, he was believed to have escaped, and his spouse, being suspected of aiding him, was sent to take his place. In the dead of the night, she fancied she beheld a spectre. Her husband stood before her! She recognized him. They shared their provisions till they had been long enough together to devise an ingenious plan of escape. It succeeded. Andronicus fled to the Danube. Thence, after many perils, he found his way to Russia, and there rendered such important services to the Greek emperor, as to secure his pardon and return to Constantinople.

Again he fell under the displeasure of Manuel, who banished him to Cilicia in Asia Minor, but with a military command. Here his romantic amours brought him into new difficulties, to escape the consequences of which, he undertook a pilgrimage to Jerusalem. New adventures with the queen dowager of that city plunged him into a deeper sea of troubles, and a price was set upon his head. He fled from Jerusalem to Damascus, thence to Bagdad and Persia, and at length settled among the Turks in Asia Minor—the implacable foes of his country. At the head of a band of outlaws, he made predatory excursions into the empire, and acquired an extensive renown, as a bandit, throughout the East. The attempts of the emperor to secure him were unsuccessful, but his wife and two children were taken and sent to Constantinople. After a while, he succeeded, by manifestations of penitence, in obtaining his pardon. He prostrated himself at the foot of the throne of Manuel, and was dismissed to a place of exile, at the eastern extremity of the Euxine Sea. The death of the emperor was followed by a civil war at Constantinople. The friends of Andronicus fed his ambition with hopes. He gathered a military force, and marched to Constantinople, where he assumed to be the guardian of Manuel's infant son, Alexius. This unfortunate child and his mother were soon disposed of. The mother was thrown into the sea, and the child was strangled with a bowstring. After surveying the dead body of the murdered infant, Andronicus rudely struck it with his foot. "Thy father," said he, "was a knave, thy mother a harlot, and thyself a fool."

Andronicus ascended the throne A. D. 1183. The ancient proverb, "Bloodthirsty is the man who returns from banishment to power," was fully verified in him. Poison, the knife, the sea, and the flames, were the common portion of those who had incurred his displeasure. Alexius Angelus was marked as a victim. In a moment of despair, he slew the executioner who approached him, and fled to the church of St. Sophia. A mournful crowd assembled there, whose lamentations soon became curses, and whose curses quickly mounted to threats. At the dawn of the next day, the city burst into sedition, and in the general clamor, *Isaac Angelus* was raised to the throne. Andronicus was absent at one of the islands in the Propontis. He hurried to Constantinople, found it full of commotion, the palace deserted, and himself forsaken by all mankind. He attempted to escape by sea; but his galley was overtaken, and he was brought in chains before the new emperor.

Andronicus was placed astride of a camel, and conducted through the city, subjected to blows and the insults of the populace. He was then hung alive, by the feet, between the pillars that supported the figures of a wolf and a sow. All the citizens whom he had robbed of a father, a husband, or a friend, were allowed to take vengeance. His teeth, hair, an eye, and a hand were torn from him as a poor compensation for their losses. "Lord, have mercy upon me," and "Why will you bruise a broken reed?" were all the exclamations he uttered. At length his prolonged agony was terminated by two furious Italians, who plunged their swords into his body.

CHAPTER CCCLXVII.

A. D. 1185 to 1261.

Reign and Deposition of Isaac Angelus—The Crusaders attack Constantinople—Description of the City and its Capture by the Venetians—Election of a Frank Emperor of Constantinople—Division of the Byzantine Empire—The Principalities of Lacia, Nice, and Trebizond—Calamities of Constantinople—Great Fire—Decline and Extinction of the Latin Empire.

Isaac Angelus, who was placed on the throne at the death of Andronicus in 1185, was a prince of gentle disposition and effeminate manners; but he was deprived of his empire and of his eyes by his own brother, Alexius III., in 1194. His son Alexius fled to Venice, and sought for aid. The West was at that time preparing for a crusade, and the Venetians had undertaken to convey the Christian armies into Asia. Arrigo Dandolo, an old man, upwards of ninety years of age who had almost entirely lost his sight, but whose mental eyes penetrated the more deeply into political intrigues was doge of Venice and the soul of the enterprise

He persuaded the crusaders to conquer Zara, a Dalmatian city, for the Venetians. They next turned their arms against Constantinople; and the result of the enterprise appears from the following narrative, which was transmitted to the pope by an individual who attended the expedition: —

"As we could not but apprehend that we should, by our great multitude, be burdensome to the Holy Land, and as we learned that the citizens of Constantinople wished to return under the dominion of their lawful emperor, we thought it expedient to settle the disquiets that existed there, in order to secure for ourselves the necessary supplies and assistance for our future proceedings. We found the city of Constantinople uncommonly strong, the citizens in arms, with sixty thousand cavalry, and all the implements necessary for defence. The unlawful emperor had told the people that we designed to subdue them, and reduce their church to obedience to your holiness. Being stocked with only provisions for fourteen days, we were obliged to repeat our attacks without intermission. On the eighth day, we broke into the city. The emperor flying with a few of his people, we seated *Alexius IV.* on the throne of his father, after releasing the latter from his dungeon.

"The new emperor promised us two hundred thousand marks of silver, provisions for a year, and his assistance in recovering the holy sepulchre. He only desired us, on account of the Greeks, to remain in our camp, without the city. Soon after this, he suffered himself to be persuaded, by his father, to fall upon us by surprise, and to set fire to our fleet. The project was discovered. The people, afraid of our vengeance, cried out for a sovereign. The emperor, to appease us and them, sent to the discontented his kinsman *Murtzulph.* The latter betrayed and murdered the emperor and his father, and shut the gates of the city against us. There is, holy father, no city in the west like Constantinople. The walls are lofty and wide, consisting of squared stones. At every interval of five hundred paces is a stone tower, supporting another of wood, six stories high. Between the towers are bridges, full of arms and bowmen. Double and very wide fosses allow no play to our machines. Often, during the night, they sent out fire-ships against us. Our land forces alarmed Murtzulph, but he preferred to die rather than surrender.

"Murtzulph had killed the young emperor with a club, but he gave out that Alexius had died from other causes. He obtained advantages over us; but at length the ships Paradise and Pilgrim, under the command of the bishops of Troyes and Soissons, effected a landing. When the Greeks saw the whole army of the Franks pressing into the houses and into the streets, their courage forsook them. The emperor took to flight, with all the nobles, and sought refuge in the palace. We put the people to the sword in the streets till night came on. At length, our foot soldiers, without orders, rushed with irresistible force to storm the imperial residence, and made themselves masters of it; whereupon all Constantinople submitted.

"Most holy father, the quantity of gold, silver, and precious stones, and other costly things which we have found, far exceeds all that could be collected in the city of Rome and in all our Christendom. Six Venetian noblemen, with the bishops of Troyes, Soissons, Halberstadt, and Ptolemais, assembled with the legates of your holiness; and after celebrating high mass and public prayers, with the counsel and assistance of the high and mighty lord, Henry Dandolo, doge of Venice elected *Baldwin*, count of Flanders, to be emperor of Constantinople." A. D. 1204.

The conquest of Constantinople by the *Latins*, or *Franks*, as the people of Western Europe were then called, was followed by the division of the empire. Venice took possession of the Greek islands. French noblemen divided the territory of ancient Greece among them. Villehardouin, the historian of these events, became lord of Achaia, and Otho de la Roche, a Burgundian, was made duke of Athens. Three principalities were founded by the Greeks: one by Theodore Lascaris, son of Alexius III., at Nice, in Bithynia. This sovereignty governed Asia Minor under the imperial name. Two other states were founded by princes of the Comnene family. One of them was Lacia, on the eastern shore of the Black Sea, where barbarism and politeness were speedily combined in a most curious manner. Trapesus, or Trebizond, was the capital of this state, and its princes subsequently assumed the title of emperor. The other state was established in Acarnania and Ætolia, by a prince of the house of Angelus.

But Constantinople suffered the most dreadful calamities at the time of the Latin conquest. Three conflagrations desolated the city, and consumed more houses in it than were contained in the three largest cities in the rest of Europe. All the horrors of military license — all that a thirst for gold, religious hatred, or the rage and brutality of an unrestrained soldiery could inflict — the city of Constantine was doomed to suffer. What ever the flames spared was the prey of the brigands, whom pillage had only made more ravenous. An irreparable loss, which has been felt to the present day, was that of the libraries which had been gathering for many ages in this great capital, and which fell a prey to the flames.

Baldwin, the Latin emperor, became, in the first year of his reign, a sacrifice to the greatness which he had acquired; he was insidiously slain by Johannicus, king of the Bulgarians, a people who, about twenty years before, had recovered their freedom. The empire devolved upon his brother *Henry*, and from him to his brother-in-law, *Peter de Courtenay*, grandson of Louis VI. of France. The Latin empire speedily declined; the customs of the emperors were not in harmony with the manners of the Greeks, and their power obtained no consolidation.

CHAPTER CCCLXVIII.

A. D 1261 to 1453.

Decline of the Byzantine Empire — Progress of the Turks, the Pisans, and the Genoese — Establishment of the Turks in Europe — Degradation of the Greek Emperor — Apathy of the Western Christians — Accession of Mahomet II. — Preparations for Attacking Constantinople — Condition of the City — The Emperor Constantine Palæologus — His noble Declaration to the Turkish Sultan.

From the end of the Latin empire, in 1261, to the final conquest by the Turks, in 1453, — a period of one hundred and ninety-two years, — ten emperors reigned at Constantinople. The duration of the empire for so long a space of time, was not owing to the ability of the sovereigns, or the power of the people to resist the causes of their decline and overthrow, but to the circumstance that the attacks of their enemies were constantly directed to other objects. The history of this long period of time possesses little interest, and need not be detailed. The fourteenth century was an age of gross superstition and clerical tyranny. Heresies, not unlike those at the same time prevailing in the West, disturbed the repose of the East. Beside these dissensions, the Turks were continually growing stronger, as the power to resist them declined.

The Pisans, the Venetians, and the Genoese, established within the suburbs of Constantinople, were no less dreaded than the Turks. The Genoese had gradually expelled their rivals in commerce, and had enclosed their settlement, on the north-east side of the port Galata, with walls, and thus secured their position by fortresses. Their strength, and the imbecility of the emperor *Cantacuzene*, in 1348, encouraged them to seize a pretext for hostilities, and the Greeks were compelled to seek the alliance of the Venetians.

In February, 1351, a memorable battle was fought, under the walls of Constantinople, by the hostile fleet of the Genoese on one side, and the Greeks and Venetians on the other. The latter were defeated, leaving the Genoese the sovereigns of the sea. The maritime war of the two Italian republics continued, with little intermission, for two hundred years.

About the middle of the fourteenth century, the Turks had established themselves in Europe by crossing the Hellespont to the Thracian city of Galliopolis, at the outlet of the Sea of Marmora, about one hundred miles south-east of Constantinople. This city was considered as the key of Greece, and even of Europe. Possessed of this stronghold, the Turks extended themselves northwardly toward the Black Sea, circumscribing the remnant of the Greek empire to a space of fifty miles by thirty, of which Constantinople was the extreme easterly point. The seat of government of the Turks in Europe was Adrianople, about one hundred and fifty miles north-west of Constantinople. At this time, Amurath I. was sultan of the Turks, having dominion on both sides of the waters which separate Europe from Asia. It is supposed that the only reason why he did not crush the whole Greek empire at a blow, was the apprehension that he might thereby combine all the west of Europe against him. He contented himself with treating the feeble emperor of the Greeks as his vassal.

In fact, the last days of the empire had already come, if a new and unexpected event in the East had not prolonged its miserable existence for half a century. This was the invasion of the Tartars under Tamerlane, or Timour, by which the storm of war was averted from Constantinople, as we have already related. The Turkish sultan, Bajazet, instead of reigning in the capital of the Cæsars, as he had hoped, became the captive of the Tartar chief. But it was evident that this was only a temporary respite to the Greeks; and all the hope that now remained to them was, to engage the Christians of the west to unite in defending and preserving the empire. The emperor *Manuel* undertook this embassy. The principal inducements held out to the West, were the union of the Greek and Latin churches, and the consequent admission of the supremacy of the pope. But the states of the west were too much occupied with their own concerns, to listen to the proposals of Manuel; and the points of difference between the two churches were irreconcilable. The attempt was renewed, in 1438, by the emperor, *John II.*, the son of Manuel, but resulted only in mortification and disappointment to the Greeks

CHAPTER CCCLXIX.

A. D. 1451 to 1453.

Mahomet II., Sultan of the Turks — Preparations for the Siege of Constantinople — Firmness of the Emperor Constantine Palæologus — Magnitude of the besieging Army and Fleet — Weakness of the Greek Force — First Assault of the Turks.

Mahomet II. became sultan of the Ottomans in 1451. He was young, enterprising, and ambitious, and from the moment of his accession to the throne, bent all his thoughts to the conquest of Constantinople. The provinces had been subdued, one after another, till, at length, the walls of the capital comprised all that was left of the Byzantine empire. The emperor John had died in 1448, and left the throne to *Constantine XI.*, surnamed *Palæologus*. Mahomet did not wait for a pretext to begin the war, but immediately commenced the erection of a castle on the Hellespont, opposite to Constantinople. As this was an infringement of the treaty existing between the two powers, Constantine remonstrated against the proceeding, but without effect, and the fortification was completed with the utmost despatch. During the winter which followed, the emperor, who saw that a war was unavoidable, made the best preparations for defence which his slender means would allow, while the Turks were busily occupied in collecting their forces for the assault of the city.

Constantinople was surrounded, both on the land and the sea side, by strong walls. On the land side, the walls were double, four miles in extent, and having a deep ditch between them. The Turks had no vessels capable of attacking the city from the sea, and, therefore, at first directed their operations toward the western wall. Gunpowder and cannon had shortly before this time been introduced into Western Europe, but the Turks had not yet learned the use of them. During the winter of 1452, a Dane or Hungarian, named *Urban*, had deserted from the Greek service, and carried the knowledge of casting cannon to the Turks at Adrianople. Here he produced a brass piece, capable of throwing a stone of six hundred pounds weight. Two months were occupied in the laborious operation of transporting this cannon to the neighborhood of Constantinople. Other smaller pieces, cast by the same artificer, made up a formidable train of artillery. Beside these instruments of destruction, the Turks made use of the ancient machines of war, as the catapulta, the balista, the tower, &c.

The Turkish armies, gathered from all quarters for the grand assault on Constantinople, amounted to upward of two hundred and fifty thousand men. Their navy comprised three hundred and twenty sail, but none of these were large ships, and the greater number were mere boats. The Turkish army had been trained during a long preparation for this great effort promises and threats were alike used, and the sultan appealed especially to the spirit of fanaticism, the doctrine of fate, and the rewards of paradise, which the founder of the Moslem faith had prescribed as the surest means of conquest. The Greeks, on the other hand, had little to rely upon. Constantinople contained one hundred thousand inhabitants, but among these, only seven thousand fighting men could be found, and of these, two thousand were Genoese, commanded by John Giustiniani. The pitiable picture of this last and devoted remnant of the *Romans*, as they still called themselves, is relieved and dignified by a single object — the character and conduct of Constantine Palæologus. He was then fifty years of age. In his hopeless condition, expecting no succor from the west, shut up by sea as well as by land, certain to perish by famine, if he could defend himself against the sword of his enemy, the world might have justified him in making the best terms he could for his miserable subjects, if not for himself. Nearly a year before the siege began, he wrote to the Turkish sultan in the following words: "Since neither oaths, nor treaty, nor submission, can secure peace, pursue your impious warfare. My trust is in God alone. If it should please him to mollify your heart, I shall rejoice in the happy change. If he delivers the city into your hands, I submit without a murmur to his holy will. But until the Judge of the earth shall pronounce between us, it is my duty to live and die in the defence of my people."

CHAPTER CCCLXX.

A. D. 1453.

Siege of Constantinople — Sultan Mahomet's Railway — Last Preparation of the Emperor — General Attack of the City — Death of the Emperor — Capture of Constantinople — Superstition of the Inhabitants — Fate of the Remnant of the Greek Empire — Consequences of the Fall of Constantinople.

THE siege of Constantinople began on the 6th of April, 1453. The Turks attacked the western wall, and attempted to batter it down with their cannon and catapults. This was the post of danger, and here Constantine animated his little army by his presence and example. By the close of the day, the Turks had succeeded in demolishing the tower of St. Romanus, in the outward wall; but after a fierce conflict at the breach, they were repulsed. The emperor and Giustiniani passed the night upon the spot; and the next morning, the sultan perceived, with grief and astonishment, that the wooden tower which he had forced over the ditch had been burnt by the Greeks, the ditch cleared, and the tower of St. Romanus again strong and entire. The reduction of the city now appeared to be hopeless, unless a double attack could be made on the west, and from the port on the north-east side. This harbor was defended not only by the Greeks, but by a bar at its mouth. It was necessary to transport vessels over land, that the Turks might have a fleet to act upon its waters; and a project was conceived by the sultan of conveying his light vessels, by means of a *railway*, ten miles, from the Bosphorus to the upper part of the harbor, where the water was too shallow to permit the approach of the heavy ships of the Greeks. The railway was built of plank and timber, and made slippery by tallow. Eighty of the Turkish vessels, with almost incredible labor, were thus transported along a line north-east of the suburbs of Pera and Galata, and safely launched in the port.

With the aid of this fleet, the Turks constructed a raft or platform, which could be floated to the base of the wall, and sufficiently strong to support heavy cannon and scaling-ladders. Forty Greek youths, who attempted to burn these works, were taken and massacred. Constantine retaliated by exposing on the walls the heads of two hundred and fifty Turkish prisoners. After upwards of fifty days spent in the vicissitudes of attack and defence, the Turks made preparations for the last general assault by land and water. The 29th of May was fixed upon for their final effort. Constantine expected this fatal attack. He summoned his officers to the palace on the evening of the 28th, and by his advice and exhortations prepared them for their duties and dangers. His last speech was the funeral oration of the Roman empire. All appeared to be sensible of the desperate extremity in which they were placed. They wept, they embraced, and regardless of their individual families and fortunes, they devoted their lives to their country, and each commander departed to his station. The emperor entered the church of St. Sophia, — soon to be converted into a Mahometan mosque, — and partook of the communion; after which, he reposed for some moments in the palace, and then mounted his horse, to be in readiness to meet the enemy.

At the dawn of day, on the 29th of May, 1453, the general assault was made by land and water. The massy walls of the city were shaken by the ponderous engines of the Turks, and the fierce onset of countless assailants. Thousands fell under the missiles which were shot by the defenders from the walls; but the breaches in the Turkish ranks were immediately filled by new assailants. All was blood, horror, and confusion. The Greeks and their Genoese allies fought with desperation, although they were outnumbered by their enemies perhaps fifty fold. At length, they began to sink under fatigue. Giustiniani was wounded and withdrew from the fight. This example struck a panic into the rest; but the emperor, to the last moment, bravely performed all the duties of a general and a soldier, and was long seen at the head of his little band of Greeks, fighting against overwhelming multitudes. His fear was, that he might fall alive into the hands of the Turks; and his last exclamation was, "Cannot there be found a *Christian* to cut off my head?" He cast away his imperial robe, and fell by an unknown hand, upon a mountain of the slain.

The Turks scaled the wall of the city on one side, and entered by a gate on the other. The inhabitants, perceiving that all was lost, fled to the church of St. Sophia, and crowded every part of that vast edifice. A tradition had prevailed among them that the Turks would enter the city, and proceed as far as the Column of Constantine in the square, before the church; that an angel would descend with a sword, and deliver it to an old man, seated at the foot of the column, saying, "Take this sword, and avenge the people of the Lord!" that the Turks would immediately be driven back across the Bosphorus, into Asia. This belief appears to have been common to all classes, for the church included every rank of inhabitants in the city. While they waited for the descent of the angel, the Turks broke into the church, and seized the unhappy victims, who were immediately bound in couples, and dragged off to slavery. More than 60,000, of both sexes and all ages, shared this fate. The whole city was plundered, and the wealth of it abandoned by the sultan to his soldiers. The numerous libraries of Constantinople, being of no value to the barbarian conquerors, were either destroyed or dispersed, and many relics of ancient literature were irrecoverably lost.

The sultan made his triumphal entry into the city on the evening of its capture. He visited the church of St. Sophia, and arrested the hand of a Turkish soldier, who was beginning to break up its marble pavement. He ordered the Christian ornaments to be torn down, and the walls to be purified, after which the building was consecrated as a mosque. He had determined, from the first, that Constantinople should be the capital of the Ottoman empire; and after the tumult of the conquest was quieted, he invited the Greeks, who had escaped from the city, to return, assuring them their life, liberty, and the unmolested enjoyment of their religion. These promises were faithfully kept by him and his successors for a period of sixty years. The eastern point of the city was cleared, to make room for the sultan's palace and gardens, and on this spot is now the seraglio of the Ottoman ruler. From this time, Constantinople has continued to be the metropolis of the Turkish empire.*

The downfall of the imperial city is commonly regarded as the end of the Byzantine dominion. The imperial name and authority, however, still existed in the family of the Comneni, at Trebizond, on the Black Sea, while the Palæologi continued to hold the greater part of the Peloponnesus. Trebizond was conquered by Mahomet, in 1462, and the emperor David Comnenus was put to death at Constantinople. The Peloponnesus was subjugated about the same time. Mahomet adorned Constantinople with new magnificence, and the architecture of the city assumed an Oriental character.

The capture of Constantinople, although a great calamity, was not without beneficial effects on the rest of Europe. It became the means of spreading knowledge throughout the kingdom of the West. Many literary and scientific men, who fled before the Turkish arms, found a refuge in Italy, to which country they carried many valuable works of ancient literature, both in the Greek and Latin languages. The manuscripts, thus happily preserved from destruction, were multiplied by the invention of printing, then of recent date, and by degrees, found their way into every part of Europe

---

CHAPTER CCCLXXI.

Government of the Byzantine Empire — Pomp of the Emperor and his Officers — Description of Constantinople — Manners, Customs, Education, Amusements, &c., of the Inhabitants — Army and Navy — The Greek Ships — Fire-Signals.

THE government of the Byzantine empire was formed upon the most arbitrary model. The sovereign was the sole fountain of honor and authority. All ranks, both in the palace and the empire, depended upon the titles and offices which were bestowed and resumed by his sole will and pleasure. For a thousand years, — from the time of Vespasian to that of Alexius Comnenus, — the Roman emperor assumed the title of *Augustus* to himself, and gave that of *Cæsar* to his associate in the empire, or to his brothers and sons. Alexius, in order to bestow a dignity superior to that of Cæsar upon his brother Isaac, invented the new title of *Sebastocrator*, compounded of two Greek words, signifying *emperor* and *Augustus*. This dignitary was exalted above the Cæsar on the first step of the throne, and was distinguished from the sovereign only by some peculiar ornaments.

The emperor alone could array himself in purple buskins, and the close diadem, or tiara, which was copied from the fashion of the Persian kings. The buskins of the Sebastocrator and Cæsar were green, and both wore open coronets or crowns. The mode of adoration, or falling prostrate on the ground, and kissing the feet of the emperor, was borrowed by Dioclesian from the Persian court, and was continued to the end of the empire. This humiliating reverence was exacted from all who entered the royal presence, even from the kings of France and Italy, and the Latin emperors of Rome. Liutprand, bishop of Cremona, describes his visit to Constantinople in the tenth century, as ambassador of Otho, emperor of Germany. When he approached the throne, the birds on a golden tree began to warble their notes, which were accompanied by the roaring of two golden lions. He was compelled to fall prostrate, and touch the floor three times with his forehead. When he rose, the throne had been hoisted by an engine, from the floor

---

* *Emperors of the Byzantine Empire.*

Date of Accession. A. D.		*Date of Accession.* A. D.	
395.	Arcadius.	911.	Constantine VII.
408.	Theodosius II.	919.	Romanus I.
450.	Marcian.	940.	Constantine VIII.
457.	Leo I.	957.	Romanus II.
474.	Leo II.	964.	Nicephorus II.
480.	Zeno.	969.	John Zimisces.
491.	Anastasius I.	975.	Basil II.
518.	Justin I.	1025.	Constantine IX.
527.	Justinian I.	1030.	Romanus III.
565.	Justin II.	1034.	Michael IV.
578.	Tiberius.	1041.	Michael V.
582.	Maurice.	1054.	Theodora.
602.	Phocas.	1055.	Constantine X.
610.	Heraclius I.	1056.	Michael VI.
641.	Constantine III.	1057.	Isaac I.
650.	Heraclianus.	1059.	Constantine XI.
660.	Constans II.	1067.	Romanus III., Diogenes.
668.	Constantine IV.	1071.	Michael VII.
685.	Justinian II.	1075.	Constantine XII.
695.	Leontius.	1078.	Nicephorus III.
698.	Tiberius III.	1081.	Alexius Comnenus.
705.	Justinian II., restored.	1118.	John Comnenus.
711.	Philip Bardanes.	1143.	Manuel Comnenus.
713.	Anastasius II.	1180.	Alexius II.
716.	Theodosius III.	1183.	Andronicus.
718.	Leo III.	1185.	Isaac II., Angelus.
741.	Constantine V., Copronymus.	1194.	Alexius III.
775.	Leo IV.	1204.	Baldwin.
780.	Constantine VI., Porphyrogenitus.	1206.	Henry.
811.	Michael I.	1217.	Robert.
813.	Leo V	1230.	Baldwin II.
820.	Michael II.	1261.	Michael Palæologus.
829.	Theophilus.	1283.	Andronicus II.
841.	Harun.	1328.	Andronicus III.
842.	Michael III.	1341.	John I.
867.	Basilius I.	1392.	Manuel.
886.	Leo VI.	1424.	John II.
900.	Alexander.	1448.	Constantine XIII., Palæologus.

to the ceiling, and the emperor appeared in new and more gorgeous apparel. Every morning and evening, the civil and military officers of the empire were admitted to the presence of the sovereign, who signified his commands by a nod or a sign; but no one was allowed to speak or sit down in his presence. When he appeared in public, the streets were cleared and purified; the pavement was strewed with flowers; the most precious furniture of the inhabitants, gold and silver plate, and silken hangings, were displayed from the windows and balconies.

Constantinople was undoubtedly the richest and most magnificent city in the world. The Franks were struck with astonishment whenever business, religion, or curiosity led them from the west to visit the Byzantine capital. Fulk, of Chartres, who saw it in the tenth century, exclaims, "O, what a vast city is Constantinople! and how beautiful! How many monasteries it contains, and how many palaces built with wonderful art! How many manufactures are here, amazing to behold! It would be astonishing to relate how this city abounds with all good things; gold, silver, and cloths of various kinds, for every hour ships arrive in its port laden with all things necessary for the use of man." Geoffrey de Villehardouin, a French nobleman of high rank, and accustomed to all the magnificence then known in the west, describes, in similar terms, the astonishment and admiration of his fellow-soldiers, who beheld Constantinople for the first time. "They could not have believed," he says, "that there was a city so beautiful and rich in the whole world. When they viewed its high walls, its lofty towers, its rich palaces, and its magnificent churches, all appeared so great, that they could have formed no conception of this sovereign city unless they had seen it with their own eyes."

Rabbi Benjamin, a Jew of Tudela, in Navarre, passed through Constantinople, on his way to the East, about the year 1160. He describes it still more minutely. "This city," he remarks, "is exceedingly populous, being a great resort for merchants from all parts of the world, both by sea and land. Nothing can compare with it but Bagdad, that mighty city of the Ishmaelites. Here is the famous temple of St. Sophia, which contains as many altars as there are days in the year, and riches, beyond all estimation, derived from offerings brought from various countries, so that the wealth of the building has no parallel in any other temple in the world. In the centre of the temple are pillars of gold and silver, huge chandeliers, lamps, and other ornaments of these precious metals, more than any man is able to reckon. The emperor, beside possessing the palace left him by his ancestors, has lately built him another on the sea-shore, called *Bilbernæ*. The pillars and walls of this building are overlaid with beaten gold and silver, and on these are engraved the wars made by him and his ancestors. There is also a golden throne adorned with precious stones, with a golden crown, hanging by chains of gold over it. This is so enriched with pearls and precious stones, that no man is able to compute the cost of the whole. The riches of this palace are absolutely incredible; the towers being filled with scarlet and purple garments, and gold.

"The revenue of Constantinople, derived from commerce and the markets, is said to be twenty thousand crowns a day. The Greek inhabitants of the city are exceedingly rich in gold and precious stones. They dress in the most magnificent style, their garments being made of crimson intermingled with gold, or embroidered with needle-work; and they all ride upon horses, as if they were the children of kings. The country abounds with all sorts of fruit, and has plenty of corn, flesh, and wine, and there is not a finer spot to be found in the whole world. The inhabitants are totally given to luxury and enjoyment, and seem to me more like women than men, through their extreme love of pleasure. No Jews dwell within the city, but there are about twenty-five hundred of this nation, who occupy one of the suburbs, called *Pera*. Some of them are merchants, and very rich. No Jew is allowed to ride on horseback, except Solomon, the Egyptian, who is physician to the emperor, and by whose exertions the Jews have been relieved in their captivity; for the Jews are very much hated by the Greeks, who insult and beat them in the streets. The tanners use them worst of all; for when they dress their hides, they pour the dirty water into the streets before the doors of the children of Israel."

Of the domestic manners of the Constantinopolitans we have some sketches furnished by the theological writers of the early age of the city. Balls, weddings, and religious processions afforded copious sources of amusement. Carriages were drawn by white mules, with trappings of silver. The public races in the Circus, or Hippodrome interested all classes, and created factions in the state, which took sides with the blue or green charioteers. Attendance at church was regarded very much as a matter of fashion. When a famous preacher was to occupy the pulpit, he collected a throng equal to those of Whitfield or Wesley, in England. A burst of eloquence or pathos produced "rounds of applause" from the audience, as if the church had been a theatre. We may add, that the churches were beset with pickpockets, and that ladies very often returned home lightened of their jewels. A full attendance at church was sure to be followed by numerous arrests by the police, and commitals to prison. We have these, and many more curious particulars of the same sort, from Chrysostom, who wrote as early as the year 400.

The Greeks of Constantinople were very superstitious. Children were christened in a ridiculous manner. A number of lamps were lighted, and labelled with names; the infant was named after the lamp which burnt longest, this being deemed an omen of longevity. Afterward the child was furnished with a multitude of charms and fascinations, consisting of amulets, bells, and crimson thread. The powers of witchcraft and the "evil eye" were anxiously counteracted. Nurses and maids took mud out of the bath, and smeared it over the forehead of the child, and this was deemed to possess potent efficacy. Another mode equally fashionable, was to hang texts from the gospe round the children's necks.

Education received some systematic attention from the Constantinopolitans at an early period. Boys were sent to public schools at four years old. They continued at school till their fifteenth year. The course of study comprised reading, writing, grammar, arithmetic, and geometry. At college, the chief mode of teaching was by lectures. Instruction was given in logic, rhetoric, Latin, ethics, medicine, and law. Constantinople was regarded as having the best law school in the Roman empire, except Berytus. Physicians ranked high, and some were made senators. Every division of Constantinople had its physician appointed, and salaried by the government. The fees were only such as the patient chose to give.

The Greeks of the Byzantine empire were not a martial people Their wealth enabled them to purchase the service of poorer nations, and to maintain a naval power. The Sclavonians, the Turks, the Bulgarians, and the Russians were hired to man their ships, and fill the ranks of their armies. Since the time of the Peloponnesian and Punic wars, the science of naval architecture appears to have declined in the hands of the Greeks and Romans. The *dromones*, or light galleys of the Byzantine empire, had only two tiers of oars; and the whole crew, as in the infancy of the art, performed the double service of mariners and soldiers. They were provided with bows and arrows, which they used from the upper deck, and with long pikes, which they pushed through the port-holes from below. The principles of maritime tactics had not undergone any change since the time of Thucydides. A squadron of galleys advanced in a crescent, and strove to impel their sharp beaks against the sides of their antagonists. A machine for casting stones and darts was built of strong timbers in the middle of the deck, and the operation of boarding was effected by a crane that hoisted baskets of armed men. Signal flags were used by day, and lights by night, to convey orders. On land, fire-signals were repeated from one mountain to another, over an extent of five hundred miles; and when the Saracens attacked Tarsus, in Cilicia, the news was conveyed to Constantinople in a few minutes.

The history of the Greek empire presents a long list of historic and theological writers, but none of great celebrity.

Ragusa.

CHAPTER CCCLXXII.

A. D. 500 to 1368.

Foundation of Ragusa — The Republican Constitution — Attack of the Croatians and Saracens — Acquisition of the Tower — Change in the Government — Usurpation of Damiano — Revolution and establishment of Venetian Influence at Ragusa.

THIS little republic, which existed more than a thousand years on the shore of the Adriatic, without attracting very particular notice from the states of Western Europe, still deserves a place in our history. Its territory comprised a strip of sea-coast on the north-eastern side of the Adriatic, about forty miles long and two or three miles wide. The city of Ragusa is a seaport, formerly called *Lausium, Rausium*, or *Ragusium*. It dates from the sixth century A. D. when the ancient city of Epidaurus, in the Roman province of Illyria, was destroyed by a horde of Sclavonians. The fugitives from this city built on an adjoining rocky peninsula, a new town, which received the name of *Lausium*, from *lau*, a rock. This place was attacked in its infancy by the same wild hordes which had destroyed Epidaurus; but the priests found means, on this occasion, to mitigate the fury of the barbarians, who contented themselves with levying a contribution. In the seventh century, the population of the new commonwealth was much increased by fugitives from the ruins of Salona and the Illyrian mountains. The town was enlarged, and strengthened with walls and a citadel.

A republican constitution was established in Ragusa, at the very commencement of its career. The legislative body consisted of a general council, comprising the members of the principal families. From this council, an executive senate was formed by lot. The president of the senate was chief magistrate, with the title of *count*, which was afterward exchanged for that of *rector*. The election took place annually. On occasions of special importance, the people were called together in what would now be called a *mass meeting*. Undue ambition was unknown, and it was the wish of all to preserve their freedom. On one occasion, they sent to Greece for a man of high reputation for wisdom, and made him their rector. By his help, they concluded a treaty with the government of Constantinople.

The surrounding country possessed but little fertility, and the people of this small commonwealth were thrown upon the resources of their own industry. Under circumstances nearly similar, the Romans had become the conquerors of the world. The Ragusans made no conquests, but became a people remarkable for industrious habits. Their city was the market for the productions of the neighboring province of Bosnia, and they established manufactures, which contributed greatly to their opulence. They derived some advantage from their connection, by treaty, with the Byzantine emperors, who were able to protect, but not to oppress them. They also made a treaty with a neighboring prince of Bosnia, by which they obtained an accession of territory. This, at the time of its transfer to the Ragusans, was little better than a wilderness; but the industrious possessors, by their skill in agriculture, soon converted it into a garden. They applied themselves also to maritime trade, built vessels, and became powerful at sea. Stephen, king of Dalmatia, ceded to them a tract of territory; and after his death, his widow Margaret, in consequence of some disturbances which broke out in her country, took refuge in Ragusa, where she became a nun. Bogoslav, king of Croatia, a relative of Margaret, marched with an army against Ragusa, and laid siege to the city, but was compelled to retire after devastating the territory. The Ragusans displayed their valor in defence of their homes on another occasion, in 867, when they were attacked by the Saracens from Africa, who took several towns on the coast of the Adriatic, and laid siege to Ragusa for a whole year. The inhabitants at length expelled them from their territory and pursued them across the Adriatic into Italy, as far as Benevento and Capua.

About this time, the Ragusans made an acquisition which added much to the security of the commonwealth. A strong tower at the entrance of their harbor had been in the possession of a Rascian nobleman, and threatened both the freedom and the subsistence of Ragusa. By adroit management, the commanders of the fortress were gained over to the republic, and admitted into the government, in consequence of which the Ragusans became masters of the tower. This fortunate acquisition was afterward celebrated by an annual festival; for trifling affairs are important to such small communities. Nearly about the same time, a new influx of Sclavonian families added to the population; the Latin language gradually fell into disuse, and the Sclavonian took its place.

In process of time, the government underwent a change. The assemblies of the people were discontinued, and the power came chiefly into the hands of the nobles, who consisted of the descendants of the founders of Ragusa and Bosnian chiefs; yet the community continued at peace and highly prosperous. In the thirteenth century, a tyrant made his appearance on the stage. The rector Demeianus, or Damiano, having held his office for a year, managed, by means of his connections, wealth, and popularity, contrary to all precedent, to obtain a reëlection — the Ragusans having previously adhered rigidly to the "one term principle." At the expiration of his second term, he continued to prevent the assembling of the great council, whose function it was to elect his successor. Damiano, therefore, held the government four years; for so scrupulous were the Ragusans in observing established forms, that they allowed the laws to be subverted on their account. Damiano now began to play the tyrant, and threw into prison the most noble youths of the house of Bobali, who were zealous supporters of freedom; but they contrived to make their escape.

Damiano had strengthened himself by gaining partisans in Ragusa, both among the patricians and the populace. A conspiracy was formed against his tyranny through the instrumentality of Peter Benessa, his son-in-law, who preferred the freedom of his country to the splendor of his family. The senators were assembled in secret, and as it was not easy to overthrow the usurper without foreign aid, they resolved to apply to Venice. Benessa went to that city, on pretence of commercial affairs, and made a treaty with the senate of that republic, by which it was agreed that Damiano should be expelled on condition that Venice should appoint the rectors of Ragusa. Two Venetian galleys put to sea, with the professed object of conveying presents to Constantinople. They touched at Ragusa, where Damiano entertained the captain, and was invited to dine on board the commander's galley on the following day. As soon as he was on board, Benessa summoned the citizens to arms in the cause of freedom, while the Venetians weighed anchor and carried off the usurper, who, being overwhelmed with mortification and rage, dashed out his brains against the walls of the cabin, A. D. 1210.

For a century and a half following this event, Ragusa was governed by Venetian rectors, who were taken from among the first patrician families of Venice, and held office for two years. The republic, in other respects, was entirely independent, and enjoyed its own laws. The Venetians, however, encouraged the spirit of faction in Ragusa, restored the popular assemblies in order to turn the attention of the people from the senate, and augmented the numbers of the latter body by new appointments, in order that it might contain individuals who should owe their dignity to Venetian influence. In 1320 the Ragusans made a commercial treaty with the emperor of Constantinople, by which, for the payment of five hundred ducats a year, they were admitted to free trade with all the Byzantine territories on the same footing as native subjects.

CHAPTER CCCLXXIII.

A. D. 1368 to 1814.

Overthrow of the Venetian Influence — Connection of Ragusa with Hungary — Treaty with Orchan — Tribute to the Turks — Neutrality of the Ragusans between the Turks and Christians — Overthrow of the Republic, and Annexation to Austria — Government, Population, Manners, Customs, &c., of the Ragusans.

The Venetian administration continued till 1368, when a war having broken out between Venice and Hungary, the Venetians were compelled, by the success of the Hungarian arms, to renounce their authority at Ragusa. By this event, the republic became restored to full independence. In gratitude for this, the Ragusans agreed to pay a tribute of five hundred ducats yearly to the king of Hungary, and to hoist his flag on their ramparts by the side of their own. A protector was necessary to Ragusa on account of its commerce in the Adriatic, which, since the Greek emperor had ceased to maintain a fleet in that sea, had been exposed to the attacks of the Genoese and the Venetians, who disregarded the neutrality of the small states, and committed all sorts of violence. The connection with Hungary soon ceased, and the Ragusans turned their attention to Orchan, the Turkish leader, whose power was already so great on the Asiatic coast, the Hellespont, the Propontis, and the Black Sea, that all commercial nations were obliged to conciliate his favor. In order to reconcile the people to an alliance with the Mahometans, a nun was induced to declare that this measure had been revealed to her as the will of God. A treaty, in consequence, was made in 1330, by which the Ragusans agreed to pay the Turkish monarch five hundred sequins a year, in return for which the republic was taken under his protection, and its commodities were exempted from duties. This sum, with presents to the Turkish nobles, continued to be paid till the end of the republic in 1806.

After the capture of Constantinople, and the increase of the Turkish power in Europe, the tribute of the Ragusans was increased. During the long wars of the sixteenth century, between the Turks and the Christian powers, the Ragusans found it a most arduous task to preserve their neutrality, as the fleets of the belligerents repeatedly visited their coasts, and plundered their territory without scruple. They were charged by the Christians with favoring the Turks, and by the Turks with being partial to the Christians, though their only study was to keep on good terms with both parties. Charles V. pressed several of their galleys into his service, and confiscated their merchant vessels. When the Venetians, the Papal admiral, and the Genoese commander, Andrew Doria, combined their fleets in the Adriatic against Hayraddin Barbarossa, in 1538, it was seriously debated among the leaders whether they should not begin by attacking Ragusa, and bringing it under subjection to Charles V.; but Doria opposed this measure, declaring that he had come to fight infidels, and not his brother Christians.

The Ragusans, in this critical emergency, sent a learned ecclesiastic to Rome, in order to justify and explain their conduct to pope Paul III. By a representation of the necessities of their condition, with their territory placed, as it were, in the very jaws of the Ottoman power, and having a scanty and rocky soil, which did not afford them the means of subsistence, they made an impression on the pope, who promised them his protection. By means of envoys and presents to the various powers, and by maintaining a most prudent and discreet conduct, the Ragusans managed to steer their little bark safely through that most stormy period. Ragusa became a city of refuge. Emigrants from all countries found hospitality there. Christians flying from the Ottomans, Florentine patriots exiled by the fall of their republic, Italians from every quarter, men of learning and genius, found there a good reception. The city was a sort of neutral ground, a stepping-stone between Christendom and Turkey; and much intercourse and correspondence were carried on through this channel, which could not be transacted direct with Constantinople.

During the seventeenth and eighteenth centuries, after a better understanding had been established between the Porte and the Christian powers, Ragusa continued to enjoy its independence and neutral security, and no Turkish soldier was allowed to set foot upon its territory. The sultan's protection was of importance to the republic, by securing its flag from the attacks of the Barbary pirates. In this respect, the Ragusan merchant ships had the advantage over those of most of the Mediterranean states, and they acted as carriers in that sea, between the Levant and the ports of Western Europe. In the early hostilities between the United States and Algiers, the negotiations and communications were carried on by Ragusan vessels.

For nearly twelve hundred years, Ragusa had preserved its independence more or less complete, and had withstood the attacks of numerous tribes of barbarians. It remained as an advanced post of European civilization on the borders of wild Bosnia, and fierce Albania, and its freedom and its flag were respected by all the states of Christendom. It fell, however, in the general crash of principalities and powers that followed the French revolution. In the quarrel between France and Russia, in 1806, about the possession of the district of Cattaro, one of the spoils of the republic of Venice, the French occupied Ragusa with their troops. Napoleon, in 1808, abolished the republic, and incorporated the territory of Ragusa with the province of Dalmatia. On his overthrow, in 1814, the Austrians took possession of Dalmatia, and that territory, including Ragusa, has ever since formed a part of the Austrian empire.

The people of this republic were divided into four orders—patricians, citizens, ecclesiastics, and plebeians. The patricians intermarried only with one another, or with noble families of other countries. They exercised no trade or profession, but lived either on the rents of their lands and houses, or on the interest of the money which they lent to the merchants and manufacturers. The patrician boys were remarkable for their forwardness and impertinence, and it was a proverb in the republic, "Deliver us from the flies of Zara and the boys of Ragusa." The citizens were chiefly engaged in trade, either as merchants or shopkeepers. All others were ecclesiastics or plebeians. The patricians, in the latter days of the republic, had the government entirely in their hands. They were all members of the general council, who elected the rector and the ecclesiastical officers. Sometimes the rector was changed every month. His authority was great; nothing could be done without his consent. He never appeared in public, except at popular festivals, and on occasions of public business. He wore a mantle of purple damask, with red shoes, which were the insignia of supreme power in the Roman empire. His body-guard consisted of twelve men, unarmed. The Ragusans were most rigid observers of etiquette and legal formalities. The length of a councillor's robe was fixed by law; and when Tuberoni Cerva entered the council hall with a robe of illegal length, the superfluous part was cut off by executive authority — a disgrace which affected him so violently, that he quitted public life, and entered into a monastery.

The Ragusan people, during the long career of their republic, appear to have been, in general, a contented, thriving race. The upper classes were well behaved, equitable, and civil; and though the patrician youths were accustomed to carry their measures with a high hand, and beat the other boys in the street, yet we are informed, by the faithful chronicler of these matters, that the citizen and plebeian youngsters always took their revenge by flogging the little aristocrats when they caught them in dark lanes. The various powers of the state were tolerably well balanced in Ragusa. Even the pope was taught to know his place, and allowed only to appoint an archbishop out of two candidates selected by the council. The Ragusans, from the earliest ages, belonged to the Western or Roman church.

The city of Ragusa stands upon the sloping sides of two hills, and is defended by walls, ditches, and castles. The streets are mostly narrow. The houses are well built, of freestone, and are spacious and commodious. The cathedral and government palace are large and fine structures, and the latter has splendid halls and galleries. Without the walls are numerous gardens and country-houses, with plantations of orange and other fruit-trees, and handsome fountains. There is an almost continuous suburb along the western coast for three miles. The population of the city was once thirty thousand. At present, it is not much above six thousand. Many able and learned men have been born at this place; among others, the mathematician Boscovich, Father Kunich, long professor of classical literature at Rome, and the learned Banduri.

The Ragusans are reckoned among the best sailors in the Mediterranean, and bear a high character for honesty and steadiness. Ship-building, manufactures of soap, liquors, and tobacco are the chief branches of industry in Ragusa. Two miles west of the city is the fine harbor of Gravosa, with docks for ship-building, and fine country houses around. Timber is imported from the opposite coast of Monte Gargaro, in Italy. The maritime trade of Ragusa was almost annihilated by the occupation of the country by the French in 1806, but it has since somewhat revived. The language of the country is a dialect of the Sclavonian; but all the educated people speak Italian: this tongue and the Latin are the literary languages of Ragusa. The little island of Meleda constituted a portion of the territory of the republic. It contains six villages. The population of the whole district is about forty thousand.

Turkey in Europe.

CHAPTER CCCLXXIV.

Origin of the Ottoman Empire — Its Extent and Political Divisions.

The Turkish or Ottoman* empire began remotely with the White Huns of Scythia; but the commencement of the present kingdom is usually referred to Solyman, chief of a branch of the Seljukian Turks, who settled in Asia Minor in the thirteenth century. Gradually growing in strength, this power swallowed up the greater part of the territories of the Saracens in Asia and Africa, and finally, crossing into Europe, wrested from the Byzantine empire, one after another, its finest provinces. Nothing was left of that mighty kingdom but Constantinople; and this, in 1453, was captured, and became the seat and centre of the Ottoman dominion. This is the only instance in which an Asiatic people has permanently established itself in Europe.

At the beginning of the present century, the Ottoman empire included nearly all the territories originally belonging to the Byzantine throne. It is now considerably reduced. Greece has become free. All the African provinces are practically independent. Of the Asiatic provinces, Asia Minor, Syria, a part of Armenia, Koordistan, and Mesopotamia, remain, though the supremacy over them is considerably lessened in modern times. Referring the reader to our account of Asiatic Turkey, we proceed to give a sketch of the European portion of this empire.

Turkey in Europe is bounded on the north by the Austrian empire, the three Principalities, and Russia, from all which it is chiefly separated by the Save and the Danube; east by the Black Sea, the Straits of Constantinople, the Sea of Marmora, the Dardanelles, and the Archipelago; south by Greece, and west by the Ionian Sea, the Gulf of Venice, and the Austrian empire. It extends from 39° to 48° north latitude, and from 16° to 30° east longitude, comprising an area of one hundred and fifty thousand square miles, and a population of fifteen millions.

A chain of mountains, forming a continuation of the great Alpine system, extends from west to east, through the northern part of Turkey, from Dalmatia to the Black Sea. The western part of the chain is called the *Dinaric Alps*; the eastern part is called the *Balkan*, or *Hæmus*. On the southern frontier of Servia, a branch of this chain shoots off to the south, stretching, under various names, through Greece. This range, called *Mount Pindus*, embraces numerous celebrated summits, among which are Parnassus, Helicon, Olympus, Pelion, Ossa, &c.

The Maritza, — the *Hebrus* of ancient geographers, — the Albanian Drino, the Axius, or *Vardar* of the moderns, the Achelous, now the *Aspropotamos*, and the Peneus, are the chief rivers.

The Archipelago, or Ægean Sea, along the territories of Turkey in Europe as well as in Asia, is strongly indented by numerous capes and headlands. The series of seas and straits which connect the Ægean with the Black Sea, are, first, the Straits of the Dardanelles, or the Hellespont; then the Sea of Marmora; then the Bosphorus, entering into the Black Sea, on which Constantinople is situated. This divides Asia from Europe, its width being from half a mile to two miles.

The climate is more severe than would be inferred from the latitude. In the recesses of the highest mountains, snow lies the greater part of the year. Other and more southerly portions enjoy a mild and delicious climate. In some parts the seasons are intensely hot.

A great portion of the country is covered with forests: cattle are extensively reared in the northern

* For the early annals of the Turks, and their history so far as it belongs to Asia, we refer the reader to our view of *Asiatic Turkey*, page 354: for the early history of the territories belonging to *Turkey in Europe*, he can consult our sketch of the *Byzantine Empire*, page 799. If the reader is desirous of tracing the remote annals of the Turks, we refer him to page 393.

Wallachian Woman.

Croatian.

Croatian Woman.

parts. The wolf, wild-boar, chamois, stags, &c., abound in the wooded districts. The horse of Turkey is small, but active; the ass and mule are much used. A great quantity of wool is produced. Olives, grapes, maize, are cultivated, but only a small part of the territory is subjected to husbandry. In the southern parts fine fruits are produced, as oranges, lemons, figs, almonds, &c. There are mines of iron, lead, and copper. On the whole, this is a country of great natural advantages, but the influences of the government and religion tend to induce general indolence and imbecility.

The political divisions adopted by European geographers are unknown to the Turks, who, in their administrative divisions, blend the Asiatic with the European parts of the empire. They divide the whole empire into two *beglerbegships*, the one comprising the European and parts of the Asiatic dominions, whose capital is Sophia; the other including the rest of the empire.

In the brilliant period of the Ottoman empire, it was further divided into forty-four *eyalets* or principalities, which were subdivided into *sangiacs*, or *broas*, (banners;) the former under the government of viziers or pachas of three tails, (that is, horse tails, carried on spears, as marks of rank or dignity,) and the latter under mirmirans, or pachas of two tails.

The divisions of Turkey in Europe are generally considered to be the following: —

Eyalets.		*Capitals.*
Roumelia,	(comprising the Thessaly, Macedonia, Albania, Thrace, &c., of European writers,)	Sophia.
Silistria,	(greater part of Bulgaria, and the eastern part of Macedonia,)	Silistria.
Bosnia,	(comprising Turkish Croatia, Bosnia, and Hertzegovana, a part of Dalmatia,)	Bosna. Serai.
The Isles,	(comprising Thasos, Samothraki, Imbros, Lemnos, Chios, Samos, Metelin or Lesbos, with Rhodes, and other islands along the coasts of Asia Minor; a part of these latter properly belong to Turkey in Asia,)	Gallipoli.

Principality of Servia. — This is an hereditary constitutional monarchy, with an independent administration, though it is tributary to the Porte. Area of the state. twelve thousand square miles; population, not far from one million. Semendria, on the Danube, with twelve thousand inhabitants, is the capital. Belgrade, the principal city, remarkable for its vast and strong military works, is the principal town; population fifty thousand. The Servians belong to the Sclavonic stock: under the Romans, they formed the province of Mœsia Superior; in the thirteenth and fourteenth centuries, Servia formed an independent kingdom, which was conquered by the Turks in the middle of the fifteenth century. In 1801, the Servians, under Czerny George, revolted, but were reduced to submission in 1813. After some new attempts to recover their freedom, their demands were finally granted in 1820, and they became a separate state, paying, however, an annual tribute, and receiving a Turkish garrison into Belgrade. The country seems to be pretty well governed; justice is impartially administered, and elementary schools are established in the various districts.

Principality of Wallachia. — This also is tributary to the Porte. It has an area of twenty-eight thousand square miles, and a population of more than two and a half million souls. The prince, or *hospodar*, is appointed for life. Bucharest, the capital, is a large city, with eighty thousand inhabitants. Tergovist, formerly an important town, has much declined, and at present has but five thousand inhabitants. The Wallachians, or, as they call themselves, the *Rumani*, are of the Greco-Latin stock. They are descended from the ancient *Vlachi*, in Thrace, a Christian nation belonging to the Greek church, and who used a kind of Roman dialect. They form the population of Wallachia, Moldavia, and of many of the interior provinces of the Ottoman empire. The whole nation of Wallachians is supposed to embrace four millions of souls.

Principality of Moldavia.—This likewise is tributary to the Porte. It has a population of little less than a million and a half, on an area of fifteen thousand square miles. The capital is Jassy, with forty thousand inhabitants. Moldavia formerly made part of Wallachia; the inhabitants are chiefly Wallachians, with some Jews and Gypsies: no Turks are allowed to settle in the country. The government is similar to that of Wallachia, the administration being separate and independent.

Group of Turks.

CHAPTER CCCLXXV.

A. D. 1453 to 1566.

TURKEY IN EUROPE. — *Effects of the Conquest of Constantinople, in Europe — Hunyades and Scanderbeg — Bajazet and Zizim — Reign of Selim the Cruel — Turkish Conquests — Reign of Solyman the Magnificent — Conquest of Hungary — Intrigues of the Harem.*

WHEN Constantinople fell before the arms of Mahomet II., Italy trembled for its safety. Pope Nicholas V., and, after him, Pius II., sent the most urgent entreaties to all the western Christians to unite their forces against the victorious progress of the Turks. Pius even determined to animate this new crusade by his own presence; but he was prevented by death from executing his purpose. Two Christian princes, however, arrested the progress of the Ottoman arms. John Hunyad, or Huniades, commanded the Hungarian armies, and met the hosts of Mahomet at Belgrade, on the southern frontier of Hungary. A battle fought at this place, in 1467, resulted in a victory to the Christian arms, and saved Hungary. The impression which this defeat produced on the sultan remained to the day of his death, and the Ottoman arms made no further progress in that quarter for many years. The *waywodes* of Moldavia defended themselves with so much valor, that Mahomet was contented with their nominal submission. In another quarter, George Castriot, prince of Epirus, or Albania, better known by the name of *Scanderbeg*, which in Turkish signifies *Alexander the Great*, possessed a small district among the mountains of that country, of which Croia was the capital. The Turks invaded his territory, and besieged Croia; but Scanderbeg, at the head of a small but faithful band of followers, resisted successfully the mighty armies of the invaders, and compelled them to raise the siege.

On the death of Mahomet II., in 1481, a dispute for the succession arose between his two sons, Bajazet and Zizim, each of whom had his partisans among the janizaries. *Bajazet* prevailed in Constantinople, and took possession of the throne. Zizim raised an army in Bithynia, and made himself master of Prusa. Bajazet despatched his vizier, Ahmed, against him with a strong force, and Zizim was compelled to fly, with his mother and two children, into Syria, and from thence to Egypt, both these countries then being under the dominion of the Mameluke sultans. Zizim was hospitably received by the sultan, who endeavored to persuade him to give up his ambitious schemes, but without effect; and Zizim next resorted to the king of Caramania, a petty province of Asia Minor, which had long been famous for its hostility to the Ottoman government. The two princes took the field against Bajazet, but were defeated; and Zizim fled to Rhodes and sought an asylum with the Christian knights, who were then at war with the sultan.

Zizim was favorably received at Rhodes. Bajazet made advantageous offers of peace to the knights, on condition that his brother should be given up. This they refused; but, being anxious to conclude a treaty with the sultan, they persuaded Zizim to retire to Italy. The pope kept him a prisoner at Rome for several years. He had handsome apartments assigned him in the palace of the Vatican, and was treated with all the respect due to his rank, but not allowed his liberty. Several of the Christian kings were desirous to have the custody of the royal captive, as a check upon the Turkish sultan. At length, Charles VIII. of France, in passing through Rome on his expedition against Naples, in 1494, caused him to be released. Zizim, however, died a few days afterward, not without suspicions of poison. Bajazet, being thus relieved from all danger of a competitor for his throne, employed himself in enlarging his dominions and cultivating literature. His latter days were imbittered by the behavior of his son Selim, who was fierce and warlike, and in high favor with the soldiers. By their aid, he compelled his father to resign the crown to him, in preference to his elder brother, Achmet. Bajazet, bowed down with age and infirmities, quitted the capital, attended by about five hundred domestics, and took the road to Adrianople, but died before reaching that place, being poisoned, it was supposed, by his physician, at the command of his son.

Selim, surnamed the *Cruel*, ascended the throne in 1512. His first measure was to lead an army against his brother Achmet in Asia. Achmet was defeated, made prisoner, and strangled, by order of Selim. Shortly afterward, he put a second brother to death in the same manner. Achmet left two young sons, one of whom sought refuge in Egypt, while the other fled to Persia; and, as both were kindly received by the respective sovereigns of those countries, Selim declared war against them. The Persians were defeated at the battle of Tauris, and Egypt was conquered, as we have already related in the history of those countries. Egypt became a Turkish province, and was governed by a pacha and princes called *beys*. In the course of eight years, Selim added the whole of Egypt, Palestine, and Syria to his empire. He died suddenly, it is said, in the same village where his father was poisoned by his command, A. D. 1520.

Solyman, surnamed the *Magnificent*, succeeded his father Selim. His reign is regarded by the Turks as the most splendid in all their history, not only on account of the conquests made by this prince, but from the power and grandeur to which he raised the Ottoman empire by his vigorous government and the great increase of his maritime force. The Turkish dominion, at his accession to the throne, comprised Egypt, Syria, Palestine, Greece, Albania, Servia, Bosnia, and Macedonia. The first conquest made by Solyman was Belgrade, a city on the southern frontier of Hungary, which had long been an object of contention between the sovereigns of Hungary and Turkey, on account of its commanding situation. He next captured Rhodes from the knights of St. John, as we have related in the history of that island. After these conquests, Solyman returned to Constantinople, where he applied himself to the business of legislation. Many of his laws are still in use, and bear the title of the *Canons of Solyman*. Among them was one which abolished the barbarous custom of putting to death all the male relatives of the sultan, which was formerly done to prevent them from aspiring to the throne. Some of the sovereigns had, for this reason been guilty of the cruelty of putting to death their own brothers and sons. Even infants had been strangled immediately after their birth.

When Solyman had regulated the internal affairs of the empire, he recommenced his war with Hungary. Lewis II., a young man only twenty-two years of age, was then king of Hungary, and little able to contend with the warlike and experienced sultan of Turkey. The two armies met at Mohacz, on the Danube, A. D. 1526. Solyman gained a great victory. The king and most of the Hungarian nobles were killed. The whole kingdom was left at the mercy of the conqueror, who advanced as far as Buda, plundering the country, and carrying away multitudes of the inhabitants into slavery. For fifteen years after this event, Solyman carried on a war with the Austrians, and, at one time, marched with a large army to the gates of Vienna, from which he was repulsed with great loss. In the decline of his life, Solyman grew tired of warfare, and lived in peace among his people. To the surprise and mortification of the whole empire, he married one of his slaves, a beautiful but ambitious woman, named *Roxalana*, who had gained so great an influence over his mind, that he was ruled by her will. In order to raise her own son to the throne, she plotted the death of the sultan's eldest son, Mustapha, by inventing a story of a conspiracy, and charging him with a design to dethrone his father. The sultan gave ear to the tale, and caused Mustapha to be put to death. The fraud was discovered when too late, and Solyman died a prey to remorse, A. D. 1566.

CHAPTER CCCLXXVI.

A. D. 1566 to 1798.

Selim II.—Battle of Lepanto—Amurath III.—Treaty with England—Mahomet III.—Achmet I.—Mustapha I.—Revolutions at Constantinople—Amurath IV.—Ibrahim—Mahomet IV.—Siege of Vienna—Solyman III.—Decline of the Turkish Empire—War with France.

SELIM II. acquired the throne by the crime of his mother. He made peace with the Austrians and Persians, with whom his father had been contending. But, notwithstanding his dislike for war, he was desirous of gaining renown by some important conquest. He therefore turned his eyes toward the beautiful Island of Cyprus, which was then in the possession of the Venetians. Under pretence that the islanders had ill treated some of his people who were going on a pilgrimage to Mecca, he demanded of the Venetians that it should be given up to him; and this being refused, he invaded and conquered it, in 1571. The Venetians and Spaniards equipped a large fleet to oppose the progress of the Turks, which they placed under the command of Don John of Austria, brother to Philip II., king of Spain. They encountered the Turkish fleet in the Bay of Lepanto, in the Morea, and the Christian fleet gained a complete victory, A. D. 1572. Cervantes, the author of Don Quixote, fought in this battle, and lost one of his hands by a blow from a Turkish sabre. The victory of Lepanto gave liberty to many thousands of Christian slaves, who were chained to the oars of the Turkish galleys; and it was celebrated with great rejoicings all over Chrisendom. After this loss, Selim sunk into the indolence common to the Oriental sovereigns, and died in 1575.

Amurath III, the successor of Selim, is described as a mild prince, and so great a lover of justice and good order, that he was accustomed to go out in disguise to see that his commands were obeyed. An embassy was sent to him by Queen Elizabeth of England, and permission was obtained to establish English consuls and trading-houses in the Ottoman empire. This was the foundation of the English company of Turkey merchants. The opening of this trade was a great advantage to the people of England, who were enabled to procure spices, coffee, carpets, raw silk, and a variety of useful and elegant commodities from the Levant. They also learned from the Turks the art of dyeing very fine colors.

Mahomet III. succeeded Amurath in 1595. The empire now began to decline. The sultan made pleasure his chief business, leaving the government to his mother, who was by no means equal to the task. Most of the provinces were under the dominion of pachas, who oppressed the people for the purpose of enriching themselves. The country was desolated by plague and famine, and the tributary princes of Moldavia and Wallachia revolted, and transferred their allegiance to the emperor of Germany. The wars in Hungary were renewed, and carried on with great disadvantage to the Turks. Mahomet died, in 1603, of the plague, and left the throne to his son, *Achmet I.*, a youth fifteen years of age, who had been shut up in a prison during his father's reign. The Hungarians and Persians carried on war against Turkey in the reign of Achmet, though the sultan did not head his own troops, but spent the greater part of his time in his harem, which contained upwards of three thousand females. He built a stately mosque near the church of St. Sophia, which still remains, constituting one of the chief architectural ornaments of Constantinople. Achmet died in 1617.

Mustapha, the brother of Achmet, was next placed upon the throne; but, being unfit for the government, he was deposed, after a reign of four months, in favor of *Osman*, the son of the late sultan, a boy of twelve years of age. Ambitious of being distinguished as a hero, he marched with an army into Poland, where, in consequence of his rashness and ignorance of the art of war, he was defeated, and compelled to make an ignominious peace. This caused an insurrection at Constantinople, which ended in the restoration of Mustapha and the death of Osman, who was strangled in the castle of the Seven Towers — a state prison belonging to the seraglio. The pachas took advantage of these confusions to rebel; and such a scene of anarchy ensued, that the chief men of Constantinople met together and deposed Mustapha a second time, who was sent to the Seven Towers, and *Amurath IV.*, his nephew, was placed on the throne. He was fierce, arbitrary, and cruel; but he restored order in the state, and punished the rebellious janizaries. The extravagant acts of folly which he committed have furnished subjects for many an Eastern tale. He was immoderately given to wine — an indulgence expressly forbidden by the Koran. When in a state of intoxication, he was guilty of all kinds of absurd and furious actions. He would traverse the streets with a drawn sword, to kill any one whom he might find smoking — a practice which he had forbidden, because he disliked the smell of tobacco. Sometimes he would amuse himself by shooting with a bow in all directions, regardless of whom he might kill. His attendants trembled at the very sound of his footsteps, and the people in the streets would hide themselves at his approach. He died, from excessive drinking, in 1640.

Ibrahim, the brother of Amurath, succeeded him; but the close confinement in which he had been kept for several years had so impaired his intellect, that he was totally unable to direct the affairs of the empire. He was therefore deposed, after a reign of nine years, and strangled in the prison where he had spent the early part of his life. *Mahomet IV.*, his son, a child seven years of age, succeeded him, in 1655. As soon as he was old enough to exercise his own will, he removed the court to Adrianople. In a war with Austria, an Ottoman army, commanded by the grand vizier, marched into Hungary, and approached near to Vienna, but was obliged to retreat. The Turks, however, conquered the Island of Candia from the Venetians, in 1669, after they had besieged it for thirteen years.

In the mean time, the Turks became involved in a war with Austria on the subject of Hungary. The emperor Leopold, by flagrantly violating the privileges of his Hungarian subjects, — as Austrian emperors have always been wont to do, — provoked a formidable revolt, which was headed by Count Tekeli, a leader of great courage and resolution. He called upon the sultan for assistance. Mahomet prepared one of the most formidable armaments that the Ottoman empire had ever sent against Christendom. Leopold, convinced that his own resources were not equal to the emergency, formed an alliance with John Sobieski, king of Poland. Before the Polish army could take the field, the Turkish forces, commanded by the grand vizier Kara Mustapha, invaded Austria. Vienna was besieged; its fortifications crumbled away under the fire of the Turkish artillery; the suburbs were destroyed, and the garrison were about to surrender. At this critical moment, the Polish army, under Sobieski, arrived in sight of Vienna. Mustapha led the main body of his forces to attack the Poles, while a detachment of twenty thousand made an assault on the city. But the courage of the garrison was revived: the assailants were repelled; a panic seized the Turks; they broke at the first charge of the Polish cavalry, and fled in such confusion that they abandoned their artillery, baggage, and treasures. Even the consecrated banner of Mahomet became the prize of the victors, and was sent as a trophy to the pope.

Mahomet was deposed in 1687, and *Solyman III.*, his brother, placed on the throne. He was succeeded, at the end of three years, by his brother *Achmet II.*, who, after a reign of eight years, was followed by his nephew *Mustapha II.* Under this monarch, the Ottoman empire became again, for a brief space, formidable to Christendom. The danger was averted by Prince Eugene of Savoy, who proved himself one of the greatest generals of Europe. He took the command of the Austrian armies, and, in 1697, met the Turkish army, under Mustapha, at Zenta, in Hungary. The Turks were overthrown with terrible slaughter; fifteen thousand were killed and eight thousand drowned in the River Theiss. All their artillery, baggage, and ammunition, a countless quantity of standards, the sultan's magnificent pavilion, and the great seal of the Ottoman empire, remained the prize of the conquerors. This victory was followed by the peace of Carlowitz, by which the sultan gave up all his conquests in Hungary, except Temeswar and Belgrade, ceded Azof to Russia, and the Morea to the Venetians.

Achmet III. mounted the throne, in **1703**, in consequence of the deposition of Mustapha. In his reign happened the battle of Pultowa, between the Swedes and the Russians, and the flight of Charles XII. to Bender, in the Turkish dominions. Prince Eugene defeated the Turks at Peterwaradin, and captured Temeswar and Belgrade. Achmet was dethroned in **1730**, and his place occupied by *Mahomet V.* who recovered Belgrade and the whole province of Servia from Austria. He died in **1754**, and was succeeded by his brother, *Osman III.* He was followed, after a reign of three years, by his nephew *Mustapha III.*, who became involved in wars with Russia, by which the Ottoman empire was much weakened. He died in **1774**, and left the crown to his brother *Abdul Hamid.* The empire was now in a rapid decline, and the sultan was compelled to cede to Russia the Crimea and other territories on the Black Sea. *Selim III.* came to the throne on the death of Abdul Hamid, in **1789**. The empire was now plunged deeper than ever in troubles. Rebellions broke out in Servia, Bosnia, and Albania; the pacha of Syria declared himself independent; Arabia was nearly overrun by the Wahabees; the beys of Egypt were engaged in a civil war, and the united forces of the Russians and Austrians were pressing upon the northern frontiers of the Ottoman dominions. The invasion of Egypt by Bonaparte caused the Porte to declare war against France in 1798.

CHAPTER CCCLXXVII.

A. D. 1798 to 1863.

European Discipline introduced into the Turkish Army — Deposition of Selim — Reign of Mustapha IV. and Mahomet VI. — Massacre of the Janizaries — Greek Insurrection - War with Russia — Battle of Navarino — Accession of Abdul Medjid — New Turkish Constitution — Decline and present Condition of the Empire — The Crimean War.

Amidst these perplexities, Selim judged it wise to strengthen both his army and his navy; and as he had enjoyed many opportunities of observing the superiority of European tactics, he formed a new regiment of soldiers, who wore the European uniform, and were instructed in the French military discipline. They were called *Nizami Djedid*, or the "new order," and barracks were built for them near Constantinople, to the great discontent of the janizaries, who were extremely jealous of these new troops. The Turks in general also disliked them, because they wore a Christian dress. In **1806**, a new war broke out with Russia, in which the British took part against Turkey. A British fleet blockaded the Dardanelles. The janizaries rose in rebellion, deposed the sultan, and placed on the throne his cousin *Mustapha IV.*, who reigned two months at Constantinople, in the midst of the greatest confusion. Mustapha Pacha, an adherent of Selim, raised an army of forty thousand Albanians, and marched to Constantinople for the purpose of restoring him. On reaching the walls of the seraglio, he was shocked with the sight of the dead body of Selim, who had been put to death by order of the new sultan.

The pacha Mustapha deposed his namesake, and proclaimed his brother *Mahomet VI.* The first year of his reign was disturbed by an insurrection of the janizaries, who set fire to the palace of the grand vizier, and blew him up with gunpowder. The troubles were quelled by the concessions of the sultan in abolishing the reform in the army. The Russians, in the mean time, stripped the empire of a great part of Moldavia and Bessarabia. Ali Pacha of Albania made an alliance with Napoleon, and became almost independent of the Porte; and the Greeks rose in insurrection, in 1820. The history of these events, with that of the revolt of Mehemet Ali of Egypt, will be found in other parts of this work. The janizaries being found constantly turbulent and intractable, the sultan determined to rid himself of these troublesome stipendiaries by a general massacre. Accordingly, in 1826, they were inveigled into a convenient spot amid the streets of Constantinople, where they were shot down to a man. Such was the end of this ferocious and formidable band of Mahometan mercenaries which had been, for centuries, one of the firmest supports of the Ottoman throne.

The war with the Greeks having been carried on with shocking cruelty on the part of the Turks, the governments of Russia, Great Britain, and France, interposed their mediation. But this being scornfully rejected by the Porte, the combined squadron of these three powers attacked and destroyed the whole Turkish fleet in the Bay of Navarino, on the twentieth of October, **1827**. The naval strength of the Ottoman empire was crushed forever by this blow. The Greeks established their independence. A war between the Turks and Russia broke out in 1828. The former were defeated by the Russians under Diebitsch, who captured Adrianople, the second city in the empire. A peace followed in the ensuing year, by which Turkey made great concessions. At this period the Ottoman empire became further weakened by the successes of Mehemet Ali, who finally rendered Egypt substantially independent of the Porte. Mahomet VI. died June 30, 1839.

He was succeeded by the present sultan, *Abdul Medjid*, who was then eighteen years of age. He appointed Kosrou Pacha grand vizier. This minister began to abolish the new costumes, and all the reforms introduced under the preceding reign; but he was prevented from carrying out his views to any great extent by the influence of Redschid Pacha, who had been sent as ambassador to France and England, and returned to Constantinople with a great admiration of European manners and institutions. This enlightened Turk, having been appointed grand vizier, induced the sultan to continue the reforms, and also to give a constitution to the empire based upon a European model. This scheme, so creditable to the sultan, was carried into effect on the 3d of November, 1839.

On that day, a general congress was convened by the sultan's order on the Plain of Roses, near Constantinople. Here, under the shelter of pavilions and kiosks, which had been erected for the occasion, were collected all the pachas of the Ottoman empire — the patriarchs of the Greeks and Armenians, the foreign ambassadors, the chief rabbi of the Jews, and a grea number of other persons of distinction. In the presence of the assembly, Redschid Pacha read aloud a *hatti sherif*, a state paper, which embodied a constitution, or Turkish bill of rights, granting among other privileges, security of life and property to all persons of whatever religion. Other reforms, tending to the amelioration of the condition of the subjects of Turkey, have been introduced from time to time, by the present amiable and enlightened sovereign. Although these have served to remove the great barriers to intercourse between the Ottoman and Christian nations, they have not materially strengthened the empire, which seems to have within itself the elements of decay.

In 1841, by the interference of the combined powers of Russia, Prussia, Austria, and Great Britain, the Porte was compelled to grant to Mehemit Ali the hereditary possession of the government of Egypt, thus making that country permanently independent of the Ottoman empire, although the paramount authority of the sultan is still acknowledged as a mere form, by the pacha of Egypt. In the same year, by a treaty concluded at London between the chief European powers, foreign vessels of war of all nations were excluded from the Dardanelles.

From the time of Solyman the Magnificent, the Turkish empire may be regarded as having been in a constant decline. During that age, the Ottoman power was considered as the superlative of every thing rich or great, politic or dangerous. Infinite numbers, valor approaching to enthusiasm, discipline surpassing any thing then known, and that steady ambition which never for a moment loses sight of its object, appeared to menace all the Christian states with speedy ruin. It is a very remarkable fact, that during the most flourishing and powerful state of the empire, the most distinguished Ottoman statesman and commanders were apostates from Christianity. Out of ten grand viziers during the reigns of Soloman and his successor Selim I., eight were of that character, and the renegade pachas of Turkey were of almost every nation—Albanians, Bosnians, Italians, Hungarians, Russians, Greeks, &c. Through the united valor, cunning, and want of principle exhibited by these apostates, and the talents and the faculties for government of the natives of the conquered provinces, the colossus of the Ottoman empire rose to its height, and trampled on the necks of the nations, who with renegade and slavish spirit, preyed on their own vitals.

The decline of the Ottoman power was perceptible in the course of the seventeenth century, and proceeded rapidly in the eighteenth. The rigor of that discipline by which the Turks had rendered themselves so formidable, was insensibly relaxed. With the great body of the people, the pride of conquest seems early to have extinguished the spirit of enterprise, and a kind of stately indolence soon began to grow over the national character. Luxury, and the indulgence in opium, spread widely among this sensual race, and exerted a powerful influence in enervating both the mind and the body. The sultan resigned himself to the luxuries and indulgences of the harem. The first irresistible impulse of Mahometan aggression upon Christendom gradually ebbed away. The frontier provinces were incessantly engaged in feuds and contests with invading enemies. Anarchy and turbulence rent the very heart of the empire. When the European powers began to make war with regular armies, they easily repelled those tumultuary bands which followed the Turkish standard. Above all, when Russia began to develop the strength of her gigantic empire, the Ottoman ascendency received its death blow. The Turks have now ceased to be formidable. The empire becomes weaker and weaker every day, and but for the recent interference of France and England, would ere this have been swallowed up by Russia.*

---

*In 1853, this country became the occasion of what is called the *Eastern War*, which shook all Europe with its agitations. Louis Napoleon, desirous of gratifying the Pope, as well as his Catholic subjects, sent M. Lavalette to Constantinople, with an idea of obtaining certain advantages for the Latin over the Greek Church, in respect to the "Holy Places in Palestine." The Czar of Russia, seeing what was going forward, and feeling that the privileges which he claimed and had long exercised were in jeopardy, dispatched Prince Menschikoff, March 1, 1853, to Constantinople with instructions to make propositions and urge remonstrances against the schemes of France. This was resented, and on the news reaching St. Petersburg, in June, the Czar immediately declared his intention of occupying the Danubian provinces—Moldavia and Wallachia—claiming to do so in virtue of a provision in existing treaties between the two countries.

France and England professed to view the growing power and ambition of Russia with apprehension, and regarding its present conduct as hostile to the peace of Europe, united for the protection of Turkey. Besides these general motives, each of these powers had special inducements to engage in the conflict. Louis Napoleon desired to establish himself on his throne, by some achievements which would gratify his people, and secure the respect of Europe, while England wished to break the power of Russia in the east, so that she might engross the trade of Central Asia, hitherto in the hands of Russia.

Peace or war is easily obtained, when the hearts of kings desire it. The latter, being the choice of the two leading powers in Western Europe, of course soon followed.

On the 2d of July, 1853, the Russian army entered the principalities: on the 5th of October, the sultan made a declaration of war, giving the Russians fifteen days to evacuate these provinces. A force of 120,000 Turks was raised and placed under Omer Pasha, who took up his head quarters at Shumla. We have not space to detail the events which ensued; it must suffice to say generally, that both powers continued to pour troops into the disputed territories, and that numerous bloody conflicts followed. Among these, were the battle of Oltenitza, which took place November 3d, and 4th, 1853, in which the Russians 30,000 strong, were bravely and successfully resisted, by a smaller number of Turks; the destruction of a considerable number of Turkish vessels of war—seven frigates, one steam frigate, and five smaller craft—in the harbor of Sinope, November 30th; and the battle of Citate, on the 6th of January, 1854, in which the Turks, after an obstinate fight, gained a brilliant victory. To this we may add the siege of Silistria, which, commencing on the 14th of April, continued till about the 1st of July, when the Russians in consequence of the threatening movements of the allied armies, now advancing toward the scene of warfare, abandoned the siege and commenced their retreat, which ended in the final evacuation of the principalities.

On the part of the allies, the chief events were as follows: On the 27th of March, 1854, Queen Victoria announced to Parliament, that she felt bound to afford active assistance to the sultan, her ally, against unprovoked aggression. The Emperor Napoleon, having now become the ally of England, made a similar announcement. From this time, the armies and navies of these two powers coöperated, as well in the Baltic, as in the Black Sea, and its borders, in combating Russia.

On the 23d of March, 1854, Odessa was bombarded by the allied fleets, and the Russian defenses there destroyed, the former losing a vessel of war, the Tiger, of 18 guns. Admiral Napier, with the English fleet, was joined in the Baltic by the French squadron in April—the whole force amount

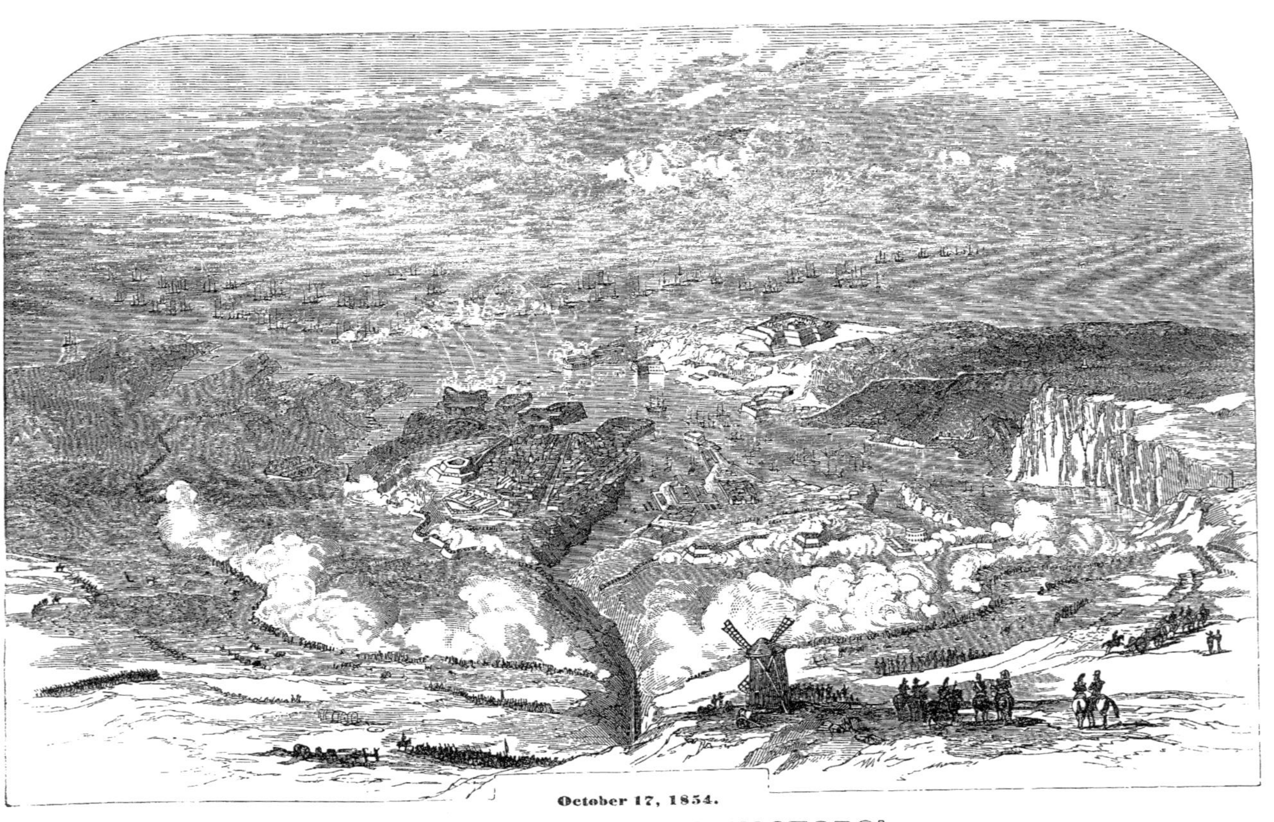

October 17, 1854.

BOMBARDMENT OF SEVASTOPOL.

CHAPTER CCCLXXVIII.

Cities, Population, Government, &c., of European Turkey.

CONSTANTINOPLE, the capital of the Turkish empire, occupies a commanding position, which we have already described in speaking of its foundation by Constantine the Great. The physical outlines of the city remain of course the same as when it was inhabited by the Roman emperors; but the appearance of the place, in respect to its architecture, has undergone a great change. With the exception of the walls on the land side, and the church of St. Sophia, there are few of the imperial structures remaining. This has been owing to the barbarism and laziness of the Turks, who, instead of procuring stone for building, fresh from the quarry, pulled down the edifices of the Greeks to construct their own. In this manner, temples, palaces, and churches have been metamorphosed into mosques, minarets, and fountains, or cut up for tombstones.

The general appearance of Constantinople, form without, is very splendid and picturesque. The ground is hilly, and all the elevated sites are covered with mosques, and other public buildings, intermixed with lofty cypress-trees. The declivities of the hills are crowded with houses and terraced streets. The multitude of buildings painted with different colors, the gilded domes, and the elegant and slender minarets crowned with shining crescents, impress the beholder with a lofty idea of the beauty and magnificence of the city. The interior, however, as in almost all the Turkish cities, disappoints expectation. With the exception of one very long avenne, the streets are narrow and crooked. The houses are mostly of wood. None of these are allowed to exceed twenty-six feet in height, which gives the streets a very mean appearance.

The most striking edifice is the church of St. Sophia. Its interior, though defaced by the Turks, retains much of its ancient grandeur. The exterior, owing to the heterogeneous additions which have been made to the original structure, presents only a pile of unsightly masses. Many of the mosques erected by the Turks are distinguished by grandeur and beauty; most of them are built of white marble. The public fountains are numerous, and some of them, with their pure white marble fronts, elaborate arabesque ornaments, and Chinese roofs, are very beautiful objects. On the eastern point of the city stands the seraglio, containing the palace and gardens of the sultan. This is a space of one hundred and fifty acres, covered with pavilions, mosques, gardens, and cypress groves. So many glittering domes, raising their lofty heads above the gardens and trees, produce a very beautiful effect at a distance.

The streets of Constantinople are mostly deserted and silent, all the activity and business of the city being concentrated in the bazaars. These are long and wide galleries, communicating with each other in an irregular manner, and covered with arches or domes. Toward the evening, the coffee-houses, which are very numerous, are much thronged. The suburbs of the city are very extensive and populous: the principal are Galata, Pera, and Scutari. The two first stand on the northern side of the Golden Horn, and the last on the Asiatic side of the Bosphorus. The trade of Constantinople is very active, and carried on with almost every part of the world. The population of the city proper is about half a million; including the suburbs, it is computed at eight hundred thousand.

Adrianople, the second city in European Turkey is situated in the interior, about one hundred and thirty five miles north-west of the capital. It is a very ancient city, having been founded, or rather enlarged and improved, by the emperor Adrian, in the second

ing to sixty-seven vessels of war. On the 15th of August, the Bomarsund forts at Hango, were bombarded by the allies, and having surrendered, were demolished. An attack upon Kronstadt, eighteen miles west of St. Petersburgh, and the great defense of that city was meditated and threatened. It is situated on a small island; its fortifications, upon a survey by the allies, were found to be so formidable, that the idea of attempting its capture was abandoned.

The Russians, having evacuated the principalities, various negotiations for peace took place — which, however, proved fruitless. In the meantime, Austria marched a large army into and occupied these territories, with the approbation of the allies and the secret satisfaction of Russia. The great struggle between the allies and Russia, was drawn to a focus in the Crimea, whither the former, under General St. Arnaud, commander of the French, and Lord Raglan, commander of the English, were conducted in September, 1854. On the 19th, a terrible battle took place on the river Alma, the allies having just landed and being 40,000 strong, against the Russians, with an inferior force. The latter were defeated with great slaughter, and then retired to Sebastopol. The allies marched upon the latter place, and passing round it, took up a position at Balaklava, on the south.

The struggle at this point, now attracted the attention of the civilized world. While the war was yet going on, the Czar Nicholas died at St. Petersburgh, March 2d, 1855, and his son Alexander succeeded him. Marshal St. Arnaud had died on the 29th of September, 1854, and Lord Raglan expired on the 28th of June the following year. The siege was vigorously pressed by the allies, 200,000 strong, and the defense was sustained with equal pertinacity. Balaklava and Inkermann became the scenes of frequent conflicts, and the hills and valleys around Sebastopol, were strewn with vestiges of murderous strife. The chief command having been given to General Pelissier, and the siege having been protracted for nearly a year, the final assault was made on the 5th of September, 1855. At this moment, all being in readiness, the French opened a cannonade along a line of four miles in length. These directed their attack upon the Russian fort called the Malakoff. The English and other allies, made a simultaneous attack upon other parts of the defenses. Night and day the tremendous assault was continued, till the morning of Sunday, the 9th, when it was announced that the Russians had retreated to the southern side of the city, leaving the enemy to occupy the fortress of Sebastopol.

This event proved decisive. In January, 1856, the Emperor Alexander signified his acceptance of the terms of accommodation proposed by the allies. In February, the fourteen representatives of the seven European powers held their first sitting at Paris, and on the 3d of March, the general treaty was signed, which brought peace to Europe, the main features of which were, an agreement to maintain the integrity of the Ottoman empire, the throwing open of the Black Sea to the marine of all nations, and the free navigation of the Danube. There were also various minor stipulations for the adjustment of boundaries between Russia and Turkey, and the internal administration of the latter country in respect to its christian subjects.

This rapid sketch gives but a faint idea of the extent of this great struggle. There were not much short of a million of men in arms and engaged in the war. It involved nearly every European state, either directly or indirectly, in the vortex of its agitations. Western Asia was the theater of numerous conflicts, and the capture of Kars in Asia Minor, by Russia, was not only an event of importance in a military point of view, but it was attended by suffering from famine on the part of the besieged city, the story of which is indescribably affecting. In addition to all this, the Eastern war, and especially the siege of Sebastopol, must be regarded as affording the most formidable display of military power that the history of the world has recorded. The waste of human life and of treasure has never been equaled in so short a space of time.

View of Constantinople

century. Its streets are narrow and irregular; but it has a large number of mosques and public baths. The most remarkable building is the mosque of Selim II., built chiefly of materials brought from the ruins of Famagosta, in Cyprus. It consists of one great apartment, like a theatre, terminating in a cupola, and surmounted by four tall minarets. A large aqueduct supplies the baths, fountains, and mosques with water.

Mufti, Ulema, &c.

Many remains of Roman buildings are also to be found here. Adrianople has manufactures of silk, woollen, cotton, and leather, and carries on some commerce by means of the River Maritza, which is navigable from this place to the Archipelago. Its exports are manufactured articles, fine wool, leather, wax, &c. The population is about one hundred thousand.

The government of the Ottoman empire is despotic. The *sultan* is nominally absolute; there is no political body in the state having the power to check his will. The constitution is but a grant of the sovereign, and may be recalled at his pleasure. He is expected, however, to reign conformably to the religious and civil principles inculcated in the Koran, and to the traditions handed down from Mahomet. The *ulema* is the assembly or corporation of learned men, comprising the professors of divinity, of law, and of other sciences. A member of the *ulema* is called a *mollah*, or man of law.

Costumes of Officers about the Court of the Sultan.

The *mufti*, or chief doctor of law, is president of the ulema. The *kanun-nameh* is the legal code of institutions and decisions which have been made from time to time. The council of state, or assembly of chief officers who give advice to the sultan, is called the *divan*. The government is sometimes called the *Sublime Porte*, either from the harbor of the Golden Horn, or from the great gate of the sultan's palace. The *grand vizier* is prime minister. The *reis effendi* is secretary of state.

The inhabitants of the Ottoman empire are divided

into two great classes—the Turks, or Osmanlis, who are the ruling race, and the Rayahs, or the ancient inhabitants of the countries conquered by the Turkish arms. The Rayahs are mostly Christians, as Greeks, Armenians, Sclavonians, &c. They pay the capitation or poll-tax, which the Turks do not pay. They are far more numerous than the Turks, in the European territories. The Turks themselves can hardly be said to have a home or a country in Europe. Since their first establishment on the west side of the Bosphorus, to the present day, they have never, in any considerable degree, intermixed with the nations which they conquered. They have continued a distinct and separate people, oppressing their vanquished subjects, often with cruelty and scorn, and even regarding them as a degraded race, unworthy of exchanging with their conquerors the civilities of social life. Throughout Europe, they may be regarded only as military colonists. They form the garrisons in the fortresses, or live on their incomes, or pay from the government, or on the money which they extort from the Rayahs—though this species of oppression is, in a measure, abolished by the new constitution. It may be remarked, too, that the spirit of hostility to the Christians is gradually giving way, on the part of the Turks, before the influence of intercourse and the spread of intelligence.

Spain.

CHAPTER CCCLXXIX.

Geographical Description, Ancient and Modern.

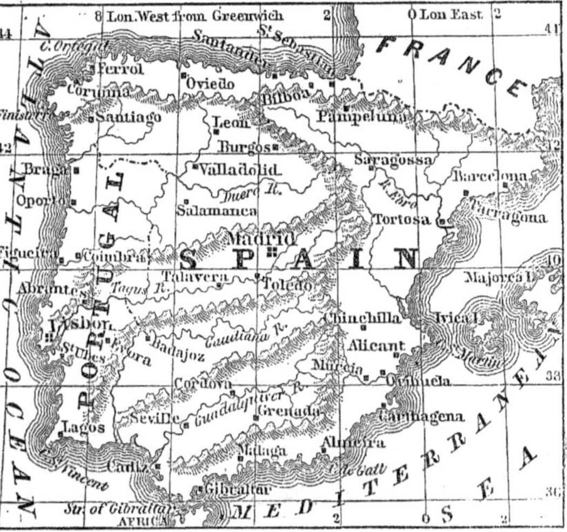

SPAIN, called by the natives *España*, is bounded north by France and the Bay of Biscay, west by Portugal and the Atlantic Ocean, and south and east by the Straits of Gibraltar and the Mediterranean Sea. It extends from 36° to 44° north latitude, and from 3° 20′ east to 9° 40′ west longitude. Its greatest length from east to west is six hundred and forty miles; its breadth, five hundred and twenty-five; area, one hundred and seventy thousand square miles. Population, seventeen millions.

The peninsula, which comprises Spain and Portugal, is covered by a range called the *Hesperian Mountains*, comprehending three separate groups—the southern, the central, and the northern. The southern group stretches from Cape St. Vincent, on the Atlantic, to Cape de Gata, on the Mediterranean, and includes the three great ranges of the Sierra Nevada, the Sierra Morena, and the Sierra of Toledo. The Sierra Nevada, or Snowy Range, contains the loftiest summits in the peninsula, some of which are covered with perpetual snow. The highest peak, that of Mulhacen, has an elevation of eleven thousand six hundred and sixty feet.

The central group consists of two chains, one of which extends along the northern bank of the Tagus, from its source to the rock of Cintra, near its mouth, and the other stretches from the sources of the Ebro, south-easterly to Cape Palos. Between these two chains lies an elevated plain, from twenty-two hundred to twenty-eight hundred feet high. The former chain contains many summits from six thousand to ten thousand feet in height; the latter is less elevated.

The northern group consists of a single chain, the Pyrenees, stretching across the peninsula, from Cape Creus to Cape Finisterre, on the Atlantic. The term *Pyrenees* is sometimes confined to the eastern part, which separates France from Spain, and terminates at Fontarabia; the more westerly portion being known under the name of the *Andalusian Mountains*. Many of the peaks rise to the height of ten thousand or eleven thousand feet; the loftiest, La Maladetta, is eleven thousand four hundred and twenty-five feet high. They yield great quantities of timber, and are rich in minerals. Seven passes or defiles admit the passage of wheel carriages, and there are upwards of one hundred practicable for foot passengers. On the south, towards Spain, the declivities of the Pyrenees are precipitous, and have a barren aspect. On the north, towards France, they are less steep and rocky, and afford abundant pastures for sheep and cattle, and many rich forests. Montserrat is an isolated and rocky mountain peak, thirty-three hundred feet high—nineteen miles northwest of Barcelona. Upon this is a famous monastery of the Benedictines, to which pilgrimages were formerly made. The top of this mountain is generally enveloped in clouds; but when fair, the view is exceedingly diversified and beautiful.

Spain is not a well-watered country. The chief rivers are as follows: the Douro, which flows westerly through Portugal, and empties into the Atlantic, after a course of five hundred miles; the Tagus, which also flows through Portugal, and passing by Lisbon, enters the Atlantic, after a course of six hundred miles; the Ebro, and the Guadalquiver, which flow into the Mediterranean Sea

Scene among the Balearic Isles.

The Balearic Isles, in the Mediterranean, consisting of Majorca, Minorca, and Ivica, are the chief islands belonging to Spain.

In general, the climate of Spain is mild. The southern portions, on account of their position, are hot, but the heat is moderated by sea breezes. On the higher portions, at the north, there is considerable snow in winter. Andalusia is renowned for the beauty of the sky, and the prevalence of fair weather. The provinces along the Mediterranean are delightful. Among the fruits are oranges, lemons, figs, grapes, dates, olives, pomegranates, and pistachio nuts; also prunes, peaches, chestnuts, &c.; maize, rice, oil, sugar, silk, as well as the common grains, are produced. The forests yield a variety of oaks, among which are the cork-tree, the evergreen oak, &c.

In ancient times it appears that Spain was renowned for its minerals—the Greeks, Phœnicians, Carthaginians, and Romans coming hither to obtain these articles. It is curious that what Spain was to the ancient world, her colonies become to the modern world—in the supply of minerals. At the present day, though the actual amount of metals obtained from the mines of Spain is not great, it is still supposed that they contain rich treasures of mineral wealth. The most productive mines are those of lead in Granada; the quicksilver mines of Almaden, in La Mancha. Salt, iron, tin, and antimony are found in various places.

Among the wild animals are the wild-boar, bear, wolf, deer, and many smaller quadrupeds. Among the birds are the flamingo and the bustard. Insects are more numerous and in greater variety, than in most other parts of Europe.

Among the animal products of Spain, the horse is entitled to particular notice. The Arabs, when in possession of the country, stocked it with their finest breeds, and though the race has degenerated, it still shows many of the points by which it was originally distinguished. In beauty, grace, and docility, the horses of Andalusia are said to be superior to those of England; but it may be doubtful whether they are equal to the same amount of labor. In fact, the number of good horses is rapidly decreasing, chiefly owing to the preference given to mules for domestic and agricultural purposes. The importation of horses to improve the breed, and the exportation of colts are alike forbidden; it is said that the "number of horses bred at present is quite inconsiderable, notwithstanding the decrees, premiums, and encouragements of every kind that have been offered by government. The celebrated breed of the sovereigns of Spain at Cordova is nearly extinct; in the Serricinia de Ronda (once the Cleveland of Spain) only miserable animals called *serranos* are now reared. The wealthiest Andalusian nobles have only two or three indifferent saddle-horses, and there is scarcely a horse in the whole country fit for the draught of artillery." Great numbers of mules are bred in Old Castile, being sent till they come to their full size to the rich pastures of Estremadura, whence they are supplied to the rest of Spain. The asses are very different animals from those seen in England and America, being of a large size, carefully bred, and in strength, docility, and sure footedness, nearly equal to the mules.

The political divisions of Spain are as follows:

Old Provinces.	*New Provinces.*
Andalusia	Cordova, Jaen, Granada, Almeira, Malaga, Seville, Cadiz, Huelva.
Aragon	Saragossa, Huesca, Teruel.
Asterias	Oviedo.
New Castile	Madrid, Toledo, Ciudad Real, Cuenca, Guadalaxaria.
Old Castile	Burgos, Logrono, Santander, Avila, Segovia, Soria, Valladolid, Palencia.
Estremadura	Badajoz, Caceres.
Catalonia	Barcelona, Tanagona, Lerida, Gerona.
Gallicia	Corunna, Lugo, Orene, Pontevedra.
Leon	Leon, Salamanca, Zamora.
Murcia	Murcia, Albacete.
Valencia	Valencia, Alicante, Castellon de la Plana.
Navarra	Navarra.
Alava	Vittoria.
Biscay	Bilbao.
Guipuzcoa	St. Sebastian, Balearic Isles, Canary Isles.

Cuba and Porto Rico, in the West Indies, are the most important colonies.

Madrid, the capital of the kingdom, stands in the midst of a barren plain, two thousand feet above the level of the sea. It possesses numerous splendid buildings, and some parts have an air of magnificence

CHAPTER CCCLXXX.

2200 B. C. to A. D. 419.

Ancient History of Spain — The Celtiberians — The Phœnicians and Carthaginians — Native Tribes — Roman Conquest of Spain from the Carthaginians — Spain as a Roman Province.

In this remote peninsula of the west, with its many mysterious and sequestered nooks, its thousands of lovely and picturesque localities, its grand and beautiful scenery, the early poets of Eastern Europe delighted to place their Hesperia, the land of beloved and departed spirits, the ever-blooming gardens of the blessed. They therefore sometimes named the country after Hesperus, the star of evening, which, in those charming climates, sheds a mild but splendid radiance above the western horizon, and might well be fancied to illumine a better and a happier world. Such were the dreams of poetry. History, also, ere it emerges from fable, relates that the earliest colonists of Spain were from Atlantis, an immense paradisiacal island, supposed to be now sunk in the Atlantic Ocean. Equally baseless is the tradition of some Spanish writers, that their romantic country was settled twenty-two hundred years before the Christian era, by Tubal, a son of Noah.

The Greeks called the country *Iberia*, from its most prominent aboriginal tribe, the Iberi. These were attacked by the Celts, and, after a long and obstinate resistance, the two nations agreed to unite, share the country in common, and adopt the name *Celtiberi*, to express their united interests. The warlike Celtiberians were formidable both as cavalry and infantry. When the horse had broken the ranks of the foe, the riders dismounted, and fought on foot. The dress of the warriors was a coarse woollen mantle, greaves of hair, an iron helmet with a red feather, a round buckler, and a two-edged sword of the finest temper. The land and its harvests were equally distributed, and death was the penalty for grasping more than one man's share. These hospitable people believed that the entertaining of a stranger called down the direct blessing of Heaven. But they sacrificed human victims, and obtained auguries by inspecting the entrails.

The women wore iron collars, with rods of the same metal rising behind the head, and bending over it toward the front; upon these they hung their veils, a usual ornament, as it still is with the Spanish ladies. They pulled out the hair from their foreheads, and rubbed them with oil, a shining forehead being considered a great beauty. It was a part of the duty of the annual assembly of the aged Celtiberians to examine what the women had made with their own hands during the year, and a reward was given to her who had done her work best. But the fierceness of barbarians is observable in the fact that a lover's best means of obtaining the preference over his fellow-suitors was to present the fair, to whose hand he aspired, the head of an enemy slain in battle.

The Phœnicians traded (1000 B. C.) with the inhabitants of Spain, exchanging iron, beads, trinkets, and a variety of similar articles, for silver. At first, they found silver very plentiful, even the common utensils of the country being made of it; and, after lading their vessels with it, they are said to have made anchors of it, that they might carry away more. This they exchanged for its weight in gold, in Arabia — thus obtaining a profit of at least one thousand per cent. The Phœnicians founded factories upon the coast, and these in spite of the jealousies of the natives, increased to colonies. The most ancient of these was Tarshish, or Tartessus, including a town, island, and country at the mouth of the Guadalquivir, then called *Bætis.* The next was Gadix, still a flourishing city, called *Cadiz* — its ancient name slightly modified.

The Carthaginians intruded upon this Phœnician trade, but were long unable to extend their power further than had been done by their unscrupulous predecessors. But finally they obtained a firm foothold, and occupied that fine portion of Southern Spain called by them *Bætica*, and afterward named *Andalusia* and *Grenada.* Rhodians, Phocæans, Samians, and other Greeks, forced themselves, also, into this lucrative trade, and actually founded factories on the coast. Greek writers, alone, give us any accounts of the aborigines of Spain. It seems there were a multitude of isolated communities, seventeen of which are enumerated,* — each with its peculiarities of character, customs, and manners, just as we should expect from the physical structure of the country, formed, as it is, into a network of rugged mountains.

Spain was the common battle-ground of Rome and Carthage, in their contest for the dominion of the west. The rapine and cruelty of the Carthaginians had prevented alliances and friendly intercourse with the natives of the interior; but the coasts acknowledged the sway of foreign masters. Saguntum, a Greek city near the mouth of the Ebro, was in alliance with Rome, whose boundary was the Ebro. Hannibal, the general of Carthage, by taking Saguntum, precipitated the second Punic war, 218 B. C. The citizens, seeing further resistance hopeless, destroyed themselves, with their wives, children, and effects, in a common conflagration. But Hannibal, notwithstanding this awful catas-

* Near Cape Finisterre were the *Artabri;* the *Bracari* had their chief town at Braga; the *Lucences*, at Lugo. These three tribes formed the *Callæci*, who gave name to the modern Galicia. On the east of them were the *Astures*, in what is now part of the Asturias. Their capital was at Astorga. Further east were the *Vaccæi*, the least barbarous of the Celtiberians. In Biscay, and part of the Asturias, were the fierce *Cantabri;* they went to battle two upon one horse. North of the Ebro were the *Vascones*, ancestors of the Gascons. The *Jacetani* were scattered over the Pyrenean slopes of Aragon. In Catalonia dwelt the *Ceretani*, *Indigetes*, *Ausetani*, *Cosetani*, and others. South of the Ebro were the *Arevaci*, in Segovia, and the *Pelendones*, in Soria and Moncayo. The *Edetani*, one of the most powerful tribes, peopled the space between the Ebro and the Albaracino Mountains. A not less formidable nation, the *Ilercaones*, lived between the Upper Jucar and Lower Ebro. The *Carpetani* were about Toledo, and the *Oretani* to the south of them. The *Olcades* dwelt upon the Jucar; the *Bastitani*, in the centre of Murcia, whence they often made incursions into Bætica. The *Contestani* were settled from Cape Palos to the Jucar. In Portugal, the *Cynesii* were the earliest known inhabitants of Algarve. The *Celtici* lived between the Gaudiana and the Tagus; the *Vettones*, round the mountains of Gredos. The *Lusitani*, a nation of freebooters, who caused the name *Lusitania* to be given to the province, were settled in Estremadura. Their food was flour and sweet acorns, and their drink beer; they were active, patient of fatigue, swift of foot, and advanced to battle in a measured dance. The *Bastuli Pœni* dwelt in Bætica, on the Mediterranean shore; the *Bæturi*, on the shore of the ocean, at the mouth of the Bætis. The *Turdetani* inhabited the southern slopes of the Sierra d'Aracena, and were the earliest civilized and most enlightened of the tribes. Silver abounded in their country.

trophe, still gathered plunder enough for his object, and advanced upon Italy. Assisted by the natives, three Carthaginian generals routed and cut to pieces the Roman armies in Spain, under the brothers Publius and Cneius Scipio, who were both killed.

The son of Publius, Publius Cornelius Scipio, afterward named *Africanus*, about twenty-one years old, was now sent into Spain with a Roman army. It was a trying moment to the Romans; for Hannibal had just wrested from them nearly all Italy, and annihilated their army at Cannæ. Such, however, was the ability of the young Scipio, that, in four years, the Carthaginians were completely driven out of Spain; tribe after tribe of the natives was conquered, and the whole country submitted to Rome. But this submission lasted only while compelled by overwhelming force; revolt after revolt, to quell which tasked the resources of the ablest generals of Rome — brought on long and cruel wars; and the country was not thoroughly reduced, or Romanized, till the time of Augustus, when, reduced to a Roman province, its language, manners, and customs, became assimilated to those of the rest of the empire.

An interesting incident — the theme of a fine poem — is told of the young Scipio, at his taking of New Carthage, now called *Carthagena*, the day after fifty-four thousand of the enemy had been slain in battle. At this city were collected hostages from all the tribes, the flower of the noble youth of Spain, and maidens from their most distinguished families. By the right of war, all this bright array of beauty belonged, as slaves, to the victor. The most charming of these was selected for the general himself. In the words of the poet:

"Soft as she passed along, with downcast eyes,
Where gentle sorrow shed, — and now and then
Dropped o'er her cheek the trickling tear, —
The Roman legions languished, and hard war
Felt more than pity."

Scipio, on questioning her, discovered, through her blushes, that she was betrothed to a beloved prince, who

—— "forgot his chains,
His lost dominions, and for her alone
Wept out his tender soul."

Suddenly, inspired with a virtue foreign to his general character, the Roman commander called for her lover and parents. The anxiety of the captives was intense. The army looked curiously and dubiously upon the unwonted scene. The chief now broke the anxious silence. "Know," said he to the prince, "that Romans can conquer their hearts as well as their enemies. Take, then, thy lovely bride, and with her thy liberty and kingdom; and, when you behold these charms with transport, be a friend to Rome."

"Ecstatic wonder held the lovers mute,
While the loud camp, and all the clustering crowd
That hung around, rang with repeated shouts.
Fame took the alarm, and through resounding Spain
Blew fast the fair report, which more than arms
Admiring nations to the Romans gained."

The tragedy of the fall of Numantia (133 B. C.) enacted by the cruelty of Scipio Æmilianus, excites far different feelings. Investing the city with strong fortifications, manned by an army of sixty thousand, against one tenth of that number who defended the place, the cautious general resolved to reduce his intrepid foe by famine. The furious efforts of the besieged against his fortifications were useless; and hunger began its fatal work. The vilest aliments were eagerly devoured, and even the corpses of the dead. In vain did the Numantians beg an honorable peace, in vain urge their own generosity on five preceding occasions when armies of Rome lay at their mercy; in vain did they request a fair field, that they might die with honor. The cold-hearted Roman declared that he was content to wait the effects of famine. This reply filled the city with the wildest fury, increased to horror by intoxication. A frenzied mass of men and women rushed out upon the Roman intrenchments. Some were killed, the rest driven back. Æmilianus had ordered them to be spared, sardonically observing that, "the more mouths there were, the sooner would their food be exhausted." Despair now reigned triumphant. Some took poison, some fell on their swords, some set fire to their houses, and perished in the flames. Others, hastening to the square, engaged, two by two, in mortal strife. The vanquished was immediately beheaded, and his corpse thrown into a huge fire. Parents, children, relatives, and friends, meanwhile, fell to destroying each other, or, with shouts of triumph, rushed into heated furnaces. Not an individual survived. Ruins, blood, solitude, and horror, feasted the eyes of the brutal victor, as he surveyed his diabolical work.

The sway of the Romans was not without its advantages in Spain. They built fine cities, made good roads, and taught the natives, whom they obliged to assist, not only to become architects, engineers, masons, carpenters, &c., but more skilful agriculturists, also, by adopting implements before unknown. The people, as was the fact in Gaul and Britain, thus became a peaceable race of farmers, shepherds, and artisans, protected by Roman garrisons and governors. So they remained during four centuries, when the power of Rome began to decline, and the emperors were obliged to abandon, by degrees, their foreign possessions, which were thus left unprotected, after being rendered unable to protect themselves.

CHAPTER CCCLXXXI.

A. D. 419 to 714.

Spain under the Goths — Gothic Conquest Government — Annals — Decline and Ruin of the Empire.

The Roman legions being withdrawn, the people found themselves unable to cope with the vigorous warriors of the north, who now began to press upon them, pushed southward by the same causes which had precipitated them upon the central provinces of the Roman empire. Wave after wave of fierce, half-naked hordes, succeeded each other, all alike attracted by the sunny climes and fertile harvests of the south, and the treasures of wealth that ages of peaceful industry had accumulated there. Like birds of prey, these ravening vultures of the cold and barren north fought with each other for the lands and the plunder they had wrested from their common victim — the effeminate Roman.

Thus, in the beginning of the fifth century, the Suevi, Vandals, and Visigoths, invaded the peninsula almost unresisted, and, mixing with the Celts and Iberians, produced, with the addition of the Moors, long after, the different traits the physiologist still observes in Spain. The *Suevi* descended the Duero, under Ermeric, and made Braga their capital. The *Vandals*, under Genseric, fixed themselves in the centre of the kingdom, choosing Toledo for their chief city. But they had been settled here only fifteen years, when the *Visigoths*, conquered in Gaul, abandoned Toulouse and, penetrating Spain, compelled the Vandals to fly into Africa — not, however, before their short residence in Bætica had changed its name to *Vandalousia*, whence the modern name of that delightful region, *Andalusia.* The Visigoths, under Ataulph, now settled in Spain, founding the Gothic monarchy, A. D. 419.

They were a brave, hospitable, but unenlightened people, priding themselves on their independence, and taught to think war the only pursuit befitting the dignity of freemen. They, therefore, had great contempt for trade, and all the arts of peace; so that their conquest of Spain threw it back into barbarism, for the Visigoths took the land, and, according to the laws of war, made slaves of the people. If they gained a territory, they divided it into lots of various sizes, each warrior having a share assigned to him according to his rank, with a sufficient number of slaves to till it; and these slaves were the conquered people. The dress of the Goths was of many colors, and reached nearly to the knee. It was made with short sleeves, so that their arms and legs were bare; but their feet were covered with short boots, and their hair hung in twisted locks upon their shoulders.

In religion, the conquering nation were Christians of the Arian sect, at enmity with the Catholics; but in 587, Recared, king of the Goths, adopted the tenets of the Catholic Christians, and most of his subjects followed the example of their sovereign. From that time, the clergy possessed great power in Spain, where they held the first place in the national assemblies; and, in fact, there is no country in the world in which the priesthood have always maintained so much influence.

The Goths seem to have adopted the Latin language, spoken by the conquered people. They lived in a plain and frugal manner. Their mode of building was rude, though, in after ages, the name *Gothic* was given to a style of architecture which, in several respects, still commands the admiration of modern taste. As soon as the Goths were firmly settled, they began to found religious establishments; and so prevalent was the bias, in those stormy days of violence, towards a life of monastic peace, safety, and seclusion, that monks and nuns, in time, formed the chief part of the population.

The Gothic monarchy in Spain lasted about three hundred years; during which the descendants of the original conquerors had spread themselves over the whole country, and were, in fact, the Spaniards of that age — the former population having become extinct, or existing only in a state of depression, or of slavery: so that the Spanish name for a gentleman is *hidalgo*, a contraction of *hijo del Goda* — "son of a Goth."

The throne was elective; and whenever the king died, the people assembled to choose a new one, a candidate from the royal family having the preference. On the appointed day, the electors, chiefly bishops and nobles, repaired to some large, open place, followed by an immense concourse of people, where the candidates for royalty presented themselves; and he who had the most voices in his favor was declared king. As soon as the election was decided, the new monarch made a solemn oath to govern with justice and valor; after which, he was lifted on a shield above the crowd, and proclaimed amid loud acclamations. In course of time, however, this rough ceremony — originating in the habits of a conquering camp of warriors towards a victorious general — was discontinued; and the later Gothic monarchs were crowned by a bishop with a crown of gold, and invested with purple robes. Thus arrayed, and seated on a magnificent throne of silver, the sovereign received the homage of his subjects.

Ataulph, the first king, was satisfied with the little kingdom of Catalonia; but his followers, desiring further conquests, put him to death, and elected a king, Sigeric, so fierce and cruel, that he too was assassinated, and a brave chieftain, named *Wallia*, chosen in his stead. Wallia conquered all Spain and Portugal, and the south of France, fixing his capital at Toulouse. Theodored, his successor, was killed at Chalons, in a great battle with Attila, king of the Huns, A. D. 451. Of his three sons, who reigned successively, Euric, the youngest, distinguished himself by composing the first code of laws the Goths had ever known. Before this, they had been governed by traditional customs.

Alaric, son of Euric, succeeded his father, and held his court at Bourdeaux. Clovis, king of the Franks, determined to expel the Goths from France, made war upon him, and he was slain in battle. *Almeric*, the infant son of Alaric, was placed on the throne, through the influence of his grandfather, Theodoric, the Gothic king of Italy. He sent out an army to defend the rights of the child, appointed a minister to govern for him till he should be of age, and induced Clovis to give him the hand of his daughter Clotilda in marriage. The nuptials were celebrated in due time, Almeric ascended the throne and removed his court to Seville, then the chief town in Spain. But he did not live happily with his wife, as they were of different sects in religion, the king being an Arian, and the queen a Catholic. In consequence of their perpetual quarrels, the queen complained to her brother, Childebert, king of France, who went to war with Almeric, conquered and slew him, and took his sister back to her own country, A. D. 531.

A long list of kings occupied the Gothic throne for one hundred and forty years after the death of Almeric; few of them distinguished for virtue, or any elements of greatness. *Leovigild*, however, is an exception: he ruled seventeen years, with equal wisdom and justice, made some excellent laws, and maintained at his court a degree of splendor unparalleled by his predecessors. His son *Recared*, who ascended the throne in 587, was a Catholic, and introduced the Catholic religion, as has been already remarked.

During these reigns, the Spanish provinces were governed on a feudal system, by dukes, who ranked next in dignity to the king. Each city had a governor, who was accountable for his conduct to the duke of the province; and the small towns, or villages, were under the control of magistrates, whose business it was to see that the laws were not violated in their particular district.

The Goths had now been settled in the peninsula for two hundred and fifty years. The easy lives they led, in this warm and fruitful climate, had made them indolent and effeminate; self-indulgence had extinguished the martial ardor which gave success to their ancestors, and had effaced from their characters many of the noble traits which distinguished the original Goths

Thus this degenerate race, not being occupied either by war, commerce, or learning, naturally fell into vices, from want of useful and active employment. Vice, become extensively prevalent, is the sure forerunner of national ruin. It is generally not difficult to trace the effect to the cause; in this case, the connection is flagrantly evident.

In the absence of public virtue and patriotism, the unscrupulous selfishness of those who had power and wealth within their grasp, manifested itself upon the death of Recared II., A. D. 621. A multitude of usurpers quickly succeeded each other on the throne, to which they raised themselves by the most violent and wicked means. There was, however, enough of spirit yet left in the people to become weary and disgusted with the misgovernment thus forced upon them. They, therefore, determined to select some good man, who would, if possible, restore the kingdom to order.

There dwelt, at some distance from Toledo, which was then the capital, a noble Goth, named *Wamba*, who, being fond of a retired life, seldom visited the city, but passed his time in cultivating his farm. Every one was acquainted with his talents and virtues, and it was generally agreed that he was the very man the exigencies of the state required; a deputation was, therefore, sent to him to offer him the crown.

At first, he was very unwilling to accept the proffered honor, saying, that he was "an old man, unaccustomed to the bustle of public life, and preferred his rural pursuits to the splendor of a court"—and offering many other excuses. The deputation listened patiently for some time, when the chief of the deputies—a man of energy, decision, and something of the ancient Gothic fierceness—thus addressed him: "In casting our eyes upon you, most noble Wamba, we have been actuated by a desire to promote the public welfare; therefore it is your duty to sacrifice your inclinations to the good of your country; and, if you refuse to do so, we must consider you in the light of an enemy." In saying these words, he drew his dagger, and threatened to kill the modest and noble farmer, if he would not accept the crown. Wamba was, therefore, obliged to comply, and his election proved highly advantageous to the nation. He exerted all his talents for the benefit of the people, made many good laws, and suppressed the disorders which had brought the country to the brink of ruin. For at least a half century, his virtues, and those of his successors, were able to avert the impending disasters of Gothic Spain.

The Arabs of Africa, active with their new-born fanaticism, and encouraged by the disorders of the kingdom, had begun to make incursions upon the coasts of the empire, and were shortly to become its most formidable enemies. Wamba fitted out a fleet against them, and fought a battle by sea,—the first naval engagement recorded in Spanish history, destined at a future time to chronicle maritime enterprises, which made the Spaniards rulers of the sea, and masters of half the world. After a few years, Wamba—weary of the cares and fatigues of royalty, or perhaps hopeless of ultimately saving his country—retired into a monastery,* leaving the crown to a nobleman, named *Ervigor*, who was, in every way, worthy to succeed him. He, too, became a monk; and after two more sovereigns had worn the crown, it was placed on the head of *Roderic*, the Last of the Goths.

The Arabs, crouched on the opposite coasts of Africa, like the lion of their deserts, had long watched their enticing prey, and only waited a favorable moment to bring it within their grasp. The vices of Roderic gave them this precious opportunity, and they eagerly availed themselves of it. This last of the Gothic kings had trampled on the family honor of Count Julian, a Spaniard of noble birth, but haughty and revengeful, who was governor of Mauritania, a province held by the Spaniards on the African side of the Straits of Gibraltar. A father's desire of vengeance on the man who had ruined the virtue of his daughter, overcame the scruples of the patriot, the fidelity of the governor, and even Spanish loyalty. Count Julian entered into a league with the Arabs, and, having admitted two of their great generals, Muza and Tarik, into Mauritania—as we have elsewhere related—assisted Tarik to cross over into Spain, with a vast army of Saracens, who fought a memorable battle with the Spaniards on the plains of Xeres.

The combat between the Christians and Saracens lasted three days, when the victory was decided in favor of the latter; but Roderic, the king, disappeared. In vain was his body sought for amongst the slain He was never heard of afterwards, and his fate, to this day, remains a mystery. With him ended the empire of the Goths, A. D. 714. Founded in usurpation and blood, continued in a cruel slavery of the conquered—in persecution, and religious bigotry—its fate, sealed by one of the bloodiest battles on record, excites little sympathy. It deserved, as it received, a bloody death.

CHAPTER CCCLXXXII.

A. D. 711 to 787.

Establishment of the Moors in Spain—Abderahman I.—Moorish Character and Manners.

The rapid conquest of Spain by the Saracens has been noticed in our history of the Arabs, as also the check they received from Martel, in the centre of France. The unoccupied lands, and those which had been deserted by their former inhabitants, were distributed among the Arab chiefs, and the towns were soon filled with merchants and persons of consequence, who came in great numbers from Africa and Arabia, bringing with them their wives, families, and property, with many of the luxuries of the Eastern nations, which had hitherto been unknown in Europe. The manners that were now introduced into Spain may be learned from that faithful transcript of Oriental life, the Arabian Nights.

For more than forty years, the newly-acquired territory was considered as a part of the dominions of the Eastern sovereigns of Islam, who sent emirs, or viceroys, from Damascus, to conduct the administration; but these rulers, and the governors appointed by them, were, for the most part, so cruel and oppressive, that at length, all the principal sheiks assembled together to consult upon the means of establishing a better mode of government. They were determined that se

* Some writers assert that, having fallen into a state of insensibility, Wamba, who was thought to be dying, was, according to the custom in such cases, hastily shaven, and enveloped in a penitential habit; that is, made a monk. On his recovery, the obligation to adopt the monkish profession was considered imperative, though it had been involuntary.

fine a country — abounding in all the treasures of the earth, and capable of being converted into a rich and powerful empire — should no longer be ruined by mismanagement; therefore they agreed that it would be far better to declare themselves entirely independent of the sovereign of the Mussulmans, and elect a khalif of their own, who would live amongst them, and protect their rights.

This scheme was rendered the more easy of accomplishment by the revolution which had placed Abbas on the throne of Damascus. The Arabian States had submitted to the usurper; but the Moors of Spain refused to acknowledge him. *Abderahman*, or *Abd er Rahman*, one of the sons of the dethroned khalif, had escaped the massacre of the Ommiade family, as related at p. 339, by being absent on a hunting excursion. As soon as the melancholy tidings reached him, he took refuge among the Bedouins of Arabia and afterwards among those of Africa. His misfortunes, his learning, his gentle manners and handsome person, soon endeared him to the inhabitants of the deserts, who many times saved him from the enemies of his house, by whom he was closely pursued.

Habib, governor of Barca, though he owed every thing to the Ommiades, was now the most active in hunting down its fugitive heir. One night, a troop of his cavalry surrounded the tents of the Bedouins, and demanded if they had not among them a young Syrian, describing accurately the person of the prince; for the khalif had anxiously forwarded the description to all the emirs of his empire. Recognizing their guest in the person sought, and shrewdly suspecting that the visit of Habib's horsemen boded no good, the Bedouins replied that the youth had been hunting with some companions, but might be found in a valley which they pointed out at some distance. No sooner were the troopers departed, than the faithful Bedouins awoke their guest, and told him what had passed. With tears in his eyes, he thanked them for this proof of their affection, and, attended by some of the most resolute youths of the tribe, fled farther into the desert. After various adventures, he arrived safely in Mauritania, where he was joyfully welcomed by a noble sheik, to whom he was related.

This amiable and talented young prince seemed the only person likely to unite the distracted interests of the Spanish Moors. His story was made known to the assembled sheiks by one of their number "Let Abderahman be our sovereign!" was the united wish of all. The sheiks at once sent deputies to the prince, who neither disguised nor diminished the difficulties with which he would have to contend, but assured him of their own fidelity, and of the obedience of the Arab, Syrian, and Egyptian tribes. "Noble deputies," the prince answered, "I will unite my destiny with yours; I will go and fight with you. I fear neither adversity nor the dangers of war. If I am young, misfortune, I hope, has proved me, and never yet found me wanting." He added that he was bound to mention the matter to the friends who had received him under their protection, and ask their counsel. "Go, my son," replied an aged sheik, his kinsman; "the finger of Heaven beckons thee! Rely on us all, the cimeter alone can restore the honor of thy line." The youth of the whole tribe were eager to accompany him; but he selected only seven hundred and fifty well-armed horsemen for this arduous expedition.

Abderahman landed on the coast of Andalusia in the early part of the year 755, as already noted. The inhabitants of that province, sheiks and people, received him with open arms, and made the air ring with their acclamations. His appearance, his station, his majestic mien, his open countenance, won upon the multitude. His march to Seville was one continued triumph. Twenty thousand voices cheered his progress. Twenty thousand cimeters, wielded by vigorous hands, were at his disposal. The surrounding towns immediately sent deputies with their submission, and the offer of their services. The viceroy of the Damascus khalif, in consternation, flew from province to province, to muster a force sufficient to oppose this triumphal march. But he was overthrown; and, in the short space of a year, Abderahman had triumphed over all his enemies, formidable as they were both for valor and numbers, and found himself seated securely on the Spanish throne, at Cordova.

Such was the beginning of the Moorish empire founded at a time when England was divided into the seven or eight kingdoms of the Saxon heptarchy; and it continued, for several centuries, the most wealthy and magnificent, as well as the most civilized state in Europe. Abderahman commenced his reign by making such regulations as were likely to secure good order and prosperity to the kingdom. He could not make new laws, because the laws of Mahometans are such as Mahomet gave them in the Koran, and are never altered; but he took care to appoint good and just magistrates in all the towns, and released his Christian subjects from the payment of a great part of the tribute money hitherto exacted from them, which materially bettered their condition. He also gave encouragement to commerce, and employment to laborers, by having dock-yards built all along the coast — a great advantage to a country whose cities were filled with merchants, trading to all parts of the world then known.

He improved his capital by a thousand works of art. He narrowed the bed of the Guadalquivir by stupendous embankments; the space thus rescued from the waters he transformed into extensive gardens, in the centre of which arose a tower, commanding a vast prospect. Expert architects, masons, and workmen abounded among the Arabs; nor could the skill of a people who had once been familiar with Roman art have entirely vanished from Spain. Summoning to his aid all the architectural talent of the age, Abderahman built at Cordova one of the most superb mosques in the world, which remains to this day, a splendid monument of the interesting and enlightened people over whom he ruled. It was supported by three hundred and sixty-five marble columns, had nineteen bronze gates of curious workmanship, and was lighted by four thousand seven hundred lamps, kept continually burning.

The khalif is said to have been the first who transplanted the palm-tree into the congenial climate of Spain. The Orientals have a strong sympathy for trees, and are in the habit of connecting the planting of them with interesting personal and family events. The Arabic poets compliment the taste of their amiable monarch, by representing him as alive to such refined feelings, as he contemplates the graceful tree and thus apostrophizes it. "Beautiful palm! thou art, like me, a stranger in these places; but the western breezes kiss thy branches, thy roots strike into a fertile soil, and thy head rises into a pure sky. Before the cruelty of Abul Abbas banished me from my native land, my tears often bedewed thy kindred plants of the Euphrates; but neither they nor the river remember my grief. Beautiful palm! thou canst not regret thy country!"

The kingdom of Cordova comprised Valencia, Murcia, Grenada, Andalusia, Portugal, and almost the whole of Castile. Under some of the more powerful sovereigns, these limits were extended. Under Abderahman, they included Catalonia, Aragon, and Leon; even the Asturians paid him tribute; so that, with the exception of the precarious authority of Charlemagne in Catalonia and Aragon, the whole peninsula south of the Pyrenees was subject to the Moors. But they had great difficulty in maintaining those parts even of their acknowledged possessions which bordered on the plains at the foot of the Asturias, as the Christians, who had taken refuge in those mountains at the time of the conquest, were increasing in numbers every year, and by carrying on an almost incessant warfare against the conquerors, were gradually extending their territories. The wars between the Christians and Saracens, indeed, continued, with few intervals of peace, during the whole period of Moorish dominion.

Yet, notwithstanding their national animosity, a Spaniard would sometimes marry a Moorish maiden; and many a young, misbelieving warrior braved innumerable difficulties and dangers for the sake of obtaining his Christian bride. Such marriages were generally preceded by numerous romantic adventures, as may readily be imagined, since they were always opposed by the relations of both parties; beside which, the ingenuity of the lover had to be exercised in contriving means of seeing and conversing with the lady of his choice. Their correspondence was sometimes held by means of flowers, which, in the East, it is customary to arrange in such order as to convey the same meaning as a written billet; an idea or word, universally understood, being assigned to each flower.

The Moors were an industrious race of people, and the agriculture of Spain, during their occupation of the country, was in a most flourishing state. They introduced plantations of sugar, rice, and cotton, in the cultivation of which they were assisted by negro slaves. We are indebted to them for the elements of many useful sciences, particularly that of chemistry; the first paper made in Europe was manufactured by them. Their carpets, silks, gold and silver embroidery, and manufactures in steel and leather, were long unrivalled; they introduced the simple figures we use in arithmetic — an unique specimen of a universal alphabet, as far as it goes. They taught mathematics, astronomy, philosophy, and medicine; and were altogether so superior in knowledge to the Europeans in general, that many Christians of all nations went to study in the Arabian schools of Cordova.

In making choice of that city for the capital of his kingdom, the khalif displayed an excellent taste, as the surrounding country was most delightful, adorned with groves of orange and citron, which were reflected in the clear waters of the Guadalquivir, on whose picturesque banks were extensive gardens, with their gay kiosks, and palaces ornamented with all the agreeable and striking characteristics of Saracenic architecture. The Oriental fondness for gardens was connected, among the Arabs, with the study of botany — a favorite pursuit, which made them acquainted with the medicinal qualities of herbs. Thus, like the Jews, they became famous as physicians.

The domestic manners of the Spanish Moors differed very much from those of Europeans, as well as from the simplicity of the primitive Arabs, for they had adopted much from the Persians, Syrians, and Turks. The ladies lived in seclusion, having their own separate apartments, where no male visitors, except their husbands, were admitted. They were taught to work embroidery, and to play upon the lute; but their minds were left totally uncultivated, and they spent the greater part of their time in adorning their persons. They wore the large Turkish trousers, short open robes, and long veils, their dresses being often richly embroidered with gold and beads, in imitation of pearls. Their seats were low cushions, and mats, or carpets spread on the floor; and their meats were served by slaves, on tables raised only a few inches from the ground. They drank no wine, because wine is forbidden by the laws of the prophet; but they made a kind of sherry of the grape, were very fond of coffee, and drank sherbets, or the juice of fruits prepared with water and sugar. They did not eat much meat, but excelled in the art of making pastry and confectionery of all kinds, which usually constituted the chief part of every repast.

The costume of the men was a long, loose robe, over large trousers, fastened round the waist with a girdle of embroidered leather, in which they carried a dagger. Sometimes the robe was of cloth, sometimes of silk, and the turban was either of silk or muslin, frequently embroidered with gold.

The government of the khalifs was of a patriarchal kind, which regards the sovereign as the father of a large family, whose children are at liberty to approach him, and address their complaints to his own ear. The Moorish sovereigns had the power of choosing their own successors, and some left the crown to a younger son, in preference to an elder one, if they thought the former would make the better monarch.

CHAPTER CCCLXXXIII.

A. D. 787 to 1492.

Moorish Kings of Cordova — Annals of the Kingdom — Abderahman III. — Prosperous State of the Kingdom — Its Decline and Fall — Rise, Decline, and Fall of the Kingdom of Grenada.

Mahometan Spain found in Abderahman I. the hero and legislator she needed, to lay broad and deep the foundations of her prosperity. His youngest son, *Hixem*, surnamed the *Just and Good*, was equally devoted to the welfare of his people. *Alhakem the Cruel*, son and successor of Hixem, had a troubled reign. As circumstances developed his character, it was found to combine two traits not uncommonly united — love of luxury and love of blood. Three hundred heads at one time, and four hundred at another, were taken off, under pretexts more or less just, to gratify the latter, and the interests of the state and happiness of his people were neglected in the indulgence of the former.

He passed the whole of his time, indeed, shut up in his palace with his female slaves, listening to voca and instrumental music, or witnessing the lascivious dance. Devolving the cares of royalty on his son, in 815, that he might more unreservedly enjoy its sensual pleasures, he surrounded himself with a well-paid guard of five thousand men, for greater safety against his outraged people. To meet this new expense, new taxes were laid, and the cruelty with which those who resisted the levy were punished, excied a riotous rebellion. In a few minutes, the streets of the capital were strewed with the dead bodies of the mob; three hundred suffered the dreadful torture of impalement. The suburbs were levelled, and their inhabitants exiled; eight thousand refugees fled to Fez, fifteen thousand to Alexandria, in Egypt. These held the city till bribed to proceed to Crete, where they founded the city of Candia. Remorse now seized the cruel Alhakem; solitude was intolerable to him, sleep almost impossible. He would call up his singers and dancers in the dead of night, and send for his ministers and judges. When the latter had listened and looked on, waiting long and in vain to be informed of the public business which required their attendance,—he would coolly bid them go home. This whimsical tyrant died in 821.

In the reign of his son, *Abderahman II.*, a magnanimous and beloved prince, the Northmen, or Sea-kings, barbarously ravaged the coasts of Spain and Portugal, even destroying the half of Seville. So terrible were these marauders, that they were generally allowed to retire to their ships unmolested. Drought and locusts followed for two years, and a famine ensued, which the king alleviated by importing corn from Africa. A rule of succession was enacted in the early part of this reign, that prevented the many miseries which had heretofore arisen from the uncertainty of the law as to the heirship to the throne. This king beautified and adorned his capital, and introduced abundance of pure water by leaden pipes. He also attracted men of genius, learning, or talent to his court, both natives and foreigners, by unexampled liberality.

Mohammed I. next ascended the throne, in 852—a man of letters, and a friend to genius, but a persecutor of his Christian subjects. His son and successor, *Almondhir*, reigned but two years, being killed in battle with Calib, son of the rebel Omar ben Hafs. *Abdalla* next succeeded to the sovereignty; but at his death, the formidable adventurer, *Calib*, who could marshal an army of sixty thousand men, reigned at Toledo, over the half of Mahometan Spain. Omar, the father of Calib, had been a laborer of Ronda, but after annoying the country as a petty robber in Andalusia, he went into the Pyrenees, and became a king. Both he and his son after him set the whole force of the state at defiance.

Abderahman III., grandson of Abdalla, next filled the Spanish throne, with glory to himself and Spain, A. D. 912. His reign is called the *golden age* of the Moorish empire. While a prince, he was the universal favorite of the nation, from his mild manners, generosity, and astonishing progress in learning. By universal acclamation, he was hailed as "prince of believers," and "defender of the faith of God;" he was thus the first of his family to assume the spiritual honors of the khalifate. He deemed it his first duty to exterminate the audacious rebels who had so long distracted the empire; he therefore sent his famous uncle, Almudafar, with a select force of forty thousand men, against Calib, who was defeated on the banks of the Jucar, losing seven thousand men; three thousand of the royal troops were also slain. The whole kingdom was then speedily brought back to its allegiance; and soon after the khalif conquered the kingdom of Fez, in Africa. He was also engaged, in the first part of his reign, in wars against the Christians.

But the glory of this great prince was not acquired by warlike exploits alone, as he was still more fond of cultivating the arts of peace. His virtues were rewarded by the affection of his people and the prosperity of the nation. In his internal administration, he was distinguished for great capacity of mind, for unbounded liberality, for unrivalled magnificence, and for inflexible justice; yet had he been less prosperous, he might have been more happy. It was this prince who remarked that, during his fifty years of empire, he had known but fourteen days of true enjoyment! His taste and luxury were exhibited in the foundation of a palace and city, about six miles from Cordova, in honor of his favorite wife, which he named, after her, *Zehra*, or *Azhara*. In the city was a mosque which rivalled that of his great namesake at Cordova. The roof of the palace was supported by above four thousand pillars of variegated marble; the floors and walls were of the same costly material. The chief apartments were adorned with exquisite fountains and baths; and the whole were surrounded with the most magnificent gardens, in the midst of which rose a pavilion of extensive prospect, resting on pillars of white marble ornamented with gold. In the centre of the pavilion, a fountain of quicksilver constantly played, reflecting, in a new and wondrous manner, the rays of the sun.

Abderahman III. showed himself capable of a sublimity of justice, which, as in the similar example of the Roman Brutus, mankind are ever at a loss whether to admire or detest. The king had designated his second son, Alhakem, for his successor; upon which his elder son, Abdalla, entered into a conspiracy for the assassination or perpetual imprisonment of the heir apparent. The plot was discovered, and the would-be fratricide confessed his guilt. His injured brother now pleaded for Abdalla, who, it was asserted, had been misguided by evil counsellors. The answer of the king was worthy of "the proudest Roman of them all." "Thy humane request," said he, "becomes thee well, and if I were a private individual, it should be granted, but *as a king*, I owe both to my people and my successors an example of justice. I deeply lament the fate of my son; I shall lament it through life; but neither thy tears nor my grief shall prevent the punishment of his crime." The prince was strangled; and though the stern father acted from a sense of duty, he was never happy afterward. Who but must feel for the good man, in listening to the pathetic verses he addressed to a friend. "The days of sunshine are past—dark night approaches, the shadows of which no morn will ever dissipate!"

This reign, as has been intimated, is termed the most brilliant period in the history of the Spanish Arabs. Commerce flourished and riches were accumulated in an unexampled degree; a powerful navy was formed and maintained in full activity; the arts and sciences were cultivated with ardor, for their professors were rewarded with princely liberality; many splendid public works were undertaken in the principal towns of Mahometan Spain; power was the friend of industry, of merit, and of poverty; and the king's fame was so widely diffused as to bring rich embassies even from Constantinople. Thus, at two hundred years from its birth, the kingdom had grown to the height of its prosperity. Its merchants were very rich; its manufactories of silk, woollen, cotton, and linen were numerous, and furnished employment for tens of thousands of the people; plate and jewelry, of its own manufacture, were every where in common use; the land was rendered fertile by assiduous and skilful irrigation. Rice, sugar, and cotton were extensively cultivated, and the landholders or farmers were much more thriving than they were in the feudal days of the Gothic kings, who always exacted, as a tribute, one third of the produce of the land; whereas the khalifs only required a tenth.

The commerce of the Saracens in the Mediterranean was much more extensive than that of the Christians, and their naval power much superior. The king built a larger vessel than had ever been seen before, which he loaded with valuable merchandise, to be sold in the East. It came back laden with goods for the khalif's use, and brought, also, a number of beautiful female slaves, skilled in music and dancing, to enliven the royal banquets. The opulence of this flourishing kingdom was so great, that the governors of the provinces, and the judges, vied with the king himself in the magnificence of their palaces and gardens; like him, they were surrounded by artists, poets, philosophers, and others, who were distinguished by their superior talents; and these they entertained in the most sumptuous manner. Many public libraries and academies, for science and literature, were established in all the great towns. At this period, also, when the practice of medicine was almost unknown elsewhere, the physicians of Cordova were held in such high estimation, that princes came to the court of the khalif to be cured of disease.

Alhakem, the next king, (A. D. 961,) emulated the virtues of his predecessor — a thing rare in the annals of flourishing empires. He was averse to war, fond of tranquillity, and immoderately attached to literature. His agents were constantly employed, throughout the East, in purchasing scarce and curious books: he himself wrote to every author of reputation for a copy of his works, for which he payed royally; and wherever he could not purchase a book, he caused it to be transcribed. The catalogue of his library, though unfinished, numbered forty-four volumes. On his accession to the sovereignty, in order that he might devote his chief time to the public administration, yet not neglect interests so dear to him, he confided to one of his brothers the care of his library, and to another the duty of protecting literary institutions, and of rewarding the learned. His reign is the Augustan age of Arabic literature in Spain.

Even this good prince was once guilty of an act of tyranny; but the sequel is much to his praise. Desiring to enlarge a garden, he endeavored to purchase the adjoining field. The owner refused to sell; whereupon the khalif took it by force. The owner complained to the cadi, who, taking a sack, slung it across the back of a mule, and proceeded to the lot, where he found the khalif busy pointing out a site for a pavilion. He begged to be allowed to fill his sack with earth. When he had done so, he respectfully requested the khalif to assist him in lifting the sack to the back of the mule. The khalif, thinking it some jest, goodnaturedly attempted to lift one end of the sack, but found it too heavy. "O prince," said the cadi, "if thou canst not now lift so small a portion of the field thou hast usurped, as is contained in this sack, how wilt thou bear the weight of the whole of it upon thy head in the judgment day!" The king thanked his intrepid monitor, and restored the field.

Hixem II. succeeded to the throne at the age of eleven years, and the queen mother appointed, as regent, her secretary, a man of great genius, valor, and activity, best known by his surname of *Almanzor*, "the conqueror." This title was given him from his successes against the Christians. It is said that he won fifty-four battles, and at length died of chagrin, at a great age, in consequence of losing one. This great sovereign — for he acted as such — was not only a most able general and valiant soldier, but an enlightened statesman, an active governor, an encourager of science and the arts, and a munificent rewarder of merit. His death (A. D. 1002) was fatal to Cordova.

During the next two hundred years, the empire, after reaching the zenith of its glory, declined, and came to ruin, its fine capital falling into the hands of the Christians. The annals of this period are, in general, but a bloody record of battles, sieges, and treasons, rebellions, persecutions, and petty successes of rival chiefs, which indicate the decline of the national spirit, and the lack of a central, controlling energy, — in short, the convulsions of a body whose "whole head is sick, and whose heart is faint."

The most prominent cause of ruin was the parcelling of the empire into petty chieftaincies, which were made hereditary in the families of the successful partisans, who obtained the fief at first.* Thus the nation retrograded from a central government, — powerful enough to protect the rights of all, with its subordinate powers properly distributed, — back to the barbarian, or feudal system, which had brought, and was bringing, upon Europe such terrible evils, through the slavery and degradation of the many, and the clashing selfishness of the blind and wilful few.

Hixem III., called by the people to the throne, (A. D. 1026) against his own wishes, endeavored to deserve the affection of his subjects, to redress wrongs, encourage industry, administer justice impartially, relieve the poor, and repress the exactions of the local magistrates. The governors resisted, and he took the field against them; but they were too powerful for him, and he was compelled to treat with open rebels. He failed where success was impossible; and the fickle mob, imputing it to him as a crime, paraded the streets, demanding his deposition. He gladly retired

* The imbecile Hixem II. had been thrown into prison by a usurper, and was supposed to be dead; but one of the chiefs produced him to the populace, and using him as a puppet, was intrusted by him, because of certain successes, with the privilege of changing revocable into hereditary fiefs. Some of the most powerful of the governors were, by this novelty, drawn for a time into Hixem's interest; but from this moment each looked forward to a separate and independent sovereignty. Suleyman, the rival of Hixem, used the same ruinous means against his opponent. By giving the governors of Calatrava, Saragossa, Medina Cœli, and Guadalaxara, the hereditary and irrevocable possession of their governments, he secured their powerful aid. This was the signal for the creation of numerous independent and rival kingdoms, and consequently for the ruin of Mahometan Spain. Its strength against the Christians lay in its union: when disunited, it fell an easy prey, in detail. Carried away by their reckless passions, the Moorish chiefs rushed blindly to this fatal result.

o private life: the remembrance of his virtues, however, long survived his power; and Arabic writers all represent him as too good for his age. With him ended the khalifate of the west, and the noble race of Omeya, or Moawiyah, in **1031**. The empire seemed to sink at once. Not thirty years had elapsed since the great Almanzor wielded the resources of Africa and Spain, threatening the entire destruction of the Christians, whom he had driven to an obscure corner of the vast peninsula. Now, Africa is lost; the Christians hold two thirds of the country; the petty but independent governors — the boldest of whom trembled at the name of Almanzor — openly insult the ruler of Cordova, whose authority extends little farther than the walls of his capital. "Assuredly," says an historian, "so astounding a catastrophe has no parallel in all history!"

From this period, A. D. **1031**, to the establishment of the kingdom of Grenada, in A. D. 1228, there was no supreme chief of Mahometan Spain, if we except the fleeting conquerors, — the Almoravides and Almohades, — who arrived from Africa, and the fabric of whose dominion was as suddenly destroyed as erected. The portion of country free from the progressive approaches of the Christian sovereignties fell under the government of petty kings, whose obscure broils we have not the patience to detail, nor would the reader have patience to follow the tedious recital.

The Kingdom of Grenada, from the romantic interest thrown around it in its prosperity, and the melancholy story of its fall, deserves a larger space than our plan can accord to it. Its history claims attention, also, as it has employed more than one elegant pen of America; and her most fascinating writer has strewn the flowers of taste over the tomb of Grenada, waking an echo, in every feeling bosom, to the "last sigh of the Moor."

Before the year 1238, the original Spaniards had, by constant perseverance, in reducing state after state, reconquered nearly the whole of the land of their fathers. Aragon, Navarre, Castile, and Portugal, were all large and powerful states. In short, the whole peninsula was under the dominion of Christian princes, except the beautiful and fertile province of Grenada, in the south, scarce inferior to the Cordovan kingdom, except in extent of territory. Grenada indeed, foiled, for two centuries and a half, all the attacks of the Christians of Spain, till the several Christian states became consolidated in a powerful and overwhelming empire, which could no longer be resisted.

Mohammed I., ben Alhamar, one of the kings of Southern Spain, seemed alone to possess the ability to withstand the Christians; and when Valencia was taken from the Moors, his power was increased by a body of fifty thousand Mahometans, who left the city and placed themselves under his sway. This king fixed his court at Grenada, and fortified the city, A. D. 1238, resolving to extend, or at least preserve his dominions against the rebellious Moorish governors on the one hand, and the Christians on the other. He paid tribute to Ferdinand III., king of Leon and Castile; but his successors refused to acknowledge allegiance, and the usual wars were renewed.

Though energetic and intrepid, Mohammed I. was mild and conciliating; he was prudent, yet of comprehensive views and magnificent tastes. He repaired the frontier fortresses of his kingdom, which extended from Algeziras to Almeria, and as far inland as Jaen and Huescar. Every Mussulman was, by the constitution of the state and of society, a soldier: he had, however, no regular pay. The king of Grenada not only kept up a standing army, on regular pay, but, in addition, allotted to each soldier a piece of ground on the frontier, large enough to maintain himself, his family, and his horse — the dear friend of the Arab. These little farms thus served as a barrier against the enemy, more effectual than walls; for the soldier fought to protect his own family and hearthstone.

Thus secured externally, the kingdom, under the good government of Mohammed I., soon became as renowned as Cordova had ever been for agriculture, commerce, arts, manufactures, — especially silk, — and for wealth and industry. Prizes were awarded to stimulate all the mechanic arts, and especially to the best weavers of silk and growers of wool. Warehouses, hospitals, poorhouses, markets with fixed prices, schools, colleges, and good inns were seen on every hand. The fine palace of the Alhambra, built for his residence, is still a grand object of attraction to travellers. The capital was also beautified with baths, fountains, delightful public walks, gardens, and every convenience, all paid for, not by tax, but from the king's gold and silver mines. Every town was divided into wards, with an inspector over each; patrols guarded the streets at night, and the gates of the cities were closed at a certain hour of the evening; courts of justice were held every day by the impartial sovereign; and, above all, charity — not only in sharing money, fruits, grain, flocks, and merchandise, with the needy, but in humane attentions to the sick, and in hospitality — was generally practised by the people, happy in thus performing the duties enjoined by their religion.

Eleven sovereigns had reigned in Grenada: the twelfth was a usurper, and the story of the thirteenth, *Jusef III.*, is singular. His brother, the previous king, imprisoned him and usurped the throne for ten years: at the end of that period, he was taken dangerously ill; and, anxious that his son should succeed him, he sent orders to his brother's keeper to put his prisoner, Jusef, to death. The keeper had contracted an affection for the disinherited prince, and was engaged at chess with him when the fatal letter arrived. Jusef, judging of its contents by the agitation of his friend, requested to be allowed to play out the game, and he would then yield up his life. Before the game was finished, however, another messenger came, to announce that the usurper was dead; and the reprieved victim ascended the throne as Jusef III. Taught, probably, by adversity, he was an excellent king: his court was renowned for splendid tournaments; and many hot-headed young men from France, and other countries, where duelling was forbidden, came to Grenada to settle their disputes by single combat. It is said that the Moors first introduced tournaments into Europe, as they did bull-fights into Spain.

From the time of Jusef III. to the fall of Grenada, the wars in Spain continued with very little intermission, and the damage done to the country was lamentable, indeed irremediable. It was the object of both Christian and Mahometan to ruin each other's land; and for that purpose soldiers, called *taladores*, were employed, whose business was, not to fight, but, while the rest were engaged in battle, to lay waste the surrounding country, cut down the fruit trees, root up the vines, destroy the grain, and ravage all the gardens so that the land, wherever they came, was converted into a dreary desert; and doubtless the effects of this suicidal policy are seen in the desolate tracts with which Spain abounds at the present day.

Numerous romantic adventures occurred in these perpetual border wars — the subjects of many a pretty ballad still sung by the Spanish peasantry, as they sit under their trees on a summer's evening. The following relation is a specimen of the pleasing character of these popular tales. A Spanish reconnoitring party captured a young Moor of rank, richly dressed, and mounted on a superb Arabian charger. When brought to the Christian governor, to the astonishment of all, the prisoner burst into tears, at the same time stating himself to be the son of the alcalde of Ronda. "Tears are unbecoming a soldier, especially thee," said the governor, sternly, knowing the alcalde to be one of the bravest of the brave. "Alas!" replied the prisoner, "it is not for myself I weep. I love a maiden more beautiful than the sun, and dearer to me than life. This very evening she was to have become my bride, and will not know the reason of my absence." Pitying his grief, the governor gave him permission to go and take leave of his betrothed, on condition that he would return the next day. What was his surprise to see the youth enter his presence the next morning with his lovely bride, who had insisted on sharing captivity and slavery with him! Pleased with the youth for his fidelity to his word, and with the maiden for her devoted and disinterested affection, the governor restored them both to liberty.

Literature and the elegant and useful arts were carried to a high degree of excellence by the Spanish Moors, while the rest of Europe remained sunk in barbarism. The munificence and taste of their sovereigns were most ostentatiously displayed in their public edifices, palaces, mosques, and hospitals, and in the construction of commodious quays, fountains, bridges, and aqueducts, which, penetrating the sides of the mountains, or sweeping on lofty arches across the valleys, rivalled in their proportions the works of ancient Rome.

Grenada had been prosperous and happy for nearly two hundred years, when a desperate civil war broke out, in consequence of a dispute between two princes for the throne. On the other hand, the Christian kingdoms of Spain had, just at this period, ceased their enfeebling quarrels, and become united in one, under Ferdinand of Aragon and Isabella of Castile, who were now desirous of including Grenada also under their dominion, so that it might embrace all Spain. The civil war favored their design; yet the distracted kingdom of the Moors defended itself so bravely, even after losing city after city, that it was not till 1492 that its capital was taken, and the kingdom of Grenada thus finally reduced.

Abu Abdalla, or Boabdil, its king, seeing no hope of effectually defending the city, which had suffered severely by the rage of the contending parties, capitulated, on condition that the Moors should be allowed to exercise their own religion, and be governed by their own laws. On these terms, the gates were opened, and the last of the Moorish sovereigns went forth to finish his days, an exile in Africa, A. D. 1492, January 4th. A hill is still pointed out, whence Abu Abdalla took his farewell look at the charming abode of so many kings, — the home of his youth; and the height yet bears the name of "The last Sigh of the Moor."

CHAPTER CCCLXXXIV.

A. D. 718 to 1863.

Origin of the Spanish Monarchy — The Cid — Free Cities — Orders of Knighthood — Ferdinand and Isabella — Charles V. — Philip II. — Modern History of Spain.

Ferdinand and Isabella.

We have seen that, in 1492, the Spanish monarchy extended over every part of the peninsula. It will now be necessary to look back, and consider of what materials, and by what means this kingdom was built up. Nearly eight hundred years before, we find a remnant of Christians — Goths and Spaniards together — betaking themselves to the mountain fastnesses of North-western Spain, and in these rude homes of independence, fortifying themselves against their fierce invaders from the south, as did the primeval Spaniards and their descendants take refuge here against invaders from the coast, the east, and the north.

Few at first, the number of individuals who took shelter in these solitudes was increased gradually by multitudes, as the Mahometan excesses became more frequent and intolerable; for neither prompt submission, nor treaties, could guaranty the conquered from plunder, persecution, and massacre. Finding themselves growing stronger, the exiles resolved to found an infant state. "The care of the sacred relics, carefully conveyed hither on the reduction of Toledo the presence, not only of prelates, but of nobles descended from the blood of the Goths; that devotion to a good cause, that sense of duty, which adversity never fails to create and confirm; and the necessity of self-preservation, — united these refugees in an indissoluble bond." A. D. 718. They elected for their king *Pelayo*, of the royal Gothic house, whom they inaugurated after the ancient form. At the given signal a buckler was brought; and

> ——— "eight, for their strength and stature chosen,
> Came to their honored office. Round the shield
> Standing, they lower it for the chieftain's feet,
> Then, slowly raised upon their shoulders, lift
> The steady weight. Erect Pelayo stands,
> And thrice he brandishes the shining sword.
> Th' archbishop to the assembled people cries,
> 'Spaniards, behold your king!' The multitude
> Then sent forth all their voice, with loud acclaim!

Full soon was the temper of this band of patriots, heroes, exiles for liberty and religion, severely tried. A conquering general of the enemy sought them in their retreats with a large force. On the heights of Coradunga and in the cavern of St. Mary, the small but resolute band of Pelayo was concealed, waiting for the attack. As the Arabs clambered up the steep ascent to the cave, huge rocks and stones were thundered down upon their dense ranks, by which they were precipitated into the narrow valley below. Thousands were crushed; the assailants were defeated; and the Christians, sallying forth from their hiding-places, inflicted a terrible loss on the fugitives. Two more successful battles established the infant kingdom of *the Asturias*, called afterward, from its capital, the kingdom of *Oviedo*.

The origin of the kingdom of *Navarre* is very obscure. Its counts were probably dependent on the Asturias, and at times on the Arabs and Franks. Charlemagne conquered it in A. D. 777–8. Sancho Iñigo was the first independent count — A. D. 873.

Sixty years after the Moorish conquest, the nobles and people of *Castile* disowned allegiance to Cordova, and became allies and vassals of the king of Oviedo, who lent them aid to throw off the Moorish yoke. Under this king, the country was distributed to several petty chiefs, called *counts of Castile*. *Ordonio II.* had removed his court from Oviedo to Leon, which thenceforth gave name to the kingdom. Becoming jealous of the great power of the counts, he invited them to a council, and treacherously assassinated them. This base cruelty so exasperated the Castilians, that they revolted, and under a ruler called a *count*, became independent of Ordonio, who was too much occupied in defending himself against the mighty Almanzor, to attempt the recovery of Castile.

Among those who assisted in the final and fatal defeat of that Moorish conqueror, in 1002, was *Sancho the Great*, king of Navarre, who had married the sister of the count of Castile. The count died without children, and Sancho took possession of Castile in right of his wife. He thus became the most powerful prince in Spain, for he had already united a large part of Aragon to his dominions of Navarre.

At his death, Sancho divided his empire among his three sons, of whom *Ferdinand I.* received Castile, and took the title of *king*. In 1037, by marrying the heiress of Leon, and thus uniting that kingdom with his own, he made Castile the principal state in Spain; it is called, in history, the "kingdom of Castile and Leon," and furnished the well-known symbols of the *lion* and the *castle* seen on Spanish coins. Ferdinand I. died in 1065, and was one of the greatest and best of the Spanish kings.

The Spaniards, at this time were much inferior to the Moors in civilization; their unequal laws were based on the Gothic. Their institutions, therefore, continued to be feudal. Commerce, arts, and manufactures, except those of weapons, were very backward among them. The barbarous duel and trial by combat were allowed, but the romantic profession of chivalry did not yet exist.

There were knights, however, who made themselves famous throughout the world for valor and magnanimity; among whom none was more renowned than *the Cid*, Don Rodrigo Diaz de Bivar, the hero of many

The Cid.

popular tales and ballads. When yet a boy, he fought a powerful and experienced warrior, who had insulted his father, cut off his head, and brought it home at his saddle-bow. This so rejoiced the heart of the warlike old man, that, although custom did not allow children ever to be seated in presence of their parents, he placed his son above himself at his own table. The Cid was champion of Castile, and very successful against the Moors, so that his exploits earned him the honor of knighthood from his king. At the accession of *King Alfonso VI.*, after the assassination of his brother, the Cid called upon the king to expurgate him self, by oath, of any connection with the murder. This alienated the monarch from the hero, who, on some after-pretext, was exiled from court. Followed into banishment by a numerous band of retainers, he resolved to conquer a kingdom for himself; and having wrested Valencia from the Moors, he became its king, or Cid. His exploits reconciled his sovereign to him, and he returned to court. The rest of his life is filled with wondrous deeds of valor against the Moors.

Such is the received account of this hero of romance; but its accuracy has been doubted by modern historical sceptics. While the Cid was living, his reputation was sufficient to keep the Moors in awe; but when he was dead, their courage revived, and they boldly attacked the Spaniards, even in Valencia, the city where his remains were laid. The story goes,—and it may serve as a specimen of the tales of the Cid,—that the Spaniards went forth to meet them, and behold, a warrior, with the well-known dress of the Cid, but with the aspect of death, was at their head! The Moors recognized his features, and fled, in superstitious horror, fancying that a miracle had been performed in behalf of the Spaniards. The truth was, however, that the Christians had taken him from the tomb, set him on his war-horse, and thus, even after h's death, he achieved a victory over his foes! This inciden sufficiently attests the wonderful power which the Cid's name exerted, as well over his countrymen as over their enemies.

Two singular institutions of this period claim a passing notice—the establishment of free cities, and the founding of certain orders of knighthood. The cities and towns of Spain, in general, were under the power of feudal despots. But, in consequence of the desolations of war, several extensive territories had become a complete desert; a king is said to have marched in one of these tracts for fifteen days, without observing a sign of cultivation or a human abode. The kings of several small states, therefore, decreed that whoever would take up these waste lands, settle on them, and build villages, should be free from all the tyrannous exactions of feudal service and taxes of every kind. They were also made sanctuaries for criminals. Many of them thus became large and populous towns, full of the spirit of freedom. They also originated and built up a wealthy and independent middle class.

Several religious orders of knighthood, similar to that of the Knights Templars, had their origin about the same time with the free cities. The object of all the orders was, to support the Christian religion against the misbelievers, and expel them from the country. None could belong to them but men of noble birth; and the various orders were distinguished by different ensigns; as, for example, the knights of Alcantara displayed a green cross on the shield; those of Calatrava, a red one; and those of St. James of Compostella,—the famous patron saint of Spain, *Santiago*, or *San Diego*,—a cross in the form of a sword.

The tradition of the founding of the latter order is characteristic of the manners of the times. A number of young Castilian noblemen, having brought themselves into difficulties by their extravagance, agreed to form a band of robbers, and took possession of a ruined castle among the mountains of Leon, where they amassed a store of wealth, by plundering the travellers who passed that way. At length, repenting of their crimes, they made a vow to expiate them by devoting the remainder of their lives to the service of Christianity, and, accordingly, performed such feats against the Moors, that the king of Castile made them all knights, and, by their own desire, created for them a new order, that of the knights of St. James. Their duty was to defend the tomb of the saint, at Santiago—a kind of Mecca of Christian pilgrimage,—and protect the pilgrims, who visited it in infinite numbers from all parts of Spain and Europe.

It was during the period of the holy wars, which lasted two hundred years, that the first Moorish empire, that of Cordova, was gradually subdued by the Spaniards, who were occasionally aided by bands of crusaders on their way to the Holy Land. The Scotch earl of Douglass, who was carrying the heart of King Bruce to Palestine, fell in one of these campaigns. Alfonso VI. conquered all the country as far as Madrid; rebuilt the towns that had been destroyed in the wars; made the ancient Gothic capital, Toledo, an archbishopric again, and formed the province of *New Castile*. One of his daughters married a French count, who received from her father the north of Portugal as her dowry; from which time, (A. D. 1095,) Spain and Portugal may be considered as separate countries.

Ferdinand III. completed the conquest of Cordova, (A. D. 1248,) leaving only Grenada to the Moors. The beautiful capital, Cordova, was destroyed during the siege: nothing of its ancient grandeur remains but the splendid mosque, which is now a Catholic church. The many noble qualities of Ferdinand III. were stained with cruelty and bigotry. Multitudes of Jews were burnt alive in his reign, and even by his own hand. He founded the University of Salamanca, instituted a parliament of the nobles and clergy, and made a code which is the foundation of the present laws of Spain. His court was famous for the splendor of its tournaments: it was at one of these that Edward I. was captivated by the graces of the princess, Eleanor, whom he made queen of England, and where she introduced some of the elegant Moorish fashions.

Among the more noted kings of Spain, of the ensuing period, we may name *Alfonso X.*, celebrated for his learning; *Alfonso XI.*, one of the most powerful princes of his time; *Pedro the Cruel*, to whom Edward III. of England betrothed his daughter,—though she died previous to the marriage. Pedro married Blanche of Bourbon, whom he imprisoned, and, it is supposed, poisoned he was guilty of many other murders. *John I.* admitted four commoners to the council of the state; such was the increasing consequence of the middle classes *Henry III.*, returning hungry from the chase, was obliged to wait for his supper till the game he had killed was cooked, as the tradespeople would not trust his steward. Angry at this, when told that his nobles were feasting sumptuously with the archbishop of Toledo, he personally satisfied himself of the fact by gaining clandestine admittance to the table. He then feigned a dangerous illness, the report of which brought all his nobles and the archbishop to the palace where they were reproached with their peculations and detained in custody till they had given back to the crown their ill-gotten lands and fortresses.

After the death of Henry III. ensued a period of anarchy and misrule, during which the Holy Brotherhood was instituted,—a private association for the redress of grievances and the righting of the wronged—something like the self-constituted "Regulators" of our western frontiers. During the civil wars, Henry IV. was deposed and Alfonso enthroned, who however, died suddenly, and Henry was restored, on condition that he named for his successor his sister *Isabella.* This was the renowned princess who married Ferdinand, heir to Aragon.

On the death of Henry IV., in 1474, this illustrious pair, *Ferdinand* and *Isabella*, ascended the united throne of Castile and Aragon, as joint sovereigns; and thus commenced a new and glorious era for Spain, and, indeed, for the world. Among the objects accomplished in this eventful reign, were, the conquest of Grenada, bringing all Spain under one monarch; the discovery of America by Columbus; clearing the country of banditti, by demolishing the castles that harbored them; the curbing of the tyranny of the nobles by a revival, with extended powers, of the holy

Embarkation of Columbus.

brotherhood. This now became a horse patrol, or mounted and armed police, who brought all suspicious persons, of whatever rank, before duly-appointed judges, being supported by a tax on the citizens. Finally, the Catalonian barons were compelled, during this reign, to emancipate their serfs, as the nobles of the other provinces had done, thus mitigating the feudal vassalage.

Queen Isabella was a woman of extraordinary talent; she shared the government equally with her husband, was amiable in domestic life, kind to her subjects, always prudent, pious, and charitable. Ferdinand was equally prudent, but not so liberal, either in his ideas or his actions. They were both strict in the administration of justice, and punished crimes without distinction of persons. That magistrates might be restrained from malversation, chief judges, called *corregidores*, were sent round to every town, with authority to examine into their conduct. But these benefits were much counterbalanced by the establishment of that detestable tribunal, the Inquisition, a court instituted first in Spain, at Seville, in **1481**, for the purpose of exterminating the heretics — a term applied to the Jews, and others not Roman Catholics. This all-pervading spiritual tyranny has greatly injured the Spanish character. It was not finally abolished till A. D. **1836**. The expulsion of the Moors from Spain, was also a miserable policy, which deprived the state of hundreds of thousands of industrious members, skilful artisans, agriculturists, and merchants.

Ferdinand died some years after his wife, in **1516**. After her death, he unjustly invaded and took possession of Navarre, and obtained the kingdom of Naples by no less dishonest and dishonorable means, as we have elsewhere noticed. The crown devolved, at his death, on his grandson, *Charles V.*, also emperor of Germany. After his election to the latter dignity, Charles was very seldom in Spain, but left its administration to Cardinal Adrian; and, in consequence of taxes for wars in which they had no interest, the Spaniards revolted. The king was, therefore, compelled to visit Spain, where, however, he acted with great clemency. One day, when some officious person offered to tell him where one of those who had been condemned to death was concealed, he replied, "You had better tell the unfortunate gentleman where I am."

Charles abdicated his throne, in **1558**, in favor of *Philip II.*, his son, the husband of Queen Mary of England. He reigned from A. D. **1558** to **1598**. Spain was now at the culminating point of her prosperity. The bigoted Philip hated every religion but the Catholic; and his persecutions of his Dutch subjects lost him Holland. As England had aided the Dutch in achieving their independence, and was also a bulwark of Protestantism, Philip determined to invade that country. For this purpose he made immense preparations; all Spain resounded for years with the din of warlike armaments, and, at last, a fleet put to sea of one hundred and twenty vessels, boastingly called the *Invincible Armada*. But part of it was destroyed by storms, and part defeated by the English fleet; so that the result was exceedingly mortifying to Spanish pride.

The galling oppression of this gloomy tyrant aroused, about the same time, a revolt among the descendants of the Moors, who might be reckoned among the most valuable of the citizens of the empire. On Christmas day, **1567**, these Moriscoes, or Christianized Moors, assisted by Moors from Africa, suddenly came forth armed, massacred the priests in a most barbarous manner, then the magistrates, and next vented their fury on every Christian they met. A civil war ensued of unequalled atrocity on both sides, which ended in the complete subjugation of the Moriscoes, who were compelled to scatter themselves over the country, and were soon lost among the Christian population.

Philip II. succeeded, in default of other heirs, to the crown of Portugal, in **1583**, and to all her colonial possessions. He thus became the most powerful monarch of his age. But his Portuguese subjects hated the government of Spain. The Philippine Islands were colonized with Spaniards during this reign Philip II. was the first Spanish sovereign who made Madrid his capital. At the distance of thirty miles from the city he built the famous palace of the Escurial, the model of which is said to have been the gridiron on which St. Bartholomew was martyred. It has eighty staircases, seventy-three fountains, eighteen hundred and sixty rooms, eight organs, and twelve thousand windows and doors.

Philip III. ordered all the Christian Moors to leave the kingdom in thirty days, and to carry nothing with them. During the enforcement of this cruel edict, six hundred thousand industrious citizens were driven out penniless — an irremediable loss, and followed by the rapid decline of the country which thus acted so unnatural a part to her children. Commerce, agriculture, and manufactures retrograded, till, from being the foremost nation of Europe Spain is now ranked among the most impotent. *Philip IV.* lost Portugal, which asserted its independence, and proclaimed the duke of Braganza, king.

Charles II, a weak prince, ruled by his ministers and bishops, succeeded in 1665. At his death, in 1700, occurred the ruinous war of the "Succession," the two claimants of the throne being Philip, grandson of Louis XIV., nominated by Charles II., and Charles, archduke of Austria, son of the granddaughter of Philip III. The English, Dutch, Portuguese, and some of the Italian states sided with the archduke. During this contest the English took Gibraltar from the Spaniards, and Holland passed to Austria. When the archduke succeeded to the throne of Germany, he gave up his claim, and *Philip V.* ascended the Spanish throne. He was the first monarch of Spain of the house of Bourbon, and a very arbitrary prince.

Ferdinand VI. succeeded in 1746, and reigned thirteen years, leaving the throne, at his death, to his brother Charles, king of Naples, who gave up that crown on ascending the Spanish throne as *Charles III.* The only event which disturbed the peace of his reign was a riot at Madrid on account of a decree — designed to prevent assassinations — against large hats and cloaks. The order was so offensive to the people, that it was countermanded. The Jesuits, who were supposed to have instigated the riot, were banished from Spain, three hours only being given them to get ready. They afterward received from the Spanish government a pension of a shilling a day in Italy, where, at first, they had been refused admittance. The king also put a stop to the *autos da fé*, or burning of heretics, by the Inquisition, and colonized the Sierra Morena,* hitherto a barren waste of heath and forest, although in the middle of the country.

In 1789, *Charles IV.* came to the throne. Just after his accession, the French revolution occurred; and the king, obliged to side with the French republicans, was involved in a war with England. The combined French and Spanish fleets were defeated, off Trafalgar, by the British fleet, under Nelson, A. D. 1805, the year after Napoleon became emperor. Spain was now much declined from her former power, and her armies were neither so brave nor so well officered and disciplined as they once were. Bonaparte expected little opposition in his views of aggrandizement from Charles, who was a weak monarch.

In 1808, it was rumored that the French had entered Spain, and that the royal family intended to follow the recent example of Portugal, and emigrate to America. Godoy, called *Prince of Peace*, from having negotiated the peace with France, supposed to have advised the step, was mobbed, and fled; the people thronged the roads to prevent the royal family from quitting the country. The disturbances increased, and the king became so alarmed, that he resigned his crown to his son, *Ferdinand VII.* Father and son now set off, with a French guard, to meet Napoleon at Bayonne, and Madrid was taken possession of by French troops. At Bayonne, Charles and Ferdinand were compelled to resign all pretensions to the Spanish crown, which Napoleon immediately conferred on his brother Joseph.

The Spanish patriots obtained troops and aid from England; and now ensued the "Peninsular War," one of the most bloody and romantic on record. Sir Arthur Wellesley, now duke of Wellington, commanded the English forces during the first and last part of this conflict, which resulted, in 1813, in the expulsion of the French from the country. Battles were fought in every province; the towns were besieged, the villages set on fire; the cities were plundered, and the people reduced to the lowest state of poverty and wretchedness. Thousands must have perished from want, had it not been for the charity of the clergy, who, during this period of distress, exerted themselves in the most benevolent manner to relieve the wants of the sufferers.

Ferdinand was released by Napoleon, and hastened to reoccupy his throne; but, in his attempts to restore the old order of things, sowed the seeds of great mischief. These have been producing an ample harvest of public and private injustice, revolutions, massacres, and assassinations, up to the present time. Napoleon had abolished the Inquisition, thrown open the monasteries, set the monks to productive labors, sold the church lands, and suppressed all remains of the oppressive feudal system; so that the peasantry were no longer vassals to the great landholders, but were at liberty to establish inns, mills, bakehouses, and fisheries for their own profit, instead of that of their proud and indolent lords. The Cortes passed certain laws, called the *Constitution of the Cortes of* 1812, which were very advantageous to the people. These the king not only refused to sanction, but imprisoned or exiled many of the chief members of the Cortes; he also destroyed the liberty of the press, by appointing a censorship. Mexico and the South American republics soon declared their independence of Spain; and only Cuba, Porto Rico, the Canaries, Philippines, and a few places of less importance, are now left to the empire out of all her vast foreign possessions.

Ferdinand VII. died in 1833, leaving an infant daughter but three years of age, the present queen, *Isabella II.*, whose mother, Queen Christina, was appointed regent of the kingdom during the minority. Don Carlos, brother of Ferdinand, claimed the crown on the ground of the salic law, which excluded females from the throne. A civil war ensued, which has reduced the country to the brink of ruin, disorganizing and demoralizing society to a frightful extent. The clergy and the North supported Don Carlos; Madrid and the South, Isabella. In 1836, the constitution of the Cortes was restored by the queen regent, the religious orders were suppressed, and the Spaniards now enjoy a considerable degree of freedom.

In 1840, four regents were appointed, of whom Espartero was at the head, and Queen Christina retired to Italy. The liberal and energetic government

* Poor peasants of Germany were induced to settle here by grants to each settler of land, free of rent, for ten years, a cottage and bakehouse, seed, farming tools, ten cows, an ass, some pigs, and some poultry. These settlements are now the neatest and most prosperous villages in Spain.

of the regents has quieted the country. In the year 1846, Queen Isabella was married to the Sicilian prince of Trapani, and her youngest sister, the infanta, to the duke of Montpensier, son of Louis Philippe, then king of France. Occasional disturbances from factions, instigated by Don Carlos, occurred, and in 1854 a revolution took place, which compelled Queen Isabella to sign a liberal constitution. Her mother, Christina, was obliged to fly as well as the ministers. A reaction however, took place in 1856; the new constitution was repudiated, and the old order of things restored.*

CHAPTER CCCLXXXV.

General Views — Spanish Character — Government and Laws — Power — Religion — Language and Literature.

To the early writers of Greece, Spain was the land of romance and fable. It has continued to be, down to the present moment, a fairy land of polite literature. Secluded from the rest of Europe by position, and connected, by wonderful events, with Africa and the Orientals, it has never been a great thoroughfare for the commerce of European ideas, but has maintained a peculiar character, combining traits of both the Oriental and Occidental mind. The internal capabilities of Spain are immense. Her soil, climate, ports, and people — every thing offers a foundation for greatness. Her children are distinguished for their chivalrous qualities, their pride, their scorn of sordid views, their sense of honor, their capacity for intellectual attainments, their inflexible virtues.

Intrusted with powers bounded by precedent, or by conscience alone, — powers which, in other hands, might have proved fatal to the community, — the kings of Spain, with a few striking exceptions, have not been tyrants. Her nobility and gentry are not more distinguished for illustrious descent than for unsullied honor and boundless generosity. Many of her ecclesiastics, excepting the useless and profligate friars, — her secular priests especially, — would honorably sustain a comparison in learning with those of any country, and have generally been not only patriots, but often among the foremost defenders of popular rights, as understood by monarchists. Her citizens, even her rustics, are distinguished for native intelligence, for an honest hereditary pride, for the virtues of hospitality, of simplicity, of sincerity, in a degree almost without

---

* VISIGOTHIC KINGS IN SPAIN.

Date of Accession
A. D.

411. Ataulphus.
415. Sigeric, (a few days.)
415. Wallia.
420. Theodored.
451. Thorismund.
452. Theodoric I.
466. Euric.
483. Alaric.
506. Gesaleic.
511. Theodoric II.
522. Almeric.
531. Theudis.
548. Theudisel.
549. Agilan.
554. Athanagild I.
567. Liuva I.
570. Leovigild.
587. Recared I.
601. Liuva II.
603. Witteric.
610. Gundemar.
612. Sisebert.
Recared II., three months.
621. Swintila.
631. Sisenand.
636. Chintila.
640. Tulga.
642. Chindaswind.
649. Receswind.
672. Wamba.
680. Ervigor.
687. Egica.
701. Witiza.
709. Roderic.
711. Theodomir.
743. Athanagild II., in Valencia, and tributary to Moors.

SUEVIC KINGS.

409. Hermenric.
438. Rechila.
448. Rechiarius.
457. Maldras.
460. Frumarius.
464. Remismund. This was the last independent king; besides, are
550. Carriaric.
559. Theodomir.
569. Mir.
582. Eboric.
583. Andeca. He was dethroned by Leovigild, who destroyed the Suevic government in 584

VANDALIC KINGS.

409. Gunderic.
425. Genseric. He passed to Africa with his whole nation.

MOORISH SOVEREIGNS.

Emirs.

711. Tarik, Musa.
714. Abdelasis.
715. Ayub, Alhaur.
721. Alsama.
722. Abderahman.
724. Ambisa.
726. Hodeira, Yahia.
727. Othman, Hodeira ben Alhaus, Alhaitam.
728. Mohammed.
729. Abderahman. (2d time.)
733. Abdelmelic.
736. Ocba.
741. Abdelmelic. (2d time.)
742. Baleg, Thalaba.
743. Husam.
744. Thueba.
746. Yussuf.

Kings.

755. Abderahman I. ben Moawyah.
787. Hixem I.
796. Alhakem I.
821. Abderahman II.
852. Mohammed I.
886. Almondhir.
888. Abdalla.
912. Abderahman III.
961. Alhakem II.
976. Hixem II.
1012. Suleyman.
1015. Ali.
1017. Abderahman IV.
1018. Alcassim.
1023. Abderahman V., Mohammed II.
1026. Hixem III.

Reguli of Cordova.

1031. Gehwar.
1044. Mohammed ben Gehwar.
1060. Mohammed Almoateded.
1069. Mohammed Almostadir.

Almoravide Dynasty. (African.)

1094. Jusef.
1107. Ali.
1144. Taxfin.

Almohade Dynasty. (African.)

1147. Abdelmumen.
1163. Jusef.
1178. Yacub.
1199. Mohammed.
1213. Abu Yacub.
1223. Abulmelic, Abdelwahid
1225. Almamon, Abu Ali.

Kings of Grenada.

1238. Mohammed I.
1273. Mohammed II.
1302. Mohammed III.
1309. Nassir.
1313. Ismail.
1325. Mohammed IV.
1333. Jusef I.
1354. Mohammed V.
1359. Ismail II.
1360. Abu Said.
1391. Jusef II.
1396. Mohammed VI.
1408. Jusef III.
1423. Mohammed VII.
1427. Mohammed VIII.
1429. Mohammed VII., (restored.)
1432. Jusef IV., Mohammed VII., (restored.)
1445. Mohammed IX.
1454. Mohammed X.
1463. Muley Ali.
1483. Abu Abdalla.
1484. Abdalla el Zagal.

CHRISTIAN KINGS.

Of the Asturias and Leon.

718. Pelayo, of the Gothic royal family.
737. Favila.
739. Alfonso I.
757. Fruela I.
768. Aurelio.
774. Mauregato.
788. Bermudo I.
791. Alfonso II.
842. Ramiro I.
850. Ordoño I.
866. Alfonso III.
910. Garcia.
914. Ordoño II.
923. Fruela II.
925. Alfonso IV.
930. Ramiro II.
950. Ordoño III.
955. Sancho I
967. Ramiro III.
982. Bermudo II.
999. Alfonso V.
1027. Bermudo III.

Kings of Castile.

1026. Sancho I., (king of Navarre also.)
1035. Fernando I., (also king of Leon.)
1065. Sancho II.
1072. Alfonso VI.
1109. Urraca, queen, and her husband Alfonso VII. of Leon.
1126. Alfonso II., (emperor.)
1157. Sancho III.
1158. Alfonso III.
1214. Enrique I. (Henry.)
1217. Fernando III.
1230. Also king of Leon.

Kings of Leon and Castile

1252. Alfonso X.
1284. Sancho IV.
1295. Fernando IV.
1312. Alfonso XI.
1350. Pedro the Cruel.
1369. Enrique II.
1379. Juan I.
1390. Enrique III.
1406. Juan II.
1454. Enrique IV.
1474. Isabel and her husband, Fernando V., who was, in
1479, Fernando II. of Aragon.
1504. Juana and Philip I (Austrian.)
1512. Navarre united to Castile.
1516. Aragon united to Castile.

SPANISH SOVEREIGNS.

Austrian Dynasty.

1516. Carlos I., (Charles V., emperor.)
1558. Philip II.
1598. Philip III.
1621. Philip IV.
1665. Carlos II. (Charles.)

Bourbon Dynasty.

1700. Philip V.
1746. Fernando VI.
1759. Carlos III.
1789. Carlos IV.
1833. Isabella II.

example. The character of the lower classes is, however, demoralized by the great prevalence of the lawless habits of the smuggler, who plies his adventurous employment in almost every part of Spain.

Spanish Smugglers.

Though composed of many mingled races, there is yet a degree of unity in the Spanish character, the general traits of which we have enumerated. But, in the midst of this unity, there is a variety in the several provinces. Every where the character is strongly marked; but its shades are said to differ, in comparison, between different portions of the same nation, more than those of some separate kingdoms in other parts of Europe. This is owing to the low state of industry, natural barriers and want of roads, all preventing that freedom and frequency of intercourse which give uniformity of character to nations differently situated. The more unfavorable peculiarities of disposition in the several regions of Spain have been thus graphically described. The Biscayans are haughty, irascible, and passionate; the Galicians are melancholy and unsocial, but industrious and brave; the Catalonians are impetuous and indocile, but energetic and indefatigable; the Aragonese are devoted to their country, and attached to their ancient customs; the Castilians are grave and proud; the Estremadurans, insolent and vain; the Andalusians, arrogant; the Murcians, dull; the Valencians, gay.

Such is the substance of the Spanish character. In its leading traits, it is noble and lofty; but, unhappily, pervading ignorance and poverty, the result of continued political and religious oppression, have debased a large portion of the people, especially in the towns and cities. Such, indeed, has been the influence of the government upon the national spirit, that, for several centuries, Spain has been a feeble and insignificant power in the great balance of Europe.

The present government is a constitutional monarchy, and gives hope of restoring Spain to its proper place among the nations. Under the present constitution, essentially that of 1812, no one can be imprisoned without a fair trial; property cannot be confiscated at the will of the sovereign; the taxes are so regulated, that all persons contribute in proportion to their means; the liberty of the press is established and men of merit are eligible to any honorable employments, although they may not be of noble birth. The deputies of the cities are elected every three years, and the *Cortes*, composed of the nobility, higher clergy, and these deputies, meets regularly once a year.

The Cortes is an institution peculiar to Spain. The first mention of deputies of the people is in the Cortes of Leon, A. D. 1188, and of Castile, the same year. Thus, at the convocation of the states at Burgos, forty-eight towns were represented by deputies selected by lot. Popular representation, therefore, existed in Spain a half century earlier than in Germany or England. Assemblies of the Cortes were very frequent in the reign of Ferdinand IV. Deputies of thirty-two towns fraternized, in 1295, in defence of popular rights against brute force; and, in 1315, the nobles and deputies from a hundred communities confederated for the same purpose. But the Cortes was ineffectual to suppress the flagrant disorders of the times, which could only be quieted by the consolidation of the royal power in the hands of Alfonso XI. He exchanged the Teutonic for the Roman jurisprudence.

Our limits will not allow us to trace further the growth of the Spanish constitution, which was "in an especial degree the work of accident,"—the natural growth of time and circumstances. We can only remark that the fourteenth century was the brightest period of municipal glory and of popular representation. But even then the representation was very imperfect; and, in the next century, after being confined to eighteen cities, the Cortes became a mere convenience of the sovereign, for registering the royal decrees and raising supplies, like the present Russian senate. It was the same in the time of Ferdinand and Isabella.

The office of *Justiza* was another peculiarly Spanish institution. By the ancient constitution of Aragon, the person of him who held this was sacred, and his jurisdiction was almost unbounded. He was the supreme interpreter of the laws, and arbiter in the last resort; it was even his prerogative to inspect the conduct of the king. He combined the offices of the Athenian ephori and the Roman tribunes. A succession of able men gave dignity and stability to the office. The Justiza, therefore, became of great use as an arbiter between king, nobles, and people, liege and vassal, the weak and the powerful, the state and the individual. But the origin and extent of this officer's authority is much disputed.

The only religion tolerated in Spain is the Roman Catholic. Its priests and friars we have already characterized, as also that frightful instrument of spiritual tyranny, the Inquisition. The Spaniard seems more naturally religious than most nations, and Spain has generally been the paradise of priests. Ecclesiastics have accumulated enormous estates; and, though much of the church property has passed to other hands, the revenues of some of the sees are still extravagant Pilgrimages and processions have been and are favorite modes for the manifestation of devotion. Many religious orders have been instituted in this devout country, among which none was more noble and god like in its object than that of the Order of Mercy for the Redemption of Christian Captives, founded in 1198. In forty years, it numbered six hundred houses, all engaged in freeing captives from the miseries of slavery—the usual fortune of the vanquished in war

A system of popular education cannot be said to exist in Spain. But, though there has been a great deficiency of schools for the people, the universities of Spain have been famous in past ages, and an attention to popular education is on the increase. Little progress, however, is to be expected, so long as religious despotism lies at the foundation of society.

The Spanish language is remarkable for dignity and melodiousness. It is formed of Latin, Gothic, and the tongues of primeval Spain, with copious additions from the Arabic. In the eighth and ninth centuries, teachers of Latin were procured from Spain, to teach that language in Italy. The sixteenth century was the Augustan age of Spanish literature. Cervantes, Calderon, Lope de Vega, Ercilla, Quevedo, are some of its great names. The Don Quixote of Cervantes had great effect in moulding his own age, and is still read

Cervantes.

and admired. Lope de Vega is a dramatist of incredible fecundity, and, with Calderon, is remarkable for brilliant poetical language and fertility of invention. The Araucana, an epic poem of Ercilla, celebrating the Spanish contest with the indomitable Araucanians of South America, still holds its place among the few epics that are read. Spanish writers, in all departments, are so numerous, that it is impossible here even to name those of merit in each. Their works commence as far back as the close of the twelfth century, when the Castilian language, the standard of the Spanish, took a permanent form. The earliest Spanish composition extant is the poem of the Cid, which dates about A. D. 1200.

It is difficult to estimate the political power of Spain at the present moment. It would depend greatly on the universality and depth of the sentiment that called her energies into action. Her cities, an important element of national power, are reviving, and begin to resume a flourishing aspect, denoting that her moneyed ability is increasing. The principal of these are interesting in an historical point of view. Madrid was founded in the midst of an arid country, and Philip II. is supposed to have committed a great mistake in not making Lisbon his capital, instead. The city, though possessing many stately edifices, has rather a gloomy air, chiefly from the long, dead walls of its numerous convents. It numbers little less than half a million of people. Barcelona, the most liberal of the cities of Spain, has one or two fine streets, and a busy, energetic, and liberty-loving population, mostly engaged in manufactures and the Mediterranean trade. Cadiz, at the other extremity of the kingdom, is also renowned for its freedom of thought—the result of commerce and enterprise. It long held the monopoly of the colonial trade, and now does most of the business of Spain upon the Atlantic. Carthagena is at present of little consequence; but Malaga, so renowned in Moorish story, retains much commercial importance, especially from the rich vineyards in its neighborhood. Toledo figures in ecclesiastical history. Cordova, Seville, and Grenada, are famed in the wars with the Moors. These are still flourishing and beautiful cities, full of interesting historical associations. Pampeluna and Saragossa have added to their ancient warlike

Gibraltar

renown by modern deeds of heroism. Gibraltar, considered one of the strongest fortresses in the world, has a town below it, with considerable commerce. Both fortress and town belong to the English. Several seaports on the Bay of Biscay enrich the frugal, energetic, and industrious people in that quarter by their fisheries. Wool, silk, olives, grapes, wines, and soap, are the chief articles of produce which give activity to the cities and towns of Spain.

This misgoverned country has been exhausted not only by foreign, but by civil war. Yet her force may be only slumbering. The former glory of her people denotes a strength of character from which, when thoroughly aroused, great things may reasonably be expected. Liberty,—freedom of body, will, and worship,—might yet give to Spain a glory infinitely beyond that which the gold of Mexico and Peru produced.

The navy (1863), contains 250 vessels; the army, 200,000 men; the revenue has risen to one hundred millions per annum. There is reason to hope that the malign influences, civil, social, and religious, which have so long operated to retard the due development of the Spanish race, have now, in a great measure, ceased, and that, under the salutary operation of her present more liberal constitution, — perfected as we trust it may be by future modification, — Spain may become something worthy of herself — proportionate, in happiness and grandeur, to the high natural endowments of her people, and to the long and severe education she has experienced.

CHAPTER CCCLXXXVI.

The Gypsies — Their Origin and History — Their Manners, Habits, and Condition, in various Countries — General Characteristics.

OUR account of the Spanish peninsula would be incomplete without a notice of that remarkable race, the Gypsies, who have long existed in this country, isolated from the rest of the community. They are also found in several other countries of Europe; but the accounts we have of those of Spain, where they are said to number some forty or fifty thousand individuals, are most complete.

Every where, the Gypsy race live a vagabond life in the spirit of one of their rude songs: —

"Too much rest is rust;
There's ever cheer in changing;
We lose by too much trust;
Let's be up and ranging."

They generally reside in tents, which they pitch in bye places; and, when the resources of the neighborhood are exhausted, — that is, when every henroost they can reach is robbed, and every movable thing they can stealthily lay hands on is pilfered; when the men have jockeyed all who will deal with them in horses, and prescribed for all men and animals who will be doctored by them; and when the fortunes of all the silly people of the vicinity have been told by the women, — the vagrant troop suddenly decamp from their filthy lair, greatly to the relief of the inhabitants in the vicinity. Though probably one of the most beautiful of races by nature, — as might be inferred from the beauty of their infants even now, — yet habitual exposure to the burning rays of the sun, the biting of the frost, and the pelting of the rain and snow, destroys their beauty at an early age, and their ugliness at an advanced period of life is no less remarkable than the loveliness of their infancy.

Itinerant Gypsies.

For a period of more than four hundred years, this singular people have been strolling, with little change, over Europe, like foreigners and strangers. Their "hand against every man, and every man's hand against" them, they are the Ishmaelites of civilization. Africa makes them no blacker, nor Europe whiter; they neither learn to be lazy in Spain, nor diligent in Germany; they neither reverence Christ in Christendom, nor Mahomet in Turkey. The year in which they first made their appearance in Europe is nowhere recorded; but it is clear they did not originate in that quarter of the globe. In Russia, they are styled *Zigani*; in Turkey and Persia, *Zingarri*; in Germany, *Zigeuner*; and in Spain, *Zincali*, supposed to mean *blacks of Zend*, or *India*. Indeed, some learned men trace them to the neighborhood of the River Indus, and suppose them to have been Hindoos of a very low caste, driven from their native country by Tartar invaders. In Spain, they are also called *Gitanos*, and in England, *Gypsies*, from a general belief that they were originally Egyptians. The French call them *Bohemians*, as they first attracted attention in Bohemia, though they had previously been long wandering in the remote parts of Sclavonia. In their own language, they call themselves and their language *Rommany*, a word of Sanscrit origin, signifying *The*

Husbands. The unchangeableness of their manners and institutions points to a very ancient and an Oriental origin.

In 1417, they are mentioned near the North Sea, and the next year in Switzerland; in 1422, in Italy, and, a few years after, in France and Spain. They did not travel in a single body, but in separate hordes, each having its leader, sometimes called a *Count*, as, in England, their chief is still called *King of the beggars.* Others gave themselves out for dukes and kings of Lesser Egypt. People believed them to be Egyptians and pilgrims, who were constrained to wander on some religious account. The Gypsies told fabulous stories, to spread this belief, and these were received with such credulity, that they were every where allowed free passage. Even in Spain, the Inquisition overlooked these practical pagans, being, probably, intent on hawking at richer, and therefore more profitable game. In Hungary, too, they were no less free, though in the midst of slaves. The early golden age of the Gypsies, alluded to above, lasted half a century, when their impostures were exposed, and they were discovered to be inveterate vagabonds and robbers by profession. From this period, they began to suffer persecution.

In Russia, the Gypsies are found in all parts of the country except St. Petersburg, from which place they have been banished. In most of the towns, they support themselves by trading in and doctoring horses; but the greater part of them lead an unsettled life upon the vast grassy plains, which afford them pasturage for herds, and plenty of wild game. Fortune-telling and robbery are among their employments. They resist cold to a wonderful degree; and it is not uncommon to find them encamped in the midst of snow, in slight canvas tents, when the weather is twenty-five or thirty degrees below zero. But among the Gypsies of Moscow, there are many who inhabit stately houses, go abroad in elegant equipages, intermarry in good society, and are not behind the higher order of Russians, either in appearance or mental acquirements. This arises mostly from the perfection the female part of this colony have acquired in the vocal art.

In Hungary the habits of this people are abominable; their hovels are sinks of filth, their dress is rags, and their food the vilest aliments. Yet no people are merrier. They sing and dance perpetually, and play the violin with great skill. They are addicted to horse-dealing, and are likewise tinkers and smiths in a small way. Thieving and fortune-telling are added to their occupations in this country, as everywhere else. Napoleon brought several of them, in his army, from Hungary into Spain,; and many interesting scenes ensued between them and their compatriots, the Gitanos, who were astonished at the proficiency of their brethren in the art and mystery of thieving, and looked up to them, consequently, as superior beings.

The race appeared in England three centuries ago; but a persecution, aiming at their extermination, was raised against them; and the gallows, that prominent characteristic of English civilization, groaned under the weight of Gypsy carcasses. But these days passed by, and the miserable remnant crept forth from the secret holes where they had burrowed, increased in numbers, and, each tribe or family taking a particular circuit, fairly divided the land, as a foraging ground, among them. The men are horse-jockeys, devoting their leisure to tinkering; they are always to be found at the prize-fight and race-course. The women tell fortunes. Both sexes are arrant cheats and thieves. They usually pitch their tents in some green lane, or on the side of a common, near a village,

A Gypsy Fortune-teller.

under the shelter of a high bank, trees, or a hedge The English Gypsies are the handsomest of their race, they speak English with fluency, and, in their gait and demeanor, have the ease and grace of the free sons of the wild.

In France, the police have nearly rid the country of them. In Italy, they are not allowed to remain two nights in any one place. They are scattered, though not in great numbers, over Germany, Denmark, and Sweden. Many of the race are found in Turkey, especially at Constantinople, where the females frequently enter the harems of women of rank, pretending to cure children of the "evil eye," and to interpret dreams. They also appear in the coffee-houses as dancing-girls, and peddle precious stones, and sometimes poisons. They are common in Moldavia, Wallachia, and Servia.

The Gypsies of Spain, for many years after their arrival in that country, made no change in the usual vagabond habits of the race, except that they became, from the disordered state of society there, even more unprincipled, reckless, lawless, and mischievous, than elsewhere. They were often in league with the *contrabandistas*, or smugglers. A large band of them would encamp in the neighborhood of a remote village, scantily peopled, and remain there till, like a swarm of locusts, they had consumed every thing they could in any way appropriate, or until driven off by the officers of justice. Then followed a hurried march. The women and children, mounted on lean but spirited asses, scoured along the plains. Ragged and savage-looking men, wielding the scourge and goad, scampered at their side or close behind, whilst a small party, on strong horses, armed with rusty matchlocks and sabres, brought up the rear, threatening the distant foe, and now and then saluting them with a hoarse blast from the Gypsy horn.

"Let us for a moment suppose," says a recent author "some unfortunate traveller, mounted on a handsome mule, or a beast of some value, meeting, unarmed and alone, such a rabble rout at the close of the day, in the wildest part, for example, of La Mancha. We will suppose that he is journeying from Seville to Madrid, and that he has left behind him the gloomy and horrible passes of the Sierra Morena. His bosom, which for some time past, has been contracted with dreadful forebodings, is beginning to expand; his blood, which had been chilled in his veins, is beginning to circulate warmly and freely; he is fondly anticipating the distant inn and savory omelet. The sun is sinking rapidly behind the wild mountains in his rear; he has reached the bottom of a small valley, where runs a rivulet, at which he allows his tired animal to drink; he is about to ascend the side of a hill; his eyes are turned upward; suddenly he beholds strange and uncouth forms at the top of the ascent; the descending sun slants his rays upon red cloaks, with here and there a turbaned head, or long, streaming hair. The traveller hesitates; but, reflecting that he is no longer in the mountains, and that, in the open road, there is no danger of banditti, he advances. In a moment, he is in the midst of a Gypsy group, and there is a general halt. Fiery and snakelike eyes are turned upon him, full of intense expression; he hears a jabbering, in a language unintelligible to his ears. At length, an ugly-looking urchin springs from the crupper of a halting mule, and, in a lisping accent, entreats charity in the name of the Blessed Virgin. The traveller, with a faltering hand, produces his purse. In an instant, a huge, knotted club, from an unseen hand, strikes him headlong from his mule. Next morning, a naked corpse, smeared with blood and brains, is found upon the road; and, within a week, a simple cross marks the spot, and records the event, according to the custom of Spain. Such are the anecdotes related by the Spanish writers of these people."

The Spanish Gypsies have, however, to a considerable degree, renounced their wandering life. They have insensibly become more civilized by residence in towns: mental culture is not entirely neglected, and their education and acquirements are said to be, on the whole, not inferior to those of the lower classes of Spaniards. Nor during the wide-spread disorganization of society consequent upon the ferocious civil wars in which the peninsula has been so frequently involved, have these settled Gypsies returned to the usual roving and marauding habits of their people.

Among the characteristics common to the Gipsy race in general, beside those of rejecting agriculture and regular service of every kind, filthiness, jockeying, pilfering, iron-working, tinkering, and fortune-telling, already enumerated, — it may be remarked that they have many Oriental notions, are strongly attached to their own peculiar habits of life and modes of thinking, are destitute of the Christian ideas of morality except in regard to female chastity, and live as atheists without worship or a belief in the immortality of the soul. They invariably preserve every custom or fancy which has once been current among them, be it ever so noxious or absurd, while any affection which has once predominated in their minds, retains its dominion for ages. Their marriage festivals are boisterous, bizarre, and often ruinously extravagant. The themes of their rude poetry, which generally consists of single verses, scraps, or catches, are, of course, the various incidents of Gypsy life, cattle-stealing, prison adventures, assassination, revenge, &c. Amongst these effusions are sometimes found tender and beautiful thoughts; but they are few and far between, like the occasional flower or shrub adorning the rugged crags and gloomy dens in which most of the race love to harbor.

Portugal.

CHAPTER CCCLXXXVII.

Origin of the Portuguese Monarchy — Its most renowned Kings — Flourishing Period — Decline — Present Condition — General Views.

Portugal occupies the western part of the Spanish peninsula: it is three hundred and fifty miles long, and about one hundred and twenty broad. The climate, face of the country, and products, are similar to those of Spain. The Tagus is the principal river. Lisbon, the capital, is situated on its northern bank, ten miles from its mouth. The following are the political divisions of the country: —

Provinces.	*Population*, 1862.	*Chief Cities.*
Minho,	860,479	Oporto.
Tras-os-Montes,	324,295	Villa Real.
Beira, Upper,	1,036,629	Coimbra.
" Lower,	149,964.	
Estremadura,	755,122	Lisbon.
Alentejo,	305,404	Evora.
Algarve,	152,784	Faro.
Population of Portugal,	3,584,677	

The commercial enterprise of Portugal formerly gave her rich colonies in every quarter of the world: at present, these are reduced to the Azores, Madeira, Cape Verd, and Guinea islands, Angola and Mozambique in Africa, and Goa, Dilli, Macao, &c., in Asia.

As Portugal, geographically considered, is but an appendage to Spain, so in its history it is blended with that country till the eleventh century. Its ancient name was *Lusitania;* its modern name of *Portugal* was derived from *Oporto*, one of its principal towns. The history of the country, while a portion of Spain, will be found in our account of that kingdom. The history of Portugal, as an independent state, will now be given.

The government of Portugal from the Minho to the Tagus, and the right of conquering as far as the Guadiana, were conferred, A. D. 1095, by Alonso VI. of Castile, on *Henri* of Besançon, who in 1072 had married the king's illegitimate daughter Teresa. Whether this territory was given in full sovereignty, or merely as a feudal fief, is much disputed: the latter is most likely.* The administration of Henri, or

* For three centuries, most of Northern Portugal had been subject to local governors, dependent on the counts of Galicia; yet the Mahometans sometimes seized on the strong fortresses, and kept possession of them as long as they could. Thus Coimbra, Viseu, and Lamego, which had been reduced by Alfonso I. and his immediate successors, were recovered, in 997, by the great Almanzor. In 1027, King Alfonso V. of Leon fell before Viseu, the siege of which was in consequence abandoned; but, in 1057, both it and Lamego were recovered by his son-in-law Ferdinand I., and Coimbra the following year. In 1093, Santarem, Lisbon, and Cintra were reduced by Alfonso VI., the famous conqueror of Toledo, whose arms were generally so successful against the misbelievers. As these conquests were continually exposed to the irruptions of the Almoravides, they were disposed of in 1095, as stated in the text.

Count Henrique, as he was called, was vigorous, and his triumphs over the Moors, in concert with his father-in-law and alone, were numerous and important. He died in 1112, leaving the chief towns of Portugal enriched, by his liberality, with many ecclesiastical structures.

Teresa, widow of the deceased count, assumed the government during the minority of his son *Alfonso I.* Violence, unbridled passions, and unnatural jealousy toward her son, distinguished her conduct, and Alfonso was at length obliged to take the reins of government from her by force, which he did in A. D. 1128. He was a formidable enemy to the Moors, and obtained a signal victory over them at the battle of Ourique, in 1139; after which signal success, he assumed the title of *king*.

The count had assembled an army at Coimbra, to reduce the Almoravide fortresses of Southern Portugal. The Mahometan governor of Badajos summoned all his brethren of the neighboring provinces to arms, procured a vast reënforcement from Africa, and advanced to the plains of Ourique, forty miles north-east of Lagos, where the Christians had penetrated and lay encamped. Despondency seized the Christians when they beheld the immense host of their foes, covering hill and valley, far and near. But Alfonso I., who had chosen and fortified a strong position on an eminence, was able, by the force of personal courage and conduct, to banish the misgivings of his troops, and inspire them with his own unconquerable spirit. Their religious enthusiasm was aroused by a tale of wonder. The count, on the eve of battle, we are told, opened the Bible, and the first passage which struck his eye was the victory of Gideon: suddenly he fell asleep, and saw in vision the Savior of men, who promised him victory on the morrow, and prosperity to the sixteenth generation. Certain of the crown of victory or that of martyrdom, the soldiers of the count were now roused to the highest pitch of fanatic valor, and routed the enemy after a furious battle. Two hundred thousand Mahometans are said to have been left dead on the field of battle!

Alfonso was several times assisted in his enterprises by armies of crusaders going to the Holy Land. A fleet of them, under William Longsword, king of England, assisted him in recovering Lisbon. The incidents connected with the taking of Evora are characteristic of the times. Giraldo the Dauntless, fleeing from justice, became a bandit in the wilds of Alemtejo, and was long the terror alike of Moors and Christians. Remorse at last prompted him to retrieve his past life by some act which should procure him pardon. Noticing that Evora was negligently guarded, he watched an opportunity for taking the redoubt on a gentle eminence which protected the gate. The guard was a Moor, who, while he slept, left his daughter to watch the gate. She too fell asleep, and Giraldo, stealing up the hill, cut off the heads of both father and daughter, and held them up as a signal to his comrades below. A few of these now advanced to the gate of the city, and showed themselves, while the chief force lay in ambush. The garrison, enraged to be braved by so small a band, rushed forth tumultuously, and pursued the Christians, who fled as they approached. The party in ambush now seized the unguarded gate, spread along the streets, forced the houses, and inflicted horrible carnage, till the people consented to submit to Alfonso. The king rewarded this exploit with the pardon of the banditti, and made their chief governor of the captured city.

The taking of Santarem presents a picture of woe darker in its shading than was common even in those bloody ages. The fortifications were strong, and stratagem was therefore resorted to. A small band of resolute men were sent, at the dead of night, to scale the walls: having done this, they opened the gates to the Christian troops, who rushed in. The struggle which ensued, amid the darkness of night, the clash of weapons, the yells of fighting and the groans of dying warriors, with the shrieks of women and infants, who were indiscriminately butchered — constituted a scene of horror which the fell demon of war alone could delight to witness!

Dom Fuas Roupinho was one of the most celebrated heroes of these wars. He was one of the captains, under Sancho, the son of the king. Many stories like the following are told of him. Returning one day to his fortress with a small band, he found it furiously assailed by a numerous body of the enemy. His followers wished to attack them in flank, but Dom Fuas, thinking his garrison valorous enough to hold out, restrained his soldiers. At nightfall, the Moors, fatigued with the day's fighting, retired to their tents. "Now," said the fierce captain to his band, "God hath put these infidels into our hands." They descended the hill, softly as the mountain mist, fell on the sleeping Moors, and slaughtered them with impunity: very few escaped. The valor of Dom Fuas caused the king to intrust him with a fleet, and he was no less successful on a new element, destroying the navy of the enemy, and even insulting the coast of Barbary.

During the reign of *Sancho I.*, who succeeded his father, Alfonso I., in 1186, Portugal suffered from the wrath of the pope, and from pestilence, and famine. The first was caused by the king's marrying a daughter to her cousin, Alfonso IX., king of Leon, and placed both Portugal and Leon under the papal interdict; the two other scourges were attributed by the superstitious people to the same cause. The last eight years of his reign were tranquil, and were spent by Sancho in efforts to encourage population, relieve distress, and provide for the true happiness of his people.

His successor, *Alfonso II.*, refused to give to his brothers the vast sums of money left them by their father's will, and seized two fortresses, which had been given to his sisters, afterwards deified as Saints Teresa and Sancha. But the pope arranged that the fortresses should be held for the sisters by the Knights Templars, and, at the death of the princesses, should revert to the crown. This king was so corpulent, that he effected little in war against the Moors. Miracles, favoring the Christians, were not wanting, however, according to the old chroniclers, when he did battle for the cross.

The story of the taking of the important fortified town of Moura, in this reign, is singular and romantic. Saluquia, a lady of rank, was betrothed to the noble Moor Brafama, and this town was to be her dowry. At the time appointed for the wedding, two Christian hidalgos, having dressed up a troop of their followers as Moors, surprised and massacred the bridegroom and his attendants as they were approaching the fortress. They then rode into the town, on the tower of which Saluquia stood waiting the arrival of her destined husband, and shouted out to her in Arabic that they escorted the happy Brafama. The maiden ordered the gates to be opened; but, as soon as she saw the carnage which ensued, suspecting the truth, and disdaining to become the captive of her lover's murderers, she threw herself headlong from the tower. Ever after the tower was called *Moura*, or "the Mooress."

Alfonso II. taxed the possessions of the church, in which he was plainly right, and obliged the churchmen to lead their vassals to battle in person, in which he was as plainly wrong. The archbishop of Braga remonstrated, and finally anathematized the king and his counsellors, for doing which he was deprived of his revenues, and compelled to flee the kingdom. Pope Honorius III. sent three Castilian bishops to insist on ample reparation. On its refusal, they excommunicated the king, and interdicted the kingdom the performance of all the rites of worship and religion. The afflicted people urged a reconciliation; the king yielded, was absolved, and the interdict removed. But, in the midst of this affair, the king died. His son and successor, *Sancho II.*, (A. D. 1223,) dared not retract the concessions his father had made, but busied himself in fighting the Moors, and that very successfully. Taking fortress after fortress, he won from them the possession of Algarve. The king, however, was of a weak constitution and feeble mind, though not vicious. Great disasters afflicted his kingdom, and the native historians have stigmatized his memory; principally, no doubt, on account of his hostility to the immunities of the clergy. It is certain that his creatures oppressed that body at times. It appears also that the king did not repress the feuds and excesses of his barons, and treated the remonstrances of his people with contempt. Pope Innocent IV., therefore, gave the crown to his brother, *Alfonso III.*, who was assisted to usurp it (A. D. 1245) by the Castilians. Bigamy of the king, and ignoble disputes with prelates and the military orders, marked this reign; and, as often has happened, the usurper, though at first lavish of promises and favors, showed himself, when his throne was established, a rapacious and unprincipled tyrant.

King *Dinis*, who next ascended the throne, A. D. 1279, though the son of Alfonso III., was one of the best of the Portuguese monarchs. Finding himself, like his predecessors, embroiled with the church, and perceiving that it must eventually triumph against him,—for, in these ages, papal encroachments were systematic, uniform, and always successful,—he sought to gain conditions by voluntary submission. He therefore convoked his prelates, and arranged articles of mutual concession and reconciliation with the church. He experienced trouble from the rebellion of a brother, and the quarrels of a natural and a legitimate son—a just punishment for having himself fomented the rebellions which distracted the neighboring kingdom of Castile.

This king reigned forty-five years. He was a great friend to literature, and founded the universities of Lisbon and Coimbra, which were soon crowded with students, most of whom were intended for the profession of law, as commerce was considered degrading to young men of high birth. Trade, however, was beginning to flourish, and the king took great pains to promote industry by encouraging it and manufactures, also. In this reign the order of Templars was abolished.

The son of the king, *Alfonso IV.*, had often rebelled, and was abetted by most of the idle and spendthrift young men of the kingdom. He even neglected the exhortations of his dying father, and, instead of attending to business, gave his whole time to the chase Soon after his accession, which occurred in 1325 some very important business had been delayed while the king was absent, for a whole month, on a hunting excursion. Upon his return, the ministers told him that if he continued to spend his time in such frivolous pursuits, they must choose another king. Alfonso who had entered the council chamber in his hunting dress, covered with dust, quitted the room in a very angry mood; but, on reflection, he saw that he was wrong. Changing his attire for a dress more suitable to a state council, he returned, and, ascending the throne with a dignified air, declared that he would thenceforth conduct himself, not as a sportsman, but as a king. He kept his word, and the country, during his reign, was as prosperous as in the time of King Dinis.

But Alfonso was a stern, unfeeling man, as appears from his conduct to Inez de Castro, whose tragical fate is still held in sad remembrance. She was a young and beautiful Castilian lady, who was secretly married to the king's eldest son, Don Pedro; but as the prince was afraid to acknowledge this alliance to his father, he kept his wife concealed in a retired dwelling near Coimbra, where he visited her as often as he thought he could do so without exciting suspicion. But some of the courtiers discovered the secret, and revealed it to the king, who sent directly for the prince, to ask him if it were true. Don Pedro assured his father that they were mistaken; but, as he positively refused to marry any other lady, every one felt convinced that Inez was his wife. The nobles, jealous of the family of De Castro, and fearful the children of Inez might dispute the crown with Pedro's son by a former wife, conspired against the life of the disowned bride, and the king joined them.

Accompanied by three of his barbarous counsellors, the monarch came to the retreat of their victim, during the absence of her husband on a hunting excursion. Poor Inez, pale and trembling, led her three children toward her stern father-in-law, who entered the apartment alone, with looks denoting the purpose of his visit. Kneeling at his feet, she entreated him not to injure her; and when he saw her so young and lovely, surrounded by his own grandchildren, his heart was softened, and he went away without doing her any harm. His companions reproached his infirmity of purpose, and he told them to go and do what he had left undone. Without staying to give him time to change his mind, they hastened to the house of the unfortunate princess, who now pleaded for mercy in vain, and in a few moments her voice was silenced forever.*

When Don Pedro returned from hunting, his grief and fury at the deed of cruelty knew no bounds. He raised a formidable army, and, not being able to possess himself of the person of the assassins, he destroyed their estates, and laid waste the provinces in which they were situated. But, on their banishment, he disbanded his army, and became reconciled to his father, who died, shortly afterward, full of remorse, A. D. 1357. The outraged prince now ascended the throne as *Pedro I.*; and, giving way to his uncontrollable desire of revenge on the murderers of his beloved Inez, proposed to the king of Castile, with

* In 1361, Pedro I. vindicated the memory of this lady by an oath that she was his lawful wife, taken before the convention of the states; his chamberlain and a bishop likewise swore that they were witnesses of the marriage. Pope John XXII.'s bull of dispensation for it was also produced.

whom they had taken refuge, an exchange of the fugitives from justice in their respective kingdoms. He thus got two of the assassins into his power, and put them to death with horrible tortures. The third, Pacheco, escaped in the dress of a beggar, whom he had often relieved. The grateful mendicant passed, unsuspected in his rags, through the wicket of one of the gates of the town where Pacheco lived, and which had been shut while that nobleman was abroad in the forest, to prevent his getting news of the intended arrest at his return to the city. Encountering his benefactor in the wood, the beggar persuaded him to exchange clothes with himself, and accompany the first body of muleteers he should meet into Aragon. He did so, arrived safely in Aragon, and subsequently went to France, whence he returned, after a time, to his own country.

The savage delight of the king in witnessing the torments of the two accomplices of Pacheco, has probably given him the title by which he is known — *Pedro the Cruel.* The atrocity perpetrated upon his wife, indeed, would be little calculated to teach him mercy. He horsewhipped a bishop for concubinage, and punished adultery with death. He also, to restrain the extravagance and swindling of his nobles, punished those who bought or sold on credit, by stripes for the first offence, and death for the second.

An inferior officer of the law one day complained that a gentleman, on whom he had served a process, had struck him and plucked him by the beard. Pedro turned to the presiding judge, and said, "I have been struck, and my beard has been plucked by one of my subjects." The judge, who understood the appeal, caused the culprit to be arrested and beheaded.

Perceiving that lawsuits were frequent, tedious, and expensive, and shrewdly divining the reason, he purged his court of all advocates and proctors, of all who had a manifest interest in litigation, and reduced all processes to a simple statement of the case by the parties concerned, and of the sentence by the judges, reserving, however, to himself the privilege of deciding appeals. The result was an incredible diminution of lawsuits — as diseases decreased when the physicians were expelled from Rome. Pedro was liberal of rewards, and devoted to music and dancing.

Ferdinand I., son of Pedro by his former wife, Constanza, succeeded his father. He was fickle, impulsive, idle, irresolute, and his very benevolence made him the dupe of designing men. He was the tool of his ambitious and totally unprincipled wife Leonora, an adulteress, forger, and murderess, whose wickedness occasioned him so much mental suffering, that, joined to constitutional weakness, it brought him to a premature grave. His reign was one of the most deplorable that ever afflicted Portugal.

By the death of Ferdinand, in 1583, his daughter Beatrix, queen of Castile, was the true heir to the throne. But it had been stipulated on her marriage, that, if Ferdinand died, a regency should be appointed till Beatrix had a son capable of reigning, and that son must be educated in Portugal. But she had no child at the king's death; her husband, Juan, therefore, claimed the crown in her right, much to the vexation of the Portuguese, who liked neither Juan nor the regent, Leonora, appointed by the late king's will. The populace clamored for Joam, son of Pedro and Inez; but he and his brother now languished in the dungeons of Castile. Finally, another *Joam*, an illegitimate son of Pedro, and grand master of a military order, usurped the regency, which was proffered to him by the people. He was cool, prompt, courageous, and unrestrained by conscience. By granting amnesty and freedom to criminals and prisoners of all kinds, he swelled the ranks of his army, and murder, plunder, rape, and sacrilege, were its constant attendants. The Castilian king invaded Portugal, but unsuccessfully; and the states proclaimed the grand master, king, A. D. 1385. He was the founder of a dynasty which reigned till A. D. 1580.

By his queen Philippa, daughter of the English duke of Lancaster, Joam, or *John I.*, had five sons, all of whom were brave and adventurous princes, especially Don Henry, the third brother, who distinguished himself not only in battle against the Moors of Africa, but by his attention to philosophy, astronomy, and navigation; so that he became the father of maritime discovery among the Portuguese. His object was to find a way round Africa to India; but this was not accomplished till more than a hundred years after. His vessels, however, went as far as Guinea. In the reign of King *John II.*, in 1487, as elsewhere stated, Diaz reached the Cape of Good Hope. This John II. was so excellent a monarch, that he was called the *Perfect Prince.* His great object was to reduce the power of the feudal lords by elevating the middle classes. He therefore examined into the titles of their fiefs and privileges, many of which, being found to be wrongfully obtained, were nullified, and thus several towns and villages were freed from vassalage. Many charters of liberties were also granted to towns; and the king took from the nobles the right of acting as magistrates and judges on their own estates, which gave them power over the lives, persons, and property of their vassals. He ordained, instead, that every man should have a fair trial by an independent court of justice. Such laws would, of course, tend to develop the latent energies of the nation; and it was not long before Portugal rose to be the leading maritime power of the world. The great fault of John II. was his religious intolerance, especially toward the Jews, whom he enslaved and treated with every indignity.

He beheaded the leading noble of his kingdom — the duke of Braganza — who treasonably opposed his reforms; he also banished his powerful family. The nobles now conspired and sent assassins to murder the king. He met the wretches as he ascended the great staircase of the palace alone; and being already aware of the plot, and divining their intention from a sudden signal made by one of them, he demanded, "What is the matter?" with a presence of mind and a commanding air peculiar to himself. "Nothing," replied the assassin, "but that I was near falling." "Beware of falling," rejoined the king, with his usual coolness, and walked on — thus baffling the attempt of the villains. A few days after, while he was in church, he was surrounded by the conspirators again, and again escaped by his imposing presence, as no one of them dared to strike at so much majesty. But their fate approached. Sending for his cousin, the duke of Viseo, the leader of the conspirators, as if on confidential business, he asked him carelessly, after a few moments of indifferent conversation, "Cousin, suppose you knew a man who had sworn to take your life, what would you do?" "I would hasten to take his," replied the duke. "Die, then," replied the king, and plunged a dagger into his heart. Other nobles were executed and the treason suppressed.

In 1491, John's only legitimate son and heir was killed by a fall from a horse. For some time, the king refused to be comforted; his vigorous mind seemed prostrated. His people touchingly condoled with him, gently reproved his grief, and told him he must live for them, since in each of them he had still a son. "The happiness of my subjects is indeed," he replied, "my only consolation. I will labor for their good; but let them pardon me; nature is weak, and I am but a man." This great prince died in 1495. The success of his administration was unrivalled: he introduced industry and comfort among his people, added largely to the national resources, and was, in many respects, the greatest monarch that ever swayed the sceptre of Portugal.

Under *Manuel*, his successor, the passage to India round the Cape of Good Hope was discovered, by a Portugese navigator,. Vasco de Gama, A. D. 1497. After a dangerous passage, he landed at Calicut, on the coast of Malabar, then the emporium of the trade of Hindostan. Its foreign commerce was in the hands of the Arabs, who here purchased spices, precious stones, silks, cottons, cloths, muslins, &c., which passed into Italy by the way of Alexandria. The Arabs became jealous of the Portuguese, at once, and prejudiced the king of the country against them, so that they barely escaped with life, and returned to Portugal after an absence of more than two years. Vasco De Gama was received with as much joy as Columbus had been in Spain, on his return from America. Manuel fitted out a fleet of thirteen ships, under Cabral for the Indies; he discovered Brazil on his way, which, according to the right of discovery, now belonged to Portugal. When the fleet arrived at Calicut, its people were soon so much prejudiced against the strangers by the Arabs, that fifty of them were killed; whereupon the Portuguese fired the town and the Arab vessels, and went to another part of the country. Many settlements were made, missionaries were sent out, and a career of conquest entered upon by Alboquerque and others, which we have detailed in our history of India.

Mistress of the Indian and African trade, her resources fully developed, and the energies of her people aroused, Portugal was now at the height of her prosperity, and Manuel was one of the greatest sovereigns of Europe. He was the first European prince who sent an embassy to China, and opened with it a direct trade: that country was in fact unknown to the West as a great empire, till Portuguese vessels visited Canton in 1516.

At the accession of *John III.*, in 1521, the Spaniards and Portuguese had girdled the earth with their power. While gold was to be obtained by fighting for it, they grew rich, for they were practised in warfare, and were willing to go abroad and make rapid fortunes by plundering the natives of the new world; but as these means were rapidly exhausted, and they would not substitute the slower but surer pursuits of industry, their prosperity was not lasting.

John III. was of a gloomy disposition, and established the Inquisition in Portugal, to force the Jews to embrace Christianity. He was also much attached to the Jesuits, who, under his patronage, converted whole tribes of savages to their religion, such as it was, and taught them the arts of civilized life. *Sebastian*, grandson of the king, was but an infant when John died, A. D. 1557; and during the regency of an aged and timid great uncle, Cardinal Henry, the state lost many of its possessions in Africa and India in less time than it had cost to gain them. On coming of age, Sebastian, with the headstrong rashness of youth, resolved on an expedition to Africa, to restore a prince of Morocco to his throne, and also to recover the territories that had been lost to his kingdom. Deaf to the advice of all his best friends, he embarked with as many troops as he could raise,—quite inadequate, however, in numbers. He was accompanied by most of the young noblemen of Portugal, none of whom were destined ever to return; for they were all killed or made captives in a desperate battle that was fought soon after they landed. Most of them fell by the side of their youthful king, who was seen to rush into the thickest of the fight. A body was found, supposed to be his, but so disfigured as to leave its identity quite doubtful. This was taken back to his country, and buried with magnificence. But the common people of Portugal, even down to the present day, believe that their chivalrous king is still confined in some enchanted castle of the Moors, and will one day return and restore the faded glory of the kingdom.

Cardinal Henry now reigned two years, and on his death, there was no direct heir to the throne, and much bloodshed and quarrelling ensued. It was at last decided that *Philip II.* of Spain had the best right to the crown, and he was proclaimed king; and for sixty years the two kingdoms were united under one sovereign, as England and Scotland are now; but the Portuguese disliked to see their kingdom secondary and ruled by a viceroy. Philip too, being at war with Holland, forbade the Portuguese to furnish the Dutch with India goods; and this, by inducing that nation to trade to India themselves, greatly injured the Portuguese commerce with that wealthy region.

A revolution, planned and executed by some of the leading nobles and clergy, restored the independence of the country, after twenty-three years' fighting. A native sovereign of the house of Braganza was placed on the throne, under the name of *John IV.*, A. D. 1640, thus founding the dynasty which rules Portugal at the present day.

We have space to detail but a few of the events which checker the uniform tendency to decline, noticeable in what remains to be recorded of Portuguese history. *Alfonso VI.*, a king of depraved tastes, profligate habits, and headstrong perversity, was deposed through the management of his French wife. She accused him of impotency, obtained a divorce, and was married to his brother *Pedro*, who ascended the throne, A. D. 1668. *Joseph* introduced salutary reforms, founded schools where Aristotle was forsaken for Bacon, abolished slavery, and merited the bronze statue his people erected to his memory. He was the best monarch Portugal could boast since Philip I.

In the reign of Joseph a most awful calamity occurred at Lisbon, November 1, 1755. The morning of the day was bright, beautiful, and cloudless, when the ground suddenly began to tremble, and the walls of the houses to rock. Men, women, and children rushed shrieking into the streets, and in a few moments many houses fell with a tremendous crash, and frightful chasms opened in the earth, stopping those who were endeavoring to save themselves by flight. The utmost terror, confusion, and despair prevailed every where; and in a few minutes, the fine city of Lisbon was entirely destroyed. The splendid cathedral, churches, convents, palaces, public buildings of all kinds, were, in a moment, a heap of rubbish: twenty thousand persons were destroyed. A conflagration added to the horrors of the earthquake. During the whole of that melancholy winter, the people of Lisbon had no better dwellings than the tents they had erected in the fields. Without food or clothing, they must have perished but for charity. The English parliament granted a large sum of money, and grain, wearing apparel, blankets, &c., were contributed for their relief. Spain, too, rendered every assistance in her power.

Joseph had no son, and his daughter, *Maria*, succeeded him, in **1777**. She had married her uncle. When she became insane, her son, *John VI.*, was made regent, just as the French revolution commenced, 1789. On the refusal of the Portuguese to break their alliance with England, who had reduced them almost to the condition of an English colony, Napoleon sent Junot to invade the country, A. D. 1807. The royal family fled to Brazil—an event more fully noticed in our history of that country. The next year, the British drove the French from Portugal, and the Portuguese took an active part against the latter during the peninsula war. In 1820, an insurrection broke out in consequence of the residence of the royal family in Brazil—a constitution was formed, and Brazil was separated from Portugal, in 1822. The king returned to Lisbon; and since these events, discord, revolution, and civil war have distracted the kingdom. *Miguel*, the king's brother, a bloody tyrant, seized the throne in 1828, and overthrew the constitution. He was expelled by Pedro, his elder brother, emperor of Brazil, who confirmed his own daughter, *Maria II.*, on the throne, A. D. 1834. Pedro V. succeeded her in 1837, and Luis I., in 1861. The latter died in 1863.

The monks, by giving their support to Miguel, had incurred the displeasure of Pedro, who suppressed all the monasteries and convents in the kingdom, and confiscated their property. The Cortes, at his death, divided the lands into small lots, and sold them to laboring people on easy terms—a measure which must strongly tend to revive the prosperity of the nation. The monks, friars, or *padres*, the most idle, profligate, and ignorant portion of the religious communities, are described as "a class who have practised more knavery, and corrupted more morals, than all the world beside. Without principle or regularity of conduct, consisting of the dregs of society, assuming the monkish habit merely to escape a life of drudgery, suffered to prowl wherever they please, using the mask of religion to extort money from the weak, to seduce the wives and daughters of such as afford them hospitality,—they are, and have ever been, a curse to every nation which harbors them." The clergy have a better character.

The people of Portugal are more homogeneous than those of Spain: the rural population are friendly, hospitable, temperate, and polite, but the general character is inferior to the Spanish. In Algarve, a wild and desolate country, the latest rescued from the Arabs, the natives still have a Moorish cast. They are exceedingly ignorant and superstitious, believing every old castle to be enchanted and guarded by some Eastern fairy, till the Moors shall be restored again to their ancient empire and all the splendor of former days. The Spaniards and Portuguese, though of kindred blood, language, and religion, are still mutually hostile to each other. The former have a saying to the effect, that if you take from a Spaniard all his virtues, you make of him a good Portuguese.

The commerce of the kingdom is yet extensive. Wines, oil, oranges, lemons, and other fruits, are exchanged for the linen and woollen cloths, silks, muslins, hosiery, furniture, cutlery, hardware, &c., which are made better and cheaper elsewhere. Portuguese manufactures are generally inferior to the Spanish. The mechanic arts are clumsily practised. Carpenters, masons, smiths, &c., are below our standards of excellence; but the goldsmiths and jewellers of Lisbon exhibit much expertness. The peasantry are extremely poor. Banditti are very numerous in every part of the country—pupils schooled in their employment, doubtless, by the civil wars. They often carry off persons of consequence for the sake of the ransom. Assassinations are so frequent, that, in several districts, the government has suspended "*the guarantees*," an act similar to our *habeas corpus*.

It would be difficult to estimate the resources and power of Portugal, situated as she is at present. A strong government might perhaps bring into the field an army of twenty thousand men. Her navy is inconsiderable. Shorn of all her foreign possessions, with a few exceptions, already noticed, the maritime energy of the nation is but the shadow of what it once was.

The language resembles the Spanish, and is superior to it for conversation. The Portuguese love to speak of it as the "eldest daughter of the Latin." This daughter of Rome has been the servant of the Goths and the Moors; still, however, the mother tongue predominates more in Portugal than in any other part of the world. The Portuguese has the same proportion of Arabic as the Castilian, but it has escaped all guttural sounds.

Literature has obtained some triumphs in this language; but the Lusiad of Camoens, a religious epic describing the exploits of the Portuguese, is almost the only book now thought of when Portuguese literature is mentioned. The country, however, has produced an eminent dramatist, Gil Vicente, and several able historians. No other nation possesses such excellent chroniclers; of these, Lopez, De Barros, and De Couto are the most distinguished.

Kings of Portugal.

Date of Accession.
A. D.
1139. Alfonso I.
1185. Sancho I.
1211. Alfonso II.
1223. Sancho II.
1248. Alfonso III.
1278. Dinis, (Dionis.)
1325. Alfonso IV.
1357. Pedro I.
1367. Ferdinand.
1383. John I.
1433. Duarte, (Edward.)
1438. Alfonso V.
1481. John II.
1495. Manuel, (Emanuel.)

Of the Ancient Dynasty.
1521. John III.
1557. Sebastian.
1578. Henry.

Date of Accession.
A. D.
1580. Philip I. (II. of Spain.)
1598. Philip II. (III. of Spain.)
1621. Philip III. (IV. of Spain.)

House of Braganza.
1640. John IV.
1656. Alfonso VI.
1683. Pedro II.
1707. John V.
1750. Joseph.
1777. Maria I.
1789. John VI.
1826. Regency of Pedro.
1828. Miguel (usurper).
1834. Maria II.
1837. Pedro V. 1861. Luis I.

France.

CHAPTER CCCLXXXVIII.

Geographical Sketch, Ancient and Modern.

THIS country, so celebrated for its fertility,* for the vivacity and refinement of its people, and the large influence the nation has exercised over the fortunes of Europe, especially in modern times, is bounded on the north by the English Channel, Belgium, and Prussia; on the east by Baden, Switzerland, and Sardinia; on the south by the Mediterranean and Spain; on the west by the Atlantic. Its length is about six hundred and sixty by six hundred miles wide; its extent two hundred and ten thousand square miles. The population is thirty-seven millions, or one hundred and seventy-six to the square mile.

The great central chain of mountains is the Cevennes These branch off in various directions under different names. The loftiest peaks are about six thousand feet high. To the east, between France and Switzerland, are the Vosges and Jura mountains; to the southeast, between France and Sardinia, are branches of the Alps; between France and Spain, at the south of the former, are the Pyrenees.

France is watered by various rivers, of which the principal are the Seine, Rhone, Loire, Rhine, Garonne, and Gironde. The Seine is a very crooked stream, four hundred and eighty miles long, its general course being from southeast to northwest. It passes by Paris, and enters the English Channel at Havre. The Rhone, three hundred miles long, rises in the Alps, enters France on the east, and empties into the Mediterranean by four mouths at Marseilles. The Loire, five hundred and fifty miles long, rises in the Cevennes, drains the centre of France, and empties into the Bay of Biscay. The Garonne, three hundred and sixty miles long, rises in the Pyrenees, and empties into the Gironde. The latter is a mere estuary, and empties into the Bay of Biscay.

The Rhine, the Moselle, and the Meuse, have but a portion of their course in France. The other principal rivers are the Somme, flowing into the English Channel; the Charente, and the Adour, into the Bay of Biscay; the Var, into the Mediterranean; the Marne and Oise, tributaries of the Seine; the Allier, Sarthe, and Mayenne, of the Loire; the Lot and Tarn, of the Garonne; and the Isere and Durance, of the Rhone. The lakes of France are few in number and small in extent.

On the north is an arm of the sea, called by the

* In general, the aspect of France, as presented to the eye of a traveller, is less beautiful than that of many other countries. The following is a description furnished by Inglis, an Englishman, who went on foot through the country a few years since. "All panegyric upon the loveliness and laughing fertility of France is rhodomontade. There is more of the beautiful and picturesque in many a single county of England, or even of Scotland, than in all the scattered beauties of France, were they concentrated within a ring-fence, excepting always the Pyrenees, which I cannot help looking upon as a kind of separate territory—the mere boundary between France and Spain; but at all events the Pyrenees must be excepted.

"I have travelled through almost every part of France, and truly I have found its beauties thinly sown. If the banks of some of its rivers be excepted—the Seine, the Loire, the Rhone, and the Garonne—some parts of Normandy, and the departments of the Pyrenees, France is an unromantic, uninteresting, unlovely land; and even in these favored parts, such as the vaunted Orleannois, where shall we find the green meadows that lie along the banks of our Thames, Avon, or Severn? or upon which of them shall we pause to admire those romantic views—that charming variety of rock, wood, and mountain, that characterize the banks of the Tamar, the Wye, the Derwent, the Swale, the Wharff, or the Dove? These are nowhere to be found. * * *

"I pity the man who crosses France in any direction. Thousands know how ennuyant is the journey from Calais to Paris; but they who never travel further, suppose that lovely France, panegyrized by so many, lies beyond. No such thing. Let them continue their journey by whichever road they please, and they will find but little improvement. * * * Chateaux also we have in these provinces (those of the L)—but oh, how different from the chateaux of which we read in the romance writers, and which never existed but in their imaginations! The chateaux are for the most part *boxes* upon a large scale, staring-houses with wings, and a parapet-wall in front, covered with vases of flowers. In short, we find the whole a delusion, and our minds revert to the green acclivities of our own hills, our oak forests, our lakes and rivers, and the beauty and fertility that, along with the picturesque, mingle in an English landscape."

But if the indiscriminating panegyrists of France have gone too far on the one hand, Mr. Inglis has no doubt somewhat overshot the mark on the other. Mr. Maclaren, than whom there can be no better authority, says that from Chalons-sur-Marne to Avignon, the Rhone flows through one of the most beautiful, picturesque, and delightful regions in the world. And there are some other districts in France, the scenery of which will bear a comparison with that of any other country.

British the *English Channel*, but by the French *La Manche.* It is subject to high and impetuous tides. The Bay of Biscay, or Gulf of Gascony, lies on the west of France, and north of Spain. The Lion's Gulf — incorrectly written *Gulf of Lyons* — is a part of the Mediterranean, so called from the violent agitations of its waters.

In the Bay of Biscay are the small islands of Oléron, Ré, Noirmoutier, and Belle Isle; a little farther north is the isle of Ouessant or Ushant. The islands of Alderney, Guernsey, and Jersey, in the English Channel, are politically attached to England. On the southern coast are the Hyères. Corsica, which has been already described, belongs to France; it lies in the Mediterranean, about fifty miles from the Italian, and one hundred from the French, coast.

The face of the country in France is greatly diversified. It has been geologically described as a vast basin, the circumference and centre of which are of primitive formation, the intermediate spaces being filled with tertiary and secondary kinds. In the mountains of the Cervennes, there are the traces of extinct volcanoes, lava streams, &c., showing that, in remote ages, this territory was the scene of volcanic activity. Similar traces are met with on the banks of the Rhine, in the Vosges, and in the department of the Var.

The northern and western coasts of France consist largely of immense downs or sand banks; and even where they are formed by cliffs, the shore is seldom bold enough to be approached with safety; the harbors, therefore, are few. On the Mediterranean shore, the coast of Languedoc is dangerous, but that of Provence abounds in good harbors.

A large part of the soil of France is very superior, though there are many tracts of mountains, heaths and gravel beds, all unproductive. In general the fertility of France seems to have been overrated. Probably one-third part of the territory is not under cultivation, or in any considerable degree productive. The borders of the rivers are generally very fertile.

The climate of France is probably not excelled by that of any other country in Europe. In general, the air is pure and the winters mild, though the difference of latitude, elevation, &c., makes great differences in temperature. At the south, olives, lemons, oranges and figs are produced; in the middle regions, the vine yields in abundance, and here the finest wines are made in great quantities; in the north, the cereal grains, and such fruits as cherries, currants, apples, and pears, come to perfection.

The northern portions are subject to cold and moisture during the winter. In Normandy, snow falls in small quantities, and the rivers are sometimes frozen for two or three months. At Paris, there are light falls of snow, and the Seine is frozen over every four or five years. At Marseilles, the climate is like that of Virginia.

The vegetable products of France are very numerous, the useful plants, as well as the ornamental, having been largely introduced from various parts of the world. Forest trees are extensively cultivated for fuel. Since the revolution of 1793, the lands have been, over a great part of France, very minutely divided. It is said that there are eight millions of landed proprietors in the country. This division is visible in the territories of the north, and especially between Havre and Paris. Very many of these landed estates consist of an acre, a half an acre, or even less, and as each tract is especially devoted to a distinct crop, the whole landscape is striped or chequered like a piece of printed calico. This minute division of the land is supposed to have kept the agriculture of France in a backward state, inasmuch as the small proprietors have neither the enterprise nor the means for making improvements.

One remarkable fact is, that around the towns, the whole lands are under a kind of garden cultivation. Kitchen vegetables are reared in great perfection. In the vine countries, the cultivation of the grape engrosses the attention of the people, yet it is observable that here the great mass of the people are poor, ignorant and depressed. Those parts of France which have long been celebrated as the regions of the vine, in general, present a country and a people as little gratifying to philanthropy, as other less favored parts of the earth.

One of the greatest wants of the northern parts of France is fuel. The coal beds are numerous, but they are in the interior, and as yet no easy means of transportation are afforded. Lead, copper, iron, silver, and other minerals are found, but they are not extensively wrought.

The wild boar is still hunted in the forests of France: bears and wolves are not uncommon. In some of the mountainous districts, these attack and kill persons whom they find alone and unprotected. Children often fall a sacrifice to them, during the winter season, when they are pinched for food. The other wild animals are those which are found in other parts of Central Europe.

The manufactures of France are exceedingly varied, and of great amount. There are numerous canals, and the railroads, radiating from Paris, extend to all parts of the country.

The history of France begins with the wars of the Romans against this country, two or three centuries before the Christian era. It was conquered by Julius Cæsar about 50 B. C. For nearly five hundred years it was under the dominion of the Romans, who built cities, and introduced their arts and civilization into the country. In A. D. 480, Clovis, a Frankish chief, laid the foundation of a kingdom, which has continued to the present day.

The Greeks called this country *Galatia;* the Romans, *Gallia.* The first inhabitants were the Belgæ, who occupied what is now called *Belgium*, and were mingled with the adjacent German tribes; the Gauls, or Celts, who peopled the north; and the Aquitani, who dwelt in the southwest. The latter, bordering on Spain, were blended with the tribes of that country. Ancient Gaul was, therefore, considered as divided into three parts, occupied by these three great nations; but after the conquest by the Romans, the country was divided into four parts, called the *Four Gauls.* These were as follows: —

Divisions.	*No. of Provinces.*	*Chief Cities.*	*Modern Names.*
Gallia Narbonensis,	Five,..	Nemausus,	Nismes.
		Tolosa,	Toulouse.
		Narbo,	Narbonne.
		Viennensis,	Vienne.
		Avenio,	Avignon.
		Gratianapolis,	Grenoble.
		Massilia,	Marseilles.
		Telo Martius,	Toulon.
Gallia Aquitania, ..	Three,	Avaricum,	Bourges.
		Augustonometum,	Clermont.
		Augustoritum,	Limoges.
		Burdigala,	Bourdeaux
		Lapurdum,	Bayonne.

Divisions.	*No. of Provinces.*	*Chief Cities.*	*Modern Names.*
		Lugdunum, ...	Lyons.
		Augustodunum, ...	Autun.
		Alesia,...............	Alise.
		Agedincum,..........	Sens.
GALLIA LUGDUNENSIS,	Four,	Autricum, ...	Chartres.
		Lutetia,...............	Paris.
		Augustobona, ...	Troyes.
		Rotomagus, ...	Rouen.
		Aræegenus,............	Bayeux.
		Brivates Portus,.......	Brest.
		Augusta,.............	Treves.
		Divodurum...........	Metz.
		Verodunum, ...	Verdun.
		Durocortorum, ...	Rheims.
		Durocatalaunum, ...	Chalons.
GALLIA BELGICA, ...	Five,..	Cæsaromagus,........	Beauvois.
		Turnacum,...........	Tournay.
		Colonia Agrippina,.....	Cologne.
		Lugdunum Batavorum,	Leyden.
		Moguntiacum,........	Mentz.
		Confluentes,..........	Coblentz.
		Argentoratum,........	Strasbourg.

It will be understood that this last division embraced portions of Belgium, France, and Germany. Of the three great races or nations, who appear to have possessed ancient Gaul, the Celts were, by far, the most numerous. These, like the Belgæ and Aquitani, were each divided into a great number of tribes, as were the Indians of our country when it was first discovered. These were all conquered by the Romans, and subsequently by the Franks, who overran the territory, driving before them and almost annihilating the people who were then found in possession of the soil. The history of these events will be given in the following chapters.

France, at the present time, is divided into eighty-six departments,* which are subdivided into arrondissements, cantons, and communes. Its whole extent is above two hundred thousand square miles; the population, thirty-seven millions.

* It was formerly divided into thirty-three provinces or governments, the names of which are connected with many historical events, and are still in popular use. The following are the names of the ancient provinces, with the present departments:—

NORTHERN PART.

Ancient Provinces.	*Departments.*	*Capitals.*	*Pop.1861*
Flanders,...........	North, ...	Lille, ...	131,827
Artois, ...	Pas de Calais.	Arras,............	
Picardy,............	Somme,..........	Amiens, ...	
Normandy, ...	Lower Seine,......	Rouen, ...	102,649
	Eure, ...	Evreux, ...	
	Calvados, ...	Caen, ...	
	Manche............	Saint Lo,.........	
	Orne, ...	Alençon, ...	
Isle of France, ...	Seine,.............	PARIS, ...	1,696 141
	Seine and Oise.....	Versailles,........	
	Seine and Marne,..	Melun, ...	
	Oise, ...	Beauvais,.........	
	Aisne,....	Laon, ...	
Champagne,........	Ardennes,.........	Mezieres,.........	
	Marne, ...	Chalons-sur-Marne,	
	Aube, ...	Troyes,...........	
	Upper Marne, ...	Chaumont, ...	
Lorraine, ...	Meuse, ...	Bar-le-Duc, ...	
	Moselle, ...	Metz, ...	
	Meurthe, ...	Nancy, ...	
	Vosges, ...	Epinal, ...	

CENTRAL PART.

Orleannois,.........	Loiret, ...	Orleans, ...	
	Eure and Loir, ...	Chartres, ...	
	Loir and Cher, ...	Blois,.............	
Touraine, ...	Indre and Loire, ...	Tours, ...	
Berry, ...	Indre,.............	Chateauroux, ...	
	Cher, ...	Bourges,..........	
Nivernais,..........	Nievre,............	Nevers,...........	
Bourbonnais, ...	Allier,............	Moulins,..........	
Marche, ...	Creuse,...........	Gueret, ...	
Limousin,..........	Upper Vienne,.....	Limoges, ...	
	Correze,..........	Tulle, ...	
Auvergne	Puy de Dome, ...	Clermont, ...	
	Cantal,...........	Aurillac	

CHAPTER CCCLXXXIX.

800 B. C. to A. D. 741.

Ancient Gaul—Its first Inhabitants—Irruption of the Barbarians—Pharamond—Clovis—The Merovingian Kings.

ANCIENT *Gaul* included the whole of the present France and Belgium, with part of Holland, Prussia, Bavaria, and Switzerland. The *Gauls*, or *Celts*, at the north, and the *Iberians*, or *Aquitani*, in the south, seem to have been the first inhabitants of France proper. Although these two people lived in close proximity to each other, they were dissimilar in language, habits, and manners, and were never confederated together. The Celts, united in large bands, were lovers of noise and feasting, had all the habits of warlike life, undertook distant expeditions, and engaged in adventurous battles: the Iberians, on the contrary, are represented by Strabo as a people divided into small tribes, patient and laborious, attached to their mountainous country, and digging and cultivating the soil, in order to procure metals and produce grain. It is remarkable that the languages spoken by these two people should have descended to us through distant ages. The Iberian is in fact preserved in the *Basque* of the Biscayan country, and in the contiguous parts of Spain; and the Celtic is, after more than two thousand years, the native language of the peasants of Lower Brittany, in France, and those of Ireland, and also of Wales, in Great Britain.

WESTERN PART.

Ancient Provinces.	*Departments.*	*Capitals.*	*Pop.1861*
Maine, ...	Sarthe,...........	Le Mans, ...	
	Mayenne, ...	Laval,............	
Anjou, ...	Maine and Loire, ..	Angers, ...	
Brittany, ...	Ille and Vilaine,...	Rennes, ...	
	Côtes du Nord,....	Saint Brieuc, ...	
	Finisterre,........	Quimper,.........	
	Morbihan, ...	Vannes, ...	
	Lower Loire,......	Nantes,...........	113,625
Poitou, ...	Vienne, ...	Poitiers, ...	
	Two Sevres,.......	Niort, ...	
	Vendee,..........	Bourbon Vendee, ..	
Aunis, Saintonge and Angoumois, ...	Lower Charente,...	Rochelle, ...	
	Charente, ...	Angoulême, ...	

EASTERN PART.

Alsace,............	Upper Rhine,......	Colmar, ...	
	Lower Rhine, ...	Strasbourg, ...	82,014
Franche Comté,.....	Upper Saône,......	Vesoul,...........	
	Doubs,............	Besançon, ...	
	Jura, ...	Lons-le-Saulnier, ..	
Burgundy,.........	Yonne,...........	Auxerre, ...	
	Côte d'Or,........	Dijon, ...	
	Saône and Loire, ..	Macon,...........	
	Ain, ...	Bourg,...........	
Lyonnais, ...	Rhone,...........	Lyons, ...	318,803
	Loire, ...	Montbrison, ...	

SOUTHERN PART.

Languedoc, ...	Upper Loire, ...	Le Puy, ...	
	Ardeche, ...	Privas, ...	
	Lozere, ...	Mende, ...	
	Gard, ...	Nîmes, ...	
	Herault,..........	Montpellier, ...	
	Tarn, ...	Alby,.............	
	Aude, ...	Carcassonne, ...	
	Upper Garonne,....	Toulouse,.........	113,229
Roussillon, ...	East Pyrenees,.....	Perpignan,........	
County of Foix, ...	Ariege,...........	Foix, ...	
Guyenne and Gascony,...............	Dordogne,........	Perigueux,........	
	Gironde, ...	Bourdeaux, ...	162 750
	Lot and Garonne,..	Agen, ...	
	Lot,..............	Cahors	
	Tarn and Garonne,	Montauban, ...	
	Aveyron,.........	Rhodez, ...	
	Landes, ...	Mont-de-Marsan, ..	
	Gers,.......... ..	Auch, ...	
	Upper Pyrenees,...	Tarbes,...........	
Bearn,.............	Lower Pyrenees,...	Pau, ...	
Dauphiny,.........	Isere, ...	Grenoble,.........	
	Drome,............	Valence, ...	
	Upper Alps, ...	Gap,.............	
County of Venaissin,	Vaucluse, ...	Avignon, ...	
Provence, ...	Lower Alps, ...	Digne,...........	
	Mouths of Rhone,..	Marseilles,........	200 910
	Var, ...	Draguignan, ...	
Corsica, .	Corsica .	Ajaccio, ...	

Celtic Village.

The Celts, more powerful, because more numerous and united, drove the Iberians beyond the Pyrenees. Still later, the Phœnicians landed upon the coast of Gaul, attracted by the riches of her mines; and the Ionians of Phocis founded Marseilles, making it the seat of a rich colony, in the year 590 B. C. Previous to this last event, a new Celtic tribe had been added to the Gallic Celts. In respect to this — amid the obscurity that envelops these distant ages — the most generally received opinion is, that the Cimmerians, or Cimbri, who also belonged to the Celtic race, separated from it in remote antiquity, and spread themselves along the Rhine and Danube, and advanced even to the borders of the Euxine Sea. Toward the seventh century B. C., a great movement and a general shock among the people of Southern Asia forced these Cimbri of the Euxine to fall back upon the west; and after a struggle of half a century with their brethren, the Celts, they established themselves principally in the north-west of Gaul, between the Seine and the Loire — about 630 B. C.

From this time, the influence of these new comers prevailed in Gaul. It was they who brought from the confines of Asia to the extremity of Europe that druidical religion which has left so many monuments to excite the surprise of the beholder; a religion of terror and sombre mystery, which had its temples in the forests, under the shadow of the oak, or on the tempest-beaten sides of the hills; and which mingled with the barbarous practice of human sacrifices some ideas of the immortality of the soul and the existence of another world.

The Celts and the Cimbri, henceforth confounded under the name of *Gauls*, early measured swords with the Romans. While Rome was still an unknown town, preparing in her humble cradle for the conquest of the world, the Gauls passed the Apennines, and fell upon the devoted city, which was delivered, as already related, into their hands by the terrified inhabitants. For two centuries, the Gauls were the most terrible and powerful enemies of Rome. When Hannibal carried his army into Italy, it was by the aid of the Gauls that he conquered at Thrasymenus and at Cannæ. These soldiers fought against Rome with such fury, that it seemed, says the historian, that they were carried away by a blind and instinctive hatred against the future conquerors of their country.

About 150 B. C., the Romans, profiting by divisions existing between certain Gallic tribes, penetrated into the country, and in thirty years were masters of its south-eastern portion. They were prevented from pursuing their conquest by a formidable invasion of the Cimbri and Teutones, of which we have given an account in the history of Rome. These tribes were annihilated by Marius: the men were mostly killed on the field, while the women cut the throats of their children, or fastened themselves to the horns of their oxen, by which they were goaded to death. The barbarians were thus destroyed. But it was for Julius Cæsar, the most illustrious name in Roman history, that the final conquest of this country was reserved. After an eight years' struggle, Gaul surrendered to this victorious general. In his Commentaries, Cæsar describes the Gauls as cheerful and light-hearted, with feelings quick and impetuous, but not deep or lasting. They lived by hunting and fishing; their arms were bows, arrows, and axes. Their dress consisted of tight trousers, with a mantle thrown over their shoulders. They had no churches, but the people assembled in the midst of thick forests, where their priests, called *Druids*, offered sacrifices to the God whom they worshipped. The city of Paris was but a collection of huts, made of mud and clay, like Indian wigwams.

The final conquest of Gaul by Cæsar took place in the year 50 B. C., after nine campaigns, in which, it is said, a million of men were slain. The Romans governed it for more than four centuries without disturbance. The country was rapidly transformed by contact with the customs and laws of Rome. The name of Gaul was replaced by that of Gallo-Roman. The fusion between the two people is still evident in France The basis of the French language, laws, and administration is derived from the Romans. The mixture of the two races, Italian and Celtic, is still visible in the inhabitants. The history of Gaul, during the Roman domination, presents few prominent points and few great names. Its annals belong rather to the empire than to France. There were present at Rome Gallic orators, Gallic *savans*, Gallic generals. Rome, in exchange, sent her refinements, and soon after her

Ancient Celtic Warriors.

Merovingian Sovereigns.

superstitions and corruption. We have already spoken in full of the irruption of the barbarians upon the Roman empire in the fifth century, A. D., and its downfall in 476. Gaul shared the fate of Rome; it was overrun by these terrible missionaries of Heaven, and its destinies became finally separated from those of Italy.

About A. D. 376, the Huns, who lived to the north of the Caspian Sea, upon the confines of China, began to march toward the western world. At their approach, even barbarians were terrified. They were represented to the Romans as animals walking on two feet, and as being descended from sorcerers and demons. Nothing could resist the shock of these hordes. Sweeping before them all other nations, they displaced the Alans, and put the Goths in motion; the people of Germany themselves were soon thrown into disorder, to the very borders of the west.

The Burgundians, or Bourguignons, were the first of these who established themselves in Gaul, A. D. 413. Originating, like the Vandals, the Suevi, and the Lombards, on the borders of the Baltic Sea, they had aided the Romans in their wars against the Germans; and for several years they remained encamped in the Alps, between the sources of the Rhine and those of the Danube. The Burgundians, on whom history throws but little light, were remarkable for their height, as well as for the mildness of their manners, and the simplicity of their minds. They were, for the most part, engaged in domestic employments, especially carpentry, finding in peace and industry resources that other barbarians found only in war and pillage.

The Visigoths were the next settlers, and, like the Burgundians, appeared but little hostile to the Gauls. The barbarism of their manners was tempered by contact with the Romans. Historians represent them as an active and intelligent people, alive to the beauties of art and the grandeur of Roman civilization. Both these tribes had come with their wives, children, and herds, searching for a country, in place of the one they had lost. Another tribe, called *Franks*, now made incursions upon the Gallic territory, but for a very different purpose. This nation inhabited a country now comprehended in Franconia, Hesse Cassel, and Westphalia. But little is known of their origin or of their history at this period. The general belief is, that they were led into France about 420, by a king named *Pharamond*. They were rude and belligerent, and after a successful war, divided the conquered land among themselves, making slaves of the people they subdued. Pharamond was succeeded by two other kings, named *Clodion* and *Meroveus*. The Franks were not firmly established in Gaul, however, till the time of Clovis. These early sovereigns obtained the name of *Merovingians*, from Meroveus, the successor of Pharamond and were called the *long-haired* kings, from their flowing locks, which afterward became a mark of nobility Though there are great doubts as to the historical existence of Pharamond, Clodius, and Meroveus, there are none as to Clovis. Here the page of history becomes clear and certain. He conquered the rest of the country, changed the name of Gaul to that of *France*, and made Paris his capital.

On Christmas day, 496, he was baptized at Rheims, and was thus the first Christian king of France. The phial containing the oil with which he was consecrated is preserved to this day, and is called the *sacred phial*. Clovis may be considered the founder of the French monarchy, for he first combined the fragments of the several nations which now occupied France, into one. He established many just and humane laws. He formed the *Salic code*, one provision of which is still in force, excluding females from the throne of France. From the time of Clovis to the present day, there has never been a *sole queen* of France, though the wife of the king is called queen. He passed thirty years in perpetual wars, living in the midst of his soldiers, more like a general or chief of banditti than a king. To secure his authority, he caused the heads of many of his relations to be shaved; and afterward, lest time should renew the long hair, — the emblem of royalty, — he put them to death.

Clovis died in 511, and his kingdom was divided between his four sons, *Thierry I.*, *Clodomir*, *Childebert I.*, and *Clothaire I.* They began their joint reigns in 512. Clothaire survived them all, and died in 561. His four sons, *Charibert I.*, *Gouthran*, *Chilperic*, and *Sigebert*, succeeded him. Sigebert married Brunhault, daughter of the king of Spain, and Chilperic married Fredegonde, the daughter of a peasant. The quarrels between the two queens deluged France with blood. Gouthran outlived all his brothers. and died in 593. The kingdom was then divided between *Childebert II.*, son of Sigebert, and *Clothaire II.*, son of Chilperic. Two sons of Clothaire II. succeeded these sovereigns in 628, — *Dagobert I.*, and *Charibert II.* Dagobert became sole king in 631, by the murder of his brother. He was guilty of many

Clovis, with his Army.

atrocious crimes, but was distinguished for his justice in the execution of the laws. He waged many successful wars against the Saxons, Sclavonians, and Gascons; but he stained the splendor of his victories by

Dagobert.

cruelty and licentiousness. After he had conquered the Saxons, he caused all those whose stature exceeded the length of his sword to be put to death. France, during his reign, rose to some degree of consideration.

Dagobert died in 638, and the monarchs who succeeded him were called *Fainéans* or *Sluggards*. They took no part in the government, but passed their lives in indolence, and all the power fell into the hands of the ministers, or, as they were called, the *Mayors of the palace*. In 688, Pepin d'Heristal, mayor of the palace, assumed the whole power. The kings succeeded each other as mere crowned puppets, the mayor possessing the real authority. Pepin died in 714, and was followed in his office by his son Charles, surnamed *Martel*, or "the Hammer," from the weight of his blows in battle. He saved the kingdom from the Saracens, as we have related in their history. On the death of *Thierry II.*, in 737, he dispensed with the ceremony of appointing a nominal king, and mounted the throne himself. In 741, he bequeathed the kingdom to his sons *Pepin* and *Carloman*, who assumed the title, as well as power, of kings, and thus put an end

Charles Martel.

to the Merovingian dynasty, or race of Clovis, who had occupied the throne from 481 to 741.

CHAPTER CCCXC.

A. D. 741 to 986.

Pepin the Short — Charlemagne — The Carlovingian Kings.

THE division which Charles had made did not last long. Pepin, though called *the Short*, from his diminutive stature, was active and ambitious, and soon persuaded Carloman to enter a convent. He strengthened his own power, and caused himself to be proclaimed king and was the founder of a new race of monarchs. He was anointed with oil from the sacred phial — a ceremony which has ever since been performed at the coronation of the kings of France. The country now attained to great strength and consequence. Pepin's fame reached even Constantinople; and the sovereign of the Eastern Empire sent him many magnificent presents. The comforts and luxuries of life had become more common: fairs were held at stated points all over the kingdom. At these fairs merchants from Italy and the countries of the south were present, with foreign goods for sale.

The manners and customs of these times, throughout Europe, were greatly influenced by the *Feudal System*, of which we shall speak briefly here, referring the reader to a fuller account in the history of Germany, in which country the system had its origin. The kings of the early ages were generally great warriors, who led their own armies to battle, and were always attended by their nobles. These nobles, instead of receiving money for their services, were paid in land, granted by the king, on condition that they should do him homage, and fight in all his wars with a certain number of soldiers. These lands descended from father to son, but could not be inherited by females, as they could not fulfil the conditions of tenure. The noblemen to whom lands were thus granted were called *crown vassals*, and the lands were called *fiefs*: these were generally very extensive, so that the lords were able to give small estates out of them to barons of a lower degree, who did them homage and service, as they, in their turn, were bound to serve the king. Thus every man in the kingdom was the vassal of some superior, who was called his *liege lord*: the serfs, or bondmen, were considered a part of the estate on which they were born, and were sold or conveyed with it, like the sheep or cattle. In the course of time, the liege lord acquired absolute power over the lives and property of his vassals. Feudalism rested, therefore, upon the vassalage of the mass, to a few lords or nobles, who were proprietors of the land.

Pepin died in 768, leaving his kingdom to his two sons, *Charles* and *Carloman*. The latter survived only two years, and Charles thus became sole master of the empire of the Franks. He acquired the name of *Charlemagne*, or "Charles the Great," and from him the dynasty, founded by his father, is called the *Carlovingian*. He was the most celebrated warrior of his age; fifty-three expeditions were undertaken during his reign, among which the wars against the Lombards, the Saxons, and the Saracens were the most conspicuous. The first, after a contest of three years, resulted in the subjection of Lombardy, in 776: this country was given by Charlemagne as a distinct kingdom to his son Pepin. The war against the Saxons was one of the most severely contested that had yet been waged by one nation against another: it lasted thirty-three years, and was principally carried on in the territory of the barbarian Saxons themselves; for Charles, instead of waiting for them on his own borders, crossed the frontiers and sought them out in their retreats. With indefatigable perseverance, employing priests and missionaries when arms had failed, he finally subdued them, after eighteen campaigns. The only defeat he ever sustained in his long military career, was in an expedition against the Saracens in Spain.

It required no less genius to administer the government of his immense dominion than to subdue the various nations who were now incorporated into the body of this gigantic empire. He fixed his court at Aix-la-Chapelle, — now in Prussia, — from whence he could easily watch the barbarous nations he had conquered: he was drawn in that direction, also, by his tastes, sympathies, and family recollections. He was a German, having been born at the castle of Salzburg, in Bavaria, and in all his actions showed his predilection for German customs; but in the administration of his kingdom, he was obliged to seek guidance and examples from higher sources. In Germany, he would have found none but barbarous governments, and authority exercised in confined limits, and over nomadic and uncivilized tribes; while from the south shone the example of the best ages of the Roman dominion, from which he borrowed such ideas as could be transferred to his own ruder people. Following the Roman system in the government of the provinces, he intrusted the direction of his distant territories to prefects, whom he called *dukes*, or *counts*. It was their duty to attend to the raising of troops, the administration of justice, and the collection of taxes. To guard against the fraudulent exercise of power, Charlemagne created a body of royal envoys, or inspectors, who made, from personal observation, periodical reports to the sovereign, on the state of the country, and the conduct of his representatives. He convoked thirty-five national assemblies during his reign, in which were discussed the laws, by whose aid Charlemagne hoped to bring his various people under one legislation, civil and religious. He failed, signally, however, to blend together so many races, each of which had its peculiar laws, customs, and gods. Impossible as was his design, it may still be deemed an honor to have attempted it

Charlemagne.

Charlemagne was one of the most learned men of his age, though his knowledge would be considered very limited in our day. In the midst of the active labors which occupied his life, he still found time to study grammar, history, theology, astronomy, legislation, and music. He applied himself to the task of awakening among his subjects a taste for literature and literary pursuits. The monks were almost the only people who possessed any learning, and but few of the nobility could even read. Charlemagne established schools for the young, founded the University of Paris, endowed monasteries, and encouraged professors, whom he paid liberally. At this period — in the year 800 — he was crowned emperor at Rome. Historians affirm that this was done withou. his consent, while he was present at a mass celebrated in the Vatican. The pope, it is said, while engaged in the sacred office, advanced suddenly toward Charles, and, pouring the holy oil upon his head, pronounced him Emperor of the West. It is more probable that it was a scheme arranged between the pope and himself; at all events, since the fall of the empire of the West, no sovereign had appeared with power at all comparable to his. He lived fourteen years after his coronation; yet old age never for an instant diminished the prodigious activity of his life.

The reign of Charlemagne forms the link between ancient and modern history, and marks the period when learning and the arts were first encouraged in France: he may be considered the principal regenerator of Western Europe, after the fall of the Roman empire. The French, as well as the Germans, have a just pride in this monarch for his many personal virtues, his justice, his zeal in the cultivation of the sciences, and his extreme earnestness to soften the manners of his subjects. He died at Aix-la-Chapelle, in January, 814, uttering, in a low and faltering tone, " Into thy hands, O Lord, I commend my spirit." This happened in the seventy-second year of his age, and the forty-seventh of his reign. His body was deposited in a vault of his chapel. It was placed upon a throne of gold, dressed in the imperial robes, with the crown on his head, and his sword by his side: the Bible was placed upon his knees; but under his vestments was the hair shirt of the penitent, and he still bore the pilgrim's purse, which he had carried in all his pilgrimages to Rome. At his death, the empire extended to the Ebro on the south, to the Eyder and Vistula on the east and north, and to the sea on the west. It included Italy, the whole of Germany, with the present Hungary, Bohemia, Poland, Prussia, half of Spain, and all France.

Louis le Debonnaire, son of Charlemagne, succeeded his father, but possessed neither his wisdom nor energy. He was twice deposed by three of his sons, but was restored by a fourth, the youngest of the family. He died in 840, and his empire was divided among his sons. Lothaire, the eldest, received, for his share, Italy and part of Germany, with the title of emperor; Louis, called the *German*, took the rest of Germany; and *Charles the Bald* was crowned king of France. The Normans, or Northmen, — a race of barbarians who inhabited the northern parts of Europe, Sweden, Norway, and Denmark, — now began to make themselves the terror of the neighboring countries. They were skilful seamen and formidable enemies; they sailed along the coasts, and, steering their barks up the rivers, proceeded to burn and plunder the farms and villages wherever they came, so that no property was secure. France was the principal scene of these depredations. This state of things continued during several reigns, when an event took place that transformed the Northmen from a band of robbers into a great and powerful people.

Louis II., son of Charles the Bald, and surnamed *the Stammerer*, from an impediment in his speech, succeeded his father, but reigned only two years, and died in 879. The kingdom was divided between his two sons, *Louis* and *Carloman*. They did not live long, and the crown of France was bestowed, by the nobles and bishops, on *Charles the Fat*, son of Louis the German. He was already emperor of Germany, and thus the whole empire of Charlemagne, with the exception of Provence, was reunited under his grandson. To the imbecility of this sovereign the Normans owed the rise of their power. They fell upon France with greater fury than ever before. In 886, they laid siege to Paris. This city was still a small place, and was almost unguarded, the king and the court being then at Pavia, in Italy. It was defended, however, by the bravest men in France, with Eudes, count of Paris, at their head. This general despatched repeated messages to the king, imploring him to send troops to the relief of the beleaguered city; and it was only after Paris had stood a siege of four years, that Charles made his appearance with his army. But, instead of preparing for battle, he yielded to his present fears, and sent for the Norman chief, offering him a large sum of money to quit the kingdom, at the same time giving him permission to march into another part of the country, to ravage and lay it waste. The mortification and disgust of his subjects were such, that they renounced their allegiance to him, and he was formally deposed. Deprived of his rank, and deserted by all the world, he became a wretched outcast in his own dominions, and would have died of want, but for the charity of a priest, who supplied him with food and raiment as long as he lived.

Count Eudes was chosen to succeed him, and reigned for ten years. He was constantly occupied in opposing the incursions of the Normans, who were bent upon gaining a foothold in the country. He died in 898, and *Charles*, son of Louis the Stammerer, and surnamed *the Simple*, from his incapacity, ascended the throne. The weakness of his intellect rendered him unfit to govern, and he was a mere puppet in the hands of ambitious nobles. He gave the Normans full possession of a part of France then called *Neustria*, but afterward *Normandy*, on condition that Rollo, their chief, should embrace the Christian faith, and do homage for his new domain. The terms were accepted; but a slight demur arose as to the ceremony of kissing the king's foot — a degradation to which the haughty chieftain did not choose to submit. He at last consented to do it by proxy, and ordered one of his soldiers to perform the act of obeisance for him. But it seems that the rude Norman did not relish the humiliation more than his master. Instead of kneeling to salute the royal foot, as was the custom, he caught it up, and lifted it so quickly to his lips, that the king lost his balance, and fell from his throne. This act of disrespect was overlooked, however, and Rollo and his followers were baptized, and settled in their new dominions. Rollo was the first duke of Normandy and became the ancestor of a long line of English kings, being the great-grandfather of William the Conqueror. He gave up his predatory habits, established schools, and framed wise laws. His followers, in one or two generations, became assimilated to the French in language, manners, and customs. Normandy, under the administration of Rollo, became, in a short time, the most fertile and flourishing province of France.

Charles the Simple gave so many proofs of his incapacity for government, that he was deposed by his subjects in 922, and died in 928. The crown was offered to Hugh the Great, nephew of Eudes, who declined the title in favor of his brother-in-law, *Raoul*, but retained the authority. Raoul died in 935, and the sceptre was again offered to Hugh, who still refused, and sent to England to recall the son of Charles the Simple, who had been an exile in that country since the deposition of his father. Hugh received him with the greatest respect, and caused him to be crowned by the title of *Louis IV.* He was sometimes, also, called *d'Outremer*, or *the Stranger.* He died in 954, after a reign of eighteen years, unmarked by any important events. Hugh died two years after him, and was said to be the most powerful man that never wore a crown. He was almost an absolute sovereign, but never bore the title of king. He was married three times, and each of his wives was a king's daughter. All his wealth and power were inherited by his son, Hugh Capet.

Louis d'Outremer was succeeded by his son, *Lothaire*, who reigned from 954 to 986. This period is destitute of striking incidents. *Louis V.*, his son, surnamed *the Sluggard*, next ascended the throne, but held the power but a few months. There were now none of the race of Charlemagne in a condition to support their right to the throne, and *Hugh Capet*, employing his wealth and influence as a means of advancement, mounted it himself. Thus ended the Carlovingian dynasty, which had lasted two hundred and seventy-six years. Under the later sovereigns of this race, the kingdom, which, during the reigns of Charlemagne and Louis the German, included, as we have stated, Italy, Germany, Prussia, France, and part of Spain, was reduced to a little territory around Rheims and Paris. The greater part of France, at this period, consisted of fiefs belonging to the nobles, who held themselves quite independent of the king; and Hugh, though he had gained a crown, exercised authority over a very small portion of the country which was nominally his. The great barons acknowledged themselves as his vassals, but would not submit to his control, and each considered himself the absolute lord in his own dominion.

CHAPTER CCCXCI.

A. D. 986 to 1108.

Capetian Kings — Introduction of Chivalry — The first Crusade.

There were now seven principalities or states, all independent of the crown: Burgundy, Aquitaine, Normandy, Gascony, Flanders, Champagne, and Toulouse. The insignificance of the royal authority is well demonstrated by the reply of one of these self-created lords, who, on being asked by Hugh, "Who made you a count?" returned for answer, "Who made you a king?" This state of things did not please Hugh and his successors, who made it their grand object to lessen the power of their haughty vassals. This was not accomplished, to any great extent, till the reign of Philip Augustus, two centuries later. Hugh, however, was a wise ruler, and, by his public measures, gave permanency to his dynasty, which was, till the recent French revolution, the oldest sovereign house in existence. It has given one hundred and eighteen monarchs to Europe; viz., thirty-six kings of France, twenty-two kings of Portugal, eleven of Naples and Sicily, five of Spain, three of Hungary, three emperors of Constantinople, three kings of Navarre, seventeen dukes of Burgundy, twelve dukes of Brittany, two dukes of Lorraine, and four dukes of Parma. After having been deprived of four thrones and again restored to them, this family stood forth as the first and most ancient support of the European principle of political legitimacy.

Hugh resided at Paris, which, from that time, became the regular seat of government. After a reign of ten years, he died in 996, leaving one son and three daughters. The tenth century, which was now drawing to a close, has been termed the *iron age*, as being the period most disgraced by murders, cruelty, immorality, and irreligion. The conquest of Egypt by the Saracens, in the seventh century, had cut off the communication between that country and Europe, and papyrus, upon which all books were written, was no longer to be had. Every thing was therefore written upon parchment; and this was so dear, that the works of the Romans were erased, to give place to some new composition. A moderate fortune was insufficient for the purchase of a single volume. A countess of Anjou paid, for a copy of a small religious work, two hundred sheep, five quarters of wheat, and the same quantity of rye and millet.

Hugh Capet was succeeded by his son, *Robert the Pious.* In regard to this king, we have little information; and this is in part owing to a very curious circumstance. It was very generally believed that the world was to last only a thousand years from the commencement of the Christian era, and this period was now close at hand. No one felt inclined to write the annals of a world which was so soon to end; the serious and pious became still more devout, and retired to seclusion, where they spent their time in prayer and repentance. The gay and the thoughtless determined to make the most of what yet remained, and plunged more deeply into the whirl of dissipation. So the world went on, and, as the year 1000 approached, a general gloom and dread prevailed. Most of the lands were no longer cultivated, and useful labor in a great measure ceased. The fatal day arrived and passed; and, when the dreaded year had come and gone, and 1001 had succeeded, the people gradually took courage, and returned to their labors. Thus ended this singular superstition.

From the little information which we have of the son of Hugh Capet, we infer that he was more fit to be a monk than a king. He was noted for his piety, his charity to the poor, and the mildness of his temper. But, with all his virtues, he made a very indifferent sovereign. He had married a wife to whom he was most tenderly attached. Being distantly related to her by blood, however, the pope, Gregory V., sent an order to Robert and his wife Bertha to separate. This they refused to do, and the enraged pope passed a sentence of excommunication upon the royal couple, who were instantly deserted by the alarmed court. The kingdom was put under an *interdict;* that is, none of the offices of religion could be performed in the country. The churches were shut, and no one could be baptized or married. Even the dead were hurried to the grave without the rites of burial. Robert was importuned on all sides to yield, and the monks finally prevailed, through the superstitions of the king. He consented to a separation, and Bertha went into a convent. In 1002, Robert married a second wife, Constance of Provence.

Most extraordinary anecdotes are told of the fancy indulged by this king in the choice of his associates

He preferred the society of beggars to that of the queen and her friends, and kept three hundred of them constantly in his palace. He took care to conceal them, however, from Constance. One day he had hidden a beggar under the table at dinner, and, from time to time, when the queen's eyes were turned another way, adroitly threw him a piece of meat. When dinner was over, the beggar was gone, and, strange to say, the gold ornaments of the king's mantle were missing also. When not with his friends, the beggars, Robert spent his time in the company of monks, and in making pilgrimages. As he was returning from one of these, in **1031**, he was taken sick, and died at Milan, in the sixtieth year of his age, and thirty-fourth of his reign.

His son, *Henry I.*, succeeded him. On the accession of the Capetian, or third race of French kings, the monarchy, previously elective, became hereditary, and descended from father to son. In order to render this succession more certain, the first six kings caused their eldest sons to be consecrated. Still, in the ceremony of consecration, a form was used, which served to perpetuate the remembrance of the right of election in the minds of the people. They were asked if they consented to receive the new sovereign; but as they always returned an affirmative answer, and as no account had been taken of the possibility of their refusing to accept the proposed king, it is fair to suppose that this apparent consultation of their pleasure was a mere formality, and that their decision had little influence upon the result.

Henry's accession to the throne was disputed by Constance, his mother, who wished to secure it for her youngest son. She excited a revolt against him, which Henry quelled with the assistance of Robert the Magnificent, or, as he was sometimes called on account of his crimes, Robert the Devil, duke of Normandy. Constance was placed in a convent, where she died. Henry satisfied the ambition of his brother by giving him Burgundy, and liberally rewarded Robert. This latter prince, oppressed with remorse for his sins, set out on a pilgrimage to Jerusalem, having just made the nobles swear fealty to his son. Robert died in the Holy Land, and several Norman barons united in an attempt to wrest from his son, William, his inheritance, and share it among themselves. But William, though young, gave early proof of the great abilities which afterward distinguished him, and with the aid of Henry, king of England, maintained his rights. The French king soon grew jealous of the rising power of the young duke, and invaded Normandy. He was repulsed with great loss, and obliged to make peace. This attempt, however, was never forgotten, and it laid the foundation of the animosity which henceforth subsisted between the French and English monarchs; for it was soon afterward that William of Normandy, better known as *William the Conqueror*, became king of England by his victory over Harold, the last of the Saxons.

Henry I. died in **1060**, after a reign of twenty-nine years. He was an insignificant personage, and the French historians of the period seem almost to have forgotten that such a sovereign was in existence. He was eclipsed in power by some of his nobles, and thrown into still deeper shade by important events in which he took no part. The people made more rapid strides toward improvement than they had ever before done. A new class of men appeared at this epoch, whose influence and example produced an immense change in the manners of society. They introduced order, refinement, and courtesy among a people of such rude habits, that they could hardly be called civilized, though they had advanced considerably beyond the barbarism of the original Franks. The members

Knight Errant.

of this institution were called ***knights errant***, and the system itself *chivalry*.

It must be remembered that, at this period, injustice and oppression were common: the laws were set at defiance by turbulent barons, who were continually at war with each other. The knights errant came forward as the protectors of those who were unable to defend themselves. They devoted their swords to God, and swore never to use them but in the cause of the weak and oppressed. This romantic spirit was rapidly extended, and chivalry soon became a regular profession; every noble aspired to the honor of becoming a knight. Men of noble birth, only, were admitted into the order. Beside his nobility, however, the candidate for knighthood was required to be courteous, generous, and respectful to his superiors, and to ladies; these qualifications being absolutely necessary in all aspirants to chivalric honors. An important consequence of this was, that more care was bestowed upon the education of youth; politeness, truth, and obedience were cherished in those who were being instructed in the observances of chivalry. The first step in social advancement had now been made; something besides mere brute strength was necessary in order to gain distinction, and it was no longer a received maxim that might makes right.

The ceremonies of admission to the order were singular. The candidate, having arrived at the age of twenty-one, and having given evidence of possessing the necessary qualifications, was placed in a bath; his sins were thus supposed to be washed away. He was then clothed, first in a white tunic, then in a crimson vest, and lastly in a complete suit of black armor: the white tunic typified the purity of the life he was vowing to lead; the crimson vest denoted the blood he would be called upon to shed; and the black armor was an emblem of death, for which he must always be prepared. His dress was then completed by a belt, and a pair of spurs, which were to denote his readiness to hasten where duty called him. Lastly, his sword was girded on; and this part of the ceremony was accompanied by an exhortation to be brave and loyal. The whole was concluded by a blow on the shoulder from the blade of a sword, intended as a memento to fix strongly in the mind of the knight the engagements he had entered into.

On the completion of the ceremonies, the newly-made knight was at liberty to roam about the world in search of adventures. Many a daring deed was performed by these men, whose chief glory consisted in surmounting difficulties and dangers. They were bound by a vow to defend their country, their religion, and their liege lord; to protect women and children; and to be always ready to fight in aid of the oppressed. They paid no taxes, were not vassals to any one, and were always welcome guests wherever they arrived; every castle gate was freely opened at the approach of a knight errant, and he was hospitably entertained as long as he chose to stay.

Although this institution had taken its rise in a desire to befriend the weak and defenceless, yet its indirect consequences extended beyond this object. It refined the manners of the nobles, and introduced habits of expense, that gave a stimulus to industry. Trade was greatly increased, and talent and invention were encouraged. The traffic of the country was no longer confined to roving pedlers; the towns were again peopled; the streets were filled with shops and warehouses; and the merchants became rich, and were enabled to engage in foreign commerce. The condition of the country people and farmers was also improved. Though they still labored for the benefit of their lords, and therefore could not grow rich, they were subject to fewer personal injuries. The knights errant had entered into an agreement that no one should be permitted to molest the laborers in the field, or deprive them of their implements of industry.

Though chivalry often carried the feelings of love and honor to fanatical excess, yet it did much good by purifying and refining the fountains of action: the reverence paid to them also prevented mankind from relapsing into barbarism, the inevitable tendency of things in an age when the feudal system lay at the foundations of society. The influence which chivalry exerted upon poetry was very great. The *troubadours* in the south, the *trouvères* in the north of France, the *minstrels* in England, and *minniesingers* in Germany, sung the achievements of the knights who received and entertained them hospitably. By the intercourse with the East, which grew up during the crusades, fairies, and all the wonders of enchantment, were introduced from that quarter of the world into the romantic or chivalric poetry. It was not long after the introduction of chivalry, that the knights had an opportunity of distinguishing themselves as the champions of religion. Under *Philip I.*, who succeeded his father, Henry, in 1060, the first of the *Crusades* took place. The origin of these famous expeditions is as follows.

From the earliest days of Christianity, the custom of making pilgrimages to the shrines of saints, or other places that were deemed holy, had been common throughout Europe. A journey on foot to some sanctified spot in Italy or Palestine, was thought to be the surest mode of making expiation for sin. In the time of Charlemagne, the roads of France were so thronged with pilgrims of both sexes, of all ranks and ages, journeying from England to Rome, that a large portion of the king's revenue was derived from the tolls that they paid on their way. At a later period, the pilgrims extended their journey to Jerusalem, a much longer and more perilous undertaking. While Palestine remained a part of the Eastern empire, the devotee found no difficulty in thus discharging his religious vows. Under the rule of the Saracens, also, access to the holy city was freely granted to the pilgrims, on the payment of a small tax. But at the period of which we are speaking, Jerusalem had fallen into the hands of the Turks, and pilgrimages became not only perilous and expensive, but often resulted in death captivity, or martyrdom. The clergy were insulted, stripped, and thrown into dungeons. Many Christians found in the Holy Land were treated with the greatest cruelty.

All Europe was fired with indignation at the treatment the pilgrims received at the hands of the Turks A monk, called *Peter the Hermit*, who had himself been to Jerusalem, and had been an eye-witness of the atrocities of the Turks, obtained permission of the pope to exhort all Christian warriors to take up arms against the infidels in the Holy Land. Covered with rags, and barefooted, he travelled from court to court, from castle to castle, from city to city. He was listened to as a prophet, and the people, inspired with enthusiasm similar to his own, enlisted with fervor in the sacred cause. The symbol of enlistment was a cross of red stuff sewed to the shoulder of the cloak; hence the name *crusade*, or *croisade*.

Peter the Hermit.

The whole of France was now like a troubled ocean. The passion of the age was for war and adventurous enterprises. The barons sold and pledged their lands to obtain the means of joining the expedition; while the citizens seized the opportunity of buying titles and privileges, now that they were so cheap. The pope promised a full remission of sins to all who assumed the cross; and thousands of hardened offenders, whose crimes, in the ordinary course of things, could only have been expiated by long and severe penance, preferred the more agreeable method of going to war, and fighting for the redemption of the holy sepulchre. If they succeeded, a fortune in this world seemed secure; if they died, a crown of martyrdom was promised in the

POPE URBAN BLESSING THE CRUSADERS.

next. Incited by these alluring temptations, more than a million of persons had soon pledged themselves to the crusade A large proportion of them were beggars, women, and children. Such as these, who had no preparation to make, refused to wait for the rest, but started, to the number of three hundred thousand, Peter the Hermit and Walter the Penniless, marching at their head.

Among this motley assemblage, there were but eight horsemen; and the expedition was in all other respects equally unprovided. They were ignorant of the distance they had to go, and of the countries through which they must pass; and when they had crossed the frontiers of France, and heard a strange language spoken, they imagined themselves at their journey's end. The children inquired at every town if that was Jerusalem. Their conductors, who were totally ignorant of the way to Palestine, led their deluded followers through Hungary, sometimes pursuing the track of an animal, or the flight of a bird. This miserable army of adventurers supposed that God would employ miracles to supply their wants, and that they should be fed like the Israelites in the wilderness. But finding themselves disappointed of the quails and manna they expected, they were forced to levy contributions upon the countries through which they passed. The inhabitants rose against them, and gave them battle. Nearly the whole of this vast multitude fell victims to the fury of their assailants. Almost all who had escaped death by hunger, fatigue, or pestilence, fell by the sword, half way between the city they went to rescue and the homes they left behind. Peter and Walter were among the few survivors: they waited at Constantinople for the better disciplined and more efficient forces which were preparing to depart when they left France.

This great armament, amounting in the whole to more than three hundred thousand fighting men, had assembled from different nations, but chiefly from France. It was organized in three divisions; Godfrey of Bouillon, a warrior of high renown, commanding the first; Hugh, brother of Philip, Robert of Normandy, and many other princes, sharing the direction of the second; while the third was led by Raymond of Toulouse. It is not our purpose to follow the crusaders in their wild career. They swept through the Eastern empire, making the emperor of Constantinople tremble on his throne. Presuming upon the holiness of their cause, they treated him and his subjects more like slaves than allies. The evils of having no commander, to assume the direction of the entire undertaking, soon became apparent. The moment a city was captured, a dispute arose as to whom it should belong. At length, the different leaders separated, each to fight on his own account, and to gain a kingdom for himself. Some were successful, while others were never heard of afterward; a few still remained faithful to their vows; but of the mighty host that left Europe, only a small remnant, under Godfrey of Bouillon, arrived within sight of the holy city. Jerusalem was taken by assault on the 15th of July, 1099, and the standard of the cross was planted on its walls. Godfrey was elected king of the city, and assumed a crown of thorns, instead of gold, as the appropriate symbol of his authority.

From this time crusading was held in high repute: several expeditions were led by the greatest sovereigns in Europe, and there was scarcely a knight or noble in any country who did not engage in these wars. There were seven of these wild expeditions in the course of the next two centuries. After immense sums had been expended, and more than two millions of Europeans had perished in the cause, they were abandoned. We shall speak more particularly of these several attempts to redeem the holy sepulchre, in their appropriate place. Notwithstanding the loss of life which attended them, they were not without their advantages: the people of Asia were more refined than those of Europe, and were acquainted with many arts of which Europeans were ignorant. A knowledge of these was introduced by the crusaders from Asia into Europe, and many refinements disseminated by them throughout the West.

CHAPTER CCCXCII.

A. D. 1108 to 1328.

Philip Augustus — Persecution of the Albigenses — Reign of St. Louis — Destruction of the Knights Templars.

PHILIP I. died in 1108, after a slothful and disgraceful reign of forty-eight years. At his death, the power of the monarch of France had reached its lowest state of debasement, for it only extended over a district of one hundred and twenty square miles, of which Paris was the capital city. Philip showed some consciousness of his own unworthiness, for he desired that he might not be interred in the Abbey of St. Denis, the usual burial-place of the French kings, being, as he said, too great a sinner to lay his bones by those of the great martyr. He was succeeded by his son *Louis VI.*, to whose love of justice a new class of persons — the *citizens* — owed the foundation of their freedom, wealth, and importance. Until this period, there had been no middle rank, the whole population consisting of the nobles and their dependants. The traders were not free — carrying on trade for their own benefit — but were, for the most part, poor mechanics, who were the serfs and vassals of the feudal lord within whose domain they resided. Louis saw that none would labor with energy and success while their profits were taken from them by rapacious tyrants, and determined upon a plan to remedy the evil. He put the citizens in a situation to defend themselves, by granting charters to many of the towns. The people thus acquired the right of electing their own magistrates, and of forming a militia in defence of their rights. They were freed from servitude, and were no longer at the mercy of capricious and cruel masters.

This plan of the king was strenuously opposed by the nobles, whose power it so much abridged; but the barons had already lost much of their influence in consequence of the holy wars. Many of them had been absent for years in Palestine; and others, to raise money for the crusades, had sold their estates and pawned their titles and privileges. From this time, the cities improved in wealth and consequence, and the citizens became a respectable and influential class Art, science, and commerce flourished; waste lands were brought under cultivation. Freedom soon spread from the towns into the country districts, and the peasants were, at length, no longer bought and sold with the trees that grew on the soil. The people, by these concessions, were strongly attached to the king, and his power was thus greatly augmented. He was enabled to keep the nobles in a state of subjection: many of these were no better than captains of lawless banditti, who rode about the country with a train of armed ruffians at their side. The king made war upon the most notorious of these titled robbers, laid siege to their castles, and compelled them to lead more orderly lives for the future.

Louis died August 1, 1137, sincerely lamented by the great mass of his subjects, whose friend and protector he had always been. His son, *Louis the Young*, was his successor. This prince was naturally amiable, but without much talent. He married Eleanor, sole heiress of Aquitaine, and this extensive territory was thus united to the crown. Soon after he ascended the throne, Thibault, count of Champagne, rebelled against him; and in the course of the war which followed, the king set fire to the cathedral of Vitry, in which thirteen hundred persons had taken refuge: they all perished in the flames. Louis was so shocked at this dreadful deed, that he gave up the war, and, to make some atonement, vowed to make a pilgrimage to Jerusalem. Thus originated the second crusade. The king of France was joined by Conrad, emperor of Germany, each monarch being at the head of a numerous and splendid army. It was a most ill-fated enterprise. Each army, consisting of about two hundred thousand men, was cut to pieces by the Turks, before the expedition reached Asia. About a hundred warriors only arrived in Palestine, among whom was Louis. He was ashamed to return, and his self-accusations completely changed his temper. His cheerfulness forsook him, and he became peevish and morose. He quarrelled with his wife, Eleanor, and obtained a divorce from her. She married Henry Plantagenet of Normandy, who subsequently became king of England. He thus obtained a dominion in France, with the title of *duke of Aquitaine*.

A curious illustration of the manners of this age is furnished in an account of a royal marriage at the court of Navarre. The princes and princesses were entertained by a combat between two blind men and a pig. The men were armed with clubs, and the pig was to be the prize of whichever could knock it on the head. But the pig, having the use of his eyes, could generally avoid the blows which were aimed at him; and the blind men, instead of hitting the pig, frequently hit one another; and in this, it seems, consisted the chief diversion of the sport to the spectators.

Louis VII. died in 1180, leaving his throne to his son, *Philip II.*, better known in history as *Philip Augustus.* France was quiet at his accession, and he devoted much time to beautifying Paris, his capital. He extended its limits, introduced water into the city by an aqueduct, built the Louvre, and paved some of the streets. These pacific employments did not long interest him, and he endeavored to excite dissension between England and France. Henry, king of England, was anxious to preserve peace, and Philip was foiled. He then tried his artifices upon the sons of Henry, and took Richard, the eldest, under his protection. They became intimate friends, drinking out of the same cup, living in the same tent, and sleeping in the same bed. On the death of his father, Richard became king of England, with the title of *Richard I.*, and surnamed *Cœur de Lion.* The two princes agreed to engage in a new crusade. The great object of life seemed at this period to be fighting against the infidels. All the knights and nobles of France and England were eager to join the expedition. No pilgrims — none but soldiers — were permitted to take part in the enterprise: it was, therefore, the most effective of the crusade armies that ever left Europe.

The friendship of the two kings soon gave way to hatred. Richard was the most famous knight of the age; and the praises lavished upon his heroic qualities so wrought upon the jealous heart of his rival, that he deserted the crusade at Acre, and returned to Europe. He now made an attack upon Normandy, which was still an English possession; but it was not till after the death of Richard that he succeeded in wresting it from foreign rule. He also gained many other valuable fiefs, which added much to the power of the crown; for every fief that was conquered put an end to the sway of some feudal lord, and increased the dominion of the sovereign. As he extended the empire he improved it also, by the encouragement he gave to learning, commerce, and the arts.

The latter part of the reign of Philip was disturbed by his persecution of a religious sect of Christians, called the *Albigenses*, who had long dwelt in the peaceful valleys of Provence and Languedoc. They had grown rich by commerce carried on through the Mediterranean Sea, and had imbibed a taste for poetry by their intercourse with the Arabs, who possessed an empire in Spain. They lived upon the territory of Raymond, count of Toulouse, who had suffered them to enjoy their religions opinions unmolested. The pope, who was intolerant of the slightest difference in spiritual belief, excommunicated Raymond, and proclaimed a crusade against the Albigenses. It was one of the most cruel and exterminating wars mentioned in history. Thousands of the devoted sect were massacred without mercy. Rewards and indulgences were promised to all who would help to destroy them They were totally subdued, and the southern provinces were annexed to the crown of France. It was at this period that the terrible court of justice called the *Inquisition* was instituted. This tribunal was afterward introduced into other Catholic countries; but it was in Spain that its proceedings were conducted with those horrible cruelties which have given so fearful a celebrity to its name.

Philip Augustus died in 1227, having reigned forty-four years, during which he had nearly doubled the extent of his territory, and so far crushed the feudal power of the nobility, that it never afterward gained an ascendency. The reign of his son *Louis VIII.* was short, and principally spent in prosecuting the war with the Albigenses. It was said of him that he "was the son of an excellent father, and the father of an excellent son." He died in 1226, leaving several sons, the eldest of whom, Louis, was only twelve years of age. His mother, Queen Blanche, was appointed to manage the affairs of the state during his minority. By her decision and promptitude, she maintained the power till her son had reached the age of twenty-one when she resigned the regency.

Louis IX., or *St. Louis*, was one of the best kings that ever ruled the French nation. He was mild and forgiving, and at the same time brave and firm. He drew his revenues from his estates only, and not from the purses of the people. He had not been long on the throne when he was attacked by a violent illness

His body was racked with pain, and the power of speech was taken away. When he was able to speak, he made a vow to lead a crusade against the infidels, and, on his complete recovery, prepared to start upon the expedition. He devoted six years to putting his kingdom in order, and then sailed for Egypt. Never was there a more disastrous undertaking than this. The army was hemmed in by the waters of the Nile, and the greater part perished by disease, famine, or the swords of the infidels. The king and his chief officers were made prisoners, but were released on payment of a large ransom. Louis went to Palestine, but returned to France on hearing that his mother had died of grief at his misfortunes. He was received with joy and respect; but it was remarked that he still wore the cross upon his shoulder.

He now devoted himself to repairing the damages France had sustained during his absence. He substituted trial by a court of justice for the barbarous custom of trial by combat, or *wager of battle*. He heard the complaints of the poor, and redressed their wrongs, sitting in the open air, at the foot of an oak, which is still standing in the forest of Vincennes. After a wise administration of the government for sixteen years, he had brought his kingdom into a state of complete tranquillity, and had recruited his finances. Every thing seemed favorable to the execution of his favorite project — another crusade. He embarked with a crowd of nobles in July, 1270. He directed his course toward Africa, in the wild hope of converting the king of Tunis. He was immediately attacked by the Turks; and while he was occupied in taking measures of defence, a plague broke out in his camp, and carried off vast numbers of his soldiers. The king himself was soon seized with the epidemic. When at the point of death, he caused himself to be lifted from his bed, and laid upon a heap of ashes on the floor. He expired in the forty-fourth year of his reign, in the midst of a scene of horror difficult to describe. The few that remained of the unfortunate crusaders embarked for France with Prince *Philip*, who succeeded his father. He was called the *Bold*, or *Hardy*, from having survived the calamities of Tunis. Thus ended the seventh and last crusade, in 1270.

Nothing happened during the reign of Philip the Bold of great importance. He died fifteen years after his accession, and was succeeded, in 1285, by his son *Philip the Fair*. This king occupied the early part of his reign in making what are called *sumptuary laws;* that is, laws for the purpose of preventing persons from spending more than they could afford, and of forcing them to live within their means. Only two meals were allowed in the day — dinner at ten, and supper, the principal meal, at five. One dish of meat at dinner and two at supper were allowed. On fast days, herrings supplied the place of more solid food. The law was soon evaded by placing several kinds of meat on one dish. The dress of the various classes of citizens was regulated by law. Ladies and gentlemen were often seized at balls and taken to prison for being too finely dressed. A man's rank might be known from the length of his shoes. The points were turned up before, like a cow's horn; and it was the proximity of these frightful appendages to the knee, that determined the rank of the wearer. The clergy exclaimed against this absurd fashion, and a succeeding king forbade the custom. So shoes twelve inches long were proscribed; but others, twelve inches wide, at once made their appearance. The inexorable edict of fashion ordained that what was taken from the length must be added to the breadth.

Philip loved money, and was deterred by no scruples of conscience from any method of obtaining it. He increased very much the possessions of the French crown. He married Jane, heiress of Navarre; and upon the death of the count of Toulouse, without heirs, his territories came to the king. He formed a plan with the pope for the suppression of the Knights Templars, and the inheritance of their wealth. Their devotion to

Knights Templars.

the defence of the pious pilgrims, had excited admiration throughout the Christian world. They had, many of them, returned from the East, and were living magnificently in their own castles all over Europe. Every Templar in France was arrested on the same day. They were thrown into dungeons, and put to the torture, until many, in their agony, confessed crimes of which they were never guilty. The grand master of the order, De Molai, was burned alive. It is said that, while on the scaffold, he summoned the pope to appear at the eternal throne of justice, to answer for his murder, in forty days, and the king in four months: certain it is, that both died within the stated times.

Philip the Fair died in 1314, and left three sons, all of whom came to the throne in succession. The first, *Louis X.*, caused the slaves to be released from bondage, who thus became freemen. This was not done from motives of humanity, but for the purpose of raising money. Freedom was offered to all the serfs upon the payment of a small sum. But many preferred their money to their liberty; so the king hit upon the singular expedient of forcing them to be free, whether they would or not. The great nobles followed the example of the king, and slavery was abolished throughout France. Louis died in 1316, leaving only one child, a daughter. The Salic law forbade females to succeed to the throne; and this was the first occasion which had occurred for several centuries for applying this rule. Many were disposed to question its validity; but the parliament confirmed it, and *Philip V.*, brother to Louis X., was made king. He died after an uninteresting reign of six years, and as he left only daughters, was succeeded by his brother *Charles IV.* This king died in 1328, leaving no male heirs. The crown passed from the direct line of Hugh Capet to *Philip of Valois*, another branch of the Capetian family, called the *House of Valois*.

CHAPTER CCCXCIII.

A. D. 1328 to 1430.

Wars between England and France — Battles of Cressy and Poictiers — The Jacquerie — Insanity of Charles VI. — Battle of Agincourt — Joan of Arc.

THE event just mentioned was the origin of a long series of wars between France and England. The title of Philip of Valois to the throne was disputed by Edward III., of England, who claimed it for himself, in right of his mother, who was a daughter of Philip the Fair. It was evident, however, that Edward could not thus inherit a kingdom which, by the Salic law, could never have been hers. The mother, who had no right to the throne, could transmit none to her son. Edward was very ambitious, and made his claim, however unfounded, a pretext for invading France: a war ensued which lasted, with some intermissions, above a hundred years. The king of England led a powerful army into France: he was accompanied by his son Edward, called the *Black Prince*, from his dark armor and black plume of feathers.

On the 27th of August, 1346, was fought the famous battle of Cressy, which terminated so fatally to the French. The havoc was terrible. There were left upon the field two kings, eleven high princes, eighty great nobles, twelve hundred knights, and more than thirty thousand private soldiers. Cannon were used for the first time as engines of destruction in this battle, the invention of gunpowder being then of recent date. The English brought with them six of these machines; but they were clumsy and unmanageable. Philip fought bravely, but was obliged to flee. Edward now laid siege to Calais, which, being upon the the French coast, was called the *gate of France*. The city surrendered after a twelvemonth's resistance. Peace was soon after made between France and England. Neither of the rival monarchs had money enough to carry on the war, and they agreed to a truce of ten years. Petrarch, the Italian poet, who visited France at this period, says of it, "The country appeared every where desolated with fire and sword. The fields lay waste and uncultivated. The houses were falling to ruins, except here and there a fortress. Paris looked forlorn and desolate. The streets were overgrown with weeds, and the people seemed sad and downcast." The whole of France was reduced to a deplorable state of wretchedness by famine and the plague; and in this time of general calamity, troops of banditti marched openly about, robbing the dying and the dead, and committing all sorts of depredations.

It was during the reign of Philip of Valois that the heir to the crown assumed the title of *Dauphin*, from the following circumstance: the lord of the large province of Dauphiné was obliged to sell his lands to pay his debts; which he did with the less reluctance, as he had no children to inherit his possessions. The king of France, who had long been anxious to attach this territory to his domains, purchased it, promising that the eldest son of the king should always bear the title of *dauphin*. This was, till the period of the revolution, the distinguishing title of the king's heir. In a similar manner, the eldest son of the king or queen of England is called the *prince of Wales*.

Philip died in 1350, and *John*, his eldest son, ascended the throne. His reign was one of the most disastrous in French history. Hardly had the ten years' truce expired, than the Black Prince again made his appearance in France. In the hope of stopping his progress, John assembled all his forces, and met him at Poictiers. Edward had but eight thousand men with him, who were quickly surrounded by the enemy's army, numbering some sixty thousand soldiers. The event was far different from what either party could have anticipated. During the conflict, a panic seized the French troops, and the English gained a complete victory. The prisoners taken by the English were more numerous than their whole army. John, on being captured, gave up his sword to some English barons, and was conducted with courtesy and respect to the tent of the king. He was sent to England, where he was detained in captivity for four years. During his absence, from a superstitious hope that it might aid his release, a wax taper was placed in the church of Notre Dame, and kept burning till his return. It was six miles in length, and might have encircled the city of Paris. It was wound, like a rope, around a large wheel.

During the king's detention in England, France was in a state of perpetual confusion. The dauphin was appointed regent. But he had not the energy necessary to preserve order; and the nobles, having no one to restrain them, endeavored to reduce their tenants again to the condition of serfs. They burnt the homes of the peasants, and drove them, like beasts, to seek a shelter in woods and forests. The hatred of the poorer classes toward the rich was increased by a new tax imposed upon the peasantry, for the purpose of raising money to ransom the prisoners of high rank, who had been taken at the battle of Poictiers. They naturally felt but little interest in redeeming their oppressors from captivity. With one accord, the peasants and laborers armed themselves against the nobles, vowing to destroy every person of high birth in the kingdom. They seized scythes, pitchforks, and every weapon they could lay their hands on. Their numbers hourly increased, and they swept onward like a flood, destroying and laying waste wherever they went. Many acts of barbarity were committed by them, till, at length, the insurrection was quelled by a famous knight, named Gaston de Foix, who, with a few followers, killed several thousand of the rioters. This insurrection is known by the name of *La Jacquerie*, as the French peasant was frequently called *Jacques Bonhomme*, or Goodman James.

As soon as quiet was reëstablished in the country, the dauphin endeavored to obtain his father's release Edward's conditions were severe, however, and hostilities again ensued. He marched into France with a large army, journeying leisurely along from place to place, amusing himself with his hawks and his hounds Suddenly he was overtaken by a violent storm, the most terrific, say the chronicles of the period, since the deluge. The thunder and lightning were incessant; the hailstones were of such size, and fell with such violence, that six thousand horses of the English army were killed. The king was so struck with the terror of the scene, that he made peace at once, and released his royal captive. The conditions of his deliverance were, a large ransom, to be paid in three instalments, and the leaving of his sons and thirty of his nobles as security for the fulfilment of the contract. Two of the hostages, sons of the king, vexed at the delay in paying the ransom, broke their parole and fled. John, to avoid the suspicion of being concerned in this breach of faith, returned to England, and surrendered himself to Edward. He died at London, April 8, 1364.

The dauphin now became king, as *Charles V.* The English still occupied the south-west of France, and Charles was naturally anxious to rid himself of such troublesome neighbors. He therefore summoned Edward of England to appear and do homage to him as his vassal. This Edward was bound to do, as lord of Gascony. He refused, however, and Charles declared him a rebel, and his possessions in France forfeited. A successful war against Edward terminated the difficulties between the two nations, and tranquillity was restored to France. The English were driven out of the country, and, in a few years, had nothing remaining, of all their conquests in France, but Calais, and the towns of Bourdeaux and Bayonne, in the south. Charles reigned sixteen years, and his prudent government procured for him the surname of the *Wise.* He formed libraries and encouraged learned men. He caused the works of many of the old Greek and Latin authors to be translated into French. The manner in which this was done, may be inferred from the fact that a contemporary writer represents the original authors as loudly complaining of the ignorance of their translators, who made them say things which they had never thought of.

The pictures of this age were curious productions. The painters probably distrusted their own powers; for a label was put into the mouth of every figure, that the meaning of the painting might not be mistaken. Some of these singular performances still exist. The first public clock in France was made, at the desire of Charles, by a German. It was placed in the tower of the palace, and excited much wonder by its regularity and precision in striking the hours. The famous prison of the Bastile was built at this period. Charles died in 1380, from the effect of poison, administered by the king of Navarre.

The Bastile.

Charles VI., called also the *Well-beloved*, was only thirteen years old at his father's death. He was affectionate and obliging, and never forgot a kindness, nor a promise which he had made. He had an extraordinary facility in remembering a face that he had once seen, or a name which he had once heard. Spite of his good qualities, however, his reign was one of the most disastrous in French history. During his minority, his uncles, the dukes of Anjou, of Berry, and of Burgundy, successively took the head of the government as regent; and under their administration, France quickly returned to a state of disorder and of civil dissensions. The duke of Anjou, to whom Joanna, queen of Naples, had bequeathed her possessions, assembled a large army, and marched into Italy. The expedition was most disastrous; the army was destroyed, and the duke died in poverty and distress. The duke of Burgundy determined to invade England in 1386. He collected together a fleet of one thousand three hundred and eighty-seven vessels. Every gentleman connected with the expedition had an attendant called a *pillard*, or robber, whose business it was to plunder for his master's benefit. The attempt signally failed: the fleet was detained till the stormy season commenced, when a large part of it was dashed to pieces against the rocky coasts of the neighborhood.

Charles came of age in 1388, and assumed the conduct of affairs. The first acts of his government gave good promise for the future. But he soon began to give unmistakable signs of insanity. The first fit seized him as he was journeying through a forest on his way to Brittany. He was taken with a sudden frenzy, and, drawing his sword, rushed madly upon his attendants, who all fled at his approach. A violent mental derangement followed, which finally settled into complete lunacy, which clouded the rest of his life. For thirty years, he had his reason only at short intervals. Though decorated with the outward signs of royalty, he was an object of contempt and neglect to those around him. The queen abandoned him and her children to the care of servants, and, using all the revenue for her own amusement, left them destitute of the absolute necessaries of life. It has been generally supposed that cards were invented to amuse Charles during his lucid moments: this is hardly probable, as it is stated by some authorities that a law was made before his time to prevent gambling, in which cards and dice were expressly mentioned.

The insanity of the king rendering it impossible for him to administer the government, the duke of Burgundy, his uncle, and the duke of Orleans, both contended for the regency. Hence arose the civil wars between the two houses, that for many years made the whole country a scene of tumult and bloodshed. At last, Henry V. of England took advantage of the troubled state of France to gratify his ambition. He revived the claim made by Edward III. to the French crown, and on that pretext invaded the kingdom. The *oriflamme*, or sacred banner of France, was unfurled. This standard, it was pretended by the monks of former times, was brought down from heaven to Clovis. It was believed that the safety of the kingdom depended upon its preservation. Henry ravaged the country without opposition, and met the enemy for the first time at Agincourt. On the 26th of October, 1415, the French experienced a more disastrous defeat than that of Cressy or Poictiers. Through want of skill in their general, they were drawn into a marsh, where they sunk to their knees at every step. After a terrific battle, the field was yielded to the English, and a

French herald appeared before Henry, begging permission, on the part of the French, to bury their dead. "What is the name of yon castle on the hill?" asked Henry of the herald. "The castle of Agincourt," he replied. "Then," said the king, "let the place where the battle was fought be called the *field of Agincourt.*"

The French Herald before King Henry.

Henry was acknowledged regent and heir to the crown. He married the princess Catharine, daughter of the poor old king; and these proceedings the unconscious Charles was made to sanction. The unhappy king died at Vincennes, October 21, 1422.

Henry V. died almost at the same time, leaving a son only a few months old. The duke of Bedford was appointed regent of France. The dauphin, son of Charles, now resolved to make a desperate effort for the recovery of his dominions. The southern provinces took his part, while those of the north obeyed the duke of Bedford. The war thus renewed desolated the whole face of the country. The lands lay uncultivated; the wolves, made bold by hunger, found their way into Paris, and actually attacked the citizens. For a long time, the English party maintained its advantage over the dauphin. Of all France, nothing remained to him but the city of Orleans; and in 1428 the English laid siege to that place. The young prince now thought his cause lost and his fortunes hopeless, when one of the most singular occurrences in history turned the tide in his favor. This was the appearance of Joan of Arc, called the *Maid of Orleans.*

This interesting girl was the daughter of poor parents, and was born in the little town of Domremy. From her infancy she had been taught to look upon the English with abhorrence, and the scenes of desolation which were enacted before her, were the daily conversation of those with whom she associated. Politica and party interests were thus forced upon the mind of Joan. She was, by her own account, about thirteen years old, when a supernatural vision first appeared to her. From that time, voices continued to haunt her, and to echo the enthusiastic and restless wishes of her own heart. These voices were her visitors and advisers, and prompted her to quit her native place, take up arms and drive the foe before her, and thus procure for the dauphin his coronation at Rheims. When she was seventeen years old, and the fortunes of Charles were at the lowest ebb, she went to him, and offered to deliver Orleans from the fate which was hanging over it, and cause him to be crowned king. The courtiers thought her mad; but Charles, after some hesitation, accepted the offer. Joan was arrayed in a full suit of armor, was furnished with an escort of troops, and received the rank of a military commander.

Her fame had gone before her. She and her soldiers were suffered to pass unmolested through the enemy's camp, and to enter Orleans. The English soldiers were seized with a horror of fighting against Heaven. She carried with her a convoy of provisions to the besieged, whose hearts were raised from despair to a fanatical confidence of success. The English, who, in every previous encounter, had defeated the French, felt their courage paralyzed by the presence of this simple girl. Wherever she led the attack, they threw down their arms and fled. Many deserted; so that a proclamation was issued in England against all who should abandon the cause "for fear of the mayde." Joan was wounded several times, but never killed any one, or shed any blood, with her own hand. The siege of Orleans was raised, after a series of great achievements on the part of the French; and in one week after the arrival of Joan, the beleaguered city was relieved. She then declared herself ready to perform the second part of her mission.

Rheims was at a great distance, and in the hands of the English. Charles's troops were few, and the road was guarded by strong fortresses. But he yielded to the importunity of his protectress, and set out on the journey. Every town along the route submitted without striking a blow, and his progress resembled a triumph. At Rheims he was presented with the keys of the town. The coronation of the dauphin was performed in the cathedral of that city, with the holy oil of Clovis. During the ceremony, the Maid of Orleans stood by the altar, in complete armor, her banner in her hand.

When the ceremony was finished, she threw herself at the feet of the king, now Charles VII., and said, "O noble king, now that the pleasure of God is done, and I have raised the siege of the city of Orleans, and have caused you to be crowned in your city of Rheims, let me be taken back to my father and mother." She seemed no longer sustained by her previous enthusiasm, and felt that her mission was accomplished. But the king desired her to stay with the army till the English were driven out of France. After a series of successes, she was in one instance defeated, and finally was captured in a sally against the enemy, in 1430. She fell into the hands of the duke of Bedford. Though every law of honor dictated that she should be treated as a prisoner of war, she was brought to trial as a sorceress and heretic. The clergy who tried her were in the interest of Bedford, and condemned her to die. A pile of wood was prepared in the market place at Rouen, and, encircled by a body of judges and ecclesiastics, she was burned to death, and her ashes were thrown into the Seine. Public opinion afterward turned in her favor, and the judges who condemned her were hooted at by the populace every time they appeared in the streets The judgment of God seemed to fall

Statue of Joan of Arc.

upon them, for they all died violent deaths. In 1454, a revision of the sentence took place: Joan was pronounced innocent, and a statue to her memory was erected on the spot where she perished. Her family was also ennobled by the king, whose fortunes she had so essentially promoted.

CHAPTER CCCXCIV.

A. D. 1430 to 1572.

Reign of Louis XI.—Foreign Wars—Francis I.—The Field of the Cloth of Gold—Wars with the Emperor of Germany—Charles IX.—Catharine de Medicis—Massacre of St. Bartholomew.

NOTWITHSTANDING the capture of Joan of Arc, the English daily lost ground in France. One city after another submitted to Charles. Six years after the death of the Maid of Orleans, he made his public entry into Paris, after an absence of seventeen years. The regent, Bedford, died of vexation at the successes of the French, and the English soon possessed no territory in France but the city of Calais. Under the good government of the native sovereign, France was gradually restored to prosperity. A dreadful famine, however, desolated the country in his reign. So great was the mortality in Paris, that the wolves roamed about the nearly deserted streets, and carried off children before the eyes of their parents. Charles VII. reigned thirty-nine years. He died of starvation, in 1461, refusing to take food, on account of suspicions that his son, afterward *Louis XI.*, intended to poison him.

Louis was in Burgundy when he heard of his father's death. He was crowned at Rheims, and proceeded from thence to Paris, where he excited the indignation of all good persons by his unworthy acts. He very much resembled the Roman emperor Nero in point of cruelty, and was, besides, mean, base, selfish, and treacherous. He dismissed all his father's counsellors, and gave places of authority only to such as were too mean to dispute his will. His prime object was to establish a despotic government; and, as this could only be done by destroying the power of the nobility, he determined, from the commencement of his reign, to rid himself of all those whose influence might interfere with his views. With this intention, he imprisoned many of the chief nobles, while their retainers were seized and hanged on trees in the forests. Others were shut up in cages, and exhibited like wild beasts. The nobles, who had once possessed more power than the king himself, made a show of resistance, and armed their vassals; but Louis was artful enough to induce them to lay down their arms, by making promises which he never meant to perform. The court had now none of that splendor that had previously distinguished it. The nobles that remained at liberty were few, and these were afraid of speaking their sentiments freely. The royal residence was more like a prison than a palace: the king was himself distinguished by the shabbiness of his hat and coat.

The fashions of this age were curious. In the reign of Charles VI., it had been necessary to make the doors wider, to admit the head-dress of the ladies, six feet broad. The same doors were now made higher, to give passage to an extraordinary structure, three feet high. This was in the form of a turban, tapering toward the top, and wreathed round with a handkerchief of silk, or other light material, the corners of which hung to the ground. Men wore jackets stuffed at the shoulders, to make them appear broad. The hair was worn so long, that it covered the eyes and face. The noble authors of the time complain that citizens and even servants, had jackets of silk, satin, and velvet, and that almost all wore peaks to their shoes a foot long.

The reign of Louis XI. was disturbed by continual wars between the king and Charles the Bold, duke of Burgundy. Of all the great fiefs that formerly existed in France, two only were now unattached to the crown: these were Brittany and Burgundy. The latter included a country equal in extent to the dominions of Louis, for it comprehended all the Netherlands, the duchy of Burgundy, and Artois. Louis looked upon the duke in the light of a rival sovereign, rather than as a vassal noble. The enmity and jealousy of these two princes furnish the leading events of this reign. In 1475, Edward IV. of England entered France with a powerful army, and claimed the throne. Louis resorted to his customary arts in such cases, and by fair promises and cajolery, purchased the good will of Edward's ministers, and finally bribed the monarch himself to return to England. The English soldiers were well feasted at the expense of Louis, who sent several cartloads of wine and other incentives to hilarity and good will to the English camp. He requested a personal interview with Edward, and the two kings met upon a bridge, in the centre of which was a large wooden grating, almost breast high. They embraced through the openings of the grate, and swore to observe faithfully the treaty which had been made, after which they passed some time in familiar discourse.

The duke of Burgundy died soon after this in a war with the Swiss, leaving an only daughter, Mary of Burgundy, who ought to have inherited his dominions; but Louis declared, that by the Salic law, she was excluded from inheriting any estates within the boundaries of France. He therefore took possession of them himself, and thus the great fief of Burgundy became united to the crown. Edward IV. of England was now dead, and Louis was rid of his most dreaded rival. But his constitution was broken down, and the fear of death and assassination filled him with indescribable horror. He shut himself up in his castle of Plessis, where even his own daughters were forbidden

Louis XI. and Tristan L'Hermite, his Hangman.

to visit him without invitation. Any person who approached without making himself known was shot. The avenues of this abode of misery were lined with gibbets instead of trees, and one of the three familiar associates of the king was his hangman. The others were his barber and physician. The latter pretended that it had been predicted to him that his death should take place a few days before that of the king. Louis therefore watched over the life of the physician with anxious care, and loaded him with presents. Battles between rats and cats were his principal amusement. He drank the blood of young children, in the hope of instilling youth and health into his veins. Terrible and marvellous medicines were compounded for him. The nearer death approached, the more his dread of it increased. He tried to keep it off by the arts of superstition, and hoped to deceive God as he had men. He wore relics and amulets about his person, and little leaden images surrounded his cap. When near his end, he prayed that he might die on a Saturday. This wish was gratified. He expired Saturday, May 20, 1483.

The great end and aim of Louis was to annihilate the pretensions and power of the feudal princes. He pursued this object with indefatigable perseverance, and was signally successful. Yet he cannot have the credit of aiming at any good object. He crushed the nobles, only to engross their power himself. The feudal system, indeed, disappeared with him, but absolute monarchy took its place, and continued to the revolution. The increase of territorial dominion was never his policy. When the Genoese offered to take him for their sovereign, he answered, "The Genoese give themselves to me, and I give them to the devil!" He labored incessantly to establish the French unity as he understood it — one territory and one sovereign. He never committed useless crimes, but never hesitated to perpetrate any act, if necessary to gain his ends. He was not cruel by nature, but exercised cruelty without remorse. He avoided intercourse with the great and good, and accomplished every thing by paltry means. He transformed his lackeys into heralds, his barbers into ministers. The executioner was his familiar spirit. He lived in the midst of scaffolds, prisons, iron cages, and chains, and died surrounded by quacks, hermits, and astrologers. There was no great man in his reign, and little virtue. Fear supplanted every other feeling. The people were as submissive as galley slaves.

Louis XI. left one son and two daughters. The son, afterward *Charles VIII.*, though in his fourteenth year, was not allowed to assume the reins of government. He was placed under the guardianship of his eldest sister, Anne of Beaujeu. The princes of the royal family, and particularly the duke of Orleans, did not readily submit to this arrangement; and, having made an unsuccessful attempt to displace Anne, fled to the court of Brittany. This was the only fief that now remained independent of the king. Upon this territory the rulers of France had already cast longing eyes, and Anne was glad of a pretext for war. The Bretons were defeated in the battle of St. Aubin. The duke of Orleans was taken prisoner, and the duke of Brittany did not long survive the defeat. His daughter, sole heiress of the duchy, was thirteen years old at this time, but possessed discretion far beyond her age. She was advised to settle all difficulties by marrying Charles, whom she looked upon as the natural enemy of her family. He entered her capital city in disguise, however, visited the princess, and pleaded with such effect, that he won his cause. They were married in 1491. Thus, after the lapse of several centuries, France was again united under one sovereign. The last remnant of the feudal system was now incorporated in the monarchy, and the kingdom was at a high pitch of power. The country was at peace, and civil wars were at an end. The energy and desire for continual excitement, which had thus far exhausted themselves in internal struggles, now led the French across the frontier, carrying war into foreign countries.

In 1494, the king resolved to enforce the claims he had upon Naples, by virtue of Charles of Anjou's bequest to Louis XI. He invaded Italy with an army of eighteen thousand men. The king of Naples and the Italian princes imagined that the whole would end in idle talk, and took no measures of defence. "It seemed," says an old historian, "as if God had blindfolded their eyes, and tied down their hands, and raised up this young king to chastise them, who came with a small force and a brainless council." Every city opened its gates at his approach. After a sojourn of three months in the kingdom, a powerful league, formed against him, forced him to return to France. He broke through the hosts of the enemy, who had gathered in strong numbers to oppose his passage. He was stripped of all his conquests in Italy in as short a time as he had taken to gain them. He died in 1498, in the twenty-eighth year of his age. His amiable manners rendered him a great favorite, and acquired for him the surname of the *Courteous*.

Charles left no children, and was succeeded upon the throne by Louis, great-grandson of Charles V. We have hitherto spoken of him as the duke of Orleans; but he now received the title of *Louis XII.* It was feared, that he, having in turn, become the strongest, would wreak his vengeance upon the partisans of Anne of Beaujeu. But when asked to remove an old general from the army who had taken him prisoner at the battle of St. Aubin, he replied, "It does not become the king of France to revenge the quarrels of the duke of Orleans." He was surnamed the *father of his people*, as he diminished the taxes, and regulated the expenses of the government with great order and economy. He obtained a divorce from his wife Joan, and married Anne of Brittany, the widow of Charles VIII. During the greater part of his reign, he was fighting in Italy, not only for the recovery of Naples, but for the duchy of Milan. His wars were unsuccessful, for, after conquering Naples, he lost it by the treachery of Ferdinand, king of Spain; and, though he entered Milan twice as a conqueror, he was finally obliged to give up his Italian claims

In 1513, a new enemy appeared in Henry VIII. king of England. He invaded France, and gained a battle in Picardy, which was called the *battle of the spurs*, being, on the part of the French, more a flight than a battle. But Louis was weary of fighting. He made peace with all his enemies; and, on the death of Anne of Brittany, which happened in 1514, he married Mary Tudor, sister of Henry. She was only sixteen years old, and fond of gayety and keeping late hours. To please his young bride, Louis gave up his regular and quiet habits of life: he relinquished his former custom of dining at eight o'clock in the morning and retiring at six in the evening. He adopted fashionable hours, and frequently sat up till midnight. These altered habits disagreed with his health, and brought on a fatal illness. He died in 1515. He left no sons, and his crown passed to his cousin Francis, count of Angoulême.

The French historians regard this as the commencement of the modern history of France; a new era seems to burst upon the world at the beginning of the sixteenth century. America had just been discovered in the west, thus offering science new seas to explore and new worlds to examine. The Greeks, driven from their home by the Turks, had brought into the west the treasures of their arts and of classic antiquity. The art of printing, now just beginning to develop itself, seemed discovered on purpose to multiply and spread these riches. The feudal system had been destroyed, and the reformation, which follows closely on these events, announces the end of the middle ages, and the beginning of an era of light and intelligence.

Francis I. was, at his accession, in the twenty-first year of his age. He was handsome and well formed, his air and demeanor were chivalrous and princely, while his gay and open character won all hearts He was desirous of raising France to an equality with Italy in point of wealth and refinement. He assembled around him the most learned men and the most celebrated artists of his time. He founded colleges for the study of Greek and Latin, and spared no expense to advance the art of printing, which was now making great progress. He wished to be considered the greatest man of his time. There was another sovereign in Europe, however, who would brook no rivalry This was Charles V., king of Spain and emperor of Germany. He was more powerful than Francis, for his dominions comprised Germany, Spain, the Netherlands, and the rich countries of Peru and Mexico. Both these princes thought that two suns could not shine in the same hemisphere, and all their efforts were directed toward eclipsing each other. Their wars disturbed the whole of Europe as long as they lived.

It was in consequence of their quarrels that a meeting, usually called the *Field of the Cloth of Gold*, took place, near Calais, between the king of France and Henry VIII. of England. The former, being very anxious to cultivate the favor of the English monarch, invited him to this entertainment. The two kings met each other on horseback, and, after a ceremonious salutation, dismounted and entered a splendid pavilion

They then began, with great gravity, to discuss the affairs for which they were ostensibly met. But they soon grew weary of such serious matters, and, leaving them to their ministers, spent eighteen days in tournaments, feastings, and other amusements. On one occasion, Francis sportively turned Henry out of bed

Henry and Francis.

at the point of the sword. They parted on the best terms imaginable. Henry went from this scene of gayety to Gravelines, a small town on the northern coast of France. Here Charles V. contrived to meet him, and so far counteracted the seductions of Francis, as to obtain from him a promise to remain neutral in the approaching contest between him and his rival.

The flames of war were soon kindled. The first attempt of Francis was unsuccessful. His best general, the Constable of Bourbon, abandoned his cause, and joined the standard of Charles. He was received with open arms, and a plan was formed, in connection with Henry VIII., for the invasion and division of France. This invasion, however, proved abortive; and Francis, elated at Bourbon's discomfiture, led an army into Italy, and laid siege to Pavia. The city was relieved by a numerous force under Bourbon and Lannoy, who attacked the French fortifications. The French troops were seized with a panic, and one of the royal family fled from the field, and never stopped till he reached Lyons, where he died of shame. Francis was taken prisoner, and gave up his sword to Lannoy. He was conveyed to Madrid, where he fell dangerously ill. Charles V. refused to see him, and this chilling indifference to royal misfortunes aggravated the malady of the French king. Charles at last consented to visit him, and the kindness of his manner hastened Francis's cure. After fifteen months' captivity, he received his liberty, but on very stringent conditions, for the execution of which his two sons remained as hostages. These conditions Francis never performed, on the pretext that promises made in prison are not binding.

He now incited the various Italian powers to revolt against the authority of Charles, and, when they had compromised themselves by taking up arms, abandoned them to the vengeance of the emperor. In acting thus, he hoped to obtain of Charles some modification of the treaty of Madrid. The treaty of Cambrai, in 1529, was the reward of his perfidy. By this agreement, Francis agreed to marry Eleanor, sister of the emperor, and to pay a large ransom for the release of his two sons. Both of these conditions he performed. But neither Charles nor Francis could long be contented without the excitement of war. They

The Constable of Bourbon

were almost constantly engaged in quarrels from 1536 to 1544, when a treaty was concluded at Cressy. Francis died in 1547, in the thirty-second year of his reign.

Henry II., his son, immediately succeeded him. He resembled his father in many parts of his character. The introduction of the reformed religion at this period excited a general ferment, and caused breaches and divisions in all orders of society. The opinions and doctrines of Luther were made known, by the art of printing, in all Christian countries. In France, those who adopted them were called *Huguenots:* the origin of the name is not known. The king died in 1559, leaving the country in a most deplorable state, from the effects of long civil wars. *Francis II.* assumed the government at the age of sixteen. He persecuted the Huguenots with the utmost cruelty during his short reign of seventeen months. Yet, in spite of the cruelties they suffered, their numbers daily augmented, till whole towns were of the Protestant persuasion.

On the death of the young king, a younger brother, *Charles IX.*, succeeded to the throne; but, being only nine years old, the government was conducted by the duke of Guise, a haughty, ambitious nobleman, and a profound enemy to the reformation, and Catharine de Medicis, the mother of Charles. This woman, celebrated for her crimes, intrigues, and talents, was a Florentine of high birth; she became early familiarized with the vices of dishonest politicians. She united in her character the most discordant and contradictory qualities. She was by nature cruel, and yet fond of refinement and the humanizing arts of life. She was both avaricious and profuse. She looked upon deceit and dissimulation as wisdom and policy. She never acted with sincerity, and never was known to lose her presence of mind. She trained her sons in the arts of deceit, and, when she became regent, during the minority of Charles IX., encouraged him to abandon himself entirely to pleasure. He was placed under the care of the mareschal de Retz, an accomplished master in every kind of vice.

The young king, thus left to himself, had the misfortune to be only taught what was bad. De Retz, however, could never make him a drunkard. He once prevailed on him to drink to intoxication; but he was so much disgusted with having been in this condition, that he was ever after remarkably abstemious. He was by nature ardent, and did every thing with a vehemence of spirit. When he danced, it was with such impetuosity that the ladies of the court dreaded him for a partner. He loved all kinds of hard labor, and took great pleasure in working at a blacksmith's forge. Catharine and the duke of Guise were now solely bent on the acquisition of power. The latter first provoked the Huguenots to take up arms and openly declare war against the Catholics. A spark set the whole kingdom in a blaze. Several Huguenots, while at their devotions in a barn, were insulted by the servants of the duke of Guise, who chanced to pass by. An affray ensued, in which the duke himself was wounded with a stone. His servants made a desperate onset upon the Protestants, and killed several of them. The latter, believing the assault to have been a premeditated commencement of hostilities, at once rushed to arms.

Such was the beginning of the dreadful religious wars which for so many years desolated France. They were carried on with a ferocity almost unexampled; all family and social ties were torn asunder; every town became a fortress, and countrymen and fellow citizens cut each other's throats in the streets. Catharine, who was a zealous Catholic, and bore a personal feeling of hatred to every Protestant, spent two years in contriving the most diabolical plot recorded in history. This was nothing less than the slaughter of all the Huguenots in France. The king, at first, shrank from so enormous a crime; but, at last, gave a reluctant consent, exclaiming, in a paroxysm of rage mingled with seeming insanity, "I consent, provided you kill them all, and leave no survivor to reproach me." Catharine wished to include Henry, king of Navarre, afterward Henry IV., in the number of victims, on account of his attachment to the Protestant religion; but Charles refused to sacrifice those of his own blood.

The night of the 24th of August, 1572, was fixed upon for the massacre. The striking of the great bell of the palace, at Paris, was to be the signal. As the appointed hour approached, the king, less hardened than his mother, was in the greatest agitation, and trembled from head to foot. To prevent the possibility of his retracting his consent, she gave the signal before the appointed hour. The admiral Coligny, a venerable, religious man, was the first victim. The cry, "Kill! kill!" now resounded through the streets. The greater part of the Protestants were surprised in their beds. For eight days, blood flowed in the streets, and corpses lay in heaps in the gutters. While these events took place in Paris, similar scenes occurred all over France. One Catholic boasted of having bought thirty Huguenots, for the purpose of torturing them. Charles himself, who, after the sight of blood, had forgotten his scruples and hesitation, shot the flying victims, as they passed the windows of the Louvre. Henry of Navarre only saved his life by abjuring Protestantism. The next day, a hawthorn bloomed for the second time that year, in the cemetery of the Innocents: this was interpreted by the fanatics as an indication of the pleasure of Heaven, and the slaughter recommenced. One hundred thousand persons were sacrificed in this ruthless butchery, which was called the *massacre of St. Bartholomew*, from the day on which it began. Many Catholics also perished, the victims of mistake, or of private animosity.* The wish of Charles that none should survive to reproach him, was not fulfilled: two millions yet remained. The civil war was renewed with greater fury than ever. The Protestants felt themselves strengthened by the sympathy of all whom bigotry had not rendered callous to every feeling of humanity, and the authors of this unparalleled crime had the mortification to discover that it had been perpetrated in vain.

CHAPTER CCCXCV.

A. D. 1572 to 1642.

Death of Charles IX., and Accession of Henry III. — Henry the Great — The Edict of Nantes — Louis XIII. — Cardinal Richelieu — His Policy and Character.

From the day of St. Bartholomew, the health of Charles rapidly declined. His nights were restless and disturbed, and his sleep unrefreshing. He was frequently overheard bewailing his atrocities, with tears and groans. His mother, Catharine, forced from him a commission of regency during the interval which must elapse between his death and the arrival of his brother from Poland, over which country he had been chosen king. Charles died in 1574, in the twenty-fourth year of his age, and the thirteenth of his reign. Henry, who was at Cracow, in Poland, departed secretly in the night, without taking any measures for the government during his absence. On arriving in France, he was crowned as *Henry III.* The first year of his reign, he manifested a disposition to govern for the good of his subjects; but every flattering trait of character soon vanished. He occupied his time in devising new fashions of dress. He painted his face white and red, and wore plasters at night to improve his complexion. He stained his hair, to hide the natural color, which was red. The dye which he used failed of its intended purpose, but was not entirely without effect, for it destroyed the hair, and left him bald. He used to sit in a closet, his sword by his side, with a basket round his neck, in which reposed a litter of small puppies. In this position he amused himself by playing at cup and ball.

While he thus neglected his duties, his unhappy kingdom continued a prey to civil war. Brother was

* It appears that the pope of Rome, Gregory XIII., took a lively interest in this massacre. He went in solemn procession to church, to give thanks for the slaughter of the heretics, and even caused a medal to be struck in commemoration of what he deemed a glorious event. Copies of this medal are still extant. On one side is the name of the pope, with his image; on the other is an angel presenting a cross to a group of persons being slain. The inscription is in Latin — "*The slaughter of the Huguenots*, 1572."

armed against brother; there were as many hostile powers as there were towns. Relations deliberately murdered each other; the lands, when cultivated at all, were tilled with the sword in one hand, and the plough in the other. The effect of this state of things on the minds of the people was melancholy indeed. Their hearts were rendered callous by familiarity with scenes of blood, and became insensible to all difference between right and wrong. The Protestants, who were increasing rapidly in numbers, extorted from Henry the privilege of holding public worship wherever they pleased, except at Paris. This concession was so displeasing to the pope, with other Catholic sovereigns of Europe, that they entered into a confederacy called the *holy league*, determining to deprive the Huguenots of their newly-acquired advantages. But all their threats could not induce the king to alter his decree. Catharine, who belonged to the alliance, died soon after, her death being hastened by her remorse for the ruin and misery which her schemes had brought, and were still bringing, upon her race. Henry III. was assassinated in the year 1589, by a monk named *Clement.* In him the house of Valois became extinct, having occupied the throne for two hundred and sixty-one years. There were thirteen monarchs of this race, of whom it may be said that they were, for the most part, brave, magnificent, and lovers of the fine arts. They expelled the English, united Dauphiny, Burgundy, Provence, and Brittany, to their dominion, and left to their successors a large and compact territory. But they were, on the other hand, with few exceptions, arbitrary and ambitious, and trampled, without scruple, on the rights of the people.

On the death of Henry III., the holy league refused to acknowledge Henry of Navarre as his successor, on account of his religion; for although he had renounced his Huguenot faith, during the massacre of St. Bartholomew, to save his life, he immediately returned to it on being released from danger, not considering himself bound by an oath thus forced upon him. His right of inheritance was incontestable. He was descended from Robert of Clermont, sixth son of St. Louis: the princes of this family were the only ones who had survived amid the rapid extinction of all branches of the royal family. The holy league, however, caused his uncle, the cardinal of Bourbon, to be proclaimed king. The Protestants declared that they would own no other sovereign than Henry, and that they were ready to die in his service. A terrible war followed, which lasted five years; the Huguenot army suffered many hardships from want of food and clothing. Queen Elizabeth several times sent Henry supplies of troops and money from England; but notwithstanding this, his clothes were often worn out, and he and his soldiers had nothing to eat but black bread. In 1590, the league lost their phantom of a king, and in the same year, Henry laid siege to Paris. But he could not prevail upon himself to bring the horrors of a bombardment upon the city, and though it was completely in his power, he refused to adopt the violent measure of an assault. He endeavored to reduce the inhabitants by famine. The Parisians, after having consumed all their provisions, devoured their dogs and cats, and even children, and ground the bones of the dead to make bread. Henry, touched with pity, allowed his soldiers to lift food, on the ends of their lances, to the besieged, and, when he found that hunger could not force them to submission, retired, and left the inhabitants unmolested. He is said to have given as a reason for his conduct,—"I would rather never have Paris, than possess it by the death and ruin of so many persons. I do not wish the city to become a cemetery, nor do I wish to reign over the dead." It now seemed evident to Henry and his counsellors, that there was only one course which could restore peace to this distracted country; and this, after due reflection and consultation, he concluded to adopt. He renounced the reformed religion, and July 25, 1593, made his profession of Catholicism in the church at St. Denis. He was crowned as *Henry IV.* in the early part of the following year.

He at once proclaimed a pardon to all the French who had borne arms against him, and the whole country submitted to his authority. Thus France saw the termination of those troubles with which she had been distracted during a period of thirty-seven years. The rights of the Huguenots were secured to them by a decree called the *Edict of Nantes.* Before this, no Protestants could be magistrates, or hold any offices of trust in the state, except in their own towns; but they were now admitted to the same privileges as other citizens; they were allowed to build churches, and to enjoy, equally with the Catholics, the favor of the king, and the protection of the laws. Twelve years of peace now allowed Henry to repair, in some sort, the evils done to France during forty years of massacre, of foreign and civil war. Order in the finances succeeded the waste and prodigality of previous administrations. He paid by degrees the debts of the crown. The peasants of the present day repeat a wish of Henry the Great, "that they might have a chicken in the pot every Sunday;" a trivial expression, perhaps, but one which well expresses his paternal sentiments. Forts were repaired, magazines and arsenals replenished, and the high roads well taken care of; the administration of justice was reformed, and the two religions subsisted together in peace. An ambassador, who had seen France in other days, remarked, on one occasion, to the king, that he no longer recognized the country which he had once found so languishing and unhappy. "Ah," said Henry, "that was because the father of the family was not then at home; he is here now, and his children prosper." In all that he did, the king found a most able assistant in Sully, his friend and minister. He was a Huguenot, and the pope labored hard to make him change his religion; but Sully's answer was, that he would never cease to pray for the conversion of his holiness.

Henry, now that his kingdom was at peace at home and abroad, formed the plan of constituting Europe upon a new basis, and uniting all Christendom into a sort of Christian republic, in which each state should be secure from the aggression of any other. But his projects were brought to a sudden termination. Reports had for some time prevailed that the king would not live long. On the 14th of May, he started in his coach with six noblemen, for the arsenal, the residence of Sully. At the crossing of a street, he was stopped by a row of vehicles passing in a different direction. A wretch, named François Ravaillac, who had time to see which was the king, jumped upon the wheel of the coach, reached over, and stabbed him twice in the breast. Henry drew a long sigh, and died without speaking. The courtiers assembled in great agitation, to determine what should be done The heir apparent was only nine years old, and the queen, his mother, Marie de Medicis, was declared regent. The consternation and public grief were universal; the king was mourned for as a father. He is the only king of the old monarchy whose memory is

Assassination of Henry IV.

still cherished with affection in France. Ravaillac, his murderer, was seized and tortured for an hour upon the rack: he bore it with the most patient calmness, without once uttering a groan, and declared to the last that he had no accomplice in the crime. He was afterward torn asunder by four horses.

The untimely death of Henry was a great misfortune to France, for his son Louis was a mere child, and subsequently displayed no signs of the virtues which had so eminently distinguished his father; and the queen regent was a weak and foolish woman, who squandered with profusion the treasures amassed by the late king. Sully withdrew from the court, and spent the rest of his life at his castle on the banks of the Loire. De Luynes, the tutor of Louis, soon became minister, and in fact governed the country. He was so arrogant and conceited, that it was said of him, that there were three most difficult things in the world — to square the circle, to find the philosopher's stone, and to speak with the duke de Luynes. Paris was the scene of constant robberies and murders; not a night passed without bloodshed; gentlemen and noblemen thought it no crime to stand at the corners of the streets and waylay the passers by, sometimes to steal a cloak, or snatch the well-filled purse of a citizen. As the king approached to maturity, strong hopes were entertained that he would display more energy, and govern the kingdom as his father had done. But these anticipations were disappointed. De Luynes died in 1621, and his place in the king's confidence was immediately filled by the celebrated Armand du Plessis Richelieu.

This extraordinary man was of noble birth, and had been educated for the church. By his abilities and cunning, he put himself in a situation to succeed the duke de Luynes, and from that period to his death, in 1642, was the despotic ruler of France. He became prime minister in 1629, assumed the government of the state, and the control of the army, usually taking the field in person. He steadily devoted all his powers to the gratification of two passions — an insatiable love of power, and an inordinate vanity. The great events of his administration were the overthrow of the aristocracy, and the humbling of the Huguenots or Protestants.

The siege and capture of Rochelle, a stronghold of the Huguenots, is the most memorable incident of the times, and well exemplifies the great ability, remorseless energy, and indefatigable perseverance of Richelieu. The minister decided upon the destruction of the town, while the inhabitants, as resolved as he, made preparations to defend themselves to the last extremity. Rochelle was a seaport town, on the Bay of Biscay. In former sieges, the people had received supplies from the English. Its situation rendered it difficult to cut off these supplies, which were always sent by water. Richelieu, however, to effect this, caused a gigantic mole to be erected across the mouth of the harbor: this structure was twice overthrown by the winds and the waves. He commenced it anew, without hesitating, reading daily in Quintius Curtius the description of Alexander's celebrated mole before the city of Tyre. During the progress of the siege, the king, now *Louis XIII.*, came himself to the scene of action.

The inhabitants, encouraged by the example of the duchess of Rohan, the daughter of Sully, submitted to the greatest misery. She herself and her daughter ate no other food during three months than horse-flesh, with a small bit of bread each day. The mayor of the city was implored by starving wretches, who were on the point of expiring, to give up the city. He replied, "Why should we submit, while there is one man left to shut the gates?" At length, however, famine triumphed over the resistance of the people. All hope of aid from England had failed, and the city surrendered. There were only four thousand survivors left out of a population of twenty-six thousand. Many more died from the avidity with which they swallowed the first food which was offered them. On the very next day after the surrender, a violent storm arose, and buried in the waves, for the third time, the fatal mole which had been the means of reducing the city. The capture of Rochelle was a fatal blow to the Protestants throughout France. Bereft of hope, all the towns which remained to them, yielded one by one, and the cause of religious freedom was crushed.

Richelieu now devoted his energies to repressing the power of the house of Austria. The French gained some increase of influence in these wars, but little accession of territory. The health of the minister was in the mean time failing. Worn down by disease, he still attended the court, being carried on the shoulders of his guards, in a machine covered with damask. He yet hoped to survive the king, and was laying plans to secure the regency, when he died, in the fifty-seventh year of his age, after having indicated Cardinal Mazarin as his successor.

No one can doubt the vast abilities of Richelieu as a statesman; but, regarding his career from our own time, he seems to have been the author of innumerable calamities to his country. In crushing the nobility, he sought only to remove an obstacle to the complete ascendency of the crown: in destroying the Protestants, he quenched the fire of mental independence, and annihilated the very sources of individual truth, honor, and dignity. From that time, all became servile and accommodating to the priesthood and the crown. *Louis XIV.* soon succeeded, and completed what Richelieu had begun. The centralization of all power in the crown was, in his view, the perfection of government. This was expressed by him in a brief apothegm — "I am the state." Here is the key to the melancholy events which have followed, drenching France in blood, and staining her annals with the crimes of successive revolutions.

In his personal character, Richelieu was fond of display and magnificence. He commenced the edifice known as the *Palais Royal*, built the church of the Sorbonne, and founded the celebrated establishment called the "Garden of Plants." He was not only greedy of the praise of his contemporaries, but covetous of posthumous fame. He patronized men of letters, that his name might be immortalized by their pens. He founded the French Academy, — an institution which exists to this day, — for the express purpose of improving the French language. No words or phrases are considered good French unless approved of by its members. The king survived his ambitious minister but five months. He appointed his wife, Anne of Austria, regent, and then prepared for death with composure. He died in 1642, in the thirty-third year of his reign.

CHAPTER CCCXCVI.

A. D. 1642 to 1783.

War of the Fronde — Louis XIV. — Revocation of the Edict of Nantes — Louis XV.

CARDINAL MAZARIN, who succeeded Richelieu as minister, was in every thing either his reverse or his inferior. Richelieu was haughty and overbearing, and beat down all opposition: Mazarin was supple and insinuating, and affected gentleness of manner. The Germans and Austrians hoped to derive great advantage from the death of Richelieu and the disorders which usually attend a minority; but Condé, the general who was now at the head of the army, by a splendid series of victories, compelled the emperor of Germany to conclude the treaty of Westphalia, in 1648. Mazarin was glad to make peace, for he found his domestic troubles quite enough to absorb his attention. He was an Italian, and his foreign accent subjected him to constant ridicule. He became speedily unpopular, and the people resisted the execution of his orders, and barricaded the streets. This was the commencement of a long disturbance, called the *War of the Fronde*, from the French word *fronder*, to browbeat or censure. Ridicule was, at first, the only weapon made use of, and songs and epigrams were, for a time, the most deadly artillery employed. Pillage and devastation soon followed; cornfields were trampled down by the cavalry in the presence of their owners. Ladies took part in these troubles. Mademoiselle de Montpensier, cousin to the king, was an active leader on the part of the Fronde. Influential nobles sold themselves to the party who best paid their services. Some were bought with money and places, others with the hand of some rich heiress; and, when they had obtained what they wanted, were quite ready for another change. The agitation continued for four years, Mazarin at one time being at court, and at another in exile, but governing the queen as absolutely in one place as in another.

The young king was at this period approaching maturity, but was purposely kept ignorant of public affairs by Mazarin. But, on the death of this minister, in 1661, he declared his resolution to take the reins into his own hands. From that time till the last moment of his life, he was not only the nominal but the real head of the state, and kept all his ministers under strict control. His reign lasted seventy-three years the first eighteen, the period of his minority, Mazarin ruled in his name. His early manhood was an epoch of comparative triumph and glory, while his old age was marked by a melancholy series of reverses. He was fond of war, and, at different periods of his life, was engaged in quarrels with almost every country of Europe. He invaded Holland with a large and well-disciplined army: having ample munitions, two able ministers and Turenne for a general — such were the advantages with which Louis entered upon his schemes of conquest. In three months, three provinces and forty strong places were taken. Inevitable ruin seemed to await the republic. Fifty thousand families prepared to seek a refuge in the East Indies; and thus the miserable glory of having desolated what was then the richest and most prosperous country in Europe would have been the only reward of the conqueror. But the emperor of Spain at this time openly declared for Holland, and Louis recalled his troops and abandoned his conquest.

Military glory was the great object of the ambition of the king, but he was far from overlooking the improvement of his territories. He had never forgotten the part which the Parisians had taken in the disturbances of the Fronde, and hence removed the court to St. Germain, and afterward to Versailles. He erected at the latter place the most splendid palace in Europe. He expended two hundred million dollars upon its buildings and grounds. His minister, the celebrated Colbert, labored assiduously to promote the prosperity of the country; and, to further this end, endeavored to render France independent of other nations by introducing the manufacture of many articles which were previously imported. Fine cloths had hitherto been brought from England; but, by his judicious patronage, their fabrication was established in France. By encouraging the growth of mulberry-trees, he enabled the silk manufacturers to dispense with the importation of raw silk. The art of making plate glass was imported from Venice, of carpets from Turkey and Flanders — and the French soon excelled their masters. A machine for weaving stockings was introduced from England; tin, steel, porcelain, and Morocco leather, hitherto brought from foreign countries, were now prepared in France.

Louis XIV., though himself illiterate, was a liberal patron of men of letters. Corneille, Molière, and Racine, dramatic writers; Boileau, La Fontaine, and Voiture, poets; Montesquieu and Fontenelle, philosophers; Bossuet and Fenelon, ecclesiastics — all flourished in his reign. The king gave pensions to the eminent men of letters throughout Europe, and thus secured to himself more adulation from men of real learning than any prince of modern times. Madame de Sévigné also lived at this period. Her letters furnish a lively picture of the times, and are considered as models of epistolary writing.

In 1685, Louis married the celebrated madame de Maintenon, the widow of a deformed old poet named Scarron. She was so poor at the time of her marriage with this author, that Scarron said her dowry consisted of "two large eyes full of fun, a fine shape, a pair of beautiful hands, a great deal of wit, and four dollars." His death did not leave her much richer than before; but, being attached to the court in the capacity of governess, she fascinated the king by her elegance of deportment and her agreeable conversation. She never received the title of queen, and assumed no airs of greatness, in consequence of her elevation. The king often transacted business with his ministers in her apartment, while she sat by sewing or reading. Sometimes he would ask her opinion, saying, "What does Madame Sobriety think?" But she carefully avoided all ostensible interference in affairs of state, though there is reason to believe that she covertly exerted a good deal of influence, and engaged in political intrigues.

More than a hundred years had now elapsed since the massacre of the Huguenots, and sixty since the siege of Rochelle. Many, who were infants at this latter period, had become grandfathers, and many, then unborn, were now the parents of large families. The Protestants again formed a considerable part of the population of France, and had built about seven hundred churches in various parts of the kingdom. Louis was a bigoted Roman Catholic, and believed that he followed the will of Heaven in murdering those who would not adopt his creed. Colbert, who had always protected the Huguenots, was dead, and the influence of the present ministers now coincided with the inclination of the king. The edict of Nantes, which secured liberty of conscience to the Protestants, was revoked, and they were deprived of the privileges they had enjoyed, and the laws which had shielded them from harm. A more cruel persecution was commenced against them than any they had before experienced. Missionaries were sent into every province to endeavor to convert them to Catholicism, and dragoons followed these to second their efforts. The latter established themselves in the houses of those who refused to obey, plundered their property, and wasted their fields. They next attacked the persons of the Protestants, pursued them into the forests, and massacred them without mercy. Men were thrown into dungeons, and females were hurried into convents, from which they never emerged except upon renunciation of their religion.

These severities induced many families to seek a new home in countries where they might worship God according to the dictates of their own hearts. All who should attempt to escape, however, were menaced with certain death; the guards were doubled on the frontiers, and the peasants were ordered to attack the fugitives wherever they met them. Those who were taken, were stripped of what they had saved from the general wreck, were loaded with chains, and often put to the torture. Notwithstanding the vigilance of the government, no less than half a million found means to escape, carrying into other countries their money, their skill in manufactures, and their habits of industry. A large number took refuge in America, and settled in the region now known as North and South Carolina. France never recovered from the blow which her industry thus received. The Huguenots were quiet and peaceable citizens, and carried on exclusively many branches of trade. The art of preparing tin and steel was known only to them, and the knowledge of it was thus lost to the kingdom. It was said of this period, "France is like a sick person, whose legs and arms have been cut off, as a remedy for a disorder which mildness and patience would have totally cured." History says little of the French Protestants from this time. Liberty of conscience was not secured to the country till the great revolution.

From this time to the year 1711, Louis was almost continually at war, and during the latter portion of this period, suffered a series of defeats and calamities. In 1688, the abdication of James II. and the *Revolution in England* placed the Prince of Orange on the throne of that country. James came to France, where he was hospitably received by Louis. A movement soon after taking place in Ireland, for the purpose of restoring the crown of Great Britain to James, he sent to the assistance of the insurgents a fleet of six thousand men. These met with a decisive defeat in the battle of the Boyne, July, 1690. Another war, which lasted fifteen years, took place on the death of the king of Spain, arising from a dispute among the several nations of Europe, as to whether he should be succeeded by Philip, the grandson of Louis XIV., or by Charles, the archduke of Austria. After much bloodshed and misery, the war ended in favor of Philip. Peace followed by the treaty of Utrecht, in 1713.

Although the "war of the succession" had been carried on in Spain, Germany, and Italy, it had cost the French nation many lives and much money. The kingdom was reduced to wretchedness and poverty. The king was seventy-six years old, and visibly drawing near his end. He reflected and meditated much, and a succession of domestic misfortunes, which now fell upon him, induced in him a religious train of thought. He began to see that he had mistaken the true aim of life, and all the ends for which his power had been given. In his last sickness, in 1715, he displayed a fortitude tempered by humility, such as few exhibit. He recollected his own weaknesses, and had the magnanimity to confess them. He died September 1, 1715, being within four days of seventy-seven years of age.

In his last years, Louis was always surrounded by a numerous throng of courtiers: to these abject slaves, a frown was a punishment almost insupportable, and banishment from the court a sentence of death. The individual who was permitted to hold a candle while the king was undressing, became an object of general envy.

Louis XIV. being dressed in the presence of his Courtiers.

The character of this sovereign is marked with contradictions. That he had some great qualities is not to be denied: he certainly acquired an extraordinary ascendency over the generation with which he lived. He was called by the French *le Grand Monarque*, and was deemed not only the greatest sovereign, but the most accomplished gentleman, of any age or country. A very different estimate is now put upon his character, both public and private. His policy was selfish, having no other object than his own glory: it was short-sighted, and laid the foundation of incalculable mischief and misery. The personal qualities of the king, were showy, and imposed on those around him. His art, in mere manner, was great: his real character consisted of a vanity and self-appreciation which sacrificed every thing to their inordinate appetite for gratification.*

The only one of the sons of Louis XIV. who had survived infancy had died in 1711, leaving three sons —the duke of Burgundy, Philip, king of Spain, and the duke of Berri. The king of Spain had renounced the succession to the throne of France, and the dukes of Berri and Burgundy were already in their graves. A son of the latter, afterward *Louis XV.*, great-grandson of Louis XIV., thus became heir to the throne. He was at this period but five years old, and a regency was, therefore, necessary. This was assumed by Philip, the duke of Orleans. One of the most remarkable events of this period was the Mississippi scheme of John Law. The extravagances of Louis XIV. had consumed all the resources of the state. The treasury was empty, and its creditors were clamorous for payment. Law proposed to the regent a plan of a bank, which should pay off the debts of the state in paper money. The profits of the bank were to be made by trading to the country in the valley of the Mississippi. Measures were taken with a view to reduce the value of gold and silver coin in comparison with the bank notes, which were never to fall below the value expressed upon them. All who had gold or silver, therefore, made haste to exchange it for bills. The officers of the bank could not satisfy the demand. The inhabitants of the provinces flocked to Paris with their metallic money, and besieged the doors of the bank. Such a concourse had never been seen at the capital before. Multitudes sold their houses and lands to purchase stock in the bank which promised to make enormous profits. Every class—clergy and laity, peers and plebeians, statesmen and chimney-sweeps and even ladies—turned stockjobbers, outbidding each other with such avidity, that, in November, 1719, the price of shares rose to more than sixty times the sum for which they had originally been sold. On one occasion, Law was taken sick, and the shares of the company immediately fell eight per cent., and, upon the rumor of his convalescence, rose again even beyond their former price. This splendid scheme, after a short-lived popularity, suddenly exploded, involving thousands of families in its fall. The institution was bankrupt, and its shares were worthless. The gold and silver disappeared; the bills of the bank alone remained, and half France was ruined. Law sought safety in flight, and, after wandering about Germany, died in Venice, in 1729.

The regency expired in 1722; but the duke of Orleans, as prime minister, continued to carry on the government. Louis XV. had but little natural capacity; and, knowing himself to be a king, and his will to be a law to those around him, always refused to study his lessons. His governess, who was aware that to whip the king would be little short of high treason, procured a child of poor parents to be the companion of his studies. Whenever Louis was idle or said his lessons badly, this unfortunate boy was whipped in his stead. The young king was remarkably handsome, and, though fond of low company, vicious and frivolous, he acquired much of the outward show of royalty, and became dignified and majestic in air and manner. Several unimportant wars disturbed the early part of his reign: peace was restored to the country by the treaty of Aix-la-Chapelle, in 1748. The few years which followed the peace were among the most prosperous that France had ever known. Manufactures and commerce flourished, and the colonies, particularly St. Domingo, made rapid advances in wealth. Under the patronage of the king, the sciences, especially mathematics and astronomy, were much cultivated. But in matters of taste, such as

* "Concerning Louis XIV. the world seems at last to have formed a correct judgment. He was not a great general; he was not a great statesman; but he was, in one sense of the word, a great king. Never was there so consummate a master of what James I. would have called kingcraft—of all those arts which most advantageously display the merits of a prince, and most completely hide his defects. Though his internal administration was bad, though the military triumphs which gave splendor to the early part of his reign were not achieved by himself, though his later years were crowded with defeats and humiliations, though he was so ignorant that he scarcely understood the Latin of his mass book, though he fell under the control of a cunning Jesuit, and of a more cunning old woman, he succeeded in passing himself off on his people as a being above humanity; and this is the most extraordinary, because he did not exclude himself from the public gaze, like those Oriental despots whose faces are never seen, and whose very names it is a crime to pronounce lightly.

"It has been said that no man is a hero to his valet; and all the world saw as much of Louis XIV. as his valet could see. Five hundred people assembled to see him shave and put on his breeches in the morning. He then kneeled down at the side of his bed, and said his prayer, while the whole assembly awaited the end in solemn silence, the ecclesiastics on their knees, and the laymen with their hats over their faces. He walked about his garden with a train of two hundred courtiers at his heels. All Versailles came to see him dine and sup. He was put to bed at night in the midst of a crowd as great as that which had met to see him rise in the morning. He took his very emetics in state, and vomited majestically in the midst of all the *grandes* and *petites entrées*.

"Yet, though he constantly exposed himself to the public gaze in situations in which it is scarcely possible for any man to preserve much personal dignity, he to the last impressed those who surrounded him with the deepest awe and reverence. The illusion which he produced on his worshippers can be compared only to those illusions to which lovers are proverbially subject during the season of courtship. It was an illusion which affected even the senses. The contemporaries of Louis thought him tall; Voltaire, who might have seen him, and who had lived with some of the most distinguished members of his court, speaks repeatedly of his majestic stature; yet it is as certain as any fact can be, that he was rather below than above the middle size. He had, it seems, a way of holding himself, a way of walking, a way of swelling his chest and rearing his head, which deceived the eyes of the multitude. Eighty years after his death, the royal cemetery was violated by the revolutionists; his coffin was opened; his body was dragged out, and it appeared that the prince, whose majestic figure had been so long and so loudly extolled, was in truth a little man.

"His person and his government have had the same fate. He had the art of making both appear grand pageants, in spite of the clearest evidence that both were below the ordinary standard. Death and time have exposed both the deceptions. The body of the great king has been measured more justly than it was measured by the courtiers, who were afraid of looking at his shoe-tie.

"His public character has been scrutinized by men free from the hopes and fears of Boileau and Molière. In the grave, the most majestic of princes is only five feet eight. In history, the hero and the politician dwindles into a vain and feeble tyrant, the slave of priests and women—little in war little in government, little in every thing but the art of simulating greatness."—*Macaulay.*

architecture and dress, the reign of Louis XV. deserves but little credit. A love of gaudy and frivolous ornament was every where visible. In dress, hoops and high heels were in all their glory. Paint, both red and white, was liberally applied to the face, neck, and hands; the hair was profusely anointed with pomatum and other unguents, and then filled with powder to the very roots.

In 1754, a war commenced between the French and English colonies in America. The details of this contest, as far as it concerns the United States and Canada, will be given in the history of those countries. The war did not extend to Europe till 1756, and is commonly called the *seven years' war*. Its most important consequence to France was the loss of Canada, which was given up to the English. The expenses attendant upon this struggle added greatly to the distresses under which the people were already suffering; and, at the death of Louis XV., in 1774, indications were beginning to appear of that discontent which led to the startling events of the next reign. Infidelity and licentiousness pervaded all classes.

The accession of the new king, *Louis XVI.*, grandson of Louis XV., a prince "who, in the most corrupt court, had led an uncorrupt life," was hailed with universal joy. He immediately applied himself to redress the grievances of the people. He dismissed the faithless ministers, and banished the dissolute companions of Louis XV. The happiness of his people seemed to be the main object of his solicitude. But his good qualities could not compensate, in the eyes of the Parisians, for certain personal deficiencies. He was clumsy in his gait and untidy in his dress; his countenance was also heavy and unpleasing. He did not look like a king, and took more pleasure in forging locks and keys in his workshop than in presiding over *fêtes*. His unpopularity was increased by his marriage, four years before his accession, with Marie Antoinette, daughter of Maria Theresa, empress of Germany. The French disliked the Austrians, and feared the influence of the princes of the house of Austria, so nearly allied to the queen, in the government of France.

Dr. Franklin arrived at this period in Paris to solicit the assistance of France in the war which the United States were then carrying on against England to gain their independence. This was urged upon Louis as a most favorable opportunity for weakening the old rival of France. But, as a king, Louis had no sympathy with rebels, as the colonists were called, and no desire to encourage subjects in resisting their sovereigns. But the popular will was strong, and Louis yielded so far as to recognize the independence of the United States by treaty. This was considered by England as a declaration of war against her. The contest which followed was carried on principally upon the sea, and with variable success, but, on the whole, favorable for France. Peace was concluded at Versailles, in January, 1783, by which she recovered nearly all the possessions she had lost during the former war, except Canada.

The Mob proceeding to Versailles

CHAPTER CCCXCVII.

A. D. 1783 to 1794.

French Revolution — National Convention — Convocation of the States General — Execution of Louis XVI. and Marie Antoinette — Rise and Fall of Robespierre.

THE FRENCH REVOLUTION — the most startling event in European history — followed close upon the American war. The expenses of the part France had borne in the struggle had added to the public debt, and the discontent of the people was daily increasing. In 1783, M. de Calonne, minister of finance, brought forward a measure, which, equitable as it was, was not proposed till every other expedient for raising money had been tried in vain. This was, to make the landed property of the clergy and nobles bear its due share of the public burden. This measure could not be carried into execution without the consent either of those bodies themselves or of some great national council. The assembling of the States General, in which all the orders of the state were represented, was the most natural resource. This, however, was deferred, and an assembly of Notables was called. These were persons summoned from all parts of the kingdom, selected by the king himself, and chiefly from the higher orders of the state. These refused to listen to the measures brought forward by Calonne, and he was obliged to resign. His successor was equally unsuccessful. In pursuance of the advice of M. Necker, who now became minister of finance, the States General were summoned to meet at Versailles on the 1st of May, 1789.

The session opened with great splendor. The assembly was composed of the three estates of the kingdom, as they were called — the clergy, the nobles, and the people. The popular party were joined by some of the two other estates. These then declared themselves the sovereign legislators of the kingdom, and assumed the title of *National Assembly.* The nobles perceived that, unless some decided steps were taken by the king, all would be lost. They accordingly entreated him to dissolve the states general. On the morning of the 20th of June, the president and members of the national assembly were prevented from entering their hall by the king's guards, and were told that the room was being prepared for a royal session, and that a meeting of the three estates would be held there for the purpose of hearing a speech from the king. The members, irritated at this treatment, hurried to an old tennis court, and, in spite of a violent storm, held their meeting, and resolved that the assembly should continue its sessions till they had formed a constitution for their country.

The king, yielding to the influence of the queen, began to collect troops about Paris and Versailles. All confidence in his discretion was now gone. The only reliance of the people was upon Necker: he was, however, soon removed from office, and ordered to leave the kingdom. Paris burst into a flame at this unexpected event. The people collected in vast crowds. The opponents of the queen and court placed upon their hats the tri-colored cockade, and all who did not adopt this badge were subjected to insult, or even death, as enemies of the people. The soldiers were ordered to disperse these assemblages, but refused to fire upon their countrymen. Uniting with the citizens, they formed themselves into a militia by the name of the *National Guard*, and chose Lafayette to be their general. Hostilities against the royal authority were openly commenced on the 14th of July, 1789, by an attack on the Bastile — a gloomy prison, which had long been the instrument of tyranny in the hands of the government. It was taken by the people from the government troops who defended it. Not one stone was suffered to remain upon another, and its keys were afterward sent to General Washington. The place where the Bastile stood was converted into a beautiful square, in the centre of which is placed the "Column of July," — crowned by an image of Liberty. It had now become evident that opposition to the popular will was vain, and Necker was recalled. The national assembly proceeded with earnestness in the work of reforming abuses. Every exclusive right and privilege throughout the kingdom was at length abolished.

The National Guard.

The royal family lived at this period at Versailles. On the 6th of October, an immense mob, led by the fishwomen of Paris, rushed to Versailles, and made an assault on the palace. All its inmates would have been sacrificed if General Lafayette had not interposed to protect them. By his advice, the king complied with the demands of the mob, and returned to Paris. The constitution prepared by the national assembly was formally ratified by the king, on the anniversary of the destruction of the Bastile. Three hundred thousand persons, the ladies all dressed in white, were present at the ceremony which took place in the Champ de Mars. In presence of this immense multitude, the king, the members of the national assembly for themselves, and Lafayette in behalf of the national guard, swore to observe and defend the constitution.

The scenes of bloodshed that occurred daily at Paris, and the murder of such officers and servants as remained faithful to them, soon impressed the king with the idea that the royal family was no longer safe at Paris. The Parisians were almost constantly in arms, and once or twice some of the more violent broke into the palace, threatening the life of the queen. At last the unhappy monarch resolved to try to make his escape. The details of the flight of the royal family and of their recapture form one of the most melancholy pictures of fallen greatness in history. They travelled in disguise and in mean-looking carriages, under the protection of surreptitious passports. In spite of all

Oath of Ratification of the Constitution.

their precautions, they were discovered at a little inn near the frontiers of Germany, where they stopped to change horses. The unfortunate fugitives were taken back to Paris, and replaced in the Tuileries, where they were watched with the utmost vigilance. The remainder of the story of Louis XVI. may be told in a few words. His enemies had determined he should die, and procured his suspension from the office of king. The royal family were committed as prisoners to an old, gloomy building, formerly belonging to the Knights Templars, and known still as the *Temple.* They were not allowed the use of pen, ink, or paper, for fear they should correspond with their friends without: they were constantly subjected to insult and vexation; every thing was done to make their imprisonment irksome. But they bore their trials with an unshaken magnanimity. Not a murmur or a complaint ever escaped them.

On the 20th of September, 1792, the national assembly gave place to the National Convention. On the first day of its session, the convention decreed that ' royalty was abolished in France." In nearly all propositions which were submitted, the voice of this assembly was unanimous. But, in regard to the treatment of the royal family and some other measures, there were two parties. The most moderate were the *Girondists*, so called because the chief members among them were from the department of the Gironde: the other party was called the *Mountain*, the seats occupied by them rising one above the other in rows. It is better known, however, as the *Jacobin party*, the members of it belonging to that club. Their great object was to take away the life of the king. They were not so numerous as the Girondists; but, by their threats, terrified the more moderate into the adoption of the most violent measures. A sort of court was instituted, before which prisoners of each sex and of all ages were brought, in mockery of all the forms of justice. The number of persons put to death by this court in Paris alone during the month of September, 1792, amounted to several thousand.

On the 25th of December, 1792, Louis was ordered to appear before the convention: he was there accused of acts of tyranny during his reign, and of treason against the state for endeavoring to escape out of the kingdom. He was found guilty upon these charges, and sentence of death was passed upon him by the pitiless tribunal. He was executed on the 21st of January, 1793. He ascended the scaffold with a firm and dignified step, and his behavior there partook of the calm fortitude which had distinguished him through all his scenes of suffering. He asserted his innocence, but was prevented from saying more by drums placed there to drown his voice. He died in the thirty-ninth year of his age, a victim to the follies and vices of those who had preceded him. Marie Antoinette was also tried, condemned, and beheaded. She met her fate with fortitude and composure.

No sooner was the fate of Louis XVI. known in England, than war was declared against France. The Austrians had been in arms against the republicans from the beginning of the revolution. On the 1st of February, 1793, the convention had made a declaration of war against England and Holland, and, a fortnight afterward, against Spain. Among the French the greatest enthusiasm prevailed. All were desirous to contribute in some way to the common cause Those who had no money brought their personal ornaments, and deposited them in the great hall of the convention. Those whose age or sex rendered them unfit for actual fighting, employed themselves in providing for the wants of the soldiers. Before the end of 1794, all Holland was conquered, and remained from this time till the close of the wars of the revolution, dependent upon France.

From the time of the king's death, the Jacobin

party obtained a complete ascendency in the convention. Robespierre, Danton, and Marat were the heads of this party, and ruled the country with absolute sway. Robespierre soon found means to rid himself of his various rivals, and became sole ruler of France. The period during which he controlled the government has been called the *Reign of Terror*. Tribunals were established not only in Paris, but in every country town, which condemned to death all who in any way incurred his displeasure. The slightest word in favor of monarchy was a sufficient cause for imprisonment; and few, upon whom a prison's gates had once shut, ever saw the light of day again, except on the way to the place of execution. The prisons were filled with persons, of both sexes, suspected of being enemies to the revolution. Women working in the fields, and young peasant girls, were often dragged to loathsome dungeons for humming the air of a loyal song, or speaking with pity of the victims who had perished. In some of the more populous towns, the prisoners were brought into a large, open space, and fired upon by the soldiers till all were dead.

Marie Antoinette on the Scaffold.

In the mean time, the foreign wars rendered it necessary to increase the army, and this gave rise to a new species of oppression, called the *conscription*. This was a law made by the convention to oblige all single men between the ages of eighteen and twenty-five to become soldiers, however contrary to their inclinations. The inhabitants of a province in the west of France, called La Vendée, refused to obey this edict, and openly declared themselves royalists. A war was immediately commenced against them, and the peace and happiness of the region, so long undisturbed, were now cruelly invaded. The country was laid waste, the castles and cottages were burned to the ground, an nearly all the inhabitants either driven away or destroyed.

Titles had already been abolished, and every vestige of nobility was at length banished from France. The terms *citoyen* and *citoyenne*—"citizen" and "citizeness" — were used instead of the more aristocratic titles *Mr* and *Mrs*. Most of the nobles had either emigrated or perished by the guillotine. The clergy now became the objects of persecution. Robespierre openly declared that Christianity should be abolished in France and all churchmen, unless they renounced their faith were threatened with death or imprisonment. The churches were shut up, and thousands of priests fled for safety to England and Italy. Others were murdered in a manner too horrible to describe. Robespierre was the chief instigator of these barbarities: he had become the leader of the Jacobin party, by exceeding his fellows in love of bloodshed. There was nothing in his personal appearance which indicated his disposition. During the most sanguinary period, he was distinguished by the delicate and affected fastidiousness of his dress. A muslin waistcoat, lined with rose-colored silk, and a coat of the softest blue, was his favorite costume. The measures which he adopted to secure and strengthen his power, proved the means of his destruction. He had obtained the execution of many influential men of his own party, to rid himself of dangerous rivals. The surviving members of the convention at length united for their common safety. On the 28th of July, 1794, Robespierre was made prisoner, and on the next day he was executed. The news of his death was received with joy throughout France, and indeed throughout the civilized world

The character and career of Robespierre have been a riddle to historians. He began public life by endeavoring to obtain the abolition of capital punishment. We have no reason to doubt his sincerity in this, nor in his early devotion to the cause of human liberty. Many of his writings and documents are full of views and doctrines now fully acknowledged in this country, if not by the world. A just estimate of his character leads to the belief that, being deficient in principle, he was borne away by the excitement of great events, until his judgment fell before ambition, and at last his reason gave way to a species of monomania. Nothing can more strongly illustrate and enforce the danger and iniquity of intrusting men of unsound moral and religious character with high public interests — than the career of Robespierre and his atheistical associates. If we mistake not, most of the political troubles of France, from that day to this, have arisen from the want of religious principle in its public men.

Some time previous to this, a young girl, named *Charlotte Corday*, a native of Normandy, hearing of the dreadful crimes committed in Paris by the leaders of the convention, took the strange resolution of assassinating one of them, and actually travelled alone to the capital to execute her design. She was herself a republican, and rejoiced at the fall of the monarchy; but she believed that Robespierre and his colleagues injured the cause of liberty by their tyranny: she wrought herself up to a degree of enthusiasm that bordered on insanity, and having arrived at Paris, selected Marat for her victim, as being the worst of the three. She obtained an interview by pretending to have papers to deliver to him; and as he took them from her hand, she plunged a knife into his bosom, and he instantly expired

The infatuated girl, who believed she was performing a meritorious act, was condemned to death, and, to the last moment, declared that she felt no regret at what she had done, but was rejoiced at having rid the world of such a monster.

CHAPTER CCCXCVIII.

A. D. 1794 to 1814.

Rise of Napoleon Bonaparte — His Marriage — The Directory — Bonaparte First Consul — Passage of the Alps — Napoleon Emperor — His Abdication and Banishment to Elba.

Whilst the great mass of the French people had quietly submitted to the government of the convention, attempts at resistance were made in some places by the friends of liberty, in others by the partisans of the king. Among the disaffected was the city of Toulon, which surrendered to an English fleet, commanded by

Napoleon, at the Age of Twenty-two.

Lord Hood, on condition that it should be held for Louis XVII. An army of the convention soon appeared before its walls. The cannon of the besiegers were directed by one who was destined to act a prominent part in the affairs of the world. This was Napoleon Bonaparte. The extraordinary ability he displayed at the siege of Toulon drew upon him the notice of many persons of consequence. The city was taken by his skill and bravery. He was placed at the head of the army stationed about Paris, called the *Army of the Interior*.

It was at this period that he married Josephine, widow of the count de Beauharnois, who had incurred the displeasure of Robespierre, and had been put to death only four days before the fall of that tyrant. In the mean time, most of the nations that had been at war with the revolutionists with a view to the restoration of the French monarchy, finding their efforts unavailing, gave up the contest, and made peace. The grand duke of Tuscany, the kings of Spain, Sweden, Denmark, and Prussia, and the Swiss Cantons, all acknowledged the new republic; but the English, the Austrians, and the Russians, and some of the Italian states, remained at war with France.

The National Convention, in whose name so much crime had been committed, terminated its disgraceful career, October 27, 1795. A new form of government was established. The legislature consisted of two bodies, — the Council of the Ancients, and the Council of Five Hundred. The executive power was intrusted to five persons, called the *Directory*. In the spring of 1796, three great armies took the field. Two, which were to act in Germany, were under the command of Generals Moreau and Jourdan. Bonaparte was appointed to the command of the third army

Josephine.

and was sent to conquer Italy. His career in that country has been sketched in the history of the several Italian states. His victories followed one another in rapid succession, and in less than two years placed the greater part of the peninsula in subjection to France. He destroyed five Austrian armies, which were sent against him, one after another. The eyes of all Europe were now riveted upon him. He had become the terror of old empires, and the founder of new states. Such sudden elevations had occasionally happened amid barbarous nations, but were hitherto unheard of in civilized Europe. He directed his course toward Germany, and in less than twenty days defeat ed the Austrians in ten combats. A suspension of arms for five days was granted by Bonaparte, and the preliminaries of a treaty of peace were signed at Leoben, April 18, 1797. Peace was finally settled by the reaty of Campo Formio, October 17 of the same year. The emperor of Germany gave up to France the Netherlands, and all his German dominions beyond the Rhine, making that river the boundary between France and Germany. A large part of Italy was formed into a new state, called the *Cisalpine Republic.*

Napoleon in Italy.

The command of the expedition to Egypt, of which we have given a full account, was now offered to Bonaparte. After splendid and decisive victories, he closed his career in that country by the battle of Aboukir, July 25, 1799. He returned to France in October of the same year. During his absence, the emperor of Germany, yielding to the solicitations of England, had renewed the war. Russia, also, had taken up arms against France. The French met with many reverses, and discontent arose among the people. The news of the return of Bonaparte was received as the harbinger of better success. His progress from the sea-coast to Paris was one of triumph. The legislative councils were holding their sessions at St. Cloud, about six miles from Paris. On the 10th of November, 1799, Bonaparte, accompanied by a large body of officers, entered the hall of the Council of Five Hundred. Its members were compelled to disperse, and the Directory was dissolved. A new government was formed, Bonaparte being at its head, with the title of *First Consul.* This event is called, in French history, the 18*th Brumaire*, and may be considered as the termination of the revolution — an event characterized by acts of bloodshed and crime which affect the mind with horror. Its agitations were not confined to France: they extended to other countries; and as the monarchs of Europe combined to crush the spirit of liberty which spread throughout their dominions, a series of wars ensued which deluged all Christendom with blood. On whom does the responsibility of such measureless evils rest? Certainly not on the oppressed millions, struggling for deliverance from miseries too great to bear, but on the despotisms which caused them. The French revolution has at least taught the world that there is retribution for corrupt kings and selfish dynasties. It has done more; for it has exploded the profane doctrine that certain men, appointed of Heaven, and having royal blood, exercise sovereignty by divine right. It has at once taught the people their power, and monarchs their responsibility; and though all the benefit that might have been hoped has not been realized, yet it is clear that the event of which we speak was the threshold of a new era in the history of Europe, which will not close till it shall be established, both in opinion and practice, that the good of the mass is the true end of government, and that the people are the only legitimate and secure depositary of political power.

One of the first acts of the consul was to propose peace to Austria and England: it was declined by both powers. On the 6th of May, 1800, he left Paris to place himself at the head of an army of sixty thousand men, which had been assembled with great secrecy in Switzerland. On the 15th of the same month, the celebrated march known as the *Passage of the Alps* commenced. At the little village of St. Pierre, every thing resembling a road ended. An immense and apparently inaccessible mountain, called St. Bernard, reared its head among general desolation and eternal frost. Precipices, ravines, and a boundless extent of snow, which a breath of air might cause to roll down the side of the mountain in masses capable of burying armies in their descent — seemed to forbid access to all living things except the chamois. The cannon were placed in the trunks of trees hollowed out for the purpose. Each was dragged by a hundred men. The carriages were taken to pieces and fastened to the backs of mules. The musical bands played from time to time at the heads of the regiments, and in places of unusual difficulty, the drums beat a charge, as if to encourage the soldiers to encounter the opposition of nature itself. The men had no refreshment, save when they dipped a morsel of biscuit in the snow. At the convent of St. Bernard, the monks distributed bread and cheese, and a cup of wine, to each soldier as he passed. The descent of the mountain was even more difficult than the ascent. It was, however, accomplished without any material loss. On the 16th of May, the advanced guard of the army ook possession of the village of Aosta, in Piedmont. The appearance of the army, descending from the Alps by ways hitherto deemed impracticable, seemed like terrible enchantment to the Austrians. On the 14th of June, the great battle of Marengo was fought, and won by the French. This decided the fate of Italy. In less than two months, Bonaparte regained all that the French had lost in that country during his absence in Egypt. On the 3d of December, the Austrian army was entirely defeated at Hohenlinuen, by the French under Moreau. Peace was made with Austria by the treaty of Luneville, February 9, 1801. On the 27th of March, 1802, peace was concluded at Amiens between France and England.

The office of consul was originally to be held only for a term of years; but the French now made Bonaparte consul for life, with the privilege of appointing his successor. The possession of absolute power did not satisfy his ambition; he wished also for some title which might express it. In 1804, he was made hereditary emperor of France, and crowned with great solemnity, in the church of Notre Dame, at Paris. Charlemagne had been obliged to go to Rome to procure investiture as emperor; Napoleon resolved that the pope should now come to France to perform the ceremony. Pius VII. administered at Paris the usual oath to Napoleon, who repeated it after him. The crown was blessed by the pope, and Napoleon, with his own hands, placed it on his head. The Cisalpine republic was formed into the kingdom of Italy, of which the emperor was invited to become sovereign. At Milan, on the 26th of May, 1805, he placed on his head the iron crown, said to have been worn by the ancient kings of the Lombards.

Our space will not permit us to give a detailed account of the great events which now followed in rapid succession. Sometimes several powers joined against Napoleon; and again one or more of them were in alliance with him. Every new treaty brought a fresh accession of territory to France. In the early part of 1805, Austria and Russia had declared war against Napoleon. He entered Germany in October, and on the 13th of November took possession of Vienna, the proud capital of the house of Austria. On the 27th of the same month the Russians and Austrians were completely defeated in the renowned battle of Austerlitz. In the treaty of peace which was signed soon after, at Presburg, his title, as emperor of the French, was acknowledged. A large portion of the continent of Europe was now at his feet. He set up kings and put them down again at his pleasure. He placed his brother Joseph upon the throne of Naples. Louis Bonaparte, another brother, was made king of Holland. Hanover, the hereditary possession of the kings of England, was bestowed upon the king of Prussia, as a reward for the neutrality which he had kept in the war. Fourteen of the least powerful German princes united together under the title of *Confederation of the Rhine*, and placed themselves under the protection of Napoleon.

This vast accumulation of power on the part of the emperor gave great alarm. Austria was too much broken down to attempt any further resistance. But Prussia had not yet tried her strength with the conqueror. Frederic declared war. Napoleon speedily set his troops in motion, and on the 14th of October 1806, gained the decisive victory of Jena, and on the 25th of the same month, entered Berlin, the capital of Prussia. Proceeding in his victorious career, he defeated the Russians successively in the battles of Eylau and of Friedland. A part of the conquered territory was formed into the new *Kingdom of Westphalia*, which Napoleon gave to his brother Jerome. As there were now no more kingdoms to win in the north of Europe, Napoleon next turned his attention to the south. A French army entered Lisbon, the capital of Portugal, November 30, 1807. In the following year the king of Spain himself resigned his crown to the emperor who bestowed it on his brother Joseph, and the now vacant dignity of king of Naples was conferred on Murat, who had married a sister of Napoleon.

But the powers of Europe which had been humbled by the conqueror did not rest quietly, and only waited for a favorable opportunity to throw off the yoke. In the spring of 1809, the Tyrolese revolted, the Westphalians expelled Jerome, and Prussia seemed on the point of joining her forces with those of Austria in a decisive movement to recover their independence. But the French emperor, returning instantly from Madrid, led his army into the heart of the German territory. The victories of Eckmuhl, Essling, and Wagram soon followed. Vienna was again taken, and the continent was a second time prostrate at the feet of Napoleon. He dictated the "peace of Vienna," October 14, 1809. Napoleon now allied himself by

Maria Louisa and the young King of Rome.

marriage with the most ancient and illustrious family in Europe. For reasons of state, he separated from Josephine, and was united to Maria Louisa, a daughter

* This celebrated battle commenced on the 5th of July, 1809. The whole of this day the Austrian line was attacked at various points, with the greatest impetuosity, by the French army, supported by an immense train of artillery, with many batteries of the heaviest calibre. The Austrians maintained their position. The next day the contest was renewed, with increased energy, by the French. At last the left wing of the Austrians was penetrated, and they were compelled to retreat with an immense loss in killed and wounded. The French also suffered severely. This was one of the hardest fought battles in which Napoleon was personally engaged.

Cossack: Scene on the Way from Moscow

of the emperor Francis II. On the 2d of April, 1811, a son was born, to whom was given the title of *King of Rome.* In 1812, Napoleon invaded Russia with an army of four hundred thousand men. The details of this disastrous campaign we must leave to the history of Russia. On the 18th of December, Napoleon arrived at Paris; the remnant of his splendid army, numbering barely fifty thousand, followed him across the snows of the north, their uniforms replaced by women's pelisses, or what rags they could pick up, their feet bare and bleeding, or protected by bundles of filthy cloths instead of shoes.

Napoleon's days of prosperity were now at an end. All the powers of Europe formed a league against him — the emperors of Russia and Austria, the king of Prussia, Bernadotte, king of Sweden, who had formerly been a general in the French army, the kings of Bavaria and Wirtemberg, and other princes of the confederation of the Rhine. But with these fearful odds against him, Napoleon did not lose his courage or his military genius. Europe was filled with wonder at the fertility of his resources. He contended in a series of battles on German territory, but was unable to arrest the advance of the enemy. A battle was fought on the heights near Montmartre, the result of which left Paris exposed to the foe. On the 31st of March, 1814, Alexander of Russia and Frederic of Prussia took possession of that capital. A proclamation was at once issued, making known the determination of the allies to replace the Bourbons on the throne. Napoleon had yet an army at Fontainebleau. The soldiers were devotedly attached to him, and would have followed him with joy once more to battle. But the marshals and officers, considering the contest as hopeless, would not listen to the proposal. Napoleon, hoping that by his abdication he might secure the throne to his son, formally renounced his right on the 4th of April, 1814. This was of no avail. The allies decided that he should be confined to the Island of Elba, situated in the Mediterranean Sea. He was to retain the title of emperor; was to be allowed all the honors usually belonging to that dignity; was to have his army and his navy; but all upon a scale proportionate to the size of his empire. This was about sixty miles in extent, and contained about twelve thousand inhabitants. This arrangement was carried into effect. His empress, Maria Louisa, with her infant son, were sent to Vienna.

Paris presented a curious spectacle during its occupation by the allied troops — soldiers of many nations, Russians, Austrians, and barbarians from the deserts of Scythia, all quartered as it were in one vast camp. In the wide streets, the soldiers had constructed huts, at the doors of which some of them might be seen cooking their food, or patching their grotesque garments. The horses, tied to the trees in the beautiful gardens, were busily employed in stripping off the bark. Around were piles of warlike accoutrements, and arms of every description, from the bows and arrows and long lances of the barbarians, to the pistols and sabres of the more civilized warriors. The Parisians themselves maintained the greatest composure. The boulevards and public gardens presented the same gay scene as if no enemy were quartered upon the place. While the cannon of the enemy were to be heard thundering in their neighborhood, they remained perfectly at their ease, trusting to the skill and good fortune of the emperor. When this failed them, and the enemy were actually within their gates, still they seemed content. They who had so recently shouted "Long live Napoleon," now shouted as loud, "Long live Louis XVIII."

The Battle-Field.

CHAPTER CCCXCIX.

A. D. 1814 to 1863.

Battle of Waterloo — Revolutions of 1830 *and* 1848 — *France a Republic — Napoleon III.*

The fall of Napoleon restored peace to all nations, and was the cause of general rejoicing. By this unexpected turn of fortune, many princes who had been driven from their thrones were restored to them: among these were Ferdinand VII. of Spain, the king of Sardinia, and Pope Pius VII. A congress was assembled at Vienna, consisting of the allied sovereigns and most of the German princes, to make a new territorial arrangement of Europe, and to fix the boundaries of every state. Louis XVIII., brother of Louis XVI. — who had been in exile since the revolution — was called to the throne of France. He was hardly settled in his dominions, when Napoleon secretly quitted Elba, and, with less than a thousand men, landed in France. Hundreds flocked to his standard in every department through which he passed. The news of his return, and of his unopposed progress toward Paris, brought dismay to the Bourbons and their adherents. The king and his court fled from the capital, and on the same day Napoleon entered the city. The whole of the army, with the exception of a few officers, and almost the whole of the civil authorities, embraced his cause. One of the first acts of the restored emperor was to endeavor to induce the allied powers to acquiesce in his restoration. But they unanimously declared their determination to enter into no treaty with him, and both sides made the most gigantic preparations for war.

Early in June, a combined English and Prussian army was quartered in the neighborhood of Brussels, under the command of Wellington and Blucher. Napoleon, at the head of one hundred and fifty thousand men, marched against them. On the 18th of June, 1815, was fought the battle of Waterloo,* which terminated forever the splendid career of Napoleon. On the 20th, he arrived a fugitive at Paris. On the 29th, he left it for Rochefort, intending to take refuge in the United States. On his arrival, he found the harbor closely guarded by the English ships. Preferring to trust himself to the generosity of the British nation, rather than run the risk of being taken prisoner in an attempt to escape, he went voluntarily on board an English vessel. On the 24th of July, he arrived in England. He was not allowed to land, nor was he permitted to have any intercourse with the people on shore. He wrote to the prince regent of England, requesting permission to reside in the country, under the protection of its laws. But the government looked upon him as too dangerous a person to be allowed to live at large. He was banished to St. Helena, a small, rocky island in the South Atlantic Ocean. He was detained a close prisoner here for the rest of his life. The strictest watch was kept, that he might not escape. The shores were lined with troops, and ships of war were constantly sailing in sight of the island. Great numbers in France cherished hopes that Napoleon would effect his escape, and once more reappear in the country; but these were annihilated by his death, on the 5th of May, 1821.

Louis XVIII. now returned to Paris: his situation, however, was an embarrassing one. He was very unpopular. His unwieldy person contrasted unfavorably with the energetic form and miraculous activity of Napoleon. He was now an old man, and unequal to contend with the difficulties that surrounded him. He restrained the freedom of the press, and various measures were adopted tending to increase the power of the government. Though he was inclined to moderate measures, the influence of the old monarchists prevailed: they were continually urging him to place restrictions upon the liberty of the people. Still the welfare of the country seems to have been his sincere object throughout his reign. His death, which happened September 16, 1824, placed the government in the hands of his brother

* This battle, the most celebrated in modern times, was fought at the little village of Waterloo, ten miles southeast of Brussels. Lord Wellington commanded the forces of the allies, and his triumph over Napoleon gave him a place among the most renowned men of the age. The battle of Waterloo was not only important from its political consequences, but it will ever be memorable for its murderous destruction of life; about eighty thousand men being killed and wounded in the engagement.

Louis XVIII.

the Count d'Artois, who took the title of *Charles X.* The arbitrary disposition of this monarch lost him the confidence of the people. His measures showed a decided hostility to the freedom of the press and to the popular party. To strengthen the influence of the crown, a large number of new peers were created. The chamber of deputies was dissolved in the hope that the new members might be more favorable to the administration. The result of the election was, contrary to all expectations, to weaken the power of the ministers, who resigned in consequence. Persons of more liberal politics were appointed, but they had not the confidence of the king; and in 1829 Prince Jules de Polignac was placed at the head of the cabinet. The very name of Polignac was hateful to the people, on account of the influence which this family was supposed to have exerted over the unfortunate Marie Antoinette. The chamber was again dissolved, and at the ensuing elections, a still larger number of liberals were chosen. This body was also dissolved before its members came together, and a new mode of election was resorted to.

The discontent of the people now began to be openly manifested. Mobs collected in the streets of Paris, and large bodies of people were every where in motion. On the 28th of July, a severe contest commenced between the soldiers and the people. The former were exposed to a harassing fire from the windows; stones, tiles, and any other missiles that could be found, were hurled upon their heads from the tops of the houses. A lady is said, with the assistance of her maid, to have thrown a piano-forte from her window into the midst of the troops below. The night was spent by the people in throwing up barricades across the principal streets. Carriages and omnibuses were overturned, the pavement was torn up and formed into mounds, and these were strengthened with planks, and pieces of furniture. About noon of the 29th, the troops of the line declared for the cause of the people. The king retired to Rambouillet, and on the 2d of August abdicated in favor of his grandson, the duke of Bourdeaux. No attention was paid to this act. The mob prepared to march in thousands to Rambouillet, but the king made his escape to England, and died in 1836 in Austria. The few who yet remain faithful to this family now look upon the duke of Bourdeaux, nephew of Charles X., called *Henry V.*, as their lawful sovereign. These constitute the present party called *Carlists.*

A government was now to be established in France Lafayette, though at heart a republican, gave his opinion in favor of a monarchy with limited powers. This was determined upon by the leaders. After much deliberation, it was resolved to offer the crown to *Louis Philippe*, a descendant of that Henry the Great whom the French had always idolized. He had been educated with liberal principles, and had fought for them at the beginning of the revolution. He had been obliged to emigrate to avoid the fury of the Jacobins, and supported himself and two younger brothers by teaching mathematics in Switzerland. He had also spent some time in the United States. From 1800 to the fall of Napoleon, he had resided in England.

On the 9th of August, 1830, he was invited to become — not the *king of France*, as the old monarchs had styled themselves — but the *king of the French;* thereby implying that the country belonged to the people, and not to the king. He accepted the office with the conditions imposed by the charter, thus solemnly promising never to infringe upon the rights of the people; engaging that they should enjoy full liberty in religion; that the press should be free, and that the privilege of voting for members of the legislature should be extended to a larger number of the people. The old nobility, and the new, that had been created by Napoleon, were to be equally acknowledged; but the king was to have the power of bestowing the rank of *peer* on as many persons as he considered it expedient to ennoble, who would then have the right of sitting in the Chamber of Peers. The title of peer, was not however, hereditary.

Funeral Car of Napoleon.

In 1841, an expedition was fitted out to bring back to France the mortal remains of Napoleon Bonaparte. This was done, in compliance with the wish of the nation, by order of Louis Philippe. The Prince de Joinville, who was intrusted with this interesting mission, was sent to St. Helena in the frigate La Belle Poule. The body of the emperor was taken from the tomb, and was borne back in state to France: his remains were deposited with all the honors befitting a great monarch, with vast and imposing ceremony, amid the sighs and tears of millions, in the Hôtel of the Invalids. The funeral car was drawn by sixteen horses, covered with cloth of gold and adorned with white plumes.

After the accession of Louis Philippe, the country continued undisturbed by foreign wars, except the operations in Algiers, already noticed. During his reign, manufactures were increased to a great extent, and agriculture, as well as commerce, were much

Alphonse de Lamartine.

improved. His measures for many years seemed to realize the hopes of those who had called him to the throne. But as he advanced in his career, and age admonished him that the reins must soon drop from his hands, he became haunted with a desire to found a dynasty on the old and exploded principles of legitimacy. This involved the necessity of engrossing the powers of the government in the hands of the monarchy, which was done by increasing the public offices to an immense extent, by maintaining a vast standing army, and by corrupting both branches of the legislature. During this process, the public debt became swollen to a frightful magnitude, the press was gradually crippled, and personal liberty abridged. Under these circumstances, many sagacious men of liberal principles became alarmed, and a powerful opposition displayed itself in the chamber of deputies, and through the press.

In 1847, a desire for general reform, and especially for the extension of the electoral privilege to a larger number of persons, became widely spread among the people. *Reform banquets*, as they were called, were held in various parts of the kingdom, to discuss the principles of suffrage. The ministry pronounced these meetings illegal, and when, in February, 1848, one was proposed to be held in Paris, they issued a proclamation formally denouncing it. The Parisians took arms against what they deemed the tyranny of the king. The revolution of 1848, which is fresh in the minds of our readers, followed this event. In many respects it resembled the revolution of 1830; it was, like that, accomplished in three days and with little bloodshed, ending in the abdication of the king in favor of his grandson. Louis Philippe, escaped, like Charles X., to England. A Provisional Government was formed, at the head of which was Lamartine, the poet and historian. This government proclaimed a Republic, and the principle of universal suffrage. A National Assembly was chosen by the people under a system of election elaborated by Lamartine and his associates. This assembly met May 4, 1848; and set about the prime object of its creation — the formation, discussion, and adoption, of a Constitution for republican France. In the mean time, it discussed and voted the laws which the new position of the country rendered necessary, while their execution was confided to an Executive Commission of five persons. A formidable insurrection broke out in June, which compelled this commission to resign. Absolute authority was granted to Eugene Cavaignac, the minister of war. After four days' severe fighting, the revolt was quelled. Cavaignac, however, continued in power till the election of a president.

The constitution was voted in the fall of 1848, and on the 10th of December, a president was chosen by the people. The two principal candidates were Cavaignac and Louis Napoleon Bonaparte. The latter was successful, receiving about three quarters of all the votes cast.* He took the oath of office some days after, in the hall of the National Assembly. He immediately entered upon his duties, but in December, 1851, he violently overturned the Constitution, and the following year he was declared Emperor, under the title of Napoleon III. He overturned the constitution by a violent and bloody revolution, called the *Coup d'Etat.* This placed the dictatorial power in his hands, which he has since held, though with some specious forms of law. On the 2d of December, 1852, he was publicly proclaimed emperor of the French, under the title of Napoleon III. On the 30th of January, 1853, his marriage with Eugenie de Montijo, countess de Teba, was celebrated at Notre Dame. On the 10th of March, 1856, she had a son, who was named king of Algeria.

Louis Napoleon took a prominent part in the Eastern war, which he is believed to have prosecuted for his own purposes of ambition. Throughout the struggle, the French army took the lead among the allied forces, and the French general, Pelissier, has the chief credit of the final capture of Sebastopol.

Napoleon III. gives constant occupation to his army. In 1859, he took the part of Sardinia against the encroachments of Austria, and the bloody battles of Montebello, Magenta, and Solferino followed. He has maintained a garrison at Rome, and while sending smaller expeditions against Syria, China, and other countries, invaded Mexico in 1862 with 30,000 men. A fuller account of these events will be found under the appropriate heads.

* Louis Napoleon is the third son of Louis Bonaparte, brother of the emperor and king of Holland, and Hortense, daughter of Josephine and Eugene Beauharnois, her first husband. He was born at Paris, in 1808. His birth was announced with all the honors considered due to royalty. At the fall of Napoleon, when the family was banished from France, his mother removed to Germany, and afterward to Switzerland, where he commenced a course of military studies. The death of the duke of Reichstadt, in 1832, gave an impulse to his ambitious hopes. His first revolutionary attempt at Strasburg, in 1836, completely failed, and he was made a prisoner. He was pardoned by Louis Philippe, on condition of his emigration to the United States. The illness of his mother occasioned his return the following year. From this period till 1840, he resided in England. In that country, he projected a descent upon Boulogne, in the hope of revolutionizing the country: the expedition failed, and ended in his being again taken prisoner. For this effort, he was condemned to perpetual imprisonment at the Château of Ham. After six years' confinement, he escaped in the guise of a workman. England again became his refuge, and from thence he witnessed the downfall of the Orleans family in 1848. While in England, he was elected a member of the assembly, and took his place; from which he was elected to the chief magistracy.

Kings of France.

Merovingian Kings.

Date of Accession.
A. D.

481. Clovis. From this point is dated the foundation of the French monarchy.
512. Thierry I., Clodomir, Childebert I., Clothaire I., sons of Clovis, reigned jointly.
561. Charibert I., Gouthran, Chilperic, Sigebert, sons of Clothaire, reigned jointly.
593. Childebert II., son of Sigebert, Clothaire II., son of Chilperic. } Joint kings.
595. Theudebert, Thierry II., sons of Childebert II., reigned jointly with Clothaire II. till 613, when Clothaire became sole king.
628. Dagobert I., Charibert II., sons of Clothaire II.
638. Sigebert II. Clovis II.
655. Dagobert II., Clothaire III., Thierry III., Childeric II., Clovis III., Dagobert III., Fainéans, who bore the title of kings till 714, under the government of Pepin d'Heristal.
714. Chilperic II., Clothaire IV., Thierry IV., Fainéans, under the government of Charles Martel.
737 Charles Martel ruled alone till 741.
741. Pepin the Short as mayor till 751, and from 751 to 768 as king.

Carlovingian Kings.

768. Charlemagne, son of Pepin.
814. Louis I., the Good-natured.
840. Charles I., the Bald.
877. Louis II.
879. Louis III. and Carloman.
886. Charles II., the Fat.
888. Eudes.
898. Charles III., the Simple.
923. Raoul.
936. Louis IV., the Stranger.
954. Lothaire.
986. Louis V. In him ended the Carlovingian race.

Capetian Kings.

987. Hugh Capet.
996. Robert I., the Pious.
1031. Henry I.
1060. Philip I.
1108. Louis VI., the Fat.
1137. Louis VII., the Young.
1180. Philip II., Augustus.
1223. Louis VIII., the Lion.
1226. Louis IX., or St. Louis.
1270. Philip III., the Bold.
1285. Philip IV., the Fair.
1314. Louis X.
1316. Philip V., the Long.
1321. Charles IV., the Fair.

Charles the Fair left no male heirs, and the crown passed from the direct line of Hugh Capet to Philip of Valois, grandson of Philip III.

Valois Branch of Capetian Kings.

1328. Philip VI.
1350. John I., the Good.
1364. Charles V., the Wise.
1380. Charles VI., the Well-beloved.
1422. Charles VII., the Victorious.
1461. Louis XI.
1483. Charles VIII., the Courteous.
1498. Louis XII., the Father of his People.
1515. Francis I.
1547. Henry II.
1559. Francis II.
1560. Charles IX.
1574. Henry III.

In Henry III. the house of Valois became extinct, and the crown passed to Henry IV., a descendant, in the tenth generation, of the sixth son of St. Louis.

Bourbon Branch of Capetian Kings.

1589. Henry IV., the Great.
1610. Louis XIII.
1643. Louis XIV.
1715. Louis XV.
1774. Louis XVI.
1815. Louis XVIII.
1824. Charles X.

The revolution of 1830 caused the crown to pass from the Bourbon branch of Capetian kings to the Orleans-Bourbon branch — Louis Philippe being a descendant, in the fifth generation, from the brother of Louis XIV.

Orleans-Bourbon Branch of Capetian Kings.

1830–1848. Louis Philippe I.

Sons of Louis Philippe.

Ferdinand, duke of Orleans. He was heir apparent to the throne of France, but was killed, in 1842, in jumping from his carriage, the horses of which had taken fright. His son, the count of Paris then about four years old, became heir apparent.

Louis, duke of Nemours.

Francis, prince of Joinville.

Henry, duke of Aumale.

Antonio, duke of Montpensier.

The revolution of 1848 overturned the monarchy in France, and put an end to the Capetian dynasty.

The Bonaparte Family.

Charles Bonaparte, a lawyer of Ajaccio, in Corsica; died in 1785.

Sons of Charles Bonaparte.

Joseph, king of Naples, and afterward king of Spain.

Napoleon, the emperor.

Lucien, who would accept of no crown under the conditions imposed by his brother.

Louis, king of Holland.

Jerome, king of Westphalia.

Son of Napoleon.

Napoleon François, duke of Reichstadt, and king of Rome. He died in 1832.

Son of Louis.

Louis Napoleon, now (1863) Emperor of the French.

In case the monarchy should be restored in France, Henry V., duke of Bourdeaux, grandson of Charles X., will be the representative of the direct Bourbon line. His supporters are called *Carlists*, or *Legitimists.* The count of Paris represents the Orleans-Bourbon branch; and his chances for the succession have much improved of late years.

CHAPTER CCCC.

General Views of France — Government — Cities — Manufactures — Commerce — Army — Navy — Arts — Sciences — Literature — People — Origin — Genius — Influence on other Nations — Manners and Customs.

France, after having been a monarchy for nearly fourteen centuries, and during several short periods a republic, is now an empire. Louis Napoleon, who, as we have said, overturned the constitution he had sworn to maintain, caused himself to be elected emperor, in 1852, and took the title of Napoleon III. The government rests almost entirely in his own hands, though certain bodies called a senate and assembly meet from time to time, and vote such laws and such sums as are required by the Emperor, through another body called the council of state. The constitution, such as it is, is his work. He appoints the senators himself. The members of the assembly are elected by the people, but few but "government candidates" are ever returned. The eighty-six departments (eighty-nine since 1862, three new ones having been made from Savoy and Nice), form so many districts, which severally elect representatives in proportion to their population.

There is no state religion in France. Out of thirty-seven millions, only two millions are regarded as Protestants; the rest are deemed Catholics. In the remote provinces, and the rural districts generally, the mass of the people are devoted to the Catholic church, and still observe its rites and ceremonies; among the educated classes, a general scepticism prevails, even among those who attend mass and confessions. The philosophy of Epicurus seems to furnish the general system of morals. Convenience is the basis of the code, and each man interprets it for himself, and we may add, for the most part, with discretion. It would appear however, that mankind need a law which springs from a source above themselves; and that no people can reach and maintain the highest state of civilization without it. The greatest obstacle to the progress of France, especially under her new political aspects, is the want of an inflexible test of truth and falsehood, — of right and wrong; and the consequent absence of those sturdy virtues, especially among the more intelligent classes, which are indispensable to a patriotic discharge of the multiplied duties belonging to citizenship. As the people, however, became corrupted through despotism, — using even religion as its instrument of degradation, — we have reason to believe that, the surest way to restore to them a true system of morals is to give them political independence.

The cities of France need no extended description here. Paris, the capital, is, doubtless, the most agreeable city in the world. It abounds in magnificent edifices, palaces, promenades, public gardens, fountains, and places of amusement. The houses are, for the most part, built of freestone, obtained from quarries beneath the city. These vast excavations, called the *catacombs*, have been used as a depository of the bones of the dead, where they have been arranged in a fanciful manner. The palace of the Tuileries has been the chief residence of the kings of France. The national library comprises four hundred thousand volumes. The national museum contains a most magnificent display of paintings and statuary. The national gardens embrace the most extensive and complete collection of specimens in the animal, mineral, and vegetable kingdoms, in the world. This gay city, which at first seems only made for pleasure and amusement, will be found to contain within its walls some of the most scientific and profound scholars that any country or age has produced.

Paris is the great centre of intrigue, politics, learning, and power. It also sets the fashions for Europe and America. An immense trade is here carried on in articles of dress, by tailors and mantuamakers. The female fashions are frequently changed, and every few months there is a new cut for male attire. Yet, while they are so fickle in the metropolis, in many parts of France the fashions are unchangeable. People may at all times be seen in Paris, from different parts of the country, attired in the costumes which prevailed there a century ago.

Besides Paris, there are many other large and celebrated towns in France. Lyons is renowned for its rich silk goods, and gold and silver stuffs; Marseilles, as a seaport; Bourdeaux, for its wines; Brest and Toulon, as naval stations; Rouen, for its manufactures; Montpellier, as the resort of invalids; Versailles, for its palace; Strasburg, for its cathedral, the spire of which is one of the loftiest artificial constructions in the world; Rheims, for its church, in which the kings of France were formerly crowned.

The manufactures of France are extensive and greatly varied; the commerce * is increasing, but it is much inferior to that of England and the United States. The army contains about six hundred thousand men. The navy comprises four hundred and seventy-eight armed vessels, of which three-fourths are steamers. The number of men afloat is over 60,000.

In many of the arts and sciences the French have taken the lead in Europe. In chemistry, mineralogy, botany, and the natural sciences generally, they have surpassed all other nations, not only in philosophical research and discovery, but in rendering science available in the common concerns of life. The genius of the nation seems to embrace opposite qualities — quickness and sensibility of intellect, with the greatest powers of abstraction. We see them excelling in the fine arts and philosophy, — in painting, music, sculpture, architecture, on the one hand, — and mathematics and metaphysics, on the other. With a curious aptitude for details, they are still equally successful in systematic and scientific arrangement; with a genius for trifles, toys, and trinkets — for bijouterie and millinery, they have an equal genius for the higher exercises of the understanding, as displayed in literature and politics — the two great fields of human thought and action

* In no country are the lands so minutely divided as in France. It is said that there are five millions of landed proprietors in the country. There is, however, a great deal of poverty, especially in the large cities.

The great distress arising from poverty has led many philanthropic minds in Europe to seek a remedy. Saint Simon and Fourier in France, and Owen in England, imagined that they had found a panacea for these evils in a new organization of society, the main object of which was to secure a right and opportunity to labor at fair wages. In France, the investigations upon this subject have resulted in a political party called *socialists*, who exercise great influence upon the affairs of the country. Amid many dogmas deemed fanciful or fanatical, they avow attachment to the recent constitution, and a desire to propagate their opinions by argument and the ballot-box. It cannot be denied that the facts they have collected and circulated have been useful to the laboring classes, in various parts of Europe, and in this country.

The brief historical sketch we have given will sufficiently verify the latter part of this observation.

A just estimate or a thorough understanding of the French nation, cannot be attained but by recurring to its early annals. The people have an intense nationality, melting them into one spirit, yet still retaining the marked peculiarities of the separate provinces, in a state of high originality derived from the blood of their remote ancestry. This, though a seeming paradox, is easily certified as a matter of fact.

In every part of France, the French language prevails. Every where we see vivacity, politeness, loquacity, — a turn for quick observation and sharp reflection, — a fondness for music and the dance, for women and war, for coquetry in one sex, and gallantry in the other. Every where we see the distinct traces of that genial temperament and happy mixture of thought and feeling, of sense and sentiment, characteristic of this nation. At the same time, the traveller in Brittany will find the people relatively poor, hard, untamable and resistant. "Along the sea-coast," says Michelet, "nature expires, and humanity becomes cold and mournful. In the islands of Sein, Batz, and Ushant, the wedding festival itself is sad and severe. The girls unblushingly make the marriage proposal; woman there becomes harder than man, and in the Ushant Isles, she is taller and stronger."

In Poitou, we shall find a mixed and contradictory, yet original character. It was of a native of this country, that an ancient writer says, "He was a good Christian, a good knight, and he travelled a long way over the world deceiving the ladies!" It was in this same Poitou, that many of the sturdy Protestant families resided, which took refuge in Rochelle, and were cut off in the celebrated siege and sack of that city — an event which took out of France a large part of its best blood, and may be regarded as one of the main causes of that religious and moral flaccidity which constitutes the greatest defect in the French national character. In Poitou, we shall also find La Vendée, a country lost in woods and hedges, where the peasants, startled from their solitude by invasion during the first French revolution, suddenly stood up a nation of heroes. In Poitou, also, is the Upper Limousin, where the people, dwelling amid rocks of lava, and living on rough wine and bitter cheese, — are harsh, sour, and semi-barbarous, appearing in strange contrast to the people of the lower districts, who are renowned for their vivacity, cheerfulness, and wit.

The provinces bordering upon the Pyrenees are checkered by the variety of races which first peopled them. At the town of Tarbes, for instance, you may see ten thousand people on a market day, gathered from the country for sixty miles around. Here will be remarked the white cap of Biorre, the brown one of Foix, and the red one of Roussillon; here is the flat hat of Aragon, the round one of Navarre, and the peaked one of Biscay. Languedoc is a country of vines. Placed at the angle of the south, it has frequently suffered from jarring races and religions; and hence the murderous energy, the tragic vivacity, of the people. "The strong and hard genius of Languedoc," says Michelet, "has not been sufficiently distinguished from the quick-witted levity of Guyenne, and the hot-headed petulance of Provence: yet there is the same difference between Languedoc and Guyenne, as between the men of the mountain and the Girondists; between Fabre and Barnave; between the smoky wine of Lunel and claret. Belief is strong and intolerant in Languedoc, often, indeed, to atrocity so is disbelief. Guyenne, on the contrary, the country of Montaigne and Montesquieu, has floated betwixt belief and doubt. Fenelon, the most religious of its celebrated men, was almost a heretic. Things grow worse as we advance toward Gascony — the land of poor devils, exceedingly noble and exceedingly beggarly — joyous and reckless, not a man of whom but would have said, like their Henri IV., 'I am going to take the desperate leap.' Such men risk all to succeed, and do succeed. The Armagnacs allied themselves with the Valois; the Albrets blending with the Bourbons at last gave kings to France.

"Provence has both resisted and sheltered all nations. All have sung the songs and danced the dances of Avignon and of Beaucaire; all have stopped at the passes over the Rhone, and the great crossways of the high roads of the south. The saints of Provence built bridges for them, and began to fraternize the west. The sprightly and lovely girls of Arles and Avignon — in continuation of their good work — have taken by the hand the Greek, the Spaniard, and the Italian, and have led off the farandola with them whether they would or not. Nor have these strangers wished to reëmbark. They have built, in Provence, Greek, Moresco, and Italian towns — and have preferred the feverish countenances of Fréjus to those of Ionia and Tusculum; have wrestled with torrents, turned the shelves of the hills into cultivated terraces, and extorted grapes from the stony ridges which yielded only thyme and lavender."

Proceeding in a similar typographical survey of France, we shall remark in Dauphiny, in Franche Comté, in Lorraine, and Ardennes, — in Burgundy, Champaigne, and Picardy, a special, local character, so distinct as to be universally recognized. It is only in Paris, the capital, that the whole is formed into one homogeneous mass; and even here the streaks of local and provincial peculiarity are not absolutely lost. The Parisian mind presents at once the most complex and the highest form of French genius. It would seem that the result of the annihilation of local provincial policy must be altogether negative; but it is not so. "From all these negations of material, local and special ideas, results a living generality, a positive fact, a lively strength." "'Tis a great and marvellous spectacle, which meets the eye as it wanders from the centre and the extremities, and embraces within its glance that vast and powerful organism where different parts are so fitly approximated, opposed or blended together — the weak with the strong, the positive with the negative — to see the eloquent and winy Burgundy betwixt the ironical naïveté of Champaigne, and the critical, polemical, and warlike ruggedness of Franche Comté and Lorraine; to see the Languedocian fanaticism between the Provençal lightness and the Gascon indifference; to see the grasping desires and spirit of conquest of Normandy restrained between resisting Brittany and thick and massive Flanders."

It is a curious fact that in Paris there are comparatively few Parisians — natives of the city. A French essayist, in describing a Parisian house of seven stories, distributes the occupants as follows. First, there are two druggists from the provinces, in the lower story; next, in the *entre-sol*, is a dentist corn-doctor from

Italy, a corset-maker from Carcassonne, and a Genoese speculator. On the rear floor is a Norman notary, with eight clerks, all from the provinces. Next is a deputy from the south, with his whole family, desirous to see how he looks in the Chamber. Next is a wet nurse, and a young man who appears under the guise of an American traveller. Next is an Italian tenor singer, who practises his *voce de petto* twelve hours a day, with a *littérateur* from Leipsic, and a Spanish marquis, named Don Beltram de las Marismas, de las Campanadas, de las Cardonas, de las Blagadas, — whose life is one continued cigarette. Next we have a lawyer from Perigord, an English tourist, making sketches of France in his room, and a university student from Germany. Next there is an aged Swiss, deeply immersed in alchemy; a Jew, who stands for the artists as model for King Priam, King Lear, the apostles and saints generally. His daughter is model for Niobe, the Graces, Venus, &c. Next is a young Bavarian girl, who gets seventeen sous a day for polishing gaiter buttons; her neighbors are, a gilder from Nantes, and a Hungarian who breeds maggots under his bed, from putrescent meat, which he sells to fishermen of the Seine, for bait. The garret — the eighth story — is occupied by the servants, who are from Picardy, Burgundy, Brittany, &c. Finally, the peak of the roof is inhabited by water-carriers, errand-runners, carriage-openers, gas-lighters, and those who get a living by picking up the ends of cigars!

The same writer tells us that particular provinces seem to supply the capital with particular professions: thus, the masons are from Creuse and Limousin; the chimney-sweeps, water-carriers, errand-runners, tinners, and tinkers, are from Auvergne and the vicinity; the tailors and boot-makers are from the region of Strasburg; the nurses are from Burgundy, &c.

That these sketches are not mere fancies, is evident from a reference to well-known facts. We shall find that nearly all the celebrated authors, artists, politicians, and *savans*, are from the provinces. Thus, to enumerate only a few of the living Parisian authors: Dumas is from Villers-Cotterets, Victor Hugo from Besançon, Balzac from Touraine; Eugene Guinot and Thiers are from Marseilles; Jules Janin is from St. Etienne; Gautier from Tarbes; the three Aragos are from Estagel; Lamartine is from Maçon; Guizot from Nismes; Madame George Sand from Berry; Lamennais from Brittany, &c. &c.

Here, then, is France; at once homogeneous and fragmental, national and provincial. There is no land where the people are more universally devoted to the central idea of country than this. *La Belle France* is the object of general idolatry; yet, as we have said, the local peculiarities remain strongly marked. France is like a painting, having one grand design, yet showing the separate threads of the canvas behind, and beyond the colors which give unity to the surface. The solution of this phenomenon is found in the early history of France. The Celts — a noisy race, "which overran Europe sword in hand, from a vain and uneasy desire to see, know, and busy themselves with every thing" — were still a genial, social people. These formed the basis of the present population, and gave tone and color to the texture of society. They were broken into many bands and tribes, and settling in different parts of the country, perpetuated their peculiarities, often deriving from the soil and climate the instruments by which these were preserved, and perhaps exaggerated.

Considering the Celtic stock as the basis of the modern Gallic nation, we must nevertheless remember the mixture of Grecian blood at Marseilles and the contiguous country; of Norman, in what still bears the name of Normandy; of Roman, infused during nearly five centuries of Roman dominion; and finally of German, in the migrations of the Burgundians, Visigoths, and Franks. This mixture of nations has been highly advantageous to France. It seems a general law that the simple, original races are rather designed to break the soil than reap the harvest of civilization. The pure Caucasian — if we take the people inhabiting the country which gives name to the race, as its example — has never advanced beyond barbarism; the Mongolian, in his native land, is little better than a savage; the Malay, the Negro, and the American Indian, have never, by themselves, shown a capacity for improvement beyond a very limited degree. The first nations, unmixed, always seem to remain children. With them the physical is predominant. The historian speaks of those which early peopled Europe, "with large, fair, soft, succulent bodies," as the infants of a nascent world. It is by grafting that the finest fruits are produced. The crab-apple will remain a crab forever if its sap be not mingled with that of other kinds. The pippin is the result of a long and careful crossing of varieties. Thus it is, among the mixed races of mankind, that we see the intellectual gaining an ascendency over the material; it is among nations in whose veins is mingled the blood of various kindreds and tongues, that are found the highest examples of intellectual and moral endowment. What was even England, with its Anglo-Saxon race, till the infusion of French-Norman blood? Do not all the monuments of which she boasts take their date since the conquest? In early ages, war — the instinct of uncivilized man — effected the mixture which Providence seems to have designed as the instrument of human improvement; in a more enlightened age, adopting the spirit of the gospel, which extends its blessings alike to Jew and Gentile, it should be the aim of every good man to soften the hostility of races, and promote the progress of society, by mingling all into one fraternity of states and nations.

The means by which the separate tribes of France have been formed into a nation, are to be found in the lively sympathy and social instinct of the Gallic nation, derived, as we have intimated, from their Celtic ancestors. Through this, the separated provinces, differing at first in habit, climate, and language, have comprehended and assimilated with each other. While along her border, France presents "against England hard Brittany and tenacious Normandy; to grave and solemn Spain opposes scoffing Gascony; to Italy, the fire of Provence; to the massive German empire, the deep and solid battalions of Alsace and Lorraine; to Belgian inflation and rage, the cool, strong wrath of Picardy — with the solemnity, reflection, and aptitude for civilization of Ardennes and Champaigne": thus encircling herself by a living wall, at once defensive and repellent, — she is bound together by the cement of a universal spirit of nationality. In no country has local and private life remained so independent as in France; yet nowhere has the common love of country been more generally diffused or firmly established.

While thus the genial spirit of the Gallic race has

spread itself over France, it has not stopped at its borders. "I cannot," says Guizot, "but regard France as the centre, the focus, of the civilization of Europe. It would be going too far to say that she has always been, upon every occasion, in advance of other nations. Italy, at various epochs, has outstripped her in the arts; England, as regards political institutions, is by far before her; and perhaps, at certain moments, we may find other nations of Europe superior to her in various particulars; but it must still be allowed that whenever France has set forward in the career of civilization, she has sprung forth with new vigor, and has soon come up with, or passed by, all her rivals.

"Not only is this the case, but those ideas, those institutions which promote civilization, whose birth must yet be referred to other countries, have,— before they could become general, or produce fruit, before they could be transplanted to other lands, or benefit the common stock of European civilization,— been obliged to undergo in France a new preparation; it is from France, as from a second country more rich and fertile, that they have started forth to make the conquest of Europe. There is not a single great idea, not a single great principle of civilization, which, in order to become universally spread, has not first passed through France.

"There is, indeed, in the genius of the French, something of a sociableness, of a sympathy — something which spreads itself with more facility and energy, than in the genius of any other people. It may be in the language, or the particular turn of mind, of the French nation; it may be in their manners, or that their ideas, being more popular, present themselves more clearly to the masses, and penetrate among them with greater ease. In a word, clearness, sociability, sympathy, are the particular characteristics of France — of its civilization; and these qualities render it eminently qualified to march at the head of European civilization."

The force of these observations has been evinced by the sympathy of the southern nations of Europe with the political revolutions in France. In 1789, in 1830, and in 1848, the billows which agitated the masses of Paris, heaved and swelled in the bosom of the million throughout Belgium, Italy, and Southern Germany. While England remains in a state of sullen isolation, France breathes her spirit over one fourth of Europe. It was a recognition of this fact, doubtless, that led Coleridge, while giving vent to his national spleen, to do some justice to France. "The French," said he, "resemble gunpowder: individually, they are smutty and contemptible, like the single grains; but as a nation, they are terrible like the mass when it explodes."

In general it may be stated, that the French nation is the most intelligent, frugal, industrious, and temperate, in Europe. Though easily excited, they are, individually, remarkable for living within their income — thus showing self-control and habits of order. In the revolution of 1789, maddened by oppression, and debased by a corrupt dynasty, many of the people seemed to delight in scenes of blood and terror. In the more recent revolutions of 1830 and 1848 — and especially in the latter — the lower classes of Paris have shown unparalleled humanity and moderation — conclusive proofs of the civilizing influence of even the partial political liberty they have enjoyed.

From these observations, it will readily be seen tha an American in France, who has previously known the French only from descriptions by the English, is forcibly struck with their unfairness; the descriptions in many points, have not even the resemblance of caricatures. It seems to be the instinct of the English to hate the French, and this accounts sufficiently for the calumny. Goldsmith hit not only on the English feeling, but he exemplified the national prejudice, in making one of his characters say, "I hate the French because they are slaves, and wear wooden shoes." It is true that this prejudice is returned by the people of France. A hatred of England is a national characteristic. Even the enlightened Michelet says that "wool and flesh are the primitive foundations of England and the English race. Their greatest man — Shakspeare — was originally a butcher!"

Julius Cæsar described the ancestors of the French as the most polished barbarians he had conquered, and what the ancestors were among the barbarous, the descendants now are among the refined. Strabo describes the ancient inhabitants as so jealous of their honor that each one of them felt it incumbent upon him to resent an insult offered to his neighbor. Like the English, the French are not without pride, though it is not like that of the English, personal, but national; the dignity of the individual vanishes before the glory of France. Glory is the passion of the French, and if the national honor be advanced, a private, or even a public calamity is little heeded. This passion for glory has had ample gratification, though at a tremendous sacrifice of human life.

The French are more sensible to the emotions of joy than of sorrow; they feel the good and forget the evil. The present outweighs the future, and the existing impulse is the ruling one. This is the instability which the English call insincerity. This also produces a facility of adaptation to circumstances that enables them to bear reverses better than any other people, and that makes them feel at home wherever they are — in courts or camps, or among the wildest savage tribes. It is noted in America that the French settler in the forest becomes identified with the Indian sooner than any other European. The natural cheerfulness of the French is sustained by a general urbanity that exists in no other country; their politeness is both a feeling and a habit.

The cheerfulness of the French is not boisterous or occasional; it is constant, and connected with great kindness of feeling. There is so little separation of families, that the manner of life seems almost patriarchal, and several generations often live under the same roof. It is a common and delightful sight to behold the whole family group, from youth to age, come out and enjoy themselves at some holiday or *fête*. Wherever the French congregate, there is a spirit of enjoyment spread over them; there are joy and animation on every face. Wrangling or intoxication is almost unknown in France. Dancing is as much the expression of joy as weeping is of grief; and a traveller cannot go far, in France, without beholding a village dance, to which, as there are no refreshments, the national cheerfulness is the only incentive. One of the most agreeable circumstances in French society is, that aged people of both sexes are among the most cherished members, whether at a village festival or Parisian *soirée*.

The British Empire.

View of London

CHAPTER CCCCI.

Description of the British Isles — Knowledge of them by the Ancients — Their general History — Formation of the United Kingdom of Great Britain and Ireland — Extent and Population of the British Empire.

The British Isles lie on the western coast of the continent of Europe. On the south they are separated from France by the English Channel; on the east, a wide expanse of sea, called the *German Ocean*, separates them from Holland, Denmark, and Norway; on the north and west, their shores are washed by the Atlantic Ocean. They are thus very favorably situated for defence in war, and for commerce in peace. They consist of two large islands — Great Britain and Ireland — with many smaller ones, principally scattered along the northern and western shores of Great Britain. This latter island, the largest of the group, is five hundred and eighty miles in length from north to south, and three hundred and seventy in its greatest breadth. It is generally regarded as divided into England, Scotland, and Wales; which three countries, though now united into one kingdom, exhibit peculiarities characterizing them, as in several respects, distinct. Ireland lies west of Great Britain. It is two hundred and thirty-five miles long, and one hundred and eighty-two broad. The climate of the British Islands is cool and moist: in the north, rain and mist are abundant. The soil of Great Britain is but moderately fertile by nature: in the north, it is rocky and sterile: a very skilful agriculture, however, and the general industry of the people, has made the greater part of it highly productive. Ireland has a richer soil, but the husbandry is inferior to that of England.

These islands appear to have been known to the ancient Phœnicians, who visited them for commercial purposes; but we know little or nothing of the condition of the country or the inhabitants at that early period. The Romans first became acquainted with these regions after their conquest of Gaul, when Julius Cæsar invaded Britain: they established their dominion in the southern half of the island, but Ireland and the north of Scotland remained unsubdued. England, Scotland, Wales, and Ireland continued under separate governments for many centuries. England gradually obtained the preëminence, and finally absorbed all the others. Ireland was conquered in the twelfth century and Wales in the thirteenth. Scotland and England became united under one sovereign in the seventeenth century, and the two kingdoms were combined into one at the beginning of the eighteenth. In 1800, Ireland was united with Great Britain, and the whole monarchy received its present name of the *United Kingdom of Great Britain and Ireland.*

The British Islands form the central part of this empire, London being its capital. The following shows the extent and population of the empire, as well as its several divisions: —

	Square miles.	*Pop.* 1861.	*Pop. sq. m.*
Whole extent of England and Wales	58,320	20,205,504	346
" " Scotland	31,324	3,061,251	94
" " Ireland	32,512	5,764,543	117
Sailors and soldiers abroad		275,900	
Total of British Isles	122,156	29,307,198	258

Beside these divisions, Great Britain has possessions in the four quarters of the globe, so that it is said the sun never ceases to shine upon its territories and its people. From the extent of its dominions, commerce and language, from its naval and military power, and its vast resources, this empire must be deemed the greatest the world has known. The population of the whole empire probably exceeds two hundred and twenty-five millions, distributed in the following manner:

	Population.
British Islands, including the islands of Alderney, Guernsey and Jersey, on the French coast, Gibraltar, Malta, and Heligoland,	29,400,000
North American Colonies. — Canada, the North-western Territory, New Brunswick, Nova Scotia, Cape Breton, Prince Edward's Island, Newfoundland, Honduras, Bermuda,	3,400,000
West Indies and South America. — Jamaica, Trinidad, Barbadoes, Antigua, Dominica, Grenada, St. Lucia, St. Vincent, the Bahamas, British Guiana,	1,200,000
African Colonies. — Mauritius, St. Helena, Gambia, Sierra Leone, Cape of Good Hope,	950,000
Colonies in Asia. — East India Company's Territories and Government Colonies in India or Hindostan, Ceylon, Farther India, Singapore, Hong Kong,	190,000,000
Australia, Van Diemen's Land, New Zealand, &c.,	1,200,000
Whole population,	225,950,000

Having given this general description of the British empire, we shall now proceed to detail its history, embracing under the head of England, the general course of events, with separate narratives of Wales

Scotland and Ireland, reaching to the several periods at which these became lost in the history of the empire. We shall close our sketch by a glance at its present political condition.

CHAPTER CCCCII.

55 B. C. to A. D. 827.

ENGLAND. — *The Ancient Britons — Julius Cæsar's Invasion — Agricola's Conquest — The Roman Dominion in Britain — Vortigern — The Saxon Emigration and Conquest — Introduction of Christianity — The Heptarchy — Establishment of the Kingdom of England.*

Landing of Cæsar.

ENGLAND appears so prominently in the history of the British Islands, that in common language we often speak of *England* as embracing the whole empire, and the English as meaning the entire people. Yet England occupies only the south-eastern and central parts of the Island of Great Britain, — Wales lying on the west, and Scotland on the north. The Thames, one hundred and sixty miles in length, flows into the German Ocean, and is navigable for ships to London — sixty miles. The Severn rises in Wales, and flows into the British Channel, after a course of two hundred miles.

The surface of England is diversified: the western portion is in parts mountainous, though none of the peaks rise over three thousand five hundred feet in height; the central part is hilly; in the eastern counties there are extensive plains and marshes. The soil is not naturally fertile, but with the exception of some barren heaths and plains, the whole is cultivated like a garden. The mineral treasures of England — tin, copper, iron, coal — are great, and have largely contributed to the wealth and power of the empire.

The ancient name of *Britain* is supposed to have originated with the Phœnicians, who visited it eight or ten centuries before the Christian era, for tin; and hence they called it *Britain*, or "the country of tin." The name of *Albion*, or "white country," was given to it on account of its high chalky cliffs along the southern coasts. The title of *England* comes from the Angles, who settled in the country during the seventh century, and, blent with the Saxons, gave the title of *Anglo-Saxons* to the English race.

The earliest inhabitants of Britain, so far as we know, were mainly of that great family, the chief branches of which, distinguished by the designation of *Celts*, spread themselves over Middle and Western Europe. The Welsh and Danish traditions indicate an emigration, also, from Jutland; and the name of *Cymry*, given to the immigrant people, has been supposed to point out their probable identity with the Cimmerians who, being expelled by the Scythians from their more ancient seats north of the Euxine, traversed Europe in a north-western direction, and formed new settlements near the Baltic and the mouth of the Elbe. Some of these barbarians reached Britain by the same route which was afterward traversed by the Saxons and Angles. The Celts crossed over from the neighboring country of Gaul; and Welsh traditions speak of two colonies, one from the country since known as Gascony, and another from Armorica. At a later period, the Belgæ, actuated by martial restlessness, or the love of plunder, assailed the south and east coasts of the island, and settled there, driving the Celts into the inland country. These Belgæ were a branch of the great Teutonic family. Thus the early settlers of Britain were the Celts from France, the Cymric Celts from Jutland, and the Belgæ, confined to the south-eastern coasts.

Cæsar is the first writer by whom any authentic particulars respecting this island are given. Stimulated probably by the desire of military renown, and of the glory of first carrying the Roman arms into Britain; provoked, also, as he tells us, by the aid which had been furnished to his enemies in Gaul, especially to the Veneti, — the people of Vannes, in Bretagne — and other maritime people of Western Gaul, he determined upon the invasion of the island. As a preliminary step, he summoned to his camp a number of the merchants who traded to the island, — who alone of the Gauls had any acquaintance with it, — and to them he addressed various inquiries. Their caution, however, or their ignorance, prevented his learning much from them. Failing in this quarter, one of his officers — C. Volusenus — was sent to reconnoitre; but he did not venture to leave his ship and trust himself on shore among the natives. Cæsar, no way deterred by his want of information, collected a fleet, and disposed his force with a view to the descent.

He found the country, as he tells us, "inhabited by those who, according to the existing tradition, were the aborigines of the island; the sea-coast, by those who, for the sake of plunder, or in order to make war, had crossed over from among the Belgæ, and who, in almost every case, retained the names of their native states, from which they emigrated to this island — in which they made war, and settled, and began to till the land. The population is very great, and the buildings very numerous, closely resembling those of the Gauls. The quantity of cattle is considerable. For money they use copper, or rings of iron of a certain weight. Tin is produced in the middle districts, and iron near the sea-coast, but the quantity of this is small: the copper which they use is imported. There is timber of every kind which is found in Gaul, except beech and fir. The people deem it unlawful to eat the hare, and the hen, and the goose: these animals, however, they breed for amusement. The country has a more temperate climate than Gaul, the cold being less intense.

"Of all the natives, those who inhabit Cantium—Kent—a district, the whole of which is near the coast, are by far the most civilized, and do not differ much in their customs from the Gauls. The inland people for the most part do not sow corn, but live on milk and flesh, and have their clothing of skins. All the Britons, however, stain themselves with woad, which makes them of a blue tinge, and gives them a more fearful appearance in battle: they also wear their hair long, and shave every part of the body except the head and upper lip. Every ten or twelve of them have their wives in common, especially brothers with brothers, and parents with children; but if any children are born, they are accounted the children of those by whom first each virgin was espoused."

From the accounts, it appears that the towns were confused assemblages of huts, generally scattered among woods, and defended with ramparts of earth. The Britons were divided into many tribes, or nations, and were in a state of barbarism, even when compared with the rude Gauls of the continent. The use of clothes was scarcely known in many parts of the island. Those of the south wore rude coverings made of the skins of wild beasts. The chief weapons were swords and lances. The warriors used chariots,

Savage Britons

drawn by horses, some of which were armed with scythes. In manners they were fierce, cruel, and bloodthirsty. Such, at least, is the description given of them by the first Roman visitors.

The Druids

The Druids appear to have been the priests, lawgivers, and judges, among the Celts of Gaul, Spain, Ireland, and Britain. These taught the worship of deities resembling the Mercury, Mars, Jupiter, and Minerva of the Greeks. They were held in great veneration by the people, and ranked even above princes and chiefs. They worshipped in groves, or in temples composed of huge stones usually arranged in circles, the remains of which are still found in France, England, and Ireland. The people assembled in vast crowds to witness their civil adjudications and their religious rites. The latter were attended with human sacrifices. The Druids were the instructors of the young, to whom they taught legendary and mystical lore, in the form of poetry. Some of them were professed bards. None of the order paid taxes, or engaged in war. The persons sacrificed were usually criminals, and the greater the torture of the victims, the more the gods were supposed to be pleased. One method of sacrifice was to put the victim in wicker baskets, and then set them on fire. The decrees of the Druids in civil as well as religious matters, were regarded with the greatest respect: indeed, these priests seem to have acquired the same ascendency over the people which was exercised by the priests of ancient Egypt and India. Hence Druidism is supposed to have been of Eastern origin.

Cæsar, after a fierce conflict with the natives, landed near Dover, and took possession of the country. He did little, however, to subdue the people, and the Romans made no permanent conquests in the island till the reign of Claudius, a century afterward. The subjugation of the Britons was a work of time and difficulty: some parts of the island never submitted to the Roman arms. Agricola, who held the chief command of the Roman forces in Britain under Vespasian, (A. D. 79,) defended the northern frontier from the fierce Picts and Scots, by a wall or chain of posts extending across the narrowest part of the island, from the Frith of Forth to that of the Clyde. In the year 120, the emperor Adrian built additional walls in this quarter, which were increased in 138 by the emperor Antonine. The northern part of Scotland, and the mountainous regions of Wales, were never conquered by the Romans. Many of the Britons escaped to Wales from the Roman dominion, and these preserved from generation to generation their implacable enmity to the conquerors.

The Romans appear to have extirpated all the national institutions of that part of Britain which yielded to their arms. The ancient religion of the natives disappeared, and the temples of the Druids fell to ruin. Very curious remains of these structures are to be seen, at the present day, at Stonehenge, on Salisbury Plain, in the south of England. These remarkable relics comprise two circular and two oval ranges of stones, having one common centre. The outer circle is one hundred and eight feet in diameter, and, when entire, consisted of thirty-eight upright stones, eighteen or twenty feet in height, and connected at the top by stones laid across. The two interior ranges are composed of stones thirty feet in height. This structure is supposed to have been a druidical temple of the remotest antiquity. It is now in a state of

Stonehenge restored.

decay, many parts of it having been thrown down and carried away. The accompanying cut represents it in its perfect state.

The Romans maintained themselves in Britain about five hundred years. During this period, they introduced their laws, customs, arts, and sciences among the inhabitants. Their power was maintained by the presence of Roman legions, and these the Britons were compelled to support. Early in the fifth century, the declining condition of the Roman empire made it necessary to abandon the province of Britain, and the legions were withdrawn. The Britons were immediately assailed by the Picts and other barbarous nations of the north, whom the legions had hitherto kept from ravaging the southern parts of the island. In their distress, the inhabitants applied to the Roman general Ætius, in Gaul. Their petition was entitled *The Groans of the Britons*, and contained this expressive passage: "The barbarians chase us into the sea, and the sea throws us back on the barbarians. We have only the hard choice left us of perishing by the sword or by the waves." The Romans, however, were too busily engaged in defending themselves from the Franks to attend to the safety of the Britons, who were thus left at the mercy of the wild barbarians of the north. Unable to protect themselves, they deserted their habitations and fields, and sought shelter in the forests, where they suffered equally from famine and the enemy.

At length, by the advice of Vortigern, one of their kings, or chieftains, the Britons applied for aid to the Saxons. These were a tribe or nation of Germans, who, in company with the Angles, another German tribe, had, from small beginnings, gradually extended their sway from the mouth of the Rhine to the coast of Jutland, or modern Denmark. Their piratical fleets, at this period, scoured the seas of Western Europe and invaded the maritime cities of Gaul. Spain and Britain were frequently plundered by their corsairs, or put under tribute. Among the chiefs of these tribes, none enjoyed

LANDING OF THE SAXONS IN ENGLAND

greater authority than the two brothers, Hengist and Horsa, who claimed to be descended from Woden, the tutelary god of the nation. To these leaders the application of Vortigern was made. They readily accepted the invitation, and, accompanied by about sixteen hundred of their countrymen, landed in Britain, A. D. 449. The Picts and Scots were subdued with so little difficulty, that the Saxons soon conceived the design of conquering the island for themselves.

Saxon Warriors.

Accordingly, instead of returning home, they invited over fresh hordes of their countrymen, and a long war ensued, in which the Saxons and Angles triumphed over the Britons in almost every encounter, and finally drove the miserable remnant of the nation to seek refuge in the mountains of Wales and Cornwall. The struggle lasted nearly a century and a half, and ended in establishing in South Britain seven Saxon kingdoms, called the *Heptarchy*. These kingdoms were Kent, Sussex, Wessex, East Anglia, Mercia, Essex, and Northumberland. The Angles were the most numerous of all the Saxon tribes in the island, in consequence of which, the Saxon territory in Britain obtained the name of *Angle-land*, or *England*, as we have before stated.

The aboriginal Britons had not been converted to Christianity during the rule of the Romans. This religion was first established in Britain, in the kingdom of Kent — the earliest and long the most powerful of the Saxon monarchies. Ethelbert, king of Kent, though a pagan, had married a Christian princess, Bertha, the daughter of Charibert, one of the successors of Clovis, king of the Franks, and had promised to allow her the free exercise of her religion. Bertha acquired much influence over her husband and his courtiers, and, in his reign, Pope Gregory the Great sent missionaries into Britain, A. D. 597. Augustin, the chief of this mission, was honorably received at the court of Ethelbert, and began to preach the gospel to the people of Kent. The rigid austerity of his manners, and the severe penances to which he subjected himself, acted powerfully on the minds of a barbarous people, and induced them readily to believe the pretended miracles which he wrought for their conversion. Ethelbert, and the great majority of his subjects, were soon received into the church. St. Augustin was the first archbishop of Canterbury; and soon after his appointment to this dignity, the abbey of Westminster was founded by Sebert, king of the East Saxons. The first stone church in England was erected at York.

The kingdoms of the Heptarchy were almost constantly involved in wars with one another; but these contests are entirely devoid of interest, and the history of the separate kingdoms is little more than a list of obscure names. An exception may be made in favor of Offa, king of Mercia, who labored zealously to extend the papal power in England, and founded the magnificent monastery of St. Albans. Charlemagne sought his friendship and alliance. The kingdom of Mercia had nearly obtained the sovereignty of the Heptarchy, when Egbert ascended the throne of Wessex, A. D. 799. He broke down the Mercian power, established his influence in the other states, and united the whole of the Anglo-Saxon dominion into one kingdom. This important event in English history took place A. D. 827, nearly four centuries after the first arrival of the Saxons in Britain. *Egbert* may therefore properly be styled the first king of England.

CHAPTER CCCCIII.

A. D. 827 to 901.

Warlike Character of the Saxons — Reign of Alfred — Invasion of the Danes — Distress of Alfred — His Adventures — England partitioned between the Saxons and Danes — Invasion of Hastings — Manners, Customs, Occupation, &c., of the Saxons — The Guilds — The Saxon Language.

Alfred in the Danish Camp.

The Saxons were chiefly devoted to war. They were bold, hardy, restless, and energetic; but the barbarous state of manners prevalent at that period

Alfred in the Neatherd's Cottage.

Alfred and the Earl of Berks

prevented them from turning their mental and physical powers to any useful account. Agriculture afforded but little employment, and that little was mostly confined to the servile class. Foreign commerce was hardly known, and there were very few products of industry or art to afford materials for trade. The Saxons had ceased to be pirates; they had no literature; and, though they had Christianity among them, its influence in improving their morality was hardly perceptible. Their nobles and princes were enterprising, ambitious, covetous, and brave. The natural tendency of such a people must be toward war. Accordingly, we find this to have been the common occupation of the Anglo-Saxons during the existence of the Heptarchy.

The consolidation of the Saxon power by Egbert gave peace to the nation, and laid the foundation for a gradual improvement in the manners of the people. Egbert reigned prosperously, and was succeeded, in 836, by his son *Ethelwulf.* The fourth son of this monarch was *Alfred the Great*, who ascended the throne in 871. He is the most famous of all the Saxon kings of England. At the age of five, he was sent by his father to Rome; yet, such was the barbarism of those times, that he was unable to read before his twelfth year. After this time, he became a diligent student. The circumstances of the period, however, were little favorable for study. A swarm of barbarians from the shores of the Baltic, under the names of *Danes* and *Northmen*, had, about this time, filled the maritime regions of Western Europe with slaughter and devastation. They first appeared in England in the latter part of the eighth century, and were vigorously repulsed by the inhabitants. When they were defeated in one quarter, they directed their course to another, ravaging and destroying every thing. Though often repelled, they were never discouraged, but always returned with increasing numbers, till they firmly established themselves in the Islands of Thanet and Sheppey, at the mouth of the Thames from whence they made constant incursions into the neighboring country. They overran, gradually, the greater part of England, built castles and fortified posts to secure themselves in the possession of the country, and treated the inhabitants with barbarous oppression and cruelty.

The first seven years of Alfred's reign appear to have been inglorious, and he lost the confidence of his people. In his first conflicts with the Danes, he was so unsuccessful, that he was compelled to abandon his army, and wander in disguise through the western part of England. Here he found shelter in the hovel of a neatherd, or cattle-keeper, in whose service he remained for some time, employed in the humblest labors. A popular story represents him as employed one day, in tending the cakes which were baking on the hearth. The king, absorbed in thought, let the cakes burn, and received a sharp rebuke from the housewife for his carelessness. On one occasion, as Alfred, in company with an associate to whom he had revealed himself, were roaming about the country, they heard a tramp of horsemen approaching. Fearing that they were Danes, they hid themselves among the bushes; but, on coming in sight, Alfred discovered them to be the earl of Berks, a Saxon nobleman, with a number of attendants. The earl, seeing Alfred by the wayside, inquired the road to Taunton. The king informed him. The earl, struck with the sound of his voice, demanded who he was, when Alfred, drawing him away from his followers into the thicket, took off his peasant's cap, and displayed, to the astonished earl, the well-known face of the Saxon king. The earl informed him that he was about to assemble his retainers, and take up arms against the Danes. They arranged their measures together, and the earl departed on his enterprise. Alfred returned to the neatherd's cottage, waiting for a favorable moment to attack the enemy. At length, he found means to assemble a few followers in the Island of Æthelingay, in the River Thone, which runs into the British Channel. From this place, he made frequent and successful attacks upon the Danes. He once ventured into their camp, in the disguise of a harper, and found them indulging in indolence and careless security. Having learned their numbers and the strength of their position, he rejoined his followers. He then summoned the Saxons to meet him at Selwood Forest, from whence he led them against the enemy. Struck with surprise at the sudden appearance of an English army, and terrified at the name of Alfred, they made but a feeble resistance; and Alfred obtained a complete victory. A treaty was at length made, by which England was divided between the Saxons and the Danes.

The country now enjoyed a period of tranquillity. Alfred rebuilt and fortified London, repaired the ruined cities, and erected castles and fortresses in different parts of England. He established a regular militia, and built a fleet of one hundred and twenty ships for the protection of the coast. A Norman sea-king, or piratical chieftain, named *Hastings*, had been, for some years, the terror of France and England, by the audacity and success of his attacks on the maritime towns of these countries. He invaded England in 891, and persevered for six years in an attempt to subjugate the Saxons. This aroused the military genius of Alfred, who resisted him with such perseverance and effect, that he at length expelled the invader from the island. This may be regarded as the period of Alfred's highest military renown. During the remaining five years of his reign, he established his dominion over all England, and was regarded with respect and esteem by the people of Wales, though that country remained independent of his authority.

Alfred established schools in England, and, in order to encourage the common people in the business of educating their children, he sent his own son to be taught among them. He compelled his nobles to build castles to defend the country from the Northmen. He was inflexible in selecting only such persons for public offices as were competent to perform their duties. Earls, governors, and ministers, who had been illiterate from their infancy, were required to learn reading and writing, or lose their employments. He was severe in the administration of justice. The institution of juries has been ascribed to Alfred; but this is doubtful. He hanged two judges for sentencing men to death without the verdict of the juries. Alfred also divided England into counties. He reformed the laws, and, having signalized himself as the greatest warrior, legislator, and scholar, of the age, died in 901.

The Saxons, in Alfred's time, were divided into nobles, ecclesiastics, freemen, and slaves. The last were born to servitude, and sold like cattle. The manners of the people exhibited a mixture of barbarism and rude luxury. The princes, nobles, and rich men and women wore ornaments of gold, and were fond of personal decoration. The houses were mere huts. Horses, cattle, sheep, and swine were abundant. Cider and mead were common drinks. Gold seems to have been abundant among the Saxons—a fact not easily accounted for, as they had little foreign trade. Vessels from the continent visited London as early as the sixth century; but it does not appear that the island produced any thing for exportation.

The Saxons had various mechanical arts. Implements of husbandry, hunting, and war-swords, spears, helmets, shields, &c., were made by their own artificers. A blacksmith was held in high esteem. They had one custom which distinguished them from all other nations of that age. They formed fraternities,

Group of Saxons.

clubs, or *guilds*, as they were called. The members contributed to a common fund, which was used for charitable purposes among themselves and the families of such as were deceased. Guildhall, the London town house of the present day, may have had an origin in these associations. England is remarkable, at the present time, for associations of this nature. The Saxons were superstitious, but not more so than their contemporaries. Their amusements were hunting, feasting, and listening to the songs of their bards, who sung or recited ballads to the music of the harp.

The Saxon language forms the basis of the modern English. Before Alfred's time, it was hardly, if at all, used in writing. Latin was the common language of books and documents; but books and writings of any sort were rare among the Saxons. Alfred was himself an author. One of his works was a translation of Boethius from Latin into Saxon. This work is extant at the present day.

CHAPTER CCCCIV.

A. D. 901 to 1087.

Edward the Elder—Edwin—Legend of St Dunstan—Danish Conquest of England—Sweyn—Canute—Harold Harefoot—Hardicanute—Edward the Confessor—Harold—Battle of Hastings—The Norman Conquest—Reign and Institutions of William the Conqueror.

EDWARD the Elder succeeded his father Alfred. He spent the greater part of his reign in wars with the Danes, who made constant encroachments upon the Saxon territories. During the reign of his immediate successors, the power of the Danes increased; but the military events of these times are uninteresting. In the reign of *Edwin*, about the middle of the tenth century, lived St. Dunstan, whose extraordinary character has made him noted in the history of England, as well as in popular tradition. He was born at Glastonbury, in 925. He learned all that was then to be known of

Sportsmen in the Twelfth Century.

mathematical science. He excelled in music, painting, engineering, and in working gold, silver, copper, and iron. His great knowledge caused him to be accused of demoniacal arts, although he was a Benedictine monk. He lived in a cavern in the side of a hill, where he passed the time in religious exercises and working metals. One night, the neighbors were alarmed by a terrific howling which proceeded from this spot. Dunstan informed them, the next morning, that the devil had been tempting him, and had thrust his head in at the door of his cavern; whereupon the saint had seized him with his tongs by the nose, and caused him to roar, as they had heard. This absurd story, which was fully believed by Dunstan's contemporaries, may serve as a specimen of the credulity of that age. Dunstan obtained such influence by the sanctity of his character, as to make the king, the nobles, the prelates, and the whole kingdom, submissive to his will. He effected a complete revolution in church affairs; and the power which he established endured for centuries.

Canute reproving his Flatterers.

The Danes continued their wars with the English. In 993, Sweyn, king of Denmark, and Olaus, king of Norway, sailed up the River Humber, with a strong force, and spread their ravages on all sides. This warfare continued for several years, till, in 1014. *Sweyn* was acknowledged king of England. *Canute*, one of his successors, conquered Norway, and compelled Malcolm, king of Scotland, to acknowledge him as his feudal sovereign, A. D. 1030. He possessed great wealth, which he expended in a magnificent pilgrimage to Rome. This is the monarch who is said to have placed his chair on the sea-shore, and commanded the waves to retire. Some historians relate this as an instance of the vanity and folly of a mortal who happened to hold an earthly dignity. Others describe it as a lesson which the discerning monarch taught to the flatterers around him.

Harold, surnamed *Harefoot*, succeeded Canute in 1035. His short reign was stained by a massacre of the Saxons, and the usurpation of the territories of their princes. *Hardicanute*, the last of the Danish kings of England, came to the throne in 1042. His reign was marked by violence and tyranny; and, at the end of two years, he died in the midst of a carousal, at the wedding of a Danish lord. By this event, a favorable opportunity was offered to the English for shaking off the yoke of their conquerors. Sweno, the eldest son of Canute, was king of Norway, and residing in that country at the time of his father's death. The eyes of the nation were turned toward Edward, a Saxon prince, who happened to be at court at this critical moment. By the influence of Earl Godwin, the most powerful nobleman in the south of England, *Edward* was placed on the throne. He was a person of weak intellect, and more fit for a cloister than a court. His austerity of manners obtained for him the surname of *Saint*, and *Confessor*, from the monkish historians of that age. Godwin, whose daughter the king had married, exercised great influence over him. Edward died, after an inglorious reign, in 1066, the most eventful year in all the history of England.

As a specimen of the manners and political customs of this age, we may instance the story of Lady Godiva. A nobleman, named *Leofric*, possessed a castle at Coventry, and, according to the practice of those days, used his military power to extort money from the people of the town and neighborhood, in the shape of tolls and duties. These were very oppressive to the people of Coventry, who petitioned in vain to be relieved from them. Leofric had married the beautiful Lady Godiva, the sister of the sheriff of Lincolnshire. This lady made frequent entreaties to her husband in favor of the citizens, but without effect, till one day he peevishly told her he would grant her request, provided she would ride through the town without any clothing. To this she agreed, and accomplished the performance with no other covering than her long tresses, which served her for a cloak. Leofric, it is said, repented of his rash proposal, and commanded every person to retire from the streets and the windows during the lady's progress, under pain of death; but one curious person obtained a glance which has obtained him the appellation of "Peeping Tom." The town of Coventry obtained a charter of freedom by this occurrence; and it is commemorated, at the present day, by an annual procession, in imitation of Lady Godiva's progress.

Procession in Honor of Lady Godiva.

Edward the Confessor left no children. By his will, he bequeathed the crown to William, duke of Normandy, one of his kinsmen. This bequest was disputed by *Harold*, the son of Godwin, who asserted his right to the throne of England. Harold was a Saxon, and was warmly supported by the nation, notwithstanding the will of Edward. William had, for some time, entertained a jealousy of Harold, believing he would endeavor to circumvent him in his claims upon the English crown. During a visit which Harold made to Normandy some time previous to the death of Edward, he had been treated with much attention by William, who induced him to take an oath before the bishop to assist William in his measures for securing the possession of the throne of England. Notwithstanding this, no sooner was the throne vacant by the death of Edward, than Harold took immediate possession, and prepared to defend his claim by the sword. William made similar preparations, and, in the autumn of the same year, set sail from Normandy, with a large fleet and army, for the invasion of England. He landed on the southern coast, and encountered the army of Harold at Hastings, about sixty miles south-east of London. On the 14th of October, 1066, was fought the battle which decided the fate of England. The field was furiously contested. At one time, victory appeared certain for the English; but, by pushing forward with too much confidence, they lost the day. Harold and his two brothers were killed, the English fled in every direction, and the victory of the Normans was complete. All England submitted immediately to the conqueror.

William the Conqueror assumed the crown. This revolution not only subverted the reigning dynasty in England, but it caused a thorough change in the population, laws, language, manners, and social institutions of the English. The consequences are felt, in a remarkable degree, to this day, not only in Great Britain, but all over the civilized world, and particularly among the races of English descent. At first, the Norman conquest appeared a great calamity. Saxon liberty was overthrown; the people were oppressed. William gave almost all the landed property in England to his Norman followers. The vanquished nation was treated as a troop of slaves. The conqueror introduced the feudal system into the country. All England was divided into baronies, or great tracts of territory. These were conferred upon the Norman chiefs, with the condition of stated services and payments to the king. The barons, in their turn, parcelled out their land, with similar obligations, among their vassals or knights. Many of the Saxon nobles retained their titles, and some degree of authority; but they were excluded from the first rank of the nobility. William attempted to abolish the Saxon language entirely; he ordered that the schools should teach only French and Latin. No tyrant, however, is able to extirpate a language. French became the legal tongue, and the dialect of the court and fashionable company; but the bulk of the people continued the use of the Saxon, which finally conquered the Norman French, and, by combining a portion of that language with itself, formed the modern English tongue. The whole substructure remained Saxon.

William's reign was marked by the compilation of the *Doomsday Book*, an official survey and record of the quantity and valuation of the lands in the kingdom, with the names of the owners. This remarkable volume is still preserved. He also instituted the *curfew*, or the regulation for putting out fires, at the ringing of a bell, shortly after sunset. This was intended not only as a police regulation, but to prevent nocturnal assemblages for the purpose of conspiracy. One of the most odious acts of William was the making of the "New Forest," near Winchester, where he expelled from the lands all the inhabitants on an extent of thirty miles of territory, to form a hunting-park for his own diversion. Several towns and villages, comprising twenty-two churches, were destroyed for this royal pastime. The present game laws of England owe their origin to William the Conqueror.

CHAPTER CCCCV.

A. D. 1087 to 1272.

William Rufus — Henry I. — Stephen Henry II. — Murder of Thomas à Becket — His Canonization — Conquest of Ireland — Richard Cœur de Lion — John — Magna Charta — Henry II. — The Commons first summoned to Parliament.

William II., surnamed *Rufus*, from his red hair succeeded to the throne of England on the death of his father, in 1087. The history of this period consists of little beside the record of tyrannical power on the part of the crown, and of resistance, and sometimes rebellion, among the powerful lords, combined with the encroachments of the papacy, and the oppression and humiliation of the great mass of the people. William Rufus, however, adorned his kingdom with many fine architectural structures; one of which, Westminster Hall, remains at the present day. He was killed accidentally while hunting in the New Forest, A. D. 1100. *Henry I.*, surnamed *Beauclerc*, succeeded him and attempted to conciliate his subjects by relaxing the severity of the Norman laws. He was followed on the throne, in 1135, by *Stephen*, whose reign was disturbed by civil wars. *Henry II.* succeeded, in 1154. His reign is famous for the martyrdom of Thomas à Becket.

This individual was an ecclesiastic, who, from an humble origin, rose to be a great favorite with the king; and received such high honor and emoluments, that he was able to live in a more sumptuous style than any

Assassination of Thomas à Becket

nobleman in the kingdom. Henry undertook certain measures to limit the power of the clergy, which, at that time, was most exorbitant in England. Becket secretly resolved to oppose this movement, but he took care to conceal his sentiments till he was made archbishop of Canterbury, the dignity of which office gave him more authority in religious affairs than was possessed by the king himself. He now attempted to increase his popularity with the people by adopting strict and austere manners. He gave up hunting and hawking, and all those sports and gayeties which had made him so agreeable a companion to the king. He lived upon bread and water, wore a penitential shirt, and subjected himself to the usual monkish mortifications of that day. In consequence of this, he was regarded as a saint by the mass, and was enabled to counteract the measures of the king with great effect.

Elated by the success of his scheme, Becket conducted himself with such insufferable arrogance, and behaved so insolently to the king, that Henry was highly provoked, and one day exclaimed, in a fit of peevishness, "Shall this fellow, who came to court on a lame horse, with all his estate in a wallet at his back, trample on me and the whole kingdom? Will none of those lazy, cowardly knights, whom I maintain, rid me of this turbulent priest?" These expressions were understood by some of the noblemen as a hint for them to murder the archbishop: accordingly, they hastened to Canterbury, and stabbed him to the heart in the cathedral, A. D. 1170. Henry was greatly shocked, or professed to be so, when he heard of this deed. He wrote to the pope, offering to perform any penance that he might think fit to impose, in order to atone for the murder. He declared his willingness to serve for three years against the Moors and Saracens, either in Spain or the Holy Land. The pope ordered him to pass a day and a night at the tomb of Becket, without food, and to be scourged by the monks. This humiliating penance was performed. Becket was canonized, and a hundred thousand persons visited his shrine in a

Harold's Oath

single year. Miracles were believed to have been wrought by his relics; and the pilgrimage to Canterbury continued for centuries.

Henry conquered Ireland, and annexed it to the English crown. His authority also extended over the duchy of Normandy, the county of Anjou, and the finest provinces of North-western France. He reformed the administration of justice, and protected the Jews, who were sadly oppressed in almost every part of Europe. In his reign, the noblemen and other eminent persons of London were in the open practice of robbery, for which purpose they often combined in bands of a hundred or more. Henry made vigorous attempts to suppress these proceedings. The first cook-shop or eating-house, was opened in London during his reign; it is mentioned in history as one of the improvements of the age.

Richard I., surnamed *Cœur de Lion*, or the "Lion

Richard Cœur de Lion trampling upon the Austrian Banner.

hearted," from his bravery, succeeded Henry in 1189. He is famous in the history of the crusades, and we have already had occasion to mention some of his exploits. Richard lived very little among his people, and did hardly any thing for the good of the country; but he was fond of daring deeds and romantic enterprises, which have made him one of the most celebrated of all the monarchs of England. Half the period of his reign was passed in a crusade to Palestine, and the other half in wars with his neighbors, or rebellious subjects in Normandy. During his crusade, he was involved in frequent quarrels with the other Christian leaders, whom he offended by his lofty behavior, and the superiority which he assumed over them. On one occasion, having planted his banner in the centre of the camp of the crusaders, in token of his supreme command, the archduke of Austria took offence, and erected his own by its side. Richard immediately tore down the standard of Austria, and trampled it under his feet. On his return to England from the Holy Land, Richard attempted to pass through the territory of the archduke; but he was made prisoner, and kept in confinement till a large sum of money was raised in England for his ransom. He was finally killed by an arrow at the siege of the Castle of Chalus, in France. The first lord mayor of London was elected in this reign. Robin Hood, the famous outlaw of Sherwood Forest, also lived during this period.

John, the brother of Richard, succeeded him in 1199. He usurped the throne, by imprisoning and putting to death his nephew, Prince Arthur. John was universally detested for his tyranny and oppression. The barons conspired against him, and compelled him to sign the Great Charter, which is regarded as the foundation of English liberty. This instrument redressed many of the feudal grievances, abolished many of the arbitrary prerogatives of the crown and established private rights by placing the life, property, and liberty of the subject under the protection of the law. The Great

Prince Arthur in Prison.

Charter, otherwise called *Magna Charta*, was signed at Runnymede, near Windsor, June 15, 1215.

John also involved himself in a quarrel with the pope respecting the power of making ecclesiastical appointments in England. The pope placed the kingdom

John and the Barons at Runnymede.

under an interdict, which, in that ignorant and superstitious age, was regarded as a most dreadful calamity. The churches were shut up; no bells were rung; no prayers said over the dead; all amusements were stopped, &c. After resisting for three years, John submitted, and resigned his crown to the pope, with the understanding that he should receive it back as a vassal of the papacy. Philip Augustus, king of France, took advantage of John's humiliation to deprive him of almost all his continental possessions.

Henry III. succeeded John in 1216. England was never in a more miserable state than during his long reign of fifty-six years. The king was but ten years of age at his accession; and the kingdom was distracted by contests for the crown, civil wars, ecclesiastical contentions, usurpations, and oppressions, to which were added wars with Scotland, France, and Wales. At one time, the earl of Leicester became possessed of sovereign authority as the head of a committee of peers. He introduced an important change into the constitution by summoning the commons to parliament in 1265. This body had previously comprised only the nobles, prelates, and knights. In this reign, coal began to be used in England; it was at first prohibited by law as a nuisance, on account of the smoke. Carpets were also first used in this reign, but they were only seen in the royal palace. For many centuries afterward, the floors of houses were strown with rushes. At the end of his long reign, in which he had been only a puppet in the hands of others, Henry was succeeded by *Edward I.*, A. D. 1272.

CHAPTER CCCCVI.

A. D. 1272 to 1382.

Edward I. — Conquest of Wales and Scotland — Wallace and Bruce — Friar Bacon — Edward II. — Battle of Bannockburn — Edward III. — Wars with France — Richard II. — Wat Tyler's Rebellion — Usurpation of Henry of Lancaster — John Wiclif.

Edward I., surnamed *Longshanks*, was a warlike and enterprising prince. The principal events of his reign were the conquest of Wales, and the attempt to subjugate Scotland. His great ambition was to unite the three kingdoms of Great Britain into one monarchy. Wales was regarded as owing an acknowledgment of sovereignty to England; and Edward, pretending that the homage had been withheld by Llewellyn, prince of Wales, invaded that country, and conquered it after an obstinate resistance from the inhabitants. Scotland offered him an equally plausible pretext for interference. The direct line of inheritance to the crown had failed; and three competitors, Baliol, Bruce, and Hastings asserted their several claims. To avoid a civil war, they agreed to abide by the decision of Edward. He declared in favor of Baliol, having made a previous agreement with him that Scotland should be held as a feudal dependency of England. Baliol became king of Scotland, but soon grew weary of the authority exercised over him by Edward, and made an effort to recover his independence. He was defeated, taken prisoner, and compelled to abdicate the crown, A. D. 1296. Scotland submitted to Edward, but many insurrections broke out in that country from time to time. William Wallace, the Scottish hero, led the insurgents, and gained a victory over the English at Stirling. He was made regent of Scotland; but after a while, he was defeated and taken prisoner by Edward, who caused him to be put to death at London.

Edward expected that this act of severity would intimidate the Scots; but the event proved otherwise The execution of Wallace aroused a spirit of revenge in the hearts of his countrymen, who soon found another leader in Robert Bruce, the son of Baliol's competitor. The war speedily turned in favor of the Scots; they took all the castles occupied by the English, expelled them from Scotland, and proclaimed Bruce as their lawful king. Edward marched with a strong army against them; but, before reaching Scotland he was taken sick, and died in Cumberland, A. D. 1307.

The reign of Edward was distinguished as the age of Roger Bacon, commonly called *Friar Bacon*,* a person whose genius was far in advance of that unenlightened period. He made great discoveries in science, and was acquainted with the use of magnifying glasses, and some of the principles of chemistry. The invention of gun powder has been ascribed to him, but this is erroneous Many of his inventions and suggestions might have been of great benefit in advancing civilization, had they

Costumes of the Time of Edward I.

not been discountenanced by the ignorance and prejudices of the times.

Edward II. had made a solemn promise to his father on his death-bed, to carry on the war against the Scots but he had neither the will nor the power to execute it. His supplies, both of men and money, failed him and for some time he abandoned himself altogether to indolence and pleasure. At the end of seven years however, he was enabled to collect a large army, with which he marched into Scotland. Bruce, with an

* Roger Bacon was born at Ilchester, in Somersetshire, in 1214. He was educated at Oxford, in the scholastic learning of the times, but his bold and inquisitive mind led him to extend his studies into a much wider realm of knowledge. His discoveries in natural philosophy, while they attracted general admiration, caused him to be looked upon with envy and jealousy by the monks of his fraternity. A report was industriously circulated that he held converse with evil spirits, and practised magical arts. This rumor was conveyed to the pope, and under pretence that Bacon was attempting to introduce innovations which might disturb the peace of the church, he was forbidden to deliver lectures to the students in the university, and at length imprisoned. The true reason seems to have been, that Bacon was one of the first to discover and censure the corruptions of the Romish church His writings contained severe comments on the ignorance and immorality of the clergy, and he even wrote a letter to the pope on the necessity of reformation. After being set at liberty, he was again imprisoned by papal authority, and the reading of his works was prohibited. He remained in prison ten years, when he obtained his liberty through the intercession of some English noblemen. He died in 1294.

army of Scots, met him on the field of Bannockburn, where a battle was fought which ended in the complete overthrow of the English, A. D. 1314. This event secured the independence of Scotland. After several years more of misgovernment, Edward provoked a rebellion of his barons. Queen Isabella, his wife, joined the rebels, and raised a body of troops in the Netherlands for their support. The king fled to Wales, but was pursued and made prisoner. After an imprisonment of nine months, he was cruelly murdered in Berkeley Castle, A. D. 1327.

Edward III. was but fifteen years of age when he

Warriors of the Times of Edward II. and III.

came to the throne, and in the early part of his reign, the administration of affairs was intrusted to a regency. In the tenth year began a series of hostilities with France, the consequences of which continued for more than a century. Edward laid claim to the crown of France by right of his mother, who was of the royal family of that country; but by the Salic law her title was void. Edward, however, invaded France, and bloody wars ensued; still England remained prosperous at home. It was during this reign, which continued fifty years, that the parliament established the three fundamental principles of the English government; namely, the illegality of raising money without the consent of parliament; the necessity of the concurrence of both houses to enact a law; and the right of the commons to investigate abuses, and impeach the ministers of the king for maleadministration.

In 1345, Edward raised a large army, and invaded France, accompanied by his son Edward, surnamed the *Black Prince.* He ravaged the country along the banks of the Seine, and approached to the gates of Paris. In that age, there was no systematic method of supplying an army with provisions by magazines, and a war consisted principally of a series of marauding excursions, in which the contending parties subsisted by ravage and plunder. The English soon exhausted the neighborhood of provisions, and famine compelled them to retreat through Picardy, toward Flanders. When the army reached the River Somme, a branch of the Seine, they found all the bridges broken down. The French, in the mean time, had collected an immense military force, and were rapidly pursuing them. The English were now in imminent peril of being overwhelmed by their enemies, for the whole army was in most weak and famishing condition, and the French outnumbered them in the proportion of eight to one. In this distress, Edward ordered a proclamation to be made throughout the neighborhood, offering a reward of a hundred gold nobles to any one who would discover a passage across the river. A French peasant

Gobin Agace and Edward III.

named *Gobin Agace*, tempted by the offer, came to the king, and informed him of a ford at a certain place in the stream. The king gave orders for the army to march, and set out accompanied by the peasant. They found a body of French posted at the ford, whom they dispersed by a sudden attack, and the whole army immediately crossed the Somme in safety. A battle was afterward fought at Cressy, A. D. 1346, which is one of the most famous in the English annals. The French, under the command of Philip, their king, were defeated with immense slaughter. In the English army were six pieces of cannon; and this is the first mention of firearms in the wars of Europe. The cannon first used by the English and French were not cast, but made of iron bars hooped together. Stones were used for balls. Shakspeare speaks of *gun-stones*, from which it appears that cannon-balls of metal were not known in his time, nearly three hundred years later.

Richard II., the grandson of Edward, and son of the celebrated Black Prince, came to the throne in 1377, before he had attained to his twelfth year. His reign was most unfortunate. The early part was distinguished by the rebellion of Wat Tyler, A. D. 1381. The people, being grievously oppressed with taxes and feudal services, rose in insurrection, under the guidance of Wat Tyler, a blacksmith, whose daughter had been grossly insulted by a tax-gatherer. They gained possession of a considerable part of London, where

The King receiving a Message from Wat Tyler.

they committed all sorts of riotous acts. The rebellion appeared so formidable, that the king came to a parley with Tyler, and demanded what the people wanted. Tyler replied that they wanted the abolition of feudal bondage, freedom of trade in fairs and markets, and the repeal of the custom of services for holding land; so that the country people should be free from vassalage, and no longer be bound to the soil on which they dwelt. These demands were so reasonable, that the king promised they should be granted. But while the negotiations were going on, Tyler was treacherously slain by Walworth, the lord mayor of London. The insurgents, having no leader, dispersed; the promises of the king were forgotten, and great numbers of people were hanged for participating in the rebellion.

England was in a most wretched state during this reign. The king was a man of very feeble mind and vicious inclinations. In his advanced age, he grew so tyrannical and extravagant, as to excite the general hatred of his subjects. His misgovernment at length provoked a rebellion. Henry of Lancaster duke of Hereford, put himself at the head of the malecontents. Richard, finding his cause hopeless, surrendered to his haughty cousin, and was forced to abdicate the crown, A. D. 1399. His subsequent fate is not exactly known. He was imprisoned in Pontefract Castle, but the circumstances of his death are involved in mystery. During this reign, symptoms of religious reformation began to appear in England. The corruptions of the church of Rome were denounced by John Wiclif, an English priest. His doctrines were investigated and condemned by a national synod, in 1382; but they had taken fast hold of the people, and some of his disciples carried them to the continent, where they continued to flourish in spite of persecution.

In this reign, a small body of Scots, under Lord James Douglas, invaded England. The son of the earl of Northumberland, known by the popular name of *Harry Hotspur*, which he acquired by his fiery

Battle of Otterbourne.

temper and impetuous valor, challenged Douglas to single combat. The Scot obtained the victory, and bore off the lance and pennon of his antagonist. On his retreat to Scotland, he was pursued by Hotspur, with a body of knights, and a battle was fought at Otterbourne, in which the chivalrous courage of both nations was displayed to the full extent. Douglas was killed, after exhibiting feats of the most daring prowess; the English were completely overthrown. This battle is described in lively terms by the old chronicler and historian, Froissart, who delighted in recounting deeds of courage and feats of chivalry. Hotspur afterwards quarrelled with King Henry, and joined the Welsh, who had revolted under Owen Glendower.

CHAPTER CCCCVII.

A. D. 1382 to 1509.

Henry IV. — Wars of the Red and White Roses — Henry V. — Wars in France — Henry VI. — Edward IV. — Richard III. Battle of Bosworth — Henry VII. — Lambert Simnel and Perkin Warbeck — Spirit of the English Government — Commencement of the Navy.

Battle of Shrewsbury: Prince Henry saving his Father

Henry IV. was a usurper, but highly in favor with the people; and the first acts of his reign were well calculated to make them acquiesce in his claim to the crown. But his usurpation led to the civil wars of the *Red and White Roses*, or the houses of York and Lancaster. Henry was the first reigning prince of the house of Lancaster, whose badge was the red rose. The rival house of York adopted the white rose as their symbol; and the contests of these two houses for the crown filled England with bloodshed and turbulence for many years. The whole of Henry's reign was occupied in struggles to keep himself on the throne. The great lords were much divided in opinion as to the legality of his title. At the first parliament, they broke out into a furious quarrel. Forty gauntlets of defiance were thrown upon the floor, and the angry words *liar* and *traitor* resounded through the hall. Civil war ensued, and many heads fell under the axe of the executioner.

Henry sought to strengthen himself by courting the ecclesiastics. Religious persecution began in his reign. Wiclif was dead, but his disciples were burnt at the stake. The Welsh, led on by Owen Glendower, rebelled, and were joined by the Percies of Northumberland, a noble family who had assisted Henry in obtaining the crown, but were not rewarded for their services according to their expectations. The rebels were overthrown at the battle of Shrewsbury, A. D. 1403. King Henry fought in person at this battle, and was thrown from his horse, and about to be made a prisoner, when he was rescued by his son, Prince Henry.

Henry V. succeeded his father in 1413. This monarch is the "Prince Hal" in Shakspeare's drama. In early life, he was given to dissipation, and spent his time with wild companions, in the commission of every sort of extravagance, sometimes robbing on the highway. On coming to the throne, he abandoned his irregular habits, and acted in a manner becoming his station. He revived the English claim to the crown of France, and invaded that country, where he gained the battle of Agincourt, and captured Paris in 1415. He died near that city in 1422, having made arrangements by treaty and marriage for the union of the two crowns in the person of his son.

Henry VI. acceded to the throne before he was a year old. His reign exhibits a perpetual series of misfortunes and civil wars. His relations quarrelled about the administration during his minority. The duke of Bedford was appointed by parliament regent of the kingdom, under the title of *Protector of England*, and under his administration began a series of wars with the French which ended in the expulsion of the English from almost all their continental possessions. The loss of trophies so gratifying to the national vanity, alienated the affections of the people from the house of Lancaster; and this dislike was increased by the haughtiness of Henry's queen, Margaret of Anjou. In the civil wars which ensued, she was exposed to great vicissitudes of fortune and hairbreadth escapes. At the battle of Towton, in Yorkshire, A. D. 1461, Margaret's army was totally defeated by the Yorkists under Edward, the competitor of Henry for the throne. This battle was decided by a violent snow-storm, which blew in the faces of the queen's soldiers, and prevented them from aiming their arrows. No quarter was given, and thirty thousand Lancastrians were put to the sword. The queen fled to Scotland with her husband, whose incapacity for government caused him to resign the management of every thing to his wife. He gathered another army, and returned to England, but was again defeated at the battle of Hexham. The cause was now so desperate, that she was compelled to separate from her husband, and both shifted for themselves in the best way they could. The king, after lying concealed for some time, was taken prisoner, and committed to the Tower of London.

The queen fled with her son to a forest, where she was attacked by robbers, who stripped her of her rings and jewels, and treated her with great indignity. The robbers then fell to quarrelling about the division of their booty, and the queen seized this opportunity to escape with her son. She wandered for some time up and down in the forest, without knowing what to do. At length she saw another robber approaching her with a drawn sword in his hand. Finding escape impossible, she suddenly adopted the resolution of throwing herself upon his protection. She advanced toward him, and, presenting her son, accosted him with these words: "Here, my friend, I commit to your care the son of your king, the prince of Wales." The robber was so struck with astonishment at this encounter, that he dropped upon his knees, and offered to devote himself to her service. The queen proceeded with him to his hut, where she remained concealed for some time. when an opportunity was found of escaping to the sea-shore, from whence she procured a conveyance to Flanders.

Queen Margaret and the Robber.

The civil wars of the roses raged with great fury in England. After much blood had been shed, the White Rose triumphed. Henry was deposed, and *Edward IV.*, of the house of York, was placed on the throne in 1461. His reign was sullied by cruelty and debauchery. After his death in 1483, the crown was usurped by *Richard III.*, duke of Gloucester, commonly known as the *Crook-backed Tyrant*. His character has been rendered odious by Shakspeare's tragedy, and the histories written in the reign of his successor; but there is good reason to believe that his crimes have been exaggerated. He is represented as

Murder of the young Princes.

having murdered his nephews in order to secure himself on the throne. But the claims of the Lancastrian family were revived by Henry Tudor, earl of Richmond, who took up arms against Richard, and defeated him at the battle of Bosworth, A. D. 1486. Henry married the daughter of Edward IV., and ascended the throne without opposition — thus extinguishing forever the hostility between the rival houses of York and Lancaster.

Henry VII. crowned on the Field of Bosworth.

Henry VII. was an able monarch, but severe, cautious, and avaricious. His chief policy was to encourage trade, and break the power of the nobility; and in these designs he clearly saw the true tendencies of the age. There were many insurrections during his reign. Two impostors, named *Lambert Simnel* and *Perkin Warbeck*, at different times assumed the title of duke of York, and pretended to have escaped from the Tower of London, where the sons of Edward IV. were supposed to have been murdered by order of Richard III. Both of these adventurers raised strong parties in England, and were countenanced by persons of distinction; but Henry succeeded in repressing the rebellions, and capturing the impostors. Simnel was made a scullion in the royal kitchen, and Warbeck was put to death. The reign of Henry was, on the whole, prosperous. The nation enjoyed repose after long convulsions. The government was arbitrary, but the people acquiesced, preferring this to the license of the civil wars. In this reign we may place the chief origin of that almost idolatrous notion of royal prerogative which was entertained by the kings of England till the final expulsion of the Stuarts, at the revolution of 1688.

Henry VII. not only began the development of the internal resources of the country by the promotion of trade, but he may be regarded as the founder of the British navy. Before his time, the government had no other mode of raising a fleet than by hiring or impressing the ships of merchants. Henry built a ship of war of extraordinary size, which was named the *Great Harry*. This cost him fourteen thousand pounds — an enormous sum for those days. His treasury contained at his death nearly two millions of pounds, which he had saved by various methods of parsimony and extortion. The royal coffers were then the only treasury of the state; and the savings of the monarch were deemed the gain of the nation.

CHAPTER CCCCVIII.

A. D. 1509 to 1558.

Henry VIII. — Cardinal Wolsey — Anne Boleyn — Quarrel with the Pope — Sir Thomas More — Henry's numerous Marriages — War with France — State of England in the Time of Henry VIII. — Abolition of Slavery — Edward VI. — Establishment of the Protestant Religion — Queen Mary — Persecutions — Loss of Calais — Death and Character of Mary.

HENRY VIII. succeeded his father in 1509. He was young, and at first a great favorite with the people, whom he gratified by his fondness for show and magnificence. The hoards of his father were soon squandered in pompous diversions. In an interview which took place between Henry and Francis I. of France, near Calais, such extravagant pomp and luxury were displayed on both sides, that the place obtained the name of the *Field of the Cloth of Gold.* Henry's vanity made him the dupe of crafty foreigners. The pope and the king of Spain inveigled him into a war with France from which he derived no profit. The Scots invaded England, but were defeated by the English under the earl of Surrey, at Flodden Field, A. D. 1513.

One of the most famous characters of this period was Cardinal Wolsey, who was the son of a butcher, but rose by his talents to be Henry's prime minister, and the richest subject in the kingdom. The aggrandizement of this haughty prelate was for a long time the main object of the king, who made him his personal favorite. Wolsey governed England nearly twenty years; for the king left all the public business to his management, and devoted himself to sports and revelry. Wolsey was a great encourager of learning, and founded several colleges. The Protestant reformation had now begun in Germany; but Henry was so hostile to the doctrines of Luther, that he wrote a work in Latin against the new opinions, which gave the pope such gratification, that he bestowed upon him the title of *Defender of the Faith.*

Henry had been married seventeen years to Catharine of Aragon, a Spanish princess, who had been the wife of his brother, when he was smitten with the charms of Anne Boleyn, a young lady of his court. He wished to divorce his queen that he might marry Anne. The pope refused to sanction the divorce; whereupon Henry caused it to be decreed on his own responsibility, and Anne Boleyn became queen of England. Wolsey opposed the measure, and thus caused his own ruin; for he was soon after disgraced, stripped of his immense wealth, and banished to a monastery, where he died of a broken heart. Henry then entirely withdrew his allegiance to the papal government. He convened a parliament in 1534, in which it was declared that the king was the only head of the church of England; that, for the future, the pope should have no authority in the realm; and that the tax of Peter Pence, instituted in the time of the Saxons, for the benefit of the papal treasury, should be abolished. The parliament granted to the king all the revenues which had formerly been paid to the pope; and the clergy, assembled in convention, passed a vote declaring that by the law of God the Roman pontiff had no more jurisdiction in England than any other foreign bishop.

By these proceedings England was rendered forever

Costumes of the Sixteenth Century.

independent of the Romish church. Yet the Catholic religion was still maintained. Henry was a determined foe to the Protestants, and caused many of them to be burned at the stake. Sir Thomas More, the chancellor of England, was executed for refusing the oath of supremacy to the king. The monks employed all their influence to inflame the people against the government, which induced Henry to suppress the monasteries. His young queen having given offence and excited his jealousy by some levities of conduct, Henry, who was totally destitute of feeling, caused her to be tried, condemned, and beheaded. He then married Jane Seymour, and, on her death, took for his fourth wife Anne of Cleves, a German princess, whom he found so unsuitable to his taste, that he dismissed her by a divorce shortly afterward. His fifth wife was Catharine Howard, who met with the same fate as Anne Boleyn, and from the same charge. His sixth wife was Catharine Parr, who was fortunate enough to outlive her husband.

Henry invaded France with an army of thirty thousand men, in **1546**, and captured Boulogne; but a peace, soon after, put an end to his schemes of conquest. He was engaged also in wars with the Scots, which consisted of mutual inroads and devastations. In the latter part of his life, the violent temper of the king was so much aggravated by disease, that his oldest friends fell victims to his caprice and tyranny. He died in 1547. His character was marked by avarice, cruelty, and self-will. He had so completely broken the spirit of the English, that, like Oriental slaves, they admired the very acts of tyranny by which they were degraded. Yet even in his despotism he was strangely inconsistent. He liberated the English nation from papal oppression, and thereby provided a corrective, for his own arbitrary principles of government. He also gave liberty to his bondsmen, saying that, as all men were free by nature, it was cruel and unjust to deprive them of the freedom which God had given them. This example was followed by the nobles who held men in bondage, and the last remains of slavery disappeared from the land without the enactment of any law for this purpose.

Previous to the time of Henry VIII., the common garden products of the present day were not raised in England. Potatoes were unknown. Carrots, turnips, lettuce, celery, &c., were imported from Holland; but in the latter part of this reign, the cultivation of these articles was introduced into the kingdom. Hops were also brought from Flanders into Kent, and currants were transported from Italy into England.

Edward VI. succeeded his father. He was but nine years of age on coming to the throne; and being feeble and sickly during the whole of his life, he can hardly be looked upon as a sovereign, since the government was altogether in the hands of other persons. In this reign, the Protestant religion was established by law in England. But the troubles occasioned by the minority of Edward, and the ambition of his guardians, prevented the reformed church from being placed on a firm foundation. He died at the age of sixteen, A. D. **1553**. The crown was claimed by four females—Mary and Elizabeth, the daughters of Henry VIII., Mary Stuart, queen of Scots, and Lady Jane Grey. The last mentioned of the competitors assumed the title of queen of England; but the nation declared in favor of Mary, and Lady Jane resigned the crown after a reign of ten days, and was beheaded on the scaffold.

Court Costumes of the Time of Queen Mary.

Mary ascended the throne, and soon after married Philip II., king of Spain — an alliance most odious to the people of England. Philip was a morose and bigoted Catholic, and Mary resembled her husband. Before she was proclaimed queen, she had promised full religious toleration to the people. But no sooner was she firmly established in power, than a sanguinary and merciless persecution was begun against the Protestants. Hundreds of these, including women and children, were burned at the stake. Among these were John Rogers, prebendary of St. Paul's, Bishops Hooper, Ridley, and Latimer, and Archbishop Cranmer

England was filled with scenes of horror, which disgraced human nature, and rendered the religion from which this persecution sprang an object of general detestation. In these cruelties, the Catholic bishops Bonner and Gardiner, were prominent actors. The reign of Mary was every way unfortunate and disgraceful to the English. In 1557, the French took Calais, which had been in possession of the English since the time of Edward III., and which was important to them, not only as a means of invading France, but as a place of deposit for the merchandise which they exported to the continent. The mortification occasioned by this disaster, and the knowledge that she was hated by her subjects, had such an effect upon Mary, that she died of grief in 1558. Her character was a compound of the most odious vices — bigotry, obstinacy, tyranny, malignity, and revenge. Her administration is known in history as the *Bloody reign of Queen Mary.*

CHAPTER CCCCIX.

A. D. 1558 to 1603.

Reign of Elizabeth — Rivalry of the Protestants and Catholics — Fate of the Queen of Scots — War with Spain — The Invincible Armada — Leicester and Essex — Death of Elizabeth — Her Character — Government — Literature — Trade, Society, Manners, &c., of the English in the Reign of Elizabeth.

Queen Elizabeth.

ELIZABETH mounted the throne amid the general joy of the nation. Her accession was the crisis of the Reformation in Great Britain. She was the daughter of Anne Boleyn, whose marriage with Henry VIII. had not been sanctioned by the Romish church. In consequence of this, her title was not recognized by the Catholics, and the king of France permitted his daughter-in-law, Mary, queen of Scots, to assume the royal arms and title. Elizabeth secured herself by entering into secret alliance with the heads of the Protestant party in Scotland, who succeeded in withdrawing that kingdom from its allegiance to the pope. Elizabeth was naturally regarded by the Protestants of Europe as their head, while Philip II. of Spain was the great champion of the Catholics. Hence England became the counterpoise to Spain in this age, as France had been in the preceding.

Elizabeth was endowed with a strong and masculine mind; and though her temper was unamiable, and her manners far from gentle, she selected able ministers, and understood how to promote the best interests of the nation. By frugal management of the public treasure, and great affability of behavior in public, she acquired a degree of popularity such as no other English sovereign ever attained. Yet her disposition was haughty and imperious, and her treatment of the unfortunate queen of Scots is justly regarded as a deep stain upon her memory. That accomplished and beautiful princess, being compelled to abandon her kingdom by a civil war, took refuge in England. Elizabeth, who hated her for her beauty, and dreaded her as a rival, kept her eighteen years in prison, and then caused her to be put to death on a charge of conspiracy, A. D. 1587.

When the inhabitants of the Netherlands revolted against the tyranny of Philip II. of Spain, Elizabeth afforded them assistance. Sir Philip Sidney, whose pastoral writings and chivalrous character made him the national favorite in the reign of Elizabeth, distinguished himself by his feats of arms in the Netherlands, and met his death in battle, A. D. 1586. Elizabeth's aid to the Netherlands led to a war with Spain, and Philip conceived the design of conquering England. He fitted out a large fleet, which the Spaniards, in their vainglorious confidence, named the *Invincible Armada.* This was the largest fleet ever known, both for the number and size of its vessels. The alarm of the English at the approach of this danger was exces-

Sir Philip Sidney.

sive. People came forward with offers of money, arms, and ships, for the public service. A considerable fleet and army were soon prepared to meet the invaders, and all private quarrels were forgotten in the general danger. In July, 1588, the great Armada was discovered approaching the coast. The ships formed a line seven miles in extent, and sailed up the British Channel in the form of a crescent. The English sent fire-ships among them at night, which threw them into disorder, and a battle ensued, which lasted the whole of the following day. The Armada was defeated, and attempted to return to Spain by sailing round the British Isles to the north. Near the Orkneys, a violent storm dispersed the fleet, and wrecked a great number of the vessels. Not more than one half the Invincible Armada returned to Spain. Such was the disastrous result of this mighty enterprise.

A Beau and Belle of Queen Elizabeth's Time.

Elizabeth remained single during the whole of her life. She received numerous proposals of marriage from the surrounding princes and the more eminent of her own subjects; she uniformly declined these offers, but with such gentle refusals as commonly encouraged her suitors to persevere in their hopes. She had many favorites, two of whom, the earls of Leicester and Essex, are well-known characters in history. Leicester was a bad man; but the queen was so much attached to him, that it was believed she would marry him. He had a beautiful young wife, whom he had married privately, and kept concealed at one of his country mansions. It is supposed she was murdered by his orders, that she might not stand in the way of his preferment with the queen. The earl of Essex was a young nobleman of great talent and spirit, but too rash to preserve the capricious favor which he had gained. After many adventures, he made an extravagant attempt to raise a rebellion in London, for which he was tried and beheaded. Elizabeth was nearly seventy years of age, yet she had cherished a romantic fondness for Essex. She never recovered from the grief occasioned by his death, but from that time sunk into a profound melancholy, of which she died, A. D. 1603.

The character of Queen Elizabeth exhibits strong contrasts. As a monarch, she displayed great qualities; as a woman, many frailties and weaknesses. She was resolute and decided in her public policy, but she wanted heart, sympathy, and sincere feeling. The love of fulsome adulation, and the readiness with which she submitted to the praises of her imaginary beauty, even in her old age, constitute a very ridiculous point in her character. She was also pettish and irascible, and in her sallies of anger, would box the

Shakspeare reading to Queen Elizabeth.

ears of those around her, whatever their rank or dignity might be. The English people, however, who experienced the benefits of her administration without being injured by the defects of her private character, have always cherished her memory with fondness, and still speak with enthusiasm of the "golden days of good Queen Bess."

During Elizabeth's reign, the government was administered on very arbitrary principles; yet the country made great advances in wealth, prosperity, and national importance. Commerce and agriculture rapidly developed the resources of the nation. Literature shone out with a brilliancy never before equalled, for this was the age of Shakspeare, Spenser, and Ben Jonson. The genius of the people, if not the wisdom of the government, surmounted every obstacle, and placed England in the very highest rank among the European states. The reign of Elizabeth is memorable, among other things, for the institution of the poor laws, the introduction of coaches into England, and the first establishment of paper-mills. The manners of the English occupied a midway station between the barbarism of the feudal ages and the refinements of modern times. Bull-baiting, cock-fighting, and many other inhuman sports of this character, were practised on Sundays, and attended by ladies of rank and fash

Style of Building in the Reign of Elizabeth.

ion. When the citizens of London went abroad in the evening, they were attended by their servants or apprentices, who carried lanterns and clubs for their defence. Forks were unknown at table, and meat was conveyed to the mouth with the fingers.

CHAPTER CCCCX.

A. D. 1603 to 1625.

Accession of James I. — The Gunpowder Plot — Incapacity of the King — Fate of Sir Walter Raleigh — Misgovernment of James — The Puritans flee to America — Negotiations for a Spanish Marriage — Condition of London in the Reign of James.

Lord Bacon.

By the will of Elizabeth, the crown was conferred upon James VI. of Scotland, the son of the unfortunate Mary Stuart. He took the title of *James I.* of England. By his accession, the crowns of England and Scotland were united under one head, and an end was put to the wars which had so long existed between the two countries. The early part of his reign was distinguished by one of the most extraordinary events in history, namely, the *Gunpowder Plot.* The English Catholics had indulged great expectations at the death of Elizabeth, believing that James whose mother had been of their religion, would either restore or tolerate the Catholic faith in his dominions. In this they were disappointed. James avowed the most decided resolution to uphold the Protestant religion, which so exasperated the Catholics, that a number of the most unscrupulous and fanatical of them laid a plot to destroy both the king and the parliament. The plan was, to convey a large quantity of gunpowder into the building in which the parliament assembled, and on the day when the session opened — upon which occasion the king would be present — to blow up the edifice, so that the enemies of the Catholic religion might be destroyed at a single stroke. This atrocious design was adopted, and Guy Fawkes, a Spanish officer, undertook to superintend the business, and apply the match. The conspirators hired the vaults beneath the Parliament House, under the pretence of selling firewood. Beneath the piles of wood they secreted thirty-six barrels of gunpowder; these were covered with fagots, and the doors were thrown open to prevent suspicion. The train was prepared so that the whole could be fired in an instant.

The plot would have succeeded, but for the anxiety of one of the conspirators to save his friend. A few days before the time appointed, Lord Monteagle, a member of the House of Peers, received an anonymous letter advising him to stay away from parliament on the 5th of November, **1605**, the day fixed for the opening of the session, and assuring him that a terrible blow was about to fall upon certain persons, and yet that they "should not see the hand that hurt them." This letter excited suspicion: it was shown to the king, who conjectured that some mischief was intended by gunpowder. At midnight before the day appointed, a party of armed men visited the vaults, and seized Fawkes, who was found with a dark lantern and matches, ready to fire the train. The other conspirators were absent in Warwickshire, where, being confident of the success of the plot, they took arms, and endeavored to excite a rebellion. They were quickly overcome, and the leaders, including Fawkes, were

Guy Fawkes and his Associates.

tried and executed. It is impossible to imagine what would have been the consequence if this diabolical attempt had not been thus happily frustrated. The 5th of November, or *Pope's Day*, as it has ever since been called, is still observed as a holiday in England, on which occasion the boys burn Guy Fawkes in effigy. Previous to the American revolution, it was celebrated in the same manner in this country.

James was a weak-minded man, and entertained the most extravagant notions of the royal prerogative. He imagined himself a consummate master of diplomacy, which he called *kingcraft;* but he was the dupe of every crafty courtier. His incapacity for government rendered England contemptible in the eyes of all Europe. He possessed much learning, but it was little more than musty pedantry. He wrote many volumes, among which were a book in defence of monarchy; a book upon demonology, in which he firmly believed; and another, entitled a *Counterblast to Tobacco*, which commodity had lately been introduced into England, and which James abhorred.

There was another plot in the reign of James, the object of which was to depose the king, and place on the throne Lady Arabella Stuart. This was also defeated. One of the persons concerned in it was the celebrated Sir Walter Raleigh, who was punished by an imprisonment of thirteen years in the Tower of London, where he wrote his History of the World. At length, he obtained his release by paying a sum of money, and declaring that he knew of a rich gold mine in the Spanish province of Guiana. The king allowed him to go on an expedition in quest of this; but Raleigh had invented the whole story, and was obliged to return to England without accomplishing any thing either profitable or reputable. The Spanish court complained of the invasion of their territory by Raleigh; and James, who wished to conciliate that nation, put Raleigh to death on the scaffold.

James gave great dissatisfaction to the English by his unkingly behavior, his parsimony, and his inattention to the duties of his station. He was over-fond of eating, drinking, hunting, and cock-fighting. He sold privileges and titles of all kinds, for money. He injured the commerce of the country by monopolies and practised all sorts of mean, huckstering arts to fill his purse. Yet he was so poor and so bad a paymaster, that his servants have been known to stop his treasurer in the street, and insist on being paid their wages, and shopkeepers refused to trust him further till their outstanding bills were settled. He persecuted the Puritans, and drove them to New England, which

Christmas Carol in the Time of James I.

country was first settled by them during this reign. Virginia had been visited by the English in the reign of Elizabeth, but the first permanent settlements were made under James. This monarch also made an attempt to civilize the Irish, who, under long oppression and persecution, had become a wild and barbarous race, constantly at war with the English residents, who could not keep them in subjection. He transported numbers of settlers into the province of Ulster, who carried useful arts and manufactures into that country. Lord Bacon, to whose philosophical writings the world is so much indebted, held the office of chancellor in this reign.

James had a strong desire to marry his son Charles to the daughter of the king of Spain; but, after much negotiation, this project failed, though the prince made a journey to Spain for the purpose of seeing his destined wife. The close of this reign was signalized by violent disputes between the king and the parliament, which prepared the most fatal consequences for his successor. The streets of London were now, for the first time, paved with stone, each inhabitant being required to pave before his own house. The citizens were also ordered to build the fronts of their houses of stone or brick. In this reign we find the first mention of steam engines in England: they are supposed by some to have been brought from Italy.

The custom of observing festivals did not disappear with the Catholic religion. During the Christmas holidays all business was laid aside, and no one, from the sovereign to the beggar, thought of any thing but merriment and feasting. Christmas was celebrated in various ways; particularly by a fantastic and joyous procession in honor of the *sirloin*, emblematical of good cheer. On New-Year's eve, the young people in country towns carried round, from house to house, a large bowl called the "wassail-cup," filled with spiced ale, and every one who tasted of it was expected to give something to the bearers. The wassail cup is sent round at the table of the lord mayor of London to this day.

CHAPTER CCCCXI.

A. D. 1625 to 1642.

Accession of Charles I. — State of Public Opinion — Arbitrary Character and Behavior of Charles — Resistance of the Commons Petition of Right — Court of High Commission and Star Chamber — The Cavaliers and Roundheads — John Hampden and the Ship Money — Invasion of the Scots — Execution of Strafford and Laud — Attempt to seize the Five Members — Flight of the King from London.

Hampden.

Charles I. succeeded his father in 1625. His temper was arbitrary and imperious, and he was educated in the most extravagant notions of royal prerogative. He imagined that, as a king, he had a right to unlimited authority over the nation, and that the only privilege of parliament was that of giving a sanction to his decrees. In this belief he was encouraged by his courtiers, who expressed only such opinions as were calculated to flatter the monarch. The love of liberty and the spirit of resistance to the encroachments of arbitrary power had grown remarkably during the reign of James; but Charles, who was utterly blind to the progress of ideas, thought only of ruling the nation like an Eastern despot. He first involved himself in a quarrel with the parliament about a requisition of money to carry on foreign wars. The grant was refused, and the king proceeded to raise money by imposing taxes of his own authority, and in violation of the constitution. All the disputes between Charles and the house of commons had one source and one object: the king was determined to act without control, and the commons were determined to resist him, and maintain their proper share of the government of the country.

Charles had married Henrietta, the daughter of Henry IV. of France, a vain and haughty woman — selfish and bigoted. She encouraged her husband in those sentiments of despotism which led to his final ruin. The Puritans were persecuted, and great numbers of them emigrated to New England. Those who remained at home became more resolute and zealous under persecution; and the hostility to the royal government increased every day. So strong was the opposition in the house of commons, that Charles, in order to quiet the nation, agreed to an ordinance called the *Petition of Right*, which would have secured the foundations of a constitutional monarchy, in which the rights both of the monarch and the people would have been respected. But the king, in violation of this instrument, continued to levy taxes without the consent of parliament; and, when the remonstrances of the commons became too energetic, he dissolved the parliament, in 1629, with a determination never to call another till he found the people more obedient.

Religious disputes aggravated these political animosities. When the ecclesiastical authority was wrested from the pope, the people of England had submitted to a jurisdiction no less arbitrary in the king, who had absolute power in church affairs. An ecclesiastical tribunal, called the *Court of High Commission*, was established under the immediate direction of the crown and carried into practice the tyrannical spirit of Charles without any scruple. The king was also encouraged in his designs against the liberty of the people by his ministers. The chief of these were Thomas Wentworth, earl of Strafford, a deserter from the popular party, and Laud, the archbishop of Canterbury. Both were men of arbitrary principles. Strafford was quite unscrupulous in the use of means to gain a favorite end: Laud was one of the most bigoted of high churchmen. Under the evil counsels of these persons Charles gave full sway to his despotic inclinations. In defiance of the Petition of Right, he imposed taxes without the authority of parliament, and gave such extensive jurisdiction to the Court of High Commission, and another arbitrary tribunal called the *Star Chamber*, that the ordinary constitutional administration of justice almost entirely ceased.

Charles, however, had his adherents, who justified and defended his tyrannical measures, and the whole nation took sides either with the king or with the commons. The partisans of the king were denominated *Cavaliers*. They were distinguished by their showy attire, wearing ringlets over their shoulders, silk doublets with slashed sleeves and laced collars, a broad beaver hat with feathers, an embroidered sword belt, and a short cloak generally thrown over one shoulder. The popular party bore the name of *Roundheads* They cropped their hair close, and dressed in the plainest manner, wearing coarse cloth of gray. black, or brown, and a high-crowned hat. The enmity of the two parties rose to such a height, that a civil war seemed inevitable. Yet Charles blindly persisted in those arbitrary measures which had been the original cause of trouble. He issued an order forbidding the Puritans to leave the country; and drew upon himself the resentment of the whole Scottish nation by attempting to make the people of that country conform to the rules of the church of England.

The English nation was still further aroused to a sense of its rights by the conduct of John Hampden, who refused to pay an illegal tax imposed by the king. under the name of *ship-money*. Hampden's case was argued before the judges; and although the royal influence was so strong over these officers that they decided against him, yet the nation saw on which side lay the constitutional right. The popular animosity was now greatly inflamed against Charles. The Scots invaded England, and defeated the English forces. Charles, in his perplexity, summoned a parliament. The house of commons immediately impeached Strafford and Laud for high treason. They were tried and condemned. The king signed the warrant for the execution of Strafford, who was beheaded in 1641. Laud was executed four years after. Charles, however, was utterly insincere and faithless in all his promises to regard the rights of the nation and the privileges of the house of commons. He continued to practise every species of intrigue and duplicity. At length, a treacherous attempt made by him to arrest four of the chief members of parliament caused so violent an excitement and indignation, that the king, overwhelmed with shame and terror, fled from London to Hampton Court, while the people of the city escorted the obnoxious members in triumph back to the house of parliament.

CHAPTER CCCCXII.

A. D. 1642 to 1651.

Civil War — Rise of Oliver Cromwell — Battles of Marston Moor, Newbury, and Naseby — The King made Prisoner — His Trial and Execution — The Commonwealth — Charles II. declared in Scotland — Cromwell's Campaign against the Scots — Battles of Dunbar and Worcester — Escape of Charles II. from England.

Cromwell.

A civil war could no longer be averted, and Charles set up his standard at Nottingham, August 25, 1642. He justified his taking up arms by asserting that the commons wished to deprive him of the very substance of his kingly authority. The commons, on the other hand, maintained that they were willing to allow him every degree of power compatible with the nation's rights. It is certain that the king had been in the wrong from the very beginning, and that at this crisis he had lost all credit with the people by his repeated acts of bad faith. When the civil war began, many of the nobility and gentry took the king's side: th yeomanry, tradesmen, and the people of the town joined with the parliament. Armies were raised on both sides. The earl of Essex, General Fairfax, and Oliver Cromwell distinguished themselves in the parliamentary army; but Cromwell soon eclipsed all the others by his military genius. At first, before Cromwell rose to notice, the king's troops had the advantage; and the parliament, to strengthen their cause, entered into an alliance with the Scotch Covenanters, who had taken arms to resist the introduction of Episcopacy into their country.

At length, Cromwell took the command of the parliamentary army, and met the royalist forces, under Prince Rupert, at Marston Moor, in July, 1644. Fifty thousand combatants here engaged in an obstinate and bloody battle, which ended in the total defeat of the royalists. Another army was collected, and defeated by Cromwell at the battle of Newbury. The king was now reduced to such extremities, that the parliament might have forced him to unconditional submission, had that body been united; but, at this crisis, dissensions began to arise among the commons on the subject of church government. One party inclined to Presbyterian forms; their opponents preferred a more popular organization, and took the name of *Independents.* The Presbyterians had the majority in parliament, but their rivals were more numerous in the army, and among them was Cromwell. He gained a third victory over the royalists at Naseby, which added to the strength of the Independent party. Charles unable to keep the field, threw himself on the mercy of the Scots; and, having opened negotiations with their leader, ventured, on the faith of some loose promises, to present himself in their camp, where he was made a prisoner. All the towns and fortresses which had held out in his name speedily surrendered to the parliament.

The civil war was now at an end; but fresh difficulties arose in the attempts to establish a new government. The Scots abandoned the king to the parliament, who attempted to negotiate with him for a restoration of his authority and the establishment of a constitutional government. Charles made many solemn promises, which seemed a sufficient foundation for a scheme of settlement; but it was soon discovered by an intercepted letter written by him to his wife in France, that he had made these promises only to deceive the people, and intended to break them at th first convenient opportunity. Finding himself distrusted, he made his escape, and fled to the Isle of Wight; but he was captured, and fell into the hand of Cromwell, who, from this moment, became mas'er of his fate. Charles was conducted to London, and declared guilty of treason by the parliament. A specia high court of justice was organized for his trial in Westminster Hall, where, after the usual forms, he was condemned to death. He was beheaded in front of the royal palace of Whitehall, January 30, 1649 Such was the end of Charles I., who, though tried and sentenced by a court not strictly legal, must be allowed to have fallen a victim to his own tyrannical disposition and bad faith.

England became a commonwealth by the death of the king. The house of lords was abolished, and the whole government vested in the house of commons. Cromwell was the most powerful man in the nation. He proceeded with an army to Ireland, where a rebellion had broken out against the English, and quickly reduced the whole island to submission. He next took the field against the Scots, who had proclaimed *Charles II.*, son of Charles I. At Dunbar, Cromwell gained a complete victory over the Scottish forces, and Charles fled to England, where he collected an army. Cromwell marched against him, and, on the 3d of September, 1651, overtook him at Worcester, where he gained another decisive victory, which he called his *crowning mercy*, as it completely crushed the royal party in England. Charles narrowly escaped being taken prisoner at this battle. He was obliged to disguise himself and wander about the country. During a period of forty-five days, he was exposed to constant danger, and at one time concealed himself in a tree, which afterward bore the name of the *royal oak*. Many persons were intrusted with his secret, but they all preserved it faithfully, although a large reward was offered for his apprehension. At length, he reached the coast of the Channel. As he was sitting upon the beach, a rude fisherman, with a pipe in his mouth, sat down by his side. The companions of Charles, in great alarm lest he should be discovered, entreated the man not to puff his pipe "so near that gentleman." "Pooh!" said

Battle of Worcester: Flight of Charles.

the fisherman; "a cat may look upon a king!" Charles escaped in safety to France.

Return of Charles II.

CHAPTER CCCCXIII.

A. D. 1651 to 1685.

Dissolution of the Long Parliament by Cromwell — He is made Lord Protector — His Administration — War with the Dutch and Spaniards — Death of Cromwell — Administration of his Son Richard — Restoration of Charles II. — His disgraceful Reign — Plague of London — Great Fire — Popish Plot — Ryehouse Plot.

Cromwell, having attained to the summit of influence with the people, excited the jealousy of the parliament, who attempted to control him by disbanding a portion of the army. But Cromwell's authority over the soldiers was unlimited; and one of the most extraordinary displays of their implicit obedience to his will, and also of his own determined and energetic character, was the manner in which he dissolved the *Long Parliament*—so called because it had sat without interruption for twelve years — the longest time that any parliament has ever continued in England without an election. On the rejection of a petition for the payment of the army, Cromwell proceeded, with a file of soldiers, to the hall where the parliament was sitting, turned the members out of doors, and put the key in his pocket, A. D. 1653. He afterward convened a new parliament, composed of his own partisans. A constitution was framed, by which Cromwell was appointed chief magistrate of the commonwealth, with the title of *Lord Protector*.

Cromwell governed the English commonwealth with talent and energy. He exercised all the power of a king; but he made wise laws, and defended the national honor and interest abroad. War broke out with the Dutch and the Spaniards; but the English navy maintained a superiority during the whole of Cromwell's administration. Admiral Blake defeated the Dutch, and chastised the Algerines and Tunisians. Admiral Venables took Jamaica from the Spaniards. In 1656, the parliament made Cromwell a formal offer of the crown It is supposed he would willingly have accepted it; but the republican party was too strong, and his own family made very urgent remonstrances. He therefore declined the title of king, and contented himself with the protectorate for life, with the power of appointing his successor. After having governed England with great ability, he died on the 3d of September, 1658, the anniversary of the battles of Dunbar and Worcester. On his death-bed, he nominated his son Richard as his successor.

Richard Cromwell succeeded peaceably to the power and title of his father. Had he possessed but an ordinary portion of energy and talent, it is thought the commonwealth of England might have been continued to the present day; but he exhibited only timidity and indecision in public affairs. His incapacity became so apparent, that he soon resigned his authority. The officers of the army now constituted the government, and great confusion ensued. General Monk, who commanded the English army in Scotland, managed to turn this conjuncture to his own advantage. After temporizing in various ways, and carrying on a secret correspondence with the royalists, he declared for *Charles II.* By his influence, a parliament was convened which restored the royal authority, and Charles II. landed in England, and took possession of the throne in 1660.

Great rejoicing took place in England on the accession of Charles; and such was the infatuation of the people, that all the popular liberties which they had gained, at the price of so much blood, from the tyrannical Charles I., were abandoned, in the most heedless and insensate manner—to the arbitrary caprice of his son. Their folly was severely punished. The reign of Charles II. is the most disgraceful in English history. This monarch was a shameless profligate, who did not scruple to betray the national interests, honor, and religion, for money to squander upon his debaucheries. He persecuted the dissenters from Episcopacy, and revived the exploded political doctrines of passive obedience and non-resistance to royal authority. For a bribe in money from Louis XIV. of France, he made war upon the Dutch, and agreed to a plan for imposing the Catholic religion, by force of arms, upon the English people. The Dutch fleet sailed up the Thames, and burnt the English shipping in the river. London was thrown into great alarm; but the English reasserted their superiority in the following year, by a victory over the Dutch on the coast of Holland. New Amsterdam, in America, was conquered from the Dutch, and named *New York.*

In 1665 occurred the great plague of London, which destroyed seventy thousand inhabitants of that city in the course of a year. In the following year happened the great fire of London, which raged four days, and destroyed thirteen thousand buildings in the heart of the city. This fire was occasioned by accident; but the religious animosities of the time caused the people to suspect the Papists; and these people were charged with being the authors of the calamity, in an inscription on the Monument which was erected to preserve the memory of the dead. This inscription was effaced by public authority a few years since. The destruction of the old church of St. Paul's, during the fire, gave occasion for the foundation of the present magnificent cathedral, which was designed and executed by Sir Christopher Wren.

The scheme of the king to force the Catholic religion upon the nation, and the cruel persecutions which his agents practised against the Scotch Covenanters, spread a gloom over the country, and inclined the people to take alarm at every symptom of danger. This dispo-

Sir Christopher Wren.

sition was increased by the success of the tyrannical and bigoted Louis XIV., of France, who had just obtained a great advantage over the Dutch by the treaty of Nimeguen, which secured him an augmentation of power very dangerous to the neighboring kingdoms. In this state of mind, the nation was alarmed with a story of a *Popish Plot.* An impostor, named *Titus Oates*, invented a tale of a conspiracy by the Jesuits for the overthrow of the Protestant religion and the murder of the king. The remembrance of the Gunpowder Plot caused the whole of this wild story to be believed, and the nation went mad with terror and excitement. Many persons were brought to trial, and executed, as parties to the imaginary plot, and the belief in its existence continued for several years. Another affair that led to tragical consequences was called the *Ryehouse Plot.* The despotic character of Charles's government caused a number of persons to associate for the purpose of considering what means could be applied to resist the progress of arbitrary power. Lords Russell and Shaftesbury, and Algernon Sidney, were among them. Their meetings were held at a country seat called the *Ryehouse.* Some of the inferior members of this confederacy entertained a design of putting the king to death; but the leaders had no such intention. The plot was discovered. Sidney and Russell were tried for conspiracy; and, though no legal evidence was found against them, they were condemned and executed, A. D. 1683.

James II., the brother of Charles, succeeded him in 1685. He was known to be a Catholic, and was therefore unpopular. But, as he had promised that he would not interfere with the established religion of the kingdom, he was permitted quietly to ascend the throne. But he was bigoted, narrow-minded, and faithless. No sooner had he found himself firmly established in authority, than he began to take measures to render his power despotic, to overturn the national religion, and substitute the Catholic in its place. But the attachment of the English people to the principles of the Protestant reformation was so strong, that James met with the most determined opposition. The duke of Monmouth, an illegitimate son of Charles II., a weak-minded but vain and ambitious man, attempted to enforce his claims to the throne by pretending a secret marriage between his mother and Charles. He was encouraged in this design by many disaffected persons, and, in concert with the earl of Argyle, projected an invasion of England and Scotland. Argyle began the enterprise by landing, with a small force, in Scotland; but he soon found the country was not so ripe for revolt as he had believed. Surrounded by enemies, he attempted to force his way into the disaffected part of the western counties; but his followers gradually abandoned him. He was taken prisoner, and carried to Edinburgh, where he perished upon the scaffold. In the mean time, Monmouth had landed in the west of England, where he was received with great enthusiasm. Encouraged by the proofs of attachment shown him by the people, he ventured to attack the royal army at Sedgmoor. But the cowardice of Lord Grey, who commanded his cavalry, and the incapacity of Monmouth himself, proved fatal to the insurgents. They were routed with great slaughter, and Monmouth, after fleeing from the field of battle, and wandering about the country for several days in great distress, was taken prisoner. James, with the most unfeeling brutality, induced his unhappy nephew to degrade himself by an abject supplication for life, and then caused him to be beheaded on the scaffold.

The cruelties exercised on all persons suspected of sharing in this insurrection, by the inhuman Colonel Kirke, and the still more infamous Judge Jeffries, were of the most shocking description. They spread a general consternation throughout the western counties, but, at the same time, excited a secret spirit of hostility to the tyrannical king. Encouraged by the success with which he had suppressed this rebellion, James began to display his design of overturning the Protestant religion, in the most undisguised manner. The laws of the kingdom were set at defiance, and every despotic measure was practised which could assist in promoting the king's grand object. The independent spirit of the nation was roused, and a conspiracy was formed for expelling him from the throne, and placing the crown on the head of the prince of Orange, who was the stadtholder or president of the republic of Holland. He was of the Protestant religion, and had married Mary, the daughter of James; he commanded a respectable influence on the continent, and the main object of his policy was to build up a barrier against the dangerous power and encroachments of Louis XIV. of France.

The conspiracy embraced a large number of the most respectable noblemen and men of influence in England. William readily entered into the design. He raised a large military and naval force in Holland, and landed in the west of England in November, 1688. At first, he was joined by so few partisans, that he began to think of returning; but the delay of the people in taking his part was owing to the terror which the sanguinary proceedings of Kirke and Jeffries had produced in that quarter. In a few days, the nobles and leading men of England flocked to him from all quarters. The adherents and favorites of James abandoned him one by one, and the prince of Orange marched unobstructed to London. James, finding himself utterly deserted, escaped to France, flinging the great seal of England into the Thames as he crossed the river in his flight.

William III. ascended the throne of England by this revolution. His reign is commonly called the reign of "William and Mary," and the crown was settled by parliament on the king and queen jointly; but the queen had no share in the government. Before the coronation, William was required to sign an act called the *Bill of Rights*, which was designed to secure the people from any more such encroachments on their liberty as had been made by the monarchs of the Stuart line. By the conditions of this bill, no taxes were in future to be levied, nor money raised in any way, without the consent of parliament. Elections were to be free. The king was not to have the power of altering or suspending laws. The cruel punishments which had disgraced the preceding reigns — such as the use of instruments of torture, cutting off ears, noses, &c. — were to be abolished, parliament was to meet more frequently, &c. By the Bill of Rights, and the measures which immediately followed it, the liberty of the press was secured, toleration in religion established, and the popular rights placed on a firm foundation. In the possession of these free institutions, the English nation acquired a far greater respect and influence among the continental powers than they had ever before enjoyed. William's connection with Holland, and the efforts of James to regain his throne led to wars with France, which resulted in the increase of the naval power of England, as well as the beginning of a funded national debt, which has since been constantly increasing. The Bank of England was established in 1694.

Anne.

Anne, the second daughter of James, succeeded to the throne on the death of William, in 1702. She was married to Prince George of Denmark, who was a very stupid man, and had no share in the government. The parties of Whig and Tory, which arose in the reign of Charles II., had for some time divided the whole nation. The Whigs had favored the prince of Orange, and caused the revolution of 1688. Their main policy was to curtail the power of the crown. The Tories were for enlarging it. These characteristics have continued to the present day; though the Whigs have been at times, the government party, and the Tories in opposition.

Europe was at this time occupied with the wars of the Spanish succession, in which Louis XIV. attempted to secure the crown of Spain to his own family. The English, Dutch, and Austrians entered into an alliance to check the ambitious projects of the French monarch. The duke of Marlborough commanded the English armies, and proved himself the greatest general of that age. He gained many victories over the French in Germany, among which those of Blenheim and Ramillies are the most celebrated. The continental wars were highly expensive to England, but were very little profitable to the nation. The only conquest of permanent importance, in this reign, was that of Gibraltar, which was taken from the Spaniards in 1704, and has ever since remained in the hands of the English. The union of the two kingdoms of England and Scotland was accomplished in 1707. The two nations received equal rights and liberties; the Scotch parliament was abolished, and the kingdom of Great Britain, as it was now called, was represented in a single parliament, sitting at London. The reign of Queen Anne was the age of Pope, Swift, Addison, Gay, and many other eminent writers.

CHAPTER CCCCXIV.

A. D. 1714 to 1760.

Accession of George I. — Rebellion of 1715 — South Sea Bubble — Administration of Sir Robert Walpole — Accession of George II. — War with Spain — Disasters in South America — Anson's Voyage — Rebellion of 1745 — Battle of Culloden — Peace of Aix-la-Chapelle — The Seven Years' War — Chatham's Administration — The New Style.

George I

George of Brunswick, a German electoral prince, became king of Great Britain, with the title of *George I.*, on the death of Anne, in 1714. This succession had been previously arranged by act of parliament, in order to annul the claims of the exiled family of Stuart, who continually urged their pretensions; it is commonly styled the *Hanoverian* succession, from the principality of Hanover, of which George was the sovereign. A change of parties was caused by this reign. The Whigs, who had been in opposition, now became the court party. They used their power to crush their political adversaries, and, by impeachments for high treason, drove the chief members of Queen Anne's ministry into exile. The Jacobites, as the partisans of the Stuarts were called, seized this opportunity to raise a rebellion in Scotland. They took up arms in 1715; but this attempt was speedily suppressed.

This reign is distinguished, in a singular manner, for the financial scheme called the *South Sea Bubble*, A. D. 1720. It was projected by Sir John Blount, and its main features were copied from Law's famous Mississippi scheme at Paris. The South Sea Company was originally formed for trading to the Pacific Ocean. Blount proposed that its business should be enlarged by combining the public stocks with its other dealings. The company, by assuming all the government securities, were to become the sole creditors of the nation—an arrangement which was expected to give them great advantages in the transaction of business. It does not appear that the people fully understood the nature of the operations by which the concerns of the company were to be rendered so profitable; but the project met with immediate success, from its novelty, and the imposing representations that were made of it. The holders of public stock willingly assented to the proposal of exchanging it for shares in the South Sea Company. The shares immediately rose in price, and people ran wild in stock speculation. Partly from the general credulity, and partly from dishonest acts practised by the contrivers of the project, it was believed that South Sea stock would pay a dividend of fifty per cent. on the par value. In consequence of this, the price rose to ten times the original cost. Change Alley, in London, was crowded from morning to night with a motley and tumultuous throng, in which ladies, noblemen, and the lowest of the populace, were mingled in entire forgetfulness of every thing but money making. Prodigious fortunes were made by stock jobbing, and other extravagant speculations were started, which, for a short time, had a similar success. This state of things, however, could not continue long. Suspicions began to be excited that the affairs of the South Sea Company were unsound. Some cautious holders of stock sold out. A panic immediately followed, and the value of the stock was discovered to be altogether imaginary. The price fell as rapidly as it had risen. Thousands of persons who were rolling in wealth found themselves suddenly reduced to beggary, and a general bankruptcy would have ensued, but for the prompt interference of parliament. Punishment was inflicted on the chief contrivers of the fraud, among whom were many individuals of rank and station.

During this reign, England was engaged in no foreign wars of any consequence. Sir Robert Walpole was prime minister. He was a corrupt politician, but he rendered a service to the nation by preserving peace. George I. never became popular with the English, and never felt at home among them. He died in 1727.

George II., his son, who succeeded him, was also a German by birth. The early part of his reign was passed in tranquillity, and the country prospered by a constantly increasing trade with foreign nations. Walpole remained at the head of the ministry, and preserved peace till 1739, when the troubles which grew out of the English trade with America brought on a war with Spain. Fleets were sent out to attack the Spanish American colonies. Admiral Vernon captured Porto Bello, and Lord Anson sailed round Cape Horn, to cruise against the Spaniards in the Pacific. The enterprises of the English, however, all resulted disastrously. Vernon was repulsed in an attack on Carthagena, and a large armament, designed for the conquest of the Spanish Main, was compelled to return to England, with the loss of 15,000 men. Anson succeeded in getting only half his squadron round Cape Horn. In the Pacific, he met with great losses, and at length, only one ship remained of all his fleet. With this, however, he was fortunate enough to make prize of a rich Spanish galleon, which in some measure compensated for the cost of the expedition. The English made no further attempts upon South America. Walpole was compelled to resign office in 1739.

Dr. Johnson.

This period is distinguished by some of the brightest names in English literature and science — Hume, Gibbon, Robertson, Dr. Johnson, Goldsmith, Fielding, Richardson, Gray, &c. Literature, which had previously depended for support chiefly upon the countenance of men of rank, now began to acquire a popular character, and the patronage of a much more numerous class of readers. The profession of an author also began to be profitable. An able writer could live by his own labor, and found himself released from that servility to the great which forms so strong a characteristic in the dedications and flatteries of preceding writers.

The new ministry entered into the war of the Austrian succession in support of the empress queen of Hungary, Maria Theresa. They augmented the army, sent large bodies of troops into the Netherlands against the French, and granted subsidies to the Danes, the Hessians, and the Austrians. George II. fought in person at the battle of Dettingen, in which the French were defeated, in **1743**; but his incapacity rendered this victory of no profit to the English or their allies. The policy of the ministry, in supporting the continental connections of Great Britain, led to new expenditures, and an alarming increase of the national debt.

While the king was upon the continent, in **1745**, a rebellion in favor of the Stuart family was projected in Scotland. Charles Stuart, the pretender, having been encouraged in this design by the king of France, Louis XV., landed in Scotland with a small French force, and set up his standard. He was joined by a considerable party of Highlanders, who supported his cause with great enthusiasm. He descended from the Highlands, and made himself master of Edinburgh. Sir John Cope, who commanded the English forces in Scotland, marched against the rebels, and a battle was fought at Preston Pans, in which the English were completely routed. Had the pretender acted with decision and energy, it is supposed he might have marched to London, and seized the government. But he wasted his time in idle pageantry in Edinburgh, which gave the English ministry time to send to Flanders for troops. The pretender at length took the field, invaded England, and advanced to Derby. The English force had now collected in considerable numbers, and he was compelled to retreat to Scotland. After various movements, the English army, under the duke of Cumberland, encountered the insurgents at Culloden. The latter were defeated, and the victors gave no quarter, putting the Highlanders to death in cold blood. These cruelties were continued for many weeks. The country of the insurgent clans was laid waste with fire and sword. The men were hunted like wild beasts on the mountains; the women and children, driven from their burned huts, perished by thousands on the barren heaths. During five months, the pretender remained concealed in the Highlands, and among the Western Isles of Scotland, though a reward of thirty thousand pounds was offered for his head, and more than fifty persons were intrusted with his secret. At length, after suffering incredible hardships, he escaped to France. The vengeance of the government fell heavily on his adherents, and numbers of the leaders were tried and executed. Their heads were placed over Temple Bar, in London, where they remained for many years.

The war on the continent of Europe was brought to a close by the treaty of Aix-la-Chapelle, in **1748**. But Great Britain and France soon became involved again in hostilities, on the subject of the boundaries of their colonies in North America. This war, which began in America in **1754**, extended to Europe, and is known in the history of that country as the *Seven Years' War* In **1756**, a general panic spread throughout England on the prospect of an invasion from France. Hanoverian and Hessian troops were hired to defend the country. The French captured Minorca from the English; and Admiral Byng, who commanded the English squadron destined for the relief of the place, having displayed a want of courage in engaging the French fleet, was tried by a court martial, and shot.

The wars carried on by the English in America and India during this period, were attended with very important results; but the particulars will be found in the histories of those countries. It is sufficient to state here, that Clive established the British power in India, and Wolfe conquered Canada from the French. In the latter part of the reign of George II., Mr. Pitt, afterwards Lord Chatham, was at the head of the British ministry, and by his great abilities largely contributed to the success of the British arms. In this reign, the New Style was introduced into England, greatly to the dissatisfaction of many ignorant people, who complained that they had been cheated of eleven days by it. A member of parliament lost his election in consequence of having voted for the New Style.

During this reign, turnpikes were first established in England, and the roads in general, which had previously been in a most imperfect and neglected state, were systematically improved. Music became a fashionable study, under the auspices of the great Handel, who resided fifty years in England. Internal improvements of many sorts were introduced, and, among others, that of internal navigation by means of canals, which has since been carried to a prodigious extent in Great Britain, with most signal advantage to trade and industry. It was in this reign that the old gates of London were pulled down, and that city was united to Westminster. The society of arts, manufactures, and commerce was instituted under George II.

CHAPTER CCCCXV.

A. D. 1760 to 1815.

Accession of George III. — Dispute on the Subject of Neutral Property — Increase of the National Debt — Administration of Lord Bute — American War — Administration of Lord North — Riots in London — General Peace — French Revolution — Continental Wars — Peace of Amiens — War with Napoleon — Battle of Waterloo — General Pacification.

Burke.

GEORGE III. became king of Great Britain, by the death of his grandfather, in 1760. The war on the continent continued but three years after his accession, being closed by the treaty of Paris, February 10, 1763. The result of the seven years' war was, that Austria and Prussia assumed the first rank among the European powers. France lost her political preëminence, and England abandoned her influence in the European system, maintaining an intimate relation only with Portugal and Holland. By the war in the colonies, England obtained a complete maritime supremacy. She monopolized the commerce of North America and Hindostan, and gained a decided superiority in the West India trade.

During the seven years' war, a question arose which led to very important discussions. France, unable to maintain a commercial intercourse with her colonies, opened the trade to neutral powers. England declared this traffic illegal, and relying on her naval superiority, seized neutral vessels and neutral property bound to hostile ports. The return of peace put an end to the dispute for a season, but it became the subject of angry controversy in every future war. This question lay at the bottom of the difficulties which produced the rupture between the United States and Great Britain in 1812.

The wars of George II. and of the early part of the reign of George III. led to another consequence, by no means foreseen at the time. The internal condition of the kingdom improved rapidly by the extension of the funding system. The national debt was increased to the sum of one hundred and forty five millions sterling; but the loans required for the war were generally raised in England. Thus the pecuniary affairs of the government became intimately connected with those of the people, and the increase of the national debt more closely united the rulers and the ruled in the bonds of a common interest. This altered state of things scarcely excited notice, though it has been the chief source of the permanence and stability displayed by the government of Great Britain, while revolutionary movements threatened to subvert all the other dynasties of Europe.

Early in this reign, the church of England saw the

John Wesley.

beginning of a new sect within its domain, which, by slow degrees, attained to great and permanent importance, not only in England, but in other countries This was the sect of Methodists, founded by John Wesley, a preacher of learning and piety, educated in the church of England, but who left that communion for the purpose of promoting a religious reform He was aided in this effort by George Whitefield, who exhibited extraordinary eloquence as a popular preacher. Both Wesley and Whitefield visited America in the prosecution of their great object, and the sect of Methodists, by their exertions, became widely and firmly established on both sides of the Atlantic.

A spirit of faction now began to trouble the councils of Great Britain. While there was any reason to apprehend danger from the house of Stuart, the Brunswick dynasty was necessarily thrown for support on the Whigs; for the Tories were, from principle, much disposed to favor the claims of the exiled family. But when all fears of the pretender had disappeared, the Tories obtained the royal favor. Personal friendship induced George III. to place the earl of Bute at the head of his cabinet. His influence excited the jealousy of the Whigs, who had long monopolized the favor of the king and the nation. The new minister took advantage of his influence over the king to procure places and pensions for a great many of his countrymen, the Scotch, and especially for his own relations; in consequence of which he became so unpopular that the king was compelled to dismiss him. It was believed, however, that he privately retained his influence in the cabinet, and thus no small portion of his unpopularity was inherited by his successors.

The ministry attempted to tax the American colonies, and by persevering in this attempt, against the remonstrances of the Americans, brought on the war which resulted in the independence of the United States. This war began in 1775. The history of it will be given in that part of our work relating to America. France, Spain, and Holland also became involved in the contest; but England had no armies employed on the continent of Europe. The transactions in India have already been described. Lord North was at the head of the cabinet during the American war. In 1780, London was disturbed by dreadful riots, occasioned by the repeal of the penal laws against the Catholics. The populace, excited by Lord George Gordon, a half-crazy person, committed every sort of outrage under the cry of "No Popery." For several days, London was completely at the mercy of the mob. Some Catholic chapels were burned, and many private houses destroyed. Religion, however, seems to have been but a pretext for the commission of these outrages; the rioters being generally incited by a desire for plunder and wanton mischief. Tranquillity was restored by the interference of the troops.

Lord North, finding it impossible to carry on the American war any longer, resigned his office. The marquis of Rockingham took his place, and negotiations were opened with the Americans. Peace was made with them, and the independence of the colonies acknowledged in 1782. A general peace was concluded in the following year.

The domestic affairs of Great Britain, during this reign, were far surpassed in importance by the foreign transactions in which the nation became engaged. Great Britain, like every other part of Europe, partook in the general agitation caused by the French revolution. War broke out between England and France in 1793, and lasted with but slight interruptions till 1815. During this period, the prime ministers of Great Britain were Messrs. Pitt, Fox, Addington, Grey, Perceval, and Lord Liverpool. The military transactions on the continent have been detailed elsewhere. In carrying on this war, it was the professed object of the British cabinet to check, first the spirit of French republicanism, and next the ambitious projects of Napoleon. They regarded the contest as a struggle for national existence; and their exertions to maintain it were indeed stupendous. Immense sums of money were raised, by loans and taxation, for the support of British armies upon the continent. The British naval force was spread over the whole ocean, and gained many brilliant victories under Nelson and other able commanders. The French commerce was annihilated, and their ships of war were compelled to keep in port. The British made a most lawless use of their naval superiority, treating the weaker powers with great haughtiness and insolence, and violating the rights of neutral nations without scruple.

The close of the eighteenth century was distinguished by a scientific discovery which has proved of more benefit to the human race than a thousand victories. It was on the 14th of May, 1796, that Dr. Jenner made his experiment of inoculating the kine pock, which proved this to be a preventive of the small pox. For this great discovery, the British parliament made him a grant of thirty thousand pounds. The

Dr. Jenner.

anniversary of the 14th of May is now commemorated by a yearly festival at Berlin, the capital of Prussia.

A prospect of a general pacification presented itself in 1802. The people of England seemed to be wearied and exhausted by the war. The national debt had increased to four hundred and fifty-one millions sterling. Monetary affairs were so embarrassed that the Bank of England had been under a stoppage of specie since 1797. An enormous weight of taxation had oppressed all classes of people, and a scarcity of provisions added to the universal distress. The ministry had undertaken and pursued the war with the professed object of restoring the Bourbons to the throne of France; but this result was now apparently at a greater distance than ever. The desire for peace overcame every other consideration, and a treaty with the French republic was signed at Amiens, on the 25th of March, 1802. The British, however, refused to give up Malta, which they had agreed to do by the treaty. The mutual jealousies of the French and English brought on a renewal of the war in May, 1803. The British maintained their supremacy at sea, and defeated the French and Spanish fleet at Trafalgar, in 1805.

During the stormy period of national politics which ensued upon the breaking out of the French revolution, the British ministry was entirely under the control of Mr. Pitt, the son of the earl of Chatham, whose administrative talents and eloquence had been powerfully exhibited in the latter part of the reign of George II. and the commencement of that of George III. Mr. Pitt's administration embraced a most eventful and important period, in the course of which the relations of parties were altogether changed, and Europe was suddenly plunged into the most extensive and bloody war which it had ever known. Pitt was the soul of the confederacies that were formed among the monarchies of Europe, to resist the revolutionary spirit of France; and the overthrow of the last coalition, by the battle of Austerlitz, is supposed to have caused him a degree of chagrin and mortification which led to his death a few months afterward, January 23, 1806.

The family of this famous statesman were distinguished for talent, and also for a considerable degree of eccentricity. In this connection we may mention Lady Hester Stanhope, a niece of Mr. Pitt. She left England immediately after his death, and travelled over a great part of Europe. Young, beautiful and wealthy, she was courted every where with all the eagerness which rank, fortune, and female charms could inspire; but she rejected every offer, either from disappointed affections, or a romantic love of adventure. After passing seven years at Constantinople, she embarked for Syria in a vessel laden with a great part of her wealth, and jewels of high value. The vessel was wrecked in a storm on the coast of Caramania, and its treasures were buried in the waves. Lady Stanhope was saved upon a desolate island. She returned to England, and sailed again for Syria with the remainder of her fortune. She landed in that country, applied herself to the study of the Arabic language, and associated with all persons who were likely to assist her intercourse with the Arabs, Druses, Maronites, and other inhabitants of Syria. She then organized a

Lady Hester Stanhope.

large caravan, and traversed every part of that country. At Palmyra, tribes of wandering Arabs, to the number of fifty thousand, assembled round her tent; and, charmed with her beauty and grace, and the splendor of her retinue, proclaimed her queen of Palmyra. After leading a wandering life in this manner for some time, she settled in an almost inaccessible solitude among the mountains of Lebanon, not far from ancient Sidon. Here she built a castle, constructed a beautiful garden in the Oriental fashion, and lived many years in a style of Eastern splendor, surrounded by a concourse of Arab and European guards and dragomans, and a numerous retinue of females and black slaves. She maintained a friendly intercourse with the government of Constantinople, the pacha of Syria, the emir Beschir, the sovereign of Lebanon, and particularly with the Arab sheiks of the desert. She died here in the year 1839, an object of admiration to the East, and of astonishment to Europe.

On the continent, the arms of Napoleon prevailed over all enemies. His seizure of the throne of Spain induced the English to send armies into that country, which at first met with great losses and defeats. Under the command of the duke of Wellington, however, they encountered the French with success, and finally wrested both Spain and Portugal from the grasp of Napoleon. Great Britain entered with ardor into the struggle which was made to check his gigantic power on the continent, and the influence of her mighty wealth and energetic spirit was every where felt. These exertions, and the disastrous campaign of the French in Russia in 1812, led to the final triumph of the English and their allies. The capture of Paris, and the abdication of Napoleon in 1814, were followed by a general peace in Europe the same year. The return of Napoleon from Elba in May, 1815 renewed the war with France; but the grand drama was finished by the battle of Waterloo, in June of the same year, as has been already related in the history of France. A war with the United States, which had been begun in 1812, was closed by a treaty in the spring of 1815, leaving Great Britain once more at peace with all the world.

The commencement of steam navigation in Great Britain may be dated at about 1811, when a steamboat was launched upon the Clyde, in Scotland, four years after Fulton had made his successful experiment upon the Hudson. The slave-trade was abolished by act of parliament, in 1807, after having been a subject of earnest debate in that body for twenty years. Wilberforce, Granville Sharpe, and other philanthropists, distinguished themselves by their persevering labors in accomplishing this great end.

CHAPTER CCCCXVI.

A. D. 1815 to 1863.

Distress and Disturbances in England — Accession of George IV. — Troubles occasioned by the Queen — Accession of William IV. — Reform Bill — Accession of Queen Victoria — Foreign Wars — Famine in Ireland — The Chartists — Rebellion of Smith O'Brien.

THE transition from war to peace caused so complete a change in all commercial transactions, that credit was shaken, trade injured, manufactures checked, and thousands of laborers and tradesmen were thrown out of employment. These evils were more sensibly felt in England than in any other country, and led to many serious riots in the manufacturing counties, and alarming symptoms of dissatisfaction in the metropolis, where meetings were held which threatened to lead to revolution. The government adopted very severe measures, but the public tranquillity was not restored till the commercial crisis had passed. Notwithstanding the cessation of the disturbances, the people remained wretched and discontented, and the discontinuance of the war hardly relieved them from any burden of taxation. The national debt had increased to the enormous sum of eight hundred millions sterling: the interest of which remained to be paid yearly

The heavy taxes, and the stagnation of trade, pressed with destructive weight on the commercial and manufacturing classes.

George III. died January 29, 1820, after a reign of sixty years — the longest and most eventful in English history. For many years previous to his death, he had been deprived of his reason: during which time the government had been exercised by his son, as prince regent. He now ascended the throne under the title of *George IV.* He had been for some years separated from his wife, who, on the accession of her husband, returned to England to claim the privileges of her rank. The king, whose hatred of his spouse was intense, refused to admit her to any share in the ceremonies of the coronation. Great excitement was caused in England by this proceeding. The people, believing the queen had been unfairly treated by her husband, adopted her cause. The ministry, at the suggestion of the king, caused her to be brought to trial before the house of lords, for scandalous and criminal misconduct. Brougham and Denman, the ablest advocates of the English bar, pleaded her cause; and the general feeling of the nation was so strongly expressed against the measure, that it was abandoned. The queen died shortly afterward, A. D. 1821. Lord Liverpool retired from the office of prime minister in 1827, and was succeeded by Mr. Canning, who died after an administration of about three months. Lord Goderich took his place for a short time, and was succeeded by the duke of Wellington. The only other event of importance, in this reign, was the admission of the Catholics to sit in parliament. George IV. died the next year, June 26, 1830.

Lord Denman.

William IV., his brother, ascended the throne. One month after this event, the revolution of July took place at Paris. Its effect in England was very powerful. The riots and rick-burnings in the rural districts had for many years given signs of popular discontent while the general clamor for parliamentary reform had grown stronger from day to day. The popular cause in England was greatly strengthened by the overthrow of Charles X. in France; and the Tory ministry, headed by the duke of Wellington, were compelled to resign at the close of the year 1830. A Whig cabinet, with Earl Grey at the head, took their place. One of the earliest measures of the new government was the introduction of a bill for the reform of parliament, by disfranchising the boroughs which elected members without any adequate constituency, called *rotten boroughs*, and granting members to the large cities which had hitherto been without representation. After a violent opposition from the advocates of the old system, the reform bill was passed in June, 1832. This was the most important change which had been made in the form of the British government for many years. Apprehensions were entertained by the enemies of the measure, that it would lead to the overthrow of monarchical institutions in England; but such views have by no means been verified by its operation. It must be added, that the supporters of the reform bill, who expected great and immediate benefits from it, have in like manner been disappointed. The form of the legislative body has been somewhat changed, but its spirit remains the same.

Canning.

William IV. died June 20, 1837. His reign is remarkable for having been the only one in all British history in which there was no foreign war and no execution for high treason. He was succeeded by the reigning sovereign, Queen *Victoria*, who was married on the 10th of February, 1840, to Prince Albert of Saxe-Coburg-Gotha, a German. The administration of the government, however, remains solely with the queen. During her reign, Great Britain was engaged in

Kings of England.

Britons.

Date of Accession.
A. D.
445. Vortigern.
454. Vortimer.
465. Ambrose.

Saxon Heptarchy.

454. Hengist in Kent.
491. Ella in Sussex.
519. Cerdic in Wessex.
527. Erchenwin in Essex.
547. Ida in Northumberland.
575. Offa in East Anglia.
582. Cridda in Mercia.
617 Rodoald in East Anglia.
624. Edwin in Northumberland.
643. Oswyn in several kingdoms.
656. Ceadwalla in Sussex and Wessex.
688. Ina in Wessex.
707. Ethelbald in Mercia.
717. " in East Anglia and Mercia. End of the Heptarchy.
828 Egbert, first king of England.
838. Ethelwolf.
857. Ethelbald.
866. Ethelred I.
872. Alfred.
901. Edward the Elder.
925. Athelstan.
941. Edmund I.
946. Edred.
955. Edwy.
959. Edgar.
975. Edward the Martyr.
978. Ethelred II.
1016. Edmund II. Ironside.

Danish Kings.

1014. Sweyn.
1017. Canute.
1035. Harold Harefoot.
1039. Hardicanute.

Saxon Kings.

1041. Edward the Confessor.
1066. Harold.

The Norman Line.

1066. William the Conqueror.
1100. Henry I.
1135. Stephen.

House of Plantagenet.

1154. Henry II.
1189. Richard I. Cœur de Lion.
1199. John.
1216. Henry III.
1272. Edward I.
1307. Edward II.
1327. Edward III.
1377. Richard II.

House of Lancaster.

1399. Henry IV.
1413. Henry V.
1422. Henry VI.

House of York.

1461. Edward IV.
1483. Edward V.
1483. Richard III.

House of Tudor.

1485. Henry VII.
1509. Henry VIII.
1547. Edward VI.
1553. Jane Grey.
1553. Mary.
1558. Elizabeth.

House of Stuart.

1603. James I.
1625. Charles I.
1649. Commonwealth.
1653. Oliver Cromwell, Protector.
1658. Richard Cromwell, Protector.
1660. Charles II.
1665. James II.

House of Orange & Nassau.

1688. William III.

House of Stuart.

1702. Anne.

House of Brunswick, or the *Hanoverian Dynasty*.

1714. George I.
1727. George II.
1760. George III.
1820. George IV.
1830. William IV
1837. Victoria

important transactions in foreign countries, and her own colonies; as the war in Afghanistan, China, and the Punjaub, and the rebellion in Canada. The history of those events will be found in other parts of this volume. Although she maintained peace with Europe, the population of Great Britain suffered great misery from want of occupation and a scarcity of food. The chief suffering was in Ireland, where the failure of the potato crop led to a famine, in which nearly half a million of persons perished during the year 1847. The emigration from Great Britain was much increased by this calamity; and hundreds of thousands abandoned their homes for the United States. This state of suffering continued with more or less agravation for some time, but has now passed away.

In 1848, shortly after the overthrow of Louis Phillippe, considerable alarm was created in England by the Chartists, a very numerous association of people, chiefly of the lower classes, who are in favor of radical changes in the government, and a written constitution. They held meetings in immense numbers in London, and other large cities, and, for a short time, threatened to cause an overturn similar to what had taken place at Paris. The great body of the nation, however, did not countenance their proceedings, and the Chartists soon ceased to attract notice. In the same year, excited by the miseries of Ireland, an improvident attempt was made to raise a rebellion in that country, by an individual named *Smith O'Brien*, and others; but it was quickly suppressed by the government, and O'Brien, with a number of his compatriots, was tried, condemned, and sentenced to transportation. Most of them were permitted to return in 1856.

Great Britain took a prominent part in the struggle with Russia, called the Eastern war, which began in 1853. Having formed an alliance with Louis Napoleon for the protection of Turkey, she dispatched in 1854 alike to the Black Sea and the Baltic, powerful fleets and armies, under her most renowned commanders. Never before has the world witnessed such formidable movements, as the use of steam and recent improvements in the weapons of war enabled the allies to make against their enemy. The gigantic power of Russia, aided by the military genius of her generals, however, rendered them less destructive than might have been expected. The operations of the allied fleets in the Baltic, were confined to the ravages of a few insignificant towns and the destruction of some inferior forts. Kronstadt, the great seat of Russian naval force, and the citadel of St. Petersburgh, presented an aspect so formidable, as to forbid an attack.

The Black Sea became the chief theater of conflict. From August, 1854, till the close of the war in 1856, the Mediterranean Sea was crowded with every kind of sea-craft, transporting men and munitions to the allied forces. Sebastopol having become the chief object of attack, there were here gathered nearly 400,000 men on both sides, and who for nearly a year were occupied in the siege. The defenses of the Russians presented batteries seventy miles in extent, and when the final assault was made, September 5th, 1855, the French opened a cannonade along a continuous line of four miles. There has probably never been witnessed a more sublime, yet terrific spectacle than was here presented during the four days and nights in which the storm was sustained.

The result of this conflict has been already stated —pp. 822. The British government made prodigious efforts to sustain the war, but although the alliance triumphed, her share of the glory was hardly equal to her sacrifices. At the same time, her expenses and her losses were enormous. It is to be remarked, however, that the spirit of the nation was in no degree broken, but with that energy and devotion which is the foundation of British power and glory, was still ready to maintain the conflict.

Since this period, little has occurred in Great Britain that requires mention here. Prince Albert died in 1861, beloved and regretted by all. Albert Edward, Prince of Wales, has been a great traveller in the Old and New World, and married in 1863, the Princess Alexandra, of Denmark. The sufferings of the cotton-spinners, owing to the rebellion in America, have made them the object of sympathy both in England and America.

CHAPTER CCCCXVII.

Character of the English—Literature—Institutions — Arts — Amusements — Architecture — Population — Productive Industry — Chief Cities.

THE character of the English is strongly marked, and it is not surprising that among many excellent qualities, we find some which are not agreeable. They are intensely national, and hence are little qualified to do justice to other countries. Their travelers, perhaps without intending it, often misrepresent the countries they visit: the periodical press, the great vehicle for disseminating opinion and reporting the current transactions of the world, is too often prostituted to the purposes of national antipathy and individual interest or spite. It is, perhaps, a frailty of the English, that they despise the French and are jealous of us: certain it is that it is rare to find candor or sound judgment in an English writer upon either of these topics.

Loyalty is no less conspicuous in the English than their nationality: this is, indeed, the master sentiment of the majority of the people, taking precedence both of religion and patriotism. What we should deem the misfortune of the country,—its royal family and its nobility,—are, to them, objects of intense and ceaseless interest. The slightest movements, the most ordinary incidents, the simplest acts of daily life, on the part of these notable personages, are deemed worthy of daily record, and constitute the staple of numerous publications, largely patronized. If the English are annoyed at what they call our national conceit, they cannot be surprised if we regard their worship of royalty and nobility—both founded upon an illusion,* according to our theory—with at least equal dislike. The English must be respected, but they are little loved in any country: throughout nearly the whole conti-

*All monarchy and its attendant nobility, are founded in the idea that a certain family, or certain families, are endowed with royal or noble blood; that is, that nature, providence, the Deity—has made these persons of a higher and better mould than other men, and hence they may claim dominion, reverence, wealth, and privileges All this is, of

nent of Europe, they are very cordially disliked. Aside from their political power, exerted through the government, it is really remarkable how little is their influence, especially in literature, taste, art, religion, and social institutions. The personal arrogance which many of the English carry with them wherever they go, and a similar tone of haughty exclusiveness characterizing their whole intercourse with the world, will readily explain the almost universal sentiment of aversion entertained toward the nation, and the little sympathy they excite, even in behalf of their many virtues and their wise and good institutions.

The spirit of the British nation, especially in public affairs, is betrayed by the names of their vessels of war, most of them steamships of recent construction: Archeron, Adder, Alecto, Avenger, Basilisk, Bloodhound, Bulldog, Crocodile, Erebus, Firebrand, Fury, Gladiator, Goliah, Gorgon, Harpy, Hecate, Hound, Jackal, Mastiff, Pluto, Rattlesnake, Revenge, Salamander, Savage, Scorpion, Scourge, Serpent, Spider, Spiteful, Spitfire, Styx, Sulphur, Tartar, Tartarus, Teaser, Terrible, Terror, Vengeance, Viper, Vixen, Virago, Volcano, Vulture, Warspite, Wildfire, Wolf, Wolverine! That these names are as significant of British taste and feeling, as of the business to which the vessels which bear them are devoted, is manifest to all.

The national arrogance of the English is farther visible in their patriotic songs, as "Rule Britannia," in which the dominion of the seas is boldly asserted; and the national anthem of God save the King, or Queen,* which is still sung by the English on festive occasions with infinite zeal and zest. Let any one compare it with the French national song of the Marseilles Hymn,† —an object of intense horror to many an Englishman,—and mark the strain of exclusiveness, the almost profane loyality of the one, and the burning patriotism and generous philanthropy of the other. The fact that the English exert little moral and social influence upon the continent, while all Europe sympathizes with every movement of France, may be easily explained by the suggestions here given.

Among the bold and striking features of the English character, one of the most prominent is the love of liberty which pervades all classes. The liberty for which the English have contended includes the right of thinking, saying, writing, and doing what their opinions, inclinations, whims, or prejudices, may prompt. Such is the theory of English liberty, yet, to a great extent it seems an imaginary boon. It may be true that a portion of the people—the upper and middle classes—realize the liberty which they claim; but what practical freedom is enjoyed by the great mass of the nation, including the population of the three kingdoms, while they are bred and brought up in such ignorance and poverty, that it is impossible for them to move from the condition in which they are born, to choose their place of abode, their profession, their companions, their religion, or their position in society? Nevertheless, the difficulty is seen and acknowledged, and it must be admitted that both the government and the people show an earnest desire to mitigate the evils which are suffered by the poorer classes. Great improvement has lately taken place in respect to them, and further improvement is insured by the national spirit, recently displayed.

---

course, a fiction. God has made no such distinction in his creatures: equality before God is the doctrine of reason and Christianity. Royalty and nobility are, therefore, assumptions. Yet those who are interested in imposing their divine origin upon the masses, and keeping up respect and awe toward them as of this high lineage, take care to surround themselves with the most imposing circumstances. They dwell in costly edifices; they ride in gilded coaches, marked with the symbols of their lofty descent; they have names and titles significant of their several dignities; they hold little intercourse with the people, and are ever seen by them encircled by the enchantments of unapproachable distance and elevation, or boundless riches and power. The royal family are as much aloof from the mass as the veiled prophet of Khorasan. They dwell in palaces, and are surrounded with gorgeous wealth and imposing pomp. Few are allowed to approach the king or queen unless they be of noble blood. He or she is enshrined in an awful dignity, shadowed forth by that fearful, cabalistic term — MAJESTY!

Such is the system by which a fiction is imposed upon a nation. The expenses attending it are exhibited by the items given in the Statistics of Royalty, under the general views of Great Britain and Ireland, at p. 963, to which the reader is referred.

* We give the original of 1745:—

GOD SAVE THE KING.

God save great George our king!
Long live our noble king;
  God save the king.
Send him victorious,
Happy, and glorious,
Long to reign over us;
  God save the king!

O Lord our God, arise!
Scatter his enemies,
  And make them fall;
Confound their politics,
Frustrate their knavish tricks;
On him our hopes we fix
  O, save us all!

Thy choicest gifts in store
On George be pleased to pour;
  Long may he reign.
May he defend our laws,
And ever give us cause
To say, with heart and voice,
  God save the king!

† THE MARSEILLES HYMN.

Ye sons of France, awake to glory!
  Hark, hark, what myriads bid you rise!
Your children, wives, and grandsires hoary
  Behold their tears and hear their cries!
Shall hateful tyrants, mischief breeding,
  With hireling hosts, a ruffian band,
  Affright and desolate the land,
While Peace and Liberty lie bleeding?

CHORUS.

To arms, to arms, ye brave!
Th' avenging sword unsheath.
March on, march on, all hearts resolved
On liberty or death!

Now, now the dangerous storm is rolling,
  Which treacherous kings confederate raise;
The dogs of war, let loose, are howling;
  And lo! our fields and cities blaze.
And shall we basely view the ruin,
  While lawless Force, with guilty stride,
  Spreads desolation far and wide,
With crime and blood his hands imbruing?

The contradictions in the English character are remarkable. In no other country of Europe, perhaps, are there more men who act steadily upon principle; at the same time, in no other country are there so many living in an habitual and open violation of all principle, and so frequently in contempt of legal ordinances. The amount of crime, especially of late, is appalling. Domestic life is, however, cultivated more sedulously by the English than by any of the continental nations, and the sanctity of marriage is more carefully guarded. Perhaps the most estimable quality of the English is their general recognition of the great principles of justice, the source of all honorable dealings among the higher classes, and of what is emphatically called *fair play* in the humbler transactions of life. Yet England, as a nation, taking her own writers as witnesses of her guilt, has not scrupled to practise injustice, robbery, and oppression, to an extent, perhaps, unparalleled by any civilized country, except ancient Rome.

In her intellectual character, England may justly be considered as proudly preëminent. Bacon, Boyle, Locke, Newton, Davy, and numerous others, of this country, have disclosed to mankind perhaps a greater sum of important truths than the philosophers of all Europe beside. Strong, clear, sound sense appears to be the mental quality characteristic of the English in philosophical pursuits. In works of imagination, the genius of the nation is bold, original, and vigorous. In the drama, Shakspeare stands unrivalled among ancient and modern poets, by his profound and extensive knowledge of mankind, his boundless range of observation throughout all nature, his exquisite play of fancy, and his irresistible power in every province of thought and feeling — the sublime, the pathetic, the terrible, and the humorous. In epic poetry, Milton stands above all other moderns. Spenser and Dryden are alike eminent, the one for sweetness and richness of description, and the other for sprightliness of numbers and versatility of power. Pope is unsurpassed for the terseness and finish of his versification. To these may be added the names of Swift, Butler, Gray, Thomson, Cowper, Scott, Southey, Wordsworth, Byron, and many others. In historical writing, England has many illustrious names, the chief of which are Gibbon, Hume, Robertson, and Macaulay. In oratory, some of her statesmen have acquired great renown, though the general taste, both in the senate and at the bar, seems to delight rather in plain sense and cogency of argument, than in those high-wrought and declamatory flights by which the great speakers of antiquity acted on the imaginations and passions of their hearers.

The institutions for public education in England are splendid and well endowed. The two universities of Oxford and Cambridge are not only the wealthiest, but the most ancient in Europe. They enjoy, among other privileges, that of sending each two members to parliament. Public schools, in addition to the universities, are very numerous; but the education of the lower classes is much neglected by the government. It is quite certain that the leading people are averse to universal education. The fine arts have been less encouraged in England than in some countries of the continent: yet there are many noble collections of paintings and statuary in the kingdom. The most distinguished of the English painters is Sir Joshua Reynolds, who introduced an original style of portrait painting in the last century.

Sir Joshua Reynolds.

The favorite amusements of the English are those which combine the advantages of air and exercise. In former times, hunting was almost the sole business of life among the English squires; and though their tastes are now much altered, this original pastime, in all its forms, continues to be eagerly followed. Horse-racing is encouraged by the nobility and gentry with equal ardor. The races of Doncaster, York, and Newmarket, are attended by the most distinguished persons in the country for rank and opulence. Among the common people boxing was a favorite amusement: but this seems to be declining. Bull-baiting was formerly prevalent, but it is now prohibited by law.

The architecture of England presents hardly any features that are strictly national. Every style of building may be found in the country. In the cities and large towns, brick is the common material for houses. The more costly structures are of freestone. Internally, no habitations in the world equal those of the English for convenience and comfort. In the article of food, the English do not differ much from the people of the United States. The national drink is malt liquor. Convivial excess, so long the reproach of the English, is becoming more rare.

The population of England, in former times, was very imperfectly known, being calculated only from very vague surveys and estimates. In the reign of Elizabeth, a careful enumeration was made, the result of which gave four millions and a half as the number of the inhabitants. At the commencement of the present century, a regular system of enumeration by census was established, to be continued at intervals of ten years. The last census, in 1861, gave a population of about twenty millions for England and Wales.

The productive industry of England far surpasses that of any country in the world, ancient or modern. The natural fertility of the soil is not equal to that of the southern countries of Europe; but by improvements in agriculture and the industry of the people, it

---

With luxury and pride surrounded,
  The vile, infatuate Despots dare —
Their thirst of gold and power unbounded
  To mete and vend the light and air.
Like beasts of burden would they load us —
  Like tyrants bid their slaves adore:
  But man is man, and who is more?
Nor shall they longer lash and goad us.

O Liberty! can man resign thee,
  Once having felt thy generous flame?
Can dungeons, bolts, and bars confine thee,
  Or whips thy noble spirit tame?
Too long the world has wept, bewailing
  That falsehood's dagger tyrants wield;
  But Freedom is our sword and shield,
And all their arts are unavailing!

Modern Shops in London.

has been made highly productive. Almost all the valuable kinds of grain are raised in abundance, and of good quality. The manufactures of England, still more than the immense products of her agriculture, have astonished the world, and raised her to a decided superiority, in this respect, over all other nations. Her woollen and cotton cloths are worn by the inhabitants of every part of the globe, and her manufactures of metal are widely diffused.

England is the greatest commercial nation in the world. The exports of the country consist almost wholly of its manufactured produce. Cotton is the most important article; next are woollen goods and wrought metals. The imports comprise almost every article for which the necessity or the luxury of man provides a market. The interior navigation of England may be regarded as one of the prime sources of the national prosperity. The canals are very numerous, and the railways still more so. The carriage roads are unsurpassed in any part of the world for their excellence. The same may be said of the bridges.

London, the capital of Great Britain, is the largest city in Europe. It stands on the Thames, at the head of ship navigation. Its whole extent may be described as seven miles in length, and five in breadth; but different portions of this great metropolis bear different names, and are subject to different municipal authorities. The city is in general well built, paved, lighted, and supplied with water. Foreigners from the continent, who visit it for the first time, soon discover that utility, and not ornament, is the main characteristic of the place, and that the inhabitants are occupied with business rather than amusement. The main streets are tolerably spacious; but very few are straight or regular. The houses are built of a dingy-colored brick and, as the air is constantly filled with smoke, the streets have a dim and gloomy appearance. The people of fashion dwell at the west end, in which are many spacious squares. London has some grand and imposing architectural structures; but hardly any of them show to advantage, on account of the smoke, which not only obscures the distant view of the buildings, but defaces with soot every thing exposed to the air. St. Paul's church, the masterpiece of Sir Christopher Wren, is the finest building in England, and is ranked next to St. Peter's at Rome; but it is closely hemmed in by buildings, which prevent a good view of it. Westminster Abbey is a noble specimen of Gothic architecture, which contains numerous monuments of kings, warriors, statesmen, philosophers, and poets. The other buildings of note are the new Houses of Parliament, Whitehall and Buckingham Palaces, Somerset House, the Royal Exchange, the Bank, the Post-Office, Covent Garden Market, &c. Near the spot where the great fire of 1666 originated, stands the monument erected to commemorate that calamity: it is two hundred and two feet in height, and is one of the most conspicuous objects in the city. There are seven bridges across the Thames in London, and a Tunnel under the river in that part where it is navigated by large ships: this is the most remarkable work of its kind ever executed.

London is the central point of business, and the

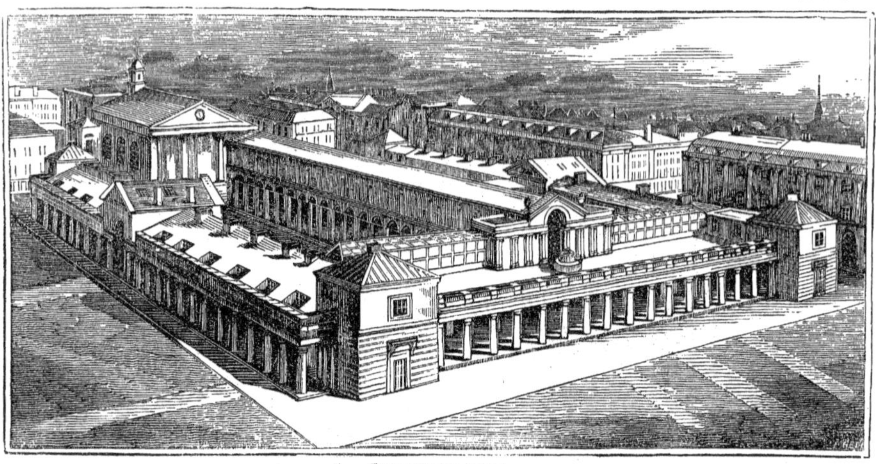

Covent Garden Market.

great money market of the empire. The Bank of England is the most gigantic institution of its kind in the world: its annual issues are about twenty millions sterling. London is also the literary emporium of the kingdom: almost all the books of importance are here printed and published. It is the centre of intelligence relating to public affairs, giving circulation to a prodigious number of newspapers and periodicals. The trade and manufactures of London embrace almost every department of human enterprise and industry. Its population in 1841 was one million eight hundred and seventy-three thousand six hundred and seventy-six. At the present moment, it is estimated at two million eight hundred thousand.

Liverpool is the chief seaport in the west of England, and the great emporium of the manufacturing districts. It is chiefly remarkable as a place of commerce, but some of its public buildings are very handsome. The most conspicuous are the Town Hall and the Exchange. The docks for the reception and unloading of merchant ships are very spacious. Numerous lines of packets run from Liverpool to various parts of the world, and the most regular and direct intercourse between Europe and America is carried on by the steam packets, which connect this city with Boston and New York. The population is about three hundred and fifty thousand.

Manchester, the centre of British industry and the manufacturing capital of the empire, is in the neighborhood of Liverpool, and connected with it by a railway. It is not a handsome city, but consists, for the most part, of narrow streets, in which manufactories

City of Bath.

and warehouses are crowded together in huge masses. The chief manufactures of Manchester are those of cotton cloth, lace, and silk. The city is remarkable for its charitable institutions, hospitals, and schools for the poor. The population is about three hundred and forty thousand. Birmingham, another manufacturing city, has a population of about three hundred thousand.

Bristol, on the Severn, was once the second city in England. It was the chief trading mart and outpost for manufactures in the west, till it was outstripped by the more rapid growth of Liverpool. It has still extensive manufactures and foreign commerce. Population, one hundred and fifty thousand. Bath, not far from Bristol, is the most beautiful city in England. Its streets are spacious, and the houses handsomely and regularly built of fine freestone. The ground on which the city stands is such as to represent it to great advantage. Bath is the resort of great numbers of invalids and wealthy idlers, who visit the place to use its mineral waters, and participate in the amusements and dissipation which are the characteristics of all fashionable watering-places in Great Britain. Among the other cities of England may be mentioned Oxford, Cambridge, and York. The two first are famous for their universities, and the last for its magnificent Gothic cathedral, called the *Minster.*

CHAPTER CCCCXVIII.

100 B. C. to A. D. 1277.

WALES. — *Description of Wales — The Ancient Welsh — The Druids — Ceremony of Cutting the Mistletoe — Remains of Ancient Druidism — Roman Invasion of Wales — Native Government — Llewellyn — Edward I.*

WALES, formerly a separate principality from England, lies in the west of Great Britain. It is bounded on the north and west by St. George's Channel; on the east by the English counties of Chester, Salop, Hereford, and Monmouth; and on the south by the Bristol Channel. It is about one hundred and eighty miles in length from north to south, and eighty in breadth. It exhibits geographically all the features of a distinct country from England, consisting of almost continued ranges of lofty mountains and precipitous crags, intersected by numerous deep ravines, with extensive valleys, affording endless views of wild and romantic scenery. The principal heights are Snowdon and Plinlymmon, the former of which is three thousand seven hundred feet in height. Lakes and streams are abundant in this mountainous region. The climate of Wales differs materially from that part of England lying in the same latitude. In general, the air is very sharp; in the mountainous regions it is bleak, but moderately mild in the vales, and those parts adjacent to the ocean, particularly in the celebrated vale of Glamorganshire. Snow is more frequent in Wales than in England, and it covers the tops of the highest mountains for many months in the year.

The ancient Welsh called their country *Cymry*, and their language *Cymraeg.* The same names are preserved in the Welsh spoken at the present day. From *Cymry* is derived *Cambria*, another name of this country. The derivation of the name *Wales* is uncertain: it has been referred to *Gael, Gaul*, and other words: it appears to have been first applied to this country by the Saxons in the sixth century. The primitive Welsh were a part of the aboriginal possessors of the Island of Britain. Their numbers were increased by the Roman invasion, which drove the Britons westward into this country. After the invaders had secured the central part of the island by forming stations and appointing garrisons, they turned their attention to the unconquered country. The Romans, on their first visit to Wales, found it possessed by three tribes of people — the *Ordovices*, *Silures*, and *Dimetæ*. They had an established government, with regular and well-disciplined troops, divided into charioteers, cavalry, and infantry. They raised corn, and their pastures were abundantly stocked with cattle, sheep, and swine. Their money consisted of rings and small plates of iron strung together.

The chief seat of Druidism seems to have been in this country. The great high priest of this religion, or arch Druid, resided in the Island of Mona, now called *Anglesea.* Here the most solemn rites of this mysterious religion were performed amidst dark groves of oak-trees, or in temples formed by circles of huge stones. Here they sacrificed human beings, consisting of prisoners taken in war, and criminals condemned to death for their offences. These miserable victims were burned in large wicker cages before the altars. Cæsar, in his Commentaries, says, "The Druids consider that the torture of those who have been taken in the commission of theft and robbery, or other crimes, is more agreeable to the immortal gods; but when there is not a sufficient number of criminals, they do not scruple to inflict this torture on the innocent. The chief deity, whom they worship, is Mercury. They have many images of him; and they regard him as the inventor of all arts, their guide in journeying, and the great regulator of trade and commerce." The power of the Druids over the people was far greater than that possessed by their princes, who seldom dared to dispute the decrees of these priests. In such a case, the offender was forbidden to attend the sacrifices — a punishment similar to the Catholic sentence of excommunication.

The Druids of Wales were believed to be skilled in magic; and their costume was calculated to strengthen this belief among a race of ignorant barbarians, whose minds were easily impressed by outward appearances. Their white robes, long beards, and the wands which they carried, might well cause them to pass for magicians in that unenlightened age. Every priest wore suspended from his neck a serpent's egg, enclosed in gold, as a charm against evil. They taught many superstitions concerning serpents, rivers, trees, fire, and other things held sacred. But their principal object of veneration was the mistletoe, when it was found growing on the oak. The great Druidical festival was held on New Year's day, when the mistletoe plant was cut with the most imposing religious solemnities. On this occasion, the Druids walked in procession, habited in their robes of ceremony, toward the oak on which the mystic plant was growing. One of them ascended the tree, and cut the mistletoe with a golden knife, while another stood below to catch the boughs in the folds of his garment, as they fell. Two milk-white bulls were then sacrificed, and great feastings and rejoicings followed. There were three solemn festivals in the year, beside that of cutting the mistletoe. One was held on the 1st of May, to pray that the fruits of the earth might prosper; another on midsummer eve, to beg a blessing on the corn then ready for reaping; and the third in October, to give thanks for the harvest. Sacrifices, feastings, songs, and music always formed part of these festivals; but one invariable mode of testifying joy was that of lighting large fires, and carrying flaming torches about the fields. Thus may be traced in the bonfires, illuminations, and fireworks of modern times, and particularly in the festivals still kept up on May day and midsummer eve, in many English villages, the remains of ancient Druidism.

The Romans, under Suetonius Paulinus, invaded Wales in the first century. They overcame the Ordovices in the north, and waged a war of extermination against the Druids. The last remnants of these people, with their followers, were driven into the Island of Mona. The Romans pursued them to their retreat, cut down the sacred groves, put the Druids to the sword, and completely extirpated the race wherever their arms prevailed. Wales, however, was a difficult region to conquer. The Silures continued the struggle for liberty in the south-east during many years, till at length, in the reign of Vespasian, the celebrated commander, Julius Agricola, was sent with a powerful army against them. He defeated the Welsh at the battle of Caer Caradoc, and completely reduced that part of the country to the Roman yoke. The affability of Agricola gained the affections of the people, and disposed them to imitate the Roman manners. He bestowed on them the privileges of citizens, received them into his armies, provided for the education of their youth, and lived among them in a style of great hospitality. Thus securing by policy what he had gained by force, he attached the country to the Roman dominions, and Cambria was dignified with the name of *Britannia Secunda.*

After the Romans withdrew from Britain, the Welsh resumed their ancient forms of government, and the country appears to have been divided into six or seven principalities. Perpetual wars were carried on with the Saxons and Angles. About the middle of the sixth century, Mælgwyn, king of North Wales, appears to have made himself supreme over all the other chieftains of the country. This government continued till the reign of Cadwallader, A. D. 703, when the strength of the Welsh was so much broken by their wars with the Saxons, that the latter made successful inroads into the country, and established their dominion here to a considerable extent.

The Danish invasion of England called off the attention of the Saxons from Wales, and left this country in a state of comparative tranquillity. The Danes afterward made some incursions into Wales, but effected no permanent conquest. After the Norman conquest of England, the Welsh refused the annual tribute which had been extorted from them by the Saxon kings as a mark of submission. William invaded their country with a powerful army, quickly reducing them to subjection, and obliged them to do homage, and take the oath of fealty to him as their superior lord. From this period, the English monarchs maintained a claim to Wales as their hereditary property.

On the death of William, the Welsh, feeling the galling yoke of their humbled condition, attempted to recover their lost independence; and joining in revolt with some refractory English barons, made an irruption into England, devastating the country with fire and sword. These outrages determined William Rufus to attempt the subjugation of the country. For this purpose he excited his barons to conquer at their own charge, under homage and fealty to him, the territories of the Welsh. These barons, who were denominated *Lord Marchers*, endeavored to secure their conquests by peopling them with English, and erecting strong fortresses to defend them from the inroads of the Welsh.

Thus was the last asylum of the Britons broken into on every side. South Wales was subdued, while North Wales, now greatly reduced, alone preserved the national character, and maintained its independence. For a long period, the inhabitants of this region, favored by the mountainous nature of the country, supported an unequal but spirited contest against their invaders. In 1237, Gryffyth, the eldest son of Llewellyn ap Jorweth, prince of North Wales, rebelled against his father. That prince applied for protection to Henry III. of England, and received it on the humiliating terms of yielding vassalage to the English crown. David, the eldest son of Llewellyn, succeeded to the throne on the death of his father, and renewed the homage to England. He made prisoner his brother Gryffyth, and delivered him to Henry, who confined him in the Tower of London, where he lost his life in an attempt to regain his freedom. Henry deprived David of the sovereignty of Wales, and bestowed it upon his own son Edward, afterward king. David sought the aid of the pope, offering to hold Wales as a dependency on the papal see. The pope absolved David from his oath of allegiance to Henry, and his commissioners cited the English king to appear before them, and answer the charge of David. Henry, it is said, quieted the pope with large sums of money.

Llewellyn, the youngest son of Gryffyth, succeeded to the throne of North Wales on the death of his uncle David. When Edward I. came to the throne of England, he summoned the Welsh prince to do homage which the latter declined, unless the king would give hostages for his safe conduct, and restore his wife, who was kept in captivity by Edward. This was refused and Edward, in 1277, proceeded to make war upon Llewellyn, in which he was assisted by David and Roderic, the brothers of the prince who had been deprived of their inheritance by him. Llewellyn defended himself among the inaccessible mountains of Caernarvonshire; but the English surrounded and blocked up his army so effectually, that after sustaining all the horrors of a siege, they were compelled to submit to the terms dictated by Edward. These were, that the Welsh should pay fifty thousand pounds, and that Llewellyn and his barons should do homage and swear fealty to the English crown, surrender a portion of their territory, and make pecuniary compensation to David and Roderic.

CHAPTER CCCCXIX.

A. D. 1277 to 1863.

Second Insurrection of Llewellyn — Invasion of Wales by Edward — Death of Llewellyn — Capture and Execution of Prince David — Subjugation of Wales — Union with England.

The English made a tyrannical use of their victory, and treated the inhabitants of the conquered provinces with great harshness. The Welsh, who were naturally choleric and irritable, again rose in arms against their oppressors. Prince David was seized with the national spirit, and made peace with his brother, promising to unite with his countrymen in the defence of Welsh liberty. Edward was not displeased with this new insurrection, as it gave him an opportunity of making his conquest final and absolute. He once more assembled his army, and advanced into Wales, A. D. 1283. The English fleet, in the mean time, attacked the Island of Anglesea, and landed in sufficient force to make themselves masters of it. This island is separated from the main land of Wales by a very narrow strait, over which the English threw a bridge of boats; but the Welsh occupied the shore with a strong army, while Llewellyn took post in an intrenched camp on the heights of Snowdon, overlooking the island. On the first attempt of the English to cross the bridge, they were repulsed with the loss of three hundred men. They were unable to pass the strait till aided by treachery. A Welshman discovered to them a ford by which he army effected a passage to the main land, without being perceived by the Welsh, and gained the rear of Llewellyn's camp.

The Welsh prince, ignorant of this treachery, descended from the heights to reconnoitre the position of the enemy. Imagining himself in perfect security, he took but a single attendant with him. Having taken a view of the shore of Anglesea, he was reposing himself in a barn, when he heard a war-cry. He asked of his attendant, "Are not my Welshmen at the bridge?" He was answered that they were. "Then I am safe," said he, "though all England should be on the other side." But the shouts and clamor soon increased, and presently he was thrown into astonishment at the sight of the English banners approaching toward him. The advanced posts of the Welsh had been attacked and routed Llewellyn put spurs to his horse, and tried to regain his camp, but was suddenly crossed in his way by an English knight, who, perceiving him to be a Welshman, but ignorant of his rank, advanced immediately upon him. A single combat ensued, and Llewellyn was struck dead by the lance of his antagonist. The knight, unconscious of the importance of his exploit, fell back to join his countrymen, who were now rapidly ascending the heights. The Welsh were drawn up in battle array, ready for the contest, but awaiting the return of their sovereign. Hour after hour passed away, but he did not appear; and, at length, they saw the squadrons of the enemy on the summits of the cliffs. Before they could recover from their surprise, they found themselves attacked on all sides. A panic spread throughout their ranks, and they fled in confusion.

When it was known that the prince was missing, the knight who had slain Llewellyn descended into the valley to see whom he had encountered. He found the dead body still on the ground, and, on examining its face, it was recognized to be the prince of Wales. Eager to reap the full reward of his exploit, he cut off the head of the corpse, and carried it to Edward, who sent it to London, placed a silver crown upon it as a mark of derision, exhibited it to the populace in Cheapside, and at last fixed it upon the Tower.

David succeeded to the sovereignty of Wales upon the death of Llewellyn; but he was unable to collect an army sufficient to meet the English in battle. He was chased from hill to hill, and hunted from one retreat to another. At length, after concealing himself under various disguises, he was betrayed in his lurking-place to the English. He was sent in chains to Shrewsbury, where Edward caused him to be tried before the peers of England. He was sentenced to be hanged, drawn, and quartered, and this barbarous punishment was carried into effect. Edward, moreover, sensible that nothing kept alive the military spirit of the people, and the remembrance of their ancient glory, so much as the traditional poetry of the country, which, assisted by the power of music, and the jollity of festivals, made a deep impression on the minds of youth, is said to have gathered together all the Welsh bards, and ordered them to be put to death. This act has been called in question. The disappearance of the bards is by some writers ascribed to the overthrow of the independent sovereignties of Wales, which deprived the wandering minstrels of all patronage and support.

The conquest of Wales is said to have given a title to the eldest son of the king of England. According to a story related by the monkish writers, Edward, shortly after the subjugation of the country, assembled the Welsh chieftains, and promised to give them for sovereign a prince of unexceptionable manners, a Welshman by birth, and one who could speak no other than the Welsh language. On their acclamations of joy, and promises of obedience, he announced to them that he conferred the principality of Wales on his son Edward, then an infant, who had been born at Caernarvon, in that country. This young prince was afterward king of England; the principality of Wales was annexed to the crown, and from that time the eldest son of the sovereign has borne the title of prince of Wales.

After the death of Llewellyn and David, all the Welsh nobility submitted to the conqueror. The laws of England, with the sheriffs and other ministers of justice not before known in Wales, were established in that country. National antipathies, however, are not easily conquered; and in order to hold the territory in subjection, Edward was obliged to erect castles of immense strength, not only on the Welsh frontiers, but in the interior. Yet these did not prevent formidable insurrections, in one of which, during the reign of Henry IV., the Welsh chieftain Owen Glendower maintained himself for years as an independent prince. By slow degrees, however, a thorough union has been effected between the inhabitants of this country and the English; and for the last three hundred years, the Welsh have been as peaceable as any subjects of the British crown.

CHAPTER CCCCXX.

Government of the Ancient Welsh — Enmity to the English — The Welsh Bards — Manners — Character — Superstitions — Language, &c., of the Welsh.

From the accounts given by the Roman writers, it appears that a monarchical form of government existed in Wales in the earliest historical times. The island was divided into several petty sovereignties, each subject to a separate prince; but in times of emergency and danger, they united under one leader, similar to a dictator among the Romans. This leader was called *Pendragon.* The power of the pendragon was temporary, but the dignity was hereditary. The right of succession to the separate governments was not so regular. Sometimes the monarch nominated his successor, with the consent of the nobles. The Welsh had a sort of parliament in very early times. Six of the most intelligent and powerful persons were summoned out of every district to assist the king in the work of legislation. The nobles were called *Uchelwyrs.* They held their lands from the crown, and each presided as lord over his particular domain. The mass of the people were in a state of villanage, and were subject to military service in war, and contributions of property.

The Welsh, for many ages after their subjugation, kept up a strong feeling of hatred against the English, which some of the English statutes against the Welsh were little calculated to remove. It was long before the people were put on the same footing with the English subjects. Severe laws were passed in the reigns of Henry IV. and Henry VI. against the Welsh bards, who kept alive the national feeling of discontent, by songs of former glory, and narratives of wrongs committed by the English; but in spite of the attempts to suppress them, the bards continued to flourish for centuries.

The Welsh bards were supposed to be endowed with powers approaching to inspiration. They were the depositaries of historical knowledge, both public and private. They possessed one talent, in particular, which endeared them more than all the rest to the Welsh nobility, namely, that of being most accomplished genealogists. They flattered the vanity of the chiefs and their followers by singing the deeds of their ancestry. No public solemnity, great feast, or wedding could take place without the presence of the bards and minstrels. A glorious emulation arose among them, and prizes were bestowed on the most worthy. The court bard was a domestic officer. He held his land free, and was entitled to a horse and a woollen garment from the king, and a linen one from the queen. At the three principal feasts of Christmas, Easter, and Whitsuntide, he sat next to the chief officer of the palace, who delivered the harp into his hand. When he accompanied the soldiers upon a foray, he had an ox or a cow from the booty. He also sung at the head of the troops when drawn up for battle. This was to remind the Welsh of their ancient right to the whole kingdom of England; for the Welsh, looking upon themselves as the only lineal descendants of the ancient Britons, regarded the English as Saxon usurpers of their territory. The topics of the old Welsh songs show the barbarous manners of these times. The bard delighted to recount scenes of turbulence, bloodshed, and rapine. The images with which he adorned his descriptions were those of the prowling wolf, the gushing blood, and the screaming kite feasting on human prey. It was not till the border wars had been suppressed by the conquest of Edward, that the inspirations of the Welsh bards dealt in more gentle themes. It was then that the mountain muse found the same delight in beauty and rural nature which she had formerly experienced only in murder and devastation.

The manners and customs of the Welsh distinguish them at this day, in some degree, from the English. They are extremely national, and though their country is not fertile, they are strongly attached to their native hills. It is rare to find a Welshman among the emigrants in foreign countries. Mountainous scenery is peculiarly friendly to those imaginary existences, which constitute the objects of superstition. This is exemplified in Wales. The belief in witchcraft is still strong here, and many are the fatal effects supposed to be produced by supernatural agents. At every house may be seen a horseshoe, a cross, or some other charm of defence. Many old women bear the odium of preventing the cows from yielding milk, and of inflicting disorders on men and cattle. The supposed witches find it profitable to encourage this belief, and never deny the charge of supernatural dealing brought against them: they thus obtain a livelihood from their imaginary power. A peculiar sort of demon is supposed to exist in this country, called *Knockers*. The Welsh miners imagine they hear them under ground, and by their noises, which represent the different stages of mining, they believe the way is found to rich veins of ore.

The Welsh language is of the Celtic family, and has a claim to very high antiquity. It is supposed to be the most primitive and uncorrupted of all the European tongues. It abounds with original words, more especially technical terms, which other languages borrow from the Greek, or express by circumlocution. This ancient tongue is spoken at the present day by the common people, though it is slowly getting into disuse. The better classes are principally educated in England, and few of them cultivate the popular dialect.

Pride of ancestry has always been a strong characteristic of the Welsh. In no other nation, except the Hebrew, has genealogy been held so important, or carried to such an extent. Family distinction is pursued into such minute and remote particularities as to excite the ridicule of all, except Welsh genealogists. So deeply is this feeling rooted in the country, that even the lowest classes of the people carefully preserve the history of their parentage, and are able to trace the names of their progenitors into the darkness of antiquity.

CHAPTER CCCCXXI.

200 B. C. to A. D. 600.

SCOTLAND. — *Geographical Description — The Caledones — Invasion of Agricola — The Picts — Invasion and Conquest of Scotland by the Irish — Saxon Colonization in Scotland — The Kingdom of Strathcluyd — St. Columba — Christianity introduced into Scotland — The Culdees.*

SCOTLAND occupies the northern part of the Island of Britain, and is about half the size of England. It consists of three distinct and very dissimilar portions — the *Highlands*, the *Lowlands*, and the *Islands*. The first, or Highland part, comprises the west and centre of Northern Scotland, constituting a region of very bleak and rugged aspect. The mountains dip almost perpendicularly into the lakes and seas on which they border; and the valleys among them are on so high a level, that they admit of no culture, except of the coarser kinds of grains. The second, or Lowland part, includes the southern extremity of Scotland, bounded by the Friths of Forth and Clyde on the north. Some of this territory is fertile; but, in general, the soil of the country is hard and unproductive. The islands comprise a considerable part of Scotland. They consist of the Orkney and Shetland Islands in the north, and the Hebrides on the west. They are rocky and barren, like the mountainous parts of the main land. and exposed to perpetual mist and rain, and the storms of the Atlantic. Some of these islands are little more than naked rocks, washed by the ocean waves, yet the resort of innumerable sea-fowl. Even these dreary regions are inhabited by natives, who spend their lives as fishermen and bird-hunters.

The lakes of Scotland, or *lochs*, as they are here called, form a characteristic feature of the country. Many of them are long arms of the sea, running up into the heart of the mountains. Among these, Loch Lomond is preëminent for its loveliness, and grandeur

Loch Katrine.

of its scenery. Loch Katrine is smaller, but is admired for a singular mixture of tranquil beauty and wild sublimity. Scott's Lady of the Lake contains a description of these regions, at once geographically accurate and highly poetical. Loch Awe is also celebrated for its scenery.

The first inhabitants of Scotland are supposed to have been a tribe of the Cimbri, an ancient people of Denmark, who migrated from that peninsula about two hundred years B.C. But this is merely conjecture. The Greek and Roman writers did not regard Scotland as a distinct country from the southern part of the island. The name of *Caledonia*, which was at one period given to it, was derived from the Caledones or Picts, a tribe of Northern Europe, who are supposed to have invaded the island from Norway, and to have driven the first settlers into the southern parts. *Caledon* means a *forester* or *savage*.

The Romans first invaded Caledonia in the reign of Tiberius. Under the command of *Agricola*, the father-in-law of the historian Tacitus, they penetrated to the Grampian Hills, where, after an obstinate battle, the skill and discipline of the legions prevailed over the rude valor of the barbarian hosts. The whole open country was abandoned to the invaders; but the inaccessible mountains of the north opposed a permanent obstacle to their progress in that quarter. The Romans formed numerous camps, to assist in the military occupation of the country. They endeavored to resist the incursions of the natives by rearing, at different periods, two walls across the island; one between the Forth and the Clyde, and the other between the Solway and the Tyne. They abandoned the country in the fifth century. The Caledonians, who were now called *Picts*, invaded the southern parts of Britain, and compelled Vortigern to call the Saxons to his assistance, as we have related in the history of England.

The name of Scotland, singular as it may seem, was derived from the Irish, who were at first called *Scots*, and their country *Scotia*. They emigrated to the western part of Caledonia in the sixth century, and soon became so numerous as to form a distinct nation from the Picts. They lived in a state of hostility with these people for two or three centuries, till, at length, in the victorious reign of Kenneth, which commenced in 836, they wrested the sceptre from Wred, the Pictish king, and established supreme sway over the whole country, which ever afterward was called *Scotland*. The Saxons had, in the mean time, occupied the south-eastern part as far as the Forth. Edwin, the Anglo-Saxon king of Northumberland, founded Edwinsburg, now *Edinburgh*. The Highlanders, to this day, call the Lowlanders *Sassenach*, or Saxons. There were also some descendants of the ancient Britons in that part of Scotland which had been possessed by the Romans, and which was called *Clydesdale*, in the kingdom of Strathcluyd. This kingdom flourished for about three hundred years, and is rendered illustrious by the name and exploits of Arthur and his knights, whose power, from the year 508 to 542, is represented by tradition as having been predominant over the south of Scotland and the north of England. The capital of this kingdom was Alcluyd, called afterward *Dun Breton* and *Dumbarton*, seated on an insulated precipitous rock, at the mouth of the River Clyde. In 757, this place was taken by the Saxons, and the kingdom subverted. The Saxons colonized the whole south of Scotland; the Lowlands became in language and manners Teutonic, and the Gael or Celts were confined to the mountain regions. The northern part of Scotland retained the name of *Pictland* till the eleventh century. The southern part was called *Valentia* and *Cumbria*.

Christianity was introduced into Scotland, according to the legends of the country, by St. Columba, or Columbkill, an Irishman, in the sixth century. He is said to have founded the monastery in the Island of Iona, one of the Hebrides, of which the ruins are still to be seen. In the neighborhood is the Island of Staffa, famous for its caverns of basaltic columns, called *Fingal's Cave*. It was here also that he was believed to have instituted an order of monks, called *Culdees*, who were subjected to very strict rules; wore sheepskin clothing, and lived by the labor of their own hands. They were the clergy of Scotland in the early days of Christianity; but as they differed in some points from the church of Rome, and did not acknowledge the supremacy of the pope, they were afterward much persecuted. St. Columba is said to have founded a

Island of Staffa.

hundred monasteries on as many islands, which were chosen in preference to the main land, that their inhabitants might be more secluded from the busy world.

CHAPTER CCCCXXII.

A. D. 600 to 1093.

Conquest of the Orkney and Shetland Islands by the Norwegians — Ancient Navigation — Reign of Duncan — Macbeth — Malcolm — Intercourse with the Norman Conquerors of England.

NORWAY, about this time, had fallen under the dominion of Harold Harfagre, a powerful warrior, who compelled many of the Danish and Norwegian princes to submit to his authority. But there were many bold chiefs who were too proud to become the vassals of the conqueror; they therefore sought their fortunes on the sea, and, by their daring deeds on this element, became the terror of all the maritime nations of Europe. Some bands of these adventurers took possession of the Orkney and Shetland Islands, which were previously inhabited by the Picts. They were followed by Harold their king, with a powerful fleet. He deprived them of the islands, which he bestowed on one of his nobles, with the title of *earl of Orkney*, on the condition that he should hold his earldom as a vassal of the crown of Norway. The first earl of Orkney was the father of Rollo, the first duke of Normandy. The Danes and Norwegians made frequent voyages to these islands, adopting the most simple contrivances to guide their course on the ocean. The compass was unknown in Europe, and the devices for navigating out of sight of land were sometimes very ingenious. A celebrated Norwegian chief, on his voyage from Shetland to Iceland, took on board his vessel some crows. When he had sailed, as he supposed, a considerable distance, and had lost sight of land, he sent up one of the crows, which immediately flew toward the point from which the vessel had departed. By this the chief was able to guess how far he had gone, as it was calculated that the bird, when high in the air, could see the land. The vessel kept on her course, and after some time another crow was sent up, which came back. This showed that there was no land in sight. A third time the experiment was tried, and the bird flew directly onward: the chief, steering according to the direction of his winged guide, arrived safe in Iceland. During a period of two hundred years, from the reign of Kenneth to that of Macbeth, the histories of Scotland recount little more than a continued series of wars with the Danes. The Saxons became subjected to the crown of Scotland; but the Scottish king held part of the Lowlands and some territories in England, in vassalage to the king of England. This was the plea on which Edward I., at a subsequent period, founded his claim to the sovereignty of Scotland. The name of Macbeth has been rendered familiar to every reader by the genius of Shakspeare. His usurpation of the throne of Scotland took place in the eleventh century. It is by no means certain that he was guilty of the crimes laid to his charge. Duncan and Macbeth were cousins, both being grandsons of *Malcolm II.* According to the rule of Scottish succession, Macbeth had the better right to the throne. *Duncan*, however, succeeded, and had reigned six years, when he was murdered while on a journey; but not at Macbeth's castle, as Shakspeare, for dramatic effect, has chosen to represent. Whether Macbeth had a hand in the murder was never proved, though he was suspected of it.

The two sons of Duncan, named *Malcolm* and *Donald Bane*, fled from Scotland; the former to the court of Edward the Confessor, in England, and the other to the Western Islands. *Macbeth* took possession of the throne. His reign was tranquil and prosperous. He was beloved by the people, and gave so much encouragement to agriculture and commerce, that Scotland never before enjoyed such plenty. Macbeth bestowed great attention upon the herring fisheries, which supplied one of the chief articles of Scottish trade at that time. After he had reigned about twelve years, he assumed the pilgrim's gown and staff, and made a journey to Rome. In the mean time, Malcolm had been endeavoring to raise a party in his own favor in England. At the court of Edward he saw a great deal of the polished manners of the French, and learned to speak their language. The Saxon monarch had been educated in France, and had introduced into his court the habits and manners of that country. Malcolm remained about fifteen years in England, which gave him an opportunity of observing the difference between the rude habits of the Scots and the refined manners of the more civilized Normans. At length, Malcolm reëntered Scotland at the head of a large army, to dispute the crown with Macbeth, who had returned from his pilgrimage. A battle was fought near Macbeth's castle of Dunsinane; the king was defeated, and compelled to retreat. He carried on the war for two years, when he was slain, and *Malcolm* ascended the throne, A. D. 1057.

When William the Norman conquered England, great numbers of the Saxons fled to Scotland; and among others, Prince Edgar Atheling, the heir of the Saxon kings of England, and his sister Margaret. She became the wife of Malcolm, and queen of Scotland. Being now allied to the Saxon royal race by the ties of relationship, as well as those of gratitude and friendship, Malcolm took up arms in their cause against William, and invaded England. The Normans, however, were too strong for him; and all that the Scots could do was to ravage the northern parts of England, and carry off the inhabitants, whom they sold for slaves. For many years afterward, there was not a village in the south of Scotland where English slaves

Distant View of Loch Awe

were not to be found. A peace ensued in 1072; and from the intercourse between the two kingdoms which followed, the Scots derived great improvement. A taste for the luxuries and refinements of life began to spread among the people; merchants were encouraged to bring into Scotland various commodities before unknown in that country. Malcolm was killed in 1093, at Alnwick, in Northumberland, in a battle with the English.

CHAPTER CCCCXXIII.

A. D. 1093 to 1214.

Conquests of Magnus the Norwegian in Scotland — Reign of Alexander I. — The Franks — Adventures of Sweyn, the Danish Pirate — Reign of David II. — Age of Chivalry — Misfortunes of William the Lion.

In the year in which Malcolm was killed, Magnus, king of Norway, invaded the Scottish islands. He landed first on Mainland, the largest of the Orkneys, where he deposed the earl of Orkney and took possession of the island. He then proceeded to the Hebrides, all of which he plundered except Iona, which was reverenced as a place of peculiar sanctity, even by the fierce and warlike Northmen. Magnus then directed his hostilities against Scotland; but after he had committed some few depredations, a peace was concluded, in which it was agreed that the Scottish monarch should resign all the islands which could be circumnavigated by a vessel steered with a rudder. When this condition was settled, the artful Norwegian caused a small boat to be conveyed to a narrow neck of land, which joins the peninsula of Cantyre to Scotland, but which is overflowed at high water. Here he sat in his boat, with the helm in his hand, till the tide came in, when he steered himself over the isthmus. In consequence of this feat, he claimed and took possession of the whole of Cantyre, as coming within the terms of the treaty.

After some revolutions which ensued on the death of Malcolm, the crown was placed on the head of *Alexander I.*, A. D. 1107. At this period, Scotland was divided into thirteen districts, each of which was under the government of a *thane*, or lord, whose power was almost independent of that of the king. Each clan had its own particular customs, and was governed by its own laws. There was no national assembly or parliament to make laws for the whole country. About this time flourished Sweyn, the celebrated Danish pirate, or Sea-king. He was lord of Gairsay, a little island among the Orkneys, where he dwelt amidst his lawless people, who seem to have been farmers at home and robbers abroad. They were accustomed to sow their fields in the spring, and then set out upon a cruise, leaving their corn to grow while they were plundering the neighboring shores. It happened, on one occasion, that Sweyn, being alone in his boat, was chased by the earl of Orkney, with whom he was at variance, and was obliged to row with all his might till he reached a small, uninhabited island, where he ran his boat into a cave and disappeared. When the tide rose, the mouth of the cave was covered with water, and Sweyn, from within, heard his pursuers wondering what had become of him. He was not seen in the Orkneys for some time, and was supposed to be dead. One day a vessel, having the appearance of a merchant ship, was seen coming from the west, with two or three men on deck. They approached the Island of Ronsay, where the earl of Orkney dwelt, and asked the news. The people informed them that the earl was gone to the other side of the island to hunt seals. The strangers steered in that direction, and soon discovered the earl with his companions. Sweyn, with a number of armed men, immediately rushed from the hold where they had lain concealed, and slew every one except the earl, whom they carried away prisoner. He was never heard of afterwards; but it is supposed he was placed in a monastery by Sweyn, who returned to his little Island of Gairsay, and was for many years the most formidable pirate of the age. He was killed at last in an attack upon the city of Dublin, A. D. 1159. The preceding narrative may serve as a specimen of the manners of those times.

David I. came to the throne in 1127. He founded the abbey of Holyrood, and fixed his residence at Edinburgh. Before his reign, Perth had been the capital of Scotland. About this time, the pirates of the

Hebrides took advantage of the weakness of the monarchy to establish among themselves a kind of independence. This was the age of chivalry in Scotland as well as in England, and there were many brave Scottish knights among the heroes in Palestine. But the country was impoverished on this account, as the richest nobles went away from Scotland to seek renown in the East, carrying all the money they could raise, instead of remaining at home to improve the condition of the land and people. Richard I. of England gave up his right of sovereignty over Scotland for a sum of money to aid him in his crusade. The population of Scotland at this time was composed of several distinct nations. The Norwegians were in possession of the islands; the Gaelic or Celtic descendants of the early inhabitants occupied the Highlands of the north, while the people of Saxon and Norman origin possessed the southern districts, and were thence called *Lowlanders*. Among these last were found the chief nobility, who had by this time become very powerful. Every Scottish baron had his strong castle and feudal domain, his vassals, retainers, and bondsmen, like the English lords. The language of the south was nearly the same as the Anglo-Saxon, while the Highlanders continued to speak the original Gaelic, to wear the ancient dress, and to live according to the rude customs of their ancestors. A great enmity existed between them and the Lowlanders, whom they considered as intruders into the land of their forefathers.

William the Lion came to the throne in 1165. He quarrelled with the king of England, and invaded that country, when he laid siege to Alnwick Castle, in Northumberland. Here he was made prisoner by some English barons, who sent him to the king. He was not liberated till he had consented to do homage for his whole kingdom, acknowledge the king of England as his lord paramount, and place in his hands the strong castles of Berwick and Roxburgh as a security for his fealty. On these hard terms he regained his freedom, and returned to Scotland as a vassal king.

In this reign, monasteries had become very numerous in Scotland, and many of them were richly endowed with lands, which were better cultivated than any other estates in the kingdom, the vassals and bondmen of the monks being secured in the possession of their farms and homesteads as long as they fulfilled the conditions on which they were held. In those days, a monastery was the surest place of refuge for those who were oppressed, and the safest lodging-house for travellers.

CHAPTER CCCCXXIV.

A. D. 1214 to 1314.

Alexander II.—Acquisition of the Hebrides—The Maid of Norway—Baliol and Bruce—Usurpation of Edward I.—Exploits of Wallace—Accession of Robert Bruce—Battle of Bannockburn.

William the Lion was succeeded in 1214 by *Alexander II.* His reign was a continued series of wars with the lords of the isles and the kings of England. He wished to reduce the former to a dependence on the crown of Scotland, and to obtain from the latter a restitution of Northumberland and other territories, which the Scotch formerly possessed in England. The Hebrides were still considered as belonging to Norway. Alexander offered to purchase them from Haco, the king of that country, but in vain. Haco declared he was not in want of money. Alexander, therefore, undertook an expedition against them, but was taken ill in the Hebrides, and died leaving a son eight years old to succeed him, under the name of *Alexander III* Haco continued to attack and plunder the coasts of Scotland, and Alexander, as soon as he came of age raised an army and marched against the invaders. He gained a great victory over them at the mouth of the Clyde, which so mortified Haco that he fled to the Orkneys, where he died of grief. His son Magnus made peace with Alexander, and sold him the Hebrides for a sum of money. The Orkney and Shetland Islands still remained under the dominion of Norway, and were inhabited principally by Norwegians.

Alexander strengthened his friendly connections with Norway, by marrying his daughter Margaret to Eric, prince of that country. The daughter of this pair is called in history the *Maid of Norway*. She became heiress of the Scottish crown on the death of Alexander, in 1286, but died on her voyage from Norway to take possession of her new dignity. This event proved a great calamity for Scotland, as it left the succession open to dispute, and various claimants arose among the relatives of the royal family. The consequence was a series of wars, which desolated the country for a long time. Among the numerous claimants for the crown, were two whose pretensions were superior to all others, so that the title finally rested between them. The one was Robert Bruce, lord of Annandale; the other was John Baliol, lord of Galloway. Edward I. of England came forward as umpire, and the Scottish nobles, being willing to avoid the miseries of a civil war, consented to leave the matter to his decision. Edward pronounced in favor of *John Baliol*, who was crowned accordingly, not as an independent sovereign, but as a vassal king, subject to the authority of the king of England—A. D. 1292.

The new monarch soon found that he had a very tyrannical master. It seems to have been the intention of Edward to provoke him by injurious treatment into a rebellion, and then to seize on his dominions as forfeited to the crown of England according to the feudal law, by which the estates of a rebellious vassal became the property of his liege lord. The scheme so far succeeded that Baliol attempted to throw off his dependence. Edward defeated him at Dunbar, and deprived him of his crown. He placed English garrisons in all the strong places, and returned to England, believing his conquest complete. But the Scots did not tamely submit to the loss of their liberty, and an able leader soon appeared in the person of William Wallace. He was a young man, of bold, adventurous disposition, and great personal prowess. His mental qualities, like those of most great heroes, have been somewhat overrated; but there is little doubt that he possessed talents of a higher order than were common among the Scottish warriors of that age. When Wallace came forward as the champion of his country, thousands gathered around his standard, and he was soon at the head of a considerable army. He gained a great victory at Stirling, and obliged the English governor to leave Scotland. The fortresses were surrendered to him and he was made regent of the kingdom, while Baliol was a captive in England.

Edward was in Flanders when the rebellion broke out. He hastened back to England, raised a large army, marched into Scotland, and defeated Wallace at the battle of Falkirk, A. D. 1298. He reëstablished his authority in the country, and most of the revolted nobles took the oath of allegiance to him. Wallace refused to submit, and for a long while maintained the contest against the English. He was at length betrayed by one whom he thought his friend, and carried a prisoner to London, where he was tried and executed for treason, A. D. 1304.

Robert Bruce, the grandson of the rival of Baliol, placed himself at the head of the Scottish insurgents, and was crowned king, at Scone, in 1306. In his first contest with the English, he was defeated and obliged to seek shelter in the woods, with a few followers. Being unsafe here, he fled to the Island of Rachrin on the coast of Ireland, where he spent some time. At length, finding the Scots better prepared to assist him, he presented himself among them, and found a considerable army ready to take the field. Edward II. of England marched against him with a force of one hundred thousand men, if we may believe the historians of that day. The Scots did not exceed forty thousand; yet so brave were they, and so highly animated by the cause in which they were engaged, that they beheld without dismay the approach of the English army, and prepared themselves for the important conflict that was to decide the fate of Scotland. A battle was fought at Bannockburn, June 4, 1314, in which Edward's army was totally defeated. This victory secured the independence of Scotland, and confirmed Bruce in possession of the throne.

Gathering of Scotch Highlanders.

CHAPTER CCCCXXV.

A. D. 1314 to 1371.

Reign and Captivity of David II.—State of Government and Society in Scotland—Manners of the Nobles—Warrior Clergymen—Slavery—Rise of the Burghers—Education—Dress.

Though the English had lost all hope of regaining their dominion in Scotland, they continued on hostile terms with that country for a long time. *David II.*, king of Scotland, invaded England while Edward III. was carrying on his wars with the French; but he was met by the English northern barons, and defeated at the battle of Nevil's Cross, A. D. 1342. David was taken captive, carried to London, and kept a prisoner in the Tower for some time. After eleven years of captivity, he was liberated by promising to pay a ransom of one hundred thousand pounds—a sum which, considering the value of money in those days, may be considered equal to ten millions of dollars at the present time.

The several nations that formerly composed the population of Scotland, had by this time become so mingled together, that they exhibited only two distinct races—the Highlanders and Lowlanders. The latter were much more polished than the former, and, as far as the unsettled state of the kingdom would permit, cultivated the useful and elegant arts, while their northern neighbors held in contempt the customs and pursuits of civilized life, regarded themselves as independent of the laws, and looked to their chieftains as their only legitimate rulers. The system of clanship prevailed in the Lowlands as well as in the Highlands, and the great nobles were, in reality, as independent of the monarch as the Highland chiefs. Each could muster his clan around him to defend his castle and his lands; and it was seldom that a clansman was found who would not fight to the last extremity for his liege lord, and obey his commands in preference to the laws of the land.

The power of a feudal superior over his vassals and bondsmen was much the same with the Scotch as with the English, and the mode of life pursued by the great was very similar in both countries. Their castles were crowded with knights, esquires, pages, and retainers of every degree. Feasting and minstrelsy were the amusements in their princely halls; while out of doors they sought the bolder pastimes of hunting, hawking, and chivalric sports. Many of the offices in noble families were hereditary, such as those of the minstrel, the baker, the brewer, the miller, and the forester. The last of these held a very important employment, as he had the care of all the game in his master's woods. It was customary for a young chieftain, on returning from his first hunting expedition, to give his hunting-suit and arms to the forester. There were perquisites attached to all the other hereditary offices. When a tenant brought his corn to be ground at the baronial mill, a certain portion was due to the baron, half as much to the miller, and a quarter to the miller's man.

The clergy of those days were hunters and warriors, and led their vassals to battle and to the chase. They were only distinguished from the lay nobles in the field by wearing cassocks over their armor. The bishops and abbots had long been the principal traders in the community, for they alone had sufficient capital to embark largely in commerce, and they at first had the exclusive right to carry on the fisheries. On all the feudal estates some of the tenants were free farmers, who hired their lands and could remove at pleasure. But a great proportion were still in bondage; nor was it till long afterward that all vestiges of slavery disappeared. The changes that took place during the wars had given liberty to many, and the masters themselves often conferred the gift of freedom on their bondmen; but the work of emancipation went on very gradually. There were slaves in Scotland till the end of the fifteenth century.

In the mean time, the *burghers* were fast rising to wealth and consequence. These were so named from the *burghs*, which were originally small colonies of traders and artisans, who in most cases had purchased their freedom from their lords. These freedmen formed themselves into trading communities, and improved their little villages till they grew into towns. To these towns privileges were from time to time granted by the kings, who knew how much the prosperity of the country depended on the encouragement given to arts and commerce. The earliest burghs in Scotland were Edinburgh and Roxburgh. The burghers gradually acquired the right of choosing their own magistrates, and of sending representatives to parliament. The chief trades were those of the blacksmith, armorer, goldsmith, tanner, dyer, and cap-maker. The Scotch smiths and armorers were not so skilful as those of England, which caused the English government to make a law that no armor should be carried into Scotland, and this was always mentioned in the passports. The Scots were then considered as foreigners by the English.

The state of education was much the same as in other countries during the feudal ages, when learning was confined entirely to the monks and clergy, and few could even read or write, except those educated for the church. There were schools in the principal towns, conducted by the monks, to which boys were sent who were designed for the clerical profession. They usually went to Oxford or Paris to complete their studies, as there was no university in Scotland till after the reign of Robert III. It is supposed that in the fourteenth century there was not a Scottish baron who knew how to write his own name. Nor was it thought any disgrace to be thus deficient, as learning was not held in much estimation by the warlike nobles of those rude times.

Every clan, both in the Highlands and Lowlands, was distinguished by the colors and pattern of the *plaid*, a garment worn by all ranks. Each clansman bore the name and wore the plaid of his chief; and thus it was known whether a man was a Douglas, a Campbell, a Macdonald, or the clansman of any other chieftain. The making of the plaids was a never-failing source of female industry, as the wool was not only spun, but dyed and woven by the people of the country.

CHAPTER CCCCXXVI.

A. D. 1371 to 1509.

Accession of the Stuarts — Private Wars Raids — Invasion of Richard II. — Destruction of Melrose — Improvements of James I. — Law against Sorners — James III. — Acquisition of the Orkney and Shetland Islands — Calamitous End of James III. — Reign of James IV.

The Bruce line of sovereigns became extinct in 1371, and *Robert II.*, of the family of Stuarts, ascended the throne. This name was derived from the office of High *Steward*, which was held by the husband of Margery Bruce. Her son Robert was the founder of the dynasty, which reigned in Scotland as long as that kingdom remained unconnected with England. The right possessed by the barons of going to war on their own account, produced constant disorders, as they were but too apt to avenge by force of arms any trifling injury offered to their vassals. Feuds of this nature often arose between the Scottish and English nobles, so that the border countries were subject to constant inroads, which were always attended with plunder and bloodshed. Every dispute was followed by a "raid," as an expedition of this kind was termed, when a large booty of cattle and prisoners was carried off. A hostile feeling was thus kept up between the two countries, which was encouraged by the king of France, who entered into an alliance with the Scottish sovereign.

On the accession of Richard II. to the throne of England, A. D. 1377, war broke out between that country and Scotland. A French army was sent to Scotland under the command of John de Vienne, admiral of France, and one of the greatest warriors of the age. Richard entered Scotland at the head of a large force, and advanced as far as Edinburgh, which was burned and plundered, nothing being spared but the monastery of Holyrood. Many other edifices were also destroyed by the invaders, and among them the beautiful abbey of Melrose. No advantage was gained by this invasion, for the country was so laid waste that the English were compelled to retreat for want of provisions. It was at this period, (1388,) that the battle of Otterbourne, or Atterburn, took place, of which we have given an account in the history of England. This affair was celebrated in the old ballads under the name of *Chevy Chase.*

James I. (A. D. 1424) made great improvements in the government. He formed the parliament of Scotland as nearly as possible on the model of that of England. He instituted regular courts of justice, and

The Battle of Chevy Chase.

thus limited the power of the lords over their vassals by taking from them the right of acting as sole judges on their own estates — a privilege long enjoyed by the feudal nobles of every country in Europe, and one that had given them absolute control over the lives and property of their dependents. By such means, James, in the course of time, accomplished his grand design of bringing the nobles under subordination, and improving the condition of the middle and lower classes. He also caused all the laws to be written in the language of the country, instead of the Latin, which had previously been the legal tongue. One of the laws enacted in this reign related to a class of beggars called *sorners*, who pretended to be gentlemen, and wandered from place to place, intruding into people's houses, where they took their seat at the table, and received what was given to them as a right rather than as a favor. They all claimed to be of gentle birth, and some of them did not scruple to ride about the country with attendants, who were beggars also. To remedy this evil, it was enacted that no such persons should be permitted to beg or insist on being entertained in any farm-houses or other dwellings. An exception, however, was made in favor of the royal or licensed beggars, known as the "Blue-gowns," or "King's bedesmen." These were men above the age of seventy, or worthy persons who had fallen into misfortunes. They were distinguished by a badge granted by the chief magistrate of the burgh; and this venerable order of privileged mendicants continued in Scotland till a very late period.

Under *James III.*, the union of the Orkney and Shetland Islands with Scotland took place by the marriage of the young king with the princess of Denmark, A. D. 1468. At this period, a belief in astrology was prevalent all over Europe; and there were few princes who did not at times seek information, with regard to future events, from men who were thought to be skilled in this imaginary science. James III. was much addicted to this practice. A soothsayer once declared to him that he should fall by the hand of his nearest of kin; whereupon he imprisoned his two brothers on a charge of treason. This act, with other measures of his administration, made him unpopular. He was a great patron of the arts, particularly that of architecture, to which he devoted the chief portion of his time. He indulged his taste for erecting sumptuous buildings to such a degree, as to increase the disaffection of the people, who found their taxes augmented by the king's expenditures. He also seized on certain revenues belonging to the church, which gave much offence to the clergy.

The power of the nobility had greatly increased in this reign, and James undertook a series of measures to reduce it. This proceeding, added to his previous unpopular acts, produced a rebellion. The nobles of the south took up arms with the avowed purpose of deposing the king, and placing his son, the duke of Rothsay, on the throne. The young prince, misguided by their evil counsels, appeared at their head, in arms against his father. The northern barons adhered to James, and the two parties met in battle array, about a mile from the memorable field of Bannockburn. The king saw his son leading his enemies against him. Either the remembrance of the prophecy, or the shock which this sight caused to his feelings, produced such an effect upon the unhappy father, that he lost all courage, and fled. As he was crossing the brook of Bannockburn, a poor woman, who was drawing water from the stream, being startled by the galloping of his horse, cast down her pitcher before him. The frightened animal suddenly reared, and threw his rider, who was severely injured by the fall. There was a mill near at hand, to which he was carried. One of the rebels, who was in pursuit of the king, hearing the woman call for assistance, rushed into the mill, and recognizing the king, instantly stabbed him to the heart. A. D. 1487. He was succeeded by his son.

James IV., notwithstanding his unnatural behavior to his father, governed the kingdom wisely, and the Scotch enjoyed an unwonted degree of tranquillity and prosperity in his reign. He gave shelter to Perkin Warbeck, the pretender to the throne of England in the time of Henry VII., and invaded England in the hope of being able to overthrow that monarch; but he found this impracticable, and made a truce with Henry, withdrawing his protection from Warbeck. James afterward formed a closer alliance with England by marrying the princess Margaret, daughter of the king. In consequence of this marriage, a treaty of peace was made between the two kingdoms, by which the town of Berwick was given up to England forever. The union of James and Margaret was an event that had great influence over the future fate of both kingdoms; for Margaret was the grandmother of Mary Queen of Scots.

CHAPTER CCCCXXVII.

A. D. 1509 to 1566.

Battle of Flodden Field — James V. — Persecution of the Protestants — Accession of Mary — The Reformation — Rivalry of Mary and Elizabeth — Marriage of Mary to Darnley — Murder of Rizzio.

As long as Henry VII. lived, peace continued between Scotland and England. But after his death, many causes of disagreement arose between King James and Henry VIII., which led to a renewal of the war. The English captured two fine Scotch vessels on the charge of piracy, though it was well known that they were ships of war, belonging to the king. James determined to invade England. All his wisest ministers endeavored to dissuade him from so rash a step; but he was bent upon indulging his resentment, and summoned all his men, capable of bearing arms, to meet him at Edinburgh, with provisions for forty days. The people obeyed with sorrow, for they saw the probability of a fatal termination to this useless undertaking. A large army was collected, and James marched into England attended by the flower of his nobility. Henry VIII. was in France, and the earl of Surrey was intrusted with the command of the forces destined to oppose the Scots. He was already in Northumberland when James crossed the border. The two armies met at Flodden Field, September, 1513. The Scots were defeated, and the king was slain with most of his nobles. The body of James was never discovered.

James V., who succeeded him, exerted himself to reëstablish peace both with England and amidst the unruly Scottish chiefs. He put himself at the head of an irregular army, composed partly of soldiers and partly of huntsmen, and made a progress through the country under pretence of hunting. He took several castles by force, and put to death those chiefs who had been guilty of illegal acts. Their lands were converted into sheepwalks by the king, who derived great profit from his flocks: this caused his uncle, Henry VIII., to call him a *farmer*. It was common, however, in that age, for all great people — kings, noblemen, bishops, abbots, &c. — to keep sheep, and send their wool to be sold in foreign countries; so that they were al traders, and many of them acquired the greater part of their wealth by their commercial dealings.

James married a French princess, Mary, the sister of the duke of Guise, who took a forward part in the persecution of the French Protestants. It was owing to his alliance with this powerful family, that he was so strong an enemy to the reformation, which at this time was making rapid progress in Scotland. James suffered the Protestants to be cruelly persecuted, and he soon became involved in disputes with Henry VIII. on the subject of religion. A war ensued, and James attempted to raise a large army; but the disaffection of his subjects was so great that his endeavors were ineffectual. Those who resorted to his standard did not yield him their cordial support, and all his military enterprises proved abortive. In an invasion of Cumberland, a body of ten thousand Scots suffered themselves to be defeated by five hundred English. Mortified by this disgrace and the contemptuous behavior of his own nobles, the king retired to Falkland Castle, where he died of chagrin, six days after the birth of his unfortunate daughter, *Mary*, Queen of Scots, A. D. 1542.

The crown of Scotland having now descended to a female infant, Henry VIII. was desirous of uniting the two countries by a marriage between the youthful queen and his son Edward. The Scottish parliament would have agreed to this proposal, but Henry wished to take upon himself the administration of the kingdom during the minority. The disputes which arose upon this point led to a declaration of war from Henry, and Mary was sent to France for safety, where she was educated, and married to the dauphin, son of Henry II. Seventeen years elapsed between the death of James V. and the return of Mary to Scotland. It was in this interval that the reformation was established in that country. In England, the Catholic religion had been abolished by authority of the king. In Scotland, the same end was accomplished by the preaching of the celebrated reformer John Knox, who was a disciple of Calvin.

The husband of Mary had become king of France under the name of *Francis II.* His death took place shortly afterward, and Mary, who was then only nineteen years of age, was recalled to her own kingdom Queen Elizabeth, who was now on the throne of England, was cousin to Mary, and the latter was regarded by many as having a better claim to the throne than Elizabeth. Mary had, therefore, been persuaded, while her husband was living, to assume the title of *Queen of France and England*, an offence which Elizabeth never forgave. The Scotch were at first much pleased with their youthful sovereign; but Mary was less satisfied with her subjects. She was a Catholic, and had been educated in French manners. Scotland was to her as a foreign land. The feelings of the people ran very strong against Popery; and the whole country was in a most unsettled condition. Domestic warfare existed between rival chieftains and in many parts there were troops of banditti who took up their abode in the ruins of old castles, or dismantled abbeys, which afforded security for themselves and their plunder.

The beginning of the queen's misfortunes was her marriage with Lord Darnley, a Scottish nobleman, who, like herself, had some claim to the crown of England. Elizabeth did every thing in her power to prevent this match. The Protestant nobles of Scotland also opposed it, as Darnley was a Catholic. An insurrection of the Protestants ensued, and Mary took the field against them, at the head of her troops. The insurgents were soon dispersed. Mary, however, became involved in domestic troubles. Darnley was a selfish, weak-minded, and ill-tempered man, and soon lost her affection. Jealousy increased her unhappiness. Every person in whose society she appeared to take pleasure, became an object of suspicion to her husband. She had a secretary named *David Rizzio*, an Italian, who was a man of education, and an accomplished musician. The queen bestowed on him a degree of favor which excited the enmity of many of the courtiers, and made him numerous enemies. Darnley's jealousy was strongly excited toward Rizzio; and one evening, when the queen and several of her ladies were at supper with him, Darnley, with some noblemen of his party, burst into the room, dragged him from the table, and stabbed him to the heart in the presence of the queen, who attempted in vain to save his life.

CHAPTER CCCCXXVIII.

A. D. 1566 to 1573.

Murder of Darnley—Marriage of Mary to Bothwell—Insurrection—Imprisonment and Deposition of Mary—Her Flight to England—Captivity and Execution—Civil War.

Mary, Queen of Scots, imprisoned at Loch-leven.

MARY fled from Holyrood House to Dunbar Castle, determined to avenge this cruel outrage. She assembled the nobles who were attached to her interest, and raised an army of eight thousand men. Darnley affected repentance for his share of the crime, and joined her against the rest of the conspirators. The principal of these were the earl of Morton and Lord Ruthven, who fled to England; while the earl of Murray, and others who had been banished for their opposition to her marriage, returned, and were taken again into favor. Among these was the earl of Bothwell, a bold, ambitious man, and a decided foe to Darnley. The queen bestowed high honors upon him, notwithstanding his hostility to her husband. Darnley, being taken ill of the small-pox, removed to a place called the *Kirk of Field*, in the neighborhood of Edinburgh. One night, just after the queen had left him on her return to Holyrood, the house was blown up with gunpowder, and Darnley was killed. It was known beyond a doubt that Bothwell was the author of this murder, and he was brought to trial for it; but, according to the custom of those times, he entered the court surrounded by a number of his friends, all well armed, and followed by a train of hired soldiers. The judges dared not venture to pronounce him guilty, and he was acquitted.

The subsequent conduct of the queen strongly indicates her participation in this crime. A few months only had elapsed, when she became the wife of Bothwell, and thus lost the respect, as well as the affection of a great part of her subjects. Her guilt was never openly proved, but the belief of it was general. The infant prince James, her son, was kept in Stirling Castle, under the guardianship of the earl of Mar. Such was the indignation of the people at Mary's disgraceful marriage, that many of the lords joined together for the purpose of expelling her from the throne. The queen and Bothwell fled to Dunbar Castle, where they assembled a few troops, intending to give battle to the insurgents. But the disaffection was so general, that Mary's own party refused to act in her behalf, unless Bothwell were banished from the country. To this she reluctantly agreed, and Bothwell went to the Orkneys. He was afterward taken prisoner by the Danes, and carried to Norway, and from thence to Sweden, where he died in the Castle of Malmoe.

When Bothwell had departed, Mary expressed her willingness to make terms with the insurgents. She was conducted back to Edinburgh, but found that she had entirely lost the respect of the people. In fact, the noblemen who had taken up arms against her had determined she should never reign in Scotland again. They sent her, under a strong guard, to Loch-leven Castle, which stands on a little island in a lake. There, after enduring some weeks of captivity and harsh treatment, she was compelled to sign a deed resigning the crown to her infant son, A. D. 1567. Mary had reigned over Scotland about seven years, and had been married three times, though she was scarcely twenty-six years old.

The earl of Murray was appointed regent of the kingdom, and the queen was kept a prisoner at Loch-leven for many months longer. At length she escaped, and was joined by several noblemen, who raised an army of five thousand men to replace her on the throne. This little army met the superior forces of the regent, Murray, at Langside. Mary's army was defeated, and she fled to England, trusting to the generosity of her cousin, Queen Elizabeth, A. D. 1568 The cold-hearted and selfish queen of England had ner thrown into prison, and treated her with all the jealousy of a personal and political rival. After holding her for eighteen years in captivity, Elizabeth caused her to be tried on a charge of conspiracy, and condemned to death. The unfortunate queen of Scots was beheaded at Fotheringay Castle, A. D. 1587. No part of Scottish history has given rise to more discussion than the character of this celebrated queen. Some writers maintain her innocence of Darnley's murder; but the general voice of history is against her. Her beauty, accomplishments, and misfortunes, have softened the judgment of mankind with regard to her errors; and she was not so much the victim of her own imprudence, as of the jealousy, malignity, and vindictive spirit of her rival Elizabeth.

The flight of Mary from Scotland was followed by another long civil war. Murray, the regent, was shot from a window as he was riding through the streets of Linlithgow, by the lord of Bothwellhaugh, in revenge for a private injury. Lord Lenox was next appointed regent, but he was soon killed in a battle with the queen's partisans; and the earl of Mar, who succeeded him, died shortly afterward, under circumstances which occasioned strong suspicion that poison had been given him at a banquet to which he had been invited by the earl of Morton, on whom the regency next devolved. The country was at this time in a very wretched state. The people were divided into two factions, called the "Queen's men," and the "King's men"—a fatal distinction, which caused fathers to fight against their sons, and brothers to contend with brothers. All peaceful occupations were suspended; commerce and agriculture were neglected; villages were burned; the prisoners taken on both sides were barbarously executed. The horrors of civil war were never more fully exemplified than in Scotland at this unhappy period. Two governments existed at the same time. The regent held one parliament at Stirling, while the queen's party held another at Edinburgh, where they kept possession of the castle. It is said that the earl of Morton held a secret correspondence with Elizabeth, and acted according to her instructions; by which means she exercised an indirect authority over Scot and while she detained the Scottish queen in prison. The cause of Mary gradually declined, till, at length, the Castle of Edinburgh was taken by the regent in 1573, which put a period to the struggle.

CHAPTER CCCCXXIX.

A. D. 1573 to 1707.

James VI.—His Accession to the Throne of England—Charles I.—Civil War—The Covenanters—Cromwell—Conquest of Scotland—The Restoration—Charles II.—Persecution of the Covenanters—James II. William III.—Union of Scotland and England.

James VI. assumed the administration of the kingdom at the age of fifteen. The earl of Morton, who for many reasons had become an object of his dislike, was accused of having been concerned in the murder of Darnley; and, although the charge was never satisfactorily proved, he was put to death, and his estates were confiscated. Mary was still languishing in imprisonment in England; but James made no exertions in behalf of his mother. He was constitutionally indolent, and a great coward. The fear of Elizabeth was sufficient to annihilate all filial feelings in his breast. The early part of his reign was disturbed by the conspiracies of discontented barons, the feuds of the border clans and the Highlanders, and the disputes of the king with the Presbyterian clergy on the subject of episcopacy. There was scarcely a nobleman in Scotland who was not in arms against some rival chief. On the death of Queen Elizabeth, A. D. 1603, James succeeded to the throne of England. The two countries remained separate kingdoms, having each its own parliament and separate laws, but administered by one king. It was now no longer necessary to defend the borders; and, as it was thought desirable to remove some of the most turbulent clans, they were sent to serve in the wars of the Netherlands, where the people were fighting to free themselves from the dominion of the Spaniards. This measure put an end to the feuds which had so long distracted that part of the country.

It was a favorite object of James to revive the order of bishops, and to compel the Scots to adopt the form of worship of the English church. All festivals had been abolished in Scotland at the period of the reformation. James was so bent upon assimilating the church government of Scotland to that of England, that he paid a visit to his native country in 1617, entirely with that view; but the attempt miscarried, and served only to make him unpopular.

James died in 1625, and was succeeded in both kingdoms by his son *Charles I.* For twelve years after his accession, Scotland remained at peace, and the condition of the people was much improved. These fair prospects, however, were blasted by the imprudent behavior of the king in England, as we have already related in the history of that country. Charles attempted to abolish the Presbyterian form of church government in Scotland, and introduce episcopacy on the model of the church of England. A rebellion was the immediate consequence, and the people of Scotland entered into a "Solemn League and Covenant" to maintain, at all hazards, the Presbyterian form of worship. This celebrated compact was signed by multitudes of the people of Edinburgh—noblemen, clergy, and citizens of all classes. Copies of it were sent to all the principal towns, where the same enthusiasm prevailed, and the people flocked to sign the covenant. The king resolved to put down the Covenanters by force of arms; the latter determined to resist him. Both sides collected their forces, and a civil war again distracted the kingdom. The king's forces were defeated, and compelled to withdraw to England. The rebellion in that country prevented him from devoting any further attention to the affairs of Scotland.

The Scotch did not agree with the English republicans; and, when Charles I. was executed, in 1649, they proclaimed his son, *Charles II.* He was then on the continent; upon his arrival in Scotland, the nobles and leading men compelled him to sign the covenant, and make a solemn promise to support the form of religion then established in Scotland, before they would take the oath of fealty to him. Cromwell marched into Scotland against the king. A large army, under General Lesley, assembled to oppose his progress. They attacked Cromwell at Dunbar, and were totally defeated. Cromwell drove the king from Scotland

and then pursued him to Worcester, as we have already related. General Monk was left with an English force, to keep possession of Scotland, and, for nine years, the country was governed by commissioners, sending a certain number of members to the English parliament.

Charles II. was restored in England and Scotland at the same time—1660. His reign in Scotland was tyrannical and oppressive. He persecuted the Presbyterians, and put to death the marquis of Argyle, who was their great supporter and had been chiefly instrumental in compelling Charles to sign the covenant. The Presbyterian clergymen were expelled from their homes, and driven to seek shelter among the caves of the mountains. The prisons were crowded with Nonconformists, or those who would not conform to the Episcopal mode of worship; and, when these receptacles were filled to overflowing, the prisoners were sent to the plantations beyond the Atlantic, and sold as slaves. It was at this period that Graham of Claverhouse, a military commander, distinguished himself by his sanguinary hostilities against the Covenanters. At first, they gained some advantages over the king's troops, defeated Claverhouse, who was sent to disperse them with a strong body of cavalry, and made themselves masters of the city of Glasgow. But, at length, a powerful army, under the duke of Monmouth, marched from England toward Glasgow, and defeated the Covenanters at the battle of Bothwell Bridge, A. D. 1679, by which the insurrection was completely suppressed.

From this period to the revolution of 1688, when James II. was expelled from the throne, and William of Orange became king of England, the history of Scotland consists entirely of the troubles occasioned by religious disputes. James ruled Scotland as tyrannically as his predecessor, and attempted to impose the Catholic religion upon the people. The accession of William, however, put an end to all these persecutions, and the Presbyterian form of worship was reëstablished. Under the reign of his successor, Queen Anne, England and Scotland were joined by an act of union, and became one monarchy, by the name of the *Kingdom of Great Britain*, A. D. 1707.

CHAPTER CCCCXXX.

Chief Cities — Agriculture, Manufactures, Commerce, Manners, Literature, Architecture, Dress, &c., of the Scotch.

EDINBURGH, the capital of Scotland, has a very peculiar situation upon three ridges, separated by deep ravines. The Old Town, which, down to the close of the last century, comprised the whole city, stands on the central ridge. The houses are here crowded into the smallest possible space, and raised, sometimes, to the height of twelve and fourteen stories. The New Town contains the residences of almost all the wealthy and fashionable classes. It is regularly built, of fine freestone, and forms one of the most elegant towns in Great Britain. The beauty of Edinburgh is enhanced by its situation, the city being overlooked, on one side, by the lofty eminence on which the castle is situated, and on the other side by a bold range of hills, the highest of which is called *Arthur's Seat.* The city strikes the eye rather by its general effect than by the architectural beauty of particular edifices. The chief structures are Holyrood House, Heriot's Hospital, and the Cathedral of St. Giles. A monument to Sir Walter Scott has recently been erected here. Edinburgh is supported principally by its courts of law, which bring numerous visitors to the place. It is a city eminently scientific and literary, and has become known, in Great Britain, under the appellation of "Modern Athens." The bookselling and publishing business is transacted here on a large scale. The trade by sea is carried on through Leith, which is the port of Edinburgh. The population is one hundred and seventy thousand.

Glasgow is the commercial capital of Scotland, and, in population, the third city in Great Britain. It is handsomely built, and its cathedral is one of the finest in Scotland. The public edifices are also remarkable for their elegance. Glasgow has a university four hundred years old, with three public libraries, and a botanic garden. The population of the city is about four hundred thousand. Greenock is the seaport of Glasgow, and has a large trade.

Paisley is a large manufacturing place, where muslins of the finest texture are fabricated. It has some fine architectural structures.

Aberdeen is called the "Queen of the North." It consists of two parts, the Old and the New City. Old Aberdeen has rather the aspect of a village, but is adorned with the fine old edifice of King's College New Aberdeen is a handsome city, built of the granite which abounds in its neighborhood: population, seventy-five thousand. Dundee is the fourth city in Scotland as to population and wealth. It has large manufactures of linen, sailcloth, &c.

Scotch Shepherd.

The proportion of cultivated land in Scotland is small, and, for a long time, the inhabitants evinced a great dislike to devote themselves to agricultural pursuits. Within a century, however, the husbandry of the country has much improved, though the natural unproductiveness of the soil is such that Scotland can never be made a fruitful country. Only about one fourth of the land is under cultivation. Vast quantities of black cattle are reared, and flocks of sheep, attended by shepherds, are seen on the hills and mountain slopes. Oats are the staple article of cultivation in Scotland, and the chief food of the rural population. Barley is also raised to some extent, but chiefly for brewing. In the Highlands, the barley is a very rude species, called *bear*, or *bigg*. The chief exported produce consists of cattle and sheep, which are sent to England in considerable numbers. The manufactures of Scotland consist principally of linen; the greater part of the raw material is imported. The fisheries are a considerable branch of industry in this country. Herring and cod abound upon the coasts. The chief commercial intercourse is with the countries on the Baltic.

Robert Burns

The Scotch are a grave, reflecting people, at the same time bold, enterprising, ambitious, and persevering. Under these impulses, they quit their native country without regret, and seek, either in England or in the countries beyond the Atlantic, that wealth and fame which they eagerly covet. The pride of birth is still prevalent, particularly among the Highland clans. Literature, soon after its revival in Europe, was cultivated in Scotland with peculiar ardor. Even in the age of scholastic pursuits, Duns Scotus and Crichton were highly famous throughout Europe. When the sounder taste for classical knowledge followed, Buchanan acquired the reputation of writing Latin with great purity. The study of polite literature was, some centuries ago, in a more advanced state in Scotland than in many other countries which have since surpassed it in that respect. The dialect which is now known as "broad Scotch" was formerly the language of a polished court and a cultivated nation.

The early Scotch writings are equal, if not superior, in delicacy of sentiment to those of modern times. Between the early and the modern period of Scotch literature, occurred an interval in which letters fell into comparative disregard.

About the middle of the last century, they revived with great vigor, and have continued to flourish in undiminished lustre to the present day. Among the Scotch writers of eminence may be mentioned Hume, Robertson, and Macaulay, in history; Reid, Smith, Ferguson, Kames, Stuart, and Brown, in moral and political philosophy; King James I., Douglas, Barbour, Allan Ramsay, Burns, and Sir Walter Scott, in poetry; and, above all, the last mentioned in romantic fiction, which he raised to a new dignity and unrivalled fame. In physical science, Scotland can boast of the names of Gregory, Simson, Black, Playfair, Hutton, and Leslie. The Scotch have, for a long time, ranked among the best-informed people in Europe. This has been owing to their parochial schools, in which poor persons are enabled to give their children an education at a small expense. There are few parents in Scotland who do not send their children to school.

The Scotch have always been a strongly religious people. In Catholic times, the Romish church enjoyed more influence, and had acquired a much greater proportion of the national wealth in Scotland than in England. But the inhabitants of the northern kingdom entered upon the course of reform with an ardent zeal, which left all their neighbors far behind. After a desperate struggle, on which, for nearly a century, the political destinies of the kingdom depended, they obtained their favorite form of presbytery, the most remote from that pompous ritual for which they have entertained the most rooted abhorrence. The principle of presbyterianism consists in the complete equality of all members of the clergy, who have each a separate parish, of which they perform all the ecclesiastical functions. The title of *bishop*, so long connected with wealth and power, was rejected, and that of *minister* substituted. The church government is exercised by presbyteries, which are formed by the meeting of the ministers of a certain district, accompanied with lay members. A minister and a body of elders constitute the *kirk session*, which is the lowest ecclesiastical judicature in this system. A *synod* is formed by the union of several presbyteries. The *general assembly* is the highest of the ecclesiastical bodies: it is composed of deputies partly clerical and partly lay, from each presbytery and borough. This assembly meets every year, and appeals are made to it upon every subject connected with religious matters. The king sends a *commissioner*, who is present at the debates, and pretends to a right of convening and dissolving it; but this right is denied by the church itself, which acknowledges no human head, and accounts itself and the state as powers entirely independent of each other. The Presbyterian system of religion was established in Scotland by act of parliament in 1696.

The people are strongly attached to their national religion. They pay much more attention to the observance of Sunday than the English. They are extremely particular with regard to the choice of their ministers, and for a long time it was customary for the presbyteries to appoint none to office who were not approved by the parishioners. On this point a very serious schism has lately taken place; and there are many seceders from the established Presbyterian government.

Sir Walter Scott.

Notwithstanding the progress of civilization, and the influence which the general diffusion of literature and commerce has exerted in the eradication of local prejudices, the Scotch have not yet properly become one people. They are still divided into Highlanders and Lowlanders — two separate classes, who, in dress, language, and the whole train of their social ideas, differ materially from each other. The Highlanders have retained many antique and striking characteristics, both physical and moral, which are obliterated in almost every other part of Great Britain. They speak Gaelic, and retain the remnants of a costume peculiar to themselves. This is the *tartan*, a cloth of mixed linen and woollen, adorned with brilliant stripes, variously crossing each other, and marking the distinctions of the clans; the *kilt*, or short petticoat, worn by the men; the *hose*, fastened below the knee; and the *bonnet*, which, in another shape, is also still worn by the shepherds of the border. The Lowlanders more nearly resemble the English in their dress and manners. Their language is English, diversified by the Scandinavian dialects.

The large towns exhibit the same sort of architecture as those of England; but the dwellings of the Scotch peasantry, especially in the Highlands, are remarkable for their rudeness. They are called *sheelings*, and are built generally of rubble-stones, plastered with mud. Part of the interior is occupied by the pigs and cattle: there is no chimney, and the smoke escapes through a hole in the roof. The beds are of fern, or heath. In regard to food, the Scotch are abstemious. The peasantry have hard fare: butcher's meat is a holiday dainty with them; and even wheaten bread is a rarity. Oatmeal, in the form of thin cakes, or porridge, constitutes the main article of subsistence. To this they add greens, or *kail*, the chief produce of their little gardens. The Scotch have some dishes which they cherish with national enthusiasm. Among these, the *haggis* holds the first place: this is a mixture of oatmeal, fat, liver, and onions, boiled in the bag which composed the stomach of an animal.

It may be said, in general, that the Scotch are eminently loyal to the British crown,* and have ceased to cherish ideas of national independence. They have a native music, simple and pathetic, expressive of rural feelings and emotions, to which they are fondly attached. The only amusements that can be deemed strictly national are football and *golf*, a game of ball and bat. Skating and *curling*, or the rolling of smooth stones upon the ice, are also pursued with great ardor during the season that admits of those amusements. The recreations of the higher ranks are nearly the same as in England. The Highlanders are fond of dancing, and have their favorite national steps and movements.

CHAPTER CCCCXXXI.

B. C. 200 to A. D. 432.

IRELAND. — *Description of Ireland — Ancient Irish — The Scots and Milesians — The Five Kings of Ireland — The Hall of Tara — The Brehons — Christianity in Ireland — Legend of St. Patrick.*

THIS island has a diversified surface, though it is not so mountainous as Scotland. The central portions are comparatively level. The northern and southern parts are of a more Alpine character. The bogs of Ireland form a remarkable feature of the country: they form large tracts, constituting a tenth part of the surface of the island. They are mostly of peat, and are from fifteen to forty feet in depth. The lakes, or *loughs*, as they are called, are small but numerous. A great part of the soil is susceptible of cultivation; and the island may be described as on the whole very fertile. The coast is generally rocky. On the northern shore

* *Kings of Scotland.*

Date of Accession. A. D.		Date of Accession. A. D.	
800.	Achaius.	1094.	Duncan II.
819.	Congal.	1098.	Edgar.
824.	Dougal.	1107.	Alexander I.
833.	Alpin.	1127.	David I.
836.	Kenneth I.	1153.	Malcolm IV.
859.	Donald I.	1165.	William.
863.	Constantine I.	1214.	Alexander II.
882.	Hugh.	1249.	Alexander III.
893.	Donald II.	1286.	Margaret.
904.	Constantine II.	1292.	John Baliol.
942.	Malcolm I.	1306.	Robert I.
953.	Indulf.	1329.	David II.
959.	Duff.	1371.	Robert II.
963.	Culen.	1390.	Robert III.
970.	Kenneth II.	1406.	James I.
987.	Constantine III.	1431.	James II.
995.	Kenneth III.	1460.	James III.
1002.	Malcolm II.	1488.	James IV.
1033.	Duncan I.	1513.	James V.
1039.	Macbeth.	1542.	Mary.
1057.	Malcolm III	1567	James VI.
1093.	Donald III.		

Round Tower.

is the celebrated group of basaltic pillars, called the *Giants' Causeway.*

The earliest inhabitants of Ireland, from which the native race now existing has sprung, appear, by the language still spoken, to have been a tribe of the great Celtic nation. Nothing certain is known of the history of this country till long after the conquest of Britain by the Romans. The speculations of ingenious antiquaries, however, have filled this void with abundance of conjectural matter. It has been said, and with some appearance of truth, that the Carthaginians and Phœnicians made voyages to Ireland, and formed settlements there, centuries before the Christian era. Many ancient structures, called *Round Towers,** are now to be seen in this country, which are supposed to be of Phœnician construction. Some regard these as Persian fire-temples; others ascribe them to the Norwegians or Danes. On this point nothing can be decided with confidence. The ancients gave to this island the names of *Ierne* and *Hibernia.*

The Irish have a tradition to the effect that, about two hundred years before the Christian era, a tribe of barbarians from the continent, called *Scoti*, or *Milesians*, emigrated through Spain to Ireland, and spread themselves over all the country; but respecting these people we have only bardic legends, which doubtless consist of a mixture of fiction and fact. Ireland obtained the title of *Scotland* from the former of these names, which has caused much confusion in the early history of the two countries. The Romans, during their occupation of Britain, made no attempt to invade Ireland, and the ancient population remained for a long time unchanged by any foreign mixture. The original Celtic is still spoken by many of the natives, with little alteration from the times preceding the English conquest. While the Romans were civilizing and improving Britain, the neighboring island remained in the same rude state in which it appears to have existed from its first settlement; unless, indeed, we admit what is claimed by its historians — that it reached a high pitch of indigenous civilization, at this period.

We are told that five chieftains ruled over the Irish in early times, called the kings of Ulster, Munster, Leinster, Connaught, and Meath. The last, however, maintained a superiority over the rest. Beside these five kings, there were numerous inferior chiefs, who also called themselves kings, and ruled their own clans with absolute authority, like the Highland chieftains of Scotland; but they were all tributary to the kings of their respective provinces. The five kings were almost always at war with each other, and were assisted by their dependent chiefs in these conflicts.

In the province of Meath was a spot called the *Hall of Tara.* This was the residence of the ancient Irish kings, and the place where the national assemblies met once a year. The lawgivers, or counsellors, were a class of Druids, called *Brehons*, who acted as magistrates and judges. They took their judgment-seats on the top of a hill, in the open air, where they heard all complaints that were brought before them, and decided every cause according to their own ideas of right and wrong. The Brehon laws related chiefly to the inheritance of lands, which was regulated in a manner that caused frequent quarrelling and bloodshed. The great object among the Irish was to obtain power over others; and as their strength depended on the extent of their territory, every chief was desirous of getting as large a portion of land as he could. Money was not known in Ireland at this period, and payments were made in cattle. The people dressed in sheepskins, and the greater part of them had no better dwellings than caves dug under the hills, or holes in the rocks. The residence of a chief was a wooden hut surrounded by a rampart of earth for a fortification.

Christianity is said to have been introduced into Ireland by St. Patrick, of whom we have the following legend: One of the Irish chieftains, having invaded

* There are one hundred and seven of these towers, or sites of towers, now known. They are of various heights, usually about eighty feet, though one rises to a hundred and twenty feet. They are very ancient, as they are spoken of by the earliest writers as very old, and of an unknown origin. They appear to have been divided into three stories, and covered with conical stone roofs. They have doors at a considerable height from the ground, and windows, or loopholes, near the top. In some the stones are nicely chiselled, in others roughly hammered.

the northern coast of France, carried off a number of captives, among whom was a youth named *Patricius*, or *Patrick*. He was sold in Ireland for a slave, and employed by his master in tending sheep. Being of a religious turn of mind, he was accustomed to wander over the mountains with his flocks, meditating on the idolatrous worship of the Irish. After six years of bondage, he made his escape to France; but he could not forget the land which he had left. He devoted himself to religious studies till he was forty-five years of age, when he applied to the pope for leave to revisit Ireland for the purpose of preaching Christianity to the natives. The pope very readily granted his request, and Patrick returned to Ireland about the year 432, with several companions who were appointed to assist him in this undertaking. Some herdsmen, who chanced to be driving their cattle near the spot where the Christians landed, were so terrified at their singular appearance, that they ran in haste to their master, and informed him that a body of pirates had made a descent upon the coast. The chieftain assembled his people, and went out to attack the invaders; but when he saw the venerable party approaching, he was so

St. Patrick.

struck with the mild and dignified countenance of Patrick, that he invited him, with his brethren, to his house. Their eloquent discourses soon made converts of the chief and his whole family. The work being thus happily begun, Patrick proceeded to Tara, where he preached before the king and all the nobles. Wherever he appeared, the people flocked around him, and became his converts. In a short space of time, the idols were all destroyed, the human sacrifices abolished, and the Christian religion established throughout the country. Such is the story commonly told of the conversion of the Irish to Christianity. It is necessary to state, however, that this account is not properly authenticated, though it is adopted by Thomas Moore in his history of Ireland, to which the reader is referred for a learned statement of the case.

CHAPTER CCCCXXXII.

A. D. 432 to 1172.

Danish Invasion of Ireland — Improvement of the Country — Brian Boru — Civil Wars in Ireland — Character of the People — Expulsion of Dermot McMurrough.

The Danes, or Northmen, invaded Ireland in the early part of the eighth century. There were so many kings in the country at this period, that we are told of two hundred being killed in one battle. The title seems to have been given to every petty chief possessed of a small piece of land and a few half-clothed followers. The Danes made several piratical inroads into the country, but do not appear to have formed any design of taking permanent possession of the island for nearly a hundred years, when they landed here in much greater force and fought pitched battles with the natives. About the year 815, they established themselves in Armagh; and in the middle of the ninth century, a Norwegian chief, named *Turges*, arrived with a powerful fleet, and subdued a great part of the country. He built fortresses and towers all round the coast, and at length assumed the title of king of Ireland. He compelled the Irish kings to pay him tribute, and imposed a tax upon all the natives which was called *nose-money*, because those who refused to pay had their noses cut off.

Not long after this, three princes of Norway, Oloff Sitric, and Ivan, came with fresh hordes of Danes into Ireland, and took possession of the three principal towns — Dublin, Limerick, and Waterford. Under the sway of these princes, the country began to experience the benefits of trade. Foreign ships, laden with corn, wine, cloth, and other articles, frequented the above-mentioned places. The invaders continued for some time on terms of hostility with the natives but in the second generation, they appear to have become friendly. About two hundred years after the settlement of the Danes in Ireland, appeared the celebrated Irish chief, *Brian Boru*. He was king of Munster, and, by repeated victories over his rivals, obtained such a preëminence as to assume the title of king of Ireland. He also gained great advantages over the Danes, and confined them to the maritime districts. He put an end to the wars between the minor kings, so that Ireland had peace under his dominion. The Danes, also, during his reign, occupied themselves solely in commercial pursuits. Brian is said to have been a liberal benefactor to the church, but the same is related of every king who receives the praise of the monkish chroniclers of Europe. There is no doubt that Brian was a brave and able prince; but the stories of his exploits, which fill the Irish tales and poems, are highly exaggerated. Many wonderful descriptions are given of the happy and prosperous state of the island under his government. A story is told of a lady who travelled alone through the country adorned with jewels, and bearing in her hand a white wand with a gold ring at the top. So well observed were the laws, that she performed the whole of her

·ourney without being robbed. A similar tale is told of Alfred the Great, and of Robert I., duke of Normandy, both of whom are said to have kept their dominions in such excellent order, that golden bracelets were hung up by the wayside, and remained untouched for three years!

Brian was killed at the great battle of Clontarf, A. D. 1014, when the Danes were defeated, and their power in Ireland was overthrown. Civil wars followed among the Irish chieftains. At length, toward the close of the eleventh century, the country was divided between two kings, one of whom was conquered by his rival; thus bringing the whole island again under the dominion of one monarch. The transactions of this period possess little interest for the reader, and there is not much known of the state of the country, or the condition of the people. The clergy and the monks appear to have possessed the learning common to the ecclesiastics of those days; but the people were exceedingly ignorant and barbarous. The peaceful pursuits of agriculture, manufacturing, &c., were disregarded, and the chiefs thought only of conquering and plundering their neighbors. The lower classes were poor and wretched in the extreme, and were supported principally by the charity of the monks. Personal freedom, however, was general; the feudal system was not introduced into Ireland, and there were no bondmen attached to the soil, as in England and Scotland. The only slaves were those who were purchased as such, or the prisoners taken in battle.

During the reign of Henry II. in England, there was an Irish chief or king of Leinster, named *Dermot McMurrough*, whose ferocity and cruelty had created him many enemies. Having grossly injured a nobleman of Connaught, named *O'Ruark*, this individual applied for redress to Roderic O'Connor, the chief king of Ireland. They joined their forces, and expelled Dermot from the country. He fled to Henry, who was then in Normandy, and had long cherished the design of conquering Ireland. This appeared to him a favorable opportunity for accomplishing it. He therefore received Dermot in a friendly manner, and agreed to assist him in recovering his kingdom of Leinster, on condition that he would consent to hold it as a vassal of the crown of England, and aid the English in conquering the rest of the island.

CHAPTER CCCCXXXIII.

A. D. 1172 to 1173.

Negotiation with the Pope for the Conquest of Ireland — Alliance of Dermot and Strongbow — Capture of Waterford — Introduction of the Feudal System into Ireland — Treaty between Dermot and Roderic — Henry invades Ireland — Conquest of the Country — Partition of the Lands by Henry.

Dermot readily accepted the proposal of Henry, who immediately wrote to the pope for permission to undertake the conquest of Ireland, promising, in case of success, to engage that the Irish should pay the annual tax of Peter pence to the pope, which they never before had done. Adrian IV. was then pope. He was an Englishman named *Nicholas Breakspear*, and the only individual of that nation who ever attained to the papal dignity. He naturally took more interest in the affairs of England than an Italian or a Frenchman would have done in his place. He not only granted permission to Henry to make the proposed conquest, but sent him a gold ring set with a fine emerald, signifying that he made him a present of the *Emerald Island.*

Dermot, having received the promise of assistance from Henry, connected himself with Richard de Clare, earl of Pembroke, a nobleman who had obtained the name of *Strongbow* from his skill in archery. It was agreed that Strongbow should furnish men for the invasion, and should be rewarded, after the conquest, by a grant of land in Ireland. It was also stipulated that Strongbow should marry Eva, the youngest daughter of Dermot, and that his heirs should succeed to the throne of Leinster. Having made this agreement, they raised a body of forces, and crossed over to Ireland, A. D. 1172. They first laid siege to Waterford, which soon surrendered by the advice of the priests, who were disposed to favor Dermot, because he was liberal in his gifts to the church. As soon as Waterford was taken, Dermot bestowed the lordship of the city and its domains upon two young Norman knights — Maurice Fitz Gerald and Robert Fitz Stephen, who had joined him in his expedition. He also bestowed fiefs on several other knights and nobles who had accompanied him; so that the feudal system was now introduced into Ireland, and the inhabitants of these baronial lands remained for ages a community distinct from the natives, both in language and manners.

The possession of Waterford was very important to Dermot, as it served him for a garrison from which he could make his attacks on the neighboring chiefs. The cruelties committed by the Normans in these excursions aroused Roderic, who was naturally neither brave nor active; and he called together an assembly of the princes and chiefs at Tara, to consult about the means of defending the country. These chieftains, instead of adopting plans to repel the enemy, quarrelled among themselves, and returned home. Roderic preferred making peace to fighting against the warlike Normans: he therefore made a treaty with Dermot, by which he agreed to acknowledge him as king of Leinster, provided he would dismiss all the foreigners in his service, and do homage to him for his kingdom. Dermot was willing to abide by these terms; but the inhabitants of Dublin chose a king of Danish origin for their chief, and refused to acknowledge Dermot. This refusal involved the affairs of Dermot and his allies in great confusion. Dublin was besieged and captured by Dermot. It afterward revolted, and was again captured. Strongbow brought over large reënforcements from England, and the war was carried on with great fury on both sides. King Henry was displeased with the proceedings of Strongbow, and issued orders to prevent him from pursuing his conquests. This measure, however, had no effect, and Henry levied an army for the purpose of invading Ireland himself. The expense of this expedition was very great; and as the king was destitute of money, he imposed a tax on all landed proprietors, called *scutage*, or *shield-tax*, because the money was paid in lieu of personal services in the army, which the landholders were bound to give, according to their feudal obligations.

When Henry had advanced on his march as far as Gloucestershire, he was met by Strongbow, who solicited a reconciliation with him. After some negotia ion, Henry agreed to pardon him, on condition that he should surrender all the seaports and fortresses which he had conquered in Ireland to the king, who, on his part, agreed that all the rest of the earl's possessions should remain to him and his heirs forever, to be held in fief of the English crown. This treaty being concluded, they both embarked, with the army, for Ireland, and landed at Waterford on the 18th of October, 1171. The arrival of the king of England in person had a wonderful effect upon the Irish, who did not make the slightest attempt to oppose him. Never was a conquest more easily effected than that of Ireland by Henry II. He had not occasion to fight a single battle, for every prince and chief in the island came forward to acknowledge his sovereignty. The form prescribed by Henry was, that each chief should do homage, surrender his domain, and receive it back again in vassalage, so that the Irish princes, who had so long ruled as independent sovereigns, were from that time vassals of the kings of England. Roderic himself, the last of the monarchs of Ireland, submitted to the same form; and Ireland has ever since been dependent on the English crown.

Henry established the feudal system in Ireland, as it existed in other countries, by granting estates to his officers for military services, homage, and fealty; and he considered it so important that land should be held by this tenure, that he obliged Strongbow to resign his principality of Leinster, which he had acquired by marriage, and accept it on a new grant for military service. Henry also gave the city of Dublin to the inhabitants of Bristol, who were a trading people, and had long carried on an extensive commerce with Ireland.

CHAPTER CCCCXXXIV.

A. D. 1173 to 1361.

Taxation of the Irish — Establishment of the English Pale — Condition of Ulster — Expedition of De Courcy — Conquest of Ulster — The Wild Irish — Building of Abbeys and Churches in Ireland — Disorders of the Country.

Henry imposed a tax upon the Irish, of a hide for every tenth head of cattle, killed. As cattle were numerous, and, in fact, constituted the chief movable wealth in Ireland, the revenue from this source was very large. Roderic still held a show of sovereignty in the country, but his authority did not extend over any part of the island possessed by the English barons, which was called the *English Pale*, and comprised the whole of Meath and Leinster, Dublin, Waterford, and the territory from the last city to Dungarvon. The Pale may therefore be considered as the English part of Ireland, and all the rest the Irish part, or *Irishie*, as it was called. In 1174, the pope's bull granting the kingdom of Ireland to Henry II., was first proclaimed in that country.

The province of Ulster, in the north, had not shared in the wars and revolutions which had devastated the remainder of the island. This province, and especially the part adjacent to Scotland, was inhabited principally by Scots, who pastured their cattle here, and lived in comparative tranquillity, till a knight named *De Courcy*, who came over from England with the new governor, Fitz Adelm, after the death of Strongbow, fancied that he was destined to be the conqueror of this unsubjugated province. De Courcy was one of those romantic knights, who, in the middle ages, were smitten with the passion for seeking adventures. His scheme of undertaking the conquest of Ulster originated in an ancient prophecy, which foretold that the kingdom of Ulster would be subdued by a white knight on a white horse, bearing birds on his shield. De Courcy was so firmly persuaded that he was the person alluded to in the prophecy, that he furnished himself with a milk-white steed, and decorated his shield with bees, which might pass for birds in a prophecy.

The governor commanded him to abandon his project, for he knew it to be the policy of Henry to allow every province to remain undisturbed that paid its tribute; but De Courcy was resolved to try his fortune. In defiance of all authority, he set off at the head of a band of soldiers for Downpatrick, the capital of Ulster. The inhabitants of the city were aroused at daybreak from their sleep by the sound of the English bugles, and starting up, saw the streets filled with armed troops. The houses were forced open and plundered, and the soldiers were soon masters of the town. O'Neil, the king of Ulster, came forward boldly to oppose the invaders, and a hard-fought battle took place, which ended in the complete overthrow of the Irish, and the establishment of De Courcy's authority in Ulster.

With this event the history of Ireland, as an independent nation, may be said to close; all which follows being rather the history of the English in Ireland, than that of the original inhabitants. The Irish were expelled from the best parts of the country, which were occupied by the invaders, who thus became the ancestors of a great part of those who are regarded, at the present day, as the Irish people. The aborigines were driven to the mountainous parts of the country, and after a few years were looked upon as an inferior race. In allusion to the barbarous manners which they had acquired, they were called the *Wild Irish.*

While Richard I. was engaged in the crusades, the greatest confusion prevailed in Ireland. The chiefs, knowing that the best English warriors were absent in the Holy Land, took advantage of this occasion to invade the English Pale. De Courcy, in the mean time, set the laws at defiance, and carried on wars at his own will and pleasure. This daring soldier built several convents, for it was the fashion of the time to atone for all sorts of evil deeds by erecting religious houses. Few noblemen at that time, and for ages afterward, remained long in Ireland without committing great crimes. The number of abbeys and churches was therefore continually increasing. Among those erected in this manner was the celebrated monastery called *Tintern Abbey:* this was built by William, earl marshal of England, who married Isabel, the daughter of Strongbow, and in consequence became earl of Pembroke. This nobleman was made governor of Ireland, and built the abbey in consequence of a vow, which he made during a storm at sea, that, if he should reach the land in safety, he would found a monastery on the spot where his foot first touched dry land. This building received its name in consequence of being inhabited by monks from Tintern Abbey in Wales.

During the long reign of Henry III., the state of

Ireland may be described as one of perpetual strife and bloodshed. The natives, who were every where becoming poorer, made many desperate efforts to rid themselves of a tyranny that was growing more and more insupportable; but without organization or discipline, they could do nothing more than set fire to the castles of the English, and murder all who fell in their way — for which they were sure to meet with fearful reprisals. In the fourteenth century, the authority of the king of England over this country was much diminished. Almost all the English possessions were in the hands of nine or ten barons, who were utterly regardless of the laws, and ruled in their own territories with all the power of despotic princes. The feudal system was now in full force among the Anglo-Irish. The barons had the right of holding courts of judicature within their own domains, and inflicting even capital punishment upon their vassals.

In a country so governed, there could not be much peace or good order. The nobles were continually at war with each other, and the natives were always in rebellion. Many of the land-owners, too, whose estates were on the borders of the English Pale, were absent in England, and took no precaution to protect their lands. Consequently, the natives made frequent inroads upon the English territories, and committted dreadful depredations. They often set fire to the churches when they were full of people, and those who escaped from the flames fell by the swords and axes of the wild Irish. Nothing was done to prevent these frightful scenes till the reign of Edward III., who made several wise laws, which diminished in some degree the disorders under which the country had been suffering.

CHAPTER CCCCXXXV.

A. D. 1361 to 1580.

The Statute of Kilkenny — Laws against the Amalgamation of the English and Irish — Visit of Richard II. to Ireland — Description of the Wild Irish — Projects of Henry VII. and Elizabeth for introducing Protestantism — First Planting of Potatoes in Ireland.

During the administration of the duke of Clarence, who was appointed by Edward III. lord lieutenant of Ireland in 1361, a famous parliament was held at Kilkenny, where an act was passed, which is known as the *Statute of Kilkenny.* The nature of this statute requires an explanation. Two centuries had now elapsed since the English first came to settle in Ireland. In that long period, although the main bodies of the two nations had remained distinct from each other, and during a great part of the time at enmity, there had been numerous intermarriages and friendships formed, so that many families descended from the first English settlers were now completely Irish, and not only spoke the Irish language, but wore the dress of the country, and acknowledged the Brehon laws. There was also a custom, called *fostering*, which prevailed in Ireland to an extraordinary extent, and formed a tie between the natives and the English that was held stronger and more sacred than the nearest relationship. It was this: The children of the English, as soon as they were born, were put out to be nursed by Irish women, who brought them up till they were of an age to be returned to their parents.

This custom, and every thing else that tended to promote a friendly intercourse between the English and the Irish, was discountenanced by the English government, and the statute of Kilkenny was made for the express purpose of preventing the intermixture of the two nations. This celebrated act declared that "fostering," and intermarriage with the natives, should be regarded as high treason, and punished accordingly; and that any man of English descent who should assume an Irish name, speak the Irish language, or adopt the laws, customs, or dress of the natives, should forfeit all his lands and tenements, or be imprisoned. The English were also forbidden by this act to entertain the Irish minstrels and bards, or to listen to their songs or tales. Nor were they to allow the Irish to pasture their cattle upon the English lands; nor to admit them into religious houses; nor to present them to any ecclesiastical benefices. Thus the Irish were excluded from every kind of benefit; for while the lower orders were prohibited from feeding their herds within the bounds of the English territories which contained the best pasturage, the higher ranks were debarred from seeking wealth and honors in the church.

Richard II. visited Ireland, A. D. 1390, with a large army, to quell the insurgents, who were every where distracting the country. But their suppression cost him no difficulty. The chiefs readily made their submission, laying aside their girdles and falling on their knees at his feet. It is remarkable that these native princes, notwithstanding their hatred of the English, and their propensity to war, were always ready, and even eager, to submit to the king of England, whenever he made his appearance among them; so great was their veneration for royalty. The disposition appears to subsist in full force at the present day.

The description given of the wild Irish of this period corresponds very nearly with those of a modern date. They were far removed from civilization, living, some in caves of the rocks, others in wigwams, like the American savages, and holding their lands mostly in common. The earth was cultivated only in small patches, and the people had no fixed dwellings, but moved about from place to place with their herds, building their wigwams wherever they found grass, wood, and water. They usually slept on the bare ground, wrapped up in a rude sort of blanket, which was worn both by men and women. Their food consisted of herbage of various kinds, milk, butter, oatmeal bread, and beef broth. The wild Irish were very superstitious; they believed in witches, fairies, charms, and spells.

When Henry VIII. had thrown off the authority of the pope in England, he attempted to make the same change in Ireland. The archbishop of Dublin received the proposition favorably, and declared against the pope. He advised the calling of a parliament to abolish the papal authority. The parliament met accordingly, and passed an act ordering that all first fruits, — that is, the first year's profits of all benefices, — and all other dues which had hitherto been paid to the pope, should in future be paid to the king, who had assumed the title of *Head of the Church.* Henry soon after sent over commissioners to suppress the monasteries, as he had suppressed them in England. Notwithstanding this, the Protestant religion was never fully established in Ireland, where the monastic orders stil existed, although their houses and lands were taken from them. To this day a large majority of the people continue to be Catholics.

When Queen Mary came to the throne, she restored the Catholic religion in Ireland, as in England, and gave back a great portion of the church lands. Queen Elizabeth reversed these proceedings, and attempted to establish Protestantism throughout the country. Laws were made requiring the people to attend Protestant churches: but Elizabeth only drove the Irish to rebellion by using force in the attempt to change their faith. The king of Spain sent assistance to the Irish rebels, who were led on by the earl of Desmond. The rebellion, however, was soon suppressed. Sir Walter Raleigh commanded a portion of the English troops in this war, and was rewarded by a grant of land from the confiscated estates of the rebels. This was a memorable epoch in the history of Ireland, for Raleigh, who had been in America, introduced the potato into his Irish plantations; and it is to this measure that Ireland is indebted for the article which has become her staple production of agriculture; though, all things considered, it has been a doubtful boon. Raleigh also attempted the cultivation of tobacco here, but the climate was found not adapted to its growth.

CHAPTER CCCCXXXVI.

A. D. 1580 to 1649.

Nocturnal Meetings — Civilization of Ulster by James I. — Insurrection of 1641 *— Massacre of the English — Civil War — Plague in Ireland.*

During the whole of Elizabeth's reign, Ireland was distracted by wars and rebellions. The natives in every part of the country were accustomed to hold meetings on the hills to discourse upon the affairs of the nation; and as these assemblies were usually held for the purpose of plotting against the English government, those who attended them always went armed. They were often surprised at these meetings by parties of English soldiers, and skirmishes took place attended with loss of life. The Irish appear always to have had a superstitious veneration for high places. Their ancient monarchs were crowned on the summit of a mount; their castles and palaces were built on elevated spots, and the national assemblies of the early ages were held on the hill of Tara, where stood the palace of the kings of Ireland in former days.

James I., on coming to the throne, projected a scheme for the colonization of the province of Ulster, which, by the forfeitures consequent upon rebellion, had become the property of the crown. He communicated his design to the citizens of London, who raised the sum of twenty thousand pounds to carry it into effect. Commissioners were sent over to take a survey of the lands, and note down proper situations for building towers and castles. It was the intention of the king to dispose of all these lands, so as to introduce arts and manufactures into the country, and promote a more friendly intercourse between the English and Irish. Until this time, no part of Ireland, except Leinster, had been divided into counties. James established these divisions in every part of the kingdom, granted fairs and markets in every county, appointed regular circuits of judges, and decreed that henceforth the laws of England should be the laws of all Ireland. The old Brehon laws were entirely abolished. In the space of nine years, James made greater progress in the civilization of Ireland than had been accomplished by all the English sovereigns who had preceded him.

But these flattering prospects were blasted in the reign of his successor, Charles I. The troubles in which that monarch become involved with his parliament, offered to the Irish a tempting occasion to rebel The plan of a general insurrection was formed by Roger O'Moore, a person who had served in the Spanish army, and who was full of zeal for the Catholic religion. He imagined that, by a sudden rising of the Catholics all over the island, the English might be expelled, and the Irish forever freed from foreign dominion. As the entire restoration of the Catholic religion was a part of his plan, he reckoned upon the assistance of the Catholic lords of the Pale, most of whom entered into the conspiracy, and concerted measures with Moore and Phelim O'Neil, the most powerful chief in Ireland. The insurrection was to begin in all parts of the country on the same day, when, upon a given signal, the forts were to be seized by the insurgents.

The secret had been preserved till the night before the execution of the plot, when it was betrayed by an Irishman named Conolly, who gave information of the intended attack upon Dublin Castle, in which were plentiful stores of arms and ammunition. Two or three of the conspirators were immediately arrested; but there was no time to stay the progress of the insurrection, which burst forth with tremendous violence, October 23, 1641. The colonists of Ulster, who had no suspicion of the existence of such a conspiracy, suddenly found themselves surrounded by mobs of infuriated Irishmen armed with staves, pitchforks, and other rude weapons, which they brandished aloft with the most frightful howlings. A massacre — one of the most barbarous and cruel to be found in history, immediately ensued. No age, no sex, no condition, was spared: without provocation and without opposition, the defenceless English were murdered in cold blood by their nearest neighbors, with whom they had long maintained a continued intercourse of kindness and good offices. Their houses were set on fire or laid level with the ground. Where the wretched owners attempted to defend themselves with their wives and children, they all perished together in the flames. Amidst these enormities, the sacred name of religion resounded on every side, not to stop the hands of the murderers, but to enforce their blows, and to steel their hearts against every movement of human sympathy. The English, as heretics abhorred of God and detestable to all holy men, were marked by the priests for slaughter. From Ulster the flames of rebellion extended immediately over all parts of the country. The English who were not massacred were turned out of their houses, stripped of their very clothes, and exposed naked and defenceless to the severities of a cold and tempestuous season. The failure of the plot at Dublin preserved in Ireland the remains of the English name. The roads were covered with crowds of wretched fugitives hastening to that city; and when the gates were opened, they presented to the view of the astonished inhabitants a scene of misery such as no human eye had previously beheld. A full recital of the horrors of this memorable massacre would be too revolting for the feelings of the reader. The number of persons who perished by all these cruelties has been estimated at two hundred thousand — a calculation liable to the exaggeration common in such

,ases, but which serves sufficiently to show the dreadful nature and extent of the calamity.

The war which followed this rebellion lasted ten years, and reduced all Ireland to extreme want and wretchedness. Where the people were not destroyed by fire and sword, they were wasted by famine and disease. The plague broke out in Ireland, and was supposed to have originated from the unwholesome food, which the people were compelled to eat. It raged more or less during the whole of this unhappy period.

CHAPTER CCCCXXXVII.

A. D. 1649 to 1780.

Conquest of Ireland by Cromwell — Emigration of the Irish — Rise of the Rapparees — Rebellion of the Irish under James II. — Restrictions on Trade — Attempts for the Relief of the Irish — Pauperism — Absenteeism.

After Charles I. had been dethroned and executed, the English parliament appointed Oliver Cromwell lord lieutenant of Ireland, and commander-in-chief of the forces in that country. This celebrated man had already given evidence of extraordinary military talents, and he went over to Ireland fully determined to put an end to the rebellion. He landed at Dublin in August, 1647, with an army of twelve thousand men. The English who had been fighting against the Irish were royalists, and Cromwell, on his arrival, was regarded as an enemy by both parties, who united their forces to oppose him. This undertaking seemed most desperate, but the great genius of Cromwell triumphed over every obstacle. He saw at a glance which was the best method to insure success, and he adopted it without hesitation or delay. Several towns had been newly fortified, that they might be able to stand a siege. Among these was the city of Drogheda, or Tredah, in which the English had a strong garrison. A siege was too slow an operation for so active a general as Cromwell, and he resolved to take it by storm. This enterprise succeeded, but the victory was dreadful; for no sooner had the cannon made a breach in the wall large enough to admit the soldiers, than they rushed in, and put the whole garrison to the sword.

This terrible example spread such consternation throughout Ireland, that Cromwell met with little opposition, and marched onward, capturing town after town. At length, he so far subdued the country, that he thought it safe to leave the completion of the work to others, while he went to suppress a rebellion of the Scots, who had taken arms in favor of Charles the Second. He gave permission to the Irish chiefs who submitted to him, to withdraw from the country with their followers. In consequence of this, forty thousand Irish emigrated to the continent, and many of them enlisted in the service of the Catholic sovereigns of Europe. Cromwell transported some thousands of the poorer sort to the West Indies, where they were put to labor on the plantations.

The conquest of Ireland resembled in many respects that of England by the Normans, when the land was taken from the natives to pay the soldiers for their services. As the dispossessed Saxons fled to the forests and formed bands of robbers, so the Irish sought refuge in their woods and bogs, from which they issued to commit ravages in the open country. These marauders acquired the name of *Rapparees*, and became so formidable that large rewards were offered by the government for their apprehension. A hundred guineas were the price of a Rapparee captain, and forty were offered for an inferior. These men, however, were not easily caught, and it was extremely dangerous to follow them, because their pursuers, who were unacquainted with the ground, were often lost in the bogs, where the surface, overgrown with grass or moss, appeared firm to the eye, and yet would prove so soft, that a person treading on it would immediately sink and be suffocated. Many of these bogs remain in their former state, and cattle are frequently lost in them at the present day.

When James II. was expelled from England, in 1688, the king of France furnished him with a fleet and an army, with which he sailed to Ireland in the hope of regaining his crown by the aid of the Irish. He landed at Kinsale, March 17, 1689. He immediately called a parliament, and issued proclamations commanding all his subjects to unite against the prince of Orange. His proceedings were very tyrannical. He dismissed from the council of state all Protestant members, forbade the Protestant worship, and ordered the people to take base coin in pay for the provisions furnished to his army. Bits of brass of the value of fourpence were stamped as five pounds. James, however, was unable to maintain himself in Ireland. The Protestants took up arms against him, and were aided by troops from England. At length, King William came over in person, and defeated James at the battle of the Boyne, June 30, 1690. James was compelled to seek refuge again in France, and the whole country submitted to William.

From this period to the reign of George III., Ireland remained at peace; but for want of good government, the blessings of peace were felt in a very limited degree. Trade revived, but such restrictions were placed upon it by the English parliament, that the Irish derived little profit from it. The laws enacted in the Irish parliament were not valid till they had been approved by the parliament of England. The Catholics were not allowed to purchase any landed property, nor to hold any office under government, and were subjected to various other disabilities. The great export trade of Ireland comprised chiefly salted provisions; but this served to enrich the merchants and graziers rather than the peasantry, most of whom had no means of subsistence but the cultivation of potatoes.

In the reign of George III., some attempts were made by the Irish parliament to create employment for distressed laborers by granting sums of money for several useful public works, as canals, roads, docks, &c. But these improvements afforded only partial relief to some of the thousands of miserable beings without food or shelter; for there were no poor laws in Ireland to provide for the aged, infirm, and destitute. Most of the great landholders were *absentees;* that is, they dwelt in England, instead of being present on their own estates, and left the management of their Irish property to agents whose chief object was to make the business as profitable to themselves as possible. They seldom showed any indulgence to the poor tenants, but forced them to pay their rents, though they were left without food for their starving children.

CHAPTER CCCCXXXVIII.

A. D. 1780 to 1863.

Enclosure of the Irish Commons — White Boys — Peep-of-Day Boys — Orangemen — United Irishmen — Rebellion of 1797 — Emmet's Rebellion — Union with England — O'Connell — Catholic Emancipation — Distress in Ireland — Famine — Smith O'Brien's Rebellion — Present Condition of Ireland.

Irish Beggars.

THE distress of the Irish peasantry was increased by the enclosure of the *commons*, on which the poor people formerly enjoyed a right of pasturage. Those who were fortunate enough to possess two or three sheep, a cow, or a donkey, fed them on the commons; but this privilege was taken away by their enclosure, for the benefit of the landholders within whose domains they were situated. In this impoverished condition, the people used to assemble in the night, and take revenge upon those whom they regarded as the authors of their misery. They pulled down the fences of the enclosed commons, by which they obtained the name of *Levellers;* but afterward they were called *White Boys*, because they wore white shirts or frocks as a uniform by which they might know each other in the night. Their outrages soon assumed an aggravated character: they murdered the tithe collectors and the receivers of the rents. The payment of tithes was regarded as a peculiar grievance, because the Catholics were compelled to pay them to the Protestant clergy. A dreadful tumult from this cause broke out in Cork and Kerry, where the peasantry marched about in large parties, calling themselves *Right Boys*, and compelling all persons they met to take an oath that they would not pay more than a certain sum, per acre, for tithes. Other bands of rioters were called *Peep-of-Day Boys.* These were associations of Protestants, who leagued together against the Catholics. They were called by this name because they were accustomed to assemble at daybreak, and sally forth against their enemies. They were afterward called *Orangemen*, from William III., prince of Orange who expelled James II. from Ireland.

In 1791, a society was formed at Dublin called the *United Irishmen.* At the head of it were many persons of rank and fortune. The secret object of this society was to collect together, in different associations, as large a number of disaffected individuals as possible, and, as soon as they felt strong enough, to make a bold effort to separate Ireland from England, and form it into an independent republic. A body of national guards was also instituted at Dublin. They adopted a green uniform, with buttons bearing a harp surmounted by a cap of liberty. These revolutionary symptoms alarmed the English government, and they employed spies, who discovered that the United Irishmen were in correspondence with the French government, with whom the English were then at war. Measures were immediately taken to anticipate the insurrection of the Irish. The English government suspended the *habeas corpus* act, and caused all suspected persons to be arrested and thrown into prison. The whole of the conspiracy was thus discovered; but this did not prevent the rebellion from breaking out in **1797.** The peasantry took arms and assembled in considerable numbers. The French government sent a squadron of ships to their assistance. The English government, however, by very prompt and decisive measures, were enabled to crush the insurrection. The Irish were totally routed at the battle of Vinegar Hill, which proved a death-blow to the rebellion in Ireland. Some years afterward a young man named *Robert Emmet* attempted to excite an insurrection at Dublin; but he was joined by only a small number of persons, and the insurgents were all made prisoners, after having created a tumult of a few hours. Emmet was tried and hanged for rebellion in **1803.**

Previous to this last event, Ireland had been united to Great Britain, forming one monarchy, by the name of the *United Kingdom of Great Britain and Ireland.* This union was effected in **1800.** Ireland gained considerable commercial advantages by it, and from the example of Scotland, it was hoped that a general tranquillity would be the result. This expectation, however, was not fulfilled. The peasantry of the south, inflamed by national jealousy, by religious animosity, and by the severe privations under which they labored, continued in a state of turbulence tending toward rebellion. The union with Great Britain though at first received with general acquiescence, soon became unpopular. In **1810,** a meeting was held at Dublin, to consider the subject of repeal. At this meeting Daniel O'Connell made his first prominent appearance as the champion of the Irish cause; and from this period he labored, without remission, as the advocate of Irish emancipation, till his death in 1847. By the constant agitation of the subject, the attention of the British parliament was drawn to the affairs of Ireland, and the penal laws against the Catholics, subjecting them to political disabilities, were gradually abolished. At length, in **1828,** the Catholic emancipation bill was passed, by which the Catholics were placed on the same footing as Protestants in their qualification for election to parliament.

This measure, however, like all others designed for the relief of the Irish, disappointed its projectors. The Irish continued miserable, and consequently restive and in **1833**, the riots and disturbances become so alarming, that the *habeas corpus* act was suspended. Considerable bodies of troops were maintained in the country to preserve peace. Some degree of quiet was restored by these means; but the condition of the poorer classes was not improved. Their chief dependence for food has long been upon the potato. For a few years past, the failure of the crops, owing to a new disease in that plant called the *potato rot*, caused the most dreadful distress in Ireland. It is computed that in 1847 nearly half a million of persons perished in that country by starvation and disease consequent upon want of food. The scenes of destitution and suffering which Ireland exhibited after the appearance of this calamity, were almost without parallel. The sympathies and charities of all civilized nations were excited by this distressing spectacle. The people of the United States sent two ships laden with provisions to the relief of the suffering Irish; and even the sultan of Turkey gave a liberal sum of money for the same purpose.

The suffering occasioned by the failure of the potato crop, was not so severe in 1849, but the emigration continued to be immense, and promised almost to rid Ireland of the Celtic race. In 1848, *William Smith O'Brien*, as already stated, made an attempt to raise a rebellion. He assumed the character of a revolutionary leader, and called upon the populace to take up arms against the British government. The people showed no general disposition to encourage him; and, after making a slight demonstration of resistance at the head of a handful of followers, he attempted to escape from the country, but was made prisoner. O'Brien and a few of his associates were tried and condemned to death; but their sentence was commuted to transportation.

The political evils under which Ireland has labored will be sufficiently apparent from what we have already related. From the earliest times, she has been in the situation of a conquered country, without ever being reconciled to the yoke or assimilated to the ruling nation. Within the last two centuries, her devoted adherence to a religion opposed to that of her rulers has been made the occasion of unspeakable misery. In consequence, also, of repeated rebellions and forfeitures, the greater part of the lands are in the possession of English and Protestant proprietors, who, having no national influence over the occupiers of their estates, hold their places only by the hated tenure of dominion and law. It is a pleasure to record, however, that late acts of parliament have materially changed the state of things, and contributed to the amelioration of the condition of Ireland and the Irish people.

The north of Ireland has been long distinguished from the rest by the superior wealth and industry of its inhabitants. These are principally manufacturers, they are of the Scottish race, and have all the prudence and forethought of that nation: the greatest part of them are Presbyterian Protestants. The south, and the region east of the Shannon are peopled by gentry of the English race, and peasantry of pure Irish extraction. The eastern counties on the coast are inhabited almost entirely by people of English descent. In the west, or wildest part of the island, are the old Irish clans, bearing still the names of their ancient chiefs, and almost as barbarous as they were a thousand years ago.

One of the most interesting parts of Ireland is Galway, in the west, where the people so closely resemble the Spaniards, and the buildings are so much in the style of those in the old cities of Spain, that travellers who are well acquainted with that country maintain that there can be no doubt of the Spanish origin of the people in this region. The peasants have the same dark complexion, large black eyes, and the peculiar expression of features that distinguish the Spanish peasantry. The resemblance of Galway to a Spanish town is increased by the number of friars that are seen walking about; and in all the places of interment are hundreds of little black crosses, such as are found in the burial-grounds of Spain.

The principal employment of the people in the west of Ireland is feeding cattle, the occupation of their ancestors from the earliest ages. Some individuals have as many as three hundred head of oxen and cows, besides sheep; so that they are in better circumstances than the agriculturists in the other parts of the country. These people, however, are an uncivilized race of beings, and so fond of fighting that their fairs and merry makings seldom end without a battle. The fairs in particular are sure to call the *shillelah*, or Irish club, into exercise. For many years past owing to the distressed and disturbed state of the country, murders have been increasing to a frightful extent in these parts, as well as in other portions of the country. The victims are generally landlords, or agents, who have ejected their tenants for non-payment of rent.

The Irish distil whiskey from barley in their little cottages, where they elude the vigilance of the excise officers. What is thus illegally made is called *potheen*. This liquor was first known in Ireland by the name of *usquebaugh*. The use of it has been carried to great excess among the lower orders, who delight in all kinds of meetings which give them an opportunity of drinking together. To this propensity perhaps may be traced the custom of *waking* the dead. Whenever a poor person dies, the neighbors assemble to drink, smoke, and lament the departure of the deceased. This is a very ancient custom, and is regarded as so indispensable, that a laborer whose relative has died, and whose children are running about half naked, will spend a month's wages in whiskey and tobacco for the men and women who come to the *wake*, which is often continued for two or three days and nights. The intemperance of the Irish has, however, been somewhat checked by the exertions of Father Matthew.

The mud cabin of the Irish peasant is the most wretched habitation that thriftless poverty ever constructed for human beings. The walls are of common mud or clay, hardened in the sun. The roof is composed of sticks and straw, and the floor is the bare ground, which is generally very damp, and not always free from pools of water. It has neither window nor chimney; and it usually contains but one apartment which is occupied by the family and the pig, if they are so rich as to possess one. A pig is, indeed, accounted

* Hatred and contempt toward the Irish, on the part of the English, has helped to make them blind to the course of true policy, and insensible to the claims of justice and humanity towards the natives of their sister isle. During the late calamitous famine in Ireland, the leading London journal openly took the ground that the only hope of that country was in a "change of men" — in other words, an extirpation of the race!

a mark of prosperity. Attached to the cabin is the potato garden, which generally furnishes the only arti-

An Irish Pig Drover.

cle of food; for few of the lower classes ever taste any thing else. The rent of a wretched cabin of this description is from thirty to forty shillings a year, exclusive of the garden. The wages of laborers are from sixpence to eightpence a day. Many go to England in harvest time to work, and during their absence their wives and children live by begging. This is the reason why a traveller in Ireland is always beset by a multitude of beggars. Yet, in spite of all this misery, the lower orders of Irish have a quickness of wit, a warmth of heart, a readiness to oblige, and a generosity that are scarcely ever met with among the same class in other countries.

The Irish landlords are in general absentees, many of whom have never seen their Irish estates. They expend no money in improvements of the land, nor do they care how their tenants are lodged, being satisfied with receiving their rent every six months from their agents. The poverty of the farmers arises in a great degree from the practice common to the great landholders of letting out their estates, for long terms of time, to a species of agents called *middlemen.* These persons underlet the land in small portions to the cultivators. The middlemen form a numerous class of the gentry in Ireland, being, in fact, the resident landholders. This ruinous system is alike injurious to the tenant and the owner. The middlemen let the land at what is called *rack rent*, that is, at a higher price than they pay for it; and many of the farmers divide the little lots which they hire, and underlet them again to the highest bidders. Wretched laborers are driven to outbid one another so as to get a small patch of ground, on which they may raise the potatoes, which are their only refuge against starvation. The lowest stage of the renting of land is styled *conacre.* This rent is frequently paid by begging, or laboring at the harvest in England.

CHAPTER CCCCXXXIX.

Government, Chief Cities, Manners, Customs, Manufactures, Agriculture, Commerce, Religion, Education, Literature, &c., of Ireland.

The government of Ireland is administered by a lord lieutenant appointed by the British crown This officer displays a portion of the state of royalty, and exercises some of the regal functions. He has his household establishment at Dublin Castle, a chancellor, a secretary, and other ministers of state. The courts of justice and the different orders of magistracy are nearly on the same footing as in England. Ireland sends one hundred and five members to the British parliament.

Dublin, the capital of Ireland, is a very handsome city. It stands at the bottom of a beautiful bay on the eastern coast, and displays a prospect, on approaching it by sea, which has been compared to that of Naples. A considerable part of the city is regularly built, exhibiting fine specimens of architecture. Sackville Street is the finest in the city. It is one hundred and seventy feet wide, and is adorned with many splendid mansions. The squares of Dublin are particularly admired for their spaciousness and regularity. The western part is called the *old town*, and bears the marks of decay. Still further west is a district called the *Liberty*, as being out of the jurisdiction of the city magistrates. It is inhabited only by the lowest orders, and exhibits scenes of filth and wretchedness not to be equalled in any other city of Great Britain. Dublin has declined since the union, when the nobles and gentry, being no longer called to attend the Irish parliament, transferred their residence to London, and their mansions in Dublin have been converted to humbler purposes. The population of Dublin is about two hundred and sixty thousand.

Cork is the second city in Ireland. The greater part of it consists of narrow and crowded streets; but there are some handsome new ones. The monastic structures, for which this city was once remarkable, have almost entirely disappeared. The present prosperity of the place is of modern growth, and arises from the provision trade, of which Cork is the chief mart. Its bay, called the *Cove of Cork*, forms one of the best harbors in the world. The population is 80,000, and, like most Irish cities, is decreasing.

Limerick, on the Shannon, is well situated for trade, and is one of the principal ports for the exportation of grain and provisions. It was formerly the strongest place in Ireland. Population, fifty thousand. Belfast and Londonderry are considerable towns in the north.

Goldsmith.

The Irish character presents very marked features many of which are praiseworthy and amiable. Hos

View in Sackville Street: Nelson's Column.

pitality is a universal trait, and is enhanced by the scantiness of the portion which is liberally shared with the stranger. The Irish are celebrated for their strong attachment to their kindred and friends, which leads them, in the midst of poverty and suffering, to support their aged relations with the purest kindness. Their faults are a deficiency in cleanliness and a want of taste for the conveniences and luxuries of civilized life. They are generally destitute of that sober and steady spirit of enterprise which distinguishes the English. The love of combat seems to be a general infirmity. The Irish do not fight single-handed, but in bands, and on a great scale. When an individual imagines himself insulted, he goes round to his companions, friends, and townsmen, and collects a multitude, who make a joint attack on the offending party. This is their practice also in America. The lighter frailties of the Irish are vanity, loquacity, a readiness to speak as well as to act without deliberation, and a hurry and confusion of ideas, which so often lead them to that peculiar sort of blunder called a *bull*. Amusement forms a copious element in the existence of an Irishman. Ample scope is afforded to the Catholics by their numerous holidays, and the Protestants vie with them in this particular. The fairs afford a grand theatre for fun and diversion. The most active sport is *hurling*, a game of ball. To this are added the amusements of horse-racing, cock-fighting, cudgelling, leaping, dancing, drinking whiskey, and knocking one another down.

The dress of the Irish peasantry consists chiefly of the native wool, worked rudely into frieze or linsey; for they seldom can afford to wear the fine linen of their own manufacture. But the most prominent feature of this attire among the lower classes, is its lamentable deficiency. In many instances, it covers little more than half the person, and presents an image of extreme poverty. Where this deficiency does not exist, an Irishman loves to display the extent of his wardrobe: when going to a fair, he puts on all the coats he has, though it be midsummer. The food of the Irish peasant is no less scanty than his dress and habitation: it consists almost wholly of potatoes, without even any other vegetable; only the better sort have buttermilk with their potatoes. In the north, oatmeal cakes and pottage are common, as in Scotland.

The manufactures of Ireland were, at first, almost exclusively confined to the north: all the attempts to establish them in the south failed till a very recent period. The chief manufacture is that of linen, which is carried on extensively in all parts of Ulster, and more or less throughout Ireland. The mode of conducting this manufacture is, in several respects, rude and imperfect. It is generally practised by individuals holding little spots of ground, the culture of which they combine with that of weaving. The same person, or at least the same family, in many cases, raises the flax, dresses it, spins it into yarn, and weaves it into cloth. Mill-spinning has been lately introduced, but it is by no means general. Cotton and woollen cloths are also manufactured in Ireland. The commerce of the island is chiefly carried on with Great Britain.

The ecclesiastical state of Ireland has been one of the chief causes of its unsettled condition. The native Irish did not share in any degree the reformation so unanimously adopted in England and Scotland. When the English church was introduced as the established religion, it threw out as dissenters the bulk of the Irish population. A large portion of the Protestants who came as colonists from Scotland were attached to the Presbyterian form. The Catholic clergy receive no stipend from government, but are supported entirely by their flocks. They are formed into a regular hierarchy, at the head of which are four archbishops. The number of Catholic priests has been estimated at fourteen hundred, beside several hundred friars. The Irish establishments for education are scanty in proportion to the population. There is only one university, that of Dublin, founded by Queen Elizabeth. The Catholics have a college at Maynooth, which the British parliament have lately assisted by a liberal grant of money. Popular education exists to a limited extent.

The literature of Ireland has a claim to consideration from its antiquity. Immediately after the introduction of Christianity, many writers arose, whose works are still extant. They consist of the lives of saints, and works of piety and discipline, which, to the inquisitive reader present many singular features in the history of the human mind. The national manners and the peculiar character of the times are rudely but justly delineated in these works. In later times, the national literature of Ireland, properly speaking, does not attract our notice ; but this country has produced great numbers of men of genius, whose names now ornament the literature of England. Swift, Goldsmith, Burke, Sheridan, Moore, and Miss Edgeworth, with a host of inferior rank among the standard authors in English were natives of Ireland.

View of Greenwich Railway, London.

CHAPTER CCCCXL.

General Views of the Kingdom of Great Britain and Ireland.

The government of Great Britain is monarchical in its form, but with a predominant infusion of oligarchy, modified by a limited representation in one branch of the legislature. It has no written form of government: that which is called the *British Constitution* is comprised in certain usages which have been handed down from remote ages, and modified by occasional legislative enactments. The government has no other guide or check than that which may be found in this vague and confused body of laws and traditions.

The monarchical element lies in the sovereign, who is hereditary. The oligarchal and republican elements lie in the parliament, which is composed of an hereditary house of lords and an elective house of commons. The king is not theoretically supposed to hold his throne by divine right, or in virtue of any indefeasible hereditary claim, though the high degree of English loyalty elevates the sovereign almost to the rank of a divinity. The nation, by its supreme council, the parliament, has dictated certain rules which control the succession.

All laws are made by a concurrence of the king, lords, and commons. The power of making war and concluding peace is lodged solely with the king. He is held to be incapable of doing wrong : all his wrong acts are supposed to be the work of his ministers, who are liable to punishment for the abuse of their power. All revenues and taxes are raised, and all money appropriated for public uses, by authority of parliament. Thus the royal prerogative is checked by the control which the representatives of a part of the people exercise over the public purse. The king can command and equip fleets, but, without the concurrence of parliament, he cannot maintain them. He can appoint men to office, but, without parliament, he cannot pay their salaries. He can declare war, but, without supplies from parliament, he cannot carry it on. He has the exclusive right of assembling parliament, but he is required by law to do so every three years. He is the head of the church, yet he cannot alter the established religion.

All English peers are members of the house of lords. The Scotch and Irish peers send only a portion of their number as representatives of the whole body The qualifications for voting for members of the house of commons varies in different towns and boroughs ;

but, in general, the rights of suffrage are much more restricted than in the United States. The king has the power of dissolving the parliament at any time, and ordering the election of new members. The established religion is Episcopacy, but every mode of worship is tolerated.

The revenue of the British empire is immense, amounting to about three hundred and twenty-five million dollars annually. Nearly one third of this amount is raised by the customs, or duties upon imports and exports, and about an equal sum by the excise, or duties upon articles consumed at home. The stamps, taxes, and post-office yield the bulk of the remainder. The principal items of expenditure are the civil list, or annual allowance for the support of the royal household, amounting to about three and a half million dollars; the army and navy more than one hundred and thirty millions; pensions, two millions; courts of justice, one million four hundred thousand, &c.

The national debt of Great Britain is about four thousand millions of dollars. This enormous amount has been accumulated by borrowing money, and anticipating each year's revenue to pay the interest. The debt is of two kinds—funded and unfunded. The unfunded debt consists of deficiencies in the payments of government, for which no regular security has been given, and which bear no interest; and of bills, or promissory notes, issued by the exchequer to defray occasional expenses. When debts of this kind have accumulated, and payment is demanded, it becomes necessary to satisfy the demand, either by paying the debt or affording the creditors a security for the principal, and for the regular payment of the interest. Recourse has been always had to the latter method, and a particular branch of the actual revenue is mortgaged for the interest of the debt. Money borrowed in this manner is said to be borrowed by funding. The public funds, or stocks, are nothing more than the public debts; and to have a share in these stocks, is to be a creditor of the nation. Three fifths of the current yearly expenditure are taken up in the payment of the interest of the national debt.

The land forces of Great Britain, under the peace establishment, amount to about two hundred and ten thousand men, chiefly stationed in Ireland and the colonies. The only means employed for raising regular troops is that of voluntary enlistment. But, in the defence of the country, the militia, comprising all able-bodied men between eighteen and forty-five, are drafted by ballot.

The naval force of Great Britain comprises six hundred vessels, about four hundred of which are generally in commission. Sailors are enlisted like soldiers; but, during war, when seamen are in high demand, impressment is resorted to; that is, sailors are taken by force in the streets and from on board merchant ships, and compelled to serve on board the men-of-war.

To an observer who looks only at the surface, Great Britain presents an object in the highest degree imposing. Its numerous colonies, its vast commerce, its stupendous military and naval power, its gorgeous court, its splendid aristocracy, its numberless institutions for art, learning, religion, and charity—are all calculated to excite in the mind of the beholder a sentiment of respect and admiration. Many persons are seduced by this external aspect of things, and ed to regard England as the great pattern of the world in religion, government, law, and society. But on closer inspection, we find that beneath this display of national glory, there is still as large an amount of misery, injustice, and corruption as in most other countries. Such, indeed, was the state of things a few years since, that the sentiment became common that the country was rapidly descending to the gulf of revolution and ruin. Speedy national bankruptcy was predicted by many sagacious individuals, as well in England as elsewhere. The centralization of government and power in London at the same time become distasteful to the colonies, some of which seemed resolved to throw off the yoke of dependence, and thus the chief instrument by which the fabric of British wealth and power has been built up, appeared likely to fall. It is to be remarked, however, that now and at the close of an expensive and destructive war,* these gloomy clouds have passed away, and at no period in modern times has Great Britain presented an aspect of more commanding power and general prosperity, than at the present moment (1863). And all this is true, while thie people are carrying a load of current expenses in the support of its goverment, which would overwhelm any other country. A few items of this account, taken from a recent English publication, we give below.†

*During the late Eastern war with Russia, both the army and navy were greatly increased; the number of steam-ships, especially, was very largely augmented. On the 23d of April, 1856, Queen Victoria reviewed the British navy at Spithead. The fleet numbered over 240 ships of war, big and little, all steamers, with the exception of two; these comprised 34,000 horse power; carried 3,000 guns, and 33,000 men; included sixteen gun-boats and three floating batteries, and extended twelve miles along the water, east and west across Spithead.

Some idea of the enormous power put forth by Great Britain in this war, may be gathered from the following statement made to parliament, May 7, 1856, by Lord Panmure: "The Eastern expedition has cost us 22,467 men. From the 19th of September, 1854, the day on which the army was first engaged in action, to the 28th of September, 1855, there were 158 officers and 1,775 men killed; died of their wounds, fifty-one officers and 1,548 men; died of cholera, thirty-five officers and 4,244 men; died of other diseases up to the 31st of December, 1855, twenty officers and 11,425 men; died of their wounds up to the 31st of March, last, 322 men—making a total loss by death of 270 officers and 19,314 men. In the same time there were discharged from the service as incapacitated from disease and wounds, altogether, 2,873 men, making a total loss of 22,467 men killed, died of their wounds, and discharged, up to the 31st of March.

"In regard to the other powers, Lord Panmure made the following statement: The losses of the French computed at 60,000 men, and the loss of the Turks and Sardinians was not reported. Of the Russians, Count Orloff admitted at Paris that the total loss of men to the Russian army had not fallen short of 500,000.

"If this estimate is correct, 650,000 men have from first to last fallen victims to the Eastern war."

Immediately after the close of the Eastern war, Great Britain became involved in conflicts with Persia, and China. These troubles (March, 1857), are still unsettled.

†THE ARISTOCRATIC SYSTEM.

"The object of government is a very simple affair. It is protection of the people, by a union of the people. All are shareholders in this great company of citizens; all have an equal interest in its prosperity; and all ought to be equally represented in it, as in other joint stock companies of far less importance. But see how things are now contrived! The aristocracy have got into their hands the entire management of the government; and as they find it works exceedingly well for them, they determine to keep things as they are. In fact, nothing short of a revolution will frighten them into compliance with the requirements of right and justice.

The British empire furnishes the highest model of Monarchy, the best specimen of Aristocracy, the most favorable example of a State Church to be found in the world; yet if we may take facts supplied by herown publications, it appears that the loyal, confiding people of the three kingdoms have hardly realized all the blessings which the vaunted "British constitution," seems to promise.

"They have possession of nearly all the landed property of the country, which they bind up in their own families by laws of entail and primogeniture. They hold possession of the church, with its revenues of nearly ten millions sterling annually, into which they thrust their brothers, sons, and toadies; for, the landed estates going to the eldest sons, the other branches must be quartered on the people, who have no means of resistance. They also keep up an enormous armed force, which, for the same reason, is officered by their relatives, who are well pensioned for figuring in red coats and gold epaulets. For them, expensive places in connection with the government are created with large retiring salaries, comfortable governorships and embassies abroad, and a host of costly offices about the court and the royal person. The people pay for all! The aristocracy levy the taxes — the people pay them. Two thirds of the entire taxation of the country are paid by that immense majority of the British empire, who have no representation whatever in the British parliament.

"*Narrow Limits and Inequality of the Representation.* — The total number of electors in Great Britain and Ireland does not average above one million for twenty-eight millions of people.

"In England, the franchise is held by only one in every nineteen of the gross population; in Scotland, by one in thirty; and in Ireland by one in forty-three.

"In England, only one male adult in seven is represented; in Scotland, only one in eleven; in Ireland, only one in seventeen.

"That is, more than seven eighths of the male adult population of Great Britain are altogether unrepresented, and are compelled to obey the laws, and to pay the taxes, made and granted by the representatives of the remaining one seventh. . . . .

"By the present system, it is so arranged that a majority of the house of commons is actually elected by one fifth of the total registered electors of Great Britain. This one fifth, or less than two hundred thousand electors, are so under the thumb of the aristocracy, that independent action is scarcely to be expected from them: slaves they are, and as slaves they act. . . . .

"By statements before the public, it appears that three millions of inhabitants of the richest and most enterprising towns in Britain are represented by only thirty-two members, whereas one hundred and thirty-two thousand inhabitants of twenty-four of the poorest and most decaying towns in the kingdom have no fewer than forty-eight representatives. These twenty-four small towns have a total population amounting to only about one half of that of Manchester; and yet they have forty-eight representatives, while Manchester has only two! These twenty-four dirty little nests of aristocratic corruption and monopoly have more voting power in the house of commons than the vast towns and cities of London, Glasgow, Bristol, Manchester, Leeds, Edinburgh, Sheffield, and Birmingham.

"Illustrations of the gross inequality of the system could be multiplied, had we space. We could enumerate a list of seventy small English boroughs, whose united constituencies amount to only twenty-six thousand five hundred, which send an equal number of members to parliament as the entire Irish people. Three hundred and sixty-seven members, or a majority of the house of commons, are elected by less than two hundred thousand electors, or about one fifth of the constituency, and one one hundred and fortieth part of the gross population of the United Kingdom. One half of the entire house are elected by towns of under ten thousand inhabitants; sixty-eight are elected by boroughs under five thousand each.

"*The Aristocratic House of Commons.* — How this system works is rendered clear enough by the complexion of the lower house of parliament, which contains about two hundred and fifty persons immediately or remotely related to the peers of the realm. It contains six marquises, seven earls, twenty-one viscounts, thirty-four lords, twenty-five right honorables, forty-seven honorables, fifty-six baronets, nine knights, eight lord lieutenants, seventy-four deputy and vice-lieutenants fifty-three magistrates, sixty-three placemen, one hundred and eight patrons of church livings; and then there are the military pensioners in addition to these, for whom large and increasing standing armies are to be kept up in time of peace, namely: three admirals, three lieutenant-generals, three major-generals, twenty-two colonels, twenty-eight lieutenant-colonels, sixteen majors, forty-three captains in the army and navy, twenty-one lieutenants in the same, and four cornets. In short, there are scarcely two hundred out of the six hundred and fifty-eight members, who have not either titles, office, place, pension, church patronage, or immediate relatives deriving large sums annually from established government abuses.

"We shall find corruption, in all its forms, the issue of this system — the grossest and rankest corruption in state and church, which this corrupt representative system is expressly contrived to uphold. And in addition to this corrupt house of commons, it is also to be kept in mind that the aristocracy have the other house — the lords — in their exclusive possession, constituted, as it is, of peers, bishops, and pensioned lawyers, whose interests are bound up with the existing system.

"When this is kept in mind, it will be no matter for surprise that there should be so many enormous public abuses to complain of — so many pensioners — so many bishops and over-paid clergy — so many ambassadors, governors, generals, and colonels — so many commissions invented — so many secretaries and under secretaries, and all sorts of officials; nor will it be wondered at if it be found that the high and titled classes, under such circumstances, have taken particularly good care to make the working classes, who are not represented, pay for the support of their system — taxing them in every thing they consume, but especially exempting landed property from the special burdens and taxes which they fix upon those who have no property but their labor.

"*Aristocratic Government.* — The object and *animus* of the entire system is but too apparent. Government in this country is not a union of the people to protect themselves, but an aristocratic contrivance to make the poor men keep the rich — to compel industry to maintain idleness — to make rich men richer, and poor men poorer.

"The aristocratic spirit pervades our entire legislation. The aristocracy control and constitute both houses of parliament. They are the governors; they make the laws; they impose the taxes; they establish monopolies; they command the army; they draw the puppet strings about the throne; they are 'the state.'

"*Aristocracy* means the *best class*. But are they so? Are they not for the most part corrupted by their inordinate wealth, and the unjust means by which it is obtained? Is not their profligacy habitual? though we admit there are illustrious exceptions. But who, that knows any thing of the peerage, does not know of their profligate loves, their gamblings in hells and at races, their depraved politics, their recklessness in running into debt, the corruption they practise at elections, and their numerous other vices?

"They are not industrious men; they are merely consumers and destroyers, game-preservers and rent-exacters. They do not teach any thing, but themselves stand much in need of being taught. They do not set any good moral example before the people; but are generally wasteful, extravagant, sensual, and often vicious and mean. They do not promote religion, but set it at nought. Though they present fat livings to priests, and patronize rich bishops, they consider themselves absolved from all engagements to religion, or its practical duties. They live in an atmosphere of fraud, flattery, falsehood, and corruption, from birth till death. The parasite tutor continues what the parasite nurse began, and toadies, sycophants, place-hunters, and the tribe of adulators who constantly hang on the skirts of 'nobility,' poison and extinguish the last remnants of manly virtue and honest independence in the aristocratic mind.

"The English aristocracy seem to be utterly ignorant of the people, and of the country which they govern. Notwithstanding the progress of the age, and the revolutions bursting out in every country in Europe, they obstinately determine to stand still. They are intent on governing us only after the old feudal fashion. They make no allowance for the earnest

We readily admit the national glory of the British empire; we do full justice to the high pitch of civilization attained by a large portion of the people; we acknowledge that the basis of English character, law, opinion, and policy is that of justice and right. We admit the greatness of the Anglo-Saxon race and name, and we glory in it. We are ready to maintain that England has been the bulwark of truth, religion, and sound principles, and the disseminator of these, through her literature, her orators, and her colonies,

minds and burning hearts of the men of this period. They have neither eyes to see, nor hearts to feel, nor brains to comprehend, the wants of modern society. They understand nothing of the tendencies of the age. The little mind they have is made up only about this — that they will stand where they are, and never, so long as they are able to resist, give up their right to plunder the people of the fruits of their industry. . . . .

"What is the number of this aristocratic class? We find this answer in the fact that the whole land of England is monopolized by not more than thirty thousand proprietors; that the soil of Scotland is monopolized by three thousand proprietors; that the soil of Ireland is monopolized by probably not more than six thousand persons. To show how this land monopoly, with its entail laws, has been sweeping round us, it may be stated that, in 1780, the number of landed proprietors in England was about two hundred and fifty thousand, instead of thirty thousand, as now; and the process of absorption is is still going on rapidly. And look at the fruits of this: an enormous population of hungry laborers engaged in gathering together wealth and taxes for the small and idle class who own the land — one million and a half of actual paupers in England, and three millions of actual paupers in Ireland, testifying to the accursed influence of this monstrous aristocratic system. . . . .

EXPENSES OF ROYALTY.

"The queen's privy purse, salaries of the household, tradesmen's bills, royal bounty, &c.	$1,960,825
Prince Albert's annuity,	150,000
" " " as field marshal and colonel,	40,000
[An appropriation of secret service money is also made to Prince Albert, to a considerable amount annually, which of course we have no means of estimating.]	
The duke of Cumberland, (king of Hanover,)	105,000
The duke of Cambridge,	135,000
The duchess of Gloucester,	80,000
The princess Sophia,	80,000
Adelaide, the queen dowager,	500,000
Duchess of Kent,	150,000
Leopold, king of the Belgians,	250,000
[This sum is still annually voted, but is not at present appropriated. King Leopold still has it as a reserve to fall back upon, in case he should have to spend the evening of his days in England with his amiable father-in-law, Louis Philippe.]	
Prince George of Cambridge,	30,000
Princess Augusta Caroline of Cambridge,	15,000
[This disgusting job was perpetrated in 1843, on the occasion of the marriage of this lady with a son of a pensioner on English bounty, the 'hereditary grand duke of Mecklenberg-Strelitz.' His father was nephew to Queen Charlotte, and because of this, the English people must pension him.]	
	$3,495,825

'*Royal Palaces and Gardens. — Expenses of Maintenance*, 1838–1842. (Parliamentary Return, March 23, 1842.)

St. James's Palace — expended from parliamentary grants,	$150,000
Royal Mews, Pimlico — parl. grants,	30,000
Kensington Palace — parl. grants,	70,000
Kensington Gardens — parl. grants,	15,000
" " crown revenues voted by parl.,	30,000
Carlton stables, exterior repair — parl. grants,	2,000
Hampton Court Palace — parl. grants,	130,000
Hampton Court Gardens — crown rev.,	20,000
Hampton Court stud-house — parl. grants,	5,000
Kew Palace and buildings — parl. grants,	35,000
Kew Gardens — parl. grants,	50,000
" " crown rev.,	65,000
Buckingham Palace — parl. grants,	170,000
" " crown rev.,	7,000
" " garden — crown rev.,	35,000
Royal Pavilion, Brighton — parl. grants,	42,000
Windsor Castle, Brighton — parl. grants,	140,000
Windsor Frogmore Mansion — parl. grants,	7,000
Windsor new riding-house and stables — crown rev.,	350,000
Windsor new kitchen garden; Frogmore do. — crown rev.,	110,000
Holyrood Palace — parl. grants,	5,000
Linlithgow Palace — parl grants,	1,000
Royal Parks. — Hyde, St. James's, and Green Parks — crown rev.,	380,000
Regent's Park — crown rev.,	130,000
Greenwich Park — crown rev.,	25,000
Richmond Park — crown rev.,	170,000
Hampton Court and Bushy Park,	75,000
Windsor Great Park and farm buildings — crown rev.,	450,000
Ascot royal stand and stables — crown rev.,	12,000
Ascot kennel for the royal stag hounds — crown rev.,	6,000
Phœnix Park, Dublin — crown rev.,	220,000
Old deer park at Kew — crown rev.,	5,000
Total public money spent in five years on royal palaces, gardens, stables, pleasure-grounds and parks,	2,942,000
If we deduct from this gross amount the sums expended on the parks in and about London — Hyde, St. James's, Green, Regent's, Greenwich, Hampton, and Richmond Parks — so aptly called the 'lungs' of London, — and also on the Phœnix Park at Dublin, and the petty sums spent in maintaining the two Royal Palaces in Scotland, or	1,175,000
There remains a sum of	1,767,000
spent on royal accommodation in five years, or an average per year of, in round numbers,	350,000
which, together with the royal salaries and expenses as above,	3,495,825
Gives the annual direct cost of royalty in England as	$3,845,825

"*The Royal Pensioners.* — But we go a little farther, and we find tacked upon the skirts of royalty a host of titled pensioners of all sorts, from the nurses and dancing-masters of royal infancy, to the ladies of bed-chambers, grooms of stole, and ushers of all sorts of colored rods. The servants of all deceased sovereigns, besides having been paid very exorbitant salaries during the period of their service, are pensioned off by a most simple process — that of dipping the official finger into the public pocket. [The shocking details under this head we omit for want of space.]

"*Salaries of the Upper Servants of Royalty. — Civil List.*

Lord chamberlain,	$10,000	Four equerries in ordinary, 3,750 each	$15,000
Lord steward,	10,000	Mistress of the robes,	2,500
Master of the horse,	10,000	Eight ladies of the bedchamber, 2,500 each,	20,000
Master of the buckhounds,	8,500	Eight maids of honor, 2,000 each,	16,000
Master of the household,	5,790	Eight lords in waiting, 3,510 each,	27,000
Vice-chamberlain,	4,620	Eight grooms in waiting, about 1,675 each,	13,400
Treasurer of the household,	4,520		
Comptroller of the do.,	4,520		
Chief equerry and clerk marshal,	5,000		

"The coachmen, postilions, and footmen of the queen alone cost $62,815 per annum, or within $20,000 of the entire salaries of the executive government of the United States! The eight lords in waiting alone receive a sum more than the annual salary of the president of the American republic! The following statement is curious: —

over the four quarters of the globe. We hope, and we believe, that in the future onward march of mankind, she is still destined to act an efficient and conspicuous part. The nation that speaks the language of Shakspeare and Milton; that has given birth to Chatham, Fox, and Burke; that cherishes the memory of Hampden and Howard, can never fall into decrepitude or cease to hold a high commission for the benefit of man till truth and justice shall triumph on earth. But admitting all this, it is impossible not to see, that

"*Expenditure of the Lord Steward (or head cook) of the Royal Household, for One Year. — Civil List.*

Bread,	$10,250	Ale and beer,	$14,055
Butter, bacon, cheese, and eggs,	24,880	Wax candles,	9,885
Milk and cream,	7,390	Tallow candles,	3,395
Butchers' meat,	47,360	Lamps,	23,300
Poultry,	18,165	Fuel,	34,230
Fish,	9,895	Stationery,	4,120
Grocery,	23,220	Turnery,	1,895
Oilery,	8,965	Braziery,	4,450
Fruit and Confectionary,	8,705	China, glass, &c.,	6,640
Vegetables,	2,435	Linen,	5,425
Wine,	24,250	Washing Table Linen,	15,650
Liquors, &c.,	9,215	Plate,	1,775
			$319,535

"*The Crown.* — We must not omit mention of the royal bauble worn by the queen on the state display of opening the houses of parliament. The following estimate of the value of the jewels in this 'magnificent diadem,' we quote from the *Polytechnic Review*: —

Twenty diamonds round the circle, $7,500 each,	$150,000
Two large centre diamonds, $10,000 each,	20,000
Fifty-four smaller diamonds, placed at the angle of the former,	500
Four crosses, each composed of twenty-five diamonds,	60,000
Four large diamonds on the top of the crosses,	200,000
Twelve diamonds contained in fleurs-de-lis,	50,000
Eighteen smaller diamonds contained in the same,	10,000
Pearls, diamonds, &c., upon the arches and crosses,	50,000
Also one hundred and forty-one small diamonds,	2,500
Twenty-six diamonds in the upper cross,	15,000
Two circles of pearls about the rim,	1,500
Cost of the stones in the crown, exclusive of the metal,	$559,500

COST OF THE GOVERNMENT.

"The cost of the civil government of Great Britain, as exhibited in the parliamentary returns, also moved for and obtained by Mr. Williams, and ordered to be printed by the house of commons, 27th July, 1843, stands as follows: —

The royal civil list — privy purse; salaries of the household and tradesmen's bills, (paid by the people,)	$1,859,000
The allowances to the principal branches of the royal family,	1,590,000
The lord lieutenant of Ireland's establishment,	152,770
The salaries and expenses of the houses of parliament,	619,235
Civil departments — salaries, &c., including superannuation allowances,	2,623,865
Other annuities, pensions, and superannuation allowances,	1,563,205
Pensions, civil list,	25,600
Total annual cost of executive,	$8,433,675

Pension List. — The most extraordinary topic in the whole range of British finances, is that of pensions. Some of these items are not a little shocking, particularly those which show the sums paid for mistresses and illegitimate children of the royalty and nobility. Other items make it appear that many of the British noblemen, of the very highest rank, receive various sums, from five to fifty thousand dollars a year, for no service rendered whatever. Some of these pensions have descended for centuries. The following is an instance selected from many of a similar kind: —

"Duke of Grafton, another hereditary pensioner, is paid annually out of the excise revenues $42,000; and out of the post-office revenues $17,000. The original pensioner was one of the numerous illegitimate offspring of Charles II.; for whose royal amours the people of this age are still called on to pay. These pensions have now been paid to the dukes of Grafton for a period of one hundred and seventy-three years; so that the maintenance of this single peerage alone has cost the English people, in hard cash, no less a sum than ten million two hundred and eighty-eight thousand two hundred and ninety dollars.

"In the majority of the pensions, they are given 'in consideration of the circumstances of the parties.' The question will occur, 'Why don't their rich and titled relatives keep them?' When a man or woman, in the humbler ranks of life, is overtaken by poverty, do they go at once to the parish board for relief? Do they not exhaust every possible resource before throwing themselves on the poor's rates? Do they not endeavor to find employment, and make an honest living? But it is not so with the proud, poverty-stricken aristocrats. They will not work — they look to the laboring classes to keep them — the interest of their titled friends is put in motion — and they secure pensions varying from five hundred to fifteen thousand dollars a year. Here, in this list, we find the sisters of the rich duke of Sutherland quartered as paupers on the country! What working-man is there in the receipt of decent wages, what shopkeeper is there, who would stoop to so beggarly a resource as a maintenance for his poor and idle relatives out of the poor's rates, levied on the hard-working and the indigent? But in the case of this aristocracy, they resort at once to the taxes without a blush. In them the extremes meet, of 'nobility' and meanness.

"The total number of government employés at present is about twenty-four thousand; of which the eight hundred and forty-one pensioners and employés divide among them above seven million and a half yearly. This does not include either the public officials in the law courts, the royal household, the colonies, or under most of the commissions, which would enormously swell the number.

"*Expenditure on the War Men.* — The amount expended annually on the military class, and their gory captains, the offshoots of the aristocracy, is positively frightful. . . . .

"Since the close of the war in 1815, no less than five hundred and forty-nine millions of pounds sterling — two thousand seven hundred and fifty millions of dollars — have been spent in keeping up our fighting establishment, mainly because the brothers and sons of the aristocracy may wear epaulets, or, what is more to the purpose, be maintained at the public cost." . . . .

As one item under this head, we give the following: —

"Grand total cost of the duke of Wellington to the country, fourteen millions of dollars!

"We need scarcely add, that the emoluments of the duke's sons, nephews, sons-in-law, and other relations, from the army, the church, and the pension list, are enormous.

"*Aristocratic Taxation.* — How is the money got to keep up all this extravagance? By a very simple process — that of thrusting the hand into the public purse, and keeping it there. The aristocracy don't ask the consent of those whom they tax; indeed, they take particular care to keep them out of their counsel as much as possible: they simply tax us, and make us pay, having at their back a tremendous posse of policemen, soldiers, and diabolical agencies of all sorts. What can we do but pay? We may grin and grind our teeth; but pay we must. . . . .

"*Exemption of the Landed Class from Taxation.* — Then, see how carefully the aristocratic classes have contrived to evade the payment of their due share of the taxation of the country. In all other states of Europe, even those considered the most 'despotic,' the chief portion of taxation is raised, as it ought to be, from the land. But in England, the land contributes little or nothing to the general taxation; the landowners have taken care of that. Thus, —

In Great Britain,	Land tax,	$5,915,000	
	Other taxes — (1847)	247,160,000	
			$253,075,000
In France,	Land tax,	116,250,000	
	Other taxes, (no income tax,)	87,500,000	
			203,750,000

the British government has not attained that perfect happiness of the people under its charge, which some of its admirers would seem to claim. The evils of the political system have been wrought into the very fabric of society, — thus corrupting even the fountains of religion and morality. The leaders of the church have been convicted of greediness and tergiversation in the national legislature, and have hardly deemed it necessary to make a show of defence. Men of the highest rank in the kingdom hesitate not to roll

In Prussia,......	Land tax,......	19,970,000	
	Other taxes,....	18,335,000	
			38,305,000
In Austria,......	Land tax,......	38,985,000	
	Other taxes,....	38,500,000	
			77,485,000

"Thus, in France, Prussia, and Austria, half of the entire revenues of the governments of those countries is derived from the land; whereas in aristocratic Britain, only five dollars in every one hundred and sixty-five raised by taxation is derived from this source. The taxes are mainly raised upon articles in daily consumption by the working classes, who are not represented; fully two thirds of the whole revenue being extorted from those who are the least able to bear the imposition of taxes; while the rich both exempt themselves, and spend the taxes so raised in the most riotous recklessness and extravagance. . . . .

"*What the Poor Man pays in Taxes.* — A case, showing the oppressive incidence of taxation, as now arranged on the poor man, was laid before parliament in 1842: —

"William Gladstone, a laborer, earned $2 75 a week, and expended $1 81 on food, as follows: one ounce of tea, two ounces of coffee, eight ounces of sugar, eight ounces of meal, eight pounds of flour, seven pints of ale, and one quarter of a pint of brandy.

The cost of these articles, free from excise and customs duties, was....................................	$0 56
Excise and customs taxes,..........................	1 25
	$1 81

"Thus, about one half of the entire wages of this laboring man, or $65 out of $140 yearly, was extorted from him by government taxation; whereas the aristocrat of $500,000 a year was not called on to contribute to the purposes of the state more than five per cent. per annum of his immense income.

"The taxation imposed on the British people is the highest in the world! Take, for example, the following instances: —

Taxation per head, for every man, woman, and child in England,....................................				$13 00
Do.	do.	do.	the United States,..	2 25
Do.	do.	do.	Russia,........	2 25
Do.	do.	do.	Austria,........	2 75
Do.	do.	do.	Prussia,........	3 00
Do.	do.	do.	France,........	6 00

"What is the gross result of the British aristocratic system? This — that on the one hand, we have a small and idle class monopolizing all the lands, monopolizing the government, and its immense patronage, regarding the right to legislate hereditarily as their birthright, imposing laws, raising taxes, and spending them to the amount of more than two hundred and fifty millions annually; and on the other hand, we have a vast industrious population, working from morn till night, often for the scantiest wages, deprived of all political power, but compelled to obey the laws, to pay the taxes, and to furnish, out of their very misery and wretchedness, the greatest part of the national revenue, which is expended in the families of the rich aristocracy themselves, all tending to the accumulation of vast aggregations of wealth on the one hand, and wide wastes of poverty and suffering on the other. . . . .

THE CHURCH.

"This is another of the costly aristocratic institutions of the country. Church revenues were originally divided into three parts, — the first part for the maintenance of the priesthood, the second for the maintenance and repair of the fabric of the church, and the third for the relief of the poor. But the clergy, aided by their patrons, the aristocracy, have contrived to throw the maintenance of the fabrics on the people in the form of church rates, and the maintenance of the poor also on the people in the form of poor rates, — while the clergy have comfortably gobbled up all! . . . .

"And here we must say, that the state church does not in any respect represent the spirit of Christianity as handed down to the disciples. It represents the spirit of Mammon, not of Jesus. Its God is money — rich benefices — hard cash. The principles of the New Testament, read from its pulpits, are openly set at defiance. Rank, practical infidelity is the practice of the church. . . . .

"The twenty-five state bishops of England divide among them annually, as shown by a late parliamentary return, the sum of nine hundred thousand dollars! The sums which they leave behind them at their death are enormous. From another parliamentary return, it is proved, as stated in the house of commons by Captain Osborne, that eleven Irish state bishops left behind them amassed wealth to the amount of nine million three hundred and seventy-five thousand dollars, accumulated within a period of from forty to fifty years! The following is the list extracted from the parliamentary return: —

"*Probates of Wills of Irish Bishops.*

Stopford, bishop of Cork,....................	$125,000
Percy, bishop of Dromore,..................	200,000
Cleaver, bishop of Ferns,....................	250,000
Bernard, bishop of Limerick,................	300,000
Knox, bishop of Killaloe,....................	500,000
Fowler, bishop of Dublin,....................	750,000
Beresford, bishop of Tuam,..................	1,250,000
Hawkins, bishop of Raphoe,................	1,250,000
Stuart, bishop of Armagh,....................	1,500,000
Porter, bishop of Clogher,....................	1,250,000
Agar, bishop of Cashel,......................	2,000,000
Making a total of........................	$9,375,000

"How great, indeed, must have been the privations of the apostolic bishop of Cashel, through which he could save two million dollars in a single life, from the tribute levied on the poorest, worst fed, and worst clad, of all the nations on the face of the earth! How much charity and Christian virtue must the prelates of Dublin, Tuam, Armagh, and Clogher, have exercised, to enable them to hoard up fortunes of from seven hundred and fifty thousand to one million five hundred thousand dollars apiece. And these are the bishops of the church of Ireland, for which we are now keeping up an army in that country of thirty-four thousand soldiers, besides an army of police, to mount guard over its safety. . . . .

"*The Revenues of the English Church.* — It is difficult to get at an exact estimate of the total revenues of the English church. Churchmen have always been exceedingly loath to give any information on this subject; they have prevaricated, and even told lies without any scruple, when the government has made inquiries on the subject. Thus, in 1835, when the ecclesiastical commission was called on to make a return of the incomes of the clergy to parliament, they gave the net revenues of the church at only seventeen million two hundred and eighty-four thousand, two hundred and fifty-five dollars. But since then the tithe commutation act has come into operation, and now it became the interest of the clergy to claim as much as possible, forgetting their previous return. What has been the consequence? That the income of the church from tithes only at once became swelled out to double the total amount they had given in a few years before; the tithe commissioners having reported, some time ago, that the tithes uncommuted amounted to twenty-five million dollars a year, and the tithes commuted to seven million four hundred thousand dollars; making a gross sum of nearly thirty-two and a half million dollars. And if the tithes yet uncommuted be rated at the same value as those commuted, the annual income of the clergy, from tithes alone, will amount to at least forty million dollars a year. . . . .

"The items may be classified as follows: —

Church tithe, estimated at....................	$40,000,000
Income of the bishoprics, (according to the bishops themselves,)........................	1,030,235
Estates of the deans and chapters,............	2,470,000
Glebes and parsonage houses,.................	1,250,000
Perpetual curacies,...........................	375,000
Benefices not parochial,.....................	162,250
Church fees on burials, marriages, christenings, &c.,	2,500,000
Oblations, offerings, and composition for offerings,	400,000
College and school foundations,...............	3,410,750

in luxury and splendor, the fruit of money taken from the public treasury, for which they offer no equivalent, and no apology but custom and the law; while at the same time half a million of people perish in their midst from destitution and famine. And yet, with all these contrasts and contradictions, Great Britian displays an energy which nothing can overcome, and a steady progress which nothing can arrest.

Lectureships in towns and populous places,....	300,000
Chaplainships and offices in public institutions, (very much underrated,) at	50,000
New churches and chapels,....................	472,500
	$52,420,735

"*Revenues of the Bishops.* — Let us see how the item appropriated by the bishops is divided; and we shall find the practical exemplification which they hold forth to their flocks, of 'laying not up treasures upon earth,' and of their injunction that 'the love of money is the root of all evil.' The following is taken from a return made to parliament in May, 1845; and from what is known of the prevarication of these gentry on a previous occasion, there is every reason to believe that the revenues are considerably understated: —

Archbishop of Canterbury,........	revenue in 1843,	$138,525
" York,...............	"	100,705
Bishop of London,...............	"	67,595
" Durham,...............	"	112,080
" Winchester,............	"	57,995
" St. Asaph,..............	"	40,420
" Bangor,................	"	37,335
" Bath and Wells,........	"	14,835
" Carlisle,...............	"	12,380
" Chester,...............	"	9,465
" Chichester,.............	"	32,595
" St. David's,............	"	23,760
" Ely,....................	"	32,430
" Exeter,................	"	5,460
" Gloucester and Bristol,..	"	26,130
" Hereford,...............	"	29,680
" Lichfield,..............	"	47,500
" Lincoln,...............	"	28,050
" Llandaff,...............	"	4,450
" Norwich,...............	"	43,825
" Oxford,................	"	12,530
" Peterborough,..........	"	20,300
" Ripon,.................	"	23,815
" Rochester,..............	"	5,510
" Salisbury,..............	"	64,395
" Worcester,..............	"	36,470
Total,...........................		$1,030,235

"As many of the bishops, however, derive salaries from sinecure livings besides their bishoprics, the sums here set down do not at all represent the sum total of their incomes. . . . .

"*The State Church of England in Ireland.* — However we may have kept patience while going over the list of enormities above detailed, we confess that we lose all patience when we come to speak of the English badge of conquest and plunder in Ireland — the blood-besmeared church of 'Rathcormac.' This church has been described by Mr. Macaulay as 'the most utterly absurd and indefensible of all the institutions now existing in the civilized world;' and by Mr. Roebuck,— a man found too fearless and honest for the aristocratic house of commons, — as 'the greatest ecclesiastical enormity in Europe.' . . . .

"The Irish church monstrosity may be displayed in a very few words. There are in Ireland eight million one hundred and seventy-five thousand one hundred and twenty-four persons, two million three hundred and eighty-five thousand of whom are absolute paupers. Three million four hundred and seventy thousand seven hundred and twenty-five persons live in mud cabins, or hovels, containing one apartment only, and of which the door is at once chimney, window, and entrance. The wages of the great mass of the population average from eight cents to twenty-one cents a day in the west and south, and from seventeen cents to twenty-four cents a day in the north. Of the total population, three million seven hundred and sixty-six thousand and sixty-six are returned as unable to read or write — for the poor Irish have been left to the 'blessings' of the voluntary system of education!

"In December, 1843, the military force in Ireland consisted of twenty-one thousand two hundred and ten soldiery, two thousand three hundred and fifty naval warriors, and nine thousand and forty-three armed police; or a total of thirty-two thousand six hundred and three men. The number has since been increased by about ten thousand additional military, and one thousand armed police, — making a total of above forty thousand armed men. — Next we come to the religious professions of the people. Of the eight million of people, seven million are Catholics, and seven hundred thousand are Episcopalians; that is, belong to the Rathcormac church. For this fraction of the Irish people, or rather the English people in Ireland, a gorgeous state church is kept up, which the wretched, impoverished, and starving Irish poor, who are Catholics, are compelled to pay for: if they refuse to pay, the church at once plays Rathcormac with them.

"*The Revenues of the 'Rathcormac Church.'*

Archbishops and bishoprics,.................	$755,638
Deans and chapters,.........................	113,121
Glebe lands,................................	460,000
Tithe composition,..........................	2,658,908
Minister's money,...........................	50,000
	$4,037,667

"It will be observed that the amount of hard cash divided by the Irish bishops amounts to seven hundred and fifty-five thousand six hundred and thirty-eight dollars annually; but this represents only a small portion of their actual gains! For there must also be added the rents and profits from six hundred and seventy thousand acres of land. . . . .

"And next, as to the work done by the parsons. Of the two thousand three hundred and eighty-four parishes, one hundred and fifty-five have no church, and not a single Protestant inhabitant; and eight hundred and ninety-five parishes have under fifty Protestant Episcopalians inhabiting them, including men, women, and children. They are not on that account, however, relieved from their payments to the church, which are still compulsorily exacted. Of thirteen hundred and eighty-five benefices, there are two hundred and thirty-three with under fifty Protestants in each. Of the three hundred dignities and prebends, seventy-five have no duties whatever to perform, and eighty-six others are mere sinecures. The dean of Raphoe receives $7455, the precentor of Lismore $2240, the archdeacon of Meath, $3655, without any duties whatever to perform, there being no Protestant souls to 'cure.' The following table of seven benefices may give an idea of the present monstrous state of things in different parts of Ireland: —

Benefices.	*No. of Protestants.*	*Clergymen.*	*Church.*	*Tithes.*
Modeligo (union),	4	0	0	$2,200
Seckeinane,......	3	0	0	1,675
Clerme,.........	17	0	0	2,800
Effin,...........	10	0	0	1,000
Gilbertstown,....	8	0	0	1,250
Mahoonagh,.....	8	0	0	2,500
Kileedy,.........	12	0	0	2,420
	62	0	0	$14,445

"Thus we have here sixty-two Protestants, who cost the people of these parishes two hundred and thirty-three dollars per head, though they have neither church nor pastor. The tithes, however, are extorted. Then we have another set of parishes in the bishopric of Cloyne, in which the cost of each Protestant Episcopalian man, woman, and child, is one hundred and forty dollars per head.

"It is scarcely necessary that we should proceed further in the exposure of this monster enormity. For the present, the above brief facts must suffice; but when we ponder them, need we feel surprise that such a system as this — thoroughly black and corrupt — unredeemed by a single good feature — should have issued in beggary and wretchedness to the Irish people, and kept that nation hanging upon the brink of rebellion ever since it has been connected with the British aristocratic government!"

CENTRAL & SOUTHERN
EUROPE
Scale of Miles
50
100
150
200
NORWAY
NORTH SEA
SWEDEN
BALTIC SEA
L. Wenner
Wetter
Skager Rack
Riga
Memel
Konigsberg
Tilsit
Wilna
Smolensk
Grodno
Dantzic
Coslin
Elbing
Elau
EAST
PRUSSIA
WEST
PRUSSIA
Soldau
Thorn
Vistula R.
R. Bug
Pripet R.
Warsaw
POLAND
Lublin
Ringkiobing
Flensburg
Bornholm
Rugen
Stettin
Colberg
Wismar
Kiel
HOLSTEIN
Lubec
Hamburg
Bremen
Oldenburg
HANOVER
Amsterdam
Rotterdam
Ostend
Antwerp
BRUSSELS
Waterloo
Namur
Cologne
Coblentz
Luxemburg
Munster
Detmold
Brunswick
Potsdam
BERLIN
Magdeburg
Frankfort
Posen
Rogasen
Kroben
Glogau
Breslau
Oppeln
PRUSSIA
SAXONY
Leipzic
Dresden
Weimar
Gotha
Cassel
Gottingen
Hesse
Mentz
Darmstadt
Frankfort
Wurtzburg
Amberg
Nuremberg
Ratisbon
Anspach
CARLSRUHE
Baden
STUTGARD
Hechingen
Augsburg
MUNICH
Passau
Prague
Culm
Tabor
Budweis
Czaslau
Glatz
BOHEMIA
MORAVIA
Brunn
Austerlitz
CRACOW
Jaroslaw
Wieliczka
GALICIA
Lemberg
Brody
Stry
Bochnia
Neusohl
Kaschau
Kremnitz
Linz
LOWER AUSTRIA
VIENNA
Wagram
UPPER AUSTRIA
Salzburg
Gran
Buda
Pesth
Debretzin
Dees
Clausenburg
Gyula
Szegedin
TRANSYLVANIA
Hermanstadt
Carpathian Mt.
Tchernowitz
Jassy
MOLDAVIA
Bender
Okna
Ismael
Fokchani
Brailow
Bucharest
WALLACHIA
Giurgevo
Silistria
Shumla
Varna
Danube R.
Dniester R.
Bog R.
Zurich
Constance
Lucerne
Geneva
SWITZERLAND
Sion
Bern
Innspruck
Bruck
Gratz
Vesprim
Platen See
AUSTRIA
Botzen
Trent
TYROL
Milan
LOMBARDY
VENICE
Verona
Padua
Mantua
Laybach
Trieste
Cilly
Agram
Essek
Petrinia
Brod
SCLAVONIA
Foldvar
Theresepol
Denta
Fiume
Turin
PIEDMONT
SARDINIA
Savigliano
Marengo
Voltri
Monaco
Nice
Parma
Modena
Bologna
Ferrara
Genoa
Lucca
FLORENCE
Pisa
Leghorn
TUSCANY
San Marino
Ancona
Fermo
Perugia
Pescara
ROME
Capua
Foggia
NAPLES
Mt. Vesuvius
Salerno
B. of Naples
Taranto
Otranto
Cozenza
Catanzaro
Reggio
Lipari Is.
Palermo
Trapani
Marsala
SICILY
Mt. Etna
Messina
Catania
Syracuse
Passaro
Malta
Valetta
Tunis
Bon
AFRICA
MEDITERRANEAN
CORSICA
Bastia
Ajaccio
Elba
Sassari
Oristagno
Cagliari
Tuelada
Zara
Mostar
DALMATIA
CROATIA
HERTZEK
BOSNIA
Serajevo
Zabatz
Belgrade
SERVIA
TURKEY
Widin
Nicopoli
BULGARIA
Sophia
Balkan Mount
Philippopolis
Adrianople
Bourgas
CONSTANTINOPLE
Silivria
Ragusa
Cattaro
Uskub
Seres
Philippi
Salonica
Berat
Mt. Olympus
Larissa
Butrinto
Joannina
Volo
Arta
Corfu
Sta Maura
Cephalonia
Zante
Missolonghi
Thebes
Patras
Corinth
Tripolizza
Navarino
GREECE
Cerigo
CANDIA
Lemnos
Metelin
ASIA MINOR
Str. of the Dardanelles
BLACK SEA
GULF OF VENICE

Germany.

Charlemagne crossing the Alps.

CHAPTER CCCCXLI.

Geographical Description — Government — Historical Outline.

GERMANY is bounded north by the German Ocean, Denmark, and the Baltic Sea; east by the Prussian provinces of Prussia and Posen, the kingdom of Poland, belonging to Russia, and the kingdoms of Gallicia and Hungary, belonging to Austria; south by the Adriatic Sea, Italy, and Switzerland; and west by France, Belgium, and the Netherlands.

The central and southern parts of Germany are traversed by several ranges of mountains. The mountains to the south of the Danube belong to the Alpine system, those on the north to the Carpathian system, which sends out numerous branches. The Hartz Mountains, belonging to the latter system, are the most northerly range. In these the celebrated Spectre of the Brocken is witnessed.* The northern part of the country is low and level, descending toward the North and Baltic Seas.

Germany is watered by five hundred rivers, sixty of which are navigable. The Danube flows through the southern part. The Weser, the Elbe, and the Oder are the principal German streams, and many of their tributaries are navigable rivers. The Rhine, which rises in Switzerland, and flows into the sea in the Netherlands, has but a part of its course in Germany.

The climate of Germany is modified by the elevation of the surface, and the exposure of the different sections. For purposes of general description, it may be divided into three regions. In the first, or that of the northern plains, the climate is humid and variable, though not cold: it is exposed to every wind which conveys fogs and storms from two seas. The northwestern plain, from its vicinity to the North Sea, is subject to frequent rains and desolating tempests, while the influence of the Baltic Sea on the north-eastern plain is less powerful, and the climate, though colder, is less variable. The second region comprehends all the central part of Germany, which is sheltered by the mountains from the variableness and humidity of the maritime climate. This zone, the most agreeable of Germany, extends from latitude 48° to 51°, but the general elevation of the surface renders it colder than other European countries of the same latitude. The third general division is the Alpine section; here the lofty heights and sudden depressions bring very different climates into contact with each other. The eternal glaciers of the Tyrol and Saltzburg are contiguous to the vine-covered valleys of Styria and Carinthia, and but little removed from the olive groves of Trieste and the ever-blooming gardens of Italy. Vines, rice, and maize thrive as far north as 54°; beyond that latitude they do not arrive at perfection. The olive and silk-worm are successfully raised only in that small part of Germany which lies south of 46°.

* The Spectre of the Brocken is an aerial figure, which has been seen and described by many travellers. One of these says, "Having ascended the Brocken—which is one of the peaks of the Hartz Mountains, in Hanover—for the thirtieth time, I was at length so fortunate as to have the pleasure of seeing this phenomenon. As I stood upon the peak of the mountain, I observed, at a great distance, a human figure of a monstrous size. A violent gust of wind having almost carried away my hat, I moved my hand toward my head, and the colossal figure did the same. I immediately made another movement by bending my body, when the figure before me repeated it. It vanished for a few moments, but again made its appearance. I then called the landlord of the neighboring inn, and, having both taken the position I had taken alone, we saw two gigantic figures, which repeated our compliments, by bending their bodies as we did, after which they finally disappeared."

The soil is generally productive. The plains in the north have, indeed, much arid land; but along the rivers are rich and fruitful soils, yielding abundant harvests. In the south, there is much barren or slightly productive land on the mountains; but the beautiful valleys and small plains rival in fertility the best alluvial lands on the banks of the northern rivers. In general, the soil in the north is heavy, and best adapted for corn; in the south, light, and best fitted for vines. The finest soil is in the central section, between the mountains and the sandy plains.

All religions are professed in Germany without restriction. Rather more than one half of the inhabitants are Roman Catholics, and above two fifths are Protestants. The Lutherans and Calvinists have been united, in many places, into one church, which takes the name of the *Evangelical Church.* There are some Mennonites, and Moravians or Herrnhutters. The Jews in Germany are about three hundred thousand.

The German confederacy was formed in 1815,* to protect the independence and secure the tranquillity of the states which entered into it. Thirty-four monarchical states and four republics, or free cities, were the parties to the federal act. The organ of the confederacy is the Diet composed of the plenipotentiaries of the sovereign members. It is constituted in two different forms: 1. The plenum, or general assembly, in which each member has at least one vote, and the great powers have several; Austria, Prussia, Bavaria, Saxony, Hanover, and Wirtemberg have each four votes; Baden, Hesse-Darmstadt, Hesse-Cassel, Denmark, (for Holstein and Lauenburg,) and the Netherlands, (for Luxemburg,) each three; Brunswick, Mecklenburg-Schwerin, and Nassau each two, and the others one each,† making seventy-one votes. 2. The ordinary diet is the other form of the assembly; in this there are but seventeen votes, the principal powers (the eleven first named above) having each one vote, and the others voting collectively. This body discusses all questions, and proposes them for adoption to the plenum, executes its decrees, and, in general, manages the affairs of the confederacy. The general assembly decides upon the propositions of the ordinary diet, makes war and peace, &c.

* The recent agitations in Europe have disturbed this arrangement, and may perhaps result in a permanent modification of the German confederation here noticed. It will be most convenient, however, in the present unsettled state of things, to base our historical and geographical notices upon this system. The following table gives a view of the German states forming the confederacy: —

POLITICAL DIVISIONS.

States.	*Rank.*	*Sq. M.*	*Pop.* 1861.	*Relig.*	*Capitals.*	*Pop.*
Austria, about one third part,.	Empire, ..	81,000	12,818,268	Cath.	Vienna, ...	476,000
Prussia, the greater part,.......	Kingdom,.	71,000	14,139,315	Prot.	Berlin,......	547,571
Bavaria,.........	...do.	28,435	4,689,000	Cath.	Munich, ...	148,201
Saxony, ...	...do.	5,705	2,255,240	Prot.	Dresden,....	128,152
Hanover, ...	...do.	14,600	1,888,070	do.	Hanover, ...	71,170
Wirtemberg, ...	...do.	7,568	1,785,952	do.	Stuttgard,...	56,108
Baden, ...	G. duchy,.	5,712	1,869,291	Cath.	Carlsruhe, ..	27,108
Hesse-Cassel, ...	Electorate,	4,386	726,686	Prot.	Cassel, ...	
Hesse-Darmstadt	G. duchy,.	3,198	856,250	do.	Darmstadt,..	
Hesse-Homburg,	Landgrav.	154	25,746	do.	Homburg,...	
Mecklenburg-Schwerin, ...	G. duchy,.	4,701	548,449	do.	Schwerin,...	
Mecklenburg-Strelitz, ...	...do.	1,094	99,060	do.	New Strelitz	
Holstein, } ..	Duchy, ...	3,168	544,419	do.	Gluckstadt, .	
Lauenburg, }		451	50,147	do.	Lauenburg, .	
Nassau, ...	..do.	1,736	449,050	do.	Wisbaden,..	
Luxemburg,.....	G. duchy,.	2,420	197,281	Cath.	Luxemburg,.	
Oldenburg,......	...do.	2,470	294,359	Prot.	Oldenburg,..	
Brunswick, ...	Duchy, ...	1,525	274,069	do.	Brunswick,..	40,635
Saxe-Weimar-Eisenach,.....	..do.	1,403	273,242	do.	Weimar,....	
Saxe-Meiningen-Hildb'ghausen,	..do.	880	172,841	do.	Meiningen,..	
Saxe-Coburg-Gotha, ...	..do.	790	153,879	do.	Gotha,......	16,609
Saxe-Altenburg,.	..do.	491	137,162	do.	Altenburg, ..	
Lippe-Detmold, .	Principal..	432	106,086	do.	Detmold,....	
Schauenburg-Lippe,........	...do. ...	205	80,144	do.	Buckeburg,..	
Schwartzburg-Rudolstadt, ...	...do.	366	70,030	do.	Rudolstadt,..	
Schwartzburg-Sondershausen,	...do.	396	62,972	do.	Sondershau'n	
Reuss-Lobenstein,.........	...do.	548	81,806	do.	Lobenstein, .	
Reuss-Greitz, ...	...do.	140	39,397	do.	Greitz,......	
Anhalt-Dessau,..	Duchy, ...	337	119,515	do.	Dessau,.....	
Anhalt-Bernburg,	..do.	336	56,031	do.	Bernburg, ..	
Anhalt-Cothen, .	..do.	316	53,000	do.	Cothen,.....	
Waldeck,.......	Principal..	455	57,550	do.	Corbach,....	
Hohenzollern-Sigmaringen,..	...do.	383	71,000	Cath.	Sigmaringen,	
Hohenzollern-Hechingen, ...	...do.	136	60,123	do.	Hechingen, ..	
Liechtenstein, ..	...do.	52	7,150	do.	Liechtenstein	
Hamburg,.......	Free city,.	149	229,941	Prot.	Hamburg, ...	
Frankfort, ...	...do.	91	83,380	do.	Frankfort, ..	
Bremen, ...	...do.	67	88,856	do.	Bremen, ...	
Lubeck, ...	...do.	142	55,423	do.	Lubec, ...	
Total, ...		247,438	44,998,75[illegible]			

The army of the confederation consists of three hundred thousand men, each state furnishing a contingent of troops proportionate to its population. There are several cities considered as federal fortresses: these are Luxemburg, Mayence, Landau, Ulm, &c

Nearly all the inhabitants of the confederacy are Germans, or descendants of the old Teutonic tribes, who have occupied the country ever since any thing has been known of its history. They call themselves *Deutschen*, and their country *Deutschland.* The language is various dialects of the German; that of the cultivated classes and of literature is the High German, which is nowhere spoken in its purity by the people. Various dialects of Low German are used in the northern districts. The Sclavonic inhabitants are chiefly in the German provinces of Austria and Prussia.

Germany has been often called the riddle of geographers; but to Americans, who are familiar with the idea of a general or national system, containing several distinct sovereignties, it is not of difficult comprehension. Germany, in its general signification, embraces the countries whose people are of German or Teutonic origin. Its boundaries are not based upon merely political divisions; and, consequently, in the German confederation only the German portions of Austria and Prussia are included.

In the history of Germany, we purpose first to give a sketch of the early settlers of the country, forming its ancient history. We then begin with the reign of Charlemagne the history of the German empire, which we trace to the era of the confederation: of this we give an account to the present time. We shall then notice the separate states of Germany.

CHAPTER CCCCXLII.

113 B. C. to A. D. 814.

History of Ancient Germany — Roman Invasions of Germany — Scythian Invasions — Annals — Charlemagne.

Ancient Germany had for its boundaries the North Sea and the Baltic, the Rhine and the Alps. On the east its limits were varied; sometimes the Germanic

† Kniphausen, however, is joined with Oldenburg, and Reuss-Schleitz with Reuss-Lobenstein, in voting.

The Spectre of the Brocken. (See p. 969.)

tribes pushed their conquests as far as the Black Sea; at other times they were driven back to the Vistula. The heaths and swamps, the cold and severe climate of this wide territory, were spoken of with horror by Romans, residents in sunny Italy. The wild tract called the *Hercynian Forest*, sixty days' journey in length and nine in breadth, stretching from Thorn on the Vistula nearly to Strasburg on the Rhine, presented a picture of gloom and dread to their imagination.

The Germanic tribes came from Central Asia, but when or how is conjectural. Little was known of them till Cæsar's time; in the next century Tacitus wrote a work upon them, and Pliny, soon after, divides them into the *Vindili*, (Burgundiones, Varini, Carini, and Gullones;) *Ingaevones*, (Cimbri, Teutones, and Chauci;) *Istaevones*, near the Rhine; *Hermiones*, in the centre, (Suevi, Hermunduri, Catti, and Cherusci;) *Peucini*, and *Bastarnæ*, bordering on Dacia. The Germans were of gigantic stature, with fair complexions, long yellow hair, and large, blue eyes, sometimes seen glaring fiercely from beneath a head-dress garnished with the grinning tusks of a boar, or the horns of a wild bull, or formed of the fur of some other beast, arranged in the shape of a hood. The religion of these fierce warriors accorded with their rude habits. They had no priesthood; they worshipped the sun, moon, and fire; the demigod Thuisco, the founder of the German race, whence we derive our words *Tuesday* and *Dutch;* the goddess Hertha, who dwelt in a sacred grove near a lake, in the Island of Rugen; Woden, the all-good, whence *Wednesday;* Thor, the god of war, who gives name to *Thursday;* and Fria, the goddess of marriage, whence *Friday*. At certain seasons, Hertha made her appearance to convert mankind: her magnificent chariot was drawn by white heifers to the shores of the island lake, where her person and chariot were washed by attendants, assisted by slaves, who were put to death as soon as the ceremony was concluded. It was believed, also, that after death, the departed heroes of the nation entered a place called *Walhalla*, or the "hall of the dead," where they passed the day in battle and the chase, and at night banqueted to the sound of celestial horns: those who had fallen in the combat of the day rising fresh and unwounded to join in the revelry, and quaff metheglin from the skulls of the slain.

In government and manners, the usual simplicity of the barbarian prevailed. When not roused by war or the chase, the men lounged on skins, slept, and caroused. The affairs of the nation were discussed at their riotous and often bloody feasts. The ancient Germanic nations were addicted to drunkenness and gaming, staking arms, houses, wives, children, slaves, and even personal liberty, on the game. There were no towns: wherever a freeman found a desirable lot, he erected a hut, and dwelt in it, with his wife, children, and domestics, as absolute lord—judging, punishing, and rewarding at will. His other serfs,—captives,—were kindly treated, lived in smaller huts, and were obliged to give the freeman a portion of the produce of the little patches they cultivated, and to defend him against his enemies. Among the household servants, were the *senischalk*, or herdsman; the *mareschalk*, or groom; and the *truchsetz*, dish-setter or sewer. These afterward became titles of distinction—"seneschal," "marshal," "sewer," or "steward"—among the grandees of the German courts. Several huts formed a *mark*, or hamlet, with a common, where the heads of families assembled once a fortnight to settle disputes, under a *graf*, or count, called *mark-graf*—"margrave." Several marks composed a *zent*; several zents a *gau;* hence the *zent-graf*, and *gau-graf*, afterward called *landgrave*. Several gaus made a people, under a *kuning*, or king, called from *kuni*, family.

The king possessed neither authority nor revenues, except those derived from his private possessions. His business was to assemble the heads of families, and propose to them such measures as he considered necessary: their approval was indicated by the clashing of arms; disapproval by a buzz, or murmur. Cattle and other things were frequently presented to the king, as marks of respect; and he had a numerous suite of freemen, as well as of slaves. His hair was longer and more flowing than that of his subjects, and on his head he wore a circlet of gold. Every freeman was a warrior, and was expected to have his arms always in readiness. The horses of the cavalry were swift and hardy, and a warrior on foot ran at the side of the cavalier, holding by the mane of his horse, and ready to leap into his place should the rider fall in battle. Their weapons were the spear, and a long two-handed sword for defence: they wore on the left arm a buckler of wood, or osier, four or five feet in length by two in width. The king was commander-in-chief, if competent; otherwise a leader was chosen from the chief men,—*fursten*, princes,— who was called a *herzog*, — dux, leader, duke. When they found themselves in presence of the enemy, the cries of the brave soldiers burst forth into a wild, fierce chant, accompanied by the braying of rude trumpets, the rattle of drums, and the clashing of spears and shields. The whole force charged in a wedge-form, with a might and courage which bore down even the stout legions of Rome.

The Romans were, in fact, never able to subdue the Germans. The two nations first met in 113 B. C., when the *Cimbri* attacked Noricum, a province of Rome on the north-eastern border of Italy. Carbo, the Roman general, remonstrated sharply, and seemed satisfied with their excuse, which alleged ignorance of the relations of alliance between Noricum and Rome. The Cimbri, thus treacherously lulled into security, were suddenly attacked by the whole Roman force: though taken at unawares, however, they fought with irresistible valor, and cut Carbo's army to pieces. Seven years after, they again defeated the Romans; but Marius, having defeated the *Teutones*, their allies, at Aix, in Provence, killing one hundred thousand of them, marched against the Cimbri, who were advancing upon Rome, and utterly routed them, also. Forty-seven years later, Cæsar, crossing the Rhine, ravaged Germany for eighteen days. 59 B. C.

In the year 9 B. C., *Drusus*, after a succession of victories, which had placed the greater part of northern Germany at the disposal of Rome, was preparing to cross the Elbe, when a woman of gigantic stature and stern aspect suddenly appeared in front of the troops, and addressed him in these words: "Thou insatiable robber! whither wouldst thou go? Depart! The end of thy misdeeds, and of thy life, is at hand." Dismayed at this apparition, Drusus immediately retreated, and within thirty days died in consequence of a fall from his horse. A little before the Christian era, however, the Romans had subdued all the territory between the Rhine, Elbe, Alps, and Danube.

But a fearful reverse awaited the Roman arms. *Varus*, the governor of the northern part of the conquered district, led an army, in A. D. 9, to suppress a distant revolt. *Herman*, a German noble, had served in the armies of Rome, and learned to detest the conquerors of his country. He was sagacious, and possessed of that rude and fiery eloquence, which gives unbounded influence over the barbarian mind. In the deep recesses of the forest, he caused his countrymen to swear the destruction of the Roman army. As Varus advanced, he found the roads blockaded with trunks of trees, whilst javelins were hurled at him by invisible enemies from the midst of the thick covert: a heavy autumnal rain made the roads slippery, and the soldiers were benumbed with cold. The baggage was burnt to relieve them; and after three days of suffering, the army reached an open space in the forest, near the present Detmold, on the Lippe. Here the great struggle began. The rain, which fell in torrents, the entangled forest, and the swampy ground, all favored the hardy and light-armed Germans. The Romans fought with their usual courage, but were soon separated, their eagle taken, and the three legions, infantry as well as cavalry, cut to pieces. Varus, seeing the day irretrievably lost, threw himself on his own sword. Of the few prisoners, some were offered up as sacrifices to the gods, and others sold into slavery

At the news of this disaster, the aged emperor of Rome, Augustus, wandered for many days through the apartments of his palace, dashing his head against the walls, and calling wildly on Varus to give him back his legions; whilst the people, thoroughly disheartened, refused to serve any more against "those terrible barbarians." Germanicus, however, led another army to the fatal battle-ground, and burned the bones of the dead, but was soon obliged to retreat before the Germans. The following year he beat them twice; yet the Romans were finally compelled to betake themselves to their ships. Germanicus was now commanded by the new emperor, Tiberius, to return to Rome, and leave the Germans to themselves.

The country now remained free from foreign aggression, and undisturbed, except by domestic quarrels, for more than three centuries. Taught by experience, however, that their strength lay in union, the people formed several confederations of smaller tribes, which, in the third century, made up the four great German nations, — the Saxons, Franks, Suevi, and Goths. The *Saxons* occupied the north; they are said to have belonged originally to the army of Alexander the Great; to have entered the mouth of the Elbe, bought of the Thuringians a tunic full of soil, and then, sprinkling it over a tract of country, claimed the whole as their own; but their early history is involved in impenetrable obscurity. The *Franks* lived westward and southward of them, on the Lower Rhine. In the middle of the third century, they invaded Gaul, Africa, and Asia Minor. The *Suevi* dwelt in the south and south-west, and called their confederation *Allemania*, or "all sorts of men," — as including divers nations; whence the French still call Germany, *Allemagne*. The *Goths* abode to the eastward, along the Danube.

In the year A. D. 376, there appeared, on the eastern frontier of Germany, a swarthy, yellow nation, of low stature, thick-set, with broad shoulders, flat noses, short thick necks, prominent cheek-bones, and small eyes; a people compared, in the rhetoric of the times to wild beasts on two legs, or the rudely carved posts of bridges. These came from North-western Asia, and were the *Huns* — terrible from their ferocious and reckless courage, their countless numbers, and their skill in horsemanship, and the use of the javelin. The origin of this people is given in the chapter of our history of Tartary, which treats of the Hunnic and Finnic races; a further notice of them will be found in our history of Hungary. Attacking the Goths, the Huns exterminated many tribes, and drove others across the Danube. But very soon after, being repulsed in an assault upon Adrianople, the remnant of the Goths united with the Huns, and then were able to overthrow the Romans in a bloody battle, which cost the life of an emperor A few years later, the Westgoths, or Visigoths, who had quarrelled with the Eastgoths, or Ostrogoths, and Huns, allied themselves with the Romans, who about this time became divided into two empires, the Eastern and Western, A. D. 395. Among the Goths at the court of the eastern emperor, was a young warrior named *Alaric*, who was elected general of their forces. Aiming at conquest, he was driven from the Peloponnesus, and repulsed from Rome, by Stilicho, a Vandal chief, commander of the forces of the eastern empire; but some ten or twelve years after, he entered Italy again, and compelled Rome to ransom itself by paying five thousand pounds of gold, thirty thousand of silver, and other valuables. The barbarians, who had so long been abused, despoiled, enslaved, and massacred by myriads "to make Rome a holiday," felt it was now their turn. The ransom was paid, but Alaric returned again and took the city, August 23, A. D. 409, as elsewhere related.

Alaric embarked for Africa; but his fleet was wrecked, and he himself died soon after, in the thirty-fourth year of his age. The Visigoths found a new leader in Alaric's brother-in-law, *Ataulf*, or *Adolphus*, who founded the Visigothic empire of France and Spain, already described in our history of Spain.

The Vandals, another German tribe, migrated to Spain, and thence to Africa; being invited thither by the treacherous Roman governor. Their king, Genseric, after ravaging the Mediterranean coasts with his fleets, took Rome in A. D. 455, and sent off its treasures to adorn his new capital of Carthage, in Africa; but most of the ships, freighted with the noblest productions of Grecian and Roman art, foundered at sea.

About the middle of the fifth century, *Attila*, or *Etzel*, a renowned warrior, who had drawn to his standard not only the whole of the Huns, but a considerable portion of the eastern Germanic tribes, declared war against the Ostrogoths, and defeated them, A. D. 449, in a series of battles. The following year, he attacked Constantinople, but was bribed to withdraw. Then the Huns marched into Gaul, where they were routed with great slaughter by the allied Goths and Romans; but the following year, they crossed the Alps, and took Aquileia, whose inhabitants fled to the swampy islands at the mouth of the Brenta, and founded Venice. At length, Attila, now called the *Scourge of God*, appeared before the imperial city, but was induced to withdraw by the bishop of Rome, and soon after died. His body was put into a golden coffin, enclosed in one of silver, and both were placed in an iron chest. His whole army followed the corpse, but near the place of burial, it was committed to slaves, who were put to death as soon as they had interred it.

Attila was, in personal appearance, the counterpart of his hideous countrymen. But the consciousness of his power imparted even to his uncouth form a dignified bearing, before which men quailed whenever he rolled his wild eyes fiercely around, as if he delighted in witnessing the terror which his looks inspired. The rude people among whom he dwelt had for ages been accustomed to worship the god of war, under the symbolic form of a sword set in the ground; and one day, an old, rusty cimeter having been brought him by a herdsman whose cow had been wounded by its point, as it lay concealed in the grass, Attila, with ready tact, placed the weapon on a lofty altar, and, summoning the people, proclaimed himself possessor of the sword of Mars, and sovereign lord of the whole earth. He thus, like several other conquerors, aroused his followers with the terrible weapon of fanaticism. So great was the influence which he acquired over his countrymen, by thus investing himself with a sacred character, that the boldest of them were unable to gaze steadily on his countenance. Attila, Alaric, &c., have been already noticed, but the history of Germany could hardly be complete without the brief sketches of these wonderful men, which we have here introduced.

Since the first great movement of the Huns, A. D. 376, France, Spain, England, and the shores of Barbary, had all received Germans, as colonists or conquerors, before the year A. D. 500. About that time, the kingdom of *Thuringia*, now the kingdom of Saxony, &c., was a powerful independent sovereignty; but it was afterward overthrown by the sons of Clovis. The *Saxons* and *Frieses*, between the mouths of the Rhine and Elbe, retained their independence many centuries longer. The *Sclavonians*, the ancient *Sarmatæ*, occupied many districts of Eastern Germany, from which they were separated by language and religion, as they are now by national prejudice. In the sixth and seventh centuries, the Sclavonians, or Slaves, possessed Mecklenburg, Pomerania, Brandenburg, Meissen, Silesia, Bohemia, Moravia, Styria, Carinthia, and two or three other districts; in all of which countries, many of their descendants remain at the present day. North of the Danube dwelt the *Gepidæ* and the *Longobardi;* afterward the *Lombards*, who took possession of, and gave name to, Northern Italy. In those districts on the Rhine and Danube which belonged to the Romans, there had sprung up a number of free cities, in which Roman luxury, architecture, language, and laws reigned without a rival. From these cities, after the recognition of Christianity by Constantine, its doctrines spread slowly over the rest of Germany.

Whenever the Germans conquered a territory, the whole, or, more generally, a portion of it, was divided by lot between the king and his followers; of whom the more powerful received the larger share. But as the influence of the chiefs not unfrequently ended with the campaign, they devised a means of retaining their authority by presenting their followers with small portions of land, which they were permitted to retain as long as they remained faithful vassals and servants of their lord. This practice, introduced by the more powerful chiefs, was imitated by others on a smaller scale; so that at length the *Feudal System* was established, and the country parcelled into multitudes of little independent sovereignties. Written codes, composed in Latin, were prevalent at the period of which we are speaking, (A. D. 500;) in these the relations of freemen and serfs, Germans and Romans, were defined; every injury, and even insult, had its suitable penalty; all trials were conducted publicly before a jury of persons of like degree with the accused. In all the German kingdoms, general assemblies of the people were held under different names; as, the *Wittenangemot*, "wise men's council," in England, and the *Märzfelder*, "fields of March," among the Franks. Peace and war were debated at these meetings; if war was decided upon, the militia, composed of every rank, were called out by the king, to appear, on pain of death, armed and equipped at an appointed time and place. In the field, each duchy and country was marshalled under the banner of its duke or count, the king being commander-in-chief.

The next great era of Germany falls under the reign of Charlemagne, at the commencement of the ninth century. The conquests of Clovis in Germany, and the ancestry and inheritance of this monarch, are sufficiently detailed in our history of France, where it will be seen that Charlemagne, on coming to the throne of the whole Frankish empire, in A. D. 771, was master of most of Western Germany. His character, lan guage, ancestors, capital, and name, were German, as was his original kingdom of Austrasia. The Franco-German monarch now commenced a career of success to which history presents few parallels; he belonged, indeed, to that class of beings who seem to be specially sent on the earth for mighty purposes.

Didier, king of Lombardy, having interfered in behalf of the claim of Charlemagne's nephew to a part of the empire, that monarch crossed the Alps, and besieged Pavia, the Lombard capital. His passage displayed the usual contrasts of pomp and wretchedness exhibited by the armies that have crossed those awful heights of eternal winter, so vainly interposed as barriers to the fierce passions of nations. The garrison of Pavia, reduced by famine, surrendered at discretion. Charlemagne sent Didier to a monastery, and placed the iron crown of Lombardy on his own head.

The following picture of the approach of Charlemagne, or *Karl*, as his contemporaries called him, — upon Pavia, is extracted from the history of the monk of St. Gall, and shows how this great warrior and statesman appeared to the generation which immediately succeeded his own. "One of the lords of the kingdom, named Ogger," says this ancient chronicler, "had incurred the displeasure of the terrible Karl, and, to escape his resentment, had taken refuge with Didier, the king of the Lombards. When it was known in Lombardy that the dreaded king of the Franks was approaching, Didier and Ogger ascended to the summit of a high tower that commanded a view of the country on all sides. At first they saw machines of war, like those that must have served the legions of Darius and Julius. 'Is not Karl with this army?' demanded the king. 'No,' replied Ogger.

"An immense troop of common soldiers came next, and the king again demanded, 'Surely, Karl is triumphantly advancing in the midst of this host?' 'No, not yet,' was Ogger's answer. 'What shall we do?' said the king in alarm, 'if he come with a still greater force than we see?' 'When he comes,' answered Ogger, 'you will see him as he is; but what will become of us I know not.' While he spoke these words, the emperor's guard, that never knew repose, began to appear in the distance. The terrified king exclaimed, 'This is Karl himself!' 'Not yet,' rejoined Ogger.

"Next to these battalions came the bishops, the abbés, the priests of the royal chapel, and the counts of the empire. Didier, believing that he saw death incarnate marshalling this troop, cried out with tears, Let us descend and hide ourselves in the bowels of the earth, far away from the frown and the fury of so terrible a foe.' But Ogger, though also trembling, — for he, too, well knew the emperor's power, — prevented his retreat, being sure that Karl was not with this troop; 'Nay,' said he, 'but when you shall see the grain shaking in the fields, and bending as before the breath of the tempest, — when you behold the affrighted Po and Tesin overflow the walls of your city with waves that are blackened with iron, — then you may believe that Karl approaches.'

"He had scarcely finished, when something like a dark cloud, lifted by the wind, was seen on the western horizon; and the sky, until then clear, became suddenly obscured. From the middle of this cloud the glancing of arms flashed forth upon the eyes of the awe-struck spectators, and Karl himself appeared — Karl, that man of iron, his head covered with a casque of iron his hands encased in gauntlets of iron, his broad chest and huge shoulders protected by a cuirass of iron, his left hand brandishing his lance of iron and his right wielding his invincible sword. The inside of his thighs, where other horsemen wore not even leather, that they might with more facility mount their steeds, was covered with scales of iron. As for buskins, the whole army wore them of iron. His buckler was of iron; the very horse was of the color and strength of iron. All who preceded him, all who moved by his side, all who followed him, and, indeed, the army, as far as the means of each individual man would allow, was equipped in a similar manner. Iron covered the fields; iron covered the roads: the rays of the sun flashed upon innumerable points of iron; and this mighty panoply of iron was borne by a race whose hearts were as hard as iron. The glancing of this iron now spread terror through the streets of the city, and every one, in his flight, reiterated the exclamation, 'O, the iron! the iron!'"

The brave, but still savage and heathen Saxons recalled Charlemagne to the north, for they would not be converted by persuasion, and he had resolved to employ force. The war continued thirty years. Though repeatedly vanquished in battle with dreadful slaughter, the Saxons, under Wittekind and Alboin, in the depths of their gloomy forests and morasses, swore vengeance and eternal hatred to the Franks, and were ever ready to rally against these oppressors. In 803, however, peace was made, and the whole Saxon territory acknowledged the Frankish king. Previous to this, in 778, Charlemagne had rescued Spain north of the Ebro from the Moors. The principal general in this expedition was *Roland*, the hero of Frankish song, who fell in a skirmish while threading the Pyrenean defile of Roncesvalles. In 787, the duke of Benevento, whose territories reached from Naples south to Brindisi, took the oath of fealty to Charlemagne: a few years later, the Avars — who had filled Hungary with their strong ring forts, built with circular walls one within another — were subdued, as were also the Poles and the Bohemians.

From the Ebro to the Theiss and Raab, from Benevento to the Eyder, all the Germanic tribes were now, for the first time, united under one head; and the empire of Charlemagne formed a vast wall against Mahometanism on the south and south-west, and heathenism on the north, north-east, and east. In the year 800, the king received from the hands of Pope Leo III., at Rome, the crown of the "Holy Germanic-Roman Empire," destined to be the symbol of German unity for a thousand and six years. Clothed with the title of emperor, Charlemagne, "the northern barbarian," now fondly imagining he had reëstablished the ancient imperial Roman throne, asked the hand of Irene, empress of Constantinople, that he might again unite the east and west, as in the days of the Cæsars; but the lady refused him with scorn. Contenting himself with the dominion of the West, the monarch now bent his efforts to incorporate all the old free states and kingdoms into one mighty empire; and with the new name, the people adopted new views and a new character. The history of the ancient Germans, therefore, ends with the supremacy of Charlemagne.

CHAPTER CCCCXLIII.

A. D. 814 to 1519.

Institutions of the "Holy Germano-Roman Empire" — Henry the Fowler — Barbarossa — Rodolph of Hapsburg — The Hussites — The Reformation.

Otho III. and Barbarossa.

THE whole fabric of Charlemagne's dominion was founded on the feudal, or vassalage system, confirmed by the popes — a system sufficiently described elsewhere. He caused all the males throughout his empire, who had attained the age of twelve years, to swear that they would in future "obey the emperor in the same manner as a vassal is bound to obey his lord." Thus the design of Clovis to subject the independent nobles to the crown was completed at one stroke. The emperor became the central point from which all acts of government emanated. Charlemagne's code of laws, "*the Capitularies*," was severe, and even cruel: to form it, he collected the laws of all the states, and laid them, one by one, before a diet composed of generals, governors of provinces, archbishops, bishops, and abbots, who gave their opinions; after which the law was confirmed or rejected. The more important letters were written by the emperor's own hand, and sealed with a seal which was set in the hilt of his sword. He would then place the letter in the hands of the proper officer, saying, "There is my order; and here," pointing to his sword, "is that which will enforce obedience to it." Yet the feudal lord of all Germany was a vassal of the pope, from whom he received the imperial crown in the character of a gift, and who was acknowledged as absolute lord of the empire in spiritual matters.

For a thousand years of Roman greatness, empire had acknowledged the *sword* alone: the religious element of the northern character was now fully infused, and the *crosier* united with the sword, as the symbol of power for the next thousand years, — to be supplanted, in its turn, by the *purse*, becoming more and more the type of empire, as the spirit of trade succeeds the crusading spirit — itself the successor of the lust of dominion which animated conquering Rome.

Charlemagne exerted himself in favor of schools for all classes. "He had established such schools," says the monk of St. Gall, the contemporary chronicler already quoted "in different parts of his dominions, to which all his subjects, rich no less than poor, were compelled to send their children, that they might receive instruction from those who were appointed to that duty. Now, it happened, on a certain day, when he was visiting one of these schools, that the children of the nobles exhibited much ignorance, whilst those of the poor gave such answers as fully contented the emperor. Placing the poor children on his right, and the rich on his left, he first addressed the former: 'I thank you, my sons, that you have obeyed my commands; continue to strive after perfection, and I will give you bishoprics and abbeys, and ye shall have favor in my sight.' Then turning, with an angry countenance, to those on his left, he said, 'Ye high-born sons of my most illustrious nobles! ye asses and coxcombs! In the pride of your birth and your possessions, you despise my commands, and give yourselves up to idleness, riot, and disorder; but' — and here he raised his hand with a threatening gesture — 'by the King of heaven! if you do not straightway make up by diligence for your former neglect, you have little good to expect at the hands of Karl.'"

Though this conquering emperor was engaged in no less than fifty-three campaigns, he yet found time to exert himself in perfecting the language and literature of Germany. For this purpose, he collected the popular songs of the various German tribes; but his son's fanaticism destroyed these precious relics. Charlemagne also directed much attention to the improvement of agriculture. His own estates were patterns of neatness, and managed according to a code of instructions written out by himself. The culture of the vine, and of fruit-trees, and the rearing of cattle, were carried on with a success which added greatly to the royal revenues. He encouraged commerce, and manufactures also, by levying none but the most necessary customs, building bridges, repairing roads, establishing fairs and markets, and bringing artisans from the commercial towns of Italy. At Frankfort, Ingelheim — his favorite residence, and Aix-la-Chapelle, his capital, buildings of extraordinary splendor were erected by command of the emperor. It is said that he was riding in the woods, when his horse plunged his foot into a hot spring, and started, so as to attract his master's attention; and thus were discovered those wonderful boiling springs which Charlemagne ever afterward used, and which have made Aix-la-Chapelle the resort of invalids from all Europe, ever since. A fair city rose on the spot, in which the sovereign built him a magnificent palace, by the help of workmen from all quarters of the world. It may be mentioned in this connection, that the famous khalif of Bagdad, Haroun al Raschid, in token of respect for the antagonist of his own enemies, the Moors of Spain, sent the Christian emperor, beside a fine elephant and costly tent, a specimen of Oriental art — a water clock, containing twelve little brazen balls, one of which fell at the end of every hour into a basin; and at the same instant, a window opened, out of which started knights, in number according to the hour, and performed their military evolutions.

Charlemagne was well proportioned, of a fine countenance, and a foot taller than ordinary men. He excelled in all bodily exercises, especially in swimming, his favorite amusement. His imperial crown is still preserved at Vienna, and would fit only the head of a giant. He was very temperate, and extremely simple in dress, except on occasions of state, when he appeared in royal magnificence. At the splendid court he held at Paderborn, in 799, his beautiful daughters delighted the people by the skill with which they managed their horses. The year before his death, after a violent illness, he rallied, and assembled the diet at Aix-la-Chapelle. Addressing, in their presence, his son Louis, who stood with him before the high altar of the cathedral, he exhorted him to fear God, and to love him; to defend the church; to be kind to his relations; to honor the priests, and love his people as his children; to choose none but men of irreproachable character for his ministers; and to keep a conscience void of offence toward God and toward man. "Wilt thou, my son," he added, "fulfil all this?" To which Prince Louis replied, "By God's help, I will." Then the emperor commanded him to take the crown from off the altar, and place it on his own head, A. D. 813.

As previously, in the case of Cæsar, and subsequently, in the case of Napoleon, a series of what the superstitious believed to be unlucky omens, were supposed to announce to the world the termination of this mighty emperor's career. "Many prodigies," says his intimate friend, secretary, son-in-law, and biographer, the knightly Eginhard, "were remarked at the approach of the king's decease;' and he, as well as others, regarded them as supernatural warnings addressed personally to himself. During the last three years of his life, there were frequent eclipses of the sun and moon for seven days in succession; a black spot was visible on the sun's disk; the gallery which Karl had constructed, at great expense, to connect the cathedral and the palace, crumbled to its very foundation on Ascension day; the wooden bridge which he had built across the Rhine at Mayence — a wonderful specimen of architectural skill, the fruit of ten years' immense labor, and which seemed destined to endure forever — was suddenly consumed by fire in the short space of three hours, and not a vestige of it remained, except what was under water. At the time of his last expedition into Saxony, against Godfred, king of the Danes, Karl, having left his tent before the sun rose, and commenced his march, saw an enormous light fall suddenly from the sky, and, in a breathless atmosphere, flare alternately to the right and left. While the army were admiring this prodigy, and wondering what it presaged, the emperor's horse fell head foremost to the ground, and so violently precipitated his rider to the earth, that the clasp of his cloak was torn off, and his sword belt broken; and he was unable to rise without the assistance of his followers, who disencumbered him of his arms. The javelin, which he chanced to have in his hand, was thrown forward more than twenty feet from the spot where he fell. The palace at Aix-la-Chapelle was shaken by a violent trembling of the earth, and the ceilings of the apartments occupied by the king were heard to crack. The mysterious fire from heaven fell on the cathedral where he was afterward buried; and the golden ball that decorated the pinnacle of the roof, struck by the flash, was broken and scattered over the house of the bishop, which was contiguous to the church. In this church, on the borders of the cornice, between the higher and lower arcades, was an inscription to the founder of the edifice, in the last line of which were the words *Carolus Princeps* — Charles, prince. It was remarked, a few months before the emperor's decease, that the letters composing the word *princeps* were so effaced as to be scarcely legible. Karl le Grand testified no fear at these portents from above, and despised them as much as if they had no connection with his own destiny."

Charlemagne* died on the 28th of January, 814, at three o'clock in the day, in the seventy-second year of his age, and the forty-seventh of his reign. As he left no directions concerning his burial, it was a matter of debate where his remains should be deposited. At length, the magnificent chapel which he had built at Aix, and placed under the invocation of the Virgin was chosen for his last and perpetual palace, as noticed in our history of France. The sepulchre, paved with pieces of gold, was perfumed; the bronze door was closed and masoned over; and a triumphal arch was erected on the spot, bearing this inscription: —

"Under this stone lies the body of Karl, the great and orthodox emperor, who nobly aggrandized the kingdom of the Franks, reigned happily forty-seven years, and died a septuagenarian, on the fifth of the kalends of February, in the eight hundred and fourteenth year of the incarnation of our Lord, at the seventh indiction."

Charlemagne passed his leisure in the society of learned men; he spoke Latin and understood Greek. Among his most distinguished literary and ecclesiastical associates was Alcuin, his spiritual adviser, an English monk, a prodigy of learning, and tutor of the emperor as well as of his family. His other intimates were the brave and intelligent Eginhard; Paul Diaconus, a learned Lombard; Bishop Turpin, the emperor's biographer, and Angilbert, his bosom friend.

In the management of his own family, Charlemagne seems to have been extremely indulgent. His daughter Emma loved her father's friend, Eginhard, and often received his visits. One morning, after having spent many hours with his mistress, Eginhard was preparing to depart, when they discovered that so much snow had fallen during the night as to render it impossible for the lover to retire without leaving the traces of his footsteps as he crossed the court. In this difficulty, Emma mounted him on her shoulders, and was carrying him toward his own apartments, when they were perceived by Charlemagne, who happened to be standing at one of the palace windows. The lovers now gave themselves up for lost; but the good-natured monarch, after reproving the presumption of Eginhard forgave them both, and granted his sanction to their marriage. Charlemagne had three sons. The eldest, Charles, and the second, Pepin, a youth of great promise, died at an early age. *Louis*, the youngest, and the most incompetent, succeeded him on the imperial throne, A. D. 814.

Louis was not fitted to sway an iron sceptre over half-barbarous subjects, and soon became the obsequious creature of the clergy. He received the name of the *Debonnaire*. He had made a will, in which he fell into the common but fatal error of dividing his dominions among his sons. The quarrels of the three brothers, and their rebellion, brought him to the grave, A. D. 840. Two of the brothers now united against the third, and, in the battle that ensued, one hundred thou-

* In the history of France, Charlemagne and his successors are noticed so far as relates to French history; here they are noticed more particularly in reference to German history. We have avoided repetition except so far as was necessary to completeness and continuity in the two histories.

sand men were slain. After this, they agreed to divide the empire between them, A. D. 843. *Lothaire*, the eldest, took the imperial dignity, with Helvetia and Lorraine; Charles the Bald had all west of Lorraine, with the title of *King of France;* and Louis, called the *German*, received the whole of Germany, with the title of king. Thus speedily was the labor of the whole life of the mighty Charlemagne brought to nought. The three empires went to the sons of Louis, of whom Charles the Fat became sole heir; thus re-uniting, for a short time, the fragments of the Germanic empire. But the subjects of Charles the Fat, disgusted with his cowardice in regard to the Northmen, deposed him, and then each nation elected its own king.

Henry of Saxony, surnamed the *Fowler*, came to the throne in A. D. 917. An archbishop offered to anoint him; but he declared it was sufficient that he was called to rule by God's grace and the choice of the people, and entreated the prelate to "reserve the oil for some more pious monarch." The kingdom had become divided into five states,—Saxony with Thuringia, Franconia, Suabia, Bavaria, and Lorraine, all which he united into one; but he was obliged to make a nine years' truce with the Hungarians, who disturbed his eastern frontier. They fought on horseback; and Henry, to improve his cavalry, ordered all whose estates qualified them, to meet for horseback exercise. Noble ladies were present at these exercises, and rewarded the successful cavaliers with their smiles. This, according to some authors, was the origin of tournaments. Thus, at the end of the truce, (A. D. 933,) Henry found himself able to meet and rout the Hungarians repeatedly, and with terrible slaughter. In 955, *Otho I.* defeated them in a battle in which sixty thousand were slain; since then, they have never invaded Germany. The Sclavonians were next reduced to obedience; and, as the Italians had already given Otho the crown of Italy, he found himself unmolested, and Germany remained prosperous, tranquil, and powerful, till his death, A. D. 973.

Otho III. succeeded his father Otho II, when but three years old. During his minority, he made such progress in his studies under Gerbert, the most learned man of his age, that he was surnamed the *Prodigy*. The duke of Bavaria attempted to wrest the succession from him, but was prevented by the loyalty of the nobles and clergy. At fifteen years of age, Otho III. was crowned king at Rome; the pope and populace, however, soon rebelled. Returning to Rome, therefore, the youthful emperor deposed the pope, and appointed Gerbert to the papacy. The year 1000 was now at hand, when it was generally believed the world would end—and every one prepared for the judgment day. Otho availed himself of the general tranquillity to make a pilgrimage to Poland; and, on his return, he opened the tomb of Charlemagne at Aix-la-Chapelle. On his visiting Rome a third time, the populace rose in insurrection; but the emperor addressed the crowd in a speech glowing with religious enthusiasm, which at once quelled the uproar.

Passing by some less important reigns, we come to that of *Henry IV.*, in A. D. 1056. This monarch set himself at open issue with the holy see, in the great struggle between the popes and the emperors which fills so large and disagreeable a portion of the history of several ages. Gregory VII. (Hildebrand) held, in so many words, that "God having placed all things under the feet of his Son, and Peter being the successor of Christ, and the pope the successor of St. Peter, it follows that all earthly principalities, and powers, and dominions, should be subject to him who is the representative of God in the world." His immediate predecessors had added to the temporalities of the Roman see, and he himself increased them; he contrived that none but the clergy should elect bishops, who must be confirmed by the pope; beside other great changes. But the most far-sighted of his schemes was the requiring all the clergy to remain unmarried. Thus their whole energies would be given to the aggrandizement of the power of the church; ecclesiastical ambition might reign within stronger minds without a rival, while weaker ones, being dependent entirely on the church for any rise in station, would become its obsequious and unscrupulous slaves. Thus father, husband, citizen, patriot, were all merged in a monster of one idea, unfit for any duties, and inadequate to any service save that of the twin tyrants, fanaticism and superstition.

Henry IV., on the occasion of the pope's interference between him and a portion of his subjects, assembled the German bishops, A. D. 1075, and deposed the pope, in a letter singularly abusive and insolent, appointing another in his stead. But he was no man to struggle successfully against Gregory VII., the master-spirit with whom he had rashly ventured to measure himself. He was excommunicated, and his subjects shrank from him as from a leper. The result of the contest was, that the monarch was obliged to appear at Canossa, in Italy, clothed in the hair-shirt of a penitent, with bare head, and feet miserably lacerated by the roughness of the road. He was insolently ordered to await the pope's pleasure in the court-yard, where he remained in the rigorous season of winter, exposed bareheaded and barefooted, for three days and three nights. But it availed him nothing. On his return, he found another emperor, a creature of the pope's, appointed by him and confirmed by the nobles. Confusion now reigned throughout the empire. There were two emperors and two popes; in every dukedom two dukes, and in every diocese two bishops. Brother fought against brother; sons were arrayed against their fathers. Henry besieged Rome for three years; and the pope took refuge with the Normans in Southern Italy. Popes Urban II. and Pascal II., after him continued the contest on the death of Gregory, and excited Henry's sons, one after the other, to rebel against him. After the death of the eldest, the second son, *Henry*, supported by the pope and the nobles. and assisted by treason in the emperor's camp, reduced his father to extremities. The latter threw himself at the feet of his inhuman child, and implored him, with streaming eyes, to have pity on his gray hairs; but the unnatural monster and his confederates were deaf to all entreaties, and compelled the old man to sign the instrument of abdication, and acknowledge his son as sovereign, by the title of *Henry V.*, A. D. 1106. Soon afterward, the broken-hearted father ended his miserable life. So abject had been his poverty, that he was obliged to sell his boots for bread. In his reign began the first crusade, A. D. 1093. In A. D. 1122, a compact was made in which the rights of the emperors and those of the popes were clearly defined.

Three years afterward, Henry V. died, and the German dukes and nobles, with their vassals and knights, assembled on the banks of the Rhine, between Mentz and Worms, for the purpose of electing his successor. The four principal nations of Germany, viz., the Saxons, Franconians, Suabians, and Bavarians, appeared at this meeting, to the number of sixty thousand, all well armed and appointed. Each chose ten nobles, who again chose one, thus reducing the number of those who were to vote at the election to four — one for each nation. *Lothaire* of Saxony was elected, A. D. 1125. To defend himself against the faction of the house of Hohenstaufen, with whom he carried on a bloody war during most of his reign, he gave up all the advantages of the compact of 1122, and held his crown, as usual, of the pope.

At his death, in 1137, two parties divided the kingdom — the *Guelfs*,* supporters of Henry, duke of Bavaria and Saxony, and the *Ghibellines*,* who elected *Conrad III.*, of Hohenstaufen, king. By him, Henry was deprived of both his dukedoms. The vassals of Henry fought manfully in his cause, and his brother, Duke Guelf, shut himself up in Weinsberg. After a protracted siege, the garrison capitulated, A. D. 1140, on condition that all the women should be allowed to depart, taking with them as much of their property as they could carry. The terms of surrender having been signed, the gates were opened, and, to the great surprise of the besiegers, the duchess appeared, bearing her husband on her shoulders, and followed by all the women of the city, similarly laden. The hill they crossed is still called *Weibertreuc*, "woman's fidelity." In 1149, Conrad III. returned from a crusade in the Holy Land, and died by poison, recommending to the electors his nephew, Frederic, called *Red-beard*, or *Barbarossa*, a Ghibelline by the father's side, and a Guelf by the mother's.

Frederic I., or Barbarossa, when he ascended the throne, was thirty years old, and a model of manly German beauty. His short, fair hair curled over a broad and noble forehead; his complexion was clear, his blue eyes full of intelligence and courage, and his lips full but delicately chiselled. Though a true son of the church, he was a determined foe to the pope's assumption of universal dominion, and was also aware that, to be effective, terms must be dictated to the pontiff at Rome. On his way thither, the Lombards implored his help against the Milanese, and he accordingly wrote the latter a letter of remonstrance. But they tore it up, and threw it in the face of his messengers. This insult they were made to rue, as we have related in our account of Italy, where the exploits of Barbarossa, south of the Alps, are noticed.† Having taken Rome, he destroyed a picture representing the German king receiving his crown as a fief from the pope, exclaiming, "You begin with painting, and follow it up by writing, in the expectation of treading us under your feet."

Returned to Germany, Frederic I. crushed the feuds of the nobles, and destroyed the castles whence many of them had long been in the habit of sallying forth, capturing peaceful travellers, especially priests and merchants, and exacting large sums of money for their ransom. The oppressed peasants also, were encouraged to seek the protection of the cities, thus building up an independent class of citizens in the place of serfs. So highly was Frederic I. esteemed abroad, that Henry II. of England wrote him a letter acknowledging his superiority, and professing his willingness to do him homage. Frederic perished by drowning, in Asia, while leading the third crusade, A. D. 1190. His body was buried at Antiochia; but the legend is still believed that he of the red beard sleeps in the cleft of a rock in Thuringia, his head resting on his hand, and his beard grown through the stone table on which he leans, to awake, at some future day, "when the ravens cease to hover over the mountain — and bring back golden times to Germany."

Henry VI., son of Frederic, was a cruel tyrant. Though but the grandson of a simple Suabian count, he wore five crowns — those of Germany, Burgundy, Lombardy, the Roman empire, and Sicily. He died in Sicily, and was buried amid universal rejoicings. Henry's son being but three years old, *Philip*, a brother of Henry, was placed upon the throne against his own wishes. He was assassinated in 1208, and *Otho IV* succeeded, who conceded the right of investiture to the pope, Innocent III., and the appointment of bishops, but soon quarrelled with him, and was excommunicated. Instigated by the pope, the nobles and states elected *Frederic II.* emperor, A. D. 1212, who had been well educated by the pope. But, not proving sufficiently obsequious, he was excommunicated in his turn. He went to Palestine, and, by his tolerant spirit, won upon the heart of the sultan, Camel, who opened to him the gates of Jerusalem, and Christians were allowed to worship in the city unmolested. Frederic II., on his return, led a life of elegant luxury in his kingdom of Apulia, which he filled with palaces and gardens. He also occupied himself in poetry, and the study of astronomy and natural history, collecting a menagerie of strange animals, and writing a natural history of birds. In the north, his empire was enlarged by the exploits and civilizing labors of the Teutonic knights, who subdued savage Prussia — and the order of the Cross and Sword, who civilized Esthonia.

The character of this interesting prince, whose mother was an Italian, united German strength and steadiness with Italian fire and elegance. He married, for his third wife, Isabella, the beautiful sister of Henry III. of England. As the bride entered Cologne, crowds of the people strewed her way with flowers, and, for many days, the richest presents were distributed to the populace. A ship, drawn by persons concealed within, which thus seemed to sail on the land, was a part of the pageant. The marriage was celebrated at Worms, with great pomp, seventy-five princes and twelve thousand knights being among the wedding guests. A general peace was proclaimed at a diet held immediately after, and all were required to refer their wrongs to the proper tribunals, instead of taking justice into their own hands, as heretofore. This ordinance was the first ever published in the German

* *Guelfs* is a corruption of *welfen*, "whelps," according to a ridiculous legend. A count bantered a woman for having three children at a birth; the woman cursed his wife so that she brought forth twelve at once, eleven of which the mother sent to be drowned. But the count met the messenger, and asked her what she had in the basket. "Puppy dogs — *welfen*," said she. However, the count lifted the cloth, and ordered the babes back to the palace, where they were carefully brought up; and their descendants, among whom are the Hanoverian dynasty of England, were called *Welfs*, or Guelfs. *Ghibellines* is said to be a corruption of *Waiblingers*, the name of a fortress.

† When Milan was taken, A. D. 1162, the pretended skulls of the Magi, or wise men of the East, deposited at Milan during the first crusade, were transferred to the cathedral of Cologne, where they are still venerated under the names of *Caspar*, *Melchior*, and *Balthasar*, the Three Kings of Cologne.

anguage, the Latin having been used up to this time, A. D. 1236.

During this romantic reign, Germany was overrun by the Mongols, as we have noticed in our history of Tartary. In consequence of his long struggles with

Frederic II. and Maximilian.

the popes, the latter part of the life of Frederic II. was an unbroken series of misfortunes. Germany was rent by frightful disorders; and the necessity for mutual protection originated the celebrated compact of the *Hansa*, or "confederacy," which included the towns of Hamburg, Lubec, Bremen, Brunswick, &c., known as the *Hanse towns*. At one time, these were eighty-five in number. In 1630, the old league was broken up, and Lubec, Hamburg, and Bremen formed a new one, as elsewhere noticed.

After the death of *Conrad IV.*, the son of Frederic II., who had succeeded to a disputed throne—the crown was offered to the highest bidder; and an Englishman, *Richard of Cornwall*, brother of Henry III., bought up the archbishop of Mentz, and obtained the election. Thirty-two wagons followed Richard into Germany, each loaded with a hogshead of gold. The archbishop of Treves, however, supported Alfonse of Castile, who offered each of the electors twenty thousand marks.

On the death of Richard, the pope and nobles sought a candidate for the office of emperor, who should be a warrior of reputation; a favorite, to a certain extent, of the people, but at the same time a zealous promoter of aristocratic interests, and blindly devoted to the papal see. Such a one they found in *Rodolph of Hapsburg*, who was crowned in A. D. 1273. After putting down Ottocar, the king of Bohemia, he cleared the country of the robber nobles, sixty-six of their castles being demolished in Thuringia, and twenty-nine of the most notorious freebooters hung in chains at Erfurt. The German peasant still delights to listen to the many tales that are told of his prowess and impartial justice. The next emperor, *Albert of Austria*, son of Rodolph, in attempting to annex part of Switzerland to the hereditary possessions of his family, excited an insurrection which ended in the independence of Switzerland. *Henry VII.*, his successor, took the patriots Charlemagne, Barbarossa, and Frederic II. for his models; but he was murdered by poison, which a monk administered to him in the sacrament of the Lord's supper, A. D. 1313. His life might have been saved, but he superstitiously refused to allow the consecrated elements to be ejected from his stomach. *Louis the Bavarian* was the last emperor who suffered the sentence of excommunication.* He had overcome his rival, Frederic of Austria, in a murderous battle which swept away the bravest of the Austrian nobility; but he afterward visited him in prison, and proposed to divide with him the imperial authority. Their signatures changed places every day, and for this purpose each had a seal engraved on which the name of his colleague was placed above his own. Louis then proceeded to Italy, deposed the pope, and put Nicholas V into the papal chair. His colleague died in 1330. In 1338, he summoned a diet, and the electors resolved, "that the German emperor was the highest power on earth, and dependent for his election on none but the princes of Germany."

Charles IV. disposed of his rival Gunther by poison; and after patient manœuvring, put an end to the alliance of Pope Urban with France, and brought him back to Rome. In 1356, there were two popes, one at Rome, the other at Avignon; and in this year Charles issued the famous *Golden Bull*,—so called from the knob, or *bulla*, of gold in which its seal is enclosed,—containing thirty chapters. It defines the privileges of the kings of Bohemia, lays down rules for the election and coronation of the emperors, restrains the cities from further encroachments upon the nobles, and establishes salutary regulations for the levying and collection of taxes. Until the dissolution of the empire, this bull was always considered the groundwork of the Germanic constitution. Charles IV. founded the first German university, at Prague, a city which he built, and the capital of his native kingdom. His example was soon followed by the Hapsburgs and the Palatine, who founded universities in Vienna and Heidelberg; others were established by the spiritual princes—the archbishops of Mentz, Treves, and Cologne, at Cologne, Erfurt, and Wurtsburg. The university at Prague soon had seven thousand students.† Bands of robbers, however, swarmed throughout Germany;

* The pope's bull ran in the following unchristian, not to say diabolical strain:—"May the Almighty God cast Louis down, and give him into the hands of his enemies and pursuers! May he fall into an unforeseen snare! Cursed be his going out and his coming in! May the Lord smite him with folly and blindness! May Heaven blast him with its lightning! May the wrath of God, and of the blessed apostles, Peter and Paul, burn against him like fire in this world and the next! May the whole earth arm itself against him! May the deep open and swallow him up quick! May his name be clean forgotten, and his memory perish from among men! May all the elements oppose him! May his house be left desolate, and all his children be driven from their dwellings, and slain by his enemies before their father's eyes!"

† Each of the universities founded in the fourteenth century, was a corporation of masters and scholars, governed by its own laws, and enjoying peculiar privileges. The whole body of academies was divided into "nations," each of which had its own officers. The rector of the university was chosen by these nations collectively, the scholars enjoying an equal right of voting with their masters. All students were allowed to wander from one university to another, and not unfrequently they supported themselves on these excursions by begging. The course of instruction was divided into four faculties, of which the first three—theology, medicine, and law—were termed *sciences*. Those who had completed their studies in either of these sciences, were admitted to the degree of *doctor*. The fourth faculty comprehended the liberal arts, seven in number, viz., grammar, rhetoric, logic, mathematics, physics, metaphysics, and moral philosophy. Proficients in these studies were termed *masters*.

and the emperor was obliged to encourage alliances of cities to suppress them. *Wenceslaus*, the next emperor, acted like a madman. On one occasion, he had three tents pitched, one black, another white, and another red. Inviting the nobles to a banquet, he introduced them, one by one, into the black tent: those who surrendered what possessions he required, he feasted in the white tent; those that refused his demands, were beheaded in the red tent. He would also set bloodhounds upon his guests, and his wife was repeatedly lacerated by these fierce animals as she lay in bed. On one occasion, he roasted the cook on a spit, who had served up an ill-dressed capon.

In **1411**, Germany had three emperors, and Christendom three popes. The arrogant and dishonored *Sigismund*, however, soon became sole emperor; and, to settle the popedom, a council was convened at Constance, consisting of the emperor, all the electors, a crowd of nobles, plenipotentiaries of foreign sovereigns, three patriarchs, thirty-three cardinals, forty-seven archbishops, one hundred and forty-five bishops, two hundred and twenty-four abbots, one thousand eight hundred priests, seven hundred and fifty doctors and several monks. It was this council of Constance that, in spite of the promise of safety, burnt at the stake the renowned martyrs John Huss and Jerome of Prague, A. D. **1415**, for heresy.* They then elected Martin V. pope, who soon succeeded in replacing the veil of thick darkness, which had been in some measure withdrawn from the abuses of the church.

The death of Huss kindled the Hussite war, in which the fierce leader Ziska repeatedly overthrew, with his peasants and women, large imperial armies, rendering Bohemia, for a time, independent. He passed hither and thither through the country, like the destroying angel, wreaking vengeance on the debauched monks and their abettors, demolishing convents, burning churches and monasteries, and carrying fire and sword into every town and village that resisted his progress. These justly-exasperated fanatics at last obliged Sigismund to guaranty to Bohemia, under certain modifications, freedom of preaching, "communion in both kinds," poverty of the priests, and appropriation of ecclesiastical property.

In 1438, *Albert of Austria* was elected to succeed Sigismund, and since then, nearly every emperor has been Austrian. He died after two years; and the incapable *Frederic III.*, the last emperor who received his crown from the pope, next reigned for fifty-three years, during which "the imperial crown had become a night-cap,"—to use the words of a quaint old author,—and full scope was given to the struggles between the temporal and spiritual powers, and the disputes of princes, great and small. Meanwhile Hungary and Bohemia detached themselves from Austria, and elected independent kings. The next emperor—*Maximilian I.*—was such a hero in person, manners and exploits, as minstrels love to celebrate in lays of chivalry; but he was unsteady, and often trifling, and the age advanced toward the great epoch of the reformation without his aid, or even consciousness of its progress. In 1516, he attempted to raise forces for a Turkish war; but a mightier contest was at hand. "We must fight," wrote a contemporary author, "not against the Turks, but against the pope;" and at the breach which Wiclif and Huss had made in the walls of papacy, both cannon and glittering steel came in play—the rough artillery of Luther's eloquence, and the polished sword-thrusts of Melancthon's elegant and scholarly pen.

* Huss taught that the pope was no greater than any other bishop; that useless holidays ought to be abolished; that the doctrine of purgatory had no foundation in Scripture; that confirmation and extreme unction were not sacraments; that auricular confession was a vain thing; that altars, priestly vestments, images, and consecrated vessels were useless, and that prayer needed not be offered up in churches merely, for, the whole earth being the Lord's, any spot of it might be used as his temple; that the sacrament of the Lord's supper ought to be received in both kinds by the laity; and that the bread and wine in the eucharist were not transubstantiated into the body and blood of Christ, but that the real body and blood were received after a spiritual and mysterious fashion

CHAPTER CCCXLIV.

A. D. 1519 to 1863.

Freedom of Conscience — Luther — Charles V. — Annals — Napoleon in Germany — The German Union, or Republic.

Charles V. in retirement.

Even a Papist cardinal acknowledges that, "a few years before the breaking out of the Lutheran and Calvinistic heresies, there existed no strictness in the spiritual courts, no discipline with regard to morals no acquisition of Christian knowledge, no respect for sacred things; in short, there was hardly a vestige of religion remaining." A Papist bishop also asserts that "most of the preachers of that day discoursed only of indulgences, pilgrimages, and alms to the monks and made things indifferent the groundwork of piety." The attempts of the abandoned Tetzel to sell indulgences or pardons for the commission of sins past or future - - in order to raise money to build St. Peter's at

Rome — brought on the crisis. Luther, the pious monk and learned professor, was fitted by nature and education to rouse the whirlwind of discussion, and guide the storm of opposition, which in the end beat down the fabric of tradition and fraud, wherein the human mind had been so long imprisoned. In October, 1517, he declared war against the sale of indulgences and other abuses by affixing to the great door of the castle church of Wittemberg a challenge to all comers, to dispute with him on ninety-five different propositions. His bold challenge fell like a spark upon powder. What thousands had thought in secret, he had dared openly to express; what hundreds of thousands had suspected, they now felt to be true.

The details of the career of Luther, aided by the gentle and candid Melancthon, would lead us into too extended a field of remark for our purpose. Suffice it to say, that Luther was summoned to Rome; but the emperor Maximilian, desirous of humbling the pope, agreed with Frederic, elector of Saxony,—who was proud of the reputation the compromised professor had acquired for his university,—that Luther must be spared. The stout reformer, therefore, met Caietanus, the general of the Dominicans, commissioned for the purpose by the pope, before the diet convened at Augsburg, A. D. 1519. The commissioner, however, on finding that Luther would not retract, refused to discuss the ninety-five propositions, and dismissed the assembly "in great wrath." The pope then excommunicated Luther, who burned his bull of excommunication, publicly, before all the professors and students of Wittemberg.

Luther.

In 1521, Luther was summoned before a diet of the empire, at Worms, by Charles V., who supposed that a discussion would put down the heresy at once. The adherents of reform and their opponents soon marshalled all Germany, and indeed most of Europe, on opposite sides. The reformers were called *Protestants*, because the elector of Saxony and other princes *protested* against the reversal, at a subsequent diet, of a decree passed by a former diet, "that every secular prince should manage the ecclesiastical affairs of his own dominions."

The Protestant Reformation led to wars which lasted the greater part of a century. The coalition of princes, called the *Smalkaldic League*, who embraced Luther's views, compelled Charles V., in 1532, and again in 1552, to grant the Protestants liberty of conscience and equal civil rights with the Catholics. But in 1618 the two parties again flew to arms, and the Thirty Years War commenced.* Tilly and Wallenstein, the imperial generals, reduced most of the Protestant territories to submission; but the cause was saved by the intervention of Gustavus Adolphus, king of Sweden. The house of Austria, which then occupied the imperial throne, was effectually crippled by his successes, and in A. D. 1648, the peace of Westphalia secured liberty of conscience and the free exercise of all religions throughout Germany — except in the Austrian dominions.

Charles V., — to return to the thread of our history — king of Spain, Naples, and Sicily, lord of the Netherlands, and of Milan, was grandson of Maximilian, and became, on the death of the emperor, in A. D. 1519, the successful candidate for the empire, over the chivalric Francis I. of France, and the Protestant Duke Frederic of Saxony. He was at the age of nineteen when he assumed the imperial mantle, after signing an instrument which secured all their rights to the princes of the empire. Two years after his election, he was crowned with great pomp, at Aix-la-Chapelle, and exchanged a wild and dissolute life for one of great regularity. He was the greatest and most powerful sovereign of his age; and reigned forty years, during most of which he was at war with his distinguished rival, Francis I. He also strenuously opposed Protestantism. In 1556, he voluntarily resigned the crown of Spain, Naples, Spanish America, and the Netherlands, to Philip II., and that of Germany to Ferdinand, and, retiring to the monastery of St. Just, in Spain, devoted himself to the simplicity and privacy of monastic life, till his death, in A. D. 1558.

* The political condition of Europe, two hundred years ago, is seen in the following sketch by Schiller: "The Romanist party was infinitely the more numerous, and more favored by the constitution of the empire: still the Protestants possessed a tract of rich territory, warlike princes and nobles, numerous armies, the sovereignty of the sea, flourishing towns, and many adherents in the Romanist states. If the Romanists had Spain and Italy on their side, Venice, Holland, and England were ready to subsidize the Protestants with their treasures, and the northern states and Turkey to aid them with their troops. Three of their princes were electors of the empire. Every thing might have been done if private interests had not been consulted rather than the public good. France had lost with her illustrious Henry all her might in the affairs of Europe. Holland was flourishing, but required all her forces for the defence of her newly acquired freedom. England, although aggrandized by the acquisition of Scotland, was deprived of that influence in Protestant Europe which had been obtained for her by the master mind of Elizabeth. The weak James I. suffered his daughter and her husband Frederic to be ruined without attempting to save them. Spain was beginning to feel the effects of that mistaken policy which had led her to neglect agriculture at home, for the sake of drawing gold from her newly-acquired possessions in America. The pope lived in constant fear of his terrible neighbors the viceroys of Milan and Naples. As head of the church, he wished success to the Romanists; but as a temporal prince, he was glad that the Protestants kept the emperor employed at home. The republic of Venice had two dangerous neighbors in Austrian Tyrol and Spanish Milan. Savoy lay between these countries and France. In the north, two powerful monarchs had made themselves respected — Christian IV. in Denmark and Gustavus Adolphus in Sweden."

Ferdinand II., the emperor of Germany through most of the Thirty Years' War, died in **1637**; and few overeigns have left behind them a name more odious. Under the cloak of religious zeal, he sent fire and sword through his native land. Heretics were exterminated, not because their doctrines were damnable, but because those who presumed to differ from their sovereign were, in his eyes, guilty of rebellion. More than ten millions of human beings were sacrificed to this unjust and cruel policy. The Jesuits had impressed upon him the infernal maxim that a land had better lie waste than harbor heretics and rebels. On this principle he acted through a long life, and reduced the fair plains and fields of Germany to the condition of a howling wilderness, through which dissolute soldiers, and half-starved, miserable peasants, in whose breasts famine and suffering had extinguished the feelings of humanity, wandered like fiends, ready to devour friends and foes alike. The year in which the emperor died, a frightful famine was added to the other horrors of war. Men disinterred and devoured human corpses, and even hunted down human beings to feed on their flesh. A pestilence was the consequence, which swept away thousands upon thousands. Hundreds destroyed themselves, being unable to endure the pangs of hunger. The license consequent on this misery utterly destroyed the morality which was once the pride and boast of Germany.

During the next century, the influence of the age of Louis XIV. greatly modified the German character, an integral part of which had hitherto been hatred of the French. In the year **1700**, Charles II., king of Spain, died, and all Europe divided itself into hostile parties on the side of France or Germany, in the war of the Spanish Succession. The rival claimants were a grandson of Louis XIV., and a son of Leopold I., the emperor of Germany. Streams of blood were shed, millions of treasure squandered, and the war ended in **1715**,—the year of the death of Anne, queen of England, and Louis XIV., king of France,—with no result beyond that of placing the contending parties in nearly the same political position they had occupied before it began.

In the first part of the eighteenth century, the Turks invaded the German empire; but Eugene compelled them to sue for peace, after the loss of their grand vizier, and the flower of their army, in the bloody engagements of Peterwardein and Belgrade. The latter of these places, together with a part of Wallachia and Servia, were ceded to Austria, but this portion was restored in **1739**. As a protection against future invasions, military colonies were placed by Eugene along the whole line of the Turkish frontier.

Charles VI. attempted to secure the succession to his daughter, *Maria Theresa*, by what is called the *Pragmatic Sanction;* that is, a guaranty of the

Maria Theresa and the Hungarian Nobles.

imperial crown to her, not only by the imperial diet, but by the principal sovereigns of Europe, most of whom acquiesced. The accession of Maria Theresa was opposed, however, by a formidable league, consisting of the kings of France and Prussia and the elector of Bavaria, who were afterward joined by Saxony, Spain, and Poland. The empress was obliged to yield up Silesia to the Prussians, and a French army overran a great part of Bohemia. Austria had taken from Hungary the right to elect her kings, and the Hungarian nobles were rather ill disposed; but when the beautiful Maria Theresa entered their diet, with her infant son upon her arm, and called on them, by their oaths of knighthood to succor a persecuted woman, they rose with one accord, drew their swords, and declared themselves ready to shed their blood in her defence. In an incredibly short space of time, they mustered a formidable army, consisting of Pandours, Croatians, and other wild hordes, whose very names were unknown in civilized Europe. Within a week, the whole of Upper Austria was cleared; and the victorious barbarians, marching into Bavaria, made themselves masters of Munich on the day that the rival emperor received the imperial crown at Frankfort. A general peace was concluded at Aix-la-Chapelle, in **1748**, conferring the imperial dignity on Maria Theresa's husband, *Francis of Lorraine*, and confirming to the queen her hereditary dominions, and Silesia to Prussia. The Seven Years' War commenced in 1756, and was ended in **1763**. It involved all Europe in misery, but left all parties in precisely the same political condition as it found them.

The manners of the imperial and German courts in the early half of the eighteenth century were luxurious and disgraceful. The money wrung from an abused and poverty-stricken people was spent by their oppressors in the most tasteless extravagance. The imperial court was conducted according to the strictest pattern of Spanish etiquette. Forty thousand persons were in some form or other attached to the establishment, and its unlimited expenditure furnished certain people with the means of revelry, whilst the profligacy of courtiers, hangers-on, and lackeys, imparted its tone to society in all ranks. Eating, drinking, and licentiousness were considered the main and only business of life. "Half Vienna was fed from the court kitchen and the court cellar." Solemn feasts, processions, and fireworks, entertained foreign visitors. The bread for the parrots of the empress was steeped in Tokay wine, of which two hogsheads were expended daily. Twelve gallons of the finest wine were also allowed daily for her possets, and twelve barrels for her baths. The court of Saxony was equally profligate, and much less dignified. Augustus the Strong died in 1733, leaving three hundred and fifty-two children. His reign was one long scene of coarse debauchery, and the most wanton expenditure, and tasteless profusion. Once, at a feast in honor of a favorite mistress, Neptune appeared on the Elbe, attended by frigates, Venetian gondolas, and gunboats, the crews of which were dressed in satin jackets and silk stockings. Turkish janizaries, Moors, and Swiss halberdiers guarded the banks; and a blazing pile of wood threw its light on an allegorical picture, which covered six thousand yards of canvas. A Gypsy party at Muhlburg cost three millions of dollars! The private treasury, or green vault, was crowded with precious stones and gold, wrought into grotesque figures, columns of ostrich's eggs, musical clocks, and hundreds of other toys, collected at a vast expense. Carpets of feathers covered the floors of the Japan palace; and one room was entirely filled with ostrich and heron plumes, which were used at the court festivals. The only portion of this gigantic toy-shop that reflected any credit on its founder was the gallery of pictures. The ecclesiastical princes were, for the most part, as profligate and debauched as the worst of the laity. A total disregard of decency was sometimes manifested even by the highest functionaries of the church. The archbishop of Cologne, during his sojourn at Versailles, gave notice that he intended to preach in the court chapel on the 1st of April: a large congregation being assembled, the preacher ascended the pulpit, and bowed gravely to the audience; then shouting, "April fools all!" he ran down the stairs amidst the laughter of the court, and the clang of horns, trumpets, and kettledrums. This was at the very epoch when the same church was carrying on a most inhuman persecution against some twenty thousand simple and virtuous peasants, of the mountains of Salzburg, not even accused of heresy, but only desirous to practise the truths of the gospel, and avoid the profanations of a corrupt priesthood! They were tortured, hunted like wild beasts, and finally banished, perfectly destitute of every thing, hurried off by force to the wilds of the north, without even being permitted to take a change of clothing. More than a thousand parents were separated from their helpless children. The only answer to every remonstrance, or cry of despair, was, "It is the emperor's will."

Francis I. died in 1765, and was succeeded by his son *Joseph II.*, who exercised little authority until the death of Maria Theresa, in 1780. Among the most important events of his reign, may be reckoned the dismemberment of Poland, and the war of the Bavarian succession. He also lost thirty-three thousand men in a Turkish war. He was an upright and excellent prince, ardently desirous of the welfare of the empire. He suppressed many hundred monasteries, and all the mendicant orders, and introduced many reforms; yet these were opposed, not only by those interested in keeping up abuses, but even by the ignorance and wilfulness of those for whose sole benefit they were designed; and the good emperor died broken-hearted A. D. 1790. *Leopold II.* then ascended the throne and died in 1792.

Alarmed at the French revolution, Leopold II. allied himself with Frederic William, king of Prussia, in 1791, to maintain the constitution of the Germanic empire, and royalty in France. This alliance gave occasion to many of the excesses of the revolutionists, and caused a powerful reaction upon Germany. In 1801, the Rhine was made the boundary between France and Germany; thus depriving the latter of a large strip of territory. On the erection of the Austrian possessions into an empire, in 1804, the ancient Germanic empire began to totter to its fall; and it was virtually dissolved, in 1806, at the formation, by Napoleon, of the Confederation of the Rhine. By this movement, sixteen German princes renounced their connection with the empire, and allied themselves to France, choosing Napoleon for their head. Soon afterward, — A. D. 1806, — the dissolution was finally consummated by the emperor, *Francis II.*, who resigned the German imperial crown, and, isolating his dominions from the rest of Germany, took the title of *Francis I., Emperor of Austria.*

On the overthrow of Napoleon, the Germanic empire was not revived; but in place of it, a confederation of

German Emperors.

Date of Accession. A. D.	
800.	Charlemagne.
814.	Louis I. the Debonnaire.
843.	Louis II. the German.
876.	Charles the Fat.
888.	Arnulph.
899.	Louis III. the Child.
911.	Conrad of Franconia.
917.	Henry I. of Saxony, the Fowler.
936.	Otho I..
973.	Otho II. the Red.
1983.	Otho III. the Prodigy.
1002.	Henry II. the Saint.
1024.	Conrad II.
1039.	Henry III.
1056.	Henry IV.
1106.	Henry V.
1125.	Lothaire.
1137.	Conrad III.
1152.	Frederic I., Barbarossa.
1190.	Henry VI.
1198.	Philip of Hohenstaufen.
1208.	Otho IV. of Brunswick.
1212.	Frederic II.
1250.	Conrad IV., William of Holland, Richard of Cornwall. Interregnum.
1273.	Adolph I. of Hapsburg.

Date of Accession. A. D.	
1291.	Rodolphus of Nassau.
1298.	Albert of Austria.
1308.	Henry VII. of Luxemburg.
1313.	Louis IV. of Bavaria, jointly with Frederic III. of Austria, the Fair.
1330.	Louis of Bavaria.
1347.	Charles IV.
1378.	Wenceslaus, (Wenzel.)
0000.	Rupert.
1411.	Sigismund.
1438.	Albert II.
1440.	Frederic III. of Styria.
1493.	Maximilian I.
1519.	Charles V.
1556.	Ferdinand I.
1564.	Maximilian II.
1575.	Rodolph II.
1612.	Matthias.
1619.	Ferdinand II.
1637.	Ferdinand III.
1657.	Leopold I. the Thick lipped.
1705.	Joseph I.
.	Charles VI.
1740.	Charles VII.
1745.	Francis I.
1765.	Joseph II.
1790.	Leopold II.
1792.	Francis II. till 1806.

he independent German states was formed, which held a diet at Frankfort periodically, to discuss matters of general interest. One third of the Austrian empire was represented in it, and, as the oldest member, her representative presided in the diet. But immediately after the French revolution of 1848, agitations took place all over Germany, and most of the princes yielded to the demands of the people for freedom of the press, representative branches in the government, &c. Several sovereigns were obliged to fly from their capitals, and the whole system of monarchy seemed tottering to its fall. A project was set on foot for uniting Germany in a grand confederation, and a parliament was assembled at Frankfort, in May, 1848, consisting of four hundred and thirty-four members, chosen by general suffrage, from various German states.

On the 24th of June, the archduke John of Austria was elected as a provisional chief of the new empire, under the title of *lord lieutenant.* He was installed July 12, and named a portion of his ministers. But in the mean time, the parliament was torn with factions, and the revolutionists seemed unable to unite upon moderate measures. About the same period, the great mass of the French people had become alarmed at the extravagances of the radicals, and a general turn of affairs against the revolutionists became visible over Europe. This tendency was favored by Russia, which now threw its weight in favor of legitimacy. Austria put down the outbreaks in Italy with a ruthless hand, and, by the aid of Russia, crushed the formidable insurrection of Hungary. The new German parliament vanished; the kings and princes who had granted liberal charters in the moment of panic, revoked them soon after, and all Germany rapidly resumed its wonted aspect of despotism. The diet of Frankfort, with some modifications, was restored about 1852.

Empire of Austria.

CHAPTER CCCCXLV.

A. D. 800 to 1863.

Geographical Description—Divisions—Origin and early Annals—Persecution of Protestantism — Rodolph II. — Revolts and Turkish Wars — Maria Theresa — Joseph II. and his Successors — Metternich — Revolution of 1848.

This empire, which at various periods has exercised so large an influence upon the fortunes of Europe, is chiefly situated between latitude 45° and 51° and longitude 9° and 26° east. On the north it is bounded by Russia, Prussia, Saxony, and Bavaria; on the east by the Russian empire; on the south by Servia, Moldavia, and the Italian States; on the west by Sardinia, Switzerland, &c. Its whole extent is estimated at two hundred and sixty thousand square miles; its population, thirty-five millions.

Various branches of the Alpine and Carpathian ranges cross it in different directions. The rivers are numerous and important. The Danube, next to the Volga, is the largest river in Europe. It rises in Baden, near three thousand feet above the level of the sea; passes Vienna, the capital of Austria, and enters the Black Sea, after a course of nearly seventeen hundred miles. It is navigable for steam packets to Vienna.

Austria is rich in minerals, especially copper, tin, lead, iron, coal, and salt. Gold, silver, and mercury are obtained in small quantities.

This empire, being made up of different countries, has of course a great variety of climates and products In the German portions, the climate is temperate, and the products similar to those of France and England Here are extensive manufactures. The internal trade by means of various rivers and canals, and an excellent system of railroads, is now extensive. Austria has but one considerable seaport, Trieste, on the Adriatic, and hence its foreign commerce is limited.

The Austrian empire embraces several divisions: viz., those provinces of which the population are of German origin; those provinces which have been derived from Poland; those which are included in ancient Hungary, and those which belong to Italy. The following table exhibits the divisions in detail, and the ensuing pages give a sketch of each country.

Provinces.	Pop. in 1858.	Chief Towns.	Pop. in '58.
Lower Austria	1,681,697	Vienna	476,222
Upper Austria	707,450	Lintz	27,628
Salzburg	146,769	Salzburg	19,000
Styria	1,056,773	Gratz	63,176
Carinthia	332,456	Klagenfurt	
Carniola	451,491	Laybach	
Goertz, Istria and Trieste	520,978	Trieste	65,874
Tyrol	851,016	Innspruck	
Bohemia	4,705,525	Prague	142,588
Moravia	1,867,094	Brunn	58,809
Silesia	443,912		
Galicia	4,597,470	Lemberg	70,384
Bukovina	456,920		
Dalmatia	404,499	Zara	
Lombardy and Venice	2,446,056	Venice	118,172
Hungary	9,900,785	Pesth	131,705
Croatia	876,009		
Transylvania	1,926,727	Clausenberg	
Military Frontiers	1,064,922		
The army	579,989		
	35,019,058		

Austria, or the Archduchy of Austria, in the time of the Romans, made part of the provinces of Noricum.* It forms the nucleus of the empire, to which the other portions have been successively attached by conquest or negotiation.

The Tyrol, traversed by the Alpine chain, resembles Switzerland, surpassing that country in its mountainous character. In early times it formed part of the ancient Rhætium, and was subdued by the Romans in the time of Augustus.

Styria is entitled a duchy. It was conquered by Tiberius, the eastern part being incorporated with Pannonia, and the western with Noricum. It was conquered by Charlemagne, and annexed to Austria in the twelfth century, with which it has since been united.

Carinthia is also a duchy, and has been an appendage of the Austrian crown since the fourteenth century. It formed a part of the ancient Noricum.

Carniola is a duchy, and has belonged to Austria for four centuries. It was part of the ancient Illyricum.

The Illyrian Coast, with the two preceding provinces, forms what is called the *Kingdom of Illyria.* This is divided into the governments of Laybach and Trieste.

Bohemia derives its name from an ancient tribe called *Boii.* After various revolutions, it became subject to Austria, in 1526.

Moravia, anciently inhabited by the Quadi and Marcomanni, became a kingdom in the ninth century, extending over Bohemia, Silesia, and part of Hungary. It was annexed to Austria, with Bohemia, in 1526.

Silesia, anciently inhabited by the Quadi, was rendered subject to Poland in the sixth century. It was conquered by the king of Bohemia in the fourteenth century. In 1745, it was divided, by the treaty of Dresden, between Prussia and Austria. It is now united with Moravia, the two forming one province.

Galicia once formed part of Hungary. In 1374, it became part of Poland. In 1773, it was annexed to Austria under the title of the *Kingdom of Galicia and Lodomeria.*

Dalmatia was anciently a part of Illyria. It belonged to Hungary till the fifteenth century, when, for a long period, it became the seat of war between the Austrians and Turks. In 1797, it was annexed to Austria.

Transylvania was long connected with Hungary but, in 1699, was annexed to Austria.

Hungary, Lombardy, and Venice, are noticed as distinct countries.

Austria takes its name from the words *oost ryck,* "east country;" and in the ninth and tenth centuries, the region of that name was the frontier of the German empire against the barbarians. It lay on both sides of the Danube, from Passau to Presburg. In 928, Henry the Fowler invested Leopold with it; Otho I. erected it into a marquisate; Frederic Barbarossa made it a duchy; the family of its dukes becoming extinct, a party invited Othocar II., king of Bohemia, to take possession of it; but Rodolph I., the emperor, refused him the investiture of the duchy, and, killing him in battle, appropriated it to his own family, whose possessions already included the Tyrol, and other parts of Switzerland. In 1283, Styria and Carniola were annexed, and Vienna became the residence of the ducal court. In the fourteenth century, the Swiss revolted, as related elsewhere. In 1438, Albert II., duke of Austria, succeeded to the crowns of Hungary and Bohemia. In 1477, Austria was erected into an archduchy, by the emperor Frederic, for his son Maximilian, with many and great privileges over the rest of the states of the empire. This prince, by marrying the heiress of Burgundy, added the Netherlands to the family inheritance. His son Philip, by marrying the heiress of Aragon and Castile, in 1496, also brought his wife's Spanish possessions to the house of Austria; and Charles, afterward the emperor Charles V., inherited them all. On his death, in 1556, Austria, Bohemia, and Hungary, passed to Ferdinand, his second son. These dominions, after being diminished by the final cession of Silesia to Prussia, in 1763, were increased, ten years subsequently, by the seizure of Galicia from Poland. Milan and Mantua had been ceded to Austria by the peace of Utrecht; but she gave up Lombardy and the Netherlands in 1797, receiving the greater part of the Venetian territory instead. Austria became an empire in 1806. In 1805, she lost all her Italian provinces, and a great part of her German possessions, and more of them still, in 1809; but the overthrow of Napoleon restored the empire with its present boundaries, as given above, leaving Austria more powerful, in respect to territory, than ever.

The history of Austria is so much identified with that of the German empire, that it will not be necessary to detail all its early events. Many of them we have given, also, in separate histories of the countries composing the Austrian empire. In the annals of her sovereigns, the singular character and conduct of *Rodolph II.* arrests attention. He succeeded his father Maximilian II. in 1576, and was of a pleasant temper, a friend of science and the arts But

* Noricum consisted of the modern Styria, Carinthia, and Salzburg, and a part of Austria and Bavaria.

unfortunately, he was weak-minded, irresolute, and entirely under the influence of Spain, of Rome, and of the Jesuits, by whom he had been educated. They knew how to plunge him into the busy idleness of erudition, that they might manage his affairs after their own fashion. Protestant preachers were banished from Austria, and the Protestant worship forbidden in all the royal cities, particularly Vienna.

When Hungary, aided by the Turks, drove the Austrians from her territory, and Sultan Achmet named Sigismund her king, (A. D. 1605,) Rodolph fell into such a melancholy state, that he no longer showed himself to his people; indeed, he became indifferent to public affairs, and began to manifest signs of mental alienation. The religions of Germany were arrayed against each other in the Catholic League and the Evangelical Union—but he took no part. His kingdom was distracted by disorders, from one end to the other; but this emperor, who had now acquired the hatred of his people through his disgust for business, occupied himself in chemical amusements, distilling essences, &c., or in cutting gems, building edifices, and observing the stars. In 1597, he had taken into his service the famous Tycho Brahe, the Danish astronomer, who, being also a superstitious astrologer, predicted to the king that he would die by the hand of some near relation. Rodolph II., therefore, feared to marry; and although he had sent his agents into almost every court in Europe, to canvass the qualifications of every marriagable princess, and transmit him portraits of the most beautiful, with notices of their character and temper, he died a bachelor.

After the silly prediction noticed above, the credulous Rodolph II., agitated by perpetual terrors, sequestered himself entirely from the world. Shut up in his palace, he became inaccessible to his courtiers; foreign ambassadors, and even his ministers, could not procure an interview. He dared no longer to frequent his chapel; and in order not to be deprived of the pleasure of seeing his horses, he caused a covered gallery to be constructed, which led from the castle to the stables. It was lighted by narrow windows, through which the rays entered obliquely, that he might promenade it without danger of being shot. Next to his horses, he loved his mistresses; but rarely was one found who could attach him for more than a week. Beside his stables and seraglio, he had a menagerie of rare animals. Sometimes he would sit motionless for whole hours, watching a clock-maker or painter at his work; and woe to the person who disturbed him in these moments of enjoyment! The first piece of furniture that came to hand flew at the head of the rash intruder. Courtiers and favorites, meanwhile, having every thing in their own hands, emptied the coffers of the state, and paralyzed every great enterprise.

The Protestant Reformation embroiled the house of Austria with several of the northern powers. The summary methods taken by the sovereigns to suppress Protestantism in the Austrian empire, indicated a cold-blooded, ruthless despotism, which made the Austrian name almost a synonyme for tyranny. In 1684, a conspiracy of the nobles was discovered in Hungary. *Leopold I.*, now emperor, put the leaders to death; and before men's minds were well recovered from the surprise and terror into which this act of despotic severity had thrown them, two hundred and fifty Lutheran ministers were summoned to Presburg, to be tried on a similar charge, and sold as galley-slaves to the Neapolitans—although no evidence of their guilt had been brought forward!

The people, thus deprived of their pastors, and persecuted beyond endurance by the Jesuits, broke out into rebellion, and in their despair invoked the assistance of the Turks; who, yielding at last to the unwearied solicitations of certain French emissaries of Louis XIV., consented to send two hundred and eighty thousand men into Hungary, under the command of the grand vizier, Kara Mustapha. A panic went before this overwhelming force, which advanced almost without opposition to the very walls of Vienna, and the city was on the point of surrendering after a siege of two months, when the commandant, Count Strahlenburg, ordered, as a last resource, a flight of rockets to be let off from the tower of St. Stephen's church. A few moments of anxious suspense followed, and then a bright flame, shooting upward from the mountain of Kahlenberg, announced to the besieged that succor was at hand. The emperor had assembled a force more rapidly than he had anticipated, and was now advancing with a large army of Germans and Poles, under the command of the Polish king, John Sobieski.

So ignorant were the Turks of military tactics, that they had neglected to occupy the passes, and were, in consequence, surprised by the imperial forces, and utterly defeated; their artillery, baggage, and treasure with the whole correspondence between Louis XIV and the grand vizier, fell into the hands of the conqueror. The following day, the king of Poland entered Vienna amidst the acclamations of the citizens, whom his valor had saved from death and slavery but the emperor, Leopold I., with the mean jealousy which belonged to his character, received him with insulting coldness, and refused to provide quarters for his army.

No sooner was Austria delivered from the Turks, than Leopold I. suffered the full weight of his vengeance to fall on the deserted Hungarians, who had been in revolt, with the famous Tekeli at their head, since 1678. Thousands of them were imprisoned, tortured, and put to death by sentence of a court presided over by Caraffa, an Italian count, and Ambringer, grand master of the Teutonic order. This tribunal was called, from its atrocious cruelty, the *Shambles of Eperies*, the place where it met. A scaffold was erected in the midst of that city, and for nine months thirty executioners were occupied in killing the victims whom the German troops brought in to be tried. The right of electing their own king was now taken from the Hungarians, and the crown of Hungary made hereditary in the family of Hapsburg. These, and other struggles between these two states, will be noticed in our history of Hungary.

The reign of *Joseph I.* was occupied with a new insurrection in Hungary, and the continuation of the war of the Spanish succession with Louis XIV. of France—an account of which will be found in our history of that famous monarch. Affairs had taken a favorable turn for the Austrians in the latter war, and the contrary in the former; when Joseph I. died prematurely, without children, at the age of thirty-three, —A. D. 1711,—leaving the Austrian throne to his brother, the archduke Charles.

The Turks, having conquered the Morea, now threatened Vienna again, and even Rome also. But the prince Eugene crossed the Danube in sight of

.neir camp of one hundred and fifty thousand men, and cut them in pieces at Peterwardein — A. D. 1716 — killing forty thousand of them, and the grand vizier, as elsewhere related. Temeswar, the last place they held in Hungary, was taken, and caused the submission to Austria of all the Banat, and a part of Wallachia. In 1717, Eugene destroyed another Turkish army, and also took Belgrade, and by the consequent peace of the next year, Austria acquired the Banat, Servia, and a part of Wallachia, Bosnia, and Croatia; but these were all restored in consequence of the dreadful defeat of the imperial army of sixty thousand men, at Grotzka, in 1739. *Charles VI.* died of chagrin the next year — the last of the house of Austria in the male line.

The acquisition of the Netherlands and the Island of Sardinia, in the early part of the eighteenth century, naturally suggested to the Austrians the thought of building up a commerce beyond seas, and a navy. Several new harbors were therefore established on the Adriatic, to attract the Levant trade and the wealth of the East; a commercial company was also formed. Another company, to carry on trade with Turkey by the Danube, gave great importance to internal commerce. In 1722, encouraged by the success of these enterprises, Charles VI. also established, at Ostend, an East India trading company. This aroused the jealousy of both the English and the Dutch, and occasioned complicated negotiations, ending in the congress of Cambray, (1724,) the convention of Ripperda, (1725,) the Hanover alliance, (1726,) the protocols of Paris, (1727,) the treaty of Berlin, (1728,) the congress of Soissons, (1729,) the treaty of Seville, (1730,) and finally the peace of Vienna, (1731.)

The calamitous war of the Austrian succession dismembered the possessions of the now enfeebled house of Austria, as elsewhere related. But the chivalrous aid of the Hungarian nobles, and the money of England enabled Maria Theresa, their queen, to withstand the coalition against her of France, Spain, Bavaria, Prussia, and Saxony; and at the end of the war, in 1746, she found herself sovereign of her hereditary dominions, her husband, Francis of Lorraine, now acknowledged emperor of Germany, being simply co-regent of the paternal inheritance with her. After striving in vain to recover Silesia from Prussia, in the seven years' war, Maria Theresa occupied herself in establishing her numerous family.* Her eldest son, the archduke Joseph, was crowned emperor of Germany in 1765, and she declared him co-regent with her in all that pertained to the military affairs of her dominions. In 1780, he succeeded her in the Austrian states, under the title of *Joseph II.*

He was a pupil of the French philosophers and political economists, and designed to carry on a series of reforms, quite analogous to the decrees of the Constituent Assembly of France, whose members were of the same school. The Austrian monarchy was then, as it is now, a composition made up of several nations, different in manners, language, and government. The feudal system existed throughout. Maria Theresa had commenced the fusion into one of the several races, but it advanced slowly: she had also attacked feudalism by moderate and successive reforms. Joseph II. was too impetuous to act with the same slowness. He wished to establish at once a unity in his states, and declared that in future there should be no separate provinces. He apportioned all the monarchy into thirteen governments, and substituted every where the absolute will of the sovereign for the authority of the nobility, and of feudal customs. He imposed the German language upon all his subjects, who actually spoke thirty different idioms. He substituted one single impost for all the various territorial contributions, abolished feudal servitude and all seigneurial rights, proclaimed the equality of all before the law, and instituted the military conscription. To develop commerce and industry, he suppressed the provincial custom-houses, opened new roads, dug canals, declared Trieste a free port, and published a tariff intended to protect Austrian manufactures from foreign competition. He limited the authority of the court of Rome, suppressed nine hundred convents, took off the censorship from the clergy, caused the system of public instruction to undergo a thorough revision, guarantied liberty of conscience to all, and restored their civil rights to Protestants and Jews. But these innovations, as we have elsewhere remarked, aroused a vast opposition in all the provinces, especially in Hungary, where they interfered with so many privileges and abuses. He also wished to consolidate the monarchy by exchanging the Netherlands for Bavaria; but the king of Prussia thought this would cause Austria to preponderate too much in Germany, and excited the king of England, as elector of Hanover, the king of Saxony, and a crowd of little princedoms with which Germany swarmed, as also the states general, to declare war against Joseph II., — A. D. 1785, — hence he was obliged to abandon his designs.

Other serious troubles soon perplexed the well-meaning emperor; for while he was engaged in a Turkish war, the Netherlands revolted, and the Austrian governor was driven from Brussels, A. D. 1789. The failing health of Joseph II., distracted by so many enemies, and a new insurrection in Hungary, prevented him from chasing the Turks from Europe, as he expected to do in a third successful campaign. Being obliged to abandon his large designs against Turkey, and to revoke his reforms in Hungary, the poor emperor, whose chief crime was that he was in advance of his age, died a short time after, his death being no doubt hastened by chagrin, A. D. 1790. "Write upon my tomb," said he, a few moments before breathing his last, "'Here lies a prince whose intentions were pure, but who had the misfortune to fail in all his projects.'"

Leopold II., his successor, with true Austrian inertia, abolished all the reforms of Joseph II., placed every thing back *in statu quo*, and set himself to opposing France and the French revolution. But the coalitions he formed against France eventuated in depriving Austria of Northern Italy, Flanders, Belgium, and Holland, and all the left bank of the Rhine, as the result of a five years' war, 1792 to 1797. Bonaparte marched to within a few leagues of Vienna, and Austria was compelled to recognize the Cisalpine Republic, and yield Belgium to France, receiving in exchange the greater part of the Venetian territory, A. D. 1797

* This royal mother procured for her second son, Peter Leopold, the archduchy of Tuscany; the third, Ferdinand, married the heiress of Modena, &c.; the fourth, Maximilian, was made assistant of Munster, and elector of Cologne. Of her daughters, Anne and Elizabeth received rich abbeys at Prague and Innspruck; Christina married the elector of Saxony; Amelia, the duke of Parma; Caroline, the king of Naples; and Marie Antoinette the dauphin of France, afterward Louis XVI.

She also acquired Western Galicia, by the third partition of Poland, in 1795. A second war against France, in 1799, in which Austria was joined by England and Russia, ended in further concessions to France, compensated in part by the annexation of Istria and Dalmatia to the kingdom. Francis II. now erected his hereditary dominions into an empire, as elsewhere remarked, A. D. 1804. The third war against France, begun in 1805, ended, the same year, in the recognition by Austria, at the peace of Presburg, of the kingdoms of Bavaria and Wirtemberg, and her surrender of the Venetian states and Dalmatia to the new kingdom of Italy, besides other cessions of territory,—in all about one hundred thousand square miles, and three millions of subjects. The next year, the German empire was dissolved by Napoleon, and Francis II. took the title of *Francis I.*, emperor of Austria alone. A fourth war, terminated by the peace of Vienna, cost her three and a half millions of subjects; while the daughter of the emperor, Maria Louisa, became the wife of Napoleon.

But after Napoleon's unfortunate campaign in Russia, Austria allied herself with England and Russia against France; and though defeated at Dresden, the allies gained the battle of Leipsic, A. D. 1813. This event resulted in the banishment of Napoleon to Elba, and left the allies to portion out Europe, which they pretended to have freed, at will; and once again the interests of the few prevailed over the interests of the many. After the battle of Waterloo, Austria took back all she had yielded, except Belgium, but annexed the new Lombard-Venetian kingdom, and gave, beside, to collateral branches of the house of Hapsburg, the grand duchy of Tuscany and the duchies of Modena, Parma, and Placenza. After this epoch, Austria, placing herself at the head of the "Holy Alliance," became the declared champion of legitimacy, and the enemy of all kinds of revolutions and reforms. These, it repeatedly lent its soldiers to put down: it established, also, an extremely severe censorship of the press, and suppressed, with atrocious severity, insignificant Italian plots; while its slavish police filled the dungeons of Spielberg with victims.

Ferdinand I. succeeded to the throne in 1835; and, though he declared an amnesty to some political prisoners, and mitigated the barbarous treatment of others, there was no beneficial change in the system of government. Where, however, he was not able to prevent any change for the better, he submitted to it with phlegmatic patience. His system was temporizing, palliative, entirely passive, and characterized by a vague and childish fear of movement, of action, and of progress. His minister, *Metternich*,—a politician without being a statesman,—seemed made expressly for Austrian politics. He knew how to think of every thing, and to grasp it from afar; he had strings to pull in every direction; and was well skilled in using women and underlings in his infinite trickeries. He excelled especially in employing money adroitly, as did Louis XIV. He had nothing great or difficult to do; he wished to maintain the *statu quo:* and thus he ruled long in the cabinets of Europe.

But when the French revolution of 1848 broke out, the wildfire of liberty ran rapidly over Europe, and even invaded Austria, the triply walled citadel of despotic legitimacy itself. Vienna became the theatre of a bloody revolt; and, March 13, Metternich fled before the popular indignation. The emperor made concessions; but these were not satisfactory, and the insurgents got possession of the capital. Ferdinand fled, and afterward resigned the crown to his nephew, *Francis Joseph I.* About the same time, Lombardy, South Tyrol, Venice, Trieste, and Bohemia revolted. This example was followed by Hungary, which finally declared itself independent, April 14, 1849.

It seemed that the Austrian empire was about to be dismembered; and, as its various kingdoms would have become so many free governments, the fate of Austria seemed to involve the fate of European monarchy itself. In this attitude of affairs, while France and England temporized, the emperor of Russia seized the critical moment, and decided the question by marching one hundred thousand men into Hungary. Austria soon gained the ascendency in Italy, and was able to complete the suppression of the revolt in that quarter. This being done, she was in a position to put her strength into the conflict with Hungary. The people there made a glorious effort, but the strife was unequal. Not a single European government came to their aid, and the patriotic Hungarians were finally overwhelmed. Austria triumphed and now holds together the discordant members of her empire.

In the late Eastern war Austria professed neutrality; but she raised an immense army, and on the evacuation of the principalities, she marched in and occupied them. She exerted herself to gain peace, and joined in the treaty of Paris, which terminated the war.

In 1858, various circumstances seemed to indicate that France and Sardinia were on the point of entering into an alliance. Austria took the alarm, and sought to strengthen her hold upon Lombardy, and even to form an Italian league. In the latter she failed. The New Year's speech of Napoleon III. leaving no doubt as to his hostile intentions, an Austrian army crossed the Ticino into Sardinia in April, 1859. They recrossed, however, and were signally defeated at Magenta, on the 4th of June. After the total rout at Solferino on the 24th of June, Austria was glad to make peace. She was allowed to retain Venice, but was compelled to resign the greater portion of Lombardy to the kingdom of Italy.

CHAPTER CCCCXLVI.

Notices of Bohemia, Moravia, and the Tyrol.

It now remains to notice the several parts of the Austrian empire as far as they have a separate history. Bohemia is one of these, which, though it has been an appanage of the royal house of Austria for four hundred years,—since A. D. 1438,—has yet a character of its own, and a history previous to that time. Its name is said to mean "home of the *Boii*," a tribe who, at an early period, subdued or ejected the aborigines, and were driven out, in their turn by the *Marcomanni.* The country is an elevated, lozenge-shaped, undulating valley, interspersed with low hills, with isolated summits, and surrounded by wild and dreary mountains.

As a kingdom, Bohemia includes the margraviate of Moravia and a portion of Upper Silesia. Previous to 1635, the Lusatias belonged to it; since then, they have been annexed to Saxony. The people are peaceably disposed, attached to their government, brave, resolute hospitable, and charitable. The great mass of the peasantry are held in servitude. Agriculture is toler ably flourishing, and manufactures more so. Prague, the capital, has many titles to historical celebrity.

The Hussites and Ziska form the chief topic of interest in the later annals of Bohemia. Their devastating struggles for religious liberty have been commemorated in our account of Germany. The Gypsy race are sometimes called *Bohemians*, as they here first attracted the notice of Europe. Our history of these singular people will be found in connection with that of Spain.

Moravia has also been involved in the destinies of the house of Austria since 1438: its independent annals are confined to a previous period. It derives its name from the River *Morava*, which passes through it. Here the *Quadi* dwelt in ancient times, who were driven out by the *Slavi*. Its kings were once powerful and independent; but in A. D. 908, the country was parcelled out among the Germans, Poles, and Hungarians. In 1086, that part of it properly called Moravia was declared a marquisate by the German emperor, Henry IV., and united with Bohemia, to whose dukes and kings it has been subject ever since.

The *Moravian Brethren*, Herrn-hutters, or Unitas Fratrum, are a religious sect, which originated in Bohemia from the remains of the stricter sort of Hussites, about the middle of the fifteenth century. In A. D. 1500, they numbered two hundred communities. In the sixteenth century, their chief residence was in Moravia, whence their name. In 1722, a part of them were reorganized under Count Zinzendorf, as the *United Brethren*, under the same general idea of establishing a Christian social organization, in conformity to the simplicity and purity of the gospel. They do not, however, allow this organization to interfere with their political or civil duties. The communities are independent and self-supported. They have distinguished themselves for their humble heroism as successful missionaries, and are now numerous throughout Europe and America, and maintain a character which for centuries has insured them the respect of society and of nations.

Transylvania, hemmed in by the Carpathian Mountains on the remotest eastern frontier of the Austrian empire, has followed the fortunes of that kingdom since 1699. It was then, by the peace of Carlovitza, incorporated in the dominions of Austria, and the transfer was acknowledged by Turkey. *Polish Austria* will be noticed in our account of Poland, whose ancient importance and tragical fate demand for it a separate history. *Hungary*, also, though long forming a part of the Austrian empire, has played so conspicuous a part in the history of Oriental Europe, both formerly and of late, that we have devoted to it, also, a distinct chapter. On the other side of the empire, the histories of *Lombardy* and of *Venice*, demanded, and have already received, a separate place in our work.

The Tyrol, long an appanage of the imperial Austrian house of Hapsburg, was disconnected from it for a short period subsequent to 1806, when it was temporarily annexed to Bavaria. The peculiarity of its situation, and of the people, entitle it to a separate notice.

The lofty mountains of Tyrol had been for centuries the dwelling-place of liberty. Subject in name to the house of Hapsburg, their inhabitants enjoyed, nevertheless, the full exercise of their republican privileges, choosing their own magistrates, and contributing to the imperial army a contingent of troops, commanded by officers of their own election, and clothed and disciplined according to the ancient fashion of their country. In return for these indulgences, the sturdy mountaineers served their emperor with the most devoted fidelity.

It was in defence of the rights of these their sovereigns, and of the inviolability of their own territory, that the Tyrolese distinguished themselves during the War of the Spanish Succession. Bavaria had sided with France against the imperialists, and in June, 1703, the elector invaded the Tyrol at the head of sixteen thousand men. Having made themselves masters of Innspruck, the main body of the Bavarians began to ascend the Brenner river, leaving a detachment under General Neuvion to follow up their advantages on the banks of the Inn. As night closed in, a line of signal fires announced to the invaders that the people were making preparations to oppose their progress. Still, Nouvion's detachment continued their march until they had reached the broken bridge of Pontelag, and were endeavoring to ford the river, when a storm of bullets from the Tyrolese marksmen — who took their aim with deadly accuracy from behind the crags which concealed them from the enemy — compelled the Bavarians first to halt, and then to retreat to the bank which they had just quitted. Scarcely had they reached their former position, when the mountains above them seemed to burst asunder, and discharge huge fragments of rock, which fell with a terrible crash on the heads of the soldiers. A general panic now seized the Bavarians, who fled in disorder toward the bridge of Zama. But here they found the bridge broken down, and the river unfordable; and being thus hemmed in on every side, and finding resistance and flight equally impracticable, they laid down their arms and surrendered to Martin Sterzinger, the Tyrolese commander. Meanwhile the elector of Bavaria, after retreating from the Brenner, had cut his way through the Tyrolese, and returned to Bavaria with the loss of two thirds of his army.

About a century later, the Tyrolese again proved that they had not lost the spirit of their brave and independent ancestry. Faithful to their hereditary loyalty, and attached as they were from choice to the house of Austria, great was their chagrin when they learnt, in 1805, that the Emperor Francis had ceded their country to Maximilian Joseph, king of Bavaria. On the 14th of January, 1806, this king issued a proclamation to his new subjects, in which he declared his intention not only of securing to them the ancient constitutional privileges which they had enjoyed under the German empire, but also of taking active measures for the improvement of their political and social condition. The last phrase was ill chosen, as addressed to men jealously attached to their institutions, and insensible of any defects which could render reform necessary or desirable; and still more unfortunate was the manner in which Maximilian proceeded to redeem his promise.

Whether in forgetfulness of his engagements to preserve their constitution, or, as is more probable, in utter ignorance of their condition and character, the king attempted to apply to the Tyrol those measures which he had found successful in his hereditary kingdom of Bavaria. But the cases were by no means parallel. In Bavaria, the people were impoverished by the exactions of indolent monks, and their morals corrupted by the scenes of clerical profligacy which they witnessed in almost every parish: in the Tyrol, the priests, few in number as compared with the exigencies of their flocks, simple in their habits, poor, and self-denying, were the friends and counsellors of the people, who were prepared to support them in their resistance to the ecclesiastical reforms of the new sovereign. The Bavarians, long unaccustomed to military service, required a measure as stringent as the conscription to bring them back to their standards, and retain them there; but the warlike mountaineers of the Tyrol had never relaxed the bands of discipline. Nor were they now inclined to receive a new system of political and judicial regulations, which, however necessary for Bavaria, were worse than useless in a country where corruption, and partiality, and legal delays were absolutely unknown. The king also disgusted his new subjects by changing the name of their country to "South Bavaria," and by the sale of the castle of Tyrol, the possessor of which, according to a time-honored prophecy, was alone entitled to their obedience.

When, therefore, Austria again raised the standard against France, and the allies of France, she might well rely on the coöperation of the Tyrolese; and in 1808, there arrived at Vienna a deputation, headed by *Andrew Hofer*, a wealthy peasant and innkeeper of the Tyrol, who had long enjoyed the confidence of his countrymen, and now pledged them to rise against Bavaria. Austria, on her part, engaged to aid them in the revolt: this was to take place during the rising of the streams in the spring, which would impede an invading army. Although this arrangement was known to many thousand Tyrolese, yet it was kept secret from the Bavarian General Kinkel, and his French colleague, Brisson.

On the night of April 9, 1809, a small red flag—the signal agreed on by the confederates—was seen floating down the stream of the Inn, and, as it passed, the tocsin rang out in the different villages, and salvos of artillery and signal-fires on the heights announced to the Tyrolese that the hour of their deliverance was come. The same simple tactics were pursued by the mountaineers as had been so successful a century before. Huge stones, fragments of rocks, and trunks of trees were collected together on the edges of the defiles through which the French and Bavarian armies were to pass. As soon as the enemy was fairly entangled in the ravine, a stentorian voice was heard far up in the clear air, "In the name of the Holy Trinity, cut all loose!" and the whole mass came crashing down into the valley below, upon the devoted heads of the invaders; whilst, at the same moment, marksmen, stationed wherever they could find a shelter, poured in a destructive fire from their unerring rifles, until, at last, the miserable remnant, bewildered and hopeless of rescue, surrendered at discretion. Eight thousand men, one hundred and more officers, and all their artillery, baggage, and ammunition, thus fell into the hands of the Tyrolese.

But Austria deserted her faithful subjects in this hour of their need: a large French force advanced to Innspruck, and the Tyrolese, hopeless of relief, seemed to yield a sullen obedience. At last, irritated beyond endurance by the outrages of the French, they flew to arms, again placed Hofer at their head, constructed cannon of larchwood bound with iron hoops, fortified their crags as before with huge rocks, and drove the French out of the country. Hofer now held the reins of government, and the Tyrolese were persuaded by the Austrian Archduke John to lay down their arms. Shortly after, Hofer, deceived by false intelligence, again raised his standard; but the spirit of his countrymen was broken. Finding it impossible to rally them, he retired to a solitary mountain, among the eternal snows. Treachery reached him even here, and he was betrayed into the hands of his enemies, who shot him, by order of Napoleon A. D. 1810. On the pacification of Europe, a few years afterward, the Tyrol was again restored to Austria.

CHAPTER CCCCXLVII.

General Views of the Austrian Empire.

The inhabitants of the Austrian empire belong to several entirely distinct races. 1. The Germans form the population of the archduchy of Austria, the greater part of that of Styria and Tyrol, and the minority in the Hungarian and Polish provinces, and in Bohemia, Moravia, and Silesia. 2. The Sclavonic race, comprising nearly one half of the population, consists of several different people: these are the Tzechs, or Bohemians; the Slowacs in Moravia and Hungary, the Poles in Galicia; the Wends in Styria, Carniola, Carinthia, and Tyrol; the Croatians, Dalmatians, &c. 3. The Uralian race comprises the dominant people of Hungary and Transylvania, or the Magyars. 4. The Latin race comprises the Italians, and the Wallachians of Hungary, Transylvania, and the military frontiers.

The Sclavonians, scattered, as we have remarked, over a great extent, are the most backward and ignorant part of the population. They are commonly employed in mere rustic labors, and many of them are still in a state of servitude. Thus, in Bohemia and Moravia, the German population conducts public affairs, transacts commercial operations, and exercises the mechanic arts, while the Sclavonians are the common laborers; and in Hungary, the Magyars, who, though in general illiterate, are a spirited and intelligent race, and fond of active employments and a military life, leave the more servile kinds of labor to the Sclavonic inhabitants. The Sclavonians, in fact, are the conquered aborigines, who were reduced to slavery or kept in a subordinate state by their conquerors. In the Polish provinces, where the Sclavonians form almost the whole population, they evince an aversion to mechanic arts and commerce, and the traders and dealers there, as in Poland, are mostly Jews.

In an agricultural country like Austria, the customs are small, and the revenue is principally raised by land and poll taxes. In the Hungarian states, the nobility are exempt from taxes. The revenue of Austria is much smaller than that of England or France, not exceeding seventy million dollars; the debt is probably four hundred million. The army is generally composed of about two hundred and seventy thousand men.

The Roman Catholic religion is professed by a very great majority of the inhabitants of Austria. The adherents of the Greek church are numerous in Transylvania, the southern part of Hungary, and in Croatia Sclavonia, and Galicia. There are many Protestants in Hungary, Galicia and the German provinces, and some Socinians, or Unitarians, in Transylvania. The number of Greek Christians is about one million five hundred thousand, that of Protestants three million and that of Catholics twenty-eight million There are

Pilgrimage to Mariazell

nearly five hundred thousand Jews, chiefly in Galicia, Moravia, Hungary, and Bohemia. All religions are tolerated in Austria. The archbishop of Vienna is the head of the Austrian church; the landed property of the church is extensive, and there are three hundred abbeys and above five hundred convents in the empire.

To show the religious character of the Catholics of Austria, we give a sketch of a pilgrimage to Mariazell: This is a small town in the province of Styria, and situated in the most romantic part of that mountainous country. A shrine and an ancient picture of the Virgin Mary, which is believed to be endowed with miraculous qualities, have given importance to the place, and annually attracted many thousands of pilgrims, ever since the finding of the picture, in the eighth or ninth century, down to our own days. These devotees wend over moor and mountain, not merely from all corners of Upper and Lower Styria, but from Carinthia, from Moravia and Silesia, from the Tyrol, from Bohemia, from Vienna, the capital, and from many other distant parts of the Austrian empire

The annual pilgrimage is regulated by the government itself, which invariably fixes the day of its departure in the hot months of July or August. An imperial proclamation to this effect, and enjoining the pilgrims to pray before the shrine of the Virgin for the prosperity of the house of Hapsburg, is put up on the great gate of St. Stephen's. On the appointed day, the devotees assemble in that Gothic cathedral at earliest dawn; at four o'clock in the morning, high mass is performed; and then the long, picturesque line, consisting of all ages and of both sexes, separated into divisions by religious banners and crucifixes, begins its toilsome march toward the rugged mountains of Styria; the pilgrims chanting hymns as they go, and having their weary steps cheered from time to time by the music of trumpets and kettle-drums, that are scattered along the line, a the head of the several divisions.

A traveller, who witnessed the scene in 1822, says that the procession which he saw leave Vienna consisted of nearly three thousand persons, who were all of the poorer classes. Females predominated; and among the young women, who were numerous, he observed many who were very pretty, and looked very graceful in their pilgrim weeds. Almost all of them were barefooted; they carried long staves entwined with flowers, and wore, for the most part, straw bonnets with enormous brims, to protect their faces from the scorching rays of the sun. This female equipment varies very much in the different provinces, each of which has its distinctive costume; and this circumstance adds to the picturesqueness of the scene, when the pilgrimages from different parts meet at their common centre — the shrine of Mariazell.

From whatever place they may come, the pilgrims always ascend the rough mountain of Mariazell, singing hymns to the Virgin. Here the young women take off their straw hats, or white linen caps, and let their hair flow in loose disorder over their shoulders; and the sturdier pilgrims, to increase their penance and the natural difficulties of the way, drag huge, heavy wooden crosses after them up the steep ascent. On gaining the summit of the mountain, and the sight of the gloomy, antique church, the pilgrims all fall prostrate, and raise a universal and long-continued shout; after which they cross themselves, rise, and approach the shrine slowly and reverentially, singing as with one voice, and making the mountains reëcho with their solemn notes. They kneel in a double row — the inner one consisting of females on their knees, and the outer one of men leaning on their staves — round a massive silver railing, which guards the sacred shrine, and pray to the picture, which they can scarcely see. At the evening hour, which, in Catholic countries, is sacred to the Virgin, at the pensive, twilight *Ave Maria*, the scenes in the church are romantic and picturesque. As the sun disappears, the young women in the inner part of the circle begin to move slowly round the railing on their knees, singing, with voices in which there is much harmony, a hymn to the Virgin; while the men, standing still, take up the burden at the end of every stanza, bending to the earth before the sacred image.

When the church service terminates, other scenes not less romantic, take place in the neighboring woods Many prefer the open air to the crowded hotels of the town, and thousands of the pilgrims bivouac in separate parties in the woods, where they pass the greater part of the night in singing, one party replying to the choruses of the other. At the earliest dawn of day, they begin to emerge, two by two, from the woods and from the town, until the mountain sides and the valley beneath seem dotted all over with white caps.

In consequence of the scandals and disorders created by the rivalry existing between the women of Gratz, the capital of Styria, and those of Vienna, Joseph II. abolished the pilgrimage from Vienna, seizing most of the treasury of Mariazell, and melting down the silver images of his mother and his brothers and sisters, hung before the shrine as votive offerings by his mother herself, the empress Maria Theresa. The pilgrimage was afterward restored and encouraged by Francis I., the late emperor of Austria.

Vienna, the capital of Austria, is pleasantly situated upon the Danube, in the midst of a fertile and picturesque region. It consists of the city proper, which is small and surrounded with walls, and thirty-four suburbs, whose spacious streets and elegant edifices form a striking contrast with the narrow streets and mean buildings of the former. Vienna contains eighteen public squares, twenty monasteries, five theatres, fifty churches, numerous scientific and charitable institutions, and very nearly five hundred thousand inhabitants. The finest promenade is the Prater, on an island in the Danube, which the rich equipages, the gay crowd, the fine walks, and the various amusements combine to render unrivalled in Europe. The imperial palace is a splendid but irregular building, containing numerous treasures of art, and a fine library of three hundred thousand volumes.

Many of the palaces of the nobles are magnificent, and enriched with galleries of paintings and sculpture, cabinets of medals, scientific collections, &c. Among the churches are St. Stephen's, a large and noble Gothic edifice, the tower of which, four hundred and fifty feet high, is one of the loftiest in Europe, and the church of the Capuchins, which contains the burial vault of the imperial family. The great hospital is remarkable for its extent, comprising seven courts, planted with trees, one hundred and eleven halls, and two thousand beds; it receives about sixteen thousand patients annually. The literary institutions are important; the university is one of the best in Europe, particularly for the medical department, and its library contains one hundred and ten thousand volumes.

In Vienna and its environs are the greatest number of botanical gardens in any place of equal extent in the world, and several of them are unrivalled by any similar establishments. Pleasure is the great occupation of the inhabitants of Vienna. In the environs are numerous parks and pretty towns. Schœnbrunn and Luxemburg are favorite summer residences of the emperor.

Other towns in the archduchy of Austria are Neustadt, containing eight thousand inhabitants, with flourishing manufactures, and connected with Vienna by a canal; Lintz, with thirty thousand, containing extensive woollen manufactures, and connected with the salt works of Gmunden by a railroad; Steyer, ten thousand inhabitants, noted for the excellence and cheapness of its cutlery, which is exported to all parts of Europe; and Salzburg, with nineteen thousand inhabitants, a cathedral, archbishop's palace, several literary institutions, and manufactures.

Gratz, a well-built town, and the capital of Styria contains a university with a rich library, and numerous other institutions for education, among which the Johanneum, or college founded by the archduke John, is the principal. Its manufactures of cotton goods, hardware, silk, &c., are extensive. Population, sixty thousand.

Innspruck, the capital of Tyrol, with ten thousand inhabitants, contains a university, and some other literary institutions. Bolzano, noted for its fairs, with eight thousand inhabitants; Trent, ten thousand inhabitants, celebrated in history as the seat of the last general council of the Catholic church, (from 1545 to 1563;) and Roveredo, with ten thousand inhabitants, a busy manufacturing place—are the other principal town of the Tyrol.

Trieste, situated upon the northern extremity of the Gulf of Venice, is the principal commercial town in the empire. Including the immediate neighborhood, with its beautiful gardens, vineyards, and country seats, it has a population of sixty five thousand souls.

Laybach, formerly capital of the duchy of Carniola and at present of the kingdom of Illyria, has an active trade, and its manufactures are extensive. A congress of European sovereigns was held here in 1820. Population, ten thousand. Idria, in the same government, derives importance from its rich mines of quicksilver. Population, five thousand.

Klagenfurt, a busy manufacturing town, with nine thousand inhabitants, was the capital of the former duchy of Carinthia. Rovigno, with a good harbor, has an active commerce, and contains ten thousand inhabitants. Pola, in the vicinity, contains some magnificent Roman ruins, among which are a temple in good preservation, a vast amphitheatre, consisting of three stories, each having seventy two arches, and capable of accommodating eighteen thousand persons, and a beautiful triumphal arch, called the *Golden Gate*.

Prague, the capital of Bohemia, is a large and flourishing city, situated on both sides of the Moldau, over which there is a splendid bridge of sixteen arches. It contains forty-eight churches, sixteen monasteries, nine synagogues, a number of elegant palaces, among which are an imperial castle, the vast palace of Wallenstein, and other public buildings. It is strongly fortified with very extensive works. The university is one of the oldest, and was long one of the most celebrated in Europe; its library contains one hundred thousand volumes. Prague is the centre of Bohemian commerce, and the depot of the active manufacturing district in which it is situated. Population, one hundred and forty thousand, of which seven thousand five hundred are Jews. It is celebrated in history as the residence of Huss, the Bohemian reformer, and the birthplace of his disciple Jerome.

Reichenberg, with ten thousand inhabitants, a flourishing town, with extensive manufactures of cotton and woollen; Budweis, six thousand, with an active trade; Joachimsthal, four thousand, noted for its mines of silver and cobalt, and the centre of a mining district, which furnishes lead and tin; Pilsen, eight thousand inhabitants, deriving an active trade from its woollen manufactures, and the mines of iron and alum in its vicinity; and Carlsbad, Tœplitz, and Seidlitz, known for their mineral waters—are the other most important Bohemian towns.

Brunn, the capital of Moravia, is a flourishing manıfacturing city, with fifty-eight thousand inhabitants. ts woollen manufactures are the most extensive in the empire. Spielberg, a fortress on a neighboring hill, s now used as a state prison. At Austerlitz, ten miles from Brunn, Napoleon gained a brilliant victory over the Russian and Austrian forces, in 1805. Olmutz, a fortified place, with thirteen thousand inhabitants, was for a time the prison of Lafayette. Lemberg, the capital of Austrian Poland, or the kingdom of Galicia, is a large and well-built city, with a population of seventy thousand souls, among whom are twenty thousand Jews. Brody, the second city, and the most important commercial town of Galicia, has twenty thousand inhabitants, of whom sixteen thousand are Jews.

There are six universities in the empire, beside those of the Italian provinces; they are at Vienna, Prague, Pesth, Lemberg, Innspruck, and Gratz. High schools and primary schools have also been established in some parts of the country; but, in general, the national education is extremely deficient.

The sovereign is styled the *Emperor of Austria;* and the government, with some diversities in the different parts, has been absolute in all, except in Hungary and Transylvania, till 1848, when a new constitution was given, as already stated.

Although Austria presents a great extent of good soil, agriculture is in so backward a state, that it is not highly productive. The processes and implements of husbandry are extremely imperfect. A considerable part of the country is covered with forests, which supply the inhabitants with fuel, coal being little used. There are extensive pastures in some of the provinces, and natural forests, which contain vast herds of cattle in a wild state. Some of the wines of Austria are highly esteemed; but the difficulties of transportation prevent them from being largely produced for exportation.

The manufactures of Austria are extensive in the aggregate; but the operations are generally carried on upon rather a small scale; and the Austrians have neither that perfection of finish nor that ingenious machinery which are to be found in the workshops of Western Europe. Woollen, linen, and cotton goods, paper, cutlery, and hardware, leather, and glass, are the most important articles of manufacturing industry.

Austria is unfavorably situated for foreign commerce Her northern provinces communicate with the sea only through the Elbe and the Vistula, by a long and difficult navigation; the eastern have navigable waters, which lead to countries not adapted for commercial operations; and the maritime coast on the Adriatic, although it has some good harbors, is separated from the interior by mountainous ranges, which render communication difficult. Trieste is the principal port, and displays considerable commercial activity. Fiume is the inlet to the Hungarian provinces, and Ragusa to Dalmatia. The inland trade of Austria is active and flourishing.

Sovereigns of Austria.

MARGRAVES.

A. D. 983 to 1156.

Leopold I., the Illustrious.
Henry I., the Rebel.
Albert I., the Victorious.
Ernest the Valiant.
Leopold II., the Beautiful.
Leopold III.
Leopold IV., the Saint.
Leopold V., the Liberal.
Henry II.

DUKES.

A. D. 1156 to 1246.

Leopold VI., the Virtuous.
Frederic I., the Catholic.
Leopold VII., the Glorious.
Frederic II., the Warlike.

1246 to 1282. Interregnum.

1283. Rodolph.
1283. Albert I. (Emperor of Germany, 1298.)
1305. Rodolph III.
1306. Frederic III., the Fair.
1330. Albert and Otho.
1339. Albert II., the Wise.
1358. Rodolph IV.
1365. Albert III. and Leopold III.
1386. Albert III.

A. D.
1395. Albert IV., the Wonder.
1404. Albert V., the Severe.
1437. Albert II. of Germany.
1439. Ladislas.
1457. Frederic IV. (emperor) and Albert VI.
1464. Frederic IV.

ARCHDUKES.

1493. Maximilian I.
1521. Ferdinand I.
1564. Maximilian II.
1576. Rodolph II.
1608. Mathias.
1619. Ferdinand II.
1637. Ferdinand III.
1657. Leopold I.
1705. Joseph I.
1711. Charles III., (Charles VI of Germany.)
1740. Maria Theresa.
1780. Joseph II.
1790. Leopold II.
1792. Francis. (Francis II. of Germany till 1806.)

EMPERORS.

1804. Francis I.
1835. Ferdinand I.
1848. Francis Joseph I

Prussia.

CHAPTER CCCCXLVIII.

A. D. 800 to 1740.

Geography of Prussia—Aborigines—Conquest by the Teutonic Knights—Made a Kingdom—Its Annals—The Great Elector—Frederic William I.

THE kingdom of Prussia, lying in Central Europe, comprises two distinct and very unequal portions, separated by the German territories of Brunswick, Hesse, Waldeck, Lippe, and Nassau. The eastern and largest portion, called Prussia East of the Weser, is bounded east by Russia; south by Austria, Saxony, and Electoral Hesse; west by Brunswick, Hanover, and Mecklenburg; and north by the Baltic Sea. The west portion, or Rhenish Prussia, is bounded east by Hesse Darmstadt, Nassau, &c.; south by France and certain German States; west by the Netherlands, Belgium, &c. Besides these, Prussia also possesses some small duchies in some of the contiguous German States.

The face of the country is generally flat or undulating, the eastern portions being bordered by the Thüringewald and Hartz mountains, and in the south by the Giant mountains. The eastern provinces belong to the basin of the Baltic; the chief rivers here are the Vistula and Oder. The western provinces belong to the basin of the North Sea, and are watered by the Elbe and its tributaries. There are various canals, connecting some of the principal rivers. The Rhine, here navigable by large vessels, and celebrated for its picturesque beauty, separates Rhenish Prussia into two nearly equal parts.

A Street in Berlin.

The coasts along the Baltic are covered with large lagoons; the east provinces contain numerous lakes. The climate of Prussia is salubrious: in the north it is cold and humid; in the south it is so mild as to produce excellent wine. A considerable part of the soil is fertile, and grain is produced so abundantly as to be exported in considerable quantities. Agriculture, the chief branch of industry, is carefully conducted: wheat, rye, oats, barley, flax, hemp, hops, tobacco, fruits, being the chief products. The vine is cultivated on the banks of the Moselle and the Rhine, in Rhenish Prussia, and here favorite wines are produced in large quantities.

The pasturage is excellent, and fine breeds of cattle are extensively raised: wool is an important product. According to a government return of 1837, the number of domestic animals in the kingdom was as follows, in round numbers: horses, 1,500,000; black cattle, 5,000,000; sheep, 15,000,000; goats, 350,000; hogs, 2,000,000. Wild-boars, wolves, foxes, stags, fallow-deer, are common; bears are more rare. The lynx, beaver, badger, &c., are often met with. Wild geese abound; bees are extensively raised. Amber is found on the shores of the Baltic. The manufactures of woollens, cottons, silk, &c., in Rhenish Prussia, are extensive, and many of their fabrics are imported into America. In Saxony and Silesia, the manufactures are also extensive. Linens and coarse woollens are made in nearly all the cottages, for domestic use. Large quantities of fine woollen cloth are produced at Aix-la-Chapelle and the vicinity. The iron manufactures are extensive and diversified, including not only articles of use, but those of ornament. For delicacy of execution and beauty of design, the fancy iron work of Prussia surpasses all other countries. The literary activity of Prussia is also remarkable, as is evinced by the great number of books annually issued from the press—particularly of Berlin and Halle. Commerce is active and extensive—the leading articles of export being grain, wool, timber, horses, zinc, flax, provisions, and linen, cotton, woollen, silk, and iron goods, with jewelry and watches.

The following are the political divisions of Prussia:

Provinces.	*Extent in sq. miles.*
East Prussia	15,000
West Prussia	10,000
Posen (Prussian Poland)	11,400
Pomerania	12,200
Silesia	15,800
Brandenburg	15,600
Saxony	10,000
Westphalia	8,000
Rhenish Prussia	10,000
Sq. miles	108,000

The whole population of Prussia is estimated at eighteen millions. It has increased rapidly of late years: in 1815, the whole number of inhabitants was but about ten millions.

The kingdom of Prussia is of modern date; its origin being referred to the *Great Elector*, as he was called, of Brandenburg, whose son assumed the royal title in 1701. Its foundations, however, were laid as far back as 1226—previous to which, it seems to have been occupied by heathen demi-savages, who lived in a wooded region on the shores of the Baltic. The *Vindili* and *Æstii* dwelt here in classic times, and the *Venedes* and other Saxons in the time of Charlemagne. In 1226, one of the kings of Poland, unable to defend his frontiers against the pagans of Prussia—who, goaded by repeated injuries from the bigoted Christians, molested them with perpetual incursions—gave a portion of the Prussian territory along the Vistula, to the Teutonic knights, on condition of their protecting Poland against those fierce and exasperated borderers. One hundred knights were sent on this errand by the grand master of their order.

The modern Prussians are mostly Germans; but the early inhabitants of their country were a tall, Vendo-Gothic race, speaking a language like that of the Lithuanians. Their eyes were blue, their hair fair and their complexion florid. Agriculture, to which they had been addicted from the earliest times, was their chief occupation. Grain, honey, the flesh of their herds and flocks, and of wild animals, were their principal food, and hydromel or metheglin their drink; beside an intoxicating liquor made from mare's milk, which they drank to excess from cups formed of the horns of the urus, or wild ox. Their dress was of skins, and of cloth, and they made iron weapons and clay utensils. These interesting people, to whom Christianity and vassalage were offered together, resisted, were attacked in detail, and miserably exterminated or enslaved by the knights, after the most obstinate and sanguinary resistance for many years.

And now was established a novel and peculiar government. The Order of Teutonic knights was, in its possessions, what the prince is in conquered countries. It regarded itself as sovereign, the source of all authority, and the proprietor of the soil. The wealthy Prussian lords, the principal ancient proprietors, called *withings*, held their hereditary family appanages, exempted from all charges, even of tithes; they owed the order military service only, both in defence of the province and in foreign wars. The most numerous class of proprietors held hereditary fiefs, as freemen, and cultivated them by hinds, over whom they exercised civil and criminal jurisdiction. The German inhabitants had lands assigned them free from tithes and corvees, while justice was administered by the mayor of the village. They paid a small capitation tax, and were held to military service. The great mass of the Prussians, reduced to serfage and attached to the soil, had no free lands, and belonged to the Order. Cities were encouraged by peculiar privileges. A deputy of the order of Teutonic knights ruled the state, responsible to the grand master and the chapter. Under this deputy, or marshal, the country was divided into commanderies, having each a castle, where resided a convention of twelve to twenty-four knights, who administered the civil affairs of the district, and led its forces. They could be displaced, and were obliged to render an annual account of their administration to the marshal.

In the fifteenth century, the territory of the order extended from the Oder to the Gulf of Finland, and contained many large cities; but their goverment had become so insupportably tyrannous, that the nobility and cities sought the protection of Poland. Wars ensued, which desolated the country, and filled it with slaughter, pestilence, and misery of every kind. To strengthen themselves, the knights elected Albert of Brandenburg, son of the margrave of Anspach, to the office of grand master. But he could obtain no support from any quarter, and being unable to prop up the declining order, it was abolished in Prussia, A. D. 1525, and the territory converted into an hereditary grand duchy, as a fief of Poland, under the elector of Brandenburg. He thus secured the means of sustaining his government. The banner of investiture was a black eagle, bearing an S in his breast. A successor of this elector was acknowledged as the sovereign of Prussia by the republic of Poland, A. D. 1657.

The Brandenburgs were a vigorous race, obstinate and arbitrary. In the war of the Protestants against Charles V., Albert of Brandenburg starved to death, in a tower at Hohenlandsburg, a crowd of hostages, among whom were eighty distinguished inhabitants of Bamberg. This ferocious tyrant was so enamored of cruelty, that when a father implored him to spare the life of one of his three sons, — were it only one, — Albert asked him which was his favorite, and, beginning with the youth pointed out by the wretched old man, put them all to death in succession, before their father's face! But his career of terror was short. He was defeated in the battle of Sievershausen, A. D. 1553, and fled wounded to France, where his excesses soon put an end to his life.

At the time the Pilgrim fathers of New England expatriated themselves to enjoy liberty of religion, and were founding their Pilgrim capital, in 1630, the Protestants of Prussia were also suffering for conscience sake, but in a far more agonizing degree. From Holland to the Carinthian Mountains, and from Prussia to the Alps of Berne, wherever the German tongue was spoken, the doctrines of Luther and of Calvin had penetrated to the hearts of the people. With the exception of Bavaria and the Tyrol, every district of Germany had, at one time or other, fought for liberty of conscience; yet there now remained no vestige of it, except in the single city of Magdeburg, in Prussia, whose brave defenders still held out against the assaults of Tilly, the ferocious general of the forces of the Germanic empire. Gustavus had arrived from Sweden; but, finding himself unsupported by the northern Protestants, he declared that, after relieving Magdeburg, he would return to Stockholm, unless he received aid. The electors of Saxony and Brandenburg held back at this crisis, and Gustavus hesitated to make an enemy of either, by an attack. Delayed by this uncertainty, he did not advance to relieve Magdeburg, but simply sent a messenger, Falkenstein, who entered the city disguised as a boatman, and took command of the feeble and dispirited garrison. The delay was fatal to the city. On the 10th of May, at four o'clock in the morning, while Falkenstein consulted with the magistrates, the enemy scaled the walls at a place where the sentinel was asleep, and before an alarm could be given, appeared in arms at the town hall. Falkenstein rushed out, and was instantly shot dead. The citizens resisted bravely till their powder failed, and then surrendered at discretion. The imperialists entered at two undefended gates, and a scene ensued too horrible for description. Some officers, who implored the brutal Tilly to have mercy on the unresisting citizens, were ordered to return in an hour: "I will then," said he, "see what can be done; but the soldier must have something for his labor and danger." In less than half the time designated, the work of blood was at its height. The furious soldiers spared neither age nor sex. Almost all the men were beheaded, and a great number of the women. Two clergymen were slain as they stood before the altar. The city was set on fire and reduced to ashes. These scenes continued until the 13th, when Tilly himself entered, and restored discipline. Four thousand persons, who had taken refuge in the fire-proof cathedral, were admitted to quarter, and for the first time during three days obtained something to eat. The terrible commander in a sort of masquerading dress, — a short jacket of green satin, and a high crowned hat, with a long red feather, which drooped over his ghastly countenance, his whole appearance that of a lunatic mountebank, — rode slowly through the town, gloating on the heaps of dead bodies, with which the streets were covered. In a letter to the emperor, he speaks of this scene of murder and desolation as the greatest victory that had been achieved since the taking of Troy and Jerusalem. "And sincerely," he adds, "do I pity the ladies of your imperial family, that they could not be present as spectators of the same!"

Gustavus now resolved no longer to spare the electors whose heartless indecision had caused this terrible calamity. Appearing before Berlin, he offered George William the choice either of instantly joining him, or seeing his capital laid in ashes. The terrified elector signed the treaty of alliance, and Gustavus garrisoned the fortresses of Berlin, Spandau, and Kustrin. The elector of Saxony also joined him, with eighteen thousand Saxons; and soon after the glorious Swede gained the decisive battle of Leipsic, A. D. 1631.

A new era commenced for Prussia with the accession of *Frederic William*, to whom history has given the name of the *Great Elector*. A. D. 1640. Formed in the school of misfortune and danger, furnished with precious experience and most valuable knowledge acquired during his stay in Holland; gifted with a penetrating mind and steady courage, Frederic William, at the age of twenty years, assumed the government of a state scarce worthy of the name, to elevate it from complete imbecility to the highest point of force and grandeur. Surrounded on all sides by formidable neighbors, jealous of each other and of him, he was obliged to conclude alliances and fight battles with each of them in turn; and it required the greatest energy and wisdom to prevent his embarrassed country from being torn piecemeal and divided between them. Yet he was able not only to preserve its integrity, but to increase its territory.

At the close of the thirty years' war, in 1648, he availed himself of a short respite from battles, to restore the exhausted strength of the state, by aiding his subjects to improve their condition. But Prussia soon became the theatre of the Swedo-Polish war, A. D. 1655. Charles Gustavus invaded and subdued Poland, and the Great Elector endeavored in vain to observe neutrality between the belligerents. Part of his domains were taken from him, and he was obliged to accept Prussia as a fief from Sweden. And when the king of Poland, John Casimir, was able again to make head against the Swedes, and encamped near Warsaw with an army of forty thousand men, — Poles, Russians, and Tartars, — the elector, with but ten thousand Swedes and six thousand men of Brandenburg, defeated him in a hard fought battle of three days' duration. A rich booty fell into the hands of the victors. It was now (1656) that the Swede, in order to secure the further coöperation of his active and shrewd ally, was obliged formally to grant the elector the sovereignty of Prussia. Excited by jealousy of the Swedish power, the German emperor, the Dutch, and the Danes joined the Poles. The elector now took the opportunity to restore peace to his own duchy. He signed a treaty with John Casimir, king of Poland, in which he gave back all he had taken from him, and promised to aid him with troops. In return, the king recognized Frederic William as absolute sovereign of Prussia, renouncing all authority over it — A. D. 1657. The Swedes, having lost much territory, made peace at the death of Charles Gustavus, — A. D. 1660, — and the elector again turned his attention to the improvement of his country. But, alarmed at the French successes in Holland, he allied himself with Austria, Denmark, and other powers, and marched to the Rhine to meet the armies of Louis XIV. Upon this, the Swedes, allies of the French, again invaded Prussia. The elector, by rapid and secret marches, was enabled to surprise his enemies, who, concentrating their forces, gave him battle at Fehrbellin, where eleven thousand Swedes, under the famous Wrangel, were defeated by five thousand six hundred Prussian cavalry, worn out by forced marches; A. D. 1675. This brilliant victory confirmed the military fame of Frederic William, and destroyed the notion of Swedish invincibility. The Swedes were finally driven from Prussia, but the gain from them was compensated by losses on the Rhine to the French, who took Cleves and Westphalia from the elector, and obliged him by a new treaty to renounce most of his conquests.

Although his attention was almost continually absorbed by long wars and an active participation in the public affairs of the other princes of Europe, the Great Elector found time, nevertheless, to occupy himself earnestly with every thing which could augment the internal prosperity of his states. From the earliest period of his long reign, a multitude of foreign colonists, attracted from Germany, Holland, and even Switzerland, by his equitable and advantageous regulations, reanimated agriculture, almost completely ruined by the Thirty Years' War. Deserts and sandy wastes were covered with harvests. Marshes were readily drained, and the banks of the Oder, the Wartha, the Wetze, and the Havel, till then sterile, became productive fields. Houses arose from their ashes, and the number of new villages was greatly increased. The elector, promptly seizing all circumstances by which he could profit, offered an asylum to twenty thousand Protestant refugees, whom the impolitic revocation of the edict of Nantes had driven from France. These strangers brought a civilization and taste for luxuries till then unknown in Prussia, created new sources of wealth, and opened new avenues of industry. The cities flourished, animated by manufactures of importance, and provided with a newly-organized police. Berlin and Potsdam were extended and embellished with promenades and imposing structures. The improvement of the great roads and the establishment of post-offices — A. D. 1650 — powerfully contributed to facilitate commercial relations in the interior. The Frederic William Canal, uniting the Spree and the Oder, was built. External commerce was also the object of the elector's solicitude; it extended itself even to the shores of Africa and America. A company was formed to establish a trade with Guinea, and a small fleet left the ports of Prussia, and built there Fort Fredericsberg, — A. D. 1681, — which was afterward sold to the Dutch. The Great Elector also reformed the ancient schools, and founded new scientific establishments, designed to extend the benefits of education to all classes of society. By an enlightened liberality, he attracted learned men and artists to his kingdom, who shed an undying lustre around his court and the universities he had founded.

In the spring of 1688, this great prince died, after ruling over Brandenburg and Prussia for forty-eight years and founding one of the mightiest European powers; though, it must be confessed, his measures were often exceedingly arbitrary. Those who opposed his encroachments on the ancient privileges of the nobles and burghers were arrested, and punished with perpetual imprisonment or death. When he felt that his end was near, he summoned his son and counsellors to his chamber, and solemnly bade them farewell. He had carried on many wars, he said; had suffered care and anxiety himself, and inflicted grievous ills on other men; "but God knoweth," continued the dying man 'in what a state I found the country at my father's death, and what I have done for it."* He then exhorted his son to follow his example, to act circumspectly, to be always prepared to defend his native land, to love his subjects, and listen to the suggestions of his faithful counsellors.

Frederic, third of the name, succeeded the elector, and, having at length obtained the emperor's consent, crowned himself *King Frederic I.* He was the reverse of his father, whose indefatigable activity was employed in aggrandizing his country, while that of the son exhausted itself in ordering the pompous ceremonial of some brilliant *fête*. The business of government was abandoned to favorites, and his only care was to increase the splendor of his court. He endeavored, by the magnificence of his costume, to conceal the insignificance of his figure; and the long curls of his peruke flowed over his back, in the vain attempt to conceal the hump which deformed it. The strictest etiquette reigned at court, even in the matter of smoking. Except in this Teutonic custom, every thing there was *à la Française*. Attracted in great numbers to his court by this French fancy of the monarch, Frenchmen were invested with functions, both civil and military; they introduced every where, among the higher classes of society, the language, literature, fashions, manners, in a word, the civilization, of their country, which prevailed, little by little also, among the middling classes of the capital. Hence the vivacity, satirical vein, and fickleness which distinguish the citizens of Berlin down to the present time. While, however, ruinous luxury reigned in the palace, a famine afflicted the country; and this was followed by a pestilence, which carried off one third of the population. A. D. 1709. The nation was so demoralized, that parents deserted children and children parents; justice and order were trampled under foot; and the people seemed to give themselves up entirely to physical enjoyments. Capital punishments for offences seemed but to increase the evil, and debauchery and crime rioted unrestrained by fear of the severe laws enacted to suppress the ever growing disorders.

The death of Frederic I. was no less singular than wretched. His third wife, Louisa of Mecklenburg, was possessed with a mania for making religious proselytes, which greatly imbittered the latter part of the king's life. He had fallen asleep, one day, in an easy chair, when his wife, in a fit of insanity caused by excess of devotion, woke him suddenly by dashing to atoms a glass door, and overwhelmed him with a torrent of the most violent reproaches. The king, frightened by the apparition of this woman,—her hair dishevelled about her shoulders, her countenance crimsoned and distorted with passion, and her person clothed in white,—imagined he beheld the famous *White Lady*, who, according to an ancient legend, always appeared in the palace of the princes of Brandenburg a short time before some member of the family was about to die. He became ill from the fright, and expired at the end of six weeks, A. D. 1713.

Frederic William I., his son and successor, brought to the throne tastes, dispositions, and habits, diametrically opposite to those of his father. He was quite as penurious as the late king had been prodigal; and instead of the showy and pompous taste of the late reign, displayed a rude plainness bordering on barbarism. He began by dismissing from his court the innumerable tribe of valets, selling off the baubles of the palace, and introducing a most rigid scrutiny and economy into all branches of the administration. The noisy and boisterous court became suddenly still and deserted; magnificence gave place to simplicity, and military parades and reviews succeeded to galas and *fêtes*. Instead of sumptuous liveries, nothing was seen moving about the precincts of the palace but the uniforms of the military staff, some of whom even performed the office of chamberlain about the person of the king. Advantageous settlements were made with Austria and France, which recognized the royalty of Prussia, and also with Holland and Sweden. For twenty-seven years, the king husbanded the resources of the kingdom, consolidated and extended by several treaties,—accumulated treasures and troops, and acted as absolute sovereign of his subjects. He exacted an obedience, instantaneous, absolute, and blind. Hard, severe, passionate, sometimes cruel, he made all about him experience the effects of his uncompromising disposition: not only his wife and children, but every functionary, from the humblest clerk to the prime minister, from the private soldier to the general—noble and simple, clergy and laity, all were made to feel that they had an inflexible *master*.

He abhorred all kinds of ceremony, and state affairs were discussed in his "tobacco college," as he called it, where every one of his intimates, perfectly at his ease, must smoke, or seem to smoke, and give his opinion with perfect freedom. A soldierly bluntness and frankness was more highly prized here, than the bland accents of polished roguery, or the siren phrases of courtly diplomacy. The politician was despised, but the soldier was listened to with respect.

The marketing of every dish that appeared on the king's meagre and abstemious table was carefully scrutinized, and the scraps of the meal anxiously looked after; but in dining with his generals, the monarch was pleased to find good cheer and even delicacies. He worked hard from morning to night himself, and required it of others. He slept very little, and always with disturbed slumbers. Inured and broken in to fatigues of all kinds, and the deprivation of the common conveniences of life, he braved the worst roads and the most tempestuous weather, requiring the same indifference and intrepidity of all his attendants. His servants never came into his presence without fear. His tyranny, indeed, passed all ordinary bounds. He kept constantly by him two pocket pistols loaded with salt, which he discharged at his domestics when they did not execute his orders with sufficient quickness. His ministers he treated as clerks, reprimanding them in the rudest and grossest terms, threatening them with terrible chastisements, and shutting them up in fortresses. Always busy, he determined the rest of the world should be as alert and active as himself; so he punished the idle with a huge cane, wielded by his own royal hand! Terror, therefore, went before him, and at his approach every body hastened out of the way

* At his accession, he found the electorate ruined, with an area of one thousand three hundred and seventy French square miles, and five hundred thousand inhabitants, a badly-disciplined army of three thousand men, four hundred thousand to five hundred thousand crowns of revenue, and an empty treasury. At his death, he left a flourishing state, one thousand nine hundred and thirty square miles in extent, one million five hundred thousand inhabitants, an army of twenty-four thousand well-disciplined and experienced veterans, two and a half millions of revenue, and six hundred thousand crowns in the treasury.

and sought to avoid his eye and his stick. In strolling about the streets during the intervals of business, or to inspect the erection of edifices here and there, he would often apply his heavy cane to the backs of fashionable loungers or loitering workmen, whom he would chase from street to street, until the unfortunates, half dead with pain and terror, fell at his feet, and roared for mercy! "Why did you run away from me, rascal?" said he to a miserable Jew, who had tried to escape as soon as he saw his well-known blue uniform faced with red. "I was afraid, and please your majesty," replied the trembling culprit. "How dare you be afraid, sir?" retorted Frederic William I., raising his cane and applying it vigorously to the man's head and shoulders; "do you not know, dolt, that I am the father of my people, and that I expect to be loved, not feared?"

The same whimsical tyranny sometimes displayed itself in his dispensation of justice. A nobleman had been condemned to close imprisonment for gross extortion. "Nonsense!" said the king, with considerable reason, to be sure: "if a poor, starving wretch steals a few miserable dollars, you put him to death; but a fellow like this, who has ruined whole families by his villany, must be spared, because he is a noble, forsooth! — let his lordship be hanged without delay." His son, afterward Frederic the Great, was seldom addressed by any title more endearing than those of *coward*, *dolt*, *coxcomb*, *puppy*, and *ass*, because his father saw fit to doubt his courage. Once he even flew at the luckless youth with his fists, and pommelled him over the face until the blood flowed in streams!

So successful was he in organizing a military force, that his successor was able to take the field with a well-appointed and exactly-disciplined army of seventy-two thousand men. But though penurious in most matters, Frederic William I. was extravagant in promotion of this his darling object. His celebrated Giant Guard was recruited at an enormous expense, and with every species of injustice, from other countries, where agents were regularly employed to kidnap the tallest men, and send them into Prussia. Peter the Great, who wanted artificers more than grenadiers, agreed to send him all the giants in his dominions, on condition of being allowed to steal and carry off an equal number of Westphalian whitesmiths! A batch of forty-three giants cost the Prussian king forty-three thousand dollars; one individual cost him nine thousand dollars. This eccentric monarch died in 1740, leaving behind him eight million seven hundred thousand dollars in the treasury, an army of about eighty thousand men, an empire increased to two thousand two hundred and seventy-five French square miles, with a population of two million two hundred and forty thousand, and a revenue of seven and a half millions of francs. Yet, though deemed the most avaricious and penurious king that ever sat on a throne, he spent eleven million crowns in efforts to encourage agriculture and repeople provinces decimated by the plague!

Frederic William aimed to found his throne firmly on a double basis of gold and steel: money and soldiers were his passions. The frontiers of the empire requiring defence were very extensive, and the age had been made venal by French politics; hence to be rigidly practical, this monarch made it his business to organize troops and amass treasure. "Money does every thing," was his favorite maxim: he called his soldiers his "dear blue children:" ignorance, brutality, and obedience composed his ideal of the hero-soldier, and incredible license was taken by his favorites, the soldiers, over their victims, the citizens. Any soldier could approach him freely at any time, and his fondness for his gigantic guard became a complete mania.

His son and successor, *Frederic II.*, called *Frederic the Great*, had a better education, a more correct taste, a greater range of thought, and a better balanced mind than his father. As a child, he manifested a ready intelligence and excellent disposition. He loved literature, drawing, and music — things entirely superfluous, and even abominable, in the eyes of his father. The rest of his tastes, also, were so contrary to the narrow views of the king, that he treated his son in the most brutal manner, descending even to kicks, and blows with fist and cane. To avoid this tyranny, the young prince endeavored to escape from the country: he was unsuccessful, however, and while a noble young friend, his accomplice, was executed before his eyes, he himself was imprisoned, and treated for a long time with the utmost ignominy. The prince at this time held the rank of lieutenant-colonel in the army, and his father ordered a court martial, that he might be tried, condemned, and shot as a deserter; but the court, in spite of the repeated orders of the tyrant, refused to pass sentence, saying they had power over the lieutenant-colonel, but not over the crown prince. Frederic laughed the distinction to scorn, and proceeded to give orders for the execution of his son.

The whole court was panic-struck at this display of unnatural cruelty, and all the foreign ambassadors joined his favorite generals in imploring the father not to imbrue his hands in the blood of his own child. Still the king persisted in his resolution; when one of the oldest of his officers, General von Buddenbrock, tearing open his vest, exclaimed, "If your majesty wants blood, take mine: but his you shall not have as long as I have life and strength to protest against it." The king relented, and the prince, having received a dying message from the beloved accomplice of his flight, urging him to submit, relaxed also from his hereditary stubbornness, and was soon after liberated, on condition of not leaving the town. Subsequently the king forgave him, and allowed him to be present at his sister's marriage. The ceremony had already commenced, when Frederic, dressed in a plain gray frock, without any order or decoration, was discovered among the servants, and dragged forward by his father, who presented him to the queen with these words: "See, madam, our Fritz is returned!" The next day, he was restored to his rank, and employed himself for months in the war office and royal demesnes. After his marriage, in 1732, he resided in the Castle of Rheinsburg, enjoying the society of his friends, and studying with infinite relish the writings of Voltaire and French translations of the classics.

CHAPTER CCCCXLIX.

A. D. 1740 to 1863.

Frederic the Great — His Successes — General Views.

In 1740, Frederic II. was called to the throne by the death of his father, and entered on the functions of government in earnest. "Our frolics are at an end," said he to the jovial companions of his revels a

Rheinsberg; "henceforth let us study how best we may fulfil the grave duties of a sovereign." Some of the early measures of his reign rendered him exceedingly popular. He was in the habit of attending to every thing himself, and led a very retired life at Sans Souci, a country place near Berlin. Except the ministers and generals, all the society at his court was French. His favorite Voltaire visited him in 1745, and again in 1750; but his conduct was vain and arrogant; and during the last visit, the two philosophers quarrelled, and Voltaire quitted Prussia in disgust.

Under the sagacious and vigorous administration of this active monarch, Prussia rose with wonderful rapidity to the rank of a first-rate power. Within ten years from his accession, an extensive tract of swampy land near Stettin, before uninhabited, contained two hundred and eighty villages, swarming with industrious mechanics and agriculturists; the Oder was made navigable by means of canals; large warehouses arose upon its banks, and intelligent foreigners embarked their capital in mercantile and farming speculations. The culture of the potato was introduced, and its general use enforced. To promote the intellectual improvement of his people, Frederic built a splendid opera house at Berlin, added many thousand volumes to the public library, and expended enormous sums in the purchase of pictures and statues.

Thus were employed the ten years of peace which succeeded to the struggles of 1744 and 1745, consequent upon Frederic's atrocious seizure of Silesia in 1742, which we have noticed in the history of Austria. The two victories over Austria in 1741 and 1742, which gained him that choicest portion of his dominions, showed him to Europe as an ambitious prince and an able captain. His martial abilities were no less conspicuous in defending his acquisition. Austria had induced England and Saxony to unite with her against Prussia. Frederic fell suddenly upon Bohemia in the summer of 1744. The approach of a large Austrian force caused him to retire upon Silesia, which he saved by the splendid victories of Hohenfriedberg and Sorr, in 1745; the latter gained by eighteen thousand Prussians over fifty thousand Austrians. Learning that the Austrian general, Charles of Lorraine, intended to surprise him in his winter quarters, he put himself at the head of his army encamped in Silesia, and gained the victory of Hennersdorf, over the Saxons. In another direction, his veteran commander, Dessau, by the victory of Kesselsdorf, opened to him the gates of Dresden. Ten days after, a treaty of peace was signed, in which Saxony agreed to pay the expenses of the war, Austria renounced all claim to Silesia, and Frederic agreed to recognize Maria Theresa's husband as emperor of Germany.

In 1756, as Maria Theresa still plotted the recovery of Silesia, Frederic entered into an alliance with England, to protect Germany from foreign invasion, and defend Hanover against the French, A. D. 1756. This alliance brought upon Prussia the enmity of France. Austria, Saxony, Russia, and France, and shortly afterward Sweden, united in a secret coalition to divide the Prussian states among themselves, leaving Frederic II. only the electorate of Brandenburg. Unterrified at this danger, which menaced the very existence of Prussia, her energetic king assumed at once the offensive, according to his wont. With his usual alacrity, he invaded Saxony at the head of sixty thousand men, and thus gave the signal for the commencement of the Seven Years' War, so favorable to the fame of Frederic. In fifteen days he was master of al Saxony. Leaving thirty-two thousand men to shut up the Saxon army in their camp at Pirna, he gained a victory over the Austrians at Lowositz with the rest of his army; and, shortly after, sixteen thousand Saxons surrendered at Pirna, which closed the campaign, A. D 1756. The next year, an army of one hundred thousand Russians invaded the eastern frontier of Prussia; an equal army of Frenchmen menaced the provinces of the Rhine; fifty thousand Swedes prepared to seize upon Pomerania; while an army of sixty thousand men, assembled by the princes of the German empire, menaced Frederic II. from another quarter. Beside these, the Austrians brought into the field two hundred thousand men. To make head against this half mil lion and more of enemies, Frederic had but one hundred and eighty thousand soldiers. Lewald was despatched with twenty-four thousand men to cover the eastern frontier against Russia; the English duke of Cumberland, with a force of Prussians, Hanoverians, Hessians, and Brunswickers, was to defend the Rhenish provinces against France, while the king himself directed his principal forces against the Austrians.

Terrible was the struggle, the very life of a powerful nation being at stake; and bravely did the young giant bear himself in the contest. Directed by the masterly intellect and unconquerable energies of Frederic II., the Prussians earned for themselves a military fame for all coming time; and their monarch fairly won for himself, throughout Europe, the appellation of *Frederic the Great;* and among his own idolizing subjects, that of *Frederic the Unique.* In March, 1757, the king entered Bohemia at four points at once, and marched his forces by four several routes directly upon the capital; and on the same day, the 6th of May, the four divisions met before Prague. A dreadful battle ensued, and victory declared for Prussia, though she left sixteen thousand of her sons dead upon the field. Marshal Schwerin fell also, who alone was "worth ten thousand men" in the king's estimation. The Austrian loss was nineteen thousand; and among the killed was Marshal Brown, one of the two chief commanders of the enemy. But an attack made by thirty thousand Prussians against twice their number, advantageously encamped on the heights of Kollin, near Prague, resulted, after a murderously obstinate battle, in the defeat of the Prussians; and Frederic was obliged to raise the siege of Prague, and evacuate Bohemia. Lewald also was defeated by the Russians at Jagaerndorf, and Cumberland shamefully capitulated to the French at Closterseven. An army of thirty thousand men was marching to join the imperial troops, in order to bear down upon Saxony, the grand *entrepôt* whence the Prussian king procured money, provisions, arms, and soldiers. Leaving thirty-six thousand men to watch the Austrians in Silesia, and ordering two of his generals to drive out the body of Croats who had got possession of Berlin, Frederic II., after a moment of despair, marched with but sixteen thousand men against the imperial army of sixty thousand. In a fierce engagement at Rosbac, (1757,) he put to complete rout both the imperialists and the French.

Meanwhile, in Silesia, Frederic lost Winterfield, one of his ablest generals. Schweidnitz, with its rich provisions and warlike stores, was given up to the Austrians; the army of the duke of Bevern was defeated at

Breslau, and that city also taken by the enemy. Hastily assembling a little army of fourteen thousand men, the unconquerable king joined them to the relics of Bevern's army, sixteen thousand men, discouraged and alarmed by defeat. Frederic raised their depressed spirits by friendly converse and sympathizing complaisance, praised their bravery, deplored their misfortunes, distributed to them wine and provisions, and thus succeeded in awakening anew their courage and enterprise, and that confidence which insures victory. With these thirty thousand men, the king had the audacity to attack eighty thousand of the enemy under Daun, and night alone saved the imperial army from complete ruin. Twenty-eight thousand Austrians fell on this bloody day of Leuthen, (Lissa.) All Silesia was now reconquered.

In the next campaign, Frederic fought a Russian army of eighty thousand, at Zorndorff, for ten hours, with fourteen thousand picked men, and the Russians were driven back. A similar indecisive engagement was fought at Hochkirch; the imperial army fell upon the Prussians at night, killing nine thousand of them. The Austrians, Swedes, and French were kept at bay, through the prodigious activity of the monarch, seconded by his able and successful generals; so that the campaign terminated, on the whole, in favor of Frederic II. Not so that of 1759, which brought with it many defeats to the Prussian arms, and left the king with but thirty thousand troops. The campaign of 1760 was no less disastrous, at first, in the affair of Landshut and the siege of Dresden; but the Prussian king was victorious at the battles of Liegnitz and Torgau. At the close of the campaign of the next year, Frederic seemed utterly prostrate; without money, without soldiers, dispossessed of his hereditary estates, and of a great part of Saxony, he himself scarcely expected to hold out through another campaign. Fortunately, his implacable enemy, Elizabeth I., empress of Russia, died in the early part of 1762, leaving the throne to Peter III., an admirer and friend of Frederic. The new emperor hastened to make peace with Prussia; and with a generosity to which history affords no parallel, restored the conquests made, without demanding the least indemnity. A body of Russian troops, even, was sent to assist the Prussians. The king of Sweden soon after followed the example of Russia in making peace. Catharine II., Peter's successor, declared for neutrality. Schweidnitz was retaken by the Prussians, who gained also a great victory at Freiburg. These events, favored by the intervention of France and Russia, induced Austria to make peace, (A. D. 1763,) and Silesia was for the third time assured to the Prussian monarchy.

The most important event of the latter part of this famous reign, was the partition of Poland, in 1772. In this matter, Frederic showed a more shameful eagerness, even, than his nefarious accomplices, and gained for his share nearly all Polish Prussia; he thus obtained a free communication between his provinces, he rich borders of the Vistula, a greater extension of his maritime commerce, and a large increase of enlightened subjects. On the other hand, Frederic's last campaign was in defence of Bavaria, over which Austria asserted unjust pretensions; but through the consummate military skill on both sides, the campaign was bloodless; and thanks to the mediation of France and Russia, Bavarian independence was maintained. In 1785, when Austria sought insidiously to aggrandize herself at the expense of Bavaria, Frederic formed the "Princes' Union," whose object was to maintain the integrity of the German empire, and the privileges of its members. Soon after, Frederic concluded a treaty of amity and commerce with our United States; and this was his last act of foreign diplomacy.

In consequence of the immense subsidies he had levied on foreign states, Prussia came out of this contest for existence free from debt, though her wars had occasioned her the disbursement of one hundred and twenty-five millions of crowns. But the country was frightfully devastated. Agriculture lacked hands — the males, even down to the age of sixteen, having been drafted in the wars of independence — and the ploughing was done by women. Commercial and manufacturing industry was deplorably prostrate. The nobility, overwhelmed with debt, were at the mercy of usurers, and on the verge of ruin. The king now bent all his vast intellectual and moral energies to the Herculean task of remedying so many woes. He had grain in his storehouses; this he distributed to the farmers for present sustenance and for seed, and gave them all the draught horses of the army. Part of a reserved fund was applied to build up cities and villages which had suffered, and to assist districts plunged in debt. Imposts were also taken off for a time. But the measure most useful to agriculture was the establishment of a "mortgage bank," which loaned the capital necessary to carry on the farms, on the security of a lien upon the lands to the bank. Manufactures were encouraged, and internal commerce promoted by a canal made to connect Stettin with Konigsberg. By promulgating a new code of laws, also, the king established justice, and decreased the expense and delay generally attending its pretended distribution. Science and genius were encouraged. But his army was an object of peculiar solicitude, and the occasion of vast expense, even in peace; and to fill his treasury, he felt obliged to resort to monopolies, and the increase of all kinds of indirect taxation.

Frederic the Great.

Frederic the Great died in 1786, after a despotic but celebrated and remarkable reign of forty-six years He left Prussia in a condition incomparably more flourishing than he found it. He increased its territory one half, and nearly trebled its inhabitants. He caused forty-two thousand families of foreign colonists to transplant themselves to the unoccupied soil of his country, and founded five hundred new settlements and villages. He added four fortresses to the twelve which he repaired and enlarged; and increased the revenue from seven and a half to twenty-eight millions of crowns; he left seventy-two millions of crowns in the treasury, in the place of eight millions seven hundred thousand, which he found there, though he had been engaged in war for eleven years, and had expended more than twenty-four millions in his various public improvements!

The great Frederic's nephew and successor, *Frederic William II.*, was unworthy of his lineage and station. Governed by obscure counsellors and shameless women, he became the puppet and satellite of the other cabinets of Europe. But in his internal administration, he promulgated a new code of laws, encouraged all kinds of industry, and constructed dikes, roads, and canals. Paid by England and allied with Austria, he marched an army of fifty thousand men to the Rhine, in 1792, to reinstate in their abused privileges the French emigrants, who were there collected, after having deserted their country in the hour of its utmost need. The result of three campaigns was a humiliating treaty with France, in 1795, which took from Prussia all her possessions on the left bank of the Rhine. Though he had engaged to defend Poland and her constitution in 1791, yet, in 1793, Frederic took a share of the spoils in the second partition of that ill-fated country among her powerful neighbors, amounting to nine hundred square miles, with eleven hundred thousand inhabitants! He also took one thousand miles more, with another million of inhabitants, at the third partition of Poland, the next year. Frederic William II. died in 1797, having not only squandered upon greedy mistresses and worthless favorites the immense treasures left by his uncle, the late king, but leaving the treasury indebted in the sum of two hundred and eighty-seven millions of crowns. His faults and follies destroyed the influence Prussia had acquired in Europe.

In strong contrast with the character of his father, the fame of *Frederic William III.*, the next king, is built on a basis even more durable than that of Frederic the Great. It was this virtuous, economical, and orderly sovereign, who so perfected the Prussian system of popular education, or the "common school system," that it has become a proverb for completeness, and a model for efficiency and thoroughness. He was able to say, ten years before his death, and prove it by the most rigid statistics, that among the fourteen millions of his subjects, there was not a child between the ages of six and fourteen years who was not receiving an elementary education more thorough and extended than was given to any large number of children in any other country in the world — than was provided by government for the children of any other nation, indeed, except the small neighboring kingdom of Saxony.

The events in the history of Prussia which grew out of the ambition of Napoleon, have been already noticed in our history of France. Hanover, taken by Napoleon in 1803, was given to Prussia by a treaty with France, in 1805. The insignificance of the Prussian king, however, tempted Napoleon to resume possession of it the next year. This so exasperated Prussia, that she declared war against France, but was very soon overrun and taken possession of by the French armies, after they had gained the battles of Jena and Auerstadt, A. D. 1806; and Napoleon installed himself, at Berlin, as master of all Prussia. By the treaty of Tilsit, in 1807, Frederic William III. lost half of his kingdom. The overthrow of Napoleon, however, in 1815, restored its previous limits. The young men of Prussia, fired with patriotism and the watchwords of liberty, had flown to arms and borne back the French invader; but the king, after his throne was once more secure, refused to give his subjects the liberal constitution he had promised in the hour of danger, and the promise was not redeemed during his lifetime. Up to the year 1847, the government continued to be a despotism, conducted with ability, indeed, but without any of those guaranties which a civilized nation should have.

Deeming that religion gives immense force to the state, the Prussian government aimed to become the religious centre of Protestantism in Germany, and to found, upon the continent, something analogous to the church and state "establishment" in England. Frederic William III. had, therefore, compelled a union of the Calvinistic and Lutheran communions into one church. And the two confessions, separated by an abyss of blood and hate for three centuries, and between which the impetuous Luther saw no possibility of reconciliation, amicably coalesced by order of the Prussian cabinet! A new liturgy, more accommodating, and in which each confession found its religious creed faintly shadowed forth, confirmed the union. The same preacher now addresses both sects in the same congregation. But, as has happened in England, the consequence is, that many, disgusted with the papistical tendencies of the established church, or wounded in their cherished predilections as to purity of doctrine and life, quarrel with their preachers, or attend no church at all, and are looked upon with an evil eye by the government; while some, also, have emigrated to America. But all has apparently yielded to the will of the monarch; Lutheranism, giving the prince ecclesiastical power, reigns; "the church has become the bride of the king, and each citizen is the fruit of their union." The curate became both a civil and an ecclesiastical officer; "professing Christians alone enjoy the rights and privileges of citizens; baptism is at once a civil and a religious rite, by which an individual acquires a title to happiness in this world and in the next, and becomes, at one and the same time, a citizen of heaven and of Prussia."

The next king in succession, *Frederic William IV.*, came to the throne in 1840; and from his previous character and education, great hopes were entertained, by the liberal portion of his subjects, that he would yield to the demands of the age; but his harsh answers to some municipalities who ventured humbly to ask him for the constitution long before promised by his father, soon dashed these hopes, and showed him to belong to the same obstinate race of autocrats as his predecessors. The system of government continued to be a sort of "political pantheism, which merged the nation in the thought and will of the prince, who was at once pontiff and king, temporal and spiritual sovereign, political, military, and religious commander-in-chief."

In the same way as the government is the church, so does it form, as it were, the immense school of Prussia, adapting itself to every age and capacity. All the establishments of public instruction are either under the immediate direction of the government, or subjected to its surveillance. Schools are scattered in all the cities, and through all the country, and connected with the government by its ecclesiastic or civil officers, who superintend them. It needs not fear the dissemination of intelligence, for it is itself the focus of the light and its supreme regulator!

Government, having thus in its hands the national faith and worship, by the church which it rules, science and intelligence, by the education it directs, possesses also the material forces of the country, by the army, which is, as it were, "the crowning work, the administrative fact, the type of all the other branches," to which it communicates that regularity and uniformity, that mechanism, which characterize the administration, and make the government one tremendous machine. In Prussia, indeed, every citizen is born a soldier; rich and poor, noble and simple, prince and subject, each and all must serve at least three years in the army. The barracks are a kind of monasteries, where the soldier is shut up and condemned to celibacy, like a monk; but the literary and scientific education of the new recruit is continued. An obedience, enforced by blows and horrible punishments, enchains the private to his officer, the subaltern to his superior, and all to the general-in-chief, the king.

Under all this rigid training, we should expect the Prussian character to be marked by a passivity and want of originality, as is the case. Ever waiting for an impulse from government, and looking to it to initiate every thing, the Prussians have the character of being the best of subjects, while lacking those essential characteristics of a good citizen — an active, self-relying public spirit, and practical efficiency in the conduct of civil affairs. The individual is apt to be lost in the machine. They are otherwise intelligent, well-educated, and probably superior in refinement of manners, especially at the capital, to most other Germans.

Immediately after the French revolution of 1848, disturbances occurred at Berlin, (March 13,) which obliged the king to make large concessions to the people. The king's brother, William I., succeeded him in 1861.

Sovereigns of Prussia.

Date of Accession. A. D.		Date of Accession. A. D.	
Dukes.			
1528.	Albert of Brandenburg.	1621.	George William.
1568.	Albert Frederic.	1640.	Frederic William, the Great Elector.
Regents.		**Kings.**	
1577.	George Frederic.	1688.	Frederic I., (Elector Frederic III.)
1605.	Joachim Frederic, (Elector of Brandenburg.)	1713.	Frederic William I.
1609.	John Sigismund, (Elector of Brandenburg.)	1740.	Frederic II., the Great.
Dukes.		1786.	Frederic William II.
1618.	John Sigismund.	1797.	Frederic William III.
		1840.	Frederic William IV.
		1861.	William I.

CHAPTER CCCCI.

WESTPHALIA. — *Historical Account — The Fem Courts — The Anabaptists — Their Outrages and Sufferings.*

ONE of the most important portions of Prussia is *Westphalia*, which has undergone such a variety of changes, that it requires a distinct historical notice. The name has been applied to tracts of country of various extent, at different times. It is now a Prussian province, with an area as large as Massachusetts, a population of nearly a million and a half, and bounded by Hanover, Brunswick, Hesse-Cassel, and Hesse-Darmstadt. In the middle ages, the name was given to that part of the great duchy of Saxony still called *Sauerland* — that is, "Red-land" — by the common people, between the Weser and the Elbe. The archbishop of Cologne received Sauerland as a fief from the Germanic empire, in 1179, under the name of *Westphalia.* In 1802, when that archbishopric was abolished, Westphalia passed as a duchy to Hesse-Darmstadt, by which power it was ceded to Prussia in 1815. It then had an area of fifteen hundred square miles.

The *Circle of Westphalia*, which belonged to the Germanic empire till the peace of Luneville, had twenty-seven thousand square miles, with two and a half millions of inhabitants. It was bounded north by the German Ocean, east by Lower Saxony, west by the Netherlands, and south by the Circle of the Lower Rhine. The Circle of Westphalia is historically interesting, as being the original seat of the Vehme, and the scene of the Anabaptist extravagances, crimes, and sufferings.

The *Vehme* — that is, "court" — or *Fem Courts* of the middle ages, were a relic of the rude efforts of barbarism to establish justice; it was the revival, in 1220, of the *frey-field gericht*, or "open field court" of former days of heathenism, whose judges were named by the priests of Mars. After the christianization of Germany, the sixteen judges were elected by certain monks. Charlemagne provided that the place of meeting should be roofed in; but it retained its old name of *Mall*, — a name, by the way, still applied to the open walk around Boston Common. The senior member acted as *graf*, or count, the junior as crier, and the remaining fourteen as jurymen. In ancient times, the tribunal — called the "king's stool" — was a green plot, sixteen feet square, measured by *rods* of the length of one side, which rods were themselves first verified as to their length by the graf, with his right foot. This was probably the origin of our rod measure. The crier then consecrated the square to justice by digging a trench in the centre: into this each of the judges cast a handful of ashes, a tile, and a coal, and it was then filled up.*

* When a criminal was to be tried, or a civil cause decided, the "free graf" and "free jurymen" assembled on the spot thus hallowed; and the crier, after proclaiming silence, addressed the graf in an uncouth rhyme, which may be translated thus: —

"Sir Graf,
By your leave,
And with submission,
I crave permission —
So tell me, I pray,
If your vassal may
This seat now place
Upon the king's seat by your good grace.

To which the graf replied in a different metre, —

"Whilst the sun shines equally
On lord and serf, on low and high,
On peasant's toil, and monarch's care,
I mighty justice will declare; —
Place the seat by measure even,
That equal judgment may be given,
And all may hear impartially
The accusation and reply"

The crier then placed the seat exactly in the middle of the square, and again addressed the graf: —

"Sir Graf, master kind,
Of your honor I you remind. —

The Vehmic tribunals of Westphalia, as revived in the time of Frederic II.,—A. D. 1220,—had an hereditary chairman, the lord of the district, or his delegate, who also appointed the jurymen, or *schöppen*. A public court was held thrice a year, and he that refused to appear before it when summoned, was tried by a portion of the judges called "the initiated," sitting in *secret tribunal*. Their sessions were generally in the halls of the episcopal palace at Cologne. The jurymen took a solemn oath of fidelity to their trust, and of secrecy, under awful penalties. They had a kind of masonic signs, grips, &c., by which they recognized each other. The accuser and accused made their statements on oath; if the latter refused to appear, he was condemned, and placed under ban. Soon after this, the corpse of the condemned was sure to be found hanging on a tree, in the trunk of which was stuck a dagger, inscribed with the mystic cipher of the Vehme, S. S. G. G.,—that is, *stick*, *stone*, *grass*, *groan*,—words, probably, of secret meaning. The *schöppen* also made circuits by day and by night, and had the right to execute upon the spot criminals caught in the fact. All the tribunals were subject to a general chapter, presided over by the emperor, or his deputy, the sovereign of Westphalia. The institution spread throughout Germany, and in the fourteenth century numbered one hundred thousand members; but it sunk into insignificance in the next century. The last fem court, held near Munster, was superseded, in 1811, by the French code.

The *Anabaptists*, as their name imports, taught that infant baptism was unscriptural, and that those thus baptized must be "baptized again," in order to become members of the Christian church. They also, in opposition to Luther, taught that resistance to unjust sovereigns was right, and looked for a kingdom of the saints on earth —a spiritual republic. This sect arose at Zwickau, and were headed by one *Klaus Storch*, a weaver, who went about attended by twelve apostles and seventy-two disciples. Expelled from Zwickau, they came to Wittemberg, and were driven thence by Luther. Munzer, one of the apostles, plundered the monasteries and the houses of the rich in Saxony, and taught the doctrine of a community of goods among Christians. His exhortations collected an army of peasants and miners, who were defeated, with the loss of five hundred men, by the united troops of the sovereigns of Saxony, Hesse, and Brunswick. Munzer himself was put to death after the battle, A. D. 1525.

In 1529, the Anabaptists committed the wildest excesses in St. Gall, Basle, Stuttgard, and Erfurt, robbing the people, going naked,—as if, being in paradise, clothes were superfluous,—and riding about, like children, on hobby-horses, broomsticks, &c. Several of the leaders were taken, and hanged by the public authorities. Munster, in Westphalia, having risen against its bishop, (A. D. 1527,) the leader of the revolt joined the Anabaptists, who thus became masters of the city, under *John of Leyden*, a tailor, and Knipperdolling, a burgomaster, his lieutenant. The new chief commenced his proceedings by running stark naked about the streets, screaming, "The King of Zion is come;" while his lieutenant shouted, "Every high place shall be brought low;" and the mob instantly pulled down all the steeples of the city. Many of the sect now flocked to Munster; but as among them there were six times as many women as men, John proposed a plurality of wives, and set the example by taking seventeen females to himself! The city was besieged by the bishop and his allies, and defended by soldiers, aided by boys who shot arrows with deadly effect, while women poured down wet lime and melted pitch upon the heads of the besiegers. Famine soon showed itself, but the fanatic leaders revelled in plenty. This being reproved by one of John's wives, he killed her, and danced round her corpse with his other wives. The city was stormed, the fanatics put to the sword, and their leaders tortured, and hung up on a tower in cages, to perish miserably.

The *Kingdom of Westphalia* was erected by Napoleon in 1807, and its sovereignty given to his brother, Joseph. It included part of Hesse-Cassel, Brunswick, and other petty states, with Paderborn, Minden, Gottingen, Magdeburg, &c., an area, in all, of fourteen thousand five hundred square miles, with about two millions of inhabitants. Cassel was its capital. Its constitution was entirely on the French model; and though previously exhausted, the country began to revive under a good administration. In 1810, Hanover was added to it, but soon taken away again. It furnished twenty-four thousand men to Napoleon's Russian expedition, few of whom returned; twelve thousand Westphalians subsequently followed him to Saxony. But in the same year, 1812, the government of Prussia was restored, and the kingdom of Westphalia abolished.

I your will obey:
So tell me, I pray,
Whether these rods be right and true,
For the poor and the wealthy too,
To measure land, estate, and gear:
Tell me, as you perdition fear."

The graf then laid the rods on the ground, and measured them with his right foot—an operation which was also performed by each of the jurymen. The crier now spoke again:—

"Sir Graf,
I ask your leave,
(If it be your good pleasure,)
That I with these your rods should measure,
Openly and without deceit,
Here the king's free judgment seat."

The graf replied,—

"Right I allow,
Wrong forbid in this cause,
Under the pains of our old known laws."

The plot having been duly measured, the graf took his seat, and delivered his charge to the jury in these words,—

"All who on this day appear:
By your consent is holden here,
Under heaven's light canopy,
Our free tribunal, openly.
Come, while sunshine yet is lasting,—
Come, while still your lips are fasting.
By rule is set the judgment seat,
The wands are proved wherewith we mete.
Judge truly then, without favor or fear:
Up, accused and accuser, while daylight is here."

Proclamation was then made, three times, that none by word or sign should presume to disturb the sittings of the court; and the jurymen, unarmed and with bare heads, took their places round the judgment seat. The accused now appeared with his sponsors. If he took an oath of innocence on the cross of the sword, and none swore against him, he was discharged; and, taking a cross-penny, cast it down before the graf, turned, and went his way:—whosoever, says at old law, "offereth him let or hinderance, hath broken the king's peace." If he acknowledged his crime, or was convicted on the oaths of a greater number than swore in his favor, the graf passed sentence of death, banishment, or fine. Criminals capitally convicted were hurried away at once, and hung on the nearest tree

Minor German States.

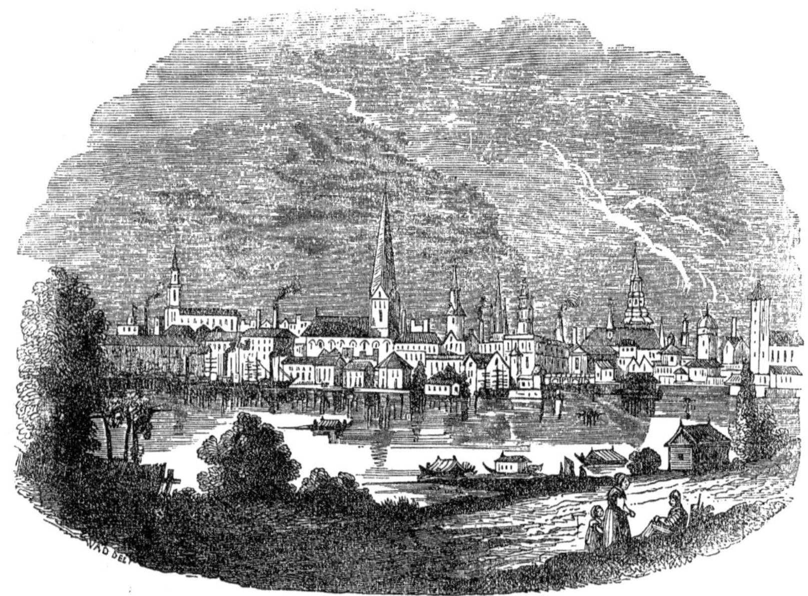

View of Hamburg.

CHAPTER CCCCLI.

Bavaria — Saxony — Hanover — Wirtemberg — Baden — Other States.

Bavaria derives its name from the *Boii* or *Boioarii* of classic Europe, whence its German appellation, *Baiern*. The original territory formed one of the most ancient duchies in Europe. It is now one half greater than in 1777, and comprises the greater part of the former Circles of Bavaria and Franconia, certain districts of Suabia, Anspach, Baireuth, Bamberg, Wurzburg, Augsburg, Eichstadt, Freisingen, and parts of Mainz, Fulda, and Spires. In 1777, the elector palatine Charles Theodore inherited it, and added to it his patrimony of four thousand two hundred and forty square miles. Bavaria now contains an area of thirty-one thousand square miles, and is second in importance, among the German states, to Austria and Prussia only. Its population is over four millions. Its climate is healthy, and few countries possess a more productive soil; yet much of it lay waste through ignorance and idleness, till the present enlightened government took measures to bring it into use. Grain, wine, and hops are its chief products. Full liberty of conscience was established, in 1818, in matters of religion. About one quarter of the population are Protestants, sixty thousand Jews, and the rest Catholics. A system of common schools exists with a thorough and efficient organization. The government is constitutional; and by the constitution of 1818, Maximilian Joseph secured to his people liberty of conscience, equality before the law and as to taxes, with a legislature elected by all classes of resident citizens, and enjoying the right of discussing and approving laws, voting the public taxes, and requiring the redress of all infringements of the rights recognized by the constitution. The revenue amounts to about thirteen and a half millions of dollars, averaging about three dollars to each individual. As to military resources, every Bavarian is liable to be enrolled in the militia after the age of twenty-one years; any one between eighteen and thirty may enlist in the regular army; and no Bavarian can settle or marry, or receive a definite appointment, till he has done all that the military law requires. The effective military force is somewhat over one hundred thousand men. There are in Bavaria two thousand four hundred and seven noble families, of which not one thousand possess landed property.

Six hundred years before the Christian èra, the *Boii* emigrated from Gaul, and, after subduing the natives, settled themselves between the upper courses of the Danube and the Alps. They were conquered by the Romans, and, in the time of Augustus, formed a part of Vindelicia. No country suffered more than Bavaria from the irruptions of the northern nations in the second century and later, which kept it in a condition of wretchedness and slavery. At last, in the fifth and sixth centuries, the *Heruli*, *Marcomanni*, *Thuringii*, and other tribes, established themselves permanently in *Noricum*, a part of the present Bavaria, adopted the name of *Boioarii*, gave that of *Boioaria* to the country, and forced the owners of the soil to abandon their native language and customs for those of the

German race. Bavaria passed from the Romans to the Ostrogoths; then to the Franks, who allowed its people to elect their own dukes from the patrician line of the *Agilolfingers.* These exercised a nearly independent sovereignty for two hundred and fifty years. *Thassilo*, the last duke, was compelled to submit to Charlemagne, A. D. 783.

In 1070, the emperor granted Bavaria to the Guelfs, and in 1180, to *Otho*, count of Wittelsbach, a native prince, from whom the present sovereigns are descended. On failure of the direct line in 1777, *Charles Theodore*, the elector palatine, came to the throne, and added his palatinate to the kingdom, as already remarked, while he ceded the district of Inn — eight hundred and forty square miles — to Austria. Subsequent changes, by adding or subtracting one and another district, left its territory to consist of the parts enumerated above. The first king of Bavaria was *Maximilian Joseph*, A. D. 1806, who left the throne to his son, *Louis Charles Augustus I.*, in 1825. This king, becoming infatuated with an adventuress, the notorious *Lola Montes*, made himself so contemptible to his subjects, in 1848, that, on March 22d of that year, he resigned his throne to his son, *Maximilian II.*, who reigns with as much moderation as can be expected, amid the despotic influences that surround him.

Louis I., lately king of Bavaria, — the most liberal of the German princes, — in order to gratify the strong feeling of nationality which exists among all who speak the German language, conceived the idea of erecting near the line of canal which connects the two great rivers of Germany, the Rhine and the Danube, a building suggestive and symbolical of Germanism, and calculated to unite together the German memories of the past, the German pride in the present, and the German hopes in the future. To recall the earliest ideas of the Germanic nations, he called it the *Valhalla*, — the "hall of heroes," — so famous in the creed of the renowned barbarians, from whom the Teutonic race is descended. This vast hall of Odin was the shadowy heaven of their fierce mythology, already noticed at page 971; its name was, therefore, appropriately given to an erection intended to commemorate the immortal men and women, deeds, arts, and ideas of Germany. The building is modelled, externally, after the Parthenon of Athens; internally it is unique, but thoroughly classic. It is one hundred and four feet high, two hundred and twenty-five feet long, and one hundred and seventy-five feet wide, and built of vast blocks of solid marble, raised on terraces of masonry. It crowns the top of a hill. The walls are eight or nine feet thick, and the roof is of bronze and iron. The inside is magnificently ornamented, and upon its sides are arranged the busts of the great men and women of the German race.

The various inhabitants of Bavaria differ very much in character; the Bavarian from the highlands near Tyrol, and the Franconian in the north part of the kingdom, being as unlike as any two Germans probably can be. The different parts of this young kingdom, indeed, have been so recently united, that it is not possible to speak of any character as common to its inhabitants. The native of Upper Bavaria is short in stature, hardy, and laborious. Many of the Bavarians are distinguished for mechanical talent.

SAXONY. — The legend as to the origin of the Saxons from the soldiers of Alexander, has been alluded to. The names earliest known among the tribes of Northern Central Europe, afterward called *Saxons* — from *sax*, a short sword — are the *Chauci*, the *Cherusci* — who routed the Romans — the *Cimbri*, and the *Teutones*. In the third century A. D., the Saxons were a numerous people, warlike and piratical, who devastated the coasts of Belgium and Britain. The latter country was invaded, in the fifth century, by two considerable hordes of these, under Hengist and Horsa. Those of the race who remained in Germany, the East and West-phalians, and Engrians, occupied a vague extent of country. Charlemagne waged a thirty years' war with the brave but savage Saxons, under their famous chief, Wittekind, duke of Westphalia, who was at length subdued, and embraced Christianity.

In 845, there was a duke of Saxony; and in the new kingdom of Germany, the Saxons were the most powerful of the six German nations — the Eastern Franks, Saxons, Frisians, Thuringians, Suabians, and Bavarians. In 919, Henry, duke of Saxony, was elected emperor of Germany, under the title of *Henry I.;* and transmitted the dignity to his son, grandson, and great-grandson. The duchy afterward passed to the Bavarian branch of the Guelf family, A. D. 1125, of which *Henry the Lion* — celebrated for his contest with the emperor — was a member, A. D. 1146–95. After several changes, *Frederic the Warrior*, margrave of Meissen (Misnia) and landgrave of Thuringia, became duke and elector of Saxony, 1424.

The union of these three countries rendered the elector of Saxony one of the most powerful princes of Germany. *Frederic the Wise* (A. D. 1486 to 1525) was celebrated as the protector of Luther from the fate of Huss, as the promoter of the reformation, and as the founder of the university of Wittemberg. At the close of the fifteenth century, Saxony was divided into three circles, Upper Saxony, Lower Saxony, and Westphalia, till 1806. At the pacification of Europe in 1815, the separate existence of Saxony, which had been faithful to Napoleon, was debated; but finally it was reduced to its present dimensions, of five thousand eight hundred square miles, with over two millions of inhabitants, by taking from it, for Prussia, some nine thousand square miles, to form the province of Prussian Saxony, and also Westphalia. The remnant was called the *Kingdom of Saxony;* and though it is the smallest kingdom of Europe, its people are the best and most universally educated. Intelligence, industry, and honesty distinguish the inhabitants.

HANOVER. — Hanover, with an area of fourteen thousand five hundred and seventy square miles, and a population of one million eight hundred and eighty-eight thousand (1861), is bounded north-west by the German Ocean, north-east by the Elbe, east and south east by Prussia and Brunswick, south-west by Lippe, Hesse-Cassel, and Prussia, and west by Holland. The valleys between its mountains are fertile, and its healthy downs pasture immense flocks. When the heath is in bloom, some sixty thousand hives are brought upon these downs, and honey is made to the value of two hundred thousand dollars annually. The revenue does not vary much from fourteen million dollars, and the military establishment numbers twenty thousand infantry, twenty-nine hundred cavalry, and eighteen thousand militia. In the latter, all males between seventeen and fifty years of age are liable to serve. There are about two hundred thousand Catholics and ten thousand Jews: the rest of the people are Protestants. The government is that of a constitutional monarchy.

A few independent tribes of hunters and herdsmen are the first inhabitants of this territory known to history. It is named as the abode of the Cherusci, who defeated Varus, the Chauci, and the Longobardi. When Charlemagne introduced Christianity here, its inhabitants were Saxons. For several hundred years, it was a part of Saxony. During the thirteenth century, of the eighty-five towns composing the Hanseatic league, thirteen were of Hanover. On the death of the English Queen Anne, the electors of Hanover, of the family of Brunswick-Lunenburg, became kings of England, and so continued, till, by the accession of Queen Victoria, the two countries were separated, as the electorate of Hanover could descend only in the male line; and the duke of Cumberland, eldest surviving brother of King William IV. of England, ascended the throne of Hanover, by the title of *Ernest Augustus*, A. D. 1837. Though bitterly opposed to reforms, he was obliged to yield to the general demand for popular rights; and, in March, 1848, granted his subjects freedom of the press, amnesty for political offences, and the convention and public declaration of the states, or representative assembly. He was succeeded by George V. in 1851.

Wirtemberg. — Wirtemberg is a kingdom, one hundred and forty miles long by one hundred broad, lying between Baden on the west and Bavaria on the east, with an area of about seven thousand five hundred square miles. Its territory is mountainous, and for the most part extremely fertile. In agricultural and manufacturing industry, as also in trade, both external and internal, Wirtemberg is highly flourishing. Its people are good natured, well educated, and robust. Its university at Tubingen has acquired great celebrity, and the number of children attending its fine system of common schools is one in six of the whole population — a proportion larger than in England and France. The revenue of the kingdom is about six millions of dollars, and the army, on the peace establishment, numbers nine or ten thousand: the war establishment enrolls about nineteen thousand men. Every subject is liable to serve six years in the army. The government has been an hereditary constitutional monarchy since 1819; previously, it was a simple monarchy. Stuttgard is the capital.

The Alemanni, those renowned enemies of Rome and conquerors of her armies, dwelt here at the beginning of the fourth century A. D.; in 496, they were subdued by the Franks, under Clovis. The country was afterward called *Suabia*, which anciently included Wirtemberg, Baden, Augsburg, and Ulm, and its dukes in time acquired the imperial crown; but the duchy of Suabia was ruined on the death of Conradin, in 1268, being frittered into petty sovereignties, which now became independent.

Ulrich I., count of Wirtemberg, one of these petty sovereigns, is the ancestor of the present dynasty of the kingdom. *Eberhard the Illustrious* had a reign of sixty years, checkered with extraordinary vicissitudes. He commenced the attempts upon the rights of the imperial cities, called the *War of the Cities* — which was carried on between the nobles and burgesses for two hundred years. Being summoned to the bar of the empire to answer certain complaints, he appeared, with a troop of two hundred horse, and declared himself to be nobody's vassal. He was placed under the ban of the empire, and his states entirely overrun, the imperialist troops committing unbounded excesses. On the emperor's death, however, he recovered all his territory, with considerable additions.

Eberhard V., after a youth of profligacy, succeeded to the throne in 1482, and faithfully devoted himself to the welfare of his kingdom, which is indebted to him for the first foundation of a representative constitution. The emperor Maximilian declared at his grave that he had "left no equal in the empire in princely virtues." A. D. 1496. *Christopher*, who began to reign in 1550, was possessed of great talents and the noblest qualities of mind and heart. It was he who completely established the Protestant religion, and founded a constitution in church and state, the main features of which remain to the present day. Situated directly between Germany and France, Wirtemberg suffered dreadful ravages in the thirty years' war, the war of the Spanish succession, and the seven years' war; and also in the hostile operations which grew out of the French Revolution. In 1797, *Frederic William Charles* ascended the throne, and was succeeded by *William*, the present sovereign, in 1816.

Baden. — The grand duchy of Baden — having six thousand square miles of surface, and more than one million people — consists of the long valley of the Rhine, from Basle to Manheim, sloping down from the Black Forest, which borders it like a ring, and broken into a number of fine and broad subordinate valleys. The soil of these is extremely fertile, and the hill-sides are covered with the richest pasturage. Its transit trade is very great, and its people are industrious and prosperous. Carlsruhe is now the capital; but the majestic ancient palace of the electors palatine is at Heidelberg. The duchy derives its name from Baden, a city so called from its warm baths, which still attract the diseased and the gay. The educational establishments of Baden are very extensive, including, beside common or primary schools, thirteen gymnasiums, four lyceums, and two universities. Since 1817, it has had a representative constitution nearly similar to that of Bavaria or Wirtemberg.

From 1052 to 1527, there were sixteen sovereigns of Baden: in 1527, it was divided into the two sovereignties of Baden-Baden and Baden-Dourlach: down to 1761, the former had eight sovereigns, and the latter nine, in the last of whom, *Charles Frederic*, who survived the last sovereign of Baden-Baden, the two were again united, as the two sovereigns had agreed they should be in either survivor. In 1801, the treaty of Luneville raised Charles Frederic to the dignity of elector, and he afterward constantly sided with France. In 1848, revolutionary agitation shook the country, but soon yielded to the general reäction. The Grand Duke Frederick came to the throne in 1858.

Other German States. — The other states, as will be seen by reference to the table at page 970, vary in extent from fifty-two square miles to five thousand seven hundred and twelve, and in population from five or six thousand to seven or eight hundred thousand. They consist of one electorate, six grand duchies, ten duchies, ten principalities, four free cities, and one landgraviate. The details of the history of all these petty sovereignties would carry us entirely beyond the limits of the present work. We can only notice them very briefly.

Hesse-Cassel is a picturesque country. It lies chiefly on the Fulda, and its branches, surrounded by Saxe-Weimar, Bavaria, Hesse-Darmstadt, Nassau, and Hanover, and between the Prussian provinces of Saxony and Westphalia. Its ancient landgraves were warlike and powerful, and it is now restored to their representative, the present elector, after forming for a while the central part of Jerome Bonaparte's ephemeral kingdom of Westphalia, A. D. 1807 to 1813. In 1848, the elector yielded to the demands for popular rights, but not till a severe riot had occurred. — *Hesse-Darmstadt* consists of two portions, separated by the River Mayne and the territory of Frankfort: it includes the famous cities of Mayence and Worms. It has now a free constitution. The two Hesses, called *Upper* and *Lower*, formed one government, mostly, from A. D. 1257 to the French revolution, with eighteen kings. Their modern sovereigns are infamous for enriching themselves by letting out the limbs, blood, and lives of their subjects for hire. Hessian mercenaries served in the American war. — *Hesse-Homburg*, between Frankfort and Nassau, owes its existence to the recent favor of Austria; it has but twenty-five thousand inhabitants. — *Mecklenburg-Schwerin* is a little larger than Connecticut, and lies between the Elbe and Baltic, Holstein and Prussia. Henry the Lion subdued it; but in A. D. 1164, it became a princedom again, its chief, *Pribislas*, having embraced Christianity. The Mecklenburgs had some twenty-two princes down to the French revolution, from which they suffered much. —*Mecklenburg-Strelitz* is not so large as Rhode Island; it is between the Prussian provinces of Brandenburg and Pomerania, with Schwerin on the north-west. It has given two queens to Great Britain. — *Kniphausen*, in Oldenburg, on the North Sea, called the *Lilliputian lordship* by humorous geographers, was recognized as an independent state, by the Germanic diet, in 1826. It has seventeen square miles, and two to three thousand population.

Holstein and *Lauenburg* have been attached to Denmark, to which the house of Holstein has given sovereigns since A. D. 1448. Here was a primitive seat of the Saxons. Holstein once belonged to the German empire, and afterward, in connection with Lauenburg, gave the king of Denmark one vote in the Germanic confederation. In 1848, it revolted, as stated in our history of Denmark, and temporarily secured an independent consideration in the new Germanic federation, after a bloody contest. Now restored to Denmark.—*Nassau*, formed by the union of territories of several branches of one family, is now nearly as large as Delaware. It lies between the Hesses and Western Prussia, having the Rhine and the Mayne on the south, and is famed for Hock and Bleschert wines. Its counts gave an emperor to Germany — Adolphus I. in A. D. 1298. — *Luxemburg* entitled whoever ruled it to a vote in the Germanic confederation; it has given four emperors to the German empire. By the revolution of 1830, it became a part of the new kingdom of Belgium, to the history of which the reader is referred Its Swiss-like mountains present scenes of savage grandeur. Its capital, Luxemburg, is one of the strongest fortresses in Europe. Its frontier position has subjected it to a variety of changes, which need not be particularized here. — *Oldenburg*, nearly surrounded by Hanover, is distinguished by the high rank of its princes, who are connected by family alliances with Russia and all the other great powers of the north. Besides the flat, marshy, Holland-like district, rich in pasture at the mouth of the Weser, it has pieces of territory in different parts of Northern Germany. It has little historic renown. It is of a size equal to Luxemburg, one fifth larger than the state of Delaware.

Brunswick is formed of three isolated territories, of unequal extent, in the midst of Hanover and Prussia, and mostly between the Elbe and the Weser. It is the appendage of one of the greatest and most ancient houses of Germany, — that of *Guelf*, whose head, Henry the Lion, contended with the house of Suabia for the empire, but was worsted, and put under the imperial ban. The kings of Britain are descended from the branch of Brunswick-Luneburg. The government continued absolute till about twenty years since, when, by a violent change of dynasty, the people obtained for themselves a representative constitution. It has produced some able generals. — *Saxe-Weimar-Eisenach* is a little state, called the Athens of Germany, and has made up for the smallness of its territory by the splendor of its intellectual triumphs. Imbedded, as it were, between Bavaria, Prussia, Saxony, and the Hesses, it could hope for little consideration in politics; but it takes the lead among the smaller states through the liberal wisdom of its dukes, who attracted to its university at Jena the greatest scholars of the age, and to its court near by, at Weimar village, such a constellation of genius as Wieland, Herder, Schiller, and Goethe — the honoring and honored intimates of its sovereigns. Its liberal press has been a great annoyance to the absolutists of Germany, and its enlightened and popular dukes were the first to give their subjects a representative constitution. — *Saxe-Meiningen-Hildburghausen* is on the Werra, and has salt, coal, and iron mines. Near it, on the north-east and south-east, is *Saxe-Coburg-Gotha*, which has given its present king to Belgium, and to England, Prince Albert, the husband of Queen Victoria. — *Saxe Altenburg* consists of two detached portions separated by Saxe-Weimar and Reuss. It claims no special historical celebrity. — *Lippe-Detmold* has a little territory famed as the locality of the destruction of the Roman army under Varus, by the Germans, already noticed. It adjoins Brunswick to the east, and is nearly surrounded by Westphalia. — *Schauenburg-Lippe* is north of the last, on the northern frontier of Hanover. One of its princes made a distinguished figure in the service of Portugal.

Schwartzburg-Rudolstadt is in the centre of Saxe-Weimar. — *Schwartzburg-Sondershausen* is farther north, in the southern part of Prussian Saxony. These two are ruled by branches of a family of great antiquity, which has vast estates in Bohemia and other parts of the Austrian territory.

Reuss-Lobenstein and *Reuss-Greitz* are contiguous territories between Saxony and Saxe-Weimar, and governed by elder and younger branches of the house of Reuss. The River Elster separates them. — *Anhalt-Dessau* is on the Mulda and the Elbe, at their junction. The ruling family is ancient, and has produced men of eminence. To branches of it belong *Anhalt-Bernburg*, west of the Saale. This lies in two detached portions, near each other. The eastern part adjoins another duchy of the family, — *Anhalt-Cothen*, which connects it with Anhalt Dessau. — *Waldeck* is composed of two hilly districts between Hesse and Hanover, Brunswick and Lippe, and owes all its importance to its mineral baths at Pyrmont. — *Hohenzollern-Sigmaringen* and *Hohenzollern-Hechingen* form con tiguous principalities to the south of Wirtemberg, between it and Baden. — *Liechtenstein* is upon the Rhine, above Lake Constance, in the Saxon Erzgebirge, with but seven thousand one hundred inhabitants. Though so diminutive, it has for its prince an Austrian nobleman who is one of the most opulent individuals of Europe, while his family is distinguished for knowledge and intelligence.

THE HANSE TOWNS. — The four cities of Hamburg, Frankfort, Bremen, and Lubec, which close our account, are free cities, under independent governments. They are the sole remnant of the Hanse towns and imperial cities.

The same policy which led the Saxon emperors to encourage the usurpations of the spiritual nobles in order to balance the overweening power of the temporal nobles, rendered them favorable to the burghers, who dwelt in towns immediately subject to the emperor, or, settling under the protection of some duke or bishop, formed what were called *Free Cities*.

In all these towns, the nucleus of the population were the free burgesses, or landed proprietors, who had built houses on their own ground, and their tenants, who, although possessing no property in the city, were proprietors of lands in some other district. To these were added a crowd of persons, originally serfs, exercising mechanical trades, or employed by the free burgesses in the capacity of household servants. These settlers, many of whom had taken refuge in the cities, to escape the tyranny of their spiritual lords, although far more numerous than the free burgesses, were viewed with great contempt by the *Geschlechte*, — "families," — who composed the aristocracy of the towns, and were neither permitted to hold public meetings, nor take any part in the management of their common affairs. In later times, however, when the traders became more powerful, they formed unions of their own, called *guilds*, each of which was governed by a guildmaster, the whole being presided over by a burgomaster, chosen out of their body. The supreme officer of the whole city was the imperial provost, generally some neighboring count, acting as commander-in-chief of the civic forces, as well as chief justice, although these two offices were sometimes separated. Under him were twelve counsellors, called *schöppen*, — aldermen, — elected by the burgesses. Their president, termed *schuldheisz*, — mayor, — at first only held a court, as his name imports, for the settlement of disputed debts; but gradually, as the emperors granted privilege after privilege to the citizens, this officer took the place of the provost, who seldom visited the town, and in some cases was even suspended from his office by an imperial ordinance. The twelve aldermen, with the mayor at their head, composed the *stadt-rath*, or town council.

Before A. D. 1250, many cities had become populous and rich. They combined to control feudal oppression, and to resist robberies and piracies. The cities along the Rhine, with some in Switzerland, maintained an armed force, at joint expense, on that river, between 1200 and 1300, and some time after. Similar causes combined nearly all the commercial cities along the northern coast of Europe, from the Baltic to the Netherlands, inclusive, and some cities in the interior of Germany. They were called the *Hanseatic League*, or the *Hanse Towns*, from *hansa*, a league, corporation, or association. In 1241, Hamburg and Lubec appear conspicuously in the league. In 1260, the number of towns, maritime and interior, was eighty-five. They sent deputies to a triennial meeting at Lubec, where their records were kept. They had a factory at London, at Bruges, at Novgorod, and at Bergen.

About the year 1361, the league received royal charters, and was favored by princes who found its naval and military power useful in controlling the feudal lords, and in suppressing piracies. The acceptable return made for this royal countenance was contributions and royal grants. The league rendered such essential service that some of its members obtained grants of perpetual freedom, and were called *free cities*, and the four named at the head of this article have so continued to the present day. The league was so powerful in 1248, that it sent forth a fleet of two hundred and forty-eight ships, and twelve thousand soldiers. It deposed a king of Sweden, and gave the crown to another. But as this league arose out of the social and political disorders of Europe, it was destined to fall, as political power acquired consistency and firmness. Sovereigns were able to subject Hanse cities to their dominion. Commerce became general, and the motives to form the league no longer continued to operate. The league ceased to exist about A. D. 1650.* The members of the congress of Vienna, A. D. 1815, though little friendly to any thing republican, considered the four cities of Hamburg, Frankfort, Lubec, and Bremen, to be so fully established as governments, and so venerable from their antiquity, that they sanctioned them as a part of the Germanic body.

CHAPTER CCCCLII.

General Views of Germany — Character of the People — Literature — Commerce, &c.

THOUGH it is easy to perceive distinctive characteristics which mark the nationality of the Prussian, the Austrian, the Bavarian, the Bohemian, and the Saxon, yet these all combine into certain general features, easily recognized as forming the German character — that character which belongs to the forty millions of souls who occupy Central Europe, and speak the German language.† Frankness, honesty, hospitality,

* Sullivan's Historical Causes and Effects.

† The popular and patriotic poet, Arndt, expresses this nationality in his stirring poem, "What is the German's Fatherland?" from a translation of which we give the following extract: —

"What is the German's Fatherland?
The Prussian land? the Suabian land?
Where Rhine's thick-clustering fruitage gleams?
Where on the Belt the seamew screams?
Not these the land:
His is a wider Fatherland.
* * * *
Bavarian or Westphalian land?
Where o'er the Dunes the wild sand blows?
Or where the Danube brawling flows?
* * * *
Is't Tyrol, or the land of Tell?
* * * *
The subject realms of Austria's crown,
That land of triumphs and renown?
* * * *
Not these the land:
His is a wider Fatherland.

What is the German's Fatherland?
O name at length this mighty land,
As wide as sounds the German tongue,
And German hymns to God are sung:
That is the land;
That, German, name thy Fatherland.

freedom from artifice and disguise, industry, application, and perseverance, a serious earnestness and straight-forwardness, are the sterling qualities which form the very respectable basis of the character of these millions. In inventive genius, they are not backward, and can claim those two inventions, printing and gunpowder, which have changed the face of the civilized world. In all the higher walks of art, Germany boasts a galaxy of names which glitter on the roll of fame: she ranks, also, with the most advanced nations in every branch of the humble arts of daily life: in mining she is first. In literary industry, also, the Germans shine unrivalled; no other country is so prolific in books.

The language is so copious, vigorous, and at the same time pliant, that it adapts itself equally to the "niceties of philosophy, the variety of conversation, and the warmth of poetry." In poetry, indeed, the German mind seems to have expressed itself more fully than in any other form — clothing its depth of feeling, its lofty, reflective, "subjective" spirit, in language strong, picturesque, and original. German poetry, as well as philosophy, however, it must be confessed, is too often obscured by mysticism. Goethe, Schiller, Wieland, Herder, Klopstock, Lessing, Gessner, Novalis, and Korner, are specimens of the variety which reigns in this department of the German intellectual character, though these are but a few of the multitude who have contributed to render the German name illustrious.

In biblical literature, her scholars are far in advance of all other nations, and also in linguistic lore: distinguished names are so numerous in these branches of knowledge, that we have no room for the list. The nation is scarcely less renowned in the department of history, especially the philosophy of history. The history of the human mind, the progressive civilization of the race, the history of literature and art, have occupied such writers as Adelung, Herder, Eichhorn, Bouterwek, and Schlegel. Among illustrious German historians we must also name Niebuhr, Wachsmuth, Von Muller, Jahn, Von Hammer, Heeren, Raumer, as leaders of a host of authors distinguished for research, patient industry, and sound judgment, even above their renowned contemporaries in other countries. Geography, twin sister to History, numbers many German names of high distinction among her votaries, at the head of whom stand Humboldt, Ritter, and Klaproth. In metaphysics, Germans have founded schools which divide the thinking world under such master minds as Kant, Gall, Fichte, Schelling, and Spurzheim; though Madame de Staël, with many others, thinks the "empire of the air" is the peculiar province of the German metaphysicians. In natural and abstract science, they have the great names of Leibnitz and Kepler; in medicine, Van Swieten and Hahnemann; in mineralogy, Werner, Mohs, and others.

That is the German's Fatherland,
Where faith is pledged by grasp of hand,
Where truth darts bright from flashing eyes,
And love in hearts warm nestling lies:
That is the land;
That, German, name thy Fatherland.

To us this glorious land is given: —
O Lord of Hosts, look down from heaven,
And grant us German loyalty,
To love our country faithfully —
To love our land,
Our undivided Fatherland."

The literary and scientific collections of Germany are the most numerous and valuable that exist in any country. Her seven largest libraries contain together over two millions of books; seven more have one hundred thousand volumes each. A lively German writer remarks, "Our activity is eminently in writing; there is nothing of any interest whatever that is not written about. To which side soever we turn, we behold books and readers. Whatever we may have in one hand, we are sure to have a book in the other. Every thing, from government down to children's cradles, has become a science, and must needs be studied. Books help to every thing. What one is ignorant of, is to be found in a book. We govern, cure, trade and travel, boil and roast, according to books. A child and a book are things which always occur to us together." It is said that upwards of four thousand new works are annually produced by the ten thousand authors of Germany. They particularly excel in works that require unwearied plodding, and infinite research throughout their worlds of books.

The amusements of the Germans are of a rather more gay and elegant description than their character would lead us to expect. Music and dancing are cultivated with extreme ardor. In dress, the Austrians and Hungarians display a pomp of array and a blaze of jewels which dazzle other nations. Among the common people there are still many fantastic fashions in apparel that have not yet yielded to the sway of French fashion, which has given uniformity to the dress of refined society everywhere. The military character is in high esteem, and the clank of iron boot-heels, the clangor of military bands, and the measured tread of stately soldiers are the common sounds of German cities.

The higher orders of German society hold themselves as separated by the most marked and decided line from the body of the nation. They are fond of titles, ancestry, and show, and hedged around by rigid prejudices of caste from all who are untitled. The petty princes surround themselves with empty pomp, and have much feudal feeling and baronial pride. The high nobles possess sovereignty themselves, or are descended from those who did; the low nobility cannot boast this. The old nobility must be able to count a line of sixteen noble ancestors, while the nobles who cannot do this belong to the young or short nobility. The patricians, or hereditary city nobles, are still another class. The body of the Germans form, perhaps, the hardest working nation in Europe, — slow, heavy, laborious. Plain and homely in their manners, simple and domestic in their habits, honesty and fidelity generally mark their transactions, and they make thriving colonists.

The most striking defect of the German character, as seen by foreigners, is a lack of practical ability in the conduct of affairs — a dreaminess and inconsequence of thought; and this perhaps arises from the habit of expecting every initiative from the government, which, indeed, in many of the states, has debarred the people from certain ranges of thought, making of them machines who are passively occupied in the routine of employment assigned them. Individuality is thus lost, and the "subject" seldom escapes from the leading strings, except to plunge into dreams and extravagances. The habit of the German mind seems to be rather to exhaust itself upon special subjects, without taking that self-relying, many-sided, enterprising, ve satile, common-sense character, which our institutions — free institutions — are calculated to develop.

The largest and wisest minds of Germany are now struggling for a wider sphere of action, and are aiming to unite the millions who speak German, for this end. Hence the desire of a common centre of political power. The government of Prussia, shrewdly profiting by this German sentiment of nationality, and the new interests arising from the development of industry consequent upon a long peace, has established a union of the German custom-houses in the different states, — the *Zollverein*, — which puts into its hands the circulation of the products of commerce, manufacture, and agriculture, and gives currency to its coin throughout all Germany.* Thus, by acquiring a vast influence over the economical interests of the Germanic countries, which it has managed to incorporate in its zollverein system, Prussia thought to assure to itself that political predominance, the object of the ambition of Frederic the Great. But it has perceived that material interests are not a sufficient bond of union, or basis of power; and, in 1849, after yielding only so far as compelled by the revolutionary storm passing over Europe, proposes a confederation as the bond of German nationality. In thus quieting the demand for reform by deliberations and seeming concessions, and flattering German feelings by a kind of union, Prussia hopes to obtain the direction of a moral power which shall give it the predominant position formerly occupied in the old Germanic empire by its inveterate rival, Austria.

The lesson taught us by European history, however, is, that no contrivances or reforms short of liberal suffrage, which shall interest the masses in the government, will give stability to European politics, develop the full power of the German character, and make it take that prominent place and influence in the civilization of the world — the amelioration of the universal family of man — which belongs to it by right of birth and race; a place, in short, by the side of the United States and England.

* The restrictedness of the commerce of the German race, in comparison with what it should be among so intelligent a people, is fully accounted for when we consider that each of its petty three hundred states in earlier times, and each of its forty or fifty sovereignties till within a very few years, were in the habit of collecting duties on articles that passed their frontiers. Thus, in passing up or down the Rhine, toll was paid at twenty-seven stations on the same article; on the Weser, twenty-three distinct tolls were exacted; on the Elbe, thirty-two! Certainly a more effectual way of strangling commerce could scarcely be imagined.

Switzerland.

CHAPTER CCCCLIII.

50 B. C. to A. D. 1863.

Geography of Switzerland — William Tell — League of the Cantons — Manners and Customs, &c.

Switzerland is an inland and mountainous country of Central Europe, having Germany on the north and east, Italy on the south, and France on the west. Its length from east to west is two hundred miles; its breadth form north to south, one hundred and thirty; and its superficial extent fifteen thousand square miles, hardly twice as great as that of Massachusetts. By far the larger portion of the country consists of mountains, comprising some of the highest summits of the Alps. It has not been inaptly remarked that "some idea may be formed of the Helvetic geography by comparing the country to a large town, of which the valleys are the streets, and the mountains groups of contiguous houses."

The Rivers Rhine, Rhone, Ticino, and Doubs, have their sources in Switzerland. The lakes of this country are remarkable for their extent, the depth and purity of their waters, and the beautiful scenery which surrounds them. The principal of them are Geneva, Constance, Neufchatel, Lucerne, and Zurich. The climate is dependent on elevation and on the cooling influence of the glaciers: † it may be said to be cold in the Alps, temperate in the plains, and hot during summer in some of the valleys. Cattle are plentiful, and form the chief wealth of the inhabitants, with the exception of those of the manufacturing districts. Among the wild animals are the ibex, the chamois, and the marmot, and, in the unfrequented tracts, bears, lynxes,

† The *glaciers* of the Alps impart one of the greatest charms to their scenery. These are formed by accumulations of snow and ice, and are often from fifteen to twenty miles long. Though every single crystal of the ice of the glaciers is perfectly white, the whole mass is of a blue color, passing through every shade from the most feeble sky blue to that of the lapis lazuli. They contrast in an extraordinary manner with the surrounding country, their lower extremities being commonly contiguous to meadows, covered with the finest grass and the most beautiful flowers, or to tracts of land clothed with magnificent trees, especially firs. *Avalanches* are more common in the Alps than in other mountains, because of the steepness of their declivities. The most common commence their descent at the highest summits, and increase in magnitude and velocity as they roll down to the valleys, sometimes overwhelming, in their headlong career, men and cattle, villages and forests, and damming up and obstructing the course of rivers. These avalanches expose travellers to the greatest dangers they have to encounter in traversing the Alps. There are certain localities on the most frequented roads in which they descend annually, and are consequently very dangerous. The snow limit of the Alps is found at an elevation of eight thousand feet above the level of the sea.

and wolves are common. Birds of prey are not unfrequent, among which is the bearded vulture, or lammergeyer, which is known to carry off lambs. This is the largest native bird of Europe. The general surface of Switzerland exceeds in rugged sublimity every other portion of Europe. The whole country consists of mountains and valleys, exhibiting the most striking contrasts of dark forests, craggy rocks, bright verdure, and eternal snow. Icy peaks rise into the air close upon the borders of fertile valleys, and luxuriant cornfields are surrounded by extensive and dreary plains of ice.

The Swiss confederacy consists of twenty-two cantons, as follows: —

Cantons.	*Pop. in 1860.*	*Capitals.*	*Pop. in 1860.*
Grisons	90,713	Coire	
Berne	467,141	Berne	29,016
Valais	90,792	Sitten	
Vaud	213,157	Lausanne	20,515
Tessin	116,343	Lugano	
St. Gall	180,411	St. Gall	14,532
Zurich	266,265	Zurich	19,758
Lucerne	130,504	Lucerne	11,522
Aargau	194,208	Aargau	
Friburg	105,523	Friburg	10,454
Uri	14,741	Altorf	
Schweitz	45,039	Schweitz	
Glaris	33,363	Glaris	
Neufchatel	87,369	Neufchatel	10,382
Thurgau	90,080	Frauenfeld	
Unterwalden	24,902	Sarnen	
Soleure	69,263	Soleure	
Bâle	92,265	Bâle	37,918
Appenzell	60,431	Appenzell	
Schaffhausen	35,500	Schaffhausen	
Geneva	82,876	Geneva	41,415
Zug	105,523	Zug	
	2,510,494		

This country was called *Helvetia* by the Romans, and was inhabited by the *Helvetii*, one of the most numerous and warlike of the Celtic tribes. About 50 B. C. the great body of the Helvetii resolved to migrate to the more fertile regions of Gaul. They were here met and defeated by Julius Cæsar with great slaughter. The survivors were allowed to return to their homes, and were henceforth in the condition of allies and tributaries of Rome. After the total conquest of Gaul, the Romans sent colonies into the country of the Helvetians, and introduced their civilization among them. The traces of its ancient subjugation to Rome are still visible in the Romanic language of a part of the country. Before the fall of the empire of the West, three German nations freed this country from the foreign domination. These were the Franks, the Burgundians, and the Ostrogoths. The Christian religion had already been introduced into Helvetia. The irruption of the Huns next swept through the peaceful valleys of the Alps, and Roman civilization disappeared. In the middle of the sixth century, the whole country was conquered by the Franks, and became a portion of their empire. It retained its ancient constitution, however: the Romans and the old inhabitants were governed by Roman laws, and each of the other tribes by its peculiar code. The Christian religion was restored, and the devastated fields were again brought under cultivation. Under Charlemagne, the arts and sciences were encouraged here.

From this period till the time of Rodolph of Hapsburg, at the close of the thirteenth century, the history of Switzerland presents but an uninteresting series of civil wars. The feudal system was especially prevalent here, and counts and dukes held the entire sway. These were from time to time made to feel their subjection to the German kings; but war with each other was their chief business, and misery the fate of the people in this distracted land. At the time when a desire to fight for the redemption of the holy sepulchre overran Europe like a tempest, many Swiss nobles went to Palestine; and thus, for a time, the country was delivered from their oppressions. The crusades, by promoting commerce, improved the condition of the cities, as a part of the troops, arms, and provisions were transmitted to Italy, through the passes of the Alps. The crusaders brought back with them new inventions in the arts. The gold and silk manufactures of the Italian and Eastern nations were imitated in Switzerland; refinement took the place of rudeness, and poetry became the favorite amusement of the nobles.

William Tell.

At this period, Rodolph, count of Hapsburg, appeared upon the stage of history. Though his provinces were small, yet his ambition was boundless, and in the course of events, he became emperor of Germany. This occurred in 1273. From him the present house of Austria is descended. For a series of generations, the daughters of this family have been celebrated for their beauty; and it is by marriage with the principal reigning families of Europe, that its aggrandizement has been effected. It was the son of this Rodolph, Albert I., who succeeded his father as emperor, that gave rise to the events connected with the history of William Tell, the "deliverer of Switzerland." The tyranny and obstinacy of this prince greatly incensed his Swiss subjects, and ultimately caused the first confederacy of the Swiss cantons He sent two governors to harass, oppress, and punish them, for their manifestations of uneasiness. These were Gesler and Landenberg. The people were now exposed to all the vexatious persecutions of petty tyrants, who were anxious to recommend themselves, by abuse of power, to the favor of an incensed master. They never appeared in public, unless surrounded by a numerous guard. Fortresses were erected in the disaffected places, into which persons of every description were thrown upon the slightest grounds of suspicion. Gesler was the slave of vanity: among other expedients to gratify this passion, he caused a pole to be erected in the market place at Altorf, and a hat to be placed upon it, to which he ordered all passers-by to pay the same respect as to his own person. The people needed no new outrage to make them feel their abject condition; but so completely were they kept in awe by the government fortresses, that they gave way to sullen despair.

On the 17th of November, 1307, three men, named *Staufacher*, *Walter Furst*, and *Melchthal*, patriots and friends of liberty, met in the field of Rutli, a retired meadow on the shores of the Lake of Lucerne. Each one was accompanied by ten chosen companions. Their object was to consult upon the necessary preparations for a general insurrection. All ideas of immediate revolt were, however, laid aside, and the first day of the new year was fixed for the rising. An event, however, took place in the interval, which nearly destroyed their hopes. William Tell, whose name will ever be celebrated in the annals of Helvetia, happened, one day, to pass through Altorf, and, seeing the pole and hat of Gesler, not only refused to bend before the fantastic ensign, but went so far as to menace it, and treat it with indignity. He was dragged before the enraged governor, who ordered him either to suffer immediate death, or pierce with an arrow an apple placed upon the head of his son, a boy about six years old. Tell hesitated for some time, but at last, confident in his unerring aim, accepted the trial. He came forward with a resolute step; the crowd trembled as he took his post. He grasped his bow, and drew the string. The arrow sped upon its errand, and the divided apple fell. Repeated peals announced the joy of the spectators, and rebounded through the adjacent rocks. The hero ran to his child, and clasped him to his bosom; then, turning to the governor, he produced another arrow, exclaiming, "Had my boy fallen, this was destined for thee!"

Gesler, mortified and enraged, ordered his guards again to seize the bold offender. After a short conflict, Tell was mastered, and was placed in a boat, to be conveyed to some distant fortress. The governor and his attendants embarked with him. Hardly had they left the shore, than the clouds which had been gathering over the summit of the mountains burst into a furious tempest. The winds lashed the waves, while around, on every side, craggy rocks arose in dreadful contrast from the level of the lake. The watermen sunk under the labor of the oar, and, commending themselves to Providence for protection, left the boat to its fate. Tell, who was a skilful pilot, was now ordered by Gesler to take charge of the vessel. He was unbound, and placed at the helm. Under his guidance, the confidence of the passengers revived. As they approached the shore, Tell boldly plunged into the flood, taking his bow with him. With one hand, he seized a projecting rock, and with the other pushed back the boat into the waves. The tempest abated, however, and the governor gained the shore. But he escaped the waves only to perish by another fate. Tell* met him on the road and, in an instant, an arrow laid him dead at his feet.

The news of this event spread like an electric spark among the friends of liberty. The insurgents rose on all sides. In the course of one day, the Castles of Sarnen and Rotzberg, in Unterwalden, those of Schwanan and Kusnach, in Schweitz, and a newly-erected fortress in Uri, were taken and given up to the flames. Every vestige of despotism was effaced with them. The welcome intelligence flew with rapidity from mountain to mountain. Every goatherd immediately threw aside his pipe and crook, and armed in the common cause. The three cantons of Schweitz, Uri, and Unterwalden, thus obtained their independence. But the house of Austria still contended for its lost privileges. The victory of Morgarten, gained by the Swiss in 1315, resulted in establishing the perpetual league of these cantons. During the next three centuries, they were continually receiving accessions of territory, by the admission of other cantons. In the early part of the sixteenth century, Turin was taken from the Milanese, and the Pays de Vaud was taken from Savoy by the Bernese in 1560. During the sixteenth and seventeenth centuries, the Swiss were distracted with religious and political feuds. By the peace of Westphalia, in 1646, the complete separation of Switzerland from the German empire was acknowledged. The republic had but little influence in foreign politics during the eighteenth century, and, until nearly its close, suffered little from foreign interference, till the epoch of that great convulsion which shook all Europe.

The French revolution agitated all the monarchical states, to which it was in open opposition. But the directory presented to the cantons a new form of constitution, which they called *unitaire*, and which the Swiss were required to adopt. As the latter clung to their old and venerated forms of freedom, an army was led into their territory, which, after encountering a brave and enthusiastic resistance, succeeded in compelling the country to submit to French dictation. Switzerland became the theatre of war between the French, Austrians, and Russians; but the first were finally triumphant. After the accession of Napoleon, the cantons made an attempt to regain their independence, which was repressed, though with some popular concessions; but Geneva and the canton of Valais were incorporated with France. On the downfall of Napoleon's power, Switzerland again became independent. The eight powers forming the congress

* The story of Tell has been sometimes called in question. Its truth, however, is attested by chapels, by the designation of the rock on which he leaped, by paintings, and other circumstances. Pilgrimages were often made to the spot where he sprang ashore, and, in 1388, about forty years after the supposed date of his death, the canton of Uri erected a chapel on the same spot, and afterward caused a eulogy to be pronounced every year in his memory. In the same year, the place was visited by one hundred and fourteen persons, who had been acquainted with him. All the old chronicles confirm this point, and Schiller, in his tragedy, follows the popular tradition. Of the subsequent events of Tell's life, very little is known. He was present at the battle of Morgarten, and is supposed to have lost his life in an inundation about the year 1350. Enough has been reserved from the records of the past to furnish a lasting lesson to tyrants, and to show that liberty may find a champion even in the wildest and most rugged scenes of nature.

TELL REFUSING HOMAGE TO GESLER'S HAT.

Swiss House.

of Vienna proclaimed, by a separate act, the perpetual neutrality of Switzerland, and the inviolability of its soil. The country has since, from time to time, been disturbed by risings of some portions of the population. Religious quarrels have caused agitation, and the French revolutions of 1830 and 1848 set the example of insurrection and turmoil. But these were transient. The people, shut up in their rocky fastnesses, seem almost isolated from the rest of the world; their politics and internal affairs are of but little interest beyond the mountains which circumscribe their action.

The Swiss confederacy is a federative state of twenty-two republics, who conduct their domestic concerns wholly independent of each other. They are all united, however, by the common tie of a federal government, called the *diet*. This is composed of representatives from the various cantons, and takes cognizance of every thing that concerns the foreign relations and general defence of the country. Zurich, Berne, and Lucerne, become alternately, each for the space of two years, the capital of the confederation. The army of the confederacy is formed out of contingents, which each canton, in proportion to its population, is obliged to furnish. It was fixed, in 1816, at sixty-seven thousand five hundred and sixteen men, of which half is a reserve. A remarkable peculiarity in the military system of Switzerland is the employment of its citizens in the service of foreign powers as a stipendiary force. Though attached to liberty themselves, seventy-five cents a day will make them flock to the banners of its most inveterate enemies. "Man and steel, the soldier and his sword," are the most remarkable of Swiss products. From Louis XI. to Louis XV., they furnished to the French service one million one hundred and ten thousand seven hundred and ninety-eight men, for which France paid over two hundred millions of dollars. This system is regularly authorized by the Swiss government. The population of Switzerland is somewhat over two millions, and rather more than half of these are Protestant.

Agriculture in Switzerland is necessarily and strictly limited by nature, many portions of the surface being absolutely inaccessible. The chief wealth of the country consists in its pastures. The meadows are mown with peculiar care and diligence. In boisterous weather, the shepherds watch all night with the cattle, encouraging them by their voices, amid the terrors of a storm upon the Alps. The country is chiefly dependent on its neighbors for a supply of grain; wine is sometimes produced on the lower declivities of the hills, and there is an ample growth of timber, principally of fir and pine. The Swiss manufactures are various and important. The greater part of the agricultural population are employed during the winter at the loom, or in other branches of manufacturing industry. In the French cantons, the making of watches, musical boxes, jewelry, &c., is most extensively carried on, while cotton and silk fabrics are the principal employment of the more northern departments. Linen fabrics, damasks, woollen cloths, paper, leather, straw plait, and iron goods are made in various places. The commerce of Switzerland is, from its inland situation, very limited, and consists chiefly in the exchange of its cattle for corn and colonial produce. A wonderful combination of industry and boldness has been displayed in carrying roads across the most rugged and precipitous Alpine barriers. The great road over the Simplon, though constructed by Napoleon for military purposes, affords very great commercial advantages.

In every district in Switzerland there are primary schools, in which are taught the elements of education—geography, history, singing, &c.; and secondary schools, in which instruction is given in ancient and modern languages, geometry, natural history, the fine arts, &c. In both these schools the rich and poor are educated together, the latter gratuitously. No child becomes able to exercise the right of citizenship, or is taken into service of any kind, without having first received the sacrament, which is administered to those only who have received a certain degree of instruction. Switzerland is, in respect to the attendance of children at school, far in advance of Great Britain, the Austrian empire, Belgium, and France. Education is at the basis of their political system. Every parish is obliged to support its own poor; but only those having the rights of citizenship are entitled to eleemosynary support.

"The great charm of Switzerland, next to its natural scenery, is the air of well-being, the neatness, and the sense of property imprinted on the people and their dwellings. They have a kind of Robinson Crusoe industry about their houses and lands; they are perpetually building, altering, repairing, or improving something about their tenements. The spirit of the proprietor is not to be mistaken in all that one sees in Switzerland. Some cottages, for instance, are adorned with long texts from Scripture, painted on or burnt into the wood in front over the door; others with the pedigree of the builder and owner. The modern taste of the proprietor shows itself in new windows, or additions to the original picturesque dwelling, which, with its immense projecting roof, sheltering or shading all these successive additions, looks like a hen sitting with a brood of chickens under her wings."*

The Swiss enjoy the reputation of being a plain, brave, honest, and simple people, among whom linger the last remnants of antique and primitive manners. Their scanty means of subsistence, the necessity of husbanding their resources, and the difficulty of increasing them, have made them sober, industrious, and economical. The distinctions of language are almost the only ones to be found among them, French, German, and a corrupt Italian dialect being each largely spoken. Chamois hunting is their national amusement. In matters of dress, the higher classes generally follow the French fashions. The national costume is confined to the females; it consists of a short petticoat, which shows the stockings as high as the knee, and a wide, flat hat tied under the chin. Sometimes the hat gives place to a strange-looking black cap, standing off the face, and in shape resembling the two wings of a butterfly. In some parts of the country, the modern invention of suspenders is not yet adopted by the men: the dress is a scanty jacket and short breeches, and there is a preposterous interval between the two garments, which the wearer makes frequent but ineffectual hitches to close.

Saturday night visits among young people constitute a peculiarity of Swiss manners. Of course, this is a favorite time for courtship. The young Swiss comes under the window of the fair lady to whom he intends paying his addresses, or with whom he wishes to become acquainted. As it is visiting night, and she expects company, she is at the window, neatly dressed, and admits or rejects the petition, which is always drawn up in regular form, generally in verse, and learned by heart. Permission being granted, the young man climbs up to the window, which is commonly in the third story; and as the houses are constructed with conveniences for this purpose, he runs little risk of breaking his neck. He sits on the window, and is regaled with gingerbread and cherry bounce. According as his views are more or less serious, or he proves more or less acceptable, he is allowed to enter the room, or is forced to remain outside. The conversation is often protracted till the dawn gives the signal for departure. Sometimes a happy lover is waylaid, on his return home, by some less favored rival, and violent battles ensue. In the mountainous region of Berne, a custom still exists for families connected by affinity or marriage, to make in common a cheese of enormous size. On it are carved the names of parties about to be married, and the same cheese often serves for the marriage of their descendants.

Geneva, the principal city of Switzerland, though comparatively small, has acquired a celebrity equal to that of the first capitals of Europe. Its situation is wonderfully picturesque; the adjacent country abounds in magnificent views, formed by the town, the lake, the numerous hills and mountains, rising suddenly from the plain in a variety of fantastic forms. This city is famous as having been the centre and asylum of the reformed religion. It possesses a public library containing eighty thousand volumes, and many other public buildings. Its university has long been distinguished as a seat of learning. Its population is about forty thousand. Berne, one of the capitals of the country, is remarkable for its romantic scenery and clean streets. Zurich is noted for its beautiful gardens and promenades, its literary distinction, and its public institutions. Basle, or Bâle, has a large trade, and its manufacture of silk ribbons is very extensive. At Lausanne Gibbon wrote the greater part of his history. Switzerland has given birth to many eminent men; but their fame sheds but little light upon their native country, having nearly all of them adopted other homes. Its literature is merged in that of Germany and France. Jean Jacques Rousseau, Lavater, Huber, Sismondi, Haller, Paracelsus, Euler, Le Sage, Necker, Pestalozzi, and Madame de Staël were all natives of Switzerland.

Swiss Girl.

* Laing's Notes.

Holland.

CHAPTER CCCCLIV.

30 B. C. to A. D. 1560.

Description of the Netherlands — Roman Conquest — The Batavi, Frisii, and Belgæ — Improvement of the Country — The Frankish Dominion — The Netherland Counts, &c. — Rise of the Free Towns.

Scene in Holland.

HOLLAND, formerly a republic, now a kingdom, is bounded north and west by the German Ocean, east by Germany, and south by Belgium. The latter country was for a long time under the same government with Holland, and shared in the same political fortunes. They were called collectively the *Netherlands*, or "Low Countries," from their geographical character; and the same history pertains to both countries for many centuries. They include the lowest part of all the continent of Europe. The northern portion, comprising the kingdom of Holland, is mostly below the level of the sea during high tides, and is defended from inundation by dikes, which the inhabitants have erected at vast expense, and which form, altogether, one of the most extraordinary monuments of human industry in the world. Belgium is also level for the most part, but is more elevated than Holland; the south-eastern part, bordering on Germany is hilly. The climate of the whole country is cool and moist, and the soil sandy and naturally sterile; yet the industry of the inhabitants has converted it into one of the richest and most populous districts of Europe. The following table shows the political divisions of the kingdom: —

Provinces.	*Capitals.*	*Population.*
North Holland,	Haarlem,	28,145
South Holland,	The Hague,	81,393
Zeeland,	Middleburg,	
North Brabant,	Hertogenbosch, or Bois de Duc,	20,489
Utrecht,	Utrecht,	54,495
Guelderland,	Arnheim,	26,382
Overyssel,	Zwoll,	19,547
Drenthe,	Assen,	
Groningen,	Groningen,	36,112
Friesland,	Leeuwerden,	25,536

In the time of the Romans, the greater part of the Netherlands consisted of dreary marshes, frequently overflowed by the sea, and thinly inhabited by people of German origin, called *Batavi* and *Frisii*. From the descriptions in the ancient writers, it appears that, when the Romans first visited this country, not a town nor village embellished the whole watery plain, nor was it enlivened by a single patch of verdure. Here and there, a few miserable huts, built on stakes or mounds of sand, which raised them above the tides, afforded an insecure shelter to the natives, who appear to have lived by the produce of the sea. South of these marshy tracts was a more elevated region, bordering upon Gaul, and including the ancient forest of Ardennes, inhabited by a race called *Belgæ*, who had towns and villages in the midst of the forest, and lived by hunting and agriculture. When Gaul was conquered by Julius Cæsar, the Belgæ also submitted to the Roman dominion: Roman colonies were settled in this country, which, with the vicinity, received the name of *Belgic Gaul*. The conquerors did not carry their arms into the northern parts, being doubtful whether they were land or sea. They made an alliance with the Batavi, who inhabited Holland; but the Frisii, or people dwelling in the extreme northern part, now called *Friesland*, refused to hold any communication with the Romans, and were left in full possession of their liberties.

The Romans remained masters of the Belgic provinces above four hundred years, during which time the inhabitants of the Lowlands learned of them the art of improving their country by digging canals to drain the marshes, and erecting dikes and embankments to keep out the sea. They were an industrious, persevering race of people, even in those early times; and their exertions were stimulated by a law which made every man the possessor of the land he redeemed from the waters. Thus the Frisii became free proprietors, instead of being vassals to feudal lords. By degrees, large tracts of territory were rendered sufficiently dry and firm to be built upon, and villages arose on every side, while fens and bogs were converted into pastures for swine and cattle. In proportion as the country grew more habitable, the population increased, and a trading intercourse was established with the Britons, which, in later years, was a source of wealth and prosperity to both nations.

In the decline of the Roman empire, Gaul was invaded and conquered by the Franks. Belgic Gaul shared the same fate, and for a long time formed a part of the Frankish monarchy. The revolutions of those days brought other German tribes to mingle with the original inhabitants of the Low Countries; so that, in the time of Charlemagne, it is probable the greater part of the population was Saxon, or at least Teutonic. Between the time of Clovis and that of Charlemagne, the whole country was greatly improved; large towns were built, and many arts and manufactures introduced from foreign countries. Ghent, Bruges, Antwerp, Bergen-op-Zoom, and many other cities, had already attained to considerable importance as trading marts. Woollen cloth was manufactured here in a style superior to that of the Franks or the English. The Christian religion was introduced, partly by the Franks and partly by missionaries from Britain and, in the early part of the ninth century, there were many churches and monasteries in different quarters of the country.

The Netherlands formed a part of the empire of

Charlemagne, who established here nearly the same form of government that existed in his French and German dominions. A governor was placed over each province, with the title of *count*, who held his dignity and the domains attached to it for life; but neither the title nor the lands were hereditary. On the death of the count, a new appointment was made. In later times, however, most of these officers, either by force or treaty, obtained from different sovereigns the right of inheritance for their children; and thus by degrees arose a number of principalities, some of which were subject to France and some to the German empire, as Flanders, Brabant, Liege, &c. The peasantry were all in vassalage to the respective lords of the domains on which they resided; but the inhabitants of the towns, who were mostly merchants and manufacturers, enjoyed all the privileges of free citizens. They elected their own magistrates, made their own laws, fortified their cities with walls and moats, and organized a regular militia; so that, in cases of danger, every citizen was a soldier, and thus they were enabled to defend their liberties against the encroachments of the nobles during the wars and usurpations of the middle ages.

All the German part of the Netherlands as far as the River Scheldt became known by the name of *Lorraine*, and was formed into two duchies, in the tenth century, by the emperor Otho II. Lower Lorraine was afterward called *Brabant*, and was the largest and most powerful sovereignty in the Netherlands. Its capital was Brussels, which is said to have derived its name from the *broussailles*, or briers, with which the spot was once overgrown. Flanders was erected into a county in the ninth century by Charles the Bald, emperor of the West and king of France, who bestowed it as a fief on an adventurous knight, named Baldwin. He, however, ran away with his daughter Judith and married her. The emperor was so incensed, that he made war upon his son-in-law; but was at length reconciled to him, and gave him the hereditary dominion of this country. The counts of Flanders, who gained so much renown in the crusades, traced their ancestry to Charlemagne, who was great-grandfather to the princess Judith.

The small territory, which now constitutes the province of Holland, appears to have had few or no inhabitants till the beginning of the eleventh century, when a nobleman named *Thierry*, who was the French governor of one of the adjoining districts, was driven from his residence by the Frisons. He took refuge with his followers on a little island, A. D. 1018. This territory was gradually enlarged by diking out the sea, and at length the emperor bestowed the sovereignty of it upon Thierry, with the title of *count of Holland*. The successors of Thierry were constantly at war with the Frisons, and many of them accompanied the crusading armies to the Holy Land. In the beginning of the fourteenth century, Amsterdam was a small town, belonging to a feudal baron, called the *lord of Amstel*, who possessed a small castle and a piece of marshy land on the bank of a river, where one of his ancestors had built a little village, consisting of a few fishermen's huts, thatched with straw. Some of the counts of Holland granted these fishermen the privilege of carrying fish through their dominions without paying toll, in consequence of which they prospered rapidly, and Amsterdam soon became a large town.

About the beginning of the fourteenth century, the dukes of Burgundy obtained, either by inheritance or marriage, the sovereignty of nearly all the Netherlands. It was at this time that the country rose to the highest pitch of manufacturing and commercial prosperity. The raw materials of France and England—countries which were then rude and agricultural—were imported into Holland and Flanders, and exported in a manufactured state. Ghent alone is said to have employed forty thousand looms. Bruges first, and then Antwerp, formed the emporium of the commerce of Northern and Central Europe. The Hollanders had erected vast dikes, which reclaimed from the ocean a much larger extent of land than they possess at present. The great bay called the *Zuyder Zee* was once a lake surrounded by land. At some period later than the tenth century, the sea burst in and overflowed an immense tract, which was lost forever. The precise date of this event is uncertain, which is extraordinary, as the calamity must have been attended by a frightful destruction of human life. The territory submerged is above seventy miles in length and forty in breadth. In the early part of the fifteenth century, another great inundation suddenly swept away upward of seventy towns and villages, with all their inhabitants.

Charles the Bold, duke of Burgundy, was killed in a battle with the Swiss in 1497. He left an only daughter, eighteen years of age, who, being the richest heiress in Europe, was sought in marriage by many aspiring princes. She chose for her husband the archduke Maximilian of Austria. By this marriage the Netherlands came under the dominion of the house of Austria, and formed one of the chief sources of the power of the emperor Charles V., who was himself a native of Ghent. He ruled the country with tyrannical sway, and left it (A. D. 1555) to his son Philip II. of Spain, a greater tyrant than himself. At this time, the Netherlands were in the highest state of commercial prosperity. Antwerp was the greatest mart of trade in Europe. In every part of the country, manufactures were in the most flourishing condition. The people of Holland had become famous for their skill in market gardening, an art which they introduced into England about this time.

Philip II. was a narrow-minded, gloomy bigot, animated only by a monkish zeal for the Catholic religion. The Protestant reformation had begun in Germany and spread into the Netherlands in the reign of Charles V., who issued some harsh decrees against those who embraced the new opinions, but did not resort to measures of severe persecution. Philip, on the contrary, determined to root out Protestantism from his dominions with fire and sword. He established the Inquisition in the Netherlands. The Protestants were imprisoned or burnt at the stake, and the political rights and liberties of the people were overthrown. Great numbers of the inhabitants emigrated to foreign countries to save their lives. Many went to England, where they were of great benefit to that kingdom by introducing the arts and manufactures of the Netherlands. The decayed towns of Norwich, Canterbury, Southampton, Colchester, and many others were converted into busy and populous places, full of silk-weavers, dyers, and woollen and linen manufacturers, while market gardens and nursery grounds were planted in the surrounding country.

CHAPTER CCCCLV.

A. D. 1560 to 1863.

Cruelties of the Duke of Alva — Rebellion in the Netherlands — Formation of the Republic of Holland — Religious Liberty — Flourishing Condition of Holland — War with England — Battles of Van Tromp and De Ruyter — Invasion of Holland by Louis XIV.

Among the Spanish governors of the Netherlands, at this time, the duke of Alva distinguished himself by his tyranny and bloodthirstiness. He was intrusted with unlimited authority by the king, and he made unsparing use of it against all persons suspected of being favorable to the new religious doctrines, or the liberties of the people. He not only allowed full sway to the Inquisition, but he instituted another tribunal, for the purpose of condemning Protestants to death, which obtained the popular name of the "Council of Blood," from its sanguinary decrees. The dreadful scenes which occurred in the Netherlands at this period have only been equalled by the horrors of the French revolution during the reign of terror. Among the many victims of distinction were Counts Egmont and Horn, both noblemen of the highest rank, and of the Catholic faith. They had been guilty of no act of disloyalty, but were put to death solely because they were friends to popular rights.

The prince of Orange and his brothers were summoned to appear before the Council of Blood; but they refused to trust themselves to its authority, and a general insurrection soon broke out. Queen Elizabeth assisted the insurgents with supplies of money, and a sanguinary and obstinate contest was begun, and protracted through a period of fifty years. The duke of Alva boasted that, during his administration, eighteen thousand persons had perished on the scaffold. Yet he was unable to subdue the independent spirit and determined enmity to Spanish dominion which animated the Netherlanders. The Dutch in the northern provinces defended themselves by opening their dikes, and laying the country under water. Their courage and perseverance, and the talent of the first two princes of the house of Orange, aided by the friendship of Queen Elizabeth, enabled them finally to achieve their independence. In 1597, the seven Dutch provinces formed a league for mutual protection and support, called the *Union of Utrecht*. By this league, they constituted themselves an independent state, with the name of the *Seven United Provinces*. They were more commonly known as the *Republic of Holland*. The remainder of the country continued under the Spanish dominion.

The Protestant religion was firmly established in the Dutch republic, but every other form of worship was olerated. The religious liberty enjoyed in this country induced great numbers of persons from France, England, and Germany, to seek refuge here from the ill usage to which they were exposed in their own countries. The Dutch provinces speedily attracted most of the manufactures, and all the commerce, which had raised the Flemish cities to such a height of prosperity. The Dutch conquered from the Portuguese, who were at that time under the dominion of Spain, the finest of their possessions in the East Indies, and rendered Amsterdam the centre of a flourishing trade with India They carried on the fisheries, especially those of herrings, on a very extensive scale, and became the first maritime people of the age. Holland owed this vast commerce partly to her peculiar situation, the industry and economy of her inhabitants, the liberal and enlightened system of policy adopted by the republic, and partly to the wars and disturbances that prevailed in most European countries during the sixteenth and seventeenth centuries, which prevented other nations from emulating the successful career of the Dutch.

Shortly after the overthrow of Charles I. in England, a feeling of hostility arose in that country against the Dutch, on account of the relationship between the house of Orange and the Stuart family. The parliament sought a pretext for going to war with Holland and soon found one in a dispute respecting the trade with America. An act was passed by the parliament called the *Navigation Act*, prohibiting the English merchants from importing or exporting goods in Dutch vessels, as they had been in the habit of doing. On pretence of enforcing this act, the Dutch ships were frequently searched, to the great annoyance and injury of the owners, whose goods were sometimes seized on suspicion, and never restored. This produced a war, A. D. 1652. In the course of nine months, seven naval battles took place between the Dutch and English fleets, the former commanded by Van Tromp, De Ruyter, and Dewitt, and the latter by Admiral Blake. At first, the Dutch had the advantage, and Van Tromp sailed in triumph down the British Channel, with a broom displayed at his mast-head, in token that he would sweep the sea clear of English ships. But this was a vain boast. In the following year, July 21, 1653, a battle was fought off Scheveling, near the Hague, in which the Dutch were defeated, and Van Tromp was killed. This was the last naval action of the war. The Dutch, disheartened by the loss of their great commander, sued for peace, which Cromwell granted on his own terms.

Charles II., on his restoration to the throne of England, made war upon the Dutch, to please Louis XIV., whose bribes he was in the habit of receiving. Several tremendous sea-fights took place, one of which lasted four days, and ended in the defeat of the Dutch. The war continued two years, during which the Dutch lost a large number of ships, and several of their best naval commanders. A short interval of peace followed, when Holland was threatened with total subjugation by Louis XIV., who made war upon that country in 1672, without the least provocation, and only for the purpose of acquiring fame as a conqueror. His armies overran all the southern part of the country, and approached within three miles of Amsterdam.

The Dutch were now in the most desperate condition. The French armies were overwhelming in number, and the English were in alliance with them; so that they had no hope of assistance from any quarter. Deputies were sent from Amsterdam to the French king, to endeavor to make terms; but that proud and arrogant monarch treated them with so much disdain, and demanded terms so humiliating to the Dutch, that they declared they would sooner die in defence of their liberties, than submit to such degradation. At first, they thought of embarking all the people, with as much of their wealth as they could carry, on board their ships, and sailing to India, thus abandoning their native country to the invaders. But this scheme was rejected; and their next resolution was to breakdown their dikes, and flood the country. This was done; and the sea, rushing in, immediately overwhelmed the land, so that Amsterdam looked like a vast fortress in the midst of the ocean, surrounded by ships of war, which came up to its very gates. The French were prevented from pursuing their conquests by this measure; but the losses and sufferings occasioned to the Dutch were enormous. Louis, having thus nearly destroyed one of the finest and most flourishing countries in Europe, and finding there was little glory to be gained in the attempt to finish the work of destruction, returned to Paris. The Dutch were assisted by some of their neighbors, who began to fear the growing ambition of the king of France; and, in the course of six years, they recovered all the places that had been captured by the French. At length, in 1678, Louis was compelled to make peace with Holland, having expended millions in the war, without gaining the slightest real advantage by his unjust and unprovoked invasion.

By these wars, and by an unwise participation in the political schemes of the continental powers, the Dutch republic became at length enfeebled. Party spirit led to mischievous factions, and, about the middle of the eighteenth century, the government suffered a change, by the establishment of the prince of Orange as hereditary stadtholder, or chief magistrate of Holland. By this measure, the original republican character of the government was effaced, and a monarchical spirit infused into it. The English had become the successful rivals of the Dutch in the East India trade, and the Dutch commerce, in every quarter, rapidly declined. At length, by a war with England at the time of the American revolution, the Dutch foreign trade was completely ruined.

The French revolution could not fail to act powerfully upon a nation so closely in contact with France as Holland. The allied powers were unable to contend with the French armies on the plains of Belgium. That country was conquered by Dumourier in 1794, and a French army, under General Pichegru, was detached to invade Holland. His approach was welcomed by a large portion of the inhabitants. Party spirit had run high for some time, and the people had been withheld from abolishing the stadtholderate only by Prussian influence. They now beheld an opportunity of doing this by the assistance of the French. The prince of Orange had his supporters, but they were feeble in comparison with the popular party; and, on the advance of the French to Amsterdam, he fled to England. The French entered the city amid general acclamations, and a new government was formed on the model of the French republic. All members of society were declared equal; the stadtholderate was abolished forever, and Holland assumed the name of the *Batavian Republic.*

The English made war upon the Dutch for their connection with France, and seized the Cape of Good Hope, Ceylon, and many other valuable Dutch colonies. The Batavian republic had but a short existence. Holland was completely under the control of the French; and, when Napoleon became emperor, he began to think of erecting thrones for the various members of his family. In 1806, Holland was made a kingdom, and Napoleon's brother Louis received the crown. He was a man of amiable temper and good intentions, but he found it impossible to rule his kingdom in conformity with the designs of Napoleon, who wished Louis to close the ports of Holland against English vessels, in order to aid his celebrated "continental system," by which he hoped to ruin the trade of Great Britain. The unwillingness of Louis to adopt this measure, which was ruinous to the Dutch merchants, caused a coolness between the two brothers, and Louis resigned his crown, July 1, 1810.

Holland was immediately incorporated with the French empire, and remained in that connection till after Napoleon's Russian campaign, in 1812. When his fortunes were evidently declining, the Dutch threw off their dependence upon France, and recalled the prince of Orange. He returned to Holland in November, 1813, and was proclaimed sovereign prince of the country. The Belgic provinces were united to Holland, and the whole erected into a monarchy, entitled the *Kingdom of the Netherlands.* Belgium was again separated from Holland, and made a separate kingdom, by the revolution of 1830, as will be seen in the history of that country. By the revolt of the Belgians, the kingdom of the Netherlands was reduced to less than half its original size. In October, 1849, William II. resigned his throne to his son, who is still king, under the title of *William III.*

CHAPTER CCCCLVI.

Chief Cities — Population — Government — Agriculture — Commerce — Manufactures — Internal Navigation — Religion — Manners, Customs, &c.

Amsterdam, the chief city of Holland, stands on the River Amstel, which flows into the Zuyder Zee. The country here is marshy, and the city is built on piles driven into the mud. It is a common complaint that a house here costs as much under ground as above. The city is, of course, a complete level; it is intersected, like Venice, by an immense number of canals, crossed by draw-bridges, and bordered, for the most part, by handsome rows of trees. The canals communicate with each other by sluices, which regulate the level of the water. The expense of keeping these in order and clearing the canals of mud are very heavy. The great industry and perseverance of the Dutch are displayed in a striking manner in their contrivances for keeping the water from overwhelming this city. The three principal streets are hardly equalled by any in Europe for spaciousness and the magnificence of their buildings. The ancient stadthouse is now the king's palace, and is one of the finest buildings in the world. Upward of thirteen thousand piles were used in laying the foundations of this enormous structure It is adorned with pillars and sculptures emblematical of commerce and trade. Amsterdam has a national museum of paintings, which contains many fine specimens of the Dutch school. The various prisons and houses of correction of this city are superior to the institutions of the same kind in other parts of Europe. The police is excellent; crimes are rare; and no beggars are to be seen in the streets. The harbor is inconvenient; but this has been, in a great measure, remedied by a canal communicating with the Helder. The commerce of Amsterdam, though much declined from what it was in the best days of the republic, is still very great, and the merchants here are among the richest capitalists of Europe. Its population is two hundred and forty-eight thousand three hundred and fifty-five.

Rotterdam is the second city in Holland. It stands at the mouth of the River Maese, and has a good harbor. It has all the best characteristics of a Dutch town, being neatly and uniformly built, with high houses and canals. It has a thriving commerce, and extensive establishments for the refining of sugar. Rotterdam was the birthplace of Erasmus, and a handsome statue is here erected to his memory. Population, one hundred and ten thousand.

Leyden is a handsome old city in the interior, surrounded by the richest meadows in Holland. It has flourishing manufactures of woollen, and a great trade in butter and cheese. Population, forty thousand. The Hague ranks only as a village, but is, in fact, one of the handsomest cities in Europe. The streets and squares are well built, and bordered with fine walks and avenues of trees. The Hague is regarded as the capital of the kingdom. Population, eighty thousand.

Utrecht is a very ancient city, famous in the Roman times as commanding a passage over the Rhine. It is also distinguished among the Dutch cities for its somewhat elevated situation. The view from its ramparts and the top of its cathedral, over the vast plains and broad waters of Holland, is extensive and delightful. Population, fifty-four thousand. Haarlem, Delft, and Dort, are also large and flourishing towns. Schiedam is famous for its gin, of which it has more than one hundred distilleries.

The population of Holland is remarkable for its density, being three hundred and twenty-four to the square mile. No country of Europe, except Belgium, surpasses it in this respect. The whole number of inhabitants is three million five hundred and seventy thousand. The births and marriages exceed in proportion those of France and Great Britain.

The government of Holland is a limited monarchy. The legislative power is vested in the states general, a popular assembly. Each province has an assembly of its own, which regulates local affairs, like the state governments of the American Union. Elections are managed in a peculiar manner. The people do not go to the polls to vote, but the ballot-boxes are carried round from house to house, and the votes are received, signed, and sealed. The upper chamber of the legislature does not consist of hereditary nobles, but of a council, the members of which are appointed by the king for life. The public debt of Holland is probably near five hundred millions of dollars.

No other country in Europe, nor perhaps in the world, produces so great an amount of valuable commodities, in proportion to its extent, as Holland; yet the soil is entirely destitute of mineral wealth. The country is one great meadow, intersected by canals, and marked every where by lines and groups of trees. The cattle are stalled in the winter, but in summer they are kept constantly grazing in the open air. The product of the dairy has been brought to such a state of improvement as to become a great object of exportation. The Dutch butter and cheese enjoy a high reputation almost all over the world. Horticulture, which is elsewhere only a recreation, has become here a business of primary importance. Besides amply supplying its own markets with culinary vegetables, Holland exports them in large quantities to Norway, and other countries where the climate forbids their culture. The city of Haarlem carries on a great trade in flowers, and exports a vast quantity of bulbous roots to England and other countries. Many years ago, the Dutch were seized with a violent passion for tulips, which they carried to such an excess, that a single flower of a particular species was sold for four thousand dollars. The speculations in tulips became a species of gambling, and the government was compelled to put a stop to the business.

The manufactures of Holland are numerous, and are advancing under the protection of the government. Woollen cloths are made at Leyden and Utrecht, silks and velvets at Haarlem and Amsterdam, linen and cotton at Haarlem, paper, leather, and a variety of other articles, in various parts of the country. Delft was once famous for its crockery, but this has now lost most of its reputation. The commerce of Holland is thriving. The exports consist of the productions already enumerated, together with refined sugar, salt, gin, beer, soap, fish, tobacco pipes, &c. Canals form one of the most remarkable features in the economical arrangements of Holland, and a leading source of her prosperity. From the level nature of the country, these are constructed with peculiar facility. The canals are almost innumerable; every town and village has one passing through it. They run through the streets of cities, enabling vessels to load and unload at the shop-doors of the traders. When frozen, they serve as highways on which the Dutch women, heavily laden, skate along, from town to town, with surprising rapidity. The largest canal is that which connects Amsterdam with the Helder. It is fifty miles long one hundred and twenty-five feet wide, and twenty-one feet deep, being navigable for ships of one thousand tons. This canal was begun in 1819, and completed in 1825.

The prevailing religion in Holland is Calvinism. The clergy receive their appointment and salaries from the government; but regard is always paid to the wishes of the parishioners. The Dutch have the honor of being the first people who established full religious toleration in their country. Holland was once famous for its men of learning, and the institutions for education are still very ample in this country. The universities of Leyden and Utrecht have long been famous. The former had once the reputation of being the first medical school in Europe, and is still highly respectable. Dutch literature is hardly known out of Holland, though this country has produced many great scholars and men of genius. Most of them, however, have written in Latin, and their productions have little of a national spirit. Grotius and Erasmus were natives of Holland, and are to be reckoned among the lights of their age. Boerhaave was the greatest medical writer of his day.

The fine arts have been cultivated with zeal and success by the Dutch, who have created a school of their own in painting. Rembrandt has treated subjects of common life and vulgar humor with great force and effect. Berghens, Cuyp, Ruysdael, Hobbima Vandervelde, and others, have excelled in the delineation of Dutch landscapes.

The general aspect of Holland is totally different from that of any other country except Belgium. The principal features of a Dutch landscape consist of meadows, rows of willows and poplars, canals, and windmills. There are no green lanes with hedges or walls, no parks or woods; many roads are quite unsheltered; but others are pleasantly shaded with trees, and every estate is bounded by canals and ditches. Every thing in this singular country seems artificial, and hence it is said that the Dutch have *built* Holland. Stone is so rare, that in many towns the streets are paved with sea-shells; and these, mixed with earth, also form most of the high roads. In their gardening, the Dutch display a taste peculiar to themselves. They clip their trees into formal shapes, and plant their flowers with mathematical precision. Their villas, or country-houses, have usually a small lawn in front, with little clumps and avenues of trees, trimmed so closely that they resemble toys. Every Dutch villa has some sentimental name attached to it, as "The Cottage of Content," "Dulce Domum," "Villa of Repose," &c., which names are generally inscribed on the gate in front.

The national character of the Dutch has taken the form natural to a trafficking and commercial people—solid, steady, quiet, laborious, eagerly intent on the accumulation of wealth, which they seek rather by economy and perseverance than by speculation. The virtue of cleanliness is carried almost to excess; and nothing can exceed the neatness and tidiness of every thing under the control of human care and industry in Holland. A drunken or ragged person is rarely to be seen, and if a beggar makes his appearance, he is immediately sent to the work-house. The tradesmen are very thrifty and careful. Credit is short, and bankruptcy very rare.

The rural population consists, for the most part, of peasant farmers, who hire the land they cultivate from the proprietors, for the owner seldom tills his own estate. The farms are usually small, and let on a lease of six years. In the larger farms, many servants are employed, who lodge with the farmer and eat at his table. In some of the farm-houses there is only one sleeping apartment for the family, where the beds are placed in niches in the wall, like the berths in a ship. In the cities and large towns, the inhabitants dress like the English: but the peasants have their local costumes, as the huge nether garments of the men, and the short jacket of the women.

Amusement is not deemed a very important matter by the Dutch. They have most of the diversions of the neighboring nations, though they do not follow them with much ardor. A great portion of their time is passed in smoking, and a Dutchman seems incomplete without a pipe in his mouth. The rivers and canals, passing through the streets, afford an opportunity of fishing from the windows. The fisheries, for which Holland was once famous, gave rise to a ceremony which is still observed. There is a particular day fixed for the commencement of the herring fishery, when the boats assemble at Vlaardingen, at the mouth of the Maese. They go in procession to the town hall, and take the ancient oath before the magistrates, that they will not begin to fish till five minutes after twelve o'clock at night on the 24th of June. After this, they hoist their flags, and go to church to offer up prayers for success. The day of the departure of the fleet is a holiday upon the river, and in all the fishing villages. The process of curing the herrings is very quickly performed, as the fish are salted and packed in barrels within a few minutes after they have been swimming in the water. The first barrel is sent off by a fast-sailing vessel to the Hague, where it is adorned with wreaths of flowers, and carried in procession, with flags and music, to the king, who makes the fortunate fisherman a handsome present in money. The next two or three barrels are also despatched to the Hague, and sold by auction, the purchaser afterward retailing them at a high price. A single herring of this first catch is

Dutch Fish Auction.

sometimes sold for a dollar, and, on account of its rarity, is regarded as a handsome present to a friend. It is common to see a livery servant carrying one or two herrings on a plate, covered with a white napkin, and accompanied by a card of presentation. The fishermen and their wives all wear the ancient national dress.

In this country, windmills meet the eye in every direction; and there is a curious custom, at Saardam, of announcing deaths and marriages by their means. When a person dies, the sails of all the mills belonging to the family of the deceased are made to stand still. When a wedding takes place, all the relatives of the bride and bridegroom decorate the sails of their mills with ribbons and garlands of flowers, and fix crowns on the points of the sails, which, thus adorned, present a very gay and fantastic appearance while in motion.

The press is under a strict control in Holland. Not a book, or newspaper, or even a handbill, can be printed without a license. No books can be used in the schools but such as are approved by the government.

Belgium.

Botanic Garden at Brussels.

CHAPTER CCCCLVII.

A. D. 1600 to 1863.

Description of Belgium — Separation from Holland — Spanish and Austrian Government — Annexation to France — Formation of the Kingdom of the Netherlands — Cities, Manners, Customs, &c. — Revolt of the Belgians — Formation of the Kingdom of Belgium.

THE kingdom of Belgium is bounded north by Holland, east by the Prussian territory, south by France, and west by the German Ocean. The greater part of the country is level, like Holland; but there are some tracts that are moderately hilly. The soil resembles that of the former country, but the air is not quite so moist. Much of what we have said in describing Holland will also apply to this country. All the northern and eastern part of Belgium resembles Holland in its general appearance, being quite level and intersected with canals in every quarter. Here also, as in Holland, the land requires the protection of dikes and embankments to shield it from inundation. The towns and illages are very numerous and thickly peopled. The southern and western provinces, bordering on France and Germany, are, however, of a different character, the surface of the country being, in many parts, undulating and overgrown with forests. Belgium is the most thickly settled country in Europe. Brussels, the capital, is a fine city. The following table shows the political divisions of the country: —

Provinces.	*Capitals.*	*Population.*
South Brabant,	Brussels,	174,829
Antwerp,	Antwerp,	111,709
East Flanders,	Ghent,	118,131
West Flanders,	Bruges,	
Hainault,	Mons, or Bergen,	
Namur,	Namur,	
Liege,	Liege, or Luttich,	96,207
Limburg,	Maestricht,	
Luxemburg,	Luxemburg,	

The revolt of the Netherlanders against the Spanish government, as we have already stated, led to the separation of Belgium from Holland in the early part of the seventeenth century. A long war reduced both these countries to a state of great suffering and destitution, when, in the year 1609, the mediation of the French caused a truce to be concluded for twelve years, during which time Holland was to be recognized as an independent nation, and the remaining provinces were to remain in the possession of Spain. This truce was the foundation of a permanent arrangement, by which the independence of Holland was secured. The Belgian provinces acquired the name of the *Spanish Netherlands*, or the *Low Countries;* sometimes they were called by the general name of *Flanders*, from the chief of these provinces. The country was so deeply impoverished by war and the oppressions of the Spaniards, that many families which had formerly lived in affluence at Brussels and Antwerp, were obliged to sell their furniture to secure the necessities of life: half the villages were so completely deserted, that the wolves roamed about them in perfect security. A long interval of peace, and an improved administration on the part of the Spaniards, restored the country to something like its former appearance; but the trade by which it had been enriched for so many centuries, was ruined: and the great cities of Flanders and Brabant never recovered the wealth and importance which distinguished them in the times of the dukes of Burgundy.

The situation of the Spanish Netherlands unfortunately exposed them to the attacks of hostile armies, and this country became the theatre of war, on which Austria and France contended for the supremacy during a series of campaigns, which extended through two centuries. By the treaty of the Pyrenees, in 1659, and that of Aix-la-Chapelle, in 1668, Spain was compelled to cede to France a portion of this country, which obtained the name of *French Flanders*, or the *French Netherlands*. During the war of the Spanish succession, the duke of Marlborough commanded the English and Dutch armies in this country. Many cities in Flanders and Brabant were besieged by them, and defended by the French and Spaniards. The battle of Ramillies was gained by Marlborough in 1706, and the French were, in consequence, obliged to evacuate all the territories which they had occupied here. By the treaty of Utrecht, which closed this war in 1713, the king of Spain relinquished his claim to the Netherlands, and they were transferred to Austria.

Under the Austrian government, the Belgian provinces recovered a considerable degree of their prosperity. The emperor, Joseph II., who came to the throne in 1780, began his reign by attempting a number of changes in this country which were not in accordance with the wishes of the people. Among these was the suppression of a number of monasteries in the Belgian cities. This occasioned a great disturbance, which soon grew into an insurrection. The Austrian troops were attacked by the people and driven out of the country. A national convention was held, and it was resolved to establish a free and independent republic, under the name of the *Belgian States*. In the midst of these proceedings, Joseph died, and was succeeded by his brother Leopold, who, by mild and conciliatory measures, induced the revolted provinces to return to their allegiance.

When the French revolutionary government made war upon Austria, they despatched an army, under General Dumourier, to invade Belgium. He defeated the Austrian army, at the battle of Jemappes, in November, 1792, and entered Brussels in triumph. In a very short time, all the Austrian territory in this quarter fell into the hands of the French. They were not suffered, however, to retain possession of it without a struggle. A large Austrian army was quickly sent into Belgium, which was joined by a Dutch and English army under the duke of York. During two years, the country was devastated by the contending parties; but at length a great victory of the French at Fleurus, not far from Waterloo, placed the country completely in their power, and Belgium was incorporated into the French republic in 1795.

The Belgians were better satisfied with the French government than their neighbors of Holland: they had long been accustomed to foreign domination, while the Dutch had enjoyed for more than two centuries all the freedom of an independent republic. The French laws were also better suited to Belgium than to Holland. Belgium constituted an important part of the French empire under Napoleon, who designed to organize a powerful naval force in this part of his dominions. He was a great benefactor to Antwerp, and restored the trade of the port, which had been ruined by the wars of the seventeenth century. He also constructed here immense docks for ship-building which still remain striking monuments of his vast designs.

This country was the theatre of Napoleon's last campaign, after his return from Elba; and here he was finally overthrown at the battle of Waterloo, June 18, 1815. Belgium and Holland were combined to form the kingdom of the Netherlands, as we have already stated. The taxes in Belgium were much increased in consequence of this union, as the Dutch government had contracted a very large national debt, which the Belgians were compelled to assist in paying. This caused great discontent. The king, moreover, did not fulfil the promises which he made at his inauguration but had assumed despotic power, in defiance of the constitution which he had sworn to maintain. He abolished the trial by jury, for which the Belgians had been indebted to the French; he issued his own arbitrary decrees, which took the place of the laws of the land; he imposed taxes without the consent of the people, and usurped authority in matters of education, by prohibiting all persons from exercising the business of teaching, even in private families, without a license. By this tyrannical act, he drove large numbers of people out of the country. Every method was used by him to underrate, depress, and affront the Belgians. Almos all honors, civil and military, were bestowed upon Dutchmen; the courts of law were all removed to the Hague; the Dutch language was made to take the place of all others in legal proceedings; and as very few of the Belgians could speak Dutch, the magistrates, judges, and all who held official situations, lost their places.

These proceedings caused a general disaffection throughout Belgium; but the king, *William I.*, was stupidly blind to the consequences which they were drawing after them. The public press, which ventured to warn him of his danger, was silenced by fines, dungeons, and banishment. Some of the most respectable and upright men in the country were punished severely for their freedom of speech. Even after the expulsion of Charles X. from France, in July, 1830, the king continued so obstinate in his tyrannical self-will, that he refused to listen to the advice of those wise counsellors, who saw the coming storm, and entreated him to avert the calamity by removing some of the causes of discontent. On the 25th of August, 1830, the people of Brussels rose in insurrection, drove out the royal troops, and made themselves masters of the city. The revolt immediately spread throughout Belgium, and the royal authority was completely overthrown. The citadel of Antwerp alone remained in the possession of the Dutch troops.

It was now quite evident that the king of Holland had entirely lost Belgium, without any reasonable hope of being able to recover it. The principal European powers, therefore, judged it best to allow the Belgians to retain the independence which they had acquired. By the acquiescence of the cabinets of Russia, Austria, Prussia, and Great Britain, the Belgians established an independent monarchy, under the title of the *Kingdom of Belgium*. The crown was first tendered to the duke of Nemours, second son of Louis Philippe of France, but was declined by him, probably under the direction of the allied powers, who did not wish the influence of France to be extended in that quarter. It was then offered to Prince Leopold of Saxe-Coburg, who, after some hesitation, consented to become king of the Belgians, and was proclaimed king at Brussels, July 4, 1831. He still (1863) remains upon the throne.

Leopold.

The king of Holland remained as obstinate as ever, and refused to accede to any of these arrangements. He persisted in the useless measure of holding the citadel of Antwerp, and it was found necessary to send a French army of sixty thousand men to besiege it. After it was nearly battered to pieces, and a dreadful destruction of human life had taken place, the citadel surrendered. This is the last event of a hostile nature that has taken place in the Netherlands down to the present day. In 1839, a treaty of separation was finally arranged, since which time both countries have enjoyed a profound peace.

Brussels, the capital of Belgium, is one of the gayest and most elegant cities of Europe. It is finely situated in a valley watered by the little river Senne; a canal connects it with Antwerp. The town hall of Brussels is one of the finest Gothic structures in existence, and has a tower three hundred and forty-eight feet high. The market-place and the park are great ornaments to the city. The latter is an extensive pleasure-ground or common, interspersed with trees, fountains, and statues. Brussels consists of two distinct parts, the old and the new town. The former is the manufacturing part, and inhabited chiefly by the working classes. It has a mean appearance, though it abounds in fine old ornamented buildings, once the residence of the nobles of Brabant, but now converted into workshops and warehouses. The new town is entirely of modern date, and from its resemblance to the French capital, has been called *Paris in miniature.* During the last century, the city was surrounded by fortified ramparts and moats; but these have been removed, and their place is occupied by fine boulevards or malls, which are planted with trees, and form an agreeable promenade. Brussels contains a university and a fine botanic garden. Population, one hundred and seventy-five thousand.

Antwerp stands at the head of ship navigation on the Scheldt. At the close of the fifteenth century, it was almost without a rival among the commercial cities of Europe; but it is now much declined. The cathedral of this place is a magnificent piece of Gothic architecture. Its noble spire is four hundred and sixty six feet high, and from its summit is exhibited a delightful view of the windings of the Scheldt, with the distant towers of Ghent, Malines, and Breda. The interior is adorned with the finest paintings of Rubens and Vandyke. Near the cathedral is a well, surrounded by an iron railing, the work of the celebrated artist Quentin Matsys, which is greatly admired for the neatness of its ornaments and the delicacy of its whole workmanship. Of late years, Antwerp has regained some of its lost commerce, and bids fair to become the chief emporium of Belgium. Population, about one hundred and ten thousand.

Quentin Matsys's Well, Antwerp.

Ghent, even in its present fallen state, is one of the noblest of the old cities of Europe. Its vast exten of walls, which, according to the boast of Charles V. could contain all Paris within them, may still be traced. It is an inland city, but is built on twenty-seven islands, most of them bordered by magnificent quays, and connected by three hundred bridges. The streets are mostly spacious and handsome, and there are many fine old churches. The general appearance of the city is of a more modern character than that of some towns in Flanders, the principal part of it having been rebuilt in the Italian style. The houses have spacious court-yards, lofty staircases, and tall windows, which have usually a small plate of looking-glass fixed on the outside, in such a position as to enable those within to see all that is passing in the street without being seen themselves. Ghent is now one of the most thriving of the manufacturing towns of Belgium. The chief articles of manufacture are cotton cloths and lace. Population, nearly one hundred and twenty thousand.

Bruges was once the rival of Antwerp in trade. It is an old-looking city, with narrow streets and lofty houses. It is famous for the manufacture of lace, an art which is taught to all the female children of the poor, in schools established for that purpose. The city is adorned with many noble churches, containing some of the finest works of the great Flemish painters. The invention of oil-painting has been ascribed to Bruges. Population, forty-one thousand nine hundred and fourteen.

Malines, or Mechlin, which was formerly celebrated for its beautiful lace, has lost much of its importance by the decline of its manufacture, owing to the caprices of fashion. This city is a venerable old place, with large antique houses and Gothic churches belonging to the middle ages. Population, twenty-two thousand eight hundred and ninety-five.

Ostend is an ancient town, once celebrated for its fortifications. It has one of the few good harbors in Flanders, and, under the Austrian sway, it became the chief seat of the limited trade of the Belgic provinces. Napoleon restored its fortifications, which were still further strengthened by the allied powers. It has now only a third of its former population, but still carries on a brisk trade with England, and has almost the appearance of an English town. Population, eleven thousand three hundred and ninety.

Liege, once the seat of a sovereign bishop, is an ancient and large city, but ill built and gloomy. It has manufactures of fine woollen cloths. Population, (1860) nearly one hundred thousand. Spa, situated in a romantic rocky region, is one of the most celebrated watering-places in Europe. The resort of visitors here, though much diminished, is still considerable, and composed of persons of distinguished rank. Ten miles south of Brussels, on the borders of the forest of Soignies, is the village of Waterloo, the scene of the last great battle of Napoleon, on the 18th of June, 1815. In the centre of the plain where the battle was

Tavern of La Belle Alliance.

fought, stands a little farm-house, or tavern, called *La Belle Alliance.* This is the spot where Wellington and Blucher met after the French were driven from the field. In memory of this great victory, a monument has been erected at Waterloo, consisting of a conical mound of earth, seven hundred feet in diameter at the base, and two hundred feet high. On the top is a pillar, sixty feet in height, supporting a lion twenty-one feet long and twelve feet high. Waterloo contains about two thousand inhabitants.

All the old towns in the Netherlands possess a peculiar interest, from the circumstance, that each has its own distinct history, and many of them, in forme days, their own sovereign princes; beside which, they offer many subjects of interesting reflection in the traces which they still exhibit of former opulence, and the rude grandeur of ancient times.

Belgium is the most densely populated kingdom in Europe, containing three hundred and ninety-three inhabitants to the square mile. The total population is four million and seven hundred thousand. The increase has been constant since the census of 1816. The government is a constitutional monarchy. The legislative body consists of a senate and chamber of representatives, both elected by the people. No privileges are attached to nobility: all persons are politically equal: the king can bestow titles, but no political privileges which are not enjoyed by the meanest of his subjects. Education is free, and religious liberty is allowed in the fullest extent.

The Belgian character is a mixture of French and Dutch. The inhabitants of this kingdom are as much distinguished for honesty and love of independence, as those of Holland; while, in respect to gayety, politeness, and fondness for luxury and show, they bear a close affinity to the French. The peasants on the French border are called *Walloons*, and are supposed to be the descendants of those warlike tribes, who, in the time of the Roman empire, inhabited the forest of Ardennes, and were known by the name of *Belgic Gauls.* Their language is peculiar to themselves, being neither Dutch, German, nor Flemish. Throughout Belgium, the French language is much in use.

A great part of what we have said respecting the agriculture, manufactures, &c., of Holland, also applies to Belgium. There are, however, some points of difference. The Belgian farms, like those of the Dutch, are generally small, but they are cultivated by the owners; and the laws respecting landed property in Belgium are the same as in France, when, on the death of a father, his estate is divided equally among his children. The superior class of Flemish farmers live very much in the style of the wealthy farmers of England in the last century. The servants sit down to dinner with their masters, and the whole family eat off pewter plates. The poorer class of farmers live comfortably: their cottages are strong and well built, consisting of two stories, the upper one being used for sleeping rooms, and the lower for kitchen and dairy. Agriculture has greatly improved within a few years. The Belgians are famous for the culture of flowers, in which they excel even the Dutch. In the neighborhood of the towns, every house has a beautiful flower-garden attached to it. Near Ghent are horticultural gardens, where two annual exhibitions of flowers are held. This city has become the chief market for flowers, the sale of which forms an important branch of trade.

The greater part of the Belgians are Catholics, who are very strict in their religious observances. The churches are all open as early as five or six in the morning, for the accommodation of the laboring classes, who usually go to church before they begin their work. The clergy exercise much influence over the peasantry, as in Ireland. In all the towns are frequently seen processions of priests in their sacerdotal robes, bearing images and other tokens of their faith, before which the passengers bow down. The afternoons and evenings of Sundays are spent in amusements of every kind people of rank go to the theatre, and the middle and lower classes to the tea-gardens and ball-rooms

No people in the world are so much addicted to beer-drinking as the Belgians. A single town contains forty or fifty breweries.

Music is cultivated in Belgium with almost as much enthusiasm as in Germany. Musical festivals are held every year at Bruges, Ghent, and Antwerp, where the performers are all amateurs, and prizes are awarded. This trial of musical ability excites an extraordinary degree of interest, each competitor being considered as the representative of some particular locality, where the people are all interested in his success. Every performer has his partisans, who escort him in procession to the town hall, wearing his colors, and carrying banners with emblematical devices. The taste for music is so general, even among the laboring people, that the airs sung in concert by groups of peasants, at their work, are often delightful to the most refined ear. The national love of harmony is manifested in the numerous chimes of twenty, fifty, or a hundred bells, called *carillons*, which are heard from the steeples of the churches and the towers of the town halls. The performers are good musicians, and receive high salaries for amusing the people on certain days with the music of the best composers. In some places, the different chimes are so numerous, that as soon as one set of bells is silent, another begins; so that there is scarcely an interval of time free from the sound of bells.

The manners of the upper classes in Belgium do not differ essentially from those of the same rank in the adjoining kingdoms. The people of Brussels dress in the French style, speak the French language, and make the same display of dress and equipage as is done at Paris. The ladies of Antwerp dress somewhat in the Spanish fashion, which prevailed in the Netherlands two or three centuries ago. They walk abroad in caps trimmed with rich lace, and a long black silk scarf, which is thrown over the head and shoulders, and fastened before, so that it answers the purpose both of a cloak and a hood.

Belgium has four universities — at Brussels, Ghent, Louvain, and Liege. At Brussels, the chief studies are law and medicine; at Louvain, divinity: the latter seminary admits only Catholics. The kingdom is very deficient in establishments for popular education. The fine arts have been successfully cultivated here; and Antwerp, during its prosperity, became a sort of Belgian Florence. Rubens and Vandyke were the great masters of the Flemish school. They are distinguished by splendor of coloring, grandeur of composition, and force of expression. They are deficient, however, in that pure and classic taste which is produced by the study of antique simplicity. Quentin Matsys, who, from a blacksmith, became a painter of great skill, was a Belgian. He was born at Antwerp, in **1460**, and at the age of twenty was induced to apply himself to painting by his love for the daughter of an artist of that city. The father refused to give his daughter in marriage, except to one who was as great a painter as himself. Matsys began the study of the art with great diligence, and soon gave a proof of his talent by painting a bee upon a flower piece in the workshop of the maiden's father, while he was absent. The latter, surprised at the masterly execution of the work, demanded who had done it; and, on hearing that the artist was Matsys, immediately consented that he should wed his daughter.

Denmark.

CHAPTER CCCCLVIII.

1038 B. C. to A. D. 1523.

Preliminary Description—The Fabulous and Heroic Ages of Scandinavian History.

The kingdom of Denmark embraces the following divisions: 1st, the peninsula of Jutland; 2d, the islands in the Baltic and the Atlantic; and, 3d, its dependencies, the duchies of Schleswig, Holstein, and Lauenburg. It is bounded north and west by the North Sea; east by the Cattegat and the Baltic; and south by the river Elbe. Its area is twenty-one thousand six hundred square miles; its population two millions and a half.

Its coasts are greatly indented by the sea, and the country is generally flat. Some of the northern parts are, as in Holland, below the level of the sea, and defended by dykes. On the east, the surface rises into gentle elevations. The highest part of the peninsula is five hundred feet, and of the islands four hundred feet above the level of the sea. Holstein and Lauenburg are the best watered. Zealand and Funen are the principal islands.

Next to the Elbe, which forms the southern boundary of the kingdom for eighty miles, the Eider is the most important river. The climate is humid and cloudy, but mild; the soil chiefly alluvial. The pasturage is excellent, and cattle are extensively raised; also horses, which are esteemed for military service. Agriculture has of late been much improved: wheat is raised for exportation. The sheep are numerous and of superior breeds.

Copenhagen, meaning Merchants'-port, the capital of Denmark, is an important seaport of Europe. It is built on the islands of Seeland and Amager, which are separated by a narrow arm of the sea, forming an excellent harbor. It is strongly fortified, and is the seat of the court. The city contains many noble public buildings, among which is the palace of Amalienburg, inhabited by the royal family, and also the castle of Charlottenburg. This latter is now used as an academy of the fine arts, and its parks are converted into a botanic garden. It has a library of four hundred thousand volumes. The university of Copenhagen is rich and flourishing. Copenhagen is the centre of the commerce of the kingdom, and by means of canals, large ships reach the warehouses in the centre of the city. The manufactures are not very important.

Elsinore, twenty-four miles north of Copenhagen, is situated on the east coast of the Island of Seeland

and at the narrowest part of the Sound, which leads to the Baltic. This is the passage of ships, going into the Baltic, and here is the fortress of Kronborg, by means of which these ships are compelled to pay the tax imposed by Denmark, called the Sound-dues. As this tax has no other foundation than that of usage, the various commercial nations of the world proposed to Denmark, in 1857, to abandon its collection, for a fair equivalent, in money, paid once for all. To this Denmark assented, and the sum was fixed at $19,000,000. The proportion of the United States was $393,011. The navigation of the Sound is now free.

NORWAY, SWEDEN AND DENMARK.

Among the colonies of Denmark are the Faroe Islands, northwest of the Shetland Isles — between 61° 20′ and 62° 25′, north latitude. They consist of twenty-two islands, only seventeen of which are inhabited. The coasts are steep and rugged, and the interior bleak, barren, and mountainous. The population is about eight thousand. Most of the inhabitants are occupied in catching fish and sea-fowl, and in raising sheep. The horses are small, but vigorous; wagons are not employed. Among the minerals are coal and opal. The people are of Norwegian descent: their spoken language is German, but their written language, Danish.

The business of pursuing sea-fowl along the rocky and precipitous coasts of these islands, is not only an important, but an exciting and dangerous vocation. The rocks are often perpendicular, and in order to reach the retreats of different kinds of birds, the hunter is let down over the rocks by a single rope, to the depth of five hundred or even a thousand feet. In some of the more inaccessible parts, the fowl are so unaccustomed to the intrusions of man, that they have not learned to fear him, and hence are easily taken with the hand. In general, they are secured by nets thrown over them by the fowler. Sealing and whaling employ a considerable number of persons. Among the exports are hose, tallow, fish, oil, feathers, skins, &c. It is hardly possible to imagine a life more lonesome and desolate than that of the inhabitants of these islands, yet in general they appear cheerful and happy. The government is confided to officers sent hither by the Danish crown.

The other colonies are Iceland and Greenland, in North America; the Islands of St. Croix, St. Thomas, and St. John, in the West Indies; Christianborg, and a few other forts, on the coast of Guinea; Tranquebar and some factories on the Coromandel coast, in Hindostan. The entire population of these possessions is about one hundred thousand.

It is universally admitted that the earliest inhabitants of the ancient Scandinavia — the Denmark, Sweden, and Norway of modern times — were a colony of Goths, whom we have so often mentioned, and who fixed their abode on the Euxine, above two thousand years before the Christian era. By a succession of conquests, these fierce and restless barbarians extended their dominion to the German Ocean; and afterward became famous as the subverters of the Roman empire, and the ancestors of the greater part of the nations that people modern Europe.

All the accounts given by the northern chroniclers of the transactions that happened prior to the Christian era, or rather until the arrival of Odin, must be regarded as fabulous. Saxo Grammaticus, who wrote about the end of the twelfth century, fixes the commencement of the Danish monarchy in the year 1038 B. C., and alleges the founder to have been an illustrious warrior called *Dan*, promoted to the sovereignty on account of his military talents. The correctness of this writer has been called in question by other authors.

All the ancient songs of the north agree in describing its primitive inhabitants as men of colossal stature and incredible strength. Their countenance was fierce, their hair long, matted, and shaggy. But it is to the celebrated invasion of Italy by the Cimbri and the Teutones, about 112 B. C., that we owe the first gleam of positive history which we possess respecting this populous and warlike community, at that era, almost unknown to the rest of Europe. While Rome was the theatre of intestine divisions, the alarming tidings came, that a numerous barbaric host of the Cimbri, numbering over three hundred thousand men, had overrun Gaul, and were pouring into Italy. The barbarians were at first successful in their attacks upon the Romans; but, at length, the Teutones suffered a total defeat from the Romans, under the lead of Marius. The nation of the Cimbri were afterward encountered by the army of Marius on the plain of Vercelli, and totally destroyed in the conflict. In the terrible slaughter of that day, one hundred and forty thousand are said to have fallen, and about sixty thousand taken prisoners, so that nearly the whole expedition perished in a single battle.

After this, led by the mysterious Odin, the Goths broke into Scandinavia, and appointed chiefs from their own nation over Denmark, Norway, and Sweden. Skiold is said to have been the first ruler of Denmark. His history, however, and that of his posterity, is involved in the mists of fable. All we know with certainty is, that Denmark was divided at this time into many small states; that the inhabitants gained their subsistence by piracy, and spread terror through every sea, and along every coast to which they came. When the power of the Romans began to decline, the Danes and Normans became conspicuous in the south by their incursions upon the shores, which were formerly protected by the guard-ships of the Romans.

The Normans, comprehending the people of Denmark, Sweden, and Norway, landed in England A. D. 832, and established there two kingdoms. Under Rollo, about 900, they made a descent on the French coasts in Normandy, occupied the Faroe Isles, the Orcades, the Shetland Isles, Iceland, and a part of Ireland, and thence proceeded to Spain, Italy, and Sicily. Wherever they came, they spread terror by their valor, ferocity, and rapacity. These expeditions made little change in their national government; it still continued a federative system, of many clans or tribes, each of which had its own head, and all were united under one sovereign. When the German kings of the Carlovingian race attempted to interfere with their domestic affairs, the tribes entered into a closer union, and the Norwegians and Danes formed two separate states. *Gorm the Old* first subdued Jutland in 863, and united all the small Danish states under his sceptre till 920. His grandson *Sweyn*, a warlike prince, subdued a part of Norway in 1000, and England in 1014. His son *Canute*, in 1016, not only completed the conquest of England, but also subdued a part of Scotland, and, in 1030, all Norway. Under him the power of Denmark reached its highest pitch. Political motives led him to embrace the Christian religion, and to introduce it into Denmark; upon which a great change took place in the character of the people.

Canute died in 1036, and left a powerful kingdom to his successors, who, in 1042, lost England, and, in 1047, Norway. The Danish kingdom was after this very much weakened by intestine broils. *Sweyn Magnus Estritson* ascended the throne in 1047, and established a new dynasty; but the feudal system, introduced by the wars of Sweyn and Canute, robbed the kingdom of its strength under this dynasty, which furnished not a single worthy prince except the great Waldemar, left the princes dependent on the choice of the bishops and nobility, plunged the peasants into bondage, caused the decay of agriculture, and abandoned commerce to the Hanse towns of Germany. With *Waldemar III.*, in 1376, the male line of the family of Estritson became extinct. His celebrated daughter *Margaret*, after the death of her son *Olave IV.*, (A. D. 1387,) took the helm of the Danish government, and connected with it both Sweden and Norway, by an act called the Union of Calmar, in 1397. After the extinction of the princes of the family of Skiold, the Danes elected *Christian I.*, count of Oldenburg, to succeed him, in 1448. This Christian was the founder of the royal Danish family, which has ever since kept possession of the throne, and from which, in modern times, Russia, Sweden, and Oldenburg have received their rulers. He connected Sleswig and Holstein with the crown of Denmark, but was so fettered by his capitulations, that he seemed to be rather the head of the royal council than a sovereign king. His son, King *John*, was bound by a still more strict capitulation in Denmark, 1481. In Norway, too, his power was more circumscribed. Holstein and Sleswig he shared with Frederic, his brother. King *Christian II.*, son of John, succeeded; he was a wicked and cruel, but by no means a weak prince, attempted to throw off his dependence on the states; but in doing it, he lost Sweden, which broke the Union of Calmar in 1523; and soon after, he was deprived of both his other crowns.

CHAPTER CCCCLIX.

A. D. 1523 to 1670.

The Reformation in Denmark.

Lutheranism, about the year 1527, was making its progress toward the north of Europe, and religion became the cause of a very important revolution, at this time, in the kingdoms of Sweden and Denmark. Being again oppressed, the Danes rebelled once more, and elected for themselves a governor, at the time when Christian II. was raised to the throne of the united kingdoms. Trollo, a Swedish archbishop, conspired with Christian to extinguish the liberties of his country. This prelate procured a bull from Leo X., laying the kingdom under excommunication. The affrighted Swedes returned to their allegiance, acknowledging the sovereignty of Christian. The king invited a large number of principal nobles to a feast, where Trollo, the prelate, made his appearance, and read aloud the bull of the pope; after which the king ordered his guards to seize the whole senate and nobility. Ninety-four senators, and an immense number of nobles and citizens, were thereupon put to death without mercy, and the whole city of Stockholm was a scene of carnage.

The Danes, irritated by the oppression of Christian, determined at length to throw off the yoke. His uncle *Frederic* of Holstein, headed the insurrection, and Denmark, by the voice of the nobility, pronounced a formal sentence of deposition, which they transmitted to Christian at his palace at Copenhagen. This he obeyed like a coward, as he had reigned like a tyrant. The duke of Holstein was elected king of Denmark and Norway; and Gustavus Vasa, the deliverer of his country, was rewarded with the crown of Sweden. A. D. 1527.

The bull of Leo X. had entirely alienated the minds of the Swedes and Danes from the religion of Rome. Gustavus was a convert to the opinions of Luther

Frederic, king of Denmark, concurred with him in his designs, and they found it no difficult matter to establish the reformed religion in the place of the Catholic.

Frederic II. succeeded, on the death of his father, to the crown of the united kingdom of Denmark and Norway; but his reign was soon disturbed by war. Frederic formed a compact with his uncle, the duke of Holstein, to wage war with the Dithmarschen, a western district of Holstein, and divide between them the territory of that heroic people. The force levied against them by the allied princes amounted to twenty-five thousand men, embracing the flower of Denmark and Holstein, to which the Dithmarschen could oppose but about seven thousand men. The supreme command of this expedition was given to John Rantzau, an aged and renowned warrior. The unfortunate Dithmarschen were routed after a severe campaign, and their strongholds carried by storm. They were then forced to submit to their conquerors, by a treaty ratified in 1559; on which occasion all the inhabitants came in a body to surrender their arms, and do homage to the victors. The whole number, disarmed and bareheaded, with white staves in their hands, fell on their knees, and swore, with uplifted hands, to bear true allegiance to the kings and the dukes forever, as their liege lords and sovereigns. Frederic celebrated this triumph with great splendor at Copenhagen, and, on that occasion, acknowledged Denmark to be a free and elective kingdom, and confirmed the rights of the aristocracy.

This victory was followed up by Frederic with a long and disastrous seven years' war with Sweden, which was productive of nothing but barren triumphs and mutual destruction. It was settled that a free commerce should be established between the two nations, and the Swedish navigation exempted from toll in passing the Sound. The remainder of Frederic's reign was devoted to the peaceful pursuits of internal administration. He died in 1588, at the age of fifty-four. He was succeeded by *Christian IV.*, who carried on a long and profitless warfare with the Swedes. The interruption of the Danish commerce with the ports in the Gulf of Riga, by the Swedes under Charles IX., and certain disputed territorial claims, occasioned that sanguinary struggle between the two kingdoms usually called the *War of Calmar.* On the death of Charles in 1611, the war was vigorously prosecuted by his son, the illustrious *Gustavus Adolphus*, who, in 1613, concluded it by treaty. About this period, the famous Thirty Years' War broke out. Christian IV. assumed the command of the Protestant confederates, but suffered severe repulses from the Catholic forces under Tilly and Wallenstein.

CHAPTER CCCCLX.

A. D. 1670 to 1798.

Accession of Christian V. — Assassination of Gustavus III.

The eldest son of *Frederic III.*, who had already been declared his successor, assumed the government under the title of *Christian V.* Notwithstanding the prudent measures of his father, he found the kingdom involved in confusion, and the state of affairs in a condition that presaged a reign not more pacific than the last. It was from the ascendency of Sweden, that the greatest danger was to be apprehended; and soon after his accession to the throne, Christian V. ordered war to be proclaimed against that country. The combined Dutch and Danish squadrons encountered the Swedish fleet off Bornholm, on the coast of Scania; the engagement lasted for several days, when it terminated in a complete victory on the part of the allies. The war between Sweden and Denmark was warmly waged with various losses and defeats on both sides, for several years, until at length it was concluded by treaty in 1679. Christian V., after great exertions, in which his conduct and courage were equally conspicuous, was forced to retire from the scene of action, deprived of every advantage, and disappointed in all his expectations. During the remainder of his reign, the attention of this great monarch was chiefly occupied with the internal affairs of his dominions, and the preservation of peace with the neighboring states. He expired in 1699, bequeathing to his country a high reputation for wisdom and courage.

The reign of *Frederic IV.* was passed in nearly unmolested repose. He died in 1730, bearing the character of a wise prince, too fond of enterprise, but strongly disposed to promote the welfare of his subjects. His son and successor, *Christian VI.*, was one of the most popular sovereigns that ever filled the Danish throne; and under his rule, the peace of Denmark continued to be undisturbed. Every thing was done by him to promote science, arts, and manufactures; and though oppressive taxes were repealed, he kept a fleet and army in a respectable condition, without increasing the burdens of his subjects. Historians have observed that no kingdom has been more fortunate in its princes than Denmark, though most of them were bad. The good fruits of the last reign continued to increase under *Frederic V.*, who succeeded his father. He was not less distinguished as a legislator than as a financier. Nothing was omitted that could render his dominions formidable to his enemies, or promote the happiness of his people. Of arts, science, and religion, he was the munificent patron. In the wars, which, since the accession of Christian VI., had involved almost every other state of Europe, and converted nearly the whole of Germany into a battle-field, Denmark took little part. Frederic had nearly been embroiled with Russia during the reign of Peter III., who, the moment he became emperor, resolved to revenge on the court of Denmark the injuries which had been committed upon his ancestors. In these attempts he was to be assisted by the king of Prussia. The king of Denmark prepared to resist the attacks with which he was threatened; but the death of the emperor relieved him from all apprehension, and he was able to compromise matters with Catharine II. by treaty. By this convention the empress ceded to Denmark, in the name of her son, the duchy of Sleswig, and so much of Holstein as appertained to the Gottorp branch of his family.

Frederic V. died in 1766, and was succeeded by his son *Christian VII.*, who married the princess Caroline Matilda of England, sister to King George III. The principal event in this reign was one which involved the unhappy queen in difficulties, and probably hastened her death. During the latter part of his life, Christian VII. fell into a state of derangement, and the government was carried on by the queen dowager and Prince Frederic. In 1773, the cession of ducal Holstein to Denmark, by Russia, took place according to the treaty just spoken of. This was a very important acquisition, as giving her the command of the whole Cimbrian peninsula, and enabling her, by forming a canal from Kiel, to connect the Baltic with the German Ocean.

In the continential wars of 1788–93, Denmark remained neuter, and by joining the armed neutrality, she excited the suspicions and resentment of England, and, being supposed to favor not only Russia, but France, became involved in a contest which was attended with deplorable losses. Christian VII. died in 1788, and was succeeded by his son *Frederic VI.*, whose reign was greatly disturbed by the struggles arising out of the French revolution.

CHAPTER CCCCLXI.

A. D. 1798 to 1863.

Participation of Denmark in the French Revolutionary Wars — Iceland — Manners and Customs.

DENMARK, which had long enjoyed repose, showed an aversion to mingle in the revolutionary conflicts now raging over all Europe. Yet this pacific kingdom was the first of the anti-Gallican confederates that was embroiled in hostilities with Great Britain, and ultimately suffered more injury from the effects of the war than any other of the northern powers. The causes that led to these collisions arose from an unwillingness on the part of Denmark to submit to the right of visitation and search claimed by the British in the case of neutral vessels. This claim was also resisted by other northern powers; and, in the year 1800, a confederation, opposed to the English, was formed by four nations — those of Denmark, Sweden, Russia, and Prussia. In consequence of these hostile measures, several hundred Baltic merchantmen were captured at sea or seized in British harbors. In March, 1801, a large British squadron, under Admirals Parker and Nelson, anchored opposite the harbor of Copenhagen.

Though the Danes had long enjoyed a profound peace, they were still animated with the courage of their brave ancestors to oppose this formidable armament. The very flower of Denmark, her peasantry, her scholars, and her artisans, flocked to her dock-yards and arsenals to struggle for their native land. The cannonade of the contending navies of England and Denmark was tremendous: above two thousand pieces of ordnance poured death "from their adamantine lips" within a space not exceeding a mile and a half in extent. But the heroic efforts of the Danes were all in vain, and in a short time their navy was defeated, with great carnage. Never before had the national valor shone forth with more distinguished lustre than in that terrible engagement, which, from its vicinity to the capital, had wound up the feelings of the people to the highest pitch of enthusiasm. A convention was soon afterward concluded, by which the maritime law maintained by England was recognized by Russia, Denmark, and Sweden, and amity thus restored between these formidable powers.

During the subsequent period of warfare, on the shores of the Baltic, between the French and the Swedes, Denmark wisely consulted her interests in pursuing a cautious neutrality. The restrictions imposed by France on the trade of other nations were an advantage to the Danes, by increasing their commerce, and crowding their harbors with a large share of the traffic formerly carried on by the interdicted states. It was at this flourishing period that their capital was a second time exposed to the destructive visitation of a naval armament from Great Britain. The object of this attack on the part of the English was, to thwart the designs of Bonaparte, who wished to compel Denmark to close the passage of the Sound against British shipping, and to avail himself of the aid of the Danish marine for the invasion of England. A British army of twenty thousand men, aided by a numerous fleet, shortly afterward laid siege to the city of Copenhagen by land and sea, and compelled its garrison to capitulate. The citadel and dock-yards were taken possession of, and the Danish fleet was seized and despatched to England.

While the other northern states were preparing, in 1813, to resist France, Denmark evinced no inclination to imitate their example. She had acted against Russia, and aided the views of Napoleon. Her seamen manned the French fleets, and her ships annoyed the trade of England. Her troops acted in concert with the French in that fatal campaign which terminated with the disastrous battle of Leipsic. After this period, Denmark entered into the grand alliance against Bonaparte, and engaged to furnish a contingent of ten thousand men to act against him. A treaty was formed, by which Frederic VI. of Denmark renounced, for himself and his successors, the possession of Norway and its dependencies. In June of 1814, a peace was concluded between Denmark and Russia and Prussia, by which the political and commercial relations between the former power and the two latter states were reëstablished as they existed before the wa

In Denmark, the constitution of 1660, which, thoug it conferred unlimited power on the sovereign, had been so administered as not to enslave the people, was considerably modified, in 1834, by the establishment of a representative branch of government. This change appears to have been dictated more by the enlightened spirit of the times than in consequence of any discontent felt under the existing system. The granting of this constitution added greatly to the well-earned popularity of Frederic VI. He was succeeded by Christian VIII., A. D. 1839. He died January 20, 1848; his son, Frederic VII., the present king, succeeded him.

In 1848, the duchies of Sleswig and Holstein revolted, and sought to become members of the new Germanic Confederation. Their cause was espoused by Prussia, and a war ensued between Denmark on the one side, and the Prussian forces, acting for the German parliament, aided by Sleswig and Holstein, on the other. After considerable bloodshed, the difficulty was suspended by an armistice, July, 1849, in which the following conditions were agreed to: 1. Sleswig is to have a separate constitution, and is not to be joined with Holstein. 2. A definite organization of the duchy of Sleswig shall be arranged by the contracting parties. 3. This article concerns the duchies of Holstein and Lauenburg. 4. The question of succession is reserved for future regulation. Since this time, both Schleswig and Holstein have been incorporated with the kingdom of Denmark.

The commerce of Denmark has been steadily improving since the peace of 1815, although still crippled in consequence of the heavy duties levied on foreign imports. Much attention is bestowed on navigation. At present, the number of its ships is estimated at upward of five thousand seven hundred; in burden, one hundred and forty-three thousand eight hundred tons. The total value of the articles exported in 1860 amounted to about twenty millions of dollars.

The inhabitants of Denmark are all of Teutonic origin, but belong to three distinct nations—the Danes, occupying Jutland and the islands; the Germans, in Holstein and Lauenburg; and the Frisians, upon the islets on the western coast. The Danish language is a branch of the great Scandinavian family of languages, and is closely allied to the Norwegian and Swedish. It is one of the softest European languages. The literature of Denmark contains many valuable works.

The Danes are of a middling stature and fair complexion, and, like the other inhabitants of the north of Europe, are more addicted to the use of animal food and spirituous liquors than those of the south. Excepting in the capital, they are not acquainted with the refinements of the more polished nations of Europe. Though personal slavery has been abolished among the peasantry since the beginning of the present century, there yet remain many traces of the feudal system. Having hardly any capital, the tenants pay their rent in kind, or by the labor of themselves and their cattle. The poverty of the peasants appears from the fact that many of them wear wooden shoes, and their families pass the long evenings of winter in spinning and making articles of clothing for domestic use.

Danish Peasants.

Iceland.—This island lies much nearer to America than Europe, and therefore belongs physically to the western continent; but its history and political condition have long connected it with the eastern. Being a dependency of Denmark, it deserves notice in our sketch of that country. It lies about two hundred miles east of the coast of Greenland, and contains more than 60,000 inhabitants. Its coasts are indented by bays, which are the results of rivers which flow from its mountains and glaciers. It is crossed by a range of irregular ridges and mountains, which have numerous offsets. In the interior is a celebrated collection of mountains, or *yokuls*, which are volcanic. The chief volcano is called *Hecla:* its eruptions are frequent, and in former times have been terrific. The boiling springs, called the *geysers*, in the southern part of the island, are celebrated curiosities.

Iceland is imagined by some to be the *Ultima Thule* spoken of by Virgil; but there is no good reason to suppose that it was known to the Romans. Its first discovery appears to have been in 860, when Naddodr, a Norwegian pirate, was driven upon the coast. A Norwegian colony made the first settlement here in 874: many of the emigrants were of distinguished families, who fled from Norway in the time of Harold Harfager. They established a republican government, appointed magistrates, and had their annual *allthing*, or national assembly, which was held at Shingralla, in the south part of the island. In this state they remained for nearly four centuries. About the year 1000, Christianity was established in Iceland. In the year 1057, Isleif, bishop of Skaholt, introduced the art of writing with the Latin alphabet; the Runic characters having been used till then only for inscriptions on stone, wood, or metal. Oral lessons, however, had kept up the historical traditions, and the feats of their ancestors were recorded in song. Icelandic literature began to be cultivated immediately after the introduction of writing. Literary societies were formed for the purpose of mutual instruction and education. The historical compositions called *sagas* have been since published, as well as many songs and other poetry. In 1120, the Icelanders framed the code of laws called *Grágás*.

Snorro Sturleson, a native of Iceland, and an extraordinary person, was one of the writers or compilers of the *Edda*,—a monument of the ancient mythology and poetry of the Scandinavians,—and he also wrote a history of Norway. Several monks, especially the Benedictines of the Shingeyra monastery, contributed largely to Icelandic literature. In 1264, the Icelanders, partly through intrigue and partly through fear, submitted to Haco, king of Norway, on the condition, however, of their laws and privileges being maintained. Still their subjection had a deteriorating influence upon their literary spirit, as well as on their commercial enterprise. In 1387, Iceland, together with Norway became subject to Denmark. About 1529, the art of printing was introduced into Iceland, and printing presses were established at Holum and Skaholt. In 1550, the Lutheran reformation was introduced, and led to the overthrow of the convents, and to the loss of many valuable national manuscripts.

The Icelandic language is the standard of the northern or Scandinavian dialect of the Gothic language The Swedish, Danish, and even the Norwegian, have been more or less subject to the influence of the Teutonic or German branch of the Gothic, whilst the Icelanders have preserved theirs pure as they imported it from Norway in the ninth century. This was the language called *Dönsk Tunga* in the middle ages. and was called by the Icelanders at first *Norræna*, which word corresponds to *Nairn*, or *Norse*, the corrupt dialect spoken till lately in part of the Orkneys. Since the language has been no longer spoken in Scandinavia, it has been styled exclusively *Icelandic*.

The Scandinavian or old Norse literature belongs to that early period when the Northmen were still idolaters. It consists, to a considerable extent, of sagas, or songs, which celebrate the deeds of their gods and heroes. It appears that, among the ancient Northmen, a race of minstrels called *Skalds* were the poets and historians: they followed the chiefs to the field in time of war, and resided at their courts during peace. They were often richly rewarded for their songs, and frequently received prizes. A list of two hundred and thirty of the most distinguished of these bards is preserved in the Icelandic language: among them are several kings and warriors. The ancient alphabet of Scandinavia is called *Runic*, that is, "hidden," because the priests who used it in writing held it as a mystery. It consisted of sixteen letters, and is supposed to have been derived from the Phœnicians.

Reikjavik, Capital of Iceland.

The Icelanders are the true descendants of the old Norsemen—tall, of florid complexion, flaxen hair, and open, frank countenance. The girls are often beautiful. Children are educated by their parents, with the assistance of the parish clergymen. All are taught to read; and the perusal of the Edda and the old sagas, with the recital of tales and legends, constitute a large part of the amusements of the people. The religion is Lutheran. Reikjavik is the capital, and the residence of the governor.

THE FAROE ISLES.—These are twenty-two in number, lying far to the north, and almost on the verge of the Arctic regions. They consist of steep rocks, covered with a thin soil, producing little but grass. Some of the rocks along the shore are eighteen hundred feet in perpendicular height. The weather is cold, and the summer only lasts during the months of July and August. The winds are excessively violent, preventing the growth of trees, and compelling the people to fix their houses in the valleys and ravines. Wildfowl are abundant: the horses and cattle are small. The extent of all the islands is six hundred square miles; population, eight thousand The largest island is Stromoe, twenty-seven miles long: the capital is Thorshavn.

These islands were discovered by the Norwegians in the ninth century, and were settled by that people. Since the union of Norway with Denmark, in the fourteenth century, they have belonged to the latter country. The people speak the Norwegian language with a Danish accent. They are handsome and well made, profess the Lutheran religion, and are hospitable, ingenuous, and peaceable in their manners.

Kings of Denmark.

Date of Accession. A. D.		Date of Accession. A. D.	
1000.	Sweyn.	1321.	Christopher II.
1036.	Hardicanute.	1332.	Waldemar III.
1042.	Magnus.	1375.	Margaret.
1047.	Sweyn Elpisdon.	1412.	Eric IX.
1074.	Harold.	1441.	Christopher III.
1076.	Canute the Saint.	1448.	Christian I.
1085.	Olaus.	1481.	John II.
1095.	Eric III.	1513.	Christian II.
1107.	Nicholas.	1523.	Frederic I.
1135.	Eric IV.	1534.	Christian III
1139.	Eric V.	1559.	Frederic II.
1147.	Canute V.	1588.	Christian IV.
1155.	Sweno.	1648.	Frederic III.
1157.	Waldemar.	1670.	Christian V.
1182.	Canute VI.	1699.	Frederic IV
1202.	Waldemar II.	1730.	Christian VI.
1242.	Eric VI.	1746.	Frederic V.
1251.	Abel.	1768.	Christian VII.
1252.	Christopher.	1808.	Frederic VI.
1259.	Eric VII.	1839.	Christian VIII.
1286.	Eric VIII.	1848.	Frederic VII

Sweden.

CHAPTER CCCCLXII.

A. D. 90 to 1863.

Description of Sweden — The Scandinavians — Union of Calmar — Gustavus Vasa — Independence of Sweden — Gustavus Adolphus — Charles XII. — Bernadotte — Present State of Sweden.

SWEDEN and Norway, which are now united into one kingdom, form an extensive country, stretching from the northern extremity of the temperate zone into the frozen region of the Arctic circle. Sweden Proper is bounded north by Norway, east by the Gulf of Bothnia and the Baltic, south by the Baltic, and west by the Baltic and Norway. All this country is subjected to a climate of severe cold. Even the southern districts have a rugged and repulsive aspect when compared with most other countries of Europe. Gloomy forests of pines stretch over the plains or hang on the sides of the mountains. The ground for five months in the year is buried under deep snow. Throughout the country, the signs of human industry are rare: cultivation appears only in scattered patches, and it was long insufficient to furnish bread to the inhabitants. Mountains, forests, rocky crags, broken streams of water, and numerous lakes constitute the chief features of the landscape in Sweden, which, in general, is very picturesque, though wild and savage. The extent of Sweden is one hundred and seventy thousand square miles; the population, three million four hundred thousand. The capital is Stockholm.

This country seems to have been totally unknown to the rest of the world at a time when Germany, Gaul, and even Britain and Denmark, were described with tolerable accuracy by the Greek and Roman geographers. Ptolemy and Pliny, who were the best informed of this class of ancient writers, appear to have known just enough of it to distinguish Sweden from Germany. They represent, off the coast of the

Swedish Peasants.

Inhabitants of Dalecarlia.

atter country, a large island, which they call *Basilia*, or *Baltia;* but of the extent and nature of this region they were entirely ignorant. The first inhabitants are supposed to have been a colony of Finns from the banks of the Volga and the neighborhood of Mount Caucasus. These were expelled at a very early period by the Teutones, from Germany. From these the southern part of Sweden obtained the name of *Gothland*. The whole country, in connection with Norway and Denmark, was called *Scandinavia*, or *Scania*.

This region has been called the "Storehouse of Nations," the "Northern Hive," &c., in allusion to the supposed fact that the swarms of barbarians which overthrew the Roman empire issued from the depths of Scandinavia. It appears that this is an error; for a country so completely covered with forests, and so unproductive by nature, is very unlikely to have afforded that immense population which spread itself over the greater part of Southern Europe. The country long remained in the darkness of paganism, and it was not till the eleventh century that Christianity penetrated into Sweden. The government varied at different times in the early ages; the kingdom of Sweden was separate from that of the Goths till the year 1132, when both nations were united into one monarchy under *Suercher*, king of the Ostrogoths, who was proclaimed king of the Swedes and Goths—a title which has been assumed by all his successors. It was afterward agreed between the two nations that the Swedes and the Goths should hold the sovereignty alternately—a measure which led to many bloody intestine wars.

In the latter part of the fourteenth century, *Magnus Smeck*, king of Sweden, added to his dominions the province of Schonen and the adjacent territory in the southern extremity of Sweden, which had not previously been comprehended in the kingdom. The reign of this monarch, however, put an end to the royal line of the Swedish and Gothic kings. Margaret of Waldemar, queen of Denmark, who obtained the name of the *Semiramis of the North*, by her superior talents and ambition, succeeded in gaining the sovereignty also of Sweden and Norway in 1397. The act by which this revolution was effected, or the *Union of Calmar*, has been already noticed. The Swedes were reluctant to lose their independence; and, soon after the death of Margaret, they rose in rebellion. But their repeated attempts to establish a separate kingdom were always defeated, till the cruel and tyrannical reign of Christian II. drove matters to extremity, and led the way to a new revolution in the early part of the sixteenth century.

Gustavus Vasa, or *Wasa*, a descendant of the ancient kings of Sweden, had fled from Stockholm to escape the tyranny of Christian, and concealed himself in the forests of Dalecarlia. A perfidious and bloody massacre committed by the king at Stockholm, in 1520, roused the Swedes to insurrection. Gustavus hoisted the national banner of Sweden in Dalecarlia and was soon joined by great numbers of his countrymen. He defeated the Danish troops which Christian sent against him, and met with such success in repeated battles, that, in three years from the beginning of the insurrection, he entered Stockholm in triumph. After a long struggle, the king of Denmark was compelled to recognize the independence of Sweden, and Gustavus was crowned king, A. D. 1527. With the establishment of the dynasty of Vasa, the history of Sweden as an independent and respectable kingdom may be said to commence. Gustavus introduced the Protestant reformation into the country, encouraged learning and industry, and raised his kingdom from the condition of a semi-barbarous and dependent territory to a comparatively high pitch of civilization.

The most distinguished of his descendants was *Gustavus Adolphus*. His reign, which began in 1611, was a glorious era for Sweden. This kingdom was now regarded as the main support of the Protestant cause, which was assailed by a formidable confederacy in the south of Europe. The success of the Austrians against the Protestants of Germany seemed to threaten the cause of the reformed religion with ruin. Gustavus was elected captain-general of the Protestant league. In 1630, he took the field, in Germany, with a small army of ten thousand Swedes; but around this gallant band rallied all the Protestants of Germany. Gustavus defended the Lutherans against the imperial armies with equal bravery and good fortune. He proved himself to be the first general of his age, and, by his skilful and original tactics, introduced a new era in the art of war. He carried on hostilities with ability and success against Russia, Poland, Den mark, and Austria. The splendid victories of Leipsic and Breitenfeld humbled the house of Austria, and re-established the civil and religious liberties of the German empire. At the battle of Lutzen, Gustavus fell in the arms of victory, November 6, 1632, at the early age of thirty-seven. Even after his fall, his generals continued to wage that desperate war of thirty years which resulted in compelling the Catholic league finally to renounce its pretensions. Sweden, at the peace which followed this great struggle, obtained Pomerania and other important possessions in Germany, and continued, till the end of the seventeenth century, to exercise a powerful influence on the affairs of Europe.

Charles XII. ascended the throne of Sweden in 1697. He was only fifteen years of age, and the sovereigns of Russia, Poland and Denmark formed a coalition to strip him of his territories. Charles met this formidable conspiracy with a spi[illegible] and energy that astonished all Europe. He attack[illegible] the king of Denmark with such unexpected vigor, [illegible]at he compelled him to make peace within six we[illegible]s. He next marched against the czar, Peter, and [illegible]eated him with a prodigious army of Russians, at N[illegible]va. He then invaded Poland, and proceeded from victory to victory, capturing Riga, Warsaw, and Cracow, till at the end of a campaign of two years, he placed a new king on the throne of Poland, in 1704. He next undertook the invasion of Russia, and marched southward into the territory of the Ukraine, to join the Cossack chief Mazeppa. At the battle of Pultowa, Charles was totally defeated by the Russians under the command of Peter, in July, 1709. He fled to Turkey, and remained at Bender, in that country, for five years. All his conquests were lost as rapidly as they had been gained; and Charles, on his return to his own country, was killed at the siege of Fredericshall, in Norway, in 1718. His death has been ascribed, with great probability, to treachery. The victories of Charles XII. threw a wild and romantic lustre around Sweden, which terminated, however, in the loss of her political station and greatness.

The influence of Sweden, after this period, was confined within her own limits; and she hardly ranked as a power of the second order. The only remarkable change which she exhibited in the course of the eighteenth century, was produced by the revolutions of 1772 and 1789, when *Gustavus III.* succeeded in converting the government into an absolute monarchy. On the breaking out of the French revolution, Sweden joined Great Britain in the war against France. In 1808, by a war with Russia, she lost Finland. In 1810, a connection having been formed between the Swedes and Napoleon, and an heir being wanting in the royal family, Bernadotte, one of Napoleon's ablest generals, was chosen crown prince of Sweden. This produced a great change in the political relations of the country. To conciliate his new subjects, Bernadotte restored the representative constitution of Sweden, which had been reduced to a mere shadow. Having joined the allies against Napoleon, he received Norway in compensation for the loss of Finland. On the death of the king in 1818, the crown prince mounted the throne, with the title of *Charles John.* His reign continued till 1844, and was marked by the uniform and increasing prosperity of the kingdom. He was succeeded by his grandson, *Oscar I.*, who was followed, in 1859, by Charles XV., the present king.

Stockholm, the capital of Sweden, is finely situated at the junction of the Lake of Malar with the sea. Viewed externally, it is one of the most beautiful cities in the world; but its interior disappoints the spectator. The streets are narrow and without sidewalks; the houses are very lofty. Some of the public buildings are splendid. The population is over one hundred thousand. The other principal towns are Gottenburg, Norrkoping, Carlscrona, and Calmar.

The constitution of Sweden is one of the few in Europe which has steadily preserved some portion of the representative system which had been formed in remote ages. The government has the form of a limited monarchy. The diet, or parliament, is an antique and cumbrous species of legislative body, consisting of four orders — the nobles, the clergy, the burghers, and the peasants. The popular portion is gradually increasing in strength. The Swedes are Protestants, and the established religious creed is Lutheranism.

The manners of the Swedes are simple, and travellers generally speak of them in terms of praise. They are hospitable and brave, with an urbanity which has given them the title of the *French of the North.* They are said, however, to be much given to indulgence in drink, and domestic distillation is practised all over the country. It is not uncommon to see children left to attend the stills, sucking the liquor with straws, and thus becoming dead drunk. A general laxity of morals pervades the country.

Sweden is rich in mines of iron, copper, and silver, and a great part of the population is engaged in mining. Education is widely diffused, and it is provided by law that all persons of both sexes shall be taught to read and write. There are two universities — those of Upsal and Lund. The study of polite literature is much encouraged.

We have already alluded to the Scandinavian literature in our sketch of Iceland. Among its relics, the descent of Odin, and Harold the valiant, are familiar to the reader. The Swedish popular poetry is analogous to that of Denmark; the Swedes are great singers, and are as much attached to their native songs, as are the Scotch to theirs. In science, Sweden boasts the names of Linnæus, and Swedenborg. The poetry of Tenger and the novels of Miss Bremer have recently excited an interest throughout Christendom. Taglioni and Jenny Lind — the most famous danseuse, and the sweetest singer of modern times — are both natives of Sweden.

Kings of Sweden.

Date of Accession. A. D.		Date of Accession. A. D.	
1001.	Olaus.	1397.	Union of Calmar.
1019.	Amund I.	*	*
1035.	Edmund.	1523.	Gustavus Vasa.
1040.	Hacquin.	1560.	Eric XVI.
1061.	Slurkill.	1568.	John II.
1075.	Ingo.	1599.	Charles IX.
1110	Ingo II.	1611.	Gustavus Adolphus.
1129.	Ragwald.	1632.	Christina.
1140.	Suercher II.	1654.	Charles X.
1160.	Eric the Holy.	1660.	Charles XI.
1161.	Charles VII.	1697.	Charles XII.
1168.	Canute.	1718.	Ulrica Leonora.
1192.	Swexcher III.	1720.	Frederic I.
1210.	Eric XI.	1751.	Adolphus Frederic.
1220.	John.	1771.	Gustavus III.
1250.	Waldemar I.	1792.	Gustavus Adolphus IV
1276.	Magnus II.	1809.	Charles XIII.
1281.	Birger.	1819.	Charles John.
1326.	Magnus III.	1844.	Oscar Frederic.
1363.	Albert.	1859.	Charles XV.

Norway.

CHAPTER CCCCLXIII.

A. D. 940 to 1814.

Description of Norway — Harold Harfager — Olaf Trygvason — The Sea-Kings — Union with Sweden — Present State of Norway.

Bergen.

NORWAY lies at the northern extremity of Europe. It is bounded north by the Frozen Sea, east by Sweden and Russia, south by Sweden and the Strait of the Cattegat, and west by the Atlantic. It is about one hundred and twenty thousand square miles in extent, and has a population of one million six hundred and fifty thousand inhabitants. In climate, soil, and general appearance, it is similar to Sweden, except that the cold in the northern parts is greater. Some distance off the coast, in the North Sea, is the whirlpool, known as the Maelstrom. In summer it is not dangerous, but is very much so in winter, especially when the north-west wind restrains the reflux of the tide. At such times, the whirlpool rages violently, so as to be heard several miles, and often engulfs vessels, and even whales, which venture to approach it.

The original inhabitants of Norway appear to have been a Scandivanian tribe, who lived altogether by fishing and the chase. They seem to have had, in the earliest ages, a rude sort of representative government, while they obeyed chiefs or kings, who were at once judges and high priests, but whose power was limited by national assemblies, which were composed wholly of freemen. Hardly any thing, however, is known of the Norwegians before the tenth century, at which period the country was divided into a number of petty sovereignties, which acknowledged a kind of supremacy in the kings of Sweden and Denmark.

Harold Harfager, the first of the great Sea-kings of the north, formed for himself an independent principality in the country, about the year 940, and, by a series of formidable expeditions obtained a wide distinction among the chieftains of the middle ages. Having united the several territories of Norway under his sway, he invaded the Shetland Isles, the Orkneys, and the Hebrides, with success, and established his dominion there. For many centuries, his successors, the Norwegian and Danish sovereigns, held full possession of these islands. They also gave a king to England, and formed a permanent establishment in Normandy. *Olaf Trygvason*, who reigned in Norway about the beginning of the eleventh century, obtained great fame by his bold adventures on sea and land. The Runic paganism had prevailed in all the Scandivanian countries, from the earliest period of history. Olaf attempted, by violent and sanguinary measures, to introduce Christianity in its place, in which he was partly successful. *Olaf II.*, who reigned from 1014 to 1030, surpassed his predecessor in tyranny and zeal for the interests of the clergy He was canonized by the Romish church, and is known at the present day as *Saint Olaf.* Temples were erected to his memory at Constantinople, and his tomb was visited by pilgrims, not only from Norway, but from all the rest of Europe.

In the eleventh century, the defeat of the Norwegian king *Haco*, in Scotland and the conquest of Norway by Canute of England put an end to the maritime dominion of the Sea-kings; and the Scandinavian nations, notwithstanding their immense supply of naval stores, have never since attained to more than a secondary rank among the maritime powers of Europe Norway again became independent in 1034, and the Norwegian kings are said to have governed Denmark for a time.

Toward the close of the fourteenth century, the three kingdoms of Norway, Sweden, and Denmark were united into one monarchy, as already stated When Sweden revolted against Christian II., and became an independent kingdom, Norway remained in connection with Denmark. This continued till 1814 when Norway was incorporated with the kingdom of Sweden, by the dictation of the allied sovereigns The Norwegians complained, not without reason against the compulsory transfer of their allegiance Yet the change was in some essential points beneficial. Denmark had deprived them of their free constitution, which they now regained; and the general administration of the government by the Danish kings had been such as to depress Norway, with a view of concentrating the wealth and the commerce of the kingdom at Copenhagen.

Norwegian Soldiers on Skates.

In their wars with Sweden, the Norwegians formed a military corps, which was provided with skates or snowshoes, and armed with rifle and sword. It was impossible to attack them with any success, while their efficacy in harassing and annoying the enemy was really extraordinary. Cannon shot could produce but little effect upon them, dispersed as they were at the distance of two or three hundred paces from each other. No army can protect itself against an enemy which has no need of path or road, and traverses with equal facility marshes, lakes, rivers, and mountains.

A highly republican spirit prevails in Norway, and the ancient influence of the nobility is nearly annihilated. This country has its own *storthing*, or legislative assembly, which is of very ancient date, and was restored by Bernadotte. It possesses much higher privileges than the Swedish diet. It assembles more frequently, and at its own fixed times, without any control from the king. It allows him only a suspensive veto, and can compel him to accept any law which has been voted three times by the storthing. These rights, having been once granted by Bernadotte, were found to press very hard against his prerogative, and he made many unsuccessful attempts to abridge them.

Christiana, the capital of Norway, stands on a capacious and beautiful bay, affording a most enchanting prospect. This city is almost the only one in the kingdom which is not built of wood; so that, in the course of two centuries, it has suffered but little injury from fire, while great numbers of other towns have been reduced to ashes. The buildings are mostly of stone, and of regular structure. The trade of the place is chiefly in timber and boards, of which Christiania is a great mart. It has considerable wealth, and a university. Population, forty thousand. Bergen and Drontheim are considerable seaports.

The manners of the Norwegians do not differ essentially from those of the Swedes. Their towns are not compactly built, but are composed of houses scattered widely apart, and extending over a space of several leagues. The people are industrious and frugal, and generally possess a competence of wealth: extreme poverty is unknown. The clergy are well educated, and active in promoting education among the people. The Danish language is generally spoken, though the Norwegians have their own dialect.

Kings of Norway.

Date of Accession. A. D.		Date of Accession. A. D.	
1000.	Sweyn.	1207.	Haco II.
1011.	Olaus I.	1263.	Magnus IV.
1032.	Sweno.	1280.	Eric II.
1036.	Magnus Oleron,	1299.	Haco III.
1047.	Harold Haardrade.	1315.	Magnus V.
1066.	Olaus II.	1326.	Haco III.
1070.	Magnus I.	1328.	Magnus VI.
1087.	Haco I.	1358.	Haco IV.
1087.	Magnus II.	1375.	Olaus IV.
1103.	Sigurd.	1397.	Union of Calmar
1162.	Magnus III.		

Lapland.

Scene in Lapland.

Scene in Lapland.

CHAPTER CCCCLXIV.

A. D. 1100 to 1863.

Description of Lapland — Origin of the Lapps -- Their Mythology — Conversion to Christianity -- Superstitions — Manners, Customs, &c., of the Laplanders.

LAPLAND is the most northerly country of Europe. It is bounded on the north by the Frozen Ocean, east by the White Sea, and in all other parts by Russia, Sweden, and Norway. Its limits are not very precisely ascertained, and it may be regarded as comprising three divisions — Russian, Swedish, and Norwegian Lapland. Russian Lapland consists of all that part of the country situated east of the River Tornea. Swedish Lapland is the largest and most southerly portion, and lies in the interior, west of the Tornea Norwegian Lapland is the smallest division, and consists of a narrow strip of territory along the northern and western coast. All this country is exposed to the intense coldness of a polar climate. The mountains are covered with perpetual snow. The southern part abounds with pine forests, but toward the north the trees disappear, and the country presents only the dreary spectacle of a heap of barren rocks, with here and there a patch of scanty vegetation of birchen or willow shrubs, and reindeer moss. As the greater part of Lapland lies within the polar circle, the summer may be regarded as one long day, and the winter as one long and dreary night.

The natives of Lapland are wholly ignorant of their origin as a people; but there can be little doubt that they were the first inhabitants of the country which they now occupy. Their parentage has been derived by some authors from the Scythians, and by others from the Hebrews; but the prevalent opinion is, that their immediate ancestors were the ancient Finns. The *Finni*, according to the descriptions given by Tacitus and Ptolemy, bore a close resemblance to the mountain Laplanders of the present day. They are supposed to have been the people designated by Herodotus under the names of *Cynocephali*, *Troglodytes*, and *Pygmies*. They disclaim the appellation of *Laplanders*, or *Lapps*, which is understood to have been bestowed upon them, as a term of reproach, by the Swedes, when they first subjugated the country. Etymologists are not agreed as to the precise import and derivation of the word. It is deduced by some from the Latin *lippus*, "blear-eyed," the natives being half blinded by the smoke of their wigwams. Others derive it from the Swedish word *lappa*, "a patch," in reference to the ragged garments of the Laplanders; and others refer it to the Finnish *lappi*, "exiles, or runaways," supposing them to have migrated or run away from Finland.

Some learned ethnologists have concluded that the Laplanders, Samoiedes, Esquimaux, and Greenlanders, who are all found in the same northern latitudes, must have been originally the same people. They suppose the Laplanders to have descended from the White Sea toward Norway and Sweden, while the Finns, on the other hand, ascended from Esthonia, through Finland. In the north of Norway, the Laplanders are called *Finns*, and the Finns who have penetrated into that country are called *Quans*. The Lapland language is represented as having a considerable analogy to that of the Finns; and as distinguished by certain peculiarities resembling the idiom of the Hebrew. It possesses an elegant brevity, expressing by one word what, in most languages, would require several.

Lapland has little of what can be called history; and that which is known of the inhabitants does not extend to a very remote antiquity. When they first attract our notice in the twelfth century, they appear as an independent people. Shortly after this time, their country was visited and explored by various roaming tribes of the Scandinavian race, who emigrated northerly along the coast of Norway, to which quarter they were attracted by the cod fishery of the Lofoden Islands. Settlements of the emigrants were formed here, and an intercourse was opened between the Scandinavians and the Laplanders. The latter appear to have been in a state of the most complete barbarism; entirely ignorant of agriculture, which was introduced among them by their new acquaintances. The Scandinavians soon acquired that influence over the Laplanders which civilization exercises over barbarism; and in the thirteenth century, we find Lapland regarded as subject to the kings of Norway. Little actual sovereignty appears, however, to have been exercised over this country at first; and the Swedes and Russians followed the example of the Norwegians by establishing settlements within its limits.

When the Swedes had obtained some degree of authority over the Laplanders, they attempted to convert them to Christianity. The natives, however, adhered to their ancient paganism with obstinate pertinacity. They worshipped a great number of deities, the chief of which was named *Radien Atzhie*, who, with his only son, was regarded as the creator and governor of the world. Other deities were *Beiwe*, the sun; *Maderatja*, the god of the air; *Horagalles*, the god of thunder; *Saiwo* and *Omak*, the gods of the mountains; *Saiwo Guella*, the conductor of souls to the shades below; *Jalme Akko*, or death; *Rota*, the sovereign of the infernal regions, &c. The immortality of the soul, and a future state of rewards and punishments, were a part of the Lapland religion; so that the faith of these uncouth and unlettered savages compares very favorably with the elegant mythology of the Greeks.

The conversion of the Laplanders to Christianity cannot be dated much earlier than the middle of the seventeenth century; and their religion is still so very imperfect as to consist in little more than receiving baptism, bearing Christian names, and giving a reluctant attendance upon a few of the festivals of the church. They retain much of their old superstition, even in the Christian rites which they have adopted. They regard the sacrament as a powerful charm to preserve them from evil spirits. Their belief in magic and incantation is as strong as ever, and they practise a species of necromancy by the use of the Runic drum. This is a wooden instrument hung round with brass rings, so near each other as to rattle together upon the slightest touch. The skin, or parchment, stretched over the drum, is covered with painted characters representing the different deities and other mystical figures. These drums are esteemed according to their antiquity, and are preserved with great care and secrecy. In any affair of importance they are consulted in the following manner. A ring is placed upon the drum-head, which is struck with a small hammer of deer's horn, so as to drive the ring from side to side over the painted surface; and according to the course which it takes, or the figures which it touches, the omen is interpreted as good or bad. Private families have their own drum for ordinary cases; but in the matters of public import, as an epidemic sickness among the people, or their cattle, the *Noiaads*, or privileged soothsayers, who are regularly trained to the art, hold a public consultation of the oracles. During the ceremony, the operator makes a number of frightful grimaces, and takes an unusual quantity of brandy and tobacco, which put him into a deep sleep. On awakening, he pretends to have been conveyed to one of the holy mountains, where he had an interview with the deities, whose revelations he then makes public.

Among so rude a people as the Laplanders, there can hardly be any thing like regular government. In general, they acknowledge the king of Sweden as their sovereign, and conform to such legal regulations as the Swedish authorities have established in their country. A small number are also tributary to Russia. They are not a numerous people, and are estimated not to exceed sixty thousand souls. Of this number, a considerable part are a mixed population, the descendants of Finnish colonists introduced by the Swedes. The pure Laplanders have a swarthy complexion, black, short hair, a wide mouth, hollow cheeks, and a pointed chin. Their eyes are weak and watery, in consequence, it is supposed, of their smoky habitations, or the glaring snows of winter, which often have the effect of depriving the natives of sight for several days after their return from a hunting expedition. They possess great strength of body, and are capable of sustaining enormous fatigue. They are not less remarkable for swiftness of foot and agility, and are inured from infancy to every kind of activity and exertion. Their stature is rather diminutive, but their slouching gait gives them the appearance of being shorter than they really are. Their dark complexion may be owing mainly to the smoke of their huts; for Linnæus, who visited their country, states that their skin in other parts is as white and delicate as that of any lady whatever.

The mountain Laplanders have no fixed habitations, but live in tents, which they move from place to place in quest of food for their reindeer. The huts of the maritime Laplanders are built of sods and roofed with birch bark. The floors are strewed with branches of trees, and on these are spread deer-skins, on which the family sit or lie down, as no part of the hut is sufficiently high to admit of standing upright. The fire is made in the centre of the hut or tent, and at all seasons these dwellings are constantly filled with smoke, which is regarded as the best defence against the gnats in summer and the cold in winter.

The Laplanders dress in coarse woollen cloth and skins. Their diet consists almost wholly of animal food. Those who inhabit the coast live principally on fish; the mountaineers subsist chiefly on the milk and flesh of the reindeer. These animals are the most valuable part of a Laplander's possessions, and the principal object of his care. They feed on grass during the summer, and in winter upon the reindeer moss, which grows every where in Lapland, and which the animal knows how to reach by scraping away the snow. Of these useful creatures a wealthy Laplander often possesses a thousand or more. They are not only valuable for their milk, and flesh, and hides, but they are trained to draw sledges upon the snow. These are made of birch wood, and shaped like a boat: the reindeer will travel with them sometimes at the rate of ten miles an hour.

The principal employment of the Laplanders is hunting and fishing. They use firearms, and are good marksmen. Though their life is full of toil, and apparently of suffering, their attachment to their native country is remarkably strong. They are ignorant and superstitious, but are free from most of the vices of civilized nations. They are entire strangers to theft, and generally sleep in the summer with open doors, in perfect security. Beggars are unknown among them, and the aged and infirm receive the most attentive care. During the winter, the Laplanders carry on some traffic with the Swedes, bartering skins, furs, dried fish, and venison, for woollen cloth, metals, tobacco, brandy, meal, and salt. There are no cities in Lapland, and only a few spots permanently inhabited. The traveller Acerbi, who visited this country in the last century, found the seat of government at Kautokeino, a place containing only four families and a priest. Hammerfest is a more modern settlement but it is still small.

Finland.

CHAPTER CCCCLXV.

A. D. 50 to 1808.

Description of Finland — Origin of the Finns — Their Migration to the West — Conquest of Finland by the Norwegians and Swedes —Transfer of the Country to Russia — Manners, Customs, &c., of the Finlanders.

Costumes of Finland.

The greater part of Finland was formerly attached to the kingdom of Sweden; but the whole now forms a part of the Russian empire. It is bounded north by Swedish Lapland, east by the Russian territory, south by the Gulf of Finland, and west by the Gulf of Bothnia. Connected with this region are the Aland or Oeland Islands, about eighty in number, and situated at the mouth of the Gulf of Bothnia. The present name of *Finland* was bestowed upon it by the Swedes; but the inhabitants call their country *Suomemna*, or the region of lakes and swamps. The whole eastern and central part of the territory is, in fact, intersected with lakes, rivers, and marshy tracts, among which are sandy flats, overgrown with moss, and studded with low hills. The northern and western parts are mountainous. In the south are extensive forests, chiefly of fir and pine. The lakes and marshy districts cover more than a third of the whole surface of the country: but the climate is said to be, on the whole, salubrious. Fogs are very common. In all parts, the winters are severe.

The first mention of the Finns in history is made by Tacitus, who ranks them among the Germans. Ptolemy also alludes to them, but in as indistinct a manner as Tacitus. They are supposed to be of Asiatic origin; their dominions once extended from the sources of the Obi, and the banks of the Volga, to the shores of the Baltic, as far as the northeast parts of Prussia. The period of their migration westward is unknown. Tacitus describes them as a savage race, without powerful weapons, horses, or the use of iron. Their principal occupation was hunting, and their arrows were pointed with bone. Most writers are of opinion that their original abode was among the Ural Mountains, from whence they spread chiefly westward. They are believed to be of the same race with the tribes which founded the kingdom of the Magyars in Hungary. They first appear, indistinctly, in history, in the neighborhood of Finland, as a wandering horde. They do not seem to have been of a warlike disposition, as they were easily reduced to subjection by the Norwegians, Swedes, and Russians, in succession.

The Norwegians began by the conquest of Finmark, from whence they made inroads, at various times, into the territory of the Permians, a tribe of Finns who inhabited the country near the White Sea. These invasions were ultimately arrested by the princes of Novgorod, who made themselves masters of Permia. The Mongol Tartars also checked the invasion of the Norwegians. The Russians next overran the Finnish territories; and in the fourteenth century, Stephen, one of their bishops, having planted the cross on the shores of the White Sea, overthrew the worship of the great Finnish deity, *Yomala*. The Swedes next invaded the country; and about the middle of the twelfth century, Eric the Pious, king of Sweden, converted the inhabitants of modern Finland to Christianity, A. D. 1156.

Of the subsequent history of the country, there is little to say. Sweden, by two treaties, in 1721 and 1741, ceded a part of her Finnish territory to Russia. The latter power, however, coveted the whole; and Finland, after having been the scene of many bloody battles between the Swedish and Russian armies, was completely overrun by the latter in 1808, and soon after abandoned by treaty to the czar. The country was lost by the incapacity and folly of the king of Sweden, who left its brave defenders to sink under an overwhelming force, while he was vainly endeavoring to conquer Norway, and the Danish islands in the Baltic.

The population of Finland is nearly two millions. Abo, the largest town, is situated on the River Aurajaki, and surrounded by hills and mountains. The buildings are chiefly of wood, and the chief trade of the place is in timber and provisions. It has manufactures of tobacco and sailcloth. It had once a university, founded by Gustavus Adolphus; but in 1827, a fire destroyed seven hundred and eighty buildings at Abo, with all those belonging to the university, including its library and scientific collections. In consequence of this calamity, the institution was removed to Helsingfors, another commercial town, with a fine harbor, which now ranks as the capital. The population of Abo is twelve thousand five hundred and fifty. Finland has the rank of a grand duchy of the Russian empire.

The modern Finlanders are a people of grave manners, but courageous and persevering. They can endure the severest privations, though their perseverance is sometimes little better than obstinacy. Their attachment to their national name, customs, and language, rendered them incapable of appreciating the blessings of civilization, which the Swedes were anxious to diffuse among them. Even at the present day, the Russian government is compelled to yield something to the national spirit of the Finlanders. Russia and the grand duchy of Finland are declared to be two distinct but inseparable states; a most contradictory description, but which has the effect of keeping the Finnish subjects of Russia quiet, by flattering their love for the mere name of independence.

The genuine Finns are short in stature, with flat faces, dark gray eyes, thick beard, tawny hair, and a sallow complexion. Those who inhabit the southern and western districts are scarcely to be distinguished in their manners from the Swedes, though they retain the national features. In Russian Finland, the inhabitants have a slowness of motion, a depression of spirit, and a simplicity and almost stupidity of look, which form a striking contrast with the lively aspect, alert movements, and cheerful humor of the Russians; but these circumstances may be chiefly owing to their condition as a conquered people. More hardy than the Russians, they are not so warmly clothed, and seldom wear the sheepskin. Their dress is a coat of coarse woollen stuff, made with little regard to shape, and tied round the body with a band; a pair of coarse linen trousers, straw shoes, and bits of woollen cloth or ropes of straw wrapped round their legs.

There is some mixture of the Swedish and Russian races in Finland, but the majority of the population is of Finnish extraction. Serfage does not exist here, as in other parts of the Russian empire. All the Finlanders are free. They have no nobility; but the peasant gives precedence to the citizen or merchant, and holds every officer of the crown in high respect The greater part of the people are addicted to agricultural pursuits. They also carry on the fisheries, manufacture tar, and build ships. The women are thrifty, much devoted to their domestic duties, and weave coarse linens and woollens for the use of their families. The peasants live in huts, containing a single room, like the American log-cabins, and warmed by a large stove, the smoke of which goes out either at the windows or through a hole in the roof. In the long nights of winter, these dwellings are illuminated by pine knots instead of candles. A stranger receives much attention: he is always the principal person in a company, and much pains are taken to please him. Vapor baths are used by all the Finlanders — a custom very common to the Sclavonic nations of the north. These baths are heated to the height of one hundred and fifty or one hundred and sixty degrees, and the vapor is produced by pouring boiling water on red-hot stones. When the bather is heated to an intense perspiration, he runs out of the bath, and rolls in the snow, if it be winter and upon the grass, if in summer. This practice, which would be thought fatal by any other people, is highly esteemed by the Finlanders as a means of invigorating and refreshing their bodies.

The Finns are mostly Christians. The inhabitants of the eastern districts, who were converted by the Russians, profess the Greek faith, the western Finns are Protestants. There are some tribes who still adhere to paganism. Almost every Finlander is a poet or a musician. A hut surrounded by forests and marshes, in the interior of the country, is often the residence of a bard, whose rustic and simple songs enliven all the villagers. Their poetry is of a strongly national and original cast, and is sung to the accompaniment of the Finnish lyre. There is scarcely any event, public or private, which does not find a poet to celebrate it. The manner in which verses are recited in public is derived from ancient practice. Two poets stand in the midst of a circle, and repeat lines alternately, every second line beginning with the last word of the preceding. Written literature can hardly be said to exist in Finland. There are schools in many of the towns, but public instruction is not widely extended Not one individual in a hundred can read. The celebrated Frederika Bremer, though her name is associated with Sweden, in consequence of her residence there was a native of Finland.

The Russian Empire.

CHAPTER CCCCXLVI.

A. D. 862 to 1604.

Geographical Description of Russia—Early Annals.

THE Russian empire comprises almost the entire northern part of the eastern continent, from the Atlantic to the Pacific, and embraces a territory spanning one half the globe, or about one hundred and eighty degrees of longitude. Of that portion which lies in Asia—the *Caucasian Countries and Siberia*—we have given an account. We shall now present a view of that part of the empire which is in Europe, and which, though less extensive than the Asiatic portion, is far the most populous and important in a political and historical point of view.

This portion of the Russian empire extends from the northern slope of the Caucasian Mountains, latitude 40° 20′, to Lapland, latitude 70° 16′ north, and from longitude 18° east to the western slope of the Ural Mountains, longitude 60° 45′ east. It is bounded east by Siberia and the Caspian Sea, south by Asiatic Russia, the Black Sea, Austria and Turkey, west by Moldavia, Austria, Prussia, the Baltic, and Sweden, and north by the Arctic Ocean.

The general surface of Russia may be considered as one vast plain, inclosed by the Ural Mountains on the east, the Caucasian on the south, and partly by the Carpathians on the west. Throughout this vast extent, thus inclosed, it does not present a single mountain. The highest point between the Black Sea and the Baltic is about 1,300 feet.

The rivers are numerous, the principal being the Danube, flowing into the Black Sea; the Don, flowing into the Sea of Azof; the Dnieper, flowing into the Black Sea; and the Vistula, flowing into the Baltic. The population in 1858 was 65,810,752.

The lakes are also numerous, among which Ladoga and Onega are the principal. The river Neva is the outlet of the former, and is a broad, deep river, and subject to inundations which frequently do great mischief. On this stream St. Petersburg, the capital, is situated.

The White Sea lies to the north, and is connected with the Arctic Ocean. The Gulf of Riga and the Gulf of Finland are estuaries of the Baltic Sea. The Sea of Azof is a gulf of the Black Sea on the north, and having the peninsula of the Crimea on the west.

Among the numerous islands which belong to this portion of the Russian empire are Nova Zembla, or New Land, in the Arctic Ocean, and further west Spitzbergen. The latter is a group of small islands, and is the most northerly land known on the globe. These are visited by whalers, and their numerous adventures here in contending with the climate and the white bears, have furnished many a tale of wonder and excitement. Nova Zembla consists of two large islands, with some mountains 3,500 feet high. The coasts are frequented by numerous walruses in summer. There are here subterranean stone labyrinths of great antiquity, of the origin and use of which, history gives us no information.

The climate of Russia is necessarily greatly diversified, inasmuch as its stretches through forty degrees of latitude from north to south. When spring comes in one division, another still experiences all the rigors of winter. Here the camel traverses arid, burning deserts, there the reindeer courses over heaps of snow, under which he finds a scanty supply of moss. This variety of the products and diversity in the manner of living, gives Russia advantages enjoyed by no other European country. She possesses in abundance all the articles of greatest necessity, and most of those which are considered luxuries. In general, however, it must be remarked that the climate of European Russia is cold, and some parts extremely so. It is curious to see, however, that human ingenuity successfully combats these rigors of nature. In St. Petersburg and Moscow, the winter is really the finest season. The houses are so arranged as to exclude the cold, while the people, enveloped in furs, course over the snow in various kinds of sledges—the whole surface of the earth being a sort of universal railroad.

The animals of Russia are those met with in the frigid as well as the temperate portions of Europe. To the north are the white bear and reindeer. The seacoast is thronged with seals, white bears, and walruses. The fur-bearing animals, beavers, martens, sables, &c., are common in these northern latitudes, and the pursuit of them furnishes employment to many of the inhabitants. The rivers and lakes swarm with fish. Horses are reared for exportation in some parts. It sometimes happens that a single khan, or chief of a tribe, on the river Don, is the owner of 10,000 horses!

All kinds of grain thrive in Russia; many of the provinces along the Black Sea furnish a large amount of wheat, which is distributed to various parts of Europe. Rye and oats are still more extensively produced. Flax and hemp are cultivated largely, both for home use and exportation. Tobacco is an important product in the south. The government has of late years exerted itself for the improvement of agriculture. Professorships of agriculture and model farms have been established, in connection with the universities. There are several tribes almost exclusively devoted to the rearing of bees, which is, consequently, an extensive branch of industry. Exclusive of the numerous herds which constitute the wealth of the nomadic tribes, every peasant has a few cattle, and even the beggar has generally a cow, or at least a goat. Tallow is and has long been the chief article of export. Wool is also becoming an important product.

Landed property in Russia is generally divided into estates, belonging either to the crown or the nobility. Some of the estates of the latter are very extensive. The peasants are in a state of slavery, and are bought and sold with the soil. Different systems of managing the lands are adopted by different proprietors. The greater part distribute the lands among their tenants, imposing a capitation tax upon each male peasant, by way of rent.

The richest districts are in the south, upon the Don and the Dnieper; but there is much fertile land upon the Volga. Between the Volga and the Don, in the Crimea, and between the Volga and Uralian Mountains, there are extensive steppes or dry plains, which, however, furnish pasturage for the large herds of the wandering Tartars. In Poland, the soil is generally thin and sandy, and there are many marshy tracts. In the north, there are barren steppes and morasses. Finland has much productive land.

Gold, silver, platina, diamonds, and iron are found in the Ural Mountains, but principally on the Asiatic side. Salt is obtained in great abundance from an immense number of salt lakes.

The system of canalization, favored by numerous navigable rivers and lakes, and by the seas which border Russia on three sides, has been carried to a great extent. Railroads are also in progress on a large scale. St. Petersburg, at the eastern extremity of the Gulf of Finland is the capital.

European Russia is divided into six geographical sections, as follows: Baltic Provinces, Great Russia, Little Russia, South Russia, West Russia, and Kingdom of Poland. These are subdivided as follows:—

THE BALTIC PROVINCES.

	Governments.	*Area in Sq. Miles.*	*Principal Town.*	*Population.*
1.	Petersburg, divided into 9 circles, ...	18,600	St. Petersburg,	520,131
2.	Grand duchy of Finland, divided into 8 provinces,	134,000	Helsingförs, ...	
3.	Esthonia, 4 circles, ..	7,224	Revel, ...	
4.	Livonia, 5 circles, ...	17,340	Riga, ...	72,136
5.	Courland, 5 bailiwicks, ...	10,000	Mitau, ...	

GREAT RUSSIA.

	Governments.	*Area in Sq. Miles.*	*Principal Town.*	*Population.*
6.	Moscow, 13 circles, ..	11,500	Moscow, ...	386,370
7.	Smolensk, 12 circles, ..	20,000	Smolensk, ...	
8.	Pskow, 8 circles, ...	21,960	Pleskow, ...	
9.	Tver, 12 circles, ...	23,560	Tver, ...	
10.	Novgorod, 10 circles, .	54,100	Novgorod, ...	
11.	Olonetz, 8 circles, ...	50,000	Petrozavodsk, .	
12.	Archangel, 7 circles, ..	320,000	Archangel, ...	
13.	Wologda, 10 circles, ..	161,000	Wologda, ...	
14.	Iaroslav, 10 circles, ..	17,000	Iaroslav, ...	
15.	Costroma, 10 circles, ..	30,000	Costroma, ...	
16.	Vladimir, 13 circles, ..	17,500	Vladimir, ...	
17.	Nischnei Novgorod, 11 circles, ...	20,180	Nischnei Novgorod, ...	
18.	Tambow, 12 circles, ..	24,200	Tambow, ...	
19.	Riäsan, 12 circles, ...	16,000	Riäsan, ...	
20.	Tula, 12 circles, ...	11,200	Tula, ...	57,705
21.	Kaluga, 11 circles, ...	10,560	Kaluga, ...	
22.	Orel, 12 circles, ...	17,830	Orel, ...	
23.	Kursk, 13 circles, ...	16,580	Kursk, ...	
24.	Woronesch, 12 circles,	29,400	Woronesch, ..	40,439

LITTLE RUSSIA.

	Governments.	*Area in Sq. Miles.*	*Principal Town.*	*Population.*
25.	Kiew, 12 circles, ...	16,800	Kiew, ...	60,682
26.	Czernigow, or Tschernigow, 12 circles, ..	20,000	Czernigow, or Tschernigow,	
27.	Poltava, 12 circles, ...	22,300	Poltava, ...	
28.	Slobodsk Ukraine, 12 circles, ...	29,000	Charkow, ...	45,156

SOUTH RUSSIA.

	Governments.	*Area in Sq. Miles.*	*Principal Town.*	*Population.*
29.	Ekatarinoslaf, 8 circles, ...	25,000	Ekatarinoslaf,	
30.	Cherson, ...	23,300	Cherson, ...	40,402
31.	Taurida, 6 circles with the country of the Tschernomorsk Cossacks, ...	22,500	Sympheropol,	
32.	Don Cossacks, ...	53,650	Staro Tscherkask, ...	
33.	Bessarabia, ...	16,800	Kischeneff, ...	85,547

WEST RUSSIA.

	Governments.	*Area in Sq. Miles.*	*Principal Town.*	*Population.*
34.	Wilna, 11 circles, ...	24,400	Wilna, ...	51,154
35.	Grodno, 8 circles, ...	14,000	Grodno, ...	
36.	Witepsk, 12 circles, ...	16,800	Witepsk, ...	
37.	Mohilew, 12 circles, ..	19,300	Mohilew, ...	
38.	Minsk, 10 circles, ...	37,000	Minsk, ...	
39.	Volhynia, 2 circles, ...	28,30[illegible]	Schitomir, ...	
40.	Podolia, 12 circles, ...	14,5[illegible]	Kaminiec, ...	
41.	Provinces of Bialystok,	3,400	[illegible]ialystok, ...	

KINGDOM OF POLAN[illegible]

	Governments.	*Area in Sq. Miles.*	*Principal Town.*	*Population.*
42.	Cracow, 4 circles, ...	4,800	Kielce, ...	
43.	Sandomir, 4 circles, ..	5,500	Sandomir, ...	
44.	Kalisch, 5 circles, ...	6,540	Kalisch, ...	
45.	Lublin, 4 circles, ...	6,650	Lublin, ...	18,304
46.	Plock, 6 circles, ...	6,500	Plock, ...	
47.	Masovia, 7 circles, ...	7,350	Warsaw, ...	162,777
48.	Podlachia, 5 circles, ..	7,250	Siedlce, ...	
49.	Augustowo, 5 circles, .	7,820	Augustowo, ..	

Previous to the ninth century A. D., the Europear territory of Russia was known only as a vast pla.n occupied by nomadic tribes similar to those which still traverse the vast steppes of Northern and Central Asia. The earliest history of these tribes, as far as it is now traceable, is given in our account of Tartary.

The restless Northmen navigated the gulfs which pierce far into these plains; and a Norman pirate chief, *Ruric*, cruising with his Varangians, in about the year 862, sailed through the Gulf of Finland, and, proceeding onward by lakes and rivers, discovered the native city of Novgorod — a collection of wooden huts, occupied by barbarian traders, who bartered various commodities for furs brought from the north. Having made himself master of this town, Ruric established himself here with his Norman followers, and took the title of *Grand Duke*. Other bands of his countrymen soon joined him, and finding himself possessor of a large territory, he divided it among his soldiers. He thus founded a state, which he named *Russia*,* and gave it Scandinavian laws. Another chief, one of his followers, at this time took possession of Kiev, or Kiew, whose people traded with Constantinople. This capital is thought by some to have been the residence of the Hyperborei, so renowned in classic lore for the virtues of the golden age. To this luxurious place *Igor*, son of Ruric, removed his capital; and the Normans soon had cruisers upon the Black Sea, who repeatedly attacked Constantinople.

The dukedom of Russia enlarged itself by conferring its new conquests, as feudal fiefs, upon chiefs, who extended them still further, and, founding cities, took the title of *dukes*, ruling over duchies dependent on the grand duke. *Vladimir the Great*, desirous of strengthening his alliance with the Greek emperor, asked the hand of his sister in marriage. It was granted on condition that the pagan duke would embrace the Christian faith; to which he consented, and, after his marriage, issued a decree ordering that all the heathen temples in his dominions should be destroyed, and Christian temples erected in their place. His subjects, too, were commanded to receive the rite of baptism, and, assembling in crowds on the banks of the rivers, were baptized, thousands at a time, by priests of the Greek church. Vladimir extended his empire over Lithuania, Livonia, and Galicia, founding cities and encouraging such of his subjects as were nomadic to become settled. The people of Russia were not, as in most feudal countries, merely nobles, serfs, and military vassals, but the towns were inhabited by free merchants, the country was tilled by free husbandmen, and the villages by a free and industrious peasantry, who labored for hire in the fields of those who were rich enough to have land. All these paid a tribute, or rather rent, in kind, to the noblemen on whose estates they resided, or to the grand duke, if the land was not appropriated. The army was composed of the nobles and their retainers, who were mostly of the Norman race. The traders and farmers were mostly descendants of the original inhabitants.

Vladimir died in 1015, and *Yaroslaf*, the most ferocious chief of his time, after defeating his brothers, reigned alone over a vast empire, which now stretched even to the confines of Hungary and Moldavia. Yaroslaf owed his success to an army of forty thousand men furnished him by Novgorod; for this city had now grown into a powerful commercial republic, both wealthy and populous. Their boastful saying was. "Who can resist God and the Great Novgorod!" The administration was conducted by a mayor, or burgomaster, and city councillors, called *boyars*, who were elected annually, as were also the governors of the provinces belonging to the state. Its duke had no power to act without the consent of the people, in declaring war, making peace, or levying new taxes. All such questions were decided in a general town meeting, called together by an enormous bell. Yaroslaf repaid the citizens, for their good service, in making some very wise laws; and he also founded a public school, in which three hundred children of the citizens were educated at his expense.

Russia was, at this period, as far advanced in civilization as the rest of Europe: Kiew, the capital, was a much finer city than either Paris or London. The inhabitants imitated the Greeks in their dress and style of living; used silver plate at their tables, drank the delicious wines of the Levant, gave sumptuous banquets, and furnished their houses in the luxurious manner of the East. The city is said to have contained three hundred churches.

Though frequently disturbed by civil wars and foreign invasions, little alteration took place in the interior organization of the country for two centuries. In 1223, however, a mighty host of Mongol Tartars, from the East, invaded the country, — weakened as it was by contests with the Greeks, Poles, and Hungarians, — ravaged it with ruthless violence from one end to the other, reduced its princes to abject subjection, and ruled over most of it for more than two hundred years, during which time Russia relapsed into a barbarism scarcely distinguishable from that of her conquerors. *Toushi*, son of Zingis Khan, as elsewhere related, routed the combined forces of all the Russian princes, on the banks of a river near the Sea of Azof, marched through the country, and, having enriched his army with spoil and numerous captives, returned to Asia. A few years later, his son *Batou* brought in another army, and completed the conquest, after six years of destructive warfare, in which Kiew, Moscow, and many other cities were laid in ashes. Plunder and tribute, not land and a settlement, were the sole objects of the Tartars. Their khan fixed his residence at Serai, on the Volga, surrounded by the Golden Horde, as his head-quarters were called; and established here the capital of his kingdom of Kipzak, whose history is noticed in our account of Tartary. Hence were sent out his deputies every year to collect the tribute, and hither each new grand duke was obliged to repair, to receive his investiture from the khan.

Novgorod, alone, preserved the right of electing her own rulers, though her duke paid tribute to the khan. One of these dukes was the renowned hero *St. Alexander Nevski*, who gained his fame by defending the capital from the combined armies of the Danes Swedes, and Teutonic knights; for Russia had all these enemies to contend with, beside the Tartars. He gave battle to the besiegers on the banks of the Neva, and, gaining a signal victory there, he received the name of *Nevski*, that is, "conqueror on the Neva,"

* The name is thought by some to be derived from a warlike tribe of Sarmatia, called *Ros* by the prophet Ezekiel, and afterward known to classical authors under the name of *Roxolani*, near the sources of the Tanais and Borysthenes. They frequently attacked the Roman frontiers. In A. D. 68, they surprised Mœsia; in 166, warred against the Marcomanni; and in 270, were triumphed over by the emperor Aurelian.

from the circumstance. About this time, the grand duke of Kiew was guilty of an act of rebellion, as the khan deemed it, in acknowledging the pope as head of the church, instead of the Greek patriarch. This grand duke's sister was married to the grand duke of Vladimir, who refused to pay tribute. The exasperated khan sent his armies to dethrone both, and gave their dominions to Alexander Nevski, with the title of *Grand Duke of Russia.* This monarch kept his country at peace, and employed his wealth in rebuilding its towns, and encouraging every good enterprise. He was rewarded by the grateful affections of the people, and at his death (A. D. 1261) was canonized. He is still revered as a saint, and a festival is held in honor of him. Novgorod, soon after his death joined the Hanseatic league.

For many years subsequent to the death of Alexander Nevski, perpetual warfare was kept up among the petty princes of the empire, each aspiring to the sovereignty, and each endeavoring to supplant the other with the khan, and gain his favor; so that there was as much political intrigue and party feeling at the barbarous court of the Golden Horde, as in the palaces of Christian princes. Meanwhile the capital was removed to Moscow, which was rebuilt, and the duchy named from it *Muscovy*, whence the Russians are called *Muscovites.* Kiew fell into the hands of the Lithuanians; the Poles, too, took several states from Russia. During these wars, many men left their homes, and carried away their wives and children into parts of the country that were uninhabited; and as their numbers were augmented by fresh refugees, they built villages, cultivated the land, and formed themselves into military republics. These people were called *Cossacks*, from Asiatic tribes of that name, with which they intermingled.

The Cossacks themselves are a mixed race of Caucasian and Tartar origin. We have spoken of those of Tartary in another place. Those of European Russia are named from their locations, Cossacks of the Don, of the Ukraine, and of the Black Sea. They are nearly independent, owing only military service to the czar. The houses of many of these people are delightfully situated in the midst of gardens; and at home they display many of the virtues of peace and simple pastoral and agricultural life. They are handsomer and taller than the Russians, whom they surpass also in honesty and dignity. Travellers describe them, at their capital, Tcherkask, as instructed, hospitable, generous, disinterested, humane, and tender to the poor. The Cossacks are well known in Europe as the most harassing light troops that ever exercised a predatory warfare in the train of an army. The capital of France has not yet forgotten the uncouth hordes, wrapped in sheepskin and overrun with vermin, who, in the hour of her humiliation, startled her streets with their wild demeanor. The Cossacks are governed by a vice-hetman, or headman, the eldest son of the emperor having the empty title of Hetman of the Cossacks.

Commerce flourished in Russia under the Tartar sway, and great fairs were held, which were frequented by merchants from Greece, Italy, and Asia. *Ivan I.* (A. D. 1320) was so rich, that he always had a purse of money carried before him, to distribute to the poor whom he met. *Demetrius*, surnamed *Donski*, from a victory gained by him over the Tartars, on the banks of the Don, was the first prince that attempted to expel the Tartars from the country; and he was finally unsuccessful. It was during his reign that Tamerlane, in retaliation of injuries, invaded the Kipzak empire, annexed it to his own, and, having revenged himself, passed through into its Russian provinces, and burnt Moscow, and other large towns, as elsewhere related.

In 1472, *Ivan Basilowitz*, or *Vasilievitz*, came to the throne, while Russia was still under the Tartar dominion. Like his predecessors, when an ambassador arrived from the haughty court of Kipzak, with despatches, he must ride out to meet him, and conduct him with all possible respect to the hall of state, where the most costly furs were spread for his seat, whilst the grand duke and his nobles were on their knees around him, listening in profound silence to the letters from their master. But Ivan was too proud to continue this; and when the khan's messengers arrived, he took the papers from their hands, tore them in pieces, and trampled them under his feet. He then expelled all the Tartar merchants from his capital, and prepared for war. He defeated the troops of the khan repeatedly, destroyed their head-quarters and all their settlements, and drove them from the country in about twenty years from his accession to the throne.

The fall of Novgorod occurred in the early part of this reign. A rich widow, desirous of raising a Lithuanian lover to the dukedom, bribed a strong party to revolt and dethrone the reigning duke, who applied to Ivan for aid. Ivan, contrary to their chartered rights, entered the city with a large army, seized merchandise, jewels, and money, and sent off the insurgent nobles to Moscow. On a fresh insurrection, he besieged and took the city, compelled the people to surrender their charter of liberties, and acknowledge him as their sovereign. The great bell he removed to Moscow, A. D. 1477. Novgorod now gradually declined and finally sunk into insignificance.

Ivan married, for his second wife, a Greek princess, *Zoe*, or *Sophia*, a niece of the last emperor of Constantinople, which had surrendered to the Turks about twenty-five years previously. The appearance of this beautiful and highly-educated young lady at his court, with a numerous suite of Greeks and Italians, made Ivan emulous to introduce the useful and elegant arts of Greece and Italy into Russia. Architects, founders, and miners were sent for, and that system of improvement begun which was so energetically and successfully carried out by Peter the Great. Ivan died in 1505.

Ivan IV., who came to the throne in 1533, pursued the plans of his grandfather. He assumed the title of *czar.* An English sea captain, having been driven into the White Sea, landed at Archangel, and came on to Moscow to ask that the English might trade at Archangel. As Ivan IV. had no port on the Baltic, but was obliged to use those of the Livonians, which might be shut against him at any time, he was glad to grant the captain's proposition. Great privileges were secured the English company who undertook this profitable trade. King Ivan was one of the suitors of Elizabeth, queen of England. In the early part of his reign, he organized a standing army called the *Strelitzes*, the first regular troops of Russia. His military power was also strengthened by the Don Cossacks, who voluntarily entered his service and helped him to conquer the provinces of Kasan and Astracan, so that the Caspian Sea was opened to a trade with Persia, which route was soon adopted by English merchants. In the latter part of this reign occurred the conquest of Siberia, as elsewhere stated.

Yet this Ivan, so intelligent and patriotic, treated the people of Novgorod with such cruelty, that he was called *Ivan the Terrible.* Ascertaining that they were in traitorous correspondence with the Poles, to surrender them the city, he hastened thither with his Strelitzes, closed the gates, and lined the streets with troops. A court, called the *Tribunal of Blood*, proceeded to try the delinquents. Every day, numbers were condemned by it and executed. Grief, horror, and despair reigned in every dwelling, for there was no escape, no means of resistance. The bloodthirsty despot thus raged for six weeks like an incensed tiger. Sixty thousand human beings are said to have fallen victims to his fury. Similar scenes of butchery were enacted in Tver, Moscow, and other cities.

This cruel disposition of Ivan was evident at a very early age. He was but thirteen years old when he assembled his *boyarins* to inform them that he needed not their guidance, and would no longer submit to their encroachments on his royal prerogative. "I ought to punish you all," he said, "for all of you have been guilty of offences against my person; but I will be indulgent, and the weight of my anger shall fall only on Andrew Schusky, who is the worst amongst you." Schusky, the head of a family which had seized the reins of government during the czar's minority, endeavored to justify himself. Ivan would not hear him. 'Seize and bind him," cried the boy despot, "and throw him to my dogs! They have a right to the repast." A pack of ferocious hounds, which Ivan took pleasure in rearing, were brought under the window, and irritated by every possible means. When they were sufficiently exasperated, Andrew Schusky was thrown amongst them. His cries increased their fury, and his body was torn to shreds and devoured.

All the most opulent citizens of Novgorod perished; but the city retained some importance, till Peter transferred its trade to St. Petersburg. The Poles, aided by the Crim Tartars, soon after took Moscow and burnt it, thousands of its inhabitants perishing in the conflagration. The former took refuge in a fortified monastery. But on emerging from his short retreat, his head, which had been covered with thick black curls, had become bald, his beard thin, his form emaciated, and his features wild and haggard. These were, perhaps, the effects of reflection on his murders at Novgorod; but he was more ferocious than ever, and, in a fit of passion or madness, killed his own son by striking him with an iron-headed staff. Remorse for this act hastened his death, which happened a few months afterward.

Until the time of Ivan I., the peasants of Russia were free; but slavery had been gradually on the increase, till at length the population of the country was made up chiefly of the nobles and their serfs. Yet it was not till a few years after the death of Ivan the Terrible, and in the reign of *Boris*, that the peasants were bound by law to the soil on which they were born; and it is remarkable that this degrading state of bondage should have begun in Russia, at the time when it was being gradually abolished in most other parts of Europe.

The weak *Feodor*, son and successor of Ivan IV., was the last of the race of Ruric. He intrusted the government entirely to his brother-in-law, *Boris Godoonoff*, an ambitious tyrant, who, in order to usurp the throne, murdered Demetrius, a younger brother of Feodor. Boris ascended the throne in 1598. His hated reign ceased in 1604. The state was troubled by the appearance of no less than seven persons who pretended to be Demetrius, escaped from his would-be murderers. The first of these, supported by Sandomir, king of Poland, succeeded to the throne. But his impolitic disregard of the religion of the people caused a tumult, in which he was killed. For seven years, the country, distracted by the other six pretenders, had no king. Moscow was plundered by the Poles, and Novgorod taken by the Swedes.

A few patriotic citizens, pledging life, property, wives, and children, to the cause, and headed by Prince Pojarski, and a butcher named Minin, resolved to save their country. Moscow was retaken, and *Michael Romanoff* was chosen czar.

CHAPTER CCCCLXVII.

A. D. 1604 to 1863.

Peter the Great — Catharine — Alexander — Nicholas — Alexander II.— Crimean War.

From the accession of this illustrious family, which still occupies the imperial throne, an entirely new character is impressed upon the history of Russia. From this time it ceases to be looked upon as an Asiatic and half-barbarous nation, and begins to be recognized as one of the European states. The young czar prudently bought peace with Sweden and Poland, by giving up a portion of territory to each; and during thirty-three years of a glorious reign, restored all the prosperity of the country. No prince was ever more beloved and respected. In 1645, his son *Alexis* succeeded him, a man of great talent and wisdom, who originated many of those plans which Peter the Great carried into effect. The Cossacks of the Ukraine offered him allegiance, and became an efficient military arm of the empire.

Feodor, son of Alexis, and his successor (A. D. 1676) engaged in the first war with the Turks, and abolished hereditary nobility. Disputes about precedency of family and privileges had troubled the court, and sometimes a noble would refuse to serve under another of less ancient family. The czar, therefore, ordered all the books containing pedigrees to be destroyed, and decreed that a soldier who had received a title for merit should rank with a noble of high birth, and above any one not in the army, even though he were a prince.

The accession of *Peter the Great*, (A. D. 1682,) another son of Alexis, forms a new era in Russian politics, industry, commerce, and manners. On the death of his brother Alexis, Peter was but ten years old, but his intellect was so superior to that of Ivan, his elder brother, that the two were declared joint sovereigns. The government was intrusted to a sister, Sophia, a princess of great beauty, talent, and accomplishments, but she abused her trust, and with her minister, Galitzin, was banished to Siberia. Peter, at the age of eighteen, entered vigorously upon his public duties.

The first care of the czar, now left free by the confirmed imbecility of his brother, was to build a navy, and equip an efficient army, that Russia might take the place in Europe which belonged to it. He sent some of the young nobility to Italy, Holland, and

Germany, to study the useful arts and sciences, and went himself and labored in the dock-yards of Holland, and visited those of England. Carefully preserved in the little house Peter occupied, on the Neva, there is still to be seen a boat which the czar made, with his own hands. It is called the *Little Grandfather*, as being the germ of the present powerful Russian navy.

The life and patriotic services of Peter are a theme for volumes. His faults were cruelty and despotism. Among his reforms we can only mention his efficient encouragement of the mechanic arts, then at the lowest ebb in Russia; the emancipation of females from a slavish degradation and Oriental seclusion, and their education as companions and equals with the males. He founded schools and universities; he altered the calendar to conform with that of the rest of Europe, and dated from the Christian era; he abolished the national costume; he repaired the roads and made new ones, established inns and post-offices upon them, and erected mile-stones; he dug canals connecting the great rivers, and had all the cities well lighted and watched. After a reign of forty-three years, in the last but one of which he crowned his empress, *Catharine I.*, as his successor, Peter the Great died A. D. 1724 — no modern prince having achieved so much in the same space of time. He had enlarged his empire first on the south, by the capture of Azof from the Turks, thus commanding the northern shore of the Black Sea and its ports. On the north-west, he had built St. Petersburg, to secure the commerce of the Baltic, and, by taking possession of Finland and Livonia, Ingria, and Carelia, gave his new capital a central position. On the Caspian, he had gained territories which secured much of the traffic of Persia, Tartary, and India. Through Siberia, also, he had opened a favorable intercourse with the wealthy empire of China.

Something of the solid character of this great prince may be learned from his conduct during a second journey for improvement to Western Europe. Louis XV. had made pompous preparations for his reception at Paris; but Peter, in the simplicity of true greatness, preferred lodging at a hotel. "I am a soldier," said he; "I want nothing but bread and beer: small rooms do very well for me, and I hate moving about in state, to tire so many people." He took care, however, to see all the famous manufactories of Paris, and visited the most eminent painters, sculptors, goldsmiths, and mathematical instrument makers, from whom he gained a great deal of valuable information. Always desirous of acquiring useful knowledge, he would frequently stop his carriage, when driving along the roads, and go into the fields to talk with the laborers, making them show him how they used their various implements, and taking sketches of such as were new to him. One day he happened to see a French priest working in his own field. "Look," said he, "at that good country parson: he produces cider and wine, and earns money with his own hands. Remind me of this when we are in Russia again; I will tell our priests of it."

Historians have vaunted the exploits and good deeds of Peter the Great, till his crimes and barbarities have been lost sight of in the glitter of panegyric. The monarch who could debase himself to the level of an executioner, beheading his rebel subjects with his own hand, and feasting his eyes with the spectacle of death when he himself was weary of slaying, — who could condemn his wife, repudiated without cause, to the frightful torture of the knout, and sign the order, which it is more than suspected he himself executed, for the death of his own son, — may have been great as a warrior and a legislator, but must ever be execrated as a man. Peter was certainly an extraordinary compound of vices and virtues. His domestic life will not bear even the most superficial investigation. The great reformer — we might almost say the founder — of the mighty empire of Russia, the conqueror of Charles of Sweden, was a drunkard and gross sensualist, a bad father, a cruel and unfaithful husband. Indeed, some of his acts seem inexplicable, otherwise than by that ferocious insanity manifest in more than one of his descendants. Even his rare impulses of mercy were apt to come too late to save the victim.

During Catharine's brief reign of two years, (A. D 1725–6,) the government was conducted chiefly by Menzikoff, who had been raised by Peter from a pastry cook's errand boy to be prime minister; a position he honored to the last. Thus the largest empire in Europe was ruled by two persons who had been the one a maid servant, the other an errand boy. *Peter II.* succeeded to the throne on the death of Catharine I., A. D. 1727. Menzikoff was banished, and his enemies, the old nobility, brought into power. But this reign closed in 1730, and *Anne*, duchess of Courland, a niece of Peter the Great, was made empress. She and the empire were both ruled by her tyrannical minister Biron, who is said to have banished at least twenty thousand persons to Siberia. But on the death of Anne, in 1740, who left him regent, he experienced this fate himself from certain conspirators. Another conspiracy, however, placed upon the throne *Elizabeth*, youngest daughter of Peter the Great, 1741. Her reign was prosperous; the court was maintained in great splendor; some of the nobles became the richest subjects in Europe; manufactures were improved, commerce flourished, and the beneficial effects of the progress of education were beginning to be perceived among the higher classes. *Peter III.*, nephew of Elizabeth, succeeded her at her death, in 1761; but as he made himself unpopular by attempting to introduce the Prussian discipline in the army, and other unpalatable reforms among the clergy and nobility his wife found means to raise a party against him. By these he was compelled to abdicate, and was then murdered, after a reign of less than six months, A. D. 1762. Peter's wife, *Catharine II.*, the daughter of a German prince, succeeded to the throne. He had married her at his aunt's desire, though both husband and wife had a great aversion for one another.

Catharine had a cultivated mind, and great energy and intelligence; but her private character, as a woman, was abominable. The leading events of her reign were the appointing a king of Poland; a war with the Turks, which gained her the Crimea, a large territory between the Bug and Dneister, and the free navigation of the Black Sea and Dardanelles; and a dreadful plague, which desolated Moscow. Nobles were also deprived of the power of putting their serfs to death; colonies of Germans were encouraged to settle on the waste lands of the empire; schools for girls were founded, and colleges for boys; and many other excellent institutions were established by this sagacious sovereign. A second war with the Turks was also successfully conducted by Prince Potemkin, the prime minister, general, and favorite of the czarina. It is said that, in his southern campaign, he was attended by an English gardener, with six hundred assistants, who carried numerous kinds of flowering shrubs and plants, and, keeping about a day's march in advance, formed a temporary garden on every spot where he chose to pitch his tent.

Paul succeeded his mother, Catharine II., in 1796. He liberated Kosciusko, and the rest of the Polish prisoners, and did several generous and just acts. He caused his father's body to be disinterred, and solemnly crowned the corpse—a ceremony that had not been performed during the life of Peter III. But he played the part of a suspicious tyrant, and the Russians were made to feel the dreadful annoyance of a minute despotism, whose spies seemed to be omnipresent. A conspiracy was formed, therefore, which put him to death in 1801, and elevated his eldest son, *Alexander*, to the throne.

Alexander was a mild, beneficent, and talented sovereign; anxious to promote the welfare of his country, but not without the ambition that makes a powerful ruler dangerous to his neighbors. He came to the throne at a critical period. The ukase, or royal decree, issued at his coronation, forbade the nobles from selling their serfs, without, at the same time, selling the land on which they were settled. Another law secured to every man the fruits of his own labor. Still another gave to every freeman permission to purchase land. Common schools were established for the education of the mass of the people; but the catechism taught in them, adopting the Asiatic idea of a ruler, bids the children and people look to the czar as God's vicegerent on earth, with almost blasphemous reverence.

The refusal of the emperor Alexander to enforce Napoleon's continental system, which inflicted great injuries on Russian commerce, finally led to a rupture with France. Foreseeing the storm, the czar spent the year 1811 in making preparations for the event. Napoleon did not wait to be attacked in his own dominions. He issued a declaration of war against Russia, and, on the 24th of June, 1812, entered the enemy's territory, and advanced toward Moscow. After severe fighting, the French army beheld, for the first time, the ancient capital of Russia. There lay the city before them, with its lofty steeples, its palaces imbosomed in delightful groves, and its copper domes glittering in the sun. But all was silent as the desert. Napoleon waited two hours, when he received the strange intelligence that Moscow was deserted by its inhabitants. The French troops entered the city, wondering at the silence and solitude which every where reigned. But this stillness was soon interrupted. The Russian governor, before leaving, had set the city on fire in several places, and the flames spread with frightful rapidity. The French fled before this new and unexpected enemy. The streets were arched with fire, and the hot air was suffocating. For four days, the flames remained undisputed master of the city, and consumed what it had cost centuries to raise. Winter was now approaching, and the Russian armies threatened to cut off all communication with France. There was no hope of safety but in a hasty retreat. On the 18th of October, the French army quitted Moscow. The history of this retreat is a record of the most dreadful calamities and sufferings. Men and horses perished by thousands, and the proud army of near half a million of men were buried in the snow, save a miserable remnant which followed their fugitive leader to France.

The result of this last effort of Napoleon proved that Russia might rely for safety on the patriotism of her people and the severity of her climate. After the battle of Waterloo, Poland was annexed to Russia, with a separate government, and Alexander was crowned as its king. The rest of the ten years of his life the emperor spent in laudable exertions for the benefit of his people. Yet he could not remedy a tithe of the evils springing from so many ages of despotism. A system of corruption which he endeavored to check, reigned from the pettiest post-office to the highest functionary; and Alexander died, in 1825, a disappointed man—his last days imbittered by the knowledge of a conspiracy which aimed to separate the empire into a number of independent states.

Alexander left the throne to his brother *Nicholas;* but a number of the soldiers declared for an elder brother, Constantine, whom Alexander knew to be too violent of temper to be intrusted with the government. The decision and moderation of Nicholas triumphed, though not without bloodshed. He was soon acknowledged as emperor, and duly crowned at Moscow, with imposing ceremonies. Constantine was made viceroy of Poland, where his misconduct caused an insurrection. Goaded by his tyranny and gross infraction of the constitution, a general insurrection took place at Warsaw, A. D. 1830. This was repressed by Russia, after a campaign of frightful devastation and bloodshed, September, 1831. Many thousands of Poles, of all ranks and conditions, were doomed to hopeless exile in Siberia, and thousands became wanderers over the face of the earth. The kingdom was incorporated with Russia, and has ever since been governed as a conquered province. This event, which outraged the moral sense of the civilized world, is but an example of that stern Asiatic despotism which has long governed the emperors of Russia.

During Alexander's reign, a successful war had been carried on against Persia; and, not long after the accession of Nicholas, another war broke out, owing to a dispute respecting boundaries. These contests are noticed in our history of Persia. The Persians were defeated in several battles, and their shah, Abbas Mirza, was glad to make peace in 1828, by giving up an extensive territory on the south-western shore of the Caspian Sea, in addition to the provinces of the Caucasus, which had been ceded to the emperor Alexander.

The Turkish war of 1829 arose from the interested interference of Russia, to promote the independence of Greece. The Russian armies passed the Balkan, and, after several victories, dictated terms of peace at Adrianople. The Greeks were declared free, and all Circassia was given to Russia. But the Circassians, who had been left at liberty by the Turks, being only obliged to pay an easy tribute, resisted this transfer of their allegiance, which Russia, with accustomed disregard of right, has been in vain endeavoring to enforce since 1829, as stated in our account of Circassia.

The Khivan war has been noticed in our history of Independent Tartary. Khiva, being directly on the route of the Russian trade with India, exacted heavy tolls, and enslaved and otherwise annoyed the Russian merchants. The people carried off Russian colonists, who had been likewise settled near the Caspian, and invaded the Kirghis tribes, under the dominion of Russia, exacting tribute of some, and exciting others to revolt. Hence, in 1839, the czar declared war against Khiva. One campaign failed in consequence of the difficulties of the deserts of Tartary; but, in a second, he succeeded, after a tremendous battle, (A. D. 1841,) in taking possession of the capital of the marauding Khivans. Thousands of captives, who had been kidnapped from Persia and Russia, were released, and caravans now pass unmolested, and their goods are free from tolls.

One of the most prominent events in the recent history of Russia, was that of her interference in the struggle between Austria and Hungary, 1848–9. The ostensible motive for this was the preservation of the integrity of the Austrian empire, guaranteed by the congress of Vienna; the real motive to check the march of liberal ideas, and crush the rising efforts of the enslaved millions of Europe for liberty. The events of the Hungarian campaign created a profound sensation throughout the world, and excited reflections reaching quite beyond the rights and interests of the gallant people thus trampled in the dust. The actual power of Russia, the genius and tendency of the government, and the particular character of the ruling sovereign, hence became subjects of the deepest interest with reflecting men.

From the period of the overthrow of Napoleon, Russia has been rapidly rising in political importance. Alexander I. was at the head of the Holy Alliance which was entered into by Russia, Austria, Prussia, and France, avowedly to suppress revolutionary principles. Nicholas after the agitations of 1848, became the head of the new Holy Alliance, and the main hope of legitimacy. He was doubtless entitled to this position, from the vast extent of his territory, the populousness of his empire, the facility with which his subjects were brought to execute his will, and the poitical and personal devotion to despotism he has manifested.

The history of Russia, for several centuries, has shown an unrelaxing spirit of encroachment, resulting in a constant accession of territory. No sense of right, no regard to principle, stands in the way of her march toward dominion and power. Whoever has ruled in Russia, the same policy has been pursued, as if destiny presided over the affairs of the empire. To their own subjects, while submissive and slavish, the czars have often been benignant and paternal; but toward those who showed the spirit of independence, or asserted the right to think and act for themselves, their vengeance has ever been remorseless as that of the tiger. Hence Russia has seemed to wear two faces; that of a benignant civilizer toward Asia, because the Asiatics, trained to submission, have licked the hand of their master; while toward Europe it has worn the malignant scowl of despotism, because Europeans have sometimes ventured to dream of personal liberty and national independence. The late Emper r Nicholas, combined in a remarkable degree, these opposite characteristics. He seemed desirous of promoting the prosperity of his people, and was frequently eulogized as being a good father and a good husband. His ambition, however, brought upon him a fearful retribution. He had long bent his greedy eye upon Turkey, and in 1853, as elsewhere related, (see p. 822,) entered upon a course of measures doubtless designed to subjugate and dismember that empire. This roused the jealousy of France and England, and brought on the Eastern war, which resulted in the humiliation of Russia.

While this conflict was raging, Nicholas was called to his final account—March, 1855—and hi son, Alexander, became his successor. A peace was agreed upon by a Congress at Paris, in March, 1856. Alexander II., as if to show that his empire had not been prostrated by the war, was crowned at Moscow, September, 1856, with amazing splendor—the expenses of the ceremonial reaching eleven millions of dollars!

Sovereigns of Russia.

Date of Accession. A. D.	GRAND DUKES.	Date of Accession. A. D.	
862.	Rurick.	1676.	Feodor, or Theodore
955.	Olga, regent.	1682.	Ivan V.
988.	Vladimir the Great.	1696.	Peter I.
1156.	Jurie, or George I.	1725.	Catharine I.
1157.	Andrew.	1727.	Peter II.
1395.	Tartar invasion.	1730.	Anne.
1474.	Ivan, or John III. (Basilowitz.)	1740.	Ivan VI.
	CZARS, OR KINGS.	1741.	Elizabeth.
1534.	Ivan IV.		*Family of Holstein.*
	House of Romanoff.	1762.	Peter III.
1613.	Michael Feodorowitz.	1762.	Catharine II.
1645.	Alexis.	1796.	Paul.
		1801.	Alexander.
		1825.	Nicholas.
		1855.	Alexander II.

CHAPTER CCCCLXVIII.

St. Petersburg—Laws of Russia, &c.

THIS renowned city, the modern capital of the Russian empire, founded by Peter the Great in 1703, at the influx of the Neva into the Gulf of Finland, is twenty miles east of Cronstadt. It stands chiefly on the south branch of the river, but partly also on some islands formed by the divergence of the stream. Three-fourths of it, however, are on the main land. Being situated on a flat and marshy soil, it is difficult o drainage, and is subject to destructive inundations Many of the houses are constructed of wood. Its noble public buildings, the breadth of its principal thoroughfares, and its large squares, render it one of the most imposing cities of Europe. The principal channel of the Neva is bordered by quays of granite, and on the side of the main land with a series of magnificent structures. The palaces and public monuments are among the most splendid in the world.

Moscow is nearly in the centre of European Russia, and was its ancient capital. It covers a circular area, and consists of the Kremlin, or citadel, surrounded with other quarters, the whole inclosed by walls, outside of which there are extensive suburbs. The ancient Kremlin, the residence of the czars in former times, has been replaced by the new Kremlin, completed in 1850, which is a magnificent structure, including several palaces and many fine works of art. The church of Ivan Veleki has a belfry 269 feet in height. The great bell, the largest in the world, twenty-one feet high and twenty feet in diameter, weighing 3,500,000 pounds, long buried under the soil, was raised and hung on a pedestal in 1836. Moscow is the residence of the most ancient and wealthy nobility of Russia. The manufactures are varied and extensive. It is connected by a railway with St. Petersburg. In 1812 it was occupied by Napoleon and his invading army, but the Russian general caused it to be set on fire, and thus forced the

French emperor to that retreat which at last issued in his overthrow.

Besides St. Petersburg and Moscow, there are no other towns or cities in Russia of very large population. Riga, on the Duna, is strongly fortified, and is a place of considerable commerce. Kiew, a place of great antiquity, is now the capital of Little Russia; Odessa, on the Black Sea, is noted for its commerce: Sebastopol, in the Crimea, is renowned for its protracted defence by the Russians against the allied French and English forces, in the war of 1854–5.

The laws of Russia consist of a number of ukases, or decrees, amounting to many thousands, put forth, from time to time, by its sovereigns, and are simply the declarations of the emperor's will, such being the only laws by which the country is governed. There is no parliament, and the senate, of sixty-two members, merely registers and promulgates the ukases, and gives its advice; it has no real independent political authority. The emperor may choose to consult his ministers, but he cannot be controlled by them, and is as much the master of his subjects as the noble is of his serfs, and can as easily deprive them of their lives, liberty, or property.

Next to despotism, slavery has been the greatest curse of Russia. Nicholas set the example of emancipating the peasants in 1839 by freeing all the serfs upon the crown lands, who have been, since then, free tenants. Twenty million serfs remained, and on the 3d of March, 1861, Alexander II. promised them their liberty in two years, under certain conditions. The promise was kept, and on the 3d of March, 1863, slavery ceased in Russia, great rejoicings taking place in the empire. The nobles have maintained that the serfs did not wish to be free, as they would then have to provide for themselves. If this is true, bondage has indeed entered their souls. It has done its worst work, if it has eradicated the instinct of independence, the germ of progress and only basis of private or public virtue. The same struggle seems to be going on in Russia, indeed, which, in remote ages, brought China, and, in modern times, Europe, out of the disastrous condition of feudalism. The emperors seem to be endeavoring to reduce the power of the nobles, and promote monarchism, which, by centralization of power, shall mould the empire into one homogeneous and progressive mass. Hence men are promoted from the ranks to be officers of the army, and an officer is placed on a par with a noble. Hence cities are incorporated and endowed with privileges; merchants and mechanics are honored with trusts, and encouraged by immunities; and serfs, who escape from their masters, are not delivered up. The design of this is to build up a middling class, who, holding the purse-strings of the nation, and grateful to their benefactor, shall form the left arm of his power, while his standing army forms the right. Thus far, the talents of the last two emperors have enabled them to make head against the old nobility; but, unhappily, their despotism leads them to absorb in the crown the power they take from the nobles. The effective military force of Russia is about eight hundred thousand men; but this is capable of almost indefinite increase. The navy consisted, in 1862, of 248 steamers and 62 sailing vessels, carrying 3,691 guns. The annual expenditure of the government is about 300,000,000 rubles, or $225,000,000.

Among the barbarous punishments inflicted by the government is that of banishment to Siberia.

Cossacks of the Don.

Costumes of the Bashkirs.

Tartars of the Crimea.

The laws of the empire require that all persons condemned to this must pass through Moscow on their way; and scarce a week elapses that does not witness a melancholy train of these exiles. Heavy rings, attached together by a strong chain, about two feet long, are riveted on the ankles of the men,—whether murderers, thieves, patriots, criminals civil or political, noble or simple,—and, thus encumbered, they have to perform, on foot, a journey that occupies six months. They are also chained together, in fours, by the wrists, and are escorted by a guard of soldiers, mounted and well armed. The female convicts walk together, not chained, but guarded; and the women who are not convicts, but wives of the male prisoners, ride in carts, with their children and baggage. A too freely spoken opinion may subject the most refined, educated, and excellent person, male or female, to this dreadful doom. On arriving at Tobolsk, the exiles are mostly well treated. The worst of the criminals are condemned to the mines,—the highest degree of punishment,—where they are shut out forever from the light of day, the air of heaven, and the sympathy of their fellow-creatures.

It remains only to notice the languages and literature of the Russians, and their character. But we must first remark that about eighty different idioms are spoken in Russia.* The Russian language is formed upon the Sclavonic. At least ten thousand works are now printed in it, and it is spoken by about forty millions. The czars have made great efforts to introduce literature, and, latterly, a national literature in particular. The chief scientific glory of Russia arises, it is said, from the names of Pallas, Gmelin, Euler, Bernouilli, and other Germans, whom Catharine's bounty induced to reside at St. Petersburg. French literature has, however, always been most fashionable among the nobles. Lomenosoff and Sumorokoff rank as the greatest Russian poets; and Karamsin, by his belles-lettres writings, has obtained a fame beyond even the wide bounds of his own country. The sciences have been liberally and successfully patronized by the emperors; and the scientific establishments and libraries are munificently supported.

The Russian character displays itself in its two extremes, that of the semi-barbaric nobles, and that of the serfs; for the middle class is yet but in embryo. The basis of the sixty millions of the Russian population is entirely Sclavonic; a race distinguished by a peculiar language; by a patient, cheerful, hardy obstinate, and enduring character; by a very limited extent of intellectual culture, and of the characteristics which raise man above the brute. This last deficiency is the consequence of long ages of bondage and oppression, and of the insulated position of this people, in the heart of their vast, monotonous steppes and deserts, removed from all the impulses which have rendered the western nations so enlightened and energetic. Cleanliness is not a Russian virtue. The Russians are admirably fitted for soldiers, and make thoroughly disciplined and most formidable troops.

Over three millions of the people of European Russia are of the Finnish race; Tartars inhabit the Crimea, and some of the southern steppes, and Bashkirs, a Tartar race, the south-eastern part of the country.

Poland.

CHAPTER CCCCLXIX.

Geographical Sketch—Annals of Poland.

POLAND, or "the plains," at the time of its greatest extent, embraced an area of country which now has a population, probably, of twenty millions.† But since 1832, it has ceased to exist as an independent state.

The Poles formed part of the great Sclavonic family, which stretched from the Baltic to the Adriatic, and from the Elbe to the mouth of the Dnieper. But from what particular Asiatic tribe the nation is descended, it is impossible to determine: they are probably a mixture arising from the amalgamation of natives with successive hordes of invaders from Asia. The kindred relation, through a common origin, of the Poles and Russians is striking: it is fainter among the Hungarians, from their incorporation with the Huns of Attila, and among the Bohemians, from their long intercourse with the Teutonic nations.

Prior to the ninth century, the Poles were but a multitude of independent tribes, each under its chief, or *palatine*, who combined under one leader or duke, in case of invasion. These tribes dwelt in a region bounded by Prussia and the Carpathian Mountains, the Bug and the Oder, and especially along the Vistula. Their old writers assure us that these tribes were descended from one of the immediate posterity of Noah, who settled this part of ancient Sarmatia.

Among the strange legends which enliven the early annals of this nation, it is related that one of its sovereign dukes,—*Popiel II.*,—after filling the country with debaucheries and cruelty, at length treacherously poisoned his uncles, who headed the people in an attempt to set bounds to his enormities. He would not even allow their corpses to be buried. But a horrible punishment was prepared for him by that Providence he had so long outraged. From the unburied corpses sprang a countless multitude of rats, of an enormous size, which immediately filled the palace

* Beside those of Siberia, these are as follows: the *Russian*, or Sclavonic; the *Finnic*, in Finland and Lapland; the *East Finnic*, separated by five hundred miles of territory, and bordering the Ural;—it has eight dialects, mingling the Turkish with the Finnic;—the *Esthonian*; the *Livonian*; the *Lithuanian*; the *Polish*; the *Slovac*; the *Wallachian*; the *Cossack*; the *Turkish*, with its four dialects of the (so called) Tartars of Kasan, properly Turks, and the most civilized of the Asiatic races; another dialect, spoken by some thirty thousand people mingled with the Bashkirs; the *Bashkir* dialect, spoken by some two hundred thousand people of a mingled Turkish, Mongol, and Finnic race, the guardians of the frontiers of Orenburg; the *Nogai Tartar* dialect, spoken by a remnant of the tribes who remained behind, in 1772, when their fellows migrated from between the Black and Caspian Seas to Soongaria, upon the invitation of China; the *Kalmuck*, a Mongol language, spoken by Mongols, who took the place they vacated. Beside all these, there are the *Turkish*, the *Armenian*, numerous dialects of the Caucasus, and the idioms of the many Germans, Italians, Jews, Greeks, &c., who are found in various parts of European Russia.

† Poland once included old Polish Prussia, Posen, Galicia, Cracow, the kingdom of Poland, Russian Poland, and Courland. In ancient times, Hungary was sometimes governed by the same king, and also Bohemia.

and sought out the guilty Popiel, his avaricious and malignant wife, and their children. In vain were great numbers destroyed; greater swarms advanced. In vain did the ducal family enclose themselves in a circle of fire; the boundary was soon passed by the ferocious animals, which, with unrelenting constancy, aimed at them, and them alone. They fled to another element, which availed them as little. The rats followed them to a neighboring lake, plunged into the water, gnawed into the sides of the vessel, and would have sunk it, had not Popiel landed on an island. In vain: his inveterate enemies were on shore as soon as he. His attendants now recognized the hand of Heaven, and left him to his fate. Accompanied by his wife and children, he fled to a neighboring tower; he ascended the highest pinnacle: still they followed; neither doors nor bars could resist them. His two sons were devoured first, then the duchess, then himself; and so completely, that not a bone remained of the four.

The authentic history of the Poles hardly reaches farther back than *Miecislas I.*, a feudatory of the German emperor Otho I. He was converted to Christianity, with his subjects, in A. D. 965. To a race addicted, as the Poles had been from time immemorial, to drunkenness, sensuality, rapes, plunder, and bloodshed, even at their entertainments, the severe morality of the gospel must have seemed a tyranny: especially irksome were its restraints to a people swayed by that impatience which is so characteristic of the Sclavonic nations. In fourteen years, however, Christianity gained the entire ascendency, being urged by the power of the king, and assisted by devoted missionaries, among whom was the renowned St. Adelbert. Miecislas himself owed his conversion to a circumstance not without its parallel in the history of the christianization of several nations. He had asked the hand of Dombrowka, daughter of the king of Hungary, in marriage; but both father and daughter refused so near a connection with a pagan. The duke therefore procured instructors in the Christian religion, was baptized and married on the same day, and issued an order for the destruction of the idols throughout his dominions.

In the year 1001, Poland became a kingdom under *Boleslas I.*, the successor of Miecislas, and the country came out successfully from its wars with Bohemia, the German empire, and Muscovy, its territory being greatly increased, and its power rendered formidable. The latter part of the life of this able sovereign was devoted to the good of his people. In the reign of *Boleslas II.*, the Poles were again at war with the Bohemians, Hungarians, and Muscovites. Being in possession of the luxurious capital of the latter, Kiev, the nobles who had followed their king to the wars, immersed in pleasure, seemed to have forgotten their deserted homes. Under these circumstances, most of their wives are said to have married with the serfs left in charge of the estates. A strange state of things ensued when the nobles finally returned: some of the wives were punished: but, conscious of equal guilt, most of the recreant husbands forgave their faithless partners, contenting themselves with punishing the serfs, and enslaving the spurious children.

Another enormity which occurred in this reign was the murder of St. Stanislas, bishop of Cracow. He had ventured mildly to expostulate with the king on his vices and excesses; but as this did not check them, he proceeded to excommunicate him, and finally laid the churches of the capital, Cracow, under an interdict. The king, exasperated, went to a chapel in the country, where Stanislas was officiating, and waiting till the worship was done, sent in his guards to assassinate him. This they attempted repeatedly, but were overawed. The king himself then entered the chapel, and with one blow of his ponderous weapon dashed out the brains of the faithful priest. The pope, Gregory VII., deposed the king for this foul deed, who died a fugitive and exile.

During many ages of violence, Poland offers the same scenes which form the dark history of the middle ages elsewhere. Sometimes the king was the tyrant; sometimes the nobles usurped all his power and again anarchy, wild and murderous, distracted the wretched country. A few bright spots, however, relieve the general gloom. One of these was the reign of *Casimir the Just*, in 1178, who reformed abuses, and sedulously devoted himself to the happiness of his people. In the early part of the thirteenth century, the wars of Poland with the Teutonic knights ended in the settling of many of them in Polish territory — a useful guard to the frontier. At the end of the century, the horrid state of anarchy which followed the death of *Lesko the Black*, seemed about to erase Poland from the list of nations; but it was put an end to through the election of the excellent *Prezemislas* as king, by the nobles and clergy, A. D. 1295. He built a wooden wall round Dantzic, the first instance of fortification in Poland. He applied his great wisdom promptly and well; but the evils of three centuries' growth were not easily eradicated. He was soon assassinated, and his successor, *Uladislas*, was obliged to ally himself with the Lithuanians against the Teutonic knights. These pagans had enslaved some twenty-four thousand Polish prisoners; and when the hand of the daughter of the duke of Lithuania was given to Uladislas to confirm the alliance, these were released and sent back to their country as the welcome dowry of the bride.

Casimir III., justly surnamed the *Great*, came to the throne in 1333. He restored peace to his country, and destroyed the lawless bands of robbers which infested it; improved the towns by introducing brick and stone for buildings, in lieu of wood and straw; made good roads and wise laws; and gave the peasantry the rights of property, and power to leave their masters on just causes of complaint. He encouraged trade by conferring privileges on the Jews, thus attracting many of them to Poland, where they still form a numerous class. So rich had they become in Cracow, — which had taken the place of Gnesna as the capital, — that on the marriage of Casimir's niece, one of them requested the honor of making her a wedding present, and sent her a sum of money equal to the dowry given her by her uncle. As Casimir had no children, he wished his nephew, *Louis*, king of Hungary, to succeed him; and the nobles, as it made the throne elective instead of hereditary, consented; but not till Louis had signed a deed promising that all Poles of noble birth should be released from taxes, and all offices should be given to native Poles. With Casimir and Louis ended the Piast dynasty.

On the death of Louis, his daughter *Hedwiga*, though betrothed to another, felt obliged, for her country's sake, to espouse Jagello, grand duke of Lithuania, — who was so desirous of the match, that he professed Christianity, and abolished paganism throughout his dominions, this being the only condition she exacted. Handsome, courteous, and of princely demeanor, the Lithuanian, baptized by the name of *Uladislas V.*, founded the Jagellon dynasty, which ruled Poland for several centuries. His son *Uladislas VI.* succeeded him, and, after passing through the usual troubles of a minority, was elected to the throne of Hungary. He became involved in a war with the Turks, under Amurath II., whose court was at Adrianople. Heading a vast army, the king, aided by Huniades, gained several victories over the Turks, with whom he made an advantageous peace, to continue ten years; but the pope persuaded him to break his contract, and, taking the field again, he was killed in the battle of Varna, A. D. 1444, at the age of twenty.

Casimir IV., his successor, aided by a revolt of many cities and nobles of Prussia and Pomerania, overthrew the dominion of the Teutonic knights, in a ruinous twelve years' war, in which three hundred thousand men are said to have fallen, and seventeen thousand villages and hamlets to have been burnt! On his accession, this prince refused to swear to observe the usual conditions. Compelled to be present at the Polish diets, the king was there reproached as a tyrant and traitor; but he bore their vociferations and howls of execration with provoking coolness. Finally, the chief nobility met, and in his presence resolved to depose him if he persisted in his obstinacy. He yielded, and from this moment, A. D. 1445, Poland was a species of republic — the name she already began to assume; and her kings were but the lieutenants of the diet. During this reign, a further modification of the government was introduced, in the appointment, by the nobles, of deputies, as their representatives in the diet, who received instructions from their constituents how to vote, and could not do otherwise than obey.

Sigismund I., who came to the throne in 1506, was one of the best of sovereigns; and during his long reign, the Poles enjoyed more prosperity than they had ever before known; for he patronized learning and industry, and preferred the glories of peace to those of war. At the Reformation, there was very little opposition made by the Polish government to the new religion; for Sigismund, after having vainly endeavored, by severe measures, to stop its progress, wisely gave up the attempt, contenting himself with excluding Protestants from all public offices. At this period, there were no less than fifty printing presses in Cracow alone, and books were printed in more than eighty towns in the kingdom. It was the only country where the liberty of the press was allowed. Copernicus, the astronomer, was a contemporary of Sigismund; he was born at Thorn, then in Poland, but now in Prussia.

With *Sigismund Augustus* ended the race of the Jagellos, A. D. 1572. The crown now became entirely elective, without reference to hereditary descent. An election was a matter of great excitement. All the palatines and chief nobility from every quarter of the kingdom, armed and on horseback, repaired to Warsaw, which had become the capital, each attended by a numerous train of vassals, consisting of all the gentlemen in his palatinate. The city and its environs presented an animated scene, and not unfrequently swords were drawn in support of the claims of different candidates, who were not allowed to be present themselves. In a temporary building on the plains of Vola, near Warsaw, the *pacta conventa*, or chartered conditions for the signature of the sovereign, were drawn up; and to these additions were made at the election of every new sovereign, till the king had scarcely a prerogative left him.

On the day of election, troops of horsemen assembled on the plain, which, though twelve miles in circumference, was hardly large enough. The senate and nuncios took their seats, and the nobles of each palatinate were ranged in separate bodies under their respective banners. The names of the several candidates were then declared by the archbishop, who, kneeling on the plain, repeated a prayer, and afterward went round on horseback to collect the votes, which were counted in the senate; and that prince for whom the most votes had been given, was immediately proclaimed king of Poland.

About the middle of the seventeenth century, a dangerous innovation was introduced into the diet, by which any member could stop its proceedings, prevent the passing of any law, and even dissolve the assembly, by his single "veto." To this absurd custom, so pregnant with disorders, many Polish writers attribute the ruin of their country.

But the evil lay deeper. There was no middle class of society — the only palladium of liberty in a monarchical country. The power of the nobles to quarrel with each other, or to tyrannize over the slaves upon their estates or simply to vote for a puppet king, could not be called liberty. Poland had only serfs, plunged in ignorance, and doomed to hopeless drudgery on the one hand, and nobles full of false pride, and buried in selfishness and luxury, on the other. The political evils of Poland, in ancient and modern times, may be traced directly or indirectly to this state of society.

During the unhappy reign of *John Casimir*, (1649 to 1668,) intercourse with France had introduced the elegances of civilized life into Poland; but the destructive wars with the Cossacks and Tartars injured commerce and retarded the progress of education.

John Sobieski, greatly renowned as a general, was elected king in 1674. After his death, there was an interregnum of a year, which showed the weakness of the kingdom. *Frederic Augustus I.* was elected king in 1697. Having allied himelf with Peter the Great against Charles XII. of Sweden, the latter overran Poland, and deposed its king, A. D. 1705; and in 1710, raised *Stanislas* to the throne, which had been vacant for five years. Civil war, pestilence, and anarchy, now afflicted Poland: the same year Frederic Augustus I. was restored by the diet at Warsaw. During his reign, a petty quarrel between some Lutheran children and a Jesuit student became the cause of mobs; a partial commission condemned the Protestants, who were punished by the diet in a most sanguinary manner, with circumstances of wanton barbarity, which disgraced the republic. This reign, which was one series of disasters, terminated in 1733.

At the next election, sixty thousand votes would have restored to the throne the philosophic Stanislas, now king of Lorraine, and father-in-law of Louis XV.; but the political destinies of Poland were no longer within the control of her leaders. Austria and Muscovy, with an arbitrary disregard of international law, not uncommon with those powers, forced the Poles to receive *Frederic Augustus II.* as king. His chief employments were hunting and smoking: to business of every description he had a mortal aversion. At his death, in 1763, Catharine II. of Russia took upon herself to choose the new king, and fixed

, a young Polish nobleman, said to have been a ·mer lover of hers, Count *Stanislas Augustus Pon-'owski*, whom she put upon the throne. Her reply the dissatisfied Poles was, "I wish him to be king, d king he shall be." Ten thousand Russian soldiers Warsaw enforced her imperial will, A. D. 1763. either the king nor diet was allowed any power; d in 1772, as elsewhere related, Russia, Prussia, d Austria took most of the kingdom to themselves. he amiable Poniatowski exerted himself to benefit at part of Poland which was left to him, and which, 1793 was reduced to a very small compass by a ew partition of most of its territory between Russia d Prussia. Population, in 1860, 4,764,446.

Kosciusko.

This tyranny roused the patriotic Poles to attempt e salvation of their country, under Count Thaddeus osciusko, who had served with honor in the American volutionary war, and who now sought to be the deliv-er of Poland. Cracow expelled the Russian gar-son, and a national council proclaimed Kosciusko ctator. But after some successes, a body of forty ousand Prussians, under Frederic William III., rned the tide of victory, and crushed the hopes of e patriots forever. Poniatowski was compelled to dicate his crown, and the remnant of Poland was vided between Russia, Austria, and Prussia. Thus nded this once powerful monarchy. Napoleon alone ould have restored it to life, and seems to have so esigned; but his retreat from Moscow sealed the fate f the project. In 1830, as we have already stated, a volt of the Poles against the violations of their con-itution, and other acts of tyranny on the part of e Russian Archduke *Constantine*,—though it gave occasion for the display of a noble patriotism,—only riveted the chains of Poland. She was now incorporated into Russia, thousands of her patriots were transported to Siberia, and the country was reduced to the condition of a conquered province.*

Early in 1863, the Poles made another effort to regain their independence. A relentless conscription for the Russian army was the immediate occasion of this uprising. At the present moment, the great powers of Europe, though not likely to give the Poles material aid, are strengthening them by their sympathy, and it is possible that Russia may restore Poland to something like her former position, with a sovereign taken from the family of the Czar.

Republic of Cracow.—This consisted of the city of that name, the second capital of Poland, with its territory, containing about four hundred and ninety square miles, and one hundred and ninety thousand inhabitants—lying upon the Vistula. In 1815, the congress of Vienna, in plundering Poland for the last time, could not agree whether Cracow should belong to Russia, Prussia, or Austria. They, therefore, guarantied its neutrality and inviolability as a republic, on condition that it should not harbor any who were obnoxious to either of the three powers. Its legislative assembly was composed of representatives annually chosen by the people at large, to whom were added six members for the church, and three of the senate, one of the latter presiding. It now flourished for thirty years as the active centre of a valuable commerce. But Austria, under pretence that Cracow was the resort of political agitators, crushed this republic—the last remnant of Polish independence—in 1846, and took the territory to herself, France, England, and Russia quietly submitting.

Warsaw, the capital of Poland, is situated in a vast sandy plain, on the Vistula. The city is, in general, meanly built, but in the suburbs there are handsome government buildings, with a university, and a number

---

* *Sovereigns of Poland.*

Dukes.

Date of Accession. A. D.

560. Lech I.
 Lech II.
750. Wenda, queen.
 Lesko I.
804. Lesko II.
810. Lesko III.
815. Popiel I.
830. Popiel II.
842. Piast I.
860. Ziemowit.
892. Lesko IV.
921. Zemomysl.
962. Miecislas I.
999. Boleslas I.

Kings.—*Aristocratic Republic.*

1001. Boleslas I.
1025. Miecislas II.
1034. Interregnum.
1041. Casimir I.
1058. Boleslas II.
1082. Uladislas I.
1102. Boleslas III.
1140. Uladislas II.
1149. Boleslas IV.
1174. Miecislas III.
1178. Casimir II., the Just.
1194. Lesko the White.
1202. Uladislas III.
1206. Lesko the White (again.)
1228. Boleslas V.
1279. Lesko the Black.
1289. Anarchy.

Date of Accession. A. D.

1295. Prezemislas.
1300. Wenceslas.
1306. Uladislas IV., the Short
1333. Casimir III., the Great.
1370. Louis.
1382. Interregnum.
1384. Hedwiga, queen.
1386. Uladislas V., Jagello.
1434. Uladislas VI.
1445. Casimir IV.
1492. John I. (Albert.)
1501. Alexander.
1506. Sigismund I.
1548. Sigismund II. (Augustus.)
1572. Interregnum.
1574. Henry.
1575. Stephen.
1586. Sigismund III.
1632. Uladislas VII.
1648. Interregnum.
1649. John II.
1668. Michael.
1673. Interregnum.
1676. John III. (Sobieski.)
1696. Interregnum.
1697. Frederic Augustus I.
1705. Deposed by Charles XII. Interregnum.
1710. Frederic Augustus I. restored.
1733. Frederic Augustus II.
1763. Interregnum.
1764-95. Stanislas Augustus Poniatowski.

of convents and hospitals. Its population resembles a perpetual masquerade — long-bearded Jews; monks in the garb of every order; veiled and shrouded nuns, self-secluded and apart; bevies of young Polish females in silk mantles, of the brightest colors, promenading the squares; the venerable ancient Polish noble, with mustachios, caftan, girdle, sabre, and red or yellow boots; the new generation, equipped in the highest style of Parisian dandyism; with Turks, Greeks, Russians, Italians, Germans, and Frenchmen, in an ever-changing throng. Warsaw has a considerable commerce by the Vistula, and manufactures of cloth, linen, carpets, stockings, carriages, and harness. The other towns of Poland are small. Lublin has eighteen thousand, and Kalisc twenty thousand.

The Poles are distinguished for bravery, military spirit, and impatience of control. They are honorable, hospitable, courteous, and lively, but not without licentiousness. The rich nobles live in much state and entertain their friends and strangers in a princely manner. The ladies are celebrated for their attractions. The peasants are poor, ignorant, and fanatical. They are stupid from the effects of servitude, and they have little conception of cleanliness. The Jews are the general traders, and the political freedom they enjoy in Poland has developed better traits in their character, as well as physiognomy, than are found in countries where they are much oppressed. They have, however, a tendency toward extortion; and, like the peasants, they are offensively filthy.

Hungary.

Hungarian Officers.

CHAPTER CCCCLXX.

Its Geography — Origin — Annals — Tekeli — Kossuth — Revolt of 1848–9 — *General Views.*

THE name of Hungary, or land of the Huns, is now applied to a vast territory — with its population of more than thirteen millions — bounded west by Moravia, Austria Proper, Styria, and Illyria; south by the Military Frontiers,* — of over eighteen thousand miles in area, — separating it from Turkey, but usually reckoned as part of Hungary; east by Wallachia Moldavia, and Russia; and north by the Carpathians separating it from Galicia. Its extent, according to these boundaries, and including the Military Frontiers, is about ninety thousand square miles. A part of it was included in the ancient Pannonia, and a portion in Dacia: the latter forming the bulwark and boundary of the Romans in this quarter.

The political divisions of Hungary are as follows: — 1. Hungary Proper, subdivided into four circles. 2. Sclavonia, divided into three counties. 3. Hungarian

* The Military Frontiers are a narrow strip of country, inhabited by more than a million of people of several races, and under an entirely distinct and peculiar government. It stretches for one thousand miles along the Turkish frontier, from the Adriatic to the Bukowina. It is divided into four military governments — the Croatian military frontier, the Sclavonian, the Hungarian, and the Transylvanian. All its civil officers are also military: its people hold their lands by military tenure, the men being obliged to appear armed for defence of the frontier whenever called upon, and to maintain a military organization and discipline. Sixty thousand effective troops are thus kept up without expense to the state. The military command of the whole is generally given to the ban of Croatia, or of Hungary, and its affairs are intrusted to a special board, or council, at Vienna. This frontier government was established by Austria, toward the commencement of the 16th century, as a protection against the Turks; but since that nation has ceased to be aggressive, its chief use is as a "sanitary cordon" against the plague, &c.

Ban is an old word, which means "chief," and is applied to the commander of certain half military districts, called *banats*, two of which are in Hungary: the largest of these has Temeswar for its capital, and lies between the Marosch the Theiss, and the Danube. Another banat is that of Croatia

Croatia,* including the circle of Carlstadt, formerly part of Illyria, and the Hungarian Littorale, or sea-coast.

Transylvania, sometimes included as part of Hungary, is a territory of about twenty thousand square miles, and two millions of inhabitants. It forms the eastern part of the ancient Dacia of the Romans, but became subject to Austria in **1713**. In 1765, Maria Theresa erected it into a grand principality, in which condition it has since remained. A part of the original territory is claimed as belonging to Hungary, and a part is included in the Military Frontiers. The people are Magyars, Saxons, Wallachians, Gypsies, Sclavonians, and Armenians.

Sclavonia is called a kingdom, and forms part of the ancient Pannonia. It derives its name from the *Sclavi*, who settled there in the seventh century, and formed one of the branches of the great Sarmatian family, called *Sclavonians*. In the tenth century, it came under the dominion of Hungary, and was confirmed to Austria in **1699**, by the peace of Carlowitz.

Hungary is also part of the Pannonia of the Romans. The early inhabitants were of the German stock, and were conquered by the emperor Augustus. In the fourth century, the Huns burst from Asia upon Europe like an avalanche.

In our accounts of Tartary, Germany, and Italy, (pp. **390, 761**, and **972**,) we have traced their history down to the time of Attila. With him their power fell, **A. D. 453**. A portion of them settled in the country called from them *Hungary*. Some authors state that the race of the ancient Huns were all cut off in the long war waged against them by Charlemagne, and that the territory was afterward peopled by the neighboring nations, to whom the present Hungarians owe their origin. But other and more accurate authors make the Hungarians of the present day to be descended from the ancient Huns, mingled with other races. The personal appearance of the Huns does not, it is true, favor this idea; but "the Finnic tribe, which formed the germ of the Hungarian nation, becoming intermingled, in the course of time, with Turkish, Sclavonic, and German races, may be said to have almost totally changed its external characteristics. The language of the present Hungarians, too, is composed of Finnic, Turkish, Sclavonic, and German elements."

The Goths and Gepidæ, who overthrew the Huns, yielded, in **526**, to the Lombards; and, when these removed to Italy, in **568**, the Avars entered. They extended their dominion to Bavaria, but were conquered, and compelled to embrace Christianity, by Charlemagne. In the ninth century, the *Magyars*, originally a people of Central Asia, penetrated into the country, and conquered it in ten years. Their chiefs divided the territory among them: *Arpad*, their leader, took half for his own share; the remainder was distributed among the inferior chiefs and their followers, and the ancient inhabitants became serfs. Arpad's grandson, Geysa, embraced the Christian religion; and his son Stephen, the last duke, assumed the title of *king*, in the year **1000**, and added Transylvania to the kingdom. Ladislas I. and Colomann subdued Sclavonia and Croatia, and, after many wars, Dalmatia; Bela II. obtained Bosnia; Emeric, Servia; and Andrew II. and his son Colomann, Galicia.

In 1310, *Charles*, brother to Louis IX. of France, was crowned king of Hungary, which he raised to a high degree of splendor. Charles having married a sister of Casimir, king of Poland, Louis, one of Charles's sons, on becoming king of Hungary, succeeded to the crown of Poland also, in **1370**. This prince, who is called *Louis the Great*, reigned from **1342** to **1382**, and his united kingdoms extended from the Baltic to the Adriatic.

On his death, Poland and Hungary were again separated, and internal troubles broke out. *Sigismund*, who reigned from **1386** to **1437**, lost nearly all the annexed dominions. The Turks approached the frontiers, and took part in every intestine broil. *Albert*, archduke of Austria, having married the only daughter of Sigismund, succeeded to the crown of Hungary in **1437**, but died in a campaign against the Turks in **1439**. Under *Ladislas V.* and *VI.*, these powerful enemies were successfully resisted by the brave John Huniades, whose son *Mathias I.* was made king in **1458**. He proved a very able and fortunate king, and brought under his dominion Moldavia, Wallachia, Moravia, Silesia, Lusatia, and great part of Austria,—forming an empire of two hundred and fifty-six thousand square miles in extent—about equal to the present Austrian empire.

After the death of Mathias I., in **1490**, the kingdom fell to pieces: civil commotions and bad government made it an easy prey to the Turks; and *Louis II.* lost his crown and life in the fatal battle of Mohacs, 1526. This so weakened the Hungarians, that they were unable for one hundred and sixty years to free their country from the enemies of Christendom. *Ferdinand I.* of Austria, who had married the sister of Louis II., being raised to the throne, the strength of his kingdom was indeed added to that of Hungary; but the king was obliged to leave Ofen and the finest part of Hungary in the hands of the Turks, who were not expelled till **1686**. This was partly owing to the unpopularity of the house of Austria, whose despotic habits and religious intolerance were most distasteful to the Hungarian nobles. Hence arose continued disputes and frequent insurrections, in which the insurgents even went so far, on some occasions, as to call the Turks to their aid.

This was done by the celebrated Hungarian leader Tekeli, who, with his misbelieving allies, had nearly got possession of Vienna, in **1683**, and which was chiefly indebted for its preservation to the Poles, under Sobieski, as already related. The treaty of Carlowitz (1699) delivered Transylvania and Hungary, and that of Passarowitz, in **1718**, relieved the Banat, from the Turkish yoke. The civil wars and insurrections, hitherto so pernicious, ceased in **1711**; and the house of Austria has ever since remained in the undisturbed possession of the country. Its inhabitants have also, on various trying occasions, shown themselves the most loyal and devoted subjects of their sovereigns, from the days of Maria Theresa till a recent date.

* *Croatia* is an ancient territory, bounded by the Adriatic, Illyria, Sclavonia, Dalmatia, and Bosnia. Half of it is now under Turkish sway. It appears that the first inhabitants were Pannonians: the Huns and Avars possessed it in turn; but finally the *Wends*, from Bohemia, in A. D. 640, settled here. From the name *Hrovasch*, which they gave the country, are formed the modern names *Croatia* and *Croats*. The people are warlike, and, in the secluded mountain districts, almost savage. They came under the dominion of Austria in the twelfth century, and have mostly so remained since.

Jellachich, Ban of Croatia.

Hungarian Noble and Serf.

In 1848, however, an insurrection broke out, which, going beyond the original causes of quarrel, designed no less than to separate Hungary from the dominion of Austria, and give it independence; to shake off the German yoke, and secure Hungarian nationality.

In order to understand the causes of this event, it is necessary to make a few preliminary statements. Joseph II., in an earnest desire for that system of centralization, or "bureaucratic" rule, at Vienna, which has long marked the policy of the imperial court, made many attempts to amalgamate or incorporate Hungary with Austria; but the nation boldly and successfully resisted them; and, in 1790, the diet of Presburg exacted from him an express recognition of their rights, in the tenth article of which he solemnly declared that "Hungary is a free and independent nation in her entire system of legislation and administration, and not subject to any other state or any other people, but that she shall always have her own separate existence and constitution; and shall consequently be governed by kings crowned according to her national laws and customs." Under this arrangement, Hungary has had its own legislative diet: the emperors of Austria have been successively crowned, and received, as kings of Hungary; the royal authority being committed to an officer called a *palatine*.

Of the several races in Hungary, the Magyars claimed and exercised supremacy, though they constituted not more than one third of the population. They are almost exclusively the landholders, and no others are privileged to vote for members of the diet, thus making inferior castes of the other races. Being high spirited and jealous of their rights, they have constantly resisted the encroachments of Austrian power, and are themselves, at the same time, very haughty toward the Sclavonic and Croatian masses of the kingdom. In this state of things, the policy of Austria was obvious: yielding only to the Magyars so far as necessary, she fostered the jealousy of the other races, intending at the proper time to bring it into action, in order to aid in crushing the haughty and restive Magyars.

The revolutionary movement caused by the events of Paris, in February, 1848, found the Hungarian leaders already in a state of great irritation against Austria, for her constant invasions of their constitutional rights Under its impulse, they took high ground with Austria, which resulted in a declaration of independence on the part of Hungary, (1848.) The leader in this and the subsequent movements was Ludwig Kossuth, originally an obscure country attorney, who had been active in enlightening the public mind, as editor of a journal, for which he had suffered imprisonment. The success of this remarkable man in inculcating just and elevated views, is evinced by the fact, that in April, 1849, the Hungarians made a formal declaration of independence, adopted a republican form of government, and gave equality of rights and privileges to all classes of citizens. Thus did they wipe out the memory of the oppressions inflicted by the nobles upon the inferior races, by one glorious act, entitling them to the sympathies and good wishes of every lover of human liberty.

Kossuth was chosen president, and continued to the end, with untiring zeal, to sustain the cause he had espoused. The government of Austria, for a time embarrassed by insurrections at Vienna and revolts in Italy, was at length able to direct its forces against Hungary, in which it was aided by an army of Croats, led by the celebrated ban, Jellachich. For a time, the Hungarian generals, Bem, Georgey, and Dembinsky, were successful, and afforded reason to hope for the final triumph of Hungarian independence. But this prospect was soon clouded. The emperor of Russia sent an army of one hundred and fifty thousand men into Hungary, which coöperated with that of Austria. While the other powers of Europe stood mute, the conflict drenched the soil of Hungary with blood. All that bravery and skill could do, were done by Kossuth and most of his compatriots; but the conflict was too unequal. Battle after battle was fought and city after city surrendered to the overwhelming forces of the allies. The last act in the terrible drama was the surrender of Georgey, and his army of thirty-five thousand men, to the Russian general, Paskiewitch, August, 1849. Finding further resistance hopeless, the Hungarians still in arms surrendered, while Kossuth and some of his associates sought refuge in the adjacent territory of the Turks. In keeping with the despotism of his whole conduct respecting Hungary the czar of Russia demanded of the sultan the sur-

Croatian Soldiers at Night.

render of the Hungarian exiles. This was magnanimously refused by the Turk, thus shaming Christendom with the spectacle of a loftier humanity in an infidel than that which belongs to the head of the Holy League. If the time has indeed come, when Christian sovereigns may learn lessons of civilization from the successor of Mahomet, how do they misrepresent the spirit of Christianity, and how unworthily do they fill the high places they occupy!

The submission of Hungary was followed by numerous executions of leaders of the revolt, who fell into the hands of the victors; these were ordered by the imperial court of Vienna, and consummated under the direction of General Haynau. Nor could these spectacles, which shocked the moral sense of the civilized world, satisfy the vindictive spirit of the Austrians. It has now been formally declared, that "the former constitution of Hungary is overthrown by the revolution;" all Hungarian privileges are abolished, and a system of government has been framed for the conquered country, which stifles the voice of the people; divides the territory into districts, presided over by military commanders, who have the power of preserving the public peace, of promulgating ordinances, of punishing crimes, and of licensing and regulating the press. The centralization of the system is complete; and though there are civil functionaries appointed, their sphere of action is subservient to the military rule, which is called "the exceptional state" of Hungary, but which bids fair to continue for years, and to form indeed the only constitution of the country.

About half of the Hungarian population is Catholic; two millions of the Greek church; one million Lutheran; two millions Calvinists and Unitarians. The several races are in the following proportion: The Magyars, or ruling race, were, in 1825, about four millions; the Sclavonians, the subject people, consisting of Slovacs, Croats, and Serbs, over four millions. Beside these, Hungary contained about seven hundred thousand Wallachians, six hundred thousand Germans, two hundred thousand Jews, fifty thousand Gypsies, beside Arnaouts, Greeks, Armenians, &c. There is no middle class: society consists of haughty nobles, poor peasants, and peddling traffickers. The nobles are brave, generous, and hardy, devotedly attached to every thing Hungarian, and fostering a rooted dislike to every thing German. The peasantry are almost as rude and barbarous in dress, aspect, and manners, now, as when the Romans first invaded Illyria; nor could the wagons of the Scythian camp be more clumsy than those which may be now seen crowding the streets of Presburg.

In the recent contest of 1848–9, auxiliaries were found in the Hungarian armies which remind us of their formidable Scythian ancestry. These were the wild population of the steppes and forests of the interior, particularly the horseherds, or tenders of the troops of wild horses on the plains. The swineherds and the fishermen employed themselves in constructing bridges, in their own manner, on a sort of tubs, in a style at first much ridiculed by their enemies, but found to be very effective. The swineherds were generally Servians: their weapon is a small axe, with a rather long handle; and they throw it with such dexterity, that, at eighty or one hundred paces, they rarely miss a man, and the blow is generally fatal.

The horseherds were especially dreaded by the Austrian troops, on account of the extraordinary weapon they carry and use with deadly skill. It is simply the whip, with which they are accustomed to catch any horse of the herd they may wish to tame and dispose of. The application of it in war is quite a novelty. It has a handle not more than two feet in length, while the thong measures from fifteen to twenty. A leaden ball is fixed to the end of it, and this, when thrown, acts like a lasso, curling round man or horse; or it sometimes strikes them to the earth with a crushing blow. The horseherds are so skilful in the use of this weapon, that, at full gallop, they will strike an enemy with unerring certainty on any part of the body they please. In skirmishes, an isolated foot soldier, if he fires his musket and misses, is lost; before he can attempt to reload the wild horseman rushes past, and, with the sweep of his ball-loaded thong, stretches him lifeless on the earth. There were some thousands of these men in the Hungarian armies. They often struck the Austrian officers from their horses with incredible dexterity. The wounds this weapon inflicts are described as frightful. Before it was known that these horseherds were serving in the Hungarian ranks, a great number of cuirassiers were brought into Pesth, wounded in a manner the military surgeons could not explain. The injury was neither a cut, nor a puncture, nor a gunshot wound; and the soldiers were for a long time ashamed to own that it was caused by so ignoble a weapon as a whip. It can only be used where the horseman has ample space: in any thing like "close order," it would be as dangerous to friends as foes. One of these horseherds was taken prisoner by the Austrians, and, probably to obtain an exact knowledge of the power of his weapon, he was ordered to display his skill in the camp. A stuffed figure was set up, the Austrian officers pointing out the parts he was to strike while in full career. Twice he did as directed, but the third time he introduced a startling variation: swinging his whip in a wide circle, he dashed his horse at a point of the line of soldiers round the place of exercise, broke through it, and was far on his way to the open fields in an instant, untouched by the volley of balls sent after him!

The amusements of the body of the people of Hungary consist chiefly of some national dances, particularly on occasion of the vintage, which is a season of unbounded gayety. The national military dress—the same commonly denominated *hussar*—is picturesque and martial, and has been imitated by the other European nations. The peasantry wear a broad-brimmed, varnished hat, with a low, rounded crown; they have their matted, long black hair negligently plaited, or tied in knots, a blue jacket and trousers, covered with a cloak of coarse woollen cloth or sheepskin, still retaining its wool. They live in small villages, or rather clusters of cottages, arranged on each side of the road; these are whitewashed and roofed with thatch, but the interior generally contains three tolerably comfortable apartments.

The Croats live in a manner which resembles that of the Chinese. All the members of a family reside together, under the government of the eldest male of the household; their children, with their wives and families, occupy parts of the same mansion, which is successively enlarged, to make room for the increase; seventy or eighty individuals are sometimes found in one house. This custom prevails in the Military Frontiers.

Hungary is, on the whole, a most prolific country. The vine flourishes here, and a million of acres are devoted to its cultivation. There are whole forests of chestnut, cherry, and plum-trees. In the south, the orange ripens in the open air. Tobacco is a staple of agriculture. Every species of grain flourishes.

The commerce of Hungary, notwithstanding its fine rivers, labors under great disadvantages, from the want of sea-coast, from the navigation of the Danube being frequently impeded, and from its embouchure being in possession of the Turks, whose barbarism has hitherto baffled every attempt to open a communication with the Black Sea. The inland traffic is tolerably brisk, and the roads are continually covered with animals, and with wagons, driven by the Jews, Gypsies, and other foreign races, to the two thousand fairs which are annually held throughout the country. The great centres of this internal traffic are Pesth and Debretzen. The exterior commerce of Hungary consists in the exchange of raw for manufactured produce.

Pesth, the capital of the late revolutionary government, contains 131,705 inhabitants; Presburg, forty-five thousand; Schemnitz, twenty-three thousand; Ofen, or Buda, fifty-five thousand; Zombor, twenty thousand; Maria Theresienstadt, fifty-three thousand; Comorn, twenty-three thousand; Mohacs, eight thousand. These are in Hungary proper. The chief town in Sclavonia is Essek, with twelve thousand inhabitants.

Education is in a backward state in Hungary, owing in a great degree, to the variety of languages. This latter circumstance has led to the use of Latin, in affairs of government, debates in the diet, and common conversation. The Magyars have sought to make their language the standard; but Austria has resisted and excited the natural jealousy of the Croats and other tribes against this measure and its promoters. This is one of the causes which led the Croats, under the popular ban, Jellachich, to take part with Austria in the recent struggle. Some of the Hungarian nobles are highly educated, and of very polished manners.

The Sclavonian language, supposed to be of Hindoo origin, is said to be spoken by sixty millions of people. The Russian, Polish, and Servian are the chief dialects. The latter is said to be the most polished; in this there are numerous popular ballads of great beauty. The Magyar language is regarded as of the Finnish stock, and not Sclavonian. In this there are many works of value in various departments of literature. Some of the ballads have been translated into English by Bowring.

We conclude our notice of Hungary by remarking that there seem to be in this great country the elements of a mighty nation, which it is vain to expect will ever amalgamate with the Germans. Russia doubtless desires to annex its population to her already overgrown mass; but the Hungarians have lately shown a spirit and power, which, with the growing weakness of Austria, seem likely at no distant day to insure their independence,—even against the overwhelming force of Russia, soon, probably, to find ful employment elsewhere.

Kings of Hungary.

House of St. Stephen.

Date of Accession
A. D.

997. Stephen I. (Saint.)
1038. Peter.
1041. Aba, or Owon.
1044. Peter, (restored.)
1047. Andrew I.
1061. Bela I.
1064. Solomon.
1074. Geysa I., the Great.
1077. Ladislas.
1095. Colomann.
1114. Stephen II.
1131. Bela II., the Blind.
1141. Geysa II.
1161. Stephen III.
1173. Bela III.
1196. Emeric.
1200. Ladislas II.
1204. Andrew II.
1235. Bela IV.
1270. Stephen IV.
1272. Ladislas III.
1290. Andrew III.

House of Anjou.

1302. Charobert.
1342. Louis I., (king of Poland.)
1382. Mary, ("King Mary.")

Date of Accession.
A. D.

1392. Sigismund, (emperor.)
1407. Elizabeth and Albert II
1439. Ladislas IV.
1444. Interregnum.
1452. Ladislas V.
1457. Mathias I. (Corvin.)
1490. Ladislas VI.
1516. Louis II.

House of Austria.

1526. Ferdinand I.
1563. Maximilian.
1572. Rodolph.
1608. Mathias II.
1618. Ferdinand II.
1625. Ferdinand III.
1647. Ferdinand IV.
1654. Leopold I.
1687. Joseph I.
1711. Charles.
1740. Maria Theresa and Francis I.
1780. Joseph II.
1790. Leopold II.
1792. Francis.
1835. Ferdinand V.
1848. Francis Joseph I.

CHAPTER CCCCLXXI.

GENERAL VIEWS OF EUROPE. — *History of the Early Tribes — Alphabetical List.*

EUROPE has been known to history for about forty centuries. The origin of its primeval inhabitants is uncertain; yet several reasons induce the belief that it was settled by the descendants of Japhet. The Hebrew writers speak of Europe under the name of the *Isles of the Gentiles;* but they had no knowledge of the northern part, and made little distinction between islands and the southern projections of Greece, Italy, and Spain; though, possibly, in primeval times, the Baltic and Black Sea may have been connected. Even the prying Greeks were ignorant of the northern regions of Europe; and though the Phœnicians visited the shores of the Baltic for amber, they studiously concealed the geographical knowledge they thus acquired.

About fifteen hundred years before the Christian era, we find *Pelasgians* and *Etruscans* mingled with later colonies from Asia in the south, and *Celts* in the west. The *Lapps* and *Finns* were probably upon the north, and Asiatic tribes in the centre and upon the east, quite as early; for as the steppes of Asia extend into Central Europe, the latter seems to have witnessed, through half her extent, the same shifting of tribes that we have noticed in Tartary. Successive hordes were continually displacing their predecessors, till the *Goths* were driven to Scandinavia, the Finns and Lapps to the arctic shores, and the *Celts* and feebler tribes to the islands of the Atlantic, or the mountains which bound the great plain. The rise of Charlemagne's empire, of the Polish kingdoms of Hungary, and lastly of Russia, successively checked these inundations of warriors from Asia, of which history records several; the chief of them being those of the Germanic tribes, and of the Huns. The invasions of the Tartars under the sons of Zingis, and under Tamerlane, are the last of these nomadic inroads.

The great plain is bounded on the south by the Alps and Carpathians. These we may presume to have defended the Etruscans and Pelasgi from the north-eastern swarms, and allowed them to remain settled long enough to develope the civilization they, and especially the Etruscans, early attained.

The *Pelasgians* seem to have entered Europe along the northern shores of Asia Minor, through Thrace; the *Goths* along the southern shores of Russia, from the Caucasus; the *Germans* along the northern shores of the Caspian from Central Asia; the *Scythians* from Independent Tartary; the *Sarmatians* from Mongolia; the *Avars* from Turkestan, and the *Huns* from Siberia.* Details respecting these tribes are added in the note below.

---

* The *Pelasgians* brought with them republican forms of government in politics, and in the arts those gigantic forms of architecture, called *cyclopean*, and consisting of unsculptured caverns and cairns or walled mounds of huge rocks, circles like Stonehenge, walls of vast rocks of unequal size and various shape, but admirably fitted, and often smoothly faced. Many of these structures still exist in Asia Minor and Southern Europe. Pelasgians appear to have inhabited Thrace, Macedonia, Southern Italy, many of the islands, and Greece, chiefly; in the latter country, they were succeeded in part by the *Hellenes*, a kindred race. Their name is said to mean "wandering masons," or "shepherds." The Pelasgi were both pastoral and agricultural; and baking of bread, use of the plough, measuring of land, are ascribed to their invention or teaching. The Grecian race, which made the most early and the most rapid progress in civilization and intellectual attainments, was that one in which the Pelasgian blood was least adulterated by foreign mixture, namely, the Ionians of Attica, and of the settlements in Asia Minor. And to the Pelasgic element we probably owe all that distinguishes the Greeks in history. *Phoroneus* is named as a Pelasgian king, in Argolis, in the eighteenth generation before the Trojan war.

The *Etruscans* were found chiefly in Tuscany. Their origin is uncertain; the best antiquarians consider them of Pelasgic race. They were the teachers of the early Romans in religion and civilization; and in art they held a place between the Egyptians and Greeks. Agriculture was the basis of their state; their religion was gloomy and superstitious, and the observance of omens was made a science. The early simplicity of their manners became corrupted by sensuality without refinement. They were energetic, made extensive conquests, and were bold and skilful navigators.

The *Celts* inhabited Great Britain and Ireland, France and Spain. They were divided into the Gallic, or Gaelic, who once inhabited France, and are still found in Ireland and Scotland; the *Cymric*, or Welsh, who now dwell in Wales, Cornwall, and as Bretons in Western France; the *Basque*, who lived in the south-west of France, and throughout Spain, and are now found in the Western Pyrenees. Some, however, make the Basques to be the Iberi, and a primitive and distinct people; and the Gaels, or Galli, and Cymri, to be two races of the same family; and they consider the three languages — the Basque, Scotch, and Welsh, as belonging to that great class which also embraces the Sanscrit, the second idiom of India. The name Celts, or Kelts, means "foresters;" but when and how they migrated from the East, is unknown. Some chronologists speak of a Celtic empire in Europe, under Uranus, Jupiter, &c., in B. C. 1993. The Gaels were confined to the limits of Hibernia, and the Highlands of Scotland, distinguished only in obscure border wars, or domestic broils, and the Cymri were driven from the plains of England by the Saxons; but the *Gallo-Celts* passed through a more agitated and brilliant career than any other of the races of the west. Beginning as nomads, their course embraced Europe, Asia, and Africa; their name is recorded with terror in the annals of almost every nation. They burned Rome; they wrested Macedonia from the veteran legions of Alexander; they forced Thermopylæ, and pillaged Delphi; they then proceeded to pitch their tents on the plains of the Troad, in the public places of Miletus, on the borders of the Halys, in Asia Minor, and on the banks of the Nile; they besieged Carthage, menaced Memphis, and numbered among their tributaries the most powerful monarchs of the East; they founded in Upper Italy a powerful empire, and in the bosom of Phrygia they reared another empire, that of Galatia, which for a long time exercised its sway over the whole of Lower Asia. It was to the remnant of this empire in Asia Minor that the apostle Paul wrote some "Epistles."

The early history of the *Finns* and *Lapps*, as far as known, has been given in our history of Lapland and Tartary. A part seem to have wandered along the shores of the Arctic Ocean, making little progress beyond the savage state, as Samoiedes, or Esquimaux; another part, the Huns, combining with Tartar tribes, made themselves a terrible name as devastators of Europe, and laid the basis of the powerful nation of the Hungarians.

The *Teutones*, or Germanic tribes, are first known to history as kindred tribes, inhabiting Central Europe. An Asiatic and nomadic origin is generally ascribed to them; but whence and when they migrated is unknown. Von Hammer calls the Germans a Bactriano-Median nation. Just before the Christian era, they were divided into the *Ingævones*, who lived on the ocean; the *Hermiones*, in the central parts; and the *Istævones*, in the rest of Germany; the subdivisions of these nations are given in our account of Germany.

About one hundred years before the Christian era, a barbarian torrent — the *Teutones*, *Cimbri*, &c. — was loosened — by what cause is unknown — from the farther side of the Elbe, and the mongrel horde of Germans and Scandinavians, of gigantic stature, savage valor, and singular accoutrements, descended toward the south. On their route, a number of Celtic tribes, of which the Tigurini and Tectosagæ are named, joined them. The Romans, having taken Noricum under their protection, and extended their sway to the Pyrenees, were crowding forward upon Austria and France. On the one frontier they were defeated by the Germans, on the other by the Celts. A second Roman army was defeated in France the next year, (A. D. 105;) but soon after Marius defeated the Cimbri and their confederate tribes, who sought to invade Italy from the north-east; and also the Teutones and Ambrones, at Aix, in Southern France. The loss of the barbarians in the two battles was nearly half a million.

The *Suevi* — that is, "red-haired" — were a powerful people of Eastern Germany, extending from the Baltic to the Danube. The *Langobardi*, *Semnones*, and *Angli* were some of its tribes; the *Catti*, *Marcomanni*, *Ubii*, and *Sygambri* are enumerated as others. The term Suevi, instead of being general, came in time to be applied to a part of these people who settled in a country named from them Suabia, now called Wittemberg and Baden. The *Alans* were a Scythian race, whose origin is given in our account of Tartary. In Europe, they dwelt between the Volga and Don. At one time, their power extended from Siberia to India; but the Huns, breaking in upon them, drove some into Caucasus, where they are called *Albanians;* others joined the Huns in their advance upon the Goths; others, still, incorporated themselves with the northern Germans, and shared with them the spoils of Roman France and Spain. The *Alemanni* — "all races of men" — were a confederacy from all the German tribes, who united upon the Upper Rhine to resist the Romans, in Caracalla's time. Clovis overthrew and dispersed them.

After the defeat of the barbarians by Marius, (101 B. C.) the fugitives who fled across the Rhine, formed a tribe called *Marcomanni.* During the next century, a leader united several tribes with them, forming the Marcomannic confederacy, with which he subdued the powerful kingdom of the *Boii*, in Bohemia and Franconia, and formed an empire which could send seventy thousand men into the field. The *Cherusci*, their rivals become the leading tribe through their defeat of Varus, humbled the Marcomanni. The *Cherusci* became feeble through dissensions, and the *Catti* rose to power, but were reduced by the Romans. Perpetual quarrels prevented the Germanic tribes from taking advantage of the growing weakness of Rome. At last, the *Batavi*, a tribe in the west, in Holland, gained decided advantages; and the Marcomannic war united the powerful tribes against the Romans. In this and similar wars success fluctuated between the parties. In the beginning of the fifth century, barbarians assailed the Roman empire on all sides. Vandals, Suevi, and Alans seized Spain; Burgundians invaded Gaul; Visigoths, Italy and Spain; the Ostrogoths warred upon the Visigoths, and the Langobardi upon the Ostrogoths. Thus began those movements, westward and southward, of innumerable hordes, which were called the *great migration of the nations*, and ended in the overthrow of Rome.

The Goths were called *Getæ* by the Romans, and are first spoken of as barbarians, of gloomy habits, dwelling near the mouths of the Danube Herodotus calls them the bravest of the Thracians. We have already, in our account of Tartary, named a branch of the blue-eyed and fair-haired Getæ, as founding an empire there under the Chinese name of *Yeta.* The Goths of the Scandinavian peninsula, Norway, Sweden, &c., are also called Getæ by the Romans. Tradition asserts that an Asiatic tribe came

The importance of the history of the early tribes and nations of Europe induces us to give a view of them, arranged in alphabetical order, for easy reference.

A.

ACHÆI, a main branch of the Æolic race, Greece.

ACHIVI, the same with *Achæi.*

ÆDUI, a powerful nation of Middle Gaul, 75 B. C.

ÆOLES, a main branch of the Hellenic race, Greece.

ÆQUI, a small tribe near ancient Rome.

ÆSTII, on the south-east shore of the Baltic.

AGATHYRSI, a civilized people of Hungary, 500 B. C.

ALANI, or ALANS, between the Don and Volga, and thence stretching their power to Germany and India.

ALBICI, on the mountains above Marseilles.

ALEMANNI, a confederation on the Upper Rhine, 50 B. C.

ALLOBROGES, "highlanders," Gauls of Dauphiny, Piedmont, and Savoy, second century B. C.

AMBARRI, Gauls on the Saone, France.

AMBIANI, Belgic Gauls about Amiens.

AMBRONES, "dwellers on the Rhone," France.

ANGLI, Germans of Holstein.

ANTHROPOPHAGI, ANDROPHAGI, "cannibals" of Polish Russia, 500 B. C.

AONES, the earlier inhabitants of Bœotia, Greece.

AQUITANI, Iberian Gauls of South-west France, between the Garonne and the Pyrenees.

AREVACI, Celtiberians about Numantia and Segovia.

ARGIPPÆI, a bald, sacred nation of the Sauromatæ.

ARGIVI, people of Argos, Greece.

ASTURES, in the Asturias, Spain, about Astorga.

ATREBATES, of Belgic Gaul, about Arras.

ATREBATI, on the Thames, England.

AUTERCI, three nations of Gaul.

AVARS, Oriental Finns, like the Huns; they formed a vast empire in Russia, in the sixth century.

B.

BASTARNÆ, went from Poland and Prussia to the Bog River.

BATAVI, some Catti of Holland, about Leyden.

BELGÆ, "warriors," Germans near the Seine.

BITURIGES, Gauls about Bourges and Bourdeaux.

BOII, went from Gaul to Bohemia; then to Bavaria.

BRENNI, and BREUNI, in Italy, near Lake Maggiore.

BRIGANTES, greatest and most ancient of the Britons, from Thrace; about York.

BRITANNI, inhabitants of Britain.

BRUTTII, in Southern Italy.

BUDINI, in 500 B. C., between Don and Volga.

BUHRGUNDS, BURGUNDI, from Prussia; they came to Burgundy, fifth century B. C.

C.

CALÆCI, in Galicia, Spain.

CANTABRI, in Biscay, Spain, resisted Rome two hundred years, till 19 B. C.

CARNUTES, in Gaul, about Chartres; here was the chief seat of the Druids.

CATTI, CHATTI, in Hesse, about Cassel.

CELTÆ, KELTÆ, the Gallic race of the west.

CELTIBERI, the Gauls united with the Basques in Mid-Spain.

CELTICI, in Portugal, about Beja.

CENTAURI, a mounted tribe of Thessaly, Greece.

CHAONES, in Epirus, near Dalmatia.

CHERUSCI, between Weser and Elbe; defeated Varus, A. D. 10.

CIMBRI, in Jutland.

CIMMERII, in South Russia.

CONCANI, in Spain, with Scythian customs.

CORALLI, savages near the mouth of the Danube.

CURETES, pirates who settled in Crete.

CYCLOPES, in Sicily, or mythical.

CYMRI, KYMRI, ancient Welsh.

CYNETES, CYNESSI, the westernmost people of Europe.

D.

DACI, or GETÆ, in Transylvania, Moldavia, Wallachia, and Hungary; subdued successively by the Sarmatæ, Goths, Huns, and Saxons.

DALMATES, on the Adriatic, from Thrace; bold, piratical, subdued by the Romans in the first century B. C.

DAMNII, anciently of Clydesdale, &c., Scotland.

DAMNONII, of Devonshire and Cornwall, Eng.

DANAI, the Greeks, especially the Argives.

DOLOPES, in the south-east of Thessaly, Greece.

DORIANS, the most powerful of the Hellenic tribes, Greece.

E.

EBURONES, of Belgic Gaul, about Liege and Tongres.

EDITANI, in Valencia, Spain.

EUGANEI, went from the Venetian territory westward.

F.

FALISCI, FALERII, Etrurians at war with Rome

FRANCI, FRANKS, a confederation of Germanic tribes against the Saxon tribes, commencing in the second century A. D. Clovis united them A. D. 500, to begin France.

FRISII, east of the Rhine's mouth, between the Ems, Vecht, and ocean; in Friesland &c.

G.

GALLI, the Belgæ, Aquitani and Celts between them.

GELONI, a civilized ancient people, with a vast wooden city in Southern Russia.

GERMANI, tribes of Germany from the Oxus, whose plains were called Dschermania, and originated the Persians.

GERRHI, Scythians about the sources of the Dnieper.

GETÆ, about the mouths of the Danube; of origin similar to the Goths.

GIGANTES, GIANTS, on the peninsula between the Gulf of Saloniki and Cassandria, in Macedonia.

GOTHI, GOTHS, went from Caucasus to Sweden, 500 B. C. In the third century A. D., Goths crossed the Dniester westward.

H.

HELLAS, HELLENES, Greece, Greeks; first in a district of Thessaly, 1384 B. C., then universally, as the tribe conquered Greece. The Hellenes were divided into Dorians, Æolians, Achæans, and Ionians.

HELOTÆ, HELOTS, a race enslaved by their Dorian conquerors, the Spartans.

HELVETII, between the Rhine and Rhone, Lakes Constance and Geneva, and Mount Jura.

HELVII, Gauls on the west bank of the Rhone.

HENETI, fabled to have come from Asia Minor, and settled near Venice.

HERACLIDÆ, the posterity of Hercules, who, after an exile of one hundred years, returned and subdued the Peloponnesus, forming the Hellenic invasion, 1104 B. C.

HERMIONES, the central tribes of Germany.

HERMUNDURI, a powerful people; the leading tribe of the Herminones, and east and north-east of the Alemanni.

HERNICI, near Rome, which they struggled against for two hundred years.

HERULI, driven from Sweden by Danes, they settled on the Sea of Azof; though defeated by Ostrogoths, they established a powerful em-

---

from the vicinity of Caucasus, conquered Scandinavia, under its chief, the younger *Odin*, who built a city Sigtuna, with a temple, established a worship and a hierarchy, introduced the Runic alphabet, and was, in short, the legislator and civilizer of the north. This was about 50 or 60 B. C.; or, according to some historians, in the fifth century B. C., at the time of the invasion of Scythia by Darius of Persia. This chief, Odin, was confounded with the god Odin, or Woden, who is supposed to be the same as Buddha. The people of that part of Scandinavia best known to the Romans were called *Hilleriones*, in Pliny's time, whence, perhaps, the name Holland. Tacitus names the *Suiones* as inhabitants of Sweden, long called Sueonia; and the *Sitones* of Norway, south of Lake Malar, where lay the city Siturn, or Sigtuna.

The name *Goths* appears first when, in the middle of the third century A. D., they crossed the Dniester, and devastated Dacia and Thrace, but were bought off and induced to return. They then spread eastward,—forming the Ostrogoth nation,—crossed the Black Sea, and ravaged its southern shores. In 269, they invaded Macedonia unsuccessfully; in 272, Dacia was given up to the western portion of the nation, who were called *Visigoths.* These Dacian Goths, or Visigoths, invaded Illyricum unsuccessfully, when Constantine I. was emperor; but Constantine II. settled them in Mœsia, where they embraced Christianity, and their bishop, Ulphilas, about the middle of the fourth century, wrote the translation of the Scriptures called the *Mœsogothic.* In 375, the Huns drove the Ostrogoths upon the Visigoths, who took refuge in Mœsia, but afterward invaded Thrace, and exercised great influence at Constantinople, as allies, mercenaries, or enemies. Their history under Alaric and Ataulph is given in our accounts of Italy, Germany, and Spain. The Ostrogoths, who had settled in Pannonia, after the destruction of the Huns, extended their power over Noricum, Rhætia, and Illyricum, and in 489 invaded Italy, as elsewhere related. Overthrown by Narses in 544, the Goths figure no longer in Europe, except in Spain.

A kingdom of *Gothia* existed in Scandinavia, distinct from Sweden Proper, till the twelfth century A. D., when it was united to Sweden. The Ostrogoths and Visigoths are thought to have been derived originally from Scandinavia. In A. D. 160, the *Vandals*—that is, "wanderers"—issued hence and annoyed the Romans; in 419, they passed, with the *Suevi* and *Alani*, into Spain; and thence, very soon, to Africa, whence they invaded Italy, and so ransacked Rome that their name became a proverb for ruthless destructiveness. Out of Scandinavia, too, came the Northmen, or *Normans*, who, as early as the eighth century, spread terror and devastation from their ships, over the shores of Europe, from the recesses of the Gulf of Finland to the coasts of Andalusia, in Spain. As Vikingar,—that is, "sea-kings," or pirates,—they entered every inlet for plunder; sacked cities, and at last founded powerful kingdoms in Russia, at Novgorod and Kiev, A. D. 862, &c.; in Normandy, in the tenth century; in Sicily and Southern Italy, in the middle of the 11th century. In 1066, this Scandinavian race conquered England, and infused some of its most commanding elements into the English character.

The early inhabitants of the great eastern plain of Europe remain to be noticed. This broad tract was considered a part of Scythia; afterward it received the name of *Sarmatia.* The Greek colonies of Southern Russia settled here between 1000 and 500 B. C., carried on a fur trade among these *Skuthoi*, as they called the inhabitants. In 699 to 616 B. C., *Cimmerians*, driven from the shores of the Azof, by *Scythians*, invaded Asia Minor through Colchis. The *Cimbri* of Denmark, and the *Kymri* of Wales, are supposed to be portions of the same people. In 500 B. C., Darius Hystaspes, the Persian, invaded Southern Russia; crossing the Danube, he marched to the Volga, then into Hungary; but he lost nearly all his army of eight hundred thousand men, though he could not bring the Scythians to a general engagement. He found the *Sauromates*, who afterward gave name to the Sarmatæ, south of the Don; the *Budini*, between the Don and Volga; a nation of hunters, the *Thyrsagetæ*, north of them; the *Melanchlæni*, or "black-clothed," between the Don and Dnieper—these were afterward called *Rhoxalani*, whence the Russians. On the banks of the Pripetz, a branch of the Dnieper, were the *Androphagi*, or "cannibals," without laws or tribunals; south-west were the *Neuri*; and south-east of them, on the Theiss and Marosch, in Hungary, were the *Agathyrsi*, who exhibited the remains of a high, primeval civilization.

In the middle of the second century A. D., the country from the Vistula, Carpathians and Dniester to the Volga, from the Artic Ocean to Caucasus, was called European and Asiatic *Sarmatia*, separated by the Don. Its nations were most of them confounded under one name, *Hamazobii*, that is, "wagon-dwellers," because, like Asiatic Scythians, they lived mostly in wagons. The name of Scythia was now transferred to Asia. In 565 A. D., we find the empire of the Avars filling all this great plain, from the Elbe and Danube, the Baltic and Artic Ocean, to the Black Sea, the Kouban, and the Volga. The *Finns* were in the north, the *Slavi* in the west, the *Bulgarians* on the Don, the *Gepidæ* in Hungary. About the time of Charlemagne, the *Grand Duchy of Russia* occupies a region south of Lake Ladoga, while the bordering empire of the *Khazars* fills the space between the Upper Dnieper, the Lower Dniester, the Black Sea, Caucasus, and the Volga. The Goths and the Greeks then shared the Crimea between them. In A. D. 1000, the grand duchy of Russia had absorbed nearly all the southern half of European Russia; the *Patzinakites* lay between it and the Black Sea; Esthonia, Livonia, and Poland between it and the Baltic. In A. D. 1300, the *Kipzak* empire stretched from Lake Aral and Soongaria, in Tartary, to Lithuania on the Baltic, and Novgorod on the Gulf of Finland, and the Arctic Ocean; while it had the Black Sea and Caucasus on the south.

Near the end of the fifteenth century, the great eastern plain is divided between Livonia, Lithuania, and Poland on the west, the Khanat of the Crimea on the south; that of Astrakan on the south-east; that of Kazan on the east; and Russia on the north-west. In 1725, Russia had absorbed nearly all the plain, from the Niemen and Lower Dniester eastward, except the Khanat of Krim, along the Black Sea and Caucasus which was added during the next century pire on the Danube, and in A. D. 476, under Odoacer, took Rome. The Lombards cut off many, and the rest migrated westward.

HETRURIANS, ETRUSCANS, in Tuscany.

HILLERIONES, a Scandinavian tribe.

HIPPOPODES, "horse-feet," a fleet Scythian tribe.

HUNNI, HUNS, Finnic Mongols from the Ural and Siberia; starting from the Volga and Azof in A. D. 374, they devastated Europe and gave name to Hungary, 30 B. C. to A. D. 500. The Vougoules are their descendants.

HYPERBOREI, "beyond Boreas," fabled to live beyond the cold winds, in a delightful climate, and to attain the age of one thousand years. The tradition of these people of a golden age points to a high primeval civilization in the north, when its climate was more tropical; or in Central Asia.

I.

IBERI, earliest known people of Spain, on the Ebro; the Basques are a remnant.

ICENI, ancient Britons in Suffolk, Norfolk, Cambridge, and Huntingdon; famous for a bloody revolt against Rome, A. D. 50.

ILLYRIANS, on the Drave and Saave to the Adriatic. The various tribes — Thracians probably, as they tattooed their bodies — united, and withstood Macedon and Rome.

INSUBRES, Gauls of Italy, with Milan for their capital. They greatly aided Hannibal against Rome.

IUTES, Goths in Jutland; led by Hengis and Horsa to England, A. D. 445.

J.

JAPYDES, in Illyria; warlike; conquered by Romans in the first century B. C.

JAPYGES, primitive barbarians of Southern Italy.

JAZYGES, Scythians on the Azof, and between the Danube and Theiss, in Temeswar.

L.

LACEDÆMONII, Spartans of Laconia, or Lacedæmon, Greece, 1490 to 145 B. C.

LANGOBARDI, "long-javelins," on the Elbe and Oder, in Brandenburg, from Sweden. They overran Italy, and gave name to Lombardy.

LAPITHÆ, agriculturists of Thessaly, who contended with the nomadic Centaurs, and united with them.

LATINI, LATINS, Romans originally of Latium, about Rome.

LELEGES, a primitive race of Greece, probably Pelasgic.

LEMOVICES, Gauls about Limoges, France.

LIBURNI, Illyrians about Zara and in Croatia, famed for swift galleys, and as porters.

LIGURES, Basques around the Gulfs of Genoa and Lyons, from the Rhone to the Arno; struggled eighty years for independence. Their language, the Limosin, still exists in Minorca.

LINGONES, in Vosges, the fiercest and wildest of the Gauls.

LOCRI, a people of Greece descended from the Leleges.

LUSITANI, early inhabitants of Portugal.

M.

MACEDONIANS, Kittim, or Illyrians, governed by Hellenic princes, north of Greece.

MARCOMANNI, "bordermen," in Moravia, or between the Maine and Neckar, then in Bohemia.

MARDI, on the Lippe. Another nation, near Rome, headed the social war 92 B. C., and wrested their rights from Rome.

MEDIOMATRICI, about Metz, a powerful Gallo-Belgic people.

MELANCHLÆNI, "black dressed," in South Russia, Rhoxolans, Russians.

MENAPII, between the Rhine and Meuse. In 50 B. C. they dwelt in the woods, without cities.

MOLOSSI, of Epirus, about Yanina, capital of Albania.

MYRMIDONES, of South Thessaly, followers of Achilles to Troy.

N.

NERVII, Gallo-Belgians on the Scheldt, round Bavia. Cambray and Tournay were their capitals, A. D. 375.

NEURI, Scythians at the heads of the Dniester and Bog.

O.

ODRYSÆ, a numerous and warlike Thracian tribe. The empire extended from the Abdera to the Danube, from Strymon to Constantinople.

ŒNOTRI, people of Œnotria, "wine-land," a primitive race of Southern Italy.

OPICI, the OSCI, aborigines of Italy.

ORDOVICES, in North Wales.

OSCI, aborigines of Central Italy, originating the Samnites, Lucani, Bruttii, Sabini, Hernici, Marsi, Sidicini, &c. The Oscan was long the vulgar tongue.

OSTROGOTHÆ, OSTROGOTHS, in Austria, conquered Rome A. D. 488.

P.

PÆONES, a numerous and ancient nation of Macedon.

PELASGI, the earliest known people of Greece, &c.

PHOCEANS, settled Marseilles, 600 B. C., from Phocæa in Asia Minor, giving the Greek element to the French character.

PHOCIANS, in Central Greece, descended of the Leleges.

PICTI, PICTS, "painted," or "robbers," in Scotland.

PICTONES, Gauls about Poitiers.

Q.

QUADI, in Moravia. They joined the Marcomanni against Marcus Antoninus, the Roman emperor; they are lost to history in the fifth century A. D.

QUIRITES, a complimentary name of the Romans.

R.

REDONES, Gauls about Rennes.

REMI, Gauls about Rheims.

RHÆTI, in the Grisons, Uri, Glaris, the Tyrol, &c., in Switzerland.

RHOXALANI, RHOXANI, the Ros and Alans, the early Russians, near the sources of the Don and Dnieper. During the first three centuries they occupied the southern parts of Poland, Red Russia, and Kiovia, the very seats possessed by the Russians of the ninth century.

S.

SABINI, SABINES, one of the most ancient tribes of Central Italy.

SALASSI, held passes of the Pennine Alps one hundred and fifty years against Rome.

SAMNITES, a Sabine tribe east of Rome; admirable troops, and bringing into the field eighty thousand foot and eight thousand horse. These well-disciplined foes long rivalled Rome.

SARDI, of Sardinia; named from a colonist, Sardus, said to have been son of Hercules. It is still barbarous in parts, and contains cairns of stone erected 1500 B. C.

SAUROMATÆ, people of Asiatic Sarmatia, between the Don, Volga, and Caucasus. They gave name to Sarmatia.

SAXONES, originally in Holstein. They spread and obtained extensive power in North Germany, England &c.

SCANDINAVIANS, people of the peninsula of Sweden and Norway.

SCORDISCI, Illyrian Gauls who extended their empire to Thrace and the Danube.

SCOTI, Celts of Scotland, from Spain through Ireland, whence they invaded Scotland.

SCYTHÆ, SCYTHIANS, in Southern Russia.

SEMNONES, Germans upon the Elbe.

SENONES, Gauls who invaded Italy under a Brennus, pillaged Rome, settled in Umbria, and were exterminated, 282 B. C.

SICAMBRI, a powerful German tribe around the Rhine, Sieg, and Lippe; conquered by Drusus, and transferred to the south of the Rhine by Tiberius.

SICANI, SICULI, the earliest known tribes of Sicily. The Sicani were the more ancient; the Siculi, Pelasgians, went from Latium, near Rome.

SILURES, in Southern Wales, about Caerleon. Caractacus, their prince, was subdued by Rome in the first century A. D.

SITONES, a German tribe in Scandinavia, south of Lake Malar, near the old capital Sigtuna.

SLAVI, or ANTES, a large, strong, warlike, but dirty race of Sarmatia, from the Dniester to the Don. Uniting with the Venedi, they fought the Franks; in the sixth century A. D., they crossed the Danube, and settled in Slavonia. The Bohemi, Sorabi, Silesii, Poloni, Cassubii, Rugii, &c., belonged to this race, which originated the Russians, Poles, Bohemians, Moravians, Carinthians, Slovacs, &c.

SPARTANS, of Greece, in Laconia.

SUESSIONES, Gauls about Soissons.

SUEVI, "red-haired," a German union from the Danube to the Baltic, including the Langobardi, Semnones, Angli, Catti, Marcomanni, Ubii, Sygambri, &c. Suabia was named from them.

SUIONES, in Sweden, to which they gave name

T.

TAURI, in the Crimea. They sacrificed all strangers to Diana.

TAURINI, Ligurians on the Upper Po, about Turin. Hannibal plundered it.

TECTOSAGES, a numerous and powerful race of Gauls near the Pyrenees. A part passed through the Hercynian forest, Pannonia, and Macedonia, to Galatia, in Asia Minor.

TEUTONI, TEUTONES, several united tribes of Germany, who marched south from the Elbe, and were defeated by the Romans, about 100 B. C.

THRACES, THRACIANS, an early civilized, powerful race in Turkey, to whom the Greeks, &c., were much indebted for their progress.

TRIBULLI, the most powerful tribe of the Thracians.

TRIBOCCI, Germans, about Strasburg.

TRINOBANTES, ancient people of Essex and Middlesex, England.

TANGRI, the first German tribe that crossed the Rhine.

TURDETANI, in Andalusia, where Homer places the Elysian Fields.

TUSCI, in Tuscany, the famous Etruscans. or Etrurians.

U.

UBII, a German tribe about Cologne

V.

VANDALI, VANDALS, Goths from Sweden who passed into Germany, Spain, and Africa, in A. D. 489.

VASCONES, in Navarre, about Pampeluna.

VEIIENTES, of Veii, near Rome; conquered after a ten years' siege.

VENEDI, Germans on the Vistula, near its mouth.

VENETI, HENETI, near the Po, from Asia Minor, or the north; driven to the islands by the Huns. In the fifth century A. D. they founded Venice.

VINDELICI, in Wirtemberg and Bavaria, about Augsburg.

VOLCÆ, a numerous and powerful nation of Southern France.

VOLSCI, neighbors of early Rome, with whom she contended for two hundred years.

CHAPTER CCCCLXXII.

Christianization of Europe — Greek Church — Protestantism — Feudalism — The Papacy — Crusades — Arts, &c.

HAVING thus given a glance at the early nations of Europe, we shall now trace the progress of Christianity among them. The age of Constantine (A. D. 335) saw all south of the Rhine and Danube a part of the Christian Roman empire; and, as already remarked, the light of Christianity shot its rays into the darkness of heathenism beyond, from the Roman cities, — foci of civilization, — which were situated on these two frontier streams.

About the middle of the eighth and the commencement of the ninth centuries, the pope of Rome was endowed with temporal possessions, and claimed not only supreme spiritual power on earth, but the right to bestow or take away crowns at pleasure. Charlemagne at this time upheld this power, and was sustained by it; he endeavored, as a Christian emperor, to extend both the temporal and spiritual dominion of Christianity, into Heathendom on the north and east, and Islam in the south-west. Hence he invaded

Moorish Spain, and spent thirty years in accomplishing the conversion and conquest of the pagan Saxons. The conversion of the Germanic tribes was carried forward by a branch of the church militant, the order of Teutonic knights, who conquered pagan Prussia in the thirteenth century. Christendom was further enlarged, a little later, by the subjugation of Esthonia and Livonia, through the bloody efforts of another militant order of the church — the knights of the Cross and the Sword. Poland was converted in 965—969. St. Adalbert also labored, about this time, as a zealous and successful missionary in the conversion of Hungary, Poland, Bohemia, and Prussia. And it may here be remarked that devoted Papist missionaries were for ages constant in their efforts to convert the heathen of Europe to Christianity. Norway and Sweden were evangelized in the eleventh century; Lithuania embraced Christianity, and Russia was converted to the Greek church by its intercourse with Constantinople, under Ruric and Vladimir the Great, in the ninth and tenth centuries.

The original constitution of the Christian churches, or congregations, was very simple. A bishop, so called from his "supervision," or "over-seeing," as pastor, was at the head of each, and sometimes of more than one, congregation. The bishop of Rome, the metropolis, would of course have some precedency, when the delegates of the congregations met in council. But the metropolitan bishop, the *bishop of Rome*, after a time claimed extraordinary power, even insisting that he was the successor of the apostle Peter, who, it was asserted, received the rank of vice-head of the church from the Savior! This claim was disputed, and particularly by the *patriarch of Constantinople*, who had also acquired great consideration from being head pastor in the metropolis of the Eastern empire. After a long controversy, this difference of views led, in the eleventh century, to the separation of the *Eastern*, or *Greek* part of the church, which acknowledged the patriarch of Constantinople, from the *Western*, or *Latin* part, which looked to the pope of Rome, as its chief.

The *Greek church* is now the established religion of Russia, Greece, and part of Austria. It numbers more than sixty-two millions of worshippers, six sevenths of whom are in Europe. Its churches are generally bedecked with tawdry pictures, of which the face and hands are painted, while the drapery, &c., are in basso relievo of silver and gold plates, or tinsel. It regards but two sacraments as divine — baptism and the eucharist, or Lord's supper. Its rites and ceremonies are similar to, but more simple than, those of the Roman Catholics, and most of its votaries are sunk in ignorance and superstition.

We may here remark, with regard to the other religions of Europe, that the Mahometan counts six millions of worshippers, the Papal one hundred and twelve millions, and the Protestant about fifty millions. In general terms, the Greek church may be said to occupy Eastern Europe, the Catholic Southern, and the Protestant Northern Europe.

Protestantism originated, as we have seen elsewhere, in a growing desire to rid the political world of the tyranny of Rome, and to purify religion from the corruptions of tradition, and the abuses of a sensual priesthood. The *Albigenses*, in France, had refused to acknowledge the pope's supremacy, and were exterminated with ruthless ferocity, A. D. 1226. A remnant of similar Christians the Vaudois, took refuge in Piedmont; where twenty thousand of them are still found. In the next century, the *Lollards*, or Wicliffites, in England, aimed to restore the simplicity of primitive Christianity from the Bible text. These were followed by the *Hussites*, in Bohemia, in the fifteenth century. But the reformers did not acquire sufficient power to resist the persecutions of the ruling church, the Papal, till the beginning of the sixteenth century, when kings and governments aided the enthusiasm, virtue, courage, and intelligence of individual reformers, and protected them from fire and fagot, the dungeon and the rack. By the Lutheran and other established churches, the "reformation" is now held to be accomplished; by the independent sects of Christendom, it is considered to be still and ever progressive.

There are several interesting phases presented by the history of Europe previous to the reformation. *Feudalism*, the *Papacy*, the *Crusades*, and *Chivalry*, have each exerted a vast influence, during the Dark or Middle Ages, — A. D. 500 to 1500, — nor is their influence yet at an end.

Feudalism was the necessary outgrowth of the imperfect organization of the militant tribes that overran the Roman empire. We may observe its elementary state in the present and past politico military organization of Tartary, the primeval home of the northern barbarians. Slavery of labor was the basis of feudalism, and the conquered were, of course, the slaves; the soldier was the citizen. The normal state being that of war, the man of that iron age full often

> "Lay down to rest with corselet braced,
> Pillowed on buckler cold and hard,
> Carved at the meal with gloves of steel,
> And drank the red wine through the helmet barred."

War was its only business and sole glory; literature its mock, and might its right. In feudalism originated many false ideas of honor which still prevail; contempt of any labor but that of human butchery; hereditary aristocracy, and a thousand unjust privileges and distinctions which have long cursed, and are still cursing, even the most highly civilized portions of the earth. Our own age has, however, seen one after another of the relics of feudalism yielding and crumbling away before the progress of rational liberty in Europe.

The institution of the *Papacy* was perhaps the most powerful instrument in moulding the character of the middle ages, and indeed of modern Europe. At first, the barbarians carried every thing by brute force but gradually the Christian priesthood obtained a quiet ascendency, which tempered the ferocity of the robbers. At the time of Charlemagne's death, the clergy, indeed, had acquired unbounded influence over the higher orders of society, and Rome spiritual, with her ghostly armies, had renewed the sway of Rome imperial, with her steel-clad legions. Nor was the influence of the church of Rome less with the masses. Its ranks were recruited from all classes; and the poorest hind, if he possessed talent, might rise through the grades of the priesthood to a level with the proudest nobles, and even tread on the neck of the mightiest emperors. Hence the church often stood between power and its victim, and occasionally represented the democratic elements of society. By its inferior priesthood, vowed to perpetual poverty, it reached and could move the very dregs of the people. Many of the "poor in spirit," doubtless, now yearned for greater purity of religion, a more sincere Christianity, as they perceived the hierarchy of the church corrupted by the possession of power, and immersed in the selfish luxuries of the aristocracy. But the priesthood felt that their grasp upon the higher classes was growing precarious, as intelligence dawned upon the night of barbarism. The popes, therefore, endeavored to build their sway upon a broader basis. Availing themselves of the invention of the mendicant orders of friars,—instituted to stem the corrupt self-indulgence of the age,—the pontiffs craftily granted these holy beggars unreasonable immunities and privileges. Thus they succeeded in converting a large class of that sort of men who were born fanatics, and might have become reformers, into the mightiest supporters of the system they had sworn to subvert.

As the excitement in regard to the end of the world, which agitated all minds during the tenth and eleventh centuries, subsided, the religious feeling of Europe, having gained depth and universality through the indefatigable efforts of the priesthood, and the missionary spirit of the age, found full expression in the *crusades*. The barefooted fanatic, *Peter*, travelling from realm to realm, pictured to the people, in frightful colors, the sufferings of their fellow-Christians from the persecuting infidel, who trampled on the sepulchre of the blessed Savior. Pope *Urban* seconded him, and in the spring of 1096, the *First Crusade* started for Palestine. Eighty thousand were led on by Peter, and two hundred thousand soon followed. The folly of this infatuated banditti was only equalled by their barbarity, especially toward the Jews. Two thirds were cut off by those whom they had outraged, the rest by Sultan *Solyman* on the plains of Nice. But *Godfrey* soon followed with a fine army and able generals, one hundred thousand horse, and six hundred thousand foot, and took Jerusalem, founding the kingdom of Syria and Palestine, A. D. 1099.

The *Second Crusade* was preached by *St. Bernard*, in 1147, and three hundred thousand Germans and French, under Conrad III. and Louis VII., entered Asia. Conrad was defeated at Iconium, and Louis at Laodicea, both in Asia Minor. In 1174, Sultan Saladin took Jerusalem. To recover it, the *Third Crusade* was undertaken by Philip Augustus of France, Richard I. of England, and Frederic Barbarossa of Germany, A. D. 1190. Frederic was drowned. The other two took Acre, quarrelled, and Philip returned in disgust. Richard made peace with Saladin, after defeating him at Ascalon, and, on his return, was imprisoned in Germany. In 1202, Baldwin, count of Flanders, set out with an immense army on a *Fourth Crusade*, but took possession of Constantinople, and went no farther. John de Brienne, with one hundred thousand men, invaded Egypt, to break the power of the sovereign of Jerusalem at its centre; he took Damietta, but was obliged to surrender; and thus ended the *Fifth Crusade*. St. Louis IX. of France invaded Egypt in 1248, with his queen, his three brothers, and all the knights of France; this was the *Sixth Crusade*. He was defeated and imprisoned; he, however, ransomed himself, and spent some time in the Holy Land, before returning to France. After a wise reign of thirteen years, Louis, urged on by a return of his fanaticism, undertook a crusade against the Moors, and, laying siege to Tunis, perished with his army by pestilence, A. D. 1270. Thus ended the *Seventh* and last *Crusade*. Some writers make ten, namely, in 1096, 1110, '50, '90, '95, 1209, '17, '28, '40, '48.

One of the most singular and incredible instances of the "exaltation" of feeling which was produced and sustained by the crusades, is what was called the *Children's Crusade*. In the district of Vendome, in France, in 1212, there appeared a shepherd boy, named Stephen, who exhibited a letter purporting to be a commission received from Jesus Christ himself, authorizing him to go forth and conquer the infidels in Palestine. "None," he said, "but innocent children could hope for success; for Christ had declared that of such is the kingdom of heaven." Accordingly, seven thousand urchins were led by him to the shores of the Adriatic, where they were murdered by the pirate inhabitants of that coast. These were followed by more than thirty thousand boys and young maidens, who took ship at Marseilles, and being wrecked on the coast of Africa, were either drowned or enslaved.

It was only during such phenomena as the crusades, that *Chivalry* could have attained perfection. The man of Feudalism, though he gloried in murder legalized by war, and considered the bedizened soldier as "the highest style of man," was not all fiend. The natural desire to relieve misery remained. Upon this were ingrafted the pride and taste of aristocratic life, with its code of honor. The fiery heart of the gallant Arab, exhaling itself, as from time immemorial, in songs to his peerless lady love; the loyal respect of the Teuton for the sex; a common religion widening the sympathies and consecrating them to a common purpose;—add that unappeasable thirst for glory, that yearning after superhuman excellence, so characteristic of the Teutonic race,—and we have all the elements of chivalry. Honor, courtesy, piety, disinterestedness, and gallantry were its soul, and they often produced the moral sublime in action. Chivalry, as a regularly organized European institution, dates from the eleventh century, when the crusades had first given a public opinion to the various Christian nations who met in Palestine, armed in a common cause.

The *Orders of Chivalry* were numerous, and their rules similar to those of the monks. The earliest society of the kind was in A. D. 499, when Clovis I. instituted the "Order of the Holy Urn." That of "the Oak" was established by Ximenes, king of Navarre, in 722; that of "the Genet," by Charles Martel, in 726. The earliest order of the crusades, was that of the Knights of St. John of Jerusalem. There were, beside, the orders of the Knights Templars; of "the Cross and Sword;" the Teutonic Knights; the Knights Hospitallers; of Mercy, and others. Those retained in England, even now, are the order of the Garter, instituted in 1350; of the Thistle, revived in 1687; of St. Patrick, instituted in 1783; of the Bath, revived in 1725.

The *Manners of the Middle Ages*, with a great deal that is revolting, present much that is picturesque and pleasing, and much that contrasts with the monotony and uniformity of modern life. But while the hollow and fantastic forms of chivalry prevailed in high life, cloaking almost universal licentiousness, boorish rudeness proclaimed the vulgarity of the people. The settlement of the barbarians in Gaul, Spain, and Italy put an end to literature and classical learning. Kings and princes could not write, and scarcely one of their subjects acquired the slightest tincture of letters. The rough baron thanked the holy Virgin that no son of his was so low as to be able to read or write. Even the clergy soon fell into the same depths of ignorance. France reached the lowest point at the beginning of the eighth, England at the middle of the ninth, century; and during the tenth century, literature was in a deplorable state in the latter country and in Italy. In 992, it was asserted that scarce a person in Rome knew the alphabet; not one priest of a thousand in Spain could write a letter. Superstition, brooding in this thick darkness, now gave birth to her myriad phantoms; trials by ordeal and duel showed that reason had yielded up every corner of her empire. Crimes were frequent, especially perjury, which strikes at the root of all social security. In short, the degradation of society was complete. Yet out of this chaos — ordained for the very purpose — a degree of order has arisen.

The art of arts in Europe has been that of *war*. In France, during the last five centuries, her years of war have amounted to three hundred and twenty-six, — namely, thirty-five civil, forty religious; seventy-six on her own soil, one hundred and seventy-five foreign. Her great and sanguinary battles have been eighty-four. Other countries would present as piteous a spectacle! In the sixteenth century, there were eighty-five years of war; in the seventeenth, sixty-nine; in the eighteenth, fifty-eight; making a total in those three centuries of two hundred and twelve years of war, to eighty-eight, only, of peace! The history of Greece and Rome, that is, of early Europe, is a catalogue of wars! But the explosive force of gunpowder has taken the place of the scythe-chariots, battering-rams, balistas, bow-guns, javelins, wild-fire, and all other implements of destruction from time immemorial. This change has given to intellect its proper superiority over brute force — has made the few and weak equal to the numerous and strong. Wars generally have become shorter and less bloody, and being carried on chiefly by mercenaries, whose trade it is, — the misery to families is less. The introduction of steam and electricity in war, if realized, will tend still more to establish the superiority of science over numbers, and forever insure European civilization against such an irruption of barbarism as destroyed that of Rome. War, too, is now conducted on such a scale, and its necessities are so costly, that kings cannot carry it on without the assistance of the moneyed interest; and this is ever and instinctively opposed to war and all its wastefulness and uncertainties. Power has passed from the sword to the purse; and should the bankers of Western Europe refuse to loan the great colossus of Eastern Europe the necessary funds for his wars, the arms of that tremendous power may be at once tied — his mercenaries may mutiny in their cantonments, and his ships rot in their docks!

The numerous *Inventions* which have blessed the few latter centuries of European civilization, also preclude all fear that it will again be plunged into the chaos from which we have now traced its emergence. Mental darkness can never cover the nations again, for printing has been invented. Priestcraft can never palsy the energies of the mind, for science has driven superstition from its murky corners. Despotism can never oppress the whole civilized world, for commerce has found new continents, where Liberty may fold her fostering wing over her children, unmolested. Nations can never again look upon each other as "natural enemies," for the progress of art and science, the facilities of trade and travel, have linked them in a thousand bonds of pleasant and profitable intercourse. War can never more be the great business of nations; for the middling classes, whose comforts are at stake, are the majority, and perceive now and forever the miserable absurdity of a state of warfare. Above all is our age blessed with the clear light of the gospel tens of millions of Bibles are distributed throughout the earth, and the light of these torches of truth, glowing upon millions of hearthstones, can never again be extinguished.

Thirty-six centuries ago, Europe began with the savage, the pirate, the robber — who contended with the wild beasts for the possession of the soil. She passed through centuries of infinite toils, sufferings, struggles, and triumphs, till she reached her culminating point of material civilization under the emperors of Rome. One hundred and twenty millions of human beings enjoyed all they were capable of enjoying under the peaceful shadow of her eagles. A few centuries later, and all was chaos. The philosopher, disgusted with the science which brought him only a knowledge of new forms of woe, dared not look about or beyond himself, and sunk into the sensualist, greedy of the moments of pleasure he could snatch from the misery around him. Even the Christian forsook the ranks where he should have battled for humanity, and slunk into the cloister of the monk, or the cell of the anchorite. Nearly as many centuries have again rolled over Europe; and now, to the philosopher, to the Christian, what a different prospect is presented! It is true, that evils still exist; despotism, the radical curse of mankind, holds sway over a large part of Europe, presenting its usual spectacles of unbounded wealth, high intelligence, and elegant refinement among the privileged few, contrasted with hopeless poverty, debasing ignorance, and unspeakable misery, on the part of the million. But the monarchical institutions which have created and cherished this state of things, as the best that human policy can devise, or that Providence permits, are either tottering to a speedy fall, or undergoing modifications which tend to their final, but inevitable, dissolution. The very foundations on which they stood are themselves undermined. European society has, for ages, rested upon the doctrine that God had given power to kings, priests, and nobles, and that any attempt to alter this system was both treason and impiety. This doctrine of absolute *conservatism* has given way to that of *progress*. The latter is now a common creed throughout one half of Europe. "A better day is coming," is not only the song of the sighing millions, but the faith of philanthropists, and the hobby of partisans, politicians, and statesmen. In France, monarchy is already dead, never to be permanently revived. There is neither loyalty to a dynasty nor a rich and time-honored peerage, nor a church allied to the state, nor any other of those pillars indispensable to the support of a throne. Nor can these things be created, in the present enlightened age, among a people who have learned to despise them. France, it would seem, must settle down upon a popular government, and all southern Europe will speedily follow her example. To this issue the course of events inevitably tends. Before the end is reached, there may be violent agitation; but we may hope that liberty, peace, and prosperity may soon follow, as the compensation for ages of darkness and despotism.

CHAPTER CCCCLXXIII

A. D. 1000 to 1390.

The Northmen in America — Discoveries of the Icelanders — Voyages of Biorn and Leif — Settlement of the Northmen in Vinland — Voyage of Niccolo Zeno — Discovery of Estotiland — The alleged Discoveries of the Welsh.

America, or the Western Continent, lies between the Atlantic and Pacific Oceans, extending from the fifty-sixth degree of southern latitude to the polar regions of the north. North and South America are joined together by the Isthmus of Panama or Darien, which is only forty miles in breadth in its narrowest part. Its length is nine thousand miles, and its entire extent fifteen millions of square miles. Its climate embraces that of every zone; but its eastern coast is generally colder than places in the same latitude in other parts of the world.

In this continent, the operations of nature appear to have been conducted on a larger scale than in any other quarter of the globe. Mountains, rivers, lakes, valleys, and forests strike the eye by the grandeur of their proportions. The noble streams of the Mississippi, the St. Lawrence, the Orinoco, the Amazon, and the La Plata, are without a parallel in the eastern continent. The lakes of America resemble seas in magnitude; and the immense mountain range of the Andes and the Rocky Mountains is the longest in the world.

It is quite remarkable that, while the vegetable and animal kingdoms of the western continent present aspects resembling those of the old world, there is still an almost universal difference in the species. We have oaks, elms, firs, and other trees, bearing the general characteristics of the same kinds in Europe; yet scarce an instance of identity is found in the whole range of the forests. We have deer, foxes, squirrels, &c.; yet in no case are they the same as those of the eastern continent. We have a few birds identical with those of Europe and Asia, but they are of kinds that might pass from one continent to the other.

Referring for further geographical details to our views of North and South America, we propose to give a brief sketch of the aborigines of this continent, an account of the discoveries of the Northmen, and those of Columbus and his followers. We shall then proceed to give a history of North America, and its several political divisions, and that of South America with its political divisions. These subjects will be treated in the following order: —

1. Sketch of North America. 2. Polar Regions 3. British America. 4. United States. 5. Mexico 6. Guatimala. 7. West Indies. 8. South America 9. Venezuela, Colombia, and Equador. 10. Peru. 11. Bolivia. 12. Chili. 13. Patagonia. 14. Buenos Ayres. 15. Uruguay. 16. Paraguay. 17. Brazil. 18. Guiana

With the exception of the two great nations of Mexico and Peru, the inhabitants of America, when discovered by the Spaniards, were in a savage or barbarous state, and there was a remarkable similarity in the general circumstances of their condition, throughout the whole of the regions which they occupied. Nor have these rude tribes improved in any material degree since their acquaintance with Europeans. If we compare the American Indians with the natives of Europe or Asia, we shall find that the superiority displayed by the latter in conducting the operations of agriculture, depends chiefly upon two circumstances, the use of tame animals and the possession of iron and other hard metals. But the aborigines of America had not reduced animals to subjection; and they were completely ignorant of the harder and more useful metals. Gold, with the exception of a little silver and copper, was the only metal known in America before the discovery; and the use of this was confined chiefly to ornament. The only tools in the possession of the natives were hatchets of stone; and with these the labor of a year was requisite to cut down a tree and hollow it into a canoe.

In agriculture, the progress was equally slow. The trees with which the forests were crowded, were of the hardest wood, and the shrubs so thickly interwoven, that the efforts of a whole tribe were scarcely sufficient to clear a small piece of ground, and adapt it to the purposes of cultivation. The fertility of the soil, rather than the industry of the people, secured to them an increase equal to their wants. A great many of their tribes depended for their subsistence chiefly on hunting and fishing. Among the greater part of the American savage communities the bonds of political association were exceedingly slight. The individuals inhabiting a certain district appeared to combine for temporary, rather than permanent, objects. Laws and the regular administration of justice were unknown. Their rulers were military commanders rather than political chiefs. In this respect the natives of America appear to have resembled the ancient Germans, as they are described to us by Cæsar and Tacitus.

The history of the discovery, conquest, and colonization of America by the Europeans, is peculiarly interesting. It displays the gradual progress of cultivation and commerce, amid regions abandoned to nature. The wilds of America exhibited an exact representation of what every country of the old continent once had been; but ancient history is wholly silent concerning the particulars of that process by which the wilderness of Europe and Asia was converted into a residence for civilization, industry, and the elegant arts The discovery of a new world not only excited a spirit of enterprise and adventure among the people of Europe, but gave rise to new scenes of almost every kind, and to endless opportunities for active and industrious exertion. It not only added vast domains to the empires of Europe, but improved the sciences of navigation, geography, astronomy, medicine, natural history, and their subsidiary branches of knowledge. The discovery and colonization of America may be enumerated among those important events, which have effected an extraordinary and lasting change in human affairs, which has manifested itself in the political and commercial system of the world.

The proper discovery of America is justly attributed to Columbus, as he was the first to bring the knowledge of the new world to the countries of Europe. But the claims of the Scandinavian adventurers to a still earlier discovery of the western continent must not be omitted in a history of the Western Hemisphere.

The Northmen landing in America.

The ancient *sagas*, or historical records of Iceland, contain various narratives relating to the voyages and discoveries of the Northmen to the west and south-west of that island, which render it extremely probable that these adventurous mariners discovered the western continent as early as the tenth or eleventh century. As a strictly historical fact, this matter has been the subject of much discussion. The Icelandic narrative is in substance as follows: —

About the close of the tenth century, the Icelanders had begun to form settlements on the coast of Greenland. A young Icelandic mariner, named Biorn, who had employed the summer in some distant voyages, arrived home at the end of the season, intending to pass the winter with his father, but found he had gone to Greenland. The ardent and enterprising temper of Biorn induced him to follow his parent across the stormy ocean, which he had never before traversed. For three days, the voyage was prosperous; but then the sky became overcast, a strong wind blew from the north, and the navigators were tossed about for several days, ignorant of their situation. At length, the gale abated, the clouds dispersed, and after a day's sail, they discovered an unknown land covered with woods and hills. They sailed for several days along this coast, after which the wind shifted to the south, and they steered back to Greenland, where they arrived in safety.

This adventure came to the knowledge of Leif, the son of Eric Redhead, a bold and enterprising young chief; and he determined to go on an expedition to this newly-discovered region. He set sail with a crew of thirty-five men, and following the direction pointed out by Biorn, arrived in sight of the unknown land. It had a wild and rugged appearance, and its mountains were covered with snow. Leif called this *Helluland*, or the "Land of Rocks." He came next to a flat and woody region, which he named *Markland*, or "Flat Land." Sailing onward before a north wind, he reached a delightful island near the coast. The soil of it was fertile; the ground was covered with bushes which bore sweet berries, and there was a river and a lake amply stored with salmon and other fish. The very grass dropped dew, sweet, like honey. In this agreeable abode the Northmen spent the winter. One day, a German of their company, who had been into the woods, returned leaping and dancing with joyous exultation: as they crowded round him to inquire the cause, he showed them some fruits, which, from his experience of southern countries, he knew to be grapes. On this account the country received the name of *Vinland*, or "Wineland."

The next adventurer, after the return of Leif to Iceland, was Thorwald, his brother, who, having made repeated voyages to Vinland, came at last to a promontory, with which he was so much delighted, that he made a vow to fix his abode there. While the Northmen were building their houses, there appeared three canoes covered with skins, each containing three men, whom the Icelandic historians call *Skrœllings*, or dwarfs. They attacked these savages, and killed all but one, who made his escape. A few days afterward, they were awakened by loud cries in the night, and, looking out, saw the bay covered with canoes, and clouds of arrows pouring in upon them. They defended themselves behind planks and boughs of trees, and, by their superior skill in fighting, they succeeded in repulsing their assailants. Thorwald, however, was mortally wounded; and, finding his end approaching, he gave instructions for burying him upon this promontory, so that his vow might, in a certain sense, be fulfilled.

Thorstein, the brother of Leif and Thorwald, undismayed by the fate of his kinsman, fitted out another expedition from Iceland, comprising twenty-five persons. They reached Vinland, but encountered great hardships; and Thorstein died of the scurvy shortly after his return. Another adventurer, named Thorfinn Karlsnefn, who married the widow of Thorstein, undertook an expedition on a much larger scale than any of the preceding. He fitted out three vessels, with upwards of a hundred emigrants, carrying cattle, furniture, tools, &c. They had a prosperous voyage, and, on reaching Vinland, found a large whale cast ashore, which afforded them ample subsistence. They cut down trees, and built themselves houses. A party of Skrœllings paid them a visit, who seemed to have had no connection with those previously encountered by the Northmen. These simple people were affrighted beyond measure by the lowing of a bull. The Northmen made them presents, with which they were highly pleased. They appeared to be ignorant of edge-tools; for one of them contrived to steal a battle-axe, with which he sportively struck one of his companions, as he had been accustomed to do with his rude tomahawk, but was astonished to find that he had given him a mortal wound.

Thorfinn made many voyages to Vinland, and grew rich. His latter days were spent in Iceland, where he lived in great splendor. After some time, other expeditions were made to Vinland; but the adventurers became involved in bloody contentions. Bishop Eric is said to have visited this country in 1321. Soon after this date, the communication with Vinland, from some unknown cause, entirely ceased, and the country was forgotten.

There is no reason to doubt the correctness of these narratives, but writers are not agreed as to the situation of Vinland. Some, who have very carefully investigated the whole history, and compared it with the geographical features of the North American coast, decide that Vinland is identical with Massachusetts and Rhode Island; that the main colony of the Northmen was in Narragansett Bay, and the promontory where Thorwald was buried is Point Alderton, at the entrance of Boston harbor. Many of the facts related in the history confirm these suppositions in a remarkable manner; yet the matter, on the whole, is so far doubtful as to restrain us from recording it as authentic history that the Northmen visited the shores of the United States. Some authors think Vinland to be the Island of Newfoundland, and others are of opinion, that the Northmen never sailed farther south than Labrador.

Posterior to the Icelandic accounts, there is a narrative of some celebrity, which is supposed to include an early record of the discovery of America. In the fourteenth and fifteenth centuries, Venice was the chief seat of all commercial and maritime enterprise. Among the noble families of this city, few held a higher rank than Zeno, who had filled the highest offices of the republic, and fought with distinction in the wars against the Turks. In 1380, Niccolo Zeno set sail for the north, with a view of visiting England and Flanders, but was driven by a tempest on the coast of a country which he calls *Friesland.* Here he remained some years, being very well treated by the prince of the country. During this time, four fishing vessels belonging to Friesland, being overtaken at sea by a violent storm, were tossed about for some time, when the sky clearing up, they discovered a large island, which they called *Estotiland*, and which they reckoned to be a thousand miles distant from Friesland. They landed and were conducted to a populous town, where they were introduced to the chief. Neither party, however, could understand the other, till a man was found who had been cast upon the same shore, and who could speak Latin. The Frieslanders remained some time in this country, which they found nearly as large as Iceland, and much more fertile. The inhabitants raised grain, and brewed beer. They had ships with which they navigated the ocean. The chief possessed a library, in which were Latin books, which the people, however, did not understand. The country contained many towns and castles. To the south of Estotiland lay a more extensive and fertile country, called *Drogio.* In a visit to this quarter, the Frieslanders were cast away, and fell into the hands of savages, by whom most of them were killed. South-west of these were people of more civilized manners. They had cities, temples, idols, gold, and silver, and offered up human sacrifices.

Only one of the Frieslanders returned to his own country; but the intelligence which he brought roused the adventurous spirit of Zichmi, the king of that region. He equipped a fleet, which he placed under the command of Zeno, for the purpose of exploring Estotiland. After sailing some distance to the west, they discovered land, which proved to be an island, called *Icaria*, governed by a son of Dædalus, king of Scotland. They met with a very inhospitable reception here, and, in attempting to land, a battle ensued, in which several persons were killed on both sides. Zeno, therefore, pursued his voyage to the west; but meeting with a constant succession of head winds, he bore away northward to Greenland, from whence he returned to Friesland by the way of the Faroe Islands.

This narrative is regarded by many geographers as authentic in the main points. Malte Brun, Forster, and others, consider it as beyond a doubt, that Estotiland is Newfoundland, and that the civilization and European aspect of the country described in the narrative were derived from the Icelandic colonies which had been settled there two centuries before. The very name given to it by the narrators is synonymous with *East-out-land*, and strikingly descriptive of the relative situation of Newfoundland to the American continent. The classical names of *Icaria* and *Dædalus* might excite suspicion; but nothing was more common, in those days, than to confound the barbarous names of unknown countries with those of Greek and Roman history. Zeno's narrative is unquestionably of an earlier date than the discovery of Columbus; and whatever we may think of its authenticity, it must be regarded as a very curious relation.

The Welsh are also said to have discovered America at an early period. According to this account, Madoc, a Welsh chieftain, having been compelled to leave his own country, set sail in the year 1170 with a small fleet, and directing his course westward, landed, after a voyage of some weeks, on a continent, where the inhabitants differed greatly from those of Europe. He remained here for a considerable time, after which he returned to Wales, leaving one hundred and twenty persons in the newly discovered region. He sailed again to the west, with a fleet of ten ships, but was never heard of afterwards. Such is the substance of their legend, which is little credited by historians.

Columbus approaching the Land.

CHAPTER CCCCLXXIV.

State of the World in the Fifteenth Century, to 1492 — Discovery of America by Columbus — Other Discoveries.

THE discovery of America by Columbus is the greatest event in history, from the overthrow of the Roman empire, to the present time. It may be remarked, that no period in the annals of the human race witnessed a more extraordinary coincidence of important events than the age in which the New World was first made known to the Old. Within this period are comprised the invention of printing, the use of gunpowder, the improvement of navigation, the revival of ancient learning, and the Protestant reformation. At this time, also, the principal monarchies of Europe began to consolidate, and acquire the form and strength which in general they exhibit at the present day. All these events conspired to change materially the face of Europe.

Before this period, the manners of the European nations may be described as little elevated above barbarism. Even in Italy, where the dawning of literature had somewhat softened the minds of the inhabitants, history, for a long time preceding this period, presents little but a series of treasons, usurpations, and massacres. Nothing appears of a solid and rational policy; scarcely any state was inspired by extensive views, or looked farther than to local and temporary advantages. A wild, romantic courage in the northern and western parts of Europe, and a crafty and unscrupulous ambition in the Italian states, were the characteristics of that age. The manners of the courts exhibit but very faint marks of civilization and politeness. The people had made few advances in useful knowledge. The small amount of learning which then existed in Christendom may be described as the dotage of scholastic philosophy combined with the infancy of a politer learning, but which rose hardly above the level of verbal trifling. Mathematical knowledge was little

FERDINAND AND ISABELLA RECEIVING COLUMBUS.

ltivated and less esteemed. There was no knowlge of the real form of the earth; and, in general, e ideas of a man did not extend beyond his own rizon.

As an instance of the low state of geographical owledge during the middle ages, we may mention at Cosmas, a learned Greek of the sixth century, ho had travelled extensively, and even made a yage to India, wrote a work entitled *Christian Topography*, the chief object of which was to confute the retical opinion that the earth was round, and to oppose the pagan belief that there existed a temperate gion to the south of the torrid zone. He informed s readers that, according to the orthodox system of ography, the earth is a quadrangular plane, extendg four hundred days' journey from east to west, and lf as far from north to south. This plane is enosed by lofty mountains, upon which rests the cany, or vault, of the firmament. A huge mountain the north side of the earth, by intercepting the ght of the sun, produces the vicissitudes of day and ght. The plane of the earth has a declivity from rth to south, in consequence of which the Euphras, Tigris, and other rivers running southward, are pid; whereas the Nile, by running up hill, has cessarily a very slow current. Such is the system Cosmas!

The belief that there existed a fourth division of the obe, larger than any of the others, had been encoured by some of the ancient philosophers. This was generally diffused in the early ages of Christianity, at two eminent fathers of the church, St. Auguse and Lactantius, had zealously labored to refute the eory, as inconsistent with the doctrines of the Bible. ith the cultivation of Greek literature in the fournth and fifteenth centuries, the old belief began to vive. At the same time, the rapid development of the irit of maritime discovery induced several nations, pecially the Portuguese, to search for new and unown lands. The state of navigation during the iddle ages may be understood from what is related the Northmen, who were the best sailors of those nes. The voyage from Greenland to Iceland and orway and back again, commonly required five years; d on one occasion, the government of Norway did t hear of the death of the bishop of Greenland till x years after it took place!

The Canaries, or Fortunate Islands, were the first nd discovered by the Europeans after the introducn of the mariner's compass: they became known to e Spaniards early in the fourteenth century. In the rly part of the fifteenth, the Portuguese began that ries of voyages of discovery along the western coast Africa, which they pursued, till, at the close of that ntury, they had doubled the Cape of Good Hope, d found a passage to India. During this period arose HRISTOPHER COLUMBUS, who was destined to carry e great enterprise of maritime discovery to an ext never before equalled. Columbus was a native Cogoleto, a small town in the territory of the reblic of Genoa. Before his time, the Italian states d produced many eminent astronomers, skilful pilots, d hardy navigators; yet their attention was almost clusively engrossed by the business of land conveyce, and the navigation of the interior seas of Eupe: they did not begin any enterprise of oceanic scovery. Columbus, who was born in 1447, was ed to the sea and made many voyages on the Atlantic, from the coast of Guinea to the northern seas. Some writers are of opinion that he visited Iceland, and obtained there a knowledge of the discovery of the western continent by the Northmen; but of this we have no positive evidence.

Columbus appears to have conceived juster notions of the figure of the earth than were generally entertained in his time. He possessed some mathematical science, and was well acquainted with all the facts in geography which had then come to the knowledge of the Europeans. The spherical form of the globe lay at the foundation of the theory which he formed to himself respecting the countries by which the Atlantic Ocean was bordered on the west, though the maps of that age, much more erroneous than his conjectures, caused him to mistake his immediate object. He believed, in short, that China and India lay in that part of the world where the American continent was afterward found. The true size of the globe was then unknown, and Columbus imagined that, by sailing westward, he should arrive at the coast of Asia. In the midst of the ignorance that prevailed in Europe respecting these matters, many writings and much speculation had been put forth on the subject. All these appear to have been carefully studied by Columbus. It is highly curious to observe the wavering and unexpected streams of light which penetrated through the great mass of darkness that lay before the contemplation of this remarkable man. It was a strange and fantastic mixture of ancient authority and modern report, of wild fable and demonstrated fact, of true conjecture and erroneous theory, out of which this enthusiastic yet reasonable projector undertook to extract, as well as he could, conclusions convincing to himself, and, if possible, satisfactory to others.

Having persuaded himself of the feasibility of his plan of finding land in the west, Columbus first proposed an expedition of discovery to the government of Genoa, but was repulsed as a visionary schemer. He next applied to the kings of Portugal and England, but with no better success, though the Portuguese privately sent a vessel of their own to make discoveries in the quarter pointed out by Columbus. He then applied to the court of Ferdinand and Isabella, the sovereigns of Spain; and after eight years of delay, his endeavors were crowned with success. Queen Isabella undertook the equipment of an expedition: three small vessels were fitted out, under the command of Columbus, who was made an admiral in the Spanish service. With this fleet he set sail from Palos, in Spain, on the 3d day of August, 1492. He steered first to the Canary Islands, and then directed his course west.

Columbus had no chart of the Atlantic Ocean, except the fanciful sketches of the geographers of the middle ages, who had filled this unknown space with sunken islands and continents, or covered it with a sky of impenetrable darkness. He had no directions from former navigators, and no experience of the winds and currents peculiar to those seas. His only guide was his own genius, and the indications which he discovered in the casual appearances of land birds and floating sea-weeds, most of them little to be depended on. It was in this voyage that the variation of the compass was first observed — an appearance which has never yet been explained by all the researches of science, and which made a most discouraging impression on the crews of Columbus. This intrepid commander, however, with a wonderful quickness and sagacity, pretended to discover a cause for this appearance, which, though it did not satisfy himself, was plausible enough to remove the apprehensions of his men. Expedients of this kind were daily wanting, and were as constantly supplied by the fertile genius of Columbus. At length, after a voyage of thirty-three days from the Canaries, land was discovered in the west; and on the 12th of October, the Spaniards landed on the Island of Guanahani, one of the Bahamas, which Columbus named *San Salvador*. Proceeding onward, he discovered Cuba and Hispaniola, and leaving a colony in the latter island, he returned to Spain.

He was received by Ferdinand and Isabella with the highest honors, and a second expedition was prepared, to extend and secure his discoveries. In that age, the reverence for the papal power was so great, that it was believed all the undiscovered regions of the earth belonged to the pope, who could give them away to whom he pleased. Before the departure of Columbus on his second voyage, therefore, the Spanish sovereigns made application to Alexander VI., who then occupied the chair of St. Peter, for a grant of these new dominions. The pontiff issued a bull, dividing all the unknown regions of the earth inhabited by infidels between the Spaniards and Portuguese; and for the purpose of making this division exact, he fixed as a common boundary an imaginary line, drawn from the north to the south pole, one hundred leagues west of the Azores. All the new-found territories west of this line were adjudged to belong to Spain, and all east of it to Portugal.

Columbus made four voyages to the west, in which he discovered all the principal islands which constitute the group now called the *West Indies*. In 1497, he discovered the continent of South America, near the mouth of the Orinoco. Other navigators and adventurers followed him; among them, Amerigo Vespucci, whose name has been given to the new world. Within half a century, the Spaniards had explored the coast of the western continent from Florida in the north to the mouth of the Amazon in the south. They had also crossed the Isthmus of Darien to the shores of the Pacific, and discovered the rich and populous empire of Peru. Hernando Cortez had conquered Mexico; and Pizarro and Almagro had reduced Peru to the dominion of Spain. In the mean time, a Portuguese fleet, under Alvarez de Cabral, on a voyage to India, accidentally discovered the coast of Brazil, in 1501; and in 1534, the Spaniards had pushed their explorations south of this region, and entered the mouth of the great river of La Plata.

Immediately after the discovery of the Western World, the Spaniards began the work of settlement. The first colony was established in the Island of Hispaniola. The natives were at first peaceable, and offered no resistance to the settlers; but the greediness of the Spaniards in the pursuit of gold, and their tyrannical conduct in compelling the natives to work for them, soon led to hostilities. The Indians collected a vast army; but Columbus, with a small force, attacked them in the night, and put them completely to the rout. The natives, being vanquished in battle, were reduced to hopeless slavery. The hardships to which they were subjected rapidly diminished their numbers, and the native islanders soon became extinct. When the gold became scarce in Hispaniola, it was necessary to seek new settlements for the fresh crowds of adventurers from Spain. The neighboring island of Porto Rico was therefore invaded, and its unfortunate inhabitants experienced the same fate as the natives of Hispaniola. The island of Cuba was next conquered, though it was then densely peopled: such was the unwarlike character of its inhabitants, that three hundred Spaniards were sufficient for its total subjugation. At a late date, they occupied the Island of Jamaica. Hispaniola is now independent, and Jamaica is held by the British.

When the West India Islands were found to offer no further attraction to the avarice of the Spaniards, they directed their enterprises to the continent. An expedition fitted out by Velasquez, the governor of Cuba, and commanded by Hernando Cortez, landed in Mexico in 1519. Montezuma, the emperor of the country, sent the Spaniards some rich presents, and ordered them to depart. But the gifts only inflamed their cupidity, and Cortez determined to penetrate into the country, and march to the capital of the empire. In conformity with this desperate resolution he burnt his ships, and marched toward the city of Mexico. He made alliances with some of the native tribes on his march, and reached the capital. He took the emperor prisoner, provoked a war with the Mexicans, and was expelled, with great loss, from the city; but after some time, he recruited his forces, and returned to besiege it. An obstinate and sanguinary struggle ensued, in which the capital was nearly destroyed, and an immense slaughter of the Mexicans took place. The Spaniards at length became masters of the city, and all resistance ceased. The whole empire of Mexico submitted to the conquerors, and was made a colony of the Spanish monarchy. It remained in this dependence till the early part of the present century, when insurrections broke out. At length, in 1821, the Mexicans declared themselves independent, and the Spanish dominion in this quarter was finally overthrown.

Shortly after the subjugation of Mexico by Cortez an expedition under Alvarado, one of his officers, proceeded against the neighboring kingdom of Guatimala, which was speedily subjected to the Spanish power. This country was also colonized, and remained attached to the Spanish monarch, with a slight dependence on Mexico, till 1821, when the inhabitants declared themselves independent.

Peru was invaded by the Spaniards, under Pizarro and Almagro, in 1531. The conduct of the invaders was the same as in Mexico. They advanced boldly into the country, and seized the person of the Inca, or sovereign of the empire. The natives resisted, and a bloody war took place, which ended in the subjugation of the country. From Peru, another expedition was despatched southward into Chili, which was finally conquered, though the Spaniards were never able to subdue the fierce and warlike tribe of Araucanians in the southern part of that country. Peru and Chili remained Spanish colonies till the early part of the present century. The former became independent in 1821, and the latter in 1818.

In 1535, the Spaniards, under Don Pedro de Mendoza, founded the city of Buenos Ayres; and the settlement of the remainder of this province followed in the course of the sixteenth century. This colony, including Paraguay, was attached to the viceroyalty of Peru, and remained under the Spanish dominion till 1816, when both parts of it became independent.

Venezuela, New Granada, and Guiana were settled

by the Spaniards in the course of the sixteenth century, and remained in colonial dependence upon Spain till the period when the other Spanish colonies revolted. Florida was explored by Ponce de Leon and Hernando Soto, early in the sixteenth century, and settlements were slowly established here by the Spaniards. They retained possession of the country, with little interruption, till 1820, when it was ceded to the United States.

California was partially explored by the Spaniards in the sixteenth century, and some portions of the territory were settled by them; the greater part remaining little known, or abandoned to the savage tribes who were found dwelling there. This country was attached to Mexico both under the Spanish dominion and after the establishment of the Mexican republic. In 1848, the northern portion was ceded by Mexico to the United States.

Of the whole immense dominion acquired by Spain in the Western World, nothing now remains under the control of that power but the two islands of Cuba and Porto Rico.

When Cabral discovered Brazil, in 1501, he did not ascertain whether it was an island or a continent; and this point was long a matter of doubt. No effort was made by the Portuguese to colonize the country for nearly half a century; but this apparent neglect arose from the reluctance of the king of Portugal to interfere with the pretensions of the king of Spain, as the papal grant of the newly-discovered countries, by a literal interpretation, was understood by the Spaniards as securing to them the whole western continent. At length, the king of Portugal, envious of the wealth acquired by his neighbors, sent out a small body of colonists, who founded San Salvador in 1549. These settlers found the native Brazilians, divided into a number of petty tribes, constantly at war with each other; the invaders, consequently, though few in number, were able without much difficulty to subdue the natives, one after another, by fomenting their animosities, and holding the balance between the contending parties. This course of policy was rendered necessary by the personal bravery of the Brazilian Indians, who, though ignorant of discipline, and unable to act in combination, displayed great individual courage in battle. They were skilful in the use of bows, darts, wooden clubs, and shields; and frequently gained the victory over the Portuguese in petty skirmishes. But they were unable to resist European tactics and policy, and hence they were finally subjected to the yoke of the invaders, with which they soon appeared to be contented.

The facility with which the Portuguese made themselves masters of this rich territory excited the cupidity of the other European powers, and they were successively attacked by the Spaniards, the French, and the Dutch. The last were the most dangerous enemies. They had just effected their deliverance from the despotism of Spain, under which the Portuguese themselves labored at that period; and hence they experienced but a slight resistance in their invasion of Brazil. The Dutch conquered a great part of the country, and would have retained permanent possession of it, had they not lost the friendship of the inhabitants by attempting to establish odious commercial monopolies. In consequence of this, they were expelled from all parts of Brazil, and the Portuguese, on regaining possession of this country, excluded all foreigners from intercourse with it. Brazil remained a colony of Portugal till 1821, when it was made a separate kingdom, under the Portuguese monarch. At length, in 1822, it was declared independent of Portugal, and erected into an empire, in which condition it now remains.

The French colonized Martinico and Guadaloupe, with a few smaller islands in the West Indies, early in the seventeenth century. On the South American continent, they made settlements in Guiana, where they still retain Cayenne and the territory in its immediate neighborhood. In North America, they established themselves in Acadia, Canada, and Louisiana. The first country they held till the beginning of the eighteenth century, when it was wrested from them by the English. The second was conquered by the English a few years later. The last, after various revolutions, came into the possession of the United States.

The English were the discoverers of the continent of North America. John Cabot, a Venetian, was sent by Henry VII. of England on a voyage of discovery to the west, in 1497. He discovered Newfoundland the same year, and explored a considerable extent of the coast north and south of that island. No attempts at colonization were made by the English till the reign of Elizabeth, when, toward the close of the sixteenth century, some expeditions were undertaken to Virginia. A permanent settlement was made here at Jamestown in 1607. During the same year, an attempt was made by the Plymouth company to establish a colony at the mouth of the Kennebec, but without success. In 1620, the Pilgrims landed at Plymouth, in Massachusetts Bay, and laid the foundation of the New England States. Other colonies were planted by the English along the North American coast, during the seventeenth century. New York was conquered from the Dutch in 1664, and in the early part of the eighteenth century, the whole line of coast from Maine to Georgia was in the possession of the English, who held the country till the declaration of independence, in 1776, which laid the foundation of the present American republic.

In the West Indies, the English first began a settlement at St. Lucia, in 1637. They afterward acquired, either by settlement or conquest, Jamaica, the Bahamas, Trinidad, St. Vincent, Tobago, Barbadoes, Antigua, and some smaller islands, with the Bermudas. On the South American continent, they obtained Demerara, and the neighboring parts of Guiana; and in Central America, the territory of Honduras.

The Dutch, under Henry Hudson, an Englishman, discovered the river which bears his name in 1609, and a Dutch settlement was formed on Manhattan Island, and at Albany, a few years later. The colony was called the *New Netherlands*, and the town, which has since become the city of New York, was named *New Amsterdam*. This territory was conquered by the English in 1664, and named *New York*. In the West Indies, the Dutch obtained the small islands of Curaçao, Bonaire, and a few others. In South America, they established themselves in that part of Guiana called *Surinam*, which they still retain.

The Swedes made a settlement in Delaware in 1627; but this soon fell into the hands of the Dutch. In the West Indies, they acquired the Island of St. Bartholomew. The Danes obtained the Islands of St. Thomas and St. Croix.

Thus was the New World parcelled out between the nations of Europe.

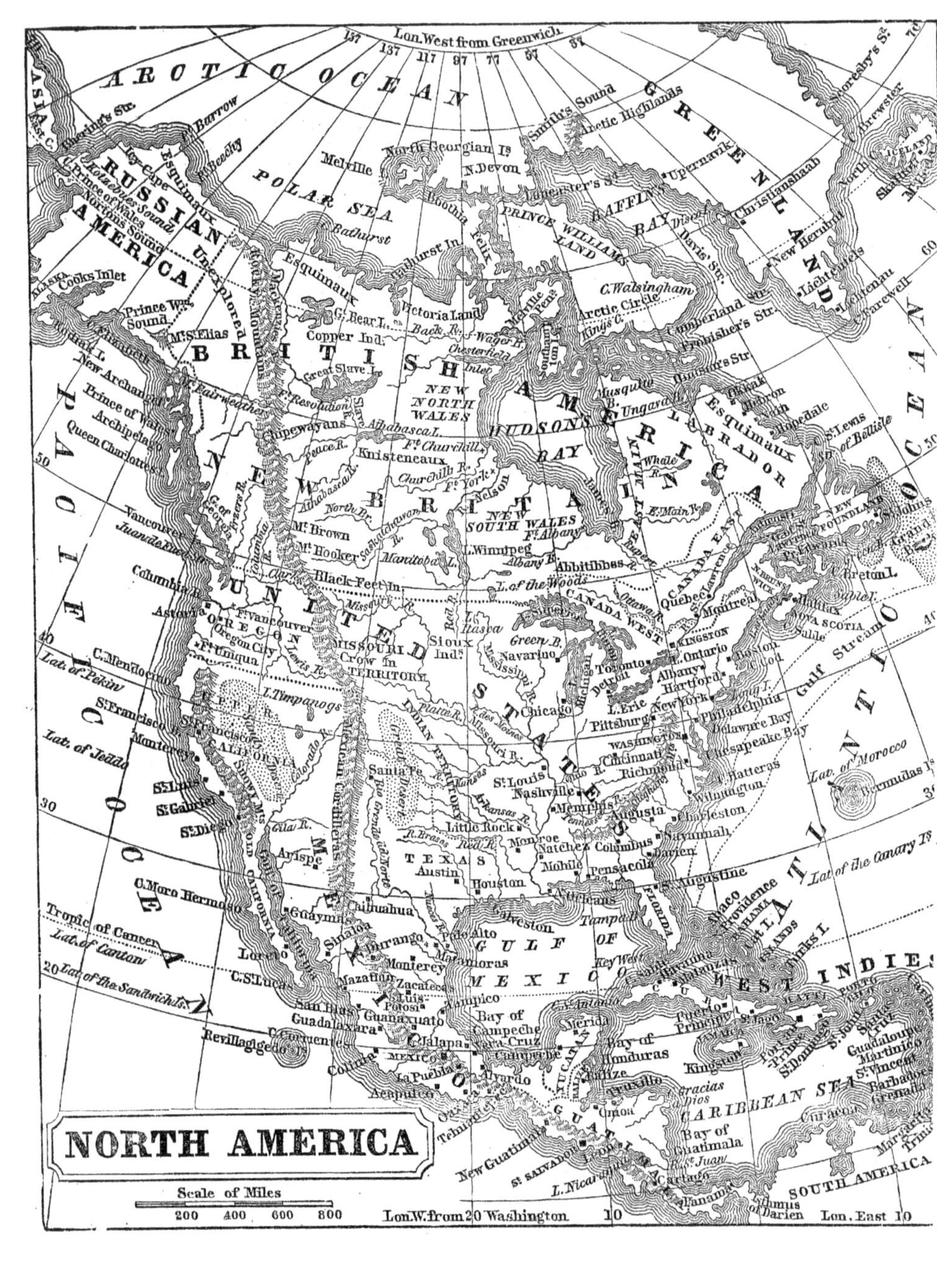
NORTH AMERICA
Scale of Miles
200 400 600 800
Lon. West from Greenwich
Lon. W. from 20 Washington 10
Lon. East 10
ARCTIC OCEAN
POLAR SEA
PACIFIC OCEAN
ATLANTIC OCEAN
RUSSIAN AMERICA
BRITISH AMERICA
NEW BRITAIN
UNITED STATES
MEXICO
GREENLAND
LABRADOR
HUDSONS BAY
BAFFINS BAY
GULF OF MEXICO
WEST INDIES
CARIBBEAN SEA
SOUTH AMERICA
OREGON
CALIFORNIA
TEXAS
MISSOURI TERRITORY
INDIAN TERRITORY
NEW NORTH WALES
NEW SOUTH WALES
CANADA EAST
CANADA WEST
NOVA SCOTIA
Tropic of Cancer
Arctic Circle
Gulf Stream
Lat. of Pekin
Lat. of Jeddo
Lat. of Canton
Lat. of the Sandwich Is.
Lat. of Morocco
Lat. of the Canary Is.
Bay of Campeche
Bay of Honduras
Bay of Guatimala

CHAPTER CCCCLXXV.

Preliminary View.

North America, which comprises about eight-fifteenths of the whole American continent, is bounded north by Behring's Strait, the Arctic Ocean, and Baffin's Bay; east by the Atlantic Ocean; south by the Gulf of Mexico and the Isthmus of Panama; and west by the Pacific Ocean. Its greatest length is about five thousand miles, and its greatest width about three thousand three hundred. Its superficial extent is eight millions of square miles.

America resembles the eastern continent, in having its northern portion, like Europe, deeply indented with seas and gulfs, while its southern portion, like Africa, presents a solid mass of land. The striking features of America are its immense range of mountains, including the Andes, nine thousand miles long; its enormous rivers, and its vast fresh-water lakes. To this we may add that the cataract of Niagara, in North America, presents the most stupendous waterfall in the world.

North America is traversed in its eastern part by the Alleghany range, and on the western by the Cordilleras and Rocky Mountains—these latter being in fact one chain, and a prolongation of the Andes, already noticed.

The central part of North America is somewhat elevated, and here the great rivers take their rise. The Saskatchewan and Mackenzie, empty into the Arctic Ocean; the St. Lawrence into the Atlantic; the Mississippi into the Gulf of Mexico, and the Columbia into the Pacific.

The gulfs, bays, and seas of North America are numerous, and some are remarkable for their extent. On the east coast, the most noted are Baffin's Bay, Hudson's Bay, Gulf of St. Lawrence, Bay of Fundy, and Chesapeake Bay; on the south, the Gulf of Mexco, which is of great extent, and a kind of Mediterranean sea. The most remarkable gulf or bay on the western side is the Gulf of California.

Both North and South America are remarkable for the vastness of the plains which mark their surface. The immense space from the outlet of the Mackenzie River to the delta of the Mississippi, and from the Rocky Mountains to the Appalachian chain, forms the most extended plain in the world. It embraces the basins of the St. Lawrence, the Mississippi, and the greater part of those of the Missouri, the Saskatchewan, the Mackenzie, the Churchill, and the Nelson. A large part of this plain, which lies north of latitude 50° north, is a bleak and barren waste, overspread with lakes, and bearing a striking resemblance to parts of Northern Asia. The more southern portion is fertile throughout, except along the western border, near the Rocky Mountains, where there is a wide space of land, for the most part a complete desert.

Two plateaus of considerable extent and elevation deserve notice. The table-land of Mexico, where is situated the capital of the Mexican States, and indeed the greater portion of the population of that country, and the Appalachian table-land, extending from the State of New York to the shores of the Gulf of Mexico. The former has an elevation of six and sometimes eight thousand feet, and the latter from fifteen hundred to twenty-five hundred feet. The central plateau, in which are the sources of the great northern and western rivers—the Saskatchewan, the Mackenzie, the Missouri, and the Mississippi, is from two thousand to three thousand five hundred feet above the level of the sea.

The peninsulas of North America are striking features of its physical formation. Among these are Labrador, Nova Scotia, Florida, and Old California The latter is seven to eight hundred miles long, traversed its whole length by a mountain chain, rising in some places to the height of five thousand feet. The intervening valleys are narrow, sandy, and sterile.

The Silver Fox.

The Raccoon.

The Rattlesnake.

The Opossum

The islands of North America are numerous, though none are of very great extent. Near the mouth of the St. Lawrence, are New Foundland, Anticosti, Prince Edward's Island, and Cape Breton. The West Indies, the most important group in this hemisphere, lies between North and South America, and can hardly be assigned to either division of the continent. In the Arctic Ocean, and along the coast of North America in the Pacific Ocean, are other islands, but none of great extent or value.

In mineral wealth, North America probably exceeds any other division of the globe, as it yields, abundantly, not only the precious metals, but also the useful minerals.

Though North America presents every variety of climate, yet this portion of the earth is almost as much noted for cold, as is Africa for heat. Along the Atlantic coast, the average temperature is about eight degrees lower than in the same parallels of latitude in the eastern hemisphere—the causes of which have been already explained. On the west coast, along the Pacific, the climate is much milder. It is to be observed that North America extends into three zones, the frigid, temperate, and torrid, and of course yields a great variety of animal and vegetable products.

Among its forests, the trees belonging to the temperate zone, attain a grandeur known in no other part of the world. There is a species of pine, in California, which rises to the height of 350 feet, with a trunk having a circumference of 70 feet. In general, it may be said, that the vegetation of the New World differs in its species from that of the Old. We have, indeed, oaks, walnuts, chesnuts, beeches, which resemble those of Europe, but they are still specifically distinct. The sugar cane was indigenous to the West Indies, but it was not used to produce sugar till after the discovery of America by the Europeans. Europe is indebted to America for the potato, Indian corn, millet, cocoa, vanilla, tobacco; and in return, America is indebted to Europe for wheat, rye, oats, barley, and rice. Our apples are superior to those of Europe, but we are indebted to Europe for the seeds which produced them.

The animal kingdom of North America presents many striking species. The bison, a kind of ox, is peculiar to this continent. Originally, it roamed over the whole of this part of America, but it is now only found west of the Mississippi. Here they are still met with in immense herds. The hunting of this animal has long been one of the chief pursuits of the Indian tribes, and of late years the white man has joined in the slaughter. Even European sportsmen now visit the western prairies to hunt the bison. The musk ox is a small variety of the ox kind, confined to the polar regions. It seems to resemble a small African buffalo. There are several kinds of bears, wolves, foxes, none of which are known in the eastern continent. The various kinds of deer, while resembling those of Europe, are specifically different.

The zoology of America, with a few exceptions as to birds, which might pass from one continent to the other, exhibits, throughout, peculiar and distinct species. We have eagles, vultures, hawks, owls, &c., but they are all, zoologically considered, different from the European kinds. It is curious to an American, in the forests of the eastern hemisphere, to hear jays, warblers, finches, sparrows, and other birds, with notes resembling those with which he is familiar, yet all different in tone, or cadence, or perhaps the whole structure of their songs.

CHAPTER CCCCLXXVI.

General Description — Discoveries — The Esquimaux — Greenland — Russian America.

THIS portion of the western world, while it repels the human race by its inhospitable and freezing climate, still attracts the imagination by the singular phenomena which it presents. In the accessible parts, winter holds sway for ten months of the year, and, farther north, the sea is converted into perpetual rock. No human foot has ventured farther than the eightieth degree of north latitude, and fancy alone can explore the hermit solitudes beyond. It is supposed that Greenland is an island; but its northern border has never been reached. On its western coast is the famous Ice Blink, an elevated sheet of ice, whose reflections seem to set the sky on fire. In these northern regions, the aurora borealis appears with its most brilliant displays. Here the sun circles around the horizon, giving a continued day for six months, and then sinks beneath, leaving the scene for six months to the dominion of night.

It might seem that this repulsive portion of the world would be abandoned by every living thing; but plants, animals, and human beings, adapted to the climate, find here their home, and a cherished abode. In the seas are the whale, the walrus, and seal; along the shores are white bears and reindeer, and a race of dwarfish savages, called *Esquimaux*, who, far from being a lean and melancholy race, are marked with oily obesity and a cheerful temperament. It is remarkable, too, that this frozen portion of the globe was known to Europe, and inhabited by Europeans, five hundred years before the prolific regions of the continent were in their possession. These regions have also, for centuries, been the theatre of adventure and discovery, and hence have a curious historical interest.

Soon after the discovery of America, attempts were made to explore its northern coasts. An idea was entertained that it rounded to a point, like South America, being connected with the Pacific by an open sea. To determine this point, many expeditions were sent hither. The first adventurers were unable to penetrate farther west than Baffin's Bay; but Henry Hudson, in 1610, steered a different course, and discovered the great bay which bears his name. Here, unfortunately, terminated his adventurous career. His crew mutinied, and set him adrift in a boat: nothing was ever heard of him afterward. Sir Thomas Button sailed in the same direction in 1612, and, finding himself in the wide expanse of Hudson's Bay, imagined he had reached the Pacific Ocean, and made full sail to the westward. To his great astonishment, he found his progress arrested by a long, unbroken line of coast, to which he gave the name of *Hope Checked.* At a still later period, Baffin sailed up Davis's Strait, and coasted along the whole extent of the shore of the great gulf beyond, which received, from him, the name of *Baffin's Bay.* The belief that this bay was completely closed by the land, deterred subsequent navigators from prosecuting their researches in that quarter.

The discoveries of Captain Cook opened new views of the extent and form of the northern extremity of America. This navigator penetrated through Behring's Straits, but the coast appeared to him to extend indefinitely to the north. It became, consequently, a general impression that America formed a huge, unbroken mass of land, approaching the north pole, and perhaps extending beyond it. This belief, however, received contradiction by the discovery of Hearne, who sailed down the Coppermine River, and found it to meet the ocean in a latitude not higher than the north part of Hudson's Bay. Soon after this, Mackenzie traced to the Polar Sea another river, twenty degrees farther west. There was now a strong presumption that a continuous sea bounded the whole of America on the north, and that there was really a north-west passage to the Pacific Ocean.

The British government, after the wars of the French revolution were closed, took up the business of northern discovery, with a determination to make every possible effort for the solution of the great geographical problem. A series of exploratory voyages was begun in vessels equipped for the express purpose of encountering the dangers of northern navigation, and the risk of detention for years in the

Frozen Sea. Captain Ross, in 1818, made the circuit of Baffin's Bay, and returned to England, with the belief that no opening existed to the west. Lieutenant Parry, the second in command to Ross, formed a different judgment, and, having satisfied the Admiralty of his grounds of belief, was sent out in 1821, with the command of a new expedition. In this memorable voyage, Captain Parry penetrated through Lancaster Sound, which he found to widen gradually, till it opened into the expanse of the Polar Sea. He did not touch on any part of the American coast, but found parallel to it a chain of large islands, and his progress through these was arrested by straits and channels encumbered with ice.

Captain Parry made two other voyages to the north, but added little to his first discoveries. In the mean time, Captain Franklin had undertaken a land journey in the footsteps of Hearne, and reached the Polar Sea, where he explored a considerable extent of coast before unknown. Another voyage by Captain Ross, and land journeys by Franklin and Captain Back, added somewhat to the geographical knowledge of the polar seas and islands; but no adventurer has yet made the entire passage from the Atlantic to the Pacific, round the northern extremity of America.

The islands discovered in these several expeditions are extensively scattered throughout the Polar Sea; but they do not present many peculiarities which call for a detailed description. Melville Island, one of the Georgian group, is the most westerly of those discovered by Parry. It is in latitude 75° north, and is about a hundred miles in length and in breadth. Here Parry's expedition spent two years, exposed to all the rigors of an arctic winter. The sun disappeared on the 4th of November, and was not seen again till the 3d of February. During this interval, the land and sea were alike covered with a monotonous surface of snow, and the thermometer averaged about twenty-eight degrees below zero. Yet the English officers, when well clothed, and no storm was blowing, were able to walk in the open air two or three hours a day; and, by judicious precautions, the health of all the crew was well preserved. In May the snow begins to melt, and in June it covers the country with pools; but it is not till August that the sea becomes open, and before October the winter has again commenced. No inhabitants were found upon these islands, nor any animals, except wolves.

North of the Danish settlements, in Greenland, Captain Ross discovered a territory which he named the *Arctic Highlands.* Here he found inhabitants. They had never before seen a civilized being, and were seized with astonishment at the sight of the ships, which they imagined to be huge birds with wings. They were found to differ from the other Esquimaux in being destitute of boats; for, though much of their food is obtained from the sea, they procure it merely by walking over the frozen surface. They have the advantage, however, of possessing iron, with which they frame instruments much more powerful than those which the other Esquimaux manufacture of bone. They differ, also, from the other Esquimaux, in having a chief or king, to whom they are much attached, and to whom they pay a tribute of seals, train oil, and fish. The cliffs on this coast present the remarkable phenomenon of red snow, the nature and origin of which have excited much controversy among the learned in Europe.

The endeavors to accomplish a north-west passage round the American continent, have been continued by the English with great perseverance. Sir John Franklin, who had previously distinguished himself in enterprises of discovery along the American shores of the Polar Sea, was sent out, in 1845, with the command of an expedition to pursue the route opened by Captain Parry. This expedition consisted of two ships, the Erebus and Terror. They carried one hundred and thirty-eight men, and provisions for four years. They sailed from England in May, 1845, and proceeded up Baffin's Bay, after which nothing was heard from them. In the autumn of 1847, three expeditions were sent in search of them; one by the way of Baffin's Bay, another through Behring's Straits, and the third over land, from the Hudson's Bay settlements. Neither of these succeeded in learning any thing of Sir John Franklin. Still other expeditions have been sent as well by the British as Americans, in search of the lost voyagers. Of these an account is given in the closing chapter of our history of the United States, page 1156, as well as a narration of the unfortunate Franklin and his companions.

Esquimaux.

The Esquimaux are thinly scattered over the regions above described, though the coasts of Labrador, and the southern shores of the Arctic Ocean, appear to be their chief abodes. As already stated, they are distinct from the other aborigines of America, and have been classed by naturalists with the Lapps, Finns, and Samoiedes of the old continent. In stature, they are below the Europeans; yet they are well formed and hardy. They are apparently of a dusky complexion; but this is said to be owing more to diet than to the natural color of the skin. Their faces are round and full, their eyes small and black, and their noses small, but not much flattened. They have the black and straight hair of the American Indians. They have various ways of building their dwellings. On the shores, where they can obtain drift wood, that material is used. In other situations, they erect tents of skins for summer, and houses of snow and ice for winter. These snow houses are very curious. They are of an orbicular shape, like the dome of a modern piece of architecture. The manner of building shows some ingenuity. Blocks of ice, or hard snow, are cut of the right size and shape, and laid in a circle of ten or fifteen feet diameter. Upon this circle is laid another course, inclining somewhat inward; and others are successively placed, till nothing remains but a small opening at the top, which is closed by a key-stone of ice. Water is then poured upon the joints of this cold masonry, which, by freezing, cements all the joints. The inside is smoothed with the knife, and a door is cut out on the southern side, which is sheltered by a covered way, or narrow entry, twenty or thirty feet long. These houses are sometimes ten feet high, and are comparatively warm and commodious. During the extreme cold of winter, they are completely dry; but, in spring, they commence thawing and dripping, and the inhabitants remove to their tents. Sometimes there are villages of these huts communicating with one another by their doors. Plates of clear ice are used for window-glass. Fires and lamps are kept burning in the huts, and the inmates sleep upon beds of skin. All the garments of the Esquimaux are made of skin; they have little variety of form, and are so full as to disguise the figure, and make the wearer appear shorter than he really is.

The Esquimaux subsist entirely on animal food, as the territories they inhabit afford very little else. They are enormous eaters, and the stories told of their powers of mastication, by the northern voyagers, are almost incredible. Every kind of fish is greedily devoured, and the more oily it is, the better. Their supplies of food are often interrupted by the vicissitude of the seasons, and other accidents, so that their life is an alternation of gluttony and fasting. Notwithstanding this apparently wretched mode of life, no people in the world are more cheerful; and they are so fond of dancing, that it seems almost their natural gait. They have dogs, which they train to draw sledges, in which they travel. They never fight, although, where they come in contact with the Indians of the continent, the latter pursue them with savage ferocity. They appear to have no government, except that of a paternal character. They have some confused notions of the supernatural world, but nothing that can be dignified with the name of religion. A Supreme Being does not enter into their conceptions.

Lichtenfels.

GREENLAND. — This is the most northerly region of the globe. It is a large island, extending from Cape Farewell, its southern point, in latitude 59° 30′, to an unknown distance in the direction of the north pole. The western coast has been explored to latitude 78°. On the eastern side, a great part of the shore is so blocked up with ice, that it has never been visited. The whole country may be described as one enormous mass of rocks, presenting high, rugged, and precipitous coasts in every quarter, open to the tempestuous Polar Sea. Land, properly speaking, cannot be said to exist in Greenland. The only thing approaching to the nature of earth, occurs along the broken crags of the inlets, or on the numerous rocky islands scattered along the coast, where are to be seen some small patches or narrow strips of thin soil. In these spots alone vegetation appears; but it is nothing more than grass, low brush-wood, mosses, and lichens. In well-sheltered valleys, birch and elder shrubs grow sometimes to the height of a man's head; and this is the nearest approach to a tree that has been made in Greenland. In the extreme south, potatoes have been raised, but all attempts to cultivate grain have been unsuccessful. The cold is so intense in winter, that even ardent spirits freeze in a room where there is a fire. In February and March, it is so powerful as to split the rocks, and cause the sea to smoke like a furnace. The winter, however, is often interrupted by thaws, which sometimes last for weeks. July is the only month in which there is no snow; though it does not lie long till October. The earth begins to thaw in June, but it is always frozen at a moderate depth. The heat is so great in the long summer days, as to evaporate the water left in the clefts of the rocks by the tide, and reduce it to a beautiful fine salt. Rain is scarce, especially in the north. It never thunders here, though lightning is frequent. The aurora borealis is very splendid, especially in winter, and always appears either in the east or south-east.

The discovery of Greenland, between the years 830 and 835, is mentioned in the Chronicle of Snorro Sturleson, a learned Icelander, of whom we have spoken in our history of Iceland. Another writer places the discovery in 770. Eric Redhead, an Icelander, having killed a powerful Icelandic chief, was obliged to quit that country, and, according to the fashion of the times, set out to discover some unknown land. He came in sight of Greenland at a point which he named *Heriolfsness.* Steering south-westerly, along the coast, he sailed round Cape Farewell, and passed the summer on an island in this neighborhood, after which he returned to Iceland. He praised the fertility of the country which he had discovered, and named it *Greenland,* in the hope of inducing adventurers to accompany him in an expedition to settle there. The country was soon visited by many Icelanders and Norwegians, and many towns were built in Greenland. The settlement increased for some time, and in the early part of the fifteenth century, it is said there were one hundred and ninety towns and villages here. Greenland, with Iceland, had at this time passed under the dominion of Denmark, and the Danish government sent out bishops to Greenland. The last of these went from Denmark in 1408, after which history makes no mention of Greenland for a long time. It appears certain that the colony became suddenly extirpated, whether from a pestilential disease, a severe winter or an irruption of pirates, never was known. When the Icelanders first visited the country, it had no inhabitants; but, in the fourteenth century, the Esquimaux — a race from which the modern Greenlanders have descended — began to make their appearance on the western coast. It is not impossible that the destruction of the colony was owing to an attack of these savages. It may be remarked, however, that a terrible pestilence, called the *black death*, ravaged all the north of Europe from A. D. 1402 to 1404.

Greenland, having thus fallen into complete oblivion, was discovered a second time by Martin Frobisher, an Englishman, in 1576, though in a second voyage, two years later, he was unable to find the land. John Davis followed the course pointed out by Frobisher, and discovered Greenland in 1585: he gave his own name to the strait which separates it from the islands to the west. William Baffin, in 1616, discovered the bay which bears his name, and sailed northward as far as 77° 30′. The Danish government, animated by the intelligence of these discoveries, began to think of their lost Greenland; and during the reigns of seven kings, they spent considerable sums in attempting to explore the eastern coast, where they erroneously supposed the ancient settlements were established; but the ice in this quarter repelled all their approaches toward the land. At length, in the early part of the last century, during the reign of Frederic IV., Hans Egede, a Norwegian clergyman, animated by religious enthusiasm, offered to proceed with his wife and children to Greenland, for the purpose of preaching the gospel to the natives. The Danish government furnished him with a transportation, and, in 1721, he landed at Baal's River, on the western coast. He built a house, and opened an intercourse with the natives, who were shy and repulsive at first, but, by friendly treatment and presents, were at length brought under his influence. Egede named his settlement *Gotthaab*, or Goodhope. In 1733, he was joined by three missionaries of the Moravian Brethren, who founded another settlement at New Herrnhut. A regular commerce with the natives was established, which was at first carried on by a company of merchants of Copenhagen, but was afterward assumed by the government, who continue to practise it on their own account.

The Danish dominion of this colony has never been disturbed. The Danish governors exercise authority only over the settlements, the natives being without laws. The articles of trade are seal-skins, furs, eider down, train oil, whalebone, and fish. A few sheep are kept by the Danish settlers, but there is hardly provender sufficient in Greenland to support them. The only domestic animal of the natives is the dog, which is used to draw sledges. White bears, reindeer, hares, and foxes, are the only wild animals. There are fourteen Danish settlements, the most northerly of which is Upernavik, in latitude 72° 48′. The number of natives holding intercourse with the Danes is about seven thousand, of whom eleven hundred are said to be Christians.

The inhabitants of Greenland consist of natives and Danish settlers, the latter amounting to between two and three hundred. The natives are of the same stock with the race of Esquimaux that extend over the whole northern coast of America. The number of those who have intercourse with Europeans is estimated at about six or seven thousand. Between the Greenlanders and Esquimaux there is a similarity of figure, dress, houses, boats, weapons, manners, and languages. The children are hardly darker than a brunette. In height, the Greenlanders seldom exceed five feet: they have flat faces, with high cheek-bones, and very full cheeks. Their eyes are small and black, but with little lustre; and their thin hair is long and dark. They have a small beard, which they carefully eradicate. A life of alternate plenty and want, in a severe climate, is so little favorable to longevity, that few males live beyond fifty years: females, who endure less hardship, sometimes attain to eighty years. In their dress, the Greenlanders make no attempt at neatness or display: protection from the cold is the only end to be attained. Seal and reindeer skins, coarse kinds of European linen, and the skins of fowls with the feathers turned inward, are the principal material for clothing. They pursue the seal, in small canoes made of skins, amid stormy seas thus displaying wonderful skill and daring. The houses are built of large blocks of stone, the interstices being filled with mud and turf. There are no chimneys, the only fire used being that of lamps. The ordinary food of the inhabitants is the Greenland salmon, and the flesh of the seal and reindeer. This constant living upon oily food gives the Greenlanders a great degree of obesity, and renders them so plethoric that they often bleed at the nose. They have some obscure conceptions of a future state, and wear amulets to defend themselves from disease and misfortune. They have no laws and no magistrates. Every thing is governed by custom, and no man has authority except over his own family. Lichtenfels is the capital, and Upernavik, on Baffin's Bay, is the most northern inhabited spot on the globe.

New Archangel.

Russian America. — This country comprises an extensive region on the north-western part of North America, of which very little is known, except along the western coast. A part of the northern coast, and lying between 150° and 155° west longitude, has never been visited. British America forms the eastern boundary. The Russian American Company have a few factories and forts on the coast and islands, but almost the whole country is occupied by various native tribes, chiefly Esquimaux. New Archangel, on the island called *Sitka* by the natives, *King George's Island* by the English, and *Baranoff* by the Russians, is the residence of the governor, and has about one thousand inhabitants. The fur trade alone gives any value to these cold and sterile regions; the sea otter, the skins of which furnish the fur, has now become comparatively scarce.

The north-western part of America was first discovered in 1728, by Behring, a German in the Russian service. Alaska was visited by the Russian fur traders about the middle of the last century. Sitka was first settled by the Russians, in 1799.

British America.

View of Quebec.

CHAPTER CCCCLXXVII.

New Britain — Canada — New Brunswick — Nova Scotia — Newfoundland — Prince Edward's Island.

British America is a territory of vast but undefined extent. It may be said, in general terms, to occupy the whole north-eastern portion of the continent, although this region consists, for the most part, of territories which the British rather claim than occupy. They are bounded north by the Arctic Ocean, east by the Atlantic, south by the United States, and west by the Pacific Ocean and Russian America. Their whole extent is nearly equal to that of the United States. The northern parts are sterile and almost desolate. The other portions are very thinly peopled, and abound with immense forests. Throughout the greater part of the southern and eastern districts, the scenery, in its primeval wildness and natural luxuriance, exhibits a picture of what the United States were two and three centuries ago, when the savage tribes were the only inhabitants of this vast domain.

The political divisions of this country are not in all cases very distinct. They consist of

	Square Miles.	*Pop.*, 1860.
New Britain, Labrador, &c.	1,860,000	5,000
Canada West	242,482	1,396,091
Canada East		1,110,664
New Brunswick	27,037	252,047
Nova Scotia, Cape Breton	15,620	330,699
Prince Edward's Island	2,173	80,857
Newfoundland	36,000	122,638
British Columbia	222,080	64,000
Vancouver's Island	12,756	25,000
	2,418,148	3,386,996

Nearly the whole tract north of Canada is either an unoccupied waste, or thinly scattered over with Indian tribes. Around Hudson's Bay are several trading stations, which have been established by the British; but with the exception of these spots, nothing like government exists in the northern portion of British America.

New Britain is the name given to the north-eastern portion of British America. It comprises the territory of Labrador and the region around Hudson's Bay. The eastern part of this country is sometimes called *East Main*, and the districts west of Hudson's Bay have received the name of *New North* and *South Wales;* but these appellations are now little used. Hudson's Bay, as we have already stated, was discovered in 1610 by Henry Hudson. It was afterward more thoroughly explored by successive navigators employed by the English Russian Company, who were anxious to find a north-western passage round the American continent. In 1668, Zacharias Gillam was sent on a voyage to this country by Charles II., at the solicitation of Prince Rupert. He was accompanied by two French merchants of Canada, named *De Grosseliers*, who had previously made an expedition from Quebec toward Hudson's Bay. Gillam passed the winter in Rupert's River, where he built the first stone fort erected in the country, which he named *Fort Charles.*

Before the return of Gillam from his voyage, the king had granted to Prince Rupert, and a company of lords, knights, and merchants associated with him, a charter dated May 2, 1669. In this charter they are styled the "Governor and Company of Adventurers trading from England to Hudson's Bay." The king ceded to them all the trade and commerce of the seas within the entrance of Hudson's Straits, together with all the countries upon the coasts. Of this extensive grant, the Hudson's Bay Company have enjoyed uninterrupted possession from 1669 to the present day, with the exception of a space of seventeen years, from 1697 to 1714, when the settlement was occupied by the French. The charter, instead of promoting the progress of discovery, is understood to have produced the opposite effect. The Hudson's Bay Company are charged with having endeavored to conceal, as much as possible, the situation of the coasts and seas connected with their territories.

The company's settlements around the whole extent of Hudson's Bay are only four, namely, Prince of Wales, or Churchill's Fort, the most northern establishment, situated at the mouth of Churchill River; York

Fort, formerly called *Bourbon* by the French, on Nelson's River; Albany Fort, called by the French *St. Anne*, on the River Albany; and Moose Fort, or St. Louis, on the southern shore of James's Bay. These settlements have a few small dependencies connected with them. The commander at each fort is styled *governor*, and the subordinate officers, in connection with him, constitute a council of government. The governors are appointed for three or five years. The trade carried on with the natives comprises furs, skins, whalebone, train oil, eider down, &c., for which the company barter fire-arms, powder, shot, cutlery, blankets, and similar goods. The profits of this trade are said to be enormous. The company are charged with transacting all their business in the greatest secrecy, always showing the utmost reluctance to expose the details of their affairs to the public view.

The British laid claim to a large portion of the territory on the shore of the Pacific watered by the River Oregon. This claim was founded on the discoveries supposed to have been made in this quarter by Sir Francis Drake. No great importance was attached to it till recently, when the settlement formed by the Americans on the west of the Rocky Mountains, drew the attention of the British government to this quarter, and their claim became a subject of negotiation with the United States government. The matter was finally adjusted by treaty, and the United States relinquished all claim to that part of the Oregon territory lying north of latitude 49 deg. In this region the British have some trading establishments, and are now projecting a settlement on an extended scale at Vancouver's Island.

Canada is bounded on the north by a range of highlands which form the southern boundary of the possessions of the Hudson's Bay Company; on the east by Labrador, the Gulf of St. Lawrence and New Brunswick; on the south by the United States; and on the west by a conventional line at or near the parallel of longitude 90 degrees west from Greenwich, which separates it from the Indian territories in that quarter. It covers an area of 344,000 square miles and includes the "Kannata" of the native proprietors, the "Aca-nada" of the pretended Castilian discoverers, and the "Nouvelle France" of the French colonists, who surrendered it to Great Britain in 1760. It was partitioned into two Provinces in 1791 and reünited in 1840.

The climate of Canada varies with the latitude, topography, and position of the several districts of country which compose it. So much of it as is situate westward of the confluence of the Ottawa with the St. Lawrence and eastward of the River St. Clair and bordering upon or in proximity to the lakes and rivers between, is favored with a climate not essentially different from that of the States of New Hampshire, Vermont, the northern part of New York and Michigan. The remaining portions are more frigid and snowy. The climate of the entire province, however, is generally salubrious, invigorating and healthful, and favorable to longevity of man and beast. The summer breezes which fan the precincts of the lakes are exhilerating and delightful.

The arability and fertility of the soil correspond with the topography and climate of the several districts. The towns which skirt the St. Lawrence above the village of Prescott, and the broader belt of counties between Kingston and Windsor, are enriched with a soil that is productive, and which, when properly tilled, yields abundant harvests of wheat, rye, corn, peas and oats. Lands to the northward of these are inferior in quality and less susceptible of cultivation, whilst those at the eastward of Prescott, including the region lately called Lower Canada, are, for the most part, too meagre and sterile to produce any but the hardier cereal crops. It should be remarked, however, in this connection, that under the imperfect system of tillage which has generally obtained in Lower Canada, it is difficult to estimate the value of lands in that region for agricultural purposes. Under the hands of the farmers of New Hampshire and Vermont they would doubtless respond in more abundant crops, and at the same time be greatly improved in appearance and value.

The settlement of this portion of the continent was prompted by the desire of his most Christian majesty, Francis I, to appropriate to himself so much of the "New World" as he was able, through the sagacity of maritime adventurers and by the law of nations respecting discovery and possession, to acquire. Having in 1524 commissioned Verazzano to traverse the Atlantic for that purpose, and having learned of him that the peninsula of Nova Scotia was uninhabited by white men, his majesty at once claimed it for his crown, by the name of Nouvelle France, and re-despatched the adventurer with instructions to penetrate the interior country drained by the St. Lawrence. The second voyage was disastrous. In 1534, Jaques Cartier, a bold and skillful mariner of St. Malo, undertook the enterprise, and after having ascended the St. Lawrence to the island now occupied by Montreal, he returned without accident, taking with him Donnaconna, an Indian king. The interest which the report of this voyage excited in the minds of the nobility, and the hopes of personal aggrandizement stimulated by it, induced an opulent nobleman of Picardy, the Sieur Roberval, to offer to bear the expenses of planting a colony in Nouvelle France, upon the condition of being himself appointed its lieutenant-general and viceroy; which proposition was accepted. Under these auspices, an expedition of five vessels was fitted out in the year 1540, and placed under the command of Cartier, who ascended the St. Lawrence to the present site of Quebec, erected a fort there, visited the rapids above Hochelaga, and after waiting a while for the arrival of Roberval, set sail for home. The viceroy subsequently arrived in a vessel laden with settlers, stores and provisions, and occupied for a time the station which Cartier had evacuated.

He then returned to France and entered the service of Charles V., where he was employed six years; after which he reëmbarked for Canada, with his brother Achille and several other noblemen, and perished at sea. This event appears to have discouraged further attempts at Colonization, until the union of parties in France, under the benignant sway of Henry IV.

The coronation of a member of the family of Bourbon was an event of great importance to the French nation, as it restored to the departments of industry and commerce that measure of public confidence without which little progress can be made in the pursuits which develop the resources of a nation. That sovereign devised ways and means for reducing the national debt, and reviving the service of the merchant-marine. Under these auspicious circumstances, the Marquis de la Roche, a nobleman of Brittany, was induced to undertake an expedition with the view of colonizing Canada. He arranged the enterprise on a scale of greater magnificence than any which had preceded it. Several large and commodious vessels were equipped and amply provisioned for the voyage. The Marquis himself was invested with authority, not only to command and to govern, but to plant colonies, erect forts, build cities, ordain laws, levy war, and create counts and barons. After taking on board a large number of persons to become settlers, and a Norman pilot to conduct the voyage, he drifted seaward with buoyant hopes of gratifying his royal patron with an early report of his complete success. But the noble marquis, like Roberval, was to be disappointed. He crossed the Atlantic; but in consequence of foul weather and angry seas, he wrecked one of his vessels, and so far shattered the rest, that he was barely able to land forty of his intended colonists upon Sable Island, to live or die, as the fates might decree, and to return, himself, in perilous discomfiture to France. Seven years afterward, and when twelve persons only of the forty thus put ashore on the island, survived, the same pilot was sent out with a vessel to take them off. It is said that the Marquis sickened and died of chagrin.

In 1600, a similar expedition was undertaken by Chauvin and Pontgrave, the former of whom sailed to, and left a party of sixteen men at, Tadoussac, and the latter with an East India voyager of the name of Champlain, came out three years afterward, and ascended the St. Lawrence to the Sault St. Louis, where their further progress was interrupted by the cataract. The next expedition was fitted out in 1608, and placed under the command of Champlain, who fixed upon an eminence distinguished by the Indians as Quebeio (Quebec) as the place for striking a permanent settlement. There he erected a spacious block-house and magazine, for the protection of his men and stores, and around it, the first substantial tenements built in Canada. There he opened a lively trade with the natives, and gave them firelocks in exchange for valuable furs. And it is said that the Indians, at that period, evinced a disposition to imitate the ways of civilization, and to cultivate, by friendly offices, the favor of the pioneers. In 1611, Champlain commenced another settlement further up the river, on an island which he named Mont-real (Mount Royal), now called Montreal, and enclosed the field first cleared, with a high earthen wall. These settlements were permanent and enduring. They were frequently assailed by the Indians, who became jealous of such encroachments upon their hunting-grounds, yet they maintained their position, and increased in population by new accessions of hardy emigrants from the mother country.

After exploring the Ottawa, and other streams issuing from the north, Champlain returned to France, where he matured further plans for prosecuting his labors, under the especial patronage of Count de Soissons, who had obtained the title of Lieutenant-General of Nouvelle France, and who delegated to him the functions of that office. Then in 1612, returning to Canada, he resumed the management of affairs, and employed four Recollet friars to conciliate and convert the natives. De Soissons was succeeded as lieutenant general and viceroy, by the Prince of Condè. In 1620, Condè surrendered his office to the Duke de Montmorency, for the consideration of 11,000 crowns. The Duke retained Champlain as his lieutenant, and the latter, during this year, brought over his family to reside with him in his new home. The first child born of French parents in the colony, was christened at Quebec, on the 24th of May, 1621. At this period, forts were erected and settlements begun at Tadoussac and Trois Rivieres. In 1622, the Duke de Ventadour, having entered into holy orders, took charge, as viceroy, of the affairs of the colony, with the view of effecting the conversion of the natives, and sent over three Jesuits, to the great displeasure of the four Recollets at Quebec.

At this period, there were a number of Calvinists actively engaged in the fur trade, under the direction of the Sieurs de Caen, uncle and nephew, who, in the rivalry and competitions of business, fell out with the Catholics, who, in turn, complained of them to the authorities. These contentions between them, portending disaster Cardinal Richlieu undertook to put an end to the difficulty by organizing a company of one hundred associates who should send three hundred Catholic tradesmen to Canada and supply them with implements, clothing and provisions for three years, and agree to have six thousand French inhabitants settled there before 1643. This, it was believed, would overslaugh the Calvinists, and place the colony in a firm and flourishing condition. To this company, and their successors forever, there was issued a royal charter, granting them the settlement at Quebec, and all the lands upon the St. Lawrence, and the rivers emptying into it, with power to confer titles, subject to the approbation of the crown; also, the exclusive right of traffic in peltries and all other commodities, for the term of fifteen years. This celebrated charter was signed in 1627. Under it, the viceroyalty was suspended, and Champlain appointed governor of the province.

In 1628, Charles I. of England, commissioned Sir David Kerkt, a Calvinistic refugee, to make a conquest of Nouvelle France, that it might be added to his majesty's other possessions in America. Kerkt appeared the following year before Quebec with an English squadron, and after one or two ineffectual attacks upon the fortress, induced the governor to surrender. Thus the English standard was raised, for the first time, upon the walls of that city, one hundred and thirty years before the battle of the Plains of Abraham. Champlain then returned to France, where he remained until the conclusion of the treaty of St. Germains, in 1632, when he was reinstated in office, and permitted to resume its exercise with ample military appointments, munitions and stores. This excellent governor died, however, in 1635, and was succeeded by Monsieur de Montmagny, who administered the government twelve years.

At this period, the ecclesiastics of the mother country evinced great solicitude for the religious welfare of the native proprietors, and coöperated with the civil authorities to convert them. The civil authorities, appreciating the value of such services in preparing the way for a stipulated peace with the natives, at once resolved to send a large number of Catholic priests into the wilderness, in advance of the columns of further emigration. The policy, once entered upon, became thenceforward a prominent feature of subsequent French colonization, from Quebec to the Mississippi. And although diverse opinions of the intrinsic merit of those early missionary labors are now entertained, it is beyond dispute that they became the foundation of that system of morals and faith which have ever since distinguished the people of Lower Canada. The Marquis de Gamache, of the order of Jesuits, founded a college at Quebec, and established an Indian school at Sillery. The Duchesse d'Aiguillon, sent out a party of Ursuline nuns to establish the Hotel Dieu, and Madame de Peltrie came out with another party, and opened the convent of St. Ursula, also, at Quebec The missionaries readily perceived that the Island of Montreal was an eligible place for religious institutions, and obtained the aid of the governor in fortifying it. In 1640, the King of France granted the entire island to the order of St. Sulspice, and appointed M. de Maisonneuve to govern it. In 1642, the spot selected for the site of the future city was consecrated and named La Ville Ma

Death of General Wolfe.

ne. In 1677, Governor Montmagny was succeeded by M. d'Aillebout, who brought with him a reinforcement of one hundred men. With this functionary came Margaret Bourgeois, who founded a seminary at Montreal, denominated The Daughters of the Congregation. In 1658, the Viscount d'Argenson was appointed Governor General of Canada, who, in 1661, was succeeded in that office by the Baron d'Avangour. In 1663, M. de Mesy was sent out by Louis XIV, not only as governor, but as King's Commissioner to examine into and revise the system of colonial government then in force. The company of "one hundred partners" were obliged to surrender their franchises to the crown, and submit to the institution of a royal government with a sovereign council, consisting of the Governor, King's Commissioner, an apostolic vicar, and four honorable gentlemen. In 1665, the Marquis de Tracy was commissioned Lieutenant General and Viceroy of Canada, who brought into the colony one thousand officers and soldiers, and a large number of agriculturists and artisans, horses and cattle. This was a valuable accession to the strength, wealth and independence of the colonists. In 1667, Tracy was succeeded by M. de Courcelles, who extended the settlements along the upper waters of the St. Lawrence, and into the interior. He was succeeded, in 1672, by the Count de Frontenac, who erected a fort at Cataraugui, and explored the country far to the westward. This viceroy managed the affairs of the colony with energy and discretion, yet he was limited in his jurisdiction. He was enjoined to permit all affairs of importance to be decided in a council to consist of the bishop, the intendant and himself, each to have an equal vote. The bishop at that time was supported by a numerous body of clergy, who were accused of desiring the supreme dictation of affairs. They opposed the sale of spirits to the savages, whilst the Count favored the traffic. The Intendant also differed with his associates. It was, therefore, found that as these parties were unable to act together, another viceroy must be appointed. The office was conferred, in 1682, upon M. de la Barre, who administered the government of the colony for the period of three years, and was succeeded by the Marquis de Denonville, an active and distinguished military officer.

Denonville was severe in his intercourse with the Indians. He neither believed nor expected that they would be conciliated. He knew they were jealous of his encroachment, and distrustful of his promises. He perceived no method of protecting the colonists from their depredations, but their reduction to subserviency and dependence. Thus reasoning, he suggested the erection of a strong fort at Niagara, and forcible measures to interdict their traffic with the English. Having, under various pretexts, enticed a number of chiefs to meet him on the banks of Lake Ontario, he arrested and put them in irons, and sent them to France to man the galleys of his sovereign. A war with the Indians ensued, during which a fort at Niagara was erected and garrisoned.

In 1689, the Count de Frontenac was re-commissioned viceroy, and restored the Iroquois chiefs carried off by his predecessor. In 1690, the English government sent a fleet, commanded by Sir William Phipps, to take Quebec, but after efforts which occupied four consecutive days, the seige was raised. Frontenac died in 1698, and was succeeded by a distinguished military officer named De Callières, who adjusted the subsisting difficulties with the Iroquois. De Callières died in 1703, and was succeeded by the Count de Vaudreuil. In 1709, Queen Anne approved of a plan for the conquest of Canada, and sent an individual named Vetch to New York, with authority and resources deemed sufficient to accomplish it; but the effort proved abortive. In 1713, the memorable treaty of Utrecht was concluded, in which France yielded her sovereignty over Acadia and Newfoundland. In 1720 and '21, the province was visited by Charlevoix, who estimated the inhabitants of Quebec at 7,000; of Trois Rivières, at 800. He mentions Seigniories below and above Quebec, the town of Montreal, and settlements begun at Frontenac, Toronto, Niagara, Detroit, and Michilimacinac, but is silent in respect to their numbers. Vaudreuil died in 1725, and was succeeded by the Chevalier de Beauharnois, who officiated twenty years, after which Count de la Galissonière, Marquis de la Jonquière, Baron de Longueuil, Marquis du Quesne, and Sieur de Vaudreuil, successively administered the government for brief periods each, and in a manner wholly incompatible with any healthy system of colonial management.

The affairs of Canada were now approaching a crisis. Great Britain had resolved to subjugate and control it. On the 8th day of September, 1760, after severe military engagements in which the commanders of both armies, Wolfe and Montcalm, had fallen, but in which the British were ultimately triumphant, it was surrendered to the victors by capitulation, subsequently affirmed by a treaty between the two powers, concluded at Paris in 1763. The conquered troops were suffered to march out from their several posts with the honors of war, and were conveyed thence to France in British vessels, under an engagement that they were not to serve again during the war. The militia, then numbering about 16,000, were permitted to return to their homes. The civic officers who desired to go, were with their families and baggage conveyed to the mother country. Religious worship, according to the ritual of the Roman church, was solemnly assured. Vested rights of property under the custom of Paris, were guarantied to the possessors. And the Indians, 7,400 of whom had been converted to the Catholic faith, who had supported the colonists against the invading army, were to be left undisturbed in the enjoyment of their fisheries and lands.

The entire population at this period, which consisted of a poor, but highly respected noblesse, a pious and devoted clergy and sisterhood of nuns, and a hardy and patriotic yeomanry, had, including the militia, increased to about 69,000; all of whom had deeply sympathized with, and most of the adult males had participated in, the defense of French dominion in Canada as the cause of their beloved country. They had never for a moment wavered in their loyalty. All that fidelity could endure they had been content to suffer; all that their strength could accomplish, they had endeavored to perform; and all that chivalry could brave, they had been willing to encounter. And they yielded only when they could bear up no longer against the force which subdued them. The fortunes of war were unpropitious, and they were finally overborne. They bowed to the stern necessity. The conquest of Canada is one of the prominent events in the history of the world.

Having become a British province, Canada was immediately impressed with a different aspect. British soldiery garrisoned the fortifications; British ensigns surmounted their towers; British subjects were invested with official authority; British laws were engrafted upon the custom of Paris, to modify the text and vary the mode of its administration, and a British appellation was affixed to the colony. It was now styled the Province of Quebec; and to the original settlers this was a surprising and somewhat humiliating transition. In the versatility of their destiny, it was reserved to them, however, to pass the ordeal of the conquest with greater fortitude than under similar circumstances is usually exhibited.

In conformity with the usages of nations making conquests, the Province of Quebec was at first, and until the subordination and loyalty of the inhabitants could be determined, placed under the rigorous sway of martial law. General Murray, the senior officer of the line after the death of Wolfe, was of right the first military governor. The general acquiescence of the people appearing probable, the general was at length invested with vice-royal authority to institute and administer such a form of civil government as would indicate the leading principles of the British constitution. Disciplined troops were quartered in the province as auxiliaries of the gubernatorial authority; English barristers were deputed to defend the policy of the new administration; Episcopal clergymen were salaried to officiate in congregations not of the Roman faith; and various agencies were employed for the work of gradually Anglicising the manners, customs and political ideas of the people. A French colony was to be converted into a British province of loyal subjects, and it was ultimately accomplished. The sagacity of the houses of Brunswick was equal to the emergency of its plans. What its fleets and armies could conquer, its polity could revolutionize and subdue.

In 1764, Grenville, chancellor of the British exchequer, suggested that the custom of Paris, hitherto in force in Canada, be superceded by the customs, laws, and forms of judicature of England, and that the duties payable to the former government be collected by the king. This initiated a system of taxation without representation, which produced uneasiness and complaint, the more justifiable, perhaps, for the reason that the judge appointed to conciliate the minds of 70,000 foreigners, had been taken from a jail, and a man totally unacquainted with their language had been created attorney-general. The fees prescribed by the governor to be paid the secretary, registrar, clerk of the council, commissary, provost-marshal, and others, were too enormous to be satisfactory; and as Catholics were ineligible to any place of trust or profit, whilst there were yet but nineteen Protestant families in the province, it was very difficult for the former to perceive the equity of the measures contrived for their government. These discontents continued, occasionally producing disorder and contumacy, until 1774, when the British parliament considered the grievance, and relaxed the rigor of the ordinance. Sir Guy Carleton was appointed governor.

The next event which marks the subsequent history of the province, was a prelude to the American revolution. The stamp act, and other measures for exacting tribute from all his majesty's colonies in America, led to much correspondence between the inhabitants of them all. Although most of the Canadians were at this period disinclined to resist the laws enacted for their governance, there were a few who counseled revolt, and advised certain members of the continental congress of their willingness to join the colonists of Massachusetts, New York, Pennsylvania and Virginia, in a general rebellion, if they could be temporarily relieved from the official surveillance then existing. This information was so far credited by the revolutionists in that congress as to influence their preliminary movements. It was perceived that it was of the highest importance to the Anglo-Saxon colonists that their neighbors in Quebec should coalesce with them in memorializing Parliament, and in resistance to the British government by arms, if arms should be resorted to in the course of their difficulties with it; and it was confidently believed that, as the province appeared to be insufficiently protected to secure its possession to Great Britain, if an army were to assail its citadel, it might be easily invaded, and the inhabitants freed from the restraints which disabled them from uni ting in a general American revolution. The sequel proved the fallacy of that opinion.

In 1775, Major General Richard Montgomery, a gallant Irish officer who had served with Wolfe at the period of the conquest, but who at this time resided in New York and sympathized with the revolutionists of that province, was placed at the head of a military expedition fitted out against Canada. After dividing his forces, and placing one division under the command of Colonel Benedict Arnold, with orders to proceed to Quebec by the way of the Kennebec River, he at once proceeded with the other by the way of Lake Champlain. On reaching St. Johns, he readily reduced that post, and soon afterward those of Chambly and Montreal, and made prisoners of their garrisons. Then proceeding down the St. Lawrence, and joining Arnold at Point-aux-Trembles, he resumed the command of the united forces, numbering about 1,200 effective men, and advanced at once upon the citadel. Governor Carleton had under arms at that point only 1,800 soldiers, of whom not more than 70 were regulars; the rest were Highlanders who had settled in the province, Canadian militia and seamen. After the issue and declension of the usual summons to surrender and an unsuccessful seige of thirty days, Montgomery prepared to storm the city on the 31st of December. Again dividing his forces into two commands, and placing one division under the direction of Arnold, he led the other in person. The two commanders were to take positions so as to advance simultaneously from opposite directions to the foot of Mountain street, to force an ingress at Prescott Gate and ascend to the upper town. In this attempt, Montgomery encountered a battery plied by British seamen and militia, and fell, mortally wounded. The troops, on witnessing the fall of their gallant leader, retreated. Arnold meanwhile, pressed his attack from the opposite side with vigor and desperate resolution, but in assailing the first barrier, received a wound which obliged him to quit the field. His party still persisted, and under the command of Captain Morgan, reduced the post, and proceeded to another, where they were surrounded, and, to the number of 426, compelled to surrender. Neither party, therefore, reached the gate, where the Governor was stationed to defend it to the last extremity.

After this repulse, Arnold succeeded to the command of the remnant of the troops, and attempted still to maintain his ground; but the severity of the weather and the indisposition of his men disabled him from effecting more than an imperfect blockade. He maintained a position, however, about three miles from the city until the ensuing May, when he raised the seige, and retreated to Montreal, where, after full consultation with his officers, he resolved to relinquish the project of conquering Canada. He finally retired from the province on the 18th of June.

The American revolution increased the population of Canada. Although a large majority of the inhabitants of the "thirteen colonies" were disloyal, there existed a minority who were loyal to the government of Great Britain; and many of the latter sought a refuge here during the contest. They were termed the United Empire Loyalists, and were commended to the especial favor of the provincial government, during and subsequent to that struggle. At the close of it, in 1783, the province received another accession of inhabitants, in the persons and families of a large number of discharged soldiers, who settled chiefly at and above Prescott, around the Bay of Quinte and along the shore of Lake Ontario. To all these, liberal grants were made—to the loyalists a supply of land, farming utensils, building materials and subsistence for two years, and the promise of a grant of 200 acres of land to each of their children, on their attaining majority—to the discharged soldiery, 5,000 acres to field officers, 3,000 to captains, 2,000 to staff officers, 250 to non-commissioned officers, and 50 to privates. These additions swelled the number of inhabitants to 130,000, of whom at least 10,000 were located at various points west of Montreal, and wrought a wonderful change in the face of the country by converting a dense and dismal wilderness into broad and arable fields. Kingston had been founded at the head of the St. Lawrence; York on the bay of Toronto; Niagara near the river of that name; and several other trading posts in the country between had grown into the importance of towns. But all the principal settlements were widely separated by intervening ranges of pathless woodlands. The royal mail from Quebec seldom reached the western settlements more frequently than twice a year. Mutual assistance in their oft-recurring difficulties with the Indians was seldom practicable. Maintenance of business relations between the settlements was scarcely possible; and social intercourse was not only interdicted by the insuperable barriers of distance, but by the inability of the inhabitants of a portion of the towns to understand the language spoken by other colonists. The French and British settlers were not only dissimilar in habits, customs and ideas, but appeared to constitute two distinct and indiffusible communities. Adhering to different systems of religious faith, venerating the institutions of a different ancestry, and animated by different ideas of duty and destiny, each of these communities was unhappy in the bonds which united them together. However loyal to the existing government they endeavored to be, the alliance was really uncongenial, and the concord unharmonious. They were a different people.

Besides these dissentient causes, there existed under the warrant of the act of 1774, an actual divorce of legal administration between the French and British inhabitants. By that document the ancient law of the colony, "the custom of Paris," had been restored to the lower settlements as "the rule of decision in all controversies relating to property and civil rights," which code had been read ministered seventeen years. The British settlers were reconciled to no jurisprudence but that of Great Britain, which had been introduced immediately after the conquest. Wherefore two distinct and dissimilar codes of legal procedure were operating in the same province at the same time, under the administration of judicial officers commissioned by the same sovereign and responsible to the same royal pleasure. And this was more than a strange anomaly. It was an irreconcilable political and judicial incongruity which menaced the existence of British power in America. This being perceived by Wm. Pitt, that sagacious minister submitted the subject to the especial consideration of Parliament, with suggestions of the propriety of a division of the province and the grant of a constitution to each community. The idea which had not at first many advocates, continued to expand in the sunlight of official favor, until 1791, when it passed into organic law. The province of Quebec was divided into Upper and Lower Canada, near the parallel of longitude 70 degrees 31 minutes west from the meridian of Greenwich, by a line commencing at the cove west of Point au Baudet, on Lake St. Francis, pursuing the western limits of the Seigniories of New Lougueuil and Vaudreil, or Rigaud, to the Ottawa river at Point Fortune and thence up the Ottawa to Temiscaming lake. During the pendency of this question, the project of a division was violently opposed on both sides of the Atlantic. The mercantile interests of the province, concentered at Montreal and Quebec, were very generally adverse to it, from the apprehension that it would infringe their western trade. So earnest were the merchants against the suggestions of Mr. Pitt, that a Quebec trader* was deputed to visit England and submit their protest at the bar of the commons. A hearing being granted, this representtive argued, that, by the act proposed the new province would be entirely cut off from all communication with Great Britain, and that as, from their situation, they could not carry on any foreign commerce, but by the intervention of merchants at Montreal and Quebec, they would have little reason to correspond with, and few opportunities of enjoying, the society of the people of Great Britain; that Niagara was the extreme western limit of cultivable lands; that the Falls of Niagara were an insuperable barrier to navigation beyond; that the few thousand loyalists upon the Catarauqui and the northern shore of Lake Ontario were too sparsely located and in settlements too detached for the enjoyment of the privileges of civil government; that as there had never been a highway robbery in that region, and as the settlers had securely slept at night with unbolted doors, there existed no necessity for criminal courts; that the embarrassments under which the inhabitants labored were the result of a bad administration of uncertain laws; and, finally, that a partition of Canada would not relieve the people of the difficulties complained of. He further represented as the real cause of provincial depression, the pride and insolence of those whose minds were corrupted by the exercise of despotic power; that the mal-administration of the government had repressed the energies, discouraged the industry, and diminished the revenues of the people; that the province was without a court-house, public school house, house of correction, or adequate prison; and that the country had, from these several causes, retrogressed to its low condition.

This and other similar arguments against the separation were earnestly pressed upon the attention of Parliament, but they were unconvincing to Mr. Pitt, and the lords and commoners acting with him. The exigencies of the case were believed to require dissimilar and somewhat extraordinary governments for the two essentially different classes of people inhabiting Canada; and the bill was therefore enacted. This law granted a constitution to the inhabitants of each district, which, although unlike in some respects, provided governments somewhat resembling, in general form, the system in force in Great Britain. Subject to the royal prerogative in its fullest cogency, it provided for the exercise of executive and judicial authority, and created legislative bodies to be composed partly of hereditary and partly of representative members. Mixed in form and varied in details to suit the circumstances of the subjects to be governed, it was, of course, not only a difficult government to administer, but doubtfully experimental in its operation. It was an anomalous system framed to meet a singular exigency in the affairs of a people of diverse lineage, faith, habits, and language, upon the idea of ultimately effecting a permanent union and affiliation. If it did not answer all the purposes of its framers, it stimulated hopes which obscured if they did not fully remove the evils which it was designed to remedy. With slight modifications and additions it was respected as the organic law of the provinces for nearly half a century, and until the reasons which called it into being lost their force against weightier arguments for union.

The divorce being effected, Governor Carleton, now Lord Dorchester, was appointed governor of the Lower, and General Simcoe lieutenant-governor of the Upper Province. The two parliaments convened simultaneously at Quebec and Niagara, on the 17th day of December, 1792. From this time forward to the date of the reünion, the two provinces were distinct in governments, and distinctive in all their leading characteristics — one being essentially French, the other essentially English. Lord Dorchester was succeeded by governors and lieutenant-governors Prescott, Milnes, Craig, Prevost, Drummond, Sherbrooke, the Duke of Richmond, Maitland, the Earl of Dalhousie, Kempt, Aylmer, Burton, Lord Gosford, the Earl of Durham, and Lord Sydenham; Gov. Simcoe by Hunter, Gore, Drummond, Murray, Robinson, Maitland, Colborne, Head, and Arthur. Presidents and Administrators intervened some of these several administrations, yet the appointments were pro tempore and of no account in the general history of the provinces.

In 1792, arrangements were perfected for the transport of a monthly mail during the season of navigation between the cities of Quebec and New York, and the result was frequently attained within the period designated. In 1795 the harvest was so deficient that Lord Dorchester prohibited the exportation of grain from the province. In 1803, the Chief-justice of Montreal declared slavery inconsistent with the laws of the country, and all negroes within the province held as slaves, were discharged from that service. In 1809, the first steam boat was launched on the St. Lawrence at Montreal, and made a passage to Quebec in sixty-six hours, with an anchorage of thirty during the voyage. In 1812, there were five newspapers published in Canada, all of which were in the lower province. The same year the Congress of the United States declared war against Great Britain, which rendered it necessary for Governor Prevost to expel American citizens from Quebec, place an embargo on shipping in the ports, and to resist military encroachments in various ways at different points along the provincial borders.

The British theory respecting allegiance, expatriation, and the right of search of American vessels upon the high seas, was repugnant to the republican sentiment of the people of the United States. The forcible exercise of that right in the case of the Chesapeake, from which four seamen were impressed, and one of them hung as a deserter, induced the congress of that government to contest it.

Great Britain thereupon proclaimed a general system of paper blockade. This called forth the Berlin decree from Napoleon Bonaparte, blockading, by the same process, the British islands. Great Britain rejoined by orders in council, blockading all ports in Europe from which the British flag had been excluded. Napoleon retaliated by the Milan decree, declaring every ship of whatever nation which should submit to search from an English vessel, liable to capture as English property. The same penalty was also denounced against all ships holding intercourse with Great Britain or her colonies. In this manner, whilst thousands of sailors were forcibly taken from American vessels to serve in the British navy American commerce was nearly destroyed by the belligerent powers. This resulted in an open declaration of

* The name of this trader was Adam Lymburner.

war on the part of the United States, which included in its scope the invasion of Canada.

Whilst affairs were thus ripening for an open conflict between the United States and Great Britain, Governor Prevost despatched a secret agent to the Eastern States, to ascertain the views of the inhabitants respecting a dissolution of the existing union. He was instructed to obtain interviews with leading men, and encourage such disaffection as he might discover to exist. The agent did not disclose the object of his mission, but carefully noted all he saw and heard respecting the subject of his inquiry, and returned the information in numerous despatches to the governor. Not being satisfactorily rewarded for these delicate and responsible services by his government, he subsequently disclosed the affair to the American cabinet, who paid him fifty thousand dollars for the correspondence. These papers were published in the United States as additional provocation for the war.

The honor of the British flag was again in controversy. The loyalty of his majesty's Canadian subjects was again to be tested. History vindicates the honorable pretension. The gentry of the Lower Province commenced the necessary hostile preparations by raising and equipping four battalions of militia, and assuming their command. The citadel of Quebec was securely garrisoned by inhabitants of the town, who were proud of the duty which they were required to perform.

The Empire Loyalists in the Upper Province rallied around the standard of General Brock. And all the military force of both provinces was assured to the government whenever and wherever the same might be needed. Canadian soil was the altar of unwavering patriotism. Neither the promises of Hull nor the overtures of Smith could seduce it. Although in no wise responsible for the war and its consequences to Great Britain, it was sufficient for Canadians to know that the British crown was interested in the question, in order to discern the path of duty. They expelled the enemy from their domain; captured armies with their commanding generals, at Detroit and River Raisin; fought the battles of Queenston, Stony Creek, Chateauguay, Chryslers', La Colle, and Lundy's Lane; and reduced by assault the towns of Mackinaw, Niagara, Oswego and Ogdensburgh—and although that national struggle added little luster to the former glory of British arms, it was greatly distinguished by illustrious examples of Canadian heroism and loyalty. Had the mother government preceded the campaign of 1812 with the structure of suitable defences in the provinces and upon the lakes, it is extremely doubtful whether an army from the United States would have made any hostile demonstrations whatever against them.

In the month of March, 1815, Gov. Prevost proclaimed the conclusion of a treaty of peace between Great Britain and the United States. The population of Upper Canada, at this period, had increased to 95,000, and that of Lower Canada to 300,000. The number of vessels afloat was 46, having an aggregate tonnage of 16,840. The annual clearance of vessels at the port of Quebec had increased to 399, with a tonnage of 86,436. In 1816 two additional steamers were launched on the St. Lawrence, and the following year one or two others were constructed. Indeed, all the navigable waters between Halifax and Mackinaw were at this time traversed with vessels of various capacities and forms in the business of internal commerce. In 1819, the Duke of Richmond, then governor-general, died, of hydrophobia, occasioned by the bite of a rabid fox, with which he was amusing himself. This sudden bereavement occasioned great lamentation and sorrow. In 1822, the subject of a reünion of the provinces was agitated, and a bill to that effect introduced into the British Parliament. It was withdrawn, however, for the purpose of ascertaining the wishes in that behalf, of the Canadian inhabitants. By this the governor was to have the power to erect townships, theretofore unrepresented, into counties, each to consist of not less than six townships, and to return a member to the assembly. The whole number of representatives for each province, who were to be freeholders of estates valued at five hundred pounds sterling above incumbrances, was not to exceed sixty; two members of the executive council of each province were to have seats in the assembly for debate; neither house was to be invested with authority to imprison for breaches of privilege until an act were passed defining it; and all written proceedings were to be indited in the English language only, and after the expiration of fifteen years the same language only should be pronounced in debate. From this time forward, until the reünion was consummated, there was an opposition party in both the provinces, each of whom sent an agent to England to advocate its views, after which the colonial secretary announced the temporary relinquishment of the project.

In 1823, there were elected to the legislative assembly of the Lower Province several members who differed with the governor respecting the control of the revenues, and who claimed for that body the exclusive right of regulating all appropriations of funds raised by taxation. They also insisted that all officers charged with the duty of receiving and disbursing public monies, were accountable to that body for the faithful performance of their duties. Pending the discussion of these questions, the receiver-general, into whose accounts these reformers had vainly demanded inquiry, became insolvent to the government, thereby indicating more clearly the necessity of the guards which they desired to place around the treasury. Two political parties on this and similar questions came into existence as the natural, if not the inevitable consequence, and various reforms in the management of public affairs were earnestly demanded. The governor, on the other hand, regarded the movement as an attempt to override the lawful authority of the government which he was bound to enforce, and thus to excite the spirit of insubordination which it was his duty to repress. An issue was therefore formed which convulsed both provinces, and finally eventuated in the abrogation of the then constitution. In 1825, Lord Dalhousie dissolved the assembly for insubordination, and withheld his approval of the election of Papineau, a distinguished leader of the reform party, to the office of speaker of a new house. Resenting this as a further encroachment on their chartered rights, the reformers utterly refused to elect another presiding officer, thereby withholding supplies altogether in the Lower Province, until the winter of 1827–8.

Meanwhile the inhabitants of the Upper Province, who had suffered losses of property during the late war, were seeking indemnity, and to that end the British government had assented to a loan of £100,000, conditioned that the province provide for the payment of one moiety of the interest. Being unable of itself to comply with these terms, the legislature applied to the government of Lower Canada to assist, by imposing additional duties on certain articles of merchandize. The effort was unn vailing, however, as the assembly of that province were of opinion that the exigency of the times would not justify the burthen. Great financial embarrassment was the consequence.

In 1827, eighty-seven thousand inhabitants of the Lower Province memorialized the king concerning the arbitrary conduct of the governor-general, arraigned him for harsh and oppressive ministrations of the laws; the misapplication of the public monies; the continuing in office of defaulting officers; the violent dissolution of the people's house of assembly; the dismissal of military officers for voting against his policy; and the reärrangement of the peace commission for political purposes. His majesty caused the document to be transmitted to the house of commons, who enacted several laws for their relief. Parliament declined, however, to relinquish the coronal power over the revenues. The precise relief invoked was therefore refused.

Dalhousie at length surrendered his commission, and Sir James Kempt was entrusted with the office. Governor Kempt assembled the legislature, accepted the election of Papineau, and addressed that body in a manner acceptable, conciliatory, and wise. He was the man for the emergency. Under his administration the executive and legislative departments were reconciled, and supply bills passed which enabled the government to proceed in concord and harmony. Representation was moreover increased from fifty to eighty-four members. But this did not satisfy the reformers.

In 1831, the assembly of the Upper Province presented a list of grievances to the governor-general, which his excellency forwarded to England with his endorsement that some of them were true. This resulted in the passage of an act vesting that body with the power of controlling the revenues—a concession that indicated a disposition in Parliament to guaranty the principles of the British constitution to his majesty's subjects in the colonies.

The Lower Province was yet agitated with questions of reform, and these were, in many instances, intermingled with jealous ideas of Catholics, respecting Protestant designs against their religion. Naturally credulous and impulsive, the habitans were easily excited to the commission of overt acts by inflammatory appeals of politicians, who counseled resistance to law as the only practicable method of obtaining relief. At an election held at Montreal on the 21st of May, 1832, the populace became heated and rebellious, and so far defied the civil authorities as to render it necessary for the latter to invoke military aid to quell disturbance. On this occasion three persons were killed. This was the first effusion of blood in the cause of constitutional reform, and but for the coincident appearance at Montreal of the Asiatic cholera, the occurrence would have been followed, doubtless, by violent retaliations. And even that terrible pestilence did not allay the malcontentment. In 1835, the assembly absolutely refused to vote any supplies, except upon the condition of assured alterations of the constitution.

Sympathizing with these movements below, the assembly of the Upper Province were disposed to avail themselves of the occasion to urge their grievances, and to insist that the judges should be independent of the crown, and that the chief justice only should have a seat in the executive council. A bill to that effect was enacted, but failed to receive the royal assent. Following the example of their brethren in Lower Canada, they declined to legislate further than to pass annual bills of supply, with designations of the persons to whom salaries should be paid, with provisoes that not more than one office should be held by the same individual. This was also disapproved; whereupon the assembly demanded the abolition of the executive, and the substitution of an elective council. This was not only disagreed to, but rebuked by Lord Stanley, then secretary of the colonial department, as disloyal contumacy and presumption. Whereupon the assembly refused to vote any supplies until the return of an agent forthwith despatched to lay their grievances before the British government. This movement resulted in the appointment of a royal commission of inquiry into the alleged grievances, in 1835, and in the proffer of conditional overtures concerning the provincial revenues.

Affairs were now at a crisis. A majority of the members of both assemblies were at direct issue with the government, and a majority of the inhabitants, at least of the Lower Province, sustained these representatives. Public meetings were held in both provinces, at which inflammatory speeches were delivered, and seditious resolutions adopted. At the Richelieu villages the tri-colored ensign was displayed as the emblem of revolution, and at St. Charles the habitans elevated the cap of liberty, and under it pledged themselves by solemn oaths to be faithful to the principles which it indicated. Gubernatorial proclamations were issued, treason reprobated, suspected magistrates and militia officers superseded, and the regular troops detailed for duty. On the 6th of November, 1837, there was another outbreak at Montreal, but no lives were lost. On the 10th, Sir John Colborne, the commander of the forces, took quarters at Montreal, and the same day despatched Captain Glasgow to take possession of a bridge near St. Johns, to prevent the armed malcontents from crossing the Richelieu. On the 16th, some of them were taken prisoners, but were recaptured by their coadjutors, in a skirmish near Longueil.

Congregating at and fortifying St. Charles, it became necessary for the government to dislodge them from that position. This was accomplished by Colonel Wetherall, at the expense of several lives, and every house in the place except one. Colonel Wetherall returned to Montreal with the liberty cap, above referred to, and several prisoners. At St. Denis an engagement occurred between the revolutionists and a party of soldiers under Colonel Gore, at which about three hundred of the former were killed. Other similar demonstrations occurred at the Lake of the Two Mountains, St. Eustache, St. Scholastique, and St. Benoit, where the peasantry were posted and fortified.

Cotemporaneous movements of a revolutionary character were going forward in the vicinity of Toronto, under the lead of Mackenzie, Egmont, and others, members of a disloyal association, styled the Provincial Convention. Through the agencies of several auxiliary societies, secretly organized in different parts of the province, and some of them beyond the provincial borders, these individuals were enabled to mature a plan of operations much more formidable and menacing than any which had preceded it. All preliminaries being arranged, this Provincial convention issued a declaration of intentions of the friends of liberty, to put down those who oppressed them; to subvert and extinguish the Canada company; to grant the public lands to volunteer soldiers in their cause; to institute a government that should be administered economically; and, in general, to "make crooked paths straight, and rough places plain." Thi document was extensively circulated within and without the province, and particularly in the adjacent States of New York, Ohio, and Michigan, where it produced an impression upon many persons, that the cause of human rights demanded their sympathy, and upon others that the magnificent offers of lands in Canada were fair inducements for perilous services in obtaining them. Then, assembling on the 4th of December, 1837, at Montgomery's, in Yonge-street, they prepared to make a descent upon Toronto. To prevent information of their movements from reaching the city, they undertook to arrest every person whom they suspected to be likely to convey it. In this proceeding they happened to discover Colonel Moodie, a distinguished officer residing near that place, on his way to the city, and thereupon fired at and mortally wounded him. Blood having been shed, it was believed that they then had no alternative but to advance speedily upon the city. Taking up a march, they entered the precincts of Toronto in the night time, whilst the lieutenant-governor, Sir Francis Head, and most of the inhabitants, were asleep. Alderman Powell discovered them, awoke Sir Francis, and rung the public bells, whilst Sheriff Jarvis, with a party of loyalists, drove the insurgents back, killing one of them and wounding another. As the lieutenant-governor had previously sent the regular soldiery to the Lower Province, he had no support but the loyal inhabitants of the town, whom he supplied with such arms as the regular troops had left behind them. They were soon joined, however, by volunteers from the neighboring districts, and particularly from Gore, whence came a large party under the command of Colonel Allan McNab, the speaker of the house of assembly. Being thus reïnforced, the governor admonished the insurgents of the consequences of their insubordination, and mildly requested them to return to their allegiance. The answer returned was, that they would do so only upon the condition that their demands should be settled by a national convention. The condition being inadmissible, the loyalists were directed to advance upon and disperse them. This order was executed on the 7th, with small arms and one field-piece. The insurgents were pursued to Montgomery's, where they were engaged, and most of them, including two of their leaders, taken prisoners. Mackenzie escaped, however, from the province into the United States. The lives lost in this encounter were very few, yet the triumph was so complete that Sir Francis deemed it discreet to discharge most of the prisoners on the spot.

Unwilling to relinquish the project of reform, Mackenzie next undertook to raise a force in the United States sufficient to compel a submission of the matters complained of to the arbitrament of a convention, or else the subversion of the government. Appealing in various ways to the sympathies of patriotic but weak and credulous men, beyond the lines, he at length succeeded in inducing several hundred men and boys to provide themselves with arms, clandestinely, if necessary, and assemble on the 13th of December upon an island in the Niagara river, above the falls. There, under the pretended command of a visionary individual named Van Rensselaer, they opened a fire on the militia and inhabitants upon the Canadian shore, and offered a reward for the apprehension of the lieutenant-governor. A small steamer called the "Caroline," which transported their munitions of war, being descried by Colonel McNab, who was then in command of the militia, it appeared to him necessary that she should be taken or sunk. He accordingly despatched Captain Drew, of the navy, with a party to make the attack, who gallantly executed the order, captured, fired and set her adrift in the current, which bore her over the falls. In this affair, an American citizen named Durfee, was killed. For this, Alexander McLeod, a British subject residing in Canada, who subsequently visited the State of New York on business, was arrested in that state, indicted, tried, but acquitted of murder. On the 14th of January, 1838, the Navy Islanders were dislodged by a few pieces of well poised artillery, after which, it is said, many of them were arrested for a violation of the neutrality laws, by Nathaniel Garrow, then a marshal of the United States.

This attempt at invasion was followed by demonstrations against Kingston, the Western District, Fighting Island, and Point Pelé, in Lake Erie, all of which were promptly repelled. In these forays, with the exception of that of Toronto, a majority of the insurgents were said to be inhabitants of the United States. On the 23d of March, Sir George Arthur arrived at Toronto to succeed Lieutenant-Governor Head, who had resigned his charge in consequence of differences between him and her majesty's government, on certain points of colonial policy. On the 29th of May, the Earl of Durham arrived in Canada, as governor-general and high-commissioner, for the purpose of adjusting, if possible, the affairs of both provinces in a proper yet satisfactory manner. On assuming the government, he discharged most of the political prisoners, except certain leaders, whom he banished to Bermuda, and permitted absent reformers to return to their homes. After a careful investigation, he made a report to her majesty's government, which has been the subject of extensive criticism, recommending the reünion of the provinces. His lordship did not remain long in charge of the government. Perceiving that his banishment of the prisoners was disapproved in England, he resigned his office and sailed for home on the 1st of November, 1838. The evening of his lordship's departure was signalized by another violent disturbance at Montreal. Several arrests were made, but the cause of difficulty being yet unadjusted, there was no enduring peace. On the 3d, a party of insurgents surprised the loyalists of Beauharnois, and took them prisoners. On the following day, whilst the inhabitants of Caughnawaga, near Montreal, were at worship, a party of rebels surrounded the church. The Indians turned out from apparent curiosity to see them, when, following the example of their chief, each wrested the musket from the hands of the rebel next him, and sounded the war-whoop. The others, being panic-struck, immediately surrendered, when the party to the number of sixty-four were tied with their own sashes and garters, and taken prisoners to Montreal. On the 10th, a portion of the 71st Regiment, and upwards of a thousand Glengary men, living on the opposite side of the river, rescued the prisoners at Beauharnois. Soon afterward an engagement occurred between a body of insurgents, who had been despatched from Napierville, to open a communication with the United States, and a party of loyal volunteers, in which the latter took several prisoners, a field-piece, and three hundred stand of arms. About this time, also, a party of American sympathisers, under the lead of a Polish adventurer, of the name of Von Schoultz, landed at Prescott, and took refuge in a wind-mill and an adjoining building. After defending themselves from this shelter until they had killed eighteen loyalists, they were taken prisoners, and to the number of one hundred and fifty-six removed to Kingston for trial by court martial

Another invasion occurred at Sandwich, where the insurgents fired the barracks, destroyed a British steamer, and deliberately killed several individuals, and among others Dr. Hume, a military surgeon. From that point they were driven back by Colonel Prince and the militia, who killed twenty-five and took twenty-six of them prisoners during the skirmish. Another party crossed the Niagara river, and endeavored to excite the people to insurrection. On hearing of the approach of troops, they set fire to an inn, took fourteen lancers prisoners, and retired from the country, leaving behind them forty prisoners, among whom were the first and second in command. Six of the Prescott invaders and the same number of Dr. Hume's murderers were executed. Among these was the brave but presumptuons Von Schoultz. In tender consideration of the juvenility of some, the infirmity of others, and the misapprehension of all who had been inveigled into the conspiracy, the English government saw fit to extend its clemency to the rest of the prisoners, immediately in some instances, and, after a temporary imprisonment, in others, that the humane principles of English liberty might be seen and appreciated. Thus terminated the second act in the solemn drama of Canadian revolution; an affair in its inception partly legitimate and partly unlawful, partly loyal and partly seditious; in its progress partly reformatory and partly subversive, partly insurrectionary and partly invasive; and ultimating in violence and civil war. Begun for a purpose not wholly inconsistent with the principles and guarantees of constitutional liberty, by representatives who did not at first meditate open rebellion, but converted by an excited populace into an angry, turbulent and reckless controversy, in which large numbers from within and without the province were subsequently embroiled, either as political aggressors or armed resistants of public authority, the embers of incipient discord kindled into a flame, which surprised and alarmed even those who had fanned them most. Changing its character with nearly every attending circumstance, and jeoparding in its course the reputation, the political fortunes, and even the lives of its leaders to an extent which they did not at first anticipate, it is yet somewhat doubtful to impartial history whether the originators of the movement were morally or politically responsible for the sorrowful consequences which encrimsoned its existence. The end finally attained in the concessions of the British government, and in the reünion of the provinces under a more liberal constitution, furnishes their best and only apology.

These disturbances of the public peace, during which all rational discussion gave way to the ebullitions of excitement, the clangor of trumpets and the din of arms, were succeeded by a season of comfortable tranquillity. Lord Durham's project of reünion formed the leading topic of general conversation and debate in both provinces, and was variously estimated by different individuals. This measure having been announced in the British parliament as the ministerial panacea for Canadian difficulties, the house of assembly of Upper Canada at once declared themselves in its favor, upon certain specified conditions. The legislative council and the Chief-justice opposed it, however, and at their instance the subject was postponed to a future session. The reasons* urged were that the bill proposed would create a representative assembly which that government might be unable, except by painful measures, to withstand, and which at no distant period would give existence to another body in which the majority would not only be opposed, in the common spirit of party, to the faithful colonial governor, but would be held together by a common desire to separate the colony from the crown; that such an organization might induce future administrations to surrender principles essential to colonial safety; that mischiefs would be likely to arise from the rivalry of Catholics and Protestants, if represented in the same legislature, that neither colony would feel that parliament had the right to change its religious character; that the two provinces united would form a territory too vast to be conveniently or safely ruled by one executive; that it would introduce into the constitution of the upper house of the legislature, principles of government unknown in any other British colony; that it would restrict the royal prerogative in making appointments of legislative counselors, and limit their terms of office; that it would permit the colonial legislature to enact laws respecting their prorogation and dissolution; and that it would entirely disarrange the judiciary, and embarrass the administration of justice. The greater portion of the crown officials were also suspicious that the abrogation of the existing system might result in displacements, greatly disadvantageous to the British crown. But in respect to this, there were different opinions.

These objections induced the British ministry to amend the bill, but did not deter them from urging its passage. It was, nevertheless, enacted to the effect that "Whereas it is necessary that provision be made for the good government of the provinces of Upper Canada and Lower Canada, in such manner as may secure the rights and liberties, and promote the interests of all classes of her majesty's subjects within the same; and whereas, to this end, it is expedient that the said provinces be reünited, and form one province for the purposes of executive government and legislation; be it, therefore, enacted by the Queen's most excellent majesty, by and with the advice and consent of the Lords, spiritual and temporal, and Commons, in this present parliament assembled, and by the authority of the same, that it shall be lawful for her majesty, with the advice of her privy council, to declare or to authorize the governor-general of the said two provinces of Upper and Lower Canada to declare by proclamation that the said provinces, upon, from and after a certain day in such proclamation to be appointed, which day shall be fifteen calendar months next after the passing of this act, shall form and be one province under the name of the province of Canada; that from and after the reünion of the said two provinces of Canada, there should be within the province of Canada one legislative council and one assembly, to be severally constituted and composed in the manner hereinafter prescribed, which shall be called the legislative council and assembly of Canada, and that, within the province of Canada, her majesty shall have power by and with the advice and consent of the said legislative council and assembly, to make laws for the peace, welfare and good government of the province of Canada, such laws not being repugnant to this act, or to such parts of the act passed in the thirty-first year of the reign of his late majesty, as are not hereby repealed, or to any act of parliament made or to be made, and not hereby repealed, which does or shall, by express enactment, or by necessary intendment extend to the province of Upper and Lower Canada, or to either of them, or to the province of Canada, and

* Reasons assigned by the Hon. Beverly Robinson, Chief-Justice of Upper Canada, in a printed communication, addressed to Lord John Russell, to be seen at length in a volume published by J. Hatchard & Son, 187 Piccadilly, London.

that all such laws being passed by the said legislative council and assembly, and assented to by her majesty, or assented to in her majesty's name by the governor of the province, shall be valid and binding to all intents and purposes within the province of Canada;" that the legislative council shall consist of not less than twenty eminent and intelligent members to be designated by the crown; that the assembly shall be composed of eighty-four members, an equal number from each of the provinces; that it shall be lawful for the legislative council and assembly to alter the divisions of counties, ridings, cities and towns, and to establish other divisions and alter the apportionment of representatives to be chosen therefrom, by a vote of two-thirds of both houses for the time being, and after presenting addresses expressing the facts to the governor; that a session of such legislative council and assembly shall be held at least once in every year, so that a period of twelve calendar months shall not intervene between the sessions; that every assembly shall continue in office four years from the day of the return of the writs for choosing the same, and no longer, subject to prorogation or dissolution by the governor; that all writs, proclamations, instruments for summoning, proroguing and dissolving the assembly, public instruments relating to the legislature, returns thereto, entries, proceedings and reports, shall be indited and printed in the English language only; that the revenues of the two provinces shall be consolidated; that the consolidated revenue fund shall be charged with the expenses of collection and management, and with forty-five thousand pounds annually toward expenses of government, and the further annual sum of thirty thousand pounds during the life of her majesty, and five years afterward; that, during the periods for which the several sums above-named are severally payable, the same shall be accepted and taken by her majesty by way of civil list instead of all other revenues arising in the province; and that three-fifths of the net product of the territorial and other revenues at the disposal of the crown be paid over to the account of the said consolidated revenue-fund, and during the life of her majesty, and five years after her demise, the remaining two-fifths shall be paid over in like manner to the same account.

It was further provided that the expenses of the collection, management and receipt of the consolidated fund should form the first charge thereon; that the annual interest of the public debt of the provinces of Upper and Lower Canada, or of either of them, at the time of the reünion, should form the second; that the payments to be made to the clergy of the united church of England and Ireland, to the clergy of the church of Scotland, and to ministers of other christian denominations, pursuant to any law or usage whereby such payments, before or at the time of passage of the act, were legally or usually paid out of the public or crown revenue of either of the provinces, should form the third; that the said sum of forty-five thousand pounds should form the fourth; that the said sum of thirty thousand pounds, so long as the same might continue to be payable, should form the fifth; that the other charges upon the rates and duties levied within the province, should form the sixth; that, subject to these several payments, the consolidated revenue fund should be appropriated for the public service in the manner the legislature might think proper, provided, always, that all bills for appropriating any part of the surplus, or for imposing any new tax or impost, originate in the assembly, and all resolutions or bills appropriating the same or any part thereof, or of any other tax or impost, should be for an object which had been previously recommended by the governor. To ensure the adoption by the provinces of this constitution, and the formation of a suitable government under it, her majesty appointed the Right Honorable Charles Poulett Thomson, formerly president of the board of trade, afterwards Lord Sydenham, to the responsible office of governor-general.

Governor Thomson came out in the autumn of 1839, and entered at once upon the discharge of his delicate trust. He found the representatives greatly divided in sentiment respecting the union, and some of them violently opposed to it. There existed, nevertheless, a conservative majority in the special council of the Lower, and in the legislature of the Upper province, in favor of the law, by whom it was considered and adopted. The result was officially announced in 1839, and was followed by a favorable election of representatives to the legislative assembly. In peaceably effecting this important substitution of civil government under the peculiar difficulties of the times, his lordship achieved for British liberty a moral triumph, and for himself an honorable and enduring fame. His administration, however, was very brief. After living to see the parliament assembled and the constitution fairly and favorably operating, he died in 1841 from injuries occasioned by a fall from his horse; and his remains, by his own desire, were buried at Kingston, at that time the seat of the new provincial government.

From one of his lordship's communications to the colonial secretary during the pendency of the preliminary resolutions in the special council of Lower Canada, some of the difficulties of his mission were clearly indicated. "No man," he observed, "looks to a practical measure of improvement. Talk to any one upon education, or public works, or better laws; you might as well talk Greek to him. Not a man cares for a single practical measure, the only end, one would suppose, of a better form of government. They have only one feeling—a hatred of race. The French hate the English, and the English hate the French, and every question resolves itself into that, and that alone. There is positively no machinery of government. Every thing is to be done by the governor and his secretary. There are no heads of departments at all, or none whom one can depend on. The wise system heretofore adopted has been to stick two men into the same office whenever a vacancy occurred, one a Frenchman, and the other a Britisher. Thus we have joint crown surveyors, joint sheriffs, &c., each opposing the other in every thing he attempts." To bring together the scattered elements of the fallen fabrics, and erect upon them a solid and orderly system of provincial government was the arduous task of the graphic author.

During this administration, amicable relations between the United States and Great Britain were seriously threatened by the arrest and trial of Alexander McLeod, in the state of New York, for killing one Amos Durfee, a citizen of that state, at the time of the capture and burning of the steamboat Caroline. Whilst upon a business errand within that jurisdiction, in January, 1841, McLeod was arrested, and indicted by the grand jury of the county of Niagara, for the crime of murder. This occasioned a diplomatic correspondence between Mr. Fox, the British minister plenipotentiary, near the government of the United States, and Daniel Webster, then secretary of state, in which the former asserted that the transaction on account of which the prisoner had been arrested, was a transaction of a public character, planned and executed by persons duly empowered by her majesty's colonial authorities, to take any steps and to do any acts which might be necessary for the defense of her majesty's territories, and for the defense of her majesty's subjects; and that, consequently, those subjects of her majesty who engaged in that transaction were performing acts of public duty, for which they were not personally and individually answerable to the laws and tribunals of any foreign country; and in the name of her majesty he formally demanded his release. To this it was replied, that the detention of McLeod was not a proper case for the interference of executive power; that his discharge should be sought in a manner conformable to the principles of law and proceedings in courts of judicature; that were such a case pending against an individual in the courts of England, the law officer of the crown might enter a nolle prosequi, or the prisoner might cause himself to be brought up on habeas corpus and discharged, if his ground of discharge were adjudged sufficient, or he might prove the same facts in his defense on his trial; that the indictment against the prisoner was pending in a state and not a federal court, but that his rights were, notwithstanding, safe; and that a tribunal so eminently distinguished as the supreme court of the state of New York might be safely relied on for a just and impartial administration of law.

McLeod then applied to the supreme court of New York for a discharge on habeas corpus. But that tribunal held that British subjects, committing homicides within that jurisdiction in time of peace, even though their sovereign avow directions and approve their acts, might, nevertheless, be criminally prosecuted; that aliens were amenable to the criminal law for offences committed, irrespective of the manner they may have entered the territory; that the right of using force does not arise in cases where the mischief exists in machination only, nor authorize retaliation for antecedent injuries; that the orders of officers of a nation at war for the destruction of life or property of an enemy within the territory of a neutral power afford no protection to persons acting under them; that sovereigns have no right to compel their subjects to enter neighboring countries to commit unlawful acts either in time of peace or war; that the jurisdiction of the court was not superseded by the avowals of Mr. Fox, nor because the prisoner's case had become the subject of executive diplomacy; that violence is never justifiable even in self-defense where the parties using it have not been themselves assailed; and that persons indicted for murder cannot be discharged on habeas corpus on proof of innocence merely, however clear the evidence may be, but must, nevertheless, abide a regular trial. It was also held that the courts of that state possess no power to order a nolle prosequi upon an indictment. The applicant was, therefore, remanded to the sheriff's custody, who confined him in a jail at Whitesboro.

This proceeding, although it indicated nothing to excite suspicion that McLeod would be released without a trial, was made the pretext for such surmises on the part of certain persons implicated in the border difficulties of 1838, and among them a mischievous fugitive from the justice of Canada of the name of Lett, and also for the contrivance of plots against his life. To get possession of his person, those individuals purloined and transported to Whitesboro several pieces of ordnance for the purpose of intimidating the jailer, and, if necessary, breaking the prison. The plan was frustrated by a proclamation of the governor of the state offering a large reward for the capture of Lett, and the following executive instructions to the sheriff of the county of Oneida: "There is much reason to apprehend that the country would be involved in war if any injury should befal Alexander McLeod while he remains in the custody of the law. The state of New York could be neither justified nor excused if any violence should reach him. Important as it is that the state should vindicate its dignity, by subjecting him to a trial for the offense with which he is charged, the honor of New York, and even that of the United States, is more deeply concerned in protecting him against danger until that vindication be accomplished. You are aware of the solicitude of this department on that subject. You are aware that the same solicitude is expressed by the president, and indeed, that it pervades the American people. I have the highest pleasure in acknowedging that you have on all proper occasions expressed, and in every proper manner manifested a deep sense of the responsibilities which, under such extraordinary circumstances, rest upon you. It is my duty now to state to you that, besides the communications of which you have heretofore been informed, very frequent letters have been received by the president, giving him notice of designs on the part of evil disposed persons to rescue McLeod and assassinate him. Although I remain of the opinion before expressed to you, that such apprehensions are without sufficient cause, yet it is certainly safer to err on the side of precaution; and no proper precaution can be omitted consistently with the respect due from the authorities of this state to those of the Union. I deem it proper, therefore, to recommend that the constabulary force assigned to attend the court should be double or treble that usually called into requisition on such occasions. You have a surplus of arms and ammunition after supplying the guard heretofore established. Let arrangements be made for placing those arms in the hands of your deputies and the constables. Should any disturbance of the peace take place, or be reasonably apprehended, you will, under the direction of the court, call out any portion of the militia of Oneida county that you may believe necessary; and to enable you to do so, the adjutant-general will be in attendance at or near Utica during the trial, and ready to render you effective assistance. Major General Scott, commanding the army of the United States, has directed the company of regular troops now stationed at Rome to be held in readiness to support you if their services should be deemed necessary. Brigadier General Wool will be near you throughout the trial, and will, whenever called upon, give you his advice and assistance if necessary. I leave it to your own prudence and discretion to determine how far you will avail yourself of the aid thus placed at your command. You will, however, allow me to remark that the spectacle in this country of a court attended by an armed force would be a scene to be much regretted. You will, therefore, be exceedingly careful to make either no military array or the least that shall be consistent with the entire security of your prisoner and the preservation of public order. For the honor of the state and country, it is to be desired that this trial, which will have all the importance and many of the features of a high state trial, may, if possible, be conducted with the simplicity which belongs to our institutions.

"If the prisoner should be convicted, you will be very careful to take such measures as shall prevent his rescue or escape. If an acquittal takes place, you will tender to him a safe conduct through the state, requiring him to proceed with as little delay as possible, and upon that route where it shall seem to you he will be least exposed to lawless violence. You will call to your aid in performing that duty the marshal of the northern district, who will officially attend you. You will also avail yourself of the aid of so many public officers and of such a guard, either civil or military, and drawn either from the militia or the regular troops before mentioned, as you may have reason to believe will be required; with such aid you will conduct the prisoner in safety to the frontier. If he refuses to leave the state or declines the protection thus tendered, your peculiar responsibilities and those of the state, so far as they have arisen from his detention, will have been discharged."

These precautions rendered the design of the sympathizers too hazardous to be carried into execution, and the same was thereupon abandoned. McLeod was tried according to usual forms of law, and acquitted on satisfactory proof of alibi, on the 12th day of October, 1841.

Lord Sydenham was succeeded by Sir Charles Bagot, who arrived in Canada on the 10th of January, 1842.

Provincial affairs had by this time so much improved as to exhibit the new system in hopeful operation. Although imperfectly organized and incompletely administered, it had strengthened the public confidence and was imparting new vigor to business. The inhabitants of the upper districts were arousing, as from a protracted slumber, to the consideration of various improvements of the times and the development of the resources of the country. Canals, rail roads, plank roads, and other new works, for travel and commerce, were building; postal arrangements were gradually extending, and labor-saving machinery for mechanical and agricultural purposes was coming into use. Colleges and academies were receiving encouragement, and common schools, for the education of the masses were rapidly increasing. And every department of industry was putting on a livelier and a thriftier aspect.

The legislative council and assembly, although yet unrelieved of the prejudices engendered by former dissensions, and yet unoblivious to old distinctions of ancestry, language and sect, were at this period tolerably well united in the purposes of legislation; all appeared desirous of giving the new system of government a fair and patient trial; all had begun to discern the dawning of a new era in public affairs; and all were ambitious to brighten the pages of their future history. The union had been ordained and accepted, but it was esteemed valuable only in the degree to which it should be perfected by legislation. And the details of necessary laws were to be determined by the exigencies of the occasion, without reference to regulations in force at the period of the separation. Nearly every provincial statute needed modification or revision, to adapt it to the altered circumstances of the people and the requirements of the times. To enact the requisite series of enabling laws, therefore, and suit them to the public interests without trenching either upon royal prerogative or the constitution, and which should be sufficiently conservative to prevent anarchy and sufficiently liberal to be popular, was a delicate, arduous and responsible task. There were civilians in both houses, however, who were competent for the duty, as voluminous public records and subsequent years of order, prosperity and peace abundantly testify.

Governor Bagot did not survive to see many of the fruits even of his own wise policy. He died at Kingston on the 18th day of May, 1843, and was succeeded by Sir Charles, afterwards Lord Metcalf, the former governor of Jamaica, who came to his charge with a high reputation as a civilian, which he had earned during his residence in the West Indies, where he had encountered and surmounted many formidable difficulties. He had, morever, greatly promoted the interests of commerce in that quarter, won the admiration and love of the inhabitants, and secured for himself the fullest confidence and approval of the government at home. He was expected by the ministry to examine, as he subsequently did, into the commerce of Canada, for the purpose of advising them fully in respect to the precise nature and extent of the grievances of which the provincial merchants were at that time generally complaining. As the revenue laws afforded little or no protection to any Canadian product, but were intended rather to augment than to diminish colonial dependence on the factories and forges of England, it had been discovered that the commerce of the province was burthened with embarrassing and oppressive restrictions. Indeed, the whole subject of imposts, both on exports and imports from the mother country, was under anxious consideration on both sides of the Atlantic, and the discussion of the topic had led to suggestions respecting free trade, commercial independence, annexation to, or reciprocity of, trade with the United States, which portended further disturbances. And his lordship found the matter greatly complicated with other kindred subjects, and among them the commercial regulations of Great Britain with her other American and Indian colonies. He was impressed at once with favorable ideas of the propriety of some form of commercial relief, but was never fully prepared to indicate a satisfactory method of effecting it to any considerable extent, without occasioning mischiefs of greater magnitude than those he desired to remedy. Hence, his excellency was after all obliged to content himself with recommending such measures for local improvement as he deemed expedient and practicable, and with affording such encouragements to industrial pursuits as he was able, until an impaired and failing constitution admonished him to relinquish his charge. He returned to England in 1845, and was succeeded by Earl Cathcart, the commander of the forces of British North America, as administrator, and in 1846, by the Right Honorable James, Earl of Elgin and Kincardine, as governor-general.

It was reserved for the Earl of Elgin to govern not only a larger number of colonists, but a greater, wealthier, wiser, and happier people, in the aggregate, than any of his predecessors. So full had been the tide of emigration from the mother country and from the United States in all the years that followed the union, that over a million and a quarter of native and adopted subjects greeted his arrival. And not only had a population thus numerous and powerful found a home in the province, but it abounded with intelligent and resolute men, who had found the golden key to the coffers of solid wealth and aggrandizement. The spell that in former days of dormant ambition was vainly taken for destiny, had been effectually broken; the rock of provincial greatness that had remained intact from the days of Cartier and Roberval, had been smitten, and the waters thereof were gushing forth; the sombre shades of mighty doubts and mightier apprehensions of evil to come had passed away, and Canada, once so insignificant on the charts of empire, and once so unimportant in the family of nations and dependencies, had aroused from her apathetic reverie, put off the ponderous sandals that clogged her progress, and, arrayed in a cheerful and more imposing habit, was standing forth as a populous, comfortable, and attractive country.

His lordship found that the several years of disquietude which preceded the union, however unpropitious they seemed to the acquisition of political knowledge, or destructive in fact to some of the elements of colonial welfare, had impressed a majority of the inhabitants with the idea that the condition of society denominated independence, could be supported only by that form of industry which feeds and clothes mankind; that other avocations were secondary in degree to that which furnishes the resources of comfort, protection and defense, and even of moral and intellectual improvement; and that, however liberal and free might be the form of civil government, the institution of itself could bring neither comfort, happiness, nor prosperity to a people too ignorant to know, or too indolent to improve, the only means of sustaining it. This really elemental, but reluctantly admitted truth, having, after several years of bad economy, found its way to the popular mind, the subject of practical and scientific agriculture was at once, by common consent exalted from a subordinate to a paramount rank in the scale of Canadian employments. And as the examples of England and of the United States, with their favorable results, had been suggestive of associated efforts for the acquisition and dissemination of agricultural information, voluntary societies for a similar purpose had not only been organized, but they were patronized and encouraged by the intelligent and enterprising portion of the people as institutions of the first importance; so that the subject of agriculture, attracting and absorbing as it had for the time the public attention, and causing a subsidence of political conflicts, which were sundering the bonds of society, was fraught not only with the pecuniary rewards of good husbandry, but in this instance with the more substantial benefits resulting from the prevalence of the idea that the way to wealth and independence lay through the avenues of productive industry.

But as the attainment of those desirable ends involved the subject of advantageous exchanges of surplus productions for imported commodities and fabrics, these improvements in the processes of agriculture added force to the objections theretofore repeatedly urged against the tariff laws and other commercial restrictions upon the colonial trade with Europe. If the tribute exacted of consumers of foreign merchandize in the form of indirect taxation were not exorbitant, it had been so imposed by differential apportionments, as to operate very unequally, not only upon different interests, but upon different localities. The monopolization of imports in Montreal and Quebec, created and sustained by British laws, was felt to be very unjust to the merchants of Kingston, Toronto and Hamilton. No valid reason was perceived why one portion of her majesty's Canadian subjects should be taxed by another, who enjoyed the advantages of nearer proximity to the seaboard. And as the western districts were contributing more than the eastern to the solid wealth of the province, any further persistence by the imperial government in a policy which lodged the supplies of Canada West into eastern ports and in the hands of contraband dealers on the south-western frontier, was felt to be incompatible with justice. These and similar complaints concerning the details of a law which in England had been regarded as difficult and perplexing, resulted, in the year 1847, in the formal abandonment, by the imperial government, of all control over the subject. The provincial legislature thereupon abolished prohibitory and differential duties on imports inland, and placed the traders of the mother country on the footing of other foreigners.

As the act of parliament of 1843 admitting American wheat into the British market at a nominal duty, as Canadian, without inquiry respecting its origin, was affording a premium of about six shillings sterling per quarter upon American exports through the St. Lawrence, and as the Welland and Beauharnois canals increased the facilities for transportation upon that noble river from the western districts and bordering states, the commerce thereon was buoyant and promising. So efficient had been the agricultural yeomanry of Canada, and so potential the influences of the premium referred to, that over half a million of barrels of flour and as many bushels of wheat were exported from Canada during the year preceding Lord Elgin's appointment. Flattering anticipations were predicated upon this rapid augmentation of profitable trade with the mother country. But as this admission of breadstuffs into the British market had been found to militate against the policy of the Corn Laws, it was impossible for the governor to preserve for Canadians the permanent enjoyment of the privilege. The imperial government was doubting the expediency of the very act which conferred it. And the influence of a governor-general, however distinguished, was not to be expected to prevail against an imperial ministry, whose policy was plainly demarked against the existing corn laws. The interests of the mother country being adverse, in this instance, to those of Canada, but nevertheless paramount, the repeal of the act in question was the requirement of a sacrifice which tasked the loyalty of her majesty's most devoted subjects. It was a privilege moreover, and not a right to enter with nominal charges the British markets with breadstuffs, and one which other weightier considerations ultimately induced the ministry to disapprove. The corn laws were repealed, and the preference which the St. Lawrence had enjoyed as the channel of American exports was, therefore, withdrawn. The new system came into full operation in 1849.

The abolition of the British corn laws, the hostility of the tariff of the United States, and the restrictions upon the navigation of the St. Lawrence, yet adhered to, fell heavily upon the Canadians. The policy which made that river a "close borough" for British shipping only; the scanty supply of vessels floating thereon; and the abundant supply of outward freights, afforded by the timber coves of Quebec, had so enhanced all other freight outward, that nothing but the premium afforded by the corn laws rendered the river transport more favorable than by New York, with the burthen of the United States tariff. When, therefore, this premium was withdrawn, and the English market was no longer the most attractive, the exports of the surplus producing sections of the province turned from their former channel to seek, by canals and railways the seaboard at New York. And so great was this diversion of exports of flour and wheat, that, in 1850, the amount sent to that emporium exceeded largely that transported seaward through the St. Lawrence.

To recompense these disadvantages as far forth as the authority reposed in him and the means at his disposal permitted, Lord Elgin and his cabinet exerted all their talents and influence in the work of developing the resources of the province, enlarging and solidifying its monetary interests, perfecting and harmonizing the various features of its domestic polity, and in the establishment of further institutions of learning. And it was the pleasure of the legislative counsel and assembly not only to concur but to coöperate with his lordship in effectuating his wise and beneficent purposes. There were enough public matters, therefore, to engross the attention of all branches of the government; and, as several progressing works of improvement were gradually withdrawing from the mother country invested funds and infusing them into the courses and operations of domestic business, to reduce the tribute to foreign factories and forges, there were also enough of private enterprises and schemes to divert the minds of all the inhabitants who were inclined to improve the golden opportunity. So that the repeal of the corn laws and the consequent diversion of trade from the St. Lawrence did not, in varying the processes of Canadian enterprise, diminish its rewards.

On the 25th of April, 1849, and whilst Lord Elgin and his cabinet were indulging the belief that the embers of former discord were so nearly extinguished that the spoliations of 1837–8 might be indemnified without danger of reviving the scenes which occasioned them, the public peace was again interrupted by the inhabitants of Montreal. The legislative council and assembly being in session in that city, whither the seat of provincial government had been removed from Kingston in 1844, and having obtained from the governor her majesty's royal assent to a bill to remunerate certain parties for their losses during the rebellion, were assailed by stones, brickbats, and other missiles projected through the windows of the parliament buildings, by a riotous assemblage outside. Being unattended with a guard of force sufficient either to disperse the assailants or repel their violence, the members of that body were compelled to evacuate the capitol and surrender it to the fury of the populace. It was then destroyed by fire, which consumed everything combustible in the structure, furniture and archives, including the public library, in which there were eighteen hundred volumes relating to the province alone, many of which, probably, can never be replaced. This affair mortified the better portion of the French inhabitants, exasperated the English, and greatly pained the governor-general and his cabinet. It was an outbreak in the midst of gratifying evidences of enduring peace. In consequence of the destruction of the parliament house the session was continued in the hall of the Bonsecours Market.

This occurrence reöpened earnest debate respecting the best location for the seat of government. As the legislatures of the former provinces left convenient halls and offices at Toronto and Quebec, where the inhabitants, relying upon the language of King William IV., "that a union of the provinces of Upper and Lower Canada was not a measure fit to be recommended to Parliament," had invested large sums in real estate which had been depreciated by the change, those places were suggested for alternate sessions; as Kingston was the place agreed upon and occupied after the union, where similar expenditures had been made in the expectation that it would remain the permanent metropolis; and as the village of Bytown, upon the Ottawa, was represented to be not only midway between the extremities of the provincial limits, but entirely exempt from the influences which had disturbed the public peace elsewhere, there were members in the legislative assembly who felt it to be their duty to suggest a removal to those localities. On the 19th of May, the Hon. Mr. Sherwood moved the assembly that an address be presented to the governor-general to the effect that it was advisable to convene the parliament alternately at Toronto and Quebec, during periods not exceeding four years at each place, and that the records and proceedings should thenceforth be made in duplicate, to the end that one copy might be deposited in the vaults of the parliament buildings at Toronto, and the other within the citadel of Quebec whereupon the Hon. Mr. McDonald moved an amendment to the effect, that, as the seat of government, after the union, was located at Kingston, and the first sessions of parliament held there; as the government purchased large and valuable tracts of land in that locality, for the purpose of erecting thereon the necessary public buildings, and which were yet available for that purpose; as the inhabitants of Kingston had expended large sums of money in providing for the expected increase of population under the assurance of its continuance as the metropolis; as the prosperity of that place had been injuriously affected by the removal to Montreal; as the position and accessibility and fortifications of that town adapted it to the uses and necessities of the government; and as the inhabitants thereof had never, whilst it was the capitol, interrupted the public peace, his excellency be recommended to appoint Kingston again as the place for convening the legislature, if in the exercise of the royal prerogative he should be pleased to remove it, from Montreal.

This amendment not prevailing, the Hon. Mr. Lyon moved to insert in the address, that the situation of Bytown presented all the advantages enumerated by Mr McDonald, and from being so literally upon the boundary line of the former provinces, it was a point where the jealousies of all the inhabitants of Canada would be most likely to be absorbed and pacified. This proposition failing, the original resolution was considered and adopted. Whereupon the governor, in the exercise of the royal prerogative, removed the seat of provincial authority, and convened the parliament first at Toronto and afterwards at Quebec.

Upon convening at Toronto the ensuing year, it became the duty of parliament to regulate the interior economy and police of the government, to extend the jurisdiction of courts, to revise and simplify many of the provincial statutes, and to consider the expediency of an effort to obtain the consent of the government of the United States to a plan for reciprocal trade in certain commodities, free of duties, between the inhabitants of the two countries. Concerning reciprocity, it was, after much debate, finally resolved, in substance, that the interests of Canada would be greatly promoted by such a treaty of commerce, and that his excellency the governor-general would render an important service by negotiating it. The resolutions being approved, the Hon. Mr. Hincks, then inspector-general of the province, was deputed by the governor to lay them before the president of the United States. But the proposition touched so many debated questions of commercial policy, and was supposed, on first impression, by statesmen in congress representing the sugar and cotton growing regions of the United States, to be calculated to affect their constituents so injuriously, that nothing more could be accomplished during that year than a formal initiation of the idea as a subject of future diplomacy, after that government should have investigated the nature, value and tendencies of the current trade of the province with the United States. Statistics on that subject satisfactory to that government were not obtained until the following year, when a voluminous report upon the trade of Canada and the lakes, prepared by the consul for this province and New Brunswick, was laid before the senate. It was not printed, however, until 1853.

Meanwhile the parliament of 1852, in a session highly distinguished in Canadian history as the "Railroad Session," further unfolded the policy of the government in respect to the subject of internal improvements. Nearly all the existing railroad charters were amended and many new ones granted. At the close of that year it was officially announced that there were 1881 miles of railway in Canada chartered, 205 miles in operation, and 618 miles in process of construction. Parliament sat at Quebec.

As improvements in agriculture and new facilities for travel and trade were developing the resources, and augmenting the wealth of the province, and affording new opportunities for profitable investments, the views of the people respecting various public interests, were undergoing a corresponding change. Among the subjects of general concern, which had come to be prominent, in the estimation of one of the existing political parties, was the embarrassed condition of large tracts of land denominated the "clergy reserves." And at the date of this record the subject remains unsettled.

The session of parliament held in 1853, was distinguished for the passage of a law amending former enactments in relation to the elective franchise and augmenting the number of representatives.

In the summer of 1854, Lord Elgin returned from England, whither he had been upon an official visit, by the way of Washington, where, with the aid of her majesty's minister plenipotentiary, he negotiated with the secretary of state of the United States, who is ex-officio minister of foreign affairs, a treaty concerning reciprocal trade, in and by which it was stipulated that all the fisheries of British America, except those of Newfoundland, and of salmon, shad and shell fish, shall be open to American citizens; that American fisheries, to the thirty-sixth parallel of north latitude, shall be open to British subjects; that all controversies between the two governments, arising out of the occupation and enjoyment of these privileges shall be settled by arbitration; that breadstuffs, flour, animals, fresh, smoked and salted meats, cotton, wool, seeds, vegetables, fruits, fish and products of fish, poultry, eggs, skins, furs, undressed stone, unwrought marble, slate, butter, cheese, tallow, lard, horns, manures, ores, coals, tar pitch, turpentine, ashes, lumber, round, hewed, or sawed and manufactured in whole or in part, firewood, plants, trees, shrubs, pelts, fish-oil, broom corn, barley, gypsum, ground or unground, burr or grindstones hewn or rough, wrought or unwrought, dye-stuffs, rags, flax and unmanufactured tobacco, the product either of Canada or the United States, shall pass the customs of both governments, free of duties; that the river St. Lawrence and the canals of Canada shall be open to American vessels; that the general government of the United States shall urge the state governments to open their canals, also, to British vessels; that both nations shall enjoy the privileges of navigation in the waters referred to, on equal terms; that Great Britain may hereafter withdraw from Americans the right of navigating her waters, in which case the American government may annul the stipulation admitting British to American fisheries, to the thirty-sixth parallel; that Newfoundland may be hereafter included within the protection of the treaty, if she desire it; and that the said treaty shall be ratified by the respective governments, within six months from the date of the convention at which it was concluded. On the 16th of June, his lordship referred the document to the provincial parliament, sitting at Quebec.

This treaty had received the approbation of neither government at the date of this record. It had elicited much discussion, however, in the public newspapers of the United States, and in such terms of favor as to indicate a general approval of the measure; but the prorogation of the Canadian parliament, hereinafter mentioned, and the questions of public policy which led to the occurrence, so far absorbed the public attention of Canadians, that few indications, either of approval or otherwise, have been manifested. It is presumed to be concurred in by a very large majority of the inhabitants.

On the 23d of June, the governor-general, in the exercise of the royal prerogative, proceeded to the chamber of the legislative council, to which the assembly had been summoned, and delivered the following speech: "HONORABLE GENTLEMEN OF THE LEGISLATIVE COUNCIL, AND GENTLEMEN OF THE LEGISLATURE ASSEMBLED: When I met you at the commencement of the present session, I expressed the hope that you would proceed without delay to pass such a law in reference to the period appointed for introducing the amended franchise, as would have enabled me to bring at once into operation those important measures affecting the representation of the people in parliament, which were adopted by you with such singular unanimity, during the last session. Having been disappointed in this expectation, I still consider that it is due to the people of the province, and most respectful to the decision of the legislature, that I should take such steps as are in my power to give effect to the law, by which the parliamentary representatives of the people are augmented, before calling the attention of parliament to questions on which the public mind has long been agitated, and the settlement of which it is desirable to effect in such a manner as will be most likely to secure for me the confidence of the people. I have come, therefore, to meet you on the present occasion, for the purpose of proroguing this parliament with a view to its immediate dissolution."

This event concludes the chequered history of united Canada—of a province inhabited by a people of diverse lineage, language and faith, and two-thirds as numerous as were the colonists of thirteen other provinces, when they became a separate power, brought together by the fortunes of war, imperial authority, and the mandates of necessity, and supporting the union with their descendants, and with new associates by voluntary pledges of assent—of a community once unambitious, indigent and feeble, but now, for the most part, enterprising, thrifty and strong—and of loyal subjects considerably divided in respect to politics and religion, but firmly united in defending and perpetuating the principles of English liberty, guarantied by their local constitution. It need not be said that the whole record is remarkable as well for the number and importance as for the singularity of the facts which it discloses. The history of Canada must forever constitute a prominent chapter in the annals of North America.*

Canada is distinguished for its munificent arrangements for the support of the Christian religion. A fund derived from the clergy reserves is shared among the several churches and denominations. Education is encouraged by the government; colleges and seminaries are supported and patronized, and good common schools exist in almost every town; and these institutions are not only improving in character and usefulness, but the people generally are impressed with the importance of affording advantages to their children, in this respect, which they did not themselves possess.

The relative growth, in wealth and consequence, of the

* The historical sketch of the province of Canada was revised in 1863.

eastern and western portions of Canada, is fairly indicated by the ratio of the increase of population. Canada East, embracing the region formerly designated as the lower province, contained a population of 423,630 in 1825, 690,782 in 1844, and 1,110,000 in 1861, whilst Canada West, embracing the region known as the upper province, contained 158,027 in 1825, 610,150 in 1844, and reached 1,396,000 in 1861, according to the most recent data which have been obtained. The west having taken position in the van of internal improvements, by which it continues to attract from the United States a formidable emigration, it may be anticipated that subsequent years will augment the difference.

The public works of Canada already constitute a distinguishing feature of the country. No where else are there canals of greater magnitude and importance. An elevation of over two hundred feet between Montreal and Kingston is overcome by seven ship-canals, varying from one mile to twelve in length, and forty-one miles in aggregate, with locks measuring two hundred feet by forty-five, and with an excavated trunk ten feet deep and from one hundred to one hundred and forty feet broad on the water surface. Another elevation, between Lakes Erie and Ontario, of three hundred and forty feet is surmounted by a ship canal twenty-eight miles in length, with locks one hundred and fifty feet long by twenty-six and a half broad, and with an excavated trunk sufficient to pass propellers and sailing craft. The locks on the St. Lawrence are capable of admitting vessels of one thousand tons burden, and those on the last mentioned work, vessels of five hundred. These artificial channels connect the navigable waters of the upper lakes with the Atlantic ocean. Another elevation of two hunhundred and ninety-two feet between the town of Bytown and the city of Kingston, is traversed by a ship canal one hundred and twenty-six miles long and five feet deep, with locks one hundred and thirty-four feet long by thirty-three broad, and uniting, by the aid of the Rideau, the waters of the Ottawa with those of Lake Ontario. The Chambly canal, between the St. Lawrence and the Richelieu, eleven and a half miles long and five feet deep, with locks one hundred and twenty feet by twenty-four, ascends an elevation of seventy-four feet. The St. Oars lock, which completes the navigation between Chambly basin and the river St. Lawrence, is two hundred feet long by forty-five broad, and relieves an elevation of five feet. The St. Ann's lock, connecting Lake of Two Mountains with St. Louis, is one hundred and ninety feet long by forty-five broad, and planes an inclination of three and a half feet. And the Burlington Bay canal opens the flourishing city of Hamilton and the country beyond, through an alluvial bar, to Lake Ontario. The cost of these works exceeded £3,000,000.

The province is also distinguished by several works of a public character, belonging to corporations, viz: The Champlain and St. Lawrence railroad between La Prairie and Rouse's Point, a distance of thirty-eight miles, connecting with the Northern, Vermont and Canada, Vermont Central, and the Rutland and Burlington railroad, and steamers on Lake Champlain; the Montreal and Lachine railroad, eight and a half miles in length, connecting the city of Montreal with the Lake St. Louis and Province line railroad above; the St. Lawrence and Atlantic railroad from Montreal eastward, and connecting at a distance of one hundred and twenty-seven miles, with an other railroad to Portland; the Lake St. Louis and Province line railroad from Caughnawaga to Mooer's, a distance of thirty miles; the Bytown and Prescott railroad (in progress) between the places indicated, a distance of fifty-three miles; the Quebec and Richmond railroad, between those places a distance of ninety-seven miles, and to connect with the railroad from the province line to Portland; the Cobourg, Peterboro and Lake Huron railroad, (in progress) from the city of Cobourg northwesterly via Peterboro to the navigable waters of the Severn river, or with Georgian Bay, a distance of over one hundred miles; the Toronto, Simcoe and Lake Huron railroad, between Lakes Ontario and Manitoulin, via Simcoe; the Rawdon and Industry railway from the village of Rawdon to Joliette college of Industry, at St. Charles Borromée, a distance of twenty miles; the Toronto and Sarnia railroad, (in progress) between Toronto and Lake Huron at the last named port, a distance of one hundred and sixteen miles; the Great Western railroad, from Niagara Falls to Windsor, a distance of two hundred and twenty-nine miles; the Buffalo, Brantford and Goderich railroad, from the frontier of the province, near Buffalo, to a point of intersection with the Great Western railroad, at the village of Paris, a distance of eighty-four miles, and thence to Goderich, a further distance of seventy four miles, and the Erie and Ontario rail road, from Niagara to Chippewa, a distance of twenty miles. Other similar works are projected, and among them, a mammoth scheme to connect, by a grand trunk line of railroad, the western districts of Canada with Halifax.

The largest city in Canada is Montreal, situate on the lofty island in the St. Lawrence of that name. It is two hundred miles distant from Kingston, one hundred and eighty from Quebec, and four hundred and twenty from New York, and contains a population, including the troops usually in garrison in that locality, of about 90,000. It is an electoral district, returning two members to the provincial parliament, and contains three banks of discount and two agencies, three savings institutions, thirty-five life, fire and marine insurance offices, four Catholic, five Episcopalian, five Methodist Episcopal, six Presbyterian, three Congregational, two Baptist, and two Unitarian church edifices, and one Jews' synagogue; one university, two colleges, two convents, two hospitals, four asylums, and one dispensary; besides a custom-house, court-house, market-hall, and other municipal buildings. Founded by the French, whose descendants have ever since predominated, the town continues to wear a Parisian aspect. And situated as it is near the confluence of the Ottawa with the St. Lawrence, and at a convergent point of several important water channels and thoroughfares, it can hardly fail to grow in population, wealth, and importance. Although not accessible, like Quebec, to the largest class of vessels, its position in the center of an area of more fertile country, with numerous approaches, renders it far more commanding. The main branch of the Ottawa, which is the timber highway to Quebec, passes north of the island and enters the St Lawrence eighteen miles below the city. About one third of its waters, however, are discharged into Lake St. Louis, and join without mingling at Caughnawaga, whence in two distinct bodies they pass over the Sault St. Louis and Norman rapids; the dark waters of the Ottawa washing the quays of the city, whilst the blue St. Lawrence laves the other shore; each preserving a distinctive appearance for several miles below. The quays are unsurpassed by any in North America. Built of solid limestone, and uniting with the locks and cut stone wharves of the Lachine canal, they display for the distance of several miles a continuous line of masonry that is very imposing. The river side, like the levees of the Ohio and Mississipi, is not disfigured by unsightly warehouses. A broad terrace, faced with gray limestone and surmounted with an iron railing, divides the city from the river, and gives to the port a neat and orderly appearance.

The water in the harbor is from ten to fifteen feet higher in the winter season than it is during the season of navigation, in consequence of accumulations of "anchor" and "bondage" ice, on the approach of winter at the delta of Lake St. Peter, forty miles below. The earliest congealments in the river being there arrested and solidified, form a barrier to other floats of the same character, and thus augment the icy accretion for miles westward, and frequently as far up as the city. This raises the water to a point at which it can effect its discharge, and generally submerges the wharves until spring, when the ice gives way and leaves the flood at its summer elevation. During this process of elevation and depression, momentary arrestations of ice occur, which raise the water to a head sometimes fearfully irresistible. The solid body of several square miles of surface crystal is suddenly lifted up and crushed against the unyielding quays, where it is deposited in enormous heaps on the terrace in front of the city. These occurrences, being natural incidents of the port, necessarily forbid its use in the winter season as a harbor of refuge.

Quebec, although the oldest, stands as the second city in size in British America, but in danger of being soon outranked by Toronto and Hamilton. Its population numbers about 50,000. It has lately been the seat of the provincial government. This city is situated at the junction of the St. Charles river with the St. Lawrence, one hundred and eighty miles below Montreal, upon two different elevations of land, and has a very picturesque and romantic appearance. It is both naturally and artificially divided into two parts, designated as the upper and lower towns, the former of which is protected by one of the best, if not the strongest fortifications upon the American continent. It is an election district, and returns two members of parliament. and contains four banks of discount, two savings institutions, sixteen fire, life, and marine insurance offices; four Catholic, three Episcopalian, one Methodist Episcopal, two Presbyterian, one Congregational, and one Baptist church edifices; two colleges, one convent, and three asylums; also many other public buildings, institutions and municipal establishments, of French and English origin. The withdrawal of British encouragement of the timber trade, by the rebatement of duties on the same article from the Baltic Sea, and the repeal of the corn laws, checked the growth of Quebec, and it now bears evidence of decadence.

The harbor of this ancient city is not unlike that of New York, as the island of Orleans, like Long Island, serves as a barrier against heavy seas and affords two channels of approach. It has a frontage of about fifteen miles on both sides of the river, which not only allows space for the necessary wharves, but it contains coves of sufficient magnitude to float forty millions of cubic feet of lumber, eighty millions of superficial feet of deals, besides large quantities of lathwood and staves. The tide is fresh, and extends ninety miles above the city, and is not fully saline within an equal distance below. The river navigation terminates at the point where pilots are taken, about one hundred and fifty miles below the city, but the river and gulf navigation to the Atlantic extends seven hundred miles. The gulf debouches into the ocean in three several places, and affords the same number of navigable channels thereto. The most northern of these, called the Straits of Belle-Isle, affords a passage to Liverpool two hundred miles shorter than the route by Cape Race, making the distance from Quebec four hundred miles less than from New York. By this channel the navigable route from the foot of Lake Ontario to any port in Great Britain does not exceed the distance thereto from New York. The middle course to the ocean is about fifty miles wide, and contains the island of St. Paul, with its two light-houses, and affords an excellent point of departure. By this, Quebec is nearer to any port in Europe than New York. The southern passage is denominated the Gut of Canso, and is invaluable to the fishing, coasting, and West India commerce.

Kingston is a city of about 20,000 inhabitants, including the troops usually in garrison there; and, although it is inferior in size, it is far from being the least in importance among the larger Canadian towns. It is situated on prominent grounds, at the head of the St. Lawrence, and is fortified with a strong fort and other military outworks, which not only protect it from invasion, but enable a very few battalions of soldiery to command the upper waters of the river. It is a less impregnable military post than Quebec, but so long as Canada remains a British province, it is one equally necessary for the government to maintain. It is an election district, returning one member of parliament, and contains the new provincial penitentiary, four banks and bank agencies, eighteen, fire, life, and marine insurance offices; two Catholic, three Episcopalian, one Methodist Episcopal, two Presbyterian, one Baptist, and one Free church edifice; two colleges, one college school, one seminary, one nunnery, two hospitals, besides a custom-house, court-house, jail, and a splendid public market and city hall. The buildings are constructed, for the most part, of the blue limestone which underlie the adjacent country, and in an ordinary but rather substantial manner. The general appearance of Kingston is that of an ancient English town, yet as there has been a recent infusion of enterprising merchants and artisans into the business circles of the place, there exist many favorable symptoms of substantial improvement.

Cobourg is a small but thriving city of about 8,000 inhabitants, situated on Lake Ontario, one hundred and five miles west of Kingston, in the county of Northumberland, and at the southern terminus of a railroad in process of construction, to connect by a lake ferriage the lines of railway from Philadelphia and New York with the navigable waters of the Georgian Bay. It has risen from the condition of a mere lake port into that of a young city, chiefly from the causes which turned the commerce of Canada out of the St. Lawrence, and suggested reciprocal trade with the United States. Located at a harbor less affected by ice than any other upon the northern shores of the lake, and one susceptible of being kept open for steamers during the greater portion of winter, it is confidently expected by the inhabitants of the place that it will become one of the most important commercial towns in that section of the province. It is the capital of the united counties of Northumberland and Durham, and contains two bank agencies, ten fire, life, and marine insurance offices; one savings institution, seven churches, one college, one theological seminary, one academy, two grammar schools, four flouring mills, and one of the largest woolen mills in the province, employing about two hundred hands, and manufacturing about one thousand yards of goods per day

Toronto, formerly York, is the largest city in Western Canada, numbering at present about 14,000 inhabitants, of whom nearly one fifth are from the United States. It is located on an extensive and beautiful bay of Lake Ontario, one hundred and sixty-five miles west of Kingston, and fifty miles east of the flourishing city of Hamilton, whose enterprising and ambitious citizens are resolved to lead in the march of improvement. Thus advantageously situated for commerce, in the front of a deep and expansive region of productive farms, irrigated by streams affording hydraulic privileges, and at the converge of numerous thoroughfares, completed and prospective, it has had an uninterupted and healthy growth to its present consequence, which has impressed it with a liveliness of aspect and a solidity of form which render it attractive for residence and business. The city is an electoral district, returning two members of parliament, and contains four banks, one savings institution, thirty-two fire, life, and marine insurance offices; four Episcopalian, four Methodist Episcopal, three Catholic, one Scotch, one Presbyterian, one Congregational, two Disciples, one Baptist, and one African Baptist church edifices; one university, three colleges, one academy, one normal school, two grammar schools, one convent, parliament buildings, provincial asylum, two hospitals, two dispensaries, one custom-house, one court-house, and jail, six large hotels, besides numerous other buildings and establishments for religious, literary, charitable, and educational purposes. The buildings are generally of brick.

Hamilton, at the head of Burlington Bay, and of the Lake Ontario and River St. Lawrence navigation, and in the heart of the best settled portion of the province, from the commercial eligibility of its situation, the rapidity of its recent growth, its present size and beauty, and the grandeur of its prospects, is styled "the Queen City of Canada." It was laid out in 1814, contained a population of 2,509 in 1839, 5,000 in 1840, 10,248 in 1850, and the same is supposed to have reached 20,000 in 1862. It is the county seat of Wentworth and Halton, and an electoral district returning one member of parliament. It is the head-quarters of the bank of British North America, and of the Gore bank, and one of the places of business of the Bank of Upper Canada, the Commercial bank of Midland District, and of the bank of Montreal. It also contains the office of the Great Western Railroad company, two savings institutions, eighteen fire, life and marine insurance offices, thirteen churches of different religious denominations, and some of them very imposing, six academies, one ladies' seminary, one Catholic benevolent school, one orphan school, eight hotels, one court house and jail, a custom-house, post-office, market-house and town-hall. Hamilton is also enriched with various manufacturing establishments, the machinery of which is moved by steam power, of which there are several flouring mills, saw mills, planing mills, foundries, machine shops, and an extensive broom factory. And in the rear of the city, there are inexhaustible strata of both freestone and limestone, which are freely resorted to for materials for substantial and ornamental buildings. The facings of the bank buildings, post-office, and many private residences, are admirable specimens of walls constructed of stone from these quarries.

The villages of Canada are numerous, and in the upper country they are generally thrifty and promising. Such of them as enjoy marine or railway facilities for commerce with Europe or the United States, concentrate the greatest wealth and population. And wherever they are accommodated with hydraulic privileges, and conveniently accessible to the lakes and the St. Lawrence, they are enlivened with exhibitions of active and profitable business. Ottawa became the capital in 1859.

New Brunswick lies south-east of Canada, between that country and Nova Scotia. The greater part of it is a wilderness, but its soil is naturally rich. It is well watered, and favorably situated for commerce and the fisheries. The history of the province is embodied in that of Nova Scotia, of which it formed a part till 1785. The first settlement attempted here by the British was in 1762, when a few families from New England established themselves on the River St. John. During the war of the revolution, several other families removed from New England to this territory, and settled the town of Sunbury. At the peace of 1783, there were not above eight hundred inhabitants in this region; but during the following year, four thousand two hundred loyalist emigrants from the American states arrived here; and in 1785, a royal charter constituted the settlements a province, by the name of *New Brunswick.* Its history from this period embraces few events of a nature to be recorded in history. The boundary between New Brunswick and the state of Maine was long a subject of controversy between the British and American governments; but this was at length adjusted by the treaty of Washington, in 1842. Within a short period of the present year, (1863,) the inhabitants of New Brunswick have become, to a considerable extent, dissatisfied with their colonial condition, and are now anticipating, in common with the Canadians, some essential changes in their political system. The government of New Brunswick consists of a legislative assembly, a council, and a governor. The population is two hundred and seventy thousand. St. John, the capital, has ten thousand inhabitants.

Nova Scotia is a peninsula, separated from New Brunswick by a very narrow isthmus and the Bay of Fundy. Its Atlantic coast is broken into innumerable small bays, harbors, and inlets. The face of the country, in general, resembles that of New Brunswick. The French visited this region in the latter part of the sixteenth century, and gave the peninsula the name of *Acadia*, which it retained for a long time. They carried on a profitable fur trade with the Indians; and in 1604, De Monts, a French Protestant, formed a settlement at Port Royal, on the Bay of Fundy; but this was destroyed a few years afterward by Captain Argall, an Englishman. In 1621, James I. of England made a grant of the country to Sir William Alexander, and its name was changed to *Nova Scotia.* French and Dutch settlers resorted here in considerable numbers; and in 1632, the whole country was ceded to France. Oliver Cromwell, in 1654, sent an armament, which conquered all the French and Dutch settlements; but by the treaty of Breda, Nova Scotia was again relinquished to the French. During the war between England and France, in 1690, a force from Boston, under the command of Sir William Phipps, captured Port Royal, and took possession of the whole province which, by a new charter, was added to the government of Massachusetts; but in 1697, the peace of Ryswick restored the country to France. In 1704, it was again invaded by an expedition from Boston, and in 1710, Port Royal was captured by a British force At length, by the treaty of Utrecht, in 1713, Nova Scotia was finally ceded by France to Great Britain.

After the acquisition of this country, the settlemen

of it was long neglected by the British. Very few persons, except trading adventurers, resorted to Nova Scotia, and the establishments were much harassed by the Indians. On one occasion, they captured sixteen or seventeen vessels that were lying at anchor in the harbor of Canseau. The conquest of Cape Breton, in 1745, by the New England troops, gave more security to the inhabitants of Nova Scotia; and in 1749, the English laid the foundation of Halifax.

The Indians continued to give them much annoyance, and as it was suspected that the French Acadians were inclined to assist the savages in their hostilities, the British government determined to remove them from the province. They did not readily submit to this measure, and the orders for their expulsion were executed with little regard to humanity. Their villages were burnt to the ground, and their farms laid waste. The wretched inhabitants, deprived of shelter, were compelled to fly to the woods, or escape into the adjoining provinces, or surrender as prisoners, and be dragged out of the country. Such was the deplorable fate of nearly twenty thousand French Acadians. This calamity affords the groundwork of a poem by Mr. Longfellow.

Halifax, on account of its excellent harbor, became a naval station, and the head-quarters of the British forces in America; and by this means, the city acquired a degree of importance before unknown. During the war of 1812, the commerce of the United States suffered much annoyance from the proximity of this rendezvous of British cruisers. The present population of Nova Scotia, including Cape Breton, is three hundred and thirty thousand.

The government of Nova Scotia is formed upon the usual colonial model. Halifax, the capital, has one of the most commodious harbors in the world, and the most extensive dock-yard in British America. The inhabitants consist chiefly of military officers and merchants. For some years, the trade and prosperity of the place have been declining. The population has diminished from twelve thousand to nine thousand. Halifax is still important as the intermediate port at which the British steampackets touch on their passage between Liverpool and the United States.

The Island of Cape Breton, between Nova Scotia and Newfoundland, was occupied by the French in 1714. It was first used as a fishing station; but about 1720, they erected strong fortifications at Louisburg, which soon became so important, as a military and naval station, as to acquire the name of the "Gibraltar of America." This formidable place was captured by the New England troops in 1745; but it was restored at the peace of Aix-la-Chapelle, in 1748. It was captured again by the British and New England forces in 1758, and has remained a British possession to the present day. It was at first attached to the government of Nova Scotia, and afterward placed under a distinct government; but in 1820, it was finally reannexed to Nova Scotia.

Newfoundland is an island lying at the mouth of the Gulf of St. Lawrence. It is the nearest to Europe of all the American territories. It is of a triangular shape, being about three hundred miles in extent on each side. The coast is broken and indented by broad and deep bays and harbors. The general aspect of the land is wild and rugged, especially when viewed from the sea. Instead of those noble forests of tall trees, with which so many parts of North America are covered, Newfoundland exhibits only a thick growth of stunted trees and shrubs. Some tracts, however, are well fitted for pasturage. This island has scarcely any history. It was the first North American territory discovered by Europeans, and the last to be explored. John Cabot, as we have already stated, discovered Newfoundland in 1497; but the interior was never penetrated, and nothing was known of the island, except the harbors, and some few places at a little distance inland, till about 1825. The rugged and forbidding appearance of the country offered no inducements for settlers to establish themselves here; and those who visited the shores were attracted by the cod fishery, which is more productive here than in any other part of the known world.

The French laid claim to Newfoundland on a pretence of priority of discovery, alleging that the fishermen of Biscay frequented the banks near this island before the time of Columbus. They made, however, no attempts to settle on the island for a long time after the discovery by Cabot. But so early was the value of the Newfoundland fishery discovered that within twenty years after the voyage of Cabot, upward of fifty vessels, of different nations, were found employed here in taking cod. The English soon outnumbered all the others, and formed settlements on the island. Their sovereignty was recognized by the treaty of Utrecht, which reserved, however, to the French the right of fishing on the banks. This was confirmed by the treaty of Paris, in 1763, when the small islands of St. Pierre and Miquelon were granted to them for curing and drying their fish.

At the commencement of the revolutionary troubles in America, the British parliament passed an act prohibiting the people of New England from fishing at Newfoundland; but at the peace of 1783, it was agreed that the citizens of the United States should enjoy unmolested the right to take fish on the banks of Newfoundland, in the Gulf of St. Lawrence, and on the coast of Newfoundland, and the neighborhood. The American right of fishing extends to within three miles of the shore. they are allowed also to dry their fish on any of the neighboring coasts unoccupied by British settlers.

Newfoundland now contains one hundred and twenty thousand inhabitants, almost all fishermen, scattered along the southern and eastern coast, in sixty or seventy fishing stations. St. John's, the capital, is one of these. The houses are of wood; and the town has repeatedly suffered by fires. The population varies according to the season; the stationary amount is about eleven thousand. Newfoundland has a legislature of its own, and the government does not differ from those of most of the other British American colonies.

Prince Edward's Island, formerly called *St. John's*, lies in the Gulf of St. Lawrence, near Nova Scotia: it was settled by the French, and captured by the British in 1758. Under the British dominion, it was first attached to the government of Nova Scotia; but in 1773, it was erected into a distinct colony. Its government is like that of the other British provinces. The population is not far from eighty thousand. Charlottetown, the capital, has about three thousand five hundred inhabitants.

The people of this island are engaged in agriculture, the fisheries, ship-building, and the timber trade. It has a number of excellent harbors and fishing stations

United States.

CHAPTER CCCCLXXVIII.

Preliminary View of the United States.

THE United States occupy the middle portion of North America, from the Atlantic to the Pacific Ocean. Consisting of thirteen States, three-fourths of a century ago, they are now thirty-four in number, not including the District of Columbia, and also eight extensive territories, being rapidly filled with people. They lie between 24° and 49° north latitude, and 67° and 125° east longitude; the southern boundary being the Gulf of Mexico and the States of Mexico, with British America on the north. The greatest extent of the country from north to south is about seventeen hundred miles, and from east to west three thousand two hundred miles. The entire frontier, including the sea and land, is about ten thousand miles

Two ranges of mountains traverse this immense territory, the Alleghanies on the east, and the Rocky Mountains on the west, their general direction being north and south. These divide the country into three regions: the Atlantic slope, lying east of the Alleghanies; the Pacific slope, lying west of the Rocky Mountains; and the great valley of the Mississippi, lying between these two ranges of mountains.

The Alleghanies are not a regular and continuous chain, but rather a plateau, upon which rise a series of mountains, separated from each other by valleys, generally of considerable elevation. The highest peaks are those of the White Mountains, in New Hampshire, rising six thousand four hundred feet above the level of the sea. In Vermont, the highest peaks of the Green Mountains are five thousand feet high; in New York, the Catskills are four thousand feet. In Pennsylvania and Virginia, the ranges extend in several long parallel ridges, some points rising to the height of three or four thousand feet.

The Rocky Mountains are a continuation of the Cordilleras of Mexico, and are on a scale of greater magnitude as to height and length. Their average distance from the Pacific may be considered as six hundred miles. Between these and the seacoast there are various minor ranges. That called the Maritime Range is the most noted.

The Mississippi Valley embraces a vast extent of country, a large portion of it of the greatest fertility. Here is the longest river in the world, some of its tributaries being equal to the great rivers of the Eastern Continent. Along the eastern borders of the Mississippi, civilization spreads over the surface; on the west, a large portion is occupied by the Indians, or only sparsely settled by hunters and trappers.

The Pacific slope is highly diversified, presenting wide deserts, lofty mountains, extended plains, and large rivers, with many curious and striking phenomena of climate and vegetation. Here also the precious metals abound, giving to this region an interest such as has rarely attached to any other country.

The coasts of the United States are bordered by three seas—the Atlantic, the Gulf of Mexico, and the Pacific. The eastern coast is intersected by numerous bays, though none of very great dimensions.

None of the great lakes lie wholly within the territory of the United States except Michigan; a part of Ontario, Erie, Huron, and Superior, are within the British provinces.

The principal rivers of the United States may be thus classed: those of the Mississippi Valley, which flow into the Mississippi, or into the Gulf of Mexico; those of the Atlantic slope, which empty into the Atlantic; and those of the Pacific slope, which flow into the Pacific.

The principal animals of North America are found within the limits of the United States. The largest of our quadrupeds is the bison, still found in considerable quantities upon the western prairies. The grizzly bear, the fiercest of his tribe, and the most formidable wild animal on this continent, inhabits the borders of

Animals of North America.

the Rocky Mountains. The moose, elk, or wapiti, Virginian deer, and mule deer, are found in different localities. Foxes, wolves, badgers, wolverines, beavers, raccoons, opossums, and other quadrupeds, still inhabit certain districts. The wild turkey, the noblest of our birds, is common in the western States. We have grouse, pigeons, and other game-birds in abundance. By comparing the animals of North America with those of South America, we shall see that in the latter there are many species unknown to our portion of the continent.

The different portions of the United States present almost every description of soil and climate. The vegetable productions include cotton, tobacco, rice, and maize; and here, indeed, the chief supplies of these articles are furnished. The annual value of the agricultural products of the United States is about twenty-five hundred millions of dollars.

The useful as well as the precious metals are furnished by inexhaustible mines. Among the most prominent are lead, coal, iron, gold, copper, and quicksilver. Most other minerals are also abundant. The annual product of the gold mines is about one hundred millions of dollars. The annual mineral product of the country is about one hundred and fifty millions.

The manufactures are of vast extent and diversity. The annual value of the cotton fabrics is one hundred and fifteen millions of dollars; of wool, sixty-nine millions; leather, seventy-two millions; iron, seventy millions; paper, seventeen millions. The total annual value of all the manufactures is nearly two thousand millions.

The exports for the year 1860 were three hundred and seventy-five million dollars, and the imports, three hundred and thirty-six million dollars. Our shipping amounts to about five and a half million tons.

The population of the United States is now (1863) at least thirty-two millions. In 1820, it was less than ten millions; in 1830, about thirteen millions; in 1840, seventeen millions, &c.

In canals, railroads, and electric telegraphs, the United States surpass every other country.

The revenue of the United States is derived from duties on imported goods and the public lands. The annual expenditure of the government is about eighty-five millions of dollars. The whole public domain includes over one thousand millions of acres.

No country equals the United States in the number of its schools for popular education, in the number and excellence of its school-books, nor in the cheapness and number of its newspapers and other periodical publications. The annual circulation of the latter is over thirteen millions of copies.

The army of the United States includes about ten thousand men; the navy seventy-four vessels of war, of all kinds. (1860)

The United States are all united under a general government called a Federal Republic; that is, a republic in which several separate republics are federated, or united into one. The legislative power of the United States is vested in the hands of Congress, which consists of two branches—the Senate and House of Representatives. The executive power is vested in the hands of a President, who, with various subordinate officers, administer the government, and are therefore called the Administration.

The great business of the general government is, to manage the affairs of the country with foreign powers, to provide for its defence against insurrection and invasion, and to attend to all the general affairs of the country, which may not happen to be the business of a particular State. The President, with a Vice-President, is elected by electors chosen in the several States. He holds his office for four years, and resides at Washington in a building belonging to the government of the United States, called the President's house. He is assisted by four subordinate officers, called Secretary of State, Secretary of the Treasury, Secretary of War, and Secretary of the Navy, to which may be added the Postmaster-General.

Congress meets at Washington every winter, and transacts its business at the capitol. Two senators are sent from each State, consequently the Senate consists of sixty-eight members. The House of Representatives has two hundred and forty-one members. Senators are chosen for six years, and members of the House of Representatives for two years. These two bodies meet in separate apartments in the capitol, and their deliberations are always distinct.

The Judiciary of the United States consists of several judges, who hold courts separately in various parts of the Union, and every winter they are united in one court at Washington, called the Supreme Court, to hear and adjudge such questions as may come up

Animals of South America.

before them. There are also local district judges, which hold courts, but do not form part of the Supreme Court at Washington. The business of the United States courts is to decide disputes, which may grow out of the laws of Congress.

PROGRESS OF THE UNITED STATES IN SIXTY-SEVEN YEARS—FROM 1793 TO 1860.

	1793.	1860.
Number of States	15	34
Members of Congress	135	309
Population of the United States	3,929,328	31,445,080
" of Boston	18,038	177,812
" of Baltimore	18,503	212,418
" of Philadelphia	42,520	562,529
" of New York	33,121	805,651
" of Washington	....	61,122
" of Richmond	4,000	37,910
" of Charleston	16,359	40,578
Receipts of the Treasury	$5,720,624	$86,835,900
National expenditure	$7,529,575	$84,578,584
Importations	$31,000,000	$362,163,941
Exportations	$26,109,000	$400,122,296
Tonnage of the merchant marine	520,764	5,853,568
Extension of the United States in square miles	805,461	2,819,811
Army	5,120	10,000
Militia	....	3,245,198
Marine of the United States—ships of war	none.	76
" " guns	"	1,783
Treaties with foreign powers	9	101
Lighthouses	12	467
Expenses of the same	$12,061	$916,000
Surface of the capitol	half an acre	8 acres.
Miles of railroads in operation	none.	33,222
Cost of same	....	$1,192,000,000
Miles of railroads in course of construction	....	18,000
Number of postoffices	209	28,586
Miles of post routes	5,642	240,594
Revenue of the Postoffice	$104,747	$8,518,367
Expenses of the Postoffice department	$72,040	$19,170,609
Number of miles of transportation	....	54,455,454
Colleges	19	221
Newspapers and periodicals	....	928,000,000
Factories	....	128,000
Capital of the same	....	$1,050,000,000
Value of the annual product	....	$1,900,000,000
Emigrants from Europe to the United States, annually	10,000	125,000
Annual product of coal-mines (tons)	....	15,500,000

The territory of the United States, which is now estimated at 2,819,811 square miles—nearly equal to all Europe—has been derived from various sources: the original colonies, the purchase of Louisiana of the French, and Florida of the Spaniards; the annexation of Texas, and a large tract obtained of Mexico, by the treaty of 1848.

EXTENT, POPULATION, &C., OF THE UNITED STATES.

Names of States.	*Population.*	*No. of Slaves.*	*Extent in sq. miles.*	*No. inhab to sq. m.*
	1860.	1860.		1860.
New England States.				
Maine	628,279	....	31,766	20
New Hampshire	326,073	....	9,280	36
Vermont	315,098	....	9,056	35
Massachusetts	1,231,066	....	7,800	176
Rhode Island	174,620	....	1,046	175
Connecticut	460,147	....	4,730	115
	3,135,283		63,678	
Middle States.				
New York	3,880,735	....	50,519	77
New Jersey	672,035	18	8,320	84
Pennsylvania	2,906,115	....	46,000	75
Delaware	112,216	1,798	2,120	56
Maryland	687,049	87,189	11,124	63
	8,258,150		118,083	
Southern States.				
Virginia	1,596,318	490,865	61,352	26
North Carolina	992,622	331,059	45,000	22
South Carolina	703,708	402,406	30,213	23
Georgia	1,057,286	462,198	58,088	17
Florida	140,425	61,745	59,268	2½
Alabama	964,201	435,080	50,722	18
Mississippi	791,305	436,631	47,156	16
Louisiana	708,002	331,726	41,255	17
Texas	604,215	182,566	237,504	3
	7,558,082		680,558	
Western States.				
Arkansas	435,450	111,115	52,198	8½
Missouri	1,182,012	114,931	67,380	16
Tennessee	1,109,801	275,719	45,600	25
Kentucky	1,155,684	225,483	37,680	30
Ohio	2,339,502	....	39,964	57
Indiana	1,350,428	....	56,243	24
Illinois	1,711,951	....	53,924	32
Michigan	749,113	....	33,809	25
Wisconsin	775,881	....	55,405	14
Iowa	674,948	....	50,914	13
Minnesota	173,855	....	81,259	2
Kansas	107,206	2	78,418	1½
	11,765,881		652,794	
District of Columbia	75,080	3,185	60	120
Pacific States.				
California	379,994	....	155,500	2½
Oregon	52,465	....	80,000	⅝
	432,459		235,500	
Territories.				
Washington	11,594	....	176,141	
Nevada	6,857	....	45,812	
Utah	40,273	29	131,220	
New Mexico	93,516	....	220,000	
Colorado	34,277	....	105,818	
Nebraska	28,841	15	122,007	
Dakota	4,887	....	318,128	
Idaho (constituted since census)	....	....	....	....
			1,119,126	
Grand totals	31,445,080	3,953,760	2,819,811	11

CHAPTER CCCCLXXIX.

A. D. 1600 to 1643.

DISCOVERIES AND SETTLEMENTS. — *New York — Virginia — Plymouth — Massachusetts Bay — Connecticut — Rhode Island — Pennsylvania — Delaware, &c.*

THE present United States of America had their foundation in English colonies, the first of which was planted in Virginia, in 1607.

We have already noticed the manner in which America was discovered, and parcelled out between the European powers. The English discovered the coasts of North America as early as 1498, but it was almost a century before any serious attempt was made to occupy the country. The first of these proved unsuccessful, and the spirit of colonization in England was consequently checked for a considerable period. But it revived early in the following century. In 1602, Bartholomew Gosnold sailed in a small bark from Falmouth, with thirty-two persons, for the northern parts of Virginia, with the design of commencing a plantation. He steered due west, instead of sailing by the Canaries and the West Indies, and was the first English commander who came to the country in a direct course. After a passage of seven weeks, they discovered land on the American coast, and sailing along the shore, the next day beheld a headland in latitude 42°, where they came to anchor. Taking a great number of cod at this place, they called it *Cape Cod.*

Subsequently, pursuing his voyage, Gosnold discovered and named *Martha's Vineyard*, entered Buzzard's Bay, and finding a fertile island, he gave it the name of *Elizabeth*, in honor of the queen. The hostility of the natives prevented his men from settling there, and they all returned home.

Although one hundred and nine years had passed away since the discovery of North America by the English, and twenty years had elapsed since the first attempt of Sir Walter Raleigh to establish a colony in Virginia, yet not an individual of that nation was now to be found in all the country. The period, however, of English settlements at length arrived. A new patent was sought by several gentlemen, at the instance of Mr. Richard Hakluyt, from King James, for the colonizing of two plantations on the main coasts of America. This Mr. Hakluyt was at that time prebendary of Westminster, and the most active and efficient promoter of English settlements in the new world; and to him England was more indebted for its American possessions than to any other man of that age.

The king, accordingly, by a patent dated the 10th of April, 1606, divided that portion of North America which is included between latitude 34° and 45° into two nearly equal districts, granting the southern part, or the first colony of Virginia, lying between 34° and 38°, to a company of merchants called the *London Company;* and the northern, or second colony of Virginia, embraced between 41° and 45°, to another body called the *Plymouth Company.* The intermediate district, from 38° to 41°, was open to both companies, who were authorized to make settlements, on the condition that they were not within one hundred miles of each other, and were vested with the right of territory along the coast fifty miles each way

Preparations were made by the London and Plymouth Companies to take possession of the territories which had been thus assigned to them. The latter company in 1607, sent out a colony of one hundred planters, who landed at the mouth of the Kennebec River. It continued there, however, but a short time, and sought refuge from its sufferings by returning to England. This was the earliest and only attempt to settle the northern colony till 1620.

The effort in regard to the southern colony was more successful, after the lessons of experience taught by the adventures of Sir Walter Raleigh, in 1584. In the succeeding century, this colony had for its father the celebrated Captain John Smith. In the love of adventure and glory, and in the exhibition of a chivalric daring and courtesy, he was unequalled by any man of that age. He came over in 1607, under Captain Christopher Newport, with three ships, having on board one hundred and five men. They made an accidental discovery of the noble Chesapeake Bay, having been driven by a storm in that quarter. Sailing up the Powhatan River, to which they gave the name of the *James*, they fixed their residence fifty miles from its mouth, and there erected a few huts. This spot, which received the name of *Jamestown*, though now undistinguished except by its traditionary memories, was the first of the English settlements in the new world.

The form of government for the infant colony was highly unfavorable. Among other obnoxious features, there was no division of property; and for five years all labor was to enure to the benefit of the joint stock. Religion was established by law according to the form of the English church at home. The council was nominated by the king; and under his commission its organization was effected soon after their arrival. Captain Smith was eventually placed at the head of the colony, although at first the choice fell on the worst man in the company — Edward Wingfield.

The usual fate of colonies was experienced here notwithstanding the energy and faithfulness of Smith. Sickness and death soon made dreadful havoc among the emigrants; added to this was the ever-annoying hostility of the Indians. In making explorations into the country, Smith, after many acts of daring, fell into the hands of the natives. Powhatan, the chief, or emperor, of the savage confederacy in these regions, condemned him to die. The deed would have been actually committed but for the magnanimous interference of Pocahontas, the young daughter of Powhatan, who with her own head shielded that of Smith from the uplifted clubs of the savages. The decree of death was reversed, and Smith was permitted to live. His knowledge of the savage character, and his consummate address, were of great service to the dispirited colony, and they were carried through the first two years, though not without losses, and disasters, and difficulties, yet so as to hold on their way, with the additions made to them, from time to time, from the mother country.

Under various leaders, and with various fortunes the colony passed its novitiate down to the year 1620, about which time, they had the dawn of civil liberty, in the calling of the first general assembly under Governor Yeardley. The colonists, until then, had been nothing more than the servants of the company. In the mean while, the excellent Pocahontas, who had rendered the most important

Pocahontas rescuing Captain Smith.

services to the colony at the risk of her life, and who had been perfidiously seized by the English, was providentially connected in marriage with an Englishman by the name of John Rolfe. In company with her husband, she went to England, received Christian baptism, bore a son, and sickened and died at the early age of twenty-two years. From her, through that son, flows some of the best blood in Virginia.

An important event in American history is the discovery of the Hudson River. That occurred in 1609, and under circumstances which gave to two nations claims to its waters and the adjoining territory. These afterward led to serious conflicts between the rival powers. The discoverer was Henry Hudson, an Englishman by birth, but engaged in the service of the Dutch East India Company. Notwithstanding the opposition of the English court, the Dutch were fortunate in erecting forts near the sites of the present cities of Albany and New York. The Hudson, in respect to navigation, has proved to be of more consequence than any other of the American rivers. The largest state and city of the Union are connected with its waters, and half the commerce of the nation centres in the noble bay which it helps to constitute. The Dutch traders, who had settled on the Island of Manhattan, the site of the present city of New York, found themselves within the limits of the northern colony of Virginia, and, when possession of the country was demanded in the name of the British sovereign, readily acknowledged the supremacy of King James.

The first settlement in New England occurred in 1620, and was the next in the order of time to that of New York. The coast between Penobscot and Cape Cod had been explored with great care, by Captain Smith in 1614. He presented a chart and description of it to Charles, prince of Wales, who, thus learning its character and features, was pleased to call it *New England*, a name which has since been applied to the country east of the Hudson. It was settled by the English Puritans, a class of people who were desirous of worshipping God in a manner more simple than was observed in the established church. As they were not allowed to do this while they continued its members, they agreed upon a separation from the church; and for the sake of peace and more liberty of conscience, they removed to Holland, which at tha time was a land of religious toleration.

The date of the removal, or rather flight, of the band of Puritans to Amsterdam, was 1607. Their pastor, the Rev. Mr. Robinson, accompanied them After staying a number of years in Holland, they embarked for America, where they hoped to avoid certain evils which they experienced in Holland, and also to build up a state based upon the principles of the Bible. They left Leyden, where they had latterly resided, for England, in July, 1620, and sailed from Plymouth on the 6th of September, in the Mayflower. After a boisterous passage, they discovered the land of Cape Cod, on the 9th of November. The next day, they entered the harbor now called *Province-town*. As they found themselves beyond the limits of the company's patent, even before landing they formed themselves into a "civil body politic, under the crown of England, for the purpose of framing just and equal laws, ordinances, acts, constitutions, and offices," to which they engaged all due submission and obedience. "This simple but august compact was the first of a series by which the fetters of a vast system of political oppression have been broken Here was assumed, for the first time, the grand pri-

Landing of the Pilgrims upon Plymouth Rock.

ciple of a voluntary confederacy of independent men, instituting government for the good, not of the governors, but of the governed." This compact was signed by forty-one persons, and John Carver was, by general consent, chosen their first governor.

After exploring, for more than a month, the adjacent waters and land, the Pilgrims finally disembarked on "Plymouth Rock," Monday, December 21, 1620 — a day ever to be observed in the annals of New England. The Mayflower was brought into the harbor in the course of a few days, and on the 25th they began building. The severity of the climate and of their toils, however, swept off half of their number before spring. Their governor and his wife were among the victims. The survivors submitted piously to the dispensation, and with stout hearts, though with feeble hands, addressed themselves, the coming year, to the great work of founding a nation of freemen and of Christians.

It was deemed, by the Pilgrims, a special providential favor, that, previously to their arrival on these shores, the Indians in and around Plymouth had been nearly exterminated by a wasting disease. The settlers were consequently less troubled by the aggressions of this savage race, for several years, than the colonists of Virginia. Indeed, they found steadfast friends in several of the natives, particularly Samoset and Massasoit, of the tribe of Pokanokets, the latter being their sachem. So far as this tribe was concerned, there was a treaty of alliance between them and the English, which remained inviolate for more than half a century. With other tribes, particularly the Narragansetts, there was occasionally some difficulty. In one instance, Canonicus, the old hereditary chieftain of that confederacy, meditated a war against the whites. This intention he expressed by sending to Governor Bradford a bunch of arrows with a rattlesnake's skin. The governor, in return, stuffed the skin with powder and ball, and after sending it to Canonicus, heard no more of war.

In another instance, a conspiracy, which had been revealed by Massasoit, was summarily suppressed by an attack on the house where the leading conspirators had assembled. This enterprise was committed to the intrepid Miles Standish, who, with only eight men, went into the enemy's country, and, finding the band together in consultation, put the whole to death. In the course of ten years after its first settlement, Plymouth numbered three hundred inhabitants, many of their brethren of the church at Leyden having come over to join them. The excellent Robinson had died in the mean time, to the great grief of the Pilgrims, having never come to his wished-for home in America. The church had been served by Elder Brewster, and continued so to be for several years after. The settlement was not marked by any striking vicissitudes, until, in common with other settlements which were springing up in every direction, Indian hostilities were awakened against the English throughout the country. These separate establishments come now under review.

A colony at some distance north of that of Plymouth was commenced in 1628, under John Endicott, a sterling Pilgrim, as their leader. He brought with him his family and other emigrants, amounting to one hundred in number, and settled on a spot then called *Naumkeag*, now Salem. This was the beginning of the colony of Massachusetts Bay. The settlers were like those of the parent colony — Puritan non-conformists, who desired greater liberty in matters of religious worship and doctrine. Associated with Endicott was Mr. White, a pious minister of Dorchester, in England. John Winthrop, Isaac Johnson, Matthew Cradock, Thomas Goff, and Sir Richard Saltonstall were religious persons in London, who were associated with the original grantees of the patent conveying the right of territory. These gentlemen finally bought out the patent. Endicott was said to be "a fit instrument to begin this wilderness work; of courage bold, undaunted, yet sociable, and of a cheerful spirit, loving or austere, as occasion served."

Treaty with Massasoit.

The next year, (1629,) the Massachusetts Company was confirmed by King Charles in their title to the soil, and at the same time received the powers of civil government. They were incorporated by the name of the *Governor and Company of Massachusetts Bay in New England.* A form of government for the colony was soon after settled, and Mr. Endicott was chosen governor. Subsequently, in the same year, it was determined by the company in England, that the government and patent of the plantation should be transferred from London to Massachusetts Bay. At the same time, a new election of officers of the colony took place: John Winthrop was chosen governor, and Thomas Dudley deputy governor. Soon after their appointment, they sailed with a large company, some of whom settled at Mishawam, — Charlestown, — others at Shawmut, — Boston. A company of three hundred had sailed a short time before.

Previously to the arrival of Governor Winthrop, the settlement had suffered severely from sickness brought on by the change of situation, scantiness of provisions, and severity of weather. Eighty of the inhabitants had died: among these were some of the principal men. In respect to provisions, the people were providentially relieved in the midst of their want. Among the towns that were commenced by means of the recent company, and the removal of others to the new places, were not only Boston and Charlestown, but Watertown, Dorchester, Roxbury, and Lynn. The first General Court of the colony was held at Boston, on the 19th of October, 1630. Shawmut was called *Boston*, in honor of Mr. Colton, the then famous minister of Boston in England, of whose coming to America they had doubtless entertained hopes.

Of the eight hundred and forty people who came with Governor Winthrop, two hundred, at least, died from April to December; and about one hundred persons, totally discouraged, returned in the same ships to England. Among those who were removed by death was the excellent Lady Arabella, coming from "the family of a noble earldom to a wilderness of wants." She was inadequate to the trials of so great a transition. She was taken sick soon after her arrival at Salem, and there died. Her husband, Isaac Johnson, "a prime man, having the best estate of any," felt her loss severely, and himself soon sunk into the grave "He made a most godly end, dying willingly."

The Massachusetts colony, during several subsequent years, were occupied in regulating the body politic, and in extending their settlements, until it became expedient to remove to a distance, and commence other colonies. In this way Connecticut and New Haven were settled. Rhode Island was partly thus colonized, though the immediate occasion of the settlement of the latter was an instance of religious persecution or intolerance. The state of things in England still drove away many of the most valuable of her people. In 1633, a noble freight of three hundred was brought over, among whom were the fathers of Connecticut, — Hooker and Haynes. In 1635, not less than three thousand arrived, among whom were Hugh Peters, and the younger Henry Vane, — afterward so conspicuous in English history.

Roger Williams, a clergyman of Salem, being banished on account of his religious views, though these embodied the true principles of religious liberty, for the first time clearly asserted, became the founder of Rhode Island, in 1636. He settled with a few followers in a place where his wanderings ended, and with pious thanksgiving named it *Providence.* In 1638, the territory of Roger Williams received an accession of inhabitants, in the most respectable of the banished followers of Mrs. Hutchinson. These were headed by William Coddington and John Clarke, — the latter a Baptist. By the influence of Mr. Williams, they obtained from Miantonomoh, a chieftain among the Narragansetts, the noble gift of Aquetnec, the island since called *Rhode Island.* Here a gov-

Roger Williams emigrating.

ernment was established on the principles of political equality and religious toleration; and Coddington was made chief magistrate. Thus Rhode Island, through the influence of her founder, has the honor of being the first colony in the new world to set the example of civil and religious liberty.

In the settlement of Connecticut, a controversy arose as to the first discoverers of that part of New England. Both the Dutch and English claimed this honor, though the former probably had the juster title. Both purchased and effected a settlement of the lands upon the Connecticut River nearly at the same time. The Dutch were finally dispossessed, or rather yielded their claims to the English. The first house erected in Connecticut was at Windsor, in 1633. It was designed merely as a trading house, the materials of which were transported in a vessel from Plymouth, up the Connecticut River. The Dutch, however, had previously erected a small trading fort on the river, where Hartford now stands. The consequence of these interfering attempts was a threatened collision, but it was happily avoided.

Many of the settlers of Plymouth and Massachusetts Bay had for some time been looking for a new home farther west, on the rich lands of the Connecticut. At the head of these was Thomas Hooker and his church. In August, 1635, a few pioneers from Dorchester selected a place at Windsor, near the Plymouth trading house; and another party from Watertown fixed on Pyquag, — Wethersfield. Accordingly, in October of the same year, sixty men, women, and children commenced their journey through the wilderness to Connecticut River. On their arrival, they settled at Windsor, Hartford, and Wethersfield. Such, however, were their trials, from the severity of the weather, and from want, that the most of the party, having an opportunity, returned in a vessel to Massachusetts. A few remained through the winter, subsisting on the most scanty fare — as malt and acorns. This was a company in advance of Mr. Hooker. During the same year, John Winthrop, son of the governor of Massachusetts, arrived from England with a commission as governor of Connecticut, under Lord Say and Seal, and Lord Brooke, to whom the council of Plymouth had sold a patent of the territory.

The next June, 1636, the Rev. Messrs. Hooker and Stone came with their company to Connecticut It was a tedious journey of a fortnight, during which they subsisted on the milk of their cows. They settled chiefly in Hartford. Messrs. Hooker and Stone became the pastors of the church in that place. Of Hooker it is said, that, "so attractive was his pulpit eloquence, from the fervor with which he breathed out his holy soul, and from the great flexibility of his manner, tones, and copious imagery, by which he adapted himself to all subjects and all occasions, that in England he drew crowds, often from great distances, of noble as well as plebeian hearers." A portion of his congregation had preceded him to New England. Amid these intense labors and sufferings in their new abode, they found the consolations of religion, as the Pilgrims every where were wont to find it. The meek and excellent Haynes was chosen chief magistrate.

Connecticut, in her early history, suffered far more from Indian hostilities than her sister colonies of Plymouth and Massachusetts. Scarcely had they been settled before a plot was formed to exterminate the English, especially those of this colony. The most warlike of all the native tribes, the Pequods, held possession of the territory on the Connecticut. In different ways they had killed thirty of the settlers, and there was no doubt of an intention, on the part of the Pequods, to massacre the whole. The General Court, May, 1637, declared war against them, and raising one hundred and fifty men from the three towns of Hartford, Windsor, and Wethersfield, sent the valiant Captain John Mason, with seventy-seven whites, together with two or three hundred friendly Indians, to the Pequod fort at Mystic. A terrible and bloody fight ensued, which ended in the entire destruction of the fort, and of the enemy within it. The victory was followed up by the pursuit of the remaining Pequods, as they collected from their haunts; and at Fairfield another victory was obtained, which completely overwhelmed the tribe. Its very name was declared extinct.

The expedition against the Pequods made the English acquainted with Quinipiac, — New Haven, — and the next year (1638) led to the settlement of that town. This and the adjoining towns soon after settled, were denominated the *Colony of New Haven.* The leaders

Emigrants going to Connecticut, in 1636.

of this colony were Theophilus Eaton and John Davenport, Puritans of much distinction in England. Eaton was possessed of a large estate, and had held high public trusts. Davenport was an eminent minister in London. The company arrived at Boston, July 26, 1637; but, desiring a residence in a different part of the country, they left Massachusetts, explored the coast, and fixed on Quinipiac as the locality of their separate establishment. Here, after some temporary arrangements, they formed themselves into a body politic, and adopted a form of government, in 1639. Eaton was chosen governor.

In 1627, Delaware began to be settled by the Swedes and Finns — a number of whom were sent over by Gustavus Adolphus. They occupied the east side of Delaware River, calling the country *New Sweden*. A tract of land was purchased by the Dutch on the west side of the river, near Cape Henlopen, in 1639. The opposing claims of the Swedes and Dutch created dissensions afterward among these settlers.

In the southern portion of America, settlements were made at a somewhat later date, except Virginia, as already narrated, and Maryland. Of the latter state Lord Baltimore was the founder. Antecedently to the date of his charter, it was a portion of the territory of Virginia. By that instrument it was separated, and declared subject only to the crown of England. Lord Baltimore was created its absolute proprietary, and was empowered, in part, to make laws for the province, and to administer them. He appointed his brother, Leonard Calvert, governor of the province, and concurred with him in the equipment of vessels for the conveyance of a numerous body of emigrants, chiefly Roman Catholics, and many of them persons of rank and fortune. The expedition arrived at the Potomac early in 1634, and came to an anchor under an island, which was named *St. Clement*. Here a cross was erected, and possession taken "in the name of the Savior of the world, and of the king of England." Calvert gave a satisfactory consideration to the Indians for the territory of which he had taken possession. The colony, commencing under favorable auspices, with a liberal charter, and religious freedom, flourished for many years under Lord Baltimore.

In 1639, Sir Fernando Gorges obtained of the crown a distinct charter in confirmation of his own grant, which had first been given in 1623, of all the land from Piscataqua to Sagadahock, styled the *Province of Maine*. Of this province he was made lord palatine, with the same powers and privileges as the bishop of Durham, in the county palatine of Durham. In virtue of these powers, he constituted a government within his province, and founded an inconsiderable village; but the settlement did not flourish.

The discovery of the Hudson, in 1609, has been spoken of, as also the settlement of some Dutch traders on Manhattan Island. It was not until 1614 tha New York was founded. It was then that a company of merchants came there by permission of the States General. The next year, the adventurers sailed up the Hudson, and built a small fort on an island near Albany. Amid the factions by which Holland was torn, settlers came over about the years 1620 and 1621, and cottages clustered around Manhattan Fort, then called *New Amsterdam*, and Peter Minuets was constituted its first governor. In the latter year, a treaty of peace and commerce was made with the Pilgrims of Plymouth. By the year 1630, many settlements were formed on the river, under the system of *patroons*, or lords of the manor, according to which whoever should conduct fifty families to New Netherlands, should hold absolute property in the lands colonized, to the extent of eight miles on each side of the river, and as far interior as the situation might require. In 1635, the Dutch were curtailed of the territory they claimed on Connecticut River, by the settlement of the Pilgrims there, and also, by the Swedes, of that on the banks of the Delaware.

About the year 1643, the barbarities of Governor Keift, in the treatment of the Manhattan Indians, — who, on account of a slight quarrel he had with them, were murdered, men, women, and children, to the number of eight hundred, — awoke the cry of savage vengeance, from tribe to tribe. It was no matter of wonder that the Dutch villages were in flames, and the inhabitants fleeing back to Holland. The interference of the Mohawks, who were friendly to the Dutch, at length put an end to the revolting scenes of murder and bloodshed

In Virginia, from 1620 to 1641, the settlements experienced a variety of fortune, though considerable progress was made from time to time. In August, 1620, a Dutch ship brought into James River twenty negroes, and sold them as slaves. This was the commencement of the gigantic evil of slavery in North America. In 1622, a terrible massacre of the English was made by the savages, under the conduct of Opechancanough, the brother and successor of Powhatan. Three hundred persons of each sex, and of every age, were butchered without pity or remorse. This constituted nearly one fourth of the whole colony. Providentially, Jamestown and the adjacent settlements escaped, else not a single white would probably have been left. A converted Indian revealed the plan in season to save so considerable a proportion of the English. A bloody war arose from this tragedy; and so complete was the retaliation upon the Indians, that the colonists were for a long time freed from savage molestation.

CHAPTER CCCCLXXX.

A. D. 1643 to 1671.

Colonial Period. —*Affairs of Virginia — Confederacy of the Four New England Colonies — Charter of Rhode Island — Connecticut — Eliot — New York — New Jersey — Delaware — Carolina.*

Most of the principal sections of the Atlantic slope had now been discovered, and settlements of greater or less extent been made. Virginia, New England, New York, New Jersey, Delaware, and Maryland, had been trodden by the foot of civilized man, and, at many important points, small towns or villages were commenced. Several of the places which have since proved to be the seats of commerce, wealth, and power, had been selected and settled. The career of colonial dependence had begun, and to most of the colonies it was a long one, alternated by prosperity and disasters, by peace and war. Pennsylvania, and the colonies south of Virginia, of the "Old Thirteen," came into being at a somewhat later date, so that this point of time which we select as the commencement of the colonial period does not embrace the latter; but we have adopted it, as forming a convenient limit of that state of things which may be denominated *discovery and settlement*, in the great majority of the colonies. Events which relate to the rise of the more newly settled colonies will be duly detailed in the present division of our work.

In Virginia, at this period, (1643,) under the administration of Sir William Berkeley, a great share of political liberty and prosperity was enjoyed. But the scene was changed the following year, in respect to their relations with the savage tribes around. The aged Opechancanough made a second attempt to cut off, simultaneously, the scattered whites. It ended, however, in the destruction of three hundred Indians, together with their chief, before the latter had an opportunity to strike an effectual blow.

The next important event in the history of Virginia was a rebellion consequent on the passage of the navigation act. This was a plan by which England monopolized the commerce of the colonies, to the great detriment of the latter. They were not allowed to ship articles abroad except to England, and then they could sell only at such prices as the English chose to give. The Virginians were aroused to a high pitch of resentment, and they broke out into open defiance of the public authorities. They found a leader in Nathaniel Bacon, a well-educated lawyer, young, bold, and ambitious. As they were in the midst of a war with the Indians at the same time, they desired to organize for self-defence, and chose Bacon for their commander. Governor Berkeley, however, refused him a commission for this purpose, and he then assumed the office without it. The aristocracy — such was the distinction of rank in Virginia — were on the side of the government, and instigated the governor to declare Bacon and his adherents rebels.

Popular liberty, however, prevailed, and the flames of civil war were lighted up. The royalists were pursued by Bacon to the Rappahannoc, where the inhabitants, hitherto of Berkeley's party, deserted, and joined the standard of insurrection. Bacon had quelled the Indians; he had now his enemies at his feet; but, in the midst of his successes, he suddenly died. His death frustrated the hopes of his adherents, and, as they were broken and dispersed, they were easily captured one after another, and twenty of the best citizens of Virginia were successively put to instant and ignominious death.

In New England, a steady progress was made in the growth and extension of settlements at this period; but these were encompassed with dangers. To provide against them, whether from without or within, a union was contemplated. This was effected in May, 1643, in Boston, where two commissioners from each of the four colonies, Plymouth, Massachusetts, Connecticut, and New Haven, had assembled. Articles of confederation were drawn up, which were eventually signed by all. They adopted the style of the "United Colonies of New England." Rhode Island was not a member of the confederacy, as she would not consent, according to requisition, to become an appendage to Plymouth. Matters pertaining to their protection and general welfare, both in respect to morals and religion, were discussed at the meetings of the delegates, though they were not empowered to make laws in reference to the individual colonies. These were left to their own independent action. The beneficial effects of this confederacy were felt long after the immediate object was gained. It nominally ceased to act at the expiration of forty years. It rendered the colonies ever after formidable to the Dutch, as well as to the Indians.

During the supremacy of the Long Parliament in England, the northern colonies, in which the Puritan elements so much abounded, remained unmolested in respect to interference on the part of the mother land. It was a time of peace and prosperity. Roger Williams was sent to England as agent for the Rhode Island and Providence Plantations, and returned with a free charter of incorporation, dated March, 1644. An extended charter, including the islands, was afterward obtained by the same agent, in connection with John Clarke. Williams continued the benefactor, as he was the founder, of the colony, and lived to a good old age, having set an example, in his own small domain, of that liberty of conscience in religion which now obtains throughout the vast extent of the United States.

The English navigation laws, which provoked a rebellion in Virginia, were in New England considered so wholly unjust, that they were evaded, and the people there, as far as possible, chartered their own vessels, and traded at such ports as they pleased.

Upon the restoration of Charles II., (1660,) his authority was acknowledged in New England, though he seemed little favorable to the colonies. Yet, even then, Connecticut obtained her charter, through the address and persuasive arts of Winthrop. It was a charter granting more ample privileges than any other which had been obtained from the English government. It included New Haven; but that province, not having been consulted, justly felt aggrieved and slighted, as it was required to yield up its separate existence. The expediency, if not the necessity, of the measure, however, forced itself on the consideration of the people of that colony, and they consented to a union with Connecticut. Winthrop was chosen governor — an appointment which he received many years in succession. Attempts soon began to be made by the government at home, by means of commissioners appointed by the king, to control, if not to humble, the colonies; yet those attempts were not, for the present, successful. Massachusetts, in particular, was firm in resisting every exercise of such a power.

This was the period of the conversion of numbers of the Indians to Christianity, through the labors of Mr. Mayhew and the devoted Eliot. Upheld by the United Colonies, these men labored indefatigably for the welfare of the savage race, so that, in 1660, here were ten towns of converted Indians in Massachusetts. A lasting monument of the zeal and unwearied diligence of Eliot was his translation of the Bible into the Indian tongue; though now, both the Indian and his language have passed away.

About the year 1654, many emigrants came to New Netherlands from among the oppressed, the unfortunate, and the enterprising of other colonies and of European nations. The inhabitants, thus increasing in numbers, sought a share of political power, and, attempting to command it through a general assembly, were summarily rebuked, and the members of the latter sent home, by the governor, Stuyvesant, with the remark that he was not to be directed " by a few ignorant subjects." Popular liberty, though checked here, advanced in the adjoining provinces; consequently, these made a more rapid progress, and crowded upon the Dutch.

In 1664, Charles II. granted to his brother, the duke of York and Albany, the territory included in the several colonies of New York, New Jersey, and Delaware. The same year, the duke despatched an expedition, under the command of Colonel Richard Nichols, to the colony at Manhattan, which had, for many years, denied the right of the English to control it. When the expedition arrived at Manhattan, in the course of the year, it demanded a surrender of the territory to his English majesty. The Dutch governor at first refused to surrender; but, finding himself without the means of resistance, and learning that many of the people were desirous of passing under the jurisdiction of the English, at length complied with the demand, and the whole country came into the hands of the English. In compliment to the duke, the two principal Dutch settlements were now named *New York* and *Albany*. The wise and healthful administration of Nichols continued for three years followed by another administration of a like character, under Colonel Lovelace.

New Jersey, which, from 1624 to 1626, had been visited and settled in a few places by the Danes, the Dutch, and the Swedes, was from 1655 to 1664 held under the power of the Dutch, who had subdued their rivals. At the latter period, the territory passed into the hands of the English, the duke of York having conveyed it to Lord Berkeley and Sir George Carteret. In 1665, Berkeley and Carteret formed a constitution for the colony, and appointed Philip Carteret governor Elizabethtown was made the seat of government.

Delaware, as we have seen, was first settled by a number of Swedes and Finns in 1627; but it was subsequently included in the grant of the duke of York, above spoken of. At this time, it was in the hands of the Dutch; but an expedition was sent against it under Sir Robert Carr, to whom it surrendered October 1, 1664. Soon after this event, it was put under the authority of the English governor of New York, and was considered a part of the province of New York.

In the year 1663, the most southern portion of the Atlantic slope — that is, the space included between the thirty-sixth degree of north latitude and the River St. Matheo — was erected into a province by the name of *Carolina*. This name was given in compliment to Charles IX., king of France, under whose patronage the coast had been discovered in 1563. This tract was conveyed by charter of Charles II., king of England at this time, to Lord Clarendon and seven others. These persons were made absolute proprietors of the territory, and invested with ample authority to settle and govern it. A confirmation and enlargement of the charter was obtained two years after. In this, the whole territory, now divided into the two Carolinas Georgia, and the Floridas, was embraced.

Planters from Virginia, and emigrants from other places, had previously — that is, in 1650 — established themselves in Albemarle county. This settlement was placed by the proprietors under the superintendence of the governor of Virginia. The other colony was to the south of this, on Cape Fear, or Clarendon River. It was erected into a county by the name of *Clarendon*. This county was settled in 1665 by emigrants from the Island of Barbadoes, after it had been mostly deserted by adventurers from New England, who had originally planted themselves there. Sir John Yeamans, who was from the island, was appointed governor, and a separate government granted, similar to that of Albemarle. In 1666, the settlement contained eight hundred inhabitants. A political constitution was at first framed for Carolina by the celebrated philosophers, Shaftesbury and Locke; but as it was highly aristocratical in its features, constituting three orders of nobility, it ill comported with the condition of the settlers, and it was in vain that the agents of the proprietors sought, in succeeding years, to enforce it upon them. " These dwellers in scattered log cabins in the woods could not be noblemen, and would not be serfs."

The first proprietary governor of Carolina, William Sayle, brought over a colony, with which he founded old Charleston. His colony was, upon his death in 1671, annexed to that of Governor Yeamans. Subsequently, the city was removed to the present site of Charleston — for a long time the capital of South Carolina.

CHAPTER CCCCLXXXI.

A. D. 1671 to 1688.

King Philip's War — Affairs of Maine and New Hampshire — Settlement of Pennsylvania — Revocation of the Charters in the Northern Colonies.

King Philip.

IN the annals of New England, the bloodiest page, perhaps, is that which records what is called *King Philip's War.* Philip, as he is generally called, though his Indian name was *Metacom,* was the younger of the two sons of Massasoit. His accession to the chieftainship of the Pokanokets occasioned more than usual joy to his subjects. His popularity qualified him to become a formidable foe to the whites, upon his avowed intention to avenge the wrongs which he conceived they had inflicted upon him. He labored unweariedly, for several years, to unite the native tribes in one great effort to cut off the entire English population. But the difficult task he accomplished only in part. Several of the tribes refused to join him; some fought against him; and of those who went with him at first, many withd...

Seizing the occasion of the execution of some of his friends on the part of the Plymouth government, Philip and his warriors, on the 24th of June, 1675, attacked Swansey, in Plymouth. The place, however, was defended, and the Indians, in their turn, were pursued, but could not be overtaken. They left the marks of their route in the ruins of burnt buildings, and the heads and hands of the captured English, which were suspended on poles by the wayside. It was through the impatience of Philip's young warriors, that the attack on Swansey was made, as Philip himself did not feel fully prepared to commence operations. But having been thus committed, there was no retreat, and it was determined, on his part as well as that of the English, to prosecute the war with the utmost vigor.

The English army, marching into the country of the Narragansetts, forced that tribe to make a treaty of peace, 15th of July, 1675, and, following the Indian king to a swamp at Pocasset, near Mount Hope, attacked him there, — but with no special effect. The leaders of the English on this occasion were Captain Fuller, and the celebrated Benjamin Church, who was then a lieutenant. After being farther pursued, Philip, with his brave band, made his quarters with the Nipmucks, and kindled the flame of war in the western plantations of Massachusetts. Indeed, the spirit of vengeance which he breathed seemed almost every where to animate the Indian bosom at this period. The day previous to Philip's arrival among the Nipmucks, a party under Captain Hutchinson were waylaid near Brookfield by these Indians, and several of them were slain. The town, also, was burnt.

The fatal affair of Bloody Brook followed on the 18th of September of the same year. This was the saddest of all the occurrences in Philip's war, in its bearing on the whites. A corps of the young men, selected from the vicinity of Boston, were all cut off, except seven or eight, in an ambush at a brook, since called by the above name, in South Deerfield. The company consisted of eighty men, with several teamsters, at the time conveying provisions from Deerfield to Hadley. The Indians were in great numbers, and had previously been engaged in several assaults upon the whites and their settlements on Connecticut River. Subsequently, in October, they burnt Springfield, and made an attack on Hadley. From the latter place they were repulsed by the Connecticut and Massachusetts forces.

The condition of the colonists at this period was one of great suffering and danger. In every place where an advantage could be taken, the Indian was present, whether in the little settlement or the secluded dwelling — in the public road or the unfrequented bypath. The Indian was acquainted with every haunt and every place of exposure. The gun and the tomahawk, the knife and the fagot, did the work of death and destruction wherever the white man could be found with inadequate protection, and both by night and day. Men, women, and children were indiscriminately massacred. The voice of lamentation and woe resounded through the wide wildernesses of Massachusetts. The midnight was frequently illumined by the light of the settler's blazing dwelling and out-houses. Such were some of the effects attendant on savage warfare!

A hard-fought and bloody battle took place on the 19th of December, in an attack on a fort of the Narragansetts, which was in a swamp in what is now South Kingston, Rhode Island. Captain Benjamin Church was one of the commanders on this occasion. From the difficult and dangerous entrance to the fort, many of the English, and especially of the officers, were killed; but after the interior of the fort was entered, a terrible destruction of the foe ensued. A thousand Indians were killed, and about six hundred wigwams were burnt. As it was in the depth of winter, many who escaped from the battle perished through hunger and exposure to the weather, while they endeavored to cover themselves with boughs, or burrow in the ground, and to sustain life on acorns and nuts. Conanchet, the leader of the Narragansetts, who had seduced this people to the violation of their treaty with the whites, was some time after taken prisoner; and though promised life and freedom if he would enter into a treaty of peace, he bravely preferred death.

The fortunes of Philip were now on the wane; and the English, in the union of the several colonies who made a common cause against him, followed up the war with energy. He was pursued from place to place, Captain Church being indefatigable in his efforts to secure or kill him. At length, the object was obtained. After being driven from swamp to swamp, he was shot on the 12th of August, 1676, by an Indian whose brother Philip himself had slain, on account of having proposed submission to the English. The result of the war, which was in effect now terminated, was decisive. The Pokanokets were nearly exterminated. The Narragansetts were greatly diminished and enfeebled. All the Indians on the Connecticut River, and most of the Nipmucks who survived, fled to Canada, and a few hundreds took refuge in New York. Those who fled to Canada afterward served as guides to the parties of hostile French and Indians, who so murderously harassed the colonies from time to time. War affects the conqueror as well as the conquered; and New England lost, during its continuance, thirteen towns, which were entirely destroyed by the enemy, six hundred dwelling-houses reduced to ashes, and about the same number of inhabitants killed, beside all the other innumerable evils incident to such a state of things.

A controversy which had subsisted for some time between the government of Massachusetts and the heirs of Sir Ferdinand Gorges, in respect to the province of Maine, was settled in England in 1677, and adjudged to the latter. Massachusetts, however, immediately purchased the title, and this territory, from that time till 1820, remained a part of Massachusetts.

In 1679, a commission was made out, by the order of the English king, for the separation of New Hampshire from the jurisdiction of Massachusetts, and its erection into a royal province. As early as 1629, the territory called *New Hampshire* had been granted by the Plymouth Company to John Mason. The settlements having become considerable, in 1640 the patent holders agreed to assign their right of jurisdiction to Massachusetts. The colony of New Hampshire remained under the government of Massachusetts until it was separated under the king's commission, as above stated. The form of government sent over by the king, ordained a president and council to govern the province, together with an assembly to be chosen by the people. The president and council were appointed by the crown. Their first chief magistrate, Edward Cranfield, a greedy speculator, became so unpopular by maladministration, that upon complaints made against him to the king, he was recalled. He had been but the tool of Mason, and the dupe of his own insane visions.

Mason died in 1685, leaving his two sons heirs to his claims on New Hampshire. The people earnestly petitioned to be united again with Massachusetts, but their wishes were frustrated. Samuel Allen, who had purchased of the heirs of Mason their title to New Hampshire, was appointed governor of the colony, and in 1692 assumed the government.

William Penn.

The settlement of Pennsylvania took place in the month of October, 1681. It received this name from William Penn, its illustrious founder. The patent conveying the territory embraced a portion both of Maryland on the south and of Connecticut on the north. The dispute about boundaries between the latter state and Pennsylvania continued no less than a century, when it was finally adjusted. The patent provided for the king's supremacy, and for obedience to British acts regarding commerce. It gave power to the proprietor to assemble the freemen, or their delegates, as he should judge best, for levying moneys, and enacting laws not contrary to the laws of England.

Mr. Penn, the patentee, was the son of Vice-Admiral Penn, and at a very early period of life was converted to the Christian faith and hope, in a manner somewhat uncommon. He was suddenly affected "with an inward comfort, and an external glory in the belief of God, and his communion with his soul." He eventually embraced the tenets of the Quaker sect, and ever retained, in a measure, the impressions thus made upon him. His father was both grieved and displeased, and spared no efforts to induce him to renounce those peculiarities of manners and practice which his religious views had impelled him to adopt. But neither his temporary abode at the university, nor foreign travel, nor occasional exclusion from the paternal roof, effected any reformation of his eccentricities. In the maintenance of his peculiarities, he at length violated the public law, and was thrown once and again into prison. He, however, outlived the reproach he had incurred: his father, who was proud of his talents, and by no means wanting in affection, befriended him from time to time; and becoming allied in marriage to a most respectable family, the public bestowed upon him unequivocal marks of confidence.

To America he now turned his thoughts, with a view to colonization, for he had at heart the relief of his suffering, persecuted brethren, the Quakers; and founding his expectations of a patent upon the large claims which his father, now deceased, had against the crown, he received the expected boon, and immediately put his projects into execution. He arrived with his emigrants at New Castle in November, 1682. The first assembly was held on the 4th of December of the same year, and by its first enactment, all the inhabitants, of whatever extraction, were naturalized. But while religious freedom was established among the people, all officers and electors must be believers in Jesus Christ. He soon after held a great council with the Indians, in which he gave them suitable instructions, and appealed to God that it was the strong desire of his heart to do them good. A treaty of peace and friendship was then executed; the native chiefs pledging for themselves and their tribes "to live in love with him and his children as long as the sun and moon should endure." The purchases of land, which had been previously made according to direction, were confirmed, and at the same time, additional purchases were made.

The plan of his capital, Philadelphia, was drawn by Penn the same year, and the building of it soon commenced; so that by the year 1684, when he left his province for England, the city contained three hundred houses and two thousand inhabitants. Between Penn and Lord Baltimore there was a want of agreement in respect to territorial boundaries, the latter having attempted to possess himself of certain land, by ejecting the settlers on their refusal to pay him quit-rent; but Penn remonstrated, and retained the jurisdiction.

Massachusetts, having been complained of for her violation of the navigation act, was, by a decision in the High Court of Chancery, declared to have forfeited her charter, and that henceforth her government should be placed in the hands of the king. But before Charles had time to adjust the affairs of the colony, he died, and was succeeded by James II. Soon after the accession of the latter, similar proceedings took place against Connecticut and Rhode Island. These colonies presented addresses of a dutiful and loyal character, which the king chose to construe into an actual surrender of their charter, and accordingly, in 1686, sent over, first Sir Joseph Dudley, but soon after, his successor, Sir Edmund Andross, as governor-general. In this latter personage, with a council, were vested all the powers of government.

Thus the colonists, after all their hardships and dangers in settling a wilderness, had no other prospect before them than the extinction of their chartered and dearly-bought privileges, and were left to the tender mercies of a capricious despot, to assign to them their portion of freedom, protection, and the products of their own labors. Sir Edmund's course, though commenced with liberal professions, terminated in acts of downright oppression and exaction. Restraints were laid upon the freedom of the press and marriage contracts, and the fees of all officers of the government were raised oppressively high. This was a dark day to the New England colonies, following, after so short an interval, the horrors of an Indian warfare; but relief was preparing for them in the assumption of the English crown by William and Mary, in 1688. The colonies were filled with rejoicing at this event, as, from the character and capacity of William, they had much to hope for from the new dynasty.

CHAPTER. CCCCLXXXII.

A. D. 1688 to 1713.

King William's War — Taking of Schenectady — Expedition to Quebec — Queen Anne's War — Northern Expeditions — Affairs in the South — Pennsylvania, New York, and New Jersey — Witchcraft.

The revolution which followed the accession of William and Mary restored their liberties to the colonists; but it involved them in a war both with the French and Indians, which lasted about seven years, viz., from 1690 to the peace of Ryswick, in 1697. This is known in the American annals as *King William's War*. It originated in the sympathies of the French king with the banished James II., and affected both the English and French colonies.

The scene opened in the determination of Governor Frontenac, at Quebec, to invade the northern English colonies. He fitted out three expeditions in the depth of winter; one against New York, a second against New Hampshire, and a third against the province of Maine. The first, consisting of about three hundred men, in February, 1690, fell upon Schenectady. The season was severely cold, and the snow so deep that it was supposed impossible for an enemy to gain access to the place; the inhabitants were accordingly less on their guard than usual. The enemy, divided into small parties, invested each house at the same moment, and the people, being asleep at the time were wholly in the power of the foe. Upon a preconcerted signal, the war-whoop was given, and immediately the work of fire, pillage, and bloodshed, commenced. Sixty persons were massacred, and twenty-seven were carried away captive; while the remainder, fleeing almost naked from their burning dwellings, were in many instances maimed by the cold, or frozen to death.

The second party of French and Indians proceeded to Salmon Falls, in New Hampshire, burnt that pleasant settlement, and butchered fifty of its inhabitants. The third party, from Quebec, in like manner, destroyed the settlement at Casco Bay, in Maine, killing and capturing one hundred people.

These events spread an alarm, and aroused a spirit of indignation in every quarter. A convention of the colonies was held in New York on the 1st of May, 1691. Important measures were there resolved upon; but one of the projects, which was for General Winthrop, of Connecticut, to proceed up Lake Champlain, and attack Montreal, failed, for the want of supplies from New York. Another scheme was the invasion of Canada from Massachusetts. This was effected, but only partial success attended it. Sir William Phipps sailed from Boston with thirty-four sail, took Port Royal, reduced Acadia, and thence proceeded up the St. Lawrence, for the purpose of capturing Quebec. But although the place was summoned to surrender, it was deemed inexpedient to attack it, when Sir William learned, as he soon did, the failure of Winthrop. The fleet, on its return to Massachusetts, suffered severely from a storm, and only a part reached the desired haven.

It was a source of humiliation to New England that the expedition to Quebec proved a failure, and the consequences in other respects were disastrous. The Indians called the *Five Nations*, settled along the banks of the Susquehannah, and in the adjacent country, who were in alliance with Great Britain, and had been a defence to the colonies against the French, became dissatisfied with the English on account of their inactivity, and manifested a disposition to make peace with the French. Attempts were made with some success, in an expedition against the French settlements in the north, under Major P. Schuyler, to arrest the disaffection of the Five Nations. But though New York thus obtained some security, the eastern colonies, particularly New Hampshire, suffered severely.

Formidable preparations were now made to strike an effectual blow at all the northern colonies, by a powerful French fleet, which was to coöperate with the forces of Frontenac — ravaging the whole sea-coast as well as the interior; but fortunately the fleet arrived too late in the season to accomplish the purpose; and thus the colonies were saved from a wasting war, if not from absolute destruction. In the treaty of Ryswick, between France and England, which soon followed, (December 10, 1697,) it was agreed, in general terms, that a mutual restitution should be made of all the countries, forts, and colonies taken by each party during the war.

This peace, however, continued but five short years. In May, 1702, England, now under Queen Anne, declared war against both France and Spain, and the contests of the parent states involved their settlements in America. The former war had produced an untold amount of suffering to the colonies. The atrocities committed by the French and Indians were almost unparalleled in history. Tomahawking, burning, roasting strangling, were but common occurrences, whenever the foe could secure their prey. No pity was felt for the captive and the sufferer. Whole families were carried off, and women and children subjected to the brutalities of savage warfare. The effects of the conflict now under consideration, commonly calle *Queen Anne's War*, were scarcely less disastrous. They fell principally on New England, as New York, through its friendly relations with the Five Nations, was in general well protected. The tragedy of Deerfield will furnish an example of the events of this melancholy period. It occurred on the night of the 28th of February, 1704.

An outline of the story is here given, as it appears in a note of Holmes's American Annals. "On information from Colonel Schuyler, of Albany, of the designs of the enemy against Deerfield, the government, on the application of Mr. Williams, minister of the town, had ordered twenty soldiers as a guard. On the night of the 28th of February, and until about two hours before day, the watch kept the streets, and then incautiously went to sleep. The enemy, who had been hovering about the town, perceiving all to be quiet, first surprised the garrison house. Another party broke into the house of Rev. Mr. Williams, who, rising from his bed, discovered near twenty entering. Instantly taking down his pistol from his bed tester, and cocking it, he put it to the breast of the first Indian who came up; but it missed fire. Three Indians then seized him, and bound him as he was, in his shirt. Having kept him nearly an hour, they suffered him to put on his clothes. Some of the party took two of his children to the door, and murdered them; as also a negro woman. His wife, who had lain in but a few weeks before, and his surviving children, were carried off with him to Canada. In wading through a small river, the second day, Mrs. Williams, unequal to the labor, fell down; and soon after, at the foot of a mountain, the Indian who took her slew her with his hatchet at one stroke. About twenty more prisoners, giving out on their way, were also killed. The army, with their prisoners, was twenty-five days between Deerfield and Chambley, depending on hunting for support. The most of the persons who arrived at Canada, were at different periods redeemed. In 1706, Mr. Williams and fifty-seven others were redeemed, and returned home."

Queen Anne's war was terminated by the treaty of Utrecht, in 1713, by which England secured Acadia. The frontiers, during this protracted contest, were constantly exposed to attacks from a savage foe, and the whole eastern country experienced the evils of a heavy military service, and a constant lookout by night and day, lest the inhabitants should be murdered or carried away captive. The progress of settlemen and improvement was effectually checked. It happened that of four expeditions by the English against Canada, three signally failed; so that deep mortification was added to losses and sufferings. In the third expedition, under Colonel Nicholson, Port Royal, in Nova Scotia, was taken, October 24, 1710, after a few days' resistance. Its name, in honor of Queen Anne, was changed to *Annapolis*.

Some portion of the southern country shared also in the distresses of Queen Anne's war. Carolina, then the frontier of the American colonies on the south, upon the breaking out of the war, engaged (1702) in a military expedition against the Spanish province of St. Augustine. The enterprise proved unsuccessful; and, as a heavy debt was incurred, the assembly adopted the expedient of a paper currency, as the means of cancelling it. This filled the colony with tumult and dissension. The expedition was conducted by Governor Moore, of the Southern Carolina. In 1703, he was more fortunate in an attack upon the Appalachian Indians, whose hostility had been instigated by the Spaniards. He proceeded into the midst of the Indian settlements, and laid in ashes their towns between the Altamaha and Savannah. Some of the captives were treated with great injustice and cruelty by the selfish governor, who appropriated their labors, or the avails of their sale, to his own use.

The French and Spaniards now threatened the English province in their turn, with a view to annex it to Florida. An invasion of Charleston was attempted in 1707, under Le Feboure, with four armed sloops, having about eight hundred men on board. Owing to the decisive steps taken by the new governor, Johnson, the enemy was repulsed, and the threatened calamity averted. It is said that Johnson, upon being summoned to surrender, and having been allowed four hours in which to return his answer, informed the messenger that he did not wish a single minute.

In 1712, a plot was laid, by the Tuscaroras and other Indians of North Carolina, to exterminate the entire white population. It so far succeeded, that one hundred and seven settlers, Palatines of Germany, who had recently come to this country, were massacred in a single night. A few who escaped gave the alarm, and, information of the danger of the remaining settlers reaching Charleston, Captain Barnwell, with six hundred militia and three hundred and fifty friendly Indians, explored their way through the intervening wilderness, and came to their relief. They boldly attacked the Indians, killed three hundred, and took one hundred prisoners. This success of the whites was followed up till the Tuscaroras sued for peace, having lost one thousand men in the course of the war.

The peace of 1713, between England and France, relieved the apprehensions of the northern part of the country, and put a welcome period to an expensive and harassing war. The eastern Indians, hearing of the treaty, sent in a flag, and desired peace. They were met at Portsmouth by the authorities of Massachusetts and New Hampshire, to whom they gave their submission, and entered into terms of pacification.

In 1699, William Penn again visited his beloved province of Pennsylvania. He found much complaint and disaffection respecting the government, and accordingly, in 1701, granted a new and liberal charter. Although this did not remove the discontents of the people, it was accepted by the assembly. Penn, having established a government, with a foresight and wisdom never exceeded by any human legislator, finally quitted the scene of his toils and his glory, and returned to England to pass the remainder of his days.

In 1698, Richard, earl of Bellamont, was appointed to the chief magistracy of the province of New York. He was particularly instructed to put an end to the piracy which prevailed at that period. As no appropriations were made by the colonial governments for this purpose, a private adventure against pirates was agreed upon, and one William Kidd was recommended to the earl, as a man of integrity and courage, who well knew the pirates, and their places of rendezvous. Kidd undertook the expedition, and sailed from New York; but he soon turned pirate himself. After a time, he burnt his ship, and returned to the colonies There is a vague tradition still existing, that he brought home large quantities of money, which he caused to be concealed in the earth. He was apprehended at Boston, sent to England for trial, and there condemned and executed.

In West Jersey, from the year 1695 to 1698, there was little regular government, owing to the disputes among the settlers, and the interfering claims of the proprietors themselves. In this state of things, at the latter period above named, the proprietors surrendered the right of government to the crown, and Anne united it with the east province. The whole was now called *New Jersey*, and was joined to New York, so far as to be ruled by the same royal governor. Of the governors who were appointed for the few subsequent years down to 1727, two of them, Lord Cornbury and Mr. Burnet, were so unacceptable to the people, that upon their complaints, they were recalled by the government at home.

It was during the latter part of the seventeenth century, that the delusion respecting witchcraft reached the highest pitch of extravagance. The colonists brought it with them from England, and it was no more their fault than that of the age. It seems, indeed, a wonder and a disgrace that a community so enlightened as the Pilgrims were in other respects, should have come under the power of a fanaticism at once so puerile and so malign. But so it was; and not until about twenty persons were executed on the charge of witchcraft, and hundreds more were imprisoned and accused, — causing general terror and distress, and threatening the subversion of all social order, — was the evil seen in its true light, and the whole ascertained to be an imposture and a delusion. As soon as the frenzy ceased to receive countenance from those in authority, it passed away, almost as suddenly as it had arisen, leaving to future times a fearful warning against such popular insanity. The principal seat of the baneful disorder was Salem, in Massachusetts though it soon extended into other parts of the province.

CHAPTER CCCCLXXXIII.

A. D. 1713 to 1736.

Border War — Carolina, and Change of Government — Massachusetts — Louisiana, and Massacre by the Indians — Settlement of Georgia.

The peace of 1713 was of short duration. The Indians became dissatisfied on account of the encroachments of the English upon their lands, and their failure to erect trading houses for the purchase of their commodities; and being, at the same time, excited by the French, were aroused to war. This, in July, 1722, became general, and continued to distress the eastern settlements until June, 1725. At the latter period, a treaty was signed by the Norridgewocks, Penobscots, and other tribes, and was afterward ratified by commissioners from Massachusetts, New Hampshire, and Nova Scotia. This proved to be a durable peace. the English trading houses flourished as the stipulations with the Indians were more strictly fulfilled, and the eastern boundary of New England remained undisturbed.

In Carolina, scarcely had the war with the Tuscaroras terminated, when the province was threatened with a conflict of greater extent and severity. The Yamassees, a powerful band of Indians, with all the native tribes from Florida to Cape Fear River, formed a conspiracy for the total extirpation of the whites in the southern country. The 15th of April, 1715, was determined upon as the day of general onslaught. But the governor took such discreet and timely precautions, as, with a favoring Providence, in a measure averted the calamity; the colonies were saved, though at the expense of the lives of nearly four hundred of the inhabitants during the war.

In 1719, the government of Carolina, which till now had been proprietary, was changed; the charter was declared by the king's privy council to have been forfeited, and the colony was thenceforth taken under the protection of the crown, in which condition it remained until the breaking out of the American revolution. This change was followed, in 1729, by another, nearly as important. This was a stipulation between the proprietors and the crown, that the former should surrender to the latter their right and interest to the government and soil for the sum of seventeen thousand five hundred pounds sterling. This agreement being carried into effect, the province was divided into North and South Carolina, each having a distinct governor.

In Massachusetts, a dispute of long continuance took place between that province and the home government respecting the salary of the royal governor. The mother country desired that the salary should be fixed, and not be dependent on the voluntary appropriations of the colonial assemblies: thus early did she guard against the possible assertion of independence, by making it the interest of the magistrate to favor the crown rather than the province. This was a system, indeed, which was designed to affect all the colonies, and which was carried in them all, except Massachusetts. In that province, the struggle which commenced about the beginning of the century, lasted till 1730, when Governor Belcher acquiesced, by the consent of the crown, in a policy which had been in vain attempted with his predecessor, — that of paying him an unusually large sum for present use, without binding the province for the future.

By means of discoveries and settlements on the valley of the Mississippi, the French laid claim to the extensive territory of Louisiana. In 1718, three ships came over, bringing eight hundred emigrants, who founded a city, and, in honor of the regent of France, named it *New Orleans*. Some settled among the Natches Indians, where the city of Natchez now stands. The French subsequently took possession of the various western routes from the St. Lawrence to the Mississippi; and Chicago, Vincennes, and Kaskaskia were, in the early part of the eighteenth century, growing settlements. The French government, intending to connect this vast territory by a line of military posts, at length excited the alarm of the English, and, at a later period, the interfering claims caused an appeal to arms.

In 1729, the Natches, who had at first received the settlers kindly, formed an extensive conspiracy to massacre the French colonists of Louisiana. The French commandant at the post of the Natches had been somewhat embroiled with the natives; but these now contrived to excite the belief that the French had no allies more faithful than they. The plot having been laid, they appeared in great numbers about the French houses on the 18th of November, pretending to the people that they were to have a great hunt. Afterward, they smoked the calumet in honor of the French commander and his company. Each having taken the post assigned him, a signal was given, and instantly the general massacre commenced. Nearly two hundred persons were killed. Of all the people at the Natches, not more than twenty French and five or six negroes escaped. One hundred and fifty children, and eighty women, with nearly as many blacks, were made prisoners. This massacre of the French, however, was avenged the following year, and the nation of the Natches, the most illustrious in Louisiana, was exterminated. The principal part of them were transported as slaves to St. Domingo.

In 1732, a number of Englishmen, from combined motives of patriotism and humanity, projected the settlement of the vacant lands in the southern portion of the chartered limits of Carolina. By this measure, it was intended to obtain possession of an extensive tract of country; to strengthen the province of Carolina; to relieve from the miseries of poverty many people in England and Ireland; to open an asylum for persecuted or oppressed members of the Protestant faith in different parts of Europe; and to attempt the conversion and civilization of the native Indians. Actuated by these benevolent considerations, James Oglethorpe and others made application to King George II. for a charter. The king, by letters patent, on the 9th of June, 1732, granted them seven eighths of all the lands from the most northern stream of the Savannah, along the sea-coast, to the most southern stream of the Altamaha, and westward from the heads of those rivers, in direct lines, to the south seas, — erecting that territory into an independent and separate government. This, in honor of the sovereign, was denominated *Georgia*.

With the settlement of this territory, which was commenced in 1733, under Oglethorpe, by one hundred and sixteen persons, was completed that of the thirteen veteran colonies, which fought the war of the revolution, and whose emblematic stars and stripes still decorate the banner of American independence.

The settlement of Georgia was expedited by the proposal to give a lot of fifty acres to each actual settler. For this purpose, eleven townships, of twenty thousand acres each, were laid out on the Savannah Altamaha, and Santee Rivers. Emigrants were not wanting to avail themselves of so advantageous an arrangement. A body of Scottish Highlanders settled on the Altamaha, and one of Germans on the Savannah. Soon after the declaration of war by England against Spain, in 1739, Oglethorpe was appointed to the chief command in South Carolina and Georgia It was not long before he projected an expedition against St. Augustine. With assistance from Virginia and Carolina, he marched at the head of more than two thousand men for Florida; and, after the capture of two small Spanish forts, — Diego and Moosa, — he sat down before St. Augustine. But although he received aid from several twenty gun ships, he was finally forced to raise the siege, and return with considerable loss. This unfortunate affair produced a serious increase of the public debt, and a temporary distrust of their commander, on the part of the people.

In 1742, the Spaniards, as they had not yet relinquished their claim to the province, invaded Georgia in heir turn. A Spanish armament, consisting of thirty-two sail, with three thousand men, under command of Don Miguel de Montano, sailed from St. Augustine, and arrived in the River Altamaha. The expedition proved to be a failure, although it was fitted out at great expense.

From the humanity by which Oglethorpe's administration was marked, slaves were at first not allowed to be brought into the province; but as this interdiction proved injurious to the pecuniary interests of the province, — since the adjoining colonies carried on their plantations by slave labor, and as even the pious Moravians and Methodists, under the eloquent Whitefield and the conscientious Wesleys, advocated conformity to the practice around them, — the pernicious system was suffered to take root in a colony distinguished by the peculiar humanity in which it was founded.

The tribe of the Natches in Louisiana, as we have seen, had been extinguished by being conquered and sold into slavery. But the Chickasaws were now the dread of the Louisianians. This tribe occupied a fine tract east of the Mississippi, and on the head of the Tombigbee. The French, in 1736, made war upon them, but seem to have met with little success. Notwithstanding the exertions of the French, the country was left in the possession of the Chickasaws. They guarded it from the occupancy of the French, and, as the event proved, kept it for the English.

CHAPTER CCCCLXXXIV.

A. D. 1736 to 1763.

Old French War — Destruction of a French Fleet — French and Indian War.

War having been proclaimed, in 1744, between England and France, M. Du Quesnel, governor of Cape Breton, sent about nine hundred men, under Duvier, who surprised and took Canso before the war was known at Boston. The place was burnt; and the conditions granted to the prisoners were, to be carried to Louisburg, and to continue there one year, and thence to be sent to Boston or Annapolis. To guard against the incursions of the French and Indians, five hundred men were impressed, of which number three hundred were for the eastern frontier, and two hundred for the western. The ordinary garrisons were reënforced, and munitions of war collected in considerable quantities.

It being deemed desirable, on many accounts, for the English to come into possession of Louisburg, the capital of the Island of Cape Breton, — a place which had been fortified with great care and expense, — Governor Shirley, of Massachusetts, meditated an attack upon it. Without waiting for the naval assistance which he had sought from England, he communicated his designs to the General Court of the colony, upon a promise from them of secrecy. The proposal, seeming to them too hazardous and expensive, was at first rejected; but having accidentally been discovered through the prayer of a member of the governor's family, the wishes of the people were expressed in favor of it, and the measure was finally carried in the court by a majority of one voice.

The only colonies that took part in this enterprise, though they were all invited as far south as Pennsylvania, were Massachusetts, Connecticut, New Hampshire, and Rhode Island. It seemed almost a Quixotic attempt — the plan for the reduction of a regularly constructed fortress being "drawn by a lawyer, to be executed by a merchant at the head of a body of husbandmen and mechanics." Yet it succeeded through several favoring circumstances. Sir William Pepperell, a merchant of Kittery, was the commander of the expedition. The land troops amounted to upward of four thousand: these were joined by other forces from England, which had now arrived, under the command of Commodore Warren. Batteries were erected before the town, and an assault eventually resolved upon. The French commander discouraged by adverse events, and by these menacing appearances, consented to capitulate upon a summons to surrender; and on the 16th of June, 1745, articles were accordingly signed. After the surrender of the fortress, the French flag was kept flying on the ramparts, and several rich prizes were thus decoyed and taken.

The French were exasperated at this loss, and sent a powerful armament, under D'Arville, with orders to ravage the whole coast of North America. With forty ships of war, beside transports, and between three and four thousand regular troops, it effected nothing, having been broken up by tempests, disease, and other disasters. The colonists considered this result as a merciful interposition of Heaven, being relieved by no agency of their own from a terror and apprehension such as had never been experienced, perhaps, by any threatened invasion from abroad. In October, 1748, a treaty of peace between England and France was signed at Aix-la-Chapelle, according to which a general restitution of places captured by the belligerent powers was made, and Cape Breton with the rest. It was a deep mortification to the inhabitants of New England, that what they termed, not unjustly "their own acquisition," should be restored to France. The Old French War, which thus terminated, had been highly injurious to the American colonies. Impoverishment and distress had been brought upon them by losses in their commerce, and through the seizure of their vessels on the coast by privateers. The supply of a currency by bills of credit, issued to cancel the debts incurred during the war, brought also the most serious evils in its train. The depreciation of the paper was so great that its value amounted but to five per cent. of its nominal amount.

Peace brought with it its indemnities and blessings. Commerce again flourished, population increased, settlements were extended, and the public credit revived. It continued, however, only eight years. In 1756, war was declared by Great Britain, under George II., against France; and a similar declaration was made on the part of France, under Louis XV. against Great Britain. This is commonly called the *French and Indian War*, the general cause of which was the alleged encroachments of the French upon the frontiers of the colonies in America belonging to the English crown. The particular occasion of it proved to be the alleged intrusion of the Ohio Company upon the territory of the French. This association, by an act of parliament in 1750, constituting it, obtained a grant of six hundred thousand acres, on or near the Ohio River, for the purposes of trade with the Indians, and of settling the country. In the prosecution of their object, they incurred the jealousy of the

French, and were forbidden further encroachments on the territory. The French followed their interdiction by fitting military movements, stationing their troops at convenient distances from the central government at the north, secured by temporary fortifications.

At the instance of the Ohio Company, thus threatened with the loss of their trade, the governor of Virginia sent a messenger to the French commandant on the Ohio, to demand the reasons of his hostile movements, and to require the evacuation of the French forts in that region. That messenger was George Washington, then in his twenty-second year. At this early age, he was called into the service of his country, and exhibited those high qualities, by which he at length reached the summit of human renown. His mission was accomplished with unequalled ability, amid dangers and difficulties the most appalling, having a party of only eight men, and traversing a wilderness of five hundred miles in extent. It is needless to say that the French refused to yield to the demands of the governor of Virginia.

As the use of force was now resolved upon, without any formal declaration of war, the Virginians were given to understand that they were to prosecute their claims by an appeal to arms. Accordingly, a regiment was raised in the province, which, with a small additional force from South Carolina, was placed under the command of Washington, as colonel. This force marched, in April, 1754, toward the Great Meadows, lying within the disputed territories, for the purpose of expelling the French. Not far from this place, he surrounded an encampment of the enemy, and defeated them. Receiving soon an addition to his troops, he advanced toward the French Fort Du Quesne, now Pittsburg, with the intention of dislodging the enemy. After proceeding a short distance, however, he learned that they had been reënforced from Canada; upon which he reluctantly relinquished the enterprise. With his four hundred men, he was subsequently attacked by fifteen hundred French, under M. de Villiers; but, though he fought bravely for several hours, his force was so inconsiderable that he was under the necessity of capitulating, though on the most honorable terms.

Washington on his Expedition to Fort Du Quesne.

In the exigencies arising out of the French hostilities, the mother country proposed a union among the colonies; the plan of such a union was drawn up by Benjamin Franklin, but it failed of being carried into effect. At this juncture, the British ministry adopted an artful project to make the colonies consent to taxation; but this met with no success. As no alternative was left, the crown resolved to carry on the war with British troops, and such auxiliary forces as the colonial assemblies might voluntarily furnish, to which scheme the Americans gave their cordial assent.

In the following year, (1755,) General Braddock was sent over from England with fifteen hundred troops. He was appointed to lead one of the four expeditions which, subsequently to his arrival, in a convention of the colonial governors, were agreed upon. This was against Fort Du Quesne; and it proved to be disastrous beyond any military event that the American annals had hitherto recorded. Brave, but ignorant of Indian warfare, — skilful, but undervaluing the wiser counsels of Washington, Braddock rushed into the midst of the wilderness without proper precautions. When fallen into an Indian ambuscade, he fought, or attempted to fight, as if he were pitted against a regular European army. He undauntedly stood their attack, but had no means of reaching the enemy, who were promiscuously firing upon him from the thick woods. He constantly sought to preserve a regular order of battle. The consequence was, that, being fair marks for the Indian gun or arrow, great numbers of his soldiers fell. Men and officers, especially the latter, who were singled out, were shot down. Of the officers on horseback, Washington alone escaped unhurt.

As soon as Braddock had received a mortal wound, his troops fled in confusion: Washington covered their retreat with the provincials The defeat was total; three fourths of the officers, and nearly half the privates, being killed or wounded. After this affair, the whole frontier of Virginia was open to the depredations of the French and Indians.

A second expedition, which had been agreed upon was designed to attack Crown Point, a French fort on the western shore of Lake Champlain. In this

General Abercrombie's Fleet crossing Lake George.

the northern colonies were concerned, whose troops, amounting to more than four thousand, were collected by the last of June, 1755, at Albany. They were led by General William Johnson and General Lyman. At Albany, they were joined by a body of Mohawks, under their sachem, Hendrick. The army arrived at the south end of Lake George the latter part of August. While here, intelligence was received that a body of the enemy, two thousand strong, had landed at South Bay,—Whitehall,—under command of Baron Dieskau, and were marching toward Fort Edward, for the purpose of destroying the provisions and military stores there. A party of twelve hundred men, commanded by Colonel Ephraim Williams, of Deerfield, Massachusetts, was detached to intercept the French, and save the fort. Dieskau, however, succeeded in routing this detachment by having drawn it into an ambush. It would, in all probability, have been wholly cut off, had not the action been precipitated through an accidental meeting of two Indians. Hendrick, the Mohawk sachem, was hailed by a hostile Indian: "Whence came you?" "From the Mohawks," he replied. "Whence came you?" rejoined Hendrick. "From Montreal," was the answer. This brought on the action sooner than was intended,—as Dieskau had ordered his flanking parties to reserve their fire until a discharge was made from the centre. As it was, the loss of the Americans was considerable. Colonel Williams and Hendrick were among the slain. The troops retreated, and joined the main body. Here they awaited the approach of their assailants, rendered more formidable by success.

Johnson was prepared to meet the confident, elated French commander. The attack made by Dieskau was vigorously repulsed, and the enemy, in turn, sought safety by flight. The Americans pursued the retreating army, under General Lyman,—Johnson having been wounded early in the action. The former bore his part in the successes of the day, though Johnson contrived to carry off all the honors. Dieskau was mortally wounded, and died soon after. This battle of Lake George was of great consequence to the English. In the elevated tone of feeling which it inspired, it seemed to be an indemnity for the mortification experienced in the defeat of Braddock. The conquering army, however, stopped short of Crown Point, which was not attacked at this period.

The third expedition was against Nova Scotia; it was directed by Generals Monckton and Winslow, with three thousand men. They sailed from Boston the 20th of May, 1755, and in a few days arrived in the Bay of Fundy. Here they were joined by three hundred British troops, and a small train of artillery; proceeding against Fort Beau Sejour, they invested and took possession of it, after a bombardment of four or five days. General Monckton, advancing farther into the country, took other forts in possession of the French, and disarmed the inhabitants. Thus, with the loss of only three men, the English possessed themselves of the whole of Nova Scotia.

A fourth expedition—that against Niagara—was committed to Governor Shirley. He did not arrive at Oswego until late in the summer of 1755; and, being obliged to wait for supplies, he found the season was too far advanced for crossing Lake Ontario. He left seven hundred men, under Colonel Mercer, to garrison the fort, and then returned to Albany. It was not till the next year (1756) that war was formally declared between France and England, although a state of warfare had existed for two years in the colonies.

In the spring of 1756, Governor Shirley was succeeded by General Abercrombie; and after him Lord Loudon came over as commander-in-chief of all his majesty's forces in America. The plan of operations for the campaign included an attack upon Niagara and Crown Point, which remained in possession of the French. But the reduction of neither of these important posts was accomplished, or even attempted this year, owing chiefly to the indecision and improvidence of Abercrombie.

Dieskau had been succeeded by the marquis de Montcalm, a commander of great ability and energy. In the month of August, 1756, this officer, with eight thousand regulars, Canadians, and Indians, invested the fort at Oswego—one of the most important posts held by the British in America—and in a few days took it. Upon the receipt of this intelligence, Lord Loudon despatched orders to General Winslow, on his march to Crown Point, not to proceed. The campaign of 1757 was sufficiently mortifying to the English; nor was that of the following year at all less so, notwithstanding the great preparations made by the British parliament to prosecute the war. Troops raised by the colonies for an expedition against Ticonderoga and

General Wolfe and his Army ascending the Heights of Abraham.

Crown Point were ordered by the commander-in-chief to proceed against Louisburg; but so dilatory was he in his measures, that the place, by means of fresh reënforcements, became too strong for the English to attempt it, and the expedition was given up.

The French, in the mean time, were urging on their victories. Montcalm, finding the English troops withdrawn from Halifax for the reduction of Louisburg, seized the occasion to make a descent on Fort William Henry, on the north shore of Lake George. After a gallant defence of six days, the garrison surrendered on the 2d of August, 1757, thus giving to Montcalm the command of the lakes and of the western frontier. Contrary to stipulation, the Indians were suffered to rob and murder the prisoners without restraint. Nearly half of a New Hampshire corps of two hundred men, was missing after this massacre.

The celebrated Lord Chatham was fortunately placed at the head of administration in 1758, under whose auspices the British arms recovered their wonted splendor. An almost constant train of victories ensued in the contests of the English with the French in America. A large number of troops were raised in New England, and were ready to take the field in the early part of the year. There were three expeditions proposed — the first against Louisburg, the second against Ticonderoga, the third against Fort Du Quesne. The attack on Louisburg, by a fleet of twenty ships of the line, eighteen frigates, and an army of fourteen thousand, under the command of Brigadier-General Amherst, and, next to him, of General Wolfe — was completely successful. The fortress surrendered on the 26th of July, with nearly six thousand prisoners, and one hundred and twenty cannon. At the same time, Isle Royal, St. Johns, with Cape Breton, fell into the hands of the British. The latter were now masters of the coast, from the St. Lawrence to Nova Scotia, and were able to obstruct the communications of Canada with France.

The expedition against Ticonderoga, on the western shore of Lake Champlain, in July, under General Abercrombie, was a failure, and the principal exception to the general tide of success on the part of the English. In the attack against the fort, nearly two thousand men were lost in killed and wounded, and then the troops were summoned away. Some amends were made for his defeat by the taking of Fort Frontenac, on the western shore of the outlet of Lake Ontario, by a detachment of three thousand men, under Colonel Bradstreet. This was important as contributing to the success of the expedition against Fort Du Quesne.

The conduct of that expedition was assigned to General Forbes, who collected for the purpose eight thousand effective men. The attack, however, was not made, as the fort was deserted by the garrison the evening before the arrival of the English army. The place thus quietly taken possession of was named *Pittsburg*, in honor of Mr. Pitt. The successes of this year prepared the way for the still greater ones of the next. The campaign of 1759 had for its object the entire conquest of Canada. It was arranged that three powerful armies should enter the country by different routes, and attack all the strongholds of the French, nearly at the same time. Ticonderoga and Crown Point, Niagara and Quebec, were the more prominent points for assault.

General Amherst, the successor of Abercrombie led one division against Ticonderoga, which he reached on the 22d of July, and which soon surrendered

Against Crown Point no blow was struck, for the enemy fled before the arrival of the English. General Prideaux took command of the second division of the main army destined against Fort Niagara, and arrived there on the 6th of July without molestation. The place was immediately invested, and on the 24th of the month, a general battle was fought, which decided the fate of Niagara, and placed it in the hands of the British.

In the mean time, General Wolfe was engaged in the most important enterprise of the campaign, — the reduction of Quebec. His force amounted to eight thousand men. In June, first landing on the Island of Orleans, a little below the city, he made several attempts to reduce the place, but without success. He then conceived the almost desperate project of ascending with his troops a precipice of from one hundred and fifty to two hundred feet, by which the Plains of Abraham, lying south and west of the city, could be gained, and thus the enemy reached in a less fortified spot. This was effected about an hour before daylight. Wolfe was the first man who leaped on shore from the boats which conveyed his troops to the place. When he perceived the difficulties around him, he said to some one near, "I do not believe there is a possibility of getting up, but we must do our endeavor." His men followed, and, escaping the French sentinels by a stratagem, and surmounting the dangers of the ascent up the precipice, they at length reached the heights.

There, on the morning of the 13th of September, Wolfe met the French army under Montcalm, who, till that hour, was not aware of the presence of his enemy in so advantageous a position. After a severe and bloody contest, in which both of these brave commanders fell, the victory was decided in favor of the English. A thousand Frenchmen lay dead on the field of battle and a thousand others were taken prisoners. The loss of the English in killed and wounded amounted to about six hundred. The capitulation of the city was signed within five days after the battle, under the direction of General Townsend. Favorable terms were given to the garrison, for Townsend knew that the resources of the French were still very considerable.

In the early part of the following year, the French army under M. de Levi, being reënforced by Canadians and Indians, engaged the English in a bloody battle, but failed to regain the city. Vaudreuil, the governor, finding that he was threatened with the entire force of the English, surrendered all the French possessions in Canada on the 8th of September, 1760. At this event, universal joy spread through the colonies, and public thanksgivings were expressed to the Ruler of nations. The southern colonies suffered, however, at this period, from the Cherokees; but in 1761, the latter were signally defeated, and compelled to sue for peace. By the treaty of Paris, 1763, Nova Scotia, Canada, the Isle of Cape Breton, and all other islands in the Gulf and River St. Lawrence, were ceded to the British crown.

CHAPTER CCCCLXXXV.

A. D. 1763 to 1774.

REVOLUTIONARY PERIOD. — *Attempts of the British Parliament to tax America — The Stamp Act — Opposition on the Part of the Colonies — First Congress in America, &c.*

We come now to the period of the Revolution. There seems to have been originally no intention, on the part of the American colonists, to become independent of the mother country. Previous to the treaty of Paris, in 1763, by which such splendid accessions to the British empire in America were secured, no adequate causes existed for a separation, — at least, as the colonists were disposed to view the subject. Had there been a desire or an intention to compass such an end, there were grounds indeed to which they might have appealed as a justification or excuse. Their connection with the empire had, in many instances, been attended by oppressions and losses; by wars, and consequent burdens; by onerous restraints imposed upon them, especially as to their commerce, and by the maleadministration, the peculation, and despotic conduct of the royal governors. Yet these circumstances had been passed over, and it was not until the subject of revenue and taxation was seriously, and as a system, taken up by the government at home, that the people in America thought of resistance and separation. Then it became a vital question with the colonies.

The American people could not approve of external duties imposed by the home government, for raising a revenue; yet they were ready to submit to such duties, provided they were not immoderate or vexatious, as in the case of the law called the *sugar act*. This was an act, passed in 1764, by which a duty was laid on "clayed sugar, indigo, coffee, &c., &c., being the produce of a colony not under the dominion of his majesty." The people of America saw in this act a principle of injustice which might prove destructive to their rights; but this alone would not have led them to permanent disaffection or resistance. It was internal taxation which they most decidedly reprobated, and this was attempted by the British parliament. The principle that taxation and representation were inseparable, was in accordance with the theory, the genius, and the precedents of British legislation; and this principle was new, for the first time, intentionally invaded. The colonies were not represented in parliament; yet an act was passed by that body, the tendency of which was to invalidate all right and title to their property.

The particular act now referred to was the "stamp act," of March 23d, 1765, which ordained that instruments of writing, such as deeds, bonds, notes, &c., in the colonies, should be null and void, unless executed on "stamped" paper — for which a duty should be paid to the crown. This was designed as the commencement of a system of taxation. In the house of commons, the measure met with strenuous opposition, particularly from Colonel Barré, whose eloquence on the occasion has often been rehearsed.

No sooner was intelligence received of the passing of the stamp act, than a general feeling of indignation spread through America. Resolutions were passed against it by most of the colonial assemblies. That of Virginia, being then in session, acted promptly, in view of the exigency, passing resolutions which strongly expressed their opposition to the measures of the British parliament. To this they were urged by a sense of their own wrongs, as well as by the eloquent and impassioned appeals of Patrick Henry, then a young lawyer, and member of the house of burgesses.

The General Court of Massachusetts, almost simultaneously with the proceedings in Virginia, and before the latter were known in the former colony, adopted measures to produce a combined opposition to the oppressive measures of parliament. Letters were addressed to the assemblies of the other colonies, recommending that a congress, composed of deputies from each, should meet for the purpose of consulting in respect to the general welfare. Most of the colonies, notwithstanding some opposition at first, took an interest in the proposal, and their delegates, on the first Tuesday in October, 1765, assembled in the city of New York. Their first measure was to draft a bill of rights, the most essential of which were an exclusive power to levy taxes, and the privilege of trial by jury — the existence of both being now perilled. The next measure was to prepare an address to the king, and petitions to both houses of parliament. Similar petitions from the colonies not represented at New York were also forwarded to England. Virginia, North Carolina, and Georgia were prevented by their governors from sending delegates to the congress.

Faneuil Hall, Boston, where the revolutionary meetings were held.

Previously to the 1st day of November, when the stamp act was to begin its operation, there had been tumultuous meetings in Boston, in which more or less violence was committed on the buildings and other property of certain obnoxious individuals, as the lieutenant-governor, the distributer of stamps, &c. But when the day arrived, the scene was imposing: the bells tolled, many shops and stores were shut, and effigies of the authors and friends of the odious act were carried about the streets, and afterward torn in pieces by the populace. Similar exhibitions of public indignation and concern were made in Newport, Providence, Portsmouth, New York, Philadelphia, and other places. The merchants and traders of New York,

Philadelphia, and Boston entered into non-importation agreements, with a view to obtain a repeal of the law. By the 1st of November, not a sheet of stamped paper was to be had, in most of the colonies.

Although the resignation of the stamp officers laid the colonists under an inability to do business according to parliamentary laws, yet they proceeded as before, and determined to brave the consequences. Vessels sailed from ports as they were wont; and the courts of justice, though suspended for a time in most of the colonies, at length undertook to proceed without the use of stamps. In England, a change in the ministry occurred about this time, which was deemed a favorable augury for the Americans; and an examination of Dr. Franklin, in the early part of the following year, before the house of commons, had the effect also of enlightening the British ministry on the subject of taxation in America. Accordingly, a bill to repeal the stamp act was brought before parliament, which, being advocated by some of its most influential members, particularly Mr. Pitt and Lord Camden, was carried, against a strong opposition. Its salutary effect, however, was destroyed by an accompanying declaratory resolution, which insisted that "parliament had a right to bind the colonies in all cases whatsoever."

The joy which the Americans felt in view of the repeal of the stamp act, though damped by the "declaratory bill," was sincere and deep; and had parliament ceased to meddle with their internal concerns, all cause of ill feeling from what had taken place would have passed over and been forgotten. But under a new ministry, in 1767, although Mr. Pitt, now earl of Chatham, was at the head of it, a second plan for taxing America was introduced into parliament, namely, by imposing duties on glass, paper, pasteboard, painters' colors, and tea. The composition of the new ministry was unfortunate, in having several members in it who were hostile to America. The discussion of the bill took place during the absence of Mr. Pitt from the house, as he was confined in the country by indisposition. Wanting his powerful opposition, it passed both houses, and received the royal assent on the 29th of June. During the same session, were passed two other acts; the one establishing a new board of custom-house officers in America, and the other restraining the legislature of the province of New York from "passing any act whatever" until they should furnish the king's troops with several required articles.

These acts, as soon as they were known, excited great alarm in the colonies. They became matters of thorough discussion among the first minds in the land, and many an able pen was employed in the defence of American rights. This was particularly true of the Letters of a Pennsylvania Farmer, written by John Dickinson. The new duties were considered by the Americans only as a new mode of extorting money from them by way of taxes, and the same feelings produced by the stamp act were awakened. As these duties, moreover, were appropriated to the support of crown officers, and to the maintenance of troops in America, it only added to the serious apprehensions which already existed. It had long been a favorite object of the British cabinet, as we have before stated, to establish in the colonies a fund, from which the salaries of the governors, judges, and other officers of the crown should be paid, independent of the annual grants of the colonial legislatures. On this subject, the house of representatives in Massachusetts maintained, with equal firmness, their former resolution. They also denounced the appointment of commissioners of customs, as a dangerous innovation, and an unnecessary increase of crown officers. While they claimed the rights of Englishmen, they, at the same time, disclaimed all ideas of independence of the parent country. The house, moreover, at the same session, addressed a circular letter to the colonies, stating the difficulties that were likely to arise by the operation of the late acts of parliament, and requesting their coöperation for redress.

The other colonies approved of the proceedings of Massachusetts, and joined in applying to the king for relief. The circular letter created alarm in the British cabinet. They considered it as an attempt to convene another congress, in order to concert measures of opposition to the authority of parliament. The ministry viewed with peculiar dread any union and concert among the colonies, and using every effort to prevent it, sought to neutralize the effect of the circular; but in vain. The ministerial mandate to disregard its recommendations was promptly set at defiance among the several colonies. In the mean time, the new board of commissioners of the customs entered on the duties of their office at Boston. This occasioned a collision between the people and the public authorities, in relation to a vessel laden with wines, which arrived at the port of Boston, May, 1768. As the duties had been evaded for the most part, and a discovery of the fact was subsequently made, the vessel was seized for a false entry, and removed to the neighborhood of a man-of-war for protection. A mob of the people of the city was immediately raised, who took summary vengeance on the custom-house officers by acts of personal violence, and by damage done to their houses. This proceeding, however, was disapproved by the council of the town.

The expectation of an armed force from Great Britain to aid the executive officers of the government in the performance of their duties, and to keep the public peace, only served to increase the alarm, discontent, and opposition that had begun so extensively to prevail, as well as to call forth some degree of preparation to meet the coming crisis. It was keenly felt that all these proceedings on the part of the mother country were unconstitutional, and in violation of the principles of British liberty, and were designed to oppress and humble the colonies. When two regiments of British troops arrived in the harbor of Boston, about the last of September, the magistrates and people of the town would not provide for them; the governor was obliged to secure for them such quarters as he could find. Boston, as might have been expected, now became a scene of confusion and misrule. Quarrels arose between the citizens and soldiers, and it is a matter of surprise that these did not sooner break out in bloody contests.

This state of things in the colonies provoked the parliament to a measure utterly subversive of liberty and the constitution. This consisted in giving authority to the governor of Massachusetts — and the same was in its nature applicable to the other colonies — to take notice of such persons as might be guilty of treason, or misprision of treason, that they might be sent to England and tried there. This was a step quite beyond endurance; and instead of intimidating, as was intended, it served to unite the colonies in a determination to defend their rights.

It is proper here to mention that, during the session of parliament in 1769, an attempt was made to obtain a repeal of the act imposing new duties, for it had become somewhat unpopular in Great Britain itself; yet Lord North, afterward placed at the head of the administration, desired to see America humbled at their feet, before such a measure of leniency should be passed in her favor. Yet in the subsequent session of 1770, while combinations still existed in America, and while the colonies had made no submission, the obnoxious act of 1767 was repealed, except in regard to the article of tea. This was by no means satisfactory to the Americans; but it served in some measure to tranquillize their minds. Still, as the troops were continued at Boston, and the other revenue acts and the acts of trade were yet enforced by the new board of commissioners, a state of extreme irritation was kept up in Massachusetts, and collisions and quarrels were perpetuated in Boston.

These contentions were carried to such a length, that at last a guard, under the command of a Captain Preston, fired upon the Bostonians in a quarrel, and eleven persons were either killed or wounded. This tragical event happened on the evening of the 5th of March, 1770, and aroused a deep spirit of vengeance. The perpetrators of the deed, however, were all acquitted upon trial, except two, who were found guilty of manslaughter; but the anniversary of the event, called the *Boston Massacre*, was observed for a long time afterward, with great solemnity. Fresh causes of irritation arose in Massachusetts, which it would exceed our limits to narrate; but it may be observed, in the language of an able historian, that "the half-way measures of the administration, since the repeal of the stamp act, had not and could not satisfy the Americans. No half-way measures, indeed, could avail. They might palliate, but could not cure the evil. The relinquishment of the *right*, as well as the *practice*, of taxing, and of regulating the internal concerns of the colonies, would alone satisfy them. On these points no compromise was possible."

Salaries given to the governor and justices of the Superior Court in Massachusetts, independent of any provincial grant which had yet been accorded, produced intense dissatisfaction, and the flame was kept up by prolonged disputes between Governor Hutchinson and the assembly, concerning the supremacy of parliament. In this state of things, the leading patriots of America now began seriously to contemplate the mighty struggle which seemed forced upon them. Great Britain was determined not to relax, and the colonies were equally resolved not to submit. For them to remain long in this condition appeared impossible.

It was, doubtless, with a view to the contingency of opposition by force of arms, that committees of correspondence between the colonies were proposed and appointed, so that unity of action might be insured. The hostility of the people of Massachusetts

Throwing the Tea into the Harbor.

was increased, about this time, (1773,) against the governor and lieutenant-governor, by the discovery and publication of certain letters which these gentlemen had sent to England in some previous year, on the subject of American affairs. These letters, by their exaggerated statements, and recommendation of coercive measures, greatly widened the breach between the two countries; and Massachusetts, by her assembly, sent a petition to the king for the removal of Governor Hutchinson and Lieutenant-Governor Oliver. But the royal assent was not obtained.

During these transactions in America, the British ministry were devising a plan for introducing tea into the country, notwithstanding the non-importation agreements among the colonists. The plan which they devised was likely to succeed, could they get the tea landed. But though the East India Company shipped large quantities of it, such was the vigilance employed, that neither at Philadelphia nor New York could it be introduced among the citizens. In Boston, it was feared that, as the loaded vessels lay in the harbor, the tea would be landed in small quantities. To prevent this, several men, dressed in the habit of Indians, boarded the ships during the night, and threw their cargoes into the water. The contents of three hundred and forty-two chests of tea were thus destroyed.

When the news of these transactions reached Eng

and, a deep feeling of resentment was excited in the minds of the ministry. A bill interdicting all commercial intercourse with the town of Boston, and also the landing and shipping of goods at that port, passed both houses of parliament, and received the sanction of the king on the 21st of June, 1774. The charter of the colony, so long the eyesore of the ministry, was the next object of attack, and several fundamental alterations of it were effected. Among other things, they materially changed, or totally repealed, the laws relating to town meetings and the election of jurors. The people now felt that they were stripped of some of their dearest rights and privileges. In New England, from the first settlement of the country, the town meetings had been cherished by the inhabitants. Here they had been wont to meet, not merely as men and citizens, but as Christians; making regulations not only for the ordinary internal police of their communities, but for the vital purposes, also, of providing for the education of their children, and of settling and maintaining their clergy.

The British government passed several other most unjust, coercive measures, which need not here be detailed; the effect of which was, to produce a keen sense both of injury and insult on the part of the colonists, and only increased their determination to resist the authority usurped over them. To carry the plans of the government into effect, General Gage was appointed governor of Massachusetts, and was received by the inhabitants of Boston with their usual courtesy; but he found them supremely indignant in regard to the late acts of ministerial oppression and tyranny, particularly the "port bill." The other colonists did not hesitate to make common cause with the people of Massachusetts, and in various ways expressed their sympathies for the sufferings of the people of Boston. In Virginia, the 1st of June, the day the port of Boston was to be shut, was appointed as a day of "fasting, humiliation, and prayer."

The necessity of another general congress, and a more intimate union of the colonies, was now perceived by all; and in the course of the summer, delegates were appointed, either by the regular assemblies, or by conventions of the people, in all the colonies except Georgia, to attend a congress to be held in Philadelphia in September. All the colonies except Massachusetts, though firmly opposed to the late claims of the parent country, were still very desirous of a reconciliation, yet with the security of their rights. But the feelings of the Massachusetts people had become too much imbittered and alienated to seek any redress, except by force of arms. They were willing, however, to yield to the desire of the other colonists, and to make a trial of other measures. John Adams is reported to have said in conversation with one of his associates, after their appointment, "I suppose we must go to Philadelphia, and enter into non-importation, non-consumption, and non-exportation agreements; but they will be of no avail; we shall have to resist by force."

CHAPTER CCCCLXXXVI.

A. D. 1774 to 1776.

Second Congress — Oppressive and coercive Measures of Parliament — Fruitless Attempts at Reconciliation — Preparations of the Colonists for Defence, &c.

The second general congress since the peace of 1763 met at Philadelphia on the 5th of September, 1774. They chose for their president Peyton Randolph, one of the delegates from Virginia; and for their secretary Charles Thompson, a citizen of Philadelphia. By this most able congress, whose measures became so important, the conduct of Massachusetts was first of all approved, which was highly gratifying to the people of that colony. They also recommended the continuance of contributions for the relief of the sufferers at Boston. During the session of this congress, a constant communication was kept up by means of expresses between Boston and Philadelphia. They next appointed a committee to state the rights of the colonies, the violations of these, and the means of redress. The declaration was drawn up in an able and candid manner, and it was agreed to pursue the following peaceable measures, viz.: 1. To enter into a non-importation association; 2. To prepare an address to the people of Great Britain, and a memoria to the inhabitants of British America; and, 3. To prepare a loyal address to his majesty.

The addresses, as they were published, can never be read without being admired, not merely for the firmness with which the rights of the country were maintained, but for unexampled elevation and dignity of sentiment, as well as energy and elegance of diction. These state papers were drawn up with an ability which evinced the high standing of the members of that august assembly, as scholars as well as statesmen. Lord Chatham declared that though he had studied and admired the free states of antiquity, the master spirits of the world, "yet, for solidity of reasoning, force of sagacity, and wisdom of conclusion, no body of men could stand in preference of this congress." The address to the king breathed the finest spirit of affec-

Meeting of Congress.

tion, loyalty, and obedience. After having despatched its business, congress dissolved on the 26th of October, with a recommendation that another congress be held on the 10th of May, 1775, unless their grievances before that time should be redressed.

The proceedings of the congress were approved by the colonies; and doubtless a large proportion of the people agreed with the major part of the delegates to that body, that the pacific measures adopted would be successful. But others thought differently; even in congress, Patrick Henry and Mr. Adams dissented from the opinion of Richard Henry Lee, George Washington, and the larger number of the members. The former gentlemen felt persuaded that the contest must ultimately be decided by force.

In the British house of commons, on the 20th of January, 1775, Lord Chatham made a motion for the recall of the troops from Boston. He accompanied this motion by one of his most eloquent speeches, but though supported by several distinguished members, it was rejected by a large majority. He was not, however, prevented, by the known determination of the ministers to coerce obedience, from presenting to the house, soon after, a conciliatory bill; but that also was decisively rejected. As parliament was now resolved to enforce obedience at the point of the bayonet, that body, at the request of the king, augmented both the army and navy; and with a view the more effectually to embarrass New England, and starve her into obedience, restricted her trade with the other parts

Battle at Lexington.

of the empire, and prohibited her fishing on the banks of Newfoundland. Most of the other colonies, soon after, were restricted in like manner. This was a measure as impolitic as it was cruel, and nerved the Americans to a more determined resistance.

At this period, earnest attempts were made in England, by certain friends of America and of peace, to produce a reconciliation between the mother country and the colonies. These attempts were in the shape of indirect negotiations with Dr. Franklin, then in England; but though concessions in the plans proposed were made on both sides, yet they were not so considerable as to suit both parties. According to Dr. Franklin's remark, "Massachusetts must suffer all the hazards and mischiefs of war, rather than admit the alteration of her charters and laws by parliament. They who can give up liberty to obtain a little temporary safety, deserve neither liberty nor safety." The alteration of the laws and charters of the colonies, and other acts, involving direct claims of sovereignty, which could not be admitted but at the sacrifice of all justice and freedom, would not be abandoned on the part of

Siege of Boston.

Britain, and could not be yielded on the part of America. An apparent defection in New York encouraged the ministry to hope that the confederacy of the colonies was broken; but as that province, like all the rest, claimed an exemption from internal taxation, the petition of its assembly was denied a hearing before parliament. New York could then but make common cause with the other colonies. No attention was paid, in America, at this time, to a circular of the British secretary of state, forbidding the election of delegates to the congress in the following May. These were chosen, eventually, from the whole thirteen colonies.

The preparations of the Americans for defence increased with the increase of danger. The manufacture of gunpowder, arms, and ammunition of every kind, was encouraged. In Massachusetts, in particular, all was vigilance and activity. Every person capable of bearing arms was to be ready at a moment's warning, and arms and provisions were collected and deposited at the towns of Worcester and Concord. Though a desperate conflict seemed inevitable, the people of Massachusetts, as well as the other colonies, were determined not to be the first to commence the attack; but were resolved to repel by force the first hostile aggression on the part of the British commander. An opportunity soon offered to bring their resolution, as well as courage, to the test. On the 18th of April, 1775, a detachment of troops moved from Boston to destroy the warlike and other stores deposited at Concord; and the next day, the battle of Lexington and Concord followed, in which the British first commenced actual hostilities, by firing on the militia collected at the former place.

The people of Massachusetts redeemed the pledge they had often given to defend their rights at the hazard of their lives. The British were repulsed, and compelled, with no inconsiderable loss, to return to Boston. The news of this engagement soon spread through the colonies. All New England was in arms, and thousands speedily marched toward the scene of action. The provincial congress of Massachusetts immediately resolved that an army of thirteen thousand men should be raised, and the other New England colonies were requested to furnish an additional number for the defence of the country. The treasurer was directed to borrow one hundred thousand pounds for the use of the province; and they declared that the citizens were no longer under any obligations of obedience to Governor Gage. Even after this, the people could truly profess to be the loyal and dutiful subjects of their king, as they were able to prove, and did prove in a statement to their agent in England, Dr. Franklin that the British troops were the aggressors in the fight at Lexington. The loss of nearly three hundred men. however, on the part of the British before they reached Boston, and that of nearly one hundred on the part of the Americans, was too considerable to allow the minds of either party to be content without other contests for supremacy.

In this state of public affairs, the meeting of congress, on the 10th of May, 1775, was quite opportune, as the results of its deliberations, also, were of the highest importance. Congress unanimously determined that the "colonies be placed in a state of defence;" at the same time, however, an ardent wish was expressed for a restoration of former harmony between the parent country and themselves. For this purpose, a dutiful petition to the king was resolved upon. On the 15th of June, George Washington, a member of their own body, was appointed commander-in-chief of the army then raised, or to be raised, for the defence of the country. This appointment he accepted with his characteristic modesty, diffidence, and disinterestedness. At the conclusion of his short but manly address to congress on this occasion, he observed, "As to pay, sir, I beg leave to assure the congress that, as no pecuniary consideration could have tempted me to accept this arduous employment at the expense of my domestic ease and happiness, I do not wish to make any profit from it. I will keep an exact account of my expenses. These, I doubt not, they will discharge, and that is all I desire." With all due solemnity, the congress assured him that they would sustain him. and adhere to him with their lives and fortunes in the cause of the country.

The novel situation in which the American people were now placed rendered it peculiarly proper for

The House still at Cambridge occupied by General Washington as his Head-Quarters.

them to declare to the world the causes which induced them to take up arms. This was done by their representatives, on the 6th of July, in a full and eloquent statement of the various acts of the British parliament, in violation of their rights, and the hostile proceedings of the administration to enforce them. They concluded their declaration by a devout appeal to the God of nations in the following terms: "With an humble confidence in the mercies of the supreme and impartial Judge and Ruler of the universe, we most devoutly implore his divine goodness, to protect us happily through this great conflict, to dispose our adversaries to reconciliation on reasonable terms, and thereby relieve the empire from the calamities of civil war."

General Washington arrived at Cambridge on the 2d of July, and there took command of the American army. Every preparation was made for the defence of the country that its means afforded. Regular enlistments were commenced, and congress recommended that all effective men in every colony, between sixteen and fifty years of age, be formed into a regular militia, be well armed and disciplined, and that one fourth part of them be selected for *minute-men*, to be ready to march at the shortest notice. A committee of safety, also, was recommended to each colony, for the security and defence of the respective colonies. These recommendations had the force of laws. Several plans of reconciliation were proposed about this period, but none of them were adopted by the American congress.

During the session of congress now held, Dr. Franklin submitted to its consideration articles of confederation and union among the colonies. These, though not acted upon definitely, were made public, and have been considered as containing the plan of union afterward adopted by congress and submitted to the colonies for their approbation. After the commencement of hostilities in Massachusetts, the disputes between the royal governors and the colonists became more serious. The people, in most instances, took possession of the public arms and ammunition, and even the public money, and assumed the powers of government. But, notwithstanding all these measures for self-defence, their views did not yet extend to a separation from Great Britain, except in the last extremity.

As arms were necessary in the event of further resistance, an enterprise was planned in Connecticut, early in May, 1775, to procure a partial supply of these, as well as to secure an important military post in this country. This was the taking of the fort of Ticonderoga, which was effected by Colonel Ethan Allen and Benedict Arnold. The garrison, then consisting of about forty men, was surprised early on the morning of the 10th of May. As the commandant was ordered to surrender the fort, he asked by what authority. Colonel Allen, in a singularly bold and original manner, replied, "In the name of the great Jehovah and the continental congress." A large amount of arms and ammunition was thus secured. Crown Point was taken peaceable possession of soon after by Colonel Warner.

About the last of May, Generals Howe, Clinton, and Burgoyne, with reënforcements, arrived at Boston, with fresh orders to compel the submission of the colonists — a work they believed might be easily accomplished. The battle of Bunker's Hill (June 17) soon convinced them that they had to meet bold and determined spirits, and that they must be engaged in other scenes than those of fishing and fowling, in which they had flattered themselves they should be principally employed in America. In this battle, three thousand men, composing the flower of the British army, were engaged. Their killed and wounded amounted to more than one thousand, while the loss of the Americans was less than half that number. The British were twice repulsed; but, the ammunition of the Americans having failed, they were forced to retreat. Although the ground was lost, they regarded this as a victory.

After this battle, the intelligence of which thrilled

every American heart, the enemy were so closely shut up in Boston by the army under the command of Washington, that they were compelled, through the remainder of the campaign, to content themselves with a few predatory excursions to the islands in Boston Bay and along the coasts of Massachusetts. The manner in which this sort of warfare was carried on is shown by the wanton burning of Charlestown and Falmouth.

On the 5th of September, congress met again, and entered on the arduous duties assigned them. That body, being aware of the intention of the ministry to attack the colonies by the way of Canada, resolved, if possible, to prevent this by taking possession of the fortresses in that province before reënforcements should be received from England. Though late in the season, Canada was invaded by the American forces. One detachment entered the country by the way of Lake Champlain, under the command of General Montgomery; and, after a severe action at St John's, took possession of Montreal, and arrived early in December before the walls of Quebec. Another detachment, under the command of Benedict Arnold, entered Canada by the River Kennebec and through the wilderness, suffering incredible hardships, on the route, from hunger and fatigue. Only a part of the troops arrived before Quebec to join the forces of Montgomery. This brave general fell in a desperate but unsuccessful assault upon that city.

During the invasion of Canada, the American army before Boston was unable, for want of ammunition, to engage in any offensive operations against the enemy, who held that place; and it was no inconsiderable achievement, as General Washington observed in a communication to congress, "to maintain a post within musket shot of the enemy, for six months together, *without powder*, and at the same time to disband one army and recruit another within that distance of twenty odd British regiments." Regular governments, following the example of Massachusetts, were now commenced in several of the provinces, not, however, without the apprehensions of a portion of the members of congress that this was a step necessarily leading to independence, for which they were not yet prepared. The last hopes of the colonists for reconciliation depended on the success of their second petition to the king; but no answer was given to it. The king, in his speech at the opening of parliament in October, accused the colonists of revolt, hostility, and rebellion, remarking that "the rebellious war carried on by them was for the purpose of establishing an independent empire."

Determined war was now to be waged against the colonists, and a force sent out sufficiently powerful to compel submission, even without a struggle. Accordingly, parliament passed some very extraordinary acts, unknown to the spirit of a civilized age, against her American people. All trade with the colonies was prohibited, and the colonists declared open enemies. Their vessels and persons were made liable to seizure. Persons found in captured vessels were to be put on board any other armed British vessel, and considered as having entered his majesty's service; and by this means might be compelled to fight against their own countrymen and relatives. Royal commissioners were appointed with authority to grant pardon on submission to individuals and to colonies; and thus the hope was entertained of creating divisions among them. Reprisals were now ordered by congress, and the American ports were opened to all the world except Great Britain. Congress also recommended to all the colonies to form governments for themselves, and independence became seriously contemplated by the leading minds of the country.

In the mean time, — that is, early in the spring of 1776, — General Washington adopted the plan of taking possession of Dorchester Heights, and fortifying them, as these commanded the harbor and the British shipping there. This was accordingly effected on the night of the 4th of March, without exciting the suspicion of the enemy. The surprise of the latter the next morning, cannot be easily conceived; and it was at once determined to evacuate Boston, which they now did. On the 17th, the British troops, under the command of Lord Howe, successor of General Gage, sailed for Halifax. Washington, to the great joy of all, immediately marched into the town. While these transactions were taking place in the north, an attempt was made, in June and July, to destroy the fort on Sullivan's Island, near Charleston, South Carolina, by General Clinton and Sir Peter Parker. The British, however, were repulsed, after an action of upward of ten hours, with great injury to their ships, and with the loss of two hundred killed and wounded.

The subject of Independence was brought before congress, on the 7th of June, by Richard Henry Lee, one of the deputies from Virginia, in the form of a resolution declaring that "the united colonies are and ought to be free and independent states; that they are absolved from all allegiance to the British crown; and that a political connection between them and the state of Great Britain is and ought to be totally dissolved." On the 8th, the resolution was debated in the committee of the whole. It was eloquently supported by Mr. Lee, Mr. Adams, and others, and opposed by Mr. John Dickinson. On the 10th, it was adopted in committee by a bare majority of the colonies. To afford time for greater unanimity, the resolution was postponed in the house until the 1st of July. In the mean time, a committee, consisting of Mr. Jefferson Dr. Franklin, Mr. Sherman, and Mr. R. R. Livingston was appointed to prepare a *Declaration of Independence.* On the 1st of July, agreeably to appointment, the resolution of Mr. Lee was resumed in that body referred to a committee of the whole, and was assented to by all the colonies except Pennsylvania and Delaware. The Declaration of Independence was reported by the special committee on the 28th of June, and, on the 4th of July, came before congress for final decision. It received the vote of every colony, and was signed by the several members. No greater question, probably, in the annals of the human race and having a more direct bearing on the welfare of mankind, was ever debated and decided by a deliberative assembly. It gave birth to a new empire and to a new order of things in the political world.

In the mean time, an attempt had been made at reconciliation on the part of the royal commissioners but in vain, as the terms could not be accepted by the American people. Subsequent attempts of a similar kind were made after the event of the declaration of independence; but it was then too late. The die was cast. The terms proposed in every case, as they amounted to little more than pardon on submission and return to allegiance, without a guaranty against future

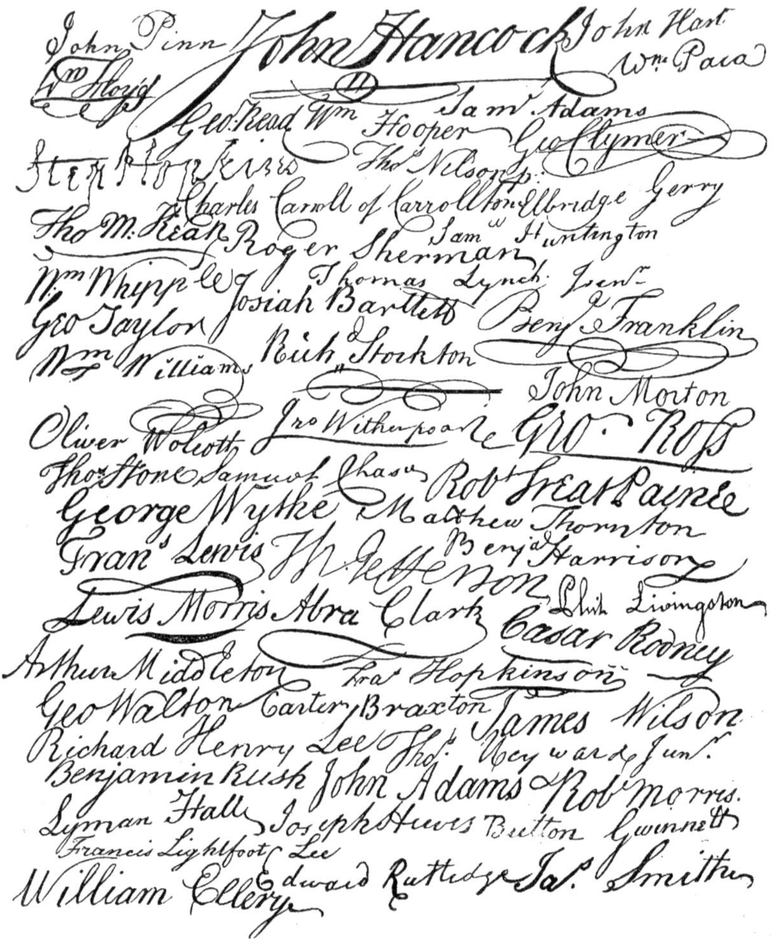

Fac-simile of the Signatures to the Declaration of Independence.

oppressions, were promptly rejected. The declaration of independence had produced a new political state in America. Allegiance was now transferred to the several states, and Americans adhering to the king or to the enemies of the states, and giving them aid, were considered as guilty of treason.

Proposals for reconciliation were soon followed by charges and commands, on the part of the royal commissioners, as the affairs of America assumed a more gloomy aspect. All persons assembled together in arms against his majesty's government were ordered to disband themselves, and return to their dwellings, there to remain in a peaceable and quiet manner. All general or provincial congresses, conventions, committees, &c., having in view the levying of money, raising troops, fitting out armed vessels, and imprisoning or molesting his majesty's subjects, were strictly forbidden. Pardons were offered to those who should return to their allegiance within a given time, of which some in the vicinity of the British troops availed themselves. To counteract the effects of such a proclamation, as far as possible, General Washington deemed it necessary soon after to issue an opposing proclamation.

It may be stated, generally, that the campaign of 1776 was unfortunate for America. The scene of military operations during this year was transferred from Massachusetts to New York. General Washington, soon after the evacuation of Boston by the British, anticipating the plan of the enemy, had removed to the city of New York with the principal part of his troops. General Howe and his army followed soon after, and, on the 2d of July, took possession of Staten Island, where he was shortly joined by his brother, Lord Howe, with a fleet and reënforcement of troops. The British army, numbering about thirty thousand strong, was more numerous and better disciplined than the American. The latter were composed of militia, or troops enlisted for a year only, and were beside unaccustomed to military life and discipline. They amounted in all to little more than seventeen thousand men.

Soon after the battle on Long Island, near Brooklyn, on the 27th of August, which resulted disastrously for the Americans, — the British having attacked that portion of Washington's army which was encamped there, — he abandoned the city of New York, and the strong places in its vicinity were taken by, or given up to, the enemy. All that had been gained in Canada the preceding year, was lost in the course of this campaign.

On retiring from New York, Washington, with his army, occupied for a short time the heights of Haerlem, and several stations in that neighborhood, during which time he had a slight skirmish with a considerable body of the enemy, who had appeared on the plains between the two camps — killing and wounding more than a hundred of them. The principal benefit of this action was its influence in reviving the depressed spirits of the whole army. Retiring from Haerlem with a portion of his forces, the American commander took up his position at White Plains. Here, on the 28th of October, after an indecisive engagement, the Americans, now greatly reduced by the return of the militia, by sickness and other casualties of war, crossed the North River, into New Jersey. On the 22d of November, the whole force under the command of General Washington did not exceed thirty-five hundred With this small number, the American general was obliged to fly before a superior force, under Lord Cornwallis; and even this remnant of an army was diminished, on its march to the Delaware, by the expiration of the term of enlistment of the Jersey and Maryland brigades. On crossing the Delaware, about the 10th of December, General Washington had only about seventeen hundred men. The object of the enemy was to get possession of Philadelphia, as soon as the ice would enable them to pass the Delaware. The loss of that city seemed inevitable. Congress, then sitting at Philadelphia, on the 12th of December removed to Baltimore for greater safety. In this gloomy and almost desperate state of public affairs, the great mass of the Americans remained firm and determined in the cause of independence.

Battle of Princeton

CHAPTER CCCCLXXXVII.

A. D. 1776 to 1779.

Capture of Hessians — Victory at Princeton — Battles at Brandywine and Germantown — Confederation of the States — Capture of Burgoyne, &c.

By an act of congress, the project of raising eighty-eight battalions to serve during the war was entered upon, and a bounty of twenty dollars was given to all non-commissioned officers and soldiers; and, in addition to this, lands were promised to those officers and soldiers who should continue in service through the war. To impart greater efficiency to the defence of the country, Washington was invested with unlimited military powers for the term of six months, unless sooner terminated by congress. He met the responsibility with his accustomed firmness and wisdom. At this period, he felt that an effort was peculiarly necessary to rouse the spirit of the nation, and to induce the enlistment of soldiers for the ensuing campaign. Such an effort he put forth in an attempt to surprise a body of Hessians encamped at Trenton. In this he succeeded, in a manner which reflects the highest credit on his military capacity. It was on the morning of the 26th of December, 1776, that he made the attack, after suffering great hardships in his march, and in crossing the Delaware in a cold and stormy night. Many of the Hessians were killed, and more than nine hundred were taken prisoners.

This enterprise produced the effect which Washington sought. It equally elevated the hopes of the Americans, and excited the astonishment of the British This victory was followed by the battle of Princeton, which was decidedly in favor of the Americans. That battle was the result of one of those bold measures which only great minds conceive and execute. Instead of encountering Lord Cornwallis, who had met him with a superior force, or attempting to retreat before him, either of which seemed equally hazardous, Washington left the enemy in their encampment, marched to Princeton by a circuitous route, and surprised the British troops at that place, all of which he effected in the night of the 1st of January, 1777, and in so secret a manner, that Cornwallis knew nothing of the movement until it was too late to afford his countrymen assistance.

At this time, the American army, notwithstanding all the efforts which had been made by congress, amounted to little more than seven thousand men. Toward the latter end of May, Washington quitted his winter encampment at Morristown; and about the same time, the British army moved from Brunswick, which had been occupied by it during the winter. Many movements of the respective armies followed, but neither seemed to have a definite plan of operation. At length, the British General Howe left New Jersey, and, embarking at Sandy Hook with sixteen thousand men, sailed for the Chesapeake. He landed his troops on the 11th of August, in Maryland. It was now apparent that his design was the occupation of Philadelphia. To prevent this, Washington immediately put his army in motion toward that city. The two armies met at Brandywine, Delaware, on the 11th of September; and, after an engagement through nearly the whole day, the Americans were forced to recede. In this battle, several foreign officers, who had embarked in our cause, and among them the brave and generous Lafayette, distinguished themselves. The latter was wounded while attempting to rally some fugitives.

It was not possible now to prevent the enemy from having access to Philadelphia, which accordingly they entered on the 26th of September. General Howe, upon occupying the city, felt the necessity of reducing some forts on the Delaware, which rendered the navigation of that river unsafe to the English. While a part of the British army was detached for that purpose, Washington attacked the portion of it which had been stationed at Germantown, six miles from Philadelphia. This attack was made on the 4th of October; but, after a severe action, the Americans were repulsed with a loss much greater than that of the enemy. Mortifying and distressing as the result was to Washington, congress saw fit to express their admiration of his plan of attack, and the bravery of the troops.

An interesting portion of American history belongs to this period, in reference to the foreign relations of the country, and particularly its efforts to secure the countenance and aid of France in its arduous struggle. The secret correspondence with the government of France; the gifts and loans with which she assisted America; her alliance and treaties with the latter, and the adroit management through which these events were brought about, and in which the great Franklin was so intimately concerned — supply a chapter of deep interest to the politician, but for which no space is allowed in this condensed narrative.

It was also about this time that the subject of a Confederation of the States was brought before congress, and articles to that effect were prepared, designed to produce and cement a perpetual union between the several states. There seemed to be a necessity for such a measure, that the line of distinction between the powers of the respective states and of congress should be clearly drawn, and thus the peace and harmony of the Union be preserved. The articles were ratified, and signed eventually on the part of all the states, though several of them at first objected.

While the military operations of the Americans, in the Middle States, wore a doubtful aspect, the northern portion of the country became the theatre of great and splendid events. The battle of Bennington, on the 16th of August, 1777, and the two battles at Stillwater — the first on the 14th of September, and the second on the 7th of October — effected the destruction of one of the finest British armies which had been sent to this country. It was commanded by General Burgoyne, who — in attempting to carry out a plan, which had been settled in England, of forming a communication between Canada and New York, and thus of cutting off New England from any intercourse with the other parts of the country — hoped to put an end at once to the confederacy and the contest. But that accomplished commander soon found himself environed with difficulties he little expected; and, at length, beaten in successive battles, surrounded on all sides with an exasperated foe, and growing short of provisions, he surrendered, on the 17th of October, his whole army, of nearly six thousand men, into the hands of the Americans. This event, as might have been expected, occasioned equal transport to the Americans, and consternation to the British, and was, in an important sense, the crisis of the revolution, as it procured from France the acknowledgment of American independence, and a treaty of alliance and commerce between the two nations.

Upon the conclusion of the campaign of 1777, the British army retired to winter quarters in Philadelphia, where they enjoyed the comforts of a wealthy city; and the American army betook itself to Valley Forge, fifteen miles from the city, where they suffered severely from hunger, cold, and nakedness. The plans of the British were changed somewhat, in consequence of the alliance of America with France. It was resolved that the royal force should evacuate Philadelphia, and become concentrated in the city of New York. The evacuation commenced on the 18th of June; but Washington, penetrating the design, had prepared to interpose what obstacles he could to its consummation. The result was, that the hostile armies came to battle on the 28th of the same month, at Monmouth, sixty-four miles from Philadelphia. The contest was most severe, and the Americans, on the whole, obtained the advantage. It was a day of excessive heat, and numbers, on both sides, perished from that cause alone. On the part of the British, three hundred and fifty-eight were killed, wounded, and missing. A smaller number were disabled among the Americans. Of the British, one hundred were taken prisoners, and one thousand deserted during the march. With this loss, the British general made good his retreat to New York on the night following the battle.

An expedition against Rhode Island, which had been in possession of the British ever since December, 1776, was concerted by Washington in the summer of 1778 but was unsuccessful, and unhappy in its results. The British force stationed at Newport consisted of six thousand troops. To meet these, a force of ten thousand men was detached, under the command of General Sullivan; but the failure of the French Count d'Estaing who had recently arrived there with twelve ships of the line and six frigates, to coöperate with Sullivan, obliged the latter to withdraw his troops. Indeed, half of his army, which consisted of militia, refused to remain, and encounter the danger, to which they were now exposed, of an attack from the British at New York. Lord Howe had just arrived with a fleet, and had craftily led on d'Estaing to give him pursuit, which was the occasion of the embarrassments of the American general. It required all the address of Washington to allay the resentments which had sprung up in the bosoms of the American soldiers, who felt aggrieved by the course of events on this occasion. The French fleet, having been shattered by a storm while in pursuit of Lord Howe, entered Boston to repair. Afterward it sailed for the West Indies, where it took Dominica from the English.

Although the expectations of success on the part of the British, in the campaign of 1778, lay in the direction of the south, yet it was not until a late period that Sir Henry Clinton was prepared to invade the states in that quarter. In November, he despatched a force of two thousand men, under Colonel Campbell, against Savannah, the capital of Georgia. The place being unprepared for defence, fell into the hands of the enemy. Four hundred and fifty Americans were taken prisoners. By this success, the state itself was virtually subdued.

Attack on Stony Point.

CHAPTER CCCCLXXXVIII

A. D. 1779 to 1783.

Predatory Incursions of the British — Reduction of Stony Point — Surrender of Charleston to Sir Henry Clinton — Defeat of the Americans in the Battle of Camden, &c.

DURING the campaign of 1779, the British seemed to aim at little more than to distress, plunder, consume and destroy — it having been, early in the year, adopted as a principle, "to render the colonies of as little use as possible to their new confederates." It was in this spirit that an expedition was fitted out from New York for Virginia. In this predatory incursion, large naval stores, magazines of provisions, and great quantities of tobacco were seized and carried off. In addition to this exploit, several towns were wantonly burned. A similar expedition was soon afterward planned against the maritime parts of Connecticut, and carried into execution by the notorious Governor Tryon. The result of this predatory attempt was the plundering of New Haven, and the burning of East Haven, Fairfield, Norwalk, and Green Farms.

The Americans, during this campaign, dispirited by means of the failure of the French fleet, and embarrassed by the daily depreciation of their bills of credit, effected but little against the enemy. Their only important enterprises were the reduction of Stony Point, forty miles north of New York, on the Hudson, and the dispersion of the Six Nations, which, with the exception of the Oneidas, had been induced by the English to take up arms against the states. The reduction of Stony Point took place July 15, and was one of the boldest enterprises which occurred in the history of the great contest. As held by the English, the place was in the condition of a real fortress, strongly defended; but the Americans, under General Wayne, with fixed bayonets, pressed through a deep morass and a double palisade, and scaled the fort, killing and making prisoners of more than six hundred men.

Toward the close of the year, Sir Henry Clinton embarked from New York with a force of between seven and eight thousand men, for the reduction of Charleston. The American troops, under the command of General Lincoln, made all the defence they were able; but it became at length apparent that the superiority was on the side of the enemy, and that the place could not be maintained. Acquiescing in the necessity of a surrender, General Lincoln presented terms of capitulation, which being accepted, the American army, of five thousand men, together with the inhabitants of the place, and four hundred pieces of artillery, were surrendered to the British. Soon after this occurrence, Sir Henry Clinton left four thousand men, for the southern service, under Lord Cornwallis, and returned to New York. The presence of the British in different parts of South Carolina was intended to overawe the inhabitants, and to enforce their submission to the royal government. These purposes however, were but indifferently accomplished. The brave General Sumpter made several attacks upon the enemy, and with considerable success. In one instance, he nearly annihilated a British regiment. In the mean while, a considerable body of American troops was advancing through the Middle States for the relief of the south.

General Gates, the hero of Stillwater, was now placed at the head of the southern army, General Lincoln having been superseded. This army, however, amounted only to four thousand men, and was inadequate to the defence of that portion of the country. As it approached South Carolina, Lord Rawdon, who commanded on the frontier under Lord Cornwallis, concentrated the royal forces at Camden, one hundred and twenty miles north-west from Charleston. Here Cornwallis, on learning the movements of the Americans, joined him. The American and British forces met on the morning of the 16th of August, 1780. The battle which ensued proved disastrous to the Americans, chiefly through the failure of the militia. A large body of the Virginia militia threw down their arms and fled, as they were approached by the British infantry with fixed bayonets. This example was followed by a considerable part of the North Carolina militia; but the continental troops played their part manfully. They yielded only when forsaken by their brethren, and when it was impossible, from want of numbers, to maintain their ground. Such was the battle of Camden; and scarcely was there a more bloody conflict during the revolutionary struggle. So far as could be ascertained, between six and seven hundred Americans were killed, and thirteen or fourteen hundred wounded and taken prisoners.

This sad result threw a temporary gloom over the American people; but the face of affairs soon after began to be more bright and cheering. The insolence and rapacity of the enemy, upon experiencing ephemeral success, only inspirited the real friends of independence to more strenuous and unremitted efforts. The campaign of 1780 was indeed disastrous in the south, nor in the north were affairs in a train at all favorable. The year passed away in the endurance of the alarms and distresses incident to a state of warfare, even where there occur no great and ruinous battles. At the north, in particular, the continued predatory incursions of the enemy brought to the inhabitants the usual amount of loss, disappointment, and suffering. There were, however, a few occurrences of a different complexion, as, for instance, the arrival of M. de Ternay at Rhode Island, on the 10th of July, from France. He brought a squadron of seven sail of the line, five frigates, and five smaller armed vessels, with several transports, and six thousand men, all under the command of Lieutenant-General de Rochambeau. The joy and expectations excited by this event cannot be easily conceived; but these were not fully borne out, as the superiority of the British fleet prevented that of the French, and the French army, for a considerable time, from coöperating with the Americans.

The latter part of the year 1780 was signalized by the treason of Arnold, the American general, who by his bravery had endeared himself to the American people. In consequence of his wounds, he was obliged to retire from active service, and was appointed to the post of commandant of Philadelphia. Here the energies which had been expended in war were devoted to gambling, luxurious living, and every species of expensive pleasure. To supply the means for such a mode of life, various expedients were resorted to, and some not the most creditable. At length, by his exactions as a public officer, he was brought to trial before a court martial, by whose sentence he received the reprimand of Washington.

In this condition of his affairs, Arnold, now bankrupt in character as well as in fortune, was prepared for any desperate undertaking, especially if it should bring gold into his private coffers. Where could the supply be found but from Britain? This thought, as well as the desire of revenge upon congress and his country, prompted him to the act which has consigned his name to eternal infamy. He made known his intention indirectly to Sir Henry Clinton, and by the latter was directed to seek the command of the fortress at West Point, in order that, as the most important place to be secured by an enemy, he might deliver it to the British. Having obtained this post, he adopted such measures as were calculated to effect the object in view. Happily for America, the plot was discovered in season to prevent the ruinous consequences that must have ensued. Major Andre, an elegant and accomplished young man, the aide-de-camp of General Clinton, who had been intrusted by him with the negotiation on this subject, was taken, and, after a fair trial, was executed on the 2d of October, as a spy.

We are under the necessity of passing over many interesting details relating to this affair. Andre was taken by three humble soldiers of the militia, whose names were John Paulding, David Williams, and Isaac Van Wert, and who, though plied by every argument and every bribe that might be expected to influence men of that class, resolutely refused to give him up. They were well rewarded by their country for this act of noble patriotism. It may be added, that the necessity of putting Andre to death, and upon the gallows, according to the example which had been set by the British, was deeply regretted on both sides of the Atlantic; Britain has found it difficult to forget, or even to forgive the act, but America stands justified before an impartial world. It was a matter of much chagrin and disappointment that Arnold escaped, and received from the British the reward of his villany and treachery. This reward was ten thousand pounds, and the rank of a brigadier-general. An exchange of Andre for Arnold would have been readily assented to on the part of the Americans; but Clinton would not consent to give up the traitor. A hazardous attempt was made by Sergeant-Major Champe to take him, but it failed.

After the battle of Camden, Cornwallis was unfortunate in the defeat of Ferguson by the mountaineers of North Carolina. The course of this officer, who had been sent into the state, had been so marked by devastation and ruin, that the inhabitants were determined no longer to submit to his atrocities. Under Campbell and others, he and his forces were completely overthrown. This event induced Cornwallis to retreat to South Carolina. Here the British troops were harassed by Colonel Sumpter on all sides. During the period of these transactions, General Gates exerted himself to collect new troops, and had greatly improved the condition of the American army in that quarter. But he had not been successful in the southern war, and, in consequence of a request from the south, he was superseded by General Greene. It was at this period, that Arnold made a descent upon Virginia, to aid the enterprises of the British in that state and in North Carolina. His favorite employment now appeared to be the devastation of his country.

America was now in an exhausted condition, and the perplexities of congress in supplying the wants of the army were nearly insuperable. They were almost without an army, and wholly without money. Their bills of credit had ceased to be of any value; and they were reduced to the mortifying necessity of declaring, by their own acts, that this was the fact, as they made them no longer a legal tender, or received them in payment of taxes. Without money of some kind, an army could neither be raised nor maintained. But the greater the exigency, the greater were the exertions of this determined band of patriots. Directions were given to their agents abroad to borrow money, if possible, on the continent. They also resorted, though reluctantly, to the unpopular measure of laying a direct tax, in order to raise money. To manage the fiscal concerns of the country, and to prevent the disorder, waste, and peculation, which had prevailed to an alarming extent, they appointed, for treasurer, Robert Morris, of Philadelphia, a gentleman of eminent purity of character, patriotism, and financial ability. His genius soon extricated the country from much of its pecuniary embarrassment. By obtaining a national bank, he secured a circulating medium of intrinsic value to the community. Abroad, Franklin procured a gift of six millions of livres from Louis XVI., and a loan of ten millions from Holland.

Before the result of these measures was fully felt, a revolt of the Pennsylvania line took place, threatening the utmost calamity to the republic. Their sufferings, from want, had induced them to assume this formidable attitude; but, by a pacific course, and by an early attention to their demands, they were pacified, and returned to their duty. But this example was contagious, and a similar revolt, a few days after, by the troops of New Jersey, was treated in a different manner. Washington saw the necessity of crushing it at once. This he did with a force so powerful as compelled immediate submission. On the leaders he inflicted condign punishment. No sedition was heard of afterward in the army. The Pennsylvania revolt occurred on the first day of the year 1781.

In the mean time, the war was carried on with vigor at the south. On the 17th of January, Colonel Morgan defeated the impetuous Tarleton in the battle at Cowpens, the latter having been detached, by Cornwallis, to oppose the American colonel, with a corps of eleven hundred men and two field-pieces. The British had three hundred killed and wounded, while the Americans had only twelve men killed and sixty wounded — an unusual disparity of loss. Morgan was immediately pursued by Cornwallis, but was saved by the sudden rise of the River Catawba, after Morgan had passed it, and before Cornwallis had reached it. It was then not fordable. On the 9th of February, the two divisions of the American army, under Greene and Huger, effected a junction at Guilford. Here a battle was fought, on the 15th of March, between Greene and Cornwallis, in which, though the Americans lost some thirteen hundred men, and were obliged to retreat, they were essentially the conquerors. Cornwallis in consequence of his losses, found himself unable to follow up his temporary advantage. He left the field, and Greene was now in a situation to pursue, harassing the rear of the enemy. But he soon altered his course, and proceeded to South Carolina. Cornwallis marched toward Petersburg, in Virginia.

In South Carolina, the British, under Lord Rawdon, who had been left in command there, were much annoyed by Sumpter and Marion; and, though the Americans were surprised and defeated in a fight at Hobkirk's Hill, they soon found themselves able to act on the aggressive. On the 10th of May, Lord Rawdon evacuated Camden. Soon after, several places held by the British were either taken or capitulated, and the fort of Ninety-Six, being found not capable of withstanding a regular siege, was abandoned. As the summer proved to be uncommonly hot and sickly, the belligerents were obliged to suspend their operations. They met, however, on the 8th of September, at Eutaw Springs, where one of the most vigorous and bloody battles of the war was fought; it was also the last conflict of any note at the south. The attack was made by General Greene, who had drawn up his forces with great skill. The British were routed, and fled; but, as they found in their flight the means of shelter, from a large house and some other objects, they rallied, and repulsed the assailants with considerable loss. As they could not well be dislodged, Greene retired from the place with five hundred prisoners. Five hundred others were killed and wounded. The loss of the Americans was six hundred. The conduct of General Greene called forth the approbation of congress, and the present of a conquered standard and a medal. Georgia and South Carolina were now recovered by the Americans, except their capitals.

As Arnold, at the beginning of the year, (1781,) was ravaging the Virginia coast, an attempt was made by Washington to obtain possession of the traitor and his force. For this purpose, Lafayette was sent toward Virginia, with twelve hundred light infantry, while the commander of the French fleet at Rhode Island despatched a squadron of eight sail of the line to cut off the retreat of Arnold from the Chesapeake. But a squadron of equal force was sent by Clinton, and, the two fleets meeting, a fight ensued, in which neither party could be said to claim the victory. The French, however, were constrained to relinquish their design.

The British armies, in the latter part of May, had formed a junction at Petersburg, and Cornwallis directed his march into the interior of Virginia, believing that the Americans were too weak and dispersed to interpose any serious resistance. Lafayette, however, who had the chief command of the separate republican troops, was able to annoy the British leader, frequently hanging upon his rear, without once coming to a general engagement, in which event the superiority of the foe as to numbers would have been disastrously felt. Cornwallis did not remain long in the interior of Virginia. He was recalled to the sea-coast by an order from Sir Henry Clinton, who had become apprehensive that the Americans and French meditated an attack on New York, and he required three thousand of Cornwallis's army to join the garrison in that city. This requisition, however, was soon countermanded, as a supply of troops had, meanwhile, been received from Germany.

Cornwallis, now near the Virginian shore, selected for his post the village of Yorktown, situated on the right bank of York River. This place he entered on the 23d of August. Washington had designed, indeed, an attack on New York; but, being disappointed as to the number of regular troops that were to have been raised, and influenced by other reasons, he suddenly changed his plan, and bent all his energies to take Cornwallis in the snare which he seemed laying for himself. Washington completely deceived Clinton, keeping up the appearance of a design upon New York. Rochambeau, with five thousand men, had joined him from Rhode Island, early in July. While the British were expecting the arrival of Count de Grasse at New York, Washington crossed the Hudson, and, contriving still further to deceive Clinton as to his ultimate object, had soon made progress too far south to be arrested by the British commander. He arrived at the head of Elk River on the 25th of August, only one hour after De Grasse entered the mouth of the Chesapeake, with twenty-five sail of the line. The mouths of the York and James Rivers were immediately blocked up, and thus all communication between the British at Yorktown and New York was cut off.

A communication was now opened with Lafayette, whose army was increased by the addition of three thousand light troops, under the marquis de St. Simon. On the 14th of September, Washington and Rochambeau joined Lafayette at Williamsburg. Cornwallis had strengthened his works, but had little hope of escape, except from Clinton. He was able, by some means, to communicate with the latter; and, though Clinton sought to make a diversion in his favor, by projecting an expedition against New London, in Connecticut, under Arnold, yet Washington was not thereby induced to quit his post at the south. Cornwallis, in the expectation of receiving succor from Clinton, called in his outposts, and withdrew within his defences, thus committing what was deemed a great error by many of his officers. They had advised his crossing the river, and regaining the open country, so as to proceed to New York. He delayed, however, and all was lost.

The combined army now moved upon him, and Yorktown was besieged. They commenced their works on the night of the 6th of October. On the 14th, two redoubts of the enemy were attacked and taken, though with loss to the allies, and particularly to the French. A vigorous sortie was made by the British on the night of the 16th, under General Abercrombie; two batteries were taken from the allies, and eleven cannon were spiked. The enemy were, however, driven back by a furious charge from the French. In this state of his affairs, Cornwallis attempted to escape in the way which, at an early period of his embarrassments, had been recommended to him, and which, had it been taken, might have been successful. He partially accomplished the object, as it was, having conveyed one division of his forces over the river, and placed a second one upon it. But, just at this crisis, the night, which had been favorable thus far, grew suddenly tempestuous. The sky became dark, and the water ruffled and agitated, and the boats were driven down the river. In this situation, they were discovered by the besiegers, who opened upon the scattered and weakened army a destructive fire. They hastened, as might be supposed, their return to the fort.

No hope of escape being left, Cornwallis was disposed to treat for a surrender. His terms were not allowed. The only indulgence that was obtained, by the most earnest persuasion, was a permission for a sloop, laden with such persons as he should select, to be allowed to pass free to New York, he being accountable for the number of persons it conveyed as prisoners of war. The whole remaining British force was to be surrendered to the allies. This was accordingly done on the 19th of October. Beside seamen, there were seven thousand men, who surrendered with sixty-two pieces of cannon, all of which fell into the hands of the Americans. Two frigates, and twenty transports, with their crews, came into the possession of the French. Clinton had set out by sea for the succor of Cornwallis on the day of the capitulation. On arriving off the capes of Virginia, he heard of the surrender, and immediately returned to New York.

Upon this event, unbounded joy filled the bosoms of the Americans. The names of Washington, Rochambeau, De Grasse, and Lafayette, were upon all lips; nor was the name of the great Deliverer of oppressed nations forgotten in his temples, as the grateful prayer and anthem were there poured forth. The war may be considered as having substantially closed upon the fall of Cornwallis. The British still held a few important posts — New York, Charleston, and Savannah; but all other parts of the country, which had been held by the enemy, were recovered into the power of congress. Only a few unimportant contests subsequently occurred. A part of the French soon after reëmbarked, and Count de Grasse sailed for the West Indies. The army under Rochambeau were cantoned in Virginia for the winter of 1782, and the main body of the Americans returned to their former position on the Hudson. Before the conclusion of the year 1781, the generous and chivalrous Lafayette had embarked for his native country. America was filled with admiration of his virtues.

England, now wearied with the war, sought the boon of peace. The way was at length opened for the attainment of this object. Commissioners were appointed by congress for negotiating peace with Great Britain. These were met at Paris by those of Great Britain, and provisional articles of peace were signed November 30, 1782; a definitive treaty was signed on the 3d of September, 1783. On the 3d of November following, the army of the United States was disbanded; Washington issued his farewell orders, and bid an affectionate adieu to the soldiers who had achieved, with him and his fellow-officers, the independence of their country. From those officers, soon after, the separation was still more tender and painful The scene will ever be held in remembrance.

CHAPTER CCCCLXXXIX.

A. D. 1783 to 1801.

Constitutional Period. — *Condition of the Country subsequently to the Revolution — Insurrections — Convention to form a new Government — Ratification of the Constitution — Washington chosen President, &c.*

From the conclusion of the war with Great Britain to the organization of the new government, America passed through a crisis scarcely less fearful than the revolution itself. It was for a long time doubtful whether the expected fruits of the great and successful struggle would be secured, or all would be lost in the disunion, anarchy, and contentions of the separate states, and beneath the load of pecuniary obligations which pressed upon them all. Great as was the exultation at first felt and expressed on the return of peace,

George Washington.

the most painful apprehensions, especially among the more reflecting, were entertained in regard to the future. Clouds and darkness rested upon it. There had been, already, intimations of the evils that might ensue from the dispositions of many in the army, particularly of some of the more ambitious officers. From this quarter had come an insidious proposal to Washington, to assume kingly authority. The temptation was repelled with the magnanimity becoming this greatest of patriots, and he hastened at the earliest opportunity, December 22, 1783, to resign to congress his commission as commander-in-chief of the American army. The disbanding of the army on the 3d of the previous month, had been a matter of difficulty, for the reasons now adverted to, aided indeed, by their unparalleled destitution and sufferings. They wished to be assured that justice should be done them by their country, and that their meritorious services should meet with a due reward. Washington pledged, for this end, all his influence with the national legislature, and with that, these heroic men were satisfied.

Congress had done what it could; but its power was limited, and its resources inconsiderable. The government was poor, and the states, having separate interests and separate views, were divided among themselves. Hence, though, by the patriotism and address of Washington, the danger arising from a suffering and discontented army was happily passed, yet there were elements, in the condition of the country at large, which portended the greatest disaster. A heavy debt encumbered the government, and a similar burden rested upon almost every corporation within it. Agriculture, trade, and manufactures, had decayed during the war, and many of the inhabitants were nearly destitute of clothing and the necessaries of life. Immediately after the peace was announced, the British sent over a great quantity of cloths, of an inferior quality, which were sold at an exorbitant price; and thus almost all the money of the country was collected and carried abroad The nation being in debt, and destitute of the means of payment, heavy taxes were necessarily imposed.

Such a state of things led, at length, to insurrections In Massachusetts, where a heavy tax was laid with a view to sustain its credit and satisfy its creditors, several attempts were made, by people convened in tumultuous assemblies, to obstruct the sitting of courts; and finally, they took up arms in opposition to the laws of the state. The discreet measures of Governor Bowdoin and his council, seconded by an armed force of four thousand men under General Lincoln, in the winter of 1786, gradually put down the spirit of resistance, and restored the authority of the laws. This rising of the people in that state, is usually styled *Shays's Insurrection*, as one Daniel Shays, a captain in the revolutionary army, was at its head. A few lives only were lost in the skirmishing which took place. Some fourteen of the rioters were convicted and sentenced to death, but were finally pardoned.

It became apparent, soon after the peace, that the general government needed greater strength. John Adams, then in Europe, suggested to congress the expediency of adopting some plan for this purpose In 1786, a convention of delegates, from five of the Middle States, met at Annapolis, who came to the conclusion that nothing short of a thorough reform of the existing government would be sufficient to ensure public peace and prosperity. The bond of federal union became weak and feeble, after the pressure of the common danger had been removed. The beginning of jealousy between the state and general governments was quite visible, and the interests of the former predominated. The local situation of some of the states was favorable for commerce, and they took advantage of it by levying contributions on their neighbors. Congress had no power to enforce the observance of treaties which it could make, or to compel the collection of money for the payment of debts which it could contract. Nothing could be more opportune, in this state of things, than the expressed convictions of the Annapolis convention. Congress approved their proceedings, and passed a resolution, recommending a general convention of delegates, to be held in Philadelphia.

This convention accordingly met in May, 1787 George Washington, one of the delegates from Virginia, was unanimously chosen its president. The convention had met, in effect, to form a system of government for a vast empire; and such an assemblage of men, for such an object, was a novel spectacle in the world. All eyes were turned upon it. It was concluded, without much difficulty, that, instead of amending the articles of confederation, a new constitution should be formed. This was a work demanding almost superhuman wisdom, prudence, and virtue; but by the divine blessing, it was accomplished. A more nearly perfect instrument than the constitution of the United States, as it was finally settled and adopted, never came from the hands of men. But the object was reached only through long and arduous debates, important mutual concessions, and the sacrifice of cherished private and state interests. The difficulties before the convention seemed nearly insurmountable, and at times there was danger of the entire failure of the object. The great party lines which have existed through the whole period of the constitutional history of this country, began then to be drawn—the division being between those who desired the strength and constraint which border on a well-regulated monarchy, and those who preferred the looser bonds and greater liberty of the old confederation. In the constitution, as it was actually framed, and as it ought to be interpreted, it is believed that the true medium was secured. Some of the members of the convention, and a portion of the community, at the time, thought that it made the government too strong, and that eventually it would overturn the liberties of America. Others feared that it created a government too weak to continue for any great length of time—indeed, that it would prove to be little better than a "rope of sand." These divisions became the foundation of the two great parties, called *Democrats* and *Federalists.*

Of the fifty-five members who composed the convention, thirty-nine signed the constitution. Some of the remaining sixteen, who were in favor of it, were called away by the urgency of their private affairs, before the constitution was ready for signatures. The new system was transmitted to congress, accompanied by a letter from Washington, recommending it as the best which the convention, in the essential difficulties of the case, could frame. There is no space here for a detailed view of the constitution, or even of its great outlines. It may only be observed, to show its difference from the articles of confederation, that it is a system reaching every individual in the community, and making them all amenable to the general laws. By the former articles of confederation, *the states* entered into "a firm league of friendship with each other, for their common defence, the security of their liberties, and their mutual and general welfare," &c. By the new constitution, as the preamble declares, "*the people*" united, and established a government, to insure domestic tranquillity, provide for the general welfare, and secure the blessings of liberty for themselves and their posterity. The convention recommended that the constitution should be submitted to state conventions, and that, as soon as the same should be ratified by a constitutional majority, which had been fixed at nine of the states, congress should take measures for the election of a president, and appoint the time for commencing operations under it. There was an immediate compliance with the requisition.

The new system came before the state conventions in 1787 and 1788. It was adopted unanimously by Georgia, New Jersey, and Delaware, and by large majorities in Pennsylvania, Connecticut, Maryland, and South Carolina. Rhode Island called no convention, and it was for a time doubtful whether the other states would assent to it, without previous amendments. At length, however, such was the urgency of the case, that small majorities were induced to yield their assent, trusting to future amendments.

The national legislature, under the constitution, convened at New York on the 4th of March, 1789, and consisted of senators and representatives from eleven states. On counting the electoral votes, it appeared that *George Washington* was unanimously chosen president, and John Adams elected vice-president. Informed of his election by a special messenger, Washington left his beloved retirement at Mount Vernon for the seat of government. On his way, he received from the people unbounded tokens of gratitude and veneration. The oath of office was administered on the 30th of April, by the chancellor of the state of New York, amid assembled thousands. It was a joyful and magnificent scene, and as the commencement of a new order of things in the political world, will be ever memorable. The president's inaugural address was replete with all that wisdom, purity, and patriotism could suggest. Immediately after the delivery of the address, Washington, with the members of both houses, attended divine service at St. Paul's Chapel. In this manner, the government commenced under the new constitution.

Congress, during its first session, was principally occupied in providing revenues for the treasury, in establishing a judiciary, in organizing the executive departments in detail, and in framing amendments to the constitution, in compliance with the suggestion of the president. The members entered at once upon the exercise of their powers under the new system. They imposed a tonnage duty, as also duties on various articles of importation. The navigating interest of the country claimed also a due proportion of their attention. Three several executive departments were established, styled departments of War, of Foreign Affairs, and of the Treasury, with a secretary at the head of each. Mr. Jefferson was placed at the head of the first, Mr Hamilton of the second, and Mr. Knox of the last. John Jay was appointed chief justice, and the associate judges of the Supreme Court were John Rutledge, James Wilson, William Cushing, Robert H. Harrison, and John Blair. Edmund Randolph was appointed attorney-general.

A day of thanksgiving was observed throughout the United States, on the occasion of the peaceable establishment of a constitution of government. Before the time of the next meeting of congress, the state of North Carolina accepted the constitution. The proceedings of the first congress—of which further mention cannot here be given—were generally approved, and the benefits of the new government speedily began to be realized.

The proceedings of the next congress, which met on the 1st of January, 1790, were marked by acts of deep importance, though perhaps by more diversity of opinion in regard to several measures. Those pertaining to the support of public credit, and particularly the assumption of the state debts, excited a long and anxious debate. The state of Virginia, through its legislature, censured the proceedings of the general government. Among other things, congress directed an enumeration of the inhabitants to be made on the first Monday of August, 1790, and established a uniform rule of naturalization, as also a fund for sinking the national debt. In May, 1790, the state of Rhode Island adopted the constitution,—the last of the old thirteen. This session did not close until August 12, 1790.

The admission of two new states into the Union was one of the first acts of the new session, which commenced on the first Monday of December following. These states were Vermont and Kentucky. The first was received on the 4th of March, 1791; the other on the 1st of June, 1792. The most important measures of this session were the establishment of a national bank, and the imposition of a tax on spirits distilled within the United States, from foreign and domestic materials. These measures did not pass without much opposition.

In the midst of the difficulties of the new government in its public councils, an Indian war opened on the north-western frontier of the states. The president had attempted pacific arrangements with the hostile tribes, but without success. Resort to force was now determined on. General Harmar was sent with a force amounting to fourteen hundred men, to effect their subjection. He succeeded in destroying the villages of the Indians, and the produce of their fields; but in an engagement near Chillicothe, he was defeated with no small loss. The successor of Harmar, Major-General Arthur St. Clair, was even more unfortunate. In a battle with the Indians near the Miami, in Ohio, he was totally defeated, on the 4th of November, 1792.

Upon the news of this disaster, the second congress, which was then in session, passed an act for raising three additional regiments of infantry, and a squadron of cavalry, to serve for three years, if not sooner discharged. This bill met with an opposition more warm and imbittered, from the opposers of the administration, than had been witnessed on any former occasion. Party spirit, with its asperities, had now become but too apparent in the national legislature, and through its members in the country at large. Dissent was plainly expressed against the plans of government adopted by Washington and his cabinet. During the next session of congress, several attempts were made to affix an odium on the measures of the president, especially through an attack on his secretary, Mr. Hamilton, by Mr. Giles, of Virginia; but these were successfully resisted.

General Washington was again elected president in 1793, by a unanimous vote, although he had consented with great reluctance to stand as a candidate for reëlection. At the same time, Mr. Adams was again chosen vice-president. It was fortunate for the United States that Washington was placed at the head of the government at this crisis. It required, in a chief magistrate, all the wisdom and firmness for which he was so distinguished, as well as all that popularity and weight of character which he had so richly deserved. The French revolution had been in progress for some time, and a war had broken out between France and England. The French, in their ardor for liberty, imagined themselves destined to carry the torch of freedom into all lands. It was evidently their intention to draw the United States into their quarrel with England. But Washington, foreseeing that such a step would compromise the interests of his country, issued, on the 22d of April, a proclamation of neutrality. The wisdom of the measure was soon apparent, although it was at first bitterly denounced by the opposition.

The American people wished, indeed, success to the French in their struggle for liberty; and the first appearance of the French revolution they hailed with a feeling of delight. But the bloody excesses of the revolutionists soon crushed the hopes that had been entertained, and at length disgusted most of the sober and reflecting people. Soon after the execution of the French king, M. Genet was sent as minister to the United States. He was a man of more passion than judgment, and more selfishness than regard of right. He seems to have considered his office as a mission to stir up the people of the United States to a war with the enemies of France.

Genet landed at Charleston, purposely avoiding an interview with Washington, so that he might be left free, for a time at least, to prosecute his plans. He at once proceeded to acts violating the rules of international law, by commissioning armed vessels from Charleston to cruise against the British. When these proceedings were known at the seat of government, Washington interposed his authority. This, Genet had the impudence to resent, and he attempted to excite a popular clamor against it, by a variety of publications appealing to the passions and caprices of the multitude. Encouraged by numbers of unthinking adherents, he became so insolent, that Washington required the French government to order him home.

Fauchet and Adet, successors of Genet, were more moderate in their conduct, but their designs were the same, and their agency mischievous in the end. During the session of congress in 1794, a resolution passed to provide a naval force adequate to the protection of the commerce of the country against the Algerine corsairs, which had become troublesome; also a law passed in prohibition of the slave trade in American ports; several measures were likewise adopted in anticipation of a war with Great Britain, growing out of her commercial restrictions, which operated unjustly on the United States. As an adjustment of these difficulties was greatly desired, Mr. Jay was appointed envoy extraordinary to the court of St. James. This gentleman succeeded in negotiating a treaty the following year. The merits of this were canvassed in the senate, at the proper time, and a majority of twenty to ten advised its ratification. The president gave it his signature, after weighing it with much consideration, and notwithstanding the formidable opposition which was made to it in the country. It prevented a war, and its effects, otherwise, were highly beneficial. In the autumn of the same year, (1795,) treaties were made with the dey of Algiers, and with a portion of the western Indians. A treaty with Spain followed soon after, by which, among other things, the navigation of the Mississippi was fully conceded. On the 1st of June, 1796, Tennessee was admitted into the Union as a state, by act of congress.

At this period, when a new election of a president was drawing near, Washington signified his intention to retire from public life. The annunciation was accompanied by a valedictory address to the people of the United States—a production as remarkable for its important political maxims, as for the expression of his inextinguishable love of his country and his kind. His advice to his countrymen cannot be too closely followed.

The successor of Washington in the government was *John Adams*, he having received the highest number of votes in the electoral college. Mr. Jefferson was chosen vice-president. Mr. Adams entered upon the presidency on the 4th of March, 1797. At this period, the country had made evident advances in commerce, wealth, the stability of its institutions, and its consideration among the nations of the earth. The wisdom, firmness, and moderation of Washington had been the means of his country's elevation and opening career of prosperity. Mr. Adams pursued substantially the same policy as that of his predecessor, and as one of the leaders in the revolution, he seemed competent to guide the helm of state.

John Adams.

The United States having come to a serious issue with the French republic, owing to the treatment of their ambassador, Mr. Pinckney, by the latter power, Mr. Adams, soon after his accession, sent three envoys extraordinary to Paris, to attempt a second negotiation. The Directory managed to delay the public recognition of them in their official capacity, but, in an indirect manner, demanded a large sum of money as a preliminary to negotiation. This being promptly refused, Messrs. Pinckney and Marshall, two of the envoys, were ordered to quit the country; but, Mr. Gerry, the third one, was allowed to remain. Attempts to negotiate with him, singly, did not succeed, and he was soon after called home by his government.

These events were followed by such French depredations on the American commerce as excited universal indignation, and the general motto was, "Millions for defence — not a cent for tribute." A regular provisional army was established by congress, taxes were raised, and additional internal duties laid. General Washington, at the call of congress, left his peaceful abode once more, to command the armies of his country. General Hamilton was made second in command. The navy was increased, and reprisals were made at sea. The French frigate L'Insurgente, of forty guns, was captured, after a desperate action, by the frigate Constellation, of thirty-eight guns, commanded by Commodore Truxton — a victory which gave great satisfaction to both political parties in America.

There being now indications of a desire of peace on the part of the French government, envoys were sent to Paris, by Mr. Adams, to effect so desirable an object. Finding the Directory overthrown, and Bonaparte at the head of the government, the envoys had no difficulty in adjusting all disputes by a treaty concluded at Paris, on the 30th of September, 1800. The disbanding of the American provisional army followed soon after.

But a great calamity had in the mean time fallen on the American people. The Father of his Country had been called from life, by a short and distressing sickness. Washington, on the 14th of December, 1799, expired at his seat at Mount Vernon, in Virginia. A nation was clad in mourning, and every possible honor was paid to the memory of him who was "first in war, first in peace, and first in the hearts of his countrymen."

In 1800, the city of Washington, in the District of Columbia, was made the seat of the general government, in accordance with a law passed by congress in 1790. For that purpose, the states of Virginia and Maryland had ceded to the United States the District, a territory of ten miles square. It may here be stated that the Virginia portion was receded to Virginia in 1846.

As the time again approached for the election of a president, the progress of popular opinion, in respect to Mr. Adams, rendered it highly improbable that the choice would fall on him. All acknowledged his abilities, his patriotism, and the services he had rendered to his country; but at the first, he was simply not preferred by the democratic party, and subsequently, he was disliked by it. The measures which most excited the opposition of that party, and which were most successfully employed against Mr. Adams as a candidate for reëlection, were several laws passed during his presidency, among which were the *alien* and *sedition* laws.

From the mode of voting, which existed at that time, it became for several days doubtful who would be president, or whether any choice would be made within the limits assigned by the constitution, as there happened to be a tie of the two highest numbers in the electoral college, and afterward a tie in the votes of the house of representatives. But the choice eventually fell on Mr. Jefferson. Aaron Burr was elected vice-president.

CHAPTER CCCCXC.

A. D. 1801 to 1817.

Mr. Jefferson President — Purchase of Louisiana — War with Tripoli — Exposure of Neutral Commerce on the High Seas — Mr. Madison President — War with England, &c.

Mr. Jefferson was inaugurated on the 4th of March, 1801. Instead of delivering a speech, in person, to the two houses of congress, as his predecessors had done, he sent to them a written message, which was read to them in succession — a practice which has since been generally followed. The message contained his political opinions, and intimations of the course he intended to pursue as chief magistrate, and was much read and commented on at the time. In the beginning of his administration, Mr. Jefferson transferred the principal offices of the government to members of the democratic party. Mr. Madison was made secretary of state.

At the opening of congress on the 8th of December, the president, in his message, recommended the abolition of the internal taxes, the repeal of the act passed in the last days of Mr. Adams's administration, a reorganization of the United States courts with sixteen new judges, and an enlargement of the rights of naturalization. These topics awakened the asperity of party feeling in a high degree; but the recommendations of the executive prevailed, and bills were passed accordingly. The year 1802 was signalized by the admission of Ohio into the Union, as an independent state. The following year became an era in our history, by the magnificent enlargement of our territory, in the cession of Louisiana to us by France. It was purchased of that nation at the price of fifteen millions of dollars. Louisiana comprised an immense region of country extending from the Mississippi to the Pacific Ocean. Of course, the free and exclusive navigation of the river was ceded with it.

Thomas Jefferson.

Mr. Jefferson was reëlected to the office of president, and took the oath required by the constitution on the 4th of March, 1805. George Clinton, of New York, was elevated to the vice-presidency. A war with Tripoli, on the southern shore of the Mediterranean, on account of depredations upon American commerce, had commenced in 1801. In the course of this war, one of the American frigates accidentally fell into the hands of the Tripolitans. By a most daring enterprise, under the direction of Lieutenant Stephen Decatur, the frigate was afterward seized in the harbor of Tripoli, by a band of Americans, under the guns of the enemy's battery. But as it was grounded, and could not be brought away, they set it on fire. The officers of the frigate had been imprisoned, and the crew treated as slaves. The cruelties of their captivity induced the Americans to put forth every effort for their relief, and to punish the barbarians. This was effected in a great measure by the exploits of Captain William Eaton. Attacking the Tripolitans on land, with a few hundred Arab troops, he brought them to terms. Prisoners were exchanged, though, as the bashaw had the greater number, he received an indemnity, in money, for the balance.

The neutrality of America, during the wars of the French revolution, brought to her wealth and prosperity — as she enjoyed the carrying trade of a great part of the world. But both of the belligerents, at length, treated neutrals with singular injustice. They were resolved that other nations should make common cause with them. For this purpose were the celebrated French and English *Decrees* issued. Great Britain issued a proclamation, May, 1806, blockading the coast of the continent from the Elbe to Brest. Enraged at this measure, the French government retaliated by the Decree issued at Berlin, November 21, declaring the British Isles in a state of blockade. This was in effect a declaration on the part of each, that no neutral should trade with the other. In November, 1807, Great Britain issued her *Orders in Council* — a measure declared to be in retaliation of the French Decree of November. These orders prohibited all neutral nations from trading with France or her allies, except upon the condition of paying tribute to England. Napoleon immediately followed this by a Decree at Milan, which declared that every vessel which should submit to be searched, or pay tribute to the English, should be confiscated, if found within his ports.

Between America and Great Britain, in particular, there were questions of the highest moment respecting the "right of search," and expatriation. The latter power, on various pretences, had long claimed and assumed the authority of searching the vessels of other nations, in order to take her native born people and this she did on the ground, that no man can change his allegiance to the government under which he was born. Britons could never be otherwise than British subjects. America held a very different doctrine, and received as her citizens the subjects of other governments, whenever they chose her protection. Being naturalized, they were, to all intents and purposes, her citizens. These, however, if British, by birth, were seized wherever the British could find them in order to man their navy; nor were these alone taken but native born Americans, in many instances. The latter was a wrong and an indignity which could not be endured, and greatly aggravated the existing difficulties between the United States and Britain.

It was in pursuance of their measures of impressment, that an outrage was committed by the British, 22d of June, 1807, on an American armed vessel, the Chesapeake, which was fired into by a British ship of war, the Leopard. As the attack, being in a time of peace, was wholly unexpected, the commander of the Chesapeake made no resistance, but soon ordered his colors to be struck. The frigate, however, did not become a prize to the Leopard, but certain men, claimed to be British subjects, were taken out of her. Great excitement was produced by this occurrence. The president of the United States, by proclamation, commanded all British armed vessels within our harbors, or waters, to depart from the same without delay, and others were prohibited from coming in. Other measures also were taken, expressive of the public sense of the injury which had been done.

By the decrees before alluded to, the commerce of America was exposed to utter destruction. Congress, though after an exhibition of much party feeling, laid an embargo (December 22, 1807) on our own vessels, as a measure calculated to be serviceable in this state of things. Mr. Monroe, the American minister in London, was instructed not only to require satisfaction on account of the Chesapeake, but to obtain security against future impressment from American vessels. The British minister — Mr. Canning — objected to the union of these subjects; but an envoy-extraordinary was sent out to the United States to adjust the affair of the Chesapeake.

James Madison, of Virginia, was elected president in 1809, and Mr. Clinton, of New York, was again chosen vice-president. The embargo, proving to be extremely unpopular in all the commercial states, was repealed on the 1st of March, 1809. As a substitute for it, congress interdicted by law all trade with France and England, and on the 12th of April, passed an act to raise an additional military force. On the 23d of April, Mr. Erskine, the British minister plenipotentiary, pledged his court to repeal its anti-neutral decrees by the 10th of June, and in consequence of an arrangement now made with the British minister, the president proclaimed that commercial intercourse would be renewed on that day; but this arrangement was not acknowledged by the king. Mr. Erskine was recalled in October, and was succeeded by Mr. Jackson. The latter soon gave offence to the American government, and all further communication with him was refused. Shortly after he was recalled.

James Madison.

The Rambouillet Decree, alleged to be a measure of retaliation for the act of congress which forbade French vessels to enter the ports of the United States, was issued by Napoleon on the 23d of March, 1810. By this, all American vessels and cargoes arriving in any of the ports of France, or of countries occupied by French troops, were ordered to be seized and condemned. On the 1st of May, congress passed an act excluding British and French armed vessels from the waters of the United States; but providing that if either of the above nations should modify its edicts before the 3d of March, 1811, so that they should cease to violate neutral commerce,—of which fact the president was to give notice by proclamation,—and the other nation should not, within three months after, pursue a similar course, commercial intercourse with the first might be renewed, but not with the other. On the 2d of November, the president issued his proclamation, declaring that the French Decrees were revoked, and that intercourse between the United States and France might be renewed. On the 10th of the same month, a proclamation was issued, interdicting commercial intercourse with Great Britain.

On the 12th of November, 1811, reparation was made by the Br sh for the attack on the Chesapeake, through the British envoy, Augustus J. Foster. The message of Mr. Madison to congress that year, on the 5th of November, indicating an apprehension of hostilities with England, the committee of foreign relations, in the House of Representatives, reported, on the 29th, resolutions for filling up the ranks of the army; for raising an additional force of ten thousand men; for authorizing the president to accept the services of fifty thousand volunteers, and for ordering out the militia when he should deem it necessary; for repairing our ships of war, and for authorizing the arming of merchantmen in self-defence. Most of these resolutions were agreed to. A bill from the senate for raising twenty-five thousand men, after much debate, was agreed to by the house.

In December, Mr. Madison communicated to congress an official account of the battle of Tippecanoe, near a branch of the Wabash, fought on the seventh of the previous month, between an army under General Harrison, governor of the Indiana territory, and a large body of Indians. In this battle, the Indians were defeated, though with great difficulty, as they had lulled the suspicions of the whites by a treacherous artifice, in offers of peace and submission. From a want of adequate means and preparation, the Americans suffered a comparatively large loss of men.

On the 3d of April, 1812, a law was passed laying an embargo for ninety days—this measure being in expectation of a war with Great Britain. On the 1st of June following, a war message was communicated to congress by the president. In it, he submitted the question, after having spoken of the impressment of American seamen, the violation of the rights and peace of our coasts by British cruisers, and other causes of difficulty, "whether the United States shall continue passive under these progressive usurpations, and these accumulated wrongs, or, opposing force to force in defence of their national rights, shall commit a just cause into the hands of the Almighty Disposer of events." On the 4th of June, a bill for declaring war with Great Britain passed the house of representatives by a majority of seventy-nine to forty-nine; and on the 17th, it passed the senate by a majority of nineteen to thirteen. The signature of the president and his proclamation of war immediately followed. A protest against the declaration of war was entered by the minority in the house of representatives. It happened that, four days after the declaration, the Decrees of Berlin having been officially revoked, the British orders in council were repealed; but other grounds of difficulty still remained

The feelings of the two parties—democrats and federalists—were wrought up to a high pitch of excitement by the declaration of war. At Baltimore, a mob attacked and destroyed the printing office of a federal paper which zealously opposed that measure of the government. In the fury of the moment, they assailed a house in which several distinguished gentlemen were collected in order to defend themselves. These, after surrendering on a promise of safety, were attacked, and being supposed to be killed, were thrown into a heap. General Lingan, a meritorious officer in the revolutionary war, was killed, and eleven others severely bruised and mangled.

The preparations for war, at the beginning, were in no respect of a promising character. The generation on the stage were mostly inexperienced in it. The army and the navy, in the days of Jefferson, had been reduced to the lowest point; the former amounting to only about three thousand men. The recent sense of danger had aroused the nation somewhat in response to the feeling which began to be awakened. Congress authorized the enlistment of twenty-five thousand men; yet but few entered the service. The want of proper officers was seriously felt, as the leading revolutionary heroes were no more. The navy at this period, was the better arm of defence, having had some experience in the recent contests with the Barbary States; but it was very small. Many enterprising individuals, in the course of the war, converted their merchant ships into privateers; but at its beginning, ten frigates, ten sloops, and one hundred and sixty-five gun boats, were all the public naval force which America could oppose to the thousand ships of the mistress of the ocean. Such were the indifferent preparations for war, at the time of its declaration!

On the 16th of August, 1812, General William Hull, governor of Michigan, to whom had been committed the service of suppressing the Indian hostilities in that country, surrendered his army to the British General Brock, without a battle, and with it the fort of Detroit, together with all other forts and garrisons belonging to the United States, within the district under his command. This was a most mortifying commencement of the contest. Hull's conduct on the occasion was afterward investigated by a court martial; but though the sentence of death was pronounced against him, it was remitted by the president in consideration of his revolutionary services, and his advanced age. This signal disaster to the American arms was, however, immediately relieved by the success of the United States frigate Constitution, in a battle with the British frigate Guerrière, Captain Isaac Hull commanding the Constitution, and Captain Dacres the Guerrière. This victory, which occurred on the 19th of August, was the commencement of a splendid series of triumphs, crowning the naval forces of the United States.

Intelligence soon reached the country of a second naval fight, which took place on the 13th of August, between the United States frigate Essex, Captain Porter, and the British sloop of war Alert, in which the latter struck to the frigate after an action of only eight minutes.

The president, according to an act of congress, having called upon the governors of states for militia to man the fortresses on the maritime frontier, the militia to be placed under officers of his own appointment — the governors of Massachusetts, Connecticut, and Rhode Island, resisted the demand "on the twofold ground that neither of the constitutional exigencies had arisen, and that the militia could not be compelled to serve under any other than their own officers, with the exception of the president himself, when personally in the field."

As a part of a concerted plan for the invasion of Canada, in three divisions — one called the northwestern army, under General Harrison, the second, the army of the centre, under General Stephen Van Rensselaer, and the third, the army of the north, under the commander-in-chief, General Dearborn — a detachment of about one thousand men from the army of the centre crossed the River Niagara, and attacked the British on Queenstown Heights. Though successful at first, General Van Rensselaer was compelled, after a long and obstinate engagement, to surrender, not having been reënforced, as was expected, by the militia from the American side. General Brock, the British commander, was killed in the battle.

On the 17th of October, the Frolic, a British sloop of war, was captured, after a severe engagement, by the Wasp, commanded by Captain Jones. The enemy was decidedly superior in force. The loss on board the Frolic was thirty killed and fifty wounded. The Frolic had no sooner come into the possession of the Americans, than it was taken, together with the Wasp, by a British seventy-four, the Poictiers. A few days after, in the same month, another splendid naval victory was gained, in the capture of the Macedonian, off the Western Isles, a frigate of the largest class, amounting to forty-nine guns, and manned with three hundred men, by Commodore Decatur of the frigate United States. The disparity in the loss of men in this engagement was very great, that of the Macedonian being thirty-six killed and sixty-eight wounded, and that of the United States being only seven killed and five wounded. Yet another naval victory was gained on the 29th of December, by the Constitution, under Commodore Bainbridge, over the Java, a British frigate carrying forty-nine guns, with four hundred men. This was the second victory obtained by the Constitution. The Java was burnt.

The scene of military operations, during the year 1813, was chiefly in the north, toward Canada. General Winchester, of the United States army, and nearly five hundred men, officers and soldiers, were made prisoners at Frenchtown, by a division of the British army from Detroit, under Colonel Proctor. With this force of the enemy a body of Indians was combined. After the surrender, nearly all the American prisoners were inhumanly butchered by the savages, although Proctor had promised that their lives and property should be secure. This calamity fell most heavily on Kentucky, as the victims of the massacre were principally among her most promising sons. The battle of Frenchtown occurred on the 22d of January. At a wide distance from this scene, two days after, an engagement took place between the Hornet, Captain James Lawrence, and the British sloop of war Peacock, off South America. This was a short action of only fifteen minutes, and resulted in the destruction of the Peacock.

Mr. Madison, having been reëlected, entered upon his second term of office, as president of the United States, on the 4th of March, 1813. De Witt Clinton was the opposing candidate. Elbridge Gerry succeeded to the vice-presidency after the death of George Clinton, who had been elected to that office.

On the 27th of April, York, the capital of Upper Canada, was taken by the troops of the United States, under the command of General Dearborn. This enterprise was conducted by General Pike, at his own request. He was conveyed, with seventeen hundred men, on board a flotilla, from Sacket's Harbor, under the command of Commodore Chauncey. On the approach of his troops toward the main work, the explosion of a magazine, previously prepared for the purpose, destroyed the lives of one hundred Americans, as also that of the gallant general himself. Before he expired, however, he was able to direct his troops to "move on!" His orders were obeyed, and the town was taken, with a great loss to the British. The spring passed without any other important event. A portion of the American coas was blockaded, and predatory incursions were made by the enemy in several places, and no inconsiderable amount of property was plundered or destroyed. Several armed vessels of the United States were prevented from sailing on a cruise, being unable to get out of port.

During the following summer, June 1st, the American frigate Chesapeake was captured by the British frigate Shannon, off Boston harbor. In this sanguinary affair, her gallant commander, Captain Lawrence, fell. On the 14th of August, the Argus, of eighteen guns, another of our armed vessels, was taken by the Pelican, of twenty guns. But in the autumn, the tide of victory returned to the Americans. On the 5th of September, the Enterprise mastered the Boxer, after an engagement of somewhat over thirty minutes. In this battle, the commander of each vessel was killed. The month of September is rendered still more memorable, as, on the 10th, a decisive victory was obtained by the American fleet over that of the British on Lake Erie. The conflict was long and desperate, as every motive which national pride and the importance of the issue could supply, actuated the combatants. It was the first instance in which an American fleet had met the fleet of an enemy. The event and the amount of the victory were couched by Perry in these concise, yet remarkable words: "We have met the enemy, and they are ours — two ships, two brigs, one schooner, and one sloop."

The Americans were now masters of the lake, and

Perry's Victory on Lake Erie

an opportunity was soon afforded for General Harrison to attack Proctor, who had hitherto been in possession of the territory in that quarter. Accordingly, on the 5th of October, a severe battle was fought between the two armies, in which the British were defeated. In this battle, the celebrated Indian chief Tecumseh, was killed. Detroit had been somewhat earlier taken possession of by the Americans, and the whole territory of Michigan was again brought under American rule. About this time, there being indications of an attack on New London by the squadron under Commodore Hardy, a portion of the militia of Connecticut was called out by their military commanders. Governor Smith, in approbation of the measure, observed to the legislature of the state, that "the government of Connecticut, the last to invite hostilities, should be the first to repel aggression." Other portions of the American coast at this period were subject to alarms and depredations from the enemy. An attempt to reduce Canada in the latter part of the year, by the combined operation of the several armies in the north and north-west, signally failed. High expectations had been indulged of its success, under generals so approved as Lewis, Hampton, Wilkinson, and Harrison; but obstacles were allowed to prevent their cöoperation, and public opinion was much divided as to the parties on whom the blame of failure should fall.

In the south, the Creek Indians, having been excited to make war against the United States, were guilty of the usual excesses and atrocities of their race during the year 1813, and until the close of the summer of 1814; when General Jackson, who conducted the war on the part of the Americans, signally defeated the savage foe. A treaty was concluded with them, August 9, 1814, on conditions advantageous to the United States. General Jackson was soon after appointed to succeed General Wilkinson in the command of the forces at New Orleans. The loss of the American frigate Essex, under Commodore Porter, in the spring of 1814, was deeply lamented in the United States. It occurred on the 28th of March, in the Bay of Valparaiso, in a fight with a superior British force — two armed vessels, which had been equipped with picked crews for the purpose of attacking the Essex. It was a most unequal engagement, and the Americans lost no credit by the result. Two other naval engagements, took place about this time, both of which issued propitiously to the Americans. The first was between the United States sloop of war

Battle of New Orleans.

Peacock, and the British brig Epervier, April 29th; and the other, the 28th of June, between the sloop of war Wasp and the English brig Reindeer.

During the entire spring, the war seemed to languish on the part of the British; but after their forces were relieved from the continental wars of Europe, they added fourteen thousand veteran troops to those that were already employed against America, and at the same time sent a strong naval armament to blockade the American coast, and ravage every accessible part of it. The northern frontier was now becoming the scene of vigorous movements. On the 3d of July, Fort Erie was taken by General Brown, after the firing of a few shots. On the 5th of July occurred the obstinate and sanguinary battle of Chippewa, in which the Americans, under General Brown, were victorious. This was the first regular pitched battle, and it was fought with great judgment and coolness on both sides. After a short interval — on the 25th of the same month — was fought the destructive battle of Bridgewater, which lasted from four o'clock in the afternoon until midnight. The Americans obtained possession of the battle-ground, but retired from it in the middle of the night to their encampment. General Brown lost in killed, wounded, and missing, from six hundred to seven hundred men. The British General Riall lost about one thousand. On the 15th of August, Fort Erie, in the command of General Gaines, was attacked by the British General Drummond; but he was repulsed with considerable loss. He abandoned the enterprise, after having pressed the siege for forty-nine days.

The seaboard was also a scene of interest and anxiety at this period. About the middle of August, between fifty and sixty British sail arrived in the Chesapeake, with troops destined for the attack of the capital of the United States. On the 23d of that month, six thousand of the enemy, commanded by General Ross, forced their way to Washington, and burnt the Capitol, president's house, and executive offices. These acts of wantonness and Vandalism involved the destruction of valuable libraries, and other articles of taste and importance which the rules of civilized warfare hold to be sacred. The enemy soon found their situation, amid a people exasperated by the scene before them, by no means safe, and they accordingly soon retired to their shipping, having lost, during the expedition, nearly one thousand men. The capture of Washington was followed, September 12th, by an attack on Baltimore, in which the American forces, militia, and inhabitants of Baltimore made a gallant defence. Being, however, overpowered by a superior force, they were compelled to retreat; but they fought so valiantly, that the attempt to gain possession of the city was abandoned by the enemy, who, during the night of Tuesday, went on board their shipping, having lost, among their killed, General Ross, the commander-in-chief of the British troops.

While these important events were transpiring in the heart of the country, at the north signal success attended the American arms at Plattsburg, and on Lake Champlain. The British army, under Sir George Prevost, amounting to fourteen thousand men, was compelled to retire on the 11th of September, from Plattsburg, and the English squadron, commanded by Commodore Downie, was captured by Commodore Macdonough on the lake. The latter was the second fleet fight, of the war, and our second victory over a British squadron. One frigate, one brig, and two sloops of war, fell into the hands of the victors. Several British galleys were sunk, and a few others escaped. Notwithstanding the recent successes experienced by the American arms, the condition of public affairs was now singularly embarrassing. The commissioners who were abroad attempting to negotiate a peace with England, according to a proposal which that country had some time before made, were little likely to succeed in their object, owing to the unreasonableness of the terms demanded: public credit was low; the national finances disordered; and the opposition to the war and to the administration, from the federal party, was unremitted. A convention from most of the New England States, amid the dissatisfaction and alarm which were felt in that quarter, as to the measures of the general government, had met at Hartford, and though it proposed no violent schemes, added to the difficulties which were experienced. The term *Hart ford Convention* has since been odious to members of the democratic party.

Notwithstanding the pending negotiations, at Ghent, between the American and British commissioners, it became apparent that serious preparations were in forwardness for the invasion of Louisiana. The attack speedily followed. In the course of the month of December, fifteen thousand troops, under Sir Edward Packenham, were landed on the coast to the east of the Mississippi, and on the 8th of January, 1815, they attacked the Americans, numbering about six thousand, chiefly militia, in their intrenchments before New Orleans. General Jackson was in command of the Americans, and had made judicious preparations to defend the place. After an engagement of more than an hour, the enemy, having lost their commander-in-chief, and Major-General Gibbs, and being weakened and dispirited by the fall of more than two thousand of their number, fled in confusion, leaving their dead and wounded on the field of battle. From the favorable position which the Americans occupied, they experienced only the very small loss of seven killed and six wounded.

The news of this victory spread rapidly through the United States, and proved to be the harbinger of peace, a treaty having been signed at Ghent, on the 24th of December, 1814. This treaty was ratified by the president and senate on the 17th of February, 1815. It is to be remarked that this was silent as to the subjects for which the war had been professedly declared. Peace, nevertheless, was hailed with joyful acclamations, for the nation was weary of war, and its waste of life, treasure, and domestic happiness. Treaties were soon after renewed with the Indian tribes.

The close of this war deserves a passing comment. Whatever may have been the wisdom of its declaration, in the existing state of the country, it was fully justified on our part by the long career of haughty aggression, which had been pursued by Great Britain. Self-respect, regard to our rights and the rights of the world, demanded of us resistance and rebuke. The usurpation of the sea, by Great Britain, as her special dominion, was a wrong not to be endured. The judgment of the world, and especially of the people of the United States, has fully borne out our government in the course they adopted. The results have been highly advantageous to the country — to its name and its position among other nations. Our victory, at New Orleans, over the veterans which had recently driven the French from Spain, with our achievements upon the sea, where the British deemed themselves invincible, taught that haughty people a salutary and abiding lesson. From that day to this, the United States have been rising in the respect of the world.

The effect of the war upon political parties was remarkable. The federalists,* who opposed it from the beginning to the end, in spite of the ability of their leaders, lost the confidence of the people, and their name henceforward became one of reproach with the democrats. Their opposition was, doubtless, carried to an unwarrantable extent, rendered the less excusable by the difficulties in which the government was involved. The democratic party, which began and sustained the war, became triumphant in the country, and, for the most part, has continued so to the present time.

Yet it was not the war alone which decided the fate of these two great parties. Federalism was founded in an honest distrust of the capacity of mankind for self-government; hence the federalists were always in opposition to the masses. It does not impugn their judgment, or their patriotism, that such was their conduct and belief; it was perhaps as much the result of good fortune as superior sagacity, that the democrats of that day hit upon the profound and glorious truth, that man is capable of self-government, — and that the people are the safest depository of power. Nothing is more certain than that, with the advance of time, our institutions have become more and more democratic, while our own confidence, and that of the world, in them, has been continually increasing. Nearly the whole government of the United States is now based upon universal suffrage; that which the old federalists deemed both dangerous and destructive, has proved to be the element of a true and reliable conservatism. Our institutions are now on the shoulders of the masses, and every citizen is interested in their maintenance. Thus, while European thrones and dynasties are crumbling to ruins, we ride out the storm, and become the refuge of those who are flying from the fluctuations and misfortunes of other lands.

Before intelligence of the peace, above noticed, could be officially diffused over the ocean, several actions took place, in which victories were obtained on both sides. A bill incorporating a national bank, under the title of the *Bank of the United States*, was passed after an animated debate in congress, and received the signature of the president on the 10th of April. Of the thirty-five millions of dollars constituting its capital, the United States were to own seven millions. The charter was to continue in force twenty years. Indiana was received into the Union as an independent state in December, 1816. Mr. Madison retired from the office of president on the 4th of March, 1817.

CHAPTER CCCCXCI.

A. D. 1817 to 1841.

Mr. Monroe President — War with the Seminole Indians — Cession of Florida to the United States — Slavery Compromise, &c.

THE fifth president of the United States was *James Monroe*, of Virginia, who entered on the duties of his office on the 4th of March, 1817. Daniel D. Tompkins, of New York, was chosen vice-president. During the administration of Mr. Monroe, not many stirring events took place, the war having happily been terminated, and the passions connected with it having subsided. Having formed a judicious cabinet, he pursued a moderate course as to political matters. To John Q. Adams was assigned the department of state. Mr. Crawford was at the head of the treasury, having been continued from the former administration. Mr. Calhoun was appointed secretary of war, and Smith Thompson was placed over the department of the

* The term *federalist* was first applied to the supporters of the federal union, established by the constitution. It was afterwards the designation of the conservative party, who feared and opposed the French revolution and democratic ideas. The conservatives of the present day have advanced so far as to adopt most of the doctrines of the democrats in Jefferson's time.

navy. With these able assistants, the president adopted measures which tended in a great measure to abate the evils which the war had introduced into the political and social system.

James Monroe.

In the summer and autumn of 1817, the president made a tour through the northern and eastern states of the Union, where he was received with distinguished courtesy and respect. Meeting congress on the 1st of December, he represented to that body the progress which the country was making in her most important interests, and particularly recommended to their notice the surviving officers and soldiers of the revolution, and the repeal of the internal duties. These recommendations were acted upon, and bills were passed providing for the indigent officers and soldiers of the revolutionary army, and for the abolishment of the internal duties. Other important bills were enacted during the session. Near the close of the year, December 11th, the state of Mississippi was admitted into the Union. In the month of April, 1818, Illinois adopted a state constitution, and in due time was admitted as a member of the Union. A treaty with Sweden was ratified on the 27th of May, 1818, by the president and senate, on the part of the United States. The ratification on the part of Sweden took place on the 24th of July, the same year.

During the year 1817, a war was carried on between the Seminole Indians and the United States, in which the former were discomfited and overthrown. Lying on the confines of the United States and Florida, and being joined by outlaws from the Creek nation, and runaway negro slaves, this confederacy of savages became exceedingly annoying to the inhabitants on our southern borders. Massacres had become so frequent that the whites had to flee from their homes for security. The flame of Indian hostility was further fanned by an Indian prophet, and by two English emissaries, Arbuthnot and Ambrister, who had taken up their residence among them for the purposes of trade. In December, a detachment of forty men, under Lieutenant Scott, having been ambushed while performing some duty which had been assigned them were all killed, except six, by a body of the Indians. General Jackson, with a body of Tennesseeans, was ordered to the spot. He soon effected the defeat and dispersion of the savages. Being convinced of the agency of the Spaniards in exciting Indian hostility, he took possession of Forts St. Marks and Pensacola, and made the two Englishmen and the prophet above spoken of prisoners. Arbuthnot and Ambrister were both tried by a court-martial, and executed.

A Convention between Great Britain and the United States was ratified by the Prince Regent on the 28th of January, 1819, and on the 2d of November following, it received the ratification of the president of the United States. The articles agreed on, among other important subjects, related to the fisheries, and the northern boundaries of the United States. On the 22d of February of the same year, a treaty was concluded at Washington by John Q. Adams and Luis de Onis, by which East and West Florida, with all the adjacent islands, &c., were ceded by Spain to the United States. A sum not exceeding five millions of dollars was to be paid by the United States out of the proceeds of sales of lands in Florida, or in stock, or money, to the citizens of the United States, on account of Spanish spoliations and injuries. During the summer of 1819, Mr. Monroe made a tour through the southern section of the country, for a purpose similar to that which he had in view in his previous journey to the north,—the inspection of the national defences, public works, arts, &c. On the 14th of December following, a resolution passed congress admitting Alabama into the Union as an independent state. In the ensuing year, 1820, March 3d, Maine became an independent state, and a member of the national Union.

On the 5th of March, 1821, Mr. Monroe, who had been again chosen president, took the customary oath of office. His reëlection was nearly unanimous. Daniel D. Tompkins was again elected vice-president.

By a proclamation of the president on the 10th of August, 1821, Missouri was declared to be an independent state, and a member of the federal Union. Two years previously, application was made to congress, by the people of Missouri, to form for them a state constitution. A bill was accordingly introduced for the purpose, a provision of which interdicted slavery, or involuntary servitude. The bill thus framed passed the house of representatives, but was rejected in the senate, and therefore failed for the time. In the session of the following year, the bill was revived. It excited a warm and prolonged debate between those who favored and those who were opposed to the restriction respecting slavery. Never had the parties in congress, perhaps, been so marked by a geographical, sectional division, or manifested feelings more dangerous to the union of the states. The whole country seemed to be actuated by a similar temper. The result was a compromise, by which slavery was to be tolerated in Missouri, and forbidden in all that part of Louisiana, as ceded by France, lying north of 36° 30′ north latitude, except so much as was embraced within the limits of the state.

In June, 1822, a convention of navigation and commerce, on terms of mutual and equal advantage, was concluded between France and the United States. About this time, also, the ports of the West India islands were opened to the Americans, by the act of the British parliament. Pirates, having for a long time infested the West India seas, and preyed upon American commerce, were at this period signally chastised by a United States schooner — the Alligator. Five American vessels were recaptured, and one piratical schooner taken. After this, congress appropriated a sum of money to fit out an expedition for the suppression of piracy. Upon the appearance of Commodore Porter with his squadron in the Caribbean Seas, the freebooters dared not show themselves, but committed their depredations on the inhabitants of the West India Islands.

In 1823, congress sanctioned the measure recommended by President Monroe, of acknowledging the independence of the South American republics. Ministers were appointed to Mexico, Buenos Ayres, Colombia, and Chili. In 1824, congress passed two important bills, which caused much debate in that body, and intense solicitude among those classes of citizens likely to be affected by them, namely — one for abolishing imprisonment for debt, and the other establishing a tariff of duties on imports into the country. During the year now spoken of, the marquis de Lafayette, now in advanced life, revisited the scenes of his early patriotic toils, sacrifices, and dangers. He became the nation's guest for many months, and visited various portions of the United States, being every where received with the utmost joy and enthusiasm. While in the country, congress voted him the sum of two hundred thousand dollars, and a township of land, which was located in Florida, as indemnity, in part, for his sacrifices and services during the revolutionary war, and as a token of their grateful remembrance of his heroic philanthropy.

During Mr. Monroe's administration, America enjoyed profound peace. Sixty millions of her national debt were discharged. The Floridas were peaceably acquired, and the western limits fixed at the Pacific Ocean. Internal taxes were repealed, the military establishment reduced to its narrowest limits of efficiency, the organization of the army improved, the independence of the South American nations recognized, progress made in the suppression of the slave trade, and the civilization of the Indians advanced. The voice of party spirit had died away, and the period is still spoken of as the era of good feeling.

The election of a successor to Mr. Monroe devolved on the house of representatives, the electors having failed to make a choice. Fears were entertained that the exigency now contemplated by the constitution, would not be passed without a dangerous excitement, and that it might shake the constitution itself. But no such effect was produced, although the result was very unsatisfactory to the minds of many, and there were loud complaints of political collusion and bargaining. *John Quincy Adams*, of Massachusetts, though he was not the highest on the list of candidates before the electoral college, was the choice of the house voting by states. He entered on the duties of his office on the 4th of March, 1825. John C. Calhoun, of South Carolina, was chosen by the electoral colleges as vice-president.

In the year 1826, and on the 4th of July, the deaths of John Adams and Thomas Jefferson took place. History, perhaps, does not present a more striking and affecting coincidence than this. That these men,

John Quincy Adams.

whose lives were identified with the independence of their country, should die together, and that too on the 4th of July, the birthday of the nation, and, still further in the year of its jubilee, — the fiftieth anniversary, — amid the rejoicings of the people, — was indeed strange and calculated to turn the thoughts of men toward that Providence, which concerns itself in the destinies of men and nations.

In 1828, the revision of the tariff agitated congress, and the warm and prolonged debates on the occasion terminated in the enacting of a law, by which protective duties were imposed on such articles of import as come into competition with certain manufactures and agricultural products of the United States. The wishes of the advocates of the protecting system were not fully met, but they had obtained an advantage which was generally appreciated in the manufacturing states.

The presidential election having been decided by the college of electors, General *Andrew Jackson*, of Tennessee, was inaugurated president, and John C Calhoun vice-president, of the United States, on the 4th of March, 1829. The president's cabinet at first consisted of Martin Van Buren, of New York, secretary of state, Samuel D. Ingham, of Pennsylvania secretary of the treasury, John H. Eaton, secretary of war, and John Branch, of North Carolina, secretary of the navy. Several changes occurred in the cabinet, subsequently. General Jackson, in his administration, proceeded on a plan of reform which he had conceived in his own mind, as necessary, and displaced from office many individuals of the opposite party in politics. Their places he filled from the democratic party The year 1829 witnessed the origin of the *state rights* or *Nullification* party in South Carolina, whose rash conduct but little recommended the principles on which it was founded. Their doctrines, however, were ably advocated in congress by Mr. Hayne of the senate and they were still more ably opposed by Daniel Webster, a member of the same body. Their speeches have been justly celebrated as models of eloquence

Andrew Jackson.

On the 19th of November, 1832, a convention met at Columbia, South Carolina, and issued an ordinance called the *Nullification ordinance*, the object of which was to set aside the acts of congress, imposing protective duties. In the event of force being applied on the part of the United States in the collection of such duties, the instrument declared that the people would hold themselves absolved from all political connection with the other states, and would forthwith proceed to organize a separate government, &c. The friends of the Union in that state, however, held their convention on the 24th of November, the result of which was the publication of a solemn protest against the ordinance. The principles of the nullifiers were reprobated in meetings held in almost every part of the United States. On the 27th of November, the legislature of the state convened at Columbia, and the governor, expressing his approval of the nullification ordinance, recommended the preparation of means to defend the state, in the event of a collision.

In this posture of affairs, President Jackson issued his Proclamation against the disorganizers in South Carolina, in which he first exposed their error, and then pointed out to them their danger. The proclamation was a well-timed and most able state paper. It was acceptable to both of the political parties of the nation. The friends of the Union, in South Carolina, placed in a most unpleasant situation, being now encouraged by the decided tone of the president, held meetings in various parts of the state, in which they declared, "We will not be forced to bear arms against the United States, be the consequences what they may." The president at once prepared for military operations against the disorganizers; but a change of tone soon took place on their part; the state authorities agreed not to oppose the collection of duties until the 1st of March, and before that period measures were taken which restored tranquillity. By an act of congress, on the 12th of February, 1833, the duties on certain articles were reduced, and the operation of the tariff was limited to the 30th of September, 1842.

General Jackson was reëlected 1833.

At an early period in his first term of office, General Jackson had recommended the removal of the tribes of Indians, residing in the southern part of the United States, under the names of the Choctaws, the Cherokees, and the Creeks, as a measure for the relief of the Southern States, and the eventual preservation of those tribes. With a view to this end, he suggested that an ample district, west of the Mississippi, and without the limits of any state or territory, might be set apart and guarantied to the tribes, each to have distinct jurisdiction over the part designated for its use and exempt from any control of the United States, except that which might be necessary to preserve peace on the frontier. Congress sanctioning the project, the president undertook their removal. With the Chickasaws and Choctaws, treaties were made, 1831—1832, by which they exchanged lands, and quietly emigrated to the country which had been selected. This was the territory next to Arkansas. But the Cherokees and Creeks were not so easily disposed of, nor was it without violent and unjust proceedings on the part of the authorities of Georgia in extending their laws over the Indian territory, that these sons of the forest were removed from the hunting-grounds of their fathers—now become almost the abodes of civilization. The teachers of Christianity had taught them knowledge in their homes, but both the instructors and their pupils were obliged to bow to the severity of law, even in its injustice.

In the attempt to remove the Seminoles in Florida, the United States became involved in a war with that race. The peremptory manner in which the object was to be effected, according to the orders of the president, very naturally displeased them. Osceola, a chief among these Indians, was treated with indignity by the United States agent, General Thompson, and, after dissembling for a while, he executed a fierce and deadly revenge. It fell first on the heads of a portion of the Indians who were true to the whites, of whom Mathla, who had made an obnoxious treaty with the Americans, was a chief. Lying in ambush with his warriors, on the 28th of December, 1835, Osceola fell upon a company of one hundred and seventeen men, commanded by Major Dade, and only thirty of them escaped. He also surprised General Thompson, at Camp King, immediately after the attack on Dade, and shot him and many others, while they were dining at a house within sight of the garrison. The Indians then retreated, unmolested by the garrison.

In the afternoon of the same day, the remaining thirty men of Dade's company, who had been at work in making an enclosure with trees, were assailed and eventually all killed. One, before he died of his wounds, was enabled, to flee by feigning death some distance, and make known the disaster. A deep sensation pervaded the country at the news of these transactions. General Clinch, in command, now made efforts to defeat and secure Osceola, but was unsuccessful. Emboldened by success, the Indians appeared simultaneously in the neighborhood of almost every settlement in Florida, destroying crops and murdering families in all directions. Every house within the distance of two hundred and fifty miles south of St. Augustine was burned to the ground. General Gaines marching to the relief of Clinch, had a battle with he Indians, and repulsed them, but was in no situation to prosecute his object, from want of provisions. This battle took place on the 29th of February, 1836.

Osceola, after parleying with General Gaines, and thus gaining time, was finally secured by General Jessup, although he came to the American general with a flag with about seventy warriors. Jessup believed him to be treacherous, and caused him with his escort, to be forcibly detained. The Indian chief died, a few months after, of a painful disease.

In 1831, Mr. Rives secured by treaty twenty-five millions of francs, as an indemnity from France for spoliations on American commerce. It had, however, nearly cost a war before the French were willing actually to pay the stipulated sum.

President Jackson had early manifested hostility to the United States Bank. The bill for the renewal of its charter — passed, by a considerable majority, in congress, in 1832 — he saw fit to veto. The funds of the government which had been deposited in that bank, he required Mr. Duane, the secretary of the treasury, to withdraw. The secretary refused to do it, and was thereupon dismissed by the president. Mr. Taney being appointed, the latter immediately complied with the president's wishes; and subsequently, by an act of congress, in 1835, the public treasure was placed in certain selected state banks. The conduct of the president in this matter was loudly condemned by many as an unwonted stretch of power, while the senate of the United States passed two resolutions, proposed by Mr. Clay, censuring the course Jackson had pursued. Subsequently, when the majority was changed, a vote was obtained to expunge the resolutions.

Martin Van Buren.

Martin Van Buren succeeded to the presidency in 1837, and at the same time Richard M. Johnson to the vice-presidency.

In consequence of the facilities afforded for obtaining money by the banks containing the public deposits, and perhaps from other causes, the community became affected with the mania of land speculation. It was carried to such an extent, that a crisis must inevitably come, and it was not long in coming. The country felt it in all its weight in the years of 1837 and 1838. The revulsion produced untold distress. All were losing money now, while before all seemed to be gaining it. In this posture of pecuniary affairs, a delegation of merchants from New York applied to the president, as a measure of alleviation, that he would immediately remit the regulations contained in the "Specie Circular" and also convene the national legislature. Mr. Van Buren did not see fit to comply with the request. The Circular in question required that the public dues should be paid in specie. This drew the gold and silver from the vaults of the banks; and as the precious metals were carried to the west, so that the speculators in land were accommodated, the merchants in the cities could not obtain the means of paying the duties on their imports. The government required specie for its dues, but did not pay it out to its creditors.

This course of things caused a dangerous exasperation in the cities. The banks in the city of New York were obliged to stop specie payment, their issues to sustain their friends having been too great. Their example imposed a similar necessity throughout the Union. This common fate was shared by the deposit banks, and the government became embarrassed. The president was obliged to assemble congress in this exigency, contrary to his previously announced intention. His proposed scheme for the relief of the government, — for he offered none for the relief of the community, — the *sub-treasury*, as it was called, was brought before congress in a bill, but it was rejected.

About this period, difficulties occurred on the northern borders of the United States, arising from the sympathies, which were felt and expressed, with the attempt made by a portion of the Canadians to obtain independence. This led to unlawful assemblages of armed people, prepared to aid any rebellion in the provinces, and thus to compromise the interests of the general government, by interference in the concerns of a nation at peace with us. Both the president of the United States and the governor of New York issued proclamations, enjoining upon the inhabitants of the frontier the obligation of observing a strict neutrality. After the affair of the Caroline, — a boat carrying one hundred and fifty Americans engaged in this unlawful enterprise, which was destroyed by the British, on board of which one American was killed, — the processes of law were attempted. Van Rensselaer the leader of the sympathizers, was arrested at the suit of the United States, but was admitted to bail M'Leod, an Englishman, was taken and tried in 1841 for the murder of the American on board of the Caroline, but was acquitted.

CHAPTER CCCCXCII.

A. D. 1841 to 1849.

William Henry Harrison President — His Death — John Tyler President — Veto of the United States Bank Bill — James K Polk President — War with Mexico, &c.

The presidential election was decided by the vote of the electoral college, and a large majority was given to *William Henry Harrison*. On the 4th of

William Henry Harrison.

March, he was inaugurated as president of the United States. John Tyler, of Virginia, at the same time became vice-president. But short was the tenure of the hero's and the patriot's office. General Harrison, who was already a man of years, expired just a month from the day of his inauguration.

Congress assembled on the **31st** of May, **1841**, in accordance with a proclamation previously issued by President Harrison, and immediately entered upon the business which required the attention of the national legislature. That business related to the condition of the revenue and finances of the country. There were also other matters of moment which demanded consideration. The first bill of importance which was adopted, was one establishing a uniform system of bankruptcy throughout the United States — a measure required by the situation of more than half a million of debtors in the country, who could not otherwise indulge the hope of satisfying the claims of their creditors, or supporting their families. Their misfortunes had generally arisen from the extraordinary state of the monetary affairs of the nation. Mr. Van Buren's sub-treasury law, which, at his repeated solicitations, had been adopted toward the close of his administration, was repealed.

It was attempted at this session to establish a United States Bank; but though a bill to that effect passed both houses, the president vetoed it, although it was a favorite measure with the party which had elevated him to the office. Another bill, with somewhat different provisions, supposed to have been framed in accordance with the wishes of Mr. Tyler, was also vetoed. These unaccountable results effected the dissolution of the cabinet All the members, except Mr. Webster, the secretary of state, resigned their places. These were immediately filled by others, the nominations to which were confirmed by the senate.

On the 20th of August, 1842, an important treaty with England was ratified by the senate. By this treaty, the north-eastern boundary was settled. This had been a troublesome and even threatening question between the United States and Great Britain.

The revision of the tariff occupied much of the attention of the second session of the twenty-seventh congress. A well-regulated tariff was deemed by the dominant party the great remedy for the evils the country was now experiencing in its diminishing revenue, sinking manufactures, and the drooping aspect of all the great branches of industry. The bill which first passed received the veto of the president, and added another to those acts which had so signally disappointed the whig party. It was contemplated on the part of some, in the despair of obtaining his sanction of any proper tariff, to close the session, and place the responsibility on the president. But the sufferings of the country forbade the idea; and another effort was put forth on the part of the friends of a judicious tariff. On the 22d of August, the same revenue bill which had been vetoed by Mr. Tyler, was passed by the house, with a majority of only two, the section concerning the land fund and the duties upon tea and coffee being omitted

John Tyler.

The third session of the twenty-seventh congress, which commenced on the 5th of December, 1842, passed several important acts relating to the repeal of the bankrupt law, to the promotion of friendly intercourse with China, and to measures carrying into effect the late treaty with Great Britain. By the last-named act, three hundred thousand dollars were to be paid, in equal portions, to Maine and Massachusetts. On the 22d of April, a message was transmitted to the senate by Mr. Tyler, announcing to that body the negotiation of a treaty with Texas, the object of which was to annex that state to the United States. This treaty, secretly negotiated, occasioned much surprise and concern, on the part of many in the community, who considered annexation as fraught with evils. On the 8th of June, a direct vote was taken on the question of ratifying the above treaty, and was decisively rejected.

On the 23d of January, 1845, a joint resolution for the annexation of Texas was carried by the house of representatives, and with amendments was passed by the senate, twenty-seven to twenty-five. The resolution admitted of an alternative as to the mode of effecting the annexation; and although it was expected, it being now at the close of the session, that Mr Tyler's successor would be called to consummate the wishes of congress, yet the former availed himself of the speediest mode of bringing Texas into the Union; and thus the annexation was accomplished before the close of his administration.

James K. Polk, of Tennessee, having been chosen president by the electoral college, was inaugurated on the 4th of March, 1845, together with George M. Dallas, of Pennsylvania, as vice-president.

At an early day of the first session of the twenty-ninth congress, joint resolutions for the admission of Texas, as a state, were introduced into the house of representatives, and were passed by a majority of one hundred and forty-one to fifty-six. A few days after, the senate also passed them. On the 30th of November, the Hon. John Slidell, who had been appointed envoy to Mexico to settle all questions in dispute between the United States and that government, arrived at Vera Cruz The latter power, however, refused to receive him in his diplomatic character, and he was obliged to return home with his object unaccomplished. The president now directed General Taylor, commanding a body of American troops in Texas, to pass the River Nueces and to concentrate them on the left bank of the De Norte. These troops had been encamped for some time at Corpus Christi, which place they left on the 11th of March, 1846, and on the 28th of that month arrived opposite Matamoras.

James K Polk.

These measures of the president created dissatisfaction in the minds of many. Such persons viewed them as both impolitic and unjust, and as necessarily leading to war with Mexico, who claimed the right to the country between the Nueces and the Del Norte. The events of the war which followed, so far as they occurred within the limits of Mexico, will be given in the history of that country; we shall therefore notice here only such as may be necessary to give continuity to our narrative. The battle of Palo Alto, which took place on the 8th of May, 1846, and that of Resaca de la Palma, on the next day, may be considered as the beginning of the struggle, which terminated so favorably to our country.

A question in relation to the boundary of the Oregon territory engaged much of the attention of congress during the winter of 1846. The British claims in this quarter clashed with our own, and for a time it was apprehended that war might ensue. But happily a proposition to make the parallel of 49° north the dividing line, was made by the British government, and accepted by the President, with the advice of the senate.

General Taylor, having captured Matamoras, and several other places in that vicinity, moved forward to Monterey, the capital of New Leon. It was found to be a strongly fortified place: the general, notwithstanding, resolved to attempt its reduction. This was effected on the 24th of September, after a severe conflict. On the 23d of February following, the celebrated battle of Buena Vista was fought, in which General Taylor, with about four thousand men, totally defeated the Mexicans, under Santa Anna, with twenty-two thousand.

The principal acts of the second session of the twenty-ninth congress had reference to the war with Mexico, and the adoption of such measures in respect to men and money, as were considered necessary to its successful prosecution. An increase of all the military forces was ordered, and in regard to pecuniary means, a supply was to be secured by treasury notes, and a loan to the amount of twenty-eight millions of dollars. The president, having recommended, at this session, an appropriation of three millions of dollars, to be employed by him in such a manner as he deemed best, in securing a peace with Mexico, an exciting debate rose thereon, which was not allayed by an amendment offered to the resolution before the house, going to the exclusion of slavery from all territory which might be acquired by the United States from Mexico, either by conquest or treaty. This celebrated resolution has been called the *Wilmot proviso*, from the name of the member who offered it, Mr. Wilmot. The resolution, after an angry debate, was passed by both houses without the proviso.

On the 29th of March, 1847, the city and castle of Vera Cruz surrendered to the combined forces of the army and navy of the United States, under General Scott and Commodore Perry. The loss of the Americans was sixty-five in killed and wounded. The battle of Cerro Gordo was fought on the 18th of April, and our victorious army, under General Scott, overcoming every obstacle, and performing extraordinary feats of skill and gallantry, advanced to the capital. On the 14th of September this was taken, after several days of sanguinary and obstinate fighting. Thus nearly the entire frontier of Mexico, with its chief cities, were in the hands of the Americans. The conflict was now at an end.

After some negotiating, a treaty of peace between the United States and Mexico, was signed at Guadaloupe Hidalgo, February 2, 1848

General Zachary Taylor and Millard Fillmore were elected president and vice-president in the autumn of 1848.

CHAPTER CCCCXCIII.

A. D. 1849 to 1852.

Taylor's Administration—His Death—Succession of Fillmore—His Administration.

Zachary Taylor.

General Taylor was inaugurated on the 4th of March, 1849. Among the first acts of his administration, was the negotiation of a treaty with Great Britain in relation to Central America, which on account of the negotiators, has been called the Clayton and Bulwer treaty. This was designed to define the policy of both countries in relation to Central America; both entered into stipulations to make no acquisitions of territory there. This treaty was ratified, but disputes as to its meaning arose between the contending parties, which for a long time created embarrassment between them.

About the same period Mr. Clayton, our secretary of state, took exceptions to certain expressions in a communication to the department, from M. Poussin, the minister of the French republic, and which resulted in his dismissal by the president. This created some difficulty with the French government, and Louis Napoleon, the president, hesitated to receive our minister, Mr. Rives. These irritations, however, were soon pacified.

From the beginning of Taylor's administration, it became obvious that the country had entered upon a stormy and threatening period of its existence. The large territorial acquisitions consequent upon the Mexican war, opened the doors of agitation which extended from one end of the country to the other. The boundless riches of the gold mines of California, suddenly drew thither a large population, and the question of its admission as a state into the union was speedily presented to the minds of the people. The annexation of Texas as well as the Mexican war, which was the consequence, was generally supported by the south under the expectation of obtaining a large acquisition of slave territory; when, therefore, it became probable that California would become a free state, great disappointment, as well as agitation, was felt in the southern states.

Mr. Clay, with that far-reaching sagacity for which he was distinguished, comprehended the coming storm, and in order to arrest or mitigate it, he with others brought forward a series of measures, which acquired the title of the "Compromise of 1850." It proposed to admit California into the Union as a free state; to organize territorial governments for New Mexico and Utah, leaving the question of slavery to the decision of the inhabitants; to define the boundaries of Texas; and to make more effectual provision for enforcing the requirements of the constitution relating to fugitives from labor. The combining of so great a variety of measures into one bill, led to its being designated as the "Omnibus." Distinguished members of the senate of both the whig and democratic parties—Webster, Cass, Douglas, Calhoun, and others—united in support of the measure.

In the midst of the congressional debate on this subject, which had now continued for seven months, President Taylor died. This event took place on Tuesday, the 9th of July, 1850, at half past ten in the evening. On the preceding Thursday, which was the anniversary of American independence, he was in the enjoyment of his usual health, and attended the celebration of the day at the Washington Monument. The oration was long, and the President listened to it with his head uncovered, exposed to a breeze which it was feared at the time might be detrimental to his health. Next morning he was attacked with cholera morbus; remittent fever supervened; the disease baffled all the skill of able physicians, and an hour and a half before midnight on Tuesday, his eyes were closed in their last sleep. He retained his reason to the last, and was perfectly calm and tranquil. His last words were, "I am prepared — I have endeavored to do my duty."

The death of an acting president of the United States is always a startling event, but owing to the peculiar circumstances of the time, the death of President Taylor caused a very profound emotion throughout the country. His funeral was celebrated with suitable ceremonies on the 13th of July. On the 10th, Mr. Fillmore, the vice president, agreeably to the provisions of the constitution, assumed the office of president. General Taylor's cabinet having resigned, he appointed a new one, as follows:

Daniel Webster, of Massachusetts, Secretary of State.

Thomas Corwin, of Ohio, Secretary of the Treasury.

James A. Pearce, of Maryland, Secretary of the Interior.

William A. Graham, of North Carolina, Secretary of the Navy.

Edward Bates, of Missouri, Secretary of War.

Nathan K. Hall, of New York, Postmaster-General.

John J. Crittenden, of Kentucky, Attorney-General.

This cabinet embodied eminent ability, large experience in public affairs, and great weight of character. The nominations were all confirmed by the senate, but Mr. Pearce and Mr. Bates were prevented by circumstances from accepting the places tendered them. After some delay, Alexander H. H. Stuart, of Virginia, was appointed secretary of the interior, and C. M. Conrad, of Louisiana, secretary of war.

A few days after Mr. Fillmore's accession, the "Omnibus bill" was brought to a vote and defeated; it was, however, afterward divided into several acts, and was thus passed. That portion of it which required the rendition of fugitive slaves was, however, violently attacked by the anti-slavery party of the North. Slaves were rescued from the custody of the United States marshals at Boston, Syracuse, and at Christiana, in the state of Pennsylvania, and in the last named of these places one or two persons were killed. The president, however, avowed his intention to execute the law. When intelligence of the proceedings of the Boston mob reached Washington, the president issued his proclamation calling upon all officers to do their duty, and prosecutions were instituted against the rioters, but the prejudices of the jury and the difficulty of identifying the criminals frequently enabled them to escape. At Syracuse one was convicted, but he died before sentence was passed upon him. After a time, however, the law was generally enforced, and opposition in a great measure subsided.

Mr. Fillmore's message on the assembling of congress in December, 1850, has been justly regarded as eminently distinguished for national spirit and statesmanlike views. He reported the total receipts into the treasury for the year ending January 30, 1850, as forty-seven millions of dollars, and the expenditures during the same period as forty-three millions. He invited the attention of congress to a great number of topics, but as there was a decided political majority against him in both houses of congress, none of his recommendations requiring legislation were adopted, except those for an asylum for disabled and destitute seamen, and for the settlement of land claims in California, and the survey of the public lands. A bill making appropriations for the improvement of rivers and harbors passed the house, but was defeated in the senate, by senators "talking against time," on the last day of the session, and preventing a vote until the constitutional term of congress had expired.

Soon after the close of this session of congress, the public prints were filled with rumors of a new expedition against Cuba, which was to sail from some of our northern ports. On the 25th of April 1851, President Fillmore issued a proclamation urging all good citizens against engaging in any such enterprise, inasmuch as it was against the law of the country, and would subject all who might be concerned in it to severe punishment. This proclamation only caused the fillibusters to be more cautious in their proceedings. Early on the morning of the 3d of August, 1851,* a steamer called the Pampero departed from New Orleans, and by the connivance of the collector got to sea, with four hundred armed men. The leader was a Spaniard by the name of Lopez, and a considerable number of the adventurers were foreigners.

After touching at Key West she proceeded to the coast of Cuba, and, on the night of the 11th and 12th of August, landed the persons on board at Playtas, within about twenty leagues of Havana.

The main body of them proceeded to, and took possession of, an inland village, six leagues distant, leaving others to follow in charge of the baggage, as soon as the means of transportation could be obtained. The latter, having taken up their line of march to connect themselves with the main body, and having proceeded about four leagues into the country, were attacked on the morning of the 13th by a body of Spanish troops, and a bloody conflict ensued; after which they retreated to the place of disembarkation, where about fifty of them obtained boats and reëmbarked therein. They were, however, intercepted among the keys near the shore by a Spanish steamer cruising on the coast, captured, and carried to Havana, and after being examined before a military court, were sentenced to be publicly executed, and the sentence was carried into effect on the 16th of August.

On receiving information of what had occurred, Commodore Foxhall A. Parker was instructed to proceed with the steam-frigate Saranac to Havana, and inquire into the charges against the persons executed, the circumstances under which they were taken, and whatsoever referred to their trial and sentence.

According to the record of the examination, the prisoners all admitted the offenses charged against them, of being hostile invaders of the island. At the time of their trial and execution, the main body of the invaders was still in the field, making war upon the Spanish authorities and Spanish subjects. After the lapse of some days, being overcome by the Spanish troops, they dispersed on the 24th of August. Lopez, their leader, was captured some days after, and executed on the 1st of September. Many of his surviving followers were killed or died of hunger and fatigue, and the rest were made prisoners. Of these none appear to have been tried or arrested. Several of them were pardoned upon application of their friends and others, and the rest, about sixty in number, were sent to Spain. These were finally pardoned by the queen, and congress provided for their expenses home. The collector of New Orleans was removed from office for neglect of duty, and the Pampero was seized by order of government, near Jackson, Florida, and tried, condemned, and sold, for a violation of our neutrality laws.

Unfortunately the ill success of this expedition, and the general reprobation of all such schemes on the part of the vast majority of the American people, have not wholly suppressed the spirit of fil-

* Prior to this, in consequence of rumors that a secret and unlawful expedition was on foot, either to invade Cuba or Mexico, President Taylor had issued his proclamation, August 11, 1849, urging all persons against engaging in any such scheme. Nevertheless, an expedition got to sea in three divisions consisting of six hundred and nine men, and these were concealed near the island of Mugeres, off the coast of Yucatan, May 15, 1850, on board the steamer Creole. On the 19th of May, under their leader, Lopez, they disembarked at Cardenas on the northern side of the island of Cuba. A skirmish ensued, and Cardenas was taken. The public treasures having been seized by the mauraders, they departed the next day and escaped in their vessel, being closely pursued by the Spanish war steamer Pizzaro. The fillibusters took refuge at Key West, where they landed, and dispersed, their steamer being seized by the United States Government.

fibustering in regard to Cuba. Several other projects of this sort have been entertained by various parties of lawless persons, but hitherto their designs have been frustrated.

In 1851 the United States frigate Mississippi was despatched to the Mediterranean, to receive Kossuth, the hero of Hungary, and his attendants, it being understood that they were about to be liberated by the Turkish government, which had held them under restraint since they took refuge in its territory, in escaping from the disastrous combat with Austria. On the 10th of September they were received on board this ship, at the Dardanelles. On the 10th of November she arrived at New York, with the exiles on board, excepting Kossuth himself, who having visited England, reached this country December 5th. He was welcomed at New York with great public demonstrations of respect, and after receiving similar homage at various places, a congressional banquet was given him at Washington, January 7, 1852. He visited our principal cities, addressing large assemblies who crowded to hear him and who listened with interest to his exciting addresses—in which he pleaded for material aid in behalf of Hungary. The enthusiasm which had thus spread over the country, soon subsided, and in July, 1852, Kossuth departed for England, taking passage under the assumed name of Alexander Smith. Since that time he has resided in England, occasionally making public addresses upon general politics, usually having a direct or indirect reference to his own country.

The forays against Cuba by armed fillibusters* from this country, attracted the attention of the European powers, and the supposed danger that the island would be wrested from Spain and fall into the possession of the United States, alarmed that jealousy of our growth which is habitual with those governments. In the early part of the year 1852 a proposal was made to the secretary of state, by the French and English ministers, to enter into a tripartite treaty, by which the three powers should bind themselves for all coming time neither to make any attempt to acquire Cuba for themselves, nor to countenance any such attempts by others. Although this proposal evinced a disposition on the part of foreign governments to an impertinent interference in our affairs, the communication of the French minister was treated respectfully. Mr. Webster addressed him a note, stating that the president would take the proposal of the French and English governments into consideration and make the question it involved the subject of mature reflection. Although the president had, with the most unflinching determination, exerted his official authority for repressing the attempts of the fillibusters, which were made the occasion of this proposal, and was opposed, for reasons of domestic policy, to the immediate acquisition of Cuba, even if it could be gained by purchase and without an interruption of friendly relations with Spain, he was nevertheless decidedly opposed to entering into any such arrangement as that proposed by France and England. He adhered to the wise policy of Washington and Jefferson, which was opposed to entangling alliances with foreign powers. He was not willing to place the government of this country in such a condition that it would be responsible to others for the proper discharge of its duty. So far as related to the acquisition of Cuba by other powers, he knew that this country had both the will and the ability to prevent it, without foreign assistance. As to its acquisition by ourselves, although we did not want it at present, he regarded it as a geographical and political necessity that it would, at some future time, fall into our hands; and he would not allow a treaty with foreign nations to fetter the march of our destiny.

The final reply of our government to this proposal for a tripartite treaty was not made until after the death of Mr. Webster. In the fall of 1852 Mr. Everett had accepted the office of secretary of state, and on the first of December, in that year, he addressed to the Count de Sartiges, by the direction of the president, a letter which ranks among the ablest and most instructive state papers ever issued by the American government.

Mr. Everett stated that the most serious attention had been given to this proposal by the president, who at the same time that he did not covet the acquisition of Cuba for the United States, considered the condition of the island as an American and not a European question, and objected to the proposed treaty, because it assumed that the United States have no other or greater interest in it than France and England. If the treaty should be assented to by the president, its certain rejection by the senate would leave the question of Cuba more unsettled than when the arrangement was proposed. This, however, would not require the president to withhold his concurrence, if no other objections existed. But the convention would be of no value unless it were lasting; and the president did not consider it within the competence of the treaty-making power to bind the government for all time to come not to make a purchase of Cuba. He was likewise unwilling to depart from the traditionary policy of the government, which had always been averse to political alliances with European powers.

After stating these preliminary objections, Mr. Everett, in his admirable letter, proceeded to set forth conditions of general policy which were adverse to the proposed alliance. The tendency of this document was to enlarge the general scope of political views in the United States, and to instruct the statesmen of foreign nations in the effect and influence of our institutions upon civilization at large. It may be considered as one of the ablest vindications of our history and our career, as well as one of the most able and candid expositions of our prospects before the world, that has ever appeared. The close of this document reflects so much light upon our history, that we deem it worthy of a place here.

"That a convention, such as is proposed, would be a transitory arrangement sure to be swept away by the irresistible tide of affairs in a new country, is to the apprehension of the president too obvious to require a labored argument. The project rests on principles applicable, if at all, to Europe, where

* We have taken the liberty to make use of several passages here from the "Biography of Millard Fillmore," published by Thomas & Lathrop of Buffalo.

international relations are in their basis of great antiquity, slowly modified for the most part in the progress of time and events, and not applicable to America, which, but lately a waste, is filling up with intense rapidity, and adjusting on natural principles those territorial relations which on the first discovery of the continent were in a good degree fortuitous. The comparative history of Europe and America, even for a single century, shows this.

"In 1752 England, France, and Spain, were not materially different in their political position in Europe from what they now are. They were ancient, mature, consolidated states, established in their relations with each other and the rest of the world—the leading powers of Western and Southern Europe. Totally different was the state of things in America. The United States had no existence as a people—a line of English colonies numbering not much over a million of inhabitants, stretched along the coast. Those of France extended from the Bay of St. Lawrence to the Gulf of Mexico, and from the Alleghanies to the Mississippi, beyond which, westward, the continent was a wilderness, occupied by wandering savages and subject to a conflicting and nominal claim on the part of France and Spain. Everything in Europe was comparatively fixed—everything in America provisional, incipient, and temporary, except the law of progress, which is as organic and vital in the youth of states as of individual men. A struggle between the provinicial authorities of England and France, for the possession of a petty stockade at the confluence of the Monongahela and the Alleghany, kindled the seven years' war, at the close of which, the great European powers, not materially affected in their relations at home, had undergone astonishing changes on this continent. France had disappeared from the map of America, whose inmost recesses had been penetrated by her zealous missionaries, and her resolute and gallant adventurers. England had added the Canadas to her transatlantic dominions. Spain had become the mistress of Louisiana, so that, in the language of the archbishop of Mexico, in 1770, she claimed Siberia as the northern boundary of New Spain.

"Twelve years only from the time the treaty of Paris was signed, another great change took place, fruitful of still greater changes to come. The American revolution broke out. It involved England, France, and Spain in a tremendous struggle, and at its close the United States of America had taken their place in the family of nations. In Europe, the ancient states were restored substantially to their former equilibrium, but a new element, of incalculable importance in reference to territorial arrangements, is henceforth to be recognized in America. Just twenty years from the close of the war of the American revoultion, France, by a treaty with Spain, of which the provisions have never been disclosed, possessed herself of Louisiana, but did so only to cede it to the United States; and in the same year Lewis and Clark started on their expedition to plant the flag of the United States on the shores of the Pacific. In 1819, Florida was sold by Spain to the United States, whose territoral possessions, in this way, had been increased three-fold in a half century. This last acquisition was so much a matter of course, that it had been distinctly foreseen by the Count Aranda, then prime minister of Spain, as long ago as 1783. But even these momentous events are but the forerunners of new territoral revolutions still more stupendous.

"A dynastic struggle, between the Emperor Napoleon and Spain, commencing in 1808, convulsed the peninsula, the vast possessions of the Spanish crown on this continent, vice-royalties and captain-generalships filling the space between California and Cape Horn. One after another asserted their independence; no friendly power in Europe, at that time, was able, or if able, was willing, to succor Spain or aid her to prop the crumbling buttresses of her colonial empire. So far from it, when France, in 1823, threw an army of one hundred thousand men into Spain, to control her domestic politics, England thought it necessary to counteract the movement by recognizing the independence of the Spanish provinces in America; in the remarkable language of the distinguished minister of the day, in order to redress the balance of power in Europe, he called into existence a new world in the west, somewhat overrating, perhaps, the extent of the derangement in the old world, and not doing full justice to the position of the United States in America, or their influence on the fortunes of their sister republics on this continent.

"Thus, in sixty years from the close of the seven years' war, Spain, like France, had lost the last remains of her once imperial possessions in this hemisphere. The United States, meantime, were, by the arts of peace and the healthful progress of things, rapidly enlarging their dimensions and consolidating their power. The great march of events still went on. Some of the new republics, from the effect of a mixture of races, or the want of training in liberal institutions, showed themselves incapable of self-government. The province of Texas revolted from Mexico by the same right by which Mexico revolted from Spain; at the memorable battle of San Jacinto, in 1836, she passed the great ordeal of nascent States, and her independence was recognized by this government, by England, by France, and other European powers. Mainly peopled from the United States, she sought naturally to be incorporated into the Union. The offer was repeatedly rejected by Presidents Jackson and Van Buren, to avoid a collision with Mexico. At last the annexation took place. As a domestic question, it is no fit subject for comment in a communication to a foreign minister; as a question of public law, there never was an extension of territory more naturally or justifiably made; it produced a disturbed relation with the government of Mexico; war ensued, and in its results, other extensive territories were, for a large pecuniary compensation on the part of the United States, added to the Union.

"Without adverting to the divisions of opinion which arose in reference to this war—as must always happen in free countries in reference to great measures—no person surveying these events with the eye of comprehensive statesmanship, can fail to trace in the main result the undoubted operation of the law of our political existence. The consequences are before the world; vast provinces, which had languished for three centuries under the leaden sway of a stationary system, are coming under the influences of an active civilization, freedom of speech and the press—the trial by jury, religious equality, and representative government, having been carried by the constitution of the United States into extensive regions in which they were unknown before. By the settlement of California the great circuit of intelligence round the globe is completed. The discovery of the gold of that region, leading as it did to the same discovery in Australia, has touched the nerves of industry throughout the world."

This fine picture of the territorial, as well as social and political development of the United States, must gratify the pride of every patriotic heart.

Millard Fillmore.

Japan also attracted attention. Some of our sailors, who had been shipwrecked and cast upon her shores, were inhospitably treated; and the president determined to attempt a negotiation with that country for their protection, and for such commercial privileges as could be obtained. With a view to open commercial intercourse with this empire, which had for several centuries been a sealed book to the various nations of the civilized world, the president ordered Commodore Aulick to the command of the East India squadron, and empowered him to open negotiations with Japan. We copy the following paragraphs from the letter of instructions to Commore Aulick, which was drawn up by Mr. Webster:

"The moment is near when the last link in the chain of oceanic steam navigation is to be formed. From China and the East Indies to Egypt; thence through the Mediterranean and the Atlantic ocean to England; thence again to our happy shores, and other parts of this great continent; from our own ports to the southernmost part of the isthmus that connects the two western continents; and from its Pacific coast, north and southward, as far as civilization has spread, the steamers of other nations, and of our own, carry intelligence, the wealth of the world, and thousands of travelers.

"It is the President's opinion that steps should be taken at once to enable our enterprising merchants to supply the last link in that great chain which unites all nations of the world, by the early establishment of a line of steamers from California to China. In order to facilitate this enterprise, it is desirable that we should obtain, from the emperor of Japan, permission to purchase from his subjects the necessary supplies of coal, which our steamers, in their out and inward voyages, may require. The well known jealousy with which the Japanese Empire has, for the last two centuries, rejected all overtures from other nations to open its ports to their vessels, embarrasses all new attempts to change the exclusive policy of that country.

* * * * *

"The President, although fully aware of the great reluctance hitherto shown by the Japanese government to enter into treaty stipulations with any foreign nation—a feeling which it is sincerely wished that you may be able to overcome—has thought it proper, in view of this latter favorable contingency, to invest you with full power to negotiate and sign a treaty of amity and commerce between the United States and the emperor of Japan."

Commodore Aulick became involved in difficulty with the Brazilian minister, who was a passenger on board his vessel to Rio Janeiro, and this resulted in his recall. It was afterwards determined to give a more imposing character to the expedition, which, consisting of seven ships, finally sailed in the autumn of 1852, under the command of Commodore Perry, who had prepared himself for the undertaking by a careful study of the whole subject, he being invested with extraordinary diplomatic and discretionary powers. The steamers Mississippi, Princeton, Susquehanna, and Alleghany, the Vermont 74, the sloops-of-war Vandalia and Macedonian, and the store-ships Supply and Southampton, were designated for the service—some of these vessels being already on the East India station. The instructions to Commodore Perry authorized him to dispatch vessels, interpreters, and all other means necessary, in his estimation, to bring about the desired results. He was directed to explore the coasts of Japan and the adjacent continent and islands; to cause views to be made of remarkable places, and soundings to be taken at entrances of harbors and rivers; and to collect information of the social, political and commercial condition of places he might visit. But the great objects of the expedition were to procure friendly admission to Japan, for purposes of trade; to effect a permanent arrangement for the protection of American seamen and property wrecked on the islands; to obtain permission for American vessels to enter Japanese ports in order to obtain supplies of provisions, &c., and to refit in case of disaster; and to establish permanent depots of coal for our steamers crossing the Pacific. If he should fail, by means of persuasion, to obtain a relaxation of the Japanese system of exclusion, or an assurance of humane treatment to our shipwrecked seamen, he was instructed to change his tone, and to inform the goverment in unequivocal terms that our government would visit every instance of inhuman treatment of our citizens with severe chastisement. He was not to use force, except in self-defense, or to resent an act of personal violence.

It was the first official act of Mr. Everett, who succeeded Mr. Webster as secretary of state, to draft the admirable letter of President Fillmore to the emperor of Japan, which constituted the grand seal, as it were, of Commodore Perry's mission. In this letter his Imperial Majesty was apprised, in language singularly felicitous, that Commodore Perry's visit had no other object than to propose that the United States and Japan should live in friendship and have commercial intercourse with each other, for mutual benefit; and his majesty was urged, in case he should not be satisfied that it would be safe altogether to abrogate the ancient laws of his empire, which forbid foreign trade, to suspend those laws for a few years, so as to try the experiment, in accordance with a custom which, he was told, prevailed here, of making treaties with foreign states for a limited period, to be renewed or not, as the parties pleased. Friendship, commerce, a supply of coal and provisions, and protection of our shipwrecked people, his majesty was assured, were the only objects of the visit of our squadron to the renowned city of Yeddo.

It is not necessary here to detail the proceedings of this important expedition; it is sufficient to say that the vessels arrived in the Japanese waters in June, 1853, and after numerous delays a treaty was signed between the commodore and commissioners of the imperial government, 31st March, 1854. This took place at the village of Yoku-hama, in the bay of Yeddo, and about nine miles from that great city. The main stipulations of the treaty were that the two ports of Simoda and Hakodadi should be open to communication with the Americans. Having visited these two places and arranged some details of the treaty, the commodore returned to America. His proceedings were regarded as very important, and England, France, and Russia hastened to secure similar arrangements with the Japanese government.

Another interesting enterprise may be properly noticed here. After various navigators had attempted in vain to discover in the Arctic seas a passage from the Atlantic to the Pacific, Sir John Franklin, a veteran in this service, was dispatched in May, 1845, to make still one more attempt. He had two vessels and one hundred and thirty-eight men. Since the early part of 1846, nothing having been heard of them, and several expeditions having been dispatched from Great Britain in quest of the missing adventurers, Henry Grinnell, a wealthy merchant of New York, feeling a deep interest in this subject, sent two vessels at his own expense in May, 1850, to the Arctic seas, under the command of Lieutenant De Haven, of the United States navy, to make search for the explorers. These proceeded to the southern extremity of Wellington Channel, where they found the graves of three of Sir John Franklin's men, made in April, 1846. After unsuccessful attempts to pass up the channel, the expedition returned. Not yet discouraged, Mr. Grinnell, in connection with the government, despatched another vessel, the brig Advance, on the same errand, under the command of Dr. E. K. Kane, the surgeon and naturalist of the first expedition. As no certain tidings were received from this expedition, the bark Relief and steam-propeller Arctic were sent under command of Captain Hartstein, May 31, 1855, by our government in search of it. On the 11th of September following, these vessels had the good fortune to meet Dr. Kane and his party on board a Danish vessel on the coast of Greenland, bound for Europe. They had lost their ship in the ice, and after incredible hardships and a series of remarkable adventures, had reached Uppernavick, in Greenland, where their dangers and difficulties ended. They left the Danish ships in which they had taken passage and returned home with Captain Hartstein. The result of Dr. Kane's* researches are exceedingly valuable, as they prove the existence of a broad open sea to the north of Greenland.

We may further state that in October, 1854, Dr. Rae, who had been connected with one of the British arctic expeditions, published an account of the discovery of the fate of Sir John Franklin and his companions. According to this statement, their ships, the Erebus and the Terror, were crushed by icebergs in 1850. Sir John and forty of his companions was seen by the Esquimaux near King William's Land, traveling afoot and dragging a boat after them. The bodies of most of them were subsequently found near the Back river, surrounded by evidences which seemed to show that some of them had been driven by hunger to Cannibalism. Dr. Rae, purchased of the Indians several articles which were brought to London, and recognized by friends as belonging to the lost members of the exploring party.

It may be added finally, that the problem of a passage through the Arctic ocean from the Atlantic to the Pacific has been determined in the affirmative, by Captain McClure, of the ship Investigator, sent in search of Sir John Franklin. Sailing eastward from Behring's Straits to a certain point where his passage was obstructed by ice, he employed sledges, and proceeded still further on the ice till he reached a place which had been visited by other navigators, Captain Parry and others. This took place in the autumn of 1853.

Of various other measures taken by President Fillmore for the extension of our commerce and the increase of practical knowledge, we have not space to speak in detail. It may be stated generally that some of our naval officers were sent to South America to survey the Laplata river and its branches. Lieutenant Lynch, with similar views, surveyed a portion of the coast of Africa, and the borders of the Dead Sea. Captain Ringgold was ordered to explore the China seas, and others to survey the valley of the Amazon. Efforts were also made to open the guano trade, which is a mo-

* It is melancholy to relate that soon after his return, Dr. Kane's constitution, shattered by his exposure and sufferings, gave way; having in vain sought restoration by a voyage to Europe, he went to Havanna, where he died February 1857. This event drew forth a general expression of regret, and numerous eulogies from scientific bodies, which recognized alike his admirable personal qualities, and the noble spirit of enterprise which he had manifested, and to which, indeed, he fell a victim

nopoly, and, in this connection, an unfortunate letter was written by the secretary of state to Mr. Jewett. Without the knowledge of the president, an order was sent to Commodore McAuley to protect our vessels in taking guano from the Lobos Islands. As soon as the president discovered the state of the case, the order was countermanded, and an arrangement was made with the Peruvian government to freight the vessels which had been sent out, at a stipulated price.

Among other important events that transpired during Mr. Fillmore's administration, we may mention the act of congress in the spring of 1851, reducing the general rate of postage to three cents, and which was subsequently amended so as to require them to be marked with stamps, as prepayment: also the purchase in the autumn of 1851, of large tracts of land in Minesota from the Sioux Indians, and the creation of the northern part of Oregon, March 1853, into a territory, by the name of Washington.

The various measures we have noticed, as has been remarked, "show that the administration of President Fillmore was characterized not less by enterprise than by wise and salutary caution, and that he fully sympathized with the progressive spirit of the age, whenever its indulgence was consistent with our obligations to others. This happy union of enterprise without rashness, of caution without timidity, entitles Mr. Fillmore to a high rank as a practical statesman."

CHAPTER CCCCXCIV.

Election of Franklin Pierce to the Presidency—His Administration—Election of James Buchanan—His Administration.

From 1852 to 1860.

In the presidential election of November, 1852, General Pierce of New Hampshire was the democratic candidate, and General Winfield Scott the whig candidate. The former prevailed. William R. King, of Alabama, was chosen vice-president. The latter, on account of enfeebled health, was unable to assume the duties of his office. He repaired to Cuba with the hope of resuscitating his constitution, but this proved unavailing. He returned to his residence in Alabama, where he died, April, 1853.

General Pierce had been elected by a large majority of the people, and he entered upon the duties of his office with a hopeful feeling throughout the country of internal peace and general prosperity. Various events, however, soon conspired to change this auspicious state of our affairs.

Among the difficulties which beset the new president, was a dispute as to the boundary between the territory of New Mexico and the contiguous Mexican state of Chihuahua. The valley of Mesilla was claimed by both parties, and by order of Santa Anna, president of Mexico, the disputed territory was taken possession of by a Mexican armed force. The controversy was settled by a treaty which conveyed the territory in question to the United States upon our payment of ten millions of dollars. The troubled condition of the government of Mexico, has, however, rendered our extended frontier along the territory of that country, the frequent scene of Indian hostility, as well as irritation with the Mexican inhabitants in the neighborhood.

The various plans set on foot by the Fillmore administration, for enlarging the boundaries of knowledge, as well as for internal improvement, were to some extent followed by the new president. In May 1853, the expedition already spoken of as projected by the preceding administration, and consisting of four armed vessels and a supply ship, commanded by Captain Ringgold, sailed from Norfolk, destined to survey the China seas. Means were also taken for the survey of several routes to our territories on the Pacific, with a view to the construction of one or more railways, to facilitate the intercourse between the eastern and western portions of our extended settlements.

In July, 1853, a Hungarian refugee named Martin Kosta, but who had been in the United States and carried an American protection, being in the city of Smyrna, was seized in obedience to an order of the Austrian consul, by the crew of an Austrian ship, and taken on board of her, with the intention of carrying him to Trieste, as a refugee. Captain Ingraham, commander of the American sloop of war St. Louis, immediately demanded his release, and this being refused, he cleared his ship for action, and threatened an immediate attack upon the Austrian vessel. This had the desired effect, and Kosta was given up to the French consul to await the action of the two governments. This gallant conduct on the part of Captain Ingraham caused a thrill of approbation throughout Europe, and was heartily approved by the American people. Congress gave expression to the general sentiment, by voting him a sword. Kosta was finally given up and returned to the United States in a government ship.

Soon after the assembling of the thirty-third congress, Mr. Douglass of Illinois, chairman of the committee on territories, introduced a bill called the Nebraska Act, the main objects of which appeared to be to erect a large portion of our western domain into two distinct territories, under the title of Kansas and Nebraska; the former being the southern and the latter the northern portion. So far the measure might have been generally acceptable, but the act contained a provision nullifying the compromises of 1820, which forever excluded slavery from the country north of latitude 36° 30.' This took the nation by surprise, and being regarded at the north as a violation not only of the compromise of 1820, but the more recent one of 1850, it caused a deep feeling of indignation. The agitation of the subject of slavery was aroused throughout the whole country. Among the remonstrances sent to congress, was one from New England, signed by three thousand ministers of the gospel. In spite of powerful opposition in congress, the bill passed the senate on the 7th of March, 1854, and on the 22d of May it was sanctioned by the house of representatives. The president was understood to have favored the measure and readily gave it his signature. Thus the foundation was laid for speedy civil war, which carried bloodshed and conflagration into the terri-

Franklin Pierce.

tory of Kansas, and caused an agitation which shook the Union to its foundation.

January 7, 1854, a treaty generally called the "reciprocity treaty," was concluded by Lord Elgin, governor-general of Canada, with the United States, by which the British American coast fisheries were thrown open to the people of this country; the free navigation of the St. Lawrence, and the Canadian lakes, was also guaranteed to us, and the products of the United States and British America, with the exception of sugar and tobacco were reciprocally admitted free of duty.

On the 28th of February, 1854, the American steamer Black Warrior, plying between New York and Nicaragua, was seized on some shallow pretense by the authorities at Havana and declared forfeited. The subject immediately attracted the attention of our government, which dispatched a special messenger to Madrid, with directions to our minister, Mr. Soulé, to demand redress. The officials at Cuba, however, became alarmed, and gave up the vessel and cargo, upon the payment of a fine of six thousand dollars—against which law the interested parties protested. This difficulty has since been adjusted.

On the 24th of May, 1854, a serious riot took place in Boston, in consequence of the seizure of Anthony Burns, a fugitive slave. The rights of the master being ascertained by the commissioner, Loring, and allowed by the circuit judge, the slave was on the 20th escorted on board the United States revenue cutter, Morris, attended by a large body of armed citizens, in the employ of the United States marshal, a company of marines from the navy yard, a body of United States troops from Fort Independence, with a brass nine pounder, a large body of militia called out by the mayor, and the whole police force of the city. No serious outbreak occurred, and the slave was taken to Virginia on board the cutter, and delivered to his master, Mr. Suttle, of that state.

On the 13th of July, 1854, the American sloop of war Cyane, Captain Hollins, bombarded San Juan, in Nicaraugua, and a small party landing from the ship, reduced the place to ashes. The reason assigned for this act was that a demand for alleged injury being made, was disregarded by the authorities. A considerable portion of the property destroyed belonged to Americans. These with others, have made a reclamation upon our government for damages. The conduct of Captain Hollins was very extensively reprobated, but he was sustained by our government.

In October of this year, 1854, our three plenipotentiaries, Mr. Buchanan at London, Mr. Mason at Paris, and Mr. Soulé at Madrid, met at Ostend in Holland, to confer together as to the policy to be pursued by our government in relation to the acquisition of Cuba. A few days after, they removed to Aix la Chapelle, in Prussia, and on the 18th made an official report to the American secretary of state, urging the acquisition of Cuba, if possible by purchase, if not by force. The following is a part of the language of this document:

"We have arrived at the conclusion, and are thoroughly convinced, that an immediate and earnest effort ought to be made by the government of the United States to purchase Cuba from Spain at any price for which it can be obtained, not exceeding the sum of $

* * * * *

"But if Spain, dead to the voice of her own interest, and actuated by stubborn pride and a false sense of honor, should refuse to sell Cuba to the United States, then the question will arise, What ought to be the course of the American government under such circumstances?

* * * * *

"After we shall have offered Spain a price for Cuba far beyond its present value, and this shall have been refused, it will then be time to consider the question, does Cuba, in the possession of Spain, seriously endanger our internal peace and the existence of our cherished Union?

"Should this question be answered in the affirmative, then, by every law, human and divine, we shall be justified in wresting it from Spain if we possess the power; and this upon the very same principle that would justify an individual in tearing down the burning house of his neighbor if there were no other means of preventing the flames from destroying his own home."

The proceedings of this congress created a great shock upon the governments of Europe, and indeed upon the views and feelings of the people of the United States. Its doctrines were not sanctioned by the administration, and are appoved by only a small portion of the country.

On the 27th of September, 1854, the Collins steamer Arctic, with four hundred and ten persons, passengers and crew, commanded by Captain Luce, and being near Cape Race, came in collision at 12 o'clock with the French screw steamer, Vesta. For a short time it was not sure that any injury had been done to the Arctic, but it was soon ascertained that her bows were stove in and she was in a sinking condition. The attempt to stop the leak proved unsuccessful, and the fires of the engine were speedily extinguished. The crew proved mutinous, and amid scenes of heart-rendering distress, terror, and despair, the ship went down at 5 o'clock. Twenty-two passengers and sixty-five of the crew were saved. The captain floated for a time on a piece of the wreck, and being taken up by a ship, was landed in Canedas. The dastardly and selfish conduct of the crew caused universal indignation.

On the 24th of October, 1854, Mr. Pierre Soulé, our minister to Spain, on landing at Calais from London on his way to Spain, and with despatches from Mr. Buchanan to Mr. Mason at Paris, was stopped by the French * police; he accordingly returned to London. Mr. Mason remonstrated, and the matter was finally adjusted, the French government saying that the order was only intended to interdict Mr. Soulé from residing in France, and not to prevent his passage to his embassy at Madrid. Mr. Soulé accordingly came to Paris on the 9th of November, and on the 11th left for Bordeaux.

Soon after the passage of the Nebraska act, which opened a vast and fertile territory to slavery, in contravention of the Missouri Compromise which had existed for thirty years, the friends of freedom in New England formed societies for aiding emigration to the new territory, in order to insure a population there who should exclude slavery by their own acts. This naturally produced a corresponding effort in the slave states, to send emigrants thither who were favorable to the institutions of slavery. The inhabitants of Missouri living along the borders of Kansas, and separated from it only by the Missouri river, sympathized deeply with the pro-slavery movement. The consequence of this state of things, was a long period of agitation in the territory of Kansas.

On the 23d of January, 1856, the Collins steamer Pacific, Captain Asa Eldridge, left Liverpool with a large number of passengers, and was never afterward heard of. Large icebergs were seen in the route of ships from England to the United States, and it is supposed she struck one of them and was immediately engulfed in the sea.

On the 9th of April, 1856, Mr. Buchanan, who had been several years our minister to England, having paid a visit to Paris, left the port of Havre for this country, his place at London being filled by Hon. George M. Dallas. On his arrival in the United States, Mr. Buchanan was received with great favor by numerous friends, and at the meeting of the democratic convention at Cincinnati, May 22, 1856, he was nominated for the presidency.

Mr. Fillmore who was traveling in Europe, was nominated by a convention of the American party,† which met at Philadelphia, in February 1856. Notice of this event reached him at Paris, and in a letter dated at that city May 21, he accepted the nomination. He arrived at New York in June, and being received with acclamations by his friends, he reiterated his acceptance of the same. He was thus the candidate of the main body of the American party, and was finally supported by a considerable number of his old whig friends.

In 1855 charges were made to our government against Mr. Crampton, the British minister at Washington, as well as the British consul at New York, Philadelphia, and Cincinnati, as having been concerned in raising recruits for the Eastern War, in contravention of our laws. Complaint of their conduct was made to the British government, but as they sustained its agents, Mr. Crampton was furnished with his passports and the consuls deprived of their exequaturs. All but one returned to England and Mr. Crampton after a time received the honor of knighthood from the queen. For some time no minister was sent to the United States, but early in the year 1857, the vacancy was filled by the appointment of Lord Napier.

In the early part of 1856, the British relief bark Resolute, which had been abandoned in the Arctic ice by Captain Kellet of the expedition under Sir Edward Belcher, was met with, floating in the northern seas by a New London whaler. She was found to have on board all the stores, equipments, and armaments she possessed when taken leave of by her crew. She had been released from her imprisonment by the melting of the ice, and had drifted a thousand miles to the south. She was purchased for forty thousand dollars, of the rescuers, by our government, and being refitted, was sent back to the British government, with an American crew under the command of Captain Hartstene of the United States navy. He arrived at Portsmouth in December, and was received with a general cheer of welcome from the people of England, as well as special attentions on the part of the government. The queen with a number of eminent persons visited the ship on the 16th. After her departure about eight thousand persons, one after another, came on board and were welcomed by the captain. For several successive days eager crowds came to see the recovered vessel and to express their gratification at the compliment paid by our government to the British nation. Captain Hartstene and his crew were entertained at a public dinner by the authorities of Portsmouth, and the captain himself was invited to dine by the queen at Osborne House. Lady Franklin, the noble wife of the lost Arctic explorer, also entertained him and his officers at her house at Brighton. A writer in one of the papers adds the following:

"The queen treated Hartstene with marked attention at dinner, and in the drawing-room. Al-

* Several motives doubtless operated on the French government, in adopting this measure. Mr. Soule was a native of France, and had been a somewhat violent republican; he had, moreover, been condemned by the tribunals for some of his writings, and it was in consequence of this that he emigrated to the United States. He, as well as his son, had been engaged in duels at Madrid, and above all, by his speeches in America as well as his participation in the Ostend conference, he had come to be regarded as a leader in the violent measures supposed to be on foot for the acquisition of Cuba. The suspicious government of Louis Napoleon might therefore regard the presence in France of such a person—as a red republican and a fillibuster, a native of the country but now clothed with diplomatic rank and influence by the government of the United States—with apprehension.

† The American party had its origin in a pretty extensive disgust at the greediness with which foreigners sought office in the United States, and the undue influence which they exercised in political affairs. The manner in which designing politicians flattered and used these foreign masses, to promote their own purposes, served to extend and deepen the feeling of discontent. The large number of important foreign appointments given to foreigners by Mr. Pierce, wrought up this feeling to its climax. About this time a secret society, bound by oaths and signs, called "Know Nothings," was organized and spread rapidly over the country. In several of the states, they carried the elections, and it seemed that they were destined to attain a political ascendency in the nation. A sudden change, however, took place in their prospects. Their councils became divided. the secret oaths and unseen combinations created alarm. The name of "Know Nothing" was abandoned and American was assumed instead. The party, however, became divided on the subject of slavery, and were known under two distinct titles, the North and the South Americans. Only a portion of these fragments actually voted for Mr. Fillmore.

terwards she came up to him and said she wished to talk with him, and remained in familiar conversation with him for an hour. On leaving the Isle of Wight there was a great display of enthusiasm; as the ship passed out of harbor, the shores were lined, and the air rang with cheers. We were escorted by a steam yacht, which is always in attendance on the ship, and the fine steam-frigate "Retribution," which was also acting as an escort, and we were towed by a government steamer. An admirality messenger is also continually in attendance on the officers. On our arrival at Spithead the ships saluted, and on entering Portsmouth harbor the transports were lined with people, cheering and waving handkerchiefs, the military bands playing national airs, and the battery saluting. The Old Victory manned her rigging and cheered. There never was such enthusiasm and exhibition of hearty feeling: it is the event of the day, and is in every one's mouth. The government have insisted that the officers shall return in the steam-frigate Retribution,* and they will probably leave on the day after Christmas. On Tuesday Captain Hartstene is invited to Lord Palmerston's country-seat."

On the 22d of May, Charles Sumner, senator of Massachusetts, was violently assaulted in the senate-chamber by Preston S. Brooks, member of congress from South Carolina. The alleged cause of this outrage was a very severe speech delivered by Mr. Sumner in the senate, May 19th, 1856, setting forth the wrongs done to Kansas, in which some reflections were cast upon South Carolina, as well as Mr. Butler, senator from that state, and uncle of Mr. Brooks. It afterwards appeared that the attack had been meditated for some time, and the assailant came into the senate-chamber, attended by a friend, Mr. Keitt, also a member of congress from South Carolina. He approached Mr. Sumner, who was writing at his desk, and suddenly, and without warning, struck him several times rapidly and with great violence, with a gutta-percha cane. Mr. Sumner sprang forward, but being pinioned by his desk could make no resistance, and fell stunned and bleeding to the floor. Several senators were in the room and saw the assault, but several of them rendered no assistance and manifested no concern in behalf of the victim. Both Mr. Brooks and Mr. Keitt were rebuked by the house, upon which they resigned their seats; but both were immediately and unanimously returned by their constituents. Mr. Sumner was long confined to his bed, and was unable to resume his seat in the senate until the end of February, 1857.

The nomination of Mr. Buchanan for the presidency by a convention of the democratic party which met at Cincinnati June 2, and of Mr. Fillmore by the delegates of the American party at Philadelphia in February, have already been mentioned. On the 18th of June, 1856, a convention of delegates assembled at Philadelphia, in pursuance of a call addressed to the people of the United States without distinction of party, who were opposed to the repeal of the Missouri Compromise and the policy of the existing administration; opposed also to the admission of slavery into free territory; in favor of admitting Kansas as a free state, and, generally, a restoration of the government to the principles of Washington. This convention nominated J. C. Fremont for president, and William L. Dayton of New Jersey, for vice-president. The supporters of this ticket assumed the name of the Republican party.

The canvass that ensued was attended with great animation, but was rather marked with thoughtful discussion than party and personal bitterness. The result was, that Mr. Buchanan received a majority of the electoral votes for the office of president, and John C. Breckenridge of Kentucky a majority for the office of vice-president. It was a remarkable feature of the election that Mr. Fillmore carried only the state of Maryland, while Fremont, the candidate of a party which had existed but a few months, received overwhelming majorities in all the free states, save New Jersey, Pennsylvania, Indiana, Illinois, and California.

Among the measures of the first session of the thirty-fourth congress which excited general attention, was one by which the pay of members, both of the house and senate, was raised from eight dollars a day to three thousand dollars a year and mileage, irrespective of the length of the sessions.

An event which caused universal sympathy was the prevalence of the yellow fever at Norfolk, and Portsmouth, Va., in the summer and autumn of 1855, which swept off many hundreds of the inhabitants. It is believed to have been unparalleled in its devastating effects, more than one third the resident inhabitants having fallen victims to the plague.

The thirty-fourth congress closed its second session on the 3d of March, 1857, having among various other important acts, made a modification of the tariff, the main features of which were, a reduction of seventy per cent. duty on brandies and some other liquors; on wines, manufactured tobacco, etc., ten per cent.; on sugar, glass, woolens, iron, manufactured silk, flannels, floor cloths, etc., six per cent.; on books and engravings two per cent.; on raw hides, brass, tin, etc., one per cent. This reduction was designed to bring down the revenue to the actual wants of the government, there having been for several years a considerable excess arising from the tariff law of 1846.

Another interesting measure of Congress, was an act in behalf of an enterprise for extending the magnetic telegraph to England across the Atlantic, the termini being a point on the eastern coast of Newfoundland and the other on the western coast of Ireland. A company for this object having been formed in England and the United States, and capitalists in both countries having favored it, our government guaranteed, on certain conditions, the sum of seventy thousand dollars a year, for ten years, the British government having entered into a similar stipulation.

We may here notice the curious and suggestive fact, that on the 17th of September, 1856, the American schooner Dean Richmond reached Liverpool direct from Chicago, with a cargo of grain, being the first vessel that ever went straight from the great lakes of the west. She was sixty days on her passage. The cost and distance were:

* This proposition was respectfully declined, and the officers and crew retnrned in an American steamer.

Towage at Welland canal,		$35
" between St. Lawrence canal,		50
" through one canal,		6
" through two canals,		9
" through three canals,		9
Montreal to Quebec,		60
Pilotage, Quebec to sea,		30
Total,		$199
Tolls on ship and cargo,		$160
Chicago to Quebec,	miles,	1,600
Quebec to Cape Race,		860
Cape Race to Cape Clear,		1,713
Cape Race to Liverpool,		2,010

It may be proper to note the death of three distinguished men, whose names were long associated with the history of the government, viz.: John C. Calhoun, Henry Clay, and Daniel Webster. The first died at Washington, March 31, 1850, aged sixty-eight. Mr. Clay also died at Washington, his decease taking place June 29, 1852, at the age of seventy-five. Mr. Webster died at his residence in Marshfield, October 28, 1852, aged seventy, having, in a manner which deeply impressed the people of the United States, given his emphatic sanction to the truth and excellence of the Christian religion.

In the summer of 1854, the disputed boundary lines between Mexico and the United States were settled.

Our chronicle of events would be incomplete, should we omit to mention the operations of an adventurer, one of our countrymen, in Nicaragua. The Central American Union being broken up, the individual states, with a small population, disturbed by elements of internal discord, were in a position of peculiar weakness and disorganization. The state of Nicaragua, especially, was a prey to rival factions. Tempted by this attitude of affairs, William Walker, a citizen of the United States then in California, and who had figured in an abortive attempt to subjugate Sonora, a province of Mexico, in the summer of 1855, appeared in Nicaragua with a small band of followers, for the purpose of conquering that country. Numerous petty conflicts ensued, with varying fortune, Walker being sustained chiefly by recruits from the United States, and opposed by the inhabitants of the country. His attitude was that of a foreigner seeking to subdue the state for his own purposes, and with no reasonable pretense of sanction by the people. For nearly two years he maintained himself in the territory, but the Costa Ricans joined the Nicaraguans, and he was expelled from the country in the spring of 1857. In November following, having collected a force of four hundred men, he embarked at Mobile, for Nicaragua, and arrived at Puerta Arenas. In December he and his men surrendered to Captain Paulding, of the United States steamer Wabash, and were carried back to the United States.

Mr. Buchanan was inaugurated as president on the 4th of March, 1857, and on the 6th his cabinet was confirmed by the senate. as follows:

Secretary of State, Lewis Cass, of Mich.; Secretary of the Treasury, Howell Cobb, of Geo.; Secretary of War, John B. Floyd, of Va.; Secretary of the Navy, Isaac Toucey, of Conn.; Secretary of the Interior, Jacob Thompson, of Miss.; Attorney-General, Jeremiah S. Black, of Penn.; Postmaster-General, Aaron V. Brown, of Tenn.

James Buchanan.

One of the first subjects which demanded the attention of the new administration was the state of things in Kansas. The avowed doctrine of the Kansas-Nebraska act, passed in 1854, was that of "Popular Sovereignty," or the right of a people of a territory to decide for themselves, whether to admit slavery or not, when they ask admission into the Union. In view of this, a movement was made, as we have already stated, in Massachusetts, by private associations, to people the territory with emigrants opposed to the establishment of slavery there: a counteracting effort was made in the South to people the territory with inhabitants in favor of slavery. The result was such as might have been anticipated: a great mass of emigrants of opposite views and feelings rushed into the territory, and were soon in a state of angry contention. Scenes of violence took place, and in 1855 and 1856 there was actual civil war, while several lives were lost, property was destroyed, and settlements broken up. After the presidential contest of the latter year, the excitement, in some degree, abated. A convention, however, which met at Lecompton September 7th, 1857, framed a constitution establishing slavery, contrary to the known wishes of a majority of the people, and the attempt of the administration to bring Kansas into the Union, under this instrument, caused a deep feeling of regret in the country.

In the autumn of 1857, there was a sudden and severe money panic, which spread over the United States, and extended even to Europe. Many of the banks suspended specie payments, though most of them resumed soon after. A very general depression of business continued, however, for two years.

In April, 1858, the Mount Vernon Ladies' Association made a contract with John A. Washington for the purchase of the Mount Vernon estate. By the untiring and skilful labors of these ladies, the large sum of $200,000, the amount of the purchase money, has been raised, and the said estate is in their legal possession.

A remarkable decision of the United States federal court was made at Washington in 1857, declaring that colored persons are not citizens of the United States; some of the members of the court also declared, incidentally, that in their opinion the Missouri compromise was unconstitutional; that congress has no power over slavery in the territories, and generally that slaves are property, in view of the constitution, and their owners may therefore claim protection for them, even in passing through free states. These suggestions are not regarded as decisions, and are believed by many to be opposed to the doctrines and practice of the government on this subject from its foundation to the present time.

On the 10th of April, 1858, Thomas Hart Benton, a distinguished Senator from Missouri, died at Washington. He had held the office of Senator for thirty years.

In the summer of 1858, the wires were laid between Valentia Bay in Ireland, and Trinity Bay in Newfoundland, for a submarine Telegraph. Numerous messages were sent both ways, and for a time it was deemed to be a successful enterprise; in a short space, however, the line failed to work, and since that time all operations have ceased. The experiment will be resumed, and confident hopes of realizing the desired object are entertained.

In 1859, intelligence was received that the steamer Fox, dispatched by Lady Franklin, had discovered that Sir John died June 11, 1847, and that his two ships, Erebus and Terror, were soon after abandoned in the ice. All his men had perished from cold and starvation. One of their boats and other remains were found on the north-west coast of King William's Island.

In this year, 1859, our minister, Mr. Ward, negotiated an important treaty with the Emperor of China, at Pekin; England and France being at war with that power.

In this year also, Oregon, the southern portion of the territory known under that name, was admitted as a state; the northern portion, called Washington, has been since organized as a territory. Some discussion ensued with Great Britain respecting the island San Juan, and General Scott was sent out to arrange matters on the spot, and the affair was amicably settled.

In 1860, the country was deeply excited by the visit of several ambassadors from Japan, who came in consequence of the treaty made by Commodore Perry with the Emperor of Japan in 1854. They were brought to Panama in the American frigate Roanoke, and from this side of the isthmus in the Powhatan. They visited Washington, Philadelphia, and New York, receiving hospitalities, making purchases, and taking down notes of machines and inventions to be developed on their return home. They brought presents to the President in acknowledgment of those sent to their emperor. They were carried back to Japan in the steam frigate Niagara. Several vessels laden with the products of Japanese industry have since arrived in this country, and doubtless some trade will be the result of the treaty and the interchange of civilities.

The Prince of Wales soon after visited Canada and the United States. He was received in the British possessions with the loyal devotion which he had a right to expect, but the enthusiasm and cordiality of his welcome in a land which had twice been at war with Great Britain, were as gratifying as they were unexpected. An era of better feeling between the two countries was confidently looked forward to; but, unfortunately, this hope has not been realized.

Late in this year, an event occurred which seemed likely to check the adventurous tendencies of a certain class of our countrymen pretty effectually. William Walker, of whose performances in Nicaragua we have spoken, invaded Honduras with a small band of followers. He was captured, tried, and summarily shot in September, 1860.

In November, a presidential election took place. The republican party, which had sprung into existence four years before, nominated Abraham Lincoln, of Illinois; the democratic party, which had split into two factions, nominated Stephen A. Douglass and John C. Breckenridge; while the so-called union party nominated John Bell. An effort was made to defeat an election by the people, and throw it into the House of Representatives, by a device called "fusion," but Abraham Lincoln was nevertheless elected by a large majority.

Abraham Lincoln.

It would be useless at the present time (1864), while we are engaged in a war for the preservation of the union of the States, to commence a record which we should have to leave unfinished. This can be better done when definite results have been attained. We therefore close our brief chronicle at this point.

Annals of the Several States of the Union.

CHAPTER CCCCXCV.

We now propose to give, for the purpose of convenient and easy reference, the annals of the several United States and Territories. Our space will allow us only to note the most conspicuous events, with very succinct sketches of a few leading characters. Maps will be given which will furnish the outlines of the physical geography of the several states.

Maine. *Annals.* — A settlement was first attempted by the Plymouth Company at the mouth of the Kennebec in 1607, but without success. The first permanent establishment was made at Saco, in 1623. Sir Ferdinando Gorges obtained a grant of the territory, and established a government here in 1639. Maine was united to Massachusetts shortly afterward. In 1652, it was separated from that state, and reunited in 1677. The French made some attempts to settle upon the islands on the coast, and also invaded the country from Canada, in company with the Indians in their wars with the English settlers; but they were finally expelled from the whole territory. In 1775, this country was distinguished for the march of the American expedition, under Arnold, across the wilderness from the Kennebec, to the St. Lawrence, at Quebec, of which an account is given in the history of the revolution. During this war, the British burnt the town of Falmouth, and took possession of the mouth of the Penobscot, where they continued till the peace, in 1783. In the war of 1812, they captured Castine and Eastport, and retained possession of these places till the peace of 1815. In 1820, Maine was separated from Massachusetts, and became an independent state. The boundary between this state and the British territory on the north-east was not clearly defined by the treaty of 1783, and afterward became the subject of a perplexing controversy between the British and American governments. These difficulties, however, were happily settled by the treaty of Washington, in 1842.

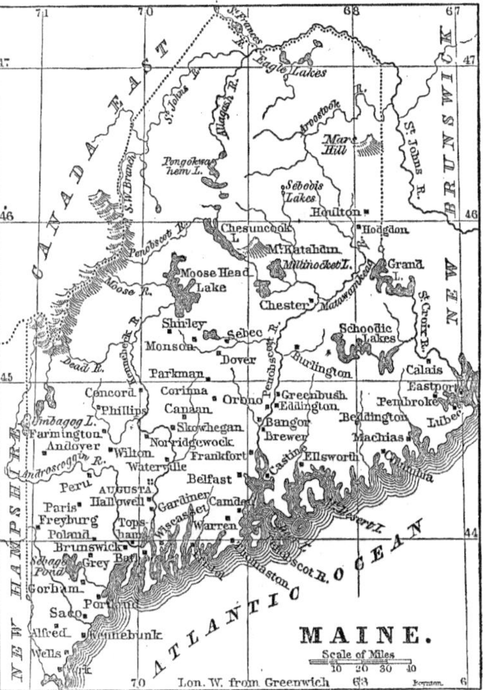

Biography. — General John Sullivan was born at Berwick, in Maine, in 1741. He was bred to the law, in which profession he had much success as a bold, energetic pleader at the bar. The breaking out of the revolution opened a career for his military talents, and as early as 1774, he was at the head of a party of Americans, who, by stratagem, gained possession of a fort in Maine, then garrisoned by British troops. In 1775, he was appointed brigadier-general in the continental army, and was stationed at Winter Hill during the siege of Boston. In 1776, he served in the expedition against Canada, and after the death of General Thomas, he took the chief command of the troops engaged in that enterprise. After the failure of the expedition, he returned to Washington's army, and was taken prisoner at the battle of Long Island, in August, 1776. In October, he was exchanged for General Prescott, of the British army. At the battle of Trenton, he commanded the right wing of the American army, and was engaged also in the battle of Brandywine. He was commander-in-chief of the expedition against Rhode Island in 1778. In 1779, he was sent by Washington on an expedition against the Six Nations of Indians in New York. He marched nearly a hundred miles through the wilderness, fell upon the savages unexpectedly, and completely dispersed them. After this, General Sullivan became involved in a misunderstanding with the board of war, and several of the members of congress, in consequence of which he resigned his command. On the restoration of peace, he returned to the practice of the law in New Hampshire, and was one of the convention which formed the constitution of that state. In 1786, he was chosen president of New Hampshire, and held the office for three years. In 1787, he was appointed district judge of New Hampshire, and died January 22, 1795.

William Phips, celebrated in the early history of New England, was born at Pemaquid, in Maine, in 1650. In early life he followed the profession of a ship-carpenter; but the love of adventure, and an ambitious temper, led him into various undertakings which gained him notice. He visited England, and induced the government to send him, with two frigates, to search for the wreck of a Spanish treasure ship which had been cast away among the Bahama Islands. He failed in his first attempt, but in a second he was so successful as to recover nearly a million and a half of dollars. For this service he was knighted by the king, and appointed high sheriff of New England. He was afterward governor of Massachusetts, and commander of several expeditions which were sent against the French in America. He died in 1694.

New Hampshire. *Annals.* — The first settlement in this state was made at Dover and Little Harbor, near Portsmouth, in 1623, under a grant obtained of the Plymouth Company, in the year preceding, by Gorges and Mason. The territory comprised in the grant was called *Laconia*, and it embraced a part of the present state of Maine. In 1629, the name of *New Hampshire* was given to this territory. In 1641, the people placed themselves under the government of Massachusetts, in which situation they remained till 1680, when New Hampshire became a separate royal province. The first legislature assembled at Portsmouth in that year.

In 1686, the authority of Andros, as we have stated in the history of Massachusetts, was extended over New Hampshire. When Andros was deposed by the people of Boston, the inhabitants of New Hampshire took the government into their own hands. They again placed themselves under the protection of Massachusetts in 1690; were again separated from that government in 1692, and once more annexed to it in 1699. In 1741, Massachusetts and New Hampshire were severed for the last time. A temporary government was established during the war of the revolution; and in 1784, a new constitution was formed this was amended in 1792.

Biography. — John Langdon, an eminent citizen of this state, was born at Portsmouth, in 1739. In early life he was engaged in mercantile business, and at one time was a sea-captain. When the revolutionary struggle commenced, he embraced without hesitation the part of the colonies. In 1774, he assisted in raising a body of troops which took possession of a fort near Portsmouth, disarmed the British garrison, and conveyed the arms and ammunition to a place of safety The British governor of the province would have seized him, but the resolute determination of the inhabitants to defend him at all hazards frustrated this intention. In 1775, he was appointed a delegate from New Hampshire to the continental congress, and in 1776, he was made navy agent. In 1777, he was chosen speaker of the assembly of New Hampshire and when funds were wanted to raise a regiment, he gave all his money, and pledged his plate and merchandise, for this purpose. With the troops thus raised, General Stark gained his memorable victory at Bennington. After the close of the revolutionary war, Mr. Langdon was president of the state of New Hampshire. In 1787, he was appointed a delegate to the convention which framed the federal constitution When the federal government went into operation, he was elected a senator from New Hampshire. In 1805, he was chosen governor of the state, and again in 1810. He died on the 18th of September, 1819 Throughout the whole of his public life, he enjoyed the highest influence in his native state, and was honored and esteemed in every part of the Union.

General John Stark was born in Londonderry, New Hampshire, in 1728. In his youth he was captured by the Indians while hunting, and detained some months in captivity. In the French war of 1775, he served in the army of Lord Howe. On the reception of the news of the battle of Lexington, he immediately repaired to Boston, and fought at the battle of Bunker Hill. He served under Washington at Trenton and Princeton; but his most important service was in the command of the American troops at Bennington, in 1777, when he gave Burgoyne's army a blow from which it never recovered, as we have stated in the history of the United States. He died in 1822.

Vermont. *Annals.* — The French, under Champlain, were the first Europeans who visited this territory; but they made no settlement within it. In 1724, the government of Massachusetts built Fort Dummer, on the Connecticut, within the territory of the present county of Windham. In 1731, the French built a fort at Crown Point, and began a settlement on the opposite side of Lake Champlain. After the conquest of Canada by the British, the settlement of the country proceeded rapidly, and the sovereignty of it was claimed both by New Hampshire and New York. The controversy was decided by George III., in favor of the latter; but the inhabitants declared themselves independent in 1777; Vermont was admitted into the Union in 1791.

Biography. — Ethan Allen, one of the most remarkable men in the history of this state, was a native of Connecticut. His parents emigrated to Vermont while he was quite young; and his education was very deficient. He soon distinguished himself by his acti e

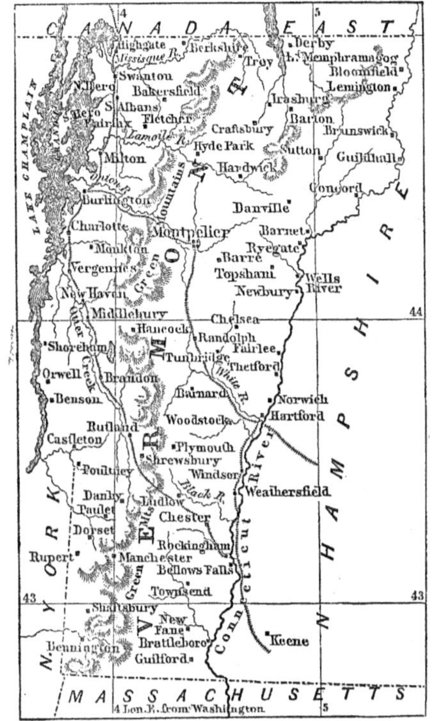

habits and energetic character. On the reception of the news of the battle of Lexington, he collected a body of two hundred and fifty Green Mountain Boys, and marched against Ticonderoga and Crown Point, both which fortresses he captured by surprise. In an attempt upon Montreal in the same year, he was taken prisoner. His captors sent him to England in irons, assuring him that he would be hanged on his arrival; but after a month's confinement in Pendennis Castle, he was transferred to Halifax, and thence to New York, which was then in the hands of the British. In May, 1778, he was exchanged for a British colonel. His health had been so much impaired by the rigors of his imprisonment, that he was unfit for active service in the army; but he was appointed to the chief command of the militia of Vermont. The British attempted to bribe him to join the Canadians against the revolted colonies, but in vain. He died on the 13th of February, 1789. He sustained through life the character of a bold and enterprising man, strongly marked by eccentricity. Although his education was limited, he was the author of several works, the most interesting of which is the narrative of his captivity. In his religious and philosophical notions, he was highly extravagant. He believed, or affected to believe, in the Pythagorean doctrine of the transmigration of souls. One of his books is entitled *Allen's Theology, or the Oracles of Reason* — the first publication of a sceptical character which appeared from the American press.

Samuel Williams, of this state, was the author of a valuable work entitled the *National and Civil History of Vermont.* Royal Tyler, of Walpole, in this state, was an author of considerable celebrity toward the close of the last century.

MASSACHUSETTS. *Annals.* — The first settlement within the territory of Massachusetts was made by the Pilgrims, at Plymouth, December 21, 1620. This settlement was called *Plymouth Colony*, and afterward the *Old Colony*, to distinguish it from the province of Massachusetts Bay, which was for some time a distinct government. The latter was begun in 1628, when a settlement was formed at Salem. In 1629, a royal charter was granted to this colony. In 1630 Boston, Dorchester, Roxbury, Cambridge, and Watertown were settled. In 1634, a representative government was established. In 1637, a war broke out with the Pequod Indians, which ended in their extermination. In 1638, Harvard College was founded at Cambridge. In 1643, in consequence of the dangers which threatened the English settlements from the hostilities of the Indians, Dutch, and French, the colonies of Massachusetts, Plymouth, Connecticut, and New Haven formed themselves into a confederacy, by the name of the *United Colonies of New England:* this continued forty years. In 1652, the province of Maine was detached from Massachusetts. In 1665, the war with the Indians, known as *Philip's war*, broke out. Brookfield, Deerfield, Hatfield, and other towns, were attacked by the Indians, and many of the inhabitants massacred. The war was closed by the defeat of the Indians, and the death of Philip, in 1676.

In 1677, Maine was restored to Massachusetts. In 1680, New Hampshire was detached from Massachusetts. In 1686, the charter of Massachusetts was taken away by James II., and Sir Edmund Andros was sent out from England as governor of all New England. He exercised his authority with such tyranny, that, in 1689, the people of Boston rose in rebellion, took Andros prisoner, sent him to England, and reëstablished the old government of Massachusetts. In 1690, the people of this colony sent an expedition, under Sir William Phips, against the French in Nova Scotia, and captured Port Royal. In the same year, an expedition under Phips was sent against Quebec, but failed of success.

In 1692, a new charter was granted by King William to Massachusetts, which extinguished the Old Colony government, and united Massachusetts, Plymouth, Maine, and Nova Scotia under one administration. In the same year, the delusion called the *Salem witchcraft* threw the colony into great terror, and caused the death of many innocent persons. In March, 1697, Haverhill was captured by the Indians, and forty of the inhabitants killed or made prisoners. In 1704, Deerfield was attacked by them, and the people killed or carried away captive. In 1745, on the breaking out of a war with the French, the government of Massachusetts sent an expedition against Louisburg, on the Island of Cape Breton, which captured that place. It was restored to the French at the conclusion of the war, and again captured by the Massachusetts forces on the renewal of hostilities in 1758.

The American revolution began in Massachusetts. The stamp act, in 1765, produced a riot at Boston, and the destruction of the stamps. In the same year, the legislature of Massachusetts proposed the calling of a general congress of the colonies. In 1768, another riot happened in Boston, occasioned by the seizure of

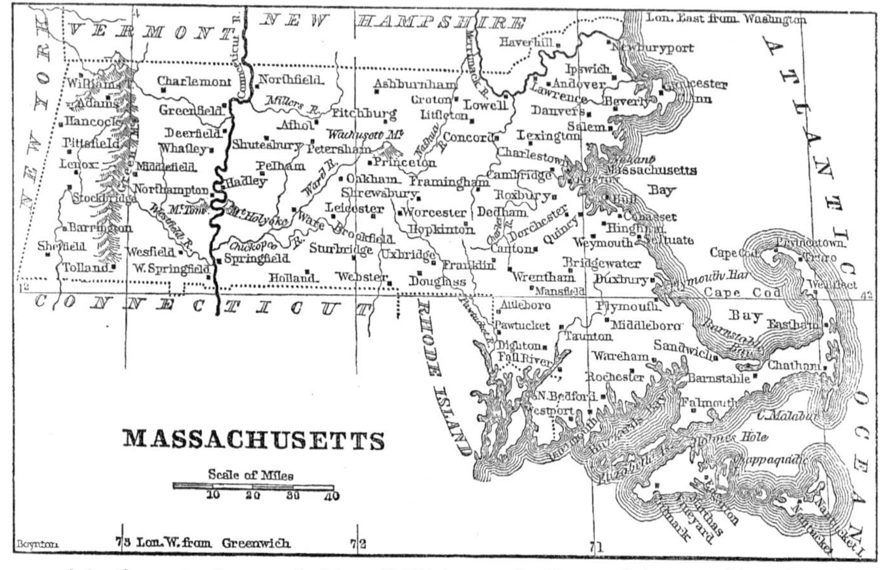

a vessel by the custom-house authorities. British troops were sent to Boston in October of the same year. On the 5th of March, 1770, occurred the collision between the troops and the people, known as the *Boston Massacre*. In 1773, the cargoes of tea sent to Boston were thrown overboard by the people, to avoid the payment of the duty, December 18. In revenge for this act, the British parliament enacted the Boston Port Bill, March 31, 1774, and the commerce of the place was destroyed. On the 20th of May, the charter of Massachusetts was taken away by the royal authority.

On the 18th of April, 1775, occurred the battle of Lexington. The people of Massachusetts rose immediately in arms, and besieged the British in Boston. On the 17th of June was fought the battle of Bunker Hill. On the 12th of July, General Washington arrived at Cambridge, and assumed the command of the American army. On the 4th of March, 1776, the Americans took possession of Dorchester Heights, and on the 17th the British evacuated Boston. The government of Massachusetts continued under the forms of the old charter. A convention to form a new constitution was held at Cambridge, September 1, 1779. The constitution was submitted to the people, ratified by them, and went into effect October 25, 1780, on which day the first legislature met at Boston. In 1786, a rebellion, headed by Daniel Shays, was raised in the western part of the state, but was quelled without bloodshed in the following year. The constitution of Massachusetts has been amended three times since its promulgation, namely, in 1821, 1831, and 1833.

Biography.—John Hancock, an eminent citizen of this state, was born at Quincy, in 1737. He was educated at Harvard College, but began life as a merchant in Boston. In 1760, he travelled in England, and was present at the coronation of George III. The death of his uncle, in 1764, left him heir to a large fortune and an extensive business, both of which he managed with great judgment and liberality. At the commencement of the revolutionary troubles, he was a member of the Massachusetts legislature, and in this station he exerted himself with so much zeal and resolution against the encroachments of Great Britain, as to draw upon himself the special indignation of Gage the British governor of Massachusetts, who, in his proclamation offering pardon to the colonists, after the battle of Lexington, exempted from this act of grace Samuel Adams and John Hancock. This circumstance only served to raise these two individuals to a greater height of popularity. Hancock was president of the continental congress from 1775 to 1779, and had the honor of signing his name first to the Declaration of Independence. After this, he held the office of governor of Massachusetts from 1780 to 1785, and from 1787 to 1793. He also acted as president of the state convention which adopted the federal constitution. He died on the 8th of October, 1793. He was the leading political character of his day in Massachusetts, and his influence throughout the Union was very great. He had little eloquence in public debate, and seldom indulged in speech-making; but his knowledge of business, his facility in despatching it, and his keen insight into the characters of men, rendered him a most efficient politician and public officer. When Washington entertained the design of bombarding Boston, Mr. Hancock advised that it should be done immediately, if necessary, although the greater part of his property consisted of houses and stores in that town. Among the other eminent men of this state may be enumerated Cotton Mather, a prodigy of learning in the early times of New England; Benjamin Franklin, whose fame is universal; John Adams, and John Quincy Adams, distinguished statesmen, and presidents of the United States. [The former died on the 4th of July, 1826, and the latter, on the 23d of February, 1848.] Thomas Hutchinson, Jeremy Belknap, and George Richards Minot, historians; Jonathan Edwards the metaphysician, Jacob Perkins, the mechanician, &c.

Rhode Island. *Annals.* — Roger Williams was the founder of the state of Rhode Island. He was banished from Massachusetts, in 1635, for entertaining doctrines which were deemed subversive of civil and religious authority. In 1636, he obtained a grant of land from the Indians, and began a settlement at Seekonk; but finding himself within the limits of the Plymouth patent, he removed, and founded Providence in the same year. The settlement was first known by the name of *Providence Plantation.* Adventurers and refugees from the neighboring colonies resorted thither, and a perfectly popular government was established. In 1638, Portsmouth was settled by William Coddington and others from Massachusetts. Newport was settled in the following year. The Providence and Rhode Island Plantations, having no charter, were not admitted into the New England confederacy in 1643. Williams, therefore, proceeded to England, and in 1644 obtained a charter from the parliament, which was then at war with the king: this united the two plantations of Providence and Rhode Island under one government. In 1647, the first general assembly met at Portsmouth. After the restoration of Charles II., a new charter was granted by him in 1663. Rhode Island quietly submitted to Andros in 1687, but on his overthrow, in 1689, the charter government was resumed.

Within this province was the chief seat of the Pequod Indians, who were exterminated by the Massachusetts settlers, as already related. At Mount Hope, near Bristol, was the residence of King Philip, and in this neighborhood he was killed.

In December, 1776, after Washington's army had retreated through the Jerseys across the Delaware, a British squadron, under Sir Peter Parker, took possession of Newport and the neighboring islands. In July, 1777, a small body of Americans, under Colonel Barton, surprised and captured General Prescot, the British commander in Rhode Island, who was subsequently exchanged for General Lee. In 1778, an expedition was undertaken by the Americans to expel the British from Rhode Island. Generals Sullivan, Greene, and Lafayette commanded the land forces, while a French fleet under Count d'Estaing prepared to coöperate in the attack by sea. Sullivan landed on Rhode Island, and laid siege to Newport; but the French fleet, being driven out to sea, and damaged by a storm, was compelled to sail for Boston to refit, and the American army found it necessary to withdraw from Rhode Island. The British retained possession till the close of the war.

The ancient charter continued in force in Rhode Island till 1844. Some endeavors to set it aside a few years previous, led to serious disturbance. A portion of the inhabitants, called the *suffrage party*, in 1843 framed a new constitution of their own, without the sanction or concurrence of the existing authorities. They chose Thomas W. Dorr for their governor, and organized a legislature. The charter government declared these proceedings illegal. The suffrage party took up arms. The charter government called out the militia, and dispersed them. Dorr fled from the state in 1843, but returned after a few months, was arrested, put on trial, convicted of treason against the state, and sentenced to imprisonment for life. In January, 1845, he was set at liberty. A new constitution was adopted in 1844.

Biography. — Nathaniel Greene, one of the ablest generals of the revolution was born near Warwick, in this state, May 22, 1742. He had no education except what he could gain from the few books which chance threw in his way; but he manifested in early life a love for the exact sciences, and in particular for the military art. In 1770, he was elected a member of the state legislature, and in 1774, he joined a company of volunteers as a private soldier. After the battle of Lexington, the state of Rhode Island raised an army, and Greene was appointed major-general. He served under Washington at Boston and New York. At the battle of Trenton, he commanded the American left wing. At the battle of Brandywine, he commanded the vanguard. He was also in the battle of Germantown and Monmouth, and was indefatigable in the service, enjoying the full confidence of Washington. In 1780, he was appointed to the chief command of the American army in the south, where General Gates had sustained serious reverses. Greene acquitted himself of his arduous duties with great ability and success, and his campaigns in the Carolinas are among the most brilliant exploits of the revolutionary war. By the victory of Eutaw Springs, he completely overthrew the power of the British in South Carolina. At the close of the war, he established himself in Georgia, where the state had made him a grant of land. He lived but a short time afterward, and died on the 19th of June, 1786, in consequence of exposure to the heat of the sun. In point of military talent, and the most important qualities of a general, he must be ranked among the revolutionary officers next to Washington.

Henry Wheaton, a native of Rhode Island, was distinguished as a statesman, a jurist, and a historian. His most popular work is the *History of the Northmen.* He was also the author of several valuable works on jurisprudence. He died in 1848.

Connecticut. *Annals.*—In 1630, this region was granted by the council of Plymouth to the earl of Warwick, who transferred it in the following year to Lord Say and Seal, Lord Brooke, and others. The English from Plymouth visited the country on the Connecticut, during the same year. The Dutch of New Amsterdam built a fort at Hartford in 1633, and the English from Plymouth established a trading house at Windsor a few months afterward. In 1635, a party of settlers from Massachusetts Bay travelled through the wilderness, and established themselves at Windsor, Hartford, and Wethersfield. In 1638, a party from Boston, led by Eaton and Davenport, began the settlement of New Haven, where they established a separate government. In 1639, the towns on the Connecticut which had previously acknowledged the authority of Massachusetts, erected a government of their own, and framed a constitution. In 1650, a treaty was made with the Dutch, by which the boundaries between the English settlements and the territories of New Amsterdam were settled. In 1662, a royal charter was granted to the colony of Connecticut, and New Haven was united to it in 1665. In 1687, Andros, who had been appointed governor of all New England, went to Hartford, and demanded the charter; but before he could obtain possession of the instrument, it was conveyed away, and hidden in a tree called the *Charter Oak.* Andros, however, assumed the government, and held his authority till he was deposed at Boston as already stated, when the charter government of Connecticut was restored. In 1693, the governor of New York attempted to establish his authority over the militia of Connecticut, but was prevented by the resolute opposition of the people. Yale College was first established at Saybrook, in 1702, and afterward removed to New Haven.

The revolution made no change in the government of Connecticut, which continued to be administered according to the forms of the ancient charter. In April, 1777, the British from New York, under General Tryon, made an inroad into Connecticut, and burnt Danbury. In February, 1779, a similar expedition, under Tryon, penetrated into the state as far as Horse Neck, where General Putnam made a miraculous escape from the enemy by spurring his horse down a precipice. In July of the same year, Tryon made a third expedition, with a force of twenty-six hundred men. He burnt East Haven, Fairfield, and Norwalk, and plundered New Haven. In 1781, a British force, under General Arnold, burnt New London, and captured Forts Trumbull and Griswold, at the mouth of the Thames. Colonel Ledyard, the commander of the latter, was barbarously murdered after surrendering, and the greater part of the garrison was put to the sword. This was the last military transaction in Connecticut during the revolutionary war. This state was one of the original members of the Union. The ancient charter remained in force till 1818, when a new constitution was established.

Biography.—Timothy Dwight, who attained to great eminence as a writer and preacher in this state was born at Northampton, in Massachusetts, May 14, 1752. He was educated at Yale College, in New Haven, and made the state of Connecticut his residence during the greater part of his life. At the age of nineteen, he began to write an epic poem entitled the *Conquest of Canaan*, which he finished in three years; but the work was not published till 1795, more than twenty years after its completion. He entered the American army, in 1777, as chaplain, and in addition to the usual duties of this station, he contributed not a little to heighten the enthusiasm of the soldiers by writing several patriotic songs, which obtained a wide popularity. In 1778, in consequence of the death of his father, he established himself at Northampton where he continued for five years, occupied in preaching, and in the cultivation of his farm. Toward the close of the war, he was twice elected a member of the legislature of Massachusetts. In 1783, he was settled in the ministry at Greenfield, in Connecticut. On the death of Dr Styles, in 1795, he was chosen to fill his place as president of Yale College. This office he held till his death, January 11, 1817. Beside several minor works, he published four volumes of Travels in New England and New York, and a system of theology.

Among the other eminent men of this state may be mentioned John Ledyard, the famous traveller; John Trumbull, the author of the Hudibrastic poem of *McFingal;* Joel Barlow, the author of the *Columbiad,* and distinguished in the public service of the United States; Ezra Styles, president of Yale College distinguished for his learning; and Noah Webster the American lexicographer.

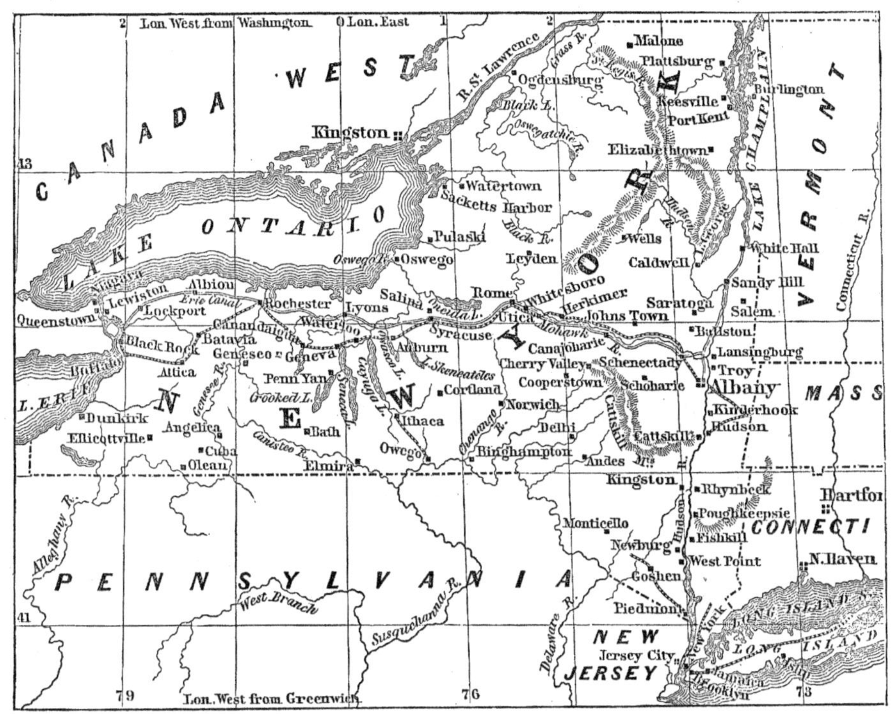

New York.—*Annals.* Henry Hudson, a commander in the Dutch service, discovered the river which bears his name in 1609. The Dutch sent ships to traffic with the natives in 1610. Argall, an English commander, captured, in 1613, a few hovels which the Dutch had built on the Island of Manhattan; and this was the beginning of the settlement of New York. In 1615, the Dutch founded Albany, which they named *Fort Orange.* The whole country claimed by them, in virtue of Hudson's discovery, received the name of the New Netherlands. The settlement on Manhattan Island was called *New Amsterdam.* In 1625, a settlement was begun at Brooklyn, on Long Island. The Dutch claimed the whole country from Cape Cod to Cape Henlopen. The English claimed it also on the plea of a prior discovery by Cabot. In 1643, the Dutch became involved in war with the Indians, and in 1651, with the Swedes, who had settled on the Delaware. The latter were compelled to submit. In 1663, a new Indian war broke out, and the village of Esopus was captured by the savages.

The English, in the mean time, had never formally abandoned their claim to the country; and in 1664, Charles II. made a grant of it to his brother, the duke of York. An English fleet was fitted out to take possession of it, although the English and Dutch were then at peace. The Dutch at New Amsterdam were altogether unprepared for defence, and submitted quietly to the invaders; the government of England was established over the whole colony in October, 1664, and its name was changed to *New York.* In a war between England and Holland, in 1673, the colony was reconquered by the Dutch; but it was restored to England in the following year. In 1683, a colonial assembly established a constitution, which they styled a *charter of liberties.*

In 1689, the colonists, headed by Jacob Leisler, a captain of militia, rose in rebellion, and deposed Nicholson, the governor. This measure was regarded by many as a usurpation. In the mean time, the French and Indians fell upon Schenectady, burnt the town, and massacred or captured all the inhabitants. Colonel Sloughter was appointed, by the king, governor of the province in 1691, and Leisler was compelled to surrender his authority into his hands. Leisler, and Milborne, his son-in-law, were tried for rebellion, condemned, and put to death the same year. In 1741, the inhabitants of New York were thrown into a great panic, by reports of a "negro plot," supposed to have been formed for burning the city. Many blacks were arrested, tried, and convicted of being in the plot. More than thirty were executed, and some of them were burned at the stake. But after the panic was over, the whole appeared to be a groundless illusion.

The threatening appearance of the French and Indians caused a convention of the colonies to be assembled at Albany, in 1754, for the purpose of treating with the Six Nations, and securing their friendship. At this convention, Dr. Franklin pressed his "Albany Plan of Union," for a confederation of the colonies under one general government. In 1755, an expedition, under General Johnson, marched against the French at Crown Point, but was defeated. In 1756, the French captured Oswego; the next year, they captured Fort William Henry. In 1758, an English army of fifteen thousand men, under Genera'

Abercrombie, marched against Ticonderoga, but without success. In 1759, the attempt was renewed under General Amherst, and Ticonderoga and Crown Point were captured.

The first colonial congress met at New York, in October, 1765, and issued a declaration of rights denying the power of parliament to tax America. On the breaking out of the revolutionary war, Ticonderoga and Crown Point were captured in 1775, by a small body of Americans under Ethan Allen. After the British were expelled from Boston, in March, 1776, Washington proceeded with his army to New York. Early in June, the British fleet appeared off Long Island, and landed a strong force there. Washington attempted to defend the island, but was defeated on the 27th of August, and compelled to retreat to New York. On the 15th of October, the British took possession of that city. On the 28th was fought the battle of White Plains. On the 16th and 18th of November, Forts Washington and Lee were captured by the British, and Washington retreated into New Jersey.

The state of New York was distinguished as the theatre of Burgoyne's campaign in 1777, which was closed by the surrender of the British army at Saratoga, on the 17th of October. After the evacuation of Philadelphia, in 1778, the British retreated to New York, which continued to be their head-quarters during the remainder of the war. Washington's army was encamped on the Hudson, and here occurred the treason of Arnold, and the execution of Andre in 1780. The British retained possession of the city of New York till the end of the war, and evacuated it in November, 1783.

New York was the scene of many of the military operations of the war of 1812. The Niagara frontier was invaded by the British, and Buffalo and Fort Niagara were captured. In 1814, a large British army, under Sir George Prevost, invaded the northern frontier, but was defeated at Plattsburg on the 11th of September, while, at the same time, the whole British fleet on Lake Champlain was captured by Commodore Macdonough. The present constitution of New York was adopted in 1821.

Biography. — John Jay, an eminent jurist and statesman of this state, was born in the city of New York, on the 1st of December, 1745. He applied himself to the legal profession, and in 1774 was sent as a delegate to the congress at Philadelphia. He drew up the address to the people of Great Britain, which is one of the most eloquent state papers of that time. In 1777, he was a member of the convention which framed the constitution of New York, and the first draught of that instrument was from his pen. In 1778, he was made chief justice of that state, and in 1779, he was appointed, by congress, minister plenipotentiary to Spain, for the purpose of obtaining from that power a recognition of the independence of the colonies, a treaty of alliance, &c.; but these attempts proved abortive, and in 1782, Mr. Jay was appointed one of the commissioners for negotiating a peace with Great Britain. In 1784, he returned to the United States, and was placed at the head of the department of foreign affairs, which post he held till the adoption of the federal constitution, when he was made chief justice of the United States. He assisted Hamilton and Madison in writing the Federalist, a series of essays on the new constitution, in which its principles were explained and defended. In 1794, he was sent as envoy extraordinary to Great Britain and negotiated a treaty with that power, which caused great excitement in the United States, and was finally rejected by the government. In 1795, he was elected governor of New York, and continued in that office till 1801, when he retired to private life. He died on the 17th of May, 1829. He was a man of varied attainments and great firmness of mind, and his writings exhibit much talent.

Among the other noted citizens of this state may be mentioned George Clinton, a general in the revolutionary war, and governor of the state; Edward Livingston, the author of a new penal code, and distinguished in national politics; Dewitt Clinton, a statesman, and the chief promoter of the canal policy in New York; Lindley Murray, the author of the English Grammar; and Charlotte Lenox, the author of several works of fiction and criticism.

NEW JERSEY. — *Annals.* This state was at first a part of the Dutch colony of New Netherlands. The Dutch built Fort Nassau, on the eastern bank of the Delaware, in 1623, but made no permanent settlement there. The earliest settlement, appears to have been Elizabethtown, which was founded in 1664. In the same year, this territory was granted to Lord Berkeley and Sir George Carteret, and named New Jersey in compliment to the latter, who had been governor of the Island of Jersey, in the English Channel. In 1672, the colonists rose in rebellion, and expelled the gov ernor. The next year, the Dutch conquered New Jersey, but restored it to the English in 1674. The government of Andros threw this colony into much trouble. In 1676, it was divided into East and West Jersey, with separate governments. For some years, the country was in an unsettled condition, without any regular government. In 1702, New Jersey was made a royal province, and united to New York. The two colonies continued under one governor, though with distinct legislative bodies, till 1738, when New Jersey was separated from New York.

New Jersey was the scene of some of the early campaigns of the revolutionary war. After the evacuation of New York by the American army, in 1776, Washington retreated into New Jersey, and at the close of the year, was compelled to cross the Delaware into Pennsylvania. On the 25th of December, he recrossed the river, and surprised the Hessians at Trenton. On the 3d of January, 1777, he fought the battle of Princeton. In the course of this year, he recovered nearly all that part of the Jerseys which had been overrun by the British. In 1778, the British evacuated Philadelphia, and retreated across the Jerseys to New York. On the 28th of June was fought the battle of Monmouth. After this, New Jersey was abandoned by the British. The present constitution of the state was adopted on the 2d of July, 1778.

Biography. — Samuel Stanhope Smith, a distinguished writer and public character of this state, was a native of Pennsylvania, but was educated at Princeton College, in New Jersey. In 1779, he was appointed professor of moral philosophy in that seminary, and contributed greatly by his labors toward restoring the institution from the dilapidated condition to which it had been reduced by the ravages of the British soldiery. In 1783, he received the additional office of professor of theology, and in 1795, he was appointed president of the college. He was one of the committee which framed a system of government for the Presbyterian church of the United States. In 1812, his declining health compelled him to resign his office of president, and he died in 1819, in the seventieth year of his age. He was a man of learning and talents. He wrote a work entitled an Essay on the Variety of Complexion in the Human Species, which displays much erudition and ingenuity. His other works are, Lectures on the Evidences of the Christian Religion, and on Moral Philosophy, a system of Natural and Revealed Religion, and several volumes of Sermons. His style has much merit for its correctness and elegance. Daniel Morgan, an able general of the revolution, was born in New Jersey. In early life he followed the occupation of a wagoner and served in Braddock's unfortunate campaign. During the revolutionary war, he distinguished himself in many campaigns; particularly at the battle of the Cowpens. He died in 1799.

Pennsylvania. — *Annals.* The first settlements in this state were made by the Swedes, from Delaware, in 1643. William Penn, in 1681, obtained from Charles II. a grant of this territory, and in 1683, he laid the foundation of Philadelphia. In 1692, the government, which was at first vested in Penn, was taken from him by the royal authority; but it was restored two years after. The charters under which the colony was governed, were granted by Penn as proprietor; and his sons held this authority till the revolution, when the proprietary claims were purchased by the state for five hundred and eighty thousand dollars, and Pennsylvania became independent.

The second continental congress assembled at Philadelphia in September, 1773. The Declaration of Independence was issued by congress at this place, July 4, 1776. In August, 1777, the British invaded Pennsylvania by the way of the Chesapeake. On the 11th of September was fought the battle of Brandywine, and on the 26th, the British took possession of Philadelphia. Congress removed to Lancaster, in Pennsylvania. On the 4th of October was fought the battle of Germantown. Washington's army passed the winter of 1777 and 1778 at Valley Forge. On the 18th of June, 1778 the British evacuated Philadelphia. In the summer of the same year, the beautiful valley of Wyoming was ravaged by the British and Indians. The present constitution of Pennsylvania was adopted in 1790.

Biography. — David Rittenhouse, an eminent astronomer, was born near Germantown, in this state, April 8, 1732. He was brought up on his father's farm, where his natural taste for the mathematical sciences soon distinguished him from his associates. While a youth, he made a wooden clock, without any scientific instruction or aid from any other person. After this, he gave himself up to mechanical pursuits and to study. With the help of two or three books, and no instructor, he mastered the mathematical sciences sufficiently to read the Principia of Newton. In the midst of his labor and study, he planned and executed an orrery, which surpassed every thing of the kind which had then been invented. In 1769, he was one of the committee appointed by the American Philosophical Society to observe the transit of Venus over the sun's disk. The reputation which he acquired by his astronomical labors attracted the attention of the government, and he was employed in many public works which required scientific knowledge and skill. He was elected a member of numerous learned societies in America and England, and in 1791, he succeeded Franklin as president of the Philosophical Society of Pennsylvania. In 1792, he was appointed director of the mint of the United States. He died June 26, 1796. Rittenhouse, like Franklin, was a self-taught man, and his ingenuity and zeal for science are abundantly conspicuous in the works which he left behind him. Other distinguished citizens of this state are Thomas Godfrey the mathematician and inventor of the quadrant called *Hadley's;* James Ralph, the author of a valuable history of England, and many political and miscellaneous works; Benjamin Rush, the celebrated physician; Robert Fulton, the first successful practiser of steam navigation; Benjamin West, the celebrated painter; and Charles Brockden Brown, the novelist.

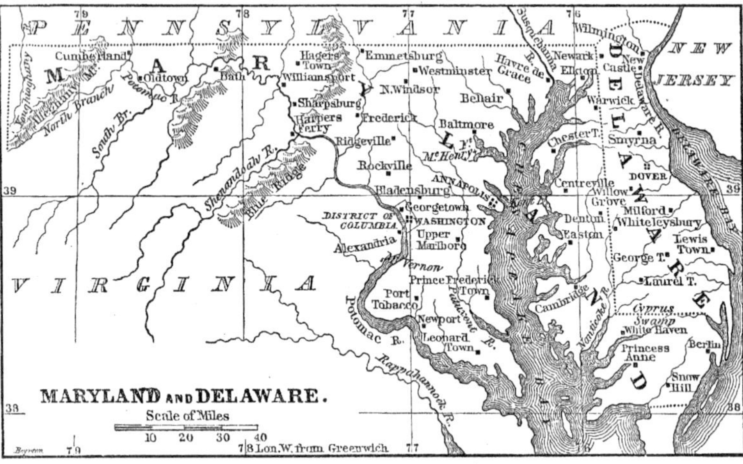

DELAWARE. *Annals.* — The Swedes, in 1638, began a settlement at Christiana Creek, near Wilmington. They claimed the country from Cape Henlopen to the Falls of the Delaware, opposite Trenton, and named it *New Sweden.* The Dutch built Fort Casimir, on the site of the present town of Newcastle, in order to check the encroachments of the Swedes in 1651; but the latter soon after made themselves masters of it. In 1655, however, the Dutch conquered all the Swedish settlements in this territory, and it became a part of the New Netherlands. Delaware was included in the grant of the territory made to William Penn in 1681, and formed a part of Pennsylvania till 1691, when it was allowed a separate deputy-governor. It was reunited to Pennsylvania in 1692. In 1703, Delaware was again separated from Pennsylvania, and had its own legislature, though the same governor presided over both colonies. The ancient forms of the government were preserved through the revolutionary struggle; and the existing constitution was framed in 1792. It was amended in 1802.

Biography. —James A. Bayard, an eminent politician of this state, was born in Philadelphia, in 1767. He was educated for the law, and settled early in life in Delaware, where he soon acquired practice and reputation. He was chosen a member of congress from this state, and distinguished himself in the affair of the impeachment of Senator Blount, in which he discussed the constitutional questions of the proceeding with great ingenuity. On many other occasions he displayed high eloquence in the debates of congress. In 1812, he strenuously opposed the declaration of war against Great Britain. In 1813, he was appointed by President Madison one of the commissioners to treat for peace under the proffered mediation of the emperor of Russia. He proceeded to St. Petersburg in 1813, but the war with France prevented the emperor from effecting his plan of mediation. The negotiations with the British were afterward transferred to Ghent; and here a peace was concluded in November, 1814, by Messrs. Adams, Bayard, Clay, Russell, and Gallatin, the American commissioners. After the ratification of the treaty, Mr. Bayard was offered the post of envoy to the court of Russia, but declined it. He returned to the United States, in 1815, in a declining state of health, and died shortly after reaching his home. His reputation as a lawyer and a political orator was equalled by very few of his contemporaries. His powers of logic were of the first order. He possessed a rich and ready elocution, commanding attention as well by his fine countenance and manly person, as by his cogent reasoning and comprehensive views.

MARYLAND. *Annals.* — This state was originally included in Virginia, and the first attempts at settling it were made at Kent Island, in the Chesapeake, in 1632. In the same year, Sir George Calvert, otherwise called *Lord Baltimore*, obtained a charter for a colony here, under the name of *Maryland.* The government was proprietary. The first settlement was made in 1634, at St. Mary's, near the Potomac, and a legislative assembly was convened here in 1635. Ten years afterward, the government was seized by a body of insurgents; but the revolt was suppressed in 1646. In 1650, the legislative body was divided into two branches — the one a popular representative body, and the other appointed by the proprietors. A civil war distracted the colony in 1655 and 1656, which was occasioned by the differences between the Protestants and Catholics. In 1658, the assembly assumed all the powers of government, excluding the governor and council; but in 1660, the old order of things was restored. In 1691, the proprietary government was annulled by King William, and Maryland was made a royal province. In 1715, the authority of the proprietors was restored, and continued till the revolution. A new constitution was adopted in 1776, which has since received several amendments.

Biography.—General John E. Howard was born in this state in 1752, and entered the continental service as a captain at the commencement of the revolutionary war. In December, 1776, he received the commission of major. He was one of the most able and efficient officers in the army of General Greene during his campaigns in the Southern States. He distinguished himself in a striking manner at the battle of the Cowpens, and may be said to have turned the fortune of the day by leading on his men to a charge with fixed bayonets — a practice for which the troops of the Maryland line became famous. Colonel Howard is said to have had in his hands, at one time, during this battle, the swords of seven British officers who had surrendered to him personally. For his gallant conduct, he received the thanks of congress and a silver medal. He fought also with great courage in the battle of Eutaw Springs, where he received a severe wound, from which he never recovered. In 1788, he was elected governor of Maryland, and occupied that station for three years. In 1796, he was chosen a senator of the United States, and continued a member of that body till 1803. When a war was apprehended with France, in 1798, and Washington was appointed to the command of the army, Colonel Howard was selected by him for the post of brigadier-general. The latter part of his life was passed in retirement. He died in October, 1827, with the reputation of one of the bravest and most deserving officers of the revolution. Otho Holland Williams, a general of the revolution, was a native of this state. He served at the seige of Boston in 1775, and in many campaigns at the south. He was adjutant-general of the southern army, from the period when General Gates assumed the command till the end of the war. He died in 1794. William Wirt, a distinguished lawyer and writer, was also a native of Maryland.

VIRGINIA. *Annals.* — James I. of England, in 1606, made a grant of a large extent of territory, comprising this state within its limits, to two English companies. Under this grant a charter was obtained, and adventurers proceeded to the country, and founded a settlement at Jamestown, May 23, 1606. John Smith, one of these adventurers, explored Chesapeake Bay, and the rivers flowing into it. A new charter was given to the company of settlers in 1609; and a third in 1612. A representative government was established, and the first colonial assembly was convened at Jamestown, June 29, 1619. A written constitution was granted by the London proprietors to the colonists in 1621.

In 1622, the Indians made a sudden attack on the settlements, and massacred three hundred and forty-seven men, women, and children. A war ensued, and the Indians were driven back into the wilderness. In 1624, the company of proprietors was dissolved by the authority of the king, who took the colony into his own hands, and it thereby became a royal government. A governor and a council were appointed by the crown to administer the authority; but the colonial assemblies continued. In 1644, another Indian massacre occurred, and hostilities continued till 1646. On the breaking out of the civil war in England, the Virginians remained faithful to the king; and a fleet was sent by the parliament to subdue them. The colonists were compelled, in 1652, to acknowledge the authority of the parliament. On the restoration of Charles II., Virginia became again a royal colony.

The British navigation act injured the trade of Virginia, and other grievances existing at the same time in the colony, the Virginians, in 1676, rose in rebellion, and chose Nathaniel Bacon for their leader. They obtained some advantages over Berkeley, the royal governor, who was compelled for a time to comply with the popular demands. But the sudden death of Bacon, in the same year, put an end to the rebel-

.ion, and several of those who shared in it were capitally punished.

Virginia was much exposed to the hostilities of the French and Indians. In 1753, the French began to erect forts within the limits of her territory, and Governor Dinwiddie despatched to their commander a letter, by the hands of George Washington, remonstrating against these encroachments. Washington brought back a reply from the French commander, refusing to withdraw his troops. War broke out, and in 1755, an army of English and Americans, under General Braddock, marched against the French post of Fort Du Quesne, now Pittsburg. They fell into an ambush, and were defeated, July 9, 1755. The frontiers were ravaged by the French and Indians, and more than a thousand of the inhabitants killed or carried into captivity. In 1758, an English and colonial army, under General Forbes, captured Fort Du Quesne, and changed the name of it to *Fort Pitt.*

Virginia remained quiet till the commencement of the revolution. In 1775, the governor, Lord Dunmore, raised the royal standard against the people. A battle took place near Norfolk, December 8, 1775, and the governor was defeated. He fled on board a ship of war, which bombarded Norfolk, and burnt that city, January 1, 1776. The royal authority was now at an end in Virginia, and an independent government was established. The British invaded the state in May, 1779, and plundered Norfolk, Portsmouth, and the neighborhood. In 1781, another marauding expedition, under General Arnold, — who had deserted the Americans, and entered the British service, — ravaged the shores of the Chesapeake, and plundered Richmond and Portsmouth. The British army under Lord Cornwallis invaded Virginia from the south during the same year, and several actions took place here. At length, Cornwallis was compelled to retreat to Yorktown, where he fortified himself, and was besieged by the American army under Washington, while the French fleet, under the Count de Grasse, blockaded the mouth of the Chesapeake. The siege of Yorktown was begun September 30, and Cornwallis surrendered his army of seven thousand men on the 19th of October, 1781. This ended the war in Virginia. This state accepted the federal constitution, and joined the Union in 1788. The state constitution was formed in 1776, and revised in 1830.

Biography. — Patrick Henry, one of the most distinguished patriots and eloquent orators of the revolution, was born in Hanover county, Virginia, May 29, 1736. He received but a slender education, and was brought up to trade and agriculture; but his success was so little encouraging, that he abandoned these pursuits for the study of law; and after a preparation of six weeks, he received a license to practise. For some years he lived in a state of great destitution, and was compelled to assist his father-in-law in the business of tavern-keeping. At length, a legal case between the clergy and the colonial government gave an occasion for the display of his eloquence, and raised him at once to notoriety. In 1765, he was elected a member of the legislature of Virginia, where he distinguished himself by taking the lead in opposing the stamp act. The boldness and eloquence which he displayed on this occasion drew the attention of the whole state, and made him the most popular man of the time. He was one of the delegates from Virginia to the first general congress in 1774. On the reception of the news of the battle of Lexington, he raised a company of volunteers, which was the first military movement in Virginia. He took a leading part in all the measures which ended in the overthrow of the royal authority in Virginia, and the convention of the colony in 1775 appointed him commander-in-chief of the forces. This command, however, he soon resigned, and was chosen the first governor of Virginia as an independent state. In 1779, he retired from office, but was reëlected at the end of the war. He was one of the convention called to act upon the acceptance of the federal constitution. Mr. Henry was hostile to the constitution, and used all his efforts to procure the rejection of it by Virginia: yet, after its adoption, he was not blind to its merits, and became one of its firmest supporters. He died on the 6th of June, 1796. His fame as a public speaker rests almost entirely on tradition; but it is probable that few men, either in ancient or modern times, have equalled him in powers of eloquence. Some of the other eminent men of Virginia are Arthur and Richard Henry Lee, both distinguished in the revolutionary councils: George Washington, Thomas Jefferson, James Madison, and James Monroe, presidents of the United States Washington died on the 16th of December, 1799 Jefferson on the 4th of July, 1826; Madison on the 28th of June, 1836, and Monroe on the 4th of July, 1831.

North Carolina. *Annals.* — Carolina was granted, in 1663, to Lord Clarendon, and other persons, and named *Albermarle County Colony.* The first settlement was made about 1660, by a company from New England, on Oldtown Creek, near Wilmington. The government was proprietary, but a charter secured the popular liberties. In 1677, the colony was disturbed by a revolt; and in 1678, the people deposed their governor, and banished him from their territory. In the early part of the last century, the population was increased by the arrival of large numbers of French Protestants, and Germans, from the countries on the Rhine, who had been driven from their homes by the devastations of war and religious persecution. In **1711**, the settlements on Roanoke and Pamlico Sound were attacked by the Indians, and one hundred and thirty of the inhabitants massacred. In 1729, the two Carolinas, which had previously been under the superintendence of the same board of proprietors, were finally separated, and royal governments, entirely unconnected, were established over them. During the revolutionary war, the contending armies made this state the scene of their operations. The battle of King's Mountain was fought in North Carolina, October 7, 1780. The present constitution was adopted in 1776.

Biography. — Hugh Williamson, a distinguished citizen of this state, was born in Chester county, Pennsylvania, May 17, 1757. He was educated for the pulpit, but from ill health was induced to turn his attention from theology to medicine. In 1760, he was appointed professor of mathematics in the college of Philadelphia. After occupying the post three years, he visited Europe, and pursued his studies at London, Edinburgh, and Utrecht. On his return to America, he devoted himself chiefly to scientific occupations, and was one of the committee appointed by the American Philosophical Society to observe the transit of Venus. His observations are recorded in the transactions of that body. He also presented to the society a theory respecting a comet which appeared about that time. In 1773, he again visited England, and was examined by the privy council respecting the state of public feeling in the colonies. It was through his hands that Franklin obtained the letters of Hutchinson and Oliver, which were sent to Boston, and became the cause of great excitement in the colonies. He next visited Holland, and returned to America in 1777. He established himself at Edenton, in North Carolina, and became a member of the state legislature, and of congress. In 1787, he was sent as a delegate to the convention at Philadelphia, which framed the federal constitution, of which he was a strong supporter. After the adoption of the constitution, he retired to private life, in which he continued to occupy himself with literary and scientific studies. In 1811, he published a work on the climate of the United States as compared with the corresponding parts of the old continent, and in 1812, a History of North Carolina, in two volumes. He died on the 22d of May, 1819. William Hooper, another eminent citizen of this state, was born at Boston, June 17th, 1742, and began the practice of the law in that town. He emigrated to North Carolina in 1767, and soon rose to distinction in the state. He was a delegate to the first continental congress, and a signer of the Declaration of Independence. He died in October, 1790.

SOUTH CAROLINA. *Annals.* — Clarendon's charter embraced all the territory from Virginia to Florida. After the first settlement in North Carolina, the proprietors, in 1670, began another on Ashley River, where they founded Old Charleston. This settlement was named the *Carteret County Colony.* Slaves were introduced into this colony the same year from Barbadoes. In 1680, the present city of Charleston was founded. A settlement was formed at Port Royal by some Scotch emigrants in 1684; but this was attacked and laid waste by the Spaniards from St. Augustine in 1686. Shortly afterward, a large number of French Protestants settled in South Carolina. From 1686 to 1693, the colony was distracted by a rebellion; the governor was deposed by the people and banished. In 1693, these troubles were partially removed by the repeal of the old government, and the establishment of a more simple and liberal form of administration. In 1702, an expedition was undertaken from South Carolina against the Spaniards at St. Augustine, which miscarried, and involved the colony deeply in debt. This led to the issue of paper money. In 1703, the Indians laid the frontier waste, but were soon reduced to submission. In 1704, the church of England was established in

South Carolina, and all dissenters were excluded from the legislature. In 1706, a French and Spanish squadron appeared off Charleston, and landed troops to attack the place, but they were repulsed. In 1715, a general Indian war broke out, headed by the Yamassees, and involving all the Indian tribes from Cape Fear River to the Alabama. The frontiers were desolated, Port Royal was abandoned, Charleston was in danger, and the colony seemed near its ruin; but at length the Indians were defeated, on the banks of the Saskehatchie, and driven into Florida. In 1719, the people of South Carolina rose in rebellion against the proprietary government, and in 1729, the country was made a royal province. In 1776, the British made an attempt upon Charleston: they landed a strong force on Long Island, near Sullivan's Island, at the mouth of Charleston harbor, and attacked Fort Moultrie, which was bombarded on the 28th of June. The garrison, however, repulsed their assailants. In 1779, the war was again carried into this state. General Lincoln commanded the American army, and an attempt was made to drive the British from Savannah, in Georgia, but without success. In 1780, a strong British force, under Sir Henry Clinton, invaded South Carolina, and laid siege to Charleston, which surrendered on the 12th of May. The royal authority was reëstablished over a great part of the state. The battle of Camden was fought on the 16th of August. General Greene took the command of the American army in the south in 1781. The battle of the Cowpens was fought on the 17th of January, that of Guilford on the 15th of March, and that of Eutaw Springs on the 8th of September. The British authority was now restricted to Charleston and its immediate neighborhood, and their troops remained quiet in that city till December, 1783, when they evacuated the state. The existing constitution was adopted in 1790, and has been repeatedly amended.

Biography. — David Ramsay, an eminent physician and historian of this state, was born in Lancaster county, Pennsylvania, April 2, 1749. He was educated for a physician, and began his practice in Maryland, from which state, after a residence of a year, he removed to South Carolina, where he soon rose to eminence. When the revolutionary troubles commenced, he took the popular side, and labored with his pen to promote the cause of independence. For some time, he attended the army as a surgeon. After this, he became a leading member of the legislature of South Carolina, and his public services were continued in that capacity to the end of the war. When Charleston was occupied by the British, they banished him to St. Augustine, where he remained in exile nearly a year. In 1782, he was elected a delegate to congress, and for a year filled the post of president *pro tempore*, during the absence of Mr. Hancock. The latter part of his life was devoted to the practice of his profession, and to literary pursuits. On the sixth of May, 1815, he was shot in the street near his own house by a maniac, and died of the wound two days afterward. Dr. Ramsay is best known by his historical writings. In 1785, he published a History of the Revolution in South Carolina, and in 1790, a History of the American Revolution. In 1801, he published a Life of Washington, and in 1808, a History of South Carolina. He left behind him, in manuscript, a History of the United States, from the first settlement of the colonies to the year 1808, and a Universal History Americanized. The former was published in three volumes, and the latter in twelve. Dr. Ramsay was a careful and diligent collector of facts, and his writings are among the best authorities for the history of our country. Among the other distinguished citizens of this state was Charles Cotesworth Pinckney, who served in the revolutionary army, and in several public stations, particularly in that of minister plenipotentiary to France during the administration of Washington. He died in 1825. Henry Laurens, a native of this state, was distinguished in the revolution. He was president of congress in 1776 '77, and '78, after which he was appointed minister plenipotentiary to Holland; but on his voyage to Europe, he was captured by the British, and imprisoned in the tower of London. After his release, he was one of the commissioners who negotiated the treaty of peace with Great Britain. He died in 1792.

GEORGIA. *Annals.* — This state remained unsettled till 1732, when General James Oglethorpe obtained a charter for establishing a colony here. The first settlement was made at Savannah. Whitefield and Wesley, the Methodist preachers, took an interest in this undertaking, for the purpose of founding an Orphan Asylum in the colony. The Spaniards in Florida occasioned much trouble to the settlers, and hostilities were carried on for some years between the two provinces. At the first settlement of Georgia, slavery was rigidly prohibited, and declared to be immoral, and contrary to the laws of England. But after some time, the inhabitants began to hire slaves of the Carolinians, and the laws against slavery were relaxed. By degrees, the prohibition was set aside, and slaves were imported into the state directly from Africa. In this manner, Georgia became, like Carolina, a planting state with slave labor. In 1752, the trustees, who had previously exercised the proprietary government, resigned their charter to the king, and Georgia was changed to a royal colony. This state was the last to join the original thirteen, which issued the Declaration of Independence. In December, 1778, the British captured Savannah, and held it till the conclusion of the war. The whole colony was reduced to their authority. In September, 1779, an attempt was made by the Americans, assisted by the French fleet under the Count d'Estaing, to recover Savannah, but without success. The state was finally evacuated by the British, in July, 1783. The present constitution was framed in 1798, and has since received amendments.

Biography.—Lyman Hall, a distinguished citizen of this state, was born in Connecticut, in 1731, and educated for the medical profession. About the year 1752, he removed, in company with forty families of New England emigrants, to the district of Medway, in Georgia. He practised his calling at Sunbury, in that state, till the commencement of the revolution. The Georgians at first did not generally embrace the revolutionary cause, but showed a disposition to submit to British authority. The district in which Mr. Hall resided, however, inclined strongly to resistance; and in March, 1775, he was chosen by his parish a delegate to the congress at Philadelphia. This parish was afterward named *Liberty*, in commemoration of the circumstance of its having been the first in the state to take the side of independence. In July, 1775, Georgia acceded to the confederacy. Mr. Hall was one of the signers of the Declaration of Independence. He continued a member of congress till 1780. When the British overran Georgia, they confiscated all his property, and compelled his family to flee from the state. At the close of the war, Mr. Hall was elected governor of Georgia. The latter part of his life was passed in retirement. He died about the year 1790. George Walton, an eminent citizen of Georgia, was born in Virginia in 1740. He was brought up as a carpenter, but after removing to Georgia, practised the profession of the law. He was a member of the continental congress, and a signer of the Declaration of Independence. He died in 1804.

Alabama. *Annals.*—This state was at first a part of Georgia, and contained, when discovered, a very numerous Indian population, which also extended into Georgia. The most considerable tribes were the Creeks, Cherokees, Choctaws, and Chickasaws. Some of these made considerable progress in civilization. In 1817, Alabama was separated from Georgia, and made a territory of the United States. In 1819, it was admitted into the Union as a state. Since this period, the Indians have been removed to the territory west of the Mississippi.

Florida. *Annals.*—Florida was discovered by the Spaniards under Ponce de Leon, in 1512; but no settlements were made here till 1565; when the Spaniards founded St. Augustine, which is now the oldest town in the United States. Very little progress, however, was made in the settlement of the country, which remained a wilderness, abandoned to the Indians. In 1763, Florida was ceded to Great Britain; but in 1783, it was restored to Spain. In 1820, the United States acquired it by treaty. In 1843, it was admitted into the Union. The Indians of Florida are numerous and warlike, and have never been entirely subdued. Ever since the acquisition of the country by the United States, Florida has been disturbed by Indian hostilities at intervals. The most noted tribe is that of the *Seminoles*, a name which signifies *runaways*; this tribe consisting of individuals who have fled from the surrounding communities. A portion of this tribe who refused to emigrate to the lands assigned them to the west of the Mississippi, carried on a war with the United States, which continued from 1835 to 1843 and in which they caused the inhabitants much annoyance. They occupied a thicket in the wilderness called the *Everglades*, from which they sallied occasionally, and made desperate attacks on the United States troops. They were at last subdued, and some of them removed to the country west of the Mississippi. The Indians who remain are still on bad terms with the settlers, and the country at the present moment (1850) is threatened with hostilities.

Mississippi. *Annals.*—This state was originally regarded as a part of the ancient French colony of Louisiana. In 1716, the French formed a settlement where the city of Natchez now stands. This colony was afterwards destroyed by the Indians in the vicinity. At the close of the French war, in 1763, the country was ceded to Great Britain. The Spaniards claimed it as a part of Florida; but in 1798, they relinquished their claims to the United States. It had then few white settlers, but in early times was the seat of a large Indian population. This was the native country of the Natchez tribe, who have given their name to one of the chief towns in the state, where their chief settlements existed when they were first visited by the French. Mississippi was admitted into the Union in 1817

Louisiana. *Annals.* — The French were the first who settled in this country, though it had probably been before visited by the Spaniards of De Soto's expedition. The French claimed the territory in consequence of their discovery of the Mississippi, and in the early part of the eighteenth century, they founded New Orleans, and gave the colony the name of Louisiana, from Louis XIV. In 1763, they ceded it to Spain; but in 1800, it was conveyed back to France by treaty. When the valley of the Mississippi began to fill up with settlers, it became very important to the United States to acquire Louisiana, in order to secure the outlet of that river. It was therefore purchased of the French by the American government, in 1803, for fifteen millions of dollars. Louisiana then comprised an indefinite extent of adjoining territory, including the present states of Louisiana, Arkansas, Mississippi, with a wide tract westward, extending to the Rocky Mountains. In 1812, the present state of Louisiana was admitted into the Union. In the latter part of 1814, the British invaded Louisiana from the Gulf of Mexico, and attempted to capture New Orleans. On the 8th of January, 1815, was fought the celebrated battle near this city, which resulted in the defeat of the British, and the total miscarriage of their expedition.

Biography. General Taylor was born in Virginia, in 1790. He entered the army at an early age; and in 1812 was in command of Fort Harrison, with the grade of captain. In the war with Great Britain, he took a prominent part, and distinguished himself in many contests with the Indians, and especially in the Seminole war. In 1845, he was placed at the head of the army of occupation at Corpus Christi, in Texas. The war with Mexico followed, throughout which he was signally victorious. He was elected president of the United States on the 7th of November, 1848. For many years, General Taylor has resided at Baton Rouge, Louisiana.

Arkansas. *Annals.* — This state belonged originally to Louisiana. In 1819, it was made a territorial government; and in 1836, it was admitted into the Union.

Texas. *Annals.* — Previously to 1690, Texas formed a remote and merely nominal part of the conquest of Cortez, inhabited by predatory Indian tribes; but in that year, the Spaniards, having driven out a colony of French who had established themselves at Matagorda, made their first permanent settlement at San Francisco. On the consummation of Mexican independence, Texas was constituted one of the federal states of Mexico, in conjunction with the adjacent state of Coahuila, a union very unpopular with the Texans, and which was productive of the first disagreement with the central government. In 1821, the colonization of Texas commenced by citizens of the United States of America. A leading pioneer in these proceedings was Stephen F. Austin, of Durham, in Connecticut. His first settlement was between the Brazos and the Colorado. In the year 1835, the separation from Mexico commenced; and in 1836, the independence of Texas was fully secured by the defeat and capture of the Mexican president, Santa Anna, at San Jacinto.* This occurred on the 21st April, 1836. In 1845, an act was passed by the congress of the United States for the annexation of Texas to the Union, and this was speedily consummated by the consent of the people of that country. It was soon after admitted into the Union.

* In this celebrated battle, General Houston was commander; nearly the whole Mexican army was annihilated. Santa Anna was permitted to go to Washington, where he had an interview with President Jackson. He was sent back to Vera Cruz in a government vessel. He lost his power in Mexico for a time, but was again made president in 1841. He was expelled in 1844, and resided for some months at Cuba. He returned to Mexico soon after, and took a leading part in the war with Mexico.

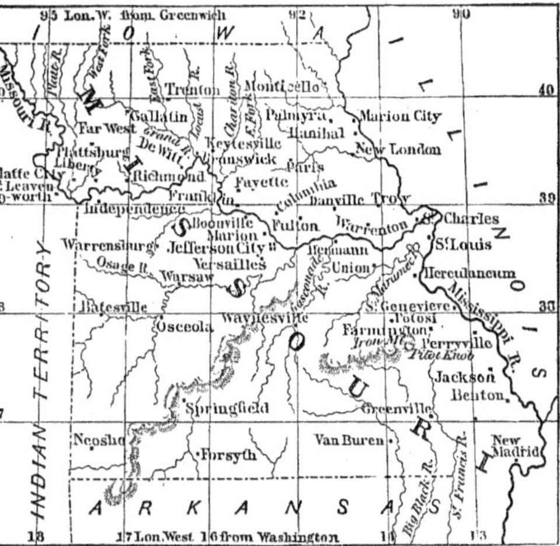

MISSOURI. *Annals.* — This state was first settled by the French in 1764, when they founded St. Louis. All this part of the country was then regarded as a portion of Louisiana. The French settlements made little progress, and there were very few white inhabitants in this quarter, when, by the purchase of Louisiana, this region came into the possession of the United States. In 1804, Missouri was erected into a territory; and in 1821, it was admitted into the Union as a state.

After Missouri had applied to congress for admission into the Union, a proposition was made to exclude slavery from the state, as a condition of its admission. A violent debate ensued. A compromise was proposed by Mr. Clay, and adopted; this tolerated slavery south of lat. 36·30 north, and prohibited it north of that line. This is called the "*Missouri Compromise.*"

TENNESSEE. *Annals.* — This state was originally a part of North Carolina. Settlements were made here about the middle of the last century, but were destroyed by the Indians. After the expulsion of the hostile tribes in 1780, new settlers established themselves here; and in 1790, Tennessee was ceded by North Carolina to the United States, and erected into a territory. In 1796, it was admitted into the Union.

Biography. — Andrew Jackson, who was for a long time a citizen of Tennessee, was born in South Carolina, March 15th 1767. At the age of twenty-one, he removed to the west district of North Carolina, which afterward became the state of Tennessee. His public career as a general and as President of the United States has been noticed in another chapter of this work. He died June 8th, 1845.

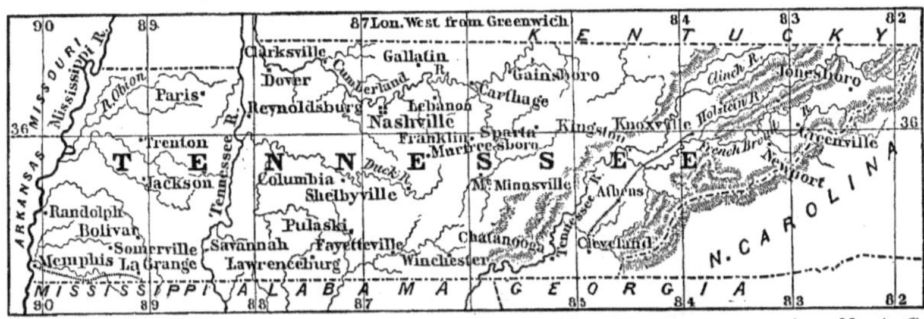

KENTUCKY. *Annals.* — The first white settler in this state was Daniel Boone, who established himself in the wilderness west of the Apalachian Mountains, about the year 1770. The territory was then regarded as a part of Virginia; but as the country became settled, that state agreed to a separation, and in 1792 Kentucky was admitted as a state into the Union. Its constitution was formed in 1799.

Biography. — Daniel Boone, the first white man who penetrated into the wilderness of Kentucky was born in Virginia in 1738, and in early life, manifested a great fondness for the adventurous pursuit of hunting in the woods. His first rambles from home were into North Carolina. From this state, he set out on an expedition across the Cumberland Mountains, with five companions, in May, 1769. Boone and one of the company were taken by the savages, but made their escape. The others returned home. Boone and his companion remained in Kentucky, and in 1773, they removed their families into that country. These were soon joined by other emigrants. Boone erected a fort in 1775 on the River Kentucky, where the town of Boonesborough is now situated: here, in 1777, he was twice besieged by the Indians, but he repulsed them. In the following year, while hunting with a number of companions, they were captured by the savages. Boone was adopted by one of the chiefs of Chillicothe, and would have been contented to remain with the Indians, had not the thoughts of his wife and children kept alive the desire to escape. After a while, he found an opportunity to effect this, and reached his home after a journey of one hundred and sixty miles, which he performed in four days, eating only one meal in all that time. Shortly afterward, his fort was besieged by a body of four hundred and fifty savages and Canadians, under British colors; but the garrison, which consisted of but fifty men, succeeded in repulsing them. Boone was engaged in many other encounters and adventures with the Indians, in which he saved his life by singular courage and dexterity. He was throughout life passionately fond of solitary roaming in the forest, and as the settlement of the country advanced, he complained that his old haunts were encroached upon by his neighbors. In 1798, he removed into Upper Louisiana, as the country on the Missouri was then called, and settled on that river, beyond the inhabited region. Here he followed his usual course of life, hunting and trapping, till his death, which took place in September, 1822.

OHIO. — *Annals.* The first settlements in this state were made by a company of revolutionary officers and soldiers, to whom the old continental congress made a grant of one million five hundred thousand acres of land. This company was organized at Boston, under the name of the Ohio company. The first emigration took place in 1786, when an association of forty-seven persons from Massachusetts, Rhode Island, and Connecticut, founded Marietta, on the 7th of April. Another settlement was made in the following year at Columbus, on the Ohio, about six miles above the spot where Cincinnati now stands. Those who established themselves here, were from the Middle States. Some French emigrants formed a settlement at Gallipolis, in 1791. Connecticut, by virtue of her charter, claimed part of the territory of Pennsylvania and of Ohio; the former she relinquished; the latter was adjusted by her receiving a tract in Ohio, which was called the *Western Reserve.* This lay along the southern shore of Lake Erie. In 1795, it was sold by Connecticut, and the money received became the foundation of her noble school fund. A settlement was made at Cleveland in 1796. The Western Reserve was mainly settled by people from Connecticut. Ohio, with a considerable part of the neighboring region, was comprised in a territorial government established by the United States in 1781, under the name of the "Territory north-west of the Ohio." Indian wars for some time checked the progress of the settlements; but the savages were at length subdued. In 1802, Ohio was admitted into the Union as a state.

Biography. — William Henry Harrison, president of the United States, and for a long time a citizen of Ohio, was born in Virginia, February 9th, 1773. He served in the army at a very early age, and was soon appointed to an important command. On the division

of the North-western Territory, he was appointed governor of the territory of Indiana. His public services have been mentioned in the history of the United States. He died April 4th, 1841, having been president only about thirty days.

INDIANA. — *Annals.* This country, which was a part of what the French called Upper Louisiana, was visited by the early French adventurers from Canada, and a settlement was formed at Vincennes, in 1730. The settlers were mostly soldiers, who had served in the armies of Louis XIV., and for thirty or forty years they remained here buried in the recesses of the wilderness, remote from civilized society, and assimilated in manners nearly to their savage neighbors. The transfer of the country to the British, in 1763, in consequence of their conquests, did not disturb them; and for a long time, no additional settlements were made in this quarter. During the revolutionary war, the French of Vincennes showed a friendly disposition toward the Americans, in consequence of which they received a grant of land, in the neighborhood of that town, at the end of the contest. Settlements of Americans began to be formed in Indiana about the close of the last century, and a territorial government was established here in 1801. The Indians gave much trouble to the settlers in this quarter, and here, in November, 1811, was fought the battle of Tippecanoe. Indiana was admitted into the Union in 1816.

progress, and the country remained mostly a wilderness. By the treaty of 1763, this region came into the possession of the British; it was, however, claimed by Virginia, and was a part of the territory ceded by that state to the United States, in 1787. In July of this year, the North-west territory was formed under a government by congress; it included Ohio, Indiana, Illinois, Michigan, and the territory of Wisconsin. In 1809, Illinois was made a separate territory. In 1818, it was admitted into the Union as a state.

MICHIGAN.—*Annals.* The French from Canada visited this state at an early period. Champlain explored the country on the shore of Lake Huron in 1615; and about 1650, the French made a settlement at Mackinaw, where they built a fort and established a missionary station. Some time after this, they erected a fortification on the strait connecting Lake St. Clair with Lake Erie, and named it *Fort Pontchartrain.* Here is now the city of Detroit. This place made a prominent figure in the early history of the French settlements, and subsequently in the wars between the French and English. In 1763, upon the conquest of Canada by the British, this country passed into their possession; but the garrison which they placed at Mackinaw was surprised

ILLINOIS.—*Annals.* This state was visited by Marquette, a French traveller, in 1673; and a few years later, settlements were formed by the French at Kaskaskia and Cahokia. These, however, made little

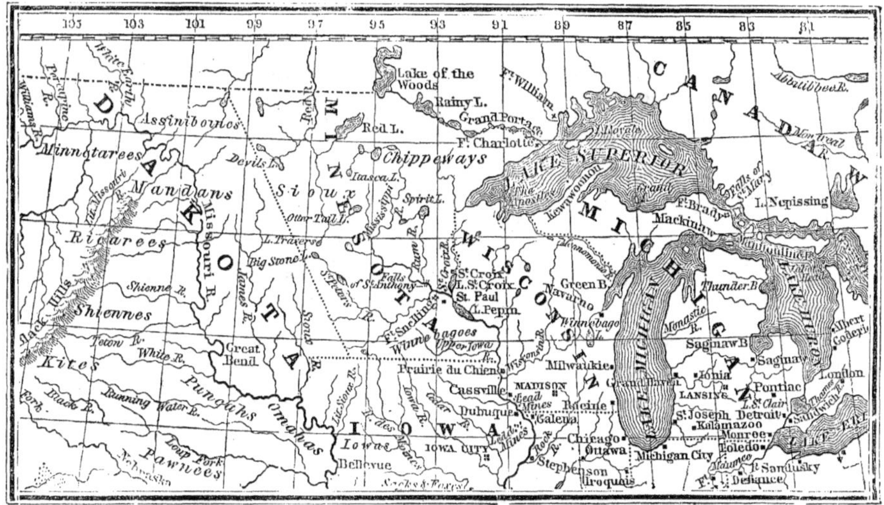

and massacred by the Indians in the same year. In 1805, Michigan was placed under a distinct territorial government. In 1812, Detroit was captured by the British, and the Indian allies of that nation committed a terrible massacre upon the Americans at Frenchtown. The enemy, however, were soon after expelled from Michigan by General Harrison. In 1836, this state was admitted into the Union.

IOWA.—*Annals.* This region, originally part of the Louisiana purchase, was erected into a territory in 1838, and became a member of the Union in 1846.

WISCONSIN.—*Annals.* This was a part of the Louisiana purchase. It was formed into a distinct territory in 1836, and became a state in 1847.

MINNESOTA.—*Annals.* This new and beautiful state derives its name from the Minnesota River. Quite a considerable portion is still in possession of the Dahcotah or Sioux Indians. It was a part of the Missouri Territory till the year 1848, when it received a distinct territorial government, St. Paul's being its capital. It was admitted to the Union in 1858.

MISSOURI T. KANSAS; **NEBRASKA.** *Annals.*—Missouri territory originally embraced the greater part of the Louisiana purchase. It contained the present Indian territory, the states of Missouri and Iowa, Minesota territory and the present Missouri territory. The latter extends from about longitude 97° on the east to the Rocky Mountains on the west. It is bounded on the north by British America, and south by the Indian territory. In 1854 a portion of the Missouri territory was erected into the two territories of Kansas and Nebraska, as elsewhere related. Kansas was admitted to the Union as a State in 1861.

Indian Medicine Man. Indian Chief. Indian Chief.

INDIAN TERRITORY. *Annals.* — This is bounded as follows: On the north by the Platte River, on the east by the states of Missouri and Arkansas, on the south by the Red River, and on the west by a desert country approaching the Rocky Mountains. It was a part of the Louisiana purchase, and was set apart, by the government of the United States, for the permanent residence of the Indian tribes that have been removed chiefly from the South-western States. Here they are to be secured in governments of their own choice, subject to no other control from the United States than such as may be necessary to preserve peace on the frontier and among the several tribes.

The population of this region amounts to about 70,000, including various tribes removed hither from countries east of the Mississippi. The *Choctaws*, *Creeks*, and *Cherokees*, formerly occupied portions of Georgia and Alabama. These, with the *Shawnees*, have made some advances in civilization. They have framed houses, cultivated lands, horses and cattle. Some of them are mechanics, and others are merchants. The missionaries have been very successful with these Indians.

Beside these there are tribes which maintain their savage modes of life. Such are the *Pawnees*, *Osages*, *Kanzas*, *Omahaws*, &c. Hunting is their chief occupation, and they frequently remove from place to place in pursuit of game. The bison, found in countless herds upon the prairies, are the chief object of pursuit with these Indians. They hunt them on horseback and on foot. In winter, they chase them on snow-shoes, and often attack them while crossing the rivers.

It is supposed that the present number of Indians within the compass of the United States is about 300,000. Their number at the period of the discovery of America, within the same territory has been variously estimated at from 500,000 to 2,000,000. At a very remote date, it appears that the valley of the Mississippi was occupied by populous nations, who had made some advances in civilization, abundant remains of which are still to be found. But these races had disappeared long before Europeans visited the country. At the time of the settlement of New England, the whole surface of the United States appears to have been more or less thickly occupied by tribes of the present Indian race. At the north they were mere savages, living in wigwams, subsisting almost wholly by the spontaneous productions of nature, by fishing, and the chase. They were in a constant state of war, which kept their numbers reduced. To the south, and especially along the borders of the Gulf of Mexico, there appears to have been large and populous tribes, somewhat farther advanced in the knowledge of the arts. They were also of a more gentle character.

At the present day, there are only a few lingering remnants of this people to the east of the Indian Territory we have just described. All the present tribes, for the most part, have lost some of their savage characteristics. Even the rudest have exchanged the bow and arrow for the rifle, and bear-skins for blankets. Those that remain are gradually fading away, and must soon disappear before the irresistible tide of emigration consisting of a superior race of men.

OREGON.—*Annals.* This state was lately bounded on the north by British America, on the east by the Rocky Mountains, south by Upper California, and west by the Pacific. Until a recent date, it was claimed both by Great Britain and the United States. It was visited in 1792 by Captain Gray, of Boston. He discovered and entered the Columbia River, to which he gave the name of his vessel. In 1804–5, it was explored by Lewis and Clark, under the direction of our government. In 1808, the Missouri Fur Company established a trading post on the head waters of Lewis' River. In 1811, the Pacific Fur Company, under John Jacob Astor, founded Astoria, at the mouth of the Columbia. At a more recent period, British fur companies also made establishments within the territory. A serious dispute arose between our government and that of Great Britain, founded upon their rival claims. The United States extended their line to 54° 40 north latitude, and the British theirs to 42°. The dispute became threatening; but happily the British government, in 1846, proposed the parallel of 49° north latitude as the boundary. This was accepted, and is now the dividing line between the two countries. Oregon Territory was recently divided into two parts, each having a territorial government. The northern part is called *Washington* territory: the southern part *Oregon*, was admitted as a State in 1859.

The chief Indian tribes of this region are the *Flatheads*, *Nez-percés*, *Wallawallas*, and *Shawnees*. Of these, there are about 20,000 They are chiefly occupied in hunting and fishing, and till lately lived on good terms with the whites. The missionaries have done them some good, but for the last few years they have displayed great hostility to the settlers.

CALIFORNIA. *Annals*. The country now embracing the State of California and the Territory of Utah, with a portion of New Mexico, was formerly called *Upper California*. It is composed of three divisions—the eastern, western, and southern. The eastern lies between the Rocky Mountains on the east and the great range of the Sierra Nevada on the west. It comprises about 200,000 square miles. With the exception of the region around the Great Salt Lake at the north, it is merely a desert of sand and mountains, occasionally surrounded with belts of verdure, and sometimes capped with eternal snow. The only white settlement is that of the Mormons, near the Salt Lake. This division nearly corresponds with the present Territory of Utah. The southern division of what was called Upper California, lies between the Gila and the Great Basin, as it is called, which forms part of the Territory just described. It is generally destitute of vegetation. This tract now belongs to New Mexico.

The western division of California extends from the summit of the Sierra Nevada to the shores of the Pacific, corresponding nearly to the present State of California. Its main feature is the united valleys of the San Joaquin and Sacramento. The western flank of the Sierra Nevada is rich in metallic treasures. It is the point to which the attention of the civilized world has been directed by the recent marvellous discoveries of gold.

In 1526, Cortez, having reduced Mexico, attempted the conquest of California, but failed: several other attempts were made by his officers, but all were unsuccessful. In 1595, a galleon was sent to make discoveries on the shore, but was lost. In 1686, the viceroy of New Spain despatched an expedition to explore the Lake of California, as the Gulf was called. The adventurers returned with an account that Old California was not an island, as had been supposed. In 1697, the Jesuits solicited and obtained permission to undertake the conquest of it. In 1765, they had in the country forty-three villages, separated from each other by the barrenness of the soil and the want of water. In 1813, California followed the fortunes of Mexico, in declaring its independence of Spain: in 1836, it was separated from Mexico, but had a kind of dependence upon it afterward. In 1846, it was taken military possession of by the United States, and May 30, 1848, it became a part of our territory by treaty with Mexico, and was admitted to the Union in 1850.

The events which speedily followed have excited the astonishment of the world. Early in 1848, it was ascertained that gold, in considerable quantities, existed along the banks of the Sacramento. Adventurers were drawn to these regions, and their most sanguine expectations being realized, others were attracted hither. The precious metal was soon found to be inexhaustible; it was discovered not only on the Sacramento, but in other localities. An immense stream of emigration was poured in upon California, not only from the United States, but from Mexico, South America, and different parts of Europe. San Francisco was speedily swelled from an insignificant village to a population of forty or fifty thousand. Other towns sprung up as if by magic. The gold regions were thronged with eager miners of almost every kindred and tongue. In about two years, gold to the value of forty millions of dollars was sent away, and it is now estimated that fifty millions a year will be realized hereafter, at least for a time.

The social condition of California presents aspects even more extraordinary than its mines. The mass of the population gathered in this territory were of course of a wild, irregular, and adventurous character. It is not to be doubted that thousands had sought refuge here from the justice of other countries. There was no enacted law: the bowie-knife and the rifle were the arbiters of almost every dispute. The people were of different origins, though by far the greater part were from the United States.

The course of events was not such as would have been anticipated by those who have no confidence in the people, and who deny the capacity of mankind for self-government. In the midst of the excitement, which existed, from the rush of emigration and the harvest of gold that all were reaping, the occupants of California discovered the necessity of government, and set about its formation. A convention was called for the preparation of a constitution. Such an instrument was speedily formed, and its wisdom and adaptation have excited admiration throughout the civilized world. Even the supercilious British press has bestowed upon it hearty commendation. This constitution was ratified by the people, and California became a state, with all the regular and established functions of government. San José, about sixty miles from San Francisco, was selected as the capital.

These events may well suggest to European politicians an inquiry whether there may not be something in our political system worthy of imitation on the other side of the Atlantic. When the people, oppressed beyond endurance, resort to revolution, in France, Germany, or Italy — the strongest minds seem to stagger as amidst the terrors of an earthquake. Statesmen, philosophers, and politicians propose schemes and theories, which are tried for a short space, and being found impracticable, are thrown aside for some form of monarchy, which has itself been a thousand times weighed in the balance and found wanting. What an example is set them by the less learned but more practical people who have been trained under our system! Separated as they are from all regular government, and under circumstances which are likely to overturn all established habits, — religion, morality, and sobriety of thought, — we see our brethren of California proceeding to the formation and establishment of a regular political system, as infallibly as the bees, assembled for the first time, proceed to build their cell according to the mathematical angle of their forefathers. Nor is this the work of a blind and uninstructed instinct. It is the result of education; it is the fruit of that plain common sense, which our political institutions are calculated to foster and diffuse among the masses. It is not because they are Anglo-Saxons, that the Californians have proceeded thus. A merely English community, under similar circumstances, would not, and could not, have formed or adopted the Californian constitution. It was because the mass had practised self-government, that the Californians succeeded in their important task. They were familiar as well with its theory as with its details, and, above all — brought up in our community — they possessed that habitual union of theory nd practice, that constant exercise of thought and ction, that just balance between the actual and the ideal, which are essential to success in all the great concerns of life. To common sense, government is a very simple affair; to the transcendental theorist, it is a riddle which defies solution.

DESERET, or UTAH.—*Annals.* Deseret is a name given to a portion of California by the Mormons, who have made a settlement and built a city near the Great Salt Lake. The history of this community is every way remarkable. They call themselves *Latter Day Saints*, and are believers in one Joe Smith, of Palmyra, in the state of New York. This person pretended that he had found in the ground certain gold plates with inscriptions which he only could decipher. His pretended translation of these is called the *Book of Mormon*, and claims to be a lost portion of the Bible. He collected some followers, and they built a temple at Rutland, Ohio, in 1830. They were driven hence, and also from Michigan and Missouri. At Nauvoo, in Illinois, they built a city, and had ten thousand votaries. They left this place about 1846, and it was purchased by Cabet and a body of French socialists. The Mormons moved toward California, and some, reaching the gold country, were among the first to discover its riches. The great body of them settled in the valley of the Bear River, near the Great Salt Lake, in the midst of a charming country. The whole community is said to number over forty thousand. They have built a city, and are constructing a temple of vast dimensions. They claim the territory immediately around them, and a large tract to the south. To this they first gave the name of DESERET—a word said to be derived from their Bible, and signifying *honey*. It was subsequently decided to call this region UTAH. Owing to its peculiar customs, the principal of which is polygamy, Utah has thus far been unable to obtain admission as a state. The territory has twice rebelled against the authority of the United States, and an army has once been sent against it.

NEW MEXICO.—*Annals.* According to Spanish authority, New Mexico extends from 32° to 42° north latitude, and from 103° to 108° west longitude, forming an area of about 200,000 square miles. It was formerly a department of Mexico, but came into our possession during the war of 1846–7, and was confirmed to us by the treaty of 1848. That portion of the territory which lies east of the Rio Grande is claimed by Texas, and its limits are therefore not yet defined. Santa Fé is the capital. The present population of this territory is small, but there are remains of ancient Spanish towns, which appear to have been large and populous. The country was conquered by the Spaniards in 1594. It was then occupied by Indian tribes: a few submitted, but others maintained a vigorous resistance for ten years. Frequent insurrections have since taken place, and an established hostility exists between the two races. New Mexico is a mountainous country, with an extensive valley formed by the Rio del Norte. Here the lands are fertile: elsewhere they are hardly capable of cultivation. Irrigation is extensively practised by the people. Horses, cattle, mules, sheep, and goats, are the chief objects of agriculture. Gold is said to be abundant, but it is not an object of great attention.

NEVADA.—*Annals.* This territory was organized in 1861, and lies between California and Utah.

COLORADO.—*Annals.* This territory was organized in 1861, and lies between Utah and Kansas.

DAKOTA.—*Annals.* This territory was organized in 1861, and includes the region to the west of Minnesota.

IDAHO.—*Annals.* This territory was organized in 1863, and lies between Dakota on the east and Washington and Oregon on the west.

CHAPTER CCCCXCVI.

General View of the United States.

We have now traced the progress of the United States, from their beginning at Jamestown in 1607, to the present time. While the origin of older nations is hidden in obscurity, our history lies open to view from the very cradle. We know the first settlers even by name; and such is the fulness of the accounts, that we are able to sympathize with their joys and sorrows, their hopes and fears, not as bands and societies only, but as individuals with whom we seem to enjoy personal acquaintance and fellowship. From this beginning we are able to follow every step in the development of our institutions, thus furnishing the most complete and certain record of a nation's rise and progress to be found in the annals of mankind.

The territory of the United States, which is now estimated at two million eight hundred thousand square miles, has been derived from various sources. The thirteen English colonies, which united in the revolutionary war, held the same territories which they now possess as states. Beside these, Virginia laid claim, by virtue of her charter, to an undefined tract to the west, including Kentucky, and what was afterward called the *North-Western Territory;* embracing Ohio, Indiana, Illinois, Michigan, and Wisconsin. These claims she ceded to the United States in 1787, making a small reservation of lands in Ohio, for the payment of certain state debts. Tennessee was originally a part of South Carolina. Alabama was mostly included in the original patent of Georgia. Maine was a part of the state of Massachusetts. Thus the whole of the present territory of the United States, east of the River Mississippi, excepting only the state of Florida and part of Mississippi, came to us as the possessions of the original thirteen English colonies.

Florida and the southern part of Mississippi were ceded to us by Spain in 1819, as compensation for spoliations upon our commerce. The Louisiana purchase, made in 1803, gave us the whole tract lying between the Mississippi River and the Rocky Mountains, including the states of Louisiana, Arkansas, Missouri, and Iowa, with the contiguous territories of Minesota, Missouri, and the Indian territory. Texas was obtained by a treaty of annexation in 1845; Oregon, by discovery and occupation; California and New Mexico, by treaty with Mexico after the war, in 1848.

The population of the United States may be considered as one half of English blood, and one quarter Irish and Scotch. The Germans are numerous, making nearly one eighth of the whole population. The rest consists of French, Spanish, and other races. This estimate is exclusive of four millions of slaves, of African descent, and three hundred thousand Indians, chiefly independent. The language of our country is English, which is spoken universally, except by foreigners; and what is remarkable, it is far more correctly spoken than by the masses in England. Our manners and customs have also an English basis, though they are modified by our condition and institutions. In physical appearance, our people have no striking resemblance to the English; the force of climate is visible in the leaner form and more oval face of our people, even in sections where the English blood is still unmixed.

The ratio of increase, hitherto, seems to show that our population doubles once in twenty-five years. In 1790, we had 4,609,724 inhabitants; in 1800 6,198,966; in 1810, 8,431,178; in 1820, 11,176,169: in 1830, 14,875,063; in 1840, 17,724,000. The census of 1860 shows the number of inhabitants at that epoch to have been 31,953,760; and since that period there is an equal ratio of increase, as emigration, and the general causes of progress in population, were never more active than at present. Taking these facts as the basis of calculation, it seems possible that the population of the United States will reach a hundred millions by the close of the present century.

It has been the custom in Europe, among the champions of monarchy, to foretell the speedy downfall of our political system, and the end of our national existence. We have outlived these predictions, and while the vaunted institutions of the old world are rushing into chaos and ruin, we see our own growing more steadfast by time; and amid the convulsions of the old world, we find millions flocking to our country as the only place of refuge, peace, and safety. The extent of our territory, the increase of our population, the multiplication of our states, each and all regarded as rocks upon which we must speedily be wrecked, have added to our political stability in the full ratio of our numerical and physical extension. We believe we have solved the problem as to whether a people are capable of self-government, and have proved that a government resting upon the assent, coöperation, and responsibility of an intelligent people, is the most stable and beneficent yet devised by man. Eighty years ago we were thirteen feeble colonies, with three millions of people; we are now thirty four, sovereign, independent states, all bound together as one nation, with thirty-one millions of inhabitants. For seventy years we have remained at peace with each other — thus setting an example which no other country has rivalled. We have spread civilization over a space equal to one half of Europe, and in every department of science, art, and literature, have contributed our share to the general stock of human intelligence and improvement. And we have done this, not only without the sympathy and favor of the leading nations of Christendom, but in spite of the special spleen and malignity of our mother country. Against her we have been obliged to contend in two wars; and what is more, against the rancorous hostility of the British press. We have been the standing target for every species of gibe and jeer — the theme of perpetual obloquy and denunciation, the chosen object of evil propnecy and malignant interpretation. If the spirit of England is somewhat changed toward us, we are bound to regard it as flowing less from a generous sympathy toward her kindred, than respect for a nation which capable of maintaining its rights.

Among the most striking monuments of our national prosperity are our cities. New York is situated on an island about fifteen miles in length, which divides the Hudson into two branches. To the south-west lies the Bay, nearly encircled by land, entered from the sea by a passage called the *Narrows.* The harbor is one of the finest in the world. The multitude of vessels which surround the city, whose masts look like a forest stripped of its leaves, with the steamboats constantly arriving and departing, give evidence of the activity and extent of the trade and commerce which centre in this great metropolis. It is, in fact, the chief city of the Western Continent, and one of the greatest commercial places in the world. Its population in 1760 was ten thousand: it is now about a million.

Boston, the metropolis of New England has about one hundred and eighty thousand inhabitants. It was begun in 1630. Philadelphia, the second city as to population in the United States, was laid out in 1684; it now contains about four hundred and seventy-five thousand people. Baltimore, the largest city in Maryland, has one hundred and seventy thousand people. Washington City, the seat of government of the United States, has a splendid situation, and several fine public edifices; but its population does not exceed sixty thousand. New Orleans is a place of immense trade, and seems destined to be one of the great cities of the Western Continent. Its population is estimated at one hundred and seventy thousand. St. Louis, Cincinnati, Rochester, Lowell, Louisville, and some other places, have advanced in population with a rapidity almost beyond example. San Francisco furnishes an instance of increase, which, to the inhabitants of the Old World, seems to be incredible. In the space of ten years it has risen from a population of 1500 to 60,000. Other towns exist in California, containing streets, hotels, banks, and expresses, where, eight years since, the primeval forests were standing.

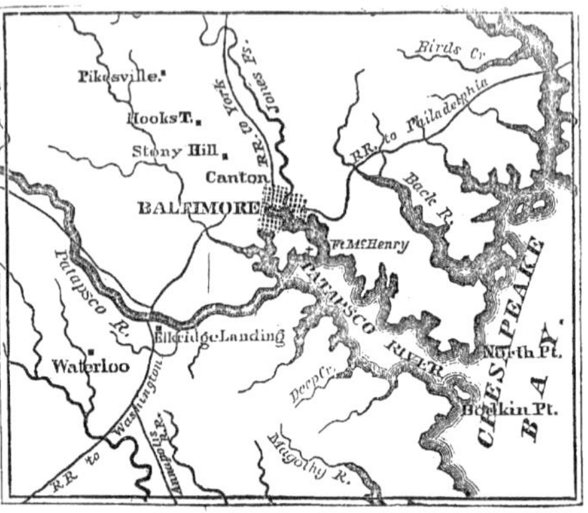

Plan of the City of Baltimore.

Plan of the City of Boston.

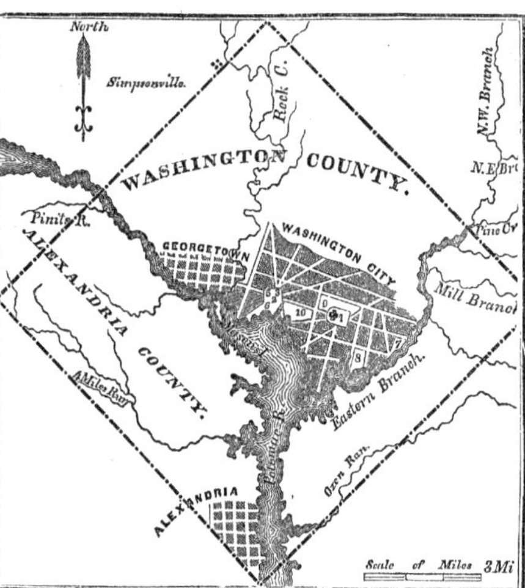

Plan of the City of Washington.

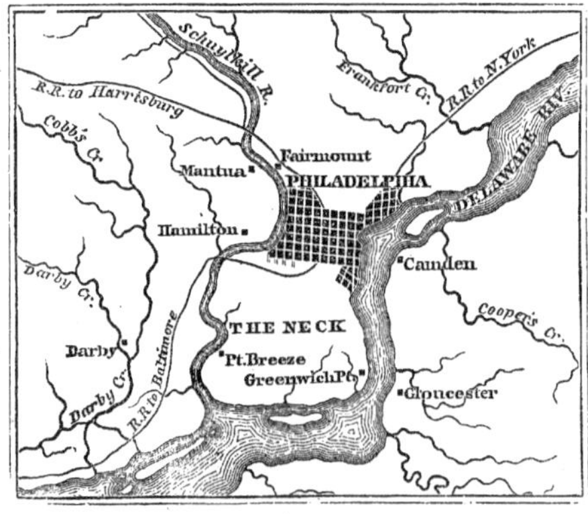

Plan of the City of Philadelphia.

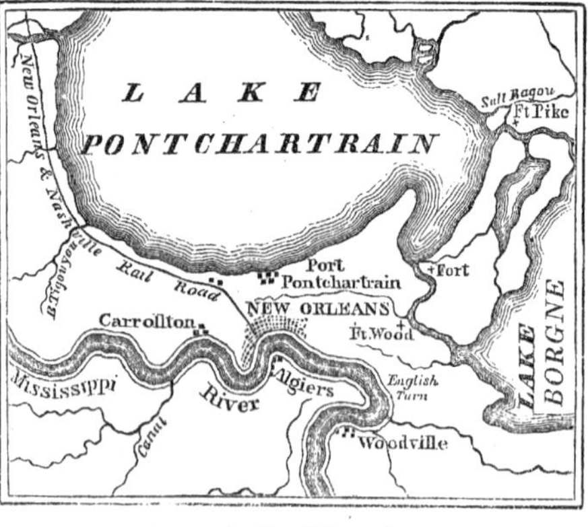

Plan of the City of New Orleans.

Mexico.

CHAPTER CCCCXCVII.

A. D. 700 to 1519.

Description of Mexico — Ancient Mexicans — The Toltecs — The Aztecs — Foundation of the Mexican Empire — Civilization of the Ancient Mexicans — Their Government and Religion — Discovery of Mexico by the Spaniards — Invasion of Cortez — The Embassy of Montezuma.

Ancient Mexicans.

MEXICO * is bounded north by the United States, east by the Gulf of Mexico, and south and west by the Pacific Ocean. The greater part of the country is elevated, and comprises a portion of that vast ridge of mountains which traverses the whole continent of America, parallel to the shore of the Pacific, known in Mexico as the chain of the Cordilleras. The middle part of this chain presents a broad table land from six thousand to eight thousand feet in height. Detached mountains occur here and there, rising above this lofty elevation into the regions of perpetual snow; among these are the volcanoes of Orizaba and Popocatepetl. The fertility of this vast table land varies with its elevation. The higher parts are barren from the want of moisture, and here the soil abounds in saline substances, which give to the wide arid plains in this quarter a resemblance to Thibet and the steppes of Central Asia. Yet a great part of Mexico must be ranked with the most fertile regions of the earth. The climate is temperate, and except in the level districts, near the sea, it is salubrious. The rivers are few in number, and small. The lakes are numerous, and appear to be the remains of others of vast extent, which formerly covered a much larger portion of this lofty plain. Mexico is rich in mines of gold and silver. Those of Guanaxuato and Real del Monte are the most productive silver mines in the world.

Mexico has its historical records for many centuries preceding the conquest of the country by the Spaniards. The first inhabitants of whom any distinct notice is taken, in these annals, were the Toltecs, a race of aboriginal Americans, or possibly Asiatics,

* The present extent of Mexico is about three hundred and twenty thousand square miles; population seven to eight millions. The capital is Mexico, which has from one hundred and fifty thousand to two hundred thousand inhabitants. The other important towns are Puebla, Guanaxuato, Guadalaxara, Vera Cruz, Acapulco, and Tampico.

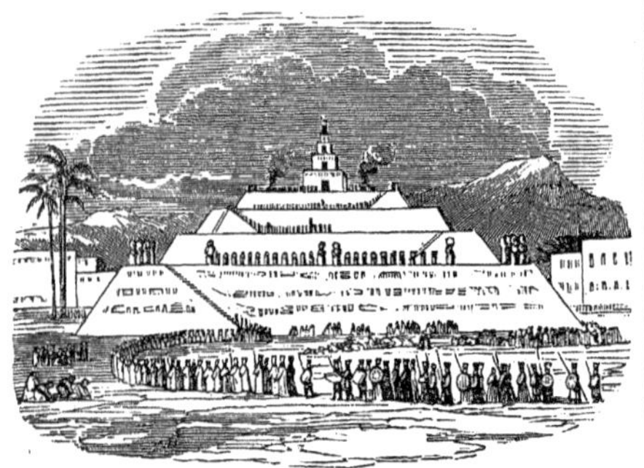

Great Temple in Ancient Mexico.

who migrated to this country from the north, about the close of the seventh century. They established themselves in Mexico, where they appear to have begun the work of civilization by the practice of agriculture, metallurgy, architecture, &c. This country then bore the name of *Anahuac*. The Toltecs held dominion over it for four hundred years, after which they disappear from history. A century afterward, another tribe, called the *Chichemecs*, invaded Anahuac from the north-west, and were followed by tribes of higher civilization; these were called *Aztecs*, *Acolhuaics*, and *Tezcucans*. In the year **1325**, the Aztecs founded the city of Tenuchtitlan, afterward named Mexico, from Mexitli, the Aztec name of the god of war. This was, in fact, the foundation of the great empire of Mexico.

When the Spaniards arrived in America, Mexico formed the most powerful and populous empire in the western world. This empire had attained, in many respects, to a considerable degree of civilization. The Mexicans built large cities, and lofty and regular pyramids. They were acquainted with the art of smelting metals and cutting stone. They had a calendar more accurate than that of the Greeks and Romans. They recorded events by paintings of a peculiar character, which were little inferior to the hieroglyphics of Egypt. Their government was monarchical. There existed a regular gradation of ranks in the empire, and the exorbitant power and pride of the nobles exhibited a strong contrast with the almost enslaved condition of the body of the people. The Mexican religion was of a most revolting and sanguinary character. Human sacrifices were offered up in vast numbers, and with the most ferocious rites. Nothing could be more hideous than their idols. Their drapery consisted of twisted snakes, and two serpents supplied the place of arms. The ornaments were all in character; a necklace of human heads and skulls was fastened together by a band of entrails. The great object of the Mexicans in battle was to take captives, in order that their deity might have abundance of victims. The Mexican temples were very numerous. Every city had several hundred; some of these were small, but many were large. They were solid masses of earth, faced with brick or stone, and resembled in shape, to a considerable degree, the pyramids of ancient Egypt. They consisted of four or five stories, regularly diminishing upward. On the top were towers and altars for sacrifices.

Ancient Mexican House

The Mexican empire was very populous, but nothing definite can be stated as to the number of its inhabitants. Mexico, the capital city, was built in a lake at a short distance from the shore. It was connected with the main land by several wide causeways of stone, one of which was seven miles long. The streets were regular, and the temples and palaces were built in a style suitable to the metropolis of a great empire. The chief square presented a busy spectacle, where every kind of merchandise was exposed for sale, and where fifty thousand people were sometimes collected together. The population of the city was estimated at three hundred thousand. The lake was surrounded by fifty other cities, and its waters were navigated by one hundred thousand canoes.

The empire of Mexico became first known to the Spaniards about the year **1517**, when Juan de Grijalva touched upon the coast, and obtained some knowledge of the wealth and populousness of the country, which he named *New Spain*. This information aroused the cupidity of the Spaniards, and an expedition was fitted out by Velasquez, the governor of Cuba, to invade this new territory. The command was intrusted to Hernando Cortez, an officer of ability and courage, but avaricious and hard-hearted, like most of the Spanish adventurers of that period. The expedition sailed from Cuba on the 10th of February, 1519, and landed in Mexico, first at Cozumel, and then at Tabasco, where Cortez took formal possession of the country. Proceeding along the coast, he arrived at St. Juan de Ulua, now Vera Cruz, on the 2d of April.

Montezuma, the emperor of Mexico, hearing of the arrival of the strangers in his country, sent ambassadors to learn their intentions. Cortez gave a haughty answer, that he would confer with no other person than the emperor himself. In the mean time, he disembarked all his men, horses, and guns, and fortified his position. The Mexicans, alarmed at the unusual appearance of the troops, the horses, the ships, and the artillery, endeavored to conciliate the Spaniards by rich presents. The ambassadors had painters in their train, who were busily employed in tracing these wonderful objects. Cortez, observing this, managed to give a greater effect to his warlike show by causing his troops to go through their manœuvres, and fire their cannon at the trees. The Mexicans, astonished at this display, fell upon their faces in terror; the ambassadors returned to Montezuma with an account of the marvels they had seen.

CHAPTER CCCCXCVIII.

A. D. 1519 to 1835.

March of Cortez toward the Capital — The Zempoallans and Tlascalans — Arrival of the Spaniards in Mexico — Montezuma made Prisoner — Expulsion of the Spaniards from Mexico — Siege and Capture of the City — Subjugation of the Mexican Empire — Spanish Government in Mexico — Revolution — Hidalgo — Iturbide — Revolt of Texas.

Montezuma.

MONTEZUMA, who was of a weak and pusillanimous disposition, felt no way inclined to admit to his presence a body of visitors, of whom he had received so alarming a description. He therefore sent a fresh embassy to Cortez, with rich presents, declining the proposed interview. But these magnificent gifts served only to stimulate the avarice of the Spaniards. Cortez resolved to temporize. He changed his camp into a permanent settlement, and patiently watched from his intrenchments the course of events. He had not long continued in this position, when he received an embassy from the Zempoallans, a tribe which had long been discontented with the government of Montezuma. He immediately entered into an alliance with these disaffected subjects, and sent an embassy to Spain to procure a ratification of his powers. He then set fire to his ships, that his soldiers, being deprived of all hope of escape, should look for safety only in victory.

Having completed these preparations, Cortez undertook the romantic and desperate enterprise of marching into the heart of an unknown country, to subdue a mighty empire, with a force consisting of only five hundred foot, fifteen horse, and six pieces of artillery His first hostile encounter was with the Tlascalans, the most warlike race in Mexico. Their country was a republic, under the protection of the empire; and they fought with the courage of men animated by a love of freedom. But nothing could resist the Spanish fire-arms. The Tlascalans, after several defeats, yielded themselves as vassals to the crown of Spain, and engaged to assist Cortez in all his future operations. Aided by six thousand of these new allies, he advanced to Cholula, a city within sixty miles of Mexico, where he was treacherously received by order of Montezuma; but having seasonably discovered that a plot was laid for his destruction, he took his revenge by a massacre of six thousand of the Cholulans.

Cortez and his Army coming in sight of the City of Mexico.

In their advance toward the capital, the Spaniards were aided by the rebellious state of the surrounding country; and after a march of some days, they obtained a sight of the city of Mexico from the mountain of Chalco. The troops were filled with exultation at the prospect, and on beholding the rich and beautiful country around them, they imagined the reward of their toils and hazards to be already in their hands. On their arrival at the entrance of the city, Montezuma went forth to meet them in all the parade and magnificence of state. He saluted Cortez in a respectful manner, and assigned to his army a lodging in the capital; this they immediately fortified in the strongest manner. The situation of the Spaniards was, however, one of great danger and perplexity. They were in a city surrounded by water; the bridges and causeways might easily be broken down, and the army, thus cut off from all communication with its allies, might be overwhelmed by superior numbers. To guard against this danger, Cortez adopted the bold resolution of seizing Montezuma, and holding him as a hostage for his own safety. This design he accomplished with the most complete success, and the emperor was carried a prisoner to the Spanish quarters.

Montezuma was detained a prisoner for six months, during which time, Cortez employed himself in collecting information respecting the country, building vessels on the lake, and dividing the gold which he had acquired among his soldiers. A danger, however, threatened him from an unexpected quarter. The governor of Cuba, anxious to share in the plunder of Mexico, sent a new armament, under the command of Narvaez, to deprive Cortez of the fruits of his victory. The latter immediately marched from Mexico, leaving a small garrison behind him, and proceeded to attack Narvaez. By a series of skilful and prudent operations, he not only overcame him, but induced his followers to enlist under his own banners. Scarcely had he returned to Mexico, when the natives rose in a general insurrection, and attacked the Spanish quarters with great fury. To appease the assailants, Cortez brought out Montezuma in his imperial robes, and persuaded him to address his subjects from the ramparts. At first they listened with respectful attention; but this was speedily followed by a shower of stones and arrows, and the unfortunate emperor was mortally wounded.

The Spaniards, after sustaining repeated attacks in Mexico, were at length compelled to retreat from the city. They were assailed furiously in their departure, and lost great numbers of men, with their artillery, ammunition and baggage, and the greater part of their gold. Having effected his escape from his enemies, Cortez fixed his head-quarters at Tezcuco, on the banks of the lake, twenty miles from the capital. The natives in this quarter became his allies, and assisted him in building a fleet, to attack Mexico by water. In this conjuncture, four vessels, fitted out by his friends in Hispaniola, arrived with a reënforcement, and Cortez immediately commenced a general assault upon the city. It was defended with great courage and perseverance by the new emperor, Guatimozin. But the Indian allies of the Spaniards now amounted to one hundred and fifty thousand soldiers, and the siege of Mexico was pushed vigorously for twenty-five days: at length, after three fourths of the city had been destroyed, the emperor attempted to make his escape, but was taken prisoner, on which the capital immediately surrendered, August 21, 1521. All the rest of the empire followed the example, and submitted to the Spaniards.

A great part of the Mexican nation, including most of the nobility and priesthood, perished in the wars and massacres of the conquest; but considerable numbers of the native population survived this calamity, and their descendants have continued to dwell in the country to the present day. The first thought of the conquerors was to seize upon the wealth of the subjugated empire, and the second, to propagate the Catholic religion among the surviving inhabitants. Missionaries were sent out from Spain, who converted great numbers of the Mexicans; and at length, the ancient religion of the country was completely extirpated. The hopes of acquiring immense wealth attracted crowds of Spanish emigrants, who gradually multiplied in a country abounding with all the necessaries of life, and Mexico became one of the most populous and wealthy of all the Spanish colonies.

As such, however, it was very ill governed. The Indians were reduced to slavery, and the Spaniards led a life of indolence. The habit of implicit submission, and the ignorance attending it, checked all spirit of enterprise, and the country slumbered under the despotism of Spain, while the principles of civil liberty were gradually pervading the English colonies, and impelling them onward in the career of national independence. A root of discontent, however, was deeply implanted in the population of Mexico. The Creoles, or Spaniards born in America, became, in process of time, the most numerous race; yet the Spanish government, with a short-sighted policy, placed all its confidence, and vested all political power, in a small body of Spaniards sent out from Europe. The discontent of the proscribed Creoles, however, might long have fermented without an explosion, had not their ties with Europe been broken by Napoleon's invasion of Spain. The first announcement of this event in **1808**, occasioned great confusion in Mexico; and at length, in **1810**, a priest named Hidalgo raised the standard of revolt. After obtaining some advantages over the royal forces, his army was defeated. Hidalgo was put to death, but the troubles were not quieted. A series of disorders and insurrections followed, the details of which would be uninteresting to the reader; but the result was the gradual weakening of the royal authority in Mexico, till in 1821, the friends of liberty made themselves masters of the capital, and Mexico became finally independent of Spain.

A congress was convened to establish a new government. Augustine Iturbide, a Mexican who had commanded the army, contrived, by a series of artful manœuvres, to get himself proclaimed emperor in 1821 He had a short and troubled reign of less than a year, when he was deposed and banished to Europe by the Mexican congress, who granted him a competent annuity for his support. In **1824**, he returned to Mexico, in the hope of recovering his throne; but was immediately arrested and put to death by order of the government. Mexico was declared a republic, and the forms of such a government were adopted throughout the country; but a constant succession of tumults, conspiracies, insurrections, and civil wars kept every thing unsettled, and ruined the prosperity of the nation. All European Spaniards were compelled to quit the territory of the republic, which was thus deprived of great numbers of the most wealthy, intelligent, and industrious of its citizens. The finances were involved in utter confusion, and all regular civil authority was at an end, while the army and its leader exercised the real control and monopolized the power of government. In 1835, the people of Texas declared themselves independent, and successfully resisted the attempts of the Mexicans to repossess themselves of the country. In the war which attended this revolution, the Texans captured General Santa Anna, the Mexican president. The result was the final separation of Texas from Mexico, and its annexation to the American Union

Bombardment of Vera Cruz.

CHAPTER CCCCXCIX.

A. D. 1835 to 1863.

War with the United States — Battles of Palo Alto and Resaca de la Palma — Capture of Matamoras and Monterey — Battle of Buena Vista — Capture of Vera Cruz — Battle of Cerro Gordo — Capture of Jalapa — Guerilla Warfare — Battles of Contreras, Cherubusco, Molino del Rey, and Chapultepec — Capture of Mexico — Conquest of California and New Mexico — Peace with the United States — War with France.

THE annexation of Texas led to a war between Mexico and the United States. The western boundary of Texas was a subject of dispute — both republics claiming the territory between the Rio Grande and the Nueces. The United States forces, under General Taylor, having occupied this territory, the Mexicans pretended to view it as an act of hostility, and a collision immediately took place. The first blood was shed on the 10th of April, 1846, when Colonel Cross of the American army, on an excursion from the camp upon the eastern bank of the Rio Grande, was waylaid and murdered by the Mexicans. General Ampudia, the Mexican commander at Matamoras, issued a proclamation commanding the American troops to withdraw beyond the Nueces. General Taylor replied by warning him not to commit hostilities, and declaring his determination to maintain his ground. He also caused the mouth of the Rio Grande to be blockaded, to prevent the Mexicans from throwing reinforcements into Matamoras. On the 25th of April, a scouting party of Americans under captain Houston were surprised by a party of Mexicans; sixteen were killed and wounded, and nearly all the survivors taken prisoners.

General Taylor, who was at Fort Brown opposite Matamoras, now perceived that it was the intention of the Mexicans to cross the river above and get into his rear, thus cutting off his communication with Point Isabel on the coast, where his magazines had been established. To defeat this manœuvre, he took up his march for the latter place. Arista, who had succeeded Ampudia in the command at Matamoras, mistaking this movement for a retreat, immediately crossed the Rio Grande at some distance above Fort Brown, and marched in the direction of Point Isabel. A heavy cannonade was opened from Matamoras upon the fort on the third of May, which was continued at intervals for a week.

In the meantime, Taylor had reached Point Isabel, placed a strong garrison there, and was on his march back to the Rio Grande, when, on the eighth of May he encountered the enemy on the plains of Palo Alto. The Mexicans were about six thousand strong, with eight hundred cavalry, and several field pieces. The Americans did not exceed twenty-three hundred. The battle commenced at two in the afternoon. The Mexican cavalry made repeated charges, but were as often driven back. The conflict lasted five hours, and was decided chiefly by the American artillery, which was served with such skill and effect that the Mexicans were repulsed at every point, and driven off the field with the loss of two hundred killed and four hundred wounded. The Americans had nine killed, and forty-four wounded. In the night, the Mexicans retreated. The victors encamped on the field of battle and resumed their march on the next day.

The Mexicans had not retreated far. After two hours march, the Americans encountered their army drawn up in a strong position, in a ravine called Resaca de la Palma. Their batteries completely swept the road approaching them, and their artillery did such execution as to render it necessary to dislodge them from this post. Captain May was ordered to charge with his dragoons. This was immediately done. The Mexican artillerymen were driven from their guns, their pieces captured, and the Mexican general, Vega, taken prisoner. The American infantry now charged the Mexican main body, and the battle was soon decided. The Mexicans broke their ranks, fled from the field, and were pursued by the American cavalry. The pursuit was continued till all the survivors of the Mexican army, were either taken prisoners or driven across the Rio Grande. In this battle, the American force did not exceed seventeen hundred men. The Mexicans had been reinforced after the action of Palo Alto, and were not less than six thousand strong. Their loss in the two battles was estimated at above a thousand. The military skill of General Taylor, and the courage of the American troops were strikingly evinced in these two victories. The veteran forces of the Mexicans were completely routed; eight pieces of artillery, a large number of prisoners, including fourteen officers, with all the baggage and stores of the enemy, fell into the hands of the Americans.

The tables were now turned upon the Mexicans, who found the war was about to be carried into their own country. Arista attempted to check the advance of the Americans by proposing an armistice, till the dispute between the two governments should be settled; but General Taylor had no authority to make such an arrangement. The Mexicans abandoned Matamoras, and the Americans took possession of that place on the 18th of May. General Taylor fixed his head quarters here during the summer. The towns of Mier, Camargo, Revilla, and Reynosa, also surrendered, and were garrisoned by the Americans. Reinforcements having joined the American army, General Taylor toward the end of August, had a force of nine thousand men at his disposal. It was determined to march upon Monterey, the chief city of New Leon. On the 20th of August, a division under General Worth, proceeded in that direction. General Taylor followed on the 5th of September, leaving a force of two thousand men upon the Rio Grande. On the 19th, the united forces of Taylor and Worth reached Walnut Springs, three miles from Monterey.

This place is situated at the base of the Sierra Madre mountains, in a position of great natural strength, and strongly fortified by art. The city is not only surrounded by fortifications mounted with heavy cannon, but it is in itself one great castle, consisting of straight streets lined with stone houses, the walls of which rising above the flat roofs, serve as ramparts and battlements. The population was about fifteen thousand, and the garrison amounted to seven thousand regular troops, with two or three thousand irregulars. Notwithstanding the strength of the place, and the superior numbers of the enemy, General Taylor was so confident of the courage of his own men, that he did not hesitate to storm the city. The attack was commenced on the 21st, by General Worth's division, and continued by the remainder of the army during all the next day. On the 23d, the assault became general, and a desperate conflict ensued in the streets of the city. Volleys of musketry from the house-tops, were poured upon the American troops, but they advanced from house to house and from square to square, till the main body of the Mexicans had been driven from the lower part of the city, and had taken shelter behind their barricades. Ampudia, the Mexican commander, finding the place untenable, proposed on the morning of the 24th, to evacuate Monterey. This was agreed to by General Taylor, and the Americans took possession of the city. The loss in the storming of Monterey was severe; the Americans had one hundred and twenty killed, and three hundred and thirty-seven wounded. The Mexican loss was never published.

General Taylor established his head quarters at Monterey, and detached General Worth to take possession of Saltillo. In the meantime, the Mexicans made extraordinary efforts to raise an army to drive the invaders from their country. Santa Anna, who had returned from his exile in the West Indies to Mexico, was made provisional president, and through his active exertions, a force of more than twenty thousand men, was assembled at San Luis Potosi in January 1847. These troops comprised the flower of the Mexican nation, and were completely equipped. It was the design of Santa Anna to fall at once upon General Taylor's army, overwhelm it by superiority of numbers, and pursue his conquering march to the Rio Grande, where all the American military posts and magazines would fall into his hands.

About the end of January, Gen. Taylor received information of Santa Anna's preparations. Determining at once to meet the approaching enemy, he left a garrison of fifteen hundred men in Monterey, and marched on the 31st, towards Saltillo. Passing this point on the 2d of February, he reached Agua Nueva, twenty miles south on the San Luis road, where he encamped till the 21st, where he learnt that the whole Mexican army was advancing upon him. The enemy had five times his force, and it was necessary to take a strong position, in order to balance in some degree, this great disparity of numbers. Taylor, therefore, fell back to the mountain pass of Buena Vista, where the bases of the heights are worn by the rains into deep gullies, opposing great obstacles to the operations of cavalry and artillery.

On the morning of the 22d of February, the Mexican army came in sight, full of the most confident anticipations of victory. Santa Anna sent a flag of truce, summoning the American commander to surrender at discretion. General Taylor returned a very laconic refusal. A skirmishing began which was carried on through the night, and the battle commenced early the next morning. The fighting was most desperate. The Mexicans trusting to their great superiority of numbers, were pursuaded that their antagonists must be overwhelmed. They returned to the onset at every repulse, and continued the contest till night. The Americans maintained their position with inflexible courage, and the Mexicans finding their assaults repelled in every quarter, retreated under cover of the night. Their loss in killed and wounded was upwards of fifteen hundred; that of the Americans about seven hundred. In their retreat, the Mexican army was almost annihilated. This battle was of great importance, in every point of view, and must be regarded as one of the main causes of our subsequent rapid success in the war.

The military operations in this quarter were closed by the victory of Buena Vista. The whole frontier of the Rio Grande was secured from attack, and the Mexicans were too much intimidated by their repeated defeats to entertain any hope of regaining what they had lost in that part of their territory. The war was now transferred to another quarter. A scheme was projected for invading Mexico in the south, and striking a blow at the capital. In pursuance of this design, a squadron of United States ships was sent to blockade Vera Cruz. A small naval force under

Commodore Connor captured Tampico on the 12th of November, 1846. The force assembled for the attack on Vera Cruz, amounted to eleven thousand men, which included a part of the army of General Taylor. The whole were placed under command of General Scott. On the 9th of March 1847, they landed near Vera Cruz, and proceeded to attack the city. After suffering a heavy bombardment, Vera Cruz surrendered on the 26th of March, together with the strong castle of San Juan De Ulloa, which constitutes its chief defence by sea.

Early in April, General Scott, at the head of an army of 10,000 men, began his march for the interior. On reaching the mountain pass at Cerro Gordo, he found the enemy posted in great force to oppose his progress. They were commanded by Santa Anna, who, after his defeat at Buena Vista, had succeeded in raising and equipping another army. His position at Cerro Gordo was very strong, and completely commanded the road. General Scott, by skilful manœuvering, gained possession of some indirect approaches to the Mexican position, and on the 18th of April he stormed the heights of Cerro Gordo. The promptness and intrepidity of the American soldiers speedily carried the day. The Mexicans were completely routed, and put to flight; three thousand laid down their arms and surrendered prisoners of war, including five generals, and a great number of other officers. The quantity of cannon, small arms, military stores and baggage which fell into the hands of the Americans was so great, that the captors were almost embarrassed with the result of victory.

Jalapa surrendered on the day following the battle of Cerro Gordo, and on the 22d of April, the Americans took possession of the castle of Perote, one of the strongest fortresses in Mexico, containing fifty-four pieces of artillery, and a vast quantity of arms and military stores. On the 15th of May, the Americans entered the city of Puebla, one of the largest in Mexico, containing eighty thousand inhabitants. The Mexicans, finding it in vain to contend with the Americans in the field of battle, organized bands of guerilla troops, who harassed the invaders by petty skirmishing attacks, in which they were sometimes successful, cutting off escorts of prisoners and scouting parties. In one of these conflicts, at the National Bridge, a body of 1400 Mexicans was defeated.

General Scott halted at Puebla till August. On the 7th of that month, he recommenced his march for Mexico, and on the fourth day, reached the great valley in which that capital is situated. The Mexican troops had occupied all the roads, and fortified their position in the strongest manner. Santa Anna issued a gasconading proclamation, declaring that the Americans should never reach the city of Mexico, except by marching over his dead body. General Scott, instead of attacking the enemy in front, ordered a road to be cut round the southern shores of the lakes of Chalco and Xochimilco, by which he turned the right flank of the enemy's position, and rendered the Mexican fortifications useless. On the 19th of August, the Americans attacked Contreras, and a battle ensued which ended in the defeat of the Mexicans. On the following day, another battle was fought at Cherubusco, with a similar result. In these battles, the courage of the American soldiers in contending against superior numbers, and the brilliant success of their skill and intrepidity were very conspicuous. The Mexican force engaged was estimated at over thirty thousand: that of the Americans at eight thousand. The route and dispersion of the Mexicans were complete; artillery, military stores, and prisoners, to a vast amount, fell into the hands of the victors, and the road to the capital was laid open. An armistice was now proposed by the Mexicans, and agreed to by General Scott, with the understanding that negotiations were to be immediately opened for a peace. The Mexicans, however, were desirous only to gain time, in the hope of assembling new forces. The negotiations, however, failed, and the armistice expired on the 6th of September.

On the 7th, the Americans attacked Molino del Rey, where the Mexicans had a cannon foundry; and, after a desperate action, captured the place. On the 12th, they stormed, and captured the castle of Chapultepec. Several more of the outposts of the city were successively attacked and taken; and finally, on the 13th of September, 1847, the American army entered the city of Mexico in triumph. The Mexicans had previously opened their jails and prisons, and turned the convicts loose in the streets. These wretches committed many assassinations upon the Americans during some days after the capture, but General Scott established such strict police regulations, that these disorders were soon quieted, and the city, during its occupation by the American troops, enjoyed a degree of security and tranquillity which it had never known under the Mexican government.

In the meantime, New Mexico and California had been occupied by the American forces. The affairs of the Mexican government were in the greatest confusion, and the negotiations for peace proceeded slowly. At length, in January, 1848, a treaty was agreed upon by the American and Mexican commissioners at Guadalupe Hidalgo; and, on the 10th of March following, it was ratified by the senate of the United States. By this treaty, upper California, and a portion of New Mexico, were ceded to the United States, for the sum of fifteen millions of dollars; all the other conquests of the Americans were restored.

Since the conclusion of the war with the United States, Mexico has returned to her former condition, and is again periodically agitated by seditions, conspiracies, and scenes of disorder. As we write (1863), a French army of 30,000 men, sent by Louis Napoleon to invade the country, upon the pretext of unpaid debts, is endeavoring, in the face of great difficulties and discouragement, to force its way through Puebla to the city of Mexico. This event seems to have united all parties in the defence of their country.

CHAPTER D.

YUCATAN. — *General Views — The Capital of Mexico — Manners and Customs of the Mexicans.*

YUCATAN revolted from the Mexican government during the civil dissensions of the republic in 1839. A Mexican force invaded the province, but was repulsed with great loss, and Yucatan assumed an independent position. Afterwards, she rejoined the Mexican union on her own terms; but the convention appears to have been little more than nominal. At the present moment (1863) it is difficult to determine whether this province belongs to Mexico or not. For a year or two past, the Indians have been in a state of insur

Mexican Antiquities.

rection, and have committed great slaughter among he inhabitants. They still remain unsubdued, the government being too weak to establish its own authority in the province.

Yucatan is particularly interesting for its antiquities, which are scattered all over the country, and present a most important field for the researches of the historian. The ruins of more than forty ancient cities have been already discovered, abounding with sculptures and curiosities of architecture. The most important are those of Uxmal, Kabah, Gabna, Kewik, Labpak, Chi-chen, Ocosingo, and Santa Cruz del Quicha.

At the village of Palenque, near the borders of Yucatan, are the vestiges of a large city, which was probably, in ancient times, the capital of an empire, whose history has perished. This metropolis remained concealed, like another Herculaneum, not under ground, but overgrown with a thick forest, in the midst of a vast desert. At length, about the middle of the last century, some Spaniards, having penetrated into the midst of the dreary solitude, discovered the remains of a superb city, eighteen miles in circuit. The solid edifices, stately palaces, and magnificent public monuments, still visible at this place, strike the beholder with astonishment. The hieroglyphics, symbols, emblems, and sculptures of various kinds, which have been discovered in the temples of Palenque, bear a strong resemblance to those of the Egyptians. Ruins of a similar character to those of Palenque are to be seen at Mitla.

Mexico, the capital of the republic of Mexico, stands on the site of the ancient city of Montezuma's empire; but the lake is so diminished that the modern capital is three miles from the shore. It is a regular and beautiful city, surrounded by a picturesque neighborhood. The streets are straight, and much of the architecture is in a correct style. The national palace, and the cathedral, in particular, are magnificent structures. The population is about one hundred and forty thousand. Puebla is a beautiful city, with a cathedral, the interior of which surpasses every other in the western world for richness of ornament. Vera Cruz, the chief seaport, is a well built city, with considerable trade, but it is unhealthy. Population ten thousand.

Mexican Antiquities.

The population of Mexico is composed of severa races. One half are Indians, the descendants of the ancient Mexicans; a million and a half are whites and the remainder a mixed breed, Spanish, Indian and Negro. The whites are natives of the country, the old Spaniards having been all expelled. They were formerly denominated *Creoles*, in contradistinction to the natives of old Spain; but this name is now discarded. Many of these are descended from the first conquerors, and possess enormous fortunes, the incomes of which they expend in ostentatious living. The Indians exhibit the general features of the other aborigines of America. They have the same swarthy or copper color, flat and smooth hair, small beard, and prominent cheek-bones. Their manners are marked by a peculiar apathy. They are grave, gloomy, and silent, throwing a mysterious air over the most indifferent actions. They have a fondness for flowers which was their characteristic in the times of Cortez. They have also a strong genius for painting and carving, and imitate with facility and success any model which is presented to them.

The higher classes in Mexico display much finery in their dress. An idea of them may be formed from the following description of a Mexican on horseback dressed for the *alameda*, or public parade of the capital. He wears a jacket, embroidered with gold, or trimmed with rich fur; breeches open at the knee, and terminating in two points considerably below it, of some extraordinary color, as pea-green or bright blue; on his head is a gold or silver bound hat. The lower part of the leg is protected by a pair of stamped leather boots, curiously wrapped round it, and attached to the knee with embroidered garters; these boots descend only as far as the ankle, where they are met by shoes of a most peculiar shape, with a sort of wing projecting on the saddle side; and the whole is terminated by spurs so enormously large that they often weigh a pound and a half. A riding-cloak is sometimes thrown over the front of the saddle, and crossed behind the rider in such a manner as to display a circular piece of blue or green velvet, beautifully embroidered. The horse is arrayed in a corresponding manner, with trappings of gilt leather, and gold and silver ornaments. These accoutrements, with a full riding dress, often cost a thousand dollars

The apparel of the ladies, strange to say, is not so showy as that of the men. They dress, commonly, in black, except on holidays; the head is generally uncovered, or has only a light veil thrown over it. They bestow great pains upon their hair, and are particularly neat about the feet, the stocking being usually of fine silk. On holidays, and other public occasions, the dress is more gay, but comparatively, not expensive; artificial flowers are worn in abundance, and ostrich feathers sparingly. The dress of the poorer classes, and of the Indians, forms a strong contrast to the preceding. The streets of the Mexican cities abound with crowds of people destitute of shoes or stockings, or shirts, and with little more covering than a dirty blanket thrown over their shoulders. The mass of the people are catholic, and the catholic religion is established by law.

Cookery is not in a very advanced state in Mexico, and the best inns in the country are described as wretched. The beef and mutton are ordinary; though this is said to be owing to a want of skill in the butchers. As to vegetables, there are few countries that can boast of such a variety, and the consumption of them is prodigious. The common bread is the *tortilla*, which in New England we call an *Indian Johnny-cake.* Wild game is abundant. The vine is not cultivated in Mexico, and wine is scarce and dear. The common drink is *pulque*, a strong liquor made from the agave plant, of which immense quantities are drunk, chiefly by the middle and lower classes, and by the Indians.

The roads in Mexico are rough, and travelling is accomplished for the most part by mules. A Mexican inn contains little or nothing beside the bare walls. If the traveller be very much fatigued, he may stretch himself at full length on the floor, or perhaps he may obtain the luxury of a table. To any thing beyond this he must not aspire; nor must he expect to find, except in the towns, any thing to eat beside tortillas.

The Mexicans are lively, and fond of amusement. Religious festivals and fireworks are their delight; and the dances, although very ungraceful compared with those of Old Spain, are always well attended. The love of this amusement is more general among the peasantry, who frequently dance throughout the whole night, with a regard to order and decency which is very praiseworthy. Their musical instruments are small guitars, fiddles, and harps, of their own making. Singing usually accompanies the fandango tunes. The amusements of the children are the same as those prevailing among us; but as they grow up, the love of gaming is instilled into them by the example of their parents, and this soon forms the most important occupation of their lives. Gaming, smoking cigars, and riding on horseback, are the chief pursuits of the men. Smoking is not confined to the male part of the population. Ladies may be seen at the theatre with a fan in one hand, and a cigar in the other, enveloped in a cloud of smoke.

The architecture of Mexico resembles, in its chief characteristics, that of Old Spain. The houses are spacious, but seldom above two stories in height. The roofs are flat, and as they sometimes communicate with each other for a considerable distance, when seen from an elevation, they look like immense terraces, the parapets by which they are separated being invisible at a distance. The frequency of earthquakes renders lofty structures insecure. Mexico abounds in churches and convents with very splendid interiors. The cathedral of the capital is celebrated for its magnificence.

Guatimala.

CHAPTER DI.

A. D. 1523 to 1850.

Description of Central America — Ancient Civilization — Conquest of the Country by Alvarado — Rebellion of the Natives — Calamities of the City of Guatimala — Spanish Government in Guatimala — Revolution — Establishment of the Republics of Central America — The Mosquito Shore.

Guatimala,* or the Republic of Central America, is bounded north by Mexico and the Gulf of Honduras, east by the Caribbean Sea, and south and west by the Pacific Ocean. It is a mountainous country, but does not exhibit any large tracts of table land like those of Mexico. The great chain of the Cordilleras, which rises to so lofty a height in the north, sinks very rapidly in traversing this region, and, as it approaches the Isthmus of Panama, becomes a mere rocky dike connecting the two continents of North and South America. The western coast of Guatimala is subject to terrific earthquakes, which have sometimes overwhelmed whole cities and destroyed thousands of people.

The history of Guatimala, and the country itself, remained very little known to the rest of the world till recent events brought them into notice; yet the records of the country appear in many respects worthy of investigation. The ancient Guatimalans had made a progress in civilization equal to that of the Mexicans. In the depths of the forests have been found the remains of ancient cities, containing monuments similar in grandeur and ornament to the great structures of Mexico. On the walls of these edifices are found well-executed sculptures, of a character denoting a common origin with that of the Mexican hieroglyphics. The Toltecs, who preceded the Aztecs as rulers that civilized Mexico, appear to have been driven southward, and to have settled in Guatimala.

After the conquest of Mexico, Cortez despatched Christoval de Olid into the country bordering that empire on the south. Olid landed on the coast of Honduras, where he founded a town, to which he gave his own name. The fame of the Spanish conquest

* Guatimala is a narrow strip of territory about one thousand miles in length. In climate, people, and products, it resembles Mexico. It is noted for its earthquakes, volcanos, and silver mines. The government is a federal republic; the country is sometimes called the *United States of Central America.* The Catholic religion, alone, is tolerated by law.

Earthquake in Guatimala.

in Mexico spread rapidly through the country, and the Guatimalans sent ambassadors to Cortez offering to become vassals of the king of Spain. Cortez accepted their offers, and sent Pedro de Alvarado, one of his officers, who had been most active in the conquest of Mexico, to take possession of Guatimala, and receive the submission of the natives. The country was then divided into many different kingdoms, independent of each other. Alvarado marched from Mexico on the 13th of November, **1523**, with a force of three hundred Spaniards, and a large body of native auxiliaries, principally Tlascalans and Cholulans. He first conquered Soconusco and Tonala. Further onward, he was met by the Quiches, who opposed his passage with resolute obstinacy. On the 14th of May, 1524, a desperate battle was fought, in which the Quiches were defeated. Alvarado then advanced into the kingdom of Kachiquel, where the Spaniards were received in a friendly manner. After reposing here for a short time, they pursued their march into the territory of the Zutugiles. On reaching a place called *Almolonga*, meaning a spring of water, they were charmed with the beauty of the spot, which lay between two lofty mountains, from one of which streams of water were running down in every direction, while volumes of smoke and fire were issuing from the summit of the other. Here they determined to establish themselves, and accordingly laid the foundation of a city which they named *St. Jago de los Caballeros de Guatimala.* This was afterward known as the "old city of Guatimala."

During the stay of Alvarado at this place, emissaries came to him from several caciques of the Pipil nation, to offer their submission. They also informed him that the natives of Escuintla, who were a very warlike race, had determined to oppose the Spaniards. Alvarado immediately proceeded to attack them. He had a large body of Kachique auxiliaries in his army; but as there were no roads in the country, they were obliged to cut their way through the woods, sometimes making a progress of only two leagues a day. At length, they reached the neighborhood of the town of Escuintepeque, without being discovered by the inhabitants, in a dark, rainy night, while the Indians were all asleep. The Spaniards made a sudden attack upon them; many fled to the woods at the first alarm, but a considerable number made a stand in some of the largest houses, where they barricaded themselves, and fought with great desperation. After a contest of five hours, the Spaniards, seeing no appearance of submission on the part of the Indians set fire to the town. Alvarado, at the same time, sent a message to the cacique, informing him that unless he immediately submitted to the king of Spain, he would cut up and destroy all the maize and cocoa fields This threat had its effect, and the Escuintepeque Indians, with the other communities in the neighborhood, acknowledged themselves the vassals of the Spanish monarch. Alvarado proceeded in his march, encountering and overcoming the natives in numerous obstinate battles during a march of more than a thousand miles, till the whole country submitted to his arms.

Alvarado remained here two years. In 1526, he returned to Cortez, leaving his brother Gonzalo to command in his absence. This officer was avaricious and cruel, and resolved to improve this opportunity to enrich himself. He issued an order that eight hundred Indians should bring him every day a reed of the size of his little finger filled with fine gold, on pain of being reduced to slavery. The unfortunate victims of his rapacity exerted themselves to the utmost, but were unable to pay the tribute. Gonzalo punished them cruelly, and threatened to put them to death. The natives, driven to desperation, rose in rebellion. A force of thirty thousand men was collected, and falling suddenly upon Guatimala, they drove the Spaniards out of the place, with the loss of many killed and wounded. The Spaniards were compelled to abandon the neighborhood till the return of Alvarado, when the war was commenced against the natives. After a campaign of very severe fighting, they were again subdued. Guatamala was erected into a province, styled an *audiencia*, having a slight dependence on the viceroyalty of Mexico. No other part of Spanish America was so completely shut out from the observation of the rest of the world as Guatimala for nearly three centuries. All the intercourse between this country and Europe was carried on through the Mexican port of Vera Cruz.

The old city of Guatimala is remarkable for the calamities which mark its history. It may be regarded as the most unfortunate city that ever existed In **1532**, the neighborhood was ravaged, and the city thrown into consternation by a wild beast of uncommon size and ferocity, which descended from the mountain called the *Water Volcano*, and devoured the cattle of the inhabitants. Alvarado was compelled to take the field against this powerful enemy; and it was only after a hunting campaign of five months, in which the whole city was engaged, that the monster was killed. In 1536, a fire broke out in the city which consumed the greater part of the buildings. A more terrible calamity occurred in September, 1541. For three days an incessant rain fell; and on the fourth, the water descended in a perfect deluge, accompanied by the most tremendous thunder and lightning. In the midst of this dreadful storm, on the morning of the 11th, the volcano in the neighborhood burst forth into flames in the most terrific manner; violent earthquakes shook the ground, and the inhabitants imagined the end of the world was at hand. An immense torrent of water then rushed down the mountain, carrying with it enormous rocks and trees. This destructive mass fell upon the city, overwhelming nearly all the houses, and burying great numbers of the inhabitants under its ruins. The city was rebuilt about a league distant from the original spot; but the inhabitants could not escape the disasters to which it seemed to be doomed. A fatal epidemic, attended with a profuse bleeding at the nose, swept away great numbers of people in 1558. Earthquakes in 1565, 1575, 1576, and 1577, threw down public buildings, and caused other serious damages. On the 27th of December, 1581, the volcano threw out such quantities of thick smoke and ashes, that the sun was entirely obscured, and lamps were lighted at noon. In 1585, earthquakes were so constant throughout the year that not an interval of eight days passed without a violent shock. For months together, the mountain was in a perpetual flame. On the 21st of December, 1586, a terrible earthquake destroyed the greater part of the city, burying the people beneath the ruins. In 1601, an unknown pestilential disorder, equal in malignity, and the suddenness of its fatal effects, to the cholera, carried off great numbers of the inhabitants.

On the 18th of February, 1651, the earth shook with a dreadful subterraneous noise. Many houses were thrown down; the tiles of the roofs flew in all directions, like straws before a gust of wind. The bells of the churches were rung by the vibrations of the steeples; great masses of rock were rolled down the mountains; and even the wild beasts were so terrified that they quitted their retreats in the forest, and fled to the habitations of men for shelter. Among these, a puma, of enormous size and fierceness, burst into the middle of the city, tore down a paper which was posted upon one of the public buildings, and then made his escape into the woods. The city was again shaken and damaged by earthquakes in 1679, 1683, 1684, 1687, and 1689. In 1686, another fatal epidemic committed great ravages among the inhabitants; and the corpses were so numerous as to be buried in a common grave. Volcanic eruptions occurred in 1705 and 1710, covering the city with impenetrable darkness at noonday. In 1717, more than one half the place was destroyed by an earthquake.

In 1733, the small-pox swept away 1500 of the inhabitants of Guatimala. In 1736, a hurricane destroyed a part of the city, burying the inhabitants under the ruins. Earthquakes and eruptions, attended by fatal effects, ensued at different times, till 1773, when the calamities of Guatimala were brought to a climax. During May and June, earthquakes were frequent. In July, so tremendous and appalling were these convulsions, that the narrators are at a loss for language to describe them. The city was dreadfully damaged, and the earthquakes continued till December with such fatal consequences, that Guatimala was reduced to a heap of ruins. The inhabitants were, nevertheless, inclined to rebuild it upon the same spot; but the Spanish government ordered them to remove to a place twenty-five miles distant, where they erected the city of New Guatimala. For many years, the site of the old city remained deserted, but very recently it has begun to rise from its ruins.

The inhabitants of Guatimala remained quiet under the Spanish government somewhat longer than their neighbors; but at length, in 1821, they declared themselves independent. The Mexicans, at first, endeavored to retain Guatimala as an appendage to their own republic; but finding the inhabitants of the latter country strongly averse to such a connection, they submitted to the separation. A government was framed in 1823, constituting a federal republic, under the name of the *United States of Central America.* The states were five, namely, Guatemala, San Salvador, Honduras, Costa Rica, and Nicaragua. The union was similar to that of our own government in form, but it was, in fact, rather nominal than real. Within the last few years the union has ceased to be in operation, and the several states act independently. Early in 1853, the president of Guatimala, Carrera, invaded San Salvador, in the hope of conquering and annexing the country. The Salvadorians, however, routed his army.

The population of Guatimala is about 1,800,000. One half are Indians, one fifth whites, and the remainder a mixed population. There are no blacks. New Guatimala, the capital, is a well-built, regular, and beautiful city, finely situated, though inferior in the beauty and fertility of its neighborhood to the old city. The houses are built low, to avoid danger from earthquakes. Population 60,000. Old Guatimala has about 18,000 inhabitants. Leon, in the state of Nicaragua, has 35,000. San Salvador has 16,000. The country abounds with ruins of ancient cities, which testify to its former populousness and the civilization and industry of the aboriginal inhabitants. At Copan are to be seen the massy stone walls of one of these cities, with gigantic statues and other sculptures in stone. These ruins are generally overgrown with thick forests, and there are doubtless many which remain undiscovered to this day.

The maritime district to the east of Honduras and Nicaragua, is a wild region, called the MOSQUITO SHORE, and inhabited by a native race, called the *Mosquito Indians.* These aborigines have never been subjugated. Their chief is called the King of the Musquitos. The British assert a claim to authority in the territory, and maintain that the Mosquito king is under the protection of the British crown. The United States have recently made arrangements for the construction of a canal across the Isthmus and through lake Nicaragua, in a territory which is affected by the British claim. This subject created some controversy between the two governments; but a treaty was made between them in 1850, which adjusted the difficulty. This will leave the proposed canal open to all nations.

The West Indies.*

Sugar Farm in the West Indies.

CHAPTER DII.

Description of the West Indies — Settlement of Cuba, Hispaniola, Porto Rico, Jamaica, &c. — History of Cuba, Hayti, Jamaica, &c.

THE West India Islands constitute an archipelago, situated between North and South America. They extend in a curve from the southern extremity of Florida, first in a south-easterly direction, and then southerly, to the mouth of the Orinoco. They are bounded north and east by the Atlantic, south by the Caribbean Sea, and west by the Gulf of Mexico. The eastern division of the group is sometimes called the Antilles, the Caribbee, or the Windward Islands. This last appellation is applied to them from the circumstance of their being exposed to the direct action of the trade winds, which always blow here from east to west.

The largest of these islands, Cuba, Hispaniola, and Jamaica, are mountainous. Most of them are highly fertile, producing nearly all of the tropical fruits and plants in high perfection. No part of the earth is better adapted to the culture of the sugar-cane than these islands, although it is not a native of the soil, but was brought from the old continent by Columbus, in his second voyage. The climate is hot, but in most of the islands it is salubrious. Dreadful hurricanes sometimes occur, which destroy the towns and lay waste the plantations.

When the Spaniards first visited these islands, they found them inhabited by two distinct races of people. All the large islands, and most of the smaller ones in their neighborhood, were peopled by a race of very mild and inoffensive character, whose manners were simple and natural, and whose life seemed to be devoted only to ease and enjoyment. They had made little progress in the useful arts, — their ingenuity not having extended further than the construction of huts, log-canoes, hammocks to sleep in, and a few other articles of household furniture. They wore very slight dresses of coarse cotton cloth, of their own manufacture. Their government was of the simplest kind. The chiefs were called *Caciques*, and ruled with patriarchal authority.

* The West Indies have been celebrated, ever since their discovery, for their rich and valuable products. Coffee, sugar, rum, tobacco, cotton, cocoa, pimento or allspice, mahogany, logwood, &c., are exported to an immense amount and the people receive, in return, lumber, fish, beef, pork, &c. An active trade is carried on between these islands and the various parts of Europe and America.

The whole population of the West Indies is estimated at 3,000,000, of whom only about 500,000 are whites. The rest are blacks, or mulattoes. In Hayti, and the British islands, the negroes are free; but in the other islands most of them are slaves. The following table gives a view of these islands: —

Islands.	To whom belonging.	Extent.	Population.	Capital.
Cuba, ...	Spain, ...	54,000	1,500,000	Havana.
Porto Rico, ...	..do..........	4,140	375,000	St. Johns.
Hayti, ...	Independent, .	28,000	800,000	Port au Prince
Jamaica, ...	Great Britain,.	6,400	346,000	Kingston.
Barbadoes, ...	..do....do ...	166	102,000	Bridgetown
Trinidad, ...	..do....do ...	1,600	45,000	Port Spain
Antigua, ...	..do....do ...	93	36,000	St. Johns.
Grenada, ...	..do....do ...	109	29,000	St. George
St. Vincent, ..	..do....do ...	131	26,000	Kingston.
St. Kitt's, ...	..do....do ...	70	24,000	Basse Terre
Dominica, ...	..do....do ...	29	20,000	Roseau.
St. Lucia, ...	..do....do ...	225	18,000	Carenage.
Tobago, ...	..do....do ...	140	14,000	Scarborough
Nevis, ...	..do....do ...	20	12,000	Charlestown
Montserrat, ...	..do....do ...	47	8,000	Plymouth.
Tortola, ...	..do....do ...	——	7,000	Road Harbor
Anguilla, ...	..do....do ...	——	3,000	——
Bahamas, ...	..do....do ...	5,500	28,000	Nassau.
Bermudas, ...	..do....do ...	——	11,000	Georgetown
Guadaloupe, ..	France, ...	675	140,000	Basse Terre
Martinico, ...	..do	370	140,000	St. Pierre.
Mariegalante, .	..do	——	11,500	Basse Terre.
Doseada, ...	..do	——	1,500	——
Santa Cruz, ..	Denmark, ...	100	34,000	Christianstad
St. Thomas, ..	....do........	40	15,000	St. Thomas.
St. Johns, ...	....do........	——	3,000	——
St. Eustasia, ..	Holland, ...	——	20,000	The Bay.
Curacoa, ...	...do.........	——	12,000	Williamstad
St. Martin's, ..	...do.........	——	11,000	——
St. Barthol'w, .	Sweden, ...	——	8,000	Gustavia.
Margarita, ...	Venezuela, ..	——	16,000	Pampatar

The other race dwelt in the Antilles, and were distinguished from their neighbors by their superior courage and martial character. They were called *Caribs*. Among themselves they lived in tolerable harmony, but were fierce and savage toward their enemies. They were skilful sailors, and capable of intense application to labor. Instead of tamely submitting to the European invaders, they bravely resisted them, and when overcome, chose rather to die than toil as slaves.

Of these two races of aborigines, the first are totally extinct, and of the latter only a few individuals are now known to exist. At the period of the discovery, he West India Islands were supposed to contain three or four millions of inhabitants. This population has been exchanged for the European and African races. The islands are all colonial possessions of the different European powers, except Hispaniola, or Hayti, which is independent.

Cuba.—This island is the largest, richest, and most important, of all the Spanish colonies in America. It is seven hundred miles long, and about ninety broad. The interior is mountainous, but it has much fertile territory. The climate is mild, and in the elevated parts very salubrious. The soil is well adapted to the cultivation of the sugar-cane and coffee, which are the staple articles of agriculture.

Cuba was discovered by Columbus in his first voyage to the west, in 1492. The appearance of the island quite enchanted him. He describes it thus: "Every thing invited me to settle here. The beauty of the streams, the clearness of the water, through which I could see the sandy bottom; the multitude of palm-trees of different kinds, the tallest and finest I had ever seen; and an infinite number of other large and flourishing trees; the birds, and the verdure of the plains, — are so amazingly beautiful, that this country exceeds all others, as far as the day surpasses the night in splendor." Columbus sent a party of men to make discoveries in the interior, thinking he had reached the shores of Hindostan or China. Here they first saw the Indians smoking tobacco.

No attempt was made to conquer the island, or form a settlement, for nineteen years. At length, in 1511, Diego Velasquez sailed from Hispaniola with a body of three hundred and seventy Spaniards, including Hernando Cortez and Bartholomew de Las Casas. They landed at Puerto de Palmas. This part of the island was under the dominion of a cacique named Hatuey. He was a native of Hispaniola, and had fled from that island to escape from the tyranny of the Spanish invaders. When he saw the sails of the Spanish fleet approaching the shores of Cuba, he summoned the chief men of the neighborhood around him, and assured them that they would be conquered and reduced to slavery, unless they made the god of their enemies propitious to them. "Gold," said he, "is the god of the Spaniards. We must not expect to prosper so long as he remains among us. He is no less our enemy than the men who worship him. They seek for him every where, and where they find him, there they fix themselves. Were he hidden in the bowels of the earth, they would discover him. Were we to swallow him down our own throats, they would plunge their hands into our bowels, and drag him out. There is no place except the bottom of the sea, that can elude their search. Let us, then, throw him into the sea that our enemies may not molest us." With these exhortations he persuaded the people to bring out all their gold, and cast it into the sea. This story, which is related by all the early historians of the West Indies, shows a refinement in cunning quite unusual in these natives.

The artifice, however, did not produce the desired effect. The Spaniards landed, and the natives collected in great numbers to resist them. The fire-arms and horses of the invaders easily dispersed the multitudes of naked Indians: they were pursued through the country and Hatuey was taken. The cruel Velasquez, in order to strike terror into the natives, ordered him to be burnt alive. A Franciscan friar attended him at the stake, and exhorted him to take pity on his own soul, and not expose it to eternal fire, which he might escape, and enjoy the happiness of dwelling in Paradise forever by being baptized. Hatuey asked him if there were any Spaniards in that delightful country. "Only the good ones," answered the friar. "The best," said Hatuey, "are good for nothing, and I will not go where there is a chance of meeting one of them." Hatuey was burned, the other caciques submitted, and Cuba was conquered without the loss of a single Spaniard. The island was very populous; the inhabitants were estimated at a million.

The thirst for gold had tempted the Spaniards into this island, but they were disappointed. The inhabitants possessed some of this metal, but they appear to have obtained it from Hispaniola. The Spaniards, believing there were mines in Cuba, tortured the natives without mercy, to obtain information from them. The miseries thus inflicted upon the unhappy islanders are shocking to contemplate. At length their sufferings and despair were so excessive, that they formed a general resolution to commit suicide; but their design was frustrated by one of their Spanish tyrants, named Vasco Porcelles, who threatened to hang himself along with them, that he might have the pleasure, as he said, of tormenting them in the next world more than he had done in this. So intense was their fear of the Spaniards, whom they believed, as well they might, to be incarnate demons, that this threat completely checked their desperate design. But it was not long before the oppressions of their masters, and the ravages of the small-pox, completely exterminated the native inhabitants, and the island was reduced to a solitude. Afterward it was slowly colonized by the Spaniards.

The city of Havana was founded shortly after the conquest. The situation was selected as a convenient place for the Spanish ships to touch at in their voyages between Mexico and Spain. In 1536, it was captured by a French pirate, who obliged the inhabitants to pay seven hundred ducats, to save it from being burnt. The day after his departure, three ships arrived from Mexico, unloaded their cargoes, and sailed in pursuit of him. But such was the cowardice of the Spaniards, that the pirate took all the three ships, and returning to Havana, compelled the inhabitants to pay seven hundred ducats more for the ransom of the Mexican cargoes. The city was afterward strongly fortified, and increased gradually as the island became settled. It was captured by the buccaneers under Morgan, in 1669. In the war between Spain and Great Britain, in 1762, it was taken by the English, but was restored to Spain in the following year. In 1796, the remains of Columbus were removed from the city of St. Domingo to Havana, where they remain at present. The population of Cuba is about 1,500,000, less than one half of whom are whites.

HAYTI. — This island has been known by different names in the course of its history. *Hayti* was the name given it by the natives. Columbus named it *Espanola*, or Little Spain. The English altered the name to *Hispaniola*. The French called it *St. Domingo*, from the city of that name, which was at one time its capital. Since the dominion of the blacks has been established here, the aboriginal name of Hayti has been resumed.

The island is about three hundred and sixty miles long, but of very unequal breadth. In soil, climate, and geographical features, it does not differ essentially from Cuba. It was discovered by Columbus in his first voyage, and here the Spaniards formed their first settlements in the western world. The town of Isabella was founded by Columbus at his first visit; but this establishment did not flourish, and a new settlement was soon after made at San Domingo. The island, on its first discovery, was very populous; but the Spaniards soon exterminated the natives, by their inhuman oppressions, in compelling them to labor in the gold mines. After the depopulation of the island, and the exhaustion of the mines, Hispaniola was comparatively neglected by the Spaniards, and all the northern and western parts became a wilderness. The woods abounded with cattle, which had been introduced by the first settlers, and now ran wild. The Buccaneers * began their career, in this island, by hunting cattle, and selling their hides to Dutch or French traders, who resorted to the ports of Hispaniola for this traffic. They next formed a piratical establishment on the little Island of Tortuga, close to the northern coast of Hispaniola. Being here threatened by the hostilities of the Spaniards, they preferred to submit to the French, and were taken under the probate protection of Louis XIV., who sent them a governor. In 1697, the western part of Hispaniola was ceded by Spain to France, and this territory was cultivated by the French settlers with great industry and success. Cape François and Port au Prince became rich and flourishing cities, with a very active commerce. When the French revolution broke out, it was estimated that the agricultural produce of the French colony of St. Domingo amounted to upward of forty millions of dollars.

The revolution, however, proved the ruin of the colony. In 1794, the slaves were declared free by an act of the National Convention. This led to a general insurrection of the blacks and mulattoes, and the white inhabitants were all massacred or expelled from the island. After some years of anarchy and bloodshed, during which all the sugar-works on the island were destroyed, a government was established among the blacks under a leader named *Toussaint l'Ouverture*. The country enjoyed a short period of tranquillity, but Toussaint was treacherously decoyed into the hands of the French, and carried to France, where he died in prison. A French army was sent out, which recovered possession of the colony; but the blacks soon rose against them under a leader named *Dessalines*, and the French were expelled in 1803. In the following year, this leader proclaimed himself emperor of Hayti; but his reign was cut short, in 1806, by the dagger of an assassin.

The independent part of Hispaniola was now divided into two states. In the north, a negro republic was formed, under Christophe, and in the south, a mulatto republic, under Petion. These rival states were perpetually at war. Christophe made himself emperor in 1811, and reigned till 1820, when the people rose in insurrection, and he committed suicide. Boyer, the mulatto president, who had succeeded Petion, immediately marched an army into the north, and the two states were united under his authority. The Spanish government, in the mean time, had ceded, in 1795, their portion of the island to France; but as the French were unable to take possession of it, the Spaniards reoccupied it in 1808. In 1809, the inhabitants declared themselves independent, and in 1822, they submitted to the authority of Boyer, who was now ruler of the whole island. The French made a treaty with the Haytian government, in 1825, by which the independence of Hayti was acknowledged, on condition of the payment of 150,000,000 francs in five annual instalments. For some years afterward the island remained in tranquillity, but troubles and civil wars soon recurred. At length, in 1849, Faustin Soulouque, a military adventurer, overturned the republic, and assumed the supreme authority, under the title of *Faustin I.*, Emperor of Hayti. In 1861, the eastern portion was betrayed into the hands of Spain by its president Santana. Early in 1863, the inhabitants rose and sought to throw off the Spanish yoke, but the effort was immediately repressed. Hayti sent its first representative to the United States in 1863.

The agriculture and commerce of this island are now greatly reduced The inhabitants raise but little more of any article than is necessary for their own consumption. Port au Prince is the capital, and the chief port of trade. It has about 30,000 inhabitants. Cape Haytien, formerly Cape François, once the most wealthy and flourishing place in the West Indies, fell into decay after the revolution On the 7th of May, 1842, the whole Island of Hispaniola was shaken by an earthquake, which completely destroyed the town of Cape Haytien, with ten thousand

* The Buccaneers first attract notice during the sixth century, in the Island of St. Domingo. They called themselves the Brethren of the Coast, or, as the French termed them, "Flibustiers." Their occupation consisted in the hunting of wild cattle, and the selling of their hides to the Dutch. They decoyed persons to the West Indies, and made slaves of them. The Spaniards made repeated attempts to exterminate them, but without success. They at last decided to destroy all the wild cattle in St. Domingo by a general chase. This had the desired effect. The Buccaneers abandoned St. Domingo, and took refuge in the small island of Tortuga. They now turned pirates, and attacked the ships of every nation. The Spaniards, however, were the grand objects of their hostility. They rapidly increased in numbers and strength, sailed in larger vessels, and carried on their enterprises with still greater audacity. They attacked and set fire to Gibraltar and Maracaybo, in South America. In 1668 they captured Porto Bello, and obtained plunder and ransom to the amount of two hundred and fifty thousand dollars. The year after, they plundered Panama, and set it on fire. In 1683, twelve hundred Buccaneers attacked Vera Cruz, and obtained complete possession of it in one night. They pillaged the city, undisturbed, for three days. They then offered to ransom the inhabitants for two millions of dollars. Half of this was paid, and fifteen hundred slaves given as hostages for the payment of the rest. The last remarkable event in the history of the Buccaneers, is the capture of Carthagena, in 1697. The war between Great Britain and France was a severe blow to them, as they were chiefly composed of the subjects of those two powers. They turned their arms against each other, and never confederated afterward. After an existence of nearly two centuries, they disappeared, leaving not a trace behind them.

Sugar Mill.

of its inhabitants, leaving scarcely a third part remaining. The present population of the island is about eight hundred thousand.

Jamaica. — This island is the largest of the British possessions in the West Indies. It is about one hundred and forty miles in length, and fifty in breadth. A ridge of mountains runs through its whole length, the lofty heights of which are interspersed with beautiful savannas. The sides of the mountains are clothed with forests of mahogany, lignum vitæ, logwood, and other trees. The soil in the level parts of the island is highly fertile, and is regarded as the best adapted to the cultivation of sugar that is to be found in the West Indies. The climate is temperate and generally healthy.

Jamaica was discovered by Columbus in 1494, during his second visit to America. No settlement was then attempted by the Spaniards, and Columbus, on his fourth voyage, in 1503, while exploring the coast of the continent, was driven by tempestuous weather, after losing two of his ships, to bear away with the two others for Jamaica. With great difficulty he reached a harbor on the northern side of the island, where he ran his ships aground to prevent their foundering. He remained upward of a year in this quarter, exposed to all sorts of hardships, the governor of Hispaniola refusing to relieve him. The Indians were at first disposed to be unfriendly; but Columbus gained their confidence by predicting an eclipse of the moon, which he knew was about to happen. They were so terrified at the phenomenon, that they submitted at once to the Spaniards, and supplied them with food during the remainder of their stay on the island.

As Jamaica produced none of the precious metals, the Spaniards treated it with neglect. About the beginning of the sixteenth century, they began a settlement here under Juan de Esquivel. This officer treated the natives with great mildness, and employed them in planting cotton, and other agricultural labors. His successors were less humane and considerate, and the same cruelties were exercised toward these unhappy beings as in Hispaniola. At this day, caverns are frequently discovered among the mountains, containing human bones, the miserable remains of the unfortunate Indians, who fled to these lonely recesses to escape the swords of the Spaniards, and here perished of hunger. The population of the island, at the time of the discovery, is supposed to have been sixty thousand. They were so completely exterminated, that at the end of thirty or forty years, not one remained.

The city of St. Jago de la Vega, now called *Spanish Town*, was founded by Diego Columbus, the son of the great navigator, about 1530. When Portugal became subjected to the crown of Spain, Jamaica was transferred as a possession to the house of Braganza, and many Portuguese colonists settled in the island. In 1596, a body of English, under Sir Anthony Shirley, made a descent upon Jamaica, and plundered the capital. A similar invasion occurred about forty years afterward. Jamaica was retained by Spain, when Portugal revolted, and became an independent kingdom, in 1640. In 1655, Oliver Cromwell sent an expedition, under Admiral Penn and General Venables, against Hispaniola. The undertaking miscarried, but the armament captured Jamaica. At that time, the island was regarded as of little value; but Cromwell determined to colonize it. The first English settlement consisted of three thousand disbanded soldiers; and Jamaica was kept under a military government till the restoration of Charles II. When the English conquered the island, the negro slaves of the Spaniards fled to the mountains, and led a life of wild freedom, under the name of *Maroons*. They were for a long time very troublesome to the English planters, with whom they maintained a state of perpetual hostility till the year 1738, when a treaty was made by which they were allowed their freedom, and the possession of fifteen hundred acres of land. Under this arrangement, they remained peaceable till 1775, when a new Maroon war broke out. The negroes were at first successful, but at length the English adopted the practice of the Spaniards in the extermi nation of the natives. They obtained bloodhounds from Cuba, by the help of which the Maroons were driven into the mountains, and ultimately obliged to submit. Large numbers of them were transported to Nova Scotia. After this, the island remained quiet, and was the seat of an active and profitable commerce. In 1834, all the slaves in the British West Indies were emancipated by act of parliament. One of the consequences of this measure has been the gradual decline of the agriculture and trade of Jamaica.

Porto Rico was discovered by Columbus in 1493; but the Spaniards made no attempt to settle it till 1509, when they invaded the island in search of gold, under Ponce de Leon. They met with no resistance from the natives, who had been fully informed of the hard fate which had befallen their neighbors in Hispaniola. At first, they submitted to the Spaniards, regarding them as superior beings; but a little intercourse having convinced them that the invaders were mere mortal men, they rose in insurrection, and massacred a hundred of them. Ponce de Leon made a vigorous attack upon the Indians, and defeated them with great slaughter. During the struggle, his forces were recruited by a fresh arrival from Hispaniola, which caused the natives to believe that the Spaniards whom they had massacred were come to life again. Struck with superstitious terror by this impression, they submitted again to the yoke, and subsequently met with the fate of the natives of the other islands, being condemned to labor in searching for gold, in which they all miserably perished. After its depopulation, Porto Rico was neglected till the beginning of the present century. A new era of prosperity then commenced, and it is now the seat of a flourishing and increasing trade. The value of the annual exports exceeds four millions of dollars. Two thirds of the commerce of this island are in the hands of the Americans. The capital, San Juan, is a well-built town, with a good harbor, strongly fortified.

Barbadoes, the most easterly of the West India Islands, appears to have had no aboriginal population. This was the earliest of the islands settled by the English. Some families established themselves here in 1627, but without any authority from the government. Two years afterward, a regular English colony was introduced by the earl of Carlisle, and their numbers were much increased by the emigrants who left England to escape from the political troubles in the time of Charles I. The English have retained possession of Barbadoes to this day.

Antigua was also uninhabited till 1628, when some Frenchmen, who fled from the Spaniards at St. Christopher's, came to reside here. No regular settlement, however, was made till 1666, in which year Charles II. made a grant of the island to Lord Willoughby, who established a colony here. Nevis was occupied by the English in 1628, and Montserrat in 1632.

St. Christopher's was first settled by the French and the English, who landed in this island on the same day, in 1625. At first, they shared it between them; but in 1702, the English expelled their neighbors, and at the treaty of Utrecht, the island was assigned to Great Britain. — The Virgin Islands are about sixty in number, but are all small. At first, they were visited by the Spaniards, Dutch, and English, solely for the purpose of catching turtle. The English at length kept permanent possession of them, and established sugar plantations. — Grenada was settled by the French in 1651, but a century afterward was seized by the British, and confirmed to them at the peace of 1763. — Tobago was settled by the Dutch in 1632. The French and English disputed with them the possession of the island, and finally, in 1763, it was ceded to Great Britain. — St. Lucia received a colony of English in 1639, but they were all massacred by the natives. The French next attempted a settlement, but with no better success. It was finally colonized by the English. — Trinidad was first settled by the Spaniards, in 1535. They retained possession of it till 1797, when it was ceded to Great Britain. — St. Vincent's and Dominica were settled by the French, and subsequently acquired by the English.

The Lucayos or Bahama Islands, as we have already related, were the first part of the western world visited by the Spaniards. After their depopulation by the conquerors, who carried off the inhabitants to work in the gold mines elsewhere, these islands fell into total neglect. In 1629, the English took possession of New Providence, but were expelled by the Spaniards in 1641. They again settled here in 1666, and were a second time expelled, in 1703. The Bahamas then became a rendezvous for pirates, who were finally suppressed by the English, under Captain Woodes Rogers. The islands were then colonized by the English, and remained quietly in their possession till 1776, when they were attacked by the American fleet, under Commodore Hopkins, who captured New Providence. In 1781, the Spaniards again made themselves masters of these islands; but they were retaken by the English, and confirmed to them by the treaty of 1783.

Martinique and Guadaloupe were settled by the French, in 1635.— Deseada, Mariegalante, St. Martin's, and the Saintes, were occupied by them at a later date. All these now belong to the French. — Curaçoa was settled by the Spaniards in 1527: the Dutch captured it in 1634, and retain it at the present day. They also acquired and still hold St. Eustasia and Saba. The Danes obtained possession of St. Thomas, St. John, and St. Croix, or Santa Cruz, and still hold them. The Swedes have the single island of St. Bartholomew.

The Bermudas are not, strictly speaking, a part of the West Indies; but for want of a more appropriate place, they may be described here. They are situated in the midst of the Atlantic, about six hundred miles from the coast of North Carolina, which is the nearest land in their neighborhood. They are upward of four hundred in number, but most of them are mere rocks. Only eight of them are of any real importance. They were discovered in 1522, by Juan Bermudez, a Spaniard, who found them uninhabited. Sir George Somers, an Englishman, was wrecked on them in 1609, on which account they were sometimes called after his name. He built here a small vessel of cedar, without any iron, except one bolt in the keel, and sailed to Virginia. The English began to settle on the Bermudas in 1612, and during the civil wars in the reign of Charles I., they became the asylum of many distinguished personages, among others the poet Waller, who, by celebrating in his verses the beauty of their aspect and the felicity of their climate, spread around them a poetic lustre. The Bermudas, however, have never been the seat of much commerce, and are chiefly important to Great Britain as a naval station.

CHAPTER DIII.

Geographical Sketch. — Political Divisions. — Historical Outline.

South America is a large peninsula, attached to North America by the narrow Isthmus of Darien. It is remarkable, in its physical structure, for its long range of lofty mountains, its numerous volcanoes, its vast plains, and its mighty rivers.

The face of the country may be divided into three parts, — the western, middle, and eastern. The western part consists of an extensive plain, or plateau, elevated nearly twelve thousand feet above the level of the sea, crowned with a vast chain of insulated peaks called the Andes, several of which are volcanic, and in constant activity. The middle portion lies to the east of this, and is several times broader. It is a great expanse of country, composed of marshy and sandy plains, furrowed by three magnificent rivers and their numerous branches. The eastern portion, embracing the maritime part of Brazil, is moderately elevated.

The climate of South America is very remarkable. In the low and level parts, near the equator, the temperature is always that of summer. The trees are clothed in perpetual verdure, the flowers are ever in blossom, and the fruits ripen at all seasons. In the elevated plains, the temperature is cool and delightful, and throughout the year, the climate has the charms of spring. On the mountains it is still colder, and at the height of fifteen or sixteen thousand feet, winter establishes a perpetual dominion. Thus, in the same latitude, and within the compass of a few hundred miles, are three distinct zones, each having its own temperature, and its peculiar classes of trees, plants, and animals.

The most remarkable animals of South America are the tapir, which resembles the hog, with a long, flexible snout, which it uses like the trunk of an elephant; the ant-eater, which feeds on ants; the llama, resembling the camel; the jaguar, which is like the African panther; and the condor, a species of vulture, and the largest bird of flight. Beside these, there are numerous monkeys, parrots, toucans, alligators, and a variety of serpents. The birds are celebrated for their glowing plumage.

The larger part of the inhabitants of South America are descendants of the native Indians; some of these are partially civilized; but large tribes still wander in a savage state. In Terra del Fuego, they are dwarfish, and seem to be among the most degraded of the human race. There are many negroes and mestizos, especially in Guiana and Brazil. The ruling people are the descendants of Europeans, chiefly Spaniards, who maintain the manners of their original country. The Catholic religion every where prevails. The people are generally ignorant; the mass are poor, but there are a few who are very rich. The country is destitute of roads and bridges, and travelling is generally performed with horses or mules. In the free states. however, there is a general tendency to improvement. South America presents great richness and variety in the vegetable kingdom. Among the native productions are, the India rubber tree, palms of various kinds, and two hundred and fifty kinds of wood useful for carpentry and dyeing. Coffee, sugar, cotton, indigo, and grains of various kinds, are abundantly produced by cultivation. The mines of South America have been celebrated for three hundred years; and they have yielded immense quantities of gold, silver, and precious gems. The annual value of these articles, still obtained, amounts to many millions of dollars, though the mines are generally less productive than formerly, and some are quite of them exhausted.

The Amazon is the largest, though not the longest, river in the world. Its branches spread over a valley nearly as extensive as the whole of Europe, and it carries as much water to the ocean as all the rivers of that quarter of the world! The other great rivers are the Orinoco and the La Plata.

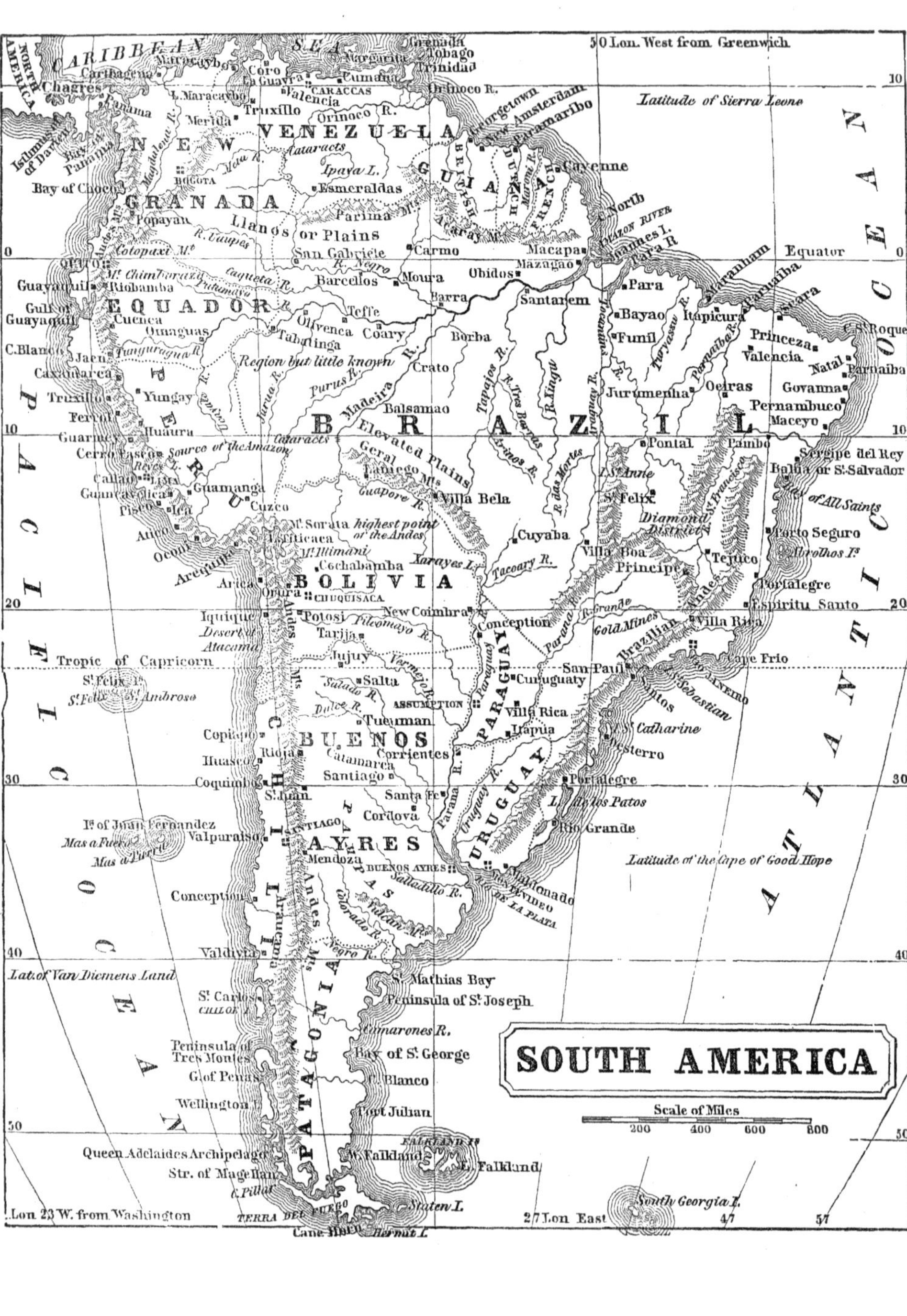
SOUTH AMERICA
Scale of Miles
200 400 600 800
50 Lon. West from Greenwich
Lon 23 W. from Washington
27 Lon. East
47
57
10
0
20
30
40
50
Equator
Tropic of Capricorn
Latitude of Sierra Leone
Latitude of the Cape of Good Hope
Lat. of Van Diemens Land
CARIBBEAN SEA
NORTH AMERICA
ATLANTIC OCEAN
PACIFIC OCEAN
NEW GRANADA
VENEZUELA
GUIANA
BRITISH
DUTCH
FRENCH
EQUADOR
PERU
BRAZIL
BOLIVIA
PARAGUAY
URUGUAY
BUENOS AYRES
CHILI
PATAGONIA
Grenada
Tobago
Trinidad
Margarita
Maracaybo
Carthagena
Chagres
Coro
La Guayra
Cumana
CARACCAS
Valencia
Orinoco R.
L. Maracaybo
Truxillo
Merida
Panama
Isthmus of Darien
Bay of Panama
Bay of Choco
BOGOTA
Magdalena R.
Meta R.
Cataracts
Ipava L.
Esmeraldas
Parima Mts
Acaray Mts
Georgetown
New Amsterdam
Paramaribo
Cayenne
C. North
Popayan
Llanos or Plains
R. Vaupes
Cotopaxi Mt
San Gabriele
Carmo
Macapa
Mazagao
Joannes I.
Para R
QUITO
Mt Chimboraza
Riobamba
Guayaquil
Gulf of Guayaquil
Cuenca
Caqueta R.
Putumayo
Barcellos
R. Negro
Moura
Obidos
Barra
Santarem
Para
Maranham
Parnaiba
Seara
Omaguas
Olivenca
Teffe
Coary
Tabatinga
Borba
Bayao
Itapicura
Funil
C. St Roque
Princeza
Valencia
Natal
Parnaiba
C. Blanco
Jaen
Tunguragua R.
Region but little known
Purus R.
Madeira R.
Crato
Tapajos R.
Tres Barras
Xingu
Tocantins R.
Araguay R.
Oeiras
Govanna
Cassamarca
Truxillo
Yungay
Jurumenha
Pernambuco
Maceyo
Balsamao
Ferrol
Huaura
Guarmey
Cataracts
Elevated Plains
Geral
Pontal
Pambo
Sergipe del Rey
Bahia or St Salvador
Bay of All Saints
Cerro Pasco
Source of the Amazon
Callao
Lima
Guancavelica
Guamanga
Pisco
Ica
Cuzco
Guapore R.
Villa Bela
R. das Mortes
St Anne
St Felix
Diamond District
Porto Seguro
Abrolhos Is
Atico
Ocona
Arequipa
Mt Sorata highest point of the Andes
Titicaca
Mt Illimani
Cochabamba
Xarayes L.
Cuyaba
Tacoary R.
Villa Boa
Principe
Tejuco
Portalegre
Espiritu Santo
Arica
Orura
CHUQUISACA
Potosi
New Coimbra
Conception
Parana R.
R. Grande
Gold Mines
Villa Rica
Cape Frio
Iquique
Desert of Atacama
Tarija
Pilcomayo R.
Jujuy
Vermejo R.
San Paul
RIO JANEIRO
St Sebastian
Santos
St Felix Is
St Ambroso
Salado R.
Salta
ASSUMPTION
Curuguaty
Villa Rica
Itapua
St Catharine
Desterro
Dulce R.
Tucuman
Copiapo
Huasco
Rioja
Catamarca
Corrientes
Coquimbo
Santiago
Portalegre
S. Juan
Santa Fe
Cordova
Uruguay R.
L. de los Patos
Rio Grande
Is of Juan Fernandez
Mas a Fuera
Mas a Tierra
Valparaiso
SANTIAGO
Mendoza
BUENOS AYRES
Salladillo R.
MONTEVIDEO
Maldonado
R. DE LA PLATA
Conception
Araucania
Andes Mts
Colorado R.
Volcan Mt
Valdivia
Negro R.
St Mathias Bay
Peninsula of St Joseph
St Carlos
CHILOE I.
Camarones R.
Peninsula of Tres Montes
Bay of St George
G. of Penas
C. Blanco
Wellington I.
Port Julian
FALKLAND IS
W. Falkland
E. Falkland
Queen Adelaides Archipelago
Str. of Magellan
C. Pillar
TERRA DEL FUEGO
Staten I.
South Georgia I.
Cape Horn
Hermit I.

The following are the present political divisions of South America: —

Countries.	Extent.	Population.	Pop. sq.m.	Capitals.	Pop.
Guiana	100,000	275,000	3	Paramaribo	28,000
Venezuela	420,000	1,565,000	3	Caraccas	25,000
New Grenada	520,000	2,200,000	4	Bogota	47,000
Equador	290,000	1,000,000	3	Quito	85,000
Peru	490,000	2,500,000	5	Lima	57,000
Bolivia	550,000	1,500,000	3	La Pas	40,000
Chili	50,000	1,560,000	30	Santiago	65,000
Patagonia					
Buenos Ayres	650,000	1,200,000	2	Buenos Ayres	120,000
Uruguay	75,000	240,000	3	Montevideo	45,000
Paraguay	340,000	1,340,000	4	Assumption	30,000
Brazil	3,340,000	7,680,000	2	Rio Janeiro	300,000

On his first and second voyages to America, the discoveries of Columbus did not go beyond the West Indies. In 1498, he came in view of the continent of South America, near the mouth of the Orinoco. Soon after, Vespucci and Ojeda explored nearly the whole circuit of the Gulf of Mexico. In 1500, Álvarez Cabral, a Portuguese, on a voyage to the East Indies, came unexpectedly in sight of the coast of Brazil. On the 29th of September, Balboa discovered the Pacific Ocean. In 1519, Magellan first circumnavigated the southern point of the continent, and passed by Cape Horn into the Pacific.

The whole of South America came into the hands of Spain, with the exception of Brazil, which was occupied by Portugal, and the small district of Guiana, which fell to the lot of Holland, England, and France. The ancient tribes of South America were of the same general stock as those of North America, and they were divided, in a similar manner, into numerous bands or nations, displaying every condition of society, from the savage to the civilized. The Spaniards proceeded to conquer the countries they discovered, robbing, enslaving, or extirpating the natives without scruple or remorse. Peru, a populous empire, far advanced in the arts, was subdued by Pizarro, in 1535, attended by acts of treachery and cruelty hardly equalled in the annals of mankind. Having been thus conquered, the several portions of the country remained as royal provinces, under the dominion of Spain and Portugal, till the present century, when they all became independent. In general, it may be said that the republics of South America have not been successful, owing, doubtless, to the fact that the Catholic religion, which is opposed to progress and general education, has prevailed in them all, and in most has been established by law.

New Grenada. Venezuela. Equador.

CHAPTER DIV.

*The Aborigines of New Grenada — Legend of Bochica — Spanish Conquest — Revolution — Republic of Colombia — Bolivar — Formation of the three Republics of New Grenada, Venezuela, and Equador.**

The republics of New Grenada, Venezuela, and Equador, or Ecuador, comprised the kingdom of New Grenada under the Spanish government; and their history is therefore combined till a recent period. Previous to the arrival of the Spaniards, the country was divided into many native governments, the subjects of which differed essentially from each other, in manners, policy, and civilization. The most distinguished of all the native tribes was that of the *Muyscas*, who were not only the most numerous, but the most civilized. Their traditions reached back to a very remote period of antiquity. The most remarkable point in their traditional history was the mysterious appearance of their great legislator, Bochica, who was believed to be the offspring of the Sun. According to the tradition, while the Indians were disputing about the choice of a king, Bochica suddenly made his appearance among them. He is described as a white man, clothed in long garments, and wearing a venerable beard. After having patiently listened to the contending parties, he advised them to choose Huncahua, which they accordingly did. This chief is said to have subdued the country from the plains of San Juan to the mountains of Opon.

The Muyscas had a regularly organized society: they lived chiefly by agriculture, and wore cotton garments. They owned property independent of each other, on which taxes were levied for the support of government. They had fixed laws, and judges appointed to execute them. The *Zaque*, or Cacique, was treated with great reverence: he was carried about in a palanquin, attended by his guards and courtiers. Flowers were strewn along the ground wherever he was to pass. The people never approached him but with

* *Venezuela* consists in part of vast *llanos*, or plains, which feed millions of horses and cattle. Two thirds of the people are negroes and mixed races; one half of the remainder are whites; and the rest are Indians, partially civilized. *Caraccas*, the capital, is on a plain three thousand feet above the level of the sea. In 1812, it was visited by an earthquake, which suddenly buried ten thousand people in its ruins. Bolivar was born at Caraccas in 1783, and died, near Carthagena, in 1831, having lost his high popularity.

New Grenada includes the isthmus of Darien; it consists of lofty mountains and elevated plains. The inhabitants are chiefly negroes and Indians, with a small population of whites. *Bogota*, the capital, is situated on an elevated plain, eight thousand feet above the level of the sea. *Carthagena* is the principal seaport.

Equador derives its name from the *Equator*, which crosses Quito, the capital. Here is Cotopaxi, one of the most terrific of volcanoes. *Quito*, situated on the ruins of extinct volcanoes, is nine thousand feet above the level of the sea. *Guayaquil* is on the gulf of the same name, and is a flourishing seaport. The productions of the soil, and the character of the people, are nearly the same as in the other Colombian states.

averted countenance, as if they imagined him a divinity, in whose face they dared not look.

This country was first discovered by Columbus in his third voyage to the west in 1498. He sailed into the mouth of the River Orinoco, along the coast of Paria, but made no settlement there. Alonzo de Ojeda, Amerigo Vespucci, and various other navigators, followed Columbus in exploring the coast in this quarter. Vespucci gave the first regular description of the country and the people who inhabited the coast. It is said that he falsified the date of his voyage, in order to make it appear that the discovery of the continent was made by him; but this is a disputed point. The description which he published caused the name of *America* to be given to this country.

In 1508, Ojeda and Diego Nicuessa obtained from the king of Spain extensive grants in this country. The northern part was named by them Golden Castile, and afterwards Tierra Firme: the English called it the Spanish Main. These two adventurers sailed from Hispaniola in 1510, to take possession of the country. Ojeda landed at Caramari, where the city of Carthagena was afterward built. Here he imprudently attacked the natives, who defended themselves with such bravery that they killed almost all the Spaniards, and reduced the remainder to great extremity; but just as they had given themselves up for lost, they were relieved by the arrival of Nicuessa. The settlement at Caramari was abandoned, and another, called San Sebastian, was begun in the Gulf of Darien. Here the colonists were soon in danger of starving, and Ojeda sailed for Hispaniola to procure supplies. He was shipwrecked on the voyage, lost all his property, and soon after died of want.

The colony being reduced to great distress, most of the settlers went back to Caramari; but meeting with reënforcements from Hispaniola, they returned to San Sebastian. Here they found their town in ruins, from an attack of the Indians. In addition to this misfortune, their ships were driven ashore; but by great exertion they were got afloat again, and the whole colony, by the advice of Nunez de Balboa, sailed to the River of Darien, where they attacked and conquered an Indian tribe, and founded a settlement, which they named *Santa Maria Antigua del Darien.* In the mean time, Nicuessa had encountered great disasters in attempting to establish a colony at Nombre de Dios. He was solicited to come to Santa Maria and assume the government. On his arrival at that place, he found the colonists involved in great dissensions; and Nicuessa, instead of being made governor, was sent o sea in a rotten vessel, and never heard of afterward.

Balboa led a small party of Spaniards into the interior on an exploring expedition. The Indians informed him that by ascending a certain mountain, he might obtain a sight of the Great South Sea. Balboa went up the mountain, and first saw the waters of the Pacific on the 25th of September, 1513. He pursued his march to the shore, and was the first who embarked on that ocean. He explored a part of the western coast of the isthmus in a canoe, and on his return made known to the Spaniards the existence of another great ocean in the west. In 1514, the province of Tierra Firme, including both the grants of Nicuessa and Ojeda, was given by another charter to Pedro Arias de Avila. Under the government of this person, Balboa was beheaded for being concerned in a evolt. In 1518, the western coast of Panama, Veragua, and Darien, was explored under the orders of Avila, and the town of Panama was founded. In 1536, the Spaniards, under Benalcazar, invaded the southern part of New Grenada, from Quito, while Gonzalo Ximenes de Quesada overran the northern district from Santa Maria. They met with much resistance from the natives, but finally succeeded in reducing the whole country to submission. It received the name of the *Kingdom of New Grenada* in 1547. At first it was governed by a captain-general: this officer was exchanged for a viceroy in 1718, restored in 1724, and again exchanged for a viceroy in 1740.

New Grenada never attained to the golden fame of Mexico and Peru, but its fine upper valleys and table lands became the seat of considerable agriculture, and a tolerably numerous and industrious population was gradually formed here. It was in this viceroyalty that the spirit of independence first broke out, after it had been long secretly forming throughout Spanish America. As early as 1781, the introduction of an oppressive tax caused a revolt, which for some time bore a threatening aspect. This time, however, the attempt was suppressed. The French revolution caused a new excitement; but the exertions of the government checked the rising spirit of independence. The discontents of the people, however, were not quieted; and General Miranda, a native of Caracas, raised a body of adventurers in the United States, and in 1806, landed with them on the northern coast of the viceroyalty, for the purpose of raising an insurrection. The people of the neighborhood were so slow to join him, that he was compelled to abandon his undertaking.

But at length a revolution burst out in 1810. The Spanish officers were deposed, and popular meetings were convened to organize a new government. At first separate republics were formed in New Grenada and Venezuela. The Spanish government, in the mean time, made the most desperate efforts to recover this revolted province. They sent successive expeditions under the command of Morillo, one of their ablest generals. Many of the large towns were captured, and the insurgents were driven to hide themselves among the rocks of the Andes and the marshes of the Orinoco. The control of the revolution, however, soon became engrossed in the hands of one individual: this was Simon Bolivar, a native of Caracas, who for many years became the most prominent and powerful man in South America, and distinguished himself by his military genius and talent for command. After repeated vicissitudes and immense bloodshed and suffering, the independent cause triumphed. In November, 1823, the Spaniards evacuated the country. Previous to this, in 1819, Venezuela and New Grenada had been united into one government, under the title of the *Republic of Colombia.*

The first general congress of Colombia met at Rosario de Cucuta in May, 1821. Bolivar was elected president. But the new republic was soon distracted by civil discords, and it became evident that a central and consolidated government was unsuited to so large an extent of territory. The people of Venezuela refused obedience to the Colombian constitution, and the disaffection spread to other parts of the country. The result of these movements was, that the republic of Colombia was dismembered, and in 1831, three separate governments were formed out of it, namely, New Grenada, Venezuela, and Equador.

Peru and Bolivia.

CHAPTER DV.

The Ancient Peruvians — Manco Capac — Spanish Conquest — Revolution — Formation of the Republics of Peru and Bolivia.

PERU,* an empire supposed to contain ten millions of inhabitants, was invaded and conquered by a small company of Spanish adventurers, under the direction of Pizarro, Almagro, and Luque. The chief leader was Pizarro: he crossed the isthmus to the Pacific, sailed along the coast, and landed in Peru in 1531. At this juncture the nation was divided by a civil war between the sons of the deceased Inca. Huascar, the elder, was dethroned by his brother Atahualpa, and detained in captivity, while his partisans were secretly maturing plans for his restoration. Pizarro advanced into the country with the professed design of acting as a mediator, but with the perfidious purpose of making himself master of Atahualpa, as Cortez had seized the unfortunate Montezuma. He prepared for the execution of his scheme with the same deliberation, and with as little compunction, as if he were engaged in the most honorable enterprise. When the Spaniards approached the capital, the Inca was easily persuaded to consent to an interview, and he visited the invaders with a barbarous magnificence, which inflamed the cupidity of the Spaniards almost beyond the power of restraint.

When Atahualpa reached the Spanish camp, he was addressed by Valverde, the chaplain of the expedition, in a long discourse, in which the priest expatiated upon the mysteries of creation and redemption, and the supremacy of the pope. He then informed the Inca that Pope Alexander had bestowed the dominion of Peru upon the king of Spain, and that the Inca must immediately embrace Christianity, and acknowledge himself a vassal of that monarch. Atahualpa, as we may well imagine, was quite astonished at a speech so absurd, and inquired where the priest had learned such wonderful things. "In this book," replied Valverde, offering him his Breviary. The Inca took the book, turned over the leaves, and put it to his ear. "This tells me nothing," he exclaimed, flinging it to the ground. The priest in real or feigned indignation, immediately cried out, "Blasphemy! blasphemy! To arms! to arms! Christians, avenge the profanation of God's word!' This solemn farce appears to have been preconcerted: all was ready for the assault; the trumpet immediately sounded a charge, and the artillery and musketry opened a heavy fire; the cavalry rushed upon the unarmed multitude, who could make no defence, and

---

* The ancient Peruvians had made great progress in civilization before the arrival of the Spaniards. According to the traditions of the inhabitants, Manco Capac and his wife Mama Oella, two unknown individuals, came among them in the thirteenth century, and first taught them the useful arts of life, — agriculture, architecture, spinning, weaving, &c. These persons founded a dynasty of princes in Peru, called *Incas*. They were believed to be the children of the sun, which luminary became the chief deity of the Peruvians, and this royal race were not permitted to intermarry with the common people. The empire founded by the Incas was very populous, powerful, and well governed. Its civilization was strongly contrasted with that of the Mexicans. Instead of the fierce spirit, the bloody wars, and the ferocious rites of religion which prevailed among the latter people, a spirit of mildness and beneficence reigned in the institutions of the Peruvians. Complete order and obedience were established throughout a dominion more than two thousand miles in extent. The land was carefully cultivated; the waters of the rivers were diverted into channels for the purpose of irrigation; mountains were formed into terraces to receive the water, and walls built to prevent it from escaping. An imperial road was constructed fifteen hundred miles in length, across the mountainous part of the country, connecting the two chief cities of Cuzco and Quito, and another of the same length, running parallel to it along the sea-coast. The architecture of the Peruvians displayed great ingenuity, as well as labor. Their ancient structures were not lofty, which was probably owing to the frequency of earthquakes in this country; but the walls were very massive, and formed of immense blocks of stone accurately jointed. Some of these enclosed enormous spaces of ground, and were divided into an infinity of apartments. In one of them, which is yet standing, there is room for five thousand men. Gold was very abundant in Peru. The two great cities of Cuzco and Quito abounded in stately buildings, many of which were lavishly adorned with gold and silver. The Peruvians had neither letters nor hieroglyphics, but made use of *quipos*, or knotted cord, to preserve the memory of events.

Modern Peru consists of lofty table lands, crossed by the Andes. The climate is mild, and the plains are fertile. The mines of Peru are still rich in gold and silver, though they have been drained for three centuries by the avarice of Europeans.

Lima, the capital, was founded by Pizarro, and is nine miles from the Pacific. It abounds in splendid churches, loaded with ornaments of gold and silver. The climate is that of perpetual summer.

Cuzco is five hundred and fifty miles south-east of Lima, and has some magnificent ruins of its ancient structures, especially of the Temple of the Sun, which was the chief seat of Peruvian worship. When taken by Pizarro, in 1534, this city contained an almost incredible amount of silver, gold, and precious stones

Atahualpa was taken prisoner. He was conveyed to the Spanish camp, while his captors, after massacring thousands of the helpless natives, loaded themselves with rich plunder.

The unhappy Inca attempted to obtain his liberty by offering an immense sum of gold for his ransom; but Pizarro, after receiving the gold, resolved to put him to death. Atahualpa was thereupon subjected to a mock trial, and then strangled. The Spaniards, after the murder of the Inca, quarrelled among themselves about the division of the spoils, and the Peruvians took advantage of the discord to raise a formidable insurrection; but this was quelled after a great effusion of blood. The leaders in the conquest came to a violent end. Almagro was put to death, on a charge of treason, by his associate Pizarro, and the latter was assassinated shortly afterward by the son of Almagro. The country was disturbed by factions, and it was not till a quarter of a century had elapsed after the conquest, that the royal authority was fully established in Peru. Most of the large cities in this country were founded by Pizarro. Among these was Lima, the capital, which soon rose to great wealth.

The Spanish authority was more firmly established in Peru than in any other part of South America. The government, also, was more iniquitous and oppressive to the conquered race. The mines were, from the first moment of the conquest, almost the only object which engaged the attention of the Spaniards. The Indians were compelled to work in them by a system of the most horrible cruelty, which destroyed every year four out of every five of the laborers. They submitted passively to the dreadful oppression till the latter part of the last century. In 1780, they rose in rebellion under Tupac Amaru, a descendant of the ancient Incas, and were not quieted until the country had been filled with bloodshed and devastation, and all its resources utterly exhausted.

Another attempt at revolution was made in Peru in 1805. The chief leader in this design was Ubalde, an eminent jurist. A considerable party entered into his schemes; but before they could be matured, the government took the alarm. Ubalde and eight of his adherents were seized and put to death, and upward of a hundred others were exiled. The particulars of this plot were never fully divulged, but it is pretty clear that independence was the object. After the suppression of this attempt, Peru remained tranquil, though the disaffection of the people was by no means removed. The neighboring provinces engaged in the war of independence at a much earlier date; and at length the Chilians, having defeated the Spaniards in the decisive battle of Maypu, in 1818, conceived the design of securing their independence, by expelling them from Peru. A naval armament was accordingly fitted out in 1819, and commenced hostilities by blockading the Peruvian ports and capturing their ships. It was commanded by Lord Cochrane, an English adventurer, and a great portion of the crew were English and Americans. In August, 1820, a land expedition of five thousand men, called the Liberating Army, under General San Martin, embarked at Valparaiso for the invasion of Peru. They landed at Pizco, about one hundred miles south of Lima, on the 11th of September. After a campaign of little bloodshed, San Martin entered Lima on the 12th of July, 1821, and on the 28th of that month the independence of Peru was formally declared. Callao, the port of Lima, surrendered in the following year. But the revolution was marked by many vicissitudes: the royalists gained some advantage over their opponents; the Peruvians solicited aid from the Colombians, and Bolivar marched into Peru with a strong force. The Spaniards were defeated in several battles, and at length were finally overthrown at Ayacucho in December, 1824. This was the last effort of Spain for the recovery of her dominion in South America, although the castle of Callao held out till January, 1826, when it surrendered to the Peruvians

View of Potosi.

Through the exertions of Bolivar, the district of Upper Peru was erected into an independent state, and named Bolivia.* A constitution was formed under his auspices, and he was appointed president of Bolivia for life. In 1826, he managed to procure the adoption of this constitution in Peru, where it added greatly to his power, as it not only confirmed him in the government of the country for life, but likewise allowed him to appoint his successor, and released him from all responsibility for his actions. This arbitrary government proved highly distasteful to the Peruvians, and they seized the occasion when Bolivar was absent in Colombia to rise in insurrection. In January, 1827, a complete revolution was effected in Peru. The Bolivian constitution was annulled, and a new government formed, combining the properties of a federal and a central system, with a president chosen for four years, a national congress, and separate provincial governments. From this time, Peru has remained distinct from Bolivia, but the country has been perpetually distracted by parties struggling for power, and by civil wars and revolutions growing out of the conflicts of these parties. The government, though nominally republican, is commonly in the hands of ambitious party leaders, struggling to maintain themselves in power.

* In Bolivia, the Andes rise to their greatest elevation; and here we find the pinnacle of Sorato, twenty-five thousand three hundred and eighty feet, or nearly five miles, in height. Here, also, is Illimani, which is little less elevated. The general surface of the country is rough and mountainous. There are extensive valleys, which are marked with fertility. The climate, in the high grounds, is cold and variable; on the plains it is mild and salubrious. Between the Andes and the ocean is the Desert of Atacama, three hundred miles in length, and extending into Chili. Titicaca, the only considerable lake in South America, is partly in Bolivia. It is remarkable as containing the island upon which Manco Capac, the founder of the ancient Peruvian empire, is said first to have appeared to the inhabitants, to teach them the arts of civilization, and the sublime worship of the sun. Potosi is situated on the southern declivity of the Cerro del Potosi, and, being thirteen thousand two hundred and sixty-five feet above the level of the sea is the most elevated town on the globe. The silver mines, the most celebrated in the world, are said to have been first discovered by a slave, who was climbing the mountain in pursuit of a wild animal.

DISCOVERY OF THE PACIFIC OCEAN BY BALBOA.

Chili and Patagonia.

CHAPTER DVI.

Caupolican.

Spanish Conquest of Chili — Wars with the Araucanians — Revolution — Formation of the Republic of Chili — Description of Patagonia.

THE Spanish conquerors, as soon as they had effected the subjugation of Peru, undertook an expedition against Chili.* In 1535, Almagro collected a force of five hundred and seventy Spaniards and fifteen thousand Peruvian Indians, and set out for the invasion. There were but two routes which led to Chili, and both were then regarded as almost impassable. The first ran along the sea-shore, across the burning sands of the desert of Atacama, which afforded neither water nor any other means of subsistence for a traveller. The other road led across steep mountains of prodigious height, covered with perpetual snows. These difficulties did not discourage Almagro, and he determined upon the latter route as being the shortest. In this attempt the invaders encountered the most dreadful sufferings; a hundred and fifty of the Spaniards and ten thousand of the Indians perished from cold. Almagro reached Chili, but the state of affairs in Peru compelled him to return without effecting the conquest of the country which he had invaded.

A second Spanish army, under Pedro de Valdivia, invaded Chili in 1541. The country was found peopled by a race of natives very different from the unwarlike and pusillanimous Peruvians. The most distinguished tribe were the Araucanians, the bravest and most martial of all the South American nations. Valdivia found his progress through the country constantly obstructed by the activity and courage of his enemies. The war of invasion lasted for ten years: some districts were overrun by the Spaniards, and the natives, harassed by repeated losses, reluctantly submitted; but most of them obstinately persisted in the defence of their liberty. The Araucanians resisted al the attempts of the Spaniards to subdue them. Their great leader was Caupolican, whose exploits have been celebrated by the Spanish poets Ercilla and Lope de Vega. His military skill would have done credit to the warfare of more civilized nations. He formed thirteen companies of a thousand men each, and arranged them according to a system of tactics invented by himself. The novelty of this mode of fighting disconcerted the Spaniards; and in one of the battles, Valdivia maintained a severe struggle against the forces of Caupolican, without gaining any advantage. The Spaniards, wearied with the length of the contest, retreated toward a defile, which they judged an advantageous place for defence; but the Araucanians did not allow them sufficient time to secure their retreat. Caupolican detached a strong body of men to march through by-ways and take possession of the defile, while he pushed on and followed close upon the retiring Spaniards with so much precaution and skill, that the whole Spanish force was surrounded and defeated. Valdivia was taken prisoner, and brought into the presence of Caupolican, who was willing to spare his life, but another chieftain struck him dead with a club. It is said that the Indians poured melted gold down his throat, exclaiming, "Glut thyself with that metal of which thou art so fond."

Valdivia had founded the city which bears his name, and those of Conception and Quillota. The Araucanians ravaged the Spanish settlements, after this victory, burning the cities and towns, and compelling the inhabitants to escape northward. The invaders would have been completely expelled from Chili, had they not received timely assistance by large reënforcements from Peru, which enabled them to defend their remaining ports, and recover some of those which they had lost. These fatal hostilities were renewed, as the Spaniards attempted to extend their conquests. Many bloody battles were fought, and for a long course of years the war was interrupted only by short truces. Caupolican was taken prisoner by the Spaniards, and put to death at the stake in the most barbarous manner; but the Araucanians were never subdued, and continue to maintain their independence in the southern part of Chili to the present day.

During the long period in which Chili remained a Spanish colony, some attempts were made by the Dutch and English to form settlements here. but with

* Modern Chili is a narrow tract along the Pacific, one thousand miles long. The climate is fine; the tops of the Andes are covered with perpetual snow. There are numerous plains with luxuriant pastures There are mines of copper, gold, and silver. Valparaiso is the principal commercial city in Chili. Conception is situated on one of the finest bays in South America. Valdivia, Chillan, Coquimbo. Copiapo, St Fernando, and Petorca, are the other most important towns.

out success. At first, the colonial authority of Peru was extended over this country but in 1567, Chili was separated from Peru, and placed under a captain-general, dependent solely on the king of Spain.

A revolutionary movement took place in Chili, as early as 1810, in consequence of the intelligence of the seizure of the crown of Spain by Napoleon. The captain-general was compelled to resign, and a general congress convened, which issued a decree permitting all persons who were dissatisfied with the change in the government to leave the country, with their property, within six months. The new government, however, were soon beset with difficulties. A royalist force was despatched from Peru to suppress the revolutionary movement. Much discord existed in the insurgent party, on which account the Peruvian army was enabled to defeat their forces, and drive them across the Andes toward Mendoza. San Martin, the governor of that city, received and supported them, and soon after put himself at the head of the revolutionary armies in that part of South America. He assembled a large force, and in January, 1817, marched across the Andes into Chili. He met the royalist army at Chacabuco, on the 12th of February, and obtained a decisive victory. He pursued his conquering march to Santiago, the capital, where he was received with acclamations. The Spanish forces were compelled to take refuge in the port of Conception.

The viceroy of Peru, however, resolved upon making a desperate effort for the restoration of the royal power in Chili. He collected all his disposable troops, and sent them to reënforce those at Conception. This combined army obtained at first some considerable advantage over the Chilians; but at length at the battle of Maypu, on the 5th of April, 1818, the Spanish army was completely overthrown, and the independence of Chili secured. At first, the authority was placed in the hands of O'Higgins, an officer in the army of San Martin, who governed with the title of Supreme Director; but in a short time he attempted to rule by a self-elected senate, and became unpopular; in consequence of which, he was obliged to resign his authority in 1823 to General Ramon Freyre. In January, 1826, the archipelago of Chiloe, which till then had remained in the hands of the Spaniards, submitted to the government of Chili. In 1827, some changes were made in the constitution; but after a period of dissension, the country became quiet, and has since been prosperous.

For several years the frontiers of Chili were disturbed by the depredations of a Spanish outlaw named Benavides, who put himself at the head of a body of Araucanian Indians, and desolated the country with fire and sword, and the commission of bloody atrocities, unsurpassed in the history of savage warfare. His continued successes, and the authority which he had acquired over the Indians, induced him to think himself a powerful monarch, and he attempted to establish a navy. He captured several English and American vessels which touched upon the coast for supplies, and made himself master of a large amount of property, arms, and military stores. The Spaniards encouraged him in his piracies and murders, and furnished him with troops and artillery. But his career of blood was at length cut short by the Chilians, who despatched an expedition against him in October, 1821. Arauco, his stronghold, was taken, his forces were defeated, and Benavides attempted to save himself by flight. He was captured shortly after, tried, and executed in February, 1822.

On the western coast of South America, four hundred miles from the coast, are a group of islands, called Juan Fernandez. These took their name from a Spanish navigator who discovered them. The Buccaneers made them a place of resort, during the seventeenth century. In 1705, a Scotch sailor named Alexander Selkirk was put on shore here, where he remained four years. His adventures gave rise to the story of Robinson Crusoe.

Patagonia, which forms the southern part of South America, is a desolate region, and can hardly be said to have a history. It was discovered by Magellan in 1518. This navigator drew considerable attention to the country, by the description he gave of the inhabitants, whom he represented as of a gigantic size. Many other voyagers, who visited Patagonia afterward, confirmed these descriptions. Captain Byron, who saw the Patagonians about the middle of the last century, stated that many of them were eight and nine feet in height. These accounts, however, were contradicted by other persons, and there is reason to think there was much exaggeration in the first descriptions. For a long time, very little was actually known of these people; but within the present century, Patagonia has been more accurately explored by various voyagers and travellers. Captain Fitzroy, of the British discovery ships Adventure and Beagle, visited this country about twenty years ago, and has furnished the most accurate account of the people, which we possess. According to his statement, the Patagonians, though not altogether the race of giants which they have been represented, are yet a people of uncommon height. The people of Terra del Fuego, on the contrary, are represented as a miserable, weak race, of small stature

United Provinces of La Plata.

CHAPTER DVII.

Catching Wild Cattle with the Lasso.

Discovery and Conquest of La Plata — Revolution and Establishment of the Argentine Republic. — PARAGUAY. — *Establishments of the Jesuits — Revolution — Dictatorship of Dr. Francia* — URUGUAY. — *Separation from Buenos Ayres — War with the Brazilians.*

THE great river called the *Rio de la Plata*,* or "River of Silver," was discovered by the Spaniards, under Juan de Solis, in 1515. Sebastian Cabot, the discoverer of Newfoundland, made a voyage to this quarter, in the service of the king of Spain, in 1530, and sailed up the river. He gave it the name of La Plata, because, among the spoils of a few Indians killed by the Spaniards, some ornaments of silver were found. He built a fortress here, and returned to Spain, leaving a garrison behind, who were all massacred by the natives.

Another expedition, led by Mendoza, laid the foundation of the city of Buenos Ayres in 1535. The Indians besieged this place, and the Spaniards, to avoid starvation, were compelled in the following year to abandon it, and proceed farther up the river, where they founded Asuncion, in Paraguay. The natives continued hostile, and the Spaniards, in order to gain their friendship, took wives from among the Indian women. By these intermarriages was begun the race of *Mestizoes*, which in process of time became so common in South America. The thirst of gold perpetuated the cruelty of the Spaniards, even after the connections which they had formed; but their search for the precious metal was fruitless. The situation of Asuncion was unfavorable for obtaining supplies from Spain. Several ships which were bringing troops and ammunition were lost in the river, and at length the settlers were compelled, by orders from the court of Spain, to return to Buenos Ayres. This city was accordingly rebuilt in 1580. Some of the native tribes in the neighborhood submitted to the Spaniards: those who set a higher value upon their liberty removed to a distance, as the Spanish settlements were extended. Buenos Ayres derived its first importance from a few cattle having strayed into the immense plains in the neighborhood, where they multiplied with astonishing rapidity amid the rich pastures. The hides of these animals soon became a great staple of commerce, and continue so at the present day.

On its first settlement this country was attached to the government of Peru. The Jesuits established their missions here in the seventeenth century, and met with great success in converting the Indians to Christianity, and reclaiming them from a savage life. In the course of a century, more than a hundred thousand of the natives of different tribes were collected together in villages and communities, where they were governed with strict discipline by their spiritual teachers. When the order of the Jesuits was suppressed in the eighteenth century, these Indian establishments were broken up or fell into decay. In 1778, Buenos Ayres was separated from Peru, and erected into a viceroyalty, including all the Spanish provinces east of the Andes; these limits embraced Upper Peru, with the mines of Potosi, which rendered the viceroyalty of Buenos Ayres the most important division of South America, next to Mexico.

The people of Buenos Ayres were among the first of the Spanish Americans who showed a disposition to throw off the dominion of the mother country. In 1806, when Spain was at war with Great Britain, the British government sent an expedition against Buenos Ayres, which captured that city by surprise. But after holding possession of it for fifteen days, the captors were compelled to abandon it. An attempt of the British to regain it was triumphantly repulsed by the inhabitants in 1808. Napoleon shortly afterward seized the throne of Spain, and endeavored by his emissaries to induce the Spanish Americans to acquiesce in the change of dynasty. But the Buenos Ayreans refused to submit to his authority; and in 1810, they organized a new government, which recognized Ferdinand VII. as a sovereign, but was in reality independent. This was followed by a long series of disturbances and vicissitudes. Monte Video resisted the authority of Buenos Ayres. It was subdued by General Artigas, who subsequently assumed the political authority in Monte Video, and made himself an independent chief.

The Portuguese of Brazil, tempted by the intestine discords of their neighbors, invaded the country and seized Monte Video, with the whole of the territory east of the river, called the Banda Oriental. This invasion was resisted by the Buenos Ayreans vigorously and successfully, and the Brazilians were compelled to evacuate the territory which they had occupied. The Banda Oriental was erected into an independent republic, and Paraguay detached itself from Buenos Ayres, under the dictatorship of Dr. Francia

* Most of the territory of Buenos Ayres consists of the pampas, which extend from the Atlantic to the Andes. They are covered with rank herbage, which affords support to immense numbers of horses and cattle. Multitudes of these are wild, and are caught by the inhabitants with a rope called a *laso*. The Gauchos are a people who inhabit the pampas, and live chiefly upon the flesh of wild cattle. They are excellent horsemen, and are so used to riding as hardly to be able to walk. The soil of this country is good, but agriculture is little attended to. Buenos Ayres, on the La Plata, two hundred miles from the sea, is the capital. It is the centre of trade for this portion of South America, and has an extensive foreign commerce. Cordova and Mendoza are places of some note

The other provinces of the viceroyalty, with the exception of Upper Peru, held a general congress at Tucuman in March, 1816, and in the following year an independent republic was established, under the title of the *United Provinces of the Rio de la Plata.* The constitution first established was similar to that of the United States; but the government has since undergone many changes, and the country has hardly, at any time, been free from civil war and public disturbances. The chief authority was long in the hands of General Rosas, who exercised all the power of a dictator; but he has recently been driven from the country.

The population of the United Provinces is abou one million eight hundred thousand. Buenos Ayres the capital, stands on the southern shore of the La Plata. It is regularly and handsomely built of brick and has a population of one hundred and twenty thousand. It is the chief seat of the commerce of this country.

Paraguay and Uruguay.

CHAPTER DVIII.

Dr. Gaspar Rodrigo Francia.

Discovery, History, and Insurrection.

THE republic of Paraguay * is bounded north and east by Brazil, south by Uruguay and La Plata, and west by La Plata and Bolivia. The northern part is mountainous; the remainder consists of savannas and wooded plains, interspersed with hilly tracts. It is one of the most beautiful and fertile portions of South America.

We have already mentioned the foundation of Asuncion in this country, as early as 1536. This settlement, however, made very little progress; and Paraguay can hardly be said to have a history for a long time after the first visit of the Spaniards. The country was included in the government of Buenos Ayres, and it obtained notice in the last century chiefly from Indian establishments formed here by the Jesuits. Before the arrival of the Spaniards, Paraguay had contained a great number of native tribes, who lived by hunting and fishing, and upon wild fruits and honey, which were found in great abundance in the forests. For more than a century the Spaniards laid waste the country by their wars with the natives, whose enmity they perpetuated by every species of cruel treatment, when the Jesuits conceived the design of gaining the friendship of the savages by a system of conciliation and friendly offices. The scheme which they finally determined on was to draw them out of the forest, in which they had dispersed themselves to escape the merciless swords of the Spaniards, and collect them in villages at a safe distance from the Spanish settlements. This scheme was crowned with great success. The Jesuits penetrated into the forests in search of the natives, and prevailed upon great numbers of them to renounce their old customs and prejudices, and to embrace the Christian religion. The establishments thus formed were models of their kind: the Indians paid implicit obedience to their spiritual direction; the utmost order and regularity of government was established among them.

The Jesuits had the wisdom to civilize the savages in some measure before they attempted to convert them to a religion which it was impossible for them to understand while under the influence of their savage notions. They did not pretend to make them avowed Christians, till they had made them feel in some degree like men. As soon as they had succeeded in gathering them into communities, they exerted themselves to provide every thing for their subsistence and comfort. In this manner, by rendering them contented and tractable, they found it much easier to persuade them to adopt the Christian religion. The Jesuits imitated the example of the Incas of Peru in the division of the land into three portions, — for religious purposes, for the public, and for individuals. They encouraged working for orphans and destitute people; they rewarded meritorious actions; they inspected the morals of the people; they promoted industry, educated the children, and taught them to sing hymns, while they marched in long processions. The use of money was unknown in the Jesuit establishments, for those who exercised mechanical trades deposited their works in the public warehouses. They were supplied with

* The soil of Paraguay is fertile, and the climate delightful. Mate, or Paraguay tea, is largely cultivated, and much used by the inhabitants. Asumption is the capital.

the common necessaries of life, from the labors of the husbandmen. After the example of the Incas, the Jesuits established a theocratical government, with an additional feature peculiar to the Catholic religion: this was the practice of confession, which in Paraguay brought the guilty person to the feet of the magistrate. Every one was his own accuser, and voluntarily submitted to punishment. The priests took great pains to learn the languages of the Indians, but prohibited them from learning Spanish. Their authority and influence, obtained in this manner, were long perpetuated over the converted natives.

The abolition of the order of the Jesuits by the pope, in the eighteenth century, caused the ruin of their establishments in the western world. In 1768, the missions of Paraguay were taken out of their hands, by order of the Spanish court, and intrusted to ecclesiastics of other denominations. This change, with the attempt to transfer many of the Indian associations to different parts of the country, led to the speedy decline and final dissolution of the communities which had exhibited such unparalleled success in the endeavor to civilize the American aborigines.

An attempt at revolution was made in Paraguay in the early part of the last century. Don Joseph de Antequera, a knight of Alcantara, having been appointed governor of this province by the administrative council, in a manner somewhat illegal, in consequence of the disaffection of the inhabitants toward his predecessor, was compelled to maintain himself by force against the authorities of Peru and Buenos Ayres, who sent armies to depose him from his office. His success against his enemies was so brilliant, that he gave himself the airs of a sovereign ruler, and it was believed that he intended to proclaim himself king of Paraguay. With a little more promptness and decision he might have secured this object; but he delayed action till the popular feeling in his favor had subsided, and an army from Peru expelled him from Paraguay. He was subsequently taken prisoner, and put to death in 1731. Several insurrections followed, and the authority of Spain was not fully reëstablished till 1735.

We have already given an account of the manner in which Paraguay became detached from the government of Buenos Ayres, shortly after the revolt from the mother country in 1810. The people of Paraguay, like those of all the other revolted Spanish colonies, began their career of independence by various puerile attempts to establish republican forms and titles in their government. They created consuls and legislative bodies; but after the lapse of three or four years, the whole state sunk under the power of one man, — Dr. Gaspar Rodrigo Francia, a native of Paraguay. He was educated by the monks of Asuncion, and afterward studied at the university of Cordova in Tucuman, where he received the degree of doctor of theology. He was never out of South America; and when the revolution began, he was in the practice of the law at Asuncion.

Francia was elected to a popular office, behaved independently, flattered no party, and professed his sole political object to be the entire separation of Paraguay from Spain, and its erection into an independent republic. He ultimately became the ruler of this country, and exercised the most despotic sway. He attempted to cut off all intercourse with other countries, and permitted no strangers who came to Paraguay to leave the country.

He perpetuated his power by maintaining an army of five thousand men, whom he attached to his interests by allowing them great license among the people, though he enforced the strictest discipline in their military services. Yet he lived in constant fear of assassination, and cooked his own food as a precaution against poison. His conduct displayed strong marks of eccentricity, and sometimes of a disordered intellect. His behavior, in general, bore a resemblance to that of Charles XII. of Sweden. He maintained his despotic government to the last, and died in 1842, at the advanced age of 84. Since this event the country has preserved its usual tranquility: the government is administered by a president elected for life, who is the civil governor, with whom is associated a military commandant.

Uruguay. — The republic of Uruguay* was formerly known by the name of the Banda Oriental, or "eastern side." It was first settled by the Spaniards from Buenos Ayres, and was regarded by them as appertaining to that colony; but the Portuguese government professed to consider it as a part of Brazil, and the claim to this territory was long a subject of dispute between the two powers. When Buenos Ayres revolted from Spain, the people of the Banda Oriental joined them. General Artigas, as we have already related, obtained the chief authority here, defeated the Buenos Ayrean troops, and assumed independent power. For nine years he maintained himself in authority; but in 1816, the government of Brazil, fearing the introduction of revolutionary doctrines into that country from this quarter, sent an army of ten thousand men, which captured Monte Video in January, 1817: the whole district submitted to the conquerors, and was incorporated with Brazil. In this state it remained till 1825, when the inhabitants rose in insurrection, and declared themselves independent. The Brazilians were expelled, and at the end of a war of two years, the emperor of Brazil acknowledged the independence of the Banda, which was erected into a republic under the name of *Uruguay*. A constitution similar to that of the United States was adopted in 1830. The government of Buenos Ayres, however, long maintained its claim to the sovereignty of this territory, and hostilities continued between the two republics till a recent period. In 1852 the commerce of the state was declared open to all the world, and this has resulted in great advantages.

* Uruguay is the smallest of the South American republics. The country is a fertile region, but badly cultivated. Monte Video, the capital, is on the north bank of the La Plata, and has a good harbor.

Brazil and Guiana.

CHAPTER DIV.

Discovery and Settlement of Brazil — Conquest and Expulsion of the Dutch. — Discovery of Gold and Diamonds — Revolution — Independence of Brazil. — GUIANA. — *Story of El Dorado.*

BRAZIL * was discovered by Alvarez de Cabral, the commander of a Portuguese squadron, on his voyage to India in 1501, as we have already stated. Cabral, however, did not ascertain whether it was an island or a part of the continent; and this long remained a matter of doubt. For nearly fifty years the Portuguese government made no attempt to establish colonies in this fine region. Their right to the territory, in fact, was regarded as very uncertain, according to the principles of international policy, as they were then understood. The pope had granted to the king of Spain the dominion over all newly discovered territories in the west, and to the Portuguese all in the east: by virtue of this grant, it was assumed that the king of Spain was entitled to the possession of the whole western continent. But as the Spaniards pursued their conquests in America, and made themselves masters of the rich empires of Mexico and Peru, the envy of the Portuguese was strongly excited by their success, and the court of Lisbon determined to take possession of Brazil. Accordingly, in 1549, a body of colonists was sent out, who founded San Salvador. Cabral had given the whole country the name of *Santa Cruz*, or the Holy Cross, agreeably to the common practice of the Portuguese and Spaniards, in bestowing religious appellations upon the territories which they discovered. But this name did not continue long. The country was found to produce in great abundance a red dye-wood, which was called brazil, from *braza*, the Portuguese word for a coal of fire. This wood was the first commercial article exported from the country, which, in consequence, soon obtained the name of the "country of brazil;" and the new name, at last, entirely supplanted the old one.

The Indians of Brazil were very different from those of Mexico and Peru. They had made little progress in civilization, and were divided into a number of petty states, or tribes, constantly at war with each other. The Portuguese were few in number, yet they found it easy to subdue the natives, by exciting animosities among the rival nations, and taking part with one after another, according as they saw the fortune of war inclining. Without resorting to this policy, it is doubtful whether the Portuguese would have been able to maintain their footing in the country, as the natives were distinguished for their bravery, and showed great skill in the use of their rude weapons, which consisted of bows and arrows, darts and clubs.

The first settlers were chiefly convicts taken from the jails of Portugal. This was unfortunate for the infant colony, and contributed to check its prosperity, as these persons were often unruly, and caused great disorders. The Spanish government also attempted to interfere, by setting up a claim to Brazil, founded on the Pope's grant. This dispute was at length settled, and the king of Spain renounced, in favor of the Portuguese, all pretension to the territory lying between the River Amazon and the River of Plate. After this arrangement, the settlement of the country advanced more rapidly. Grants of land were made to adventurers of respectable character and many of the Portuguese nobility interested themselves in a colony which now began to promise rich returns to the settlers. The government was remodelled; the cultivation of the sugar cane was introduced, and negroes were imported from Africa. Brazil soon became a rich and flourishing colony.

The other maritime nations of Europe showed an inclination to dispute the possession of so extensive a domain by the Portuguese. The French made a serious attempt to found a colony in Brazil. The Sieur de Villegagnon conducted a body of French Huguenots to Rio Janeiro in 1555, and gave this country the name of *Antarctic France*. The English made an endeavor to establish themselves at Paraiba. The Portuguese of that day, however, manifested a vast deal more courage and enterprise than their countrymen of the present time seem to possess; and their resolute and persevering attacks soon expelled the intruders from all parts of Brazil. When, however, this country was transferred, along with Portugal, to the Spanish crown, in 1580, the bravery and national spirit of the Portuguese sensibly declined; and the Dutch, who were then at war with Spain, sent out formidable expeditions, which conquered all the northern part of Brazil. They kept possession of their conquests for half a century, and by prudent management might have retained it permanently. But a course of maleadministration alienated the attachment of the Portuguese inhabitants, and about the middle of the seventeenth century, their enemies in Brazil commenced a series of attacks, by which they soon expelled the Dutch from all their conquests. After many vain endeavors to retrieve their affairs, both by arms and negotiation, the Dutch, in 1661, found themselves compelled to make a final cession of Brazil to Portugal.

The great prosperity of this colony dates from the year 1699, when gold was first discovered here. The circumstances of this discovery are variously related. It is said that an exploring party from Rio Janeiro penetrated into the interior in 1695, and found the Indians in possession of some gold dust. A few years afterward, a company of soldiers, traversing one of the inland districts, met with Indians using gold fish-hooks. Upon this information, strict search was made for the precious metal. The result was precisely similar to what has recently taken place in California: few veins of gold were found capable of being worked by mining, but the gullies, and beds of mountain torrents, yielded lumps and particles of gold in almost incredible abundance. The labor of collecting it was performed chiefly by negroes. The yearly

* Brazil is the most extensive state in America. It occupies the great basin of the Amazon, one of the most fertile regions on the globe. It embraces nearly one half of South America, and is almost equal in extent to the whole of Europe. The climate is generally mild, and the productions are rich and varied. Agriculture receives little attention. The rearing of cattle, which are produced in vast numbers, is the leading pursuit. Gold is obtained in considerable quantities; but the diamond mines are still more important. These are wrought on account of the government, and furnish the greater part of the diamonds. Rio Janeiro is the capital.

product was supposed to exceed fifteen millions of dollars.*

The southern part of Brazil, in the eighteenth century, was for some time subjected to the dominion of the Paulists, a community of freebooters, who took their name from the town of St. Paul, in that quarter. They were originally criminal convicts sent from Portugal to Brazil. On their first arrival, they were allowed to live free; but when it became necessary to subject them to the restraints of law, they ran away into the woods, married Indian wives, and broke off all intercourse with the settlers. A large number of these desperadoes collected at the town of St. Paul, which became their head-quarters. The situation of the place was such that it could be defended by a handful of men against the most powerful armies that could be sent against them. This inspired them with the resolution to make themselves independent; and their ambition was successful. Desperate and profligate characters from all quarters resorted to St. Paul. None were allowed to visit the place, except with a view of settling there; and candidates to obtain admittance were subjected to a severe trial. Those who could not pass through that kind of novitiate, or who were suspected of treachery, were barbarously murdered, as well as all who showed any inclination to quit the community. The Paulists for a long time defied the power of the Portuguese government. Their chief exploits were slave-hunts among the Indians. In these enterprises they ravaged the country in every direction, committing the most horrid cruelties. They are said to have destroyed upward of a million of the natives. These dangerous undertakings, however, diminished the numbers of the Paulists, and at length they became too feeble to maintain their independence, and were finally exterminated.

The policy of the court of Lisbon toward Brazil was narrow and illiberal, like that of Spain toward her colonies. Industry was little encouraged, and commerce was fettered by restrictions and monopolies: the attention of the government was engrossed in the search for gold and diamonds. No vessel of any foreign nation was allowed to touch at a Brazilian port, and strangers were rigidly excluded from the country or jealously watched. Trade was confined almost exclusively to the fortified ports. This state of things continued till the beginning of the present century, when a great change was effected in the political condition of Brazil by the events in Europe. The design of removing the court of Portugal to this country, as an asylum from the oppressions of powerful neighbors, had been long entertained in the mother country. The Marquis de Pombal, in 1761, had determined on such a measure, and preparations were made to transport the royal family across the Atlantic, when the Spaniards threatened to march upon Lisbon; but as the danger of invasion subsided, the project was abandoned.

The separation of Brazil from Portugal was occasioned by Napoleon's attempt to seize the latter kingdom. In 1807, a French army under Junot took possession of Lisbon. The prince regent, with all his court, abandoned the country, and sailed for Brazil on the 25th of January, 1808. The court was established at Rio Janeiro, and the inhabitants soon realized the benefits of the change. A royal charter was issued, abolishing the old, exclusive system of trade, and granting to the Brazilians free commerce with all foreign nations. Another decree permitted the free exercise of industry to all classes of people. The press, which for three centuries had been excluded, was now established in the country, and in 1808, the first book was printed in Brazil. This single fact shows the deplorable state of ignorance and darkness in which this great country had been kept by the government.

The downfall of Napoleon restored to the prince regent, then king, the dominion of Portugal; but he still lingered in Brazil, which seemed to be regarded as decidedly the most valuable and important portion of the empire. It was made a separate state in 1815, when a royal decree elevated it to the dignity of a kingdom. The whole Portuguese monarchy, under this new arrangement, was entitled the *United Kingdoms of Portugal, the Algarves, and Brazil.* This political system, however, was destined to be of short continuance. In 1817, an insurrection broke out at Pernambuco, which, though quelled for the time, left the country in an uneasy and disturbed state. The king returned to Portugal in 1821. The Brazilians had now a strong desire to separate themselves entirely from Portugal; and this was soon so openly displayed, that a constituent assembly of deputies from every part of the country was convened to take the subject into consideration. On the 12th of October, 1822, Don Pedro, son of the king, was proclaimed constitutional emperor of Brazil: all connection with Portugal was dissolved by the popular voice, and Brazil became an independent power. The king of Portugal acknowledged the independence of the Brazilians, in consideration of the sum of ten millions of dollars paid him for the loss of that part of his empire. The king was also recognized as emperor, with the succession of Don Pedro, who, in the mean time, was to govern Brazil in the capacity of regent. By the death of his father, in March, 1826, he became emperor.

The country, however, continued in an unquiet state, and prospered so little under his reign, that the people compelled him to abdicate the crown in April 1831. His infant son, Don Pedro II., succeeded him and the government was administered by a regency in his name. Since this period, Brazil has enjoyed more tranquillity than any other South American state except Paraguay, and but for the difficulties which arise from the continuance of negro slavery, this country would seem to enjoy every fair prospect of advancing rapidly in social prosperity and political importance.

* The discovery of diamonds, a few years later, added another prolific source of revenue to Brazil. No diamonds had ever been found in any part of the world except Hindostan, till, in the early part of the eighteenth century, they were discovered to exist in the Serro de Frio, in Brazil. The slaves, who were employed in seeking for gold in this quarter, used to find little sparkling stones, which they threw away along with the sand and gravel. At length many of them were collected as playthings for children. Some of them happened to be seen by Pedro de Almeyda, governor-general of the mines, who had been in the East Indies. He suspceted them to be diamonds; but it was difficult to make any one believe that such precious stones could originate any where except in the East. The court of Lisbon were unable to satisfy themselves till they sent a number of them to Holland, where they were cut by able artificers, and pronounced genuine diamonds. A vigilant search was immediately made for them in Brazil, and the result was so successful, that the Rio Janeiro fleet, in 1732, brought home diamonds to the value of many millions of dollars. This caused them to fall considerably in price; but the government took such measures as soon raised them to their original value, which they have ever since maintained. They conferred on a company the exclusive right of searching for and selling diamonds, all above a certain size being reserved for the king. These two discoveries of gold and diamonds placed Brazil on a level with the richest of the Spanish American possessions; at the same time the fertility of the soil was fully ascertained, and considerable progress was made in causing it to yield the richest articles of tropical produce

Indians of South America.

GUIANA.* — Columbus, in 1498, discovered the mouth of the Orinoco, and Pinzon made further discoveries on this coast in the following year; but the country was neglected by the Spaniards for many years. They seem to have made some attempts to explore it in 1535, but being disappointed in their search after mines, they regarded it as of little value. Afterward it became the scene of a most extraordinary delusion, in which the thirst of gold tempted the Spaniards into adventures surpassing the fictions of romance. In this quarter was supposed to be situated the fabulous region of El Dorado. Along the coast rumors prevailed of an inland country abounding in gold. It was said that a brother of Atahualpa, the Inca of Peru, fled from that country after the invasion of the Spaniards, carrying with him an immense quantity of treasures, and founded an empire in a remote part of Guiana, of which the most marvellous descriptions were given. The capital of the empire was called *Manoa*, and, according to the story, abounded to such a degree in the precious metals, that in one street there were no less than three thousand silversmiths. The palace of the king or emperor stood on an island in a lake; it was built of white stone, having two towers at the entrance, and between them a column with a large silver moon on the top, and two lions, or *pumas*, fastened to its base by chains of gold. Within was a quadrangular court planted with trees, and watered by a silver fountain, which spouted water through four golden pipes. The columns of the palace were of porphyry and alabaster; the galleries of ebony and cedar; the throne was of ivory, with steps of gold. An altar of silver stood in front, supporting a golden sun, and four lamps were kept burning before it day and night. The sovereign of the empire was called *El Dorado*, or the "Gilded One," because, according to the extravagant story, he was covered every day with gold dust, which was fastened to his skin with fragrant gum; this was washed off at night and renewed the next morning.

In those days no fiction was too absurd to gain belief among the adventurers in the western world. The Spaniards made innumerable attempts to reach this fabulous region. They marched thousands of miles through pathless woods, encountering incredible fatigues and sufferings: yet in vain. The glittering vision of El Dorado fled before them as they advanced; but they were still tempted to pursue it. The belief in the existence of this country cost the Spaniards a greater expenditure of life and treasure than all their other conquests in America. This belief was not extinct at the end of the sixteenth century. Sir Walter Raleigh made use of the fable of El Dorado to allure the English into a scheme of his own for conquering Guiana, though it is doubtful whether he believed the marvellous part of the story. In the year 1600, he sailed from England at the head of an expedition, landed in Guiana, and made an unsuccessful attempt to penetrate into the interior. The whole design miscarried, and he was compelled to return, in disgrace, to England. This affair finally brough thim to the scaffold.

About the year 1590, the Dutch began settlements in Guiana, on the River Demerara, and at other places. These fell into the hands of the French and English some time afterward, but were recovered by the Dutch, and retained by them till 1781, when the colonies on the Demerara and Essequibo put themselves under British protection. In 1787, the French again took possession of them: the British conquered them in 1796: they were restored to the Dutch in 1802, recaptured by the British in 1803, and remain in their possession at the present day.

The French formed a settlement at Cayenne in 1635; but this, after experiencing many disasters, was abandoned to the Dutch. The French renewed their attempt in 1663, and expelled the Dutch from Cayenne. The English became masters of this colony in 1667, and the Dutch a second time in 1676. The French, however, subsequently recovered possession of it, and hold it at the present day.

Guiana formerly comprised five divisions; Spanish, French, Dutch, English, and Portuguese. Spanish Guiana now forms a part of the republic of Venezuela, and Portuguese Guiana is incorporated with the empire of Brazil. The remainder is now divided between the French, British, and Dutch. The whole population is about 250,000.

* Guiana is now the only part of South America which is in a state of colonial dependence. It is divided into three parts: the eastern belongs to the French, the middle to the Dutch, and the western to the British. The interior is still in the possession of warlike tribes of native Indians, and runaway negroes, called Maroons. The country along the coast, only, is occupied by the whites. It is a low, flat, and unhealthy region, with a hot, oppressive climate It is, however exceedingly fertile

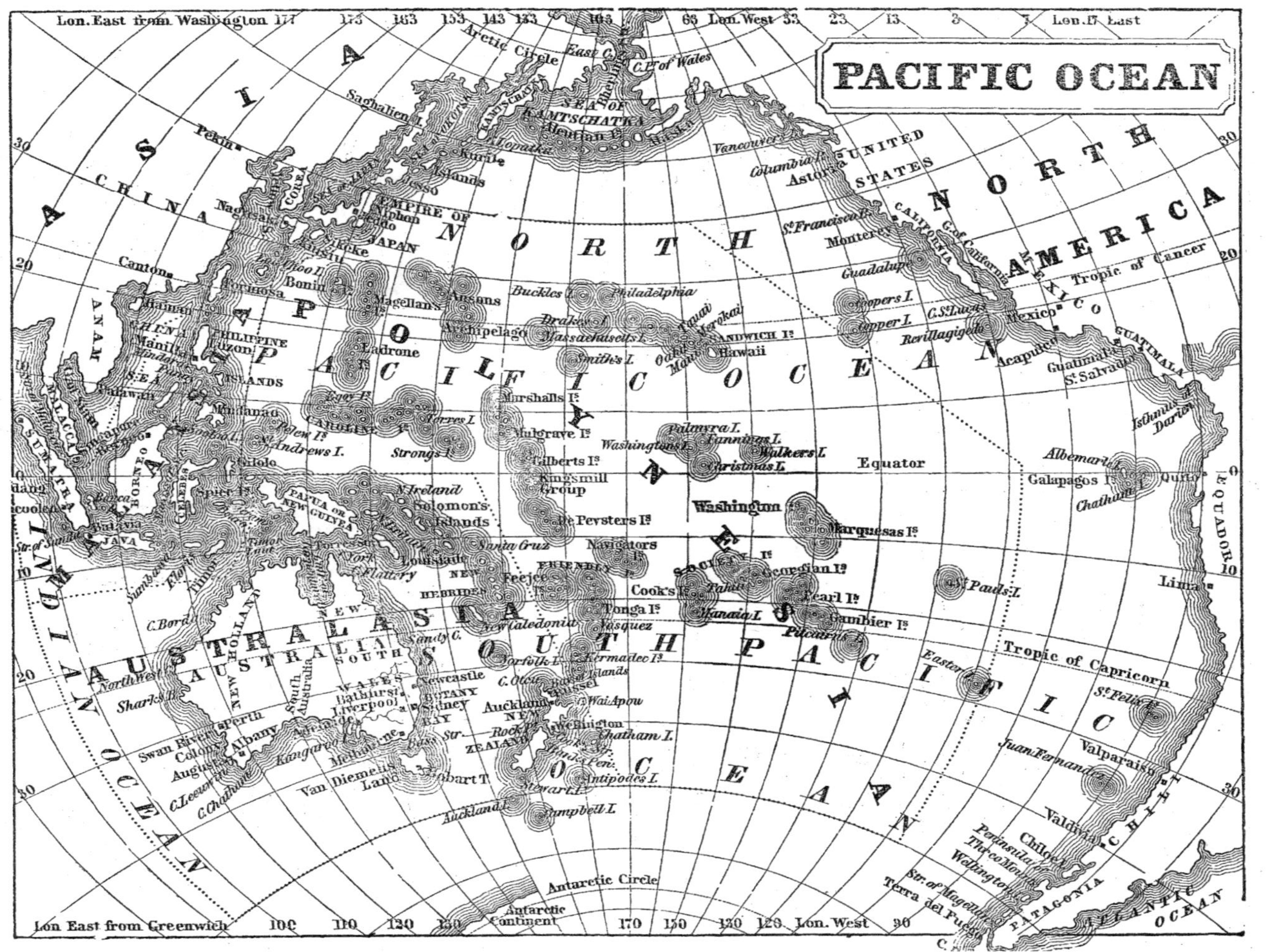
PACIFIC OCEAN
Lon. East from Washington
Lon. West
Lon. East from Greenwich
ASIA
CHINA
Pekin
Canton
COREA
EMPIRE OF JAPAN
Nipon
Jeddo
Saghalien I.
Kurile Islands
Arctic Circle
East C.
C. Pt. of Wales
SEA OF KAMTSCHATKA
Aleutian Is.
Alaska
Vancouver I.
Columbia R.
Astoria
UNITED STATES
NORTH AMERICA
CALIFORNIA
G. of California
St. Francisco B.
Monterey
Guadalupe
MEXICO
Mexico
Acapulco
Tropic of Cancer
GUATIMALA
Guatimala
St. Salvador
Isthmus of Darien
Quito
EQUADOR
Lima
NORTH PACIFIC OCEAN
Bonin Is.
Formosa
Hainan
ANAM
PHILIPPINE ISLANDS
Luzon
Manilla
Mindanao
Magellans
Ansons
Archipelago
Ladrone Is.
Buckles I.
Philadelphia
Drakes I.
Massachusetts I.
SANDWICH Is.
Oahu
Tauai
Mauai
Morokai
Hawaii
Smiths I.
CAROLINE Is.
Pelew Is.
St. Andrews I.
Torres I.
Strongs I.
Marshalls Is.
Mulgrave Is.
Gilberts Is.
Kingsmill Group
De Peysters Is.
Palmyra I.
Fannings I.
Washington I.
Walkers I.
Christmas I.
Equator
Albemarle I.
Galapagos Is.
Chatham I.
Washington
Marquesas Is.
POLYNESIA
SUMATRA
MALACCA
BORNEO
CELEBES
Gilolo
JAVA
Batavia
Timor
PAPUA OR NEW GUINEA
N. Ireland
Solomon's Islands
Louisiade
Santa Cruz
NEW HEBRIDES
Feejee Is.
Navigators Is.
FRIENDLY Is.
Tonga Is.
SOCIETY Is.
Tahiti
Georgian Is.
Cook's Is.
Pearl Is.
Gambier Is.
Pitcairn
St. Pauls I.
New Caledonia
Vasquez
Norfolk I.
Kermadec Is.
Bay of Islands
Tropic of Capricorn
Easter I.
AUSTRALASIA
NEW HOLLAND
AUSTRALIA
North West C.
Sharks B.
Swan River Colony
Perth
Augusta
Albany
C. Leeuwin
South Australia
NEW SOUTH WALES
Bathurst
Liverpool
Sydney
Newcastle
BOTANY BAY
Sandy C.
Kangaroo I.
Melbourne
Bass Str.
Van Diemen's Land
Hobart T.
NEW ZEALAND
Auckland
Wellington
Wai Apou
Chatham I.
Antipodes I.
Stewart I.
Auckland I.
Campbell I.
SOUTH PACIFIC OCEAN
St. Felix I.
Juan Fernandez
Valparaiso
Valdivia
CHILI
Chiloe I.
Wellington I.
PATAGONIA
Str. of Magellan
Terra del Fuego
ATLANTIC OCEAN
Antarctic Circle
Antarctic Continent
INDIAN OCEAN

CHAPTER DV.

Geographical Description.

THE Pacific Ocean * is studded with groups of islands, many of which are extensive and populous, and which are embraced, by geographers, under the title of *Oceanica.* The land surface is estimated at four millions five hundred thousand square miles, and the population at twenty millions. Many of the islands of the Pacific are volcanic, and send forth terrific volumes of lava, smoke, and ashes. Many, also, are evidently built up by myriads of corallines, which are sea-animals, so small as to be scarcely observed by the naked eye. Most of the islands are within, or near the tropics, and have warm climates. Some of them are exceedingly prolific. Among the peculiar vegetable products are various rich spices, sandal-wood, the bread-fruit tree, plantain, yam, and other fruits. Among the remarkable animals of Oceanica are the orang-outang, the largest species of ape; the anaconda, a gigantic kind of serpent; and the cassowary, resembling the ostrich. These are confined to the Asiatic islands. New Holland produces some very curious animals. The natives of Oceanica chiefly belong to two races — the Malays, and a kind of negro. The latter are dull and degraded, and are confined to New Holland, New Guinea, and Van Diemen's Land. The former, scattered over all the other islands of the Pacific, are active and intelligent. Most of the larger islands are now controlled by Europeans; the natives being, for the most part, in a savage state. Oceanica is divided into three portions: the *Asiatic Islands*, or *Malaysia*, *Australasia*, and *Polynesia.* Malaysia contains several important and fruitful islands, most of which are under the government of foreign nations.

The following table exhibits the principal Asiatic islands: —

	Names.	Possessed by.	Extent.	Population.	Chief Towns.
Sunda Islands.	Sumatra, ...	Natives, ...	180,000	4,500,000	Bencoolen
	Java, ...	Dutch, ...	52,000	4,280,000	Batavia.
	Banca, ...	..do..........	5,600	80,000	———
	Timor, ...	Dutch & Port.,	8,800	100,000	Lifus.
Moluccas.	Amboyna, ...	Dutch, ...	450	45,000	Amboyna.
	Ceram, ...	..do..........	4,000	120,000	———
	Gilolo, ...	..do..........	12,000	———	Saftanag.
	Banda Islands, ...	..do..........	———	———	———
	Borneo, ...	Natives, ...	300,000	3,500,000	Borneo.
	Celebes, ...	Dutch, ...	75,000	2,500,000	Macassar
Philippine Isles.	Luzon, ...	Spaniards, ...	70,000	1,200,000	Manilla.
	Mindanao, ...	....do.......	30,000	900,000	Mindanao
	Samar, ...	....do.......	800	84,000	———
	Negros, ...	....do.......	500	75,000	———

Sumatra produces great quantities of pepper and camphor, and Mount Ophir here rises to the height of thirteen thousand feet. Java, the most cultivated of the Sunda Isles, yields coffee, sugar, rice, &c. The Moluccas, or Spice Islands, are famous for producing cloves and nutmegs, which are cultivated in no other part of the world. Borneo, the largest island of Malacca, has rich mines of gold and diamonds. Celebes is inhabited in the south by an active and commercial people. The Philippine Isles are rich in sugar, rice, &c.

The following table exhibits the extent, population, &c., of the Australasian islands.

Names.	Square Miles.	White Pop.	Native Pop.	Total Pop.
New Holland	1,000,000	320,000	60,000	380,000
Van Diemen's Land, ...	22,209	50,000	3,000	90,000
New Caledonia, ...	6,108	———	40,000	40,000
New Hebrides, ...	2,291	———	150,000	150,000
Qu. Charlotte's Island, ..	1,537	———	30,000	30,000
Solomon's Isles, ...	17,610	———	100,000	100,000
Louisiades, ...	764	———	10,000	10,000
New Britain, ...	24,433	———	65,000	65,000
New Guinea, ...	305,540	———	500,000	500,000
New Zealand, ...	———	———	250,000	250,000
		370,000	1,[illegible]08,000	1,615,000

* The Pacific Ocean is the largest on the globe, and covers more than one third of the earth's surface. The width of the Pacific at the equator, extending from Equador, in South America, to the peninsula of Malacca, is nearly one hundred and eighty degrees, or one half the circumference of the globe — an extent of about twelve thousand miles. Toward the north, the two continents approach each other, and only the narrow Straits of Behring, forty miles wide, separate America from Asia, and connect the Pacific with the Arctic Ocean. The Pacific derived its name from the early navigators, who deemed it more tranquil than other seas. Though this may be its general character, yet it is subject to violent tempests, especially upon the coast of Asia. There is a general current in the Pacific, near the equator, setting from east to west, from the American to the Asiatic shore. There are also various other currents, especially among the islands and broken coasts of Asia. There are, likewise, *trade-winds* blowing constantly in one direction, and *monsoons*, blowing six months one way, and six months the other.

New Holland, the largest island on the globe—now generally called *Australia*—is held by Great Britain. It seems like a new world; for its vegetable as well as animal kingdom is unlike that of all other countries. Here is the kangaroo, an animal as large as a sheep, that sits on its hind legs, carries its young in a pocket or pouch, and leaps fifty feet at a bound. Here, also, is the bird of paradise, the black swan, and the lyre-bird, the tall feathers of the latter being shaped like an ancient lyre or harp. The natives are an ignorant and degraded race of negroes. The British have several settlements,—one at New South Wales, of which Sidney is the chief town; one at Swan River, and one at King George's Sound. Botany Bay, near Sidney, was established as a place of banishment for persons in Great Britain who had been convicted of crimes A. D. 1788; and since that period, New South Wales has been a penal colony. The recent discovery of gold in Australia, has greatly increased the importance of this country.

There are British settlements at Van Diemen's Land and New Zealand; the rest of the Australian islands are occupied by the natives. The negro races are chiefly confined to New Holland and New Guinea, as already stated. The New Zealanders are of the Malay stock, and are a vigorous and interesting people.

Polynesia comprises the numerous groups of islands lying to the east of Malaysia and Australasia. Among these groups, the principal are the Ladrones, Caroline, Mulgrave, Friendly, Society, Marquesas, and Sandwich Isles. Most of them are fruitful, and yield the bread fruit, plantain, banana, cocoa-nut, with citrons, oranges, pineapples, and other tropical productions. The natives are of the Malay race, though rendered gentle by a soft climate. They are, however, fierce and passionate when excited. They are all savages, and addicted to absurd idolatries, except so far as they have been changed by missionary efforts. The Sandwich Islands are particularly interesting, the people having been converted to Christianity and civilization by the American missionaries. Honolulu, on the Island of Oahu, is the capital, and contains 7,000 inhabitants, partly whites. On these islands are churches, books, newspapers, magazines; here also there is a thriving commerce. Pitcairn's Island is noted as having been the residence of the descendants of some British sailors, who mutinied and settled here, with some Otaheitan women, in 1790, and the surviving, 199 in number, were removed to Norfolk Island in 1856.

CHAPTER DVI.

Discoveries in the Pacific — The Antartic Continent.

THE ancients had some faint notion of the existence of islands beyond the region which they denominated Farther India; but we have no account of any voyage made in this quarter till the middle of the ninth century, when the Arab navigators, in their intercourse with China, visited some of the Islands of the Indian Archipelago. Of these voyages, however, we have no particular narrative. The islands appear to have had a native population at the earliest period, and settlements were made among them by the Malay adventurers at different times. Marco Polo, a Venetian, who travelled to China through Tartary, toward the end of the thirteenth century, returned to Europe by way of the China Sea, and the Indian Ocean. He describes two islands, which he calls *Great* and *Little Java:* these seem to be Borneo and Sumatra. At this period, the countries beyond Farther India were hardly better known than in the time of the Romans

The Portuguese, as we have seen, were the first Europeans who began the career of maritime discovery in the East. They arrived in India by the route of the Cape of Good Hope, at the close of the fifteenth century. By the year 1510, they had visited all the islands of the Malay Archipelago, as far as the Moluccas. The Spaniards, in the mean time, under Columbus and his successors, were pushing their discoveries and conquests in the West. As these two courses must necessarily meet on the opposite side of the globe, a dispute arose between the two nations as to the limits of their respective discoveries. While this point was in dispute, Magellan, a Portuguese navigator in the Spanish service, sailed into the South Sea, by the straits which bear his name, in 1519. He steered to the north-west for three months and twenty days, without seeing land, when he fell in with two small islands, to which he gave the name of *Desaventurados*, or Unlucky, as they afforded neither food nor water, when his crew were famishing for both. The smoothness of the sea, during this long voyage, caused him to bestow upon it the name of the PACIFIC OCEAN, which it is likely to retain permanently, though some geographers and historians have proposed to call it the *Magellanic Ocean.*

Having crossed the great ocean, Magellan reached the Ladrone Islands in March, 1520. He then steered westerly, and fell in with a number of islands which, he named the *Archipelago of St. Lazarus.* Afterward they received the name of the Philippines, from Philip II., king of Spain. The first island upon which the voyagers landed was Zebu. The inhabitants were at war with their neighbors, and Magellan, very unwisely taking a part in the hostilities, was killed. His ships then continued their route to the west, and discovered Borneo, the Moluccas, and Timor. After many disasters, one ship only, out of the five which began the expedition, returned to Spain round the Cape of Good Hope. The crew were greatly surprised to find they had lost a day in their reckoning,—a circumstance which every schoolboy can now account for—in circumnavigating the globe.

Magellan's voyage was succeeded by many others, conducted by navigators of different nations, to the Pacific and Indian Oceans. In 1527, New Guinea is supposed to have been discovered by a Portuguese, though the Spaniards affirm that one of their countrymen, named Saavedra, first visited the island in 1530, and gave it the name of Papua. There are good reasons also for supposing that the Portuguese were the first Europeans that discovered New Holland, which event appears to have taken place about 1535 Among the Spanish navigators of the 16th century, the most enterprising was Alvarez Mendana. His discoveries were made chiefly between 1568 and 1595. He first sailed from Peru across the Pacific and discovered an archipelago, to which he gave the name of *Solomon's Islands.*

On a second voyage to these islands, Mendana made further discoveries. In a third voyage, he carried a number of priests and soldiers,—the former to convert the natives, and the latter to reduce them to slavery; two objects, which, in the Spanish system of colonization, have always gone hand in hand. The project, in this instance, miscarried. Mendana died at Santa Cruz, one of the islands which he had discovered; and with him expired all schemes of colonization in this quarter. Subsequent navigators could not find the Solomon's Islands in the position allotted to them by Mendana; they were successively placed by geographers in parts of the Pacific very distant from each other, and at length altogether omitted in the charts. At a later date they were identified with the easternmost of the Papua Archipelago, seen by Carteret, Bougainville, and others. Mendana, in his last voyage, discovered the group now known as the Marquesas.

Quiros, a companion of Mendana, and animated by the same spirit of enterprise, sailed from Lima on a voyage of discovery in 1606. He met with an island which he called Sagittaria, evidently the one now known as Otaheite, or Tahiti: another, named by him Terra del Espiritu Santo, appears to be the principal island of the New Hebrides visited by Captain Cook.

In 1615, two Dutch commanders, Lemaire and Schouten, sailed on an expedition to the South Sea. The Dutch government had granted a monopoly of the East India trade to a company, and had prohibited all their other subjects from voyaging to the Indian Ocean, either by the Cape of Good Hope, or the Strait of Magellan. The object of this undertaking was, therefore, to discover a passage which would enable private adventurers to share in the trade to India, without infringing the law. The western continent had been traced south as far as the Straits of Magellan, but not beyond: it was then supposed that the main land extended to the south pole. Lemaire and Schouten steered south from the straits, and discovered the passage called the Straits of Lemaire, with the island to the east, which they named *Staaten Land.* Continuing their course to the south, on the 31st of January, 1615, they doubled the southern point of Terra del Fuego, which they named Cape Horn, after one of their ships. From this point they steered north-westerly across the Pacific, and discovered several islands, to which they gave the name of the *Mischievous Islands*, from the reefs and shoals which surrounded them. Here they gave up their search for a southern continent, and directed their course to the east of the Papuan Archipelago. Thence, steering west, they discovered the east coast of the island, afterward called *New Ireland.* They supposed it to be a part of New Guinea, along which island they coasted, and at length arrived at the Moluccas.

Between 1616 and 1640, several Dutch explorers visited the north and west coasts of New Holland. In 1642, Abel Jansen Tasman, a Dutch navigator, sailed from Batavia, coasted along the southern part of New Holland, and gave the name of *Van Diemen's Land* to an island, which he supposed to be a part of that island. Steering from this quarter, he discovered New Zealand, which was supposed to be a portion of a great southern continent. He then proceeded to the north, and fell in with many islands: one group, called by him *Prince William's Group*, are evidently those now known as the Feejee Islands.

Dampier, an English voyager, discovered, in 1683, the strait which separates New Guinea from New Britain. In 1721, Roggewein, a commander in the service of the Dutch East India Company, sailed round Cape Horn, in search of a southern continent. He discovered first Easter Island, a solitary rock rising from the abyss of the ocean, at an immense distance from any other land. Steering from this point to the north-west, he met with several islands, some of which are evidently those called *Palliser's Islands*, by Cook. It is remarkable, that in this voyage of Roggewein we find the first recorded notice of the luminous appearance of the sea.

The English commander Byron, in 1764, discovered some islands in the Pacific. In 1766, Captain Wallis, his companion, sailed on a second voyage, accompanied by Captain Carteret. They separated in the Straits of Magellan. Wallis discovered several islands, particularly Otaheite, which he named *King George's Island.* Carteret discovered a group, on which he bestowed the name of *Queen Charlotte*, though a part of them, at least, must have been seen previously by Mendana. Bougainville, a French commander, visited Otaheite shortly after the discovery by Wallis. He gave it the name of New Cythera. He also met with many islands which he supposed to be new discoveries, but most of them had been visited by the navigators above mentioned. On his return, he discovered the land east of New Guinea, which he named *Louisiade.* In 1769, Surville, another Frenchman, discovered land north of New Guinea, which he called the *Land of Assassins*, from the attack made upon him by the natives.

In 1768, Captain Cook sailed on his first voyage to the Pacific Ocean. He touched at Otaheite, where the British astronomers made their observations on the transit of Venus over the sun's disk. He then steered to New Holland, and explored the eastern coast of that continent, which he named *New South Wales.* He also visited New Zealand, and discovered the straits which divide it into two islands. The Society Islands received their name from Captain Cook. In 1772, Kenguelen, a Frenchman, discovered the island named *Kenguelen's Land.*

In 1773, Cook sailed upon his second voyage, with instructions to circumnavigate the globe in a high southern latitude, and to explore those parts so effectually, as to settle the question whether a southern continent existed, accessible to navigation. In this voyage he discovered Sandwich Land, and ascertained the extent of the archipelago of the New Hebrides. He also discovered New Caledonia and the Friendly Islands. His third voyage was commenced in 1776. He discovered several islands in the South Pacific, including Pitcairn's Island, and in the North, the group of the Sandwich Islands, at one of which, named Owhyhee, or Hawaii, he was killed. Vancouver was sent out, by the British government, to make discoveries in the Pacific, in 1770. He coasted along the south-west side of New Holland, called Lion's Land, for more than three hundred miles, and took possession of it in the name of the king of England.

During the present century, various English, French, and American navigators have explored almost every part of the Pacific Ocean, and rendered it quite certain that there remain no territories of any considerable extent now undiscovered, except in the immediate neighborhood of the south pole. The most recent explorations have been made in that quarter. A considerable extent of coast, denominated an *Antarctic Continent*, was discovered by Captain Wilkes, of the American exploring expedition, in 1840, and another portion, called *Victoria Land.* was visited by Captain Ross of the English expedition, in 1841

INDEX.

A.

B.

D.

E.

F.

G.

H.

I

J.

K.

L.

M.

N.

T.

U.

V.

W.

X.

Y.

Z.

THE END.

www.ingramcontent.com/pod-product-compliance
Lightning Source LLC
LaVergne TN
LVHW021223110826
845150LV00002B/229

* 9 7 8 1 4 2 5 5 6 4 1 3 1 *